Child Development
Its Nature and Course

IMPORTANT:

HERE IS YOUR REGISTRATION CODE TO ACCESS
YOUR PREMIUM McGRAW-HILL ONLINE RESOURCES.

For key premium online resources you need THIS CODE to gain access. Once the code is entered, you will be able to use the Web resources for the length of your course.

If your course is using **WebCT** or **Blackboard**, you'll be able to use this code to access the McGraw-Hill content within your instructor's online course.

Access is provided if you have purchased a new book. If the registration code is missing from this book, the registration screen on our Website, and within your WebCT or Blackboard course, will tell you how to obtain your new code.

Registering for McGraw-Hill Online Resources

TO gain access to your MCGraw-Hill web resources simply follow the steps below:

1. USE YOUR WEB BROWSER TO GO TO: **www.mhhe.com/dehart5**
2. CLICK ON **FIRST TIME USER**.
3. ENTER THE REGISTRATION CODE* PRINTED ON THE TEAR-OFF BOOKMARK ON THE RIGHT.
4. AFTER YOU HAVE ENTERED YOUR REGISTRATION CODE, CLICK **REGISTER**.
5. FOLLOW THE INSTRUCTIONS TO SET-UP YOUR PERSONAL UserID AND PASSWORD.
6. WRITE YOUR UserID AND PASSWORD DOWN FOR FUTURE REFERENCE. KEEP IT IN A SAFE PLACE.

TO GAIN ACCESS to the McGraw-Hill content in your instructor's **WebCT** or **Blackboard** course simply log in to the course with the UserID and Password provided by your instructor. Enter the registration code exactly as it appears in the box to the right when prompted by the system. You will only need to use the code the first time you click on McGraw-Hill content.

Thank you, and welcome
to your MCGraw-Hill
online Resources!

0-07-292370-9 T/A DEHART: CHILD DEVELOPMENT, 5/E

MCGRAW-HILL
ONLINE RESOURCES

REGISTRATION CODE

5T5W-TWH2-KZ6X-FC24-QF23

Child Development
Its Nature and Course

Fifth Edition

GANIE B. DEHART
State University of New York at Geneseo

L. ALAN SROUFE
University of Minnesota

ROBERT G. COOPER
San José State University

Boston   Burr Ridge, IL   Dubuque, IA   Madison, WI   New York   San Francisco   St. Louis
Bangkok   Bogotá   Caracas   Kuala Lumpur   Lisbon   London   Madrid   Mexico City
Milan   Montreal   New Delhi   Santiago   Seoul   Singapore   Sydney   Taipei   Toronto

Higher Education

CHILD DEVELOPMENT
ITS NATURE AND COURSE
Published by McGraw-Hill, a business unit of The McGraw-Hill Companies, Inc., 1221 Avenue of the
Americas, New York, NY, 10020. Copyright © 2004, 2000, 1996, 1992, 1988 by The McGraw-Hill
Companies, Inc. All rights reserved. No part of this publication may be reproduced or distributed in any
form or by any means, or stored in a database or retrieval system, without the prior written consent of
The McGraw-Hill Companies, Inc., including, but not limited to, in any network or other electronic storage
or transmission, or broadcast for distance learning.
Some ancillaries, including electronic and print components, may not be available to customers outside the
United States.

This book is printed on acid-free paper.
domestic 1 2 3 4 5 6 7 8 9 0 WCK/WCK 0 9 8 7 6 5 4 3
international 1 2 3 4 5 6 7 8 9 0 WCK/WCK 0 9 8 7 6 5 4 3

ISBN 0-07-249141-8

Publisher: *Stephen Rutter*
Senior sponsoring editor: *Rebecca Hope*
Developmental editor: *Mary Kate Hanley*
Marketing manager: *Melissa S. Caughlin*
Media producer: *Ginger Bunn*
Senior project manager: *Jean Hamilton*
Lead production supervisor: *Randy L. Hurst*
Lead designer: *Jean M. Mailander*
Cover/Interior design: *Jeanne Calabrese*
Photo research coordinator: *Alexandra Ambrose*
Photo researcher: *David Tietz*
Cover credit: *©Frank Siteman/Mira.com*
Supplement producer: *Kate Boylan*
Compositor: *The GTS Companies*
Typeface: *10/12 Times Roman*
Printer: *Quebecor World Versailles Inc.*

Library of Congress Control Number: 2003108584

International Edition ISBN 0–07–121450–X
Copyright © 2004. Exclusive rights by the McGraw-Hill Companies, Inc. for manufacture and export. This
book cannot be re-exported from the country to which it is sold by McGraw-Hill. The International Edition
is not available in North America.

To Al Price, whose excitement about teaching and passion for the well-being of children and families started me down this path.
GBD

To all of those who provide care for children.
LAS

To children around the world whose lives are impoverished by conflict and wars.
RGC

About the Authors

Ganie B. DeHart is associate professor of psychology at the State University of New York at Geneseo. She has taught undergraduate courses in child and adolescent development, applied developmental psychology, social development, atypical development, and cross-cultural psychology. Her research interests lie at the intersection of language, cognitive, and social development, especially the roles played by family and school as contexts for children's development. Her research on children's sibling and friend relationships has been funded by NIH. In 1999-2000 she was an SRCD Executive Branch Policy Fellow at the National Institute for Child Health and Human Development. Her publications have focused on sibling interaction, conflict, and pretend play. Dr. DeHart graduated summa cum laude from Brigham Young University in 1972, received an M.S. in education of exceptional children from The Johns Hopkins University in 1980, and received a Ph.D. from the Institute of Child Development at the University of Minnesota in 1990.

Robert G. Cooper is professor of psychology and Associate Vice President for Undergraduate Studies at San José State University. He has taught undergraduate and graduate classes in developmental psychology and cognitive development for over 25 years. His professional career has focused on issues in the development of cognitive skills that are particularly relevant in educational settings. His major research in the area of cognitive development, which has been supported by NIMH and NIE, concerns the development of mathematical concepts. His recent research has focused on African American and Latino/Latina youth and their pathways to college. Dr. Cooper graduated cum laude from Pomona College in 1968 and received his Ph.D. from the University of Minnesota in 1973. He has published numerous articles, contributed chapters to several books, and has been a consulting editor for various journals, including *Developmental Psychology, Cognitive Development*, and *Child Development*.

L. Alan Sroufe is William Harris Professor of Child Psychology at the Institute of Child Development, University of Minnesota (and professor of psychiatry, University of Minnesota Medical School). He has taught undergraduate child psychology classes for over 30 years and is internationally recognized as an expert on attachment, emotional development, and developmental psychopathology, having published three books and more than 100 articles on these and related topics in psychology, child development, and psychiatry journals. Dr. Sroufe graduated with highest honors from Whittier College in 1963 and received his Ph.D. from the University of Wisconsin in 1967. From 1984 to 1985, he was a fellow at the Center for Advanced Study in the Behavioral Sciences at Stanford. He has been consulting editor or associate editor for numerous journals, including *Developmental Psychology, Infant Behavior and Development, Child Development, Development and Psychopathology*, and *Psychiatry*.

Contents in Brief

Contents

Part 2 INFANCY 117

FOUR CHILDREN AS INFANTS 118

Chapter 4
First Adaptations 123

Chapter 5
Infant Cognitive
Development 159

Chapter 6
Infant Social and
Emotional Development 193

PART 3 TODDLERHOOD   229

FOUR CHILDREN AS TODDLERS   230

Chapter 7
**Toddler Language
and Thinking**   235

Chapter 8
**Toddler Social and
Emotional Development**   267

Chapter 12
**Social and Emotional Development
in Middle Childhood**   411

PART FIVE EPILOGUE: Middle Childhood

Part 6   ADOLESCENCE   445

FOUR CHILDREN IN ADOLESCENCE   446

Chapter 13
**Physical and Cognitive
Development in Adolescence**   453

Chapter 14
**Social and Emotional
Development in Adolescence**   487

Part 7   Disorders and Resiliency   523

Chapter 15
Developmental
Psychopathology   525

Preface

A number of years ago at a meeting of the Society for Research in Child Development, a group of developmental psychologists was convened to discuss the kind of textbook that was needed for the child development course. Despite the diversity of perspectives represented by the group (Urie Bronfenbrenner, Shirley Feldman, Tiffany Field, Marion Gindes, Scott Paris, and Alan Sroufe), there was notable agreement that certain key developmental ideas were not well represented in existing texts. In particular, the systematic and integrated nature of development, the mutual influences of child and context, and the way previous development influences current development seemed not to be fully conveyed. It was felt that these ideas were well established in the field but had proved difficult to build into a textbook. Facts often are easier to present than principles, and facets of development are easier to convey than the nature of development itself.

Beyond the belief that a child development text organized around coherent principles could and should be written, the working group believed that instructors shouldn't have to choose between a text that was authoritative and a text that was readable and engaging. A multifaceted view of development and a solid treatment of research and theory can be presented effectively to undergraduates by organizing material around a core set of themes within a chronological format and by presenting the material in a way that captivates the students. To do so, this text introduces three families and follows them throughout the book. These families, which are fictionalized composites of research case histories, serve as a device to illustrate graphically the role of context, the systematic interplay between child and environment, and the coherence of development. The families provide a way of showing how various influences come together to determine both normative and individual development. They let us bring life to the complex facts, research findings, and theories about child development. They also help students develop a clear understanding of the concepts of causality, continuity, and change.

The book is organized around principles and themes of development, which are reinforced continually in different ways. The developmental principles under consideration are order, continuity, and directionality. The major themes highlighted are the role of context, the issue of continuity versus change, the interplay between experiential and maturational aspects of development, the connections between social and cognitive development, and the contrast between individual and normative development. These principles and themes provide a framework for the presentation of the facts and theories of developmental psychology and a means of unifying the disparate aspects of development.

FEATURES OF THIS BOOK

Our thematic orientation inspired a number of features in the book. First, we adopted a chronological format, which seemed the best way to illustrate the orderly, organic, and integrated nature of development and to underscore our other themes and principles. Like other chronological texts, this one has cognitive and social/emotional chapters within units that cover particular developmental periods.

There are also several unique chapters. In Part One, there is a chapter (2) on contexts, which not only brings together information about the various levels and kinds of influence on the developing child (e.g., the roles of biological factors, family influence, and culture), but also sets the stage for considering the interaction of child and environment throughout the text. There is a separate two-chapter section on toddlerhood (Part Three), which spans the transition from infancy to childhood. The last chapter (15), on developmental psychopathology, focuses on abnormal behavior as developmental deviation. Not only is this chapter fascinating to students, it is also a vehicle for reinforcing the relationships among the major themes in the text and for once again relating material on normative development, individual development, and context to the experiences of the three families. Preceding each chronological unit is a vignette about our three families; these vignettes introduce the basic issues for each developmental period and carry themes forward from section to section. Each unit concludes with an epilogue, in which cognitive and social aspects are interwoven and the family stories and research are brought together.

FAMILY VIGNETTES

Our family vignettes begin with the conception of three children, each in different circumstances. One child is born to white working-class parents who have a 2-year-old daughter and strongly desire a son. The second child is born to a teenager abandoned by her boyfriend and rejected by her own single mother. The third child is an unplanned but welcome addition to an inner city, extended black family. The families represent a moderate degree of diversity; for example, none of the children is handicapped and none of the families is from a third world culture. This strategy is intended to illustrate the subtle yet dramatic influence of context while keeping the stories relevant to students.

The family stories are fictionalized, but drawn from our experience studying hundreds of families longitudinally and conducting research with countless subjects from early infancy through adolescence. Our black family was the result of collaboration with Diana Slaughter and her students at Northwestern University, who developed the characters, scenes, and dialogue during a graduate seminar entitled "Developmental Tasks of the Black Child in Urban America." Our families are abstractions from real families grappling with developmental and life issues. Their life stories are drawn from and consistent with developmental research. The capacities of the children and the issues they face at each age are those reported in the literature. Likewise, the contextual influences on individual lives are based on research; for example, the son and daughter in one of our families react differently to their parents' conflict and marital breakup—a pattern suggested by research on gender differences in responses to divorce.

As a teaching device the family vignettes serve several purposes. Reading these engaging stories, students will begin to understand major developmental issues, themes, and achievements for a given period. The stories also help make connections between developmental periods, in both normative and individual terms.

Perhaps the major content contribution of the vignettes is to convey a systems perspective to students. The concept of a system is hard to explain, but it can be illustrated. The stories will give students a feel for the direct and indirect influence of context on children, the influence of each child's particular developmental history, and the roles of children in creating their own environments. Child, family, and larger environment adapt to each other in an ongoing process. The text underscores these ideas through traditional research and theory presentation, but students will see the workings of systems in the family stories.

Once students have read the vignettes, the chapters on research and theory will be more understandable and more relevant to them. The research questions and methods will make sense, and students will be able to see more coherence in the total body of research. The goal is for our questions to be their questions; that is, the presentation of the families should raise the very questions that contemporary researchers are pursuing.

EPILOGUES

The family vignettes were written to convey important themes and critical issues. The cognitive and social/emotional chapters present contemporary research in the context of those themes and issues. Finally, integrative unit summaries, the Epilogues, explicitly tie together this material. The epilogues summarize major achievements of the period across domains, review key themes, and apply research findings to the three families' experiences. Not only does an integrated picture of the child emerge, in a way that students will remember, but cutting-edge issues in the field are also made understandable. The themes of continuity and change and the interplay between child and environment are reworked throughout the book.

ABOUT THE FIFTH EDITION

We believe that a new edition should be a new edition. While you will find the same thematic structure in this new edition and the same emphasis on going beyond isolated facts about children's capacities to an understanding of the nature of development itself, you will also find that every chapter has been revised to reflect current research and emerging trends.

Since the publication of the fourth edition there has been an outpouring of research on the human genome, cultural diversity in development, infant cognitive development, preschoolers' conceptual knowledge, peer relationships in middle childhood, and adolescent romantic relationships. In addition, important efforts are underway to understand the interaction of brain development and experience, the social context of cognitive development, and emotional development. You will find all these new developments amply covered in this edition, along with other changes that reflect extensive surveying of students and faculty.

We have added three new features to this edition of the textbook. In the margins of each chapter you will find icons for the *Child Development CD* and *Web Resources*. The *Child Development CD* icons direct you to relevant features on McGraw-Hill's *Multimedia Courseware for Child Development* developed by Charlotte J. Patterson. The *Web Resources* icons direct you to relevant websites; because Internet addresses and sites change so often, these can be accessed through a set of frequently updated links on the textbook's website. At the end of each chapter you will find a section labeled *Application and Observation*—a list of activities students can pursue outside of class.

As in the fourth edition, each chapter includes two boxes: *A Closer Look,* which provides details on one topic raised in the chapter, and *Applying Research Findings,* which illustrates how research findings may be applied to pressing societal issues. New boxes have been added on practical implications of research on early brain development, school readiness, and the developmental implications of high-stakes testing in elementary school.

We hope you will find this new edition gives you what you expect from a contemporary child development textbook, but also something more. We have added more extensive treatment of sociocultural perspectives on cognitive development to our previous coverage of information-processing and Piagetian approaches. Our coverage of social developmental theory includes cognitive social learning theory and Bowlby's attachment theory as well as traditional learning and psychoanalytic theories. You will find traditional topics such as sex-role development and conservation along with newer topics such as internal working models and theory of mind. You will find very contemporary material on day care, family conflict, and prenatal teratogens. But beyond this, we hope you will find that we have told a coherent story of the unfolding of development.

A number of people helped make this a high quality fifth edition. We would like to thank the members of the McGraw-Hill team, who were consistently supportive and responsive. We also thank Rebecca Hope, Senior Sponsoring Editor, and Mary Kate Hanley, Developmental Editor, who worked closely with us every step of the way, as well as Jean Hamilton, our Senior Project Manager, Alexandra Ambrose, Photo Research Coordinator, and David Tietz, Photo Researcher. It was great to be a part of this team.

Using recent research findings and reviewer feedback, the authors made several changes and updates in all of the chapters of the fifth edition of *Child Development: Its Nature and Course*. Highlights of these changes include:

CHAPTER 1
Added:
Issue of specificity vs. generality in development
Researchers associated with information-processing and social learning theories

CHAPTER 2
Updated:
All statistics on family and social/economic contexts
Research on maternal employment

Added:
Implications of Human Genome Project
Issues related to school readiness

CHAPTER 3
Updated:
Physical gender development (SRY gene)
Effects of teratogens
Mother-child transmission of HIV
Outcomes for low birth weight babies

Added:
Implications of Human Genome Project
Importance of folic acid before and during pregnancy

CHAPTER 4
Added:
Expanded material on brain development
Box on practical implications of research on early brain development

Impact of Back-to-Sleep campaign on motor development
Touch and pain in newborns

Updated:
Newborn imitation

CHAPTER 5
Added:
New toddler research that raises questions about infants' knowledge of objects

Updated:
Infants' understanding of number

CHAPTER 6
Updated:
Implications of infant day care

CHAPTER 7
General updating—no major additions

CHAPTER 8
Extensively updated and reorganized.

Added:
Section on beginnings of self-control and self-regulation
Section on the active role of the child—impact of child characteristics on development
Expanded material on role of brain development in social and emotional development

CHAPTER 9
Added:
Issue of specificity vs. generality in preschool cognitive development
Research on children's understanding of magical processes
Box on school readiness

Updated:
Material on adult involvement in children's memory performance, including children as witnesses

CHAPTER 10
Added:
Expanded material on self-regulation
Expanded material on moral development and internalization of standards for behavior

Updated:
Role of children's experiences in development of sex-typed behavior
Role of pretend play and imaginary companions in social and emotional development

CHAPTER 11
Added:
Box on high-stakes testing

Updated:
Interaction of heredity and environment in development of intelligence
Stability of IQ over time

CHAPTER 12
Added:
Issue of executive functioning

Updated:
Children's reactions to parental conflict and divorce

CHAPTER 13
Updated:
Processes and timing of pubertal development
Adolescent brain development

CHAPTER 14
Added:
Expanded cross-cultural perspective on adolescence
Sibling relationships in adolescence
Factors associated with dropping out of school

Updated:
Data on adolescent sexual activity and drug use
Adolescents' reactions to parental divorce and remarriage

CHAPTER 15
Added:
Expanded coverage of autistic spectrum disorders

Updated:
Genetic and biological factors in psychological disorders

SUPPLEMENTS

The following supplements listed accompany the fifth edition of *Child Development: Its Nature and Course.* Please contact your McGraw-Hill representative to learn more. To locate your representative please visit: www.mhhe.com and click on "Rep Locator."

For the Instructor

The Instructor's Manual
Denise M. Arehart—University of Colorado, Denver
This revised Instructor's Manual provides the professor with several helpful tools to organize the child development course. For each chapter, a brief summary, an outline, and a concise Chapter Review are provided. New to this edition is the integration of in-class activities for the lifespan development course created by Patricia A. Jarvis and Gary L. Creasey at Illinois State University. Discussion questions encourage the incorporation of interesting and controversial topics into lectures. A list of videos with brief content descriptions provide addition resources. The Instructor's Manual is available only in electronic format on the Online Learning Center (http://www.mhhe.com/dehart5) and on the Instructor's Resource CD-ROM.

Test Bank
Denise Davidson—Loyola University, Chicago
The Test Bank was extensively revised for this edition with an increase of conceptual questions. It includes over 1,000 text-related multiple-choice questions, as well as a variety of essay questions that encourage critical thinking. The Test Bank is available only in electronic format on the Instructor's Resource CD-ROM where it will be in Computerized Test Bank format, as well as in Word and rich text formats.

McGraw-Hill's Visual Assets Database (VAD) for Lifespan Development
Jasna Jovanovic, University of Illinois—Urbana-Champaign
McGraw-Hill's Visual Assets Database is a password-protected online database of hundreds of multimedia resources for use in classroom presentations, including original video clips, audio clips, photographs, and illustrations—all designed to bring to life concepts in developmental psychology. In addition to offering ready-made multimedia presentations for every stage of the lifespan, the VAD's search engine and unique "My Modules" program allows instructors to select from the database's resources to create their own customized presentations, or "modules." These customized presentations are saved in an instructor's folder on the McGraw-Hill site, and the presentation is then run directly from the VAD to the Internet-equipped classroom.

Annual Editions and Taking Sides
Published by Dushkin/McGraw-Hill, these collections of articles convey the latest research and thinking in child development. Helpful features include a topic guide, and annotated table of contents, unit overviews, and a topical index.
Annual Editions: Child Growth and Development 03/04
Annual Editions: Early Childhood Education 02/03
Taking Sides: Clashing Views on Controversial Issues in Childhood and Society

For the Student

Study Guide
Ganie B. DeHart—State University of New York, Geneseo
Chapter features for this revised Study Guide include multiple-choice questions, matching, short answer, and essay questions reflecting chapter material. Also included is an answer key to the multiple-choice questions with explanations of the correct answer and sample responses to the essay questions.

Multimedia Courseware for Child Development
Charlotte Patterson—University of Virginia
Packaged with your text, this interactive CD-ROM includes video footage of classic and contemporary experiments, detailed viewing guides, challenging preview, follow-up and interactive feedback, graphic, graduated developmental charts, a variety of hands-on projects, related Web sites, and navigational aides. Throughout your text, you will see notations in the margin to direct you to this CD-ROM to further enhance your child development learning experience. Its content focuses on integrating digital media to better

explain physical, cognitive, and social emotional development throughout childhood and adolescence.

Online Learning Center

This extensive Web site, designed specifically to accompany DeHart's *Child Development,* Fifth Edition, offers an array of resources for instructors and students. For students, the Web site includes a variety of interactive quizzing and exercises, key terms, chapter outlines, and summaries. New to this edition is PowerWeb. This unique tool provides you with current articles, curriculum-based materials, weekly updates, informative and timely world news, referred Web links, research tools, and study tools. A PowerWeb access card is packaged FREE with each new copy of the text. This is a great way to hone critical thinking skills and stay up to date on current events in child development.

Reviewers

Finally, we would like to thank our reviewers whose feedback helped us to reorganize and improve this fifth edition as well as previous editions.

Denise M. Arehart, *University of Colorado at Denver*
Brenda Bankart, *Wabash College*
Susan J. Bass, *Montgomery County Community College*
Elena Bettoli-Vaughan, *University of New Mexico*
Laura Hess Brown, *State University of New York College at Oswego*

Elaine Cassel, *Lord Fairfax Community College*
Nancy T. Coghill, *University of Southwestern Louisiana*
David Conner, *Truman State University*
Gary Creasey, *Illinois State University*
Candace A. Croft, *Clarke College*
Michael M. Criss, *Auburn University*
Denise Davidson, *Loyola University of Chicago*
Eric S. De Vos, *Saginaw Valley State University*
Lisabeth F. DiLalla, *Southern Illinois University*
Cynthia A. Erdley, *University of Maine, Orono*
Tiffany Field, *Nova Southeastern University, Touch Research Institute*
Dyan W. Harper, *University of Missouri—St. Louis*
Elizabeth D. Hutchison, *Virginia Commonwealth University*
Michelle Johnston Hutt, *University of Southern Maine*
Patricia Kolasa, *University of Nebraska at Omaha*
Paul A. Miller, *Arizona State University*
Peggy W. Nash, *Broward Community College*
Gerryann Olson, *Sonoma State University*
Carol L. Patrick, *Fort Hays State University*
Joe Price, *San Diego State University*
Brigette Ryalls, *University of Nebraska at Omaha*

Ganie B. DeHart
L. Alan Sroufe
Robert G. Cooper

Child Development
Its Nature and Course

1 The Nature of Development

During the years from conception through adolescence a remarkable transformation takes place—a single fertilized egg cell, smaller than the period at the end of this sentence, grows first into a human infant, and then, through successive phases of childhood, into a young adult. In the pages of this book, you will read about this fascinating set of changes. You will learn about the unfolding of many general human capacities, including the abilities to speak and reason, to feel and express emotions, and to form enduring relationships. You will also learn about the emergence of individual differences in intellectual abilities, emotional responses, and styles of social interaction.

All these changes are part of human development. During childhood and adolescence, **development** consists of age-related changes that are orderly, cumulative, and directional (Gottlieb, 1991; Valsiner, 1998; Waters and Sroufe, 1983). By *orderly* we mean that the changes follow a logical sequence, with each one paving the way for future changes and making sense in light of what went before. By *cumulative* we mean that each phase includes all that went before it as well as something more (just as baking a mixture of flour, sugar, eggs, baking powder, and salt retains these ingredients in the final product but also creates something more—cake). And by *directional* we mean that development always moves toward greater complexity.

In this book we seek not only to describe these age-related changes, but also to explain the processes that produce them. Our developmental perspective is based on three major assumptions:

- Development involves **qualitative changes**—fundamental transformations in a child's abilities or characteristics over time, as well as **quantitative changes**—increases in the *amount* of an ability or characteristic a child already has.
- Children's later abilities, behavior, and understanding of the world emerge from earlier ones in a systematic way.
- Each individual's development is coherent over time, reflecting continuity as well as change.

Taking a developmental perspective makes it possible to see how particular behaviors emerge in children, how they change in predictable ways over time, and what forms they are apt to take in the future. Children's behavior makes more sense when viewed as part of a developmental sequence rather than as isolated happenings. For instance, when you know that 1-year-olds will soon acquire language, their pointing and gesturing become more meaningful. Knowing the developmental phase a child will soon enter provides a perspective for understanding where he or she is right now. Similarly, knowing a child's individual developmental history makes current behavior more understandable and future behavior more predictable.

In this chapter we explore the nature of development and some major ideas about how it occurs. We begin by looking at several basic developmental concepts, including qualitative change and normative and individual development. Next, we present a framework for understanding the factors that shape the course of development, including genetic potentials, past development, and current environmental conditions. Then we discuss major theories that have been proposed to explain why children behave and think differently at different ages, and why children the same age do not all act the same. Finally, we summarize the methods psychologists use to study children's development.

Development:
Age-related changes that are orderly, cumulative, and directional.

Qualitative change:
A developmental change involving a fundamental transformation in an ability or characteristic.

Quantitative change:
A developmental change involving an increase in the amount of an existing ability or characteristic.

Questions to Think About As You Read

- What are your own assumptions about the nature of development and the factors that contribute to it?
- How might an understanding of basic principles of development be useful to parents and teachers?

BASIC DEVELOPMENTAL CONCEPTS

Concepts central to a developmental perspective include the notion of *qualitative change* and the distinction between *normative* and *individual* development. Let's look more closely at each of these ideas.

Qualitative Change

The mother of 6-month-old Mikey puts one end of a cloth in her mouth and dangles the other end in front of her baby, shaking her head from side to side. Mikey grows still and watches the cloth intently, a fixed expression on his face. Soberly, he reaches for it and pulls it away from his mother. Still without a smile, he puts the cloth in his own mouth and begins to explore it with his tongue.

In the same situation another child, 10-month-old Meryl, behaves quite differently. She watches with rapt attention as her mother dangles the cloth. Glancing back and forth between the cloth and her mother's face, she smiles and starts to laugh. Gleefully, she grabs the cloth away. Then, laughing even harder, she tries to stuff the cloth back into her mother's mouth.

What explains the remarkable difference between these two babies? You might think that Meryl, through practicing this game, has learned skills for playing it that Mikey doesn't yet have. Certainly learning plays some role here, but if you were to play the game over and over with a 6-month-old, the practice would lead to boredom, not laughter. Perhaps the different reactions stem from individual differences in temperament—maybe Meryl has a sunny disposition and would have laughed at the game at age 6 months, whereas Mikey is a serious child who will not laugh even when he is older. Although this explanation seems plausible when you look at only two children, it is not adequate. If you were to repeat the experiment with many babies of different dispositions, both boys and girls, you would find that Mikey and Meryl are typical of their ages. It is almost impossible to get *any* 6-month-old to laugh using this procedure, whereas most 10-month-olds will at least smile. Yet 6-month-olds already have many of the major capacities that 10-month-olds do. They recognize their mother as distinct from other people; they laugh in certain situations, such as being tickled; and they have the physical coordination to replace the cloth in their mother's mouth. Nevertheless, their reactions differ sharply from those of 10-month-olds. We are still left with the question of why.

A 10-month-old can enjoy a game of putting a cloth in his mother's mouth because he understands the relation between the cloth and his mother, and he anticipates the outcome of his actions.

A developmental perspective can provide an explanation based on qualitative change (e.g., Kitchener, 1983; Overton, 1998). Compared with 6-month-old Mikey, 10-month-old Meryl is vastly more capable; she is in a different league. Mikey does not even seem aware of the connection between the cloth and his mother. It is as if his mother recedes into the background as the cloth captures his attention. He pulls the cloth out of her mouth just as he would pull on any other object to get it. He sees no game in this at all. Meryl, in contrast, can consider both the cloth and her mother at the same time, and she responds to the relationship between them. She can remember her mother without the cloth and recognize that her mother with the cloth is discrepant from what her mother is usually like. She also knows that she can re-create the incongruity by stuffing the cloth back in her mother's mouth. She laughs because she remembers each previous state and anticipates the outcome of her actions. Far more than Mikey, she has a sense of past and future. She is beginning to understand that people and objects have permanence. Mother is still there, with or without the cloth.

The 6-month-old, of course, is having experiences that will eventually allow the 10-month-old's capacities to emerge. A 6-month-old can remember and anticipate, but these abilities are primitive compared with those of a 10-month-old. Both 6-month-olds and 10-month-olds are active learners, but 10-month-olds can learn things of greater complexity because of their greater ability to process information and their greater understanding of the world.

Behavioral reorganization:
A change in the way a developing child organizes and uses his or her capabilities; one way in which qualitative change occurs.

One way that qualitative change occurs is by means of **behavioral reorganization.** Meryl not only has more thinking and behavioral skills than 6-month-old Mikey, she also has a new way of *organizing* her thoughts and actions, of using her capabilities and fitting them together. It is because she can coordinate her memories, actions, and anticipations that she laughs at the game. The successive reorganization of thoughts and actions that occurs as children mature allows them to engage in increasingly complex behaviors.

The concepts of qualitative change and behavioral reorganization, both central to development, may become clearer if you think about how they apply to other areas of life. Consider an accounting company in which all work is done using handheld calculators. For a while the firm grows simply by adding new accountants, each of whom does the same thing (*quantitative* change). But then computers are installed. This new technology produces dramatic *qualitative* change. Not only is the firm able to handle vastly more accounts, but tasks are now performed in very different ways. Specialization occurs: some employees work on writing computer programs; others focus on inputting data; still others concentrate on interpreting the output. A more elaborate organizational hierarchy evolves. Knowledge from the old system is used in the new one, but it is now part of a totally different organization. Something similar seems to happen in many areas of human development.

Qualitative change and behavioral reorganization are evident throughout development. Parents may repeatedly tell their 8-year-old not to leave the water running because it wastes a valuable resource, only to have this message fall on seemingly deaf ears. But, to the parents' surprise, the same child comes home from school a few years later and begins to lecture them on the necessity of water conservation with the fervor of an evangelist. This new ability to grasp the significance of an issue is part of a fundamentally new perspective on the world and the future. It is not just that adolescents know more facts about water conservation than 8-year-olds. They also have a more abstract understanding of the concept of community and a greater capacity to project their lives into the future, which allows them to use the facts they know in a different way.

Normative and Individual Development

Normative development:
The general changes and reorganizations in behavior that virtually all children share as they grow older.

Individual development:
(1) Individual variations around the normative course of development; (2) continuity within a child's developmental pathway.

One major concern of developmental psychologists is describing and explaining **normative development,** the general changes and reorganizations in behavior that virtually all children share as they grow older. (*Normative* means typical or average.) To many developmentalists, however, tracking **individual development** is equally important.

Individual development has two meanings. First, it refers to individual variation around the normative course of development. If you were to chart the progress of a hundred children from birth through adolescence, you would find much variation in the ages at which they reached developmental milestones, such as walking, talking, counting to ten, and playing cooperatively with another child. This is why we can state only *average* ages at which various abilities emerge. For instance, on *average,* children recognize their reflections in a mirror at about 22 months. However, sometimes this ability emerges later, even in normal infants, and occasionally it can be seen as early as 15 months. Children with Down syndrome do not smile at the cloth-in-the-mouth game until their second year and do not recognize themselves in a mirror until about age $2\frac{1}{2}$ (Mans, Cicchetti, and Sroufe, 1978). They progress toward these achievements in the same way as other children, but at a slower pace.

Second, individual development refers to continuity within each child's individual developmental pathway over time. For example, an exuberant and confident 2-year-old is less likely to end up hesitant and withdrawn three years later than is a 2-year-old with a more negative developmental history (Arend, Gove, and Sroufe, 1979; Kagan, 2000). Even when dramatic changes in individual personality do take place, logical reasons can generally be found. Just as normative development is coherent and predictable, so too is individual development.

Each child is unique and will reach developmental milestones at his or her own rate.

A FRAMEWORK FOR UNDERSTANDING DEVELOPMENT

A fundamental challenge facing developmental psychologists is to explain how and why developmental changes come about. From the broadest perspective, development depends on three factors:

- developmental potentials provided by the organism's genes;
- the organism's developmental history; and
- current environmental conditions.

The first two factors may be thought of as existing in the organism. Every human child carries a set of genes that contains the basic guidelines for the unfolding of development. But which genes are turned on at any given time depends on the particular point in development a child has reached—that is, on the changes that have gone before. Moreover, the unfolding also depends on current environmental support. Environmental support includes all of the nutrients, sensory inputs, circumstances, and challenges the developing organism encounters. Understanding just how genes, past development, and current environmental conditions interact to produce developmental changes is a major task for the field of developmental psychology.

Origins of the Framework: Evolutionary Theory

Important clues concerning how this interaction works are found in the evolutionary theory of Charles Darwin (1809–1882). Darwin, who is considered the father of the theory of evolution, was one of the most influential scientists to ponder developmental influences (Charlesworth, 1994). His theory of evolution is not a theory of child development, but it *is* a theory of the development and adaptation of species. As such, it is a useful starting point for thinking about how development of any kind takes place.

Darwin was a naturalist who wanted a scientific explanation for the diversity of living things on earth and for their ability to exist in all kinds of environments. His careful observations of plants and animals led to one of the most important insights in all of

More on Charles Darwin

Adaptation:
A change in a species that increases chances of survival in a particular environment.

Natural selection:
The process by which traits that are well adapted to an environment are selected through reproduction and become increasingly common in a species.

Evolution:
The development of species through structural changes over time.

science: the idea that each species is equipped for survival and reproduction in its particular environment. For example, suppose lizards on two islands have different colors that match the colors of the local rocks and vegetation. Darwin would explain this kind of color difference as an **adaptation** to the environment—a change in a species that came about because it increased chances of survival. He called the process by which such changes occur **natural selection.** In natural selection, traits that are well adapted to an environment are *selected* through reproduction. Individuals with traits that help them survive in a particular setting are most likely to live long enough to reproduce and pass those advantageous traits on to their young. As a result, the advantageous traits become increasingly common in each generation, until eventually the traits are very widespread.

Suppose, for example, that sea currents carry lizards from an island made of dark rock to a sandy island where most of them are too dark to blend in with the background and are easily spotted by predators. Among the lizards that survive to reproduce are many that are slightly lighter in color. These lizards pass the genes for lighter color on to their young. In the next generation, therefore, lighter-colored lizards increase in number. So it goes, generation after generation, until eventually the lizards on the island are predominantly light-colored—a survival advantage in this particular setting. If other characteristics change as well in response to the new environment, a new subspecies of lizard could evolve. Because the earth has so many different environments, and because there is also substantial genetic diversity, natural selection has produced a huge number of species. This development of species through structural changes over time is the process of **evolution.**

The details of Darwin's theory have been criticized, especially assumptions that evolutionary change must always be so gradual and that there has been a single line of evolution from the lowest life form to humans (e.g., Gould, 2002). Nonetheless, his view that the evolution of species is based on an interaction of genes and environment is widely accepted today. You can see how our three-factor model of human development derives from it. Darwin argued that species development depends, on the one hand, on what already exists (the organism's set of genes and its evolutionary history) and, on the other hand, on the potentially changing environment in which the organism lives. Similarly, human development is also the product of genes, developmental history, and current environmental conditions.

Evolutionary theory is important to the study of child development in other ways as well. It helps focus attention on the genetically based inclinations and abilities common to all humans that have helped our species survive. These include a group-living nature and a propensity to form social ties, an ability to create complex systems of communication, a motivation to explore and discover, and an exceptional capacity to learn, reason, and solve problems. These are key areas in the study of child development. They also suggest a standard for evaluating the adequacy of environments for infants and children. Successful development

Charles Darwin with his eldest son.

Each animal has unique adaptive capacities. The cheetah is blessed with great speed. The hedgehog has prickly spines. The katydid blends well with the vegetation that surrounds it.

depends on a good fit between the environment and the genetically based inclinations and abilities of human infants. Babies have a built-in propensity to form relationships with others, but others must be regularly available for strong social bonds to develop. Children have a built-in motivation to explore and discover, but if few objects are available to look at or handle, the motivation will go largely unused. The environment must be responsive to infants' and children's predispositions and capacities.

Other Views on Heredity and Environment

Even before Darwin's groundbreaking work, people speculated on the roles of heredity and environment—also referred to as *nature* and *nurture*—in shaping human development. They were not concerned with the evolution of the human species, but rather with how individuals develop as they do. For example, the old saying "As the twig is bent, the tree's inclined" suggests that early environmental forces are critical, while the saying "The apple never falls far from the tree" stresses genetic traits inherited from parents.

Philosophical Approaches Two views of human nature from the sixteenth and seventeenth centuries exemplify contrasting ideas about the influences of nature and nurture. English philosopher John Locke (1632–1704) saw the infant as a *tabula rasa,* a totally blank slate to be written on by life's experiences. In Locke's view, children are neither good nor bad by nature, but become what they become because of their environments. If parents raise their children properly, the children will develop into responsible members of society. Today, traces of Locke's ideas can be seen in theories that stress the importance of rewards, punishments, and other learning experiences in shaping the way children act.

Shortly after Locke died, a French philosopher was born whose ideas helped establish a different point of view. Jean Jacques Rousseau (1712–1778) believed that human development unfolds naturally in positive ways as long as society allows it to do so. Parents, Rousseau argued, need not shape their children forcibly. They merely have to let human development take its natural course. In this century, Rousseau's idea of naturally unfolding development has appealed to those who focus on inherited potentials in children and to those who stress normative patterns of development, general patterns that virtually all children share. Arnold Gesell, who conducted research on children's physical and motor development at Yale University during the 1920s and 1930s, is probably the best known of those who have focused on normative patterns. Gesell's view was that these patterns unfold naturally with **maturation**—age-related physical changes guided by a genetic plan. A more recent outgrowth of Rousseau's thinking is seen in the work of those who stress the child's natural tendency to comply with the wishes of parents who have raised them in a nurturant way (e.g., Ainsworth, Bell, and Stayton, 1974; Waters et al., 1991; Kochanska, Coy, and Murray, 2001).

mhhe.com
/dehart5

More on Locke and Rousseau

Maturation:
Age-related physical changes guided by a genetic plan.

Contemporary Approaches Discussion of how heredity and environment influence development continues to this day. Some researchers focus more on heredity (e.g., Plomin et al., 1997; Scarr, 1997), others more on environment (e.g., Wachs, 1991), but all agree that both work together in guiding development (Gottlieb, 2001; McGuffin, Riley, and Plomin, 2001). There are countless examples of the interaction of heredity and environment. Having a biological parent with clinical depression predicts depression in children to a modest degree, even for children raised in adoptive homes. This suggests a genetic influence. However, the number of foster care placements before permanent adoption also predicts depression. This suggests an environmental influence. Most important, the two influences together predict depression far better than either alone (Cadoret et al., 1990). Environmental influences work hand in hand with genetic ones. The box on the next page contains a discussion of environmental and genetic influences on intelligence, an issue that has been studied extensively.

Similarities and differences between siblings also illustrate the complex interplay between heredity and environment. Identical twins, even those reared apart, are more similar than fraternal twins or nontwin siblings on such characteristics as verbal ability and shyness (Plomin et al., 1997; Waller et al., 1990). This suggests the importance of genetic factors, since identical twins have all their genes in common. However, it is important to remember that common environmental factors may have an influence even in cases of identical twins reared apart, depending on how long they were reared together before being separated, how much time they spend together after being reunited, and how similar their adoptive environments are (Joseph, 2002). In addition, other siblings share on average half the genes that differentiate them from other humans, yet they are as different in social and emotional characteristics as unrelated children (Dunn and Plomin, 1990; Hetherington, Reiss, and Plomin, 1994). This finding suggests an important role for environment. The presence of siblings pushes children to assert their individuality, and in families with more than one child each child is treated differently. Even identical twins are treated differently by parents, and differential treatment seems to influence later behavior. In one study, the member of a pair of identical twins who reported more criticism from their parents in childhood was more often depressed as an adult (Baker and Daniels, 1990).

Our own view of heredity and environment is that it is not fruitful to try to determine which is more important. Each is essential. Without genetic guidelines there can be no development, and without environmental support, development cannot proceed.

Minnesota Twin Family Study

Identical twins, especially those reared apart, have been of great interest to researchers seeking to understand the role of genetic inheritance in individual development and behavior.

APPLYING RESEARCH FINDINGS

Genetic and Environmental Influences on Intelligence

The question of how much heredity and environment each contribute to IQ differences has aroused controversy for decades. The evidence for a genetic contribution to IQ differences comes primarily from studies of twins and adopted children (Scarr, 1997). Identical twins, even if they have been reared apart, are much more similar in IQ than are any other pair of siblings (either fraternal twins or nontwins) or two unrelated individuals. Such data have been used to support the claim that heredity contributes to similarities and differences in IQ. At the same time, however, they also show a powerful role for environment. For instance, identical twins, who share identical genes, do not have identical IQs, and the difference in their IQs tends to be greater if they are raised apart. Clearly, a complex interplay of genes and environment creates IQ differences.

This complex interplay was illustrated in an early study of adopted children (Skodak and Skeels, 1949). The biological mothers had below-average intelligence (mean IQ 85.7), while the adoptive parents had above-average intelligence (mean IQ about 120). The children were placed in their new homes before 6 months of age, so the rearing environments they experienced were largely those of their adoptive families. The researchers tested the children several times over a period of years. The children's mean IQs ranged from 107 to 116—20 to 30 points above the mean IQ of the biological mothers, a very significant dif-ference. However, at age 7 the average correlation between a particular child's IQ score and the score of his or her adoptive parents was only .16, as opposed to a .36 correlation between the child's IQ and the biological mother's. (Correlations indicate the extent to which two measures are related to each other. *Positive correlations* like these mean that two measures tend to rise and fall together; the higher the correlation, the stronger that tendency.) Furthermore, the relationship between the children's IQs and the IQs of their biological mothers stayed strong as they passed through childhood, but the relationship with the adoptive parents' IQs declined over time. By the age of 13, the correlation between the child's IQ and that of the adoptive parents had dropped to .04, while the child-biological mother correlation still averaged .38.

As a group, the children's IQs were apparently raised as a result of their placement in advantageous environments. However, *individual differences* among the children were more predictable from information about their genetic inheritance than from information about variations in their adoptive parents' intelligence level. Notice, though, that the fact that their IQs were more closely related to their biological mothers' IQs than to those of their adoptive parents does *not* mean that their development was unaffected by the enriched environment in their adoptive homes.

To illustrate the critical influences of genes, environment, and past development, consider an example from the prenatal period. What happens if at an early stage in the development of a chick embryo, a piece of tissue is surgically removed from the base of a leg bud and placed at the tip of a wing bud? The transplanted tissue goes on to develop into a normal-looking wing tip. Apparently, chemical signals in the wing bud tell the genes in the transplanted leg bud tissue to direct that tissue's development into wing instead of leg. But if this same procedure is done late in the embryo's development, the leg tissue will not be incorporated into the wing. It is now too late for the new context to alter the course of development. Chemical signals in the leg bud have already triggered genes there to start the tissue differentiating into part of a thigh. What if the transplant is done at an intermediate stage, when the tissue is already committed to becoming leg, but not yet committed to becoming thigh? Amazingly, the result is a claw-like structure at the end of the wing! In other words, at this stage the tissue carries instructions to become leg tissue but no final instructions to become thigh. The new context can induce the tissue to become a tip, but only the tip of a leg. What develops depends on genes, environment, and past development. The genetic makeup ensures that the tissue will become part of a chick—it will not become a fin, for example. Genes and developmental history combine to determine that it will be part of a chick *leg*. The current context induces it to be a tip. The tissue becomes the tip of a chicken leg, a claw.

Although this experiment was done with chick embryos for ethical reasons, the same principles apply to both prenatal and postnatal human development. In humans, the development of binocular vision (the brain's integration of information received from two eyes) depends on appropriate visual experience occurring at the appropriate time. If it does not occur at the correct time, the part of the brain that would have been used to interpret binocular vision is put to other uses. Genetic information constrains how the brain develops, but much of its ultimate organization is a consequence of experience. Furthermore, brain development does not occur just by the addition of new parts or functions as the brain matures; rather, an increasingly complex organization of functions emerges with development (Schore, 1994).

Examples such as these lead us to conclude that neither genes nor environment can be considered more important in development. Changes in a group of cells, a baby's progress from crawling to walking, the emergence of a child's personality, and countless other developmental changes are all joint products of heredity, past development, and current environment.

THEORETICAL PERSPECTIVES ON DEVELOPMENT

Over the years psychologists have proposed a number of theories to explain human development. Some theories of development focus on normative development, others on how children become unique individuals. Some attempt to explain all aspects of development, others concentrate on more specific domains of development. Each emphasizes different factors and issues, thus providing different perspectives on developmental changes. Before turning to specific theories used in the study of child development, let us examine the meaning and functions of scientific theories in general.

The Nature of Theories

Theory:
An organized set of ideas about how things operate, an attempt to explain past findings and predict future ones.

As children grow older, they are increasingly able to choose appropriate gifts for others. Various theories explain this development in different ways.

A scientific **theory** is an organized set of ideas about how things operate, an attempt to explain past findings and predict future ones. Individual observations take on meaning when they are interpreted from the perspective of a particular theory.

Different theories provide different perspectives and explanations for the same set of observations. Suppose Father's Day is coming up and a mother takes her two sons shopping. The 3-year-old picks out a shiny toy truck for his father, while the 6-year-old selects a baseball cap. Both boys see Father's Day as a special occasion and want the best for their dad, but the 6-year-old's choice is far more likely to be used by the father. Why do they make such different choices?

According to the theory of the Swiss psychologist Jean Piaget, the 6-year-old's choice is evidence of a developmental decline in egocentrism—that is, a movement away from viewing the world only from one's own perspective. Piaget theorized that children become less egocentric with age: 6-year-olds are fundamentally less egocentric than 3-year-olds, who in turn are vastly less egocentric than 1-year-olds.

In contrast, part of Sigmund Freud's psychoanalytic theory holds that, beginning at around age 4, children strive to be like, or identify with, the parent of the same sex. This identification is an indirect way for children to feel they have power in the world. Viewed through Freudian theory, a 6-year-old boy who picks a cap for his father and a similar cap for himself is doing so partly because of identification with his father.

Note that each of these approaches attempts to explain a particular behavioral change in terms of more general processes of development. One of the important functions of theories is to *provide a framework for interpreting specific facts and research findings.* This makes it possible to apply existing knowledge to a range of new situations.

A second major function of theories is to *guide scientific research.* Researchers could explore an infinite number of questions about human development. Theories help them decide which questions are important to ask and how to ask them. For example, if you hold the theory that much of individual behavior is determined by heredity, you would give high priority to contrasting people with similar and dissimilar genetic makeups (identical twins versus unrelated individuals, for instance). If, however, you think early experience is a major determinant of behavior, you would conduct studies contrasting people with different childhood histories. A researcher interested in the interaction between heredity and environment might try to examine both genetic and environmental variation in the same study.

The validity of a theory can be judged on the basis of three main criteria:

- It must be sensible and consistent; that is, it must not contain assumptions that are incompatible or known to be false.

- It must help us interpret and make sense of what we know by organizing, integrating, and making understandable the body of research findings on a topic.

- It must be specific enough to be testable—in other words, we must be able to derive from the theory statements open to proof or disproof.

Of course, the validity or usefulness of a theory in the behavioral sciences usually cannot be decided by one or two critical tests. Rather, an ongoing check of research findings is needed.

Six Major Theories of Development

Consider a scene in a day care center playground. A boy climbing the ladder on a slide slips and falls, cutting his lip. His cries draw others' attention. One 2-year-old playing nearby becomes upset himself and starts crying also. Another 2-year-old offers the injured child her teddy bear, even though he shows no interest in the toy. With a clear expression of concern on his face, a 5-year-old calls a teacher and stands by while she tends to the boy. Another 5-year-old might walk away or even tease the injured child for crying, something a 2-year-old would be unlikely to do.

The reactions of these children may be explained in different ways, and different theories focus on different aspects of the situation. Some theories focus on general age-related changes. Why, for example, do 5-year-olds act so differently from 2-year-olds in this instance? Other theories focus on individual differences among children who are the same age. Why do some 5-year-olds show empathy, while others do not? Theories also differ in that some stress cognitive aspects of the children's reactions (how they think about and understand the situation), while others stress social and emotional aspects. Some recent theories attempt to combine both viewpoints, seeing them as interrelated.

In the sections that follow we introduce you to six major theories that have been used in the study of child development, showing how different theories lead to different

Each developmental theory has a different explanation for children's responses to an injured playmate.

Jean Piaget

More on Piaget

Sensorimotor period:
Piaget's term for the first two years of life, when awareness of the world is limited to what can be known through sensory awareness and motor acts.

Preoperational period:
Piaget's term for the period when children have mental representation but do not yet reason logically or systematically.

Concrete operational period:
Piaget's term for the period when children begin to use logical operations to reason about concrete objects.

Formal operational period:
Piaget's term for the period when children gain the ability to reason systematically about abstract issues and hypothetical problems.

explanations of children's behavior. The first three theories focus on cognitive development—the development of children's thinking, language, and other mental skills. The other three focus on social and emotional development—the development of children's feelings and relationships with others. The same order (cognitive development first, then social and emotional development) is also used in later chapters of the book.

Theories Stressing Cognitive Development

Piaget's Theory of Cognitive Development. The Swiss developmental psychologist Jean Piaget (1896–1980) formulated the first comprehensive theory of cognitive development. Piaget was mainly interested in normative cognitive development—that is, in changes in thinking that occur with age among all typically developing children. In particular, he studied the development of children's logical reasoning abilities. He argued that as children grow older they undergo major *qualitative* changes in how they understand and learn about the world. Older children do not just have more skills and information than younger ones, their thinking is also organized in fundamentally different ways. Just as Darwin proposed that biological adaptation leads to the emergence of new species, Piaget proposed that cognitive adaptation to the environment over the course of development leads to the emergence of new kinds of thinking.

One of Piaget's enduring contributions to developmental psychology is the view that children develop cognitively by actively constructing a system for understanding the world, rather than passively acquiring new facts. Piaget also believed that children's understanding of the world at any given stage is limited by their current cognitive structures. As they pass through the various stages of development, their cognitive structures become increasingly abstract and sophisticated.

Piaget believed that major shifts in thinking took place at approximately 2, 7, and 12 years of age. Piaget called infancy the **sensorimotor period,** because he viewed infants' awareness of the world as limited to what they know through sensory awareness and motor acts. By about age 2, infants gain the ability to use mental representation to think about the world; this new ability marks the transition into the **preoperational period,** which lasts until about age 7. During this period children can think about things not physically present, but their reasoning is not yet logical or systematic. At about age 7, children enter the **concrete operational period** when they begin to use logical operations to reason about concrete objects. Finally, around age 12 children begin to develop the ability to reason systematically about abstract issues and hypothetical problems, marking the beginning of the **formal operational period.** Table 1.1 summarizes the major developmental periods in Piaget's theory.

Table 1.1 Major Developmental Periods in Piaget's Theory

Age	Developmental Period	Cognitive Characteristics
Birth to 2 years	Sensorimotor	Infants understand the world through sensory information and motor responses.
2 to 6 years	Preoperational	Children use mental representation to reason about the world, but thinking is not yet logical.
7 to 11 years	Concrete Operational	Children can perform logical operations on concrete objects.
12 years and up	Formal Operational	Children can think logically about abstract issues and hypothetical situations.

Piaget argued that all normally developing children go through the same major periods of development, in the same order, at about the same ages, and that this process cannot be greatly accelerated through training. Knowledge and skills acquired through training would simply not be enough to boost a child to a higher cognitive level; instead, they must be organized within a new, broader cognitive structure before the next step in cognitive development can take place. Educators who apply Piaget's theory argue that instruction must be carefully designed to be appropriate to a child's current way of understanding and learning about the world.

To illustrate Piaget's theory, consider again the children on the playground. The 2-year-olds are just entering the preoperational period of cognitive development, whereas the 5-year-olds have been in this period for several years. When the ability to use mental representation first develops, children use it in an immature, egocentric way. They mentally represent things from their own perspective and have a hard time thinking about how other people might be experiencing or representing the world; they simply don't understand that other people have other points of view. The 2-year-old on the playground who offers her own teddy bear to the boy doesn't grasp that for him the bear isn't a much-loved, comforting object, as it is for her.

Five-year-olds, in contrast, are beginning to understand that the views of other people are sometimes different from their own. In a limited way they can think about what the hurt child is experiencing and what might relieve his distress. (They can also figure out what might make him feel worse; helping and teasing draw on the same cognitive capacity.) In Piaget's view, therefore, 5-year-olds do not simply have more mental skills than 2-year-olds; they think in a different way. Still, 5-year-olds have a long way to go before they think like adults, or even like older children. Their notions of cause and effect are hazy. For instance, a 5-year-old might scold the slide for hurting his playmate, something that a typical 9-year-old would never do.

The observations Piaget made and the questions he asked about children's thinking continue to influence researchers today. Indeed, it is almost impossible to overstate the impact that Piaget's thinking has had on developmental psychology (Beilin, 1994). In Chapter 5, where we describe the development of thinking during infancy, we will say more about the mechanisms Piaget proposed to explain cognitive development.

Information-Processing Theory. Psychologists working from the perspective of **information-processing theory** seek to understand thought processes by comparing them to the workings of a computer. Like a computer, a person receives input (information from the environment) and processes it, drawing on information already stored in memory. The information-processing approach is not the product of a single theorist. During the 1960s, researchers began to use concepts from computer science in their work on adult cognition (Newell and Simon, 1961; Atkinson and Shiffrin, 1969). In the 1970s the approach was adopted by psychologists studying children's cognitive skills (e.g., Klahr and Wallace, 1976). Developmental psychologists with an information-processing perspective are particularly interested in age-related changes in children's memory, problem-solving skills, and knowledge base (Klahr and MacWhinney, 1998). One of the most currently influential developmental researchers in the information-processing tradition is Robert Siegler, who has studied the rules children use in solving problems and the processes involved in mastering new problems (Chen and Siegler, 2000; Siegler, 1998).

Unlike Piaget, information-processing theorists see development in terms of *quantitative* change—gradual improvements in attention, memory, and thinking that lead to greater skill in interpreting events and a wider range of problem-solving strategies. By analyzing the steps children take in performing a mental task, these researchers seek to chart and explain cognitive changes that occur with age. Like Piaget, most information-processing theorists are interested in universal patterns of development, but the perspective can also be applied to understanding individual differences among children of the same age. Educational psychologists in particular have begun to use it this way

Information-processing theory: A theory that seeks to explain human thought processes by comparing them to the workings of a computer.

Lev Semyonovich Vygotsky

Sociocultural theory:
A theory that emphasizes the role of social interaction and specific cultural practices in the development of cognitive skills.

More on Vygotsky

Private speech:
Audible speech that children direct to themselves in regulating their own behavior.

Inner speech:
Children's inaudible directives to themselves, used for behavior regulation.

Zone of proximal development:
Vygotsky's term for the gap between a particular child's current performance and potential performance with guidance from someone more skilled.

to describe differences in children's learning abilities and styles. We will describe information-processing theory in more detail in Chapter 9, where we discuss memory and attention in preschoolers.

Information-processing theorists would explain the different responses of the 2- and 5-year-olds to a hurt playmate in terms of the children's knowledge base about the problem, their skills in using memory to store and retrieve information, and the ease and flexibility with which they apply past experiences to new situations. To help, the children must first match stored knowledge with aspects of the current situation to determine if help is needed—for instance, matching the injured boy's cries with knowledge that a child who is hurt and upset often begins to cry. The 5-year-old's greater experience facilitates these matches; some 2-year-olds might not even recognize that the situation requires help. For example, they might incorrectly associate the boy's crying with failure to get a particular toy he wanted.

In addition to deciding whether help is needed, the children must decide what kind of assistance is best. To do so, they must sort through memories of responses they have used in the past or have seen others using and decide which one is likely to work best. Because the 5-year-old has a much broader store of knowledge about possible responses to someone who is hurt, he is more likely to find a good solution. Two-year-olds might be unable to think of any solution at all (and therefore start to cry), or might try an ineffective solution (offering a teddy bear). A broader store of knowledge about possible solutions also makes 5-year-olds more flexible in responding than 2-year-olds. For instance, if no teacher were nearby, a 5-year-old could probably think of an alternative solution, such as going inside to find an adult. In contrast, a 2-year-old who thought of calling her own mother to help might not know how to modify this strategy upon realizing that her mother was not around.

Thus, according to information-processing theory, the 5-year-old's greater effectiveness in this situation stems from two things: a larger base of information and an ability to use information more effectively. Five-year-olds have stored in memory more knowledge of the meaning of events and how to do things, and they can retrieve this knowledge more quickly, use it to make more appropriate comparisons, and draw conclusions more rapidly.

Sociocultural Theory. In recent years increasing numbers of psychologists have become interested in studying children's cognitive development in its social and cultural context. **Sociocultural theory** emphasizes the role played by social interaction and specific cultural practices in the development of cognitive skills (Rogoff, 1998; Wertsch, Del Río, and Alvarez, 1995; Wertsch and Tulviste, 1994).

Much of the current research being done from a sociocultural perspective has been influenced by the ideas of a Russian psychologist named Lev Semyonovich Vygotsky (1896–1934). Vygotsky argued that children first learn cognitive skills in social settings and only later internalize them. Therefore, cognitive development can be understood only by studying the social and cultural processes in which it originates.

For example, Vygotsky argued that children learn to plan and to regulate their own behavior by gradually internalizing directives that they originally hear in social interaction with adults. First they begin to produce the directives themselves in **private speech,** audible speech that they direct to themselves. Ultimately, they become able to use **inner speech,** inaudible directives to themselves, to regulate their behavior. Young children often produce private self-directive speech when engaged in a challenging task, muttering such directions as "Got to stay inside the lines" or "First this one, *then* that one." As they master the task and become more confident of their own abilities, the self-direction becomes internal rather than external, and the audible self-directives disappear.

One of Vygotsky's most influential ideas was the concept of the **zone of proximal development,** the gap between a particular child's current performance and that child's potential performance if given guidance by someone more skilled. Vygotsky argued that the zone of proximal development is where learning and cognitive development occur, as children gradually internalize skills they could initially do only in a social setting and thereby expand their repertoire of cognitive abilities. It is important to note that the zone of proximal development does not extend indefinitely; at any point in development, there are always skills that remain beyond the child's current abilities, even with assistance. For example, 2-year-olds have limited abilities to dress themselves, but if adults hold out a pair of shorts for them to step into or guide their arms to the appropriate sleeves in a T-shirt, they can pull the shorts and the shirt on. However, no matter how much assistance adults provide, 2-year-olds will not be able to tie their own shoes.

Like Piaget, Vygotsky believed that cognitive development involves qualitative change, with children's abilities taking sudden, dramatic leaps forward as they internalize cognitive skills. In Vygotsky's theory, cognitive development does not consist simply of improving existing skills, but of fundamentally reorganizing them as they move from the external social realm to the internal cognitive realm. Unlike Piaget, Vygotsky did not believe that children have to construct their understanding of reality themselves; instead, they can benefit from the knowledge already gained by those around them. One researcher working from a sociocultural perspective commented:

Child Development CD
Piaget vs. Vygotsky

> *The young child is often thought of as a little scientist exploring the world and discovering the principles of its operation. We often forget that while the scientist is working on the border of human knowledge and finding out things that nobody yet knows, the child is finding out precisely what everybody knows.*
>
> *(Newman, 1982, cited in Rogoff, 1990, p. 42)*

A sociocultural analysis of children's reactions to an injured playmate would focus on the role of social interaction and cultural practices in the development of children's understanding of the situation. Differences in the children's responses might be explained as the result of exposure to varying cultural practices or differences in internalizing the necessary skills. The 2-year-old who cries in response to another child's injury might have been pushed beyond the limits of his individual cognitive functioning; with prompting from an adult or older child, he might be able to offer simple assistance or comfort.

The 5-year-old who went for help has had more exposure to cultural practices for comforting others and more opportunities to internalize them. This internalization might be the result of being placed in situations in which he could gain experience helping and nurturing others, or of receiving explicit instruction on the importance of helping. In either case, his behavior would reflect the value that his culture and the adults in his life place on learning to be helpful.

A sociocultural approach would also be useful for explaining cultural differences in children's responses to the playground situation. For example, in cultures that emphasize interdependence, such as Japan, even 5-year-olds would be unlikely to tease an injured child in need of help.

Theories Stressing Social and Emotional Development

Psychoanalytic Views. **Psychoanalytic theories** are perspectives on human development derived from the ideas of the Viennese physician Sigmund Freud (1856–1939). These theories attempt both to describe normative social and emotional development and to explain individual developmental pathways and variations from the norm.

After treating a number of emotionally disturbed patients, Freud concluded that abnormal behavior results from inadequate expression of innate drives—intense urges based in human biology, such as the need for sex or the expression of aggression. Out of these ideas Freud developed a theory of psychological development from infancy to adulthood. He argued that at birth the mind consists of a reservoir of primitive drives and instincts, called the **id.** Over the first few years of life, the **ego,** or self, emerges.

Sigmund Freud

Psychoanalytic theory:
Any theory of development derived from the ideas of Freud.

Id:
Freud's term for the part of the mind that consists of primitive drives and instincts.

Ego:
Freud's term for the self; the part of the mind whose major role is to find safe and appropriate ways to express instinctual drives.

Superego:
Freud's term for the conscience; the part of the mind that has internalized rules and values governing behavior.

More on Freud

Fixation:
Failure to resolve the major issues of a psychosexual stage, resulting in repeated symbolic reliving of those issues.

More on Erikson

The ego's major role is to find safe and appropriate ways to express instinctual drives. Thus, the child develops the ability to delay gratification of impulses in order to meet society's demands, particularly demands conveyed by parents. At first it is fear of punishment that encourages this new self-control, but in the late preschool years the child begins to develop a **superego,** or conscience. Now the child has made the parents' rules and values part of the self. He or she feels guilty for misbehavior and tries to be good even when adults are not around.

Returning to our playground example, Freud would argue that the 5-year-old who helps is developing the ability to control impulses. He does not become angry with the hurt boy for crying and blocking the slide. Instead, he puts aside his own immediate desires and looks for help. The boy's ego is now well developed enough to know that anger would not be a good reaction since it would probably bring a teacher's rebuke. At the same time, the 5-year-old is also developing a superego; he is internalizing his parents' rules and values and acquiring a conscience. He now feels it is wrong to ignore a hurt child, and he might feel guilty if he did so. Another 5-year-old who ignores the injured playmate and seems to feel no guilt is not as far along in developing a superego.

Freud also proposed a theory of individual personality development, how adults come to have different styles of social and emotional behavior. In Freud's early writing, personality was viewed as unfolding in a series of five stages (see Table 1.2). In each stage the child's primary motivation is to gratify the drive for sensual pleasure in a particular part of the body. All children, Freud claimed, go through the stages in the same order, at similar ages. Adult personality is a result of how much the gratification of drives is restricted or indulged in particular stages; both undergratification and overgratification can lead to anxiety and **fixation,** in which a person who fails to resolve the major issues of a stage relives them later in symbolic ways. For example, a baby who is harshly weaned from the breast may become anxious because oral gratification has been withheld, and continue to focus on oral issues later in life. He or she may become preoccupied with getting care from others or begin drinking heavily to counter feelings of loneliness. Because the earlier oral conflict is buried in the adult's subconscious, he or she is unaware of the reasons for these behaviors.

The stages and issues in Freud's theory of individual development reflect the concerns of his time and place (late 19th Century Vienna) and traumas from his own infancy and childhood (Breger, 2000). With its great emphasis on the satisfaction of innate drives for sensual pleasure, the details of Freud's original theory have little direct influence on developmental psychology today. Modern psychoanalytic thinkers have proposed broader sets of developmental issues and conflicts that people face from infancy through the various stages of adulthood. These thinkers (and even Freud in his later writings) also put more emphasis on ego development, or development of the self, and they see people as far more actively involved in determining the course of their own development. Still, certain of Freud's core ideas have been incorporated into modern psychoanalytic perspectives. Freud's legacy to modern psychology includes the ideas that emotions have a critical impact on thinking, that early relationships are vitally important, that past conflicts can be pushed out of conscious awareness but still affect a person's life, and that the same events can have different meanings to different people depending on their developmental histories (Emde, 1994).

The writings of Erik Erikson (1902–1994) on social and emotional development stem in part from Freud's legacy. Like Freud, Erikson (1963) assigned a critical role to feelings and social relationships, especially early in life, and he proposed a series of qualitatively distinct stages that occur in a certain order. But Erikson did not believe a person can become fixated at an unsuccessfully completed stage of development. Instead, each of his stages involves a developmental issue that everyone resolves in some way, although some people do so more satisfactorily than others. Erikson's issues are also much broader than Freud's. For example, Erikson saw feeding as an important arena for infant-parent interaction, but he believed that the quality of care a baby receives entails much more than feeding and oral gratification. Playing, rocking, comforting, changing,

Table 1.2 A Comparison of Freud's Psychosexual Stages with Erikson's Psychosocial Stages

Age	Freud's Psychosexual Stages	Erikson's Psychosocial Stages	Erikson's Developmental Issues
Birth to 1 year	Oral	Basic trust vs. mistrust	Infants learn to trust others to satisfy their needs and therefore develop feelings of self-worth. Infants receiving inconsistent care may grow to mistrust the people in their world.
1 to 3 years	Anal	Autonomy vs. shame and doubt	Children learn to be self-sufficient by mastering tasks such as feeding and dressing themselves. They begin to separate from their parents and conform to social rules. If parents' demands are too restrictive, harsh, or lax, children may doubt their ability to act on the world and develop feelings of shame.
3 to 6 years	Phallic	Initiative vs. guilt	Expanding on the autonomy developed in the previous stage, children initiate pretend play with peers and accept responsibilities such as household chores. Sometimes these activities create conflicts with other family members, producing guilt; excessive guilt inhibits initiative. Children can resolve the crisis by learning to balance initiative against the demands of others.
7 to 11 years	Latency	Industry vs. inferiority	Children master increasingly difficult skills, particularly peer interaction and academic tasks. Children whose industry enables them to succeed in these areas develop a sense of mastery and self-assurance. Children who do not experience mastery feel inferior and shun new activities.
12 to 18 years	Genital	Identity vs. role confusion	Adolescents build on all earlier experiences to develop a sense of identity, particularly in relation to their society. Failure to reach this goal may cause confusion in identity, the choice of an occupation, and adult roles.
Young Adulthood		Intimacy vs. isolation	Young adults strive to form strong friendships and achieve love and companionship with another person. Individuals who have not developed a strong identity in adolescence may have difficulty forming intimate relationships and experience isolation and loneliness.
Adulthood		Generativity vs. stagnation	Generativity includes responsibilities such as raising children and productivity in one's work. Adults who cannot perform these tasks become stagnant.
Maturity/ Old Age		Ego integrity vs. despair	Older adults achieve ego integrity if they can look back on their lives and view them as productive and satisfying. If they view life as a disappointment, despair results.

and bathing are also opportunities for the baby to learn about the responsiveness and dependability of parents. To Erikson the *overall* quality of care determines whether the child will develop basic trust or mistrust. Whatever the developmental outcome, the child does not become fixated, but moves on to other developmental issues.

Erikson's eight psychosocial stages and Freud's five psychosexual stages are summarized in Table 1.2. Erikson's stages are called psycho*social* because relationships with others play a prominent role in all of them; Freud's stages are called psycho*sexual* because they revolve around gratification of basic drives for sensual pleasure. The issues that define Erikson's stages have provided an important organizing scheme for describing human social and emotional development. We will discuss the first five of them in later chapters.

Social learning theory:
A theory that emphasizes the learning of behaviors through associations with different kinds of consequences, especially in a social context.

Modeling:
Learning by imitating others' behavior, especially behavior that has been observed to have positive consequences.

Social Learning Theory. **Social learning theory** is an outgrowth of earlier learning theory, which proposed that behaviors are learned through associations with different kinds of consequences. According to learning theory, children tend to repeat behaviors that have resulted in rewards or have allowed them to avoid unpleasant consequences, and they tend to discontinue behaviors that do not have one of these two outcomes. In addition, *social* learning theorists believe a great deal of learning comes about through observation of others. Through a process known as **modeling,** children often imitate behaviors that they have seen others do, especially if they observe them to have positive consequences. Social learning theorists focus on human learning that occurs in a social context, through observation and interaction with others.

Social learning theory is the product of work by many psychologists over a number of years. Perhaps the most influential social learning theorist for the field of developmental psychology is Albert Bandura (b. 1925). Bandura's early work focused on the role of imitation in children's aggression (e.g., Bandura, Ross, and Ross, 1961). More recently, he has studied issues related to children's ability to regulate their own actions (Bandura, 1997).

Like information-processing theorists, social learning theorists see development as a gradual, cumulative process. However, their focus is on social behavior rather than on thinking. Additionally, social learning theorists are more interested in explaining differences among children of the same age than in explaining differences among children of different ages. Issues that have been prominent in research based on social learning theory include identifying factors that influence the likelihood children will imitate a model and explaining the development of aggression and prosocial behavior.

Returning to our playground example, social learning theorists would say that the 5-year-old who helps the injured boy has probably seen other people rewarded for behaving helpfully and may have been praised for helping others himself. As a result, he has acquired the notion that helping is called for in this situation, and the expectation that praise comes to those who help. In contrast, a 5-year-old girl who teases the injured child may have learned that a good way to get attention from her parents is to upset her baby brother. Such attention is not as rewarding as praise, but it is better than being ignored. A 5-year-old who walks away may have been ignored or hit by children he has tried to help, causing him to associate helping with negative consequences. Alternatively, he may not have been exposed to models of helping behavior, or he may have little experience with this particular situation (for instance, he may be an only child who just entered day care). The 2-year-olds' responses may also be explained in terms of their inexperience.

In general, social learning theory is more useful in explaining specific social and emotional responses in children than it is in explaining universal patterns of behavioral change with age. In later chapters we will apply social learning theory to the issue of why some children respond to social situations differently than their peers.

Adaptational theory:
Bowlby's developmental theory, which integrates ideas from evolutionary, psychoanalytic, and cognitive theories to explain the development and impact of early attachment relationships.

Bowlby's Adaptational Theory. The English psychiatrist John Bowlby (1908–1990) sought to bring together social, emotional, and cognitive aspects of development in his **adaptational theory.** Of all the theorists we discuss here, Bowlby is the most heavily indebted to Darwin's theory of evolution. But Bowlby was also strongly influenced by Freud's psychoanalytic views on individual development, especially the importance of early relationships. In addition, his is a cognitive theory in which acquisition of mental structures fundamentally changes children's engagement with the world and children are viewed as actively processing information to guide social behavior.

Bowlby began with the idea that human babies are predisposed to behave in ways that promote closeness with their caregivers. This is part of the human evolutionary heritage, an adaptation we share with our primate relatives. Much as baby monkeys cling to their mother's fur to avoid separation, human babies, as soon as they are able, cry, call, and crawl after their caregivers to stay close to them. The tendency to form

John Bowlby and Mary Ainsworth, who developed a procedure for testing Bowlby's theory, discuss attachment research.

early attachments is biologically built in, and for virtually all children it unfolds through a sequence of stages, culminating in a reciprocal partnership with parents (see Chapter 6).

To the idea that babies are predisposed to form attachments to caregivers, Bowlby added the psychoanalytic notion that the quality of infant-adult attachment is heavily influenced by the quality of care the baby experiences. The tendency to form attachments and the stages of their development are universal, but the security of attachments varies greatly. Bowlby argued that infants who experience responsive care develop a belief that they can influence the environment and obtain care from others when needed. In time, securely attached children believe more generally that they can prevail even in the face of stress or adversity. In contrast, infants who do not receive responsive care and who are not secure in their attachments may be doubtful of their own abilities, and they may become socially isolated or aggressive.

Bowlby's theory therefore includes an important role for cognition and learning. Through hours of interaction with caregivers, infants develop generalized expectations about caregivers' responses and their own role in producing those responses. By participating in a responsive relationship, an infant learns not only that the caregiver is available and responsive but also that this is the way relationships work. Such broader patterns of beliefs are later applied in many different contexts.

Bowlby's theory would explain the different reactions to the injured child in the schoolyard in terms of attachment history. The boy who comes to the injured child's aid has probably experienced empathic and responsive care. Children who have experienced a nurturing relationship not only learn to expect and receive care but also learn more generally that when one partner in a relationship is in need, the other responds. In addition, they have confidence in their own ability to solve problems. In contrast, a 5-year-old who responds with hostility to the injured boy has probably experienced hostility, rejection, and emotional unresponsiveness himself. We will describe Bowlby's ideas more fully in later chapters.

More on Bowlby

Why So Many Theories?

We have described only a few of the theories of human development. There are many others, some of which we will discuss later in the book. Why so many different theories? Why hasn't developmental psychology produced a single theory, accepted by all?

One answer is that *different theories focus on different aspects of development* (see Table 1.3). Piaget, for example, focused on cognitive development, while Erikson focused on social and emotional development. Piaget's theory is not an alternative to

Table 1.3 A Comparison of Theories of Development

Emphasis on:	Piaget	Information-Processing	Sociocultural	Psychoanalytic	Social Learning	Bowlby
Normative/ individual development?	Normative	Normative	Both	Both	Individual	Both
Environment/ heredity?	Heredity (Species level)	Environment	Environment	Both	Environment	Both
Stages?	Yes	No	Yes	Yes	No	Yes
Early experience?	No	No	No	Yes	No	Yes
Specificity/ generality?	Domain- and culture-general	Domain-specific, culture-general	Domain- and culture-specific	Domain- and culture-general	Domain-specific, culture-general	Domain-specific, culture-general

Erikson's; each concentrates on different things. Moreover, even theories that look at the same general area of development may still focus on different factors within that area. For instance, Bowlby's adaptational theory looks at prior relationships with caregivers and the expectations derived from them in trying to understand differences in children's social behaviors. Social learning theory, in contrast, is more concerned with the particular behaviors individual children display, how they came to learn them, and the specific situations that tend to elicit them. Thus, Bowlby's theory and social learning theory differ in part because each is looking at different pieces of a large and complex puzzle.

A second reason why there is no single, universally accepted theory in developmental psychology is that *like other areas of science, psychologists' knowledge of human development is a work in progress.* As researchers have observed children and theorized about their development over the last hundred years or so, the store of knowledge about children's behavior has increased. One goal of developmental psychology is to describe the course of development, but another equally important goal is to refine existing theories, resolve discrepancies between theories, and generate new theories that are more accurate and comprehensive in scope. The theories of today are based on more data and better understanding than the theories of yesterday, but there is always room for improvement.

As developmentalists pursue the second goal, the theories they propose often turn out to have more and more in common. For example, modern social learning theory stresses the general beliefs that people acquire through their observations of others and their histories of rewards and punishments. These include beliefs about one's own ability to be effective, what Bandura (1997) refers to as *self-efficacy*. Self-efficacy, in turn, is very similar to Bowlby's notion of a person's expectations about the self. So the question is not whether people have ideas about themselves that influence their behavior. Both theories agree that they do. Instead, the question is whether these attitudes about the self are specific to particular situations and derive from particular learning experiences (as social learning theory contends), or whether they derive from the general quality of early relationships (as adaptational theory holds). The answers to such questions can come only from additional research, which in turn will no doubt raise new questions.

MAJOR ISSUES IN DEVELOPMENT

The six theories we have presented disagree on several major issues, including:

- the issue of *gradual development versus stages*—whether development is best viewed as a cumulative process of quantitative change or as a series of qualitatively distinct stages;
- the issue of *early versus current experiences*—whether early experience has a decisive impact on later development or current behavior largely reflects current experiences; and
- the issue of *specificity versus generality*—whether processes of development are domain- and context-specific or domain-general and universal.

Gradual Development versus Stages

The question of whether development occurs gradually or in stages comes up most often in relation to normative development, the general patterns of change that most children experience. Most of the debate has centered around patterns of cognitive change. As we have seen, information-processing theorists come down on the side of gradual or quantitative change. They believe that cognitive development is the result of gradual improvement in attention, memory, and problem-solving skills. Their position is based on research showing that younger children can perform certain cognitive tasks almost as well as older children if they are helped to break down the tasks into simpler steps, or if they are taught the required skills before testing.

In contrast, Piaget's stage theory holds that cognitive development consists not merely of quantitative changes in cognitive skills, but also of qualitative changes in how children think and understand the world. Older children approach problems and understand things in ways that younger children simply cannot. This position is supported by research showing that training children on advanced tasks is only modestly successful and that younger children consistently make the same mistakes on problems that older children see as easy and obvious. When asked to explain their answers, younger children's responses suggest that they think in ways fundamentally different from the way older children think. Moreover, they approach problems in different ways. For example, when asked to put a set of sticks in order by length, most preschoolers respond with a trial-and-error approach; they have no concept of *seriation* and no overall strategy for putting the sticks in order. In contrast, older children carry out the task by systematically comparing the sticks; they understand from the outset what the final result should look like, and they have a clear strategy of comparative measurement that they can use to solve the problem.

Cognitive development is not the only area in which the issue of developmental stages has arisen. The psychoanalytic theories of Freud and Erikson are stage theories, and stage theories have also been proposed for moral development and the development of peer relationships. In later chapters of the book you will notice that we sometimes describe development in terms of acquiring new and different behaviors, thinking skills, or understandings of oneself or of social relationships. Other times we describe development in terms of modifications to and extensions of existing skills or behaviors, which occur gradually. We believe that both quantitative and qualitative transitions are part of development.

The issue of gradual development versus stages is in part an issue of level of analysis. Viewing the same process at different levels of analysis can lead to different conclusions about whether it involves gradual or stagelike change. Consider the process by which H_2O changes from ice to water to water vapor. As the temperature rises, there are clear transitions between *qualitatively* different states. Yet at the same time, the change in the temperature of the material is gradual and continuous. In much the same way, children's existing skills may gradually improve until eventually a fundamentally new skill has emerged—for example, when children make the transition from crawling to walking or from being able to identify individual letters of the alphabet to being able to read words and sentences.

Early versus Current Experiences

The question of which is more important, early or current experiences, most often arises in discussions of social and emotional development. Social learning theorists attach little importance to the age at which experiences occur. They see a child's style of responding to other people as resulting from the accumulated history of reactions to the child's behavior. In fact, many view current experiences as more important than previous ones because the child is, after all, acting in the present. Jerome Kagan (1984) draws an analogy between experience and tape recordings. Each experience (the child's behavior plus any positive or negative consequences it brings) is recorded in memory. However, the *record* button in the child's mind is always turned on. If current experiences echo past experiences, the tape remains unchanged. But if current behavior leads to different consequences, the old tape is erased and a new message recorded. In support of this view, research has shown that a person's style of responding can change over time if relevant circumstances change. Moreover, the same person may behave differently in different situations (one way with family members, for example, and another way with peers) if each situation involves different consequences.

Other theorists assign greater importance to early experiences. Erikson, for example, held that each stage of psychosocial development is influenced by the previous one. For instance, how well a toddler negotiates the issue of autonomy is influenced by how much he or she developed basic trust through close relationships with adults in infancy. Lacking the emotional security of basic trust makes it harder to try out new things and accept parental guidance during the toddler years. Similarly, it is easier for young adults to form satisfying intimate relationships if they achieved a coherent identity during adolescence. This is not to say that how a developmental issue is resolved affects a person indelibly for life. There is always opportunity for change given new experiences. For example, a satisfying intimate relationship in young adulthood may help a formerly mistrustful child become a more trusting adult.

Bowlby's adaptational theory grants importance to the influence of current experiences, while still assigning a special role to early experiences. In Bowlby's view, development proceeds within the framework of previous patterns of adaptation. New situations are interpreted in light of previously formed expectations about the self and others. Fundamental change remains possible, however, for adaptations are a product of development up to that point *and* of new circumstances. Bowlby summarized this perspective using a model of a branching tree, which he adopted from C. H. Waddington (1957) (see Figure 1.1). In this model, early experience does not irrevocably determine what a child will become. The child who follows path A, for instance, might take several different routes at certain points in development. Early choices, however, do limit the alternatives available at later stages. The path-A child may branch left or right midway through development, but may not suddenly switch to path D. In Bowlby's theory, as in Piaget's, children are not passive recipients of environmental influences. Instead, they are active participants in their own development and help to create their own environments through the choices they make.

Specificity versus Generality

The issue of specificity versus generality includes two separate questions. The first question is one of *domain specificity*—are developmental processes specific to particular knowledge or skill domains or do they apply more generally to a broad range of abilities? This question has implications for how broad the scope of developmental theories

Figure 1.1
BOWLBY'S MODEL OF DEVELOPMENTAL PATHWAYS
Change always remains possible, but choices at each point are constrained by directions previously taken. Children following paths A and B may wind up quite similar in their pattern of adaptation despite different directions taken in early life. Children on paths C and D are quite different and perhaps atypical because of extreme directions continually taken. *[Adapted from Waddington (1957) in Bowlby (1973).]*

can be. The second question is one of *cultural specificity*—are developmental processes specific to particular social or cultural contexts or are they socially and culturally universal? This issue has implications for developmental theories' applicability across social settings and cultures.

The issue of domain specificity has been raised most often in connection with cognitive development, where the question is whether a theory attempts to explain cognitive development in general or focuses instead on processes specific to particular domains. Piaget's theory was intended as an explanation of cognitive development in general, proposing fundamental cognitive structures and abilities that cut across domains, such as mental representation and logical operations. On the other hand, information-processing theory focuses on more specific skills and strategies and takes into consideration children's knowledge in particular domains, such as chess and dinosaurs (e.g., Chi and Ceci, 1987). The general recent trend in developmental psychology, especially among researchers who study cognitive development, has been away from theories that attempt to account for development in general and toward theories that focus more narrowly on development in specific domains.

The issue of cultural specificity is relevant to theories in all areas of development. All of the theories discussed in this chapter were formulated in Europe and North America, and all of them reflect the assumptions and concerns of the cultures from which they come. Only the sociocultural approach explicitly addresses social and cultural context in explaining development. Piaget, Freud, and Erikson assumed that they were describing culturally universal structures and processes, but a large body of cross-cultural research suggests that only some aspects of their theories apply across Western and non-Western cultures. For example, Piaget's description of infants' behavior during the sensorimotor period holds up well across a wide range of cultures, but his assumption that abstract, scientific reasoning is the ultimate outcome of cognitive development does not transfer to cultures in which formal schooling is rare (Dasen and Heron, 1981). Freud's and Erikson's emphasis on autonomy in toddlerhood makes sense in most European and North American cultural settings, but not in cultures in which dependency is encouraged, such as traditional Japanese culture (Doi, 1992). Bowlby's adaptational theory, with its evolutionary roots, was also intended to be culturally universal. The tendency of infants to form attachments to caregivers and the biological adaptiveness of infant–caregiver attachments do seem to be universal, but the ways attachment is manifested appear to be more culture-specific. For example, what constitutes responsive caregiving varies across cultures; North American mothers tend to wait for infants to signal their needs or distress before responding to them, whereas Japanese mothers are more likely to try to anticipate their infants' needs and structure the environment to minimize distress (Rothbaum et al., 2000). Research conducted from the perspectives of social learning and information-processing theories reveals many culture-specific developmental outcomes, even though neither theory explicitly addresses cultural issues. For example, children studying the Koran in Islamic schools in Morocco become exceptionally skilled at memorizing text, but do not develop unusual skills in other areas of cognitive development or even for other types of memory tasks (Wagner and Spratt, 1987). We will further discuss issues related to the cultural context of development in Chapter 2, and we will return to them frequently throughout the book.

RESEARCH METHODS FOR STUDYING DEVELOPMENT

Developmentalists use many research methods to gather information. Some, such as laboratory experiments, are modeled after methods used in the physical sciences. Others, such as observing people in natural settings, are more similar to procedures used in the biological sciences, in which description and classification are of major importance. Each method for studying development has its strengths and weaknesses. None is more or less scientific than the others. A method's power and meaningfulness depend on how it is used. The choice of method depends primarily on the question being asked; some questions are best approached with one procedure, other questions with entirely different techniques. Many issues must be studied with a combination of methods before they are fully understood.

Experiments

Suppose you wanted to answer the question of whether newborns have a preference for looking at human faces. You might start by watching newborns in their homes to find out what they look at. If you kept track of the time they spent looking at faces, you might tentatively conclude that babies do prefer to look at faces. This tentative conclusion is an example of a **hypothesis** about children's behavior—a testable proposition, often developed to check the validity of a particular theory.

How could you decide whether faces are more interesting than other things to newborns? The best way to test this hypothesis is with an **experiment,** a study in which the researcher controls conditions and systematically manipulates one or more variables so as to rule out all other influences except the one(s) being investigated. In the baby's home controlling all of these factors would be difficult. That is why psychologists usually study such issues in a laboratory, where they can use sophisticated equipment to determine precisely where a baby is looking and can systematically vary the stimuli presented to find out what best captures infants' attention.

In this case, the researcher would show babies a number of pairs of different stimuli of equal complexity (e.g., a normal human face, a scrambled face, a black-and-white checkerboard pattern) and observe which stimulus in each pair the babies looked at longer. If the babies look longer at normal human faces than at other equally complex stimuli when given a choice, it suggests that they do indeed have a preference for faces. Further experiments could then be done to determine what features of faces account for this preference.

Laboratory experiments have both advantages and disadvantages. In a laboratory setting, researchers have great control over the conditions under which people are tested. They can eliminate or reduce variability in factors that are not of interest in the study, and they can ensure that each person is tested under highly similar conditions. In experiments in which several conditions are compared, research participants are randomly

Hypothesis:
A testable proposition, often developed to check the validity of a theory.

Experiment:
A study in which researchers control conditions and systematically manipulate one or more factors so as to rule out all influences except the one(s) being investigated.

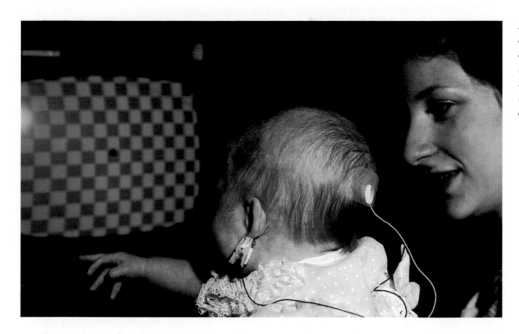

In the laboratory, researchers can control what infants experience and can measure responses precisely. Here, an infant's brain waves are being recorded as she looks at visual displays.

assigned to groups to reduce the chance that the groups will differ systematically in some way other than the factors of interest to the researcher.

However, the results of laboratory experiments are not always generalizable to everyday settings. People may behave differently in a laboratory than in natural settings, either because the lab is strange and intimidating or because they want to look good to the experimenter. In addition, laboratory settings do not always accurately reproduce the relevant aspects of everyday situations, and laboratory tasks do not always measure what they were intended to measure. *disadvantages* For example, Daryl Bem and David Funder (1978) found that children's ability to delay gratification in a laboratory (to refrain from touching an attractive toy until given permission) did not predict their ability to control impulses at school. Instead, delay of gratification in the lab predicted obedience, lack of curiosity, and submissiveness to adults in everyday situations. Apparently, the children who refrained longest from touching the toys were particularly concerned about pleasing the experimenter, rather than being particularly good at impulse control. Thus, laboratory findings may not always mean what they seem to at first. Psychologists call this the issue of **ecological validity**—the degree to which findings inside the laboratory generalize to the outside world.

When laboratory findings do generalize to everyday settings, researchers must still be cautious in drawing implications. If an experiment reveals that a certain stimulus can cause a certain response, one cannot conclude that this cause-and-effect relationship is common in the everyday world. For example, psychologist John Watson (1928) once induced a fear of rats in a little boy named Albert by repeatedly making a loud noise near the child's ear while showing him a laboratory rat. However, this does not mean that most people who fear rats do so because they have learned to associate rats with loud noises.

Another limitation of laboratory experiments is that many questions of interest to developmentalists are not open to experimentation. For instance, researchers cannot assign children to abusive conditions to observe the results, even though they are very interested in the effects of child abuse. Purposely exposing children to pain or anguish is ethically unthinkable; for this reason, Watson's study of little Albert would not be done today. Nor can researchers create certain everyday events (the birth of a sibling, a mother's decision to work outside the home) in the laboratory. This doesn't mean that these important issues can't be studied scientifically; it just means that other research methods must be used.

Ecological validity:
The degree to which experimental findings in the laboratory generalize to the outside world.

Nonexperimental Research

For research questions that cannot be studied in laboratory experiments, developmental psychologists use a variety of **nonexperimental methods.** These methods vary in the amount of control researchers have over the situation, but they all involve collecting information about people's behavior without manipulating the factors thought to be influencing it. Nonexperimental methods are also referred to as **correlational methods** because they allow researchers to examine relationships *(correlations)* among factors being studied but not to draw conclusions about causes and effects.

For example, suppose researchers observe greater conflict in families with young teenagers than in those with older teenagers and wonder whether the young teenagers might be the cause. There is no way of knowing through correlational methods whether this hypothesis is right. The fact that two factors are often found together does not necessarily mean that one *causes* the other. In England some years ago the number of storks in an area was positively correlated with the number of human births there—that is, the more storks, the more births. This does not mean that storks bring babies; instead, some third factor, related to both of the others, had to be at work. As it turned out, that factor was population density. Heavily industrialized urban areas had many large chimneys where storks liked to nest; the same areas also had large populations and consequently many babies. Similarly, some factor other than the presence of young teenagers could be causing conflict in their families.

Natural Experiments A **natural experiment** is called for when it is not possible to assign people to groups randomly, as is done in laboratory experiments. Instead, researchers compare naturally occurring groups of people. For instance, in studying communication in families with adolescents of various ages, researchers cannot take a large number of families and randomly give one-third of them a 12-year-old, one-third a 14-year-old, and one-third a 16-year-old. Instead, they must make do with the families that nature provides.

In some natural experiments, a structured task is given to members of naturally occurring groups. For example, families with adolescents of various ages could be given the task of planning a family vacation. In other natural experiments, the impact of a naturally occurring event, such as the adoption of children from Romanian orphanages by North American families, is studied.

One major advantage of natural experiments is that they allow psychologists to study issues that cannot be studied in laboratory experiments. Another advantage is that they generally provide greater ecological validity than laboratory experiments do—that is, their results are more likely to be generalizable to everyday life.

The major disadvantage of natural experiments is that they offer researchers less control than laboratory experiments. There is always the possibility that naturally occurring groups differ in unexpected ways other than the variable of interest. For instance, families with adolescents of varying ages may also vary in the amount of time they spend together; differences in family communication might be due *either* to the ages of the adolescents *or* to the amount of time family members spend together. To minimize the chance that some factor other than the adolescents' ages is influencing family communication, the researchers could select families that are similar in many ways, such as parental income, marital satisfaction, and number of children. However, it is generally impossible to find naturally occurring groups that differ *only* on the variable(s) of interest.

Naturalistic Observation One method frequently used by developmental psychologists is to observe behavior in everyday settings as it occurs naturally, a technique called **naturalistic observation.** For example, suppose you wanted to find out whether preschoolers have more conflicts during play with siblings or with friends. You could bring children into a laboratory with siblings and friends, give them tasks to complete, and count how many conflicts they had. However, the laboratory setting might change the nature of their interactions, and the tasks you gave them might not be typical of the

---

Nonexperimental methods:
Research methods in which information about behavior is collected without manipulating the factors thought to be influencing it.

Correlational methods:
Research methods that allow researchers to examine relationships among factors but not to draw conclusions about causes and effects.

Natural experiment:
An observational method in which researchers compare groups of people who differ naturally on the factors being studied.

Naturalistic observation:
A research method in which naturally occuring behavior is observed in everyday settings.

Observation in natural settings is more likely than laboratory research to capture the way children usually behave.

things they usually did together. To find out how much conflict they *typically* had with siblings and friends, you would have to observe them in a more natural setting.

This approach to research has a long history. In the 19th Century it was used by Darwin; more recently, it has been central to a field of study called **ethology,** which seeks to understand animal behavior through careful observation of species in their natural habitats. One example is Jane Goodall's research on chimpanzee social behavior. The information about free-ranging chimps that she collected through years of observation in East African forests could never have been obtained by studying chimps in a laboratory. Anthropologists have also made extensive use of naturalistic observation to study behavior in a wide range of cultural settings around the world.

Much research on human development also uses the technique of naturalistic observation. Researchers go to homes, schools, and playgrounds to watch and record the everyday behavior of children and adults. At times they try to simulate natural settings in their own research rooms. For instance, they might create an attractive playroom, bring in a group of children to play, and observe or videotape the children through a one-way mirror, so as not to interfere with their behavior.

In all the settings where naturalistic observations take place, researchers are precise and systematic in recording what they see. They count the frequencies of particular behaviors, note sequences as they occur, and rate the people observed for qualitative factors such as mood or level of enthusiasm. Sophisticated automated devices are also used for keeping records, and behavior is often audio- or videotaped for later analysis. This careful recording of data distinguishes trained psychologists from casual observers. Psychologists do not just watch and try to remember but are constantly keeping an account, usually in quantitative form (e.g., the number of times a child pushes another or offers to share a toy, or the number of times a child asks an adult for assistance or the adult gives assistance without being asked).

Naturalistic observation has the advantage of describing human behavior in real-life situations; its ecological validity tends to be high. Naturalistic observation is therefore very useful for studying many socially relevant issues. Its main disadvantage is low researcher control over the situation. Variables other than those of primary interest may influence people's behavior and affect the results of the study, and it is hard to make sure that the conditions under which different people are observed are really comparable.

Ethology:

A field of study relying on observation of species in their natural habitats, in order to understand patterns of behavior and their functions.

Survey Research Some questions of interest to developmental psychologists cannot be answered by experimental or observational techniques. Some behaviors are relatively infrequent or too private to lend themselves to naturalistic observation. In other cases, researchers are interested in people's perceptions of situations, such as parents' perceptions of their children's behavior or children's perceptions of their relationships with their friends. Often, these questions can be studied by means of **survey research,** using interviews or questionnaires to collect information.

Survey research can involve giving questionnaires to large numbers of randomly selected participants to find out the prevalence of behaviors in a population, as in the Monitoring the Future Study, an annual survey on adolescent drug use (Johnston, O'Malley, and Bachman, 2002). Or it can involve interviews with much smaller numbers of participants addressing more specific research questions, as in studies of children's perceptions of their relationship networks (Furman and Buhrmester, 1992).

Some advantages of survey research are that it provides access to information that could not be gained by any other method, and large amounts of data can be collected relatively cheaply and quickly. One disadvantage is that it provides information about people's perceptions or recollections of events rather than direct access to the events themselves. In addition, people's responses on questionnaires or interviews may be affected by a desire to appear socially acceptable, to impress, or to shock the researcher.

Combining Observation and Experimentation

To understand some aspects of development, researchers often go back and forth between experimental and nonexperimental approaches. Suppose observation suggests that family conflict is to some degree caused by parents' failure to appreciate teenagers' growing competence and desire for independence (Collins, 1990). An experiment could be done in which one group of parents was informed about these changes in adolescents and the signs that the changes were taking place, while another group of parents was not so informed. If the informed group later showed less family conflict than the noninformed group, we would have evidence supporting the observational hypothesis.

Consider another example of the complementary use of observational and experimental approaches. Based on observation, animal researchers hypothesized that the tendency of babies to cling to their mothers is a genetically based behavior that helps protect them. Staying close to the mother is not learned because she provides food; it is a built-in behavior related to the security she gives. Harry Harlow conducted an experiment to test this hypothesis. He found that baby monkeys separated from their real mothers would cling to a soft terrycloth surrogate mother that did not dispense food in preference to a wire surrogate mother that did (Harlow and Harlow, 1966). Harlow's experiment showed that feeding by a mother is not necessary for a baby to form an attachment. Other researchers built on this finding, again using observation. Observing interactions between infants and their mothers, they began to clarify how mother-infant attachments develop in natural settings.

Studying Change Over Time

One problem peculiar to developmental research is how to study changes that occur and factors that influence behavior over time. For example, developmental psychologists want to know whether entering full-time day care as a very young baby affects outcomes later in childhood. To answer this question, researchers would have to conduct a natural experiment with a long time span. They would have to assess how day-care versus home-reared children fare from infancy through a number of years in childhood and perhaps adolescence. How do developmentalists go about making such assessments?

One way is to follow the same people over a designated time period, in a **longitudinal study.** To study the effects of early day care, researchers might select one group of babies whose parents placed them in day care by the age of six months and another group whose parents raised them at home for the first year and a half. They would try to choose families similar on such characteristics as socioeconomic level, current marital status and satisfaction, and attitudes toward child rearing. In this way, they could have some confidence that the choice of day care or home care would be the major difference between the two groups. Periodically, the researchers would interview the parents and assess the children's emotional adjustment, social skills, and cognitive growth. Each assessment would allow them to compare how the two groups were developing. If they wanted to follow these children through early adolescence, this study would take about fourteen years.

A faster way to investigate this issue would be to conduct a **cross-sectional study,** in which groups of people of different ages are studied at the same time. In this case, the researchers would select a sample of children ranging in age from 1 to 14 years. Half the children at each age would have been placed in day care by age six months; the other half would have been raised at home during infancy. Again, the researchers would try to match the families on factors such as socioeconomic level and social support. Then they would assess children looked after in day care versus those reared at home in the 1-year-old group, the 2-year-old group, the 3-year-old group, and so on.

Cross-sectional and longitudinal studies both have advantages and disadvantages. Cross-sectional studies can be done more quickly and cheaply, which is often an important practical consideration. However, they are limited in what they can reveal about development. They show what children of different ages are like, but they cannot show the *process* of development, the path from one developmental phase to the next. Because cross-sectional findings are statistics about groups examined at a single point in time, they reveal nothing about individual development. The study of physical growth provides a good example. If you were to plot the average height of boys at ages 11 to 18, the resulting curve would be smooth and steady, as shown in Figure 1.2. Such a curve, however, would not be a good indicator of an individual boy's growth over these years. Individual children grow at different rates and have growth spurts at different ages; the individual growth curves in Figure 1.2 show a growth spurt for one boy between ages 12 and 13, for another between ages 13 and 14, and for a third between ages 15 and 16. Individual differences in physical growth can be discovered only by studying the same children over time.

Another disadvantage of cross-sectional studies is a problem known as a **cohort effect.** A cohort effect occurs when a difference between groups in a cross-sectional study

Cross-sectional study:
A study comparing groups of people of different ages at the same time.

Cohort effect:
In a cross-sectional study, a difference between age groups due to a peculiarity in one of the groups being studied rather than to a general developmental difference.

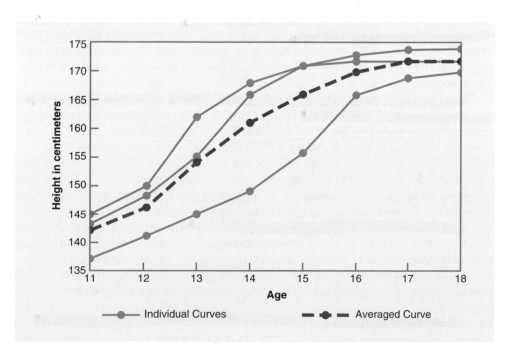

Figure 1.2
COMPARISON OF INDIVIDUAL AND AVERAGED GROWTH CURVES.
(Source: Based on information in Tanner, 1990.)

reflects a peculiarity in one of the age groups (or *cohorts*) being studied, rather than a general developmental difference. For example, children born during a period of war, civil unrest, or economic hardship often show different patterns of physical and social development than children born just a few years earlier or later (e.g., Elder, 1999). Comparing children from these cohorts might yield information about the effects of the unusual events they experienced, but it would not tell us very much about development in general.

The biggest disadvantage of longitudinal studies is that they are expensive and time-consuming. They also suffer from the problem of **subject attrition,** or the loss of study participants over time. Over the course of a longitudinal study, participants may move away, lose interest in the study, become too busy to continue their involvement, or even die.

A major advantage of longitudinal studies is that they *can* be used to track individual development over time and to examine processes of development. *Prospective* longitudinal studies, in which children are followed from early in life, before any developmental problems have appeared, provide an unparalleled opportunity to study the processes involved in individual development. By following the same children over time, researchers can get ideas about how the same capacity is shown in different ways at different ages and how changes in individual functioning occur. The box on page 33 provides details on one such study, the Minnesota Longitudinal Study.

Developmentalists rely on a combination of cross-sectional and longitudinal methods to overcome the disadvantages of each approach. Sometimes they even combine the two in the same study. For example, in an **accelerated longitudinal design,** researchers simultaneously follow several age groups over a period of time. If you started with groups of 1-, 4-, 7-, and 10-year-olds and followed them for three years, you would cover a developmental span of thirteen years in a much shorter time frame. You would be able to demonstrate that observed changes were developmental changes and not merely cohort effects if you could show that your new 4-year-olds (the original 1-year-olds three years later) were comparable to the original 4-year-old group. You could also test whether individual performance at each age was predicted by performance at the earlier age.

THE THEMES OF THIS BOOK

In this chapter we have introduced four important themes. First, *development is characterized by both change and continuity*. Change is sometimes minor and gradual, at other times fundamental and dramatic. But even in the case of major qualitative changes, there are logical connections between past and present. What was there previously is the foundation for what emerges next.

Second, *within a framework of normative development, each child shows a unique pattern of individual development*. Each child goes through the same major developmental phases, on roughly the same timetable. In other words, most children follow the norms of human development. Yet each child is also a unique individual, in some ways different from every other, because of his or her genetic makeup and developmental history. Individual development, like normative development, unfolds in a coherent manner, with continuity between past and present. A particular child's current patterns of behavior are an outgrowth of that child's previous patterns of behavior.

Third, *context plays a critical role in development*. The particular circumstances in which children find themselves influence the timing of normative developmental changes and the unique patterns of individual development. In trying to understand human development, we must consider the total developmental context, which includes genetic makeup, current environment (physical, social, and cultural), and previous developmental history.

Fourth, *cognitive and social development work together in one integrated process*. Although this book has separate chapters on cognitive and social development, that

Subject attrition:
In a longitudinal study, the loss of participants over time.

Minnesota Longitudinal Study

Accelerated longitudinal design:
A type of longitudinal study in which researchers simultaneously follow several age groups over a period of time.

A CLOSER LOOK

A PROSPECTIVE LONGITUDINAL STUDY

One example of a prospective longitudinal study is the Minnesota Longitudinal Study, which began in 1976 and has followed a group of children of low-income parents from birth into adulthood. The goal was to examine the impacts of early relationship experiences on later functioning. Over the years, the children's behavior has been studied at home, at school, in a summer day camp, and in the laboratory. They have been observed alone, with their mothers, with peers, and with other adults. They have been interviewed, and their mothers and teachers have completed questionnaires about their behavior.

Particular strengths of the Minnesota Longitudinal Study include:

- *Adequate sample size.* The 180 children in the study form a sample large enough for examination of a number of potential developmental influences, yet small enough for detailed data collection. A larger sample would allow analysis of even more influences, whereas a smaller sample would allow even more detailed observations. There are always trade-offs between sample size and comprehensiveness of measurement.
- *Duration of study.* Beginning early in life allows examination of inborn differences before they have been dramatically influenced by experience and makes it possible to test whether earliest experiences are of special importance. Following the participants to maturity allows study of outcomes of great interest that cannot be studied in childhood, such as styles of romantic relationships and psychological problems that emerge in late adolescence or early adulthood.
- *Comprehensiveness of measures.* Temperament, quality of care, IQ, language development, peer relationships, school achievement, and a variety of other domains were assessed. Without a broad range of measures, it

is difficult to draw conclusions about the influence of early experience on later development. If quality of care in infancy is found to be related to later peer behavior, for example, it is useful to be able to judge whether the link between these two variables can be explained by some third factor, such as inborn differences in temperament. (Maybe calm, easygoing babies elicit good care from their mothers and also get along well with other children later on.) With comprehensive measures, such issues can be at least partially resolved by statistically taking into consideration relevant third factors.

- *Theoretical underpinnings.* An underlying theory lends focus to a study of this size. In the Minnesota study, researchers tested hypotheses based on Bowlby's adaptational theory—for example, that children who were secure in their attachments in infancy would be more confident than other children later on. Without theoretical guidance, it would be difficult to decide which connections to investigate among the thousands of pieces of data gathered in the study.
- *Attention to context.* Assessing contextual factors for the children in the study, such as the stress experienced by their families and the social support available to them, makes it possible to think of causes of developmental outcomes in complex ways. For example, it was found that insensitive care received by some infants in this study was related to high stress experienced by their parents. When the stress lessened or support increased, parents were often able to be more responsive to their children and the children's behavior improved accordingly. Such findings make it clear that it is too simplistic to conclude that parent behavior by itself causes a particular outcome.

division is not meant to imply that these two areas are unrelated. Developmental changes in children's thinking are always closely related to developmental changes in how children interact with other people, and interacting with others frequently triggers changes in how children think.

To help illustrate these major themes, throughout this book we present three family case histories that focus on the lives of four individual children. Although the stories are fictionalized, they are based on composites of actual cases drawn from the authors' research experience, with consultation from ethnic minority psychologists. A new chapter in the case histories appears at the beginning of each part of the book. We also use the cases to illustrate specific points in the text.

When you first meet the families at the beginning of Part One, the future mothers are either pregnant or considering having a child. Each family lives in different circumstances. Throughout the book, as the four children develop from infants to adolescents, their family situations change as they go through good times and bad. You will see how changing life circumstances influence children and how individual children respond to various challenges. By getting to know these families, by seeing in a tangible way how individuals unfold within a context, we believe that you will be better able to understand the theories and findings of developmental psychology presented in this book.

At the end of each part is an Epilogue, in which we tie the content of the chapters to the lives of the children we are following. We think this structure will not only help you better remember the material you are learning, but it will also give you a more life-like and holistic picture of developing children. Although the facts and theories of child development are interesting in themselves, we believe that they can be even more fascinating when connected to the lives of four developing children.

Chapter Summary

Introduction

Development in childhood and adolescence consists of change that is orderly, cumulative, and directional. Our developmental perspective assumes that

- development involves **qualitative changes** as well as **quantitative changes;**
- children's later abilities, behavior, and understanding of the world emerge from earlier ones in a systematic way; and
- each individual's development is coherent over time, reflecting continuity as well as change.

Basic Developmental Concepts

Basic developmental concepts include qualitative change and normative and individual development.

- **Qualitative change,** found throughout development, occurs as children's skills are reorganized to produce new and increasingly complex thoughts and behaviors.
- **Normative development** refers to the general age-related changes in behavior that virtually all children share.
- **Individual development** refers to individual variation around normative development and to continuity in each child's individual developmental pathway.

A Framework for Understanding Development

Three factors—*genes, developmental history,* and *current environmental conditions*—combine to shape the course of development. Philosophers and psychologists have debated the relative roles of these factors for hundreds of years.

- Darwin's theory of **evolution** proposed that each species is equipped for survival and reproduction in its particular environment because of the process of **natural selection.** Evolutionary theory has contributed to the study of human development by identifying the adaptive significance of various human behaviors. Both the general course of human development and the

particular requirements for the adequate development of children derive from our evolutionary heritage as a species.
- Philosophical approaches to the nature-nurture question have included Locke's view of the child as a *tabula rasa* and Rousseau's concept of the naturally positive unfolding of human development.
- All contemporary researchers agree that it is important to consider genes and environment in interaction. Genetic influences can unfold only within an environmental context, and environmental influences need a base of genetic potentials to work on. Developmental history influences what potentials are drawn upon and how the environment is engaged and interpreted. The major issue today is exactly how genes, developmental history, and environment interact.

Theoretical Perspectives on Development

Psychologists have proposed a number of theories to explain human development.

- A **theory** is an organized set of ideas about how things operate, an attempt to account for past observations and to predict future ones. Theories provide a framework for interpreting specific facts and research findings and give direction to scientific research.
- The validity of a theory can be judged on three criteria:
    - It must be sensible and consistent.
    - It must organize, integrate, and make understandable a body of research findings.
    - It must be specific enough to be testable.
- Some theories of human development seek to describe and explain normative development; others focus on individual development.
- Some theories emphasize cognitive development. Piaget's theory focuses on major qualitative changes in the way children think. **Information-processing theory** focuses on gradual changes over time in memory abilities and skills

for solving problems. **Sociocultural theory** emphasizes the role played by social interaction and specific cultural practices in the development of cognitive skills.

- Other theories emphasize social and emotional development. **Psychoanalytic theory** emphasizes the power of early emotional experiences to influence later behavior. **Social learning theory** emphasizes gradual changes in behavior through direct reinforcement and observation of other people. Bowlby's **adaptational theory** combines ideas from psychoanalytic theory, cognitive theories, and evolutionary theory to explain the quality and impact of early attachment relationships.
- Developmental psychology has many theories because different theories focus on different aspects of development, and psychologists' knowledge of human development is a work in progress.

Major Issues in Development

Three major issues in developmental psychology are

- Gradual development versus stages;
- Early versus current experiences; and
- Specificity versus generality.

Research Methods for Studying Development

Researchers use a number of methods to study human development:

- In an **experiment** they systematically manipulate one or more factors in an effort to rule out all other influences on behavior except the ones being studied.

- For research questions that cannot be studied experimentally, researchers use **nonexperimental** or **correlational methods.** These include **natural experiments,** in which they compare groups that differ naturally on some factor, **naturalistic observation,** in which researchers systematically observe and record behavior as it naturally occurs, and **survey research,** in which they collect information using interviews or questionnaires.
- To observe change over time, developmentalists may use a **longitudinal study,** in which a group of people is followed over time. To study age differences, researchers may conduct a **cross-sectional study,** comparing groups of people of different ages at the same time. In an **accelerated longitudinal design,** researchers combine these two methods by following several age groups over time simultaneously.

The Themes of This Book

This book has four important themes:

- Development is characterized by both change and continuity.
- Individual development occurs within a framework of normative developmental patterns.
- Context plays a critical role in development.
- Cognitive and social development work together in one integrated process.

Review Questions

Introduction

1. What are the basic characteristics of **development?**

Basic Developmental Concepts

2. Explain and give examples of **behavioral reorganization, normative development,** and **individual development.**

A Framework for Understanding Development

3. How do genetic potentials, developmental history, and environmental conditions interact to produce developmental changes?
4. Explain how Darwin's, Locke's, and Rousseau's views are relevant to child development.

Theoretical Perspectives on Development

5. Explain the major functions of scientific **theories** and how their validity can be tested.

6. Compare and contrast the major characteristics of the six theories of human development discussed in this chapter (Piaget's theory, **information-processing theory, sociocultural theory, psychoanalytic theory, social learning theory,** and **adaptational theory**).

Major Issues in Development

7. Explain the issues involved in the questions of gradual development versus stages, early versus current experiences, and specificity versus generality.

Research Methods for Studying Development

8. Explain the differences between **experiments, natural experiments, naturalistic observation,** and **survey research,** and summarize the advantages and disadvantages of each.
9. Explain the research methods used to study behavior over time, and summarize the advantages and disadvantages of each.

Application and Observation

1. Describe your own development since infancy, since early childhood, since elementary school, since adolescence, and since starting college. If possible, look at photos of yourself at various ages. Which of your characteristics have changed? Which have stayed more or less the same? How would you explain both the changes and the stability?

2. Make two lists of traits (physical and psychological/behavioral): those that you share with other members of your family (immediate or extended) and those that are distinctive to you, compared to other family members. How do you think genetic and environmental factors have influenced the development of each of the traits you listed?

3. Think about metaphors for children and their development by completing the following sentence in as many different ways as you can: "Children are like_____." What do the metaphors you choose reveal about your assumptions about children and about development? How do your assumptions compare to those underlying the theories discussed in this chapter?

4. Try your hand at naturalistic observation. Find a setting in which you can unobtrusively observe children (of any age that interests you) interacting with each other or with their families. Possible settings include school or day care classrooms, playgrounds, fast-food restaurants, grocery stores, skating rinks, or even at home with siblings or friends. (Be sure to ask permission where appropriate.) First, simply observe one child or a group of children for 5–10 minutes and try to write down everything about their behavior that seems important to you. Next, choose one specific question you'd like to address with observation and decide what you need to record about the children's behavior that would help answer your question. Be systematic and limit what you record, perhaps by tallying how often particular behaviors occur. When you're done, describe what each observation experience was like and assess the usefulness of the information you were able to write down during each period of observation.

Beginnings

Part 1 Introducing Three Families

John and Delores Williams

"Three twenty-two . . . four seventy . . . sixty-eight cents . . . Your total is two hundred thirty-nine dollars and fifty-seven cents," the supermarket cashier said, staring blankly at Delores Williams from behind strands of dyed blond hair. Delores looked at her husband John in disbelief. "Two hundred and thirty-nine dollars," she repeated, as if to make sure he had heard. How could food for the family cost so much? Granted, 11-year-old John, Jr., ate like a horse. "Be sure to get some broccoli for dinner," John's mother, Momma Jo, had teased, knowing that JJ hated broccoli. "Then there'll be something left for the rest of us to eat." But 8-year-old Teresa hardly ate anything at all. And John's sister Denise skipped a lot of meals. She was always running off to her part-time job or one of her college courses. So how did they need $239 worth of groceries for a week? It didn't seem possible.

"Let me see that receipt," Delores demanded, as they walked toward the curb. "There's gotta be somethin' wrong. I only have twenty dollars left over to last the rest of the week! What's gonna happen when we have to start buyin' diapers and formula? Do you know how much those things cost? How are we gonna pay for this baby? What a mistake this whole thing is!"

"A mistake?" John stopped the shopping cart abruptly. "Come on now, DeeDee. This is our child you're talkin' about. We're gonna manage. Why, look how my momma managed when my poppa died. Black teachers in Mississippi didn't make nothin' in those days. But she worked hard and she did it. She saved enough to move us here to Chicago and things got better. We'll both keep workin', and Momma'll watch the baby."

DeeDee looked at him doubtfully. She didn't want to struggle like John's mother had struggled. Already she felt tired. Too tired even to try. The thought of juggling a baby, her job at the telephone company, and all the demands of the rest of the family was overwhelming. Her voice grew quiet, dis-couraged. "I guess I'm worried too about whether the baby's gonna be all right. I'm *thirty-six*. What am I doin' pregnant again?"

"Honey," John said, more gently now, "we've been over and over this. You'll get the test next month and it'll tell us everything's OK. But even if there's somethin' wrong, it don't matter. We made this baby together and together we're gonna love him, and raise him, and *pay* for him. We've just got to take things one step at a time. So stop talkin' this 'It ain't no good, it ain't gonna work' stuff. You've been playin' those tunes for weeks now. Get rid of them and start playin' some new ones."

DeeDee looked at John and started to smile, but a sudden squeal of brakes made her turn around. Already a small crowd was gathering around a young woman who lay on the parking lot pavement. Pale and dazed, she was trying to prop herself up, but her ankle was oddly twisted. Her arms and legs looked frail and thin next to her obviously pregnant belly. "The baby," she said. "My God, the baby!"

DeeDee stared. The thought of losing a baby struck her suddenly, of having a child slip away before you can even see it and hold it. Of course she wanted this baby. It was part of her already, part of both her and John. She wanted it more than anything else in the world.

The driver of the car was bending over the injured woman. "Lady, are you all right? I was just backing up. I was watching where I was going. I swear to God I was. But you fell right into the car. Are you OK? Is someone calling a doctor? For God's sake, let's get an ambulance here!"

DeeDee felt an urge to go to the woman, to try to comfort her. But what would this white woman think of a strange black woman stepping out of the crowd? DeeDee didn't care. She walked over and knelt beside her.

"You'll be OK," she said gently. "You didn't fall very hard. I think it's just your ankle. Why don't you lie back on my sweater here and try to relax. Someone's gone to call an ambulance."

The woman's head sank into the green softness of DeeDee's sweater. "Thanks," she answered gratefully, the fear starting to fade from her face. "It's just . . . this is my first baby."

"I know," said DeeDee. Her voice was almost a whisper. "You don't have to explain to me. I'm pregnant, too."

The woman looked at DeeDee and smiled. She reached out her hand and lightly touched DeeDee's wrist. And though DeeDee knew it wasn't possible at such an early stage, she had the sense that she could feel the new life inside her.

Frank and Christine Gordon

"Hey! Way to go! Strike that turkey out! What an arm that guy has," Frank Gordon exclaimed to his wife's brothers-in-law as he rose from his chair in front of the TV set to reach for another beer. Like everyone else in Pawtucket, Rhode Island, he was an avid Red Sox fan.

"Hey, Paula. Game's over. Let's get goin'," Dan shouted to his wife five minutes later.

"Yeah, we're gonna shove off too," Chuck added. "I gotta be on the job early tomorrow."

The three men sauntered into the kitchen, leaving behind a chaos of pizza boxes, beer cans, and potato chip bags. Their wives sat around the small kitchen table, laughing and talking over mugs of coffee.

"You'd think you girls never got to see each other, the way you three go on," Frank commented, as he tossed Dan and Chuck their jackets. Paula, Sarah, and Christine rose reluctantly from the table and carried their mugs to the sink. Then Paula and Sarah went into the back bedroom, each to collect a sleeping child.

"See ya soon, Chrissie," they said to their sister, as they picked their way carefully down the dimly lit back steps. As usual, Dan and Chuck were already in their cars, revving the engines, anxious to be off.

Usually on a weeknight after a ball game Frank would head for the bedroom, leaving Christine to clean up. But tonight he hung around. "You're lookin' good, Chrissie," he said, catching hold of her arm as she passed by. "You could get in trouble lookin' like that."

"I don't know that I want to get in trouble," Christine answered, with an uneasy laugh, knowing exactly what Frank had in mind. "You know I'm not so sure about having another baby just yet."

"What's not to be sure about? We have a girl; we want a boy. You've said so yourself. Maggie's gonna be two before we know it, and she needs a baby brother. It's as simple as that."

"Yeah, I know. But . . . well, I've been kind of thinking about getting a job at the dress shop where Paula works."

"Oh, geez, here we go again. Look, Chrissie, I'm not gonna get into another big thing about this. I don't want you workin' and that's that. You belong here at home with Maggie. I can support this family just fine."

"That's not really it, Frank," Christine replied. "I was watching this program on TV this morning, you know? And they were talking about how important it is for a woman to have a sense of really doing something, you know? Accomplishing something . . ."

"So selling dresses to a bunch of broads is accomplishing something and raising your own kids isn't? Is that what you're tryin' to tell me? I swear I can't figure you out. What more do you want for accomplishment? You've got a cute little girl, a decent apartment, a bunch of fancy gadgets in the kitchen. What's this job of yours gonna get us that we don't already have? Tell me that. I'll tell you what it's *not* gonna get us. It's not gonna get us a son."

"Well, I don't know," Christine answered. "You know, I just think it's something we have to talk about more."

"So we're talkin' about it now. What more do you want?"

Christine wondered what more she did want. It wasn't really something she could put her finger on. Just a vague idea about someday maybe having her own dress shop. Everyone said she had a real flair for clothes. But when she tried to picture getting from her life as it was now to running her own business, the whole thing seemed impossible. If I had really wanted to be a businesswoman, Christine thought, I wouldn't have been so quick to marry Frank right after high school.

Christine looked at her wedding picture on top of the TV. A thin, pretty girl of 19 looked back from beneath a lacy white veil. Beside her was Frank, with an air of self-assurance even at 24. The happiest day of her life, she had thought back then. Frank was so handsome he made her the envy of all her friends. Christine's father, Mike, had encouraged the match. He said that Frank was the first real man Christine had dated. "He's not like some of those college wimps you've brought home lately," he told her. "You'd be crazy not to hang onto that guy." And hang on Christine did. She built her life around Frank—around his strength, his decisiveness, his self-confidence. He made this once-shy girl feel like the most desirable woman on earth.

"You know what more I want?" Christine said, staring down at the carpet and slowly looking up. "I want us to feel real close. Remember? Like we used to?"

"Hey. We're married. Five years. How could we be closer?"

"Well, there's having another baby together, I guess," Christine answered. "Raising a little all-star for the Red Sox. What more in life could you accomplish, huh?"

"Now you're thinkin' right!" Frank said, failing to notice the lingering note of doubt in her voice.

"You're doing great, Chrissie," said the large, gray-haired nurse with the ruddy complexion and clear blue eyes. "I didn't have this easy a time until my fifth baby."

Christine's lips and mouth felt too dry from her breathing exercises to respond with more than a faint smile. But the nurse was right. This delivery was incredibly easy compared with her first. She felt enormous pressure with each contraction, but not the excruciating pain that had accompanied Maggie's birth. In fact, the whole pregnancy had been easy. Despite her large size in the last trimester, she had felt wonderful. "Sit down. Take it easy," other people would tell her, and Christine would wonder why. She felt like repainting the whole apartment, not sitting around with her feet up.

"It must be a boy," she said to the nurse, after a particularly strong contraction. "Just like his father. Can't wait to get going." She looked over at Frank, who stood by the door, looking nervous and ill-at-ease.

"We'll find out soon," the doctor said. "I can see the head crowning. Push *hard* this time, Christine. Push!"

The details of what happened next were difficult for Christine to remember later. She became totally absorbed in the act of pushing her new baby into the world. With her eyes intently focused on a small spot of sunlight on the ceiling, the voices around her seemed at a distance, muffled and indistinct. A final push, and she felt the baby emerging. Joy flooded her body, like the rush of some intoxicating drug. Then she heard Frank's voice, loud and excited: "What is it? What is it?"

"What a beautiful baby," the nurse said, as she took the baby from the doctor.

"But is it a boy? Tell me, is it a *boy?*"

Karen Polonius

When the bell rang announcing the end of class, 16-year-old Karen Polonius quickly gathered up her belongings and was the first person out the door. She practically ran down the corridor to her locker, whirled the combination, and tugged open the door. Reaching into the jumble of school books and discarded candy wrappers, she grabbed what she needed for her homework assignments and rushed out the side exit. The number 6 bus was at the corner, just ready to pull away. Karen jumped on. Now she relaxed a little. Sliding into a seat, she unwrapped a stick of gum and gazed aimlessly out the window. All too soon she reached her stop. She got off and walked the two short blocks east. Here she was. There was no more putting it off. Taking a deep breath, she pushed open the glass door and stepped inside the building. The sign overhead read: Fresno Family Planning Clinic.

Karen sat down and began nervously poking through a stack of magazines, waiting to be called. So what if she felt a little queasy in the mornings and her period was six weeks late. It might just be because she was frightened. Jeff did use condoms, after all. Except for just once or twice. But that couldn't be enough to get her pregnant, could it?

Karen felt numb as she sat in Dr. Rich's office, listening to his sympathetic voice. "As I see it, Karen, you have several choices. You can go through with the pregnancy and give up the baby for adoption. . . ." This can't be happening, Karen thought. It's *got* to be a mistake. Or maybe it's an April Fool's joke. That's it! Today's April first. Dr. Rich's voice droned on: "At this early stage there would be little risk to you in removing the products of conception, but going this route would of course depend on your personal beliefs." What did he mean "the products of conception"? Does he mean the baby? He *must* mean the baby.

The trip home was a blur for Karen. All she could remember clearly was fumbling in her bag for her keys as she stood on the doorstep in the late afternoon shadows. Thank God her mother wasn't home from work yet. She could go upstairs and try to get herself together.

"Maybe Mom won't even notice anything's the matter," Karen said to herself as she flopped onto her bed. Mom was always preoccupied these days trying to sell those dumb houses to those stupid people. Well, maybe she shouldn't knock it. It hadn't been easy for Mom since the divorce. Dad was almost always late with the support payments, and sometimes he didn't send them at all. "What did I tell you? Men are no damn good. They only think of themselves," Karen's mother would say when the end of the month came and went and no check had arrived in the mail. "I hope Mom's not right," Karen prayed, as she picked up the phone to call Jeff.

Karen wasn't sure how Jeff would react when she broke the news to him. But she wasn't prepared for what happened. Jeff, usually so cool and easygoing, panicked. And Karen's mention of possible marriage only made things worse.

"Married? Are you *crazy?* I'm not ready to get married. I don't know about you, but *I'm* going to college. And what about law school, huh? I'm not gonna ruin my life!" There was an icy silence. "I'm telling you, Karen," Jeff finally said, barely containing his anger, "if you keep trying to push this fatherhood thing on me, I'll swear it's not my kid."

So much for Mr. Wonderful, Karen thought bitterly, as she ripped the pictures of Jeff off her bedroom wall. Mom was right. Men are no damn good. But what was she going to do now? Have an abortion? No, she couldn't destroy her own baby. But what then? Adoption? Could she really give away a part of herself?

It took Karen two weeks to summon the courage to tell her mother what the problem was. By then she had decided: She was going to keep the baby.

Karen's mother was incredulous. She stood there with the potato peeler poised in midair, as if she couldn't believe what she was hearing. Then she got angry. "How could you do such a dumb thing? Didn't I tell you to be careful when you went out with that guy? Well, you can't keep the baby. That's all there is to it. The idea's *ridiculous!*"

Karen exploded. She was sick and tired of people telling her she was crazy or ridiculous. "Damn it, Mom! It's *my* body and *my* baby. For once in my life I'm gonna make a decision without other people telling me what to do. Make love! Have an abortion! I've had it with all of you. I'm gonna love this baby and this baby's gonna love me. And nobody's ever gonna hurt my baby the way they've hurt me!"

Karen was crying now and nearly hysterical. She ran out the back door, with her mother calling behind her. "Karen, come back here! Come back!"

Karen lay on her bed, the autumn sunlight streaming through the window and forming geometric patterns on the folds of the blue-flowered sheets. Only one thought occupied her mind this morning: How in the world was she going to get up? It was as if she no longer had any stomach muscles with which to pull herself into a sitting position. She decided to dangle her legs over the side of the bed and slide out. She edged her way to the side of the bed, holding her pregnant belly, as if carrying the baby in her hands. Suddenly, a small foot sharply kicked her left palm. Karen pulled her hand back quickly. She didn't like it when the baby kicked so hard. The sensation of her own flesh rippling and bulging bothered her.

Karen lay still for a minute, until the baby finally stopped moving. She was just about to resume her shuffle to the side of the bed, when an intense pain gripped her abdomen. It encircled her like a large belt being pulled tighter and tighter. Karen gasped and struggled to sit up. The baby wasn't due for another two weeks. What was happening? The pain grew worse, until it seemed to envelop her body. Karen began to panic. This wasn't the way it was *supposed* to happen. Everyone had told her labor would start slowly, giving her time to get control. This sudden, agonizing pain was not what she expected. As Karen lay gripped by the strong contraction, she felt a warm wetness slowly soaking the mattress beneath her. Oh, no, she thought. My water must have broken! How could this all be happening so fast? And then she began screaming: "Mom! *Mom!*"

Four Children in Context

One baby has already entered the world, joining a two-year-old sister, and two more are soon to be born. These four children will encounter different circumstances that will help to shape their lives. John and DeeDee's child will face economic struggles and the challenges of being black, growing up in an inner city. This child, however, will also have a very supportive family, with strong ties of love and commitment. Although DeeDee voices concern about paying for another child, she feels deep down that the baby is a cherished addition to her life.

Christine Gordon is more ambivalent about having another baby. Nevertheless, she finally agrees to become pregnant, largely in the hope of giving Frank the son he wants. Christine hopes that a son will renew feelings of closeness in her marriage. This child will enter a family-centered environment, where traditional sex roles are accepted as the natural order of things.

Karen Polonius, in contrast, does not even have a chance to try out the traditional role of wife. Her baby will be born to a mother who herself is still in many ways a child. Inexperienced at motherhood and lacking emotional support from others, Karen faces a difficult time ahead.

How the course of development is influenced by life circumstances is a major theme of this book. The fictional characters you have just met face different situations, which in turn will affect their children. All have certain things in common: they are English-speaking, live in the urban United States, and are of moderate means. Despite this common ground, however, enough differences exist among these families for them to raise children who are in many ways different from each other. By reading about the lives of these four children, we hope you can better appreciate the influence of family and other contextual factors on development.

We also hope you will better appreciate the two-way interaction between child and environment. Children are affected by the circumstances around them, but they also influence those circumstances. As a child's individual style emerges over time, that style has an impact on those who are important in the child's world. Lives unfold amid a constant interplay of person and environment. You will witness this process in the lives of our four children.

2 The Contexts of Development

If you want a seed to develop into a normal, healthy plant, you must give it appropriate soil, light, and moisture. The quality of these environmental factors, along with characteristics of the seed itself, will determine how it grows and matures. All living things develop in an environment—a *context*—and, as we suggested in Chapter 1, the nature of that context plays a critical role in development. This is as true of humans as it is of other species. Human development, both physical and psychological, requires an appropriate context for its unfolding. If that context is abnormal, development may be, too.

Evidence for this comes from the occasional discovery of a child who has been isolated from human contact for years. One such child, a boy of about 12, was found in a forest in Aveyron, France, in 1799. Newspapers called him "the wild boy of Aveyron" because his behavior was more like a wild animal's than a human's. Authorities surmised he had been abandoned years before by impoverished parents, a practice not uncommon at the time. A doctor took an interest in the boy's case and tried to civilize him. But despite intense efforts, Victor, as the doctor called him, remained abnormal in all respects, without social skills and unable to use language.

A more recent case is that of a girl named Genie. From the time she was a year old, her emotionally unstable father imprisoned her in a small room, harnessed in a sitting position during the day and bound in a cagelike crib at night. By the time she was discovered at age 13, Genie was physically deformed and underdeveloped from being kept confined. She was also seriously retarded in every area of human functioning. In time Genie made some progress in physical and intellectual development, including modest use of language, but she remained severely handicapped in establishing social relationships (Curtiss, 1977; Rymer, 1993).

Because no one knows what Victor and Genie were like at birth, it is not clear to what extent their deficiencies were caused by their early isolation or why attempts to help them had such limited success. We do not know if they remained abnormal because of inborn defects, such as mental retardation, or because of irreversible damage from early environmental deprivation. Still, their cases support the idea that human contact is essential for normal development.

Early environmental deprivation need not be so extreme to have harmful effects on development, as shown in classic studies of infants raised in institutions (Karen, 1994; Spitz, 1945). The babies in these studies were fed and kept clean, but most of the time

Child Development CD:
Physical and Emotional Neglect

This picture is from a movie about the real-life case of Victor, "the wild boy of Aveyron," who was found in a forest at about age 12.

they were left alone, with little to look at or touch. Lacking the physical and social stimulation human infants need, they soon became apathetic, unresponsive, and withdrawn.

More recent studies of children in Eastern European orphanages also show the negative consequences of early institutional rearing. Children in overcrowded Romanian orphanages typically are both physically and socially deprived. As many as twenty children may be cared for by one nurse, and the care is perfunctory, directed only to the children's basic physical needs. There is no playing with the children and almost no face-to-face interaction. As a result, the children are listless and emotionless and have numerous physical problems (Johnson, 2000). Children adopted from these orphanages have a higher than

In overcrowded Romanian orphanages, children receive little individual attention. Just like baths, bedtime, and mealtime, sitting on the potty is a group activity.

usual rate of insecure parent-child attachment relationships and are often indiscriminately friendly toward adults—behavior that makes sense in an orphanage where caregivers are constantly changing (Ames and Chisholm, 2001). They also show signs of biological effects of early deprivation, such as heightened physiological responses to stress, that may in turn influence social interaction (Gunnar et al., 2001).

Children observed in less physically deprived but socially sterile Russian institutions at first seemed precocious; they could dress themselves early and showed skill in handling objects. However, later they were aggressive with other children and quite needy of adult contact (Dubrovina and Ruzska, 1990). The effects of early institutionalization depend on the type of stimulation and care provided, its appropriateness to the age and individual nature of the child, and the availability of opportunities for normal give-and-take between infant and caregiver (Provence, 1989). The box on page 46 describes some ways of improving institutional care of infants.

Most children do not suffer early environmental deprivation, but everyone is partly the product of the contexts in which they develop. The three families we introduced at the beginning of Part One come from different economic circumstances, ethnic groups, and communities. All three families are influenced by the dominant North American culture, but their cultural backgrounds differ in some respects. Other factors in their lives, such as relationships among family members, are continually changing, and these also affect the environment in which their children are raised. In addition, the children born into these three families will each have a unique set of genes, which will further contribute to developmental differences among them. Thus, each of them will grow up with a different set of contextual influences, and as a result their developmental paths will differ in many ways.

Questions to Think About As You Read

- What aspects of the contexts provided by the Williams, Gordon, and Polonius families seem likely to be especially significant for their children's development?
- What must an environment include to be supportive of human development?

AN OVERVIEW OF DEVELOPMENTAL CONTEXTS

When we say that human development takes place in context, we are actually referring to a set of contexts. The contexts for development include human evolutionary history, the culture into which a child is born, the particular historic period in which the child

APPLYING RESEARCH FINDINGS

Helping Infants in Institutions to Develop Normally

Ongoing studies of infants in orphanages reveal devastating consequences in all areas of development, which often persist years after adoption (Holden, 1996; Johnson, 2000). Lowered IQs, severely compromised physical development (including brain development), and social, emotional, and behavioral disturbances are common. These developmental problems appear to result specifically from poor quality care. The seriousness of the effects depends on length of stay in the institution and age at adoption; those adopted before 6 months are relatively unharmed. Adequate home care prior to institutionalization also offers some protection (Johnson, 2000; Rutter, Kreppner, and O'Connor, 2001).

Studies of children from Romanian orphanages are especially informative because many children of all ages were adopted in a short period of time (1990–91) due to political reasons. Thus, healthy children were not selected first for adoption; they were just as likely as unhealthy or disabled babies to have remained in the orphanage past age 2, with devastating consequences.

Videotapes made in even the best Romanian orphanages (where conditions are sanitary and the children's nutritional needs are met) document the profound consequences of emotional deprivation. Without attentive, emotionally involved caregivers, babies are apathetic and disengaged from their surroundings; they appear to clinical observers to be depressed. They also show unusual mannerisms, such as rocking themselves. Often they don't show wariness when it would be expected. If they display positive emotion, it is like that of a much younger baby. An 18-month-old, for example, might smile at the face of a stranger in the manner of a normal 2- or 3-month-old. These infants' social relations are also abnormal, with social give-and-take notably absent; they treat others more like objects than people.

Research suggests that impersonal care is the critical cause of these symptoms. Institutions with a more homelike atmosphere, where a baby gets individualized care from the same caregiver, compromise development far less. When the number of caregivers on a unit was increased in selected Romanian orphanages and the caregivers were encouraged to interact with the infants, development proceeded much more normally (Johnson, 2000).

More extensive changes could probably prevent many of the negative consequences of institutionalization for infants. The major goals would be to provide recurrent social interaction and emotional involvement with the same small group of caregivers, to ensure continuity in care, and to provide interesting sensory experiences for the children on a daily basis. Some specific changes to accomplish these objectives (based on Provence, 1989) are listed below. Institutionalization of infants is to be avoided if at all possible and should never be considered routine. But if such settings are used in certain extreme situations, proper conditions of care must be ensured.

RECOMMENDED CHANGES FROM TRADITIONAL INSTITUTIONAL CARE TO INDIVIDUALIZED CARE

Traditional Institutional Care	Individualized Care
Feeding with propped bottle	Holding with eye-to-eye contact while feeding
Left in crib except for bathing and dressing	Given floor freedom and interaction with adults on demand
Toys suspended from crib	Interactive play with adults as well as crib toys
8-to-1 ratio of infants to caregivers (32-to-1 at night)	One-on-one contact with consistent staff members frequently throughout day and regular night staff
Confined to nursery	Varied experiences in and away from institution

lives, the child's community, the surrounding socioeconomic climate, and the child's home, family, peer group, and school. All of these influence development in complex, interlocking ways. For instance, many common features of modern North American culture, such as television sets, two working parents, out-of-home child care, and formal schooling, do not go together by coincidence; they are part of the same societal pattern, and their influences supplement one another.

Urie Bronfenbrenner (1979; Bronfenbrenner and Morris, 1998; Bronfenbrenner and Evans, 2000) of Cornell University has suggested a way of conceptualizing developmental contexts that helps to clarify how they are related to each other and how they influence development. He proposes a model of concentric rings, with each ring influ-

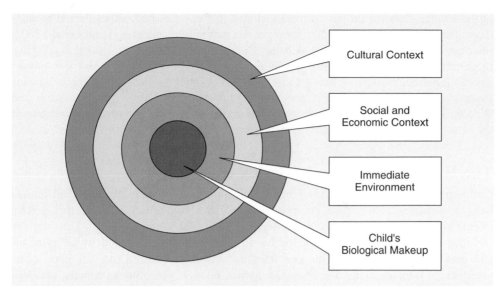

Figure 2.1
THE CHILD'S DEVELOPMENTAL
CONTEXTS
Urie Bronfenbrenner has
suggested that children's
development is influenced by
their biological heritage, by the
immediate environment, and by
the larger circumstances in
which they are brought up.

encing all the rings inside it. As you can see in Figure 2.1, the child is at the center of the rings, bringing to development a particular *biological makeup.* Surrounding the child is the first ring, the *immediate environment.* It contains all the settings, people, and physical objects with which the child has direct contact. For most North American children, this includes home, family, toys, playgrounds, peers, classrooms, and teachers.

The immediate environment does not exist in a vacuum but is embedded in a broader *social and economic context.* For instance, the materials and staff present in a classroom, the curriculum taught there, and the school's physical facilities are typically shaped by local school board decisions, community economic circumstances, and state and national educational and funding policies. Similarly, while a child may have no direct contact with a parent's boss, the boss may affect the parent's behavior at home, which in turn affects the child. These broader, indirect social and economic influences make up the second ring in Figure 2.1.

The third ring in Figure 2.1 is the *cultural context.* It consists of all the beliefs, attitudes, values, and guidelines for behavior that people in a particular society tend to share. For example, most adults in North American society believe that babies need a great deal of individual attention and that they should ideally receive much of their care from their mothers. This belief is part of our culture and affects how babies are cared for. The value that most Americans place on democracy, independence, and economic success is also part of our culture and influences what children are taught, both at home and at school.

The rest of this chapter is devoted to a closer examination of each of the rings in Bronfenbrenner's model. We will examine the impact of these developmental contexts throughout the book as we look at the major periods of child development.

THE CHILD'S BIOLOGICAL MAKEUP

The first developmental context we will consider is the child's biological makeup, which lies at the center of Bronfenbrenner's model. It includes three components:

- The evolutionary heritage shared by all humans
- The child's individual genetic inheritance
- The biological results of interactions between genes and the environment

Except for identical twins, each child has a genetic makeup that is in some ways different from every other person's. At the same time there is also great genetic similarity across individual humans, racial and ethnic groups, and even species. The research

Human Genome Project

of the Human Genome Project has demonstrated that any two randomly selected humans have approximately 99.9 percent of their genetic material in common (Venter et al., 2001; International Human Genome Sequencing Consortium, 2001). The genes that we have in common represent our common evolutionary heritage as humans. But our human genetic inheritance also overlaps greatly with that of other species; for example, humans share about 98 percent of their genes with chimpanzees (Gibbons, 1998; King and Wilson, 1975). Minor variations in genes can have such large effects in part because of the power of interactions with the environment.

The Human Evolutionary Heritage

Children do not enter the world as neutral creatures that have to be taught all human behaviors. Instead, they come equipped with a rich evolutionary heritage that greatly affects how they act (Bjorklund and Pellegrini, 2002; Charlesworth, 1994). This heritage includes some behavioral traits shared by all mammals; others shared by all primates (the order of animals to which humans, apes, and monkeys belong); and still others characteristic of humans alone. For example, human infants, like other mammals, are born with the sucking reflex needed to get milk from their mothers. Like other primates, they have an inherited tendency to seek social stimulation and to form strong attachments to caregivers. In addition, they have a built-in ability to acquire language, something unique to members of the human species.

One important feature of our evolutionary heritage is *a rather precise timetable for many developmental milestones,* from reaching for and grasping nearby objects to showing the emotion of fear. This timetable applies to babies in widely varying circumstances, a fact that suggests a strong influence of heredity (Suomi, 1977; Charlesworth, 1994).

Perhaps the most basic of all human biological givens is *a strong disposition to act on the environment,* rather than being passive. From the beginning, human infants examine and manipulate things around them. This tendency is characteristic of all mammals, but it is most pronounced in the higher primates, with their strong inquisitiveness and inclination to solve problems (Suomi, 1977; White, 1959). For example, monkeys and chimpanzees will work hard to solve a problem, such as unfastening a latch, just for a chance to watch other animals through a window (Butler, 1953). Human children, too, solve problems just for the fun of it. The satisfaction humans get from discovery has helped our species survive by encouraging exploration and invention (Breger, 1974; Harter, 1980).

Closely related to humans' curiosity is *an innate propensity for learning.* For instance, by the age of 4, children around the world are fluent in their native language. Young children, it seems, have a built-in readiness to acquire this complex skill (Lenneberg, 1967; Pinker, 1994). Our nearest animal relatives, the chimpanzees, have great difficulty learning even the rudiments of symbolic communication (Petitto, 1992).

Of course, the ease with which humans learn depends on what they are learning. Newborns can quickly learn to adjust their rate of sucking (DeCasper and Fifer, 1980) or to turn their heads from side to side in a precise sequence (Papoušek, 1967). Sucking and head turning are used in nursing and are vital for survival. Babies are born with these responses built in and are biologically prepared to learn various ways of using them. As children mature, what they can readily learn changes. The facility for learning language emerges at about 18 months of age;

A basic biological given of primates, including humans, is the strong motivation to investigate novel aspects of the environment and to manipulate objects and solve problems.

certain abstract concepts are mastered only after adolescence. A basic propensity for learning is part of children's biological inheritance, but exactly *what* they can learn at any particular time depends partly on their level of development.

As humans, children also inherit *a predisposition to be social,* to interact and form bonds with others of their species. This social predisposition is essential to their survival. Because human children take years to become self-sufficient, forming ties to others helps ensure that they get the care they need. It is therefore not surprising that babies come equipped with behaviors that tend to elicit caregiving responses from adults. Looking, listening, smiling, cooing, crying, clinging, and following are all biologically based behaviors that help establish early social relationships. Throughout development the human social predisposition can be seen again and again. The preschooler who seeks out peers to play with, the adolescent who forms a romantic attachment, and the adult who cares for children are all acting in accordance with their biological makeup.

Young children especially enjoy objects that invite action. They will often carry out the same action over and over simply for the reward of doing it.

Individual Genetic Characteristics

The inherited predispositions shared by all humans reflect genetic influences at the species level that are a product of our evolutionary history. However, as we discussed in Chapter 1, the evolution of a species can't occur without individual differences. Individual genetic differences have allowed our species to meet environmental challenges over hundreds of thousands of years. As environmental conditions change, individuals with genetic traits suited to the new conditions survive, while those lacking such traits do not.

Individual differences in genetic makeup have both direct and indirect influences on development. Consider the genetic defect that produces Down syndrome. It has direct effects by impairing mental and physical development. But it also has indirect effects; people have certain expectations of what a child with Down syndrome can do, which in turn affect the child's education, living situation, and job opportunities. Similarly, some researchers believe that genes directly influence certain aspects of behavior, such as activity level and wariness (Goldsmith et al., 2000; Kagan, 1998; Plomin et al., 1997). If this is true, these genes would also indirectly influence development through the reactions of other people to these behaviors (Chipuer et al., 1993; Scarr and McCartney, 1983).

Interactions Between Genes and the Environment

Biological characteristics do not stem solely from genetic inheritance. At birth, a child's biological makeup has already been shaped by environmental factors. Maternal health, nutrition, and drug or alcohol use during pregnancy can all affect the child's physical makeup. (We will consider these influences in more detail in Chapter 3.) After birth, the child's biological makeup continues to be influenced by a wide range of environmental factors—for example, nutrition, illnesses, and exposure to lead. In fact, everything the child experiences can have an impact on further biological development. The child's developing brain and nervous system are particularly susceptible to the effects of experience and the environment—and these, in turn, have a powerful influence on further development and behavior.

Canalization:
The extent to which genes constrain environmental influences on particular traits.

As we noted in Chapter 1, many developmentalists are interested in how genes and environment interact to produce behavior (e.g., Brown, 1999; Gottlieb, 2001). A major question concerns the degree to which genes *constrain,* or put limits on, environmental influence. C. H. Waddington (1966) used the term **canalization** to refer to these genetic constraints. In his view, some behaviors are strongly canalized, or channeled, from the beginning. For example, babies' vocalizations begin to include consonant-vowel combinations at about 4 to 6 months of age, regardless of culture or social context. Even with a great deal of environmental variation, this behavior appears in accord with a timetable that seems to be inborn. Other characteristics, such as skill in social interaction, are thought to be much more open to environmental influences.

For some capacities, canalization is relatively weak early in life, and the constraints become more rigid with age. The process is analogous to what happens when water runs down a sandy hillside. At first, the water establishes broad paths, or channels. If water continues to pour down in the same direction, some of the grooves deepen. Eventually, the channels become so deep that massive environmental change is needed to reroute them. Some human characteristics develop this way. For example, children may be born with genetic tendencies to be more or less irritable, active, or wary, but initially such tendencies are not firmly established. Genes simply provide broad dispositions for behavior, which may be either intensified or diminished over time, depending on the child's environment. Such behavior is susceptible to environmental input at first, but it becomes more difficult to change later.

For other capacities, strong genetic canalization exists early, but later there is increased openness to environmental influences. For example, institutionalization during the first four months of life has little lasting effect on children's social and emotional development, which suggests that during this period social and emotional capacities are strongly canalized. But institutionalization from 4 to 12 months, and especially beyond age 2, has a dramatic impact on social and emotional development, indicating that the older infant is more vulnerable to environmental influence in these areas (O'Connor and Rutter, 2000). Robert McCall (1981) has proposed that cognitive development also follows such a course. Until the age of 2 years, he argues, cognitive development is strongly canalized by the child's biological makeup. The range of behavior across children is narrow, and widely differing environments have relatively little impact. After age 2, however, developmental pathways diverge. Genetically determined tendencies have a decreasing impact on behavior, and children become more susceptible to variations in experience.

Over time, experience has an impact on the child's biological makeup, just as biological development gives rise to new behaviors and produces new experiences for the child. Gilbert Gottlieb (1991) has suggested that experience plays a role in the canalization of development just described. It is not simply that genes are preprogrammed to gain or lose influence over time, but also that experience changes the biological nature of the child and the way in which genes are expressed. Brain maturation underlies the emergence of many behaviors, such as the increasing perceptual abilities of early infancy and the acquisition of language in the second year of life. However, it is also clear that experience, made possible by new behavioral capacities, in turn promotes the further development of brain structures and connections (Schore, 1994, 2001b).

THE CHILD'S IMMEDIATE ENVIRONMENT

Ultimately, all the contextual factors that influence a child operate through the child's immediate environment—the people, places, and things with which the child has direct contact. The people in the immediate environment are especially important both because they interact directly with the child and because they are largely responsible for the child's physical surroundings. Parents, for example, not only play with their children but also choose their playthings. The way they do each of these things can affect the children's development.

Children's development is influenced not just by parents but by the entire family system. Often this includes grandparents and other extended family members.

In the following sections we look at several parts of the typical North American child's immediate environment. First and foremost is the family, but also important are day care, peer groups, neighborhoods, and schools.

The Family Context

The family is a dominant part of a child's immediate environment. Family members interact directly with the child every day, stimulating language development and cognitive skills. Family members provide children with their first opportunities to form social relationships. The emotional quality of these relationships can have far-reaching effects, influencing a child's curiosity, problem-solving attitude, and interactions with peers. Family members also provide models for behavior. Children imitate the people around them, especially the people they love and admire. Parents and older siblings model not only specific behaviors, but also general roles. Much of a child's understanding of what it is to be male or female, mother or father, husband or wife, comes from the family. Finally, the ways in which families are structured and the tasks children are given to do foster the development of particular characteristics. For example, children in many cultures develop the capacity to nurture by helping to care for younger siblings (Zukow-Goldring, 2002).

The Family as a System   For many years researchers who studied the family's influence on children focused almost exclusively on the role of the mother, because she traditionally had the major direct impact on young children and because the importance of maternal care was a cornerstone of psychoanalytic theory. Insofar as it underscored children's psychological need for a warm, emotionally supportive environment, this stress on the mother-child relationship was beneficial. But developmentalists came to realize that such a focus was too narrow. In some cultures, the mother is not the only caregiver, even for very young children (Harkness and Super, 2002; Tronick, Morelli, and Ivey, 1992). In many African-American families, grandmothers play an important role in child rearing (Gibson, 2002; McAdoo, 2002). The traditional view of the family's influence on children had to be expanded to include other family members besides the mother.

Even the influence of mothers on children had to be examined more broadly. Mothers never care for children in isolation; the quality of their caregiving is influenced, both directly and indirectly, by other family members. Today, the developmental influences of fathers and siblings are topics of active study, as is the broader family support system, including grandparents and other members of extended families (Bengtson, 2001). Also of great interest is the child's own role in shaping family interactions. The family is no longer seen as a set of separate relationships existing side by side, but as a complex, interconnected system (Cox and Paley, 1997; Kreppner, 2002; Minuchin, 1988; Sroufe and Fleeson, 1988).

At the simplest level, the idea of a system implies that each family member's behavior depends in part on the behavior of the others. What a mother does, for instance, depends in part on what her husband and children do, just as a child's behavior is partly determined by the behavior of parents and siblings. Notice that influences between family members always move in two directions, not just one. While characteristics of parents help to shape the behavior of their children, characteristics of the children in turn influence the parents' behavior. These **bidirectional effects** (Bell, 1968) can be seen very clearly in the development of sex-typed behavior in children. Many American parents behave differently toward their sons than toward their daughters. Toddler girls get their hair tied in ribbons; toddler boys get tossed in the air. These different styles of caregiving encourage children to act in sex-typed ways, which in turn reinforce the parents' beliefs and child-rearing practices.

Over time, bidirectional effects between children and their environment powerfully influence development. Arnold Sameroff has proposed a **transactional model** to describe the cumulative effects of ongoing bidirectional influences between parents and children, taking into account the family's social and economic context as well (Sameroff and Fiese, 2000; Sameroff and Chandler, 1975). A newborn enters the family system with certain innate tendencies. The parents, because of their own circumstances and characteristics, respond to the baby in particular ways. The baby's behavior then gradually changes, partly because of the parents' influences, partly because of maturation. These changes in the baby's behavior in turn elicit new responses from the parents, which further influence the child, and so on, in an ongoing cycle.

Sameroff's transactional model can help to answer some otherwise puzzling questions, such as why certain moderately premature infants have developmental problems. The answer does not lie solely with the babies, for in general such infants develop quite well (Greenberg and Crnic, 1988; Laucht et al., 2001). Moreover, those who later encounter developmental problems are physically indistinguishable at birth from those who do not. It seems that the premature babies who have trouble are mainly those in very low-income homes (Sameroff and Chandler, 1975). Sameroff's transactional model can help us understand what goes wrong in these cases. A premature infant requires special care and poses special challenges for parents. These demands can be overtaxing for parents already burdened with the many stresses of poverty. Thus, the baby's condition at birth interacts with the parents' psychological state, which itself is shaped by their

Bidirectional effects:
Two-way developmental influences between family members.

Transactional model:
Sameroff's model describing the cumulative effects of ongoing two-way influences between children and parents.

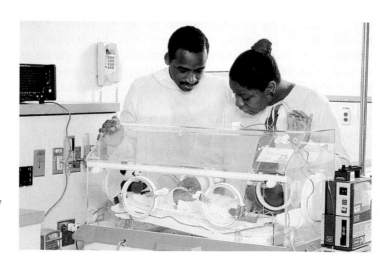

Premature infants require special care, which is most likely to be provided by parents with adequate psychological resources and social support.

economic and social circumstances. In some cases the parents become less effective caregivers, and the baby fails to thrive.

Note that it is the transaction between particular actors in a particular context that gives rise to the outcome. In middle-class families, which do not suffer the extra burdens of poverty, moderate prematurity in an infant does *not* predict negative outcomes. Studies have found that middle-class mothers of premature babies generally provide more intensive and supportive care than do middle-class mothers of full-term infants. Premature babies in these families generally catch up with full-term babies developmentally by about age 2 (Greenberg and Crnic, 1988; Landry et al., 1997). Apparently, premature infants, with their special needs, tend to elicit sensitive care from caregivers who have adequate social support and are not unduly stressed.

Characteristics of Family Systems Family systems are complex, partly because *they are made up of many subsystems* (relationships between siblings, between parents and children, between mother and father), *all of which are joined together in a coherent, interlocking network.* The various relationships in a family system fit together like pieces of a jigsaw puzzle. For example, qualities of siblings' relationships are predictable from qualities of mother-child relationships (Dunn and Kendrick, 1982a; Volling and Belsky, 1992). Similarly, one parent's relationship with a particular child is connected with all other relationships in the family. If a mother is seductive toward her son, her relationship with her daughter is often hostile and her relationship with her husband is often emotionally distant (Sroufe et al., 1985). Rather than saying that the mother-son relationship causes the mother-father distance, or that the mother-father distance causes seductiveness toward the son, we would prefer to emphasize that the network of relationships within the family is a coherent one. Close, supportive relationships between spouses generally are not found in families in which one parent is emotionally overinvolved with an opposite-gender child, and vice versa. Thus, the idea of the family as a system means more than that each individual member affects the other members. It also means that each family member is affected fundamentally by the organization of the *whole* (Sroufe and Fleeson, 1988).

In addition to being a complex and coherent network of relationships, *a family is a dynamic, open system, subject to change as well as continuity.* One way family systems change is by adding or losing members. For instance, family relationships change fundamentally when a new child is born (Cowan and Cowan, 2000). Before the birth, a family system already exists, and the child is fitted into that system more or less smoothly. How the child fits into the existing family system can even be influenced by such factors as whether the parents wanted a boy or a girl (Stattin and Klackenberg-Larson, 1991). Consider the Gordon family in our case history. Wanting a son is Frank and Christine's primary reason for having a second child. A place in the system is already prepared for the child. If the baby does turn out to be a boy, he will immediately have a role of sizable importance—he will make the family complete. But if the baby turns out to be a girl, Frank may actively show his disappointment toward both the child and his wife, and Christine may feel she has failed by not producing a boy. Or, if she has a son and the wished-for closeness with Frank doesn't result, Christine may become angry at her husband. The wishes, expectations, and needs of the Gordons will influence how they react to the baby and to each other after the baby's birth. The arrival of the new baby will alter the family system, with effects on all the individuals and relationships within it.

Family systems also change as circumstances change, as crises are faced, and as members enter new developmental phases (Conger et al., 1994; Elder, 1998). Developmentalists are particularly interested in how a child's development influences and is influenced by the overall development of the family. The Gordons' hoped-for son may initially be *given* the role of holding the family together, but as he grows older, he may actively *seek out* this role, particularly if the relationship between his mother and father worsens. As they develop, children become active participants in defining and maintaining the

mhhe.com
/dehart5

Transition to Parenthood

family system. Individual development and family development are always closely linked.

Another feature of family systems is that *they are subject to cyclical influences that can be repeated across generations.* For example, children's personality development is related to their parents' level of marital harmony (Cummings and Davies, 2002; Emery, 1999). Children's personalities in turn predict their future marital satisfaction and harmony. Family harmony or discord, in other words, tends to perpetuate itself. In one study such cycles of influence were demonstrated across four generations (Elder, Caspi, and Downey, 1986). Parenting practices, both positive and negative, also often seem to be repeated across generations (Putallaz et al., 1998; Simons et al., 1991). In the Minnesota Longitudinal Study, for example, significant continuity was found between the treatment participants received as toddlers and the treatment they later gave their own toddler-aged children (Levy, 1999). Fortunately, this cycle can be broken if a child from such a background manages to establish a solid, supportive marital relationship in adulthood.

Fatherhood

Fathers in the Family System Developmental psychologists have become increasingly interested in fathers' influences on children, which can be either direct or indirect (Booth and Crouter, 1998; Cabrera et al., 2000; Lamb, 1997). Studies of the *direct* effects of fathers on children's development have revealed that children are involved with their fathers and emotionally attached to them even in infancy (Cohen and Campos, 1974; Parke and Stearns, 1993). Such involvement intensifies during the toddler period, especially for boys. In later chapters you will read about the influences of fathers on sex-role learning, cognitive development, achievement motivation, and personality development.

Fathers also have important *indirect* influences through their impact on the behavior of mothers or siblings. There is evidence that when a father and mother are together, they tend to show more positive emotion toward their children than either does separately (Parke and Stearns, 1993). Apparently, the mere presence of a partner can affect parent-child interactions. In general, marital harmony is associated with nurturant parenting and good child adjustment (Cowan and Cowan, 2000; Parke and Buriel, 1998). So a father who maintains a positive, supportive relationship with his wife is indirectly benefiting his children. For example, when the father of an infant provides strong emotional support for the mother, her care of their infant is more effective (Belsky and Isabella, 1988). Even women who were troubled as children can become nurturant mothers if they marry supportive men (Caspi and Elder, 1988).

Fathers are commonly very involved with their toddlers, often engaging them in play.

Children of single mothers can also benefit from their mothers' relationships with men—even men who are not their biological fathers—provided those relationships are stable ones (Sroufe and Pierce, 1999). Byron Egeland and his colleagues (Erickson, Egeland, and Sroufe, 1985) followed the social and emotional development of a group of low-income children from birth through school age. One major difference they found between children whose social and emotional functioning improved over time and children who showed consistently poor functioning was that the mothers of improving children were more likely to have formed a stable partnership, either marrying or becoming involved with a man on a steady basis. In these families, the mothers' parenting may have improved because of emotional support from their partners.

Siblings in the Family System   Siblings also have both direct and indirect effects on children's development. Older siblings' direct effects on younger children come through their roles as companions, teachers, and models. In many cultures, children take on the responsibility of caring for younger siblings as early as age 5 (Zukow-Goldring, 2002). When an older sibling is present, a younger child may learn directly from that sibling's behavior. Older children also learn from the experience of having a younger sibling as they take on a new role in the family and learn to interpret the younger child's behavior (Mendelson, 1990). Interacting with a sibling, who is relatively close in age and highly familiar, may help children develop social understanding and interaction skills that they can later use in interacting with children outside the family (DeHart, 1999; Dunn, 1988). At the same time, siblings indirectly influence one another's development through the impact they have on their parents' behavior (Dunn, 1993).

Sibling influences are not the same across all families, even in families matched by the age and sex of their children. One reason is that the quality of sibling relationships varies greatly (Brody, 1998). Another is that the influence of siblings is mediated by other aspects of family functioning. For example, the impact of a younger sibling on a firstborn depends on how the family system was previously working, how the parents prepare the older child for the baby's arrival, and how the family adjusts to developmental changes in each child (Dunn, 1988; Howe, 1991; Kreppner, 2002).

You will learn more about sibling influences in later chapters. The important point for now is that many of these influences could never be discovered if researchers did not view the family as a system. Sibling relationships clearly affect children's development.

Researchers are interested in the consequences of sibling relationships and how they are influenced by other relationships in the family system.

Parents' treatment of each of their children influences the children's relationships with each other, and the sibling relationships in turn have an impact on the parents' behavior (McHale and Crouter, 1996). Each relationship touches every other, and much is missed when any one relationship is viewed in isolation.

Immediate Contexts Outside the Family

As children grow older, they increasingly find themselves in settings outside the family. Four of these have major roles in development:

- day care;
- the peer group;
- the neighborhood; and
- the school.

We will say a great deal about the influences of these settings in later chapters. Here we simply provide an introduction and raise some of the questions researchers have tried to answer.

The Day Care Setting   As the proportion of single parents has risen and more mothers have sought work outside the home, the use of day care has increased in the United States. By 2001, there were over 10 million American mothers with children under age 6 in the workforce (U. S. Census Bureau, 2002b). As shown in Figure 2.2, fewer than one in four preschoolers in the United States with employed mothers are enrolled in formal child care or school settings. The majority are in less formal settings. Nearly half are cared for by their fathers or by other relatives. About one in six is in **family day care,** an arrangement in which a group of children is cared for in the home of a nonrelative.

Since the use of day care in the United States is so widespread, developmentalists are interested in its impact. Researchers now agree that even full-time day care for toddlers and preschool children has no demonstrable negative effects. In fact, substantial evidence indicates that good-quality day care can be beneficial for children over a year old, promoting both cognitive and social development. Debate continues, however, over day care for infants *under* a year old, with strong arguments on both sides (Belsky, 2001; NICHD Early Child Care Research Network, 2001). Many important questions about

Family day care:
A day care setting in which a group of children is cared for in the home of a nonrelative.

NICHD Study of Early Child Care

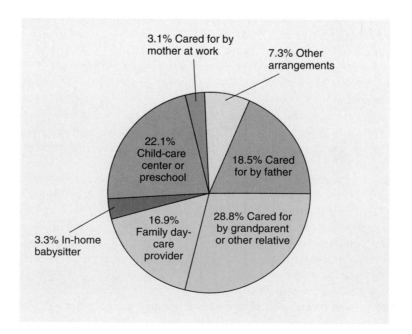

Figure 2.2
CHILD CARE ARRANGEMENTS FOR U.S. CHILDREN UNDER 5 WITH EMPLOYED MOTHERS, 1999 *(Source: U.S. Census Bureau, 2003.)*

The majority of children under age 6 in the United States now have mothers who are employed outside the home. Many of these children are cared for in family day care homes like the one shown here.

day care and its effects on children's development remain to be fully answered (Lamb, 1998). How does day care affect parent-child relationships, especially in infancy? Does the developmental impact differ depending on the age at which day care begins? Does it differ depending on the social class from which a child comes or the type of day care used? We will return to these issues in Chapter 6.

The Peer Group The peer group offers an important setting for children's development that complements and expands on that provided by the family (Hartup, 1999; Rubin, Bukowski, and Parker, 1998; Sroufe, Egeland, and Carlson, 1999). The importance of peers grows as children get older and spend more time with them. By age 11, peers occupy about as much of the average child's time as do adults; thereafter, the balance tips in favor of peers (Rubin et al., 1998). By adolescence, peers exert a heavy influence on dress, tastes, and activities. Teenagers spend seemingly endless hours with their special friends and often view activities with parents as an intrusion. What are children learning in all those hours spent with peers? What skills, values, and expectations do peers convey to one another?

One thing the peer group teaches is how to interact in equal-status, or *symmetrical,* relationships. Relationships between children and adults are inherently unequal or *asymmetrical.* No matter how warm and caring the interactions may be, the adult always retains the power to tell the child what to do. In a group of same-age peers, however, no child holds any formal authority over the others. As a result, the peer group is a critical setting for learning fairness, reciprocity, cooperation, and how to manage interpersonal aggression (Hartup, 1999; Sroufe et al., 1999).

Another powerful learning experience the peer group provides is reinforcement of the values, beliefs, and behavior standards that are part of the child's culture. Consider our culture's sex-role standards, the different behaviors expected of girls and boys. Although parents initially convey them to children, peers are their most dogmatic enforcers. This is particularly true in boys' peer groups, in which a preference for feminine toys or pastimes meets with derision even among preschoolers (Ruble and Martin, 1998).

We will first examine the peer group in Chapter 10, which deals with early childhood. In later chapters we will follow the peer group's influence into the elementary and high school years. In the process we will answer some important questions: why do some children find it easy to get along with peers while others are socially isolated or actively rejected by them? When do true friendships between children emerge, and what underlies this development? When do children begin to think of their peer groups as having boundaries—of their own friends as "we" and other children as "they"? What promotes this sense of peer solidarity? How conforming are children to their peer groups, and why does conformity seem to intensify during middle childhood and early adolescence? To what extent do the norms and values of adolescent peer groups conflict with those of parents and other adults?

The Neighborhood Every family lives in a particular neighborhood with physical and social characteristics that can affect children's development. The type and condition of housing, yards, streets, sidewalks, recreational facilities, and businesses in a neighborhood have an impact on children's activities and developmental opportunities. Even more important, children are influenced by the other people who live in the neighborhood and their activities, values, beliefs, and resources. All these factors are obviously affected by the larger social and economic context, which we will discuss shortly. However, there is evidence that the neighborhood itself exerts an influence on children's development that is separate from family influences on the one hand, and from general social and economic influences on the other (Booth and Crouter, 2001; Leventhal and Brooks-Gunn, 2000).

Children and Violence

Most of the research on neighborhoods has focused on the impact of various factors associated with community poverty, as opposed to family poverty, on children's development. For example, neighborhoods with high levels of poverty also tend to have high levels of violent crime; as discussed in A Closer Look on page 59, continuing exposure to violence as a part of daily life can have serious impacts on children's development (Osofsky, 1997; Kupersmidt et al., 2002). Having affluent neighbors is associated with positive developmental outcomes in both early childhood and adolescence, regardless of a child's own family income level (Shonkoff and Phillips, 2000). Conversely, adolescents who live in neighborhoods where there are few affluent residents with high-status jobs are at heightened risk for pregnancy and dropping out of school. These research results suggest that neighborhoods have their effects on children and adolescents by means of *collective socialization*, in which adults in a neighborhood provide role models and monitoring for local children, rather than by means of *behavioral contagion*, in which negative peer influences spread problem behaviors. The social networks that form in neighborhoods can provide support and access to resources such as jobs for adolescents. Affluent neighbors may decrease adolescents' risk for certain negative outcomes because they are able to help in practical ways, such as providing job leads, as well as in less tangible ways.

The School The school is often thought of as the child's workplace. By age 6 or 7, children in North America spend six hours a day, five days a week, in school. Children in Japan and Western Europe spend even more time in the classroom. The school is thus a potentially powerful influence on development. At the same time, both normative and individual developmental issues have an impact on schools.

Children learn much more at school than the information in their textbooks. Like the peer group, the school is a great instructor in cultural norms and values. For example, studies show that American elementary school teachers respond to their students in ways that reinforce traditional sex roles (American Association of University Women, 1998; Sadker, 1999). American schools are also strong conveyors of such mainstream values as neatness, discipline, punctuality, competition, hard work, and material success.

Gender Bias in Schools

Normative developmental considerations are reflected in school structures and activities for children of different ages. In many parts of the world, nursery schools are

A CLOSER LOOK

VIOLENCE AND CHILDREN

For many children, violence is part of the immediate environment. In inner-city neighborhoods described by some as "war zones," exposure to violence tends to begin early in life and to be chronic (Garbarino, 2001). In one Chicago study, about 60 percent of the inner-city high school students surveyed had witnessed one or more shootings, 43 percent had witnessed at least one murder, over one-quarter had been the victim of a violent crime, and nearly half reported they had been shot at (Jenkins and Bell, 1997). Similar rates have been found for children living in other large cities. Rates of both witnessing and being victims of violence are lower outside large urban areas, but even in small towns about 30 percent of adolescents report they have witnessed a shooting (Singer et al., 1995).

Exposure to violence at home is also a problem for many American children. In 2000, abuse and neglect cases involving nearly 3 million children were investigated in the United States. Strong evidence of abuse or neglect was found for 862,000 of these children; about 19 percent of the cases involved physical abuse (U.S. Census Bureau, 2000b). Many additional children witness domestic violence directed at their mothers or other family members.

What are the impacts on children who are exposed to violence? Children exposed to chronic high levels of violence often show symptoms of post-traumatic stress disorder (PTSD), a psychological disorder first identified among soldiers returning from combat (Jenkins and Bell, 1997; Kupersmidt et al., 2002). These symptoms include repeatedly visualizing and reenacting traumatic events, specific violence-related fears, and an overall sense of hopelessness. Psychological consequences also include other stress-related disorders, passivity, regression to early developmental stages, self-destructive behaviors, difficulty trusting others, and problems forming an identity in adolescence. Declines in school achievement are common.

However, one of the most common outcomes of exposure to violence is aggressive behavior toward others. This outcome helps to explain why the rates for both commission of violent crime and death by homicide among juveniles in the United States remain the highest among industrialized nations and homicide remains the leading cause of death among African-American males aged 15 to 24 (Anderson, 2002).

The effects on children of exposure to violence vary, depending on such factors as how close they were to a violent event, their relationship with the victim, and the presence of other stressors in their lives. Factors that tend to make the effects less severe include a strong relationship with parents who respond supportively and protectively, family cohesiveness, support from outside the home (either individual or institutional), and the child's own intelligence level, sense of self-efficacy, and social and problem-solving skills. Unfortunately, parents who are themselves trying to cope with neighborhood or family violence are often not able to provide the support that would help their children develop the skills needed for coping with violence.

Long-term solutions to the problems caused by exposure to violence include reducing poverty, unemployment, and family disruption. Short-term solutions include encouraging professionals who regularly deal with children exposed to violence, such as doctors and teachers, to provide support and intervention (Jenkins and Bell, 1997; Kupersmidt et al., 2002).

flexibly structured, with an emphasis on social activities. North American accreditation standards for early childhood education emphasize development appropriateness (Hart, Burts, and Charlesworth, 1997; National Association for the Education of Young Children, 1998). More formal instruction usually begins in the early elementary school years, when most children are cognitively ready for it (Sameroff and Haith, 1996). Throughout elementary school, children generally have one teacher for most academic subjects because strong teacher-student relationships are assumed to be especially important for preadolescents. In middle school or junior high, students begin to have different teachers for different subjects, but continuing to have a central teacher for some subjects eases the transition from elementary school (Clements and Seidman, 2002).

Children's development histories and individual differences make a difference in the impacts schools have on their further development. The transition to elementary school is often particularly challenging for children with disabilities and for children from low-income, minority, or non-English-speaking families. Preschool experiences with family, peers, preschool teachers, and the larger community all influence children's readiness to start elementary school, but schools also vary in their readiness to meet children's diverse individual needs (Pianta, Rimm-Kaufman, and Cox, 1999). Knowledge of basic school-related topics, such as numbers, letters, colors, and shapes, is one small part of school readiness, but children's cognitive, social, and emotional development are probably even more important (Meisels, 1999). Once children are in school, the social organization of schools and the quality of teacher-student relationships continue to influence their academic success and feelings about school (Clements and Seidman, 2002, Hamre and Pianta, 2001). We will return to these topics in more detail in later chapters.

THE SOCIAL AND ECONOMIC CONTEXT

All the elements of a child's immediate environment—his or her family, day care, peers, and school—are embedded in a broader social and economic context (the second ring in Figure 2.1). This context includes:

- the community in which a child's immediate environment exists;
- social institutions, such as local and national governments, health-care systems, and religious organizations; and
- social and economic conditions in the community and in the larger society, such as birth and marriage rates, average family size, crime rates, employment patterns, income levels, and inflation rates.

The social and economic context affects children *directly,* as when youngsters in low-income inner-city neighborhoods feel the effects of unsafe housing, poor health care, high crime rates, and overcrowding. At the same time, the social and economic context affects children *indirectly* by influencing their parents' behavior. If parents are stressed by the hardships of poverty or job loss, for example, the quality of their caregiving may diminish.

You will see the impact of differences in social and economic context in many parts of this book, especially in the stories of our three families. Later in this chapter, we discuss the special hardships that extreme poverty brings. But first we look at how American families have been affected by some widely shared changes in social and economic context.

Family Changes Caused by Social and Economic Factors

A popular TV show of the 1950s, tellingly called *Father Knows Best,* always began with the businessman father arriving at his house in the suburbs after a hard day's work. "Margaret, I'm home!" he would call out as he opened the front door. In the kitchen his homemaker wife, who had spent the day tending the house and children, was making dinner. Wiping her hands on her clean apron, she would rush to the door to greet the family breadwinner.

Few American families fit this traditional pattern today. Social and economic forces have changed the way most families live. The majority of married women with children now work outside the home. This is due partly to changing values and aspirations that have led many women to pursue careers and partly to economic circumstances that make it hard for families to manage on one salary. As Figure 2.3 shows, in the years between 1947 and 1985, the proportion of employed married mothers grew from 20 to 60 percent (Norton and Glick, 1986); by 2000 it had reached nearly 71 percent (U.S. Census Bureau, 2002b). This trend includes women with children under age 1; in 2000, nearly 60 percent of these mothers had full- or part-time jobs. Employment rates are even higher for divorced, widowed, and separated mothers.

Another change in American families that has had a significant effect on child development is an increase in single-parent families, due to divorce and births to unmarried

Statistics on Maternal Employment

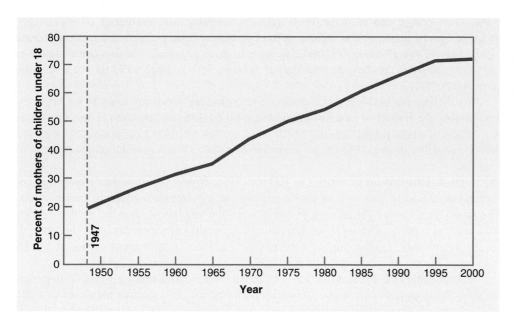

Figure 2.3
EMPLOYED MARRIED
MOTHERS OF CHILDREN
UNDER 18 YEARS,
1947–2000
The proportion of mothers in the
work force who are also raising
children has more than tripled in
50 years. *(Sources: Norton and
Glick, 1986; U.S. Census
Bureau, 2002b.)*

mothers. Between 1970 and 2000, the number of single-parent families with children under 18 in the United States more than tripled, from 3.4 to 12 million (see Figure 2.4). In 2000, nearly 27 percent of the children in the United States (19.2 million) lived with one parent (22.4 percent with their mothers; 4.2 percent with their fathers) (Fields and Casper, 2001). It is estimated that between 50 and 60 percent of children born in the

Statistics on Single Parenthood

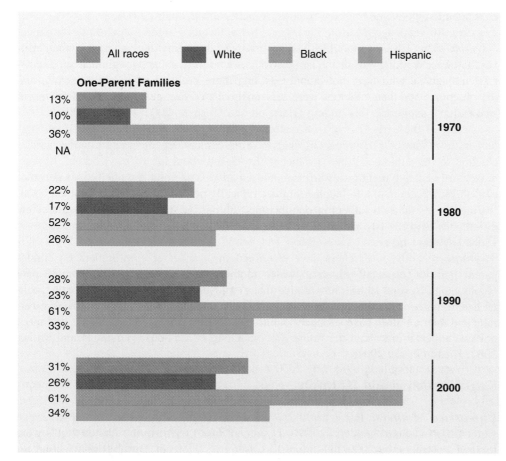

Figure 2.4
SINGLE-PARENT FAMILIES IN
THE U.S., 1970–2000
The proportion of single-parent
families in the United States has
increased greatly since 1970.
The percentage is highest for
black families, but the rate of
increase has been greatest for
white families. *(Source: U.S.
Census Bureau, 1995, 2002b.)*

1990s will spend part of their childhood in a single-parent household (Hetherington, Bridges, and Insabella, 1998). Living in a single-parent family often has severe economic consequences for children; in 2000, the median family income for two-parent families was $59,184; for families with no father present, it was only $25,794 (U.S. Census Bureau, 2002b).

To analyze the developmental consequences of these dramatic changes, we begin by considering the impact of mothers' employment on families and children. Then we look at the effects of single-parent families—both those created by births to unmarried women and those created by divorce. Finally, we consider some other kinds of nontraditional families.

Maternal Employment and Its Effects The effects of a mother's employment depend on a host of factors both inside and outside her family. Significant factors inside the family include the children's age and gender, the amount of time the mother spends at work, the quality of shared time remaining, the quality of substitute care, the strength of the parent-child relationship, and the meaning of the woman's employment to herself and other family members (Hoffman, 2000).

Some studies have found that *early* maternal employment (during a child's first year of life) is associated with slightly lowered performance on cognitive measures in early and middle childhood (Brooks-Gunn, Han, and Waldfogel, 2002; Han, Waldfogel, and Brooks-Gunn, 2001). However, maternal employment has mainly positive impacts for older children, especially girls (Hoffman, 2000). Both girls and boys tend to have less traditional ideas about gender roles when their mothers work. Daughters of employed mothers have higher academic achievement, greater independence and assertiveness, and better emotional adjustment than daughters of nonemployed mothers. For boys, research findings have been mixed, with some studies finding slight negative impacts of maternal employment on academic achievement and problem behaviors, especially for middle-class boys. Maternal employment seems to have few effects on adolescents' adjustment or academic achievement (Perry-Jenkins, Repetti, and Crouter, 2000).

Over 40 years ago, Marion Yarrow and her colleagues found that child development outcomes were related to mothers' satisfaction with their employment status, whether or not they were working outside the home. Mothers who were unhappy with their situation—especially those who were not employed—had more problems with child rearing, and the outcomes for their children were less positive (Yarrow et al., 1962). More recent studies have supported this finding (Harrison and Ungerer, 2002; Hoffman, 2000).

Much of the early research on maternal employment focused on two-parent families; in those families, the impact of maternal employment depends in part on the father's reaction to the situation. When a father is displeased about his wife's working, he may have more negative feelings toward his children and his parental responsibilities (Crouter et al., 1987). Fathers in two-income families typically perform more household and child-rearing chores than do fathers in one-income families. Overall, however, there are few differences between two-parent families in which the mother is employed and those in which she stays home.

More recently, researchers have examined the impact of employment on single-parent families, especially those in which mothers have moved from welfare to paid employment. Several studies have found that employed single mothers have better mental health, parenting behavior, social support, and coping skills than those receiving welfare, and their children have stronger cognitive skills, fewer behavior problems, and more positive expectations about the future (Brooks-Gunn et al., 2001; Gennetian and Miller, 2002; Huston et al., 2001).

Single Parenting and Its Effects

Unmarried Mothers. In the last thirty years, the rate of births to unmarried American women has increased greatly. In 1970, 11 percent of all births in the United States were to unwed mothers; by 2000, that figure had risen to 33 percent. Birthrates have risen for

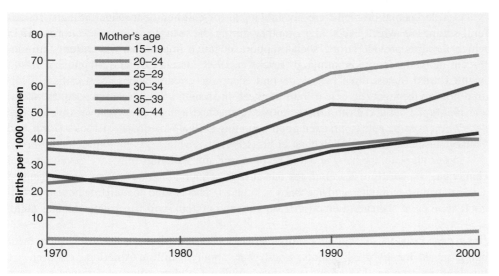

Figure 2.5
BIRTHRATES FOR
UNMARRIED WOMEN,
1970–2000
Birthrates have risen for
unmarried women in all age
groups under 40 in the last thirty
years. *(Source: U.S. Census
Bureau, 2002b; Ventura &
Bachrach, 2000.)*

unmarried women in all age groups (see Figure 2.5). In fact, the majority of the unmarried women who gave birth in 2000 (56.3 percent) were in their twenties.

Much of the concern about out-of-wedlock births has been focused on teenagers who become mothers. About 28 percent of the unmarried women who gave birth in 2000 were under age 20. The total *number* of births to teenage mothers reached its peak in the 1970s, but the percentage of teenage mothers who are unmarried has steadily increased since then (see Figures 2.5 and 2.6).

Children of unmarried teenage mothers often have developmental problems, such as cognitive lags and behavior problems, and they show higher than average rates of school failure, delinquency, early sexual activity, and pregnancy (Coley and Chase-Lansdale, 1998). However, the mothers of most of the children who have been studied have been poor, as well as young and unmarried. It is not clear which of these factors is most responsible for the children's negative outcomes, but there is some evidence that poverty may be the key factor (Brooks-Gunn and Furstenberg, 1986; Coley and Chase-Lansdale, 1998).

Child Development CD:
Teenage Pregnancy and Childbearing

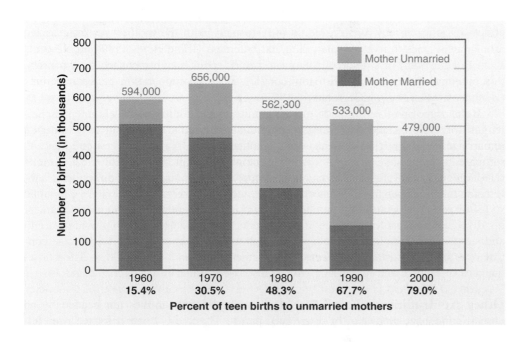

Figure 2.6
BIRTHS TO MOTHERS
YOUNGER THAN 20 BY
MARITAL STATUS, U.S.,
1960–2000
The *number* of births to
teenagers has declined since
1970, but the proportion of
teenage mothers who are
unmarried has risen steadily
since 1960. *(Sources: Ventura
et al., 1997, 2001.)*

Developmental problems are not inevitable for children of teenage mothers. In cultural settings in which becoming a mother during the teenage years is the norm and in which families provide strong social support, negative impacts on the children of adolescent mothers seem to be minimal (Erickson, 1998; Garcia Coll and Magnuson, 1999). In the United States, three factors beyond economic circumstances seem critical. Children born to teenagers do best if their mothers finish high school, receive adequate social and emotional support from others, and have reached a high enough level of cognitive development to be able to practice good parenting skills (Furstenberg, Brooks-Gunn, and Chase-Lansdale, 1989; O'Callaghan et al., 1999).

In our vignette, the baby about to be born to Karen Polonius may face developmental challenges, especially if Karen drops out of high school and continues to receive limited support from her mother and the baby's father. If she is able to finish school and find good sources of social and emotional support, the outlook will be brighter for her child.

Child Development CD:
Divorce and Child Development

Divorced Parents. Developmentalists are also concerned about the consequences of being raised by divorced parents. Each year, about 1 million American children are involved in divorce (U.S. Census Bureau, 1999). Children often experience negative effects when their parents divorce. School-age boys, for instance, tend to show a short-term decline in school achievement and to become more demanding and less obedient toward the parent who has been awarded custody of them (Emery, 1999; Hetherington and Kelly, 2002). The consequences of divorce and remarriage are diverse and complex, however. Some children prosper, others have long-lasting developmental problems, and still others show delayed effects during adolescence. These variable outcomes seem to be related to the child's age, sex, and personality, to the quality of home life and parenting, and to the resources available to both parents and child (Hetherington and Kelly, 2002; Hetherington and Stanley-Hagan, 1999).

An important question is whether the reactions observed in children of divorce are caused by the divorce itself or by the parents' conflict (Grych and Fincham, 2001; Hetherington and Stanley-Hagan, 1999). Research has shown that divorce that ends parental conflict is generally better for children than a conflict-ridden marriage, but divorce in which the parents' animosities continue is usually worse for children than a marriage with conflict. Ongoing contact with the noncustodial parent (usually the father) generally reduces the negative consequences of divorce, provided there is no serious conflict between the parents (Hetherington and Kelly, 2002). These two factors—reduced conflict and continued contact with both parents—seem to be more influential than the particular custody arrangement following a divorce. There are no major differences in the effects of joint custody versus sole custody (usually with the mother), as long as the arrangement leads to reduced quarreling and bitterness (Kline et al., 1989). Adolescents seem to adjust best to a divorce if they can avoid feeling caught between their parents; this outcome is most likely with low conflict and high cooperation between parents (Buchanan, Maccoby, and Dornbusch, 1991).

Remarriage and the formation of stepfamilies create additional developmental challenges for children and adolescents; individual children's adjustment to a parent's remarriage generally takes several years. Conflict is often higher between children and stepparents (especially stepmothers) than between children and biological parents (Hetherington and Kelly). Adjustment to a stepparent tends to be more difficult for adolescents than for younger children or postadolescents (Parke and Buriel, 1998). Optimal styles of parenting and family functioning seem to be different for stepfamilies than for nondivorced families; for example, it often works best for stepparents to provide warmth and support for discipline by biological parents rather than attempting to exercise control over children's behavior themselves (Hetherington and Kelly, 2002). The consequences of divorce and remarriage will be discussed further in Chapters 12 and 14.

Other Nontraditional Families Not all nontraditional families are headed by an unmarried teenage mother or by a divorced parent. The family context for today's chil-

Families in the United States are more varied today than ever. Many couples, both heterosexual and homosexual, become parents by adopting children from other countries.

dren includes adult career women who choose to become mothers outside of marriage, single adoptive parents, and families in which one or both parents are homosexual. Research on such nontraditional families is just beginning, but some important findings are already known. For example, studies show that homosexual parents are as involved with their children as heterosexual parents are, and they report no more problems with their children than do other parents. Moreover, being reared by homosexual parents produces no obvious differences in gender identity, sex-role behavior, or sexual orientation, and it does not appear to put a child at risk for psychological problems (Bailey et al., 1995; Flaks et al., 1995; Patterson, 2002). Other factors, such as social support, parental adjustment, and attitudes toward child rearing appear to be more important than a parent's sexual orientation per se.

Socioeconomic Status and the Family

Another important aspect of the social and economic context is **socioeconomic status (SES),** the grouping of people within a society on the basis of income, occupation, and education. Developmentalists have long been interested in how SES affects child rearing because living conditions, opportunities, and educational background all influence values, attitudes, and expectations regarding children. Researchers have found many differences in child-rearing practices between working-class and middle-class parents (Hoff, Laursen, and Tardif, 2002). For example, working-class parents in general use more physical discipline and emphasize obedience, whereas middle-class parents are more likely to reason with their children and encourage self-expression (McLoyd, 1990).

These findings do not imply, however, that the techniques favored by middle-class parents are necessarily superior. Both styles of parenting have potential drawbacks. Reasoning, when carried to extremes, can induce much guilt in children, just as physical discipline can become physical abuse. Moreover, different socioeconomic settings may demand somewhat different styles of parenting. For middle-class families, a parenting style that is firm and consistent but allows children considerable input in family rule making and decision making seems to produce the best results (Baumrind, 1989). In poor, inner-city neighborhoods, a parenting style featuring strict rules and an emphasis on obedience may protect children from the dangers of the environment (McLoyd, 1998). In less threatening settings, parents may be more free to focus on issues such as self-expression because day-to-day life is less dangerous for their children.

Socioeconomic status (SES): The grouping of people within a society on the basis of income, occupation, and education.

Figure 2.7
PERCENTAGES OF CHILDREN AND ELDERLY LIVING IN POVERTY, 1960–2000
Poverty rates for all age groups in the United States declined in the 1960s, with the establishment of antipoverty programs. That decline continued for the elderly through 2000, as programs for the elderly continued to be well funded. Meanwhile, the rate of poverty among children increased after 1970, as programs aimed specifically at children were cut back and the percentage of single-parent families increased. During the economic boom of the 1990s the poverty rate for children dropped, but in 2000 it remained more than one and one-half times the rate for the elderly. *(Sources: U.S. Census Bureau, 2002a; Dalaker, 2001. Figures for children under 6 not available before 1970.)*

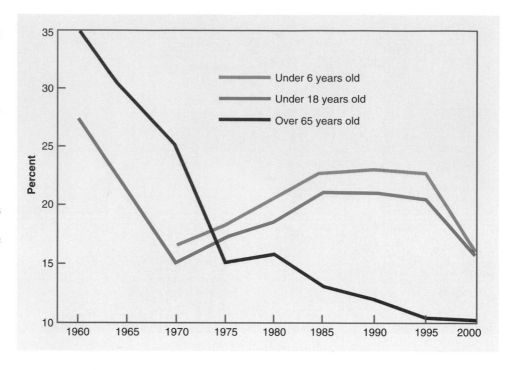

In any case, excellent and poor quality child care cut across socioeconomic lines (Egeland and Sroufe, 1981). When poor quality care does occur in low-income families, it is not caused by SES in itself, any more than the simple fact that a mother works means that her children will be cared for inadequately. Instead, poor quality child care is usually the result of a whole set of circumstances that often accompany economic disadvantage.

Child Poverty

Poverty and Child Development The United States is the world's wealthiest nation, yet 11.6 million American children lived in poverty in 2000 (see Figure 2.7). This figure includes one in six children in the United States overall; the rate is nearly twice as high for African-American and Hispanic children. As we've said, children in single-parent homes are at high risk for poverty; about 40 percent of the children in American families headed by single mothers are poor (Dalaker, 2001).

Poverty has serious consequences for child development, especially if it is persistent (Bradley and Corwyn, 2002; McLoyd, 1998). Children who grow up in poverty score lower than other children on IQ, vocabulary, and school achievement tests. They are more likely to repeat grades, be placed in special education, and drop out of high school, and they show higher rates of behavior problems and delinquency.

What is it about being poor that produces these outcomes? Inadequate prenatal care, prenatal exposure to drugs and alcohol, and low birth weight set the stage for later cognitive deficits by impairing brain development. Exposure to lead in the environment and a lack of cognitive stimulation at home further intensify negative effects on cognitive development. Social and emotional problems appear to be related more directly to high levels of family stress and harsh, inconsistent parenting (Bradley and Corwyn, 2002; McLoyd, 1998).

Poor families usually experience much more stress than middle-class families do. In addition to financial uncertainty, they are more likely to be exposed to a continuous string of negative events (such as job loss, eviction, illness, and criminal assault) and to chronic problems (such as substandard, overcrowded housing and dangerous neighborhoods). These many sources of stress can cause parents to become depressed, irritable, and distracted, resulting in punitive and erratic behavior toward their children (Bradley and Corwyn, 2002; McLoyd, 1990). When stress is coupled with social isolation, it can take

This child's drawing, with its references to drugs and injury, reflects the impact of the high levels of violence to which many poor inner-city children are exposed.

an even higher toll on the quality of child care. Thus, it is not poverty per se that causes developmental problems, but all of the factors associated with it (Ackerman et al., 1999).

At its worst, poverty can become a self-perpetuating cycle. Psychologists and social policy makers are especially concerned about the effects of poverty on the black underclass, as poverty among African Americans has become increasingly concentrated in inner-city ghettos (Wilson, 1989). Many of the industries that formerly provided employment for the black working class (automobile, textiles, rubber, steel, meat packing) have shut their plants in the last thirty-five years, and unemployment rates for inner-city blacks have soared. At the same time, middle-class professional blacks have left the inner city for more comfortable neighborhoods. As a result of this exodus, many churches, neighborhood associations, schools, and businesses have either cut back services or closed their doors. Thus, many young people growing up in the inner city lack not only job opportunities but also role models for a successful working life and institutions that could offer them encouragement and guidance (McLoyd, 1990).

Of course, some families do a good job of rearing their children under the worst of conditions. "But . . . most parents who live in poverty don't beat the odds; they reflect the odds" (Halpern, 1990, p. 14). Intervention programs, such as Project Head Start for preschoolers and other programs that begin in infancy or even during pregnancy, can make a difference in the outcomes for children born into poverty, but programs of this sort reach only a tiny fraction of the children who could benefit from them (Harris, 1996). (We will discuss intervention programs further in Chapters 5 and 10.)

Homelessness Homelessness carries a particularly strong set of risks for children. Single mothers with young children are the most rapidly growing segment of the homeless population (Bassuk and Rosenberg, 1990). In 2002, nearly 40 percent of the homeless population in U.S. cities were families with children (U.S. Conference of Mayors, 2002). Homeless women are less likely than other impoverished women to receive prenatal care, and rates of low birth weight and infant mortality are higher for their babies (Chavkin et al., 1987). Compared with children living in poverty but having homes, homeless children suffer from more health problems and are less likely to receive proper immunizations (Wright, 1990). Homeless children experience even greater life stress than other

Homeless Families

poor children, including more disruption of school and friendships, and they show higher rates of behavior problems (Buckner et al., 1999; Masten et al., 1993).

Unemployment and Family Relationships   Transitory poverty has fewer lasting impacts on children than persistent poverty does, but family stress associated with changing economic circumstances can take a toll. Unemployment and loss of income tend to affect children indirectly, through negative impacts on mothers' and fathers' psychological functioning and parenting behavior. Studies reveal that job loss is often associated with increased family conflict, heightened risk of domestic violence, and changes in the frequency and consistency of child discipline. In turn, children often develop social and emotional problems, including increased anxiety and depression and decreased self-esteem. Whether job loss or other economic strains actually have a negative impact on children depends on parents' response to the situation and on the degree of social support parents receive from spouses and other adults. Negative changes in child and family functioning are most likely if parents become depressed or irritable and if they lack social support. Researchers have found these patterns in both one- and two-parent families, in situations ranging from the Great Depression of the 1930s to the recession in the rural United States in the 1980s and individual job loss in the 1990s (Conger et al., 1994; Elder, Caspi, and Burton, 1988; McLoyd et al., 1994; Simons et al., 1992).

THE CULTURAL CONTEXT

In a nursery school in Beijing, China, a teacher is showing a group of 3-year-olds a mechanical Ping-Pong game. The toy consists of a miniature table with a net and two mechanical players who stiffly swing their paddles. The teacher explains how the new toy works and then places it on the ground so the children can see it in action. A sea of little bodies quickly surrounds the toy. Thirty pairs of eyes intently watch the performance, but not a single child moves. Those in the front do not even stretch out an arm to hold or finger the toy. The children squat quietly in a tightly packed circle, staring in delighted fascination. At the back of the circle a teacher is holding a Western child, the son of a diplomat stationed in Beijing. She lets the boy down, and without hesitation he breaks through the ranks and lunges for the toy. The teacher quickly scoops him up while the Chinese children look on (Kessen, 1975).

These differences in behavior between Chinese and Western children are largely a reflection of two different **cultures**—two different systems of beliefs, attitudes, values, and guidelines for behavior. These elements of culture help to shape the behavior of the people who share them. As a result, different cultures tend to produce different patterns of personality characteristics, cognitive skills, and social relationships (Konner, 1991; Rubin, 1998; Shweder et al., 1998).

For example, the social organization and expectations of traditional Japanese culture are quite different from those of North American culture (Doi, 1992; Rothbaum et al., 2000; Shwalb and Shwalb, 1995). Belonging to the group rather than individual assertiveness is the principal guide to behavior. Respect and agreeableness are highly valued, as are emotional maturity, self-control, and courtesy. Family bonds are very tight and relationships are closely interdependent. Newborns are viewed as initially *independent* (not bound to the group), and making them *dependent* (and part of the group) is considered an urgent task. Traditional Japanese mothers *never* part from their young children, even to go shopping. Thus, Japanese culture fosters certain personal and social characteristics that are quite different from those fostered by North American culture.

The cultural context is represented by the third ring in Figure 2.1. Family, peer groups, schools, and communities always exist within a culture and are greatly influenced by it. These influences, in turn, affect the developing child.

Culture:
A system of beliefs, attitudes, values, and guidelines for behavior shared by a group of people.

Different cultures provide different contexts for children's development. Even young Chinese children are expected to pay close attention during lessons. Fewer requirements of this type are placed on North American preschoolers.

Cultural Influences

Children born in every culture share the same human biological inheritance and the same fundamental need for care. Thus, adults in every culture face the same major tasks in rearing children:

- providing infants with the basic nurturance needed for development, and
- preparing children to function as adults in their particular social world.

The latter task involves passing along the rules, standards, and values of the culture, a process known as **socialization.** Cultures differ from each other in:

- the ways the tasks of nurturance and socialization are carried out,
- the specific rules and values that are passed along, and
- the final outcome of socialization—that is, the behaviors, beliefs, and worldviews children adopt.

Socialization:
The process by which children acquire the rules, standards, and values of a culture.

Socialization occurs not only through explicit instruction but also through the day-to-day experiences of childhood. The values important in a particular culture are often reflected in the structure of the settings in which children spend their time, which in turn produce different developmental outcomes. To Western eyes, a Chinese nursery school seems spartan because there are few toys and little play equipment. Chinese nursery school teachers initiate and organize most of the daily activities, while children listen, follow instructions, take turns, and share. This classroom structure very efficiently teaches important Chinese values of self-control, obedience, and group cooperation. In contrast, a typical North American nursery school provides a wide array of toys and equipment that children can use in their own ways. Teachers organize some activities, but much of the time is given to free play in which children choose and structure their own activities. This arrangement fosters traits considered important by most North Americans—self-expression and individuality (Tobin, Wu, and Davidson, 1989).

As another example of how the daily experiences of children implicitly convey cultural beliefs and values, consider the educational practices common in Japan (Rohlen and Le Tendre, 1996; Stevenson and Lee, 1990). Japanese culture places a high value on formal education, and Japanese students score much higher than North American students do on international tests of math and science. Starting in elementary school, Japanese children are expected to devote themselves to learning. They spend many more hours in the classroom and doing homework than North American youngsters do. In addition, many Japanese children attend special schools, called *juku,* after regular school hours to receive extra tutoring for exams or enrichment courses in subjects such as calligraphy. Because Japanese parents believe that achievement depends on effort, they are rarely satisfied with their children's academic achievement and keep urging them to work harder. North American parents, in contrast, tend to believe that academic success depends on innate ability as much as on effort, and most assume that their children are doing about as well as they can.

Children's behavior also reflects the values and demands of their culture. Some years ago, Millard Madsen at UCLA developed a series of two-person games for studying children's inclination to cooperate or compete (Kagan and Madsen, 1972; Madsen, 1971). In one game, four hands were needed to open a box. Only if the two players worked together, pushing all four latches at the same time, would either of them get a prize. In another game, two players at opposite ends of a table each held a string connected to a case containing a marble in the middle of the table, as shown in Figure 2.8. The strings could be used to pull the marble case to cups at either end of the table, and the children were allowed to keep all the marbles that ended up in their cups. The marble case was

mhhe.com /dehart5

Education in Japan

Japanese infants are seldom separated from their mothers. Coats are even available with specially designed hoods to cover babies being carried on their mothers' backs.

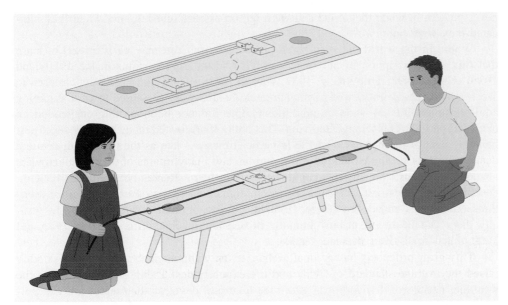

Figure 2.8
MADSEN'S MARBLE-PULL COOPERATION GAME
(Source: From M. Madsen, "Development and Cross-Cultural Differences in Cooperative and Competitive Behavior of Young Children," Journal of Cross-Cultural Psychology, 2, p. 367, 1971. Copyright © 1971 by Sage Publications, Inc. Reprinted by Permission of Sage Publications, Inc.)

held together with magnets, and if both children pulled their strings at the same time, the case would break apart and neither child would get the marble. To win any marbles, the children had to take turns pulling the strings. Madsen found dramatic differences in behavior between urban Anglo-American and rural Mexican children. The Anglo-American children, especially older ones, were far more competitive, clinging to a competitive strategy even when it had no benefit for them. The rural Mexican children were far more cooperative, even when only one of them could benefit at a time. Anglo-American and Mexican children favored different strategies, but both chose strategies that worked well—that were *adaptive*—in their own cultures.

Beatrice and John Whiting (1975) found similar tendencies in a study of children living in six different cultures in the United States, India, Kenya, Mexico, Okinawa, and the Philippines. Children in the nonindustrialized cultures were given tasks important to the well-being of their families, such as caring for younger siblings and tending goats while their mothers worked in the fields. These children showed nurturant and responsible behavior, traits suited to the roles they performed. If they failed to tend the goats, their families would have no milk. In contrast, children in the industrialized cultures were more dependent and self-centered. In complex industrialized cultures children do not need to contribute to their family's survival, so a self-centered orientation can be tolerated in them. In fact, being somewhat self-centered is actually an asset in cultures that depend on a desire for personal profit to motivate economic growth.

The notion of cultural adaptiveness also implies that the same child-rearing practice may have different meanings and therefore produce different outcomes in two different cultures. For example, in the United States, many people would hold that having children share a bed with their parents, especially past infancy, is a form of maltreatment. But in many parts of the world, including Japan, India, and the highlands of Guatemala, children routinely sleep with parents or other adult relatives without harm. Members of these cultures would view the American practice of forcing infants to sleep alone in separate rooms as abhorrent and abusive (Morelli et al., 1992). The entire cultural context must be considered before the meaning and impact of a particular practice can be determined (Shweder et al., 1998).

Cultural Change and Child Development

A culture once existed in which the most important goal in raising children was to establish strong parental control. Training the child to be obedient began in the first year. To avoid spoiling a baby, only the infant's physical needs were met. Babies' bids for attention were strongly discouraged, and sentimental treatment was avoided. Infants were

In the 1920s, parents in the United States were advised to avoid sentimental treatment of their children, to keep them on a strict schedule, and to begin training them in good habits as early as possible.

China's One-Child Policy

Subcultures:
Groups whose beliefs, attitudes, values, and guidelines for behavior differ in some ways from those of the dominant culture.

never picked up when they cried and were fed on a strict schedule, not when they indicated they were hungry.

Where in the world did such harsh practices exist? You may be surprised to learn that this is a description of our own society's child-rearing customs in the 1920s and 1930s (Grant, 1998; Truby-King, 1937; Watson, 1928). Until quite recently, children in Western societies were viewed as miniature adults and were pressured toward assuming adult responsibility as soon as possible. People did not believe children needed an extended period of nurturant caregiving. This outlook originated many centuries ago, perhaps because of the harshness of life in earlier times. As late as the nineteenth century, death at birth or during childhood was common, and many infants of poor families were abandoned because their parents could not support them. (Remember the case of Victor, described at the beginning of this chapter.) In eighteenth-century Paris, one out of every three babies was abandoned (Piers, 1978). Children admitted to foundling homes usually died. Out of 10,272 babies admitted to one Dublin institution between 1775 and 1800, only 45 survived (Kessen, 1965).

This grim prognosis has gradually changed as technological progress has steadily raised the average standard of living and life expectancies. Today, many parents in the wealthier nations of the world can afford the luxury of devoting themselves to their children's emotional welfare. In poorer countries, the physical survival of children remains the primary concern, and parents must still bend much of their effort to ensuring that their children survive infancy (LeVine, 1988).

Undoubtedly, cultural change will continue to affect parenting and child development. In some societies, cultural changes are happening very rapidly. For instance, far-reaching change is taking place in China, where a family-centered culture is being transformed into a state-centered one. Imagine the consequences of establishing universal preschool education in a society where young children have traditionally been cared for at home. Imagine the effects of a one-child-per-family policy in a culture that for centuries has considered large families a blessing. One result of the one-child policy has been for both families and the government to devote increased resources to the care and education of these single children, to ensure their optimal development. Chinese researchers and officials have been concerned that such concentrated attention might produce a generation of "little emperors"—children whose sense of privilege and individualism may not be well suited to the collective orientation of Chinese society. Research aimed at determining whether such concern is justified has produced mixed results (Chen and Goldsmith, 1991; Falbo and Poston, 1993; Jiao, Ji, and Jing, 1986; Yang et al., 1995).

Subcultures

Complex, industrialized cultures often include a number of **subcultures**—groups whose beliefs, attitudes, values, and guidelines for behavior differ in some ways from those of the dominant culture. North American societies contain a wide range of subcultures, including African Americans, Latinos, Asian Americans, and Europeans from various national backgrounds; many different Native American tribes; and numerous religious groups. Like the larger culture, particular subcultures have a major influence on child development (Entwisle, 1994).

Sometimes the beliefs, attitudes, values, and guidelines for behavior that are part of a child's subculture clash with those of the larger culture. Consider how social relations and communications are structured in a typical North American classroom (Tharp, 1989; Dalton and Tharp, 2002). Material is usually presented to the class as a whole, after which students are given time to practice on their own and receive some individual instruction. Communication follows a "switchboard" format, with the teacher asking rapid-fire questions, students answering quickly, and the teacher pronouncing the answer right or wrong before moving on to the next point. The emphasis is on individual achievement, and cooperation on homework or tests is considered cheating.

This format is well suited to children from most white, middle-class families, where the dominant cultural values of individual achievement and competition are stressed, but

In traditional Native American cultures, children learn skills holistically. Watching her mother weave, this Navajo girl learns to understand the process of weaving as a whole, rather than learning each step separately.

it is not equally suited to children from other backgrounds. For example, in traditional Hawaiian culture, older siblings care for younger siblings in small groups in which cooperation and mutual help are valued. This cultural pattern prepares children for group problem solving, but not for whole-class or individual instruction. In many Native American communities, children are taught skills holistically; boning a fish or weaving a rug would be taught as a complete process, rather than in the step-by-step manner practiced in school. Children accustomed to a holistic style of learning may find the typical classroom approach to such topics as arithmetic skills unnatural and confusing. Moreover, the oral traditions of some subcultures clash with the communication style of the typical classroom. For example, the black oral tradition includes challenge games, in which children are encouraged to take on adult roles and issue commands and reprimands. In class, this verbal game playing is often viewed as rude or impertinent (Heath, 1989).

Thus, how well a child fares in the typical North American classroom depends in part on the norms and values that the child has absorbed at home. If those norms and values are compatible with those of the dominant culture, academic success is more likely. The success of many recent Asian immigrants rests in part on subcultural values that emphasize education, expectations of academic success, and a belief that children have a moral obligation to do well for the family (Sue and Okazaki, 1990). There is now considerable evidence that when educators take subcultural differences into account, academic achievement increases (Tharp, 1989; Dalton and Tharp, 2002). We consider cultural compatibility in education practices in Chapter 11.

You will see the impact of subcultural differences in our three family stories. For example, as black Americans living in an urban center, members of the Williams family are influenced by certain subcultural norms, including reliance on an extended family (Fisher, Jackson, and Villarruel, 1998; McAdoo, 2002; Wilson, 1989). The Williamses' lives provide a good example of how subcultural influences continually interact with broader cultural forces.

Traditional Hawaiian Education

DEVELOPMENT AS CONTEXT

No discussion of developmental contexts would be complete without a mention of development itself as a context for further development. Development provides a context in two ways. First, *it gives each person a developmental history, which influences the course of future development.* This idea is central to Erikson's theory, discussed in Chapter 1.

According to Erikson, the way a child negotiates the issues of a particular developmental period depends in part on development during earlier periods. For example, toddlers must strike a balance between their emerging sense of autonomy and capacity for self-assertion, on the one hand, and the limits their parents impose, on the other. But a toddler's tendency to comply with parents' demands is forecast by the nature of the *infant*-parent relationship (Matas, Arend, and Sroufe, 1978). Part of the context for development in the toddler period is development in the preceding period, infancy. Similarly, children enter preschool with differing orientations toward their peers and teachers, and with differing expectations about their own capacities to master new situations. These differences, which are rooted in each child's developmental history, become part of the context for development in the preschool years.

Second, *development provides a context for future development because children change physically and intellectually as they mature.* The transformations in physical and cognitive capacities that occur with maturation have a dramatic influence on how children interact with their environments. Because of physical maturation, the toddler is much more mobile than the infant, much more able to get into things. This new mobility encourages parents in many cultures to impose new demands, and the child's world consequently changes. At the same time, the toddler begins to understand and use language as a result of neurological and cognitive maturation. This opens up a whole new way of dealing with the world, which greatly affects future development.

CONTEXTS IN INTERACTION

This chapter's central message has been that human development always occurs within a set of contexts:

- the child's biological makeup,
- the immediate environment,
- the broader social and economic context,
- the cultural context, and
- the context of the child's own developmental level and history.

None of these contexts exists in isolation. None exerts its influence apart from the others. All are constantly interacting, helping to shape how the child develops.

As an example of how contexts interact, consider maternal employment in the United States, discussed earlier in this chapter. As attitudes toward mothers working outside the home became more favorable (a change in the cultural context), and as economic pressures on families increased (a change in the social and economic context), the number of employed women with young children grew dramatically. This change altered the physical surroundings in which many young children spend their time and the people with whom they have regular contact (a change in the child's immediate environment). In turn, as the number of two-earner families increased, maternal employment became even more socially acceptable—a further alteration of the cultural context in which children are reared in our society. Thus, change in one developmental context goes hand in hand with changes in others, and all affect child development in an interconnected way.

Another important point to remember in thinking about developmental contexts is that certain environmental factors tend to go together (Masten et al., 1990). Economic advantage, job satisfaction, adequate food and housing, a stable home life, and social support often accompany one another, as do high crime rates, ineffective schools, unemployment, and family disorganization (Ackerman et al., 1999; McLoyd, 1990, 1998).

Remember, too, that all the environmental influences we have discussed in this chapter are funneled to some extent through the family. For instance, children are not *directly* affected by their parents' social isolation or job stress. Instead, these factors have an *indirect* influence by affecting the quality of care the children receive at home (Crouter and

McHale, 1993; McLoyd et al., 1994). Not even the influences of day care, the school, and the peer group are removed from the family. It is parents who arrange for day care, select schools for their children, and promote or fail to promote peer relationships (Rubin et al., 1998). In short, the significance that various developmental contexts have for a child is always affected by the child's family. Biological, socioeconomic, and cultural factors provide both the challenges parents face and the resources they may draw on for the task of child rearing.

Chapter Summary

Introduction

Human development is strongly influenced by the contexts in which it occurs.

- Extreme deprivation, as in the cases of Victor, Genie, and some institutionalized children, leads to abnormal development.
- Within more typical ranges, differences in developmental contexts produce varying developmental paths.

An Overview of Developmental Contexts

Bronfenbrenner describes developmental contexts as a series of concentric rings:

- the child's biological makeup,
- the immediate environment,
- the social and economic context, and
- the cultural context.

The Child's Biological Makeup

The child's biological makeup consists of:

- the evolutionary heritage shared by all human beings,
- the child's individual genetic inheritance, and
- characteristics that result from interactions between genes and the environment.

Major features of the human evolutionary heritage include:

- a timetable for developmental milestones,
- a strong disposition to act on the environment,
- an innate propensity for learning, and
- a predisposition to be social.

The Child's Immediate Environment

The child's immediate environment includes all the settings, people, and objects that directly touch the child's daily life.

- The family is a dominant part of a child's immediate environment, an interconnected *system* in which each member's behavior depends in part on the behaviors of the others.

- Important settings outside the family that are part of children's immediate environment include day care, the peer group, the neighborhood, and the school.

The Social and Economic Context

The broader social and economic context consists of social and economic conditions in the community and in the larger society. In the last forty years, social and economic factors have produced major changes in how American families live, all of which have consequences for children's development.

- The majority of American mothers now work outside the home; the effects of maternal employment on children's development depend on many factors, including family members' satisfaction with their situation.
- The rate of births to unmarried women has increased greatly since 1970. Research on this issue has focused on children of low-income, single, adolescent mothers; poverty contributes strongly to these children's developmental problems.
- Divorce also produces a large number of single-parent families; its consequences for children's development are varied and complex, depending on characteristics of the child, the parent, and their social situation.

Socioeconomic status (SES) influences children's development in many ways.

- Working-class and middle-class parents tend to use different child-rearing methods, but good and poor quality care of children is found at every socioeconomic level.
- Persistent poverty has serious consequences for children's cognitive and social-emotional development. Cognitive development is especially harmed by prenatal factors, lead in the environment, and lack of stimulation; social and emotional problems are related more directly to family stress and poor parenting.
- Homelessness carries a particularly strong set of risks for children, increasing the likelihood of a variety of problems.

- Unemployment and other changes in economic circumstances affect children indirectly, through their impacts on parents' psychological functioning and behavior.

The Cultural Context

The cultural context of child development consists of all the beliefs, attitudes, values, and guidelines for behavior shared by the people in a child's culture. Culture influences children's development by shaping the social and economic context and the child's immediate environment.

- In all cultures, adults face the same two major tasks in rearing children: nurturance and **socialization.**
- Cultures differ in the ways they carry out the tasks of nurturance and socialization, the specific rules and values passed along, and the final outcome of socialization.
- Socialization occurs through explicit instruction and through the way day-to-day experiences for children are structured in settings such as the educational system.
- Children's behavior often reflects the values and demands of their culture; in other words, it tends to be culturally adaptive.

- Changes in cultures are usually reflected in changes in child-rearing methods and in developmental outcomes.
- Many societies include a number of **subcultures,** each with their own influences on children's development. Inconsistencies between the values and norms of the dominant culture and those of a child's subculture can contribute to academic problems.

Development as Context

Development itself provides a context for future development in two ways.

- Each person's developmental history influences the course of further development.
- Changes in physical and cognitive abilities produced by maturation have a dramatic influence on how children interact with their environments and continue to develop.

Contexts in Interaction

The biological context, the immediate environment, the social and economic context, and the cultural context are constantly interacting as they influence how children develop. Certain environmental factors tend to go together. All the environmental factors that children experience are funneled to some extent through the family.

Review Questions

Introduction

1. What is known about the effects of environmental deprivation on children's development?

An Overview of Developmental Contexts

2. Describe Bronfenbrenner's model of developmental contexts and explain what is included at each level in the model.

The Child's Biological Makeup

3. Explain the three basic components of the child's biological makeup and how they interact.

The Child's Immediate Environment

4. Explain how the family, day care, peers, neighborhoods, and schools influence children's development.

The Social and Economic Context

5. Summarize the ways American families have changed in recent decades and how these changes have affected children's development.

6. Explain how SES influences children's development.

The Cultural Context

7. What is the same about child rearing across all cultures? What differs across cultures?
8. Summarize the impacts of culture on children's development.

Development as Context

9. Explain two ways in which development itself provides a context for further development.

Contexts in Interaction

10. Explain how contexts interact to influence children's development.

Application and Observation

1. Apply Bronfenbrenner's model of developmental contexts to the three families described in the vignettes on pages 38–41. Describe what each of the contexts in the model will be like for each of the babies who are about to be born, including any relevant information on the baby's biological makeup. How might the babies' development be affected by the environments into which they will be born?

2. Interview several parents of infants about their transition to parenthood. How did the arrival of a baby change their daily lives, their relationships with their partners, their relationships with their extended families, and their views of themselves?

3. Spend several hours in a preschool or elementary school classroom, observing typical classroom activities. Take note of the curriculum, classroom routine, rules, arrangement of the room, class size, adults in the room, materials and equipment, and social interactions. What formal lessons are being taught? What cultural values and norms are being communicated?

4. Interview several parents of young children about the choices they have made about work and child care arrangements. You might ask about the factors that influenced their decisions about work and child care, positive and negative experiences with current and past work and child care situations, challenges and problems they currently face, and what they think the ideal situation would be for them and their children.

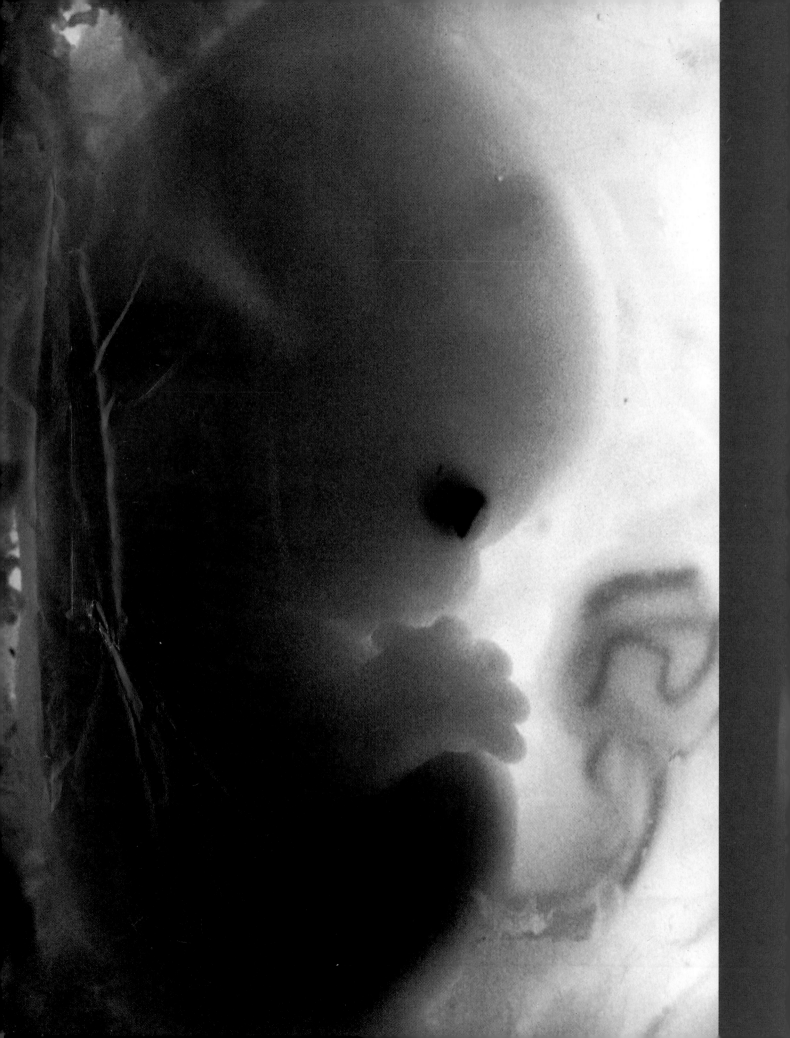

3 Heredity and Prenatal Development

Prenatal period:
The period of development prior to birth.

Differentiation:
A developmental process in which structures and functions become increasingly specialized.

If you stand outside a maternity-ward nursery, you are likely to find adults searching for family resemblances in their newborns. "Those big eyes are just like her mother's," someone might observe, or "He has his father's dimpled chin." Many family resemblances are related to genes, the chemical guidelines for development that each of us inherits from our parents. In this chapter you will learn how genes are expressed and how they interact with environmental influences. One major theme of this chapter is that *genes are only one part of a complex developmental system.* As we discussed in Chapters 1 and 2, genes guide development, but they function in a particular environment. We stress the role of context and the importance of a systems view throughout this book. That view is especially apparent when we consider the period of development prior to birth, which is called the **prenatal period.**

A second important theme of this chapter is that *development involves **differentiation,*** the process by which parts of an organism progressively take on specialized forms and functions. Differentiation always moves in the direction of greater refinement, complexity, and specialization. For instance, every human begins life as a single cell, which at first divides to produce cells that are identical to the original cell. Soon, however, the cells produced by further divisions begin to take on specialized forms and functions. Ultimately, the body will consist of such diverse cell types as red blood cells, muscle cells, nerve cells, and skin cells. Just as the one-celled creatures that first appeared on this planet differentiated into many species over millions of generations, so the initial cell that begins a human life differentiates through successive generations of cell division to produce all the parts of the body.

Human development involves more than differentiation alone. A third theme of this chapter is that, as we discussed in Chapter 1, *development involves repeated reorganization and qualitative change.* Cells undergo reorganization by migrating to form various

Parents provide a baby with a unique set of genes, and the whole family contributes to the environment in which those genes will be expressed.

tissues, and tissue cells reorganize further to build organs with intricate structures. The result is qualitative change in the developing organism. As you will see in this chapter, the embryo at five weeks after conception is fundamentally different than it was at two weeks; at eight weeks after conception it is fundamentally different than it was at five weeks. Not only have new parts been added, but the embryo has achieved new levels of organization and functioning.

A fourth theme is that during prenatal development *new structures and capacities emerge in an orderly way from those that existed before.* The pictures of human embryos in this chapter show that each stage is a logical outgrowth of the previous one, just as human development throughout childhood and adolescence is orderly, cumulative, and directional.

This chapter traces the development of a human being from conception through birth. We begin with a look at the set of genes the child inherits from his or her parents. As you will see, genes interact not only with their cellular environments but also with one another. Next, we turn to the events leading up to conception, when sperm and egg join to form a new organism. From there we take up the major stages of prenatal development, in which a single-celled organism is transformed over time into a baby ready to be born. We look in detail at some environmental influences that can disrupt prenatal development, such as exposure to certain drugs and diseases. We also examine genetic abnormalities that can cause developmental problems, and we explore methods of diagnosing them. Finally, we look at the birth of a baby, some of the problems that can arise at this time, and some cultural variations in childbirth.

Questions to Think About As You Read

- How do factors at each level in Bronfenbrenner's model affect prenatal development?
- What practical implications does information about genetics and prenatal development have for parents-to-be?

GENETIC PROCESSES

Every cell in your body contains the complete set of genetic instructions that have helped to guide your development from a single fertilized egg. These genetic instructions have led to your general human characteristics (such as hands instead of wings or fins), as well as your unique combination of variable traits (such as eye color and blood type). Your genetic instructions are stored in threadlike structures known as **chromosomes,** which are located in the nucleus, or central region, of each of your cells. Chromosomes are composed of long molecules of DNA (deoxyribonucleic acid), which have a twisted, double-helix structure that resembles a spiral staircase (see Figure 3.1). This structure gives DNA molecules the remarkable capacity to "unzip" down the middle and produce exact copies of themselves. Both the original and the copies contain blueprints for assembling the proteins that give each cell its particular structure and enable it to carry out its work. A **gene** is simply a segment of DNA that contains the code for producing a particular protein. The human **genome,** the complete DNA sequence found in each human cell, contains an estimated 30,000–40,000 genes (Venter et al., 2001; International Human Genome Sequencing Consortium, 2001) as well as long stretches of "junk" DNA, the function of which is not yet clear.

Chromosome:
Threadlike structures in which the organism's genetic instructions are stored, composed of DNA and located in the nucleus of each cell.

Gene:
A segment of DNA that contains the code for producing a particular protein.

Genome:
The complete DNA sequence for an organism.

Mechanisms of Cell Division

Your life began with one cell—a fertilized egg—containing one set of forty-six chromosomes. Copies of these original forty-six chromosomes are today found in each of the

Human Genome Project

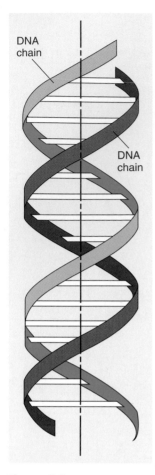

Figure 3.1
DNA, THE DOUBLE HELIX
DNA has a twisted, double-helix structure that consists of two long strands of molecules, like the railings of two spiral staircases, connected by short strands resembling steps.

Somatic cells:
The cells that make up the body, not including egg and sperm cells.

Mitosis:
The process of cell division by which the body grows and repairs itself, in which the genetic material from the parent cell is duplicated in each daughter cell.

Homologues:
Two chromosomes that form one of the twenty-three pairs of human chromosomes and resemble each other in size, shape, and the types of genes they carry.

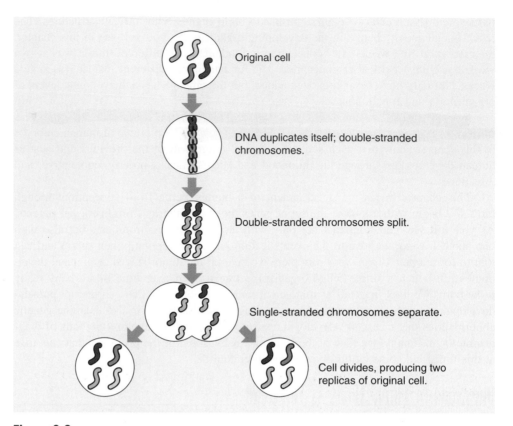

Figure 3.2
THE PROCESS OF MITOSIS
Only four of the forty-six chromosomes in the original cell are shown. *(Source: Based on information from Larsen, 2001.)*

billions of **somatic cells** that make up your body. These cells were formed by a process of cell division called **mitosis,** as shown in Figure 3.2. The process of mitosis occurs as follows:

- The DNA in the original cell duplicates itself, producing double-stranded chromosomes.
- The double-stranded chromosomes line up along the cell's center, and each one splits into two single-stranded chromosomes.
- The single-stranded chromosomes separate and move to opposite sides of the cell.
- The original cell divides down the middle, producing two new cells that are exact replicas of the original, each containing forty-six chromosomes.

Mitotic cell division is repeated again and again throughout an organism's life. It is the basic process by which the body grows and maintains itself.

Your forty-six chromosomes consist of twenty-three pairs; the two chromosomes in a pair are called **homologues.** Homologous chromosomes are similar in size and shape and contain the same types of genes. (Figure 3.3 shows a complete set of chromosomes for a normal male.) One member of each pair of homologues (twenty-three chromosomes in all) came from your mother, carried in the egg from which you were conceived. The other member of each pair (again twenty-three in number) came from your father, carried in one of his sperm.

But how did your mother's egg cells and your father's sperm cells come to have only twenty-three chromosomes, when all the other cells in their bodies have forty-six? The answer lies in a special kind of cell division that gives rise to egg and sperm cells.

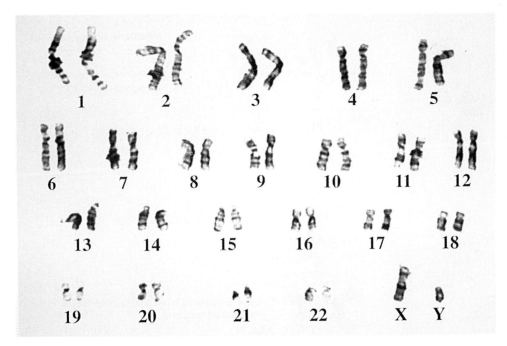

Figure 3.3
A COMPLETE SET OF
HUMAN CHROMOSOMES
This microphotograph shows
the twenty-three pairs of
chromosomes possessed by a
normal male, with an X and a Y
chromosome in the twenty-third
pair.

During this process, called **meiosis,** the number of chromosomes in egg and sperm cells is reduced to only twenty-three each, so that when an egg cell and a sperm cell unite, the fertilized egg will have the forty-six chromosomes needed for normal development. Without this important halving process, an egg cell and a sperm cell would each contain forty-six chromosomes, and the fertilized egg would contain ninety-two chromosomes, double the correct number.

The steps involved in meiosis are shown in Figure 3.4.

- The DNA in a **germ cell** (the type of cell from which egg cells or sperm cells are produced) duplicates itself, resulting in double-stranded chromosomes.

- The homologous chromosomes arrange themselves in pairs and exchange genetic material (in each pair one homologue came from the person's mother, the other from the person's father).

- The homologous chromosomes separate and move to opposite ends of the cell in preparation for cell division.

- The cell divides, with each of the two resulting cells receiving twenty-three double-stranded chromosomes (*first meiotic division*).

- The double-stranded chromosomes in these two cells split.

- These cells divide, yielding four new cells, each with a single set of twenty-three chromosomes (*second meiotic division*).

In males, all four of the new cells become mature sperm; in females, only one becomes a mature egg. But in both cases, the mature reproductive cell, or **gamete,** has half the normal number of chromosomes.

In addition to producing gametes with the correct number of chromosomes, meiosis also contributes to genetic diversity by means of two important processes: **crossing over** and **random assortment.** These two processes guarantee that each child (or each set of identical twins) inherits a unique mix of genes that no one else has ever possessed. *Crossing over* occurs during the second step in meiosis, when the homologous chromosomes in the germ cell arrange themselves in pairs. The homologues connect at various points and exchange corresponding segments (see Figure 3.5). By corresponding segments, we mean segments containing genes that code for the same characteristic, such as eye color. Since there are often several alternative forms of a gene, crossing over

Meiosis:
The process of cell division by which egg and sperm cells are formed.

/dehart5

DNA

Germ cells:
The cells from which eggs and sperm are produced.

Gamete:
A mature reproductive cell (egg or sperm).

Crossing over:
An exchange of corresponding segments of genetic material between homologous chromosomes during meiosis.

Figure 3.4

THE PROCESS OF MEIOSIS

Only four of the forty-six chromosomes in the original cell are shown. *(Source: Based on information from Larsen, 2001.)*

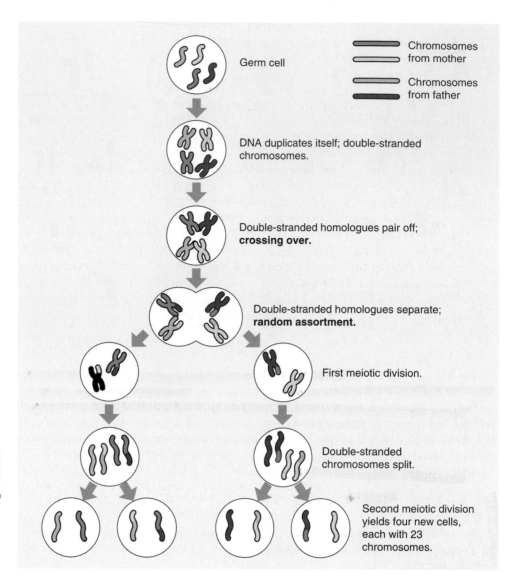

Germ cell

Chromosomes from mother

Chromosomes from father

DNA duplicates itself; double-stranded chromosomes.

Double-stranded homologues pair off; **crossing over.**

Double-stranded homologues separate; **random assortment.**

First meiotic division.

Double-stranded chromosomes split.

Second meiotic division yields four new cells, each with 23 chromosomes.

mhhe.com /dehart5

Mitosis vs. Meiosis Animation

Figure 3.5

CROSSING OVER

Variety in human offspring is greatly increased because during meiotic cell division chromosomes cross over, exchanging genetic material. *(Source: From Developmental Psychology: Theory, Research, and Applications, 1st edition, by D. Shaffer. Copyright © 1985. Reprinted with permission of Wadsworth, a division of Thomson Learning: www.thomson rights.com. Fax 800-730-2215.)*

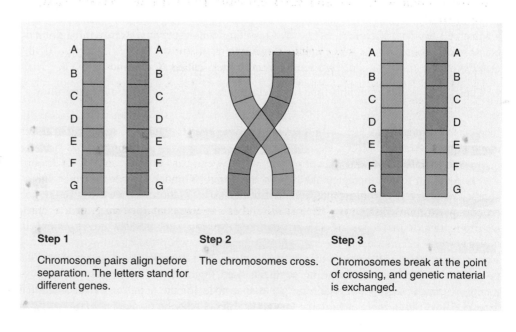

A   A
B   B
C   C
D   D
E   E
F   F
G   G

A   A
B   B
C   C
D   D
E   E
F   F
G   G

Step 1

Chromosome pairs align before separation. The letters stand for different genes.

Step 2

The chromosomes cross.

Step 3

Chromosomes break at the point of crossing, and genetic material is exchanged.

creates new genetic combinations within chromosomes. For example, a chromosome that originally contained genes that produce blue eyes may give up those genes to its homologous chromosome in exchange for genes that produce brown or green eyes. Many such exchanges make for a substantial shuffling of genes.

Further shuffling of genes occurs by means of **random assortment** when the homologous chromosomes separate and move to opposite ends of the germ cell in preparation for cell division. This sorting of homologues occurs without regard to their original sources. Purely by chance, some of the chromosomes that move to each end of the cell originally came from the person's mother, while others originally came from the person's father. Because of this reshuffling, each of the new reproductive cells contains a random assortment of chromosomes from the mother's and father's sides.

By itself, the random assortment of chromosomes during meiosis allows a man or woman to produce 8 million different chromosome combinations (all possible combinations from twenty-three chromosome pairs, or 2^{23}). Because of crossing over, the variability in an individual's egg or sperm cells is actually even greater. The chance that a couple would produce two identical children from two *separate* combinations of egg and sperm is thus less than 1 in 64 *trillion*. Except for identical twins, who develop from one fertilized egg, children of the same parents are never genetically exactly alike. On average, siblings share 50 percent of the genes that differentiate them from other humans; exactly which traits they have in common is a matter of chance.

How Genes Influence Development

Genes do not control development the way a computer program controls a computer. Instead, development is the result of an interplay between genes and the environment. Just as children's behavior is influenced by their surroundings, genes are influenced by their environments. In the normal course of development, genes are turned on or off by chemical signals in their most immediate environment, the cell. At the same time, the cell is affected by a host of environmental factors (from nutrients to drugs to viruses that enter the bloodstream). Thus, the presence or absence of vital ingredients in the cell, or the introduction of harmful substances, can influence how a gene is expressed. In addition, genes are influenced by the organism's developmental history, the cumulative effects of all the changes that have taken place so far. The development of physical gender in the prenatal period illustrates all of these points.

The Interaction of Genes and Environment: The Case of Physical Gender Development The development of human gender begins at the moment of conception, when the sperm fertilizes the egg. The new individual's gender is shaped by just one pair of chromosomes, the **sex chromosomes,** which scientists label number 23. If this twenty-third pair consists of two long chromosomes, called X chromosomes, the stage is set for the development of a female. If it consists of one X chromosome plus a much shorter Y chromosome (as shown in Figure 3.3), the development of a male is set into motion. Note that in males, with their XY pattern, the twenty-third pair of chromosomes is not completely homologous. The X chromosome contains genetic material that the Y chromosome does not have.

Since females carry only X chromosomes, they can pass on only an X to their children via the eggs they produce. Men, who have both X and Y chromosomes, produce sperm that carry X chromosomes and sperm that carry Y chromosomes. Consequently, a child's sex is determined by whether the father's sperm contained an X or a Y chromosome. Whichever type of sperm fertilizes the egg sets gender development in motion.

Conception is just the beginning of this developmental process. An XX or an XY chromosome pattern determines only whether an embryo will develop testes or ovaries— a development that does not occur until several weeks after conception. Thus, sexual differentiation is an example of how the action of genes is sometimes delayed until a critical

Random assortment:
The shuffling of chromosomes from the mother and the father that occurs during meiosis when homologues separate in preparation for cell division.

/dehart5

Sex Determination

Sex chromosomes:
In humans, the twenty-third pair of chromosomes, which determine genetic gender. Females normally have two X chromosomes, males one X chromosome and one Y chromosome.

Critical period:
A limited time during which some part of a developing organism is susceptible to influcnces that can bring about specific and permanent changes.

Gonads:
The sex glands—the ovaries and testes.

Hormone:
A chemical produced in the body that regulates physiological processes.

Androgens:
Male sex hormones.

period in development (Plomin et al., 1997). A **critical period** is a limited time when some part of a developing organism is susceptible to influences that can bring about specific and permanent changes. The critical period for sexual differentiation begins in the seventh week after conception. For the first six weeks, the primitive **gonad** (sex gland) tissues look exactly the same in males and females. In the seventh week, the presence of a particular gene on the Y chromosome (called the SRY gene, which stands for **S**ex-determining **R**egion of the **Y** chromosome) triggers part of this tissue to begin differentiating into testes, the male sex glands. If no SRY gene is present, the gonad tissues start differentiating into ovaries, the female sex glands, in another week or so. From here on, gender development in the embryo is shaped by **hormones** (chemicals produced in the body that regulate physiological processes).

Once testes are partially formed, they begin to secrete male sex hormones, or **androgens.** Androgens cause certain primitive structures to differentiate into the male reproductive tract and form a penis. At the same time, the testes secrete another hormone that causes atrophy of structures with the potential to become parts of the female reproductive system. In XX embryos, the *absence* of male hormones allows development of the female reproductive tract; female sex hormones need not be present for female sex organs to develop.

Several lines of evidence show that the presence or absence of androgens is the key factor in physical gender development (Larsen, 2001). One involves studies in which scientists have manipulated prenatal hormones in animals. If androgens are withheld at the critical point in development, genetically male embryos will develop genitals that appear female. Conversely, if genetically female embryos are given large doses of androgens, these genetic females will develop genitals that appear male. Another line of evidence involves studies of human embryos that were accidentally exposed to too much or too little androgen in the critical prenatal period. For instance, XX embryos are sometimes exposed to abnormally high levels of androgens, either because their mothers receive hormone treatments without knowing they are pregnant or because their mothers' adrenal glands secrete excessive amounts of androgens. These genetically female embryos often develop genitals that appear male. Conversely, genetically male embryos sometimes develop genitals that appear female because the cells of their bodies are insensitive to androgens and react as if no androgens were present (American Academy of Pediatrics, 2000; Money and Ehrhardt, 1972).

The key point here is that genes and environment interact to guide development. The genes in a fertilized egg are not sufficient *by themselves* to produce a male or a female. Genes contain information for guiding development, but how that information is actually used depends on the environment in which the genes operate. For instance, the presence of the SRY gene causes certain cells of the embryo to develop into testes. But note the great importance of the cells' *location*. Not all the embryo's cells differentiate into testes, even though all of them contain a Y chromosome with an SRY gene. The particular environment in which the gene operates is critical. Genes are part of a developmental system that also includes many environmental factors, as discussed in Chapters 1 and 2.

How Genes Affect One Another

Genes interact not only with the environment but also with one another. A simple example can be seen in the development of blood type (Plomin et al., 1997). Each individual inherits two genes that code for blood type, one from each parent. These genes come in several different forms; such alternate forms of genes for the same trait are called **alleles.** In the case of blood type, the alleles are A, B, and O.

Allele:
One of several alternate forms of a particular gene.

Homozygous:
Carrying two identical alleles for a particular trait.

What blood type an individual has depends on the combination of alleles he or she inherits and how they interact with one another. (see Table 3.1.) An individual who inherits the same allele from both parents—that is, who has the combination AA, BB, or OO—is said to be **homozygous** for this trait. A homozygous individual will always display

Table 3.1 Inheritance of Blood Type

Mother		Father	
Genotype:	AO	Genotype:	BO
Phenotype:	Type A blood	Phenotype:	Type B blood

Father's alleles

Mother's alleles		B	O
	A	Genotype: AB Phenotype: Type AB blood	Genotype: AO Phenotype: Type A blood
	O	Genotype: OB Phenotype: Type B blood	Genotype: OO Phenotype: Type O blood

whatever characteristic the two identical genes code for. For example, an individual with the combination OO will have type O blood. A different outcome occurs in people who are **heterozygous**—that is, who carry two different alleles for a single trait. Sometimes one allele is *dominant* and the other *recessive;* in that case, only the dominant allele will be expressed. For instance, individuals who inherit one allele for type A blood and one for type O will have blood type A because the A allele is dominant and the O allele is recessive. Similarly, an individual with a B and O combination will have type B blood because the B allele is also dominant over the O. But if an individual inherits one A allele and one B, neither allele dominates the other; the two are said to be *codominant.* Both will be expressed, and the person will have blood type AB.

The example of blood type shows that you cannot always tell an individual's **genotype** (genetic makeup) simply by looking at his or her **phenotype** (observable traits). Dominant alleles mask the presence of recessive alleles. In the case of blood types, there are actually six possible genotypes (AA, AO, BB, BO, AB, and OO), but only four phenotypes (A, B, AB, and O) because the recessive O gene can be masked by a dominant A or B.

Some recessive genetic traits are called **sex-linked traits** because they are carried on one of the sex chromosomes, the X, and are commonly expressed only in males. Examples are red-green color blindness and hemophilia. Males are vulnerable to these traits because they have only one X chromosome, inherited from their mothers. If a male's X chromosome happens to carry a gene for one of these traits, he will invariably exhibit the trait. His smaller Y chromosome doesn't carry the gene at all, so there can be no dominant allele to cancel out the recessive allele's effects. Females, who have two X chromosomes, will not exhibit the trait unless they inherit it from *both* parents, which occurs very rarely for most sex-linked traits. If a woman inherits the trait from *either* parent, however, she will be a carrier of the trait and can pass it on to her sons. Figure 3.6 shows how sex-linked traits are inherited, using hemophilia as an example.

So far we have been discussing traits that are governed by a single gene or by a single pair of alleles. Actually, such traits are not very common (Plomin et al., 1997). Most human characteristics are influenced by numerous gene pairs, often on different chromosomes. Such characteristics are **polygenic.** Examples include height, weight, skin color, and intelligence. In fact, any trait for which people show a large range of variation (in contrast to an "either/or" characteristic) is probably polygenic. We will explore two important polygenic characteristics later in the book when we discuss the development of intelligence (Chapter 11) and the mental disorder schizophrenia (Chapter 15).

Heterozygous:
Carrying two different alleles for a particular trait.

Genotype:
An individual's genetic makeup.

Phenotype:
An individual's observable traits.

Sex-linked traits:
Recessive genetic traits that are carried on the X chromosome and are commonly expressed only in males.

Polygenic:
Influenced by multiple gene pairs.

Figure 3.6
INHERITANCE OF SEX-
LINKED GENETIC TRAIT:
HEMOPHILIA

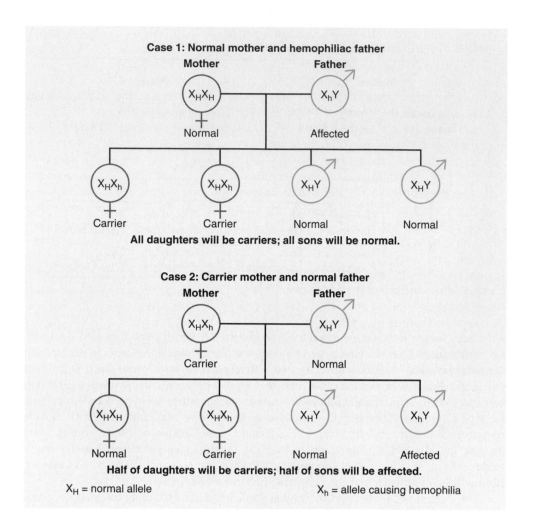

Summing Up the Influence of Genes

It is important to remember that relatively few traits are directly determined by genes acting alone (as is the case for blood type). Rather, the outcome depends on interactions of
genes and environment at particular times in development. Consider, for example, *phenylke-
tonuria* (PKU), a genetic disorder in which phenylalanine (a naturally occurring substance
found in many foods) builds up within a child's body, causing permanent brain damage and
mental retardation. This disorder occurs in children who inherit a particular recessive gene
from both parents. Fortunately, the outcome for babies with the genes for PKU can be influenced by environmental intervention. Children who test positive for PKU at birth can be
put on a low-phenylalanine diet. If the diet is started in the first six weeks of life, these children suffer few harmful effects; in most cases, they later display intelligence in the normal
range. Children who start the special diet later, however, usually have IQs below 70.

This is a clear example of both the critical period concept (the infant's first six weeks
in this case) and the interaction of genes and environment to produce developmental outcomes. The important point to remember is that *genes always act within a context that
influences how they are expressed.*

CONCEPTION

Conception Video

For thousands of years, people have understood the link between sexual intercourse and
conception, but only in the last century have they come to understand exactly what takes
place when a new life begins. Until the eighteenth century, it was believed that inside

either the egg or the sperm was a miniature person, called a *homunculus,* already fully formed. All that was needed was something to trigger the growth of this tiny person. Some believed that the sperm was the trigger for a homunculus inside the egg. Today we know that there is no homunculus. Instead, both sperm and egg contain genes that help guide the complex developmental process that results in a new human being. In this section we explore the joining of sperm and egg that initiates this process.

Like many other aspects of development, conception depends on appropriate timing of a chain of events. In most women an egg cell, or **ovum,** ripens in one of the ovaries over a period of about twenty-eight days. When the ovum is ready for fertilization, **ovulation** occurs and the ovum is released into one of the fallopian tubes, the passages that lead from each ovary to the uterus. The journey down the fallopian tube, as shown in Figure 3.7, takes several days. If the ovum is not fertilized by a sperm within the first twenty-four hours, it disintegrates upon reaching the uterus. However, if sexual intercourse occurs at the appropriate time, the ovum will meet thousands of sperm, sometimes as many as a million. From several hundred million sperm ejaculated into the vagina, these are the ones that happened to find their way into the correct fallopian tube. If one of these sperm penetrates the ovum's outer membrane, a tiny single-celled organism called a **zygote** is produced. Once an ovum has been penetrated, a biochemical change prevents other sperm from entering.

Occasionally a woman's ovaries release more than one ovum at a time. The use of modern fertility drugs has made this an increasingly common occurrence. If two ova are fertilized by two different sperm, the result is **dizygotic** ("two zygote") **twins,** also called fraternal twins. Since different ova and sperm produce each twin in a dizygotic pair, these children are no more similar genetically than any other two siblings.

Ovum:
An egg cell.

Ovulation:
Release of an ovum into one of the fallopian tubes, the passages that lead into the uterus.

Zygote:
The cell resulting from the union of a sperm cell with an ovum.

Dizygotic twins:
Fraternal twins, the result of the fertilization of two ova by two different sperm.

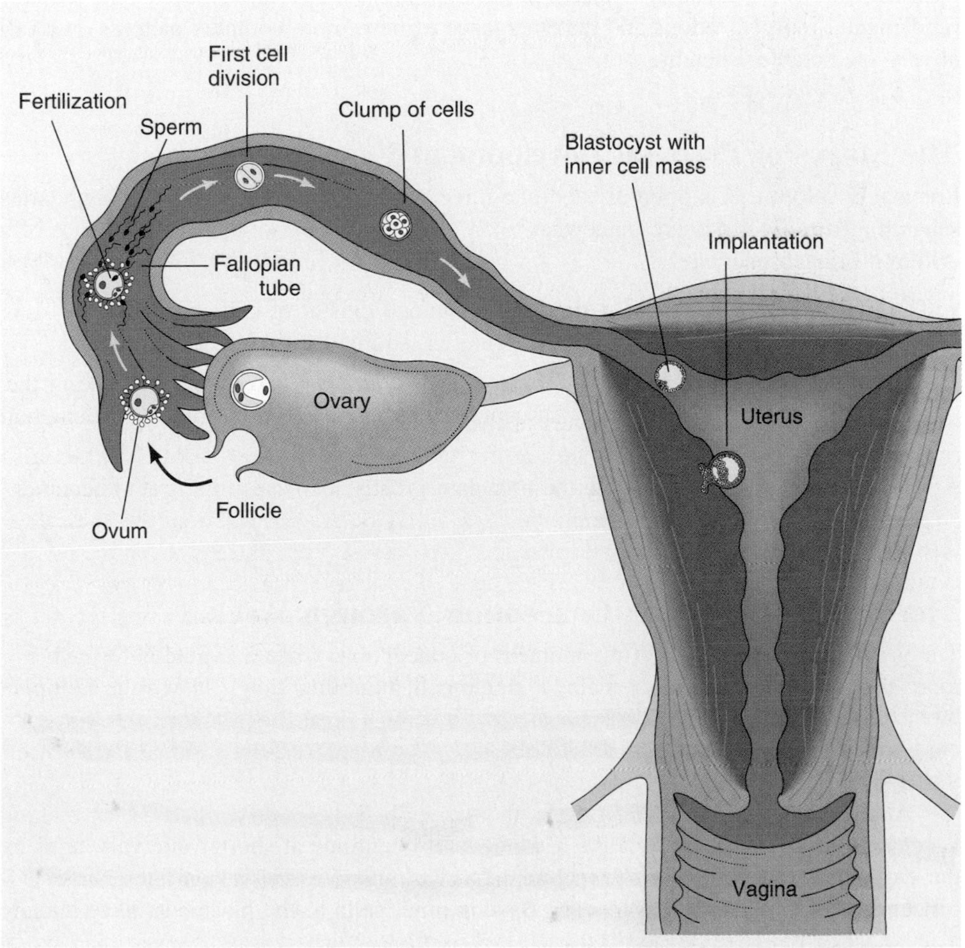

Figure 3.7
FERTILIZATION
Fertilization normally occurs at the upper end of the fallopian tube. The fertilized egg begins the process of cell division even as it is traveling to the uterus. In normal pregnancies this clump of cells will then become implanted in the uterine wall. (*Source: From E. Hall, M. Perlmutter, and M. E. Lamb. Child Psychology Today. Copyright © 1982. Reproduced with permission of the McGraw-Hill Companies, Inc.*)

Monozygotic twins:
Identical twins, the result of the division of a single fertilized egg into two separate units during its early cell division.

Sometimes a single fertilized egg splits into two separate units very early in its development, and identical twins are formed. Since twins produced in this manner are the product of only one ovum and one sperm, they are called **monozygotic** ("one zygote") **twins** and are genetically identical. As we mentioned in Chapter 1, monozygotic twins are of particularly great interest to researchers studying the interaction of genes and environment.

Conceiving a child requires the perfect timing of interconnected systems. Problems or obstacles at any point can lead to infertility, the inability to conceive a child. But as complex as human conception is, the next nine months of prenatal development are even more so. The more we learn about the intricate process of transforming a single fertilized egg into a complete human being, the more miraculous the birth of each baby seems.

PRENATAL DEVELOPMENT

The prenatal period—from conception to birth approximately thirty-eight weeks later—is a time of tremendous differentiation and rapid growth. Starting from a single fertilized egg, cells divide, migrate, and interact to take on specialized forms and functions. Out of this cellular activity emerge a human fetus and its life-support system. As you read the following sections, pay particular attention to two general principles:

Child Development CD
Prenatal Development

• increasingly complex structures develop out of initially limited resources, and

• prenatal development follows a consistent timetable, with different structures and capabilities emerging at specific, predictable times.

Both of these principles apply not only to prenatal development, but also to human development in general. We will see many examples of both in children's development after birth as well, as the capacities present at any one point in development pave the way for fundamental reorganizations and the emergence of new, more complex patterns on a relatively predictable timetable.

The Stages of Prenatal Development

Prenatal development is often divided into three major periods. Although the boundaries separating these periods are somewhat fuzzy, the developing organism is qualitatively different in each one:

• During the *germinal period,* a tiny, self-contained cluster of cells becomes implanted in the lining of the mother's uterus, and cell differentiation begins.

• During the *embryonic period,* the major organs and body parts develop, making the developing organism particularly susceptible to damage from harmful environmental influences.

• Finally, during the *fetal period,* the organism greatly increases in size and becomes a moving, sleeping, waking being.

Germinal Period Video

The Germinal Period: Conception Through Week 2

The germinal period begins at the moment of conception, when a zygote is formed. For more than a day, the zygote remains a single cell, tumbling slowly down the fallopian tube. About thirty hours after fertilization, the zygote's single cell divides in two, beginning the process of mitosis by which the entire body will develop and maintain itself throughout life.

Blastocyst:
The hollow, ball-like structure into which a zygote develops in the first week following conception.

About sixty hours after conception, the two cells of the zygote each divide, making four cells, all still structurally alike. Cell divisions continue at shorter intervals, until by the end of a week there are more than a hundred cells clustered together in a hollow ball-like structure called a **blastocyst.** By this time, cells in the blastocyst have already

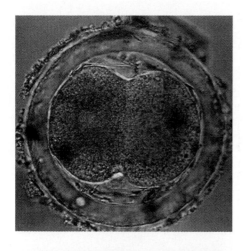
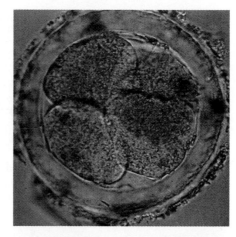
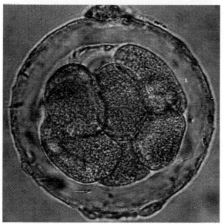
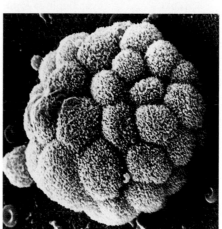

About 30 hours after fertilization the first cell division occurs. Then cell divisions continue at shorter intervals until, by the end of the week, more than a hundred cells have formed in a cluster. This hollow, ball-like structure is called the blastocyst.

begun to *differentiate* or take on specialized forms and functions. A group of cells at one end of the blastocyst, the **embryoblast** or inner cell mass, will develop into the embryo. The rest of the blastocyst, known as the **trophoblast** or outer cell mass, will form the basis of the embryo's life-support system. This early cell differentiation is an example of qualitative change. The zygote is now a fundamentally different organism than it was just a week before.

While the cells of the blastocyst are dividing and differentiating, another essential process is taking place: implantation of the zygote in the lining of the mother's uterus. About the sixth day after fertilization, the blastocyst makes contact with the uterine lining. Hormone secretions have stimulated the lining to become rich with blood, preparing it to nourish the fertilized egg. The trophoblast rapidly grows tendril-like extensions that burrow into the uterine wall. By the end of the second week, the organism is firmly attached to the uterus, drawing nutrients and oxygen from its blood vessels.

The Embryonic Period: Weeks 3 Through 8

Once the zygote is firmly implanted, it is called an **embryo.** The embryonic period, from the end of the second week after conception to the end of the eighth week, is a time of rapid cell division and differentiation. It is the period when all the vital organs and other major body structures are formed—a process called **organogenesis** (Larsen, 2001). Table 3.2 lists some of the major developmental landmarks during the embryonic period, and the photographs on page 93 show what an embryo looks like at different ages. Let's examine in detail what occurs during these important prenatal weeks, beginning with development of the embryo's life-support system.

Embryoblast:
A group of cells at one end of the blastocyst that develops into the embryo.

Trophoblast:
The cells in the blastocyst that form the basis of the embryo's life-support system.

Embryo:
The term applied to the developing organism during weeks 3 through 8 of prenatal development.

Organogenesis:
The formation of organs and other major body structures.

Table 3.2 Developmental Milestones of the Embryo

Time after Conception	Physical Changes
12–13 days	Implantation is complete.
14 days	Mature **placenta** begins to develop.
3 weeks (15–20 days)	Development of **endoderm, mesoderm,** and **ectoderm.** Central nervous system begins to form. Embryo becomes attached to wall of uterus by **umbilical cord.** Placenta develops rapidly.
4 weeks (21–28 days)	Eyes begin to form. Heart starts beating. Length is 5 mm (less than $\frac{1}{4}$ in.), growth rate about 1 mm per day. Blood vessels develop. Placenta maternal-infant circulation begins to function.
5 weeks	Arm and leg buds form.
7 weeks	Facial structures fuse (otherwise, facial defects).
8 weeks	Length is 3 cm (slightly more than 1 in.). Major development of organs is completed. Most external features recognizable at birth are present.

Source: J. Rosenblith and J. Sims-Knight (1985). *In the Beginning: Development in the First Two Years.* Copyright © 1985. Used by permission of Judy F. Rosenblith.

Embryonic Period Video

Placenta:
A mass of tissue that supplies oxygen and nutrients to the embryo and carries away waste products.

Umbilical cord:
A cord containing blood vessels that connects the embryo with the placenta.

Amniotic sac:
The fluid-filled sac that surrounds and protects the embryo and the fetus.

The Embryo's Life-Support System The support system for the developing embryo consists of three major parts: the placenta, the umbilical cord, and the fluid-filled amniotic sac. The **placenta** is a mass of tissue that forms partly from cells of the uterine lining and partly from cells of the trophoblast. Separate sets of blood vessels link the placenta to the embryo, via the **umbilical cord,** and to the mother, via the uterine wall. In the placenta, oxygen and nutrients are transferred from the mother to the embryo, and waste products are transferred from the embryo to the mother. Because the mother and the embryo have completely separate blood supplies, these transfers occur through the cell membranes of the placenta. Oxygen and carbon dioxide molecules are small enough to pass through these cell membranes, but blood cells are too large. The cell membranes also offer protection against some substances that could be harmful to the embryo. Most bacteria, for instance, are too large to pass through them. However, the placenta does not offer absolute protection. Some viruses, as well as molecules of alcohol and many other drugs, are small enough to pass through, with negative effects that we will discuss later in the chapter.

Another major part of the embryo's life-support system is the fluid-filled **amniotic sac,** which provides a closed, protective environment within which the embryo develops. Foreign substances cannot come in contact with the embryo except by way of the placenta and the umbilical cord. The amniotic fluid also cushions the embryo against minor bumps and jostling. Recall the minor parking lot accident that DeeDee Williams witnessed in the story at the beginning of this part of the book. Because of the protection of the amniotic fluid, the pregnant woman's fetus was probably unharmed. In addition, amniotic fluid helps to minimize temperature changes as the mother experiences warm and cold environments.

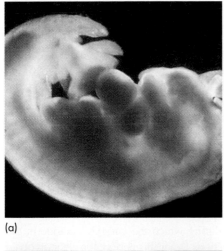

(a)

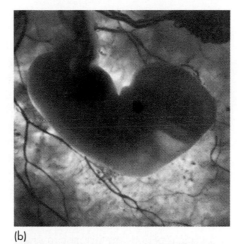

(b)

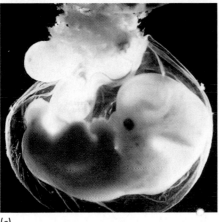

(c)

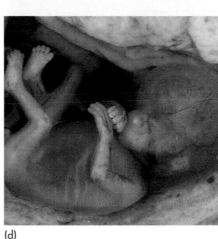

(d)

These photographs show a developing human embryo at (a) 4 to 5 weeks, (b) 5 to 6 weeks, (c) 7 weeks, and (d) 8 weeks after conception. At 4 weeks the embryo is just 1/4 inch long; at 8 weeks it has grown to 1 inch. Notice the dramatic increase in complexity of organization in just one month of pregnancy.

Embryonic Cell Differentiation While the placenta, umbilical cord, and amniotic sac are developing, the embryo itself is undergoing major changes (Larsen, 2001). During the third week after conception (the first week of the embryonic period), the new organism becomes oval in shape and then indented. This indentation is the beginning of what will become the mouth and digestive tract. Cells on the surface of the embryo migrate to this indentation and move inward to form a central layer between two other layers of cells. By the end of the week, three layers of differentiated tissues have formed: the **endoderm, mesoderm,** and **ectoderm.** *Endoderm* cells will develop into internal organs such as the stomach, liver, and lungs; *mesoderm* cells will become muscles, bone, and blood; and *ectoderm* cells will form the central nervous system, sensory organs, and skin.

The movements of cells that give rise to differentiated layers set the stage for important interactions among tissues that eventually shape the various parts of the body. These critical tissue interactions that trigger developmental changes are called **embryonic inductions.** Scientists believe they are caused by chemical substances that spread from one tissue to the other. Embryonic inductions provide another example of how the environmental context (in this case, the placement of cells) plays an indispensable role in carrying out an organism's genetic potential (McMillan et al., 1999).

In the first embryonic induction, cells of the mesoderm induce overlying ectoderm tissue to begin further differentiation into a structure that will eventually become the brain and spinal cord. This differentiation occurs because some genes in the ectoderm are turned on and others are turned off, causing the cells containing those genes to change structure and function. Scientists know it is the mesoderm that induces these changes, and not the ectoderm itself, because of studies with animal embryos. In those studies,

Endoderm:
Cells that develop into internal organs such as the stomach, liver, and lungs.

Mesoderm:
Cells that become the muscles, skeleton, and blood.

Ectoderm:
Cells that form the central nervous system, sensory organs, and skin.

Embryonic induction:
A chemical interaction between the cells of different tissues that triggers developmental changes in the embryo.

transplanting mesoderm tissue from one embryo to another at the same stage of development triggered formation of a second brain and spinal cord on the host embryo.

Another embryonic induction controls the formation of the lens of the eye. The lens develops wherever a certain outgrowth of the forebrain comes in contact with the embryo's outer surface. Animal studies show that if this outgrowth is transplanted so that it contacts the embryo's back instead of the front of its head, a lens will proceed to form in this odd location.

Timing is often a crucial factor in gene-environment interactions during the embryonic period. Suppose, for example, that the outgrowth of the forebrain that induces formation of an eye lens is transplanted from the head of a younger animal embryo to the back of an older one. The older embryo is well beyond the stage at which the lenses of the eyes normally form. Will this older embryo go on to acquire yet another lens? No, it will not. The cells on the surface of the older embryo's back are now committed to being skin, and induction of a new lens is no longer possible. The time prior to this commitment is an example of a critical period—in this case, a critical period during which the embryo's ectoderm tissue can be induced to develop in one of several directions. After this period, the cells involved have started to take on particular forms and functions and cannot reverse their development.

The Timetable for Embryonic Development   Figure 3.8 shows the critical periods in the emergence of some of the body parts in the human embryo and fetus—the peri-

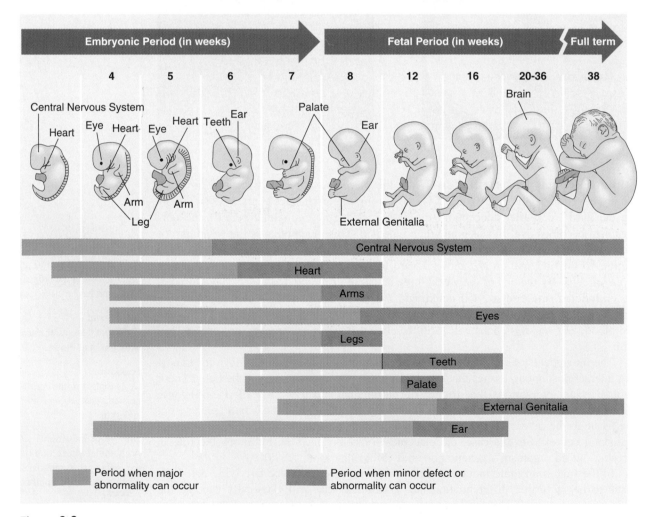

Figure 3.8
CRITICAL PERIODS IN THE DEVELOPMENT OF VARIOUS ORGANS, SYSTEMS, AND BODY PARTS
Each organ, system, and part has its own critical timetable and is most susceptible to disruption during that time. *(Source: Adapted from K. L. Moore,* Before We Are Born, *p. 96. Copyright © 1974. Used by permission of W. B. Sanders Company and the author.)*

ods during which development of each part is particularly susceptible to disruption. As you can see, embryonic development occurs in a very predictable order, according to a strict timetable (Larsen, 2001). By the end of the third week after conception, the central nervous system has started to form, and the beginnings of the eyes can be seen. By the fourth week, the heart and digestive system are appearing, and by the fifth week, limb buds that will become arms and legs are visible. Finally, in the sixth through the eighth weeks, fingers and toes start to emerge and the bones begin to harden. This sequence reveals two principles of prenatal growth:

- Development proceeds from the head downward (**cephalocaudal development**).
- Development proceeds from the center of the body outward to the extremities (**proximodistal development**).

Cephalocaudal development:
The principle that development proceeds from the head downward.

The predictable sequence and timing of embryonic development can be observed in newborns with certain combinations of problems. For example, infants with malformed outer ears also often have kidney defects, not because the outer ears and the kidneys have any direct connection, but because they are formed at the same time prenatally (McMillan et al., 1999). If something goes wrong during a critical period and an organ becomes malformed, that defect can be corrected only through surgery. The developmental process cannot be redone at some later stage. When a critical period is over, the tissues involved have differentiated, and the embryo has become a qualitatively different organism. For some body parts, such as the limbs and the palate, the critical period lasts for only a few weeks; other parts, particularly the central nervous system, take much longer to develop and thus are susceptible to damage throughout the embryonic and fetal periods. (A Closer Look on page 96 provides more specifics about prenatal brain development.)

Proximodistal development:
The principle that development proceeds from the center of the body outward.

The embryonic period is a time when many crucial changes take place, making the unborn child most vulnerable to developmental errors. Yet it is also a time when the mother may not yet realize she is pregnant. If she neglects her own health now, or ingests the wrong substances, the development of her child may be severely compromised, as you will see later in this chapter.

The Fetal Period: Week 9 to Birth

From the ninth until the thirty-eighth week after conception, when birth usually occurs, the developing organism is called a **fetus.** The fetal period differs from the embryonic period in several fundamental ways. During the embryonic period most of the major body parts are formed; during the fetal period those parts grow rapidly and become refined in structure (Larsen, 2001). Table 3.3 shows that growth in body length reaches its maximum rate early in the fetal period and then tapers off, whereas weight gains are greatest as the time of delivery approaches. Refinements in body parts occur throughout the fetal period, with each change taking place on a predictable schedule. For example,

Fetus:
The term applied to the developing organism during weeks 9 through 38 of prenatal development.

Fetal Period Video

Table 3.3 Length and Weight Gains During Fetal Period

Week	Length	Weight
8	1 in.	$\frac{1}{30}$ oz.
12	3 in.	1 oz.
16	6 in.	4 oz.
20	10 in.	1 lb.
24	12 in.	2 lb.
28	15 in.	3 lb.
32	17 in.	$4\frac{1}{2}$ lb.
36	18 in.	$7\frac{1}{2}$ lb.

A CLOSER LOOK

PRENATAL BRAIN DEVELOPMENT

Of all the organs in the human body, the brain takes the longest to mature. The central nervous system begins to form before any other organ in the body. Brain development continues throughout the embryonic and fetal periods, and it is still not complete at the time of birth. This extended period of development makes possible the great complexity of the human brain, but it also means that neurological development is susceptible to disruption by environmental influences throughout the prenatal period and early childhood.

During the embryonic period, the basic structures of the central nervous system form:

- At about eighteen days after conception, the formation of the central nervous system begins as a region of the ectoderm thickens and begins to fold in upon itself. (This occurs as a result of the first embryonic induction, which we have already described.)
- By twenty-one to twenty-two days after conception, the folds formed in the ectoderm grow together to form the **neural tube,** a tube running from the head to the tail of the embryo, which will develop into the brain and spinal cord.
- By week 4 of prenatal development, **neurons,** or nerve cells, are differentiating, and the spinal cord and major regions of the brain have started to form.

During the fetal period, **neurogenesis,** the formation of neurons, occurs at a rapid rate, estimated at about 250,000 per minute (Cowan, 1979), and the structures of the brain continue to develop:

- During weeks 10 to 20 of prenatal development most of the neurons that will make up the **cerebral cortex** are formed. The cerebral cortex is the brain's thin, highly convoluted outer layer. Neuron formation is nearly complete by about week 28 (Rakic, 1995).
- The neurons that make up the cerebral cortex are produced in a region just underneath the cortex called the *proliferative zone* and must migrate to their final positions in the cortex. The process of migration is nearly complete by about week 24 of prenatal development.
- Beginning at about week 24, **synapses,** connections between neurons, begin to form.
- At the time of birth, the volume of the infant's cerebral cortex is about one-third that of an adult's, even though it contains almost all the neurons it will ever have. Later growth comes mainly from increases in the size of neurons and in the number of connections among them (Huttenlocher, 2002).

Figure 3.9 illustrates the development of the brain during the embryonic and fetal periods.

Neural tube:
A tube running from the head to the tail of the embryo, which will develop into the brain and spinal cord.

Neurons:
Nerve cells.

Neurogenesis:
Formation of neurons.

Cerebral cortex:
The brain's thin, highly convoluted outer layer.

Synapses:
Connections between neurons.

in the fourth month the pads on the fingers and toes form; in the fifth month eyebrows and eyelashes grow; and in the seventh month the male testes usually descend into the scrotum. These refinements are very important, but they differ fundamentally from the laying down of basic structures that occurred during the embryonic period.

Another major difference between the embryonic and fetal periods is that the fetus is more responsive than the embryo. During the embryonic period, the developing organism merely floats in the amniotic fluid, moored by its umbilical cord. By the tenth week after conception, however, the nervous system is mature enough so that the fetus will flex its entire trunk if any part of its body is touched. Such a global reaction occurs even if the stimulation is directed to a specific body part. Gradually, fetal movements become less global and more specialized. After the eighteenth week, when various parts of the body are touched, the responses are very specific. Touching the sole of the foot now produces a leg withdrawal, not movement of the entire body, as occurred early in the fetal period. The fetus has achieved a fundamentally more advanced way of responding, which is thought to be due to the development of higher brain centers responsible for coordinating motor acts (Rakic, 1995). Notice how these qualitative changes in behavior are directly linked to qualitative changes in the structure of the nervous system.

Fetal movements do not occur only in response to external stimulation. By the twelfth week the fetus spontaneously moves its arms and legs, swallows, and "breathes" (inhales and exhales amniotic fluid). Still later, as the nervous system becomes increasingly refined, more precise limb and finger movements are possible.

The fetal period is also the time when behaviors become increasingly regular and integrated. The fetus develops a relatively regular sleep-wake cycle, usually adopting the

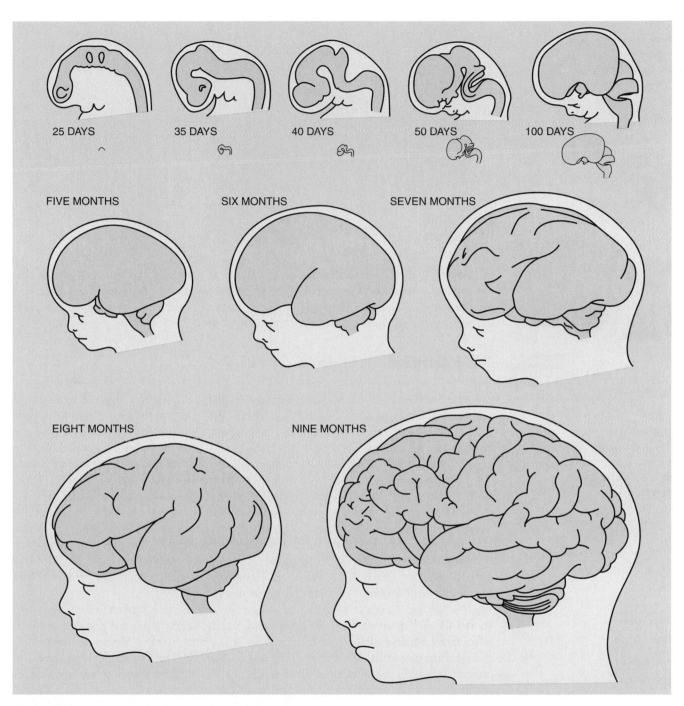

Figure 3.9
PRENATAL BRAIN DEVELOPMENT
By 25 days after conception, the neural tube has formed. By 5 months, the basic structures of the brain have formed. From 5 to 9 months, neurons form at a rapid rate, and connections between them develop. *(Source: By Tom Prentiss from W. M. Cowan, Scientific American, September 1979, p. 116. Used by permission of the Estate of Tom Prentiss.)*

same position for sleep. If the mother moves into a position that causes the fetus discomfort, it will move around until it finds a more comfortable position. At 7 months some fetuses regularly suck their thumbs or hands while they are sleeping. Their eyelids, which previously were fused shut, now separate and allow them to open and close their eyes. By the eighth month, fetuses are responsive to moderately loud sounds; they can hear and react to some of what goes on outside the womb. And, as we will discuss

During the second and third trimesters of pregnancy, movements of the fetus become increasingly evident.

in Chapter 4, there is evidence that babies can later recognize the sound of stories that their mothers read aloud repeatedly during the last weeks of pregnancy (DeCasper and Spence, 1986). All these changes are evidence that an initially passive organism is gradually being transformed into an active, adapting baby.

**mhhe.com
/dehart5**

Expectant Mother's Journal

Trimesters:
Three-month periods that correspond to changes in the mother's experience of pregnancy.

THE MOTHER'S EXPERIENCE OF PREGNANCY

From the mother's point of view, prenatal development is usually gauged in terms of the progress of her pregnancy. Obstetricians divide pregnancy into three 3-month periods called **trimesters,** which correspond to changes in the mother's experiences. Fatigue and drowsiness are common during the first trimester. Women may also experience swelling of the breasts, frequent urination, and, in many cases, morning sickness. But the intensity of these symptoms varies from woman to woman (Cunningham et al., 2001). Especially if she did not expect to get pregnant, a woman can easily misinterpret or overlook the early signs of pregnancy. Even cessation of the menstrual cycle can sometimes be overlooked, especially by women with irregular periods. In addition, some pregnant women experience intermittent vaginal bleeding, or spotting, in the first trimester, which they may interpret as an unusually light period. If a woman is taking medications or using alcohol or illegal drugs, failure to recognize pregnancy can have serious consequences for the developing child, as we will discuss shortly.

The second trimester is often the most enjoyable for the mother. Her fatigue and nausea usually disappear. The first fetal movements, called *quickening,* can usually be felt around the end of the fourth month. Soon the fetus's initial fluttering movements change into substantial movements of the body and limbs. The mother now has the extraordinary experience of feeling new life inside her. Her bulging abdomen becomes apparent, but she is not yet so large as to feel awkward or burdened.

Physically, the third trimester can be trying for the mother. The increase in size of the fetus and uterus puts pressure on her other organs. Fetal kicking can now extend for long periods, sometimes causing discomfort or keeping the mother awake at night. Some women report that by the ninth month they felt as if they had been pregnant forever; others recall late pregnancy as one of the happiest times in their lives.

PROBLEMS IN PRENATAL DEVELOPMENT

Congenital (birth) defect:
Any abnormality that is present at birth.

Given the enormous complexity of creating a human being, it seems amazing that the process can ever take place without error. In the delivery room parents commonly count the fingers and toes of their newborn to make sure everything is there. In most cases, the baby is fine. But sadly, some infants are born with abnormalities. Any abnormality that is present at birth is called a **congenital defect** or **birth defect.**

Congenital defects can arise from problems in the infant's genes, in the prenatal environment, or in both. About 25 percent of congenital defects are purely genetic in origin, and about 3 percent are due solely to environmental factors. Nearly 25 percent are caused by a combination of genetic and environmental factors. For over 40 percent of all birth defects, a specific cause is unknown (McMillan et al., 1999).

Genetic Defects

Some genetic defects involve inheritance of a single gene for some disorder. These **single-gene disorders** are also called **Mendelian disorders** because they follow the basic principles of genetic inheritance described by Gregor Mendel in the 1860s. Most single-gene disorders are the result of inheriting a recessive allele from each parent, as in the case of PKU, discussed earlier. Other examples of disorders caused by recessive genes are *sickle-cell anemia* (a painful and potentially fatal blood disorder found primarily in people whose ancestors came from West Africa and some areas around the Mediterranean Sea) and *Tay-Sachs disease* (a steady deterioration of the nervous system leading to death before age 2, found primarily in Jews of Eastern European origin and in some Cajun families in Louisiana.)

A few single-gene disorders are caused by inheritance of a dominant allele. One such disorder is *Huntington disease,* a fatal neurological disorder that often does not appear until after age 40. Because the gene for Huntington disease is a dominant allele, those who carry it inevitably develop and die from the disorder, in many cases after they have produced children. Each child of a person who develops Huntington disease has a 50 percent chance of inheriting the disorder.

Other genetic defects involve **chromosomal abnormalities,** which occur when errors in meiosis produce sperm or egg cells with extra, missing, or damaged chromosomes. Over 90 percent of all fertilized eggs with chromosomal abnormalities are miscarried. But about 1 in every 160 newborns has some sort of chromosomal abnormality (Nussbaum, McInnes, and Huntington, 2001). Some chromosomal abnormalities cause no particular developmental problems; others produce a predictable set of physical abnormalities.

The best-known example of a chromosomal abnormality is *Down syndrome,* which involves the pair of chromosomes that scientists label number 21. If the twenty-first chromosome pair fails to separate during meiosis, when reproductive cells are formed, the resulting egg or sperm will contain two twenty-first chromosomes. When this egg or sperm joins another reproductive cell at conception, the result is a zygote with three twenty-first chromosomes instead of the usual two (which is why Down syndrome is also called *tri*somy 21). About 75 percent of trisomy 21 conceptions result in miscarriage. Those babies who survive suffer multiple problems. Their physical development is abnormal in a number of ways. They are usually short, with stubby fingers, a broad face, and rather flat facial features. Many also have heart or digestive-system defects, which can cause early death.

Down syndrome is the most common genetic cause of moderate mental retardation (Nussbaum et al., 2001). Despite this, children with Down syndrome show the same sequences of development as normal children, only delayed. With supportive environments many can achieve near normal functioning, particularly if a carefully designed intervention program starts in infancy (Cicchetti and Beeghly, 1990; Hauser-Cram et al., 2001; Leonard et al., 2002). But there is no environmental cure for Down syndrome, as there is for PKU. All the damage occurs during the prenatal period, and it cannot be reversed.

Down syndrome is relatively rare, affecting about 1 in every 800 births. But the frequency increases with the age of the mother. For women aged 20 to 24, the rate is 1 in 1,400 births, whereas for women over 45 the rate is 1 in 25 (Nussbaum et al., 2001). Scientists believe that this higher incidence in older women is caused by damage to egg cells over time, due to exposure to harmful environmental factors.

Another type of chromosomal abnormality occurs when a baby receives an abnormal number of sex chromosomes, again due to an error in meiosis when the mother's egg or the father's sperm was produced. These **sex chromosome abnormalities** are

Single-gene (Mendelian) disorder: Any disorder produced by inheritance of a single gene.

Chromosomal abnormality: Any genetic defect that occurs when errors in meiosis produce sperm or egg cells with incorrect numbers of chromosomes or with damaged chromosomes.

/dehart5

Down Syndrome

Sex chromosome abnormalities: A type of chromosomal abnormality that occurs when a baby receives an abnormal number of sex chromosomes.

Almond-shaped eyes, a broad, flattened face, and poor muscle tone are prominent features of Down syndrome. Children with this condition show varying degrees of mental retardation.

among the most common genetic disorders, occurring about once in every five hundred births (Nussbaum et al., 2001). For example, males may receive an extra X chromosome (a condition known as *Klinefelter syndrome*) or an extra Y chromosome *(XYY syndrome)*. Females may also have an extra X chromosome *(trisomy X)*, or they may have only one X chromosome *(Turner syndrome)*. Many people with sex chromosome abnormalities never know they have them because they often cause no serious developmental problems. However, some of these abnormalities result in infertility (Klinefelter and Turner syndromes), some in educational problems (Klinefelter syndrome and trisomy X), and some in reduced IQ (XYY syndrome).

Environmental Influences

Teratogen:
A substance in the environment that can cause physical malformations during prenatal development.

Substances in the environment that can cause physical malformations during prenatal development are called **teratogens,** and the study of their effects is called *teratology.* Teratology reveals the critical role that environment plays in development. Teratogens usually cause abnormalities by preventing or modifying normal cell division and differentiation. Thus, teratogens generally pose the greatest danger during the critical periods of the embryonic stage, when the major body parts are forming. Because later development consists primarily of refinements of existing structures, teratogens tend to do less damage during the fetal period. This is not to say that the fetus is immune to environmental hazards. The central nervous system, for example, grows and differentiates rapidly throughout gestation, as discussed in the box on page 96, and thus can be damaged at any point in the prenatal period. Teratogens should be avoided throughout pregnancy.

In the following sections we look at some of the most common teratogens and other environmental factors that can contribute to birth defects. Sorting out the impacts of individual teratogens is often quite difficult because in many cases infants have been exposed to several potentially harmful environmental factors before birth. Applying Research Findings on page 101 examines the ways that environmental factors can combine and interact with each other to produce risks to prenatal development.

Progress toward identifying effects of specific teratogens has been made with studies in which additional risk factors are controlled, either statistically or by selecting participants who are similar in key respects, such as SES and health status. In addition, experiments in which animals are exposed prenatally to various teratogens have helped researchers identify mechanisms by which developmental damage may occur.

APPLYING RESEARCH FINDINGS

MULTIPLE RISK FACTORS AND PRENATAL DEVELOPMENT

It is difficult to separate the impacts of prenatal exposure to alcohol, tobacco, and other drugs because babies who have been exposed to one of these substances before birth have frequently been exposed to several of them (Lester, LaGasse, and Bigsby, 1998). Pregnant women who smoke often also consume alcohol, and pregnant women who use cocaine or heroin usually smoke and drink as well. In addition, smoking, drinking, and drug use during pregnancy are all associated with other pre- and postnatal **risk factors** that increase the likelihood of negative developmental outcomes. Additional prenatal risk factors include low socioeconomic status, adolescent pregnancy, limited education, high maternal stress, poor nutrition, lack of prenatal care, and exposure to HIV. Many of these continue as risk factors after birth; additional postnatal risk factors include low birth weight, poor parenting skills, chaotic home environments, and lack of social support.

Multiple risk factors can affect prenatal development in at least two ways:

- First, there are simple *additive effects*—as the number of risk factors increases, the overall risk of negative effects on development increases.
- There are also *multiplicative effects*—multiple risk factors can interact with each other in ways that modify or intensify the individual effects of each risk factor.

We have already seen several examples of the additive effects of multiple risk factors. In Chapter 2, we discussed how family context influences developmental outcomes for low-birth-weight babies. Low-birth-weight babies born to middle-class families often have no long-term difficulties; however, those born to low-SES families are at heightened risk for developmental problems. These outcomes can be explained partly by the greater resources available to middle-class families for coping with the demands of a low-birth-weight baby. In addition, the babies born to low-SES families are more likely to experience multiple risk factors both before and after birth.

Research on prenatal exposure to alcohol, tobacco, and illicit drugs has uncovered a number of multiplicative effects involving these substances and other risk factors:

- Infants whose mothers smoke heavily during pregnancy suffer a higher rate of sudden infant death syndrome (SIDS) than infants born to nonsmokers. In addition, prematurity, low birth weight, and lack of prenatal care increase the risk of SIDS for infants born to heavy smokers, but *not* for infants born to nonsmokers (Schellscheidt, Oyen, and Jorch, 1997).
- Some studies have found that the effects of prenatal exposure to cocaine and other drugs are intensified by inadequate home environments and maternal distress after birth (Chasnoff et al., 1998; Singer et al., 1997). Children with prenatal cocaine exposure adopted by middle- to upper-class families show mild to moderate effects on IQ and language development, compared with severe effects on similar children raised by their biological mothers (Koren et al., 1998).
- The effects of prenatal cocaine exposure seem to differ depending on whether a baby is born prematurely or carried to term, with premature babies showing greater increases in irritability and full-term babies showing larger growth deficits (Brown et al., 1998).

Alcohol, Tobacco, and Illicit Drugs   Most people realize that illicit drugs, such as heroin and cocaine, are harmful to an embryo or fetus. However, babies are more likely to be exposed to alcohol or nicotine before birth than to heroin or cocaine, and in many cases the effects of these legal drugs are at least as severe as those of illegal drugs. Prenatal exposure to alcohol, tobacco, and illicit drugs can affect development in at least three ways:

- by passing through the placenta and interfering directly with the development of the embryo or fetus,
- by affecting the mother physically and psychologically in ways that can have an indirect impact on the embryo or fetus, and
- by causing the baby to be born with a physical addiction.

The risk of physical addiction in newborns is greatest for narcotics, such as heroin, but it is also sometimes seen in babies who have been exposed to cocaine or nicotine (Wagner et al., 1998).

Alcohol.   In the United States, about 20 percent of newborns have had prenatal alcohol exposure, and nearly 1 percent of newborns show some degree of obvious neurological

Risk factors:
Factors that increase the likelihood of negative developmental outcomes.

Child Development CD
Prenatal Alcohol Exposure

problems as a result (Msall et al., 1998; Sampson et al., 1997). A much larger number of children may have more subtle cognitive and behavioral problems related to prenatal alcohol exposure (Sampson et al., 2000). Animal and human research make it clear that alcohol severely disrupts prenatal brain development in a variety of ways (Guerri, 1998; Jacobson and Jacobson, 2000; Streissguth and O'Malley, 2000).

The risk and severity of birth defects increase with the amount of alcohol consumed during pregnancy, but *any* prenatal exposure to alcohol carries some risk (Sampson et al., 2000). Because brain development continues right up to the time of birth, the brain is vulnerable to the effects of alcohol throughout pregnancy. As a result, doctors recommend that women abstain completely from alcohol throughout pregnancy. A woman who has consumed alcohol early in pregnancy, however, can still improve the outcome for her unborn child if she stops drinking, even if some damage has already occurred (Barr and Streissguth, 2001).

Alcohol consumption is particularly likely to cause neurological problems if the pregnant woman is a binge drinker (regularly having more than five drinks at a time) or if she drinks heavily early in pregnancy (Jacobson and Jacobson, 2000; Streissguth, Sampson, and Barr, 1989). However, infants whose mothers drink heavily *late* in pregnancy show the most severe retardation in physical growth (Jacobson, Jacobson, and Sokol, 1994).

Fetal alcohol syndrome (FAS):
A constellation of problems found among babies born to heavy drinkers.

About one in three babies born to heavy drinkers has a constellation of problems called **fetal alcohol syndrome (FAS).** Full-blown fetal alcohol syndrome occurs in about two of every thousand births in the United States (Msall et al., 1998). Babies with FAS have a distinctive pattern of unusual facial characteristics, poor growth, and central nervous system problems, such as mental retardation, irritability, and hyperactivity (Mattson and Riley, 1998). These problems cannot be corrected after birth. Even with adequate diet, children with FAS stay small and thin for their age in early childhood. In adolescence and adulthood, their unusual facial features become less pronounced, but they remain cognitively impaired and have a higher than usual rate of psychological and social behavior problems (Kelly, Day, and Streissguth, 2000; Steinhausen and Spohr, 1998).

Many children who were exposed to somewhat lower levels of alcohol prenatally do not have the facial abnormalities and growth problems seen in FAS, but they still have neurological and behavioral problems. These problems include irritability and reduced information-processing speed in infancy, lowered IQ, motor difficulties in the preschool years, problems with arithmetic and reading skills in middle childhood, and a heightened risk of nicotine, alcohol, and drug dependence in adulthood (Jacobson and Jacobson, 2000; Streissguth et al., 1989; Yates et al., 1998).

A flattened nose, an underdeveloped upper lip, and widely spaced eyes are three common physical characteristics usually seen in children with fetal alcohol syndrome.

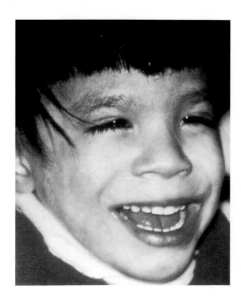

Tobacco. Prenatal exposure to maternal tobacco use is far more common than exposure to illicit drugs or heavy drinking. In the United States, surveys have found that as many as 22 percent of newborns have mothers who smoked during pregnancy (U.S. Department of Health and Human Services, 2001). Pregnant women who smoke are more likely than nonsmokers to deliver prematurely and to have babies with low birth weight; the more they smoke, the greater the risk (Rush and Callahan, 1989; Wang et al., 1997). There is also evidence that heavy smoking during pregnancy (usually defined as at least ten cigarettes per day) has a negative impact on children's later language, cognitive, and reading skills, and increases the risk of conduct and attentional disorders (Cornelius et al., 2001; Fried, Watkinson, and Gray, 1998; Mick et al., 2002; Wakschlag and Hans, 2002).

Smoking contributes to these problems directly by exposing the developing fetus to nicotine and indirectly through its impacts on the mother's body. There is increasing evidence that nicotine may affect prenatal brain development, in part by activating nicotine receptors in the brain (Hellström-Lindahl and Nordberg, 2002). Maternal smoking may further affect brain development by raising carbon monoxide levels in the mother's blood and interfering with the functioning of the placenta, both of which decrease the amount of oxygen available to the fetus (Sastry, 1991).

Cocaine. In the United States, cocaine-exposed babies are estimated to account for over half of the newborns affected by illicit drugs (Church et al., 1998). Prenatal exposure to cocaine has several effects on physical development (Church et al., 1998; Datta-Bhutada, Johnson, and Rosen, 1998). Women who use cocaine during pregnancy have a greatly increased risk of miscarriage, stillbirth due to separation of the placenta from the uterine wall, and premature delivery. Their babies tend to be small for gestational age and to have smaller than average heads.

Newborns who have been exposed to cocaine show a variety of behavioral effects, depending to some extent on how heavily their mothers used cocaine during pregnancy. Some show impaired arousal; others are irritable and tense (Chiriboga, 1998). Later in infancy they have difficulty regulating arousal during interaction with caregivers (Bendersky and Lewis, 1998). Some researchers have also found negative effects on motor development and cognitive functioning, especially for infants who received heavy exposure throughout prenatal development (Alessandri, Bendersky, and Lewis, 1998; Jacobson and Jacobson, 2000; Swanson et al., 1999).

The long-term effects of prenatal cocaine exposure are not yet clear. Some studies suggest that many of the early behavioral effects, such as irritability, diminish over time (Chiriboga, 1998). However, longitudinal studies have found evidence of continuing cognitive, attentional, and language deficits, behavior problems, and difficulty with social relationships in early and middle childhood (Bandstra et al., 2001; Delaney-Black et al., 1998; Koren et al., 1998; Richardson, 1998). These effects are especially likely when drug exposure is combined with other prenatal risks and social disruption (Accornero et al., 2002).

Heroin. The rate of prenatal exposure to narcotics, such as heroin, is lower than for other illicit drugs, but dramatic effects are often apparent at birth. Women who are addicted to narcotics give birth to babies who are also addicted and who suffer classic symptoms of drug withdrawal, including breathing difficulties, vomiting, tremors, and convulsions (Wagner et al., 1998). Addicted newborns are usually put on maintenance doses of narcotics, which are then withdrawn slowly.

Even after withdrawal from drugs, these children have problems (Ornoy et al., 2001; van Baar et al., 1994). Babies born to addicted mothers are often underweight, with small head circumference, and they remain small for their age throughout childhood. As infants they tend to be hypersensitive to sound, touch, and changes in position. Because their nervous systems are so easily overloaded, they avoid stimulation and therefore miss normal opportunities to explore and learn from their environment. Over time, this hypersensitivity can lead to learning difficulties and poor relationships with parents, who find these children unrewarding. As they grow older, children born addicted to narcotics often show behavioral problems, such as hyperactivity, and delays in cognitive and language development.

However, as with other teratogens, family environment after birth makes a difference in long-term outcomes for children exposed to heroin prenatally. Studies in the United States, Europe, and Israel have all found the worst outcomes for children raised in impoverished environments by parents who continue to use drugs. Children adopted by middle-class families at an early age show relatively normal intellectual functioning by elementary school age, with a heightened risk of attention deficit disorders the most commonly reported long-term effect (Ornoy et al., 2001).

Methadone, a drug used to wean addicts from heroin, is often given to pregnant heroin users. Treatment with methadone is usually considered preferable to continued maternal heroin use or heroin withdrawal during pregnancy (Kandall et al., 1999). It reduces pregnancy complications and does not seem to have negative effects on brain development (Nassogne et al., 1998). However, babies born to women taking methadone do suffer withdrawal symptoms after birth, and other treatment options are being tested (Fischer et al., 1998).

Medications   Just as alcohol, nicotine, and illicit drugs can have negative impacts on prenatal development, so can medications prescribed by a doctor or purchased over the counter. Because there are so many drugs whose effects are not yet known, women are often advised to avoid all drugs during pregnancy except those that have been proven safe.

Thalidomide.   Thalidomide is the classic example of a teratogen. This sedative was sold over the counter in Europe and Canada in the early 1960s as a remedy for morning sickness. The drug was kept off the market in the United States because Frances Kelsey, a physician at the Food and Drug Administration, wanted more evidence of its safety than the animal studies that had been conducted. As it turned out, what was safe for developing rats was not at all safe for human embryos. Women who took thalidomide during the first two months of pregnancy gave birth to babies with a variety of severe malformations. The particular defect depended on exactly when the drug had been taken. For example, if it was taken about three weeks after conception, the baby was likely to be born

In Brazil and other countries with a high incidence of leprosy, thalidomide is readily available and subject to misuse. This baby was born without arms or legs after his mother took thalidomide while she was pregnant.

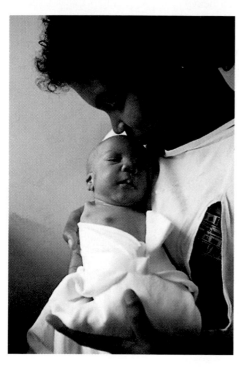

without ears. If it was taken about four weeks after conception, the child was likely to have deformed legs, or even no legs at all. However, if it was first taken later than the eighth week of pregnancy, after the major body parts had formed, no birth defects were likely (Newman, 1986). Sadly, birth defects from thalidomide are not entirely a thing of the past. Thalidomide has turned out to be an effective treatment for leprosy and for some symptoms associated with cancer and AIDS, and there have been new reports of birth defects caused by its use in some developing countries, especially in South America (Annas and Elias, 1999; Castilla et al., 1996; Stephens and Brynner, 2001).

The thalidomide episode teaches several lessons. First, drugs that are safe for some animals may not be safe for humans. Second, prolonged use of a drug is not required for it to have a negative effect on development. Some women who gave birth to babies with deformities had used thalidomide for only one or two days (Taussig, 1962). This was possible because developmental change occurs rapidly during the embryonic period, and once tissues have differentiated incorrectly there is no turning back. Third, the case of thalidomide shows how precise the timetable for prenatal development is. Dramatically different but predictable abnormalities occurred in each of the early weeks of pregnancy.

Hormones.   Both male and female hormones can cause birth defects if taken during pregnancy (Cunningham et al., 2001). As already mentioned, girls whose mothers receive androgens early in pregnancy can develop masculinized genitals. However, the most widespread problem caused by hormone treatments resulted from use of diethylstilbestrol (DES), which is a synthetic **estrogen,** a female hormone. From the 1940s through the 1960s, DES was often prescribed to prevent miscarriages. Since millions of normal-looking babies were born to women who took DES, it appeared to be perfectly safe. However, when these children became adults, problems began to appear (Hatch et al., 1998; Mittendorf, 1995). In women, the problems include reproductive tract abnormalities that sometimes interfere with pregnancy, as well as increased rates of cervical and vaginal cancer. In men, various genital abnormalities have been found. Such outcomes show that teratogens can have effects that do not become apparent for years.

Estrogen:
A female sex hormone.

Diseases   A variety of diseases are known to have harmful effects on prenatal development. Many viruses can pass through the placenta, and some can have serious consequences for the embryo or fetus. Diseases can affect prenatal development in three ways:

• Some, such as rubella, influenza, and mumps, have direct effects on the development of the embryo or fetus.

- Others, such as HIV, herpes and syphilis, are directly transmitted from mother to child before or during delivery.
- Still others, such as diabetes, affect the unborn child indirectly, through their impact on the mother's body chemistry.

Rubella. Children whose mothers had rubella (German measles) early in pregnancy have a high incidence of blindness, deafness, mental retardation, and heart defects. Birth defects from rubella have declined greatly since the rubella vaccine became available in 1969; they could be eliminated if all women in their childbearing years were immunized. How dangerous rubella is to an unborn child depends on when exposure to the virus occurs. If a pregnant woman gets rubella during the third or fourth week after conception, the probability of birth defects is 60 percent. That rate drops to 25 percent in the second month of pregnancy and to 8 percent in the third month (McMillan et al., 1999). Again we see evidence of a strict timetable for development and of greatest vulnerability during the critical period when basic structures are forming.

Rubella causes some of the same birth defects as thalidomide. Often quite different teratogens have identical effects if they are present at the same critical time in development. This makes sense given that a certain set of changes is occurring in the embryo at any particular point; anything that disrupts those changes is likely to cause similar abnormalities. By the same token, if two women are exposed to the same teratogen but at different times in pregnancy, the effects will probably differ.

HIV. The human immunodeficiency virus (HIV), the virus that causes AIDS, can cross the placenta and infect the fetus; it can also be passed to a baby by exposure to an infected mother's blood during delivery or to her milk through breastfeeding. A woman may carry the virus for up to eleven years without developing symptoms, so she may not know that she is HIV-positive when she becomes pregnant. By the end of 2002, an estimated 19.2 million women worldwide, most of them of childbearing age, and about 3.2 million children under age 15 were living with HIV (UNAIDS, 2002). About 5.5 million children had died of AIDS by that date. By far the highest concentration of children with HIV and AIDS is in Africa south of the Sahara Desert.

HIV/AIDS Worldwide

Most of the children infected with HIV acquired the virus from their mothers before or at the time of birth or through breastfeeding (UNAIDS, 2002). However, not all babies born to HIV-positive mothers are infected with the virus. Without treatment, about 15 to 25 percent of infected mothers in the United States transmit the disease to their babies; in Africa, the rate of transmission is 25 to 35 percent (Newell and Gibb, 1995). The risk of infection is greatly reduced if AZT or other antiretroviral drugs are given to HIV-positive women during pregnancy and to their babies soon after birth (Bhana et al., 2002; Connor et al., 1994). So far, there is no evidence that babies who receive this treatment suffer increased birth defects as a result (Newell and Gibb, 1995; White, Eldridge, and Andrews, 1997).

Widespread drug treatment, along with other preventive measures such as delivery by cesarean section and avoidance of breastfeeding, has greatly reduced mother-child transmission of HIV in developed countries. Between 1992 and 1997, the number of babies infected with HIV before or around the time of birth in the United States declined by two-thirds (Centers for Disease Control and Prevention, 1999). Advances in the treatment of HIV have also lengthened the life span of children who do acquire the disease, especially in developed countries (Brown, Lourie, and Pao, 2000; Lwin and Melvin, 2001). For children in the developing world who do not have ready access to anti-AIDS drugs, however, the outlook remains grim (Foster and Williamson, 2000).

The first sign of HIV infection in infants is often failure to grow, followed by repeated serious infections. Even with drug treatment, children infected with HIV often continue to suffer from impaired growth throughout infancy and childhood (Buchacz et al., 2001; Nachman et al., 2002). Brain development is often affected, resulting in problems in motor and cognitive development, even among babies whose mothers did not use drugs during pregnancy (Knight et al., 2000; Wachsler-Felder and Golden, 2002). As with other prenatal risk factors, socioeconomic status and home environment make a difference in both cognitive and social developmental outcomes for children with HIV (Battles and Wiener, 2002; Coscia et al., 2001).

Maternal Stress For years researchers have noted a correlation between high levels of stress experienced by mothers during pregnancy and such conditions as prematurity, low birth weight, and newborn irritability (Lobel, 1994). It has been hard to tell whether there was a direct causal link, however, because mothers under stress are also more likely to smoke, use drugs or alcohol, and have a poor diet. In addition, other factors that have negative impacts on prenatal development, such as poverty and adolescent pregnancy, often raise stress levels.

Recent experimental studies with rhesus monkeys provide more compelling evidence of direct negative impacts from stress. Mary Schneider (Schneider and Moore, 2000), a researcher at the University of Wisconsin, systematically exposed pregnant rhesus monkeys to stress during pregnancy, primarily by separating them from the other monkeys in their group. Their infants later showed abnormal physiological reactions to stress, especially if the mothers had experienced stress early in pregnancy. This effect appeared even for infants reared separately from their mothers, suggesting that the results were not due simply to different treatment after birth.

The results of these studies suggest that stress can affect prenatal development because it produces changes in the levels of stress-related hormones in the mother's bloodstream. These hormones alter patterns of circulation in the mother's body, potentially reducing the availability of oxygen and nutrients to the developing baby. They can also pass through the placenta and directly affect the development of the embryo or fetus.

The effects of prolonged high levels of stress should not be interpreted to mean that *any* stress during pregnancy is potentially harmful. There is no evidence that mild, occasional stress during pregnancy causes problems in prenatal development.

Maternal Nutrition Good nutrition both before and during pregnancy is important to producing a healthy baby. As with other influences on prenatal development, the presence or absence of particular nutrients may have different effects at different times. This was shown in a study of babies conceived and born during a famine in Holland toward the end of World War II. The famine greatly reduced the population's fertility rate and increased infant mortality. Moreover, if a woman was malnourished during her last three months of pregnancy, the time when the fetus normally gains the most weight, her baby was likely to be born small and thin (Stein et al., 1975).

Some researchers claim that poor maternal nutrition (particularly protein deficiency) in the last few months of pregnancy irreversibly lowers the number of brain cells a baby is born with. Several studies of children born to malnourished mothers seem to support this contention, but all these studies have flaws. The clearest evidence comes from studies of rats raised in controlled conditions. Those that experienced significant prenatal malnutrition did have fewer brain cells and also had learning deficits (Winick, 1975). But it may be unwise to generalize from rats to people. Some researchers remain unconvinced that nutrition directly affects neuron development in humans. In the Dutch study mentioned earlier, no IQ differences were found between children born during the wartime famine and children born afterward. But there is no way of knowing whether the fetuses who managed to survive the famine would normally have been more robust and intelligent than their peers. This problem is common in interpreting natural experiments; alternative explanations are often difficult to rule out.

The need for specific vitamins and minerals during pregnancy is another widely researched topic. Calcium, for instance, is essential to the formation of bones and teeth. If the mother's diet is deficient in calcium, some of it will be drawn from her own bones to meet the fetus's needs. In general, however, the fetus cannot take nutritional stores from the mother's body to compensate for deficiencies in her diet. Consequently, doctors often recommend vitamin and mineral supplements for pregnant women. But excessive vitamin intake, particularly of fat-soluble vitamins that the body can store, is also a danger. Both deficiencies and excesses of some vitamins can cause birth defects. Therefore, pregnant women should ask their doctors what nutritional supplements they should take.

One specific B-vitamin, folic acid, turns out to have a strong protective effect against certain birth defects when taken by women *before* conception, as well as early in pregnancy. Researchers have found that taking 400 micrograms of folic acid daily reduces by about 60 percent the risk of neural tube defects, such as failure of the spine to close *(spina bifida)* or absence of part of the brain *(anencephaly)* (Werler, Shapiro, and Mitchell, 1993). Beginning in 1998, the United States and Canada both required that enriched cereal grain products, including flour and pasta, be fortified with folic acid. As a result of this requirement, women's blood levels of folic acid have increased, and the incidence of neural tube defects has dropped by 20 percent in the United States (Green, 2002) and by 50 percent in Canada (McDonald et al., 2003). Because nearly half of all pregnancies are unplanned, the U.S. Public Health Service recommends that all women of child-bearing age take a multivitamin containing 400 micrograms of folic acid every day (Centers for Disease Control and Prevention, 2002).

Pregnant women who receive adequate calories and a balanced diet increase their chances of delivering a healthy baby.

Folic Acid

Maternal Age If we examine the rates of miscarriage, stillbirths, and infant deaths in the United States as a function of maternal age, an interesting pattern emerges. The rates are highest for teenagers and for women over 35. Thus, both Delores Williams and Karen Polonius might have reason to be concerned about the well-being of their babies. However, although they are at greater risk for problems than Christine Gordon, there is good reason to expect that both will give birth to healthy babies, especially if they receive good prenatal care.

There are several possible reasons why teenagers have higher rates of pregnancy failure than women in their 20s and early 30s. Teenagers' reproductive organs are not yet fully mature and may have more trouble supporting a fetus. In addition, because teenage mothers are often single and poor, as we mentioned in Chapter 2, they are less likely to receive good prenatal care and nutrition.

The potential reproductive difficulties of older than average mothers are different from those of teenagers. After about age 30, the walls of the uterus become thinner, making successful implantation of a fertilized egg less likely. In addition, since all of a woman's ova are present in immature form from the time she is born, older women's egg cells have been exposed over more years to drugs, diseases, and radiation. Such exposure may make eggs defective and unable to produce a viable fetus. As a result of these changes, women in their 30s often take longer to conceive than younger women, and some are unable to conceive without medical intervention (Dunson, Colombo, and Baird, 2002). After about age 40, declines in fertility are even greater. However, women in their 30s and early 40s who are able to become pregnant and sustain the pregnancy have almost as good a chance of bearing a normal, healthy baby as do younger women. In fact, one study of five hundred thousand women showed no association between the mother's age and the vast majority of birth defects (Baird et al., 1991). Only birth defects caused by chromosomal abnormalities, such as Down syndrome, are clearly linked to maternal age.

The number of previous pregnancies a woman has had can also influence the success of childbearing. First pregnancies at any age are more likely than subsequent ones to end in miscarriage, low birth weight, or malformations. After four pregnancies the incidence of problems again rises (Bai et al., 2002). Maternal age and socioeconomic status are contributing factors, but health complications from previous pregnancies and reproductive fatigue may also be involved.

Detection and Treatment of Fetal Disorders

Thanks to new technology, some fetal disorders can now be detected relatively early in pregnancy. **Ultrasound,** a technique that produces a computer image of the fetus by bouncing sound waves off it, allows physicians to detect structural abnormalities as small as a cleft palate. In combination with other tests, ultrasound has made it possible to diagnose more than twenty types of heart defects and heart rhythm disturbances before birth (Chervenak, Isaacson, and Mahoney, 1986). Because it is not invasive and carries little or no risk to the mother or fetus, ultrasound has begun to replace other techniques for identifying a wide variety of disorders. Ultrasound can also be used to monitor growth of the fetus and to guide instruments safely to permit the extraction of samples of amniotic fluid, fetal blood, and other tissue for diagnostic analysis.

Maternal blood tests can detect signs of some fetal disorders. For example, high levels of a substance called alpha-fetoprotein in the mother's blood may indicate a neural tube defect in the fetus. An ultrasound examination can then confirm whether a neural tube defect is actually present. Low levels of alpha-fetoprotein are a sign of possible Down syndroms and indicate the need for further testing.

Prenatal detection of Down syndrome and other genetic disorders requires a sample of genetic material from the fetus. In **amniocentesis,** a needle is inserted through the mother's abdomen to withdraw a sample of the amniotic fluid that surrounds the developing fetus (Cunningham et al., 2001). Cells that the fetus has shed into the fluid can be analyzed for chromosomal abnormalities because they contain the same chromosomes as all other cells in the fetus. The amniotic fluid can also be tested for alpha-fetoprotein to detect neural tube defects.

In another diagnostic technique, called **chorionic villus sampling (CVS),** cells are suctioned from the developing placenta via a small tube passed through the vagina and cervix or through the abdominal wall (Cunningham et al., 2001). These cells are then analyzed to determine the fetus's genetic makeup. CVS can be performed earlier than amniocentesis—usually eight to twelve weeks after the mother's last menstrual period. However, it is a more difficult procedure and is not as widely available as amniocentesis.

The burgeoning field of fetal diagnosis has made it possible to treat some disorders prenatally, with transfusions, drug therapy, and even surgery. But fetal diagnosis also has created difficult moral and emotional dilemmas for parents and for society as a whole. In the past, there was no way to predict congenital abnormalities. If a child was born with severe physical deformities or mental retardation, no one was to blame. But today we know how to detect many serious disorders prenatally, and such knowledge brings responsibility. What should prospective parents do if they discover their fetus has a serious disorder? What should society allow them to do? The controversy surrounding abortion shows there are no simple answers to these questions.

Another approach to preventing birth defects is for parents who are at high risk of producing children with a genetic disorder to receive genetic testing and counseling before they attempt a pregnancy. Because of the expense and the generally low incidence of most genetic defects, such testing is not necessary for everyone. But it can be worthwhile for couples with a family history of genetic disorders. Consider a Jewish couple of Eastern European descent worried about having a child with Tay-Sachs disease. If tests show that they both carry the recessive gene for this disorder, they know there is a 25 percent chance

Ultrasound:
A technique that produces a computer image of a fetus by bouncing sound waves off it.

Prenatal Diagnostic Techniques

Amniocentesis:
Withdrawal of amniotic fluid for the purpose of testing for chromosomal abnormalities.

Chorionic villus sampling:
A technique for analyzing the fetus's genetic makeup using cells from the developing placenta.

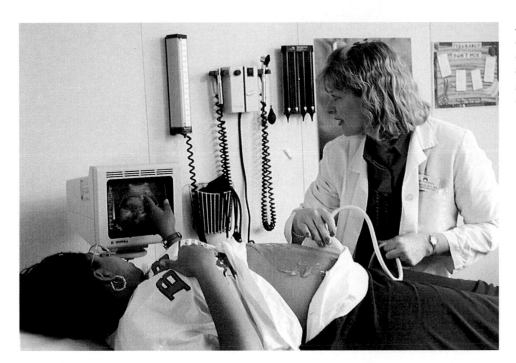

An ultrasound examination gives a pregnant woman her first look at her baby and also allows doctors to monitor the baby's growth and check for structural abnormalities.

that any child of theirs will have the fatal illness. But if only one of them is a carrier of the gene, *none* of their children will have Tay-Sachs. The many healthy, happy babies born to parents like these are testimony to the benefits of genetic testing and counseling.

BIRTH

Child Development CD
Childbirth

After nine months of gestation, human infants are ready to be born. In most cases the process is routine, as it has been for thousands of years. The fetus prepares for birth by moving into a head-down position, and the mother's uterus responds with contractions, which help move the baby through the vagina. In many cases, as with Karen in our story, one of the first signs the mother has of the impending birth is the breaking of the amniotic sac, which causes amniotic fluid to rush out of the vagina.

The Stages of Labor

Childbirth is also referred to as *labor* because of the work it entails. There are three stages of labor:

mhhe.com
/dehart5

Birth Video

- During the first stage, regular, strong contractions begin fifteen to twenty minutes apart and become stronger and more frequent as labor proceeds. This stage continues until the cervix becomes fully opened, or *dilated,* a process that may take just one hour or may last more than a day.

- For normal, head-first deliveries, the second stage of labor begins with *crowning,* when the crown of the infant's head pushes through the cervix into the vagina, and ends when the baby is delivered. Now contractions are about a minute apart and last about forty-five seconds. As the head and shoulders emerge, the head usually turns to the side. Once the shoulders are clear, the rest of the body slips out quickly. The second stage of labor usually lasts between thirty minutes and two hours.

- The third stage of labor begins when the baby is delivered and ends with the delivery of the *afterbirth,* which includes the placenta and other membranes.

The birth of a baby is often an unparalleled joy for parents.

Birth Complications

Not all pregnancies and deliveries are routine. Doctors can quickly gauge the condition of a newborn by looking at the results of a set of standard tests routinely given at one and five minutes after birth. These tests include the **Apgar scale** shown in Table 3.4. The baby's score on the Apgar is the sum of the ratings for heart rate, respiration, reflexes, muscle tone, and skin color. A score below 5 is cause for concern and requires immediate medical treatment.

Anoxia One major concern in birthing is the maintenance of a steady supply of oxygen to the infant. A long disruption in the oxygen supply, called **anoxia,** can cause damage to the infant's brain. Anoxia can occur in two basic ways. First, the umbilical cord may become pinched during delivery, constricting blood flow through it and cutting off the oxygen supply to the baby. This is most common in a breech birth, in which the infant is delivered in a bottom- or feet-first position. Such births often take longer than head-first births, and in the final stages of delivery the cord may become tangled or pinched. Second, anoxia can occur if the baby fails to begin breathing immediately after birth.

Low Birth Weight and Prematurity The question of how old or how large a fetus must be before it is able to survive outside of the womb cannot be answered precisely. It is possible for babies born as early as 20 weeks after conception (22 weeks after the mother's last menstrual period), weighing less than 500 grams (1.1 pounds), to survive, but the odds are still against them (Alexander et al., 2003). Up to the average full-term birth weight of seven and a half pounds, the heavier a fetus is, the greater its chances of survival. Since the most rapid weight gain occurs late in prenatal development (when it reaches a peak of over two ounces a day), staying in the womb for the full 38 weeks is highly advantageous. Babies born less than 35 weeks after conception (37 weeks after the mother's last menstrual period) are considered **premature.** Babies weighing less than 2500 grams (5.5 pounds) at birth are considered **low birth weight;** under 1500 grams (3.25 pounds) is considered **very low birth weight.**

Low birth weight can be due to premature delivery, retarded growth while in the womb, or both. Premature babies born after seven months of normal gestation often suffer no lasting ill effects (Greenberg and Crnic, 1988). However, babies born *small*

Apgar scale:
A scale for rating a baby's well-being shortly after birth.

Anoxia:
A disruption in the baby's oxygen supply during or just after birth.

Premature:
Referring to a baby born less than thirty-five weeks after conception.

Low birth weight:
Referring to a baby weighing less than 2500 grams at birth.

Very low birth weight:
Referring to a baby weighing less than 1500 grams at birth.

Table 3.4 The Apgar Scale

Sign	Criterion*	Score
Heart rate (beats/minute)	100 or more	2
	Less than 100	1
	Not detectable	0
Respiratory effort	Lusty crying and breathing	2
	Any shallowness, irregularity	1
	Not breathing	0
Reflex irritability	Vigorous response to stimulation (e.g., sneezing or coughing in response to stimulation of nostrils), urination, defecation	2
	Weak response	1
	No response	0
Muscle tone	Resilient, limbs spontaneously flexed and resistant to applied force	2
	Limpness, lack of resistance	1
	Complete flaccidity	0
Skin color	Pink all over	2
	Partially pink	1
	Bluish or yellowish	0

*Observations made at 60 seconds after birth.

Source: From V. Apgar, "A Proposal for a New Method of Evaluation of a Newborn Infant," *Anesthesia and Analgesia* 32:260–267. Copyright © 1975. Used by permission of Lippincott, Williams & Wilkins.

for their gestational age, even if they are carried to full term, remain at risk for later difficulties. The explanation for this is that prenatal growth retardation is usually associated with other problems, such as maternal illness, malnutrition, smoking, or drug use.

The problem of low birth weight is relatively common in our society, affecting about 7.6 percent of babies born in the United States (Martin, Park, and Sutton, 2002). It is especially common among those living in poverty. Babies who are born too small have an increased incidence of neurological problems, physical abnormalities, and lung ailments compared with babies of ideal weight.

Neonatal intensive care units have made dramatic strides in keeping low-birth-weight babies alive. As of the late 1990s, the survival rate for very-low-birth-weight babies cared for in hospitals in the United States with advanced neonatal intensive care units was over 80 percent; even for babies weighing between 500 and 750 grams, the survival rate was over 50 percent (Lemons et al., 2001). However, the rate of medical complications, such as poor postnatal growth, chronic lung disease, brain hemorrhage, and gastrointestinal problems, remains high, especially for the smallest babies. Children born at very low birth weights have a heightened risk of impaired cognitive and motor development, health and behavior problems, and low academic achievement, with the long-term risks increasing as birth weight goes down (Taylor, Klein, and Hack, 2000). As we have seen with other developmental risk factors, early intervention programs and a supportive family environment increase the chances of positive long-term outcomes for even very-low-birth-weight babies (Infant Health and Development Program, 1990).

Technological advances increase the chances that extremely premature and low-birth-weight infants will survive. Such babies are at increased risk for a variety of developmental problems.

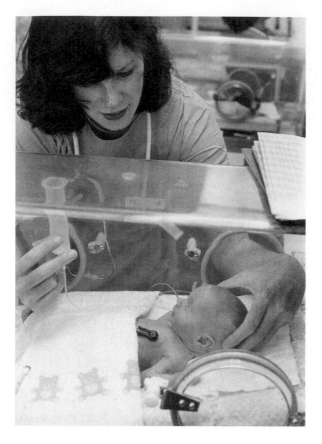

Cultural Variation in Childbirth

Although the basic biological process of labor and delivery is the same the world over, beliefs and practices surrounding childbirth vary widely (Jordan, 1993; Konner, 1991). In North America and many other industrialized cultures, most babies are delivered by physicians in hospital rooms. However, in Holland, the majority of normal births take place at home, usually with a midwife in attendance (Jordan, 1993). In many developing countries, most births occur at home with assistance from *lay midwives,* women who have years of experience delivering babies but may have no formal training. In many traditional cultures around the world, women give birth with help from female relatives or, less commonly, their husbands, but without assistance from medical personnel.

In North America the medical approach to childbirth has changed somewhat in the last thirty years. Providing hospital birthing centers with a homelike atmosphere, using nurse midwives, allowing fathers to be present in the delivery room, and permitting mothers to room in with the newborn are all part of a trend toward less medical intervention in normal deliveries. These changes have not occurred in all industrialized countries, however. For example, in Russia fathers are still barred from the delivery room and mothers and babies are kept in the hospital and away from family members for several days after delivery, for fear of infection (Konner, 1991).

Most middle-class American couples who are expecting a baby take childbirth preparation classes, and studies have found that participation in such classes can decrease anxiety about labor and delivery (Crowe and von Baeyer, 1989). One of the most common approaches used in these classes is the Lamaze method, which uses several strategies to lessen the mother's fear and pain and make birth a more positive experience. These include education about the birth process, participation of both parents in the pregnancy and delivery, and use of special breathing techniques during labor. A major advantage of natural or prepared childbirth methods such as Lamaze is a decreased reliance on painkilling drugs during labor.

In much of the world, babies are more likely to be born at home than in a hospital. Women giving birth may be assisted by relatives, by lay midwives, or—as at this birth in Gambia—by trained nurse-midwives.

Drugs commonly used during childbirth include anesthetics (which either block sensory signals or induce complete unconsciousness), analgesics (which reduce pain), and sedatives (which reduce anxiety). These drugs can affect the baby in two ways. First, they tend to lower the mother's blood pressure and the oxygen content of her blood, which in turn lowers the amount of oxygen supplied to the child. Second, most of these drugs rapidly cross the placenta and can directly affect the infant both during and after birth. The current trend in North America is to limit and carefully monitor the use of drugs during labor and delivery. General anesthetics, which cause complete unconsciousness, are now rarely used during childbirth. Regional and local anesthetics, which deaden sensations in specific parts of the body, are preferred because they have less effect on the baby and allow the mother to participate actively in the delivery (Cunningham et al., 2001).

At the same time natural childbirth has gained in popularity in the United States, there has been an increase in deliveries by **cesarean section**—that is, by surgical incision in the abdomen and uterus of the mother. Cesarean deliveries are used when heart-rate monitors indicate fetal distress, when the mother's pelvis is too small for the baby's head to pass through, or when vaginal delivery is otherwise not going well. There are clear indications that the procedure is overused in the United States; the frequency of cesarean delivery in the United States has increased from 5 percent in 1965 to 24 percent in 2001 (Martin et al., 2002). However, there is no evidence that this procedure has reduced infant mortality or birth-related damage to the nervous system. Cesarean section carries with it the risks of any major surgery and can compromise the mother's ability to deliver vaginally in future births. It also increases the risk of postdelivery complications and lengthens hospital stays. Current government guidelines set a goal of 15 percent cesarean deliveries, but progress toward this goal has been slow.

Cesarean section:
Delivery of a baby by surgical incision in the abdomen and uterus of the mother.

PRENATAL DEVELOPMENT IN CONTEXT

A major theme of this book is that development can be fully understood only by examining the context in which it occurs. That theme is very apparent in this chapter. Prenatal development unfolds in a hereditary context provided by the genes that each individual inherits from his or her parents. Those genes are guidelines for constructing a new human being—a person in many ways like all human beings, in other ways unique. At the same time, prenatal development unfolds in an environmental context—a set of hormones, nutrients, and other substances that help shape the way the genes are expressed. Some of these substances are a product of the developing organism itself, and others come from outside the womb via the placenta and the mother's bloodstream. Moreover, the environmental context is created not just by present events, but also by past developmental changes. For instance, when an embryo develops masculine genitals under the influence of male hormones, that embryo's current environment is influenced by a critical past event—either the formation of androgen-producing glands or an influx of androgens from some other source. Past development, in other words, is part of the context for present development.

The enormous importance of the environmental context in prenatal development can be seen by considering a paradox. At the moment of fertilization the new organism receives all the genetic material it will ever have. As development proceeds, these genes are duplicated each time a cell divides, and each new cell receives an identical set. Yet despite the fact that all the resulting cells share identical genetic material, they take on a remarkable variety of specialized forms and functions through the process of differentiation. How does it come about that one cell uses only certain of its genes to function as a blood cell, while another cell uses other genes to function as part of a muscle or nerve?

The answer is that some genes are activated and others are deactivated in response to environmental signals, many of which stem from interactions with other cells. Recall from Chapter 1 that the same tissue from a chick embryo could become part of a thigh, a claw, or a wing tip, depending on its location and the timing of its placement. The same process of influence by surrounding cells is what leads some cells on the surface of the new embryo to migrate into the core to form the human nervous system. You have seen the importance of the interaction of genes and the environment throughout this chapter, and you will see it again throughout this book. Development is never simply the product of a genetic blueprint; it is always influenced by previous development and current circumstances as well. This is the hallmark of all development, whether at the level of the cell, the embryo, the fetus, the newborn, the child, or the adult.

The environmental context that shapes development always has several layers, as in Bronfenbrenner's concentric rings of influence discussed in Chapter 2. During the prenatal period, some of the substances that influence development come from the developing organism itself, while others come from the mother's body via the placenta. But the environmental context of prenatal development does not stop there. The mother herself is embedded in a physical, social, and cultural environment that can greatly affect her body and the fate of her developing child.

Chapter Summary

Introduction

Four major developmental themes during the **prenatal period** are:

- genes are only one part of a complex developmental system;
- development involves **differentiation;**
- development involves repeated reorganization and qualitative change; and
- new structures and capacities emerge in an orderly manner from those that existed before.

Genetic Processes

Genes are segments of DNA located on structures called **chromosomes.** Every cell in the human body, except reproductive cells, contains twenty-three pairs of chromosomes, or forty-six in all.

Two different types of cellular division are involved in human development:

- **mitosis,** the basic process by which the body grows and maintains itself, and
- **meiosis,** a special kind of cell division that produces reproductive cells.

Meiosis serves two important functions:

- it produces egg and sperm cells with half as many chromosomes as other cells in the body, and
- it contributes to genetic diversity by means of **crossing over** and **random assortment.**

The development of physical gender is a good example of how genes operate in a particular environmental context.

- The presence of a Y chromosome causes primitive **gonad** tissue to become testes.
- If the embryo has two X chromosomes, the same tissue becomes ovaries.
- Hormones influence the further development of physical gender.

In addition to interacting with the environment, genes also interact with one another.

- In some gene pairs one **allele** is dominant and the other recessive.
- In other gene pairs codominant alleles determine how a characteristic is expressed.
- An individual's **genotype** is not always apparent from his or her **phenotype.**

Conception

The joining of sperm and egg depends on successful completion of a complicated chain of events. Twins can develop if:

- two eggs are released by the ovaries at the same time, or
- one fertilized egg splits into two embryos.

Prenatal Development

The thirty-eight weeks of prenatal development can be divided into three major periods. The developing organism is qualitatively different at each of the three periods of prenatal development.

- During the *germinal period* (from conception through week 2), the **zygote** begins the process of cell division and differentiation and becomes implanted in the uterine lining.
- During the *embryonic period* (from week 3 through week 8) a life-support system for the **embryo** develops, and all the major organs and structures of the body form.
- During the *fetal* period (from week 9 to birth) the **fetus** grows rapidly, its structures become refined, and it becomes increasingly active and responsive to its environment.

The Mother's Experience of Pregnancy

From the mother's point of view, pregnancy is divided into **trimesters.**

- The first trimester is characterized by such physical symptoms as morning sickness and fatigue.
- The second trimester is often the most enjoyable for the mother; during this time, **quickening** occurs.
- The third trimester is the most physically trying for the mother.

Problems in Prenatal Development

Congenital defects, or **birth defects,** can be caused by:

- genetic defects,
- environmental factors, or
- a combination of the two.

There are two types of genetic defects:

- **single-gene disorders,** which follow the basic principles of genetic inheritance described by Mendel, and
- **chromosomal abnormalities,** which occur when errors in meiosis produce sperm or egg cells with incorrect numbers of chromosomes or damaged chromosomes.

A **teratogen** is any substance in the environment that can cause prenatal developmental abnormalities.

- Common teratogens include drugs, hormones, and viruses.
- Teratogens can prevent or modify normal cell division and differentiation.
- Since most cell differentiation occurs during the embryonic period, embryos are especially vulnerable to the effects of teratogens.

Fetuses at risk for congenital defects can be screened by means of:

- maternal blood tests,
- **ultrasound,**
- **amniocentesis,** and
- **chorionic villus sampling.**

Birth

After nine months of gestation, the baby is pushed out of the uterus by means of contractions that become increasingly strong and regular as labor proceeds.

Major birth complications include:

- **anoxia** and
- **low birth weight** and **prematurity.**

Beliefs and practices surrounding childbirth differ widely across cultures. Recent trends in childbirth in the United States include:

- changes in the traditional medical approach, and
- an increase in the rate of cesarean sections.

Prenatal Development in Context

Prenatal development and birth illustrate the rings of contextual influence in Bronfenbrenner's model. Development is influenced by:

- genes;
- maternal nutrition, stress, illnesses, and drug taking;
- socioeconomic circumstances surrounding the pregnancy; and
- technological advances and changing childbirth practices at the cultural and societal levels.

Review Questions

Introduction

1. Explain how **differentiation** and reorganization produce qualitative change during prenatal development.

Genetic Processes

2. Describe the basic structure of human **genes** and **chromosomes.**
3. Explain the processes of **mitosis** and **meiosis.**
4. Discuss how genes and the environment interact during prenatal development.

Conception

5. Describe the process of conception and the events leading up to it.

Prenatal Development

6. List the three stages of prenatal development and summarize the events in each one.

The Mother's Experience of Pregnancy

7. Explain what is meant by **trimesters** of pregnancy and what occurs during each one.

Problems in Prenatal Development

8. Explain the major sources of birth defects and give examples of each type.
9. Discuss the use of prenatal diagnostic techniques and genetic testing and counseling.

Birth

10. Describe what happens during each of the three stages of labor.
11. Discuss the most common birth complications and their developmental outcomes.

Prenatal Development in Context

12. Explain how considering context enhances understanding of prenatal development.

Application and Observation

1. Chart the occurrence of an obvious genetically based physical trait (blood type, eye color, hair color, handedness, color blindness, etc.) in your own immediate or extended family or another family with whom you're well acquainted. What does your chart tell you about genotypes and phenotypes in your family for the trait you've chosen? Does the trait fit any obvious pattern of inheritance (dominant/recessive or sex-linked genes, for example)?

2. Read and review several popular books for parents-to-be. Based on what you've read in this chapter, how accurate and complete is the information they provide? How do they vary in the particular topics they cover? What do they reveal about current attitudes and beliefs about pregnancy and childbirth? For a broader perspective, go to the library and find advice to parents in books or magazines from earlier generations. How has the advice and information provided in these sources changed over the years?

3. Choose one ethical issue related to heredity and prenatal development (for example, the ethics of in vitro fertilization, prenatal screening for genetic disorders, the use of stem cells from human zygotes in research, or abortion). Using relevant information from this chapter, try to construct arguments for two opposing points of view on the issue you have chosen. Which of the arguments you have constructed is closer to your own position? Why?

4. Interview women from different generations or different cultural backgrounds about their experiences with pregnancy and childbirth. Topics you might cover include preparation for and sources of information about childbirth, prenatal care, labor and delivery experience, involvement of the baby's father, and breastfeeding vs. bottle feeding.

Infancy

PART 2

Part 2 Four Children as Infants

Malcolm Williams

"Let me hold him first, Momma," Teresa pleaded as her parents walked through the apartment door. "I get to hold him first 'cause I'm a girl, so I'm next to be a momma."

"What about me, girl?" laughed 21-year-old Denise, as she and the rest of the Williamses crowded around DeeDee and the baby she cradled in her arms. "Are you sayin' this boy's aunt is never gonna find herself a man?"

"My Lord. Look at that red hair!" Momma Jo exclaimed. "Where'd he get that from? Where on earth? And his eyes are so wide open, like he's takin' in everything, I never have seen a brand-new baby lookin' round like he does. Hi, sugar. Hi. I'm your gran'ma. Can I have a kiss?" Momma Jo moved the pale-blue blanket aside for a better look. As she bent closer, the baby's face puckered and he began to cry with the same piercing wails that had announced his birth the day before. "That cry is just grand," Momma Jo declared, clasping her hands together. "Just grand!"

"Sounds like I'd better keep my earphones handy," laughed 12-year-old John, Jr. His sister Teresa was speechless. She watched in fascination as the baby wriggled forcefully and turned a glowing shade of dark auburn.

"So what'll we name him?" DeeDee asked. "We've got to decide soon. Is it gonna be Muhammad, the great Ali, or Malcolm, the great leader? What do you think, Momma Jo?"

"Well, I sure don't like some pagan name like Muhammad. I prefer Malachi from the Old Testament. The prophet who foresaw the judgment day."

"Oh, Momma Jo. No one's named Malachi anymore. Other kids would tease him."

"Then name him Malcolm if that's your pleasure."

"What do the rest of you think?" asked DeeDee.

"Malcolm, 'cause he's red, like Malcolm X was," John, Jr., said with a grin.

"Yeah. Malcolm's okay," added Teresa thoughtfully.

"John, what's your pleasure?" DeeDee asked, passing the baby to him.

"My pleasure is Malcolm Muhammad Williams. The kid's a class-A fighter and he needs a name to cover him right."

"Then Malcolm M. Williams it is," DeeDee smiled, and the others nodded in agreement.

"You're one helluva kid, man," John whispered proudly into little Malcolm's ear.

In the weeks that followed, DeeDee was amazed at Malcolm's energy and alertness. By 10 weeks he fixed his large brown eyes on everything that came into view. The family responded by talking to Malcolm and bringing him a variety of objects to look at—a bright green piece of crinkly paper, an orange feather from a feather duster, a shiny lid from a frying pan that reflected light. They enjoyed his eagerness and delight at inspecting new things. At mealtime Malcolm ate at the table with the rest of the family, passed from person to person as he sucked hungrily on a bottle. Even awkward positions in Teresa's arms never seemed to disturb him. He intently studied every face that smiled and talked above his.

By the middle of his fourth month Malcolm's height and weight were above the ninety-eighth percentile on the pediatrician's chart. Although his fiery coloring had become subdued to a rich, clear brown, his activity level remained as high as ever. As he lay on his back on a blanket on the living room floor, his little arms cycled round and round and his feet kicked vigorously. He could turn himself from back to stomach in an instant. On his belly he kicked so hard, he looked like a frog swimming.

"Motor Man, I'm gonna call you," John, Jr., said one evening, catching hold of Malcolm's furiously kicking feet. "How's the little Motor Man?" Malcolm froze for an instant, then brought a fist up to his mouth. He began to suck on all five fingers so intently that the whole family started to laugh. Malcolm gurgled with pleasure and began kicking again.

The next week a freezing rain enveloped Chicago. It seemed spring would never come as ice covered the windows, but DeeDee knew Monday was the first of March and her four-month maternity leave would be over. She had thought this time would pass slowly, but life with Malcolm was like a carnival ride. He made her feel younger and more energetic than she had felt in years. The idea of going back to her job seemed dull by comparison. But the family needed the money. There was no question she had to work.

"When people call in tomorrow complainin' about their phone service, I'm gonna tell them just what I think," DeeDee told the family at the dinner table Sunday night. "Honey, I'm gonna say, of course we're slow gettin' your bill corrected. This is the phone company you're talkin' to, darlin'. What did you expect? Now if you want to see fast, come 'round to my house and see my boy Malcolm in action. . . . " At that moment Malcolm screeched in glee and beat the air with his fists. Everyone roared with laughter.

The following morning DeeDee's spirits were far less buoyant. Momma Jo carried Malcolm down to the front steps of the apartment so that she could wave his little hand goodbye as DeeDee left for work.

"Come on now, honey," John said to her gently, as she looked out the car window. "It's nothin' to cry about. He knows you're his momma. He's not gonna love you any less."

"I know," DeeDee answered. "I never thought that for a minute. It's just that I miss him so much already. Can you believe that? And I see that boy pushin' and shovin' his way into the future so fast I'm afraid I'm gonna miss it all if I'm gone too much. Do you know what I mean?"

"I know exactly what you mean," John said, covering her hand with his.

Mikey and Maggie Gordon

"Ahh-ba-ba-ba-ba-ba-ba. Ahh-ba-ba-ba-ba-ba-ba. Eeeeeeeh! Eeeeeeeh! Yo-yo-yo-yo. Ahhuuup! Ah-huuup!" THUD! Silence.

Christine Gordon opened her eyes. The green numerals on the digital clock radio read 5:45 a.m. What's he up to now? she wondered. A moment later a small figure appeared in the doorway, dimly silhouetted in the light from the street-lamp. "Mommy, Mikey's throwing stuff!" 3-year-old Maggie announced triumphantly.

"You'd better get in there, Christine. He may have fallen out of his crib." It was Frank's voice, groggy with sleep. Christine climbed out of bed and shuffled toward the door, stumbling over the family dog asleep on the floor. She went down the hall to Mikey's room, Maggie trailing behind. There he was at the foot of the crib, flinging things over the side. The thud must have been the sound of his half-empty bottle hitting a nearby wall. As usual, the crib was a shambles. Mikey had pulled the blanket and sheet completely off the mattress, dumping them in one corner. "Yi!" he said, turning to Christine and giving her his warmest eight-toothed smile. Her 13-month-old son, Michael Francis Gordon, was ready to start a new day.

Frank had been ecstatic when Mikey was born. He hung a king-sized sheet on the highway overpass he was working on. Written on it in huge blue letters were the words: IT'S A BOY!!! The next day a reporter from News Watch 10 stopped by to interview Frank. "I just want everyone to know," Frank explained, beaming into the TV camera, "that a new pitcher for the Red Sox has just been born. You should see the hands on him already! What a kid!"

Maggie had been excited about her baby brother, too. Worried that Maggie might feel displaced, Christine had talked with her often about the baby during her pregnancy and had let her feel the baby kicking. Maggie went happily off to play with her cousins when Christine and Frank left for the hospital. When Christine returned home with a red-faced, squawling, bald creature that looked nothing like her baby dolls, Maggie was a bit disappointed. But she soon fell in love with her baby brother and constantly asked when he would be big enough to play with her.

Christine picked up the future baseball star to change his soggy diaper. "Maggie, can you bring me a new diaper and the baby wipes, please?" she asked, distracting her daughter from tugging on Mikey's toes. This task completed, the three of them went down to the kitchen. As Christine began to measure coffee into the coffeemaker, Mikey stood tugging at her nightgown, chanting "joos, joos," and Maggie wandered into the living room to see if cartoons were on yet.

Through the kitchen wall Christine could hear the toilet flushing. They'd have to do something about that plumbing. Noisiest plumbing she'd ever heard. Oh, well. At least they had a house of their own now, which was what Frank had always wanted. Those nights last winter back in the old apartment had been the final straw. Mikey had been sleeping in their room because there was no space in Maggie's tiny bedroom. His presence had put a real crimp in their sex life.

"Do you think he can hear us?" Christine would whisper when they started making love.

"For Christ's sake, what does it matter? He's only 5 months old! How the hell will he know what we're doing?"

"That's just it. He may think something terrible is going on. I read that . . . "

"Nuts to what you read! I'm not gonna let some Sigfried Freud crap turn me into a monk. If it bothers you so much, why don't you let him sleep in the living room?"

"Keep your voice down! You'll wake him. There, now you've done it!" By the time Christine nursed Mikey a little and rocked him back to sleep, Frank had also drifted off—with an angry scowl creased into his face. And half the time Maggie heard the commotion and crawled into bed with them.

So a bigger place was a must or they'd end up in divorce court. Then Frank's boss told him about a deal on a rundown three-bedroom house, and they managed to scrape together the down payment. The place had peeling paint, a leaky roof, and a worn-out furnace. But at least it was a start, and Frank could do the fix-up work himself.

By 6:30, with sunlight pouring through the open windows, the Gordon family had assembled at the kitchen table. Mikey sat loftily in his high chair, banging his feet against the footrest and pressing little nuggets of Cocoa Puffs into his mouth. The sugar-coated cereal stuck to his wet fingers, making the job of feeding himself easier. Maggie, pried away from the TV set, sat at the table in her "big girl chair," trying to get her father's attention as she chattered about the cartoon she'd been watching. "Remember it's Wednesday," Christine said to Frank as she passed a spoonful of scrambled eggs in Mikey's direction. "I need the car to make a delivery to the store."

"I know, I know." Frank answered irritably. He hated to be reminded that Christine now had a job of sorts. It was such an odd job that he didn't really have much reason to object at first. It had started the Christmas before Mikey was born, when she had made matching dresses for Maggie and her sister Paula's daughter. They were red, hand-smocked, with little Christmas trees appliquéd on wide white collars. Everyone had oohed and aahed over them, and Paula had taken pictures to show to her boss at the dress shop. That had gotten the ball rolling. Paula's boss wanted Christine to make some dresses to sell on consignment. It seemed harmless enough at the time—just a little extra sewing to keep Christine busy until the baby was born. How was he to know the things she made would become such a hit? Within a few months, the store had turned a large storage closet into a special area for Christine's clothes. Frank felt he had somehow been tricked into going along with something he'd never wanted. If it wasn't for the extra money and the fact she did all the sewing at home, he would make her quit. He looked at her with growing annoyance across the kitchen table. As if on cue to break the tension, Mikey strained forward, pointing at Christine's toast and demanding "beh, beh!"

"Hey, I think he said bread!" Frank exclaimed, momentarily forgetting his annoyance. And for the next five minutes he kept pointing to the toast Christine had given Mikey, repeating "bread, bread," over and over. Mikey grinned and slapped the tray of his high chair in unrestrained delight.

That evening, Christine worked at her sewing machine in a corner of the living room while Frank watched TV from his recliner with Mikey snuggled in beside him. Maggie suddenly popped up beside Mikey. "Boo!" she shouted gleefully. Mikey laughed with delight, and soon the two were engaged in a raucous game of peekaboo, with Maggie dodging back and forth from behind the recliner and Mikey leaning over the arm, straining to see her.

"Cut it out, Maggie!" Frank demanded. "Chrissie, will ya come get your daughter? I'm tryin' to watch this program. Us men can't get any peace around here, can we, Mikey?" Frank added, addressing the little boy beside him. Father and son had become real buddies since Mikey had started to walk and talk. "Jeez. Now we've got another damn commercial!"

Mikey moved onto his father's lap and sat facing him. "Dee!" he said, looking up with bright, eager eyes. "Wanna bounce, huh?" Frank smiled, his irritation fading. Soon father and son were engrossed in their favorite game. Frank held Mikey on his lap and bounced him vigorously. Then, holding onto Mikey's arms, he suddenly spread his knees and let the baby drop between them. As Mikey squealed with laughter, Frank hoisted him back up and started all over again.

Now's as good a time as any, Christine thought. "Something happened at the store today," she started, trying to sound casual. "The owner, you know, Helen? She wants to expand the kids' clothes a bit, besides my stuff, you know. And she asked me to go on a buying trip to Boston with her. Help her pick things out. Just for a day. What do you think?"

"I think it's a rotten idea! What do ya need to do that for? You got plenty to keep you busy here. And who's gonna take care of the kids? Tell me that."

"That's no problem," Christine answered quickly. "My mom can come over for the day. And Helen's going to pay me, you know. A hundred dollars! Can you believe it? I nearly fainted."

"A hundred bucks?" Frank muttered with grudging interest. "When does she want to go?"

"Next Thursday. She's got the schedule all set up. What do you say? OK?"

"I'll never hear the end of it if I say no," Frank grumbled. "Yeah, go ahead. A hundred bucks. Why not?"

Meryl Polonius

"We'll be back with our third game of the day right after this!" the host of the TV quiz show announced with a huge artificial smile. I really should rinse out those sheets Meryl threw up on, Karen thought with a sigh, as she sat slumped on the couch. Then, after Meryl's nap, I can do a load of laundry.

In an effort to shake herself out of her lethargy, Karen slid to the floor beside her 11-month-old daughter, who was busily stacking colored rings onto a plastic post. She did this task slowly and soberly, as if diligently trying to master it. It's easy to love her at times like this when she's not fussing or screaming, Karen thought. Watching her baby's tiny fingers clumsily handling a small blue ring, Karen felt a warm glow.

Bored with the rings, Meryl looked around and crawled toward the laundry basket. "Oh no, you don't," Karen warned as she scooped her off the floor. "You'll tip it over and I'll have to pick everything up." Meryl immediately began to cry and wriggled to escape from Karen's arms. "Someone's tired," Karen declared. "It's time for your nap." Meryl cried even louder as they headed toward the bedroom. "Let's go look for teddy," Karen said, trying to soothe her daughter. "I'll bet teddy's already asleep. Shhh. You don't want to wake him, do you?" Meryl's cries turned to piercing screams. "Hey, come on," Karen pleaded, as she put Meryl in her crib. "Be good and go to sleep, and when you wake up I'll give you a cookie." Meryl's face was now a deep crimson as she screamed and pulled at the crib rail.

"Tough," muttered Karen, closing the bedroom door behind her. "You're just going to have to cry it out." Meryl's screams grated on Karen as she sat back down in front of the TV. But at least things were better than they had been right after Meryl was born. A small baby at birth, weighing just six pounds, Meryl was a fitful sleeper and a poor eater from the start. Often she would take only an ounce or so of formula and then spit it up. Karen had tried breast-feeding at the urging of Meryl's pediatrician, but she had trouble nursing and Meryl was colicky. It had taken a while to find a formula Meryl could tolerate. That had helped some, but Meryl still cried often and took a long time to settle down.

Karen had stayed out of school the previous fall. She couldn't imagine maneuvering through the halls and squeezing into the desks at school those last two months of pregnancy. After Meryl was born, Karen had been constantly exhausted from the never-ending struggle of trying to get her to keep some formula down, walking the floor with her when she cried, and staying up half the night with her. The thought of keeping up with school on top of everything else had been overwhelming. Sometimes she had found herself hoping this was all a terrible dream and any minute she would wake up. Instead of spending her time with a baby who wouldn't eat or sleep, she would be enjoying her senior year, going out with Jeff, thinking about the prom, graduation, and college.

By Christmas Karen's mother told her she had been lying around the house long enough. She had to either go back to school or get a job. Karen couldn't imagine how she could manage either one, but her counselor at the Fresno Teen Mother Project got her into a special high school program for adolescent moms. There was day care for Meryl right at the school, and Karen found it was a relief to have other girls to talk to who were going through the same things she was. It was still a hassle to get up every morning after hardly sleeping all night, get herself and Meryl ready, and make it to school anywhere near on time, but somehow she had managed to do it. She had to go to summer school to make up the semester she'd missed, but she had finally graduated in August.

After graduation, Karen had decided she needed some time off before she thought about a job or college. With school out of the way, Karen had been determined to make up for the strain the last few months had put on Meryl. Maybe now that Meryl was older, staying home with her wouldn't be so bad, Karen thought, picturing herself spending her days playing with Meryl and taking her for walks in the stroller. Anyway, it couldn't be worse than the struggle of getting out the door every morning, being in school all day, and then spending the evening dealing with a baby who was over-tired, cranky, and sick half the time. When Meryl was in day care, it seemed she always had either an ear infection or diarrhea—she caught everything the other babies came down with. If they stayed at home for a while, Karen thought, at least Meryl would be healthier. And maybe she herself could finally catch up on her sleep. Karen's mother had reluctantly agreed to the plan, as long as Karen helped with the housework and took care of Meryl herself. She had made it clear from the time Meryl was born that she wasn't about to take on the role of babysitter or substitute mother.

Now Karen wondered if staying home had been the right decision. It seemed her mother was constantly harping at her, telling her what she was doing wrong. Doing the housework and taking care of Meryl was just as exhausting as going to school had been. And Meryl was almost as hard to deal with as ever. Somehow there never seemed to be time for the walks Karen had imagined, and Meryl still wasn't an easy baby to play with.

Karen had used part of her graduation money to buy Meryl a new toy—Oscar the Grouch from *Sesame Street* in his battered garbage can. When you pressed a bulb on the side, Oscar would pop up like a jack-in-the-box. Karen couldn't wait to unwrap the toy when she got it home. She placed it in front of Meryl, who began to inspect it quietly. Then Karen pressed the bulb and Oscar leaped up, the lid of the garbage can on top of his head. Meryl startled, her lower lip protruded, and she began to cry. "Come on, honey. It's Oscar the Grouch," Karen said. "I got it just for you." Meryl turned her head away as Karen pushed the toy toward her. "Don't you *like* it?" Karen asked, moving around to stay in front of Meryl's averted face. In exasperation she made Oscar pop up one more time. Meryl wailed louder.

As the weeks rolled by, the loneliness began to get to Karen. Her mother was gone all the time, and sometimes it seemed she went days without talking to anyone her own age. Some afternoons at naptime, when Meryl wouldn't stop crying, Karen had a sudden urge to walk out the door. She could picture herself walking down the street, with the cries of her baby growing fainter and fainter behind her. Karen was horrified at these fantasies. She loved Meryl; she knew she did. But sometimes it all just seemed too much. Karen often wished that she could talk to her mother the way daughters were supposed to be able to. But whenever she tried, they always ended up fighting. Even Karen's old friends from high school seemed to have deserted her. The few who hadn't gone off to college were busy working and having fun. Sitting around with a cranky baby wasn't their idea of a good time. If it weren't for the counselor at the Teen Mother Project, Karen didn't know what she would do.

That night as Karen sat in the living room, waiting for her mother to get home, tears welled up in her eyes. "Damn you, Jeff, " she whispered, "Damn you!" Pressing Meryl's teddy bear to her face, she cried as if her heart would break.

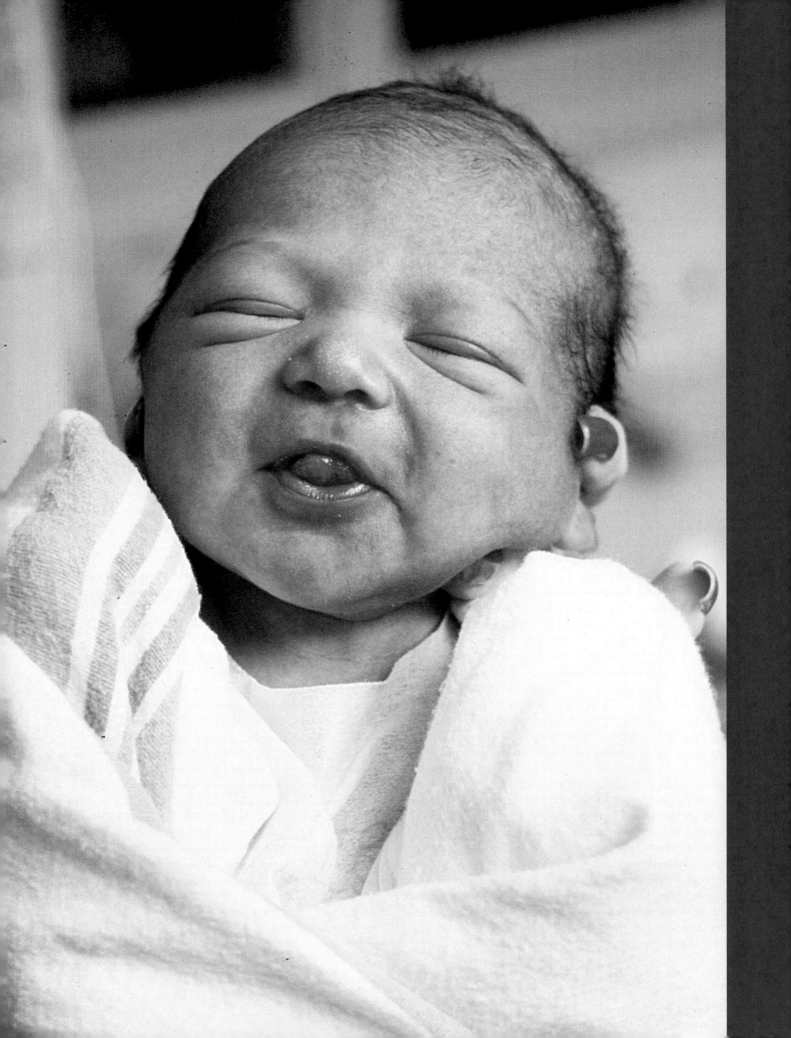

4 First Adaptations

K aren watched as Dr. Bryant gave newborn Meryl her first physical exam. Meryl squirmed on the examining table at the touch of the cold stethoscope. Her tiny face crumpled into a scowl, and she flailed her thin arms and legs.

"She may be small, Karen," Dr. Bryant said, "but she's very alert."

"She is?" Karen answered doubtfully. To her, Meryl looked totally helpless and unaware of what was going on.

"Sure," said Dr. Bryant, smiling. "Watch." And she began to talk to Meryl in gentle, soothing tones. "Hi there, little one. Hi, sweetie. Going to show your mom how smart you are, hmmm?" Meryl immediately quieted and looked up.

"She hears you," whispered Karen.

Then Dr. Bryant slowly moved a bright orange ball across Meryl's field of vision. Meryl's eyes followed it.

"She sees it!" Karen exclaimed.

"Now you try," said Dr. Bryant, encouraging Karen to move her head slowly back and forth while she talked to the baby.

"She sees me!" Karen smiled. "Does she know I'm a person? Does she know I'm her mom?"

"Not yet," Dr. Bryant answered kindly, "but she will. In a few months she'll have learned a lot about people, and she'll know you from everybody else."

As a newborn, Meryl faces the demanding developmental tasks of learning about the world and forming relationships with the people in it. Fortunately, like all newborns, she is **preadapted** to these tasks—that is, she has come equipped with built-in capacities that help her tackle them. These include a set of useful reflexes, impressive learning ability, and basic sensory and perceptual skills. Many of the abilities that newborns bring with them are already evident in some form during the prenatal period—for example, the reflexive thumb-sucking often seen in fetuses on ultrasound images. All these capacities make possible newborns' first adaptations—their first efforts to adjust to and understand the world.

The first month of life is a period of transition from life in the womb to independent existence in the outside world. As you will see in the following pages, babies change rapidly during this month as they adjust to their new surroundings. Because newborns are in many ways qualitatively different from older infants, physicians and researchers have a special term for babies during the first month of life: **neonates** (literally

Preadapted:
Equipped at birth with built-in capacities that make it possible to understand the environment and form social relationships.

Neonate:
The technical term for a baby during the first month of life.

From birth, babies have patterns of behavior that allow them to respond to their environments in an organized way.

"newborns"). A neonate's competencies, which are the building blocks of more complex behaviors, have five important characteristics:

- *They depend on prewired abilities*—abilities built into the nervous system at birth. Rapid changes and refinements in these earliest competencies often depend on both experience and maturation of the central nervous system.

- *They often meet survival needs.* For example, the sucking reflex secures nourishment, the gagging reflex prevents choking, and crying elicits care.

- *From the very beginning, they involve organized sequences of actions that serve some purpose.* For example, when Meryl turned toward Dr. Bryant's voice, this coordinated series of movements allowed her to locate the source of a sound.

- *They involve selective responses.* For example, newborns do not look with equal attention at everything around them. Instead, they tend to look at sharp contrasts, such as a pair of eyes or the border between a person's hair and forehead.

- *They allow infants to detect relationships between actions and consequences.* For example, a newborn can detect the connection between placing a thumb in the mouth and the good feelings it generates.

This chapter focuses on babies' capacities for interacting with the world during the first months of life and how those capacities change and contribute to development later in infancy. We begin with the early development of the brain, which provides the foundation for inborn capacities and their development. We continue by examining newborn states and reflexes, followed by the development of infants' learning capabilities, motor skills, sensory capacities, and perceptual abilities.

This chapter has two major themes. First, once again we focus on how *heredity and the environment work jointly to guide development.* Early development provides a good place to examine the nature-nurture issue because infant skills and behaviors are relatively limited and because their initial state is relatively untouched by experience.

Second, throughout the chapter we emphasize how *infants' initial skills, and the experiences they allow infants to have, provide the seeds for the development of more complex and flexible skills by the end of the first year.* The learning abilities, behavior systems, and sensory skills with which newborns enter the world are limited, but their very limitations guide infants to experiences that foster the development of complex skills. For example, the hearing system of newborns is quite immature, but it seems to be specially tuned to the human voice, an important factor in developing language skills and beginning to establish relationships with caregivers.

Questions to Think About As You Read

- How do infants' capacities foster interaction with the world, including other people?
- How do limitations on infants' abilities influence what they can perceive and learn?
- What practical implications do infants' early abilities and limitations have for parents?

EARLY BRAIN DEVELOPMENT

To understand newborns' abilities and limitations, it is helpful to know something about the early development of the brain—its physical growth, changes in its structure and function, and how the environment influences its development. Research in this area is

Child Development CD:
Infant Brains

challenging because opportunities for direct examination of normally developing infants' brains are limited

Researchers have used a combination of approaches to study early brain development:

- Physical growth of the brain can be measured indirectly by charting the growth of infants' head circumference or directly by examining the brains of babies who have died *(post-mortem examinations)*.

- Age-related changes in brain structure can also be studied in post-mortem examinations.

- Developmental changes in brain function in normal infants can be studied by means of *electroencephalography* (EEG), in which electrical activity in the brain is measured by electrodes placed on the scalp.

- Developmental changes in brain structure and function are increasingly being studied with various methods of brain imaging, such as *magnetic resonance imaging* (MRI) and *positron emission tomography* (PET). So far, these methods are used primarily with infants who require them for medical reasons because of practical and ethical concerns. For example, infants must be sedated to keep them still during MRIs, and PET scans involve injection of radioactive materials.

- Environmental effects on brain development can be estimated from experiments in which animals are placed in enriched or impoverished environments and from studies of children who have suffered early deprivation.

All of these methods have limitations, but together they provide an increasingly clear picture of early brain development.

Brain Growth

In accordance with the principle of cephalocaudal development discussed in Chapter 3, the head and brain are much closer to adult size at birth than other parts of the body, and they continue to grow rapidly during infancy. At birth, an infant's brain weighs 300 to 400 grams on average, which is about one-quarter of its adult weight (Morgan and Gibson, 1991). By the end of the first year, it triples in weight; it continues to grow, at a much slower rate, through adolescence. Head circumference is often used as a rough indicator of brain growth. Normal babies have an average head circumference of 34 centimeters (about 13.5 inches) at birth; by age 1, this increases to about 46 centimeters (just over 18 inches), on the way to an average adult head circumference of 52 centimeters (20.5 inches).

Changes in Structure and Function

The amazing growth in brain size during infancy is associated with considerable structural and functional development.

Developmental Timetable The various parts of the brain (see Figure 4.1) develop according to a predictable timetable, with the lower, more primitive structures completing development first:

- The spinal cord and the **brainstem,** which controls reflexes and basic survival functions such as breathing and heartbeat, are fully developed and fully functional at the time of birth.

- Some parts of the brain are relatively mature and functional at birth but continue to develop during infancy. These include the **cerebellum,** a structure involved in motor control and balance, and the **thalamus,** a structure that relays sensory information to the cerebral cortex. Also in this category is the **limbic system,** a collection of structures involved in physiological regulation, sensory integration, memory formation, and emotional responses. These structures include the **hypothalamus,** the

Brainstem:
The part of the brain that controls reflexes and basic survival functions.

Cerebellum:
A brain structure involved in motor control and balance.

Thalamus:
A brain structure that relays sensory information to the cerebral cortex.

Limbic system:
A collection of brain structures involved in physiological regulation, sensory integration, memory formation, and emotional responses.

Hypothalamus:
A brain structure that regulates physiological functions.

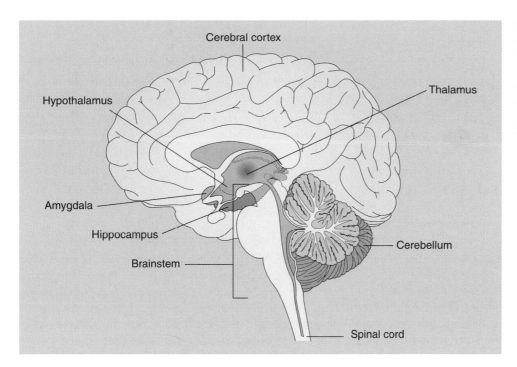

Figure 4.1
CROSS SECTION OF THE HUMAN BRAIN
(Source: From Papalia and Olds, A Child's World, 7th edition. Copyright © 1996. Reproduced with permission of the McGraw-Hill Companies.)

hippocampus, and the **amygdala.** The hypothalamus regulates such physiological functions as temperature, hunger, thirst, and sleep. The hippocampus, named for its seahorse-like shape, integrates sensory information and is essential to memory formation. The amygdala is an almond-shaped structure that is involved in memory formation and emotional responses.

- The cerebral cortex, which controls voluntary actions and higher perceptual, cognitive, and language abilities, is not fully functional at birth and has the longest period of continued development.

Developmental Processes Early brain development involves six main processes:

- neurogenesis and neuron migration,
- structural elaboration and differentiation of neurons,
- formation of connections between neurons *(synaptogenesis),*
- formation of *glial cells* and *myelination,*
- increasing connections between regions of the brain,
- pruning of excess synapses and loss of *plasticity.*

Neurogenesis and neuron migration. As you learned in Chapter 3, neurogenesis and neuron migration occur mainly during prenatal development. Most of the neurons in the cerebral cortex form by the seventh month of prenatal development (Rakic, 1995). However, neurons continue to form in the cerebellum for about the first 18 months of life (Johnson, 1997). There is also evidence from animal studies for continued neuron formation during adulthood in the hippocampus and some areas of the cortex, but the meaning of these studies for human development is not yet clear (Gould et al., 1999; Rakic, 2002).

Structural elaboration and differentiation of neurons. During cell migration newly formed neurons begin to develop *dendrites* and *axons,* which will form connections with other neurons. As shown in Figure 4.2, **dendrites** are short branching structures that receive electrical impulses from other neurons. **Axons** are longer structures

Hippocampus:
A brain structure that integrates sensory information and is essential to memory formation.

Amygdala:
A brain structure involved in memory formation and emotional responses.

Brain Maps

Dendrites:
Short, branching neuron structures that receive electrical impulses from other neurons.

Axons:
Long neuron structures that branch at the end and relay electrical impulses to other neurons.

Figure 4.2
STRUCTURE OF A NEURON
A mature neuron has a complex structure, with branching dendrites, which receive electrical information, and a long axon, which relays information to other neurons.

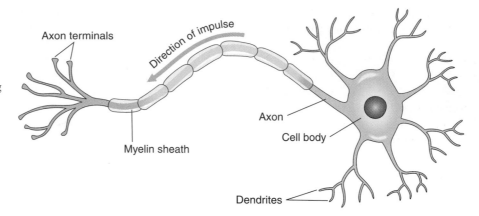

that branch at the end and relay electrical impulses to other neurons. Once neurons have migrated to their destinations in the developing brain, their structural complexity increases as dendrites form more and more branches and axons elongate, reaching out toward dendrites in other neurons. At this point neurons also begin to differentiate, or take on specific functions. Timing plays a role in differentiation; neurons that end up in the same region of the brain tend to be formed at about the same time. However, the location they end up in seems to determine their specific function, rather than the other way around, as specific genes within the neuron are turned on or off in response to chemical signals from neighboring cells.

Synaptogenesis. The development of axons and dendrites makes possible the formation of connections between neurons, or synapses. As you learned in Chapter 3, **synaptogenesis** begins before birth, but during the first 15 months of life the number of synapses increases rapidly, as shown in Figure 4.3. This happens at different ages for different parts of the cortex. For major visual and auditory areas, the increase peaks at three to four months after birth; for areas controlling higher cognitive functions, the peak occurs later in infancy (Huttenlocher, 2002).

Synaptogenesis:
Formation of synapses, or connections between neurons.

Formation of glial cells and myelination. Sometime after neurogenesis begins, a second type of brain cells called **glial cells** begins to form. Glial cells provide structural support and nourishment for neurons. Formation of glial cells begins before birth and continues to some extent throughout life, contributing significantly to the increase in brain size after birth. One important function of glial cells is the production of a fatty

Glial cells:
Brain cells that provide structural support and nourishment for neurons.

Figure 4.3
CEREBRAL CORTEX NEURONS, 1–15 MONTHS OF AGE
During the first 15 months of life, the structure of neurons in the cerebral cortex becomes increasingly complex and the interconnections among them multiply rapidly. *(Source: Reprinted by permission of the publisher from The Postnatal Development of the Human Cerebral Cortex, Vols. I-VIII by Jesse LeRoy Conel, Cambridge, Mass: Harvard University Press, Copyright © 1939, 1975 by the President and Fellows of Harvard College.)*

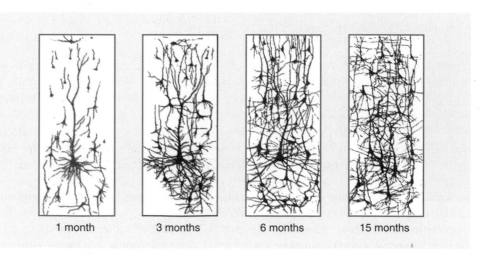

substance called *myelin*. **Myelination**—the formation of myelin sheaths around nerve fibers—helps to speed the conduction of electrical impulses throughout the nervous system. Myelination actually begins in spinal cord nerves in the fifth month of prenatal development and in lower regions of the brain in the seventh month of prenatal development. At birth, the brainstem already contains considerable myelin, but the cerebral cortex does not (Sampaio and Truwit, 2001). Myelination of higher brain regions begins soon after birth and is not complete until sometime in adolescence. In the cerebral cortex it occurs first in sensory areas, then in motor areas, and last in areas involved in higher mental functions.

Increasing connections between regions of the brain. During infancy connections between the cerebral cortex and other regions of the brain, especially the thalamus, the cerebellum, and the hippocampus, increase. At birth the lower brain regions seem to function independently, but as the cerebral cortex develops, the various parts of the brain function more interdependently (Johnson, 1997).

Pruning of excess synapses. During synaptogenesis, far more synapses are formed in the cerebral cortex than will be needed. The excess synapses are eventually eliminated, in a process similar to pruning excess branches from a tree or bush. This process begins at about 1 year of age in the major visual and auditory areas and continues into adolescence for some areas of the cerebral cortex (Huttenlocher, 2002). At birth, an infant's cerebral cortex has very high **plasticity,** the capacity for different areas to take on new functions. Pruning of excess synapses reduces the plasticity of the cortex but does not eliminate it.

Experience and Developmental Context

The rapid development of the cerebral cortex in the first months after birth helps explain many changes in infant competencies, as you will see throughout this chapter. But this development, especially the increase in interconnections among neurons and the development of specialized functions, also depends on infants' experiences (Johnson, 1998; Schore, 2001b). At the same time that the developing nervous system is fostering and constraining infants' capacities, the development of the nervous system itself is being fostered and constrained by experiences. Developmental context, both inside and outside the brain, has a strong impact on the course and outcome of brain development.

At the most basic level, interactions with other areas of the brain, as well as input from the environment, play a significant role in the development of specialized functions in the cerebral cortex (Johnson, 1998). In animal studies, tissue transplanted from one area of the cortex to another early in development takes on the structure and function of the area to which it is transplanted, not the area from which it came. The amount of various types of sensory input received through the thalamus early in development determines the size of specialized areas of the cortex. For example, as discussed later in the chapter, visual input is critical for the development of visual areas in the brain.

External environmental factors also play a major role in brain development. Malnutrition in infancy, especially if it is severe and long-lasting, can cause permanent brain damage (Shonkoff and Phillips, 2000). Depending on when it occurs, it can reduce the number of neurons formed, their size and structure, the extent and speed of myelination, or the complexity of synapse formation (Morgan and Gibson, 1991). Fortunately, if malnourished infants receive early, prolonged nutritional supplementation, much of the damage can be reversed, resulting in normal cognitive development. This is especially true if nutritional supplementation is combined with an enriched environment that provides intellectual and social stimulation. However, children may not reach the level of functioning they would have achieved with adequate nutrition.

The structure of the cerebral cortex is also influenced by the amount and type of stimulation from the environment. Rats raised in cages containing toys—objects to

Myelination:
Formation of myelin sheaths around nerve fibers, which helps to speed conduction of electrical impulses.

Plasticity:
The capacity for different areas of the brain to take on new functions.

Early Experience and the Brain

APPLYING RESEARCH FINDINGS

Practical Implications of Research on Early Brain Development

In recent years there has been extensive publicity about the research on early brain development summarized in this chapter (Thompson and Nelson, 2001). Many media accounts have implied that the first three years of life represent a true *critical period* for brain development. As discussed in Chapter 3, a critical period is a limited time when environmental influences bring about specific permanent changes in a developing organism. Once a critical period is over, the particular environmental influences involved can no longer have the same impact on development, whether positive or negative. In the case of early brain development, the argument has sometimes been made that high levels of stimulation from the environment during infancy are necessary for optimal brain development and that therefore intervention efforts must begin before age 3 to be successful.

These conclusions have major implications for new parents anxious to foster their infants' development, for prospective parents considering adoption of children who have experienced abuse or neglect, and for public policy on early intervention programs. But to what extent do research findings support popular ideas about brain development in the first three years of life?

First, the early years of life are better viewed as a **sensitive period** in the overall development of the brain than as a true critical period. A sensitive period is a time when particular experiences are especially important for development, but it is not as sharply defined as a critical period. The time period is more flexible, the environmental factors or experiences are less specific, and the outcomes are more variable. There do seem to be critical periods after birth for the development of some *specific* sensory and perceptual abilities, such as binocular vision, but not for general brain development.

Second, environmental factors have a major influence on brain development even before birth, as we have already seen. In fact, prenatal environmental influences are especially likely to produce irreversible effects on brain development—for example, neural tube defects linked to

an early lack of folic acid or developmental problems due to prenatal alcohol exposure. One of the most important ways to foster optimal brain development is to prevent exposure to harmful substances before birth and to promote good maternal nutrition and prenatal care.

Third, the first three years of life aren't the only sensitive period in brain development. Certainly, the brain goes on developing after toddlerhood and retains some plasticity throughout life. Much of importance happens later in childhood and adolescence—for instance, experiences during these years influence which synapses will be strengthened and therefore kept. Brain development after infancy builds on the foundation laid in the first years of life, but later experience can also alter the effects of early environment. The first years of life *are* important for brain development, but the window of opportunity for environmental influences does not slam shut on a child's third birthday.

Finally, early environment and early experience affect brain development in many ways. The *amount* of stimulation to which an infant is exposed is probably not the most important issue. Prolonged, severe deprivation or chronic emotional or physical trauma in the first years of life *can* have lasting impacts on brain development, with consequences for both cognitive and emotional functioning. Some basic level of sensory input is necessary for normal brain development. However, the tendency for the brain to overproduce synapses early in life seems to be biologically built in and triggered by exposure to any adequate species-typical environment—it is an experience-expectant process (Bruer, 1999). Early nutrition is important (e.g., adequate fat to support myelination, iron for general brain development). Preventing exposure to toxic substances, such as lead, is important. Providing a responsive, nurturing environment is important because it determines what *kinds* of associations are formed in the brain and influences not just cognitive but also social-emotional development, as we'll discuss in more detail in Chapters 6 and 8 (Schore, 2001b; Siegel 2001).

Sensitive period:
A time when particular experiences are especially important for development.

Experience-expectant synaptogenesis:
Synapse formation in response to input that can be expected in virtually any environment typical for a particular species.

explore and structures to climb on—develop larger brains and more dense connections between neurons than those raised in more deprived environments (Diamond, 1991; Greenough, Black, and Wallace, 1987). Similar results have been obtained from studies of children who suffer early environmental deprivation, as discussed in Chapter 2. Environmental stimulation appears to play a role both in the formation of connections between neurons and in the later pruning of synapses; connections that are used strengthen over time, while those that are not used gradually disappear (Huttenlocher, 2002).

There seem to be two processes by which experience contributes to synapse formation: *experience-expectant* and *experience-dependent synaptogenesis* (Greenough and Black, 1992). **Experience-expectant synaptogenesis** occurs in response to input that can be expected in virtually any environment typical for a particular species. It is an important process in the development of basic neurological structures, such as the human visual system. It reflects adaptation to the environment at the species level, and it produces developmental outcomes that are common to all normally developing members of a species—the distinctive songs of a particular species of bird, for example. It occurs early in development, often during specific critical periods.

In contrast, **experience-dependent synaptogenesis** occurs in response to environmental input that is specific to the individual. It is the process involved in the refinement of neurological structures and the storage of individual experiences, knowledge, and skills. It reflects individuals' adaptations to the unique features of their environments, and it produces individual differences in developmental outcomes. It continues throughout life and does not have critical periods.

Experience-dependent synaptogenesis:
Synapse formation in response to environmental input specific to an individual.

INFANT STATES

In the scene that opened this chapter, newborn Meryl started to become fussy during the physical exam, but then became alert and quiet while listening to Dr. Bryant's voice and watching the orange ball. These two states are qualitatively different, as any observer can see. One frequently used classification system identifies six infant states: two kinds of sleep *(quiet sleep* and *active sleep);* two kinds of wakefulness *(awake-and-quiet* and *awake-and-active);* and two states of distress *(fussing* and *crying)* (Brazelton, 1973; Prechtl and Beintema, 1964).

Child Development CD:
Newborn Behavior

States and the transitions between them are important in the study of infants' capabilities, because babies respond to their environments very differently depending on their state. For example, a bell sounded next to a newborn may elicit an eye movement or head turn in the direction of the sound if the baby is in an awake-and-quiet state, but not if the baby is in an active-sleep or fussing state. During the first few months of life, infants gain increasing control over their states, and the states themselves become more stable and predictable.

Sleep States

Sleep states consume a great deal of a newborn's time. The average newborn spends over 16 hours sleeping each day (Thoman and Whitney, 1989). Time spent sleeping decreases rapidly during infancy and childhood, then declines more gradually until it reaches a little more than six hours a day (Roffwarg, Muzio, and Dement, 1966). Newborns distribute sleep and awake times equally between day and night, creating difficulties for parents, especially in industrialized cultures where time and schedules are important. It usually takes months before infants sleep through the night consistently, but most middle-class American babies begin to adopt the conventional day-night sleep pattern by 8 weeks of age, as shown in Figure 4.4 (Sostek and Anders, 1981).

Although this shift may be based partly on brain maturation, infant care practices also play a role. In the United States, parents invest considerable effort in getting their babies to sleep through the night. In cultures in which parents are not so concerned about schedules, the newborn pattern of short sleep cycles distributed around the clock lasts much longer. In many cultures, infants sleep with their mothers and awaken frequently at night to nurse; mothers in these cultures typically do not regard nighttime feedings as a problem, in part because they do not need to get up to feed their babies (Morelli et al., 1992).

As mentioned earlier, there are actually two infant sleep states. One is *quiet sleep,* in which babies lie still, breathing slowly and regularly. The other is *active sleep,* in which they stir often, move their arms and legs, crinkle up their faces, breathe faster and more irregularly than in quiet sleep, and sometimes show rapid eye movements behind closed eyelids. Infant active sleep is in some ways like adult REM sleep, in which rapid eye movements (REMs) also occur (Mindell, 1993; Roffwarg et al., 1966).

Figure 4.4
CHANGES IN INFANTS'
SLEEP-WAKE CYCLE
At 2 weeks of age infants do not
follow the conventional sleep-
wake cycle of sleeping more at
night and being awake more
during the day. By 8 weeks of
age, infants in middle-class
American families have
increased the time they spend
sleeping between 10 p.m. and 2
a.m. and have decreased the time
they spend sleeping between 2
p.m. and 6 p.m. *(Source: Sostek
and Anders, 1981.)*

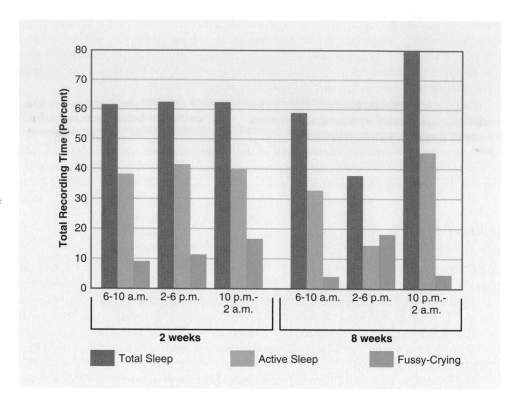

However, newborns spend a higher percentage of sleep time in active sleep (50 percent) than adults spend in REM sleep (roughly 20 percent). Newborns' active and quiet
sleep states alternate irregularly, whereas adults' stages of sleep occur in regular cycles.
In addition, the brain-wave patterns characteristic of different stages of adult sleep are
not present in newborns. These differences between newborn and adult sleep quickly
diminish, however. By age 3 months, babies generally start sleep with a non-REM
period, just as adults do, and they show the brain-wave patterns typical of adult sleep
(Mindell, 1993).

Distressed States

Compared with sleep states, the crying state occupies relatively little of a newborn's time.
Newborns usually spend less than 10 percent of their time crying (Korner et al., 1981).
Time spent crying tends to reach a peak at about six weeks after birth (Brazelton, 1962;
Hopkins, 2000). Over the first two months of life, the average infant engages in full-
blown crying only about 2 percent of the time, with another 10 percent spent fussing
(Wolff, 1987).

Infant Cries

Babies cry whenever their nervous systems are overly excited, whether that overex-
citement is due to hunger, cold, pain, or simply too much stimulation (loud noises or
even excessive touching, for example). However, the pattern of crying varies, depending on what has produced it and how upset the baby is. Three distinct crying patterns
have been reported: *Hungry cries* start with a whimper and become louder and more
sustained, *upset cries* are louder and often begin more suddenly, and *pain cries* start with
a high-pitched, high-intensity wail followed by loud crying. Most adults can distinguish
among these cries (Barr, Desilets, and Rotman, 1991), but they may be responding primarily to differences in the intensity of cries, rather than to broader qualitative differences in cries due to different causes (Hopkins, 2000). For example, even inexperienced
mothers respond most rapidly to pain cries—perhaps because they tend to be the most
intense right from their onset. However, experience both with babies in general and with
a particular baby seems to help adults interpret cries. Experienced nurses in hospital

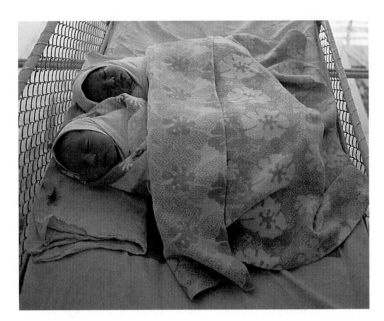

In Romania, as in many other parts of eastern Europe, young infants are typically swaddled— tightly wrapped in several layers of cloth. Swaddling has a soothing effect, probably because it keeps the baby from getting overstimulated.

nurseries are better at discriminating among different cries than are inexperienced nurses (Wasz-Höckert et al., 1968), and mothers are typically more able to interpret their own babies' cries than those of babies they don't know (Wiesenfeld, Malatesta, and DeLoach, 1981).

Caregivers often soothe crying infants, but babies also have a built-in capacity to soothe themselves. Sucking is often part of this process; allowing infants to suck on a pacifier is one effective soothing technique (Field and Goldson, 1984). Techniques with more caregiver involvement include talking softly, rocking, swaddling, and holding babies upright against the caregiver's shoulder (Korner, 1990). Not all techniques are effective with all babies, and babies differ in how easily they can be soothed by others or by themselves (Bates, 1980).

Changes in States

During the first months of life, infants' states change often, and parents are frequently involved in transitions from state to state. Parents rock their newborns to sleep, rouse them to alertness for feeding, and soothe them when they fuss or cry. By age 5 months, infants' states no longer change so often, and transitions between states are more predictable (Sostek and Anders, 1981). From this point on, parents' involvement with infants focuses increasingly on babies' behavior during awake states.

Babies vary considerably in how frequently they change states and how smoothly they make transitions between them (Matheny, Riese, and Wilson, 1985). Some babies are more easily distressed and more difficult to soothe than others. These differences appear rooted in biology, but how they develop is influenced by caregiver responses. An irritable newborn whose caregiver is soothing and responsive will tend to become less irritable over time and will gradually develop self-soothing skills. A similar baby whose caregiver is unresponsive, unpredictable, or consistently angry or rough will tend to become *more* irritable over time and will be slow to learn self-soothing.

REFLEXES IN THE NEWBORN

 Child Development CD: **Newborn Behavior**

A **reflex** is an automatic, built-in reaction elicited by a particular stimulus. Blinking when an object is poked at your eye is one example of a reflex you have had since birth. Newborns display both *permanent* reflexes, which they will retain throughout life, and

Reflex: An automatic, inborn response to a particular stimulus.

Table 4.1 Examples of Transitory Newborn Reflexes

Reflex	Description	Developmental Pattern
Sucking	When object brushes against infant's lips, rhythmic sucking occurs.	Replaced by voluntary sucking by 2 months.
Babkin	When infant is lying down, pressure on palms of both hands causes head to turn straight ahead, mouth to open, and eyes to close.	Disappears around 3 months.
Stepping	When infant is held above a surface and lowered until feet touch the surface, feet are alternately raised and lowered in a stepping motion.	Disappears around 3 months.
Grasping	Pressure on palm causes fingers to curl with a strong enough grasp to support infant's weight.	Weakens after 3 months and disappears by 1 year.
Tonic Neck	Infant placed on back tends to turn head to one side, extend arm and leg on that side, and flex limbs on the other side (like a fencing position).	Disappears around 4 months.
Rooting	When infant's cheek is stroked lightly, head turns in direction of stroked cheek and mouth opens.	Disappears around 4 months.
Moro	In response to startling stimuli, such as sudden loud noise or rapid lowering of head or body, arms are extended and then brought rapidly together and fingers close in a grasping motion.	Disappears around 5 months.
Babinski	When side of foot is stroked from heel toward toes, toes fan out and foot twists inward.	Disappears around 1 year.

transitory reflexes, which will disappear as they grow older. Reflexes enable young babies to make organized responses to their environments before they have a chance to learn. Table 4.1 lists some of the most important transitory newborn reflexes.

Survival Reflexes

Some newborn reflexes have obvious survival value. Reflexes such as blinking, sneezing, and gagging clearly aid survival by helping an infant deal with threats to the body, but because they are permanent reflexes, they are not of great interest developmentally. Developmentalists are more concerned with survival reflexes that are present at birth but disappear as the infant acquires more advanced skills.

For example, when a newborn's cheek is stroked, the baby responds by turning the head toward the side that was touched, in an apparent attempt to find something to suck. This response is called the *rooting reflex*. When an object enters a newborn's mouth, the *sucking reflex* is activated. Both these reflexes have obvious survival value to newborn mammals, who must be able to suck to get milk. The rooting and sucking reflexes allow them to obtain nourishment before they learn the connection between a nipple and food. These reflexive responses begin to change in the first few weeks of life, as infants become more skilled at nursing. This shows that the organization of behavior that reflexes provide is not totally rigid, but can be modified by experience. Between 2 and 4 months of age, a major developmental change occurs when both these reflexes disappear and give way to voluntary eating behaviors.

Other Reflexes

Some reflexes have no current survival value, but may be a legacy of our evolutionary past. For instance, when a newborn's head or body drops backward, the *Moro reflex* occurs: the arms fling out and come back toward the body's midline, with the hands curling in. This reflex resembles the response of an infant trying to grasp something to keep from falling and could have been crucial to our early ancestors' survival. Another reflex that may once have had survival value is the *grasping reflex*. When the palm of a newborn's hand is stroked, the fingers automatically curl inward as if to grasp. In fact, the grasp is firm enough to support the baby's weight. Since the grasp is reflexive, the baby cannot voluntarily let go, although fatigue will eventually weaken the grip.

Newborns appear to be able to walk when supported, but the behavior is purely a reflex that disappears before true walking develops.

Some reflexes, including grasping, involve behavior that later becomes part of more sophisticated voluntary actions. By the end of the third month, the grasping reflex declines and babies develop a voluntary grasping, usually elicited by seeing or hearing an object (Clifton et al., 1993). When Meryl is 4 months old, the sight of a bright orange ball would probably cause her to try to grasp it instead of simply following it with her eyes. Voluntary grasping allows older infants to secure and manipulate objects they wish to explore.

Another behavior seen in newborns that reappears later as a component of a skilled behavior is the *stepping reflex*. When newborns are held upright and then lowered until their feet touch a horizontal surface, they respond with a rhythmic stepping motion that resembles walking. This reflex usually disappears around 3 months of age. Months later, the same movements reappear, this time under voluntary control, as infants learn to walk.

Early in development the grasping and stepping reflexes are controlled by lower brain centers (Zelazo, 1983). As babies grow older, higher brain regions take control and begin to inhibit the reflexes; babies can now voluntarily control how they respond to stimuli that previously produced an automatic behavior. Voluntary control enables formerly reflexive actions to be integrated into more complex behaviors. This transfer of control from lower to higher brain centers is related to myelination and proliferation of connections among neurons in the cerebral cortex. The fact that several reflexes weaken or disappear at 3 to 4 months of age supports the idea that brain maturation is involved, but experience also seems to play a role. As we will discuss later, practice both slows the disappearance of some reflexes and speeds up the emergence of voluntary actions involving the same movements.

INFANT LEARNING

After Malcolm was born, his family took charge of most of what happened to him—where he lay, what he saw, what he heard. But within six months Malcolm was able to do many things for himself. He could turn over, sit up, grasp objects and put them in his mouth; he was even starting to crawl. By the time he was 1, he had acquired many other skills, including taking his first steps and saying a few words.

Developmental psychologists view such dramatic changes in behavior as the joint outcome of maturation and learning. In examining the interaction of learning and maturation, developmentalists ask questions such as: When do infants start learning? Are there limitations on what they can learn? Does the way they learn change as they grow older? The answers to these questions are of interest to parents as well as scientists. In the following sections we look at how learning abilities develop during infancy.

Habituation and Dishabituation

One of the first signs that babies are able to retain information about their environments is **habituation,** the decrease in attention that occurs when the same stimulus is presented repeatedly. When the pediatrician first spoke to Meryl, she ceased her other behaviors

Habituation:
The decrease in attention that occurs when the same stimulus is presented repeatedly.

A CLOSER LOOK

TECHNIQUES FOR STUDYING EARLY INFANT DEVELOPMENT

Developmental psychologists who study infants' earliest abilities and responses to the world share a basic problem: Young infants can't talk and don't understand language. This means they can't tell researchers what they see, hear, feel, or think, and they can't follow researchers' instructions or answer questions. As a result, experimenters have had to find *indirect* ways to measure what infants sense, perceive, and remember.

In this chapter you will read about studies using a variety of techniques developed to address this problem. Techniques mentioned include:

- *Eye movements*—Video recorders and computers can produce a detailed record of infants' eye movements as they look at a stimulus, such as a face. This record indicates something about how infants explore their environment and what features they find most interesting. One limitation: knowing where babies look doesn't tell us what they see—exactly what they pay attention to or how they organize the information they take in.
- *Preferential looking*—This method uses babies' visual preferences to measure when they can detect the difference between two stimuli. It involves placing two stimuli in front of an infant (e.g., a gray card and a card with black and white stripes), and measuring how long the infant looks at each one. One limitation: if a baby shows no preference between two stimuli, it doesn't necessarily mean he or she can't tell the difference between them—it's possible the two are equally attractive (or unattractive) to the baby.
- *Habituation/dishabituation*—Another way of measuring whether infants can discriminate between two stimuli, this method is based on one of their most basic learning abilities. A stimulus (e.g., a photo of a woman) is presented repeatedly until the baby shows signs of having lost

interest in it by decreased looking or listening. A new stimulus (e.g., a photo of a different woman or of a man) is then presented; renewed interest from the baby suggests that he or she has noticed that it is different from the previous stimulus. This method can also indicate when infants believe two stimuli are the same despite superficial differences (e.g., if they habituate to a series of photos of different women, then show dishabituation in response to a photo of a man). One limitation: when dishabituation does not occur, it does not necessarily mean the baby can't distinguish between two stimuli; it may simply mean he or she has lost interest in the experiment and is not paying attention.

- *Instrumental conditioning*—Instrumental conditioning has been used to determine what infants find reinforcing; for example, newborns have been conditioned to suck at various rates to hear a particular sound or see a particular image. It has also been used to ensure a consistent response to a stimulus of interest. For instance, infants can be conditioned to turn their heads to see an interesting mechanical toy whenever they hear a tone; their hearing can then be tested by varying the pitch or volume of the tone. One limitation: a lack of response may reflect fatigue, inattention, or individual differences in what is reinforcing, rather than a lack of the ability being tested.
- *Evoked potentials*—When a baby detects a new visual or auditory stimulus, a characteristic pattern of electrical activity appears in the brain. This provides a more direct measurement of a baby's ability to distinguish between two stimuli, using brain waves measured by an electroencephalogram (EEG). One limitation: a change in the brain's electrical activity doesn't necessarily mean the baby can make meaningful use of the information detected.

Orienting response:
The response when a stimulus is first presented, involving both behavioral and physiological changes.

Dishabituation:
Increased attention to a new stimulus after habituation to a previous stimulus.

and attended to his voice. This reaction, called an **orienting response,** includes physiological changes, such as a change in heart rate and a slight dilation of the pupils. Researchers have found that when the same stimulus is presented over and over, the orienting response disappears and the baby resumes other activities. The novelty of the stimulus apparently wears off. We know that such a decline in responding is due to learning and not fatigue, because presentation of a new stimulus again elicits the orienting response. The response to a new stimulus after decreased interest in an old stimulus is called **dishabituation.**

Habituation and dishabituation require infants to do two things. First, they must learn enough about the first stimulus to realize it is the same from one presentation to another. Second, they must compare the first and second stimuli and recognize the second one as new. Infants' tendency to become habituated has turned out to be useful to researchers interested in early perceptual and memory development. (For details on the use of habituation as a research technique, see A Closer Look above.) Research using habituation provides insight into what kinds of stimuli babies can distinguish, how many repetitions are required for a memory to form, and how long a memory will endure.

Associative Learning

Over the last seventy years, psychologists have spent a great deal of time studying **associative learning**—how infants learn that certain events tend to go together or be *associated* with each other. Two kinds of associative learning they have explored extensively are classical conditioning and instrumental conditioning.

Associative learning:
Learning that certain stimuli or events tend to go together or to be associated with one another.

Classical Conditioning   Classical conditioning is a learning process in which a new stimulus comes to elicit an established reflex response through association with an old stimulus. The Russian psychologist Ivan Pavlov (1849–1936) caused dogs to salivate by giving them food, at the same time ringing a bell. Eventually, the sound of the bell alone caused the dogs to salivate. Pavlov thus conditioned the dogs to salivate in response to a stimulus that would not normally produce that reaction.

Classical conditioning:
A learning process in which a new stimulus comes to elicit an established reflex response through association with an old stimulus.

From the 1930s through the 1950s many researchers (e.g., Wickens and Wickens, 1940) tried classical conditioning with newborns and infants under 3 months of age. Although they failed to convincingly demonstrate classical conditioning, many of these studies did demonstrate changes in behavior produced by experience. More recent studies of classical conditioning in newborns have met with greater success (e.g., Lipsitt, 1990). However, the difficulty of demonstrating classical conditioning in newborns suggests that it is not a very likely explanation for early changes in behavior. Along with a variety of other abilities, the disposition toward classical conditioning does not become well established until around 3 months of age, probably reflecting maturation of the infant's brain.

Classical conditioning by itself cannot explain emergence of *new* behavior. The response to be conditioned must already occur when the unconditioned stimulus is present. Classical conditioning simply causes an old response to be elicited in a new situation. A famous example of classical conditioning of an older infant is Watson's work with 11-month-old Albert, mentioned in Chapter 1. Watson (1928) conditioned Albert to

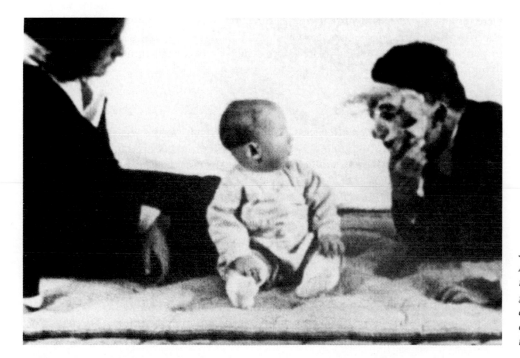

John Watson conditioned little Albert to react fearfully to white rats; the conditioned response generalized to other furry animals and eventually to furry objects, such as the mask Watson is wearing in this picture.

fear a white rat (the conditioned stimulus) by pairing the rat with a sudden loud noise (the unconditioned stimulus). Albert already possessed a fear reaction; all Watson did was make the initially neutral rat into an effective elicitor of fear. Classical conditioning may play a role in certain aspects of early emotional development, but it cannot account for the crucial acquisition of new behaviors and skills.

Instrumental Conditioning **Instrumental** or **operant conditioning** is a type of learning in which behaviors are influenced by their consequences. Consequences that increase the likelihood a behavior will be repeated are called **reinforcement.**

It is much easier to instrumentally condition newborns than to classically condition them. This suggests that human infants come prepared to notice and respond to **contingencies,** the relationships between actions and their consequences. In older children and adults, it is generally *voluntary* behaviors that are instrumentally conditioned. In newborns, researchers condition behaviors with a reflexive component, such as sucking on a nipple and turning the head from side to side (related to the rooting reflex). The relative ease of instrumentally conditioning young infants has made it a useful research technique (see A Closer Look on page 136).

As mentioned in Chapter 2, sucking rates of 3-day-old infants have been instrumentally conditioned. Newborns suck in a burst-pause pattern, a succession of rapid sucks followed by a pause. DeCasper and Fifer (1980) measured the average interval between babies' bursts of sucking on a nipple. Then they reinforced half of the babies every time their interval between bursts was *longer* than average, the other half every time their interval was *shorter* than average. The reinforcement was simply the sound of the child's mother speaking. As expected, the sucking rate of the first group of babies decreased and that of the second group increased. This experiment demonstrates not only instrumental conditioning, but also the fact that a human voice can be reinforcing for 3-day-old infants.

Instrumental conditioning is of particular interest to psychologists because it provides a means of acquiring new behaviors. One way new behaviors can be acquired is through the process of **shaping,** in which gradually closer approximations of a target behavior are reinforced. Systematic shaping can result in quite remarkable feats, even in very young infants. As mentioned in Chapter 2, Papoušek (1967) conditioned babies only a few weeks old to perform complex sequences of behavior. When the infants turned their heads in one direction, they were rewarded with a taste of sugar solution. Soon they were turning their heads repeatedly in that direction. Next the babies were rewarded only after two head turns, and again they learned the pattern. Eventually they were required to perform even longer chains of responses, such as two head turns to the right, then two to the left.

Imitative Learning

Shaping is a rather inefficient process because it depends on the chance occurrence of actions that happen to resemble desired behaviors. Fortunately, infants are also capable of **imitative learning,** in which new behaviors are learned by copying others' actions.

Imitation is a powerful mechanism for learning and a much faster way of acquiring new skills than shaping. But to acquire a new behavior, children must be able to reproduce the behavior and remember it for future use. For example, when Mikey imitates a word his father says, he must first translate the sounds he hears into a set of movements of his own lips and tongue and then store some memory of these movements.

Piaget (1962) argued that these abilities develop gradually during the first two years of life, as the capacity for mental representation emerges. According to Piaget, during the first four months of life infants can only imitate sounds and actions when an adult

---

Instrumental or operant conditioning:
Learning in which behaviors are influenced by their consequences.

Reinforcement:
Any event following a behavior that increases the likelihood the behavior will be repeated.

Contingencies:
The relationships between events and their consequences.

Shaping:
Reinforcing gradually closer approximations of a target behavior.

Imitative learning:
A way of learning new behaviors by copying others' behaviors.

By the second year of life, toddlers have become skilled at imitating others' behaviors.

repeats a behavior the infant has just produced spontaneously. For example, if a baby makes a cooing sound and an adult imitates it, the baby will often repeat the sound. Between four and eight months babies begin to imitate gestures, as long as they can see the actions they are making, and sounds they already can make on their own. Around eight months they begin to imitate actions they can't see themselves making, such as facial expressions. At about 12 months they become proficient at imitating unfamiliar actions they haven't done before on their own. Finally, at about 18 months, they are able to imitate behaviors they've seen others do in the past.

Some researchers have found evidence of apparent imitation much earlier than Piaget expected. Andrew Meltzoff and M. Keith Moore have done a series of experiments in which adults modeled facial expressions, such as sticking out the tongue and opening the mouth wide, to infants as young as 2 days old (Meltzoff and Moore, 1977, 1999). The infants produced these facial expressions more often in response to the adult models than they did spontaneously without seeing a model. Meltzoff and Moore conclude from their studies that imitation is an innate ability in infants, but this conclusion is not universally accepted. Attempts to replicate the findings have not always been successful; in fact, evidence of newborn imitation has been found mainly for sticking out the tongue (Anisfeld, 1991, 1996; Bjorklund, 1997). The same response can be elicited by other actions, such as thrusting a pen toward the baby, suggesting that there may be other explanations for the baby's response (Jacobson, 1979). Some possibilities that have been proposed are that tongue thrusting may be an innate feeding-related response to a stimulus resembling a nipple (Jacobson, 1979) or that the baby may be attempting to explore an interesting stimulus rather than attempting to imitate an action (Jones, 1996). The responses observed by Meltzoff and Moore appear to decline after about two months of age, making it seem unlikely that they are directly linked to later forms of imitation (Bjorklund, 1997).

In any case, the behaviors used in the newborn studies are all actions that neonates can already perform spontaneously. Imitation as a means of learning *new* behaviors must await further development. In fact, more than a year must pass before the baby will be able to imitate new behaviors quickly and without error. This speed and accuracy are what give imitation its special importance as a learning mechanism.

Child Development CD:
Newborn Behavior

The Concept of Preparedness

Some things are relatively easy for young infants to learn; others are difficult. Heredity seems to have endowed infants with a predisposition to acquire some behaviors but not others. This genetic predisposition is called **preparedness** (Seligman, 1970). Many developmentalists argue that some of a baby's early social behaviors are prepared responses. Examples are smiling back when an adult smiles and cooing when an adult speaks. These responses are easy for young babies; they seem biologically inclined to learn to perform them in social contexts. Other easily learned behaviors emerge in later infancy. For example, in their second six months babies readily babble the sounds of the language spoken around them. Think how complex a process it is to distinguish and reproduce speech sounds. Evolution must have prepared human babies to acquire this skill quite early. Thus, the concept of preparedness provides one way to think about the limitations on infant learning. Babies learn most easily those behaviors they are prepared to learn; they learn other behaviors more slowly or not at all.

An important aspect of preparedness is a predisposition to analyze the connection between certain behaviors and their consequences. For example, humans are prepared to recognize the connection between the taste and smell of what they eat and any subsequent feelings of nausea (Garcia and Koelling, 1966). For this reason you readily develop an aversion to foods you eat just before getting sick to your stomach, but you don't acquire a similar aversion to the people you're with or the color of the shirt you're wearing. Your brain is programmed to focus on the food-nausea connection, probably because learning to avoid food that produces illness has survival value. Babies, too, are prepared to learn certain contingencies between their own actions and the consequences produced, making instrumental conditioning of infants very easy when the association to be learned is one they're *prepared* to discover.

INFANT MOTOR SKILLS

When Mikey was born, Christine knew from experience to keep his fingernails trimmed. If his nails were allowed to grow too long, he could easily scratch his face as he moved his hands around in the poorly coordinated manner of newborns. By the time Mikey was a year old, his motor skills had improved dramatically. Now he could sit unsupported, crawl rapidly wherever he wished, pull himself up into a standing position, and take a few tentative steps while hanging onto furniture. His movements were much more deliberate and coordinated than his random flailing of arms and legs as a newborn. He could reach for and grasp an object, pick it up for inspection, and move it from hand to hand.

Figure 4.5 summarizes major milestones in motor development during the first two years, giving the average age for each. Keep in mind that normally developing children vary considerably in the ages at which they reach these milestones.

Motor Skills and Physical Growth

Infant motor skills develop in the context of dramatic physical growth. During the first year after birth, the average baby triples in weight and grows ten inches in length. Bones, which are soft and pliable at birth, become harder and more rigid. Muscle mass and strength increase. Body proportions change. At birth, the head is large relative to the rest of the body, and the trunk is long relative to the arms and legs. By the end of the first year, the head and trunk are not as out of proportion as in newborns. Just as during the prenatal period, different parts of the body grow at different times and rates.

Rapid physical growth provides a challenge for the development of motor skills; infants must learn to control the movements of bodies that are changing in size. For

Figure 4.5
MILESTONES IN MOTOR
DEVELOPMENT
Normal children vary
considerably in the ages at which
they achieve major motor
milestones. *(Source:
Frankenburg and Dodds, 1967.)*

0–2 months:
Chin up

2–4 months:
Chest up

2–5 months:
Rolls over

5–8 months:
Sits without support

5–10 months:
Stands holding on

6–10 months:
Pulls self to stand

7–13 months:
Walks holding onto
furniture

10–14 months:
Stands alone

11–14 months:
Walks well

14–22 months:
Walks up steps

example, babies must learn to reach for objects with arms that are constantly growing longer. In the discussion that follows we focus mainly on the initial acquisition of motor skills, but keep in mind that the motor system must recalibrate to adapt to physical changes throughout development.

Some Principles of Motor Skill Development

Several major principles of development that we have already encountered also apply to the development of motor skills. These principles include:

- Differentiation,
- Cephalocaudal development,
- Proximodistal development, and
- The joint role of maturation and experience.

Differentiation applies to the development of motor skills as well as it did to prenatal development of cells and body structures. A newborn's global, poorly defined motor skills develop into a set of precise skills, each adapted to a specific function. Consider infants' reactions when mouth and nose are covered by an adult's hand (Bühler, 1930). Newborns react reflexively with the whole body: arms and legs go into random motion, the

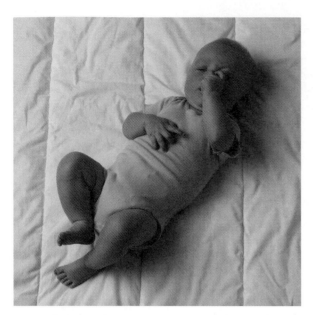

Putting babies to sleep on their backs seems to affect the timetable for developing some motor skills, but not the final outcome.

body twists, the infant wails. Such a global reaction is adaptive because it may lead to withdrawal of the hand. Some weeks later, babies respond to the same situation with more arm movements, mostly directed toward the center of the body, increasing the chance of inadvertently batting away the hand. But not until age 6 months do infants push the hand away using a directed swipe with only one arm. A month or two later, babies may even block the hand from covering the nose and mouth by using a specific anticipatory movement.

Applied to motor development, *cephalocaudal development* means that control over motor skills tends to progress from the head downward. For instance, voluntary sucking and eye movements emerge before refined walking movements. *Proximodistal development* means that control over motor skills tends to progress from the center of the body out to the extremities. For example, babies show control of head movements before arm movements, and of arm movements before hand movements. These patterns seem to be caused by different rates of development in the areas of the brain and the muscles involved in various skills.

However, as in other domains, the development of motor skills is influenced by both maturation and experience. In the early 1900s, there was great interest in charting the course of motor skill development, which was viewed as an inevitable sequence of milestones governed by maturation of the central nervous system. Contemporary developmentalists have modified this view. They argue that motor development is best understood as a dynamic system in which a number of factors—brain development, physical growth, sensory and perceptual abilities, specific motor skills, and motivation—interact in constantly changing ways (Bertenthal and Clifton, 1998). Brain development and physical growth establish only *general* behavioral tendencies. Experience is essential for these general tendencies to unfold and become refined, and to support and guide the developing organization of the central nervous system.

This view is supported by evidence that practice influences the rate of motor skill development, by the fact that there are individual differences in how babies accomplish the same tasks (Thelen, 1995), and by the fact that infant care practices can affect the timetable for the emergence of particular motor skills. For example, in the 1990s the National Institutes of Health and the American Academy of Pediatrics launched a campaign to encourage parents to put their babies to sleep on their backs rather than on their stomachs, to reduce the risk of Sudden Infant Death Syndrome. Parent surveys indicate that the campaign has been successful—the percentage of parents who put their babies to sleep on their backs has increased (Gibson et al., 2000; Willinger et al., 2000). At the same time, pediatricians began to notice that infants seemed to be reaching some early motor milestones, such as holding their heads up and rolling over, at slightly later ages than previously observed. Several systematic studies have now documented the connection between infants' sleeping position and early motor development, but there is no evidence that sleeping on their backs has permanent effects on children's motor skills (Ratliff-Schaub et al., 2001; Salls, Silverman, and Gatty, 2002).

Back-to-Sleep Campaign

The Development of Specific Motor Skills

Rather than discussing all the motor skills that emerge during infancy, we will focus on a few representative skills: controlled eye movements, reaching and grasping, and walking.

Controlled Eye Movements   Your eye movements are so automatic that you probably don't think of them as a motor skill. However, controlled eye movements are one of the earliest motor skills to develop, and they help to support further development. Without them, young infants could look only at whatever happened to be in their line of sight. They could not follow people visually as they moved about or keep their eyes fixed on something despite movements of their own heads and bodies. If infants could not control their eye movements, their ability to learn about the world would be severely limited.

Even newborns show some controlled eye movements. When they have nothing to look at, they move their eyes more often and farther than normal, as if searching for something to see (Salapatek and Kessen, 1966). As the weeks pass, babies become more effective at controlling where they look. For instance, when 1-month-olds look at a person's face, they tend to focus on border areas of high contrast. If a new stimulus appears off to one side, the baby may move his or her eyes to look at the new object. By the time the child is 2 months old, this tendency is more pronounced, and the eye shifts are more accurate (Aslin and Salapatek, 1975). Control over eye movements continues to improve until at least age 7 (Zaporozhets, 1965).

During the first months of life, babies also become increasingly skilled at visually tracking moving objects. Newborns show **saccadic eye movements,** the rapid, jerky eye movements that adults use to shift their gaze to a new object. For at least the first month of life babies typically use a series of saccadic eye movements to shift their gaze when adults would make the shift with one saccadic movement. Similarly, they use saccadic eye movements to track a moving object, rather than the smooth, continuous **pursuit eye movements** that an older infant or adult would use. By 2 months of age, smooth pursuit eye movements are common, but they can usually be applied only to slowly moving objects (Dayton and Jones, 1964). This is probably why adults tend to move their heads slowly from side to side when talking to very young infants, who cannot follow rapid side-to-side or up-and-down motions. The ability to follow more rapidly moving objects develops between 2 and 4 months of age (Aslin, 1981).

Reaching and Grasping Reaching and grasping are examples of behaviors that appear early in an infant's life, decline or disappear with development, and then reappear in more advanced forms. Newborns respond to an object within their gaze with increased arm movements in the general direction of the object, though they seldom actually make contact with it (Bertenthal and Clifton, 1998). These and other early spontaneous arm movements are generally referred to as **prereaching.** Between 1 and 4 months, infants show a decline in prereaching. Intentional reaching emerges around 4 months and gradually becomes more refined. By age 15 months, children commonly reach for things smoothly and accurately.

Researchers used to believe that the earliest accurate intentional reaching was visually guided (White, Castle, and Held, 1964). Visually guided intentional reaching requires that infants simultaneously see objects they are reaching for and their own hands so that they can adjust their hand movements appropriately. It was assumed that early experience with visually guided reaching later allowed children to reach for objects without visually monitoring their hands. We now know that extensive experience with visually guided reaching is not essential for intentional, *non*visually guided reaching to occur. At about 15 weeks of age, the same time that visually guided reaching begins, babies will reach for glowing objects in the dark, where they can't see their hands. They will also reach in the dark for objects that make interesting sounds (Clifton et al., 1993). Apparently, they can make a successful reach by combining visual or auditory information about objects with sensations about the location of their own hands in space.

This does not mean that reaching is a simple result of brain development. Esther Thelen and her colleagues (Thelen et al., 1993), who have studied early reaching in detail, conclude that reaching is refined through active exploration of the environment and the pursuit of particular goals (i.e., *wanting* particular objects). Physical maturation makes intentional reaching possible, but intentional efforts, practice, and experience transform it into a refined motor skill.

Effective reaching depends on an object being within arm's length, or on moving the rest of the body to put it within reach. This means that reaching must be integrated

Saccadic eye movements:
The rapid, jerky eye movements that occur when the gaze is shifted to a new object.

Pursuit eye movements:
The smooth, continuous eye motions used to track a moving object.

Prereaching:
Early spontaneous arm movements, sometimes made in response to an object.

Babies gradually become more accurate and coordinated in their attempts to reach for and grasp objects as reflexes are replaced by voluntary actions.

into a more complex system of body movements. Young infants reach more for nearby objects than for distant ones (Gordon and Yonas, 1976). Five-month-olds who can sit up will lean and try to reach objects that are beyond arm's length, whereas babies who cannot yet sit and lean do not try to reach in this situation (Yonas and Hartman, 1993). Similarly, a study of 8- to 10-month-olds found that they simply reach for objects that are within arm's length, but they simultaneously lean and reach for objects that are farther away (McKenzie et al., 1993). By 8 months, reaching and leaning are part of an integrated system. Babies this age do not try to reach first, fail to get the object they want, and then lean to get it; instead, they lean and reach *simultaneously* if an object is not close at hand.

The development of grasping follows a course similar to the development of reaching. It begins with a reflexive behavior that declines and is replaced by a voluntary one. Grasping skill develops gradually and follows a predictable pattern. From the beginning of voluntary grasping, infants adjust their grasp somewhat to the size, shape, and texture of objects, but with maturation and experience, their grasping becomes increasingly refined (Bertenthal and Clifton, 1998). By 3 to 4 months of age, babies can pick up objects voluntarily, but they generally use a whole-hand grasp, making it hard to pick up things that don't fit in the hand. Until about 6 months of age they have trouble letting go of objects voluntarily. By 8 months, infants can use the thumb in opposition to the fingers, but the fingers act in unison. Not until around 1 year of age are infants finally able to oppose thumb and forefinger, allowing them to grasp very small things easily.

Infant Locomotion

Walking By 7 months of age Malcolm had learned to slide along the floor on his stomach, propelled by his legs. His family was suddenly faced with all the challenges of a baby who could go almost anywhere he wanted. Nothing was safe any longer. Infants this age acquire different methods of getting around. Some push themselves by their legs; others pull their bodies along with their arms; still others sit upright and scoot across the floor on their bottoms. Later, many babies learn to creep on their hands and knees. Before their first birthday they can usually hoist themselves into a standing position and "cruise"— that is, walk along while holding onto things. Most babies take their first solo steps shortly after the age of 1, although the age at which walking begins varies greatly. The age at which a baby starts walking and the pattern of development of prior abilities, such as crawling, are unrelated to later intelligence. Thus, parents should not be concerned about early walkers who never crawled or, unless the delay is extreme, about late walkers.

The movements involved in walking are apparent in the stepping reflex, which is present at birth and starts to decline at around 2 months. As in the case of grasping, some developmentalists argue that the decline of the reflex is related to the development of connections in the brain that allow babies to control reflexive activity. It may also be that as babies get heavier they don't have the leg strength to make stepping movements. Thelen (1986) showed that the stepping reflex can still be elicited in 7-month-olds if they are supported over a treadmill. This indicates that the reflex's disappearance involves more than just the development of the ability to stop the behavior.

Thelen argues that walking depends on the ability to integrate many systems, including balance. Studies of balance in infants show that even 5-month-olds begin to make appropriate movements to remain upright when sitting, although not always successfully (Bertenthal and Clifton, 1998). After further refinement, this balancing system will later be necessary for walking.

Thelen (1981) has also illustrated the role of early rhythmic, repetitive movements in the transition from the stepping reflex to walking. As infants develop, their random and jerky movements give way to smoother, more controlled ones. For example, all normal infants show **stereotypic leg movements,** such as kicking like a frog, when they are excited. These movements, mentioned in our story about Malcolm, appear around 1 month of age and peak at 5 to 6 months. Stereotypic leg movements are not reflexes, since a wide variety of stimuli can elicit them, but they are not really voluntary actions either. Infants lying on their backs begin to kick repetitively when they reach a certain level of excitement. Interestingly, infants do not learn to control their leg movements until after the rhythmic, repetitive patterns have appeared (Rovee-Collier and Gekoski, 1979). These rhythmic patterns seem to be an important way station between reflexes and learned motor behaviors.

> **Stereotypic leg movements**
> Rhythmic, repetitive leg movements elicited automatically when an infant reaches a certain level of excitement.

The onset of walking depends partly on maturation of muscles and nervous system and partly on practice. To investigate the role of practice, researchers have studied babies in various cultures who have differing opportunities to walk. Many years ago Wayne and M. C. Dennis (1940) studied Hopi Indian babies who spent much of their first year bound to cradleboards. The babies were unbound from the boards to have their clothes changed, but otherwise they had little chance to move their legs. Toward the end of their first year, the Hopi infants were given the same freedom of movement that babies in a control group had had since birth. Surprisingly, babies in both groups learned to walk at about the same age. This and other early studies suggested that physical maturation exerted a greater influence over the onset of walking than practice did.

More recent studies have led to refinement of this conclusion. The Hopi babies had complete freedom of movement by age 1. If their movement had continued to be restricted, their walking might well have been delayed. Consider the Ache people of Paraguay, who live in a rain forest among numerous dangers. Ache mothers carry their babies around most of the time and keep young children within arm's reach for several years. Ache children do not walk well until 2 years of age (Kaplan and Dove, 1987). Apparently, prolonged restriction of movement can delay the development of walking.

Conversely, practice can speed up the development of walking to some degree. For example, the Kipsigis people of Kenya begin to teach babies to sit up, stand, and walk at 2 or 3 months (Super, 1976). Kipsigis infants start walking about three weeks earlier on average than American infants, but they aren't advanced in acquiring motor skills for which they haven't received training. This suggests that practice specific to walking can make a difference in when children take their first steps.

Additional insights come from some interesting experiments in which researchers regularly exercised babies' stepping reflex (Zelazo, 1983). The stepping reflex did not decline as rapidly as usual in these babies, and they walked somewhat sooner than infants whose stepping reflex was not exercised. Both findings are consistent with the theory that reflexes are the raw materials out of which more advanced skills are built. But even with all their practice, the experimental babies did not walk much sooner than others.

Hopi infants restrained in cradleboards learn to walk at about the same age as infants who have not been so confined.

Maturation still plays a major role in the onset of walking. We do not recommend that parents exercise their infants' stepping reflex. The time spent in this effort could be better used interacting with the baby in other ways.

SENSING AND PERCEIVING THE WORLD

When John and DeeDee brought Malcolm home from the hospital, the whole family, talking and smiling, crowded around to see him. How did the newborn perceive all this commotion? Could he see distinct faces peering into his? Could he hear different voices and tell speech from laughter? Could he smell soap on Momma Jo's hands as she touched his cheek?

Sensory Systems in the Newborn

For years people have wondered how newborns like Malcolm experience the world. Since they respond reflexively to a variety of stimuli, their sensory systems must be working. But exactly what do babies experience when they see, hear, taste, smell, and touch things around them? And what causes them to direct their senses to one thing or another?

Visual acuity:
The degree to which one can see fineness of detail.

Vision The pictures below illustrate how a mother's face may look to 1-, 2-, and 3-month-old infants. These computer-created pictures are based on estimates of babies' average **visual acuity,** the fineness of detail they are able to see. Because young infants have substantially less visual acuity than normal adults, they see much less fine detail. In fact, newborns have such poor acuity that they meet the criterion for being legally blind. Still, they use their limited visual abilities effectively to experience the world from the very beginning, and their visual acuity improves rapidly.

Infant Vision

The pictures below simulate what infants of different ages may see when looking at a person from a distance of about six inches. (Source: From Sensation and Perception, *2nd edition, by E. Bruce Goldstein. © 1984. Reprinted with permission of Wadsworth Publishing, a division of Thomson Learning. Fax 800-730-2215.)*

Determining How Clearly Babies See. How do researchers determine an infant's visual acuity when babies cannot *say* what they see? One method is to use a *preferential looking* technique developed decades ago by R. L. Fantz (1958), based on young infants' tendency to look at sharp contrasts between dark and light. Confronted with a solid gray card and a card with broad black and white stripes, even newborns look longer at the striped card. If the stripes are made progressively narrower and closer together, eventually babies no longer show a preference for the striped card, presumably when the limits of their visual acuity make the striped card look like the gray card.

Studies using preferential looking and other behavioral measures of visual acuity produce similar results. Translating these results into the ratios used to describe adult acuity, Martin Banks and Phil Salapatek (1983) estimated that at 2 weeks of age a baby's acuity is about 20/300: the child sees at 20 feet what an adult with normal vision can see at 300 feet. Five months later, a baby's visual acuity has usually improved to about 20/100. Visual acuity generally reaches adult levels by age 4–6 years (Maurer and Lewis, 2001).

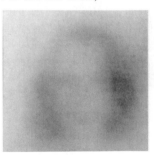

1 month

2 months

3 months

Adult

Infant visual acuity has also been studied by examining *visual evoked potentials,* the characteristic pattern of electrical activity that occurs in a baby's brain in response to a new visual stimulus. This makes it possible to tell when a baby can detect the difference between two stimuli with differing fineness of detail. Studies measuring brain activity tend to give somewhat higher estimates of infants' visual acuity than those based on behavioral measures, but they show the same general pattern of development (Atkinson and Braddick, 1989).

Young babies' limited visual acuity seems to be due to immaturity of the **retina** (the light-sensitive surface at the back of the eye), the connections between the retina and the brain, and the areas of the brain involved in vision (Maurer and Lewis, 2001). The optical quality of the lens in an infant's eye is quite good and allows a sharp image to be focused on the retina. However, the retina of a newborn has a much lower density of light-capturing cells than an adult's retina does, and the cells are not fully developed at birth. This is especially true of the **fovea,** the central region of the retina where fine detail and color are primarily detected. The form and density of cells in the fovea do not reach adult levels until sometimes after age 4. At birth, connections between the retina and the thalamus and between the thalamus and the visual areas of the cerebral cortex are not fully formed. As discussed earlier, the visual area of the cortex is not yet fully functional either. The relevant brain development is probably not completed until about age 11.

What causes infants' visual acuity to improve with age? Does this happen automatically with maturation? Although the visual system may be genetically predisposed to make the connections among brain cells needed for high visual acuity, appropriate visual experience is also necessary. Studies of cats, whose visual systems are much like humans', show that visual experience with patterned stimuli is needed to produce normal acuity. If kittens are raised in the dark, or see only diffused light, they do not develop normal acuity.

Can Infants See Colors? Determining whether young infants see colors is difficult because of the need to distinguish between color (determined by the wavelength of light) and brightness (determined by the light's intensity). When you see the difference between a red car and a blue car in a color movie, you are doing so on the basis of color. When you see a difference between the same two cars in a black-and-white movie, you are doing so on the basis of brightness. Thus, when babies who are shown two different colors look longer at one than the other, researchers have to make sure that this visual preference is based on color, not relative brightness.

By using two different colors of the same intensity, researchers have been able to show that babies cannot reliably discriminate on the basis of color alone until 7 to 8 weeks of age (Kellman and Banks, 1998). By 3 to 4 months, babies are thought to possess all of an adult's color vision abilities (Bornstein, 1978).

Hearing   It has long been known that pregnant women often feel their babies move seconds after a loud noise (Forbes and Forbes, 1927). Studies measuring fetal heart rate have shown this sensitivity to sound in fetuses 26 to 28 weeks old (Kisilevsky, Muir, and Low, 1992). In fact, hearing prior to birth is sufficiently well developed that newborns in one study showed signs of recognizing the sound characteristics of a passage from Dr. Seuss's *The Cat in the Hat* that their mothers had read out loud twice a day for six weeks prior to their scheduled delivery (DeCasper and Spence, 1986).

To measure the sensitivity of a baby's hearing, researchers monitor eye blinks, heart rate, and the brain's electrical activity as sounds are presented. They have found that for young infants to hear a noise, it must be ten to twenty decibels louder than it has to be for adults (Sinnott, Pisoni, and Aslin, 1984). (Loud voices are about twenty decibels louder than average speaking voices.) A child's sensitivity to sound gradually improves with age, but it takes twelve to thirteen years to become equal to an adult's (Maurer and

Because of their limited visual acuity, young infants pay particular attention to bold patterns with high contrast.

Retina:
The light-sensitive surface at the back of the eye.

Fovea:
The central region of the retina where fine detail and color are primarily detected.

Womb Sounds

Infants' engagement with the world around them is based partly on their steadily improving hearing abilities. By 6 months of age infants are quite sensitive to changes in loudness and pitch.

Categorical perception:
Perceiving stimuli that vary along a continuum as belonging to distinct categories.

Categorical Speech Sounds

Maurer, 1988). The ability to detect the direction from which a sound comes is also present very early, and by 18 months it reaches an adult level of accuracy (Morrongiello and Rocca, 1990).

Another issue that has been heavily studied is infants' ability to discriminate among sounds. How different must two sounds be for a baby to distinguish between them? One approach to this question is to take advantage of infants' tendency to become habituated to repeated stimuli.

In habituation studies of hearing, researchers repeatedly present one sound until the baby apparently loses interest in it. Then they change the sound. If the baby responds with renewed attention, they conclude that he or she has detected the change. Using this method, investigators have found that 6-month-olds can distinguish between sounds that differ in loudness by as little as ten decibels (Aslin, Pisoni, and Jusczyk, 1983). By the time they are 5 to 8 months old, babies are also quite good at detecting small changes in pitch (Olsho et al., 1982). Infants are sensitive to a broad range of pitches and hear high frequencies better than lower frequencies. This may be one reason why adults in many cultures use high-pitched voices when talking to infants.

Young infants discriminate among speech sounds even better than among pitches. Peter Eimas and his colleagues (Eimas, Siqueland, and Jusczyk, 1971) found that 1-month-olds can discriminate between the syllables /ba/ and /pa/. Moreover, they discriminate among sounds that fall between /ba/ and /pa/ in the same way adults do. When a computer-generated continuum of sounds between /ba/ and /pa/ is presented to adults, they do not hear it as a series of different sounds. Instead, they perceive all the sounds as either /ba/ or /pa/, with the dividing line between them at one consistent point in the continuum. Perceiving stimuli that actually vary along a continuum as belonging instead to distinct categories is called **categorical perception** (Liberman et al., 1957). When listening to sounds between /ba/ and /pa/, infants react as if they are hearing a new sound at the same point in the continuum as adults do. They show categorical perception for other speech sounds as well, suggesting that basic sensory abilities useful in learning language are biologically built in. Other research demonstrates that many aspects of speech perception change with development and depend partly on experience (Eimas, 1985).

Smell and Taste Infants' senses of taste and smell are more fully developed at birth than their vision and hearing. Newborns are very sensitive to odors and respond to them with facial expressions and body movements similar to those of adults. For instance, they respond positively to the odor of a banana, somewhat negatively to fishy odors, and very negatively to the odor of rotten eggs (Steiner, 1979). Babies can also make fine discriminations among odors, as shown in habituation studies involving very similar smells. In one study, newborns discriminated between their mothers' perfume and another perfume (Schleidt and Genzel, 1990). In another study, they discriminated between the smell of their mothers' nursing pads and those of other women (MacFarlane, 1975).

Newborns seem to be able to discriminate among sweet, sour, and bitter tastes (Crook, 1987), but their ability to sense saltiness develops gradually over the first four months of life (Kellman and Arterberry, 1998). Taste buds—receptors for the sense of taste—are present in the fetus by 13 weeks after conception (Kellman and Arterberry, 1998). From studying the tongues of premature and full-term babies, researchers know that taste buds are present throughout the mouth prior to birth and become more localized on the tongue around the normal time of delivery. Although the taste buds are relatively mature at birth, the nervous system initially processes taste information inefficiently, just as with visual information. Nervous system development related to taste is quite rapid, however, and the initial immaturity does not last long.

Touch   The sense of touch is more fully developed at birth than the other senses. Connections between nerve fibers in the skin and neurons in the spinal cord begin to form six weeks after conception, and the neurological structures involved in touch are essentially complete by about the 24th week of prenatal development (Kellman and Arterberry, 1998). Having a relatively mature sense of touch at birth is biologically adaptive because touch is involved in many newborn reflexes—rooting and sucking, for example. Early in infancy touch becomes an important means of gathering information about the physical world. When infants grasp objects and manipulate them or put them in their mouths, they are taking advantage of their well-developed sense of touch—and the large number of nerve endings in the fingers, lips, and tongue. Touch is important in state regulation from the very beginning of life; as we have seen, holding, stroking, patting, and swaddling are all effective ways to soothe crying infants. Researchers have also found that low-birth-weight infants appear to benefit from prolonged skin-to-skin contact with adults (often called *kangaroo care*), massage, and other forms of tactile stimulation (Field, 2001).

Infants and Touch

The question of whether fetuses and newborns feel pain is a significant practical issue for pediatricians and for parents. In the past, it was often assumed that newborns, especially if they were premature, did not experience pain in any real sense, and many invasive medical and surgical procedures were carried out without anesthesia or pain killers. However, it has become increasingly clear that even premature newborns and older fetuses are capable of feeling pain. The neurological structures involved in pain are in place by about the 29th week of prenatal development (Benatar and Benatar, 2001). Changes in stress hormone levels in response to painful stimuli have been observed in 23-week-old fetuses, and distinctive facial expressions that seem to indicate pain have been observed during invasive medical procedures in babies born at 26 weeks after conception (Vanhatalo and van Nieuwenhuizen, 2000). Of greatest developmental concern is the finding that repeated or intense pain during the neonatal period can have long-term effects on physiological responses to pain and stress and on the immune system (Vanhatalo and van Nieuwenhuizen, 2000). As a result, many doctors have become more aware of the need to provide pain relief to newborns, especially babies in neonatal intensive care units, who often experience repeated painful medical procedures.

Organization of Infant Sensory Behavior

Newborns use their sensory capacities in an organized way. When awake and alert, babies visually scan their environment rather than simply staring straight ahead. If they hear a sound, they direct their gaze toward it. If no sound attracts them, they scan with their eyes until they find an edge (a border of light-dark contrast). Having found an edge, they scan the zone of the edge for some time, passing back and forth over it.

As babies grow older, this pattern of visual scanning changes. For example, they begin to look at the internal features of a stimulus rather than its borders. Their sensory behavior remains organized, however. The organization of sensory behavior guarantees that infants will attend to and learn a great deal about people, since people are a rich source of the kinds of auditory and visual stimulation that attract babies' attention.

Development of Perceptual Abilities

Perception is the process by which the brain interprets information from the senses, giving it order and meaning. The fact that Malcolm can see lines and colors (sensory capabilities) does not mean that he *interprets* them as you and I do (a perceptual skill). For instance, when Malcolm looks at the faces of his family clustered around him, can he

Perception:
The process by which the brain interprets information from the senses, giving it order and meaning.

Figure 4.6
THE VISUAL CLIFF
By the time infants can crawl, they are reluctant to cross the visual cliff.

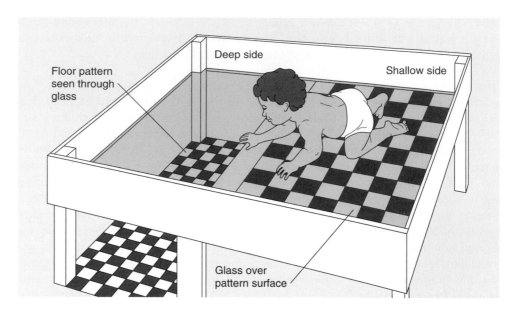

Deep side

Shallow side

Floor pattern seen through glass

Glass over pattern surface

tell that some are closer than others? Or when DeeDee turns her back to him, does Malcolm know he is still viewing the same head as before, just from a different angle?

Child Development CD:
Visual Cliff Studies

Depth and Distance Perception   When can a baby estimate how far away something is? Eleanor Gibson and Richard Walk (1960) provided a partial answer through a clever experiment using an apparatus called the *visual cliff,* shown in Figure 4.6. To construct the visual cliff, a sheet of thick glass, lighted from below to reduce reflection, is placed over a checkerboard platform with a dropoff in the middle. On the shallow side of the dropoff, the checkerboard surface is directly below the glass; on the deep side, it is several feet below. Gibson and Walk observed whether 6- to 7-month-olds, who had started to crawl, would cross the visual cliff. They found that the babies preferred the shallow side and that this preference increased with age. Babies who can crawl can also apparently perceive depth.

Joseph Campos and his colleagues (Campos et al., 1978) tested even younger babies for depth perception using Gibson and Walk's apparatus. They placed the infants facedown on each side of the visual cliff while measuring their physiological responses, such as heart rate. Babies only 2 months old could distinguish a difference between the sides. However, *fear* of the deep side was only apparent in babies who could crawl. Thus, direct experience with edges, drops, and distances probably contributes to a fear of heights in humans (Campos, Bertenthal, and Kermoian, 1992).

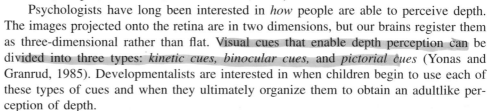

Depth Cues

Psychologists have long been interested in *how* people are able to perceive depth. The images projected onto the retina are in two dimensions, but our brains register them as three-dimensional rather than flat. Visual cues that enable depth perception can be divided into three types: *kinetic cues, binocular cues,* and *pictorial cues* (Yonas and Granrud, 1985). Developmentalists are interested in when children begin to use each of these types of cues and when they ultimately organize them to obtain an adultlike perception of depth.

Kinetic depth cues:
Visual cues in which information about depth and distance is carried in the motion of objects.

Kinetic Depth Cues.   The first visual depth cues infants become able to use are **kinetic depth cues,** in which information about depth and distance is carried in the motion of objects. Kinetic depth cues are *monocular,* meaning that only one eye is needed to perceive them. One such cue is the apparent expansion in size of approaching objects. Albert Yonas and his colleagues have found that as early as 1 month of age, babies blink more often in response to rapidly expanding shapes projected on a screen than to rapidly contracting shapes. By 3 months, they also often move their heads backward in response to the expanding shapes, and they differentiate between shapes that appear to

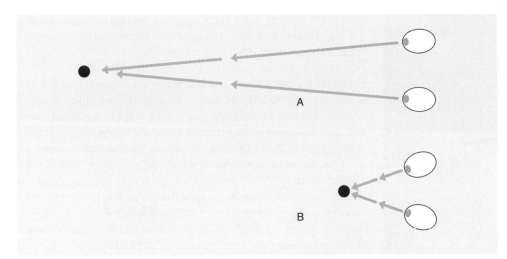

Figure 4.7
INFORMATION ABOUT
DISTANCE FROM
CONVERGENCE
(A) When viewing a distant
object, the eyes look almost
straight ahead. (B) When
viewing a nearby object, the eyes
rotate inward, toward the nose.

be about to hit them and shapes that appear to be about to miss (Yonas and Granrud, 1985). These findings suggest that some basic understanding of kinetic depth cues is present soon after birth, but the ability to interpret them becomes refined over the first few months of life as a result of experience and brain maturation.

Binocular Depth Cues. The second type of depth cues to become useful to infants is **binocular depth cues,** which result from the fact that visual information reaches the brain from two eyes rather than one. One binocular depth cue is *convergence*, which occurs when the eyes turn inward to focus on a nearby object as shown in Figure 4.7. The closer an object is, the more the eyes must angle inward. The brain uses this degree of convergence to help estimate distance. Another binocular depth cue, *retinal disparity*, results from the fact that each eye receives a slightly different image of the world. Combining the information from the two images allows the brain to interpret the scene as three-dimensional, just as combining two slightly different images produces a three-dimensional image in a Viewmaster. Infants show signs of sensitivity to both of these binocular depth cues by 3 months. By 5 months they are able to use the information from convergence and retinal disparity to detect approaching objects and to guide reaching (Atkinson and Braddick, 1989; Granrud, 1986; Von Hofsten, 1977).

A sensitive period exists during which experience has the greatest influence on the development of the ability to use binocular depth cues. Evidence for this comes from studying children born with their eyes misaligned, a condition called **strabismus.** Children with strabismus get little practice coordinating their eyes in a normal way. If the condition is not corrected, they do not receive the visual experience needed to produce connections among neurons that respond to binocular information. The result is deficient binocular depth perception. Fortunately, surgeons can correct the condition by adjusting the length of the eye muscles. Richard Aslin and Martin Banks (1978) discovered that the timing of this operation affected the later quality of binocular depth perception. People who had the operation in early infancy had binocular vision comparable to that of people born without strabismus. However, those who had the surgery after age 1 did not develop normal sensitivity to binocular depth cues. Apparently, the first year of life is a sensitive period for the development of binocular depth perception.

Development of binocular depth perception requires both maturation of an appropriate system in the brain *and* appropriate visual experience. In children with uncorrected strabismus, appropriate connections within the brain are never made because the visual experience needed to guide this developmental process is missing. Moreover, not only does visual experience shape brain development, but the reverse is also true. Infants who are born without the brain cells that respond to binocular information later develop strabismus despite having normal eye muscles. This happens because their visual system

Binocular depth cues:
Visual cues for depth and distance resulting from the fact that visual information reaches the brain from two eyes.

Strabismus:
A condition in which the eyes are misaligned and do not function together.

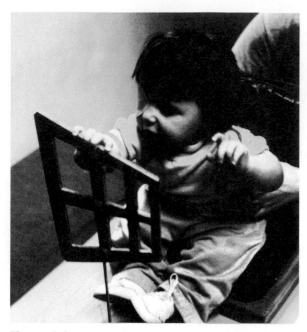

Figure 4.8
TRAPEZOIDAL WINDOW
With one eye covered, 7-month-olds reach for the long end of a trapezoidal window, suggesting they are sensitive to linear perspective.

Pictorial depth cues:
Visual cues that can be used to depict depth and distance in two-dimensional pictures.

Size constancy:
The ability to perceive an object viewed from different distances as constant in size even though its image on the retina grows larger or smaller.

Shape constancy:
The ability to perceive an object as constant in shape, even though its image on the retina changes shape when the object is viewed from different angles.

does not tell them when their eyes are properly aligned (Atkinson and Braddick, 1989). Brain development and visual experience influence each other in a circular way.

Pictorial Depth Cues. The last depth cues infants become able to use are **pictorial depth cues,** which are the cues used to depict depth in two-dimensional pictures. Like kinetic depth cues, they are monocular. In contrast to the kinetic cues, they are *static cues,* meaning they do not depend on motion for their effectiveness.

One pictorial depth cue is *linear perspective*—the fact that parallel lines seem to converge as they extend away from the viewer. Because of linear perspective, an image of a rectangular window taken at an angle will be trapezoidal in shape, not rectangular. When people look at a window that is *actually* shaped like a trapezoid, their perception of it depends on whether they look at it with one eye or two. Viewed with two eyes, it appears as what it is—an abnormal window in the shape of a trapezoid. Viewed with only one eye, it appears to be a normal rectangular window that is slanting away from the viewer (Ames, 1951). This depth effect occurs because one-eyed viewers use linear perspective to interpret what they see.

Yonas and his colleagues investigated when babies begin to use linear perspective as a depth cue by letting them look at a trapezoidal window with a patch over one eye (Yonas, Cleaves, and Pettersen, 1978) (see Figure 4.8). They found that 5-month-olds reached equally often toward both ends of the window, but 7-month-olds reached more often toward the long end—the end that would appear closer if they were using linear perspective as a depth cue. This finding suggests that infants begin to use this cue sometime between 5 and 7 months of age. Studies of other pictorial depth cues have produced similar results (Yonas and Owsley, 1987). The simultaneous onset of sensitivity to several monocular depth cues suggests that brain maturation plays a significant role in their development.

Size and Shape Constancy As Christine walks toward 13-month-old Mikey to lift him out of his crib, her image on his retina grows larger. Does Mikey think his mother is getting bigger? When she hands Mikey his bottle to drink, does he think the bottle changes shape as he views it from different angles? Mikey makes neither of these mistakes because he possesses perceptual skills called size and shape constancy.

Size constancy is the perception of an object as constant in size, even though its image on the retina grows larger or smaller as the object is viewed from different distances. Similarly, **shape constancy** is the perception of an object as constant in shape, even though its image on the retina changes shape when the object is viewed from different angles. Both these processes are crucial to perceiving the world as relatively stable.

Several studies indicate that size constancy is present even in newborns. In one study, newborns were repeatedly shown either a large or a small cube at various distances, so that *actual* size stayed the same, but the size of the retinal image varied. Then they were shown a large cube and a small cube placed at different distances so that the retinal image of both cubes was the same size. They consistently looked longer at the cube that was different in *actual* size from the one they had seen before (Slater, Mattock, and Brown, 1990).

There is also evidence of shape constancy in newborns. Slater (1989) conducted a study in which newborns were shown either squares or trapezoids displayed at varying angles, as shown in Figure 4.9. (The retinal image of some of the squares would be trapezoidal, and the retinal image of some of the trapezoids would be square.) The babies were then shown a square and a trapezoid together, both at an angle they had not previously seen. Even though they had not seen either stimulus before, the babies showed

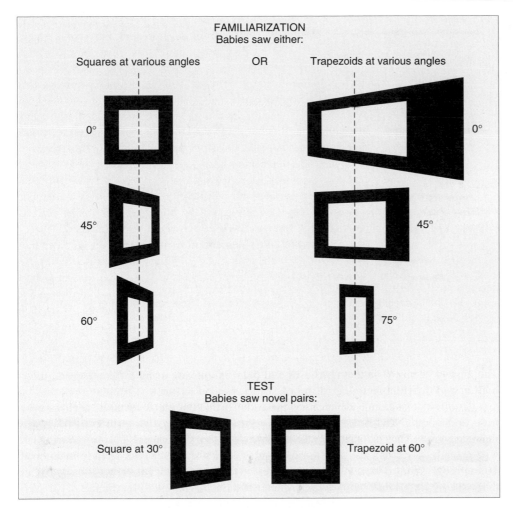

FAMILIARIZATION
Babies saw either:

Squares at various angles   OR   Trapezoids at various angles

0°   0°

45°   45°

60°   75°

TEST
Babies saw novel pairs:

Square at 30°   Trapezoid at 60°

Figure 4.9
A TEST OF SHAPE
CONSTANCY IN
NEWBORNS
(Source: Slater and Bremner, 1989, p. 62.)

a preference for the shape that was new to them. Babies who had previously seen only squares preferred the trapezoid, and babies who had seen trapezoids preferred the square.

As with less complex visual skills, newborns may have tendencies toward shape and size constancy that become more efficient and stable by 3 to 5 months. In any case, perceiving objects as relatively stable and unchanging is an important step toward an organized perception of the physical world. Understanding that the world consists of *particular* objects and people begins with the perception of constancies.

Perception of Faces Face recognition is a complex perceptual task that develops in a series of steps reflecting the influence of both brain development and experience (de Haan, 2001; Johnson, 1998). Newborns tend to track a moving facelike pattern farther than a scrambled or blank face, a preference that declines sharply between 4 and 6 weeks of age. However, when looking at figures that are *not* moving, newborns prefer abstract high-contrast patterns. Babies do not show a preference for static face-like patterns until 2 to 3 months of age.

Recognition of *specific* faces also develops gradually. There is some evidence that in the first week of life babies can recognize their mothers' faces (Pascalis et al., 1995). By age 3 months infants can recognize photographs of their mothers and prefer them to pictures of strangers (Barrera and Maurer, 1981). By 5 months infants can remember strangers' faces (Kellman and Arterberry, 1998), a task requiring very subtle distinctions.

At first glance, these findings are somewhat confusing. If newborns show a preference for tracking moving faces and quickly become able to recognize their mothers' faces, why does it take several months for more general face perception skills to develop?

Figure 4.10
DEVELOPMENT OF INFANT
SCANNING PATTERNS
When 1-month-olds look at
faces, they tend to concentrate
on the outer edges of the face.
Two-month-olds look more at
internal features, particularly the
eyes. (Blue lines indicate path of
babies' visual scanning.)
(*Source: Maurer and Salapatek,
1976.*)

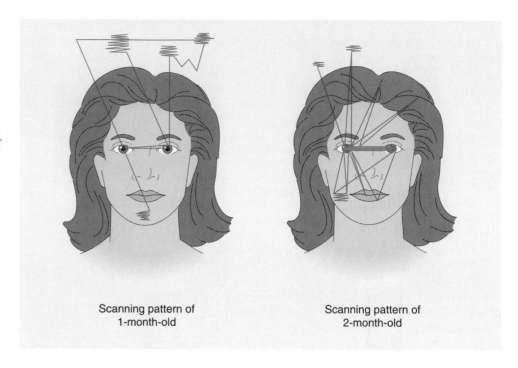

Scanning pattern of
1-month-old

Scanning pattern of
2-month-old

The answer seems to be that newborns and older infants are using different visual information and different neurological processes to respond to faces.

True face recognition depends on attention to internal facial features, such as eyes, nose, and mouth. Newborns rely heavily on outline shape in perceiving objects, presumably including faces. They can discriminate simple shapes, but they cannot discriminate a square with a circle in it from one with a triangle in it (Milewski, 1978). As already mentioned, 1-month-olds tend to look at the outer edges of faces, whereas 2-month-olds scan within the face and look at internal features (Maurer and Salapatek, 1976; see Figure 4.10). Very young infants use such general features as shape of the head and hair, rather than facial features, to recognize their mothers' faces (de Haan, 2001).

Infants' early recognition of their mothers' faces seems to be based on a general visual pattern recognition ability that does not involve the cerebral cortex (de Haan, 2001; Johnson, 1997). Likewise, their visual tracking of moving faces involves activity in lower regions of the brain, similar in some ways to newborn chicks' built-in tendency to follow adult chickens. In contrast, mature face perception depends on activity in specific areas of the cerebral cortex, which become functional in the first few months of life. The development of these areas depends in part on experience looking at faces, and infants' early tendency to track moving faces helps to provide that experience.

FIRST ADAPTATIONS IN CONTEXT

Newborns come into the world prepared in many ways for the developmental tasks they face. They have built-in responses to their environment, in the form of reflexes. They are prepared to detect contingencies—connections between their actions and changes in the environment. They have a variety of sensory capacities, and they are preadapted to attend to certain stimuli, such as light-dark contrasts and the sound of a human voice. These capacities serve them well as they explore the properties of objects and deepen their understanding of the physical world. Their preadaptations also provide them with a basis for social interaction by directing their attention to human faces and voices.

In turn, the environment provides infants with experiences that help to shape the development of their brains, their motor skills, their perceptual abilities, and the specific behaviors they learn. Other people, particularly caregivers, are the most complex, contingently responsive objects in the infant's world. Infants are biased to attend to and direct behavior toward others, who likewise are disposed to respond to infant behavior. Over time, the interactions thus set in motion form a foundation for the development of social relationships.

During the first year of life, babies face the major task of learning how to control their environment. By learning the connections between their own behaviors and subsequent reinforcements, infants gradually discover the things they can do to get what they want. In the process, the helpless newborn who merely responds reflexively to stimuli is transformed into an agent who actively controls many aspects of his or her world—a qualitative change.

Chapter Summary

Introduction

Newborns come **preadapted** to the tasks of learning about their environments and forming social relationships. The first month of life is a period of transition as **neonates** adjust to existence outside the womb.

The major themes of the chapter are:

- Heredity and the environment work jointly to guide the course of development.
- Infants' initial skills provide the seeds for development of more complex and flexible skills by the end of the first year.

Early Brain Development

Researchers have used a variety of approaches to study early brain development: measuring head circumferences, postmortem examinations, EEGs, brain imaging, animal studies, and studies of early deprivation.

In the first year of life the brain grows rapidly and changes in structure and function. Development follows a predictable timetable, with the lower structures completing development first. Early brain development involves six main processes:

- neurogenesis and neuron migration,
- structural elaboration and differentiation of neurons,
- formation of connections between neurons **(synaptogenesis),**
- formation of **glial cells** and **myelination,**
- increasing connections between regions of the brain, and
- pruning of excess synapses and loss of **plasticity.**

Brain development helps explain many changes in infant competencies, but development of the brain itself is also shaped by infants' experiences.

Infant States

Developmentalists divide the infant's rest-activity cycle into six states: *quiet sleep, active sleep, awake-and-quiet, awake-and-active, fussing,* and *crying.* The state an infant is in determines how the environment is perceived and acted upon.

Time spent in a sleep state and the pattern of sleep change during infancy, influenced by both brain maturation and cultural practices.

Babies' cries vary depending on cause and how upset they are. Experience with babies in general and with a particular baby helps adults interpret cries.

Newborns change states often and frequently need caregivers' help in making transitions. As babies grow older, they change states less often and more predictably.

Reflexes in the Newborn

A **reflex** is an automatic, built-in reaction elicited by a particular stimulus. Reflexes allow newborns to respond adaptively to their environments before they have a chance to learn.

Newborn reflexes include:

- some with clear survival value, such as the *rooting* and *sucking reflexes,*
- some that may once have had survival value, such as the *Moro* and *grasping reflexes,* and
- some that later become part of complex voluntary actions, such as the *grasping* and *stepping reflexes.*

Infant Learning

One of the first signs infants can retain information about their environments is **habituation** to a repeatedly presented stimulus and **dishabituation** to a new stimulus.

In **associative learning,** infants learn that certain events tend to go together.

- One kind of associative learning is **classical conditioning.** It is difficult to classically condition babies before 3 months of age.
- Another form of associative learning is **instrumental** or **operant conditioning.** Even newborns can be instrumentally conditioned.
- **Imitative learning** is a way of rapidly acquiring new behaviors. The ability to imitate others quickly and without error develops gradually over the first 18 months of life.

Babies have a genetic predisposition, or **preparedness,** to acquire certain behaviors. Preparedness includes a predisposition to notice **contingencies** between behaviors and their consequences.

Infant Motor Skills

Major principles of motor development include:

- differentiation,
- cephalocaudual development,
- proximodistal development, and
- interaction of maturation and experience.

Controlled eye movements are one of the first motor skills to emerge. By about 4 months, babies intentionally reach for and grasp objects. Soon after age 1, most babies start to walk. The development of many motor skills follows a pattern of early reflexive behavior that declines and is replaced by increasingly refined voluntary action.

Sensing and Perceiving the World

Newborns have a range of sensory abilities:

- They can see, although with less **visual acuity** than adults. Visual acuity gradually improves in the first year. The ability to discriminate colors develops by about 8 weeks of age.
- They can hear, but not as well as adults. They can distinguish between sounds of different loudness and pitch, and they are especially good at discriminating among speech sounds.
- They are very sensitive to odors and can discriminate among sweet, bitter, and sour tastes.
- They have a well-developed sense of touch and can feel pain.
- They use their sensory abilities in organized ways.

Infants' visual **perception** shows considerable development in the first year of life:

- Perception of depth and distance develops gradually. Babies begin to use **kinetic depth cues** between 1 and 3 months of age, **binocular depth cues** between 3 and 5 months of age, and **pictorial depth cues** between 5 and 7 months of age.
- Infants have some understanding of **size** and **shape constancy** at birth; this ability becomes increasingly stable and efficient over the first months of life.
- The way infants look at faces changes over the first months of life, and they become increasingly skilled at recognizing faces. Development of face perception is influenced by both brain development and experience.

First Adaptations in Context

Newborns come into the world biologically prepared for the developmental tasks they face; in turn, the environment provides infants with experiences that help to shape their development.

Review Questions

Introduction

1. What does it mean to say that newborns are **preadapted** to their developmental tasks?

Early Brain Development

2. How does the brain develop over the first months of life?

Infant States

3. What are the major infant states? Why are they significant?
4. How do infants' states and transitions between them change with development?

Reflexes in the Newborn

5. What are the major newborn reflexes?
6. Which are survival reflexes? Which are later incorporated into voluntary actions?

Infant Learning

7. Describe the development of **habituation, classical conditioning, operant** or **instrumental conditioning, and imitative learning.**

Infant Motor Skills

8. Describe the development of controlled eye movements, reaching and grasping, and walking.
9. How are reflexes, maturation, and experience involved in infants' motor development?

Sensing and Perceiving the World

10. What sensory skills do newborns have? How do they change with development?
11. Summarize development of depth perception, size and shape constancy, and face perception.

First Adaptations in Context

12. How do biology and environment each contribute to infants' first adaptations?

Application and Observation

1. If you have a friend or relative with an infant under 3 months old, try to elicit the rooting, sucking, grasping, and stepping reflexes as described on pages 133–135. The responses will be strongest in a newborn, but some will still be observable through the first months of life.

2. Test the idea of newborn imitation yourself, with an infant less than 2 to 3 months old (the younger the better). Hold (or have a parent hold) the baby upright facing you, being sure to support the baby's head and neck, so that the baby's face is about 10–12 inches away from yours. When you have the baby's attention, slowly stick your tongue out as far as you can and then slowly pull it back into your mouth. Wait a second and repeat several times. Try slowly opening your mouth as wide as you can and then closing it instead of sticking out your tongue. Note how often the baby sticks out his or her tongue or opens his or her mouth in response to each facial expression. (Don't be surprised if you get some tongue thrusts or mouth openings in response to the opposite behavior.) For comparison, try one of the actions tested by Jacobson (1979). Make a circle with your thumb and fingers and slowly push a red pen through it in the baby's direction, repeating as you did with the facial expressions, and note how the baby responds. Take note of other behaviors of the baby in addition to the modeled facial expressions, as well as anything else you think might be affecting the baby's performance.

3. Go to a toy store and look at toys labeled for infants under 6 months old, many of which have been developed in response to research on early infant development. How well do you think they fit what researchers have found out about young infants? How might an actual infant respond to them?

4. Observe parents and infants in several settings (for example, at home, at a family gathering, in church, in a crowded shopping mall, in an airport, at a pediatrician's office). Notice how the babies' states seem to be affected by the various settings and think about what factors might be involved. Also take note of what parents do to modify their babies' states (for example, how they respond to crying, or what they do to get their baby to respond to them or to play) and how effective the parents' strategies seem to be.

5 Infant Cognitive Development

159

One day when Malcolm was 7 months old, he crawled over to a stack of pictures his sister Teresa had drawn. He grasped the top one, wrinkling the corner as he pulled it toward him. The thick paper made a pleasant rustling sound. Malcolm dropped the first picture and reached for another, wrinkling it with two hands and shaking it. The paper rustled and flapped. Malcolm smiled and reached for a third. As he held the third picture in both hands, the paper tore down the middle with a wonderful ripping noise. Malcolm dropped one half and put the other in his mouth, feeling it grow soft and moist. Just as he was reaching for a brightly colored drawing of a little girl jumping rope, Teresa walked into the room. "Malcolm, no!" she screamed, as she ran to rescue her artwork. "Look what you've done to my drawings! You're bad! I'm gonna tell Momma!"

Why did Malcolm destroy Teresa's pictures? Was he really being bad? In this chapter you will discover that this explanation is highly unlikely. The mind of a 7-month-old does not grasp the concepts of "*my* drawings" or "bad." Malcolm cannot yet understand language, nor can he imagine how Teresa feels about what he has done. To Malcolm, Teresa's pictures are simply interesting objects to manipulate and explore. This example makes a very important point: how children perceive and interpret their experiences depends on their level of cognitive development. Malcolm is incapable of shame and remorse because his understanding of the world is as yet too limited. But he may be able to respond to the distressed tone of Teresa's voice, something he would not have done six months ago.

In this chapter we examine how infants' understanding of the world develops. We are concerned mainly with changes in *cognitive* abilities, or thinking skills, common to all normal infants. The chapter has three major themes. The first is the *orderly nature of cognitive development*. Existing specific capacities pave the way for new ones; for example, as we saw in Chapter 4, inborn reflexes are building blocks for early voluntary actions, which provide the foundation for more refined behaviors. At the same time, general capacities important for all areas of development are increasing. These include the ability to coordinate actions and to store and retrieve information efficiently from memory.

A second theme is that *infants are active participants in their own development.* They engage the environment with every means they have, practicing skills and encountering problems beyond their current capacities. On the basis of feedback from these

Infants are active participants in their own cognitive development, examining and manipulating everything that comes into their hands.

encounters and continuing brain maturation, infants develop more advanced abilities. At first they apply their new abilities automatically, but in time they become intentional planners, deliberately trying out actions and investigating their consequences. This deliberate exploration of actions and consequences moves their understanding forward at an ever-increasing pace.

A third theme is that *infant cognitive development is marked by both advances and limitations.* The trend in the last thirty years has been to attribute increasingly sophisticated cognitive abilities to infants, but there are limitations on infants' cognitive abilities as well. Advances achieved during infancy include:

- a basic understanding of the physical world, including properties of objects and relations between them;
- the ability to use basic cognitive tools, such as categorization and number, to understand the world;
- the ability to combine actions into sequences to achieve desired ends; and
- increasingly powerful and flexible memory abilities.

Cognitive limitations in infancy include:

- an emphasis on perception and action as sources of knowledge about the world,
- the absence of language and related symbolic abilities,
- limited flexibility in many emerging cognitive abilities, and
- limited memory capacity.

We begin this chapter by examining the theory of infant cognitive development proposed by Jean Piaget, which provided a starting point for more recent theories and research. We then consider challenges to Piaget's ideas, before turning to current research findings on infant cognitive development, focusing on two major areas: understanding of the physical world and memory development. We then discuss the impact of social context on cognitive development in infancy. Finally, we look at individual differences in infant cognitive development and the extent to which these differences predict future IQ.

Questions to Think About As You Read:

- How do built-in abilities and experience interact in infants' cognitive development?
- How might infants' increasing cognitive abilities affect their abilities to interact with others and form social relationships?

PIAGET'S THEORY OF INFANT COGNITIVE DEVELOPMENT

Piaget's theory provides a good starting point for discussing infant cognitive development. Piaget was the first to propose a comprehensive theory of cognitive development in infancy based on systematic observation of infants' behavior. In addition, his ideas have set the agenda for research on infant cognition. Many present-day developmentalists disagree strongly with Piaget's conclusions, but the questions he asked and the topics he studied still have a powerful influence on infancy research (Haith and Benson, 1998).

Assumptions About the Nature of Infants

As you learned in Chapter 1, Piaget called infancy the **sensorimotor period** because he believed infants' awareness of the world was limited to what they know through sensory

More on Piaget

Sensorimotor period:
Piaget's term for the first two years of life, when awareness of the world is limited to what can be known through sensory awareness and motor acts.

awareness and motor acts. Seven-month-old Malcolm is learning about the world from the effects of his own actions. He grasps a sheet of paper and watches it wrinkle, thus learning that it is flexible. He shakes the paper and hears it rustle, thus learning that it makes a pleasant sound. Malcolm's knowledge grows through the interplay of sensory skills and motor actions. His thinking does not yet include language or abstract concepts. What he knows and remembers is directly tied to what he can see, hear, feel, taste, and do.

During the first two years of life, babies begin to actively construct an understanding of the world. When Piaget said that infants are active participants in their own cognitive development, he was referring to both motor activity *and* mental activity. He believed that motor activity is essential to infants' development of understanding; passive observation is not enough. Infants do not wait for things to happen to them; instead they act on objects around them in whatever ways they can and then experience the results. Infants mentally construct an understanding of the world, not by passively absorbing information, but by actively putting together a rudimentary interpretation of how things work. At first, babies make discoveries by accident as they look around, move their bodies, and suck on whatever they can put in their mouths. Later, discoveries become more intentional as older infants deliberately try out actions and investigate their consequences.

Processes of Developmental Change

When Meryl was 6 months old, Karen offered her a sip of milk from a cup for the first time. As the rim touched her lips, Meryl started sucking to draw the milk out. The liquid spilled down both sides of her chin. With practice, Meryl soon learned how to use her lips and tongue to drink successfully from a cup. In time she much preferred drinking from a cup to drinking from a bottle.

Meryl's behavior in response to the challenge of learning to drink from a cup demonstrates two key mechanisms in Piaget's theory: *adaptation* and *equilibration*. Piaget uses these two mechanisms to account for developmental change at every age.

Adaptation is the process by which children change to function more effectively in their environment. As we mentioned in Chapter 1, this process is analogous to biological adaptation, in which new species evolve to meet environmental challenges. Piaget was referring to *individual* change, not change in an entire species. But like the evolutionists, he was interested in how behavior is modified to meet environmental challenges. When Meryl altered her style of drinking to get milk from a cup, she was *adapting* to a new situation. Without this change in her behavior, she would have continued to function poorly in this situation.

Piaget saw adaptation as the joint product of two processes: *assimilation* and *accommodation*. **Assimilation** involves applying an existing capability without modification to various situations. Newborn Meryl applied her innate sucking reflex in the same way to any object that brushed her lips—the nipple of a baby bottle, a pacifier, or even Karen's finger. The same basic response worked in all of these situations; in other words, they were all *assimilated* to Meryl's reflexive sucking response.

Sometimes existing strategies don't work in new situations. In those cases, **accommodation** becomes necessary—modifying an existing strategy or skill to meet a new demand of the environment. Meryl eventually had to modify her sucking behavior to *accommodate* different objects, such as hands, toys, and blankets. Through accommodation Meryl gradually refined her innate sucking reflex into sucking patterns suited to different objects. When she was confronted with learning to drink from a cup, further accommodation was necessary. Discovering that her existing strategy of sucking would not work with a cup, Meryl modified the movements of her lips and tongue so that the liquid wouldn't spill. Once she acquired this skill, she was adapted for drinking from a cup.

By means of assimilation and accommodation, inborn capabilities gradually develop into a variety of skills or strategies that babies can apply in many different situations. Adaptation changes not only actions but also thought. According to Piaget, infants' skills

Adaptation:
In Piaget's theory, the process by which children change in order to function more effectively in their environment.

Assimilation:
In Piaget's theory, the process of applying an existing capability without modification to various situations.

Accommodation:
In Piaget's theory, the process of modifying an existing strategy or skill to meet a new demand of the environment.

Early in infancy, babies get nourishment by applying their sucking scheme to any type of nipple they encounter (assimilation). To learn to drink from a cup, however, they must modify this scheme (accommodation).

reflect underlying cognitive structures called **schemes.** Infants' schemes are sensorimotor; they include such strategies for exploring the physical world as sucking schemes, grasping schemes, and looking schemes. In later stages of development, children's schemes or strategies for dealing with the world become increasingly abstract.

Piaget's theory also includes a mechanism to keep cognitive development moving forward: **equilibration,** a self-regulatory process that produces increasingly effective adaptations. When children are functioning adaptively, they are in a state of *equilibrium* because their behavior matches the demands of their environments. Sometimes children encounter situations that demand skills beyond their current level of development. The result is a state of *disequilibrium.* You saw an example of disequilibrium when Meryl sucked on the rim of her cup and the milk ran down her chin. Her behavior was inappropriate to the challenge she faced. Piaget argued that the natural response to disequilibrium is to try to bring things back into equilibrium by matching one's behavior to the new demands. This is accomplished through the processes of assimilation and accommodation. Meryl continued to swallow the milk that made it into her mouth, just as she had done when drinking from a bottle (assimilation), but she also gradually adjusted the movements of her tongue and lips to keep the milk from spilling (accommodation).

Sensorimotor Stages

Piaget subdivided the sensorimotor period into six stages (see Table 5.1). Development through the six sensorimotor stages entails development of increasingly complex and effective sensorimotor schemes. As infants interact with their environments, their early schemes become adapted to more and more situations.

Piaget based his initial description of the sensorimotor stages on observations of his own three children as infants (Piaget, 1952/1963). Like Darwin, Piaget was trained as a naturalist; his insightful descriptions of infant behavior demonstrate how much can be learned from careful observation of individual children.

As you read about Piaget's sensorimotor stages, remember three things:

- Piaget was describing the most advanced level of performance for each stage; early in any stage a baby is only beginning to acquire the abilities described.

Schemes:
In Piaget's theory, cognitive structures that can be applied to a variety of situations.

Equilibration:
In Piaget's theory, a self-regulatory process that produces increasingly effective adaptations.

Table 5.1 PIAGET'S STAGES OF SENSORIMOTOR DEVELOPMENT

0–1 month	Stage 1: Reflexes	Minor refinement of inborn behavior patterns
1–4 months	Stage 2: Primary circular reactions	Development of simple repeated actions centered on infant's own body
4–8 months	Stage 3: Secondary circular reactions	Development of repeated actions involving external objects
8–12 months	Stage 4: Coordination of schemes	Coordination of separate actions into goal-directed sequences of behaviors
12–18 months	Stage 5: Tertiary circular reactions	Variation of repeated actions through trial-and-error experimentation
18–24 months	Stage 6: Beginnings of representational thought	Emergence of mental schemes, as seen in deferred imitation

- The age ranges given are only approximate; different babies enter and complete each stage at different rates. What is important is the *sequence* of stages.
- Piaget's stages are only one way of describing and explaining infant cognitive development; later in the chapter, we will look at some other ways.

Stage 1: Reflexes (Birth to 1 Month) Piaget argued that in the first month of life a baby's capabilities are limited to genetically programmed reflexes, which provide a very limited range of behaviors. Development during this stage consists of minor refinements of these reflexes; no truly new behaviors emerge. Piaget used the term *reflex* in a much broader sense than most American psychologists, to refer to any built-in behavior pattern instead of automatic responses to particular stimuli. For instance, Piaget would consider Malcolm's active looking when he came home from the hospital a reflex because these eye movements are a built-in response to many kinds of visual stimuli. Piaget was also interested in standard newborn reflexes, such as sucking and grasping, as well as larger movements of the arms and hands. All of these behaviors are refined during the first month after birth, and all of them provide building blocks for development of increasingly flexible sensorimotor schemes.

Stage 2: Primary Circular Reactions (1 to 4 Months)

One evening when John was putting 2-month-old Malcolm to bed, he noticed Malcolm moving his arms in a seemingly random but rhythmic up-and-down pattern. As his right hand brushed against his face, he turned his head to the right and his arm movements became smaller. The next time his hand brushed against his face, he opened his mouth and captured it. After sucking for a while he released the hand, moved it up and down again, and then recaptured it with his mouth. Over and over Malcolm repeated this sequence. John was observing a type of sensorimotor scheme Piaget called a primary circular reaction.

Circular reaction:
A behavior that produces an interesting event, initially by chance, and is repeated.

Primary circular reaction:
A circular reaction involving an infant's own body.

A **circular reaction** is a behavior that produces an interesting event, initially by chance, and is repeated. The reaction is *circular* in the sense that the end of one sequence triggers the start of another. A **primary circular reaction** like Malcolm's is one that involves only an infant's own body, not an external object or event.

Thumb sucking frequently is learned as a primary circular reaction, just as Malcolm learned to suck his whole hand. As a baby's hands and arms move randomly, a thumb often comes in contact with the mouth, triggering the sucking reflex. You might think that once the thumb is inside the mouth the baby would go on sucking until he or she grew tired, but often this is not what happens. Piaget noticed that infants frequently pull the thumb out and attempt to repeat the actions that led to sucking on it. This is an early

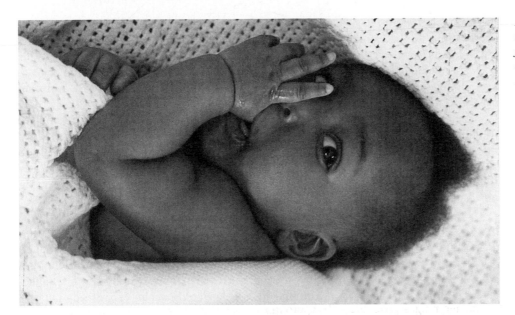

Repeatedly moving the hand to the mouth so a thumb, fingers, or fist can be sucked is a common example of a primary circular reaction.

example of infants being active participants in their own cognitive development. Babies don't just passively take in information about the world around them. Instead, their own activities generate and select information useful for development.

You may wonder why we say thumb sucking is often learned as a primary circular reaction when babies younger than stage 2 suck their thumbs and this behavior has even been observed in fetuses. Early in development, thumb sucking is a reflexive response to the accidental presence of a thumb near the mouth; it has not yet become a primary circular reaction. The inborn behaviors of stage 1 are the foundation for the primary circular reactions that develop in stage 2. These inborn behaviors, such as moving the arms and sucking, determine what kinds of events happen by accident. When babies accidentally do something that produces an interesting sensory experience, they are intrinsically motivated to try to do it again. Malcolm does not consciously think about the connection between capturing his fist in his mouth and the pleasant sensation of sucking on it. He repeats this behavior automatically, not intentionally. Piaget's stage 2 marks the emergence of new behaviors as a result of this intrinsic motivation.

Stage 3: Secondary Circular Reactions (4 to 8 Months)

At breakfast one day 6-month-old Mikey accidentally knocked a spoon off his high-chair tray. The spoon clattered to the floor, and Christine gave him a clean one. Moments later Mikey knocked the new spoon to the floor. Mikey was not trying to annoy his mother, but was simply engaging in a type of sensorimotor scheme Piaget called a secondary circular reaction.

In **secondary circular reactions,** infants actively experience the effects of their behaviors on *external objects.* As with primary circular reactions, the interesting sensory consequence is at first produced by accident, but the baby repeats the behavior, causing the consequence again.

An experiment Piaget conducted with his infant son, Laurent, shows both the skills and limitations of babies at this stage. Piaget tied a string from Laurent's wrist to a rattle suspended above his crib. If Laurent moved his arm vigorously, the rattle made a noise. By randomly waving his arms, Laurent soon caused the rattling sound. At this point he stopped, listened, and then moved his whole body so the sound occurred again. Repeating this secondary circular reaction, Laurent gradually adapted his movements until he moved only the appropriate arm. The next day Piaget again tied the string from Laurent's wrist to the rattle, but Laurent did not spontaneously move his arm. Only after his father shook the rattle did Laurent revive the previous day's circular

Secondary circular reaction:
A circular reaction involving the effects of an infant's behavior on an external object.

reaction. On the third day Piaget tied the string to Laurent's *other* wrist. Again Piaget had to reinstate the circular reaction by shaking the rattle. When Laurent began moving his arm, it was the one *without* the string. When no sound resulted, he moved his body more extensively until he heard the rattle. As Laurent repeated the circular reaction, he again adapted his movements until he eventually moved only the arm connected to the rattle.

We can say Laurent understood the connection between moving his arm and the resulting sound, but this understanding was quite limited. Even when the wrist to which the string was tied was in clear view, Laurent moved the other arm. He did not grasp the fact that the arm pulled the string, which in turn shook the rattle. Instead, he merely learned a connection between a particular behavior—moving his arm—and a particular sensory consequence—hearing the rattle.

According to Piaget, during the first year of life babies learn many such pairings between their own behaviors and sensory consequences. Another example is the early form of imitation, mentioned in Chapter 4, that emerges during stage 3. When 4-month-old Malcolm coos, DeeDee may coo back, causing him to coo again in return. Here Malcolm is learning a connection between making a certain sound and having his mother repeat it. Such circular reactions are limited to behaviors Malcolm can already perform and can actually hear or see himself produce. Malcolm cannot yet consciously mimic another person and thus acquire *new* behaviors through imitation.

Stage 4: Coordination of Schemes (8 to 12 Months)

> At 7 months, Meryl got very frustrated if she wanted a toy and some other object was blocking the way. Karen thought it was strange Meryl made such a fuss instead of moving the unwanted object, but she figured it was just Meryl's cranky nature. Two months later, one day Karen saw Meryl crawling toward the television plug. To distract her, Karen quickly placed a large toy dog in front of the socket. To her surprise, this tactic failed completely. With a sweep of her arm, Meryl knocked the dog out of the way and reached for the cord.

Coordination of schemes:
A goal-directed chain of
behaviors.

This kind of behavior reflects thinking typical of Piaget's stage 4. In this stage, infants begin to put actions together into goal-directed chains of behavior, which Piaget called **coordination of schemes.** In other words, they sometimes do a thing not for its own sake but as a means of accomplishing something else. Meryl knocked the toy dog out of the way *in order* to get to the electrical cord. Notice that this action required her to anticipate the results of hitting the dog. The ability to anticipate future consequences is a major cognitive leap forward, even though it is still limited to well-learned motor actions. Piaget saw this kind of behavior as the first clear sign of purposefulness in infants. Meryl *intended* to grasp the plug, and she knew that if she hit the dog it would no longer be in the way. By coordinating her hitting, reaching, and grasping strategies, she got what she wanted.

Piaget also argued that infants at stage 4 understand their own behavior well enough to imitate actions they seldom perform spontaneously. For instance, Piaget's 9-month-old daughter Jacqueline gradually learned how to imitate her father as he bent and straightened his index finger, something she rarely did on her own (Piaget, 1962).

Stage 5: Tertiary Circular Reactions (12 to 18 Months)

Learning to feed themselves requires babies to coordinate a series of actions to produce a desired outcome.

> One day 13-month-old Maggie was standing at the top of the stairs, her way blocked by a safety gate. As she peered over the gate with a rubber ball in one hand, the ball accidentally dropped and bounced all the way down. Maggie watched intently as the ball hit the front door. She then picked up her blue stuffed dog and dropped it over the gate, watching to see what would happen. The dog landed on the top step, somersaulted down another, and stopped when it hit the third, nose draped over the edge. Christine came out of the bedroom just in time to see Maggie forcefully hurl a shoe over the gate.

Maggie's behavior illustrates a flexible application of sensorimotor schemes that Piaget called a **tertiary circular reaction.** As with primary and secondary circular reactions, a tertiary circular reaction begins when some action accidentally leads to an interesting sensory consequence. But rather than repeating the same behavior, infants at this stage experiment. When Maggie launches various objects over the gate in a variety of ways, these trial-and-error variations allow her to discover new cause-and-effect relationships. Her understanding of the world and strategies for acting on it expand greatly as a result.

As you would expect, infants at stage 5 get into everything. They actively explore each new object, trying to discover what it can do. This exploration affords many opportunities to learn new means of reaching goals. The active exploration of stage 5 may also explain why children around 18 months of age begin to acquire simple tool-using skills, such as using a stick to dig (Flavell, Miller, and Miller, 2002). According to Piaget, the active trial-and-error approach of stage 5 infants enables them to learn to imitate behaviors they have never before performed, as mentioned in Chapter 4.

Tertiary circular reaction:
A circular reaction involving purposeful, trial-and-error experimentation with a variety of objects.

Stage 6: Beginnings of Representational Thought (18 to 24 Months)

[Piaget's 1½-year-old daughter] Jacqueline had a visit from a little boy of 18 months whom she used to see from time to time, and who, in the course of the afternoon, got into a terrible temper. He screamed as he tried to get out of a playpen and pushed it backward, stamping his feet. Jacqueline stood watching him in amazement, never having witnessed such a scene before. The next day, she herself screamed in her playpen and tried to move it, stamping her foot lightly several times in succession. (Piaget, 1962, p. 63)

This example of **deferred imitation** illustrates one of the new capabilities that mark stage 6. A day after seeing another toddler throw a temper tantrum, Jacqueline performed a good imitation of his behavior. Apparently, she had stored in memory a representation of screaming, pushing, and stamping. The ability to form mental representations like this one is a very important cognitive advance.

Piaget described stage 6 as the start of the transition from sensorimotor to **symbolic or representational thought,** the ability to make one thing stand for another. Just as reflexes provide the starting point for sensorimotor schemes, sensorimotor schemes provide the starting point for mental representations. Stage 6 toddlers start to solve problems in their heads, without having to go through the physical actions involved. Their symbolic thought is still quite limited, confined to behaviors they *could* act out. Nevertheless, Piaget saw this ability as a great cognitive leap forward.

Deferred imitation:
Imitation of observed behavior after time has elapsed, indicating an infant's ability to store a representation of the behavior in memory.

Symbolic or representational thought:
In Piaget's theory, the ability to make one thing stand for another.

CHALLENGES TO PIAGET'S THEORY

Piaget's descriptions of infant behavior were amazingly accurate, but his *explanations* for that behavior have been questioned. Major areas of disagreement include:

- the timetable for the emergence of cognitive skills,
- the existence of qualitatively distinct developmental stages,
- the range of innate abilities, and
- the source of infants' cognitive limitations.

Reassessing the Timetable for Infant Development

Research in a number of areas suggests that Piaget underestimated the skills of infants at various ages. By observing only his own children, he may have missed the earliest appearance of new skills. Developmentalists testing many infants with more sensitive measures of performance find a variety of skills at earlier ages than Piaget reported. In some cases, differences in age estimates are due to the fact that Piaget generally credited infants with a skill only when it was well developed and could be used in a variety of situations. In contrast, many of his critics have searched for the earliest evidence of the emergence of a skill.

Reassessing the Concept of Stages

Piaget offered detailed descriptions of how infants at each of his six sensorimotor stages respond to various tasks. He implied that infants who are at a particular stage with respect to one task should be at the same stage for other major tasks. Piaget believed that certain general cognitive advances characterize each stage, and these general advances should produce simultaneous progress in a number of different areas.

However, when Ina Uzgiris and J. McVicker Hunt (1975) tested a large number of infants, they found a great deal of inconsistency in each baby's achievements. An infant might be at sensorimotor stage 4 on one task, but at stage 3 or 5 on others. Piaget himself was aware of this problem, though he never provided an explanation for it. He used the term **décalage** to refer to the lack of simultaneous development in different areas.

The phenomenon of décalage has led many researchers to see cognitive development as acquisition of *separate* specific skills and understandings, rather than progress through global stages. Kurt Fischer (1980; Fischer and Bidell, 1998) argues that development entails two types of cognitive advances and constraints: some that are general, such as Piaget described, and others that are more specific. As a result, babies' progress in mastering any particular cognitive task is to some degree independent of their progress in mastering other tasks.

Reassessing Infants' Inborn Abilities

Piaget assumed that babies come equipped with only a set of reflexive behaviors and a tendency to actively engage the world. In contrast, some contemporary developmentalists, known as **neo-nativists,** have reintroduced into developmental psychology the idea that babies have a relatively broad range of innate abilities and knowledge. Some neo-nativists, such as Elizabeth Spelke (Spelke and Newport, 1998) argue that infants are born with an understanding of many basic properties of the physical world. Others, such as Renée Baillargeon (1994), suggest that they are born with fairly specific learning mechanisms that guide the development of their understanding of the world.

Reassessing Infants' Cognitive Constraints

Piaget believed infants' cognitive development was constrained by their sensorimotor cognitive structures and lack of mental representation. Some researchers argue instead that it is constrained by limits on information-processing capacity, or **working memory.** To find a hidden toy, imitate another person, or apply a familiar strategy to a new situation, an infant must use working memory to remember things, initiate actions, and control behavior. If working memory becomes temporarily filled before a task is finished, the baby faces information overload that stymies further progress. Advances in cognitive development occur as working memory capacity expands, perhaps due to brain development, or as well-practiced skills become more automatic and require less capacity (Case, 1985; Fischer and Rose, 1994).

INFANTS' UNDERSTANDING OF THE PHYSICAL WORLD

Piaget was not only interested in the development of infants' reasoning abilities, but also in their emerging knowledge of the world around them. He believed that as infants develop increasingly flexible strategies for exploring and representing their environment,

Décalage:
Piaget's term for inconsistencies in a child's cognitive development across different domains.

Neo-nativist:
A contemporary developmental theorist who believes infants have a wide range of innate abilities and knowledge.

Working memory:
The information-processing capacity available at any one time.

they use those strategies to make sense of the physical world. His ideas provided a starting point for research on infants' understanding of basic aspects of physical reality, such as concepts of objects and physical events, and basic tools for understanding the world, such as number and categorization (Haith and Benson, 1998).

According to Piaget, babies are not born with these concepts and cognitive tools. Instead, knowledge of the physical world must be constructed over time through active sensorimotor exploration. In contrast to Piaget, neo-nativists have concluded that a basic understanding of physical reality is built into babies at birth or develops very early in infancy. We will examine the evidence for these contrasting views from research on infants' understanding of the object concept, physical events, number, and categorization.

The Concept of Objects

Understanding the concept of objects is essential to an understanding of the physical world. When you look around, you do not simply see patterns of light; you see books, chairs, pencils, and so on. You know these objects have a durability beyond their colors or the shadows they cast (both of which disappear in the absence of light) and beyond your own perception (which depends on you being there). Such a realization is an important part of your understanding of reality, including your knowledge that you are distinct from other people. The interesting question for developmentalists is how and when this understanding is acquired.

A central aspect of the concept of objects is **object permanence,** the understanding that objects continue to exist when they are out of sight. Piaget provided an account of the development of object permanence over the six sensorimotor stages, describing in detail how infants of different ages respond to various tasks involving hidden objects. We will examine Piaget's ideas about object permanence before turning to the results of further research on the subject.

Piaget's Account of Object Permanence

Stages 1 and 2. In sensorimotor stages 1 and 2 (birth to 4 months), infants respond to objects with interest but seem to have no understanding of object permanence. During these stages, infants become able to track moving objects with their eyes and begin to reach for them voluntarily. However, if an object being tracked moves behind something else, the baby loses interest in it and gazes off in another direction as if it has ceased to exist. A similar reaction happens when an object is partially covered. Suppose a hungry stage 2 infant is looking at a baby bottle. Then, while the infant watches, the nipple end of the bottle is covered with a cloth so the infant can see only the bottom half. Frequently, babies this young will lose interest and begin looking at other things, as if they cannot imagine the part of the bottle that is not visible and no longer perceive the object as familiar.

Object permanence:
The understanding that objects continue to exist when they are out of sight.

Object Permanence Tasks

During stages 1 and 2 of the sensorimotor period, infants almost immediately lose interest in objects that become hidden from view.

Stage 3. In the third sensorimotor stage (4 to 8 months), infants still depend on current perceptual information for their understanding of objects, but a partial view of something is now enough to remind them of the whole. Infants this age will reach for a partially covered object. But if an object is totally covered while they watch, they will not try to reach for it after a delay of only a few seconds. Babies this age apparently need perceptual cues to remind them an object still exists, just as Piaget's son needed a perceptual cue to remember how to make an interesting sound with a rattle connected to his wrist.

Stage 4. In the fourth sensorimotor stage (8 to 12 months), infants search for hidden objects. If they see a toy being covered with a pillow, they will remove the pillow to get the toy. This behavior shows babies this age can combine sensorimotor schemes into goal-directed actions and they understand an object can be recovered after searching.

You might conclude stage 4 infants have an adultlike concept of object permanence, but studies show their understanding of objects is still flawed (Gratch, 1975). If you repeatedly hide a rattle under a cloth, an 8- to 10-month-old will find it each time. But if, with the infant watching, you put the rattle under a different cloth, he or she will keep looking for it under the first cloth, where it has always been before. Failing to find the rattle there, the baby will search randomly, perhaps finally discovering it under the second cloth—where he or she *saw* you put it. (See Figure 5.1.) This behavior is called the *A, not-B error* because infants continue to search in location A, where the object was found before, not location B, where they saw it being hidden.

Many researchers believe stage 4 infants' continued searching indicates they know the object exists and must be *somewhere* (Siegler, 1998). But looking under the first cloth shows an incomplete understanding of constraints on where the object can be.

Figure 5.1

ASSESSMENT OF OBJECT PERMANENCE

The stage 4 infant searches wherever the object was previously found. If the object is repeatedly hidden under the cloth on the infant's left, the infant immediately searches under the cloth and finds the object. When the object is hidden under the cloth on the infant's right, the stage 4 infant still searches on the left. The stage 5 infant searches wherever the object disappeared from sight. When the object is put under the cloth in the adult's closed hand, the infant searches in the adult's hand.

Stage 4:
1. Object in view
2. Object under cloth
3. Infant finds object
4. Object in view
5. Object under *other* cloth
6. Infant searches for object under first cloth

Stage 5:
1. Object is in experimenter's hand
2. Experimenter closes hand...
3. ... puts hand under cloth...
4. ... removes hand, leaving object under cloth
5. Child looks in experimenter's hand
6. Obviously upset, child quits

Piaget believed infants in stage 4 connect the reappearance of the object with an action of their own (lifting a certain cloth), and they repeat this action expecting it to bring the object back. For them the object does not have a permanence independent of their own activity.

Stage 5. In the fifth sensorimotor stage (12 to 18 months), infants no longer make the A, not-B error. Instead, they search for a hidden object wherever it disappeared from sight (see Figure 5.1). Once again it may seem they understand object permanence, but the following procedure reveals otherwise. In this sequence, you show the baby a small toy, then close your hand around it, place your hand under a cloth, leave the toy there, and withdraw your still-closed hand. Stage 5 babies will first search for the toy in your hand, where it disappeared from view. When the object isn't there, they may become upset and stop searching or may search randomly. They may or may not move the cloth and find the toy. Apparently, babies this age cannot make inferences about what happens to objects that are out of sight.

Stage 6. In the final sensorimotor stage (18 to 24 months), infants at last acquire a mature understanding of object permanence. They can now imagine movements of an object they do not actually see. In the stage 5 experiment, they immediately search under the cloth after failing to find the toy in your hand. The ability to imagine the object leaving your hand while it was under the cloth is an example of early representational thought.

Further Research on Infants' Understanding of Objects Investigators who tried to replicate Piaget's studies of object permanence found that infants generally reached the milestones for developing the object concept in the sequence Piaget observed. However, many infants reached them at somewhat earlier ages than Piaget recorded (Corman and Escalona, 1969; Uzgiris and Hunt, 1975).

Some researchers have questioned whether Piaget's tasks accurately measured infants' understanding of object permanence. They contend that babies younger than stage 4 (8 to 12 months) may understand objects are permanent but fail Piaget's tasks because they lack other skills demanded by the tasks, such as memory and manual search skills (Baillargeon, 1993). To avoid this problem, these researchers have devised tasks that reduce or eliminate the need for infants to remember the location of objects or search for them. One common approach has been to make inferences about infants' understanding of objects from their looking behavior during habituation tasks.

Present-day researchers typically use much less stringent criteria for concluding that infants understand object permanence than Piaget did (Haith and Benson, 1998). In most habituation studies, researchers do not require that all infants in an age group exhibit an understanding of the concept being tested, but only that a substantial minority of them do so. The use of research methods that catch more subtle signs of understanding than Piaget's methods allows skills to be detected when they are still emerging but are not yet well developed enough to be apparent in most situations outside the laboratory.

Perception of Partially Hidden Objects. Philip Kellman and Elizabeth Spelke (1983) used a habituation task to demonstrate that babies can make sense of partially hidden objects earlier than Piaget reported. These researchers showed $3\frac{1}{2}$- to $4\frac{1}{2}$-month-old infants a rod moving back and forth, with its central section hidden by a block, as shown in Figure 5.2. Once the babies were habituated to this sight, they were shown one of the test displays in Figure 5.2—either one long rod or two short rods, moving back and forth with no block in front of them. The babies looked longer at the two short rods than at the one long rod, suggesting they saw the original display as a single rod and found the sight of the two rods unfamiliar. However, newborns show no sign of being able to understand partly hidden objects (Slater et al., 1996). Thus, this ability seems to be acquired earlier than Piaget thought, but it does not seem to be present at birth.

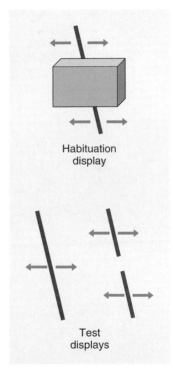

Habituation
display

Test
displays

Figure 5.2
TESTING INFANTS'
PERCEPTION OF PARTIALLY
OBSCURED OBJECTS
In Kellman and Spelke's experiment, $3\frac{1}{2}$- to $4\frac{1}{2}$-month-olds who had been habituated to the top display looked longer at the test display on the right, suggesting that they perceived the habituation display as a single rod moving back and forth behind the block. *(Source: Kellman and Spelke, 1983.)*

Evidence of Object Permanence in Stage 3 Babies. Using tests other than Piaget's, several researchers have found evidence that 4- to 8-month-olds may have some understanding of object permanence. In one study (Hood and Willatts, 1986), objects were presented to the right or the left of 5-month-olds who were prevented from reaching for them until the lights were turned out. Even though the babies could not see the objects in the dark, they reached more often to the correct side, indicating they understood the objects were still there.

Renée Baillargeon has conducted habituation experiments that suggest some understanding of object permanence as early as 4 months. All of these experiments involve observing infants' reactions to events in which an object appears to move through space occupied by a hidden object.

In one experiment (Baillargeon, 1987, 1991), babies were habituated to a screen rotating back and forth through a 180-degree arc, as shown in Figure 5.3. As the babies watched, a box was placed behind the screen in a position that should block its movement. The babies then saw two test events: a possible event, in which the screen stopped when it reached the box, and an impossible event, in which the box was surreptitiously removed and the screen did not stop. Babies as young as 4½ months looked longer at the impossible event. However, babies this age showed no expectations about *where* the screen should stop. In contrast, 6½-month-olds seemed to expect the screen to stop at a specific point, suggesting they remembered the size and location of the hidden box.

Recent research with toddlers has raised questions about young infants' knowledge about objects. Tasks analogous to the habituation tasks used with infants, but requiring action instead of looking, have been used to test toddlers' object concepts (Keen, in press).

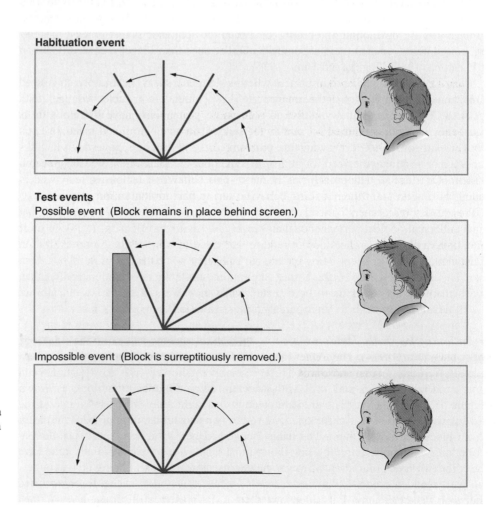

Figure 5.3
BAILLARGEON'S ROTATING SCREEN EXPERIMENT
After babies were habituated to a freely rotating screen, they saw a block being placed behind it. On the test events, they looked longer at the apparently impossible event. *(Source: Baillargeon, 1987.)*

Figure 5.4
TODDLERS' INCOMPLETE OBJECT KNOWLEDGE
Even though toddlers could see the ball rolling down the ramp and could see the barrier above the third door, they still often looked for the ball behind the wrong door. *(Source: Butler, Berthier, and Clifton, 2002.)*

In one study (Hood, Carey, and Prasada, 2000), 2-year-olds did not seem to recognize that a shelf inserted behind a screen would interrupt the trajectory of a toy dropped behind the screen. In another study (Butler, Berthier, and Clifton, 2002), toddlers watched as a ball rolled down a ramp behind a screen toward an obvious barrier. They were then asked to find the ball behind one of several doors in the screen, as shown in Figure 5.4. Even if they had watched the barrier being put in place and could see it protruding above the top of the screen, 2- and 2½-year-olds had difficulty finding the ball; only 3-year-olds could reliably pick the right door. These results suggest that even toddlers may not have a complete understanding of some characteristics of objects—or at least that they may not be able to put their understanding into action.

Explaining Infants' Search Behavior. If infants understand some aspects of object permanence as early as 4 months, one puzzle is why their search behavior lags so far behind their understanding. A possible explanation is that infants have trouble with the means-end behaviors required to search for hidden objects—lifting a cloth to allow retrieval of a toy under it, for example (Baillargeon, 1993). This explanation fits with Piaget's observation that babies do not put together goal-directed chains of behavior until sensorimotor stage 4. The emergence of means-end behaviors, including searching for hidden objects, around 8 months of age may be due in part to maturation of areas of the cerebral cortex that govern sequences of behavior (Diamond, 1991; Johnson, 1998).

However, difficulty with means-end behaviors cannot explain the A, not-B error. Babies who make this error can put together a sequence of behaviors to remove the cloth and find the object, but they have trouble shifting their search behavior to a new location. Piaget thought stage 4 infants continue to search in the same location because they connect the object's reappearance with the act of searching there. But research casts doubt on this explanation. When a hiding place is changed, stage 4 babies search only in the previous location about half the time (Butterworth, 1977). Additionally, if they are allowed to search *immediately* after an object is hidden, they always go to the right location (Gratch et al., 1974). The longer they have to wait, the more likely they are to make an error (Wellman, Cross, and Bartsch, 1986). And the older they are, the longer the wait has to be before they make a mistake (Diamond, 1988). Finally, when a baby watches an object being hidden in a new location, with six possible hiding places to choose from, the baby tends to search near the correct location (Bjork and Cummings, 1984). It seems infants are not just repeating a previously successful response. Instead, they are *trying* to remember the right location, but sometimes cannot. Memory limitations may cause them to return to the last place they remember finding the object.

Even memory limitations do not entirely explain the A, not-B error, however. Stage 4 infants often search at the location where an object was previously found even when the object is visible in its new location (Haith and Benson, 1998). One reason for this may be that it is hard for them to stop doing what has previously been reinforced; as the cerebral cortex matures, their ability to inhibit these automatic responses increases, and they stop making the A, not-B error (Diamond, Cruttenden, and Neiderman, 1994).

To summarize, recent research with infants and toddlers on the development of the object concept suggests the following:

- Piaget was fairly accurate about the *sequence* in which an understanding of the object concept is acquired, but he underestimated the *rate* of acquisition.

- Based on research using looking behavior and habituation, it now appears that infants as young as 4 months may understand in some very basic sense that objects continue to exist when they can't be seen and that one object can block the movement of another.

- However, infants' early understanding of object permanence is incomplete; they cannot make specific inferences about the size and location of hidden objects until several months later.

- Object search behavior lags considerably behind object-related looking behavior, perhaps because means-end behavior, memory, and the ability to inhibit automatic responses all develop more slowly than looking behavior.

Causality and Other Relations Between Objects

In addition to understanding properties of individual objects, infants need to understand relations *between* objects to make sense of the stream of perceptual information they receive from the world around them (Haith and Benson, 1998). Piaget laid out a gradual process by which infants came to understand causality and other relations between objects as a result of sensorimotor exploration. However, as with the object concept, some current researchers have proposed that infants are born with this understanding or develop it very early.

Research on infants' understanding of causality has focused on the causal link between one object hitting another and the movement of the second object. There is evidence from habituation studies that infants develop an understanding of this connection during the second six months of life. Alan Leslie (1984) habituated 7-month-olds to a *causal* sequence in which one brick moved across a screen, made contact with a second brick, and launched it into immediate motion. The babies showed signs of dishabituation when they then saw a *noncausal* sequence in which the first brick stopped short of contact with the second and there was a delay before the second brick moved. But they did not differentiate between two noncausal sequences—one in which there was contact between the bricks but a delay in launching the second brick, and one in which there was no contact but immediate launching.

Infants' understanding of causality seems to be situation-specific at first. Lisa Oakes and Leslie Cohen (1990; Oakes, 1994) showed babies videotapes of causal and noncausal sequences involving different types of objects. Six-month-olds differentiated between causal and noncausal events when they involved rolling balls, but not when they involved small toys. In contrast, 10-month-olds made this distinction regardless of the objects involved.

Infants and Physical Causality

Renée Baillargeon and her colleagues have studied infants' understanding of physical support, another type of relation between objects. In one study (Needham and Baillargeon, 1993), 4½-month-olds watched as a hand appeared from behind a curtain and placed a box either on top of another box or off to one side so that it appeared to be suspended in midair. The infants looked longer at the box left without apparent support than at the box left on top of another box.

Older infants show increasing understanding of the specifics of physical support. In another study (Baillargeon, Needham, and DeVos, 1992) babies were habituated to the sight of a hand pushing a box various distances along a platform, as shown in

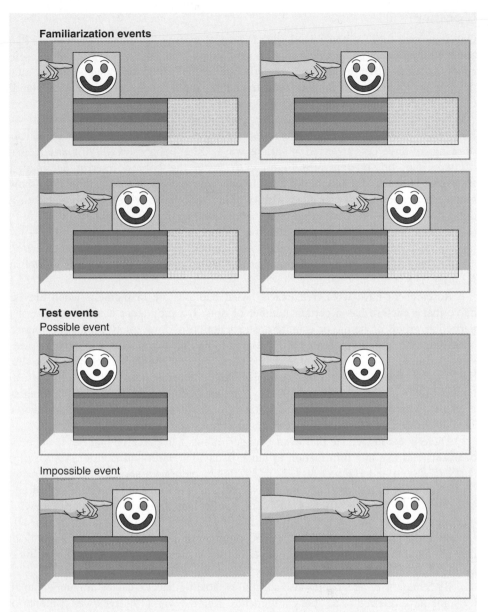

Familiarization events

Test events
Possible event

Impossible event

Figure 5.5
INFANTS' UNDERSTANDING
OF PHYSICAL SUPPORT
By 6½ months, babies look
longer at the impossible test
event than at the possible one.
*(Source: Baillargeon, Needham,
and DeVos, 1992.)*

Figure 5.5. After part of the platform was removed, the babies were shown possible and impossible test events. In possible events, the hand pushed the box to the edge of the platform and stopped. In impossible events, the hand kept pushing the box until only one edge remained in contact with the platform, but the box did not fall. At 6½ months, babies looked longer at impossible events, but the 5-month-olds made no distinction between possible and impossible events. In a study using more complex arrangements of objects (Baillargeon and Hanko-Summers, 1990), however, even 9½-month-olds did not always distinguish between arrangements that looked as if they should fall and those that did not, demonstrating that full understanding of physical support takes some time to develop.

Apparently, just as with object permanence, babies develop a rudimentary grasp of the relations between objects during the period from 4 to 8 months (Piaget's sensorimotor stage 3), but initially they can apply these concepts only in simple situations. Between 8 and 12 months (Piaget's sensorimotor stage 4), the complexity and flexibility of their understanding increases.

Number

One important tool for understanding the physical world is awareness of number. Piaget believed that a true understanding of number was beyond the capabilities of the sensorimotor period. However, research carried out over the last 25 years suggests that infants develop an awareness of number on a timetable similar to that for their understanding of many other aspects of the physical world.

Prentice Starkey and Robert Cooper (1980) used habituation to test whether 4- to 7-month-olds could recognize differences in number. They showed one group of babies drawings of three dots arranged in various ways. Other babies saw varying arrangements of two, four, or six dots (see Figure 5.6). After the babies' interest declined, the researchers changed the number of dots. Infants who had habituated to three dots showed renewed attention when presented with two dots, and those who had habituated to two dots showed renewed attention to three. But switching from four dots to six or from six to four did *not* prompt renewed attention, even in 7-month-olds. Apparently, 4- to 7-month-old babies have some awareness of number, as long as the quantities are very small. There is even some evidence that this skill is present in newborns (Antell and Keating, 1983).

Researchers have wondered exactly what babies store in memory when they perceive that a picture has a certain number of dots. Do they store a visual image of the particular group of items, or a more abstract notion of how many things are there? In one study, researchers presented 6- to 8-month-olds with two arrays of objects side by side, one array containing two objects, the other three. When the babies heard two drumbeats, they tended to look at the two-object set; when they heard three drumbeats, they tended to look at the set of three (Starkey, Spelke, and Gelman, 1983). This finding suggests that what babies remember and match in such studies is a surprisingly abstract concept of number, not just the physical characteristics of the stimuli.

There is also evidence that even younger infants can perceive number in sequences of events and use this information to guide behavior (Haith and Benson, 1998). In one study (Canfield and Haith, 1991), 2- and 3-month-olds were shown a series of pictures on two screens in a predictable numerical pattern—two on the left screen followed by one on the right screen. The 3-month-olds quickly caught on to the pattern, showing a tendency to keep looking at the left screen after the first picture and to shift their attention to the right screen after the second picture. In a follow-up study, 5-month-olds demonstrated their ability to learn a pattern of three pictures on the left followed by one on the right (Canfield and Smith, 1996).

By 5 months of age, babies also seem to be able to detect changes in number, an ability some have referred to as "baby arithmetic." Karen Wynn (1992) showed 5-month-olds

Figure 5.6

INFANT AWARENESS OF NUMBER

In Starkey and Cooper's experiment, 4- to 7-month-olds showed that they could distinguish between two and three items, but not between four and six. *(Source: Reprinted with permission from P. Starkey and R. G. Cooper, "Perception of Number by Human Infants,"* Science, 210, *pp. 1033–1035, 1980. Copyright © 1980 American Association for the Advancement of Science.)*

	Condition	Habituation Trials		Test Trial
1	Habituated to 2 dots, tested with 3 dots	A	• •	• • •
		B	• •	
2	Habituated to 3 dots, tested with 2 dots	A	• • •	• •
		B	• • •	
3	Habituated to 4 dots, tested with 6 dots	A	• • • •	• • • • • •
		B	• • • •	
4	Habituated to 6 dots, tested with 4 dots	A	• • • • • •	• • • •
		B	• • • • • •	

one doll on a stage and then placed a screen in front of the stage. Next, a hand appeared, holding a second doll, disappeared behind the screen, and reappeared with no doll. Finally, the screen was removed, revealing either one or two dolls on the stage. The babies looked longer if only one doll was present, suggesting that they expected to see two. They responded similarly if they were first shown two dolls, the hand seemed to remove one doll from behind the screen, and there were still two dolls on the stage when the screen was removed. To rule out the possibility that the babies were simply expecting *something* to change when the hand went behind the screen, Wynn repeated the procedure. This time she started with one doll on stage, showed the hand apparently leaving a second doll behind the screen, and then revealed either two or three dolls on stage. This time the infants looked longer when there were three dolls, suggesting that they expected not just any change, but a particular change in number.

The results of these studies do not necessarily mean that infants understand *number* in the sense that older children and adults do. Infants' responses may demonstrate their ability to discriminate between stimuli using general perceptual abilities rather than domain-specific numerical knowledge (Simon, 1997). Some researchers argue that infants have a more general concept of *amount,* based on perceptual cues such as the total area covered by the objects in view, rather than a specifically numerical understanding (Mix, Huttenlocher, and Levine, 2002).

Thus, babies appear to have some awareness of quantity very early in life, perhaps from birth, and the complexity and usefulness of their understanding seems to increase with age. It is important to remember, however, that their understanding of number or amount seems to be limited to sets of three or fewer; awareness of larger quantities requires further cognitive development.

Categorization

Another important tool for understanding the physical world is categorization. Categories are useful because they allow infants to group things together and to treat the members of a group as similar. Once babies are capable of categorization, they do not have to treat each object or animal or person they encounter as something entirely new; instead, they can generalize from past experience. For example, when she was 14 months old, Maggie encountered a poodle during a visit to her grandmother's house. Recognizing it as a dog in spite of its peculiar haircut, she began to play with it just as she was used to playing with her family's golden retriever puppy, chasing it and grabbing its fur. Her grandmother's poodle reacted less favorably to her behavior than her family's puppy did, giving her more information to add to her *dog* category and perhaps changing her behavior toward other dogs she might meet in the future.

Infants begin to form categories based on *perceptual* characteristics very early in life (Mandler, 1998). For example, 3-month-olds quickly habituate to a series of pictures of one type of animal and display renewed interest when shown a picture of a different type of animal (Eimas and Quinn, 1994). The categories they form are often quite specific— for example, babies habituated to horse pictures show renewed interest in pictures of cats, giraffes, and even zebras. Infants under 6 months old have also been observed to form categories involving abstract geometric patterns, men's and women's voices, human faces, and various objects, including furniture (Haith and Benson, 1998). However, these early perceptual categories seem to be based simply on detection of visual and auditory patterns; it is not accurate to say that a 3-month-old who distinguishes between pictures of horses and pictures of zebras has a *concept* of what horses or zebras are like (Mandler, 1998).

During the second six months of life, infants begin to form *conceptual* categories that cover larger domains and include greater perceptual variability than the early perceptual categories (Mandler, 1998). Jean Mandler and Laraine McDonough (1993) used an interesting variation on traditional habituation tasks to study categorization in 7- to 11-month-olds. During the familiarization phase, they gave the infants a series of objects to examine one at a time, all from the same category (either animals or vehicles). As in habituation

By about 14 months, children generalize drinking to any animal, but not to vehicles, showing that they place animals and vehicles in separate categories.

studies, infants spent decreasing time examining each new object from the same category. In the test phase, they gave each infant two new objects, one from the familiarization category and one from a new category, and observed whether the infants spent more time examining the object from the new category. Some of the objects they used were quite similar perceptually, even though they belonged to different categories—for example, airplanes and birds with their wings spread. Mandler and McDonough found that 7- to 11-month-olds consistently differentiated between animals and vehicles, but did not differentiate among specific types of animals, such as dogs, fish, and rabbits. In an extension of this study, they found differentiation among plants, animals, vehicles, and furniture in 9- to 11-month-olds, but little differentiation within these categories (Mandler, 1998).

We know less about when infants begin to use categories to make generalizations about the world. Mandler and McDonough (1996) used an imitation task to examine how broadly 14-month-olds would generalize an action across objects from different categories. They demonstrated an action, such as a dog drinking from a cup, and then gave the infants a cup, an object from the animal category and an object from the vehicle category, and watched to see whether the infant would imitate the action and which objects they would use in their imitation. They found that infants generalized drinking from a cup and being put to bed to all the animals in their study and only rarely to vehicles; in contrast, they generalized taking a doll for a ride and being opened with a key to all of the vehicles and rarely to animals. In another modeling study (Bauer and Dow, 1994), 16- and 20-month-olds generalized sequences of events to different members of the same categories originally used. For example, they were willing to reenact putting a teddy bear to bed in a crib using Big Bird and a toy bed. Interestingly, initially infants seem to generalize too broadly, assuming that fish drink or putting a baby to bed in a bathtub; not until about 18 months do they begin to narrow their generalizations to more specific categories (Mandler, 1998).

In summary, infants begin to use *perceptual* characteristics to form categories by the time they are 3 months old. By 7 months, they form *conceptual* categories that allow for considerable perceptual variability. By 14 months, they clearly *apply* categories in their behavior with objects. Their early conceptual categories tend to be rather broad, with more specific subcategories appearing at around 18 months.

MEMORY DEVELOPMENT IN INFANCY

Infant Memory

A number of years ago, one of the authors of this book and his family were in a car accident while on vacation. The author's son, less than a year old, was taken to a hospital by ambulance to have minor injuries treated. Two years later the family was driving through the town where the accident occurred. The little boy, now 3 years old, looked around and spontaneously asked: "Are we going to see the ambulance now?" Did he remember the accident from two years earlier, when he had known the meaning of only a few words, *ambulance* certainly not among them? And if babies *can* form lasting memories of things that happen to them, why do most adults recall nothing about infancy?

Recognition memory:
A type of memory in which a particular stimulus is perceived as familiar.

Recall:
Active retrieval of information from memory.

Piaget believed that infants were capable of **recognition memory**—simply perceiving a stimulus as familiar, which could be based entirely on sensorimotor information and schemes. He did not believe they could engage in **recall**—actively retrieving information from memory, which would require mental representation (Flavell et al., 2002). Research on infant memory has revealed that Piaget was partly right, but the full picture is more complicated. In the first six months of life, infants' memory abilities match Piaget's expectations, but in later infancy they go beyond what he thought was possible.

In the following sections, we first review memory development in early and later infancy. Then we examine the role of brain development in infant memory before returning to the question of why memories of infancy do not survive into later life.

Memory in Early Infancy

Babies have some memory capabilities from birth. Newborns readily habituate to repeated sights and sounds, indicating that they remember enough about a stimulus to perceive it as familiar (Schneider and Bjorklund, 1998). As mentioned in Chapter 4, newborns quickly learn to recognize their mothers' face, voice, and smell, and they can even recognize the sound patterns of a story their mothers read aloud repeatedly while they were in the womb. Most of these examples involve recognizing stimuli that were seen or heard seconds earlier or have been experienced repeatedly over a long period of time, but some evidence indicates that babies just a few days old can recognize a newly experienced stimulus for as long as 24 to 48 hours (Nelson, 1995).

Until they are about 3 months old, babies seem to have trouble storing information about *relations* between visual stimuli, even very simple relations like the angles formed by two straight lines. Cohen and Younger (1984) repeatedly showed 6- and 14-week-olds the same angle until they became habituated. Then they showed them either exactly the same angle, the same angle turned a different way, a new angle formed from lines with the same orientations as in the original angle, or a new angle formed from lines with different orientations. As shown in Figure 5.7, 6-week-olds appeared to remember the orientation of *individual* lines, not the *combination* of lines that forms an angle. They dishabituated to any angle in which the orientation of the lines changed, including the original angle turned in a new direction. The 14-week-olds, however, seemed to remember *angles* rather than the orientation of individual lines.

Studies using simple laboratory stimuli such as these help us understand why very young infants have difficulty remembering more complex stimuli, such as faces. Recall from Chapter 4 that babies don't seem to organize and store detailed concepts of particular faces until about 3 months of age.

The capacity to retain a memory for more than a few hours or days increases during the first months of life. There is clear evidence that 2- to 4-month-olds can retain a memory involving actions of their own for several weeks, as demonstrated in an interesting set of studies by Carolyn Rovee-Collier (Rovee-Collier, 1993). In these studies, babies were placed in a crib with an overhead mobile, and the mobile was attached to

Child Development CD:
Rovee-Collier Infant Memory Studies

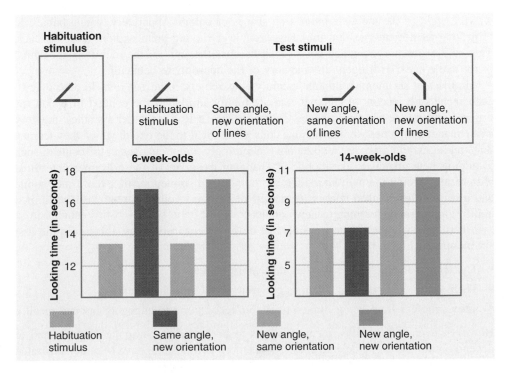

Figure 5.7
INFANT MEMORY FOR ANGLES
Cohen and Younger habituated 6- and 14-week-olds to various angles. After habituation, several angles were presented to the infants as test stimuli. Longer looking times indicated which angles were seen as different from the habituation stimulus. *(Source: Adapted from Cohen and Younger, 1984.)*

Rovee-Collier's research shows that 2- to 4-month-olds are capable of cued recall.

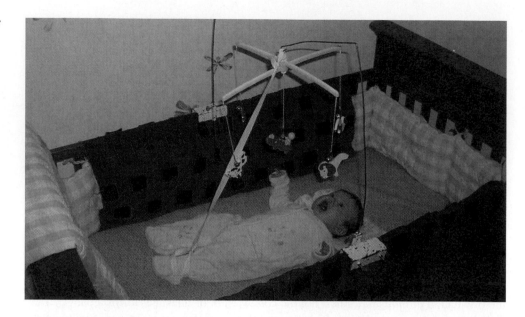

one of their legs by a ribbon. Even the 2-month-olds quickly learned that the mobile moved when they kicked. Six to eight days later, these infants showed they remembered what they had previously learned by starting to kick when they were placed in the crib with the mobile. But there were limits to how long they could remember the connection; after two weeks, they no longer spontaneously kicked when they saw the mobile.

However, it turns out that even after two weeks the memory had not totally faded. If the babies were shown the mobile the day before testing, their memory of the connection between kicking and making the mobile move could be reactivated. This finding differs somewhat from Piaget's observations of his son Laurent learning to move a rattle attached to one of his arms with a string. Just seeing the rattle suspended above his crib was not enough to get Laurent to resume moving his arm; Piaget had to shake the rattle for Laurent to remember the connection. But in both of these experiments the babies' memories were triggered by a perceptual reminder. In Laurent's case it was the *sound* of the rattle (probably its most salient feature); in Rovee-Collier's experiment it was the *sight* of the mobile's interesting shapes or colors. Apparently, young babies do form long-term memories, but they have trouble retrieving them without clear-cut cues. This kind of memory is called **cued recall** because the sight of the mobile or the sound of the rattle cues, or triggers, the memory of the appropriate behavior.

In the first six months, infants' memory is extremely *context-bound.* In other words, cued recall only occurs in contexts that are highly similar to the context in which the original experience occurred (Rovee-Collier, 1993). In Rovee-Collier's studies, memory was enhanced if babies were tested in a context identical to the one in which they learned that kicking would make the mobile move. Seemingly minor changes in the context, such as adding new objects to the mobile or changing the color of the crib liner, interfered with recall. Testing the baby in a different room also disrupted recall, even if the mobile and crib were unchanged. Babies 6 months of age and younger seem to have limited ability to generalize learning to new contexts.

In summary, babies show considerable development in memory abilities in the first six months of life:

- The length of time they can retain a memory increases.
- Their ability to remember relations between visual stimuli increases.
- They progress from being limited to simple recognition to engaging in cued recall.

However, even at 6 months, memory seems to be bound to particular contexts and to depend on immediate perceptual cues. The memory abilities that have been demonstrated

Cued recall:
A type of memory in which a familiar stimulus triggers recall of stored information.

in the first six months are consistent with Piaget's view that babies' memories are sensorimotor in nature and not true mental representations (Schneider and Bjorklund, 1998).

Memory In Later Infancy

Between 6 and 18 months, babies' memory abilities continue to improve. By the end of the first year of life, they show evidence of the ability to hold information in working memory briefly before using it to initiate some action. In addition, they show increases in the length of time they can retain memories and in their ability to engage in recall. The long-term memory skills that emerge in the second six months of life help to make possible the strong emotional bonds that infants develop with their parents at this time.

The clearest evidence for the development of working memory is 8- to 12-month-olds' gradual mastery of object permanence tasks that involve multiple hiding places. As already discussed, memory limitations are part of the explanation for the A, not-B error that is typical of babies in Piaget's sensorimotor stage 4. At 8 months, infants can find an object at a new location only after a delay of two seconds or less. The length of delay they can tolerate increases with age; by 15 months, they can still find the object after a delay of up to ten seconds (Matthews, Ellis, and Nelson, 1996). This increase indicates a growth in the ability to take action based on information held in working memory.

At the same time that infants are developing the ability to use information held in working memory for a short time, they are also increasing their ability to retain information over long periods of time (Carver, Bauer, and Nelson, 2000). One technique that has been used to study long-term memory in older infants is deferred imitation. In studies using this approach, an action or sequence of actions is modeled for babies, who are tested on their ability to reproduce it after a delay ranging from a few minutes to several months. Infants as young as 9 months show some ability to engage in deferred imitation. In a study by Andrew Meltzoff (1988), 9-month-olds watched adults demonstrate a number of actions with objects, such as pushing a button to produce a beeping sound, but were not immediately given a chance to do the actions themselves. The babies could reproduce the actions when they were shown the objects again after twenty-four hours, but not after a week.

Both the complexity of actions babies can remember and the length of time they can remember them increase with age. Eleven-month-olds can reproduce simple action sequences, such as putting a button through a slot in a container and shaking the container like a rattle, after a three-month delay (Mandler and McDonough, 1995). Sixteen-month-olds can recall longer action sequences, such as undressing and bathing a baby doll, for as long as eight months (Bauer, Hertsgaard, and Dow, 1994). These results suggest children are capable of deferred imitation much earlier than Piaget believed, if given perceptual cues to help them recall previously observed actions.

By the end of the first year infants also show evidence of *spontaneous* recall in everyday situations. In a study in which parents kept a record of infants' behavior that seemed to involve memory (Ashmead and Perlmutter, 1980), babies as young as 7 months showed evidence of memory for the usual locations of objects, such as where lotion was kept on a changing table. Older babies showed more instances of memory for unusual locations of objects, as in this example involving an 11-month-old:

> *Louise had been playing with a small doll bottle. She let it go on the floor and it rolled partially under the refrigerator. She went in her room and was playing for fifteen to twenty minutes when she found her doll and went back to where she had left her bottle, picked it up, and went back to her room (Ashmead and Perlmutter, 1980, p. 8).*

To summarize, improvements in memory abilities between 6 and 18 months include

- the emergence of working memory,
- continuing increases in how long memories are retained,

By age 1, babies show evidence of spontaneous recall by finding familiar objects when they have been left in unusual places.

- the ability to remember and reproduce increasingly complex action sequences, and
- increased ability to engage in both cued and spontaneous recall.

The memory improvements that occur between 6 and 18 months raise the possibility that infants start to use mental representation sooner than Piaget thought. During this time, memory retrieval becomes less and less dependent on perceptual cues.

Brain Development and Infant Memory

As you can see, even though memories of infancy are not carried forward into later life, infants clearly do form memories. How can this apparent paradox be explained? The answer seems to be that the term *memory* covers several rather different processes that emerge at different points in infancy and develop on different timetables. A distinction can be made between **explicit** or **declarative memory** and **implicit** or **procedural memory** (Johnson, 1997; Nelson, 1995, 1998). Explicit memory is conscious, involves mental representation of images or ideas, and can be explicitly stated or declared. Implicit memory is unconscious, involves memory for procedures or skills, and does not lend itself to explicit statement. For example, your memory of what your first bicycle looked like would be explicit or declarative; your memory of how to ride a bicycle would be implicit or procedural. You can probably form a mental image of your first bicycle, of the occasion when you received it, and perhaps even of yourself learning to ride it—all explicit memories. When you get on a bicycle and start riding, however, you do not consciously call up a memory of how to ride; instead, you simply exercise a well-learned skill—an implicit memory.

Chuck Nelson (1995, 1998) has proposed that early memory development involves several types of implicit and explicit memory systems, each of which depends on development in different parts of the brain. The types of memory that develop in the first six months of life, including those reflected in habituation and conditioning, are implicit and depend on such brain structures as the cerebellum and the hippocampus. The types of memory that develop after 6 months of age, including those reflected in advanced object permanence tasks and deferred imitation, are explicit and depend on activity in the cerebral cortex or connections between the cerebral cortex and the hippocampus (Carver, Bauer, and Nelson, 2000). This gradual development of different types of memory also helps to explain adults' inability to recall memories from infancy, a phenomenon known as **infantile amnesia.** (See A Closer Look on page 183.)

Explicit or declarative memory:
Memory that is conscious, involves mental representation of images or ideas, and can be explicitly stated or declared.

Implicit or procedural memory:
Memory that is unconscious, involves memory for procedures or skills, and does not lend itself to explicit statement.

Infantile amnesia:
Adults' inability to recall events from infancy.

A CLOSER LOOK

INFANTILE AMNESIA

Despite the fact that infants are clearly capable of forming relatively long-term memories of objects, people, and behaviors, **autobiographical memory**—enduring memory of one's own past—does not begin until after infancy. Most people's earliest memories date from around age 3½ to 4 years, although some people report memories from as early as age 2 (Schneider and Bjorklund, 1998; Usher and Neisser, 1993).

Freud was the first to use the term *infantile amnesia* to refer to this phenomenon. True to his psychosexual theory of development, Freud believed that memories from infancy are repressed because they are sexually charged and therefore not acceptable later in life. There is no evidence to support this idea; indeed, there seems to be no way to test it.

In all probability, several factors are involved in infantile amnesia. Traditionally, the basic issue has been whether infantile amnesia is a memory storage problem or a memory retrieval problem—is it that no autobiographical memories are stored during infancy, or is it that they are stored, but for some reason become unretrievable later?

As we have already seen, infants do store various sorts of memories, in some cases for relatively long periods of time. And there is evidence that 2- and 3-year-olds can remember events from late infancy. In one study, children who had repeatedly visited a university perceptual development laboratory between 6 weeks and 9 months of age showed some memory for their experiences when they returned to the lab two years later (Myers, Clifton, and Clarkson, 1987). In another study, 3-year-olds were able to remember aspects of a trip they had taken to Disney World 18 months earlier, when they were 2 years old or less (Hamond and Fivush, 1991). However, we do not know what the upper limit is for the endurance of infant memories. It is likely that immaturity of the cerebral cortex and its connections with the hippocampus interfere with *permanent* storage of memories in infancy (Bachevalier, 1991; Nelson, 1995).

The simplest explanation for infantile amnesia would be that infant memories simply decay and are lost due to the passage of time. This is unlikely because the age of earliest memories remains the same from middle childhood through adulthood; 8-year-olds and 88-year-olds both report first memories from around the same age (Nelson and Ross, 1980). Thus, it appears that some change in early childhood makes autobiographical memory possible.

At one time it was believed that the relevant change might be the emergence of language. That is, either long-term memory storage was impossible before language appeared, or memories stored by infants became inaccessible once they acquired language (Nelson and Ross, 1980). However, we now know that infants do store relatively long-term memories before they have language, and that young children who have language can still retrieve memories from before they started to talk.

It is possible that the emergence of autobiographical memory reflects a change in how memories are *organized*, rather than the emergence of an entirely new type of memory. For example, increasing language skill may help children organize memories into narratives that can be more easily retained and shared with others (Harley and Reese, 1999; Nelson, 1993). In addition, the emergence of a sense of self in early childhood may be necessary before true autobiographical memory can begin (Howe and Courage, 1997). Brain development is most likely involved, as increasingly complex connections in the cerebral cortex and between the cerebral cortex and the hippocampus make more organized and complete memories possible.

SOCIAL CONTEXT AND COGNITIVE DEVELOPMENT IN INFANCY

Autobiographical memory:
Enduring memory of one's own past.

Autobiographical Memory

Piaget argued that the role of the environment was to provide an overall context for children's active exploration, which led naturally to cognitive growth. Information-processing theorists frequently see the environment as providing specific pieces of information or contexts for practicing specific skills. However, many developmentalists, inspired by the work of Vygotsky, see both these views as far too limited in accounting for the influence of the environment.

Researchers working from a sociocultural perspective argue that adults structure the environment to foster the kind of learning they deem most important for children. This process begins in infancy and becomes increasingly pronounced as children grow older. For example, the pace of infants' cognitive development is affected by the amount and type of stimulation provided in their homes. Middle-class American parents often

Parents and Early Stimulation

surround their babies with objects designed to foster perceptual and cognitive development, such as toys and crib mobiles. Because of the value placed on academic achievement in the American middle class, some parents go even farther in attempting to accelerate their babies' cognitive development, often with limited success, as described below in Applying Research Findings. In families of lower socioeconomic status, where there is often less emphasis on academic achievement, infants tend to receive less cognitive stimulation, resulting in slower cognitive and linguistic development (Bradley and Corwyn, 2002; Hart and Risley, 1995).

Cross-cultural research on infants' sensorimotor development has found small variations in the ages at which babies can do Piaget's object permanence tasks, but striking similarities across cultures in the processes of sensorimotor development (Dasen and Heron, 1981; Gardiner and Kosmitzki, 2002). Infants around the world appear to share the same skills for exploring the world and manipulating objects. In one study French

APPLYING RESEARCH FINDINGS

Stimulation to Enhance Development

Sometimes, influenced by "experts," parents present their infants with special stimulation in hopes of dramatically advancing their cognitive development. Thus, we hear of parents reading to a baby every night even *before* birth, or buying flash cards of letters, words, or numbers to get a toddler started on the basics of reading and math.

These parents usually make two important errors in reasoning. *First,* they assume stimulation that works at one age must be good at other ages. But what fosters development in an older child does not always work for a younger one. Flash cards can help a second grader master arithmetic, but they have little value for a baby. Parents can do more to foster cognitive development through normal interactions with their babies, talking to them, responding to their vocalizations, and playing games like peekaboo. *Second,* these parents assume accelerating some aspect of cognitive development will lead to higher academic performance and a higher IQ. However, earlier does not always mean better in the long run. A child taught to read at 4 is not likely to be a better reader at 21 than a child who started reading at the more typical age of 6.

When Stimulation Programs Are Important

Special infant stimulation programs do have their place; for example, premature babies can benefit from them. These infants are deprived of the tactile and motion stimulation experienced in the uterus during the last weeks of gestation. In addition, prematurity is often associated with poverty and maternal stress, factors that can place babies at risk for developmental problems.

Successful programs for premature infants provide age-appropriate stimulation. In the weeks after birth, babies receive tactile stimulation, such as handling, rocking, and the use of water beds. Such stimulation has been found to help prevent the motor and perceptual problems that can occur in preterm infants, probably by promoting central nervous system development.

Longer-term programs typically provide more varied forms of stimulation and support. In one program, low-income families with premature babies were visited weekly at home for the first year, and the parents were helped to engage the baby in games and activities to foster cognitive, language, and social development. In the second and third years, home visits occurred twice a month, the children attended a child development center daily, and a parents' support group met six times a year. Compared with children in a control group who received only routine pediatric care and referral services, the children in this program experienced cognitive benefits. At age 2, they scored significantly higher on the Bayley Scales of Infant Development, and at age 3 they scored higher on the preschool Wechsler Intelligence Scales. This program also promoted a more effective parent-child collaboration (Gross, Spiker, and Haynes, 1997).

Why Infant Stimulation Is Effective

From a Piagetian perspective, the optimal environment for cognitive development gives infants opportunities to explore the world in ways appropriate to their current level of functioning. From an information-processing perspective, stimulation programs should provide specific experiences that fit into infants' existing knowledge structures. From a Vygotskian perspective, infants should not only have appropriately stimulating experiences, but should also develop an interaction system with caregivers that will support later social transmission of knowledge. The program described here, as well as others that have been successful (e.g., Campbell and Ramey, 1994), does all of this by simultaneously providing stimulating, age-appropriate experiences and fostering social interaction between the infant and adults.

Infants around the world manipulate objects in similar ways; for them, the physical characteristics of an object are more relevant than the object's cultural meaning.

babies and babies from the Ivory Coast in Africa handled strings of paper clips and plastic tubes in strikingly similar ways, even though paper clips and plastic tubes were not familiar objects for the African babies (Dasen and Heron, 1981). One reason for this is that the physical properties of objects are more salient for infants than their specific cultural meanings and uses.

However, infants vary in the opportunities they have for exploration and the types of objects available for manipulation. Middle-class American babies typically enjoy considerable "floor freedom" to crawl and explore the environment in their homes. American parents often go to great lengths to make such exploration possible by baby-proofing their homes with electrical outlet covers, special latches on cupboard doors, and safety gates on stairs. In many cultures located in tropical areas, babies spend very little time on the ground because of dangers such as cooking fires, insects, and poisonous snakes (LeVine, 1988). Over time, these differences in infant care practices produce differences in motor and cognitive development.

With help from adults, infants can also learn to perform specialized motor skills at an earlier than usual age. According to *The Guinness Book of World Records,* a baby named Parks Bonifay learned to water-ski before the age of 8 months. We can be fairly sure that Parks did not acquire this skill simply by being raised in an environment in which water and water skis were available for him to explore freely. Rather, we would expect that this accomplishment resulted from intense instruction from the adults around him and that waterskiing was highly valued by his family. It is also likely that Parks was already somewhat advanced in his overall motor development; most 8-month-olds could probably not be taught to water-ski, no matter how much instruction they were given.

Piagetians have argued that such direct training is not really development because it consists only of isolated skills that are not part of an integrated system for doing, thinking, and understanding. In some cases they may be correct, but there are other cases in which a skill taught early in life is culturally adaptive and becomes an important component in later development. For example, many Norwegian children begin to learn to cross-country ski as soon as they can walk and continue to develop and engage in this skill throughout life. In Polynesia, infants often learn to swim even before they can walk; for them, swimming is not just culturally valued but has obvious survival value.

The Vygotskian perspective makes several important observations that contribute to our understanding of cognitive development. First, infants frequently are more like guided tourists than like explorers as they develop cognitively—that is, what they are finding out about the world is what the adults around them already know. Second, infants in some cases can learn more rapidly from adults and in other cases are *only* able to learn things with substantial support from adults. Third, the skills that children learn from adults are almost always highly valued in those adults' social context or culture.

More on Vygotsky

INDIVIDUAL DIFFERENCES IN INFANT COGNITIVE SKILLS

Both Maggie and Mikey were active, alert babies, but they did not follow the same developmental timetable. Much to Christine's delight as a first-time mother, Maggie seemed to do everything ahead of schedule—rolling over, sitting up, crawling, walking, saying her first word. By comparison, Mikey seemed to lag a

Table 5.2 Select Items from Bayley Scales of Infant Development

Age (and Range) in Months	Item
0.1	Responds to sound of bell
0.7 (.3–2)	Eyes follow moving person
1.6 (.5–4)	Turns eyes to light
1.9 (1–4)	Blinks at shadow of hand
2.4 (1–5)	Reacts to disappearance of face
3.1 (1–5)	Reaches for dangling ring
3.8 (2–6)	Inspects own hands
4.1 (2–6)	Reaches for cube
4.4 (2–6)	Eye-hand coordination in reaching
5.4 (3–12)	Smiles at mirror image
5.8 (4–11)	Lifts cups with handle
7.1 (5–10)	Pulls string adaptively: secures ring
8.1 (6–12)	Uncovers toy
9.1 (6–14)	Responds to verbal request
10.4 (7–15)	Attempts to imitate scribble
12.0 (8–18)	Turns pages of book
12.5 (9–18)	Imitates words (Record words used)
14.2 (10–23)	Says 2 words (Note words)
16.7 (13–21)	Builds tower of 3 cubes

Source: "Bayley Scales of Infant Development." Copyright © 1969 by the Psychological Corporation. Reproduced by permission. All rights reserved. "Bayley Scales of Infant Development" is a registered trademark of The Psychological Corporation.

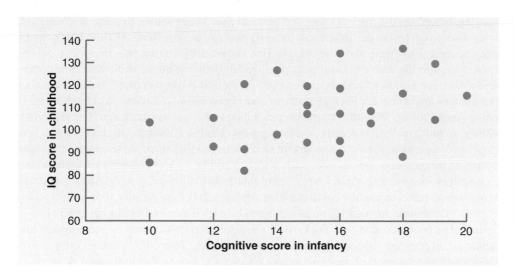

Figure 5.8
RELATIONSHIP BETWEEN INFANT TEST SCORES AND CHILDHOOD IQ
These data illustrate a correlation of .40 between a cognitive measure in infancy and an IQ measure in childhood. Note that there is so much variability that it is not possible to accurately predict an individual child's IQ score by knowing the cognitive score that child achieved in infancy.

little bit behind. When Christine consulted her baby book, she was relieved to find that he was actually reaching the major developmental milestones at fairly typical ages. Still, she wondered if the differences between them meant that Maggie would also do better in school.

Research confirms that normal babies vary considerably in the ages at which they reach various developmental milestones, and babies the same age often respond differently to the same task. Developmentalists have designed a variety of tests to measure these differences, including the Bayley Scales of Infant Development. Table 5.2 shows some of the items contained in the Bayley Scales. Notice that the items designed to assess younger babies measure attention and sensorimotor coordination, while those designed to assess older infants and toddlers are more cognitive in nature.

Just as Christine wondered about the differences between Maggie and Mikey, developmental psychologists have wondered whether a baby's performance on infant tests can predict that child's performance on cognitive tests in later periods of development. In a longitudinal study that took many years to complete, Nancy Bayley (1949) tested a group of children repeatedly from the time they were 3 months old until they were 18 years old. She found that test scores at different ages did not reliably correlate with one another until after age 4. Other studies produced similar results; scores on developmental tests in infancy and toddlerhood were not very predictive of later IQ (e.g., Honzik, 1983). Many developmentalists took this to mean that individual differences in cognitive skills during infancy were not stable. However, a more likely explanation is that infant tests such as the Bayley measure different abilities than those measured by IQ tests for older children and adults (Bornstein and Sigman, 1986; Fagan and McGrath, 1981).

More recently, researchers have found other measures of infant cognitive ability that seem to be more closely related to cognitive skills in later developmental periods. Robert McCall and Michael Carriger (1993) reviewed the results of twenty-three studies that measured infants' performance on memory tasks and then measured IQ in the same children when they were older. McCall and Carriger found moderate predictability of later IQ from early performance on memory tasks, with a correlation of about .40 between tests in infancy and later in childhood.

To illustrate what this relationship means, Figure 5.8 shows a set of data that would produce a correlation of .40 between infant cognitive scores and childhood IQ scores. In this data set, children who score higher on the infant test generally also score higher on the later test, but there are exceptions. Some children who score high in infancy score average or below average later. Others who score low or average as infants later perform well above average. Children with the same scores on the infant test receive widely

Infant Assessment

varying scores on the later IQ test; for example, the chart shows that the five children with a score of 16 on the infant test have IQ scores ranging from 90 (just below average) to over 130 (well above average). This data set illustrates two important points. First, although the data demonstrate a relationship between infant skills and later cognitive ability for *groups* of infants, the level of prediction is too low to be useful in making predictions about the intellectual skills of *individual* infants. Second, although there is some predictability from infancy to later childhood, there is no indication that cognitive ability is biologically fixed early in development. On the contrary, the data suggest that experience is critical for the development of cognitive skills, since children with the same scores in infancy can end up with such widely varying IQ scores later in childhood.

Recent longitudinal studies have found that information-processing factors, such as how long it takes infants to habituate to a stimulus and how rapidly they process perceptual information, predict IQ as late as age 11 or 12 (Rose and Feldman, 1995, 1997). John Colombo (Colombo and Frick, 1999) believes that two variables measured in the newer infant tests are particularly important for predicting future IQ: speed of information processing and capacity of working memory. Colombo argues that individual differences in these two variables may be influenced by both heredity and experience.

To summarize, traditional tests of infant cognitive abilities, which include many measures of attentional and motor skills, do not predict later performance on intelligence tests. Newer measures that focus on information-processing skills, seem to be more closely related to later cognitive abilities.

ADVANCES AND LIMITATIONS: AN OVERVIEW

At birth Malcolm responded to the world using inborn reflexes. When the side of his face was gently stroked, he automatically turned his head. When an object touched his mouth, he automatically sucked. Specific stimuli triggered specific responses, with no conscious intention by Malcolm. When we see Malcolm seven months later, the contrast is dramatic. He is purposefully reaching for and inspecting Teresa's drawings, trying out motor actions and observing the results. He is a busy, active learner trying to understand his world.

A great deal of cognitive development occurs in the first two years of life. Starting from a set of inborn abilities, babies develop an increasingly refined understanding of the world and an ever greater purposefulness in their behavior. In Piaget's terms, they gradually make the transition from a *reflexive* organism to a *reflective* organism—from responding automatically to stimuli to being able to think about, plan, and control their own behavior. These developmental trends are very important both in their own right and as preparation for the verbal world of the toddler.

Much of the research on infant cognitive development in the last forty years has been done in response to Piaget's pioneering studies. We now know Piaget underestimated the speed with which infants develop a basic understanding of the world and become capable of some form of mental representation. But we also know he got many things right in his description of infant behavior and the overall transformation that occurs during infancy. In the beginning, babies are limited to perceptual and motor information about the world, and the early memories they form are implicit and procedural in nature. Gradually, their cognitive abilities become conceptual and their memories explicit and declarative—in other words, they become able to think about the world as well as acting on it.

Looking across various areas of cognitive functioning, infants seem to make major leaps in development at about 3 to 4 months and again at about 7 to 8 months, ages that correspond to important points in brain development, as mentioned in Chapter 4. At 3 to 4 months, they begin to understand basic characteristics of objects and relations between objects, to form perceptual categories, and to remember relationships between visual stimuli. At 7 to 8 months, the complexity and flexibility of their understanding of objects increases, they begin to form conceptual categories, and the ability to hold information in working memory emerges.

But these developments do not take place in a vacuum, and they are not simply the result of preprogrammed brain development. As we saw in Chapter 4, brain development is influenced by experience and the environment. Increasing connections in the cerebral cortex make possible many cognitive advances in the second six months of life, but a stimulating physical and social environment facilitates the formation of those connections. And as we suggested at the beginning of this chapter, infants take an active role in influencing their own development. Through their efforts at mastery and the mistakes they make in the process, they learn to adapt their actions to better suit environmental demands.

Despite the great cognitive advances that take place during infancy, significant cognitive limitations remain. Infants' knowledge and cognitive skills are often fragile and not yet widely generalizable. The capacity for long-term memory remains somewhat limited. And, even though infants appear to develop mental representation earlier than Piaget thought, the acquisition of language and related symbolic abilities is just beginning.

Chapter Summary

Introduction

This chapter has three major themes:

- Cognitive development is orderly.
- Infants are active participants in their own development.
- Infant cognitive development is marked by both advances and limitations.

Piaget's Theory of Infant Cognitive Development

The following are key assumptions in Piaget's theory:

- Infants' understanding of the world is limited to what they know through sensory awareness and motor acts.
- Infants actively construct an understanding of the world.

In Piaget's view, cognitive development occurs because of two key processes:

- **Adaptation,** the process by which children change to function more effectively in their environment. It is the joint product of **assimilation** and **accommodation.**
- **Equilibration,** a self-regulatory process that produces increasingly effective adaptations.

Piaget identified six stages in the **sensorimotor period** of cognitive development:

- Stage 1 (birth to 1 month): minor refinements of inborn reflexes.
- Stage 2 (1 to 4 months): **primary circular reactions.**
- Stage 3 (4 to 8 months): **secondary circular reactions.**
- Stage 4 (8 to 12 months): **coordination of schemes.**
- Stage 5 (12 to 18 months): **tertiary circular reactions.**
- Stage 6 (18 to 24 months): emergence of **symbolic** or **representational thought.**

Challenges to Piaget's Theory

Major areas of disagreement with Piaget's theory include:

- the timetable for the emergence of cognitive skills,
- the existence of qualitatively distinct developmental stages,
- the range of innate abilities, and
- the source of infants' cognitive limitations.

Infants' Understanding of the Physical World

Piaget provided an account of the development of **object permanence.** Further research on the development of the object concept suggests:

- Piaget was fairly accurate about the *sequence* in which an understanding of the object concept is acquired, but he underestimated the *rate* of acquisition.
- Research using looking behavior and habituation suggests a basic understanding of object permanence emerges several months sooner than Piaget believed.
- However, infants' early knowledge of object properties is incomplete, and mature object search behavior does not appear until much later.

Research on infants' understanding of relations between objects reveals:

- Between 4 and 8 months, babies develop a rudimentary grasp of relations between objects, but initially they can apply these concepts only in simple situations.
- Between 8 and 12 months, the complexity and flexibility of their understanding increase.

Research on infants' understanding of number indicates:

- They appear to have some awareness of number virtually from birth.

- The complexity and usefulness of their understanding increase with age.

Research on infants' categorization skills shows:

- Infants begin to form *perceptual* categories by the time they are 3 months old.
- By 7 months, infants form *conceptual* categories.
- By 14 months, they clearly apply categories in their behavior with objects.
- Early conceptual categories are rather broad, with specific subcategories appearing around 18 months.

Memory Development in Infancy

Development in memory abilities during the first six months of life includes:

- progress from simple recognition to cued recall,
- an increase in the length of time a memory can be retained, and
- increased ability to remember relationships between visual stimuli.

Improvements in memory abilities between 6 and 18 months include:

- the emergence of working memory,
- continuing increases in how long memories are retained,
- the ability to remember and reproduce increasingly complex action sequences, and
- increased ability to engage in both cued and spontaneous recall.

The memory improvements in later infancy raise the possibility that infants start to use mental representation sooner than Piaget thought.

Early memory development involves several types of implicit and explicit memory systems, each of which depends on development in different parts of the brain:

- The types of memory that develop in the first six months of life are **implicit** and depend on such brain structures as the cerebellum and the hippocampus.
- The types of memory that develop after six months of age are **explicit** and depend on activity in the cerebral

cortex or connections between the cerebral cortex and the hippocampus.

Social Context and Cognitive Development in Infancy

Researchers working from a sociocultural perspective argue that adults structure the environment to foster the kinds of learning they deem most important for children, a process that begins in infancy and becomes increasingly pronounced as children grow older.

Individual Differences in Infant Cognitive Skills

Longitudinal studies have revealed that:

- Traditional tests of infant cognitive abilities, which include many measures of attentional and motor skills, do not predict later performance on intelligence tests.
- Newer measures that focus on information-processing skills seem to be more closely related to later cognitive abilities.

Advances and Limitations: An Overview

A great deal of cognitive development occurs in the first two years of life:

- Starting from a set of inborn abilities, babies develop an increasingly refined understanding of the world and an ever greater purposefulness in their behavior.
- Gradually, infants become able to think about the world as well as acting on it.

Infants seem to make major leaps in development at about 3 to 4 months and again at about 7 to 8 months, ages that correspond to important points in brain development.

Despite the great cognitive advances that take place during infancy, limitations remain:

- Infants' knowledge and cognitive skills are often fragile and not widely generalizable.
- The capacity for long-term memory remains limited.
- The acquisition of language and related symbolic abilities is just beginning.

Review Questions

Introduction

1. What are some major characteristics of cognitive development in infancy?

Piaget's Theory of Infant Cognitive Development

2. Explain the major assumptions and processes in Piaget's theory of infant cognitive development.

3. Describe the six stages in Piaget's theory of infant cognitive development.

Challenges to Piaget's Theory

4. What issues have other researchers raised about Piaget's theory?

Infants' Understanding of the Physical World

5. What did Piaget and more recent researchers say about the development of the object concept?
6. Summarize the development of infants' understanding of causality and other relations between objects, number, and categorization.

Memory Development in Infancy

7. Summarize the development of memory abilities in early and later infancy.
8. How is brain development involved in infant memory?

Social Context and Cognitive Development in Infancy

9. How does social context influence cognitive development in infancy?

Individual Differences in Infant Cognitive Skills

10. How well do measures of individual differences in infant cognitive skills predict later intelligence?

Advances and Limitations: An Overview

11. Summarize the major advances and limitations in cognitive development during the first two years of life.

Application and Observation

1. Try Piaget's object permanence tasks on one or more infants between the ages of 3 and 24 months. You will need a toy small enough to fit in your hand but large enough to attract an infant's attention, two napkins or washcloths, and a piece of cardboard about 11" × 13" to serve as a screen. Have one of the parents sit across from you at a small table or on the floor, holding the baby in his or her lap. Then proceed through the following tasks described on pp. 169–171: tracking a moving object, tracking a moving object behind a screen, searching for partially covered objects, searching for completely covered objects, changing hiding places, and invisible displacement of objects. Stop when the baby has failed to complete two tasks in a row. How does each baby's behavior compare to Piaget's predictions? How would you explain any differences between what the baby did and what Piaget predicted? What other characteristics of infant cognitive or perceptual development can you see in the baby's behavior?

2. Write down your earliest memory in as much detail as you can, including your best guess as to how old you were at the time. Interview several other people of varying ages about their earliest memories, including their best guesses as to how old they were. What similarities and differences do you see in the various memories you've collected from different people?

3. If you know someone with a 2- or 3-year-old, interview the parent and child about a recent salient event in the child's life (a birthday, a major holiday, a trip or other special occasion, etc.). Ask the parent to identify a major event from the past few months that the child shows signs of remembering, such as talking about it, wanting to look at pictures of it, asking when it will happen again, and so on. Tell the parent that you're interested in finding out what the child remembers about the event and that first you want to see what the child will recall without prompting. Begin with open-ended questions ("What did you do on your birthday?"). Then follow up with more specific questions ("Did you have a party? Did you have cake?"). Finally, see what the child can recall with prompting from the parent.

4. Visit a toy store and look at the toys labeled as appropriate for infants aged 6 months to 2 years. How well do they fit what researchers have found out about infants' cognitive abilities? How might an actual infant respond to them? How are they different from toys for younger infants?

6 Infant Social and Emotional Development

193

O *ne day 4-month-old Mikey woke up early from his morning nap. Cooing contentedly to himself, he began kicking. The toys on his crib gym jangled, and he kicked more. Then he waved his arms and batted a bright red ring, gurgling happily as it bobbed in response. Christine arrived and stood by the crib, smiling down at the baby. Mikey's face brightened. He broke into a broad grin and kicked his feet harder.*

Eight months later, Uncle Dan was showing 12-month-old Mikey a new mechanical toy. When he released it, it made a loud clacking noise. Frightened, Mikey turned away and scurried to Christine, raising his arms to be picked up. In Christine's arms he looked at the toy again and began smiling and pointing at it.

This chapter is about the beginnings of emotion and the emergence of infants' attachment relationships with caregivers, usually parents. Such relationships are the culmination of all cognitive, social, and emotional development in the first year of life. Initially, babies are attracted to social encounters; human faces and voices engage their interest. With development, infants learn to sustain attention, to follow complex changes in others' voices and faces, and to tolerate the excitement caused by social stimulation. Soon babies begin to go beyond reacting to others; the coordinated turn-taking of more advanced social interaction emerges. For example, when 6-month-old Mikey smiles and kicks his feet, his father or mother touches and talks to him. Mikey chortles and kicks again, and his parent smiles and touches him some more.

For Mikey to form a true attachment to Christine, he must learn to differentiate her from others. He must do more than simply recognize his mother; he must understand she is a specific, constant person. This understanding is related to the concept of object permanence discussed in Chapter 5, which emerges in the second six months of life. By the time Mikey is 8 or 10 months old, he will show he has developed this understanding by becoming distressed when Christine leaves him with someone unfamiliar. He will know his mother still exists when out of sight, and when distressed he will want her *specifically*. Given his involvement with Frank, Mikey will show many similar reactions with him.

As you learned in Chapter 5, during the second six months babies develop expectations and purposefulness. Eight-month-olds are surprised when objects magically vanish, angry when intended actions are thwarted, and joyous when goals are achieved. Events and feelings are now intimately connected; perception, cognition, and emotion are integrated (Sroufe, 1995). Experiences are categorized partly by emotions associated with them. For example, a 10-month-old may react negatively to a doctor *immediately* upon sight, evaluating the doctor in terms of the feelings he or she generated at a recent visit, without waiting to see what will happen this time.

Attachments between infants and caregivers develop in the context of this differentiating emotional and social world. By the end of the first year, infants feel secure in the presence of their caregivers, turn to them purposefully when distressed (as Mikey did when frightened by the mechanical toy), and organize play and exploration around them. Caregivers take center stage in infants' lives and provide the basis for their expectations about responsiveness of the environment.

In this chapter we trace babies' emerging capacity for social relations from the first weeks of life. First we examine the developments of the first six months, when newborns develop into active social partners who can respond to social overtures and engage in social give-and-take. Next we consider developments in the second six months, when infants acquire specific attachments to caregivers, and how such relationships affect their growing capacities for emotional expression and regulation. Then we discuss individual differences in social and emotional development, including variations in the quality of attachment relationships and in individual temperament. Finally, we turn to the overall importance of early care and consider whether early experience has special significance for development.

Babies' emotional and social development is centered around their emerging relationships with their caregivers.

Questions to Think About As You Read

- How are infants' growing social and emotional abilities related to changes in their perceptual, motor, and cognitive abilities?
- What can parents and other caregivers do to provide the best possible environment for early social and emotional development?

DEVELOPMENT IN THE FIRST SIX MONTHS

For decades researchers have probed the competencies of newborns. This research has produced two extreme views: one historical, the other recent. The historical view is associated with the nineteenth-century psychologist William James. James believed human infants were born with no perceptual or social skills whatsoever, that their world was meaningless and chaotic, a "blooming, buzzing confusion." In direct opposition is the recent view that newborns are socially advanced and can imitate complex behaviors, infer others' perspectives, and feel disappointment when social expectations aren't met (Aitken and Trevarthen, 1997; Meltzoff and Moore, 1989). In this view, even very young infants are seen as possessing desires, expectations, purpose, and will.

From a developmental perspective, neither view is satisfactory. The first is at odds with contemporary research. As discussed in Chapter 4, newborns have many competencies; their world is not meaningless confusion. The second view is a useful antidote to the first, but also runs counter to important findings. Because the brain's cerebral cortex is not fully functional at birth, it is hard to imagine how newborns could possess expectations and purpose (Nelson, 1994; Saarni, Mumme, and Campos, 1998). Moreover, we need not assume newborns are socially competent in order to account for the things they soon become able to do. We need only assume that their capacities prepare them to become part of a social system under normal caregiving circumstances. (See A Closer Look on page 196.)

A CLOSER LOOK

NEWBORN PRECOCITY

Parents and some researchers often attribute very advanced capacities to newborns. These capacities include the ability to understand emotional reactions or goals of others, a desire to share, and even the capacity for disappointment when social expectations are violated. Given the lack of development of the cerebral cortex, as discussed in Chapter 4, such capacities seem unlikely. How, then, can we explain what appear to be amazingly precocious social and emotional capacities in young infants? Usually, a simpler answer can be found in infants' more basic cognitive and perceptual capacities.

Example 1: A researcher slowly turns her head and looks at a wall on the far right. A newborn facing the researcher turns the same way. Is this to share in what the researcher is seeing? More likely, the infant is simply tracking the horizontal movement of the researcher's face.

Example 2: Four-month-olds distinguish toothy smiling faces from sad faces. This seems like a remarkable ability to interpret facial expressions, but it turns out that babies this age don't discriminate sad faces from faces showing nontoothy smiles. It is not the emotional meaning, but the greater contrast of teeth showing that allows babies this age to distinguish between the two faces (Saarni et al., 1998). Research has even shown that young infants' reactions to faces are similar whether they are upside down or right side up, because infants in the first months react to specific features rather than meaning (Walker-Andrews, 1997).

Example 3: If a parent sits stone-faced and silent in front of a 4-month-old, after a time the child will begin to fuss or even cry hard. Does this reaction indicate the baby is feeling disappointment or experiencing a violation of social expectation about his or her parent's behavior? Perhaps, but more likely something simpler is going on, especially since a similar reaction can be elicited by an unresponsive stranger's face. In fact, in babies this age *any* situation that combines highly salient and familiar elements (such as the parent's face) with unfamiliar elements (such as the unresponsiveness) tends to produce a response of wariness escalating to distress after a few minutes (Sroufe, 1995).

By age 6 months, if not earlier, the neural underpinnings of face recognition are established in the brain (de Haan and Nelson, 1999). By the end of the first year infants do have some remarkable social and emotional capacities (Thompson, 1998). They have beginning social expectations, preferences for particular people, the capacity to purposefully signal certain desires, and basic emotions such as surprise, anger, and fear. But they are not born with these capacities, and most are not yet present in early infancy. Instead, young infants produce responses that caregivers often *interpret* as social. Even though this interpretation is inaccurate, it turns out to be good for babies because it causes parents to try harder to engage them in interaction, which fosters their social and emotional development.

The Newborn as Preadapted to Social Exchanges

Newborns come equipped with certain predispositions that enable them to participate in early social exchanges, provided they receive responsive caregiving (Ainsworth and Bell, 1974; Fogel, 1993; Sander, 1975; Thompson, 1998). These predispositions, many of which were discussed in Chapter 4, *preadapt* newborns to become social. But this social potential will unfold only in a certain developmental context, much as the turning on of genes in certain cells depends on surrounding cells during prenatal development. If caregivers provide babies with appropriate stimulation and are responsive to their inborn reactions, then—and only then—coordinated social exchanges become possible and ultimately lead to genuine social partnerships (Schore, 1994).

One predisposition of newborns that preadapts them for social interaction is *a built-in ability to signal psychological and physiological needs in ways adults can interpret and are likely to respond to.* Even newborns can signal their needs by crying. Remember that babies cry whenever their nervous systems are overly excited. Newborns' cries are purely reflexive, not intentional; young babies do not cry to be defiant or get their way. Nevertheless, their cries become social signals when caring adults respond by administering to their needs. This is a subtle but important point; a newborn's behaviors serve the function of social communication only to the extent that others treat those behaviors as communications (Fogel, 1993).

Another predisposition of newborns that helps make early social exchanges possible is *the capacity to detect contingencies in the environment.* Infants notice events caused by their behaviors and repeat these behaviors (Dunham and Dunham, 1990; Papoušek, Papoušek, and Koester, 1986). Their behaviors often produce reactions from their caregivers, such as getting mother to smile and talk by looking at her and cooing. A sensitivity to these contingencies preadapts infants to become part of a social system (Thompson, 1998).

Closely related to newborns' inclination to detect and respond to contingencies is *a built-in attraction to social stimuli*. As discussed in Chapter 4, newborns are naturally attentive to light/dark contrasts and to movement. Since faces have light/dark contrasts and adults tend to smile and nod when looking at babies, newborns are drawn to faces. This attraction does not occur because newborns recognize the social significance of faces, but simply because their visual systems are especially sensitive to the kind of stimulation faces provide. Newborns' inspection of faces is further encouraged by the fact that the baby's face is usually about eight inches away from the caregiver's during early feeding, an ideal distance for newborns' limited visual acuity. Newborns are also predisposed to respond to human speech. Babies discriminate among speech sounds at a very early age, and they can hear quite well in the pitch range of human voices, including the squeaky baby-talk voice many parents use (Fogel, 1993). In addition, newborns have built-in coordination between hearing and head movements, allowing them to turn automatically in the direction of a voice and look at the speaker's face.

A final predisposition that helps the newborn become part of a social system is *the baby's inclination to fall in step with the caregiver's behavior* (Fogel, 1993). In one study, babies being given up for adoption were cared for twenty-four hours a day by one of two nurses, Nurse A or Nurse B (Sander, 1975). Nurse A did not respond as quickly as Nurse B to her babies' cries of distress, but when she did respond her caretaking was less hurried and less perfunctory. Nurse B's behavior was somewhat abrupt and fragmented. Within ten days, the infants in Nurse A's charge had more regular sleeping and eating patterns than those cared for by Nurse B. The behavior of Nurse A's babies seemed to mirror her own easygoing style. Even more striking, when infants were suddenly switched from one nurse to the other, they showed marked disruptions in sleeping and eating.

Newborns show a range of tendencies and abilities that prepare them to enter the social world very rapidly. Yet it is not accurate to refer to newborns as innately social, in the sense of being able to have organized, intentional interaction with other people. Instead, newborns are exquisitely attuned to *becoming* social, provided that responsive social partners are available. The development of this true social give-and-take is the subject we turn to next.

The Origins of Reciprocity

Over the first months of life, developmental changes take place that set the stage for the emergence of true social interactions involving mutual exchanges, or **reciprocity**, between partners. Babies stay alert for increasingly long periods, during which they actively engage the environment. At the same time, they become able to control attention, coordinate looking and reaching, and turn toward or away from stimulation *voluntarily*. Coupled with this is their ability to punctuate attentive looking with smiles, coos, and actions. Parents take advantage of these newfound capacities to build longer and more complex chains of interaction with their infants. Consider this example of John Williams interacting with 4-month-old Malcolm:

> *Hi there, big fella. Whatcha lookin' at? Can you look at me? That's right. Hey! Your ol' man's gonna getcha. Yes, he is. (Brief pause.) He's gonna getcha and gobble ya right up. What do you think of that? Come on. Come on, you little tiger. Let me see those gums. Hmmm? (Pause.) Yeah, that's right . . . that's right. (Malcolm smiles broadly and bobs his head. His father responds in kind.) Well, now, are ya gonna say somethin'? Are ya? (John nods his head and widens his eyes.) Come on! (He pauses again, and Malcolm starts cycling his arms and kicking his feet.) Come ooooon! (Longer pause. Then Malcolm gurgles happily.) Yeah, that's right! (John's smile broadens and he laughs.)*

Reciprocity:
True social interactions involving mutual exchanges between partners.

/dehart5

Parent-Infant Interaction

[Handwritten margin note: A newborns have built-in coordination between hearing & head movements, allowing them to turn automatically in the direction of a voice & look @ the speaker's face]

Parents provide the framework for increasingly complex interactions with infants.

Social learning theorists would emphasize the mutual reinforcement at the end of this sequence; both father and son derive pleasure from it, making it likely to be repeated. But the broader learning context is also important. Notice how John frames the interaction (Fogel, 1993; Stern, 1985). He waits until Malcolm seems receptive, then begins with gentle vocal and visual stimulation. He builds Malcolm's interest by varying the stimulation and gradually increasing its intensity. He takes cues from Malcolm in timing his words and actions. Equally important, he pauses and waits for Malcolm to take turns in the dialogue, and he reinforces Malcolm's vocal behavior. Detailed observational studies show that exchanges between caregivers and infants become more varied and complex through such interactions over time (Jaffe et al., 2001; Papoušek et al., 1986).

T. Berry Brazelton, who has studied parent-infant dialogues extensively, sees the caregiver as providing a *holding* framework for the baby. The caregiver holds the infant with hands, eyes, voice, smile, and changes from one form of stimulation to another. "All these holding experiences are opportunities for the infant to learn how to contain *himself,* how to control motor responses, and how to attend for longer and longer periods. They amount to a kind of learning about organization of behavior in order to attend" (Brazelton, Koslowski, and Main, 1974, p. 70).

Infants can play their part and share in the joyful outcome only if caregivers appropriately guide the interaction (Fogel, 1993; Thompson, 1998). The parent must draw forth and enhance the infant's attention and involvement, pacing and modifying the stimulation in coordination with signs from the baby, a process known as **attunement** (Stern, 1985). Attunement is part of a more general style of behavior known as **sensitive care,** which involves being aware of a baby's feelings and needs and responding to them promptly and effectively (Ainsworth, Blehar, Waters and Wall, 1978). Sensitive caregivers do not overstimulate an infant by continuing stimulation when the baby is not ready for it, nor are they chronically unresponsive. In our example, John must allow the level of tension to rise and fall in its natural course. He cannot force interactions when Malcolm is unreceptive. If Malcolm temporarily looks away to slow the pace of the stimulation, John must wait for Malcolm to indicate his readiness to continue. If John pursues him, Malcolm is likely to cry.

Caregivers vary considerably in the sensitivity of their interactions with their babies; recall Karen's unsuccessful attempts to engage Meryl with the Oscar the Grouch toy in our earlier story. (Figure 6.1 portrays the timing of caregiver and infant behaviors in sensitive and insensitive interactions.) However, sensitive care can be learned in the natural course of tending to a baby; through hours of interaction most parents become able to read the moods and signals of their infant and modify their own behavior accordingly.

Attunement:
Caregivers' adjustment of the stimulation they provide in response to signs from the infant.

Sensitive care:
A caregiving style in which the caregiver attends to the infant's needs and responds to them promptly and effectively.

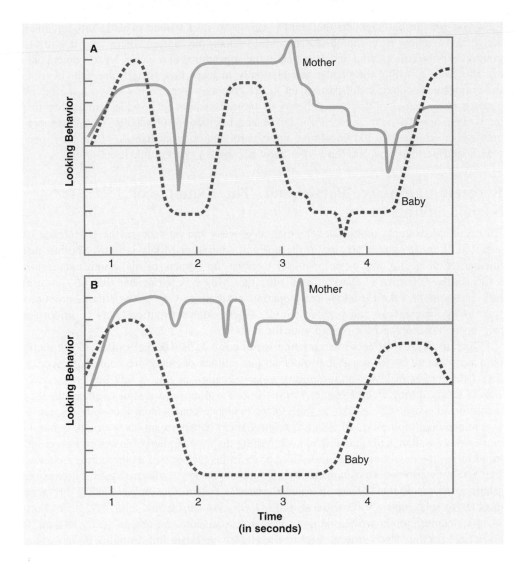

Figure 6.1
SENSITIVE AND INSENSITIVE
INTERACTIONS
These graphs show the reactions
of two different mothers to their
babies' efforts to pace the
interaction by turning away. The
dashed line shows the baby's
looking behavior. When the
dashed line is below the
horizontal center line, the baby is
looking away from the mother.
The solid line shows the
mother's behaviors (talking,
touching, making faces, etc.).
The mother in part (A) shows a
pattern of sensitive care,
reducing her stimulation when
the baby looks away; he soon
looks back to her and she
stimulates again. The mother in
part (B) keeps stimulating her
baby, which seems to keep him
away for a long time. *(Source:
Adapted from Brazelton,
Koslowski, and Main, 1974.)*

The beginnings of this coordinated interaction can be seen in the feeding of a new-born (Fogel, 1993). As mentioned in Chapter 4, newborns suck in a burst-pause pattern, a succession of rapid sucks followed by a period with little or no sucking. Lower brain regions control this pattern; the baby does not intentionally produce it. Yet caregivers often interpret the pause as a cue to respond by stroking, cuddling, or talking to the infant (Kaye and Wells, 1980). In this way, a kind of turn-taking emerges. The baby sucks, then pauses; the caregiver talks and moves; the baby starts sucking again. The caregiver behaves as if the baby's pauses were intended to elicit a response, but in fact this is only a pseudodialogue (Hayes, 1984). The caregiver single-handedly orchestrates the pattern by coordinating his or her behavior with the baby's sucking. Through such coordination, the infant is initiated into the turn-taking of human communication.

Soon the baby's involvement in social encounters becomes more complex (Papoušek et al., 1986; Stern, 1985). By 3 or 4 months, infants acquire a range of facial expressions and sounds that can be used in interactions. Babies this age also have good control of their head and eye movements, allowing them to determine what stimulation they will pay attention to. When social overtures are dull and repetitive and the baby's arousal level falls too low, he or she will search for something more interesting to look at. Conversely, when social overtures become too arousing, a baby will turn away as if to reduce the stimulation temporarily, or perhaps to process it.

Reciprocity is learned gradually, with each advancement setting the stage for the next. The process is analogous to teaching Ping-Pong to an older child (Sroufe, 1995).

First you hit the ball right to the child's paddle so it can bounce back without much active involvement from the child. The child's shots may go anywhere, and it is up to you to keep the ball moving and to maintain the appearance of a game. Next, you encourage the child to swing the paddle and gradually to learn how to aim the ball. In time, the youngster becomes a full participant in the give-and-take. So it goes with the development of reciprocity. Newborns' behavior prompts adults to provide stimulation that leads them toward more focused and organized interaction. Gradually, caregivers provide richer stimulation and encourage more participation from babies. Ultimately, genuine social partnerships develop as the baby becomes a purposeful, social being.

Becoming an Active Participant: The Example of Social Smiling

An excellent example of this developmental process can be seen in the emergence of social smiling. Imagine Christine in the hospital soon after Mikey is born. She has just finished nursing him, and as he drifts off to sleep the corners of his mouth twist up in a tiny smile. Christine is elated. She is sure that Mikey is telling her that he is warm, full, and content. Like Christine, many parents attribute to very young infants emotions such as joy, anger, fear, and surprise (Emde, 1985). Such attributions play an important role in the developing relationship with the infant.

Technically, Christine's interpretation is not correct. Newborns' smiles do not really indicate pleasure in the sense that older infants' smiles do; they are caused by spontaneous discharges in lower brain regions. One indication of this is that newborns smile almost solely during sleep (Sroufe, 1995). If their smiles were a sign of pleasure, they would occur when wide awake as well. Other evidence comes from the study of premature infants and those born without a cerebral cortex. Newborn smiles are more common in these babies than in normal children, suggesting the involvement of lower brain regions. In addition, the newborn sleep smile disappears in normal babies as the cortex matures.

You may wonder what happens during sleep to make newborns smile. The answer seems to be gentle fluctuations in arousal around a critical threshold, causing the facial muscles to relax into a little smile (Sroufe, 1995). As shown in Figure 6.2, a newborn who is sleeping lightly will smile five to eight seconds after a rattle is gently shaken. It takes time for the baby's arousal level to rise slightly and then fall, bringing on the smile.

Newborn sleep smile. Note that the mouth is closed and that there is no crinkling of the skin around the eyes.

Figure 6.2
AROUSAL THRESHOLD AND NEWBORN SLEEP SMILES
The newborn's smiles during sleep are due to fluctuations in central nervous system arousal or excitation. These may occur spontaneously, as is shown in part (A), when the infant's depth of sleep changes. Notice that following a startle reaction, it is some time before the excitation falls below the arousal threshold (the purple line) and the smile recurs. Sleep smiles may also occur following stimulation, as shown in part (B). Here a rattle is shaken, and six seconds later a smile occurs.

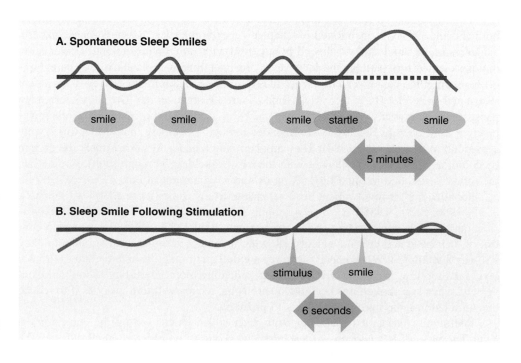

If a sleeping baby is gently shaken toward wakefulness, a series of little smiles occurs. But if a sleeping newborn is startled, causing the arousal level to shoot up, no sleep smiles occur for quite some time.

Even though Christine is technically wrong in the meaning she gives to Mikey's first smiles, she is correctly anticipating what is to come. These winsome expressions strike a chord within her, drawing her closer to her baby. Just as infants are preadapted to interact with adults, adults are preadapted to interact with infants. Over the next few weeks Mikey begins to smile when he is awake, as Christine talks to him, nuzzles him, and gently claps his hands together. She spends quite a bit of time engaged with him, partly because his smiling and cooing are rewarding to her (Stern, 1985). Like most parents, she interprets her baby's behavior as more advanced and intelligent than it really is. At 5 weeks, when Mikey grins and coos as Christine chirps at him, she assumes it is because he has a special liking for her voice. In fact, *any* gentle stimulation (music boxes, bells tinkling on his crib) can produce the proper degree of excitation to elicit a smile (Sroufe, 1995). Soon, however, Christine's voice *will* be special to Mikey.

At 8 to 10 weeks, Mikey begins to smile when Christine's face appears above his crib. He is not smiling because he knows her, as Christine might think. At this age Mikey's smiles are not reserved for his mother. He smiles when the kicking of his feet makes his mobile turn, when Maggie repeatedly presents him with the same stuffed bear, and when *any* face appears before him (Shultz and Zigler, 1970; Sroufe, 1995). These smiles are due to a form of visual mastery called **recognitory assimilation** (Piaget, 1952). With effort, Mikey is making sense of some familiar object, recognizing it as something he has seen before. In Piaget's terms, he is assimilating an event to an established scheme. The effort causes tension, which is broken by recognition, and the smile follows. Once again, fluctuations in arousal lead to a smile, but here the fluctuations are due to cognitive effort and assimilation. Turning mobiles, dangling teddy bears, and human faces can all be assimilated with effort at 10 weeks, and all produce smiles. Since these smiles are related to the meaning of the events for Mikey, it is appropriate to say that he is now smiling in pleasure. The mastery of recognition, in other words, is enjoyable to him.

Recognitory assimilation: A form of visual mastery in which the infant recognizes a familiar stimulus and assimilates it to an established scheme.

Christine's natural feeling of being special to Mikey serves to encourage further interaction. By 3 months Mikey can discriminate familiar from unfamiliar faces and prefers to look at familiar ones. By 4 or 5 months, he not only can discriminate Christine's face from other people's but also reacts specifically to her face. At this point he stops smiling at strangers, and his smiles are reserved for people he knows (Sroufe, 1995). Now his mother's and father's faces really are special to him, and his smiles are truly social.

In summary, social development during the first six months is a product of the interplay between infants and caregivers. Parents attribute meaning to interactions with their newborns, partly on the basis of the babies' responses when they talk and play with them. That meaning prompts them to continue their attentions toward their babies and to elaborate the stimulation they provide. In time, with cognitive maturation, the babies come to share in the meaning of social exchanges. By 10 weeks they feel pleasure in interacting with their caregivers; by 4 or 5 months they visually recognize their caregivers as distinct from other people. Gradually babies come to participate reciprocally in games. Thus, newborns' built-in reactions to stimulation from caregivers lead to remarkable social behavior by the end of the first six months.

Emotional Development

Emotional development includes:

- the emergence of the various emotions and
- the development of emotional regulation, the capacity to control and modulate emotion.

We will examine both of these aspects of emotional development in infancy.

By 6 months of age, infants' smiles at their parents are truly social.

Emotion:
A state of feeling that arises when a person evaluates an event in a particular way.

Child Development CD:
Visual Cliff Studies

Forerunners of Basic Emotions   An **emotion** can be defined as a state of feeling that arises when a person evaluates an event in a particular way. It usually has characteristic physiological and behavioral changes associated with it. For example, 8-month-olds placed on the "deep" side of the visual cliff, as described in Chapter 4, seem to evaluate the apparent drop-off as a dangerous situation. They show physiological and behavioral responses indicating fear—an elevated heart rate, a fearful facial expression, and frantic attempts to move to the "shallow" side. Infants who have not yet started to crawl do not appear to evaluate the situation in the same way and do not show the physiological or behavioral signs of fear.

Basic emotions emerge gradually over the first year of life as infants' emotional responses become increasingly differentiated and increasingly tied to the meaning of specific events. During the first six months, the newborn's initial reflexive, physiological responses to stimulation develop into forerunners of specific basic emotions.

From the very beginning, infants show reactions that *seem* emotional, starting with the loud cries and sleep smiles of the newborn. However, these earliest reactions are reflexive responses to the environment that reflect varying levels of arousal, rather than specific emotions (Saarni et al., 1998; Sroufe, 1995). During the first weeks of life, infants sometimes show culturally universal facial expressions associated with basic emotions such as joy, anger, and fear (Izard and Malatesta, 1987). But these early expressions are fleeting and irregular, they are not always easy to distinguish from each other, and they are not clearly related to specific events (Oster, Hegley, and Nagel, 1992). For these reasons, they probably do not mean the same thing in early infancy that they will mean later on.

By 3 months infants begin to show more specific emotional responses to events. We saw emotion when 10-week-old Mikey smiled after effortful recognition of a human face. No longer did Mikey smile merely because of physical stimulation, such as being jostled. Instead he smiled in response to the *meaning* of an event—the appearance of a familiar face. The accompanying state of feeling is a genuine emotion of pleasure. Between 3 and 6 months, infants also begin to show wariness after prolonged inspection of an unfamiliar face and frustration when prevented from carrying out an established motor routine, such as reaching for, grasping, and mouthing a toy.

However, these responses still differ from the full-blown emotions of joy, fear, and anger in several ways (Sroufe, 1995):

- The emotional reactions of 3- to 6-month-olds often require time to build up.
- The meanings attached to the events involved are very general.
- Emotional responses are still somewhat global and not well differentiated.

For example, 5-month-old Malcolm may become intensely distressed when he cannot reach a toy from his infant seat, but only after looking at it and straining to reach it for some time. His distress would not be due to desire for that particular toy; he might become frustrated if *any* motor routine were interrupted. And his reaction to not being able to reach the toy would be very similar to how he might react to a stranger's stare—crying, thrashing, and flailing his arms and legs. There are not yet clearly distinguishable responses that specifically indicate fear or anger.

The Beginnings of Emotional Regulation and Coping Babies gradually acquire the capacity to cope with or manage emotionally arousing situations. Newborns have built-in coping mechanisms, such as sleeping deeply following surgery or falling asleep in the face of repeated unpleasant stimuli (Sroufe, 1995). But such reactions are global and involuntary, and they remove the infant from interaction with the environment. By 4 or 5 months, infants can turn away from a source of stimulation, but this response is still fairly global and not well controlled by the baby. For instance, a 5-month-old will typically have difficulty turning away from a staring stranger; instead, the baby will be drawn back to the stranger's face and end up crying. Crying is a coping technique because it may bring help, but it still interrupts contact with the environment. Considerable further advances in coping skills, as well as in the emergence of basic emotions, will occur during the second six months of life.

DEVELOPMENT IN THE SECOND SIX MONTHS

As extraordinary as development is in the first six months, it is equally rapid and far-reaching in the second six. Cognitive development during this period makes babies increasingly able to recognize specific people as separate, independent entities who act and can be acted upon. It also enables a capacity for intentional behavior and a rudimentary sense of self (Saarni et al., 1998; Sroufe, 1990; Stern, 1985). These advances have important implications for the emergence of specific emotions, as well as for the capacity to regulate and control emotions.

Between 6 and 12 months, babies' social behavior becomes increasingly organized around their principal caregivers, with a purposefulness not seen in earlier months. Ten-month-old Malcolm greets his mother joyfully and seeks her out when he is distressed. These behaviors indicate he has formed a specific attachment to her, a special closeness and sense of security in her presence. This specific attachment, which also occurs with fathers and other regular caregivers (such as Malcolm's grandmother), is one of the major developmental landmarks of infancy.

Developments in the second six months are so dramatic that they can be considered *qualitative* advances. Remember from Chapter 1 the enormous difference between a 6-month-old and a 10-month-old confronted with the sight of mother with a cloth dangling from her mouth. The older baby is a fundamentally different child from the younger one. This difference was demonstrated in a classic study on the effects of hospitalization during infancy (Schaffer and Callender, 1959). Babies older than 7 months protested being hospitalized, were negative toward the hospital staff, and needed a period of readjustment after returning home, during which they showed much insecurity centered on their mothers. Apparently, disruption in the relationship with the mother was the core of the problem. Babies younger than 7 months showed none of these adverse reactions. They had not yet experienced the critical emotional changes that occur during the second half-year. In the section that follows we'll take a look at some of these changes.

Emotional Development

Emotional reactions become more frequent in the second six months of life, and they change in several fundamental ways:

- Clearly differentiated specific emotions emerge (Sroufe, 1995).
- Emotional responses become increasingly immediate, rather than requiring time to build up (Camras et al., 1992).
- All the classic facial expressions of emotion begin to appear regularly (Izard and Malatesta, 1987; Oster et al., 1992).

By the end of the first year of life, infants can recall past experiences, anticipate outcomes, and behave intentionally. As a result, their emotional reactions occur in response to events with particular meanings. Laughing while pulling a cloth from the caregiver's mouth and stuffing it back in is not based simply on recognition of the caregiver and the cloth, but on the anticipated consequences of an action. Such an immediate positive emotional reaction may be called *joy.* Likewise, an 8- to 10-month-old may immediately become upset when pursuing a ball that rolls under a couch or may react negatively to an adult in a white lab coat following a trip to the doctor for shots. Such reactions are examples of genuine *anger* and *fear,* in contrast to the more primitive emotional responses of the first six months. In the second six months, babies also show genuine *surprise* when something unexpected happens, such as a toy suddenly disappearing through a trapdoor in a high chair tray (Hiatt, Campos, and Emde, 1979).

Stranger and Separation Distress

Stranger distress:
Negative reactions of infants to strangers.

Emotional Reactions to the Unfamiliar If a stranger locks a 5-month-old in a fixed stare, the baby often peruses the stranger soberly and then starts crying after thirty seconds or so (Bronson and Pankey, 1977). A few months later (usually between 7 and 10 months), babies begin to react negatively to strangers even without prolonged inspection of them (see Figure 6.3). This **stranger distress** usually continues for two or three months, sometimes extending into the second year (Emde, Gaensbauer, and Harmon, 1976; Sroufe, 1995). The degree of stranger distress varies greatly from baby to baby. At its most intense, it has all the earmarks of real fear, with wary looks followed by turning away, pulling away, and occasional whimpering and crying. Significantly, at the same age infants first show fear in other situations, such as high places or impending collisions (Sroufe, 1995).

Research shows that distress toward strangers is not just wariness toward unfamiliar things in general. If a 10-month-old's mother does something highly novel, such as covering her face with a mask, the baby will usually squeal with delight. However, if a stranger puts on a mask and approaches, the baby will typically get upset; if the baby's mother then puts on the *same* mask, the baby will also become distressed (Sroufe, Waters, and Matas, 1974). All these events are novel, so it is not novelty alone that elicits a negative reaction. In fact, mother putting on a mask after a stranger does should be *less* novel than when mother puts on the mask first. Clearly, novel events can be either frightening or delightful, depending on how secure the baby feels in the particular context.

The context also influences reactions to strangers in general. In a standard stranger-response study, a stranger greets an infant from the doorway of a room, then gradually approaches and picks the baby up. Although babies may smile at the stranger from a distance, they often become alarmed when the stranger walks over and tries to lift them (Waters, Matas, and Sroufe, 1975). The more rapidly the stranger approaches and the more intrusively he or she behaves, the more likely the baby is to become distressed. Familiar surroundings can greatly reduce stranger distress; babies show less fear of strangers at home than in a laboratory. Stranger distress is even reduced when the newcomer uses familiar formats to interact with the infant, such as playing with a favorite

The emotional reaction of surprise emerges in the second six months of life.

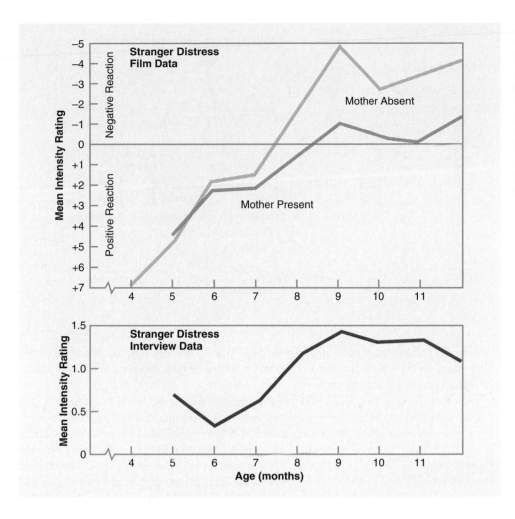

Figure 6.3
THE ONSET OF STRANGER
DISTRESS
Several studies have demonstrated
a notable increase in wariness
toward strangers in the second
half year. This developmental
trend is illustrated here in both
filmed reactions of infants and
maternal reports from interviews.
*(Source: Data from Emde,
Gaensbauer, and Harmon, 1976.)*

toy in the same way the caregiver does (Saarni et al., 1998; Sroufe, 1995), or when the infant is allowed to have control over the stranger's approach (Parritz, Mangelsdorf, and Gunnar, 1992). The caregiver's presence and reaction to the situation can also affect the infant's reaction. Infants usually show less fear of strangers when the caregiver is close by, but if the caregiver shows a worried expression, infants cry more and smile less at strangers.

In short, by about 10 months infants can make rudimentary evaluations of the threat posed by strangers and other novel events. These evaluations depend heavily on the context in which the events occur, particularly the child's sense of security and opportunities for control (Saarni et al., 1998; Sroufe, 1995). On the basis of such factors and previous experience, infants categorize an event as liked or disliked. Four-month-olds show none of this. They are made neither frightened nor joyous by mother wearing a mask, regardless of the setting or who puts it on first.

Emotional Regulation and Coping   Infants' skills for emotional regulation expand dramatically in the second six months, and their coping techniques become increasingly subtle, flexible, and serviceable (Bridges and Grolnick, 1995; Gunnar et al., 1989a). A remarkable example can be seen in the stranger-approach procedure (Waters et al., 1975). As a stranger approaches, many 10-month-olds show a pattern of brief glances down and away, followed by looking again. As shown in Figure 6.4, these gaze aversions are coordinated with heart rate acceleration, an indication of emotional arousal. As the infant watches the approaching stranger, the heart rate speeds up. Then the infant glances away, and the heart rate slows again. The infant is then relaxed enough to look at the stranger

Figure 6.4

HEART RATE AND GAZE
DURING STRANGER
APPROACH PROCEDURE
Gaze and heart rate in a standard
stranger-approach situation for a
10-month-old male infant. S
denotes "looks at stranger"; A
denotes "looks away"; and M
denotes "looks to mother."
Markers above indicate onset
and direction of looks away from
the stranger. *(Source: Waters,
Matas, and Sroufe, 1975.)*

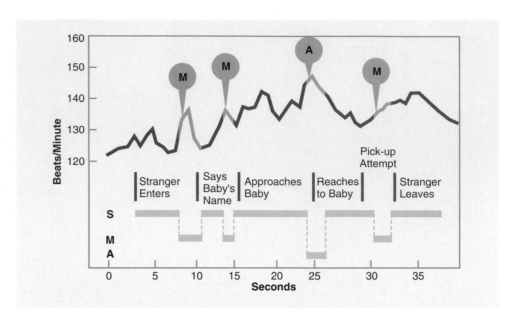

once more. Infants who show this pattern typically do not cry and are more accepting
of the stranger on a second approach. Infants who cry or turn completely away typically
are more upset on a second approach.

Another important coping technique that appears during the second half-year is purposeful signaling to the caregiver (calling, gesturing, emitting distress signals) or moving to the caregiver when threatened, as when Mikey signaled his mother to pick him
up when he was frightened by Uncle Dan's toy. Unlike crying, these techniques help the
infant maintain organized behavior and stay in contact with the environment. Regulation
of emotion in infancy is often *dyadic regulation*—that is, accomplished by caregiver and
infant together (Bridges and Grolnick, 1995). This use of the caregiver as a way of coping with novelty or threat is a hallmark of attachment, our next topic.

In summary, by late in the first year infant emotional reactions are based on the specific meaning of events, not their mere occurrence. At the same time, infants have developed increasingly sophisticated skills for coping with emotional arousal. Such complex
behavior is congruent with evidence that by this time pathways have been established
between the cerebral cortex and the limbic system, an area of the brain involved in emotion (Schore, 1994). All of this allows for a greatly increased fluidity in emotional
responding, as when Mikey was frightened by Uncle Dan's mechanical toy at one
moment, then smiling from Christine's arms seconds later.

The Formation of Attachments

Attachment:

An enduring emotional tie
between infant and caregiver.

Attachment is an enduring emotional tie between an infant and a caregiver (Bowlby,
1969/1982). The attachment relationship has special emotional qualities, which are evident not only in the baby's distress on being separated from the caregiver and joyous
greeting on being reunited, but also in the security the child seems to derive just from
being in the caregiver's presence. By age 12 months, babies want to be picked up *specifically* by the caregiver, they seek the caregiver out when they are upset, and they are
happier exploring new surroundings if the caregiver is nearby (Ainsworth et al., 1978;
Thompson, 1998).

Separation distress:

Negative reactions of infants
when the caregiver temporarily
leaves.

Hallmarks of Attachment The development of attachment follows a regular course
across diverse cultures. One sign that attachment is emerging is **separation distress.** At
about the same time infants show negative reactions to strangers, they also cry when
their caregivers temporarily leave them. These reactions occur somewhat earlier in

This infant's exuberant greeting of his arriving father is one sign of attachment.

cultures in which mothers remain in constant contact with their infants, such as the Ganda culture of East Africa (Ainsworth, 1967). However, they are seen by the end of the first year in all cultures that have been studied.

At about the same time, **greeting reactions** emerge (Vaughn, 1979). As soon as Christine appears in the doorway, Mikey smiles, squeals, bounces up and down, and stretches out his arms. He does not look, ponder his mother, and wait for some social signal. The joyous response is immediate. Apparently, Christine has become linked in Mikey's mind with special, very positive feelings. People in his world are acquiring emotional significance, just as they do for adults.

Greeting reactions:
Positive reactions of infants when the caregiver appears.

A final hallmark of attachment is **secure-base behavior.** One-year-olds show a pattern of exploration centered on the caregiver. They explore more confidently when the caregiver is present, and they monitor the caregiver's accessibility, checking back from a distance. They retreat to their secure base—the caregiver—when threatened, then venture forth again when reassured (Bowlby, 1969/1982, 1988; Sroufe, 1995).

Secure-base behavior:
Behavior in which the infant uses the caregiver as a base for exploration.

The Bases of Attachment The attachment relationship develops over the first year and continues to evolve during toddlerhood and beyond. Like other relationships, it is the product of countless hours of interaction during which caregiver and infant learn to coordinate their behavior. Attachment is distinct from **bonding,** the parent's tie to the newborn, which some argue can occur only in the first hours after birth (Klaus and Kennell, 1976). Attachment is a two-way relationship between parent and infant that develops over a long period of time. As we will see, there is ample evidence that attachment has long-term impacts on infants' development. In contrast, numerous studies have failed to demonstrate a critical need for immediate contact between parents and newborns. Even premature infants initially separated from their biological mothers usually develop normal attachment later in infancy (Easterbrooks, 1989; Rode et al., 1981). Early contact between parents and infants can be beneficial because it *starts* a relationship, but it is not absolutely critical.

Bonding:
The parent's initial emotional tie to the newborn.

Since attachment is the product of repeated interaction with a caregiver, it does not have to be the biological parent to whom a baby becomes attached. When infants are adopted early in the first year, they are just as likely as other infants to develop healthy attachment relationships (Nordhaus and Solnit, 1990; Singer et al., 1985). Moreover, infants often become attached to more than one person. Infants in Israeli kibbutzim (communal farms), who are largely tended by communal nurses but spend time each evening with their parents, become attached both to their parents and to the substitute caregivers (Sagi et al., 1994). In many cultures, babies typically become attached to both fathers and mothers (van IJzendoorn and de Wolff, 1997), though frequently they show a preference for the mother during times of threat (Cox et al., 1992). This preference probably results from the greater involvement that mothers usually have with infants. If someone other than the mother is the principal caregiver, in terms of both time and emotional commitment, that person is likely to become the child's main attachment figure.

For an infant to have several attachment figures ordered into a hierarchy on the basis of each relationship's strength makes a great deal of sense. From a learning perspective, it is reasonable that an infant who interacts regularly with more than one person will become attached to each of them, with the strongest attachment to the person who is the most involved with the child. From an evolutionary perspective, a hierarchy of attachment figures seems essential. When threatened by a predator, human infants of the distant past could not debate where to flee. They had to seek protection immediately, and having a primary attachment figure to go to helped ensure that protection would be found. Yet should this primary attachment figure die or be otherwise unavailable, infants must have the capacity for other attachments.

More on Bowlby

Many theories have been proposed to explain the processes underlying attachment formation. Early psychoanalytic theory and traditional learning theory suggested that infants became attached to the mother because she was associated with feeding. Theorists such as Erikson and Bowlby placed more emphasis on the interaction between caregiver and child. Bowlby (1969/1982) argued that the tendency to become attached has been built into humans and other primates through natural selection. According to Bowlby, all that is required for an attachment to form is that an adult be present to engage the infant; food need not be involved.

A classic set of studies by Harry Harlow and his colleagues at the University of Wisconsin supports the view that association with feeding is not the basis of attachment (e.g., Harlow and Harlow, 1966). Harlow separated baby rhesus monkeys from their mothers and raised them with various kinds of substitute mothers. In one study, each baby was raised with two substitutes, one made of stiff, bare wire, the other covered with soft terry cloth. The wire mother was equipped with a bottle for feeding. From the perspective of associative learning, the infant monkeys would be expected to become attached to the wire mother because it was associated with food. But the babies clearly preferred the terry cloth mother. They spent more time with the terry cloth mother and quickly ran to it when distressed. Apparently, for the development of an attachment, the ability to cling to the terry cloth mother and derive security from it was more important than feeding. Similarly, human infants do not become attached to their parents simply because the parents feed them. Rather, they become attached because the parents engage them in interaction.

Although all human infants become attached, not all attachments are the same. In the next section we consider differences in the security of infants' attachments, as well as other individual differences during infancy.

EXPLAINING INDIVIDUAL DIFFERENCES IN EARLY SOCIAL AND EMOTIONAL DEVELOPMENT

Observers are often impressed with the dramatic differences among babies. Some are easily aroused, cry often, and are difficult to settle. Others are placid and rarely become upset. Some are confident when facing new experiences, especially with attachment figures present. Others are timid and hesitant about anything novel. Even newborns differ in how much they sleep and cry and in how quickly they soothe themselves or can be soothed by others.

Researchers have asked a number of questions about such individual differences during infancy: How consistent are the differences? Do differences at birth predict differences at 12 months? What are the implications of individual differences in infancy for later development? Do they continue to be part of the child's personality? Finally, how are such differences to be explained?

There are two major approaches to explaining individual differences in infant behavior. One, based in Erikson's psychosocial theory and Bowlby's attachment theory, emphasizes the quality of care the infant receives and the resulting variability in the security of infant-caregiver attachment. The other emphasizes the baby's inborn temperament, based on genetic makeup and other biological influences, especially those surrounding pregnancy and birth. Although these approaches have led to two distinct lines of research, they are not necessarily in conflict with each other. Rather, they are two different perspectives on the same set of phenomena. In fact, a great deal of recent effort has been aimed at harmonizing or integrating the two views.

The Attachment Framework

In all but the most extreme cases, infants become attached to a caregiver. Mentally retarded infants become attached, though at a later age than other infants (Cicchetti and Beeghly, 1990). Blind infants and physically disabled infants become attached, with some differences in the behaviors they use to express attachment (Marvin and Pianta, 1992; Sroufe, 1995). Even abused infants become attached (Cicchetti, Toth, and Lynch, 1995). Only if there is no opportunity for ongoing interaction with a specific caregiver will there be a failure to attach, as in the case of some institutionalized infants (Johnson, 2000; O'Connor et al., 1999).

Noting the universality of attachment, John Bowlby sought to identify individual differences in attachment quality. Such differences could be seen in Harlow's studies of monkeys raised with substitute mothers. When some of these monkeys later had babies, they proved to be rejecting and punitive parents. Their infants were nevertheless clearly attached to them, but the attachments had an anxious quality, with the infants constantly trying to cling to their mothers.

Bowlby hypothesized that the quality of a baby's attachment is based on the quality of care the baby receives. When infants experience sensitive care, they become confident the caregiver will be responsive. Being able to count on the caregiver's presence and comfort gives the infant a base for exploring the environment and a ready resource in case of threat or distress. After repeated experiences in which the caregiver responds to signals, is available for communication, and alleviates stress, the baby comes to expect that such care will regularly be available. This confidence in the caregiver's availability

Toddlers use their parents as secure bases when encountering new situations.

is what Erikson means by *trust* and what Bowlby refers to as *secure attachment.* Secure attachment relationships cannot develop if care is unavailable or hit-or-miss, or if the adult actively rejects the infant's bids for attention and care. In such cases the infant will probably develop an *insecure* or *anxious attachment.*

Patterns of Attachment   To test Bowlby's hypothesis, researchers needed to measure both security of attachment and sensitivity of care, so they could examine links between the two. Mary Ainsworth, a psychologist at the University of Virginia, pioneered the study of qualitative differences in attachment (Ainsworth et al., 1978). On the basis of observations in the home and the laboratory, she identified a pattern of attachment she called *secure* and several patterns she called *anxious* (see Table 6.1). To assess individual infants' attachment patterns, Ainsworth devised a laboratory procedure known as the

Child Development CD:
Strange Situation

Table 6.1 Patterns of Attachment

Secure Attachment
Infant uses caregiver as secure base for exploration.
- Readily separates to explore toys.
- Affective sharing of play.
- Affiliative to stranger in caregiver's presence.
- Readily comforted when distressed (promoting a return to play).

Infant actively seeks contact or interaction upon reunion.
- *If distressed:* Immediately seeks and maintains contact; contact ends distress.
- *If not distressed:* Active greeting behavior; strong initiation of interaction.

Anxious-Resistant Attachment
Infant shows poverty of exploration.
- Difficulty separating to explore, may need contact even prior to separation.
- Wary of novel situations and people.

Infant has difficulty settling upon reunion.
- May mix contact seeking with resistance (hitting, kicking, squirming, rejecting toys).
- May simply continue to cry and fuss.
- May show striking passivity.

Anxious-Avoidant Attachment
Infant shows independent exploration.
- Readily separates to explore toys.
- Little affective sharing.
- Affiliative to stranger when caregiver absent (little preference).

Infant actively avoids caregiver upon reunion.
- Turns away, looks away, moves away, ignores.
- May mix avoidance with proximity.
- Avoidance more extreme on second reunion.
- No avoidance of stranger.

Disorganized/Disoriented Attachment
Infant shows inexplicable or conflicted behavior patterns that do not fit other categories.
- Sequential contradictory behaviors (e.g., contented play interrupted by extreme anger).
- Simultaneous contradictory behaviors (e.g., fearful smile, simultaneous approach and avoidance).

Infant appears dazed or disoriented.
- May show slow or incomplete movements or stilling (like deer caught in headlights).
- May show odd mannerisms (stereotypies).

Source: Adapted from Ainsworth et al., 1978; Main and Solomon, 1990.

Strange Situation. In this procedure, the baby and the caregiver (always the mother in Ainsworth's experiments) enter a playroom, which the baby is free to explore. In a series of episodes, the baby is then exposed to a strange adult with and without the mother present, is left alone briefly, and is reunited with the mother. Ainsworth found that infants' behavior in this procedure was closely related to their patterns of crying and exploration observed at home, suggesting that the Strange Situation is a valid measure of attachment.

Most infants (around 60 to 70 percent) form a **secure attachment.** These babies show a good balance between play and exploration on the one hand and a desire for proximity to the caregiver on the other. In Ainsworth's Strange Situation, they separate readily from their mothers to explore. Their responses to their mothers are emotionally positive; in play, they smile at their mothers and share discoveries with them. When the stranger enters, these babies are usually not unduly wary. They vary in how upset they are by the separation from their mothers. Regardless of their reaction to the separation, they respond positively to their mothers' return and differentiate clearly between mother and the stranger. If not unduly distressed, they show pleasure, greeting their mothers happily. If they are more upset, they quickly and effectively seek their mothers out and remain with them until reassured. Usually this comforting is smooth and rapid; before long the securely attached infants are crawling or toddling off contentedly to explore the world again.

In contrast, infants with an **anxious attachment** are unable to use the caregiver as a secure base for exploration. Such a lack of security takes several forms. One pattern is **anxious-resistant attachment.** In this pattern, infants seek a great deal of contact with their caregivers. During the Strange Situation, they are reluctant to separate from their mothers despite an array of attractive toys. When they do venture forth, even a minor stress often sends them scurrying back to their mothers. They are usually rather wary of the stranger. Typically, they are quite upset when their mothers leave, yet they cannot be readily comforted by them at reunion. Many continue to cry and fuss despite their mothers' efforts to reduce their distress. Most important, they tend to mix bids for physical closeness with *resistance* to such contact. One moment they may raise their arms to be picked up, the next moment they may squirm, push away, or kick out in anger. Their ambivalent approach to their mothers greatly interferes with their ability to get settled and begin exploring again. They behave as if they cannot get what they need from their mothers.

Anxious-avoidant attachment is quite a different pattern but equally distinct from secure attachment. Infants who exhibit this pattern in the Strange Situation readily separate from their mothers to examine the toys. Typically they are not wary of the stranger, and they do not usually cry when their mothers leave the room. What is striking about these babies is their response when their mothers return. They actively *avoid* their mothers, turning away, moving away, or studiously ignoring them; they do not behave this way toward the stranger. Normal infants may show such a pattern following a separation of several weeks from the caregiver (Heinicke and Westheimer, 1966), but not one of just three minutes. Significantly, avoidance of their mothers is even more pronounced following a second separation, during which many of the babies clearly become upset. Yet when their mothers return, these infants still do not seek them out, nor do they respond to contact with them—exactly the opposite of the behavior of securely attached infants. The more the stress of the situation increases, the more they avoid interaction with their mothers. Avoidance of the mother, like resistance, greatly interferes with the ability to become settled and return to active exploration.

Mary Main and Erik Hesse (1990) at the University of California have discussed resistance and avoidance as strategies for expressing attachment in different caregiving contexts. They describe the resistant infants as *maximizing* expression of attachment behavior in the face of inconsistent or chaotic care. If they are chronically vigilant and express attachment behavior with great intensity, perhaps the caregiver will respond adequately. The avoidant infants, in contrast, are *minimizing* expression of attachment. Since expression of attachment-related needs in the past has led to rebuff, these infants inhibit or cut off such expressions, to keep from further alienating a rejecting caregiver and to maintain some kind of proximity.

Secure attachment:
A pattern of attachment in which the infant is confident of the caregiver's availability and responsiveness and can use the caregiver as a secure base for exploration.

Anxious attachment:
Patterns of attachment in which the infant is not confident of the caregiver's availability and responsiveness and cannot use the caregiver as a secure base for exploration.

Anxious-resistant attachment:
An attachment pattern in which the infant separates from the caregiver reluctantly but shows ambivalence toward the caregiver after a brief separation.

Anxious-avoidant attachment:
An attachment pattern in which the infant readily separates from the caregiver but avoids contact after a brief separation.

Disorganized-disoriented
attachment:
A type of anxious attachment in
which the infant shows
contradictory features of several
patterns of anxious attachment or
appears dazed and disoriented.

But what happens when the caregiver is the source of threat, as in the case of abusive parents or parents whose behavior is otherwise frightening or bizarre? Infants in this situation may have an unresolvable conflict, motivated to approach an attachment figure, as other infants are, but also motivated to withdraw from a source of fear—in this case, the caregiver. These infants often cannot maintain a coherent strategy for expressing attachment and show what Main calls **disorganized-disoriented attachment** (Main and Solomon, 1990). In the Strange Situation, infants with this kind of attachment show contradictory features of several patterns or appear dazed and disoriented. They may show obvious signs of fear or confusion. Their behavior may include clear contradictions, such as approaching the caregiver but looking away at the same time. Their movements may be incomplete or very slow, or they may become motionless or show very odd behaviors. This pattern, especially in combination with avoidance, has been strongly linked to later psychopathology (Carlson, 1998).

Quality of Care and Security of Attachment   To assess the effects of quality of care on attachment security, researchers have used two approaches. One is to look at parent-infant interaction when the baby is very young and later to assess security of attachment. Numerous studies of this type have found that sensitive care is associated with secure attachment to mothers and to fathers (e.g., Ainsworth et al., 1978; de Wolff and van IJzendoorn, 1997; NICHD, 1997; Pederson et al., 1998; Posada et al., 1999). In these studies, researchers observed parent-child interactions in the home during the baby's first year of life and rated the parent's degree of sensitivity as a caregiver. When the infant was 12 to 18 months old, the researchers assessed the quality of parent-infant attachment using the Strange Situation. Across studies, the caregiver's sensitivity or intrusiveness in the early months of the baby's life predicts later secure or anxious attachment, but the infant's early behavior generally does not.

In one recent study in the United States and Chile, researchers assessed the sensitivity of caregivers interacting with their infants for six hours, both in the hospital and at home (Posada et al., 1999). Substantial correlations (.50) were found between caregiver sensitivity and later assessments of attachment security. Other studies with such extensive observation also find strong connections between caregiver sensitivity and attachment security, as well as between infants' behavior at home and in the lab (Pederson et al., 1998). For example, infants with both avoidant and resistant attachments fuss more at home than do securely attached infants, and the avoidant group shows a relative lack of close physical contact with the caregiver when in need of comforting. Such studies support the validity of Bowlby's attachment theory and the Strange Situation procedure.

Particular types of insensitive care appear to be associated with particular types of anxious attachment. Anxious-avoidant attachment tends to be associated with a caregiver who is indifferent and emotionally unavailable or who actively rejects the baby when he or she seeks physical closeness (Isabella, 1993). Anxious-resistant attachment tends to be associated with inconsistent care, including exaggerated behaviors on the part of the mother and ineffective soothing that often becomes overstimulation (Sroufe, 1988). Disorganized attachment is related to frightening or confusing behavior by the caregiver (Main and Hesse, 1990; Schuengel et al., 1999).

Sensitive care includes responding promptly to infants' cries.

The other approach to assessing the effects of quality of care on attachment is to identify parents who clearly neglect or maltreat their infants and compare their babies' attachments with those of infants whose parents don't maltreat them. Such studies have routinely found more anxious attachments in the maltreated groups (Carlson, 1998; Cicchetti, Toth, and Lynch, 1995). The specific type of anxious attachment varies and depends somewhat on the type of maltreatment. Several studies have confirmed that maltreated infants show a high incidence of Main's disorganized-disoriented pattern of anxious attachment (Carlson,

Infant Maltreatment

1998; Lyons-Ruth et al., 1990). In addition, extreme poverty and physical neglect are associated with increased anxious-resistant attachment, while anxious-avoidant attachment is more common in cases of physical abuse or emotional unavailability, a pattern in which the caregiver is emotionally unresponsive to the infant. In one study, infants experiencing emotionally unavailable care all had anxious-avoidant attachments by age 18 months (Egeland and Sroufe, 1981).

Since sensitive care involves responding promptly to the baby's cries and other signals, you might wonder whether this attention would reward crying and encourage the baby to cry more. In fact, when caregivers promptly and effectively respond to their infant's cries, the babies actually cry *less* by the end of the first year and are generally securely attached (Ainsworth and Bell, 1974). These children do not learn to be "cry-babies" through reinforcement. Instead, infants with sensitive caregivers apparently learn that their signals will receive quick and appropriate responses and that adults can be counted on to help. By age 12 months they are so confident of prompt responses that they don't need to signal alarm at the slightest stress. They know that if serious distress arises, comfort will be quickly provided. It should be pointed out that sensitive care does not mean perfect care. Parents need not always attend to the infant immediately or always do the right thing. Care only needs to be "good enough" (Winnicott, 1965).

The Context of Caregiving   If the development of secure attachment depends on the kind of care the baby receives, then factors that influence the quality of caregiving should be related to attachment. Three such factors have been investigated:

- the amount of stress in the caregiver's life,
- the social support available to the caregiver, and
- the caregiver's own developmental history.

Studies of these topics indicate that it is inappropriate simply to blame parents when attachment goes awry. Caregiving must be viewed in its broader social and psychological context, as suggested by Bronfenbrenner's model of developmental contexts, discussed in Chapter 2.

Life Stress and Social Support.   It is easier to cope with ongoing problems and everyday hassles when others are available to help and give emotional support. Those who care for infants without help and support from others also tend to experience more financial pressure and stresses of other kinds. Many studies have linked the quality of parent-infant attachment to the amount of stress and social support in caregivers' lives, as measured in interviews (Cox et al., 1989; Crockenberg, 1981; Jacobson and Frye, 1991; Thompson, 1998). If support increases or stress decreases, the quality of the child's relationship with the caregiver can improve, sometimes becoming secure when it had originally been anxious (Thompson, 1998; Vaughn et al., 1979).

Parents' Developmental History.   Several studies have now related caregivers' perceptions of their own childhoods to the quality of infant-caregiver attachment (van IJzendoorn, 1995; Ward and Carlson, 1995). Many of these studies have used the Adult Attachment Interview, developed by Mary Main and Carol George. From the ease with which adults talk about attachment-related feelings, and from inconsistencies among their statements, the degree to which they experienced responsive care and the degree to which they have resolved any feelings of being mistreated are inferred. Such reports may be obtained even before the parents' own child is born. From these reports it is possible to predict the quality of the baby's later attachment (van IJzendoorn, 1995). This is true even for parents who adopt infants, making it clear that the link is not explained by genetic similarity (Dozier et al., 2001).

Of course, how adults talk about their attachment feelings may be influenced by their current situations. Parents' current difficulties may lead them both to have problems with their infant and to report their own developmental history negatively (Roisman et al., 2002). Main notes that her Adult Attachment Interview captures adults' current state of mind concerning attachment and does not necessarily reflect their actual early attachment relationships. Some adults whose early lives were quite negative nonetheless achieve a substantial degree of understanding and emotional freedom regarding attachment. When they do, their infants are likely to be securely attached.

Other evidence of a link between parents' developmental histories and the attachment security of their own infants comes from animal studies. Such studies are only suggestive for humans, but they allow researchers to look at parenting across generations in a short period of time. Lynn Fairbanks (1989) studied mothering among vervet monkeys and found that the amount of physical contact a female monkey received from her mother when she was an infant predicted the amount of contact she later gave her own baby. Moreover, this similarity in behavior was not due to genetic similarity between mother and daughter, or to observational learning by the daughter. The amount of contact the daughter received predicted the amount of contact she later gave better than the average amount of contact the mother gave to *all* her offspring (a measure of her genetic inclination to give physical contact) or the amount of contact she was currently giving to younger siblings of the daughter (which could serve as a model for the daughter to imitate). More recently, Stephen Suomi (2002) conducted a cross-fostering study where infants were assigned to nurturant or nonnurturant adoptive mothers. Those receiving nurturant care were more caring toward their own infants when they became adults.

Infant Attachment and Later Development   Individual differences in security of attachment are thought to be important because of their implications for later development. The crux of Bowlby's theory is that different patterns of attachment reflect differences in infants' expectations, or **internal working models,** of the social world. Internal working models include expectations about the availability of the caregiver, the infant's own worthiness and ability to obtain care, and social relationships in general. An infant who experiences reliable, responsive care develops a model of the caregiver as available, of the self as worthy of care and effective in obtaining it, and of social relationships as pleasurable and rewarding. According to Bowlby, these representations are carried forward and influence later behavior and relationships, coloring the child's interpretations of events and influencing the kinds of experiences the child seeks or avoids.

Research tends to support Bowlby's theory that the quality of attachment helps to shape a child's internal working model of the social world. Attachment classifications in infancy have been shown to be related to attachment behavior in the home (Ainsworth et al., 1978; Vaughn and Waters, 1990), to be stable over time in typical samples (Waters, 1978; Weinfield et al., 1999), and to predict how well children will function later (Schneider et al., 2001; Sroufe, 2002). Curiosity, enthusiasm in solving problems, high self-esteem, and positive relations with teachers and peers have all been found to be strongly linked to the quality of early attachments. We will discuss the long-term consequences of attachment security more extensively in later chapters.

In summary, attachment theorists focus on the organization of an infant's behavior toward the principal caregiver, who becomes an attachment figure. The quality of this attachment relationship results from the history of interaction with the caregiver. That interaction, in turn, is influenced by the overall context of care, which includes the stress and social support the caregiver experiences, as well as characteristics of the particular child. The attachment relationship then provides a framework for later development and is reflected in the child's degree of self-confidence, sociability, and capacity to cope with challenges.

The Temperament Framework

Soon after Christine brought Mikey home from the hospital, she noticed that he seemed different from Maggie at the same age. Maggie had been an easy baby to deal with—Christine's mother and sisters had been amazed at how quickly she

---

Internal working model:
An infant's generalized expectations about the social world, including caregiver responsiveness, the infant's own ability to obtain care, and the nature of social relationships.

fell into a regular sleeping and eating schedule and how easily she adapted to changes. It seemed she could fall asleep anywhere, and she didn't mind being passed around from relative to relative at the family's large, noisy holiday gatherings. Mikey wasn't really difficult *to deal with, but it took a bit more time and patience to get him on a regular schedule. Every new experience, from his first bath to his first taste of strained peas, met with mild but clear protest from Mikey. But Christine soon discovered that if she soothed him, kept trying, and gave him a little time, he eventually adjusted to each new thing.*

Some researchers focus on the idea of inborn *temperament* to explain individual differences in babies' behavior of the sort that Christine noticed in Maggie and Mikey. **Temperament** refers to an individual infant's general style of behavior across contexts; it includes a variety of behavioral characteristics, such as general activity level, proneness to distress, reactivity, and inhibition (Rothbart et al., 2001). Temperament researchers generally assume that individual differences in such characteristics are biologically rooted, although they acknowledge that they can be influenced by environment as well (Goldsmith et al., 1997; Rothbart and Bates, 1998).

Early temperament research tended to focus on very specific features of behavior, such as activity and crying. In one of the first temperament studies, Alexander Thomas and Stella Chess (1977) rated infants on nine specific behavioral characteristics, as listed in Table 6.2. Using combinations of these characteristics, they categorized some babies as *easy,* some as *difficult,* and some as *slow to warm up. Easy* babies showed high biological regularity, readily approached new objects and people, and were highly adaptable and mostly positive in mood. *Difficult* babies were biologically irregular, tended to

Temperament:
An individual infant's general style of behavior across contexts.

Table 6.2 Infant Temperament Characteristics Measured by Thomas and Chess (1977)

Characteristic	Description
Activity	General degree of mobility as reflected in frequency and tempo of movement, locomotion, and other activity; from highly active to inactive.
Rhythmicity	Extent to which sleeping, resting, eating, elimination, and other body functions are regular and predictable; from regular to irregular.
Approach-withdrawal	Type of first reaction child has when encountering new situation such as an unfamiliar person, place, or toy; from approach to withdrawal.
Adaptability	Extent to which initial withdrawal response to a new situation becomes modified over time; from adaptable to nonadaptable.
Intensity	Typical intensity of child's reaction to internal states or environmental situations; from intense to mild.
Threshold	Strength of stimulus needed to cause child to respond; from high threshold to low threshold.
Mood	Typical behavior patterns related to general quality of mood; from pleasant to unpleasant.
Distractibility	Difficulty or ease with which child's ongoing activities can be interrupted; from high to low.
Persistence of attention	Extent to which child remains engaged in an activity or returns to activity after interruption; from high to low.

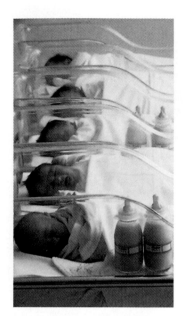

Newborns show individual differences in irritability, but these differences are not very stable over time.

withdraw from new experiences, were low in adaptability, and had intense, mostly negative moods. *Slow-to-warm-up* babies were somewhere in the middle in regularity and showed mildly negative reactions to new experiences, but tended to adapt after repeated exposure. More recent efforts have broadened the concept of temperament to include such things as tendency to express certain emotions (e.g., wariness, proneness to distress) and capacity to regulate one's own behavior (Bridges and Grolnick, 1995; Goldsmith et al., 1997; Rothbart et al., 2001).

One of the central issues in temperament research concerns the stability or consistency of behavior over time. If stable characteristics exist in infancy, perhaps these are the roots of later personality. Stability from very early in infancy would be especially important, since it would suggest that such differences are inborn. In addition, stable infant characteristics might be shown to influence the infant-caregiver relationship, with significant implications for development.

The Stability of Temperament   Early research relied heavily on parents' reports to measure babies' temperaments (Thomas and Chess, 1977). These studies did indeed find various aspects of temperament to be stable over time, but they were criticized for two reasons. First, they did not begin in the newborn period, so it was not clear that truly inborn factors were being measured. Second, parents' reports may have been biased. Early studies found little agreement between parents' reports and data obtained by other observers (Vaughn and Bost, 1999). In one study, questionnaires were given to expectant parents even before the unborn infant was moving (Rothbart and Bates, 1998). These parents' prenatal ratings (really expectations about what the baby would be like) correlated with their descriptions of the infant months later. This finding suggests that parents' expectations play a role in their reports about a baby's temperament.

More recent research, using other approaches to measure infant temperament, has been much more compelling (Rothbart and Bates, 1998). By devising questionnaires in which parents' judgments are more objective, and by combining parents' reports with those of other observers and with laboratory tests, researchers have been able to show that there are clear differences in temperament among infants. But do these differences remain stable over time?

In general, assessments of newborn behavior have not predicted later behavior very reliably, largely because behavior is so unstable in early infancy (de Weerth et al., 1999). However, by 12 months, measurements of such characteristics as frequency of negative and positive emotions and strength of reactions to sensory stimulation are quite stable and predict well to later ages (de Weerth et al., 1999; Emde et al., 1992; Rothbart and Bates, 1998). Assessments of temperament made by parents and other observers bear out this difference; there is much more agreement about temperament in older babies and children than in babies only a few months old (Rothbart and Bates, 1998; Rothbart et al., 2001). Predictions from temperament in early infancy to the preschool years and beyond have so far not been very powerful, with a few exceptions (e.g., Woodward et al., 2001).

Child Development CD:
Kagan Temperament Studies

The Biology of Temperament   Researchers have wondered whether differences in infant temperament reflect biological differences. Much is now known about the neurophysiological and hormonal systems underlying infant behavior (Gunnar, 1994; Rothbart and Bates, 1998). For example, infants who are wary in new situations have higher or more variable heart rates and blood pressure than less wary infants do (Kagan, 1992), and they are more likely to show asymmetrical electrical activity in the two sides of the frontal cerebral cortex (Calkins, Fox, and Marshall, 1996). Associations have also been found between hormone levels and a baby's emotional responses. For instance, high levels of cortisol (a hormone connected to stress) have been linked to parental reports of low adaptability and high emotional negativity, and to later crying in the Strange Situation (Gunnar et al., 1989b).

Thus, biological factors seem to be related to temperament differences observed in babies. But such correlations do not demonstrate that physiological differences are inborn or that they *cause* differences in behavior. For example, babies who are often fretful may show strong cortisol reactions or markedly variable heart rates not because these physiological changes produce fretfulness, but rather because the physiological changes are a *marker* of fretfulness. They may show cortisol responses simply *because* they are so fretful.

The Genetics of Temperament Demonstrating a genetic component for temperament would lend support to the view that the biological differences related to temperament are at least partly inborn. Many studies show more similarity in temperament between identical twins than between fraternal twins (Emde et al., 1992; Goldsmith et al., 1999; Rothbart and Bates, 1998). Since identical twins are more closely related genetically, this research suggests a genetic component for temperament. However, fraternal twins often show very little similarity in temperament, despite the fact that on average they share half of the genes that differentiate them from other people. The similarity in temperament of identical twins may be due in part to similar treatment by parents and others. This possibility is strengthened by the fact that identical twins become increasingly similar in temperament with age, but fraternal twins do not.

One study of twins reared in different homes, the Colorado Adoption Study (Plomin, 1994), found evidence of a genetic component for such personality dimensions as inhibition and negative emotions. In this study, identical twins reared apart showed some similarity in these characteristics. However, the similarity between these twins was much smaller than in studies of identical twins reared together, suggesting that environment also has an influence. Interestingly, similarities between identical twins reared apart still increase with age, suggesting that genetic factors may become more prominent after early infancy (Plomin et al., 1993).

Research with monkeys reveals the complexity of understanding temperament. Some characteristics, such as reactivity to stimulation, seem to have a genetic component, while others, such as the tendency to be nurturant, appear to be based more on experience (Suomi, 1995). Similarly, studies of human youngsters suggest some aspects of temperament have a more clear genetic foundation, while other aspects appear to be more influenced by environment (Goldsmith et al., 1999). Temperament and even brain physiology may be shaped and altered by experience (Schore, 1994); for example, the infant's capacity to stay physiologically regulated can be influenced by the caregiver's behavior (Kraemer, 1992).

By 12 months infants have a unique individual style, the product of temperament and experiences in attachment relationships. This mother describes her baby as very determined and curious.

In summary, by the end of infancy, various dimensions of behavior, often referred to as temperament, become stable, with some children more irritable, sociable, or emotionally reactive than others. By this age, there is also agreement among parents and other observers in their descriptions of particular children. However, there is little evidence for stability of behavior from the newborn period. Physiological factors are related to temperament differences, but it is not yet clear exactly how genetics and experience work together to produce these differences.

Temperament and Attachment

Attachment and temperament researchers are describing two different things. Attachment researchers are studying the quality or effectiveness of the infant-caregiver relationship.

In contrast, temperament researchers are studying the frequency or intensity of different infants' behaviors across contexts. It is important to understand both aspects of development and to consider how they might be related (Stevenson-Hinde, 1991).

For a time during the 1980s, efforts were made to explain attachment differences on the basis of temperament differences (e.g., Kagan, 1984). One argument was that differences seen in the Strange Situation were simply differences in infant temperament and did not reflect relationship differences. Perhaps anxious-resistant infants were just temperamentally irritable, and anxious-avoidant infants were aloof. But it was discovered that infants often behaved differently toward each parent in the Strange Situation (van IJzendoorn and de Wolff, 1997), that the infant's attachment classification changed with changes in level of parental stress (Vaughn et al., 1979), and that traditional measures of temperament were rarely related to attachment security (Vaughn and Bost, 1999). Measures of heart rate and cortisol reactions show that anxious-avoidant infants are not detached, but physiologically aroused (Spangler and Grossmann, 1993). Moreover, monozygotic twins are no more similar in attachment classification than dizygotic twins (O'Connor and Croft, 2001), although they are more similar in temperament. Thus, differences in Strange Situation behavior cannot be explained by infant temperament alone (Thompson, 1998; Vaughn and Bost, 1999). It seems equally unlikely that differences in care and resulting attachment quality can account for all variation in children's temperament, especially given the findings of twin studies.

To reiterate, *quality of attachment* refers to organization of behavior with respect to a particular partner, while *temperament* refers to style of behavior regardless of partner. Securely attached infants can have very different temperaments. Some are cuddly, cry a great deal, and are very active. Others cry little, are placid, and rarely want physical contact. Whatever their temperament, all securely attached infants have in common an effective relationship with a caregiver. Securely attached infants seek the contact they need with the caregiver, however little or much it may be, and that contact is effective in alleviating distress. Anxiously attached infants also can have different temperaments, which may affect how their insecurity toward the caregiver is expressed. Insecurely attached infants' doubtfulness about parent availability is probably due to the quality of care they have received, but their tendency to be outwardly angry or more passively distressed may be due to temperament (Thompson, 1998).

Not surprisingly, temperament is related to certain behaviors in the Strange Situation, but not to security of attachment itself. For example, Megan Gunnar and her colleagues (1989b) found that cortisol reactions at 9 months predicted later crying in the Strange Situation but not anxious-resistant attachment. In addition, temperament measures do not predict crying upon reunion. Thus, the baby's tendency to get upset may have some basis in temperament, but how well an infant copes with that upset in the context of the attachment relationship seems to be based on experience.

This is not to say that the two features of development are completely unrelated (Vaughn and Bost, 1999). Temperament may help to determine what constitutes sensitive care and thus fosters secure attachment for a particular infant (Sroufe, 1995). For a temperamentally placid baby, frequent stimulation may represent sensitive care, whereas for an easily overaroused infant, frequent, intense stimulation may be insensitive.

Another way temperament and attachment may be related is that, in some cases, the characteristics of a particular infant may be at odds with those of a particular caregiver. The idea that caregiver and infant characteristics may clash is called the *match-mismatch hypothesis.* There is some support for this idea. Anxious attachment is not predicted by an infant's proneness to distress or by a caregiver's need for control alone, but it is predicted by the two measures together (Mangelsdorf et al., 1990). For example, a parent with a high need to control situations may find it difficult to be sensitive to the needs of a baby who is easily upset.

A third way temperament and attachment may be related is that early infant characteristics may feed into the quality of care parents provide and thereby affect attachment quality. Two studies have shown that newborn irritability predicts anxious attachment in low-income families, with increased anxious-resistant attachment found in the United States (Susman-Stillman, Kalkoske, and Egeland, 1996) and increased anxious-avoidant attachment found in a Dutch sample (van den Boom, 1989). The cultural differences make clear that these cannot be direct temperament effects. Instead, the effects must be due to differences in how caregivers respond to babies depending on their irritability; exactly *how* the caregiving differs depends on cultural factors. For example, low-income American mothers may tend to respond to irritable babies with inconsistent care, whereas low-income Dutch mothers may respond by becoming unavailable or rejecting. In middle-class samples, no overall effect of infant irritability has been found; presumably, social support allows middle-class caregivers to compensate for infants' early difficulties (Crockenberg, 1981).

Finally, temperament can be related to attachment when an infant's characteristics tax caregivers' ability to cope. For example, extremely premature infants with serious health problems have an increased likelihood of anxious-resistant attachment (Plunkett et al., 1986), and prenatally drug-exposed babies have a heightened risk of anxious-avoidant and disorganized-disoriented attachment (Rodning, Beckwith, and Howard, 1989). These effects may occur because some of these infants cry often and are difficult to soothe, and because such difficulties are extremely stressful for parents.

In conclusion, it is useful to think about attachment developing in an interacting system of infant, caregiver, and the larger environment. Trying to decide whether quality of care or infant temperament affects development more is misguided. Infant irritability predicts caregiver insensitivity, but early caregiver insensitivity predicts later irritability even better (Engfer, 1988). Infant temperament is also predicted by parents' marital satisfaction and self-confidence (Belsky, Fish, and Isabella, 1991; Teti and Gelfand, 1991), and newborn irritability is predicted by mother's stress and anxiety during pregnancy (Molitor et al., 1984). Quality of care and infant temperament influence one another in a circular way. As a result, positive temperament and security of attachment, uncorrelated in early infancy, do converge by the preschool years (Vaughn et al., 1992).

The total context of development is more important than either the caregiver's behavior or the baby's temperament alone. For example, given Karen's ambivalence about motherhood and newborn Meryl's crankiness, interaction between the two will tend to intensify these traits. As long as Karen's situation does not improve, Meryl is likely to become a truly difficult child, even though in different circumstances her initial irritability might have been only temporary (Egeland and Sroufe, 1981; van den Boom, 1989). In contrast, Mikey might be classified as a slow-to-warm-up baby, but Christine's patience and confidence in her mothering skills help him to adjust to new experiences; over time, the way Christine responds to Mikey will help him manage his negative reaction to novelty and may actually reduce it. This is the transactional model from Chapter 2 in operation; the various parts of the system all affect one another.

THE IMPORTANCE OF EARLY CARE

As mentioned in Chapter 1, one of the most fundamental developmental issues is the significance of early experience. If development simply reflects the tally of all experiences, or if new experiences supplant prior ones, there is no unique role for early care (Lewis, 1997). On the other hand, if basic patterns of social responsiveness and emotional regulation are established in infancy, early care is of unique and fundamental importance (Sroufe, 2000).

The Sensitive Period Hypothesis

The idea that certain kinds of experience are especially important at particular points in development is known as the **sensitive period hypothesis.** For example, many developmentalists believe the quality of attachment formed in infancy sets the stage for later relationships. This is not to say attachments can form only in infancy or later relationships

Sensitive period hypothesis:
The idea that certain kinds of experience are especially important at particular points in development.

Infant monkeys separated from their parents in the first months of life are often wary and hesitant to explore. Here, a 6-month-old clings to a familiar peer rather than engaging in play.

Child Development CD:
Harlow's Monkeys

are always identical to early ones. Rather, later attachment formation may be more difficult if opportunities were absent during infancy, and the quality of early relationships may be of special importance for later development.

Studies of monkeys provide convincing evidence for the power of early experience. Monkeys who spent their early months with peers but without parents show abnormal behavior, such as marked fearfulness and clinging (Suomi, 1977). Monkeys isolated for six months are social misfits, and those isolated for the first year are completely unable to relate to others (Suomi and Harlow, 1971). Moreover, isolation for the first six months (equivalent to more than a year for humans) has more profound effects than isolation in the second six months. The social handicaps of monkeys isolated their first half-year are very difficult to overcome, even with prolonged special rehabilitation (Suomi, Harlow, and McKinney, 1972). Monkeys isolated as babies who appear to be functioning normally after years in supportive groups revert to their earlier disturbed behavior when placed in cages like those from their infancy, showing remarkable *signature stereotypies*—individual peculiar mannerisms they developed as deprived infants (Novak et al., 1992).

All the evidence suggests that humans also are adversely affected by inadequate care in infancy. In fact, because of the greater complexity of their social and emotional development, human children may be even more vulnerable to early deprivation. As discussed in Chapter 2, researchers have found a variety of negative consequences of early institutional rearing, including early physical and emotional problems, difficulties with peers in childhood and adolescence, and later problems in parenting (e.g., Gunnar, 2001; Johnson, 2000; Rutter, Quinton, and Hill, 1990). As with monkeys, the longer the early institutionalization continues—the older the age at adoption—the more serious are the child's problems (O'Connor et al., 1999). Forming close, empathic relationships seems to be a special difficulty. Parents, researchers, and policymakers have also wondered whether day care during infancy might have consequences for attachment formation. Current research findings on this issue are discussed in the box on page 221.

Cultural Diversity and Common Humanity

A consideration of infant development in cultures around the world suggests both great diversity and a core of commonality. There is diversity among cultures in styles of living, child-rearing goals, and particular behavior patterns (Bornstein et al., 1992; Hewlett

APPLYING RESEARCH FINDINGS

Day Care in Infancy

Perhaps no topic in developmental psychology has generated more controversy than the out-of-home care of infants. Touching on issues ranging from the sensitive period hypothesis (see p. 219), to the equality of women and men, the debate has sometimes been so heated that it has been referred to as "the day care wars" (see Belsky, 2001 for a review; see also Phillips and Adams, 2001; Scarr, 1998). Opinions have run the gamut from the view that nonparental care is certain to be damaging to children to the view that by itself day care in infancy poses no risk to development. What can we actually conclude from the mountain of research that has been carried out on this topic?

A moderate position seems best supported. Day care does not prevent the formation of attachment to parents, even though children also may become attached to day care providers (Thompson, 1998), nor does it inevitably lead to problems in the child or in the parent-child relationship.

On the other hand, early day care of more than 10 or 20 hours per week has been established as a developmental risk factor. This means that day care is associated with an increase in the risk of negative developmental outcomes, even though most children in day care will do well. Moreover, effects are most notable when other risk factors also are present (Belsky, 2001).

This is well illustrated by the important National Institute of Child Health and Human Development Study of Early Child Care, which has followed more than 1,200 children from birth through middle childhood (e.g., NICHD, 2001). This study found no overall impact of early day care on children's attachments to their mothers. However, when maternal care was insensitive and was combined with early day care, many more anxious attachments were found. Moreover, day care itself was found to foster less sensitive maternal care.

Likewise, while early day care by itself is only sometimes associated with later aggression or other problems, the combination of many hours per week in day care and multiple years of day care beginning early in life is most strongly related to later aggression (Belsky, 2001). Low quality day care is another risk factor that adds to the likelihood of negative outcomes. This is best demonstrated by an important intervention study (Howes et al., 1995). These investigators found that when the adult–child ratio for infant day care was changed from 1:6 to 1:4, the likelihood of later behavior problems decreased.

Our own review of the research leads us to conclude that the timing, amount, and quality of day care are all important. Given the current evidence, we would favor more child care options for parents of young infants, so that extensive day care is not their only choice. Surveys of parents indicate that they share this opinion (e.g., Farkas et al. 2000). Despite the fact that experts have sometimes told them otherwise, the majority of parents continue to believe that a full time parental presence in the home is the best option for young children and that even good day care may not be as good as what infants could get from parents.

Many countries, such as Sweden, are far ahead of the United States in providing leave from work for parents of young children. This and other options, including flexible work schedules, should be more widely available. In addition, good quality day care must be available for children whose parents need to work full-time for economic or other reasons. At present, millions of poor families in this country lack access to it (Phillips and Adams, 2001).

---

et al., 1998; Richman, Miller, and LeVine, 1992). Yet caregivers in all cultures recognize the importance of providing consistent, responsive care for young infants. Japanese mothers direct their babies' looking more to themselves than to objects and U.S. mothers do the reverse, but in both cultures mothers encourage babies to explore, imitate babies' vocalizations, and respond to their distress with nurturance (Bornstein et al., 1992). Mothers in Boston and in the Gusii tribe of Kenya both respond promptly to an upset baby, although the Gusii are more physically responsive and the U.S. mothers more verbally responsive (Richman, Miller, and LeVine, 1992).

Occasionally, variations in care have been shown to increase anxious attachment. For example, infants in an Israeli kibbutz who slept away from their mothers overnight were more likely to manifest resistant and disorganized attachment than other Israeli infants (Sagi et al., 1994). Cross-cultural variations in attachment must be interpreted with care. Infants in traditional Japanese families become extremely upset in the Strange Situation (Takahashi, 1990), but this does not mean these infants all have anxious-resistant attachments. Rather, they have almost no experience with separation, making Ainsworth's procedure inappropriate for them.

The existence of other relationships for a child doesn't seem to weaken the cultural belief that early nurturing care from the mother is important. Among the Efe foragers

NICHD Study of Early Child Care

Attachment Across Cultures

In many cultures infants are in physical contact with an adult at all times, carried in a sling during the day and sleeping with a caregiver at night.

in the Congo, for example, children have many relationships with kin, and by age 3 they spend 60 percent of their time with older children. However, up to age 2 they are primarily with their mothers, especially during the first eight months (Tronick, Morelli, and Ivey, 1992). In many cultures, mothers carry their infants at all times during waking hours and sleep with them at night (Hewlett et al., 1998; Morelli et al., 1992). Even when such constant physical proximity is not the case, as in the United States, caregivers typically respond promptly to infant distress. The universal recognition of the need for such responsive, consistent care in infancy suggests that it is vital for human adaptation.

The pervasiveness of some infant caregiving practices is a response to a common human endowment. Numerous studies show great similarity in infant emotional reactions and emotional development in the early months (Kisilevsky et al., 1998; Sroufe, 1995). However, by the end of the first year, cultural differences in experience begin to have an impact on emotional life. For example, by 11 months Chinese infants are less emotionally responsive to fear-inducing and frustrating experiences than Japanese or European-American infants, perhaps because of a tendency for Chinese families to value and encourage emotional restraint (Camras et al., 1998).

The Special Impact of Early Experience

All periods of development are important, but there is a way in which early experience has special significance. An analogy is building a house. All parts of the house are important. Without a frame there can be no roof, and without a roof any structure will soon deteriorate. But the entire building depends on a solid foundation. Similarly, basic expectations about oneself and the social world are laid down during infancy. Such expectations may guide later encounters with the world, coloring the experiences children seek and how they interpret them.

Early Experience

Psychoanalytically oriented researchers also argue that early experience is important because it cannot be readily brought to consciousness and examined, and therefore any ill effects from it may not be easily corrected (Bowlby, 1973). It is unlikely that the monkeys studied by Novak and colleagues (1992) remembered their early social deprivation, or that Suomi's (2002) monkeys remembered how they were mothered. Rather, patterns of behavioral and emotional regulation laid down in infancy were not erased by intervening experience but remained available when cued by an appropriate context.

Early experience, of course, does not determine the rest of development, and genuine change can always occur. Some children who receive inadequate early care ultimately follow a normal course of later development (Egeland, 1997; Grossmann, 1999; Werner and Smith, 2001). Research suggests that such *resilience* in development is not due to inherent invulnerability; instead, like troubled behavior, it reflects developmental processes. It may be related to the timing of changes in experience, the quality of later experiences, or both. When there is a return to healthy development, it is sometimes the case that the early experience itself was not so bad, or the child had some positive experiences to draw on. The important point to remember is that if early deprivation is not extreme and prolonged, later change remains possible.

Chapter Summary

Introduction

Social and emotional development in the first year of life culminates in the formation of attachments between infants and caregivers.

Development in the First Six Months

Newborns have certain predispositions that preadapt them to social interaction:

- the ability to signal psychological and physiological needs;
- the capacity to detect contingencies in the environment;
- the tendency to be attracted to social stimuli, including human faces and voices; and
- the inclination to fall in step with the caregiver's behavior.

Reciprocity in social interaction develops gradually. At first caregivers orchestrate social dialogues, ideally providing **sensitive care.** Infants' involvement becomes increasingly complex until they are full partners in interactions.

The development of social smiling follows a predictable timetable:

- Newborns smile because of activity in lower brain regions.
- By 8 to 10 weeks, babies smile as a result of **recognitory assimilation.**
- By 4 to 5 months, babies produce truly social smiles in response to people they know.

During the first six months, newborns' physiological responses to stimulation develop into forerunners of specific basic emotions, but differ from these emotions in several ways:

- they often require time to build up;
- the meanings attached to events are very general; and
- they are not well differentiated.

The capacity to cope with emotionally arousing situations begins to develop in the first six months of life. Early

techniques are global and involuntary, and they interrupt contact with the environment.

Development in the Second Six Months

Social and emotional developments in the second six months are so dramatic that they can be considered *qualitative* advances. During this time, emotional responses change in several fundamental ways:

- Clearly differentiated specific emotions emerge.
- Emotional responses become increasingly immediate.
- All the classic facial expressions of emotion begin to appear regularly.

Between 7 and 10 months, babies usually develop **stranger distress.** Intensity varies from infant to infant and is affected by context.

In the second six months, babies develop more flexible skills for coping with emotionally arousing situations, such as signaling or moving near the caregiver.

A major development of the second six months is the formation of specific infant-caregiver **attachments:**

- Hallmarks of attachment include **separation distress, greeting reactions,** and **secure-base behavior.**
- **Attachment** develops over many weeks and is distinct from **bonding.** The tendency to form attachments is biologically built into infants and based on infant-caregiver interaction, not on the caregiver's association with food.

Explaining Individual Differences in Early Social and Emotional Development

The attachment framework focuses on variations in the security of infant-caregiver attachment to explain individual differences in infant behavior. Almost all babies become attached to a caregiver, but the quality of attachment varies, depending on the quality of care received.

There are four major patterns of attachment:

- **Secure attachment,** characterized by a balance between exploration and proximity to the caregiver, effective comforting from the caregiver, and positive emotional responses.
- **Anxious-resistant attachment,** characterized by difficulty separating from the caregiver, distress at being left, and ambivalence toward seeking comfort from the caregiver.
- **Anxious-avoidant attachment,** characterized by ready separation from the caregiver, lack of wariness toward strangers, and avoidance of the caregiver following a brief separation.
- **Disorganized-disoriented attachment,** characterized by contradictory features of several attachment patterns or a dazed and disoriented appearance.

Each pattern of attachment is associated with a different pattern of caregiver behavior:

- Secure attachment is associated with sensitive care.
- Anxious-resistant attachment is associated with inconsistent care, exaggerated maternal behaviors, and ineffective soothing.
- Anxious-avoidant attachment is associated with indifference and emotional unavailability or active rejection.
- Disorganized-disoriented attachment is associated with maltreatment or frightening or confusing caregiver behavior.

The quality of care an infant receives is influenced by factors in the caregiver's life, including stress, social support, and the caregiver's own developmental history. Individual differences in attachment quality reflect differences in infants' **internal working models** of the social world, which in turn influence children's later experience.

The **temperament** framework emphasizes differences in behavioral style that are assumed to be inborn:

- Newborn behavior does not predict later temperament very well, but by the end of the first year, temperament becomes more stable and predictive of later behavior.
- Physiological factors are related to temperament differences, but the relative roles of genetics and experience in producing these differences are not yet completely clear.

Attachment research and temperament research provide different perspectives on infants' social development. Attachment and temperament are related to each other in several ways, and both influence the development of individual differences in infant behavior.

The Importance of Early Care

According to the **sensitive period hypothesis,** early care is of special importance for healthy emotional development. Studies of monkeys and of children in orphanages demonstrate the lasting negative impacts of inadequate care in infancy.

Although cultures around the world vary in specific child-rearing goals and practices, there is a consistent recognition of the need to provide responsive care for young infants.

Early experience has special significance because basic expectations about oneself and the social world are laid down during infancy. However, it does not determine the rest of development; later change is possible.

Review Questions

Introduction

1. What are some of the major developments in infancy that culminate in the formation of attachment relationships with caregivers?

Development in the First Six Months

2. How do newborns' predispositions and caregivers' responses work together to produce **reciprocity** in social interaction?
3. What happens in the area of emotional development during the first six months of life?

Development in the Second Six Months

4. How does emotional development continue in the second six months?
5. Explain the hallmarks of **attachment** and the process of attachment formation.

Explaining Individual Differences in Early Social and Emotional Development

6. Describe the major patterns of attachment that have been identified, the patterns of caregiver behavior associated with each, and the influences they have on later development.
7. Discuss the issue of stability and the role of biological factors with regard to **temperament.**
8. How can the attachment framework and the temperament framework be reconciled in explaining individual differences in infants' behavior?

The Importance of Early Care

9. What evidence is there that early care is of special importance for healthy emotional development?

Application and Observation

1. Interview a mother with more than one child about similarities and differences in her children's individual temperaments. Ask her to describe what each of her children was like at birth (or even before) and in early infancy. What similarities and differences did she notice in activity level, irritability, reactions to new things, cuddliness, and other temperamental characteristics mentioned in this chapter? Ask for concrete examples. How would she explain these similarities and differences? How does she think each child's current personality compares to or is connected to his or her early temperament?

2. Observe infants and/or toddlers in a day care, church nursery, play group, or other setting where you can observe several of them at the same time. What individual differences do you notice in their reactions to their environment, especially to other people? What similarities and differences do you notice in activity level, irritability, reaction to novelty, cuddliness, and other temperamental characteristics?

3. Observe morning drop-off and evening pick-up times at a day care center or day care home where infants and toddlers are cared for. How do the babies respond to separation from their parents at the beginning of the day and reunion with them at the end of the day? How do parents respond to these situations? What similarities and differences do you see across parent-infant pairs? Do you notice anything about the behavior of individual parents that seems to make these transitions go more smoothly or less smoothly? If possible, interview the day care provider and some of the parents about their perceptions of these issues.

4. Observe parents of infants of various ages interacting one-on-one with their babies. What do the parents do to provide a framework for the interactions? What do the babies contribute to the interactions? How do the contributions from parents and babies seem to change as the babies get older? If possible, observe more than one adult (either both parents, a parent and another family member, or a parent and a stranger) interacting with the same infant. How does the baby's behavior change with different interaction partners?

Part 2 Epilogue: Infancy

Development during the first year of life is rapid and dramatic. Weak and uncoordinated newborns who interact with the world largely through preprogrammed reflexes become 12-month-olds who can voluntarily reach for, inspect, and manipulate objects and can skillfully navigate by creeping or even walking. Cognitively, too, babies have made remarkable progress in their first year. They have a good grasp of object permanence and can recognize and categorize many things, categorization skills being directly linked to their improving memory abilities. Twelve-month-olds also have expectations and intentions regarding the environment, plus a growing understanding of how actions and events are related to each other. In addition, they show many specific emotions, such as joy at mastering a task, surprise at something unexpected, and anger at a blocked goal. They are now able to engage in true social give-and-take, and they have formed the close relationships with caregivers known as *attachments*.

All these advancements are closely interconnected. There are remarkable parallels between cognitive, emotional, and social development in infancy. Infant emotional reactions expand dramatically in the second six months of life. Infants show emotions that require anticipation, such as surprise, and emotions that require recall and comparison of a past event with a present circumstance, such as fear. Such changes in emotion draw upon advances in memory development and in the capacity to coordinate schemes that emerge in the second six months. In addition, emotional reactions are influenced by context—what has happened just previously, who is present, the familiarity of surroundings, and so forth—and not just by the event. In this change, as in changes in cognitive development described in Chapter 5, we see that infants in the second six months now respond to more than just their immediate perceptual experience.

Likewise, advances in social relationships and advances in cognitive development are closely connected. The beginning of social relationships is intimately tied to the cognitive ability to detect contingencies, such as the link between the child's own crying and a parent's response. At the same time, interactions with caregivers provide a wealth of new opportunities to learn about contingencies. Although attachment is viewed as an aspect of social and emotional development, it is based on the cognitive abilities to distinguish among people, to form expectations based on past interactions, and to understand that a caregiver continues to exist even when out of sight. Concurrently, social exchanges with the caregiver provide the infant with many chances to develop and practice these important cognitive skills. These examples point to the integrated nature of development. Cognitive, social, and emotional growth all proceed together.

Research on brain development during infancy reveals qualitative changes in structure and functioning. One such change occurs in the first three months, as the cerebral cortex becomes functional. This development promotes a shift from reflexive responses to voluntary control of behavior. A second major change occurs around 10 months, with maturation of important areas in the cortex and the establishment of connections between the cortex and lower areas related to emotion and memory. This development supports qualitative changes in both cognitive and social behavior. Given these changes in the brain, it is not surprising that a 10-month-old's behavior is qualitatively different from a 6-month-old's, as seen in our example of mothers and babies playing the "cloth-in-the-mouth" game in Chapter 1. At the same time, development of these brain structures is dependent on cognitive and social stimulation in the preceding months (Schore, 1994).

Four Infants

You have seen four infants begin developmental journeys toward becoming both unique individuals and members of a common human community. In many ways these children started life with the same endowments. Each had essentially the same biological equipment—the same inborn sensory and motor capabilities, the same innate inclination to seek and respond to social stimuli. None was retarded, seriously ill, or otherwise significantly impaired. All presented their parents with the task of raising a normal, healthy baby. Over the course of their first year, each went through the same set of developmental sequences, though at somewhat different rates. Each came to recognize the basic properties of objects and to form attachments around which their social, emotional, and cognitive worlds became organized. Each experienced good enough care so as not to suffer severe developmental problems.

Yet despite these shared characteristics and experiences, we also see in these four children the beginnings of four distinct individuals. Malcolm, for instance, is ahead of the others in physical maturation. He is a strong, robust baby who starts to do for himself early. Meryl, in contrast, is a rather cranky, difficult infant, easily irritated. Her feeding problems and persistent colic pose special challenges. Maggie, like Malcolm, is good-natured and exuberant, although her activity level is not as high as Malcolm's. Mikey is also a generally happy baby, but somewhat slow to warm up to new experiences. Such differences in children's habitual styles of responding can best be understood using the concept of *adaptation*, the process whereby the child and the social environment constantly adjust to each other. Let's look at our four children's caregiving environments and then examine how child and environment interact and mutually adapt.

Four Caregiving Environments

Just as our four children have basic biological traits in common, so their parents face common caregiving tasks. All the parents must meet their baby's physical needs while providing an environment with enough regularity so that the child's cycles of feeding, sleeping, and interacting with the world can become reasonably organized and stable. The parents must also provide appropriate social stimulation and be adequately responsive to their infants. To a large extent, they must shape their own behavior to that of their babies, so the babies' capacity to adapt is not overtaxed. In the process, the babies will learn that they can have an impact on the environment.

All the parents in our stories face these common tasks, but how they perform them is greatly influenced by the contexts in which they live. John and DeeDee Williams are embedded in a network of caring relationships among the members of their household. In raising Malcolm they are supported by their two older children, by John's sister, Denise, and by his mother, Momma Jo. Thus, Malcolm's early development is taking place in a system of social, psychological, and economic support that is difficult for a parent operating alone to match. In facing the challenges of urban life, Malcolm is surrounded by a buffering circle of warmth, love, and nurturance.

Mikey's situation has some of the same elements. Both parents are clearly very attached to him. Frank prizes the "all-boy" son he so wanted, and Christine is a competent, responsive mother who offers Mikey a rich social environment. Christine and Frank have emotional support from Christine's mother and sisters in raising the new baby. Although Maggie was born into the same family as Mikey, her caretaking environment was subtly different from his. As the firstborn child, she encountered parents who were not yet as experienced and confident as they were when Mikey was born. As a girl, she received less attention and affection from Frank than Mikey would get two years later. When Mikey came along, Maggie continued to enjoy support and responsiveness from her mother, who made a point of including her in the care of her new brother. But Frank's preoccupation with his new son made him even less attentive to the needs of his daughter.

One important difference distinguishes Maggie and Mikey's home environment from Malcolm's: in the Gordon household the seeds of serious conflict exist between husband and wife. Frank is intolerant of Christine's desire to pursue goals beyond being a wife and mother. Christine, although still generally accepting Frank's wishes, is beginning to realize that her talents are appreciated outside the home. She is vulnerable to feeling that her goals are being unfairly blocked by Frank. Some signs point to Mikey becoming a buffer between his parents, as when his demands at the breakfast table ("beh! beh!") distract Frank from an argument with Christine. Despite these undercurrents of tension, Mikey is developing nicely as an infant, and Maggie is continuing to build on the positive developmental foundation she gained in infancy.

Meryl's situation contrasts sharply with those of Malcolm, Maggie, and Mikey. An unplanned child, she was born to a mother who was not well prepared to respond to a baby's needs. Karen is not only young and financially dependent, she is also socially isolated—cut off from Meryl's father and her high school friends, and alienated from her mother, who might have been her one reliable resource. Staying at home with Meryl while her mother works long hours, Karen is emotionally on her own except for weekly counseling at the Teen Mother Project. Because of her own unmet needs for care and nurturance, Karen, not surprisingly, has trouble adequately nurturing Meryl. Karen is torn between her strong desire to be a good mother and her feeling of being totally overwhelmed by the task.

The Interplay Between Child and Environment

Child and environment constantly interact, each adapting to the other to achieve a temporary fit. The adjustments that are made then serve as a starting point for a new round of interactions and adaptations. A good example can be seen in Frank's early interactions with Mikey. Frank responds to his normal, healthy son as if he were the most robust, athletic infant ever born. In so doing, he draws Mikey's behavior toward increasing exuberance and a greater tolerance for rough-and-tumble play. As Mikey shows more and more "masculine" qualities, Frank's expectations about his son are confirmed and he is further encouraged to treat the baby like a "real boy." In this way, father and son interact to create the kind of child Frank so much desires. Notice how both Mikey's characteristics and Frank's behavior are involved here. It matters that Mikey is a boy and that he can tolerate Frank's level of stimulation, but Frank's reaction to Mikey is also critical. If Frank were very low-key or uninvolved with his son, Mikey would develop differently. Christine's calm, sensitive interactions with Mikey are also important in shaping his development. His early slowness to warm up to new situations elicits patient support from his mother, which moderates his negative reactions to novelty and in turn increases his ability to cope with the constantly changing stimulation found in his interactions with Frank.

Similar interactions and adaptations are taking place in our other two households. Malcolm enters the world as a loud and lively infant. Rather than being viewed as irritants, these characteristics are cherished in his family. Upon hearing Malcolm's lusty wails, Momma Jo calls them "just grand!" and John tells his son he is "one helluva kid." In this context Malcolm becomes a sociable, good-natured, easy baby, which further promotes positive responses from the members of his family. Not all infants with Malcolm's characteristics would develop this way. Without the easygoing acceptance found in Malcolm's home, what becomes sociability and exuberance could instead have become hyperactivity and a demanding nature.

Meryl and Karen provide a final example of the interaction between infant and caregiving environment. Meryl was a fretful, colicky newborn who cried a great deal. Did these characteristics cause Karen's insecurity in her role as a mother, or did Karen's insecurities, including her stress and anxiety during pregnancy, give rise to Meryl's behavior and physical distress? Clearly it is difficult to say, because the various factors are interrelated. Meryl's difficulties lower the confidence of an already insecure mother, and Karen's doubts and anxieties perpetuate and worsen Meryl's fussiness. In this case, there is a poor match between the particular infant's needs and the particular caregiver's competencies. Mother and child become locked in a negative caregiving cycle that is unlikely to be broken easily. Meryl is a prime candidate for developing the anxious-resistant pattern of attachment associated with inconsistent care.

These, then, are the initial adaptations of our four fictionalized children and their caregiving environments, all based on composites of cases in our research. They will be carried forward to become part of the developmental context during the toddler period. Meryl, Maggie, Mikey, and Malcolm now have individual styles of behavior that will affect how others respond to them. Likewise, the expectations of the people close to these children have increasingly crystallized, which will further influence the kind of care family members provide.

Many questions remain, however. Is Meryl destined to be a difficult and troubled preschooler? Under what circumstances might she evolve a more positive adaptation? If circumstances dramatically improve for Meryl, will she still be vulnerable in certain ways? What vulnerabilities might Mikey have, and how could they manifest themselves in later periods of development? How will Maggie be affected by her father's intense involvement with her younger brother and relative disengagement from her? How will the very active Malcolm fare when he enters school, where strict demands for orderliness and quiet will be imposed on him? What special challenges will he face as a black child in a densely populated urban setting? We will address these and other questions in the following units of this book.

Toddlerhood

Part 3 Four Children as Toddlers

Malcolm Williams

A breeze rippled the water in the wading pool, sending a large leaf floating slowly across the surface. The little boy leaned over the edge and stretched out his arm. He could almost touch the leaf with his fingers. He reached a little farther, then a little farther.

"Malcolm M. Williams, you get yourself away from that water this instant or you're gonna be one sorry child!"

Two-year-old Malcolm turned and looked in Momma Jo's direction. Glancing back at the water, he started to reach for the leaf one more time, but then stopped himself. Momma Jo's tone meant business. He knew better than to defy her when she sounded like that.

"That boy's just like his father was at his age," Momma Jo told an elderly woman she often sat with in the park. "You turn your back for just one second and there he's gone and got himself into a pile of mischief. Yes," she laughed softly, "a pile of mischief!" She gazed lovingly at her grandson, who was now intent on catching a small gray poodle with a rhinestone collar.

"Doggie, doggie, doggie!" Malcolm crowed gleefully, as he ran back and forth, his arms outstretched.

Momma Jo stood up and buttoned her coat against the growing chill. "Well, we best be goin'," she told her friend reluctantly. "It's gettin' dark so early these days. Winter's almost on us, that's for sure. Malcolm, honey! We're leavin' now. You let that dog be." And taking Malcolm firmly by the hand, Momma Jo started toward the park exit.

"Happy to you! Happy to you!" Malcolm sang to himself as they walked along.

"It's not your birthday anymore, honey," Momma Jo explained with a smile. "That was last week. Now you have to wait a whole year for another birthday. Then you'll be three."

"Malcky two!" the little boy said proudly with an energetic hop as they stopped at the corner. Momma Jo now had a choice to make. If she went down the street past the excavation site for the new post office, she could cut a few blocks off their normal route. But that street was deserted and filled with boarded-up buildings. It was not a safe place after dark. What could anyone want with an old woman and a baby? Momma Jo thought, deciding to risk the short walk after all. "We'll be home quicker this way," she said to Malcolm, reaching down to make sure the hood of his coat was securely tied beneath his chin. "We're real late already. Your momma's gonna worry."

"Who that?" Malcolm asked, pointing a mittened hand at four teenage boys leaning against the construction site fence. "No one we know, honey," Momma Jo answered. "Come on now, Malcolm, we're gonna walk on the other side of the street." But the four boys crossed with them, two in front and two behind. Quickly they made a circle around Momma Jo and Malcolm.

"Where ya hurryin' to, momma?" one of the four asked.

"Just let us by," Momma Jo said. 'We don't want any trouble."

"No trouble, momma," the ringleader answered. "We just wanna know what you got in that bag of yours."

"Take the bag and just let us be," Momma Jo pleaded, the tension mounting in her voice.

Malcolm looked up at Momma Jo and then at the four strangers. "Go 'way," he said quietly at first; then, louder, "Go 'way!"

The four boys looked at Malcolm and started laughing. "You heard what the man said," the ringleader hooted. "He said, go 'way!" The other three laughed louder. "Are we gonna go 'way like the little man says?"

Momma Jo put an arm protectively around Malcolm, but his attention was drawn elsewhere. "Look!" he said in his babyish voice, and his mittened hand shot up. Everyone turned to see a blue and white police car cruising slowly down the street. The four boys scattered.

"Everything all right here?" one of the policemen asked as the car stopped beside Momma Jo and Malcolm.

"It is now, officer," Momma Jo answered. "But we sure would appreciate an escort to the corner in case those four young hoodlums decide to come back."

"I'll do better than that," the policeman said. "Hop in and we'll drive you home."

"I still can't believe you were walkin' there!" John Williams said to his mother after dinner that night. "You read about things happenin' there all the time. Where was your head, Momma?"

"They're safe," said DeeDee as she cleared the dishes off the table. "That's all that matters. So let's just forget it now."

"If I had been there I would have showed them," 14-year-old JJ remarked, punching the air with his fists. "I ain't afraid of no gang turkeys."

"That's enough of that talk," his father snapped back. "Those dudes are nothin' to mess with, you hear me? You could get yourself hurt bad, boy. Hurt real bad."

"Hurt. Band-Aid. Kiss it better," Malcolm added, and John couldn't help but smile.

Later that night, as DeeDee was getting Malcolm into his pajamas, she stopped and held him by the shoulders. "I know it may be hard for you to understand," she said, "but I want you to know I'm real proud of you for stickin' up for your gran'ma today."

"Malcky go p'lice car!" Malcolm answered, still brimming over with excitement.

"I know, baby, I know," DeeDee said and hugged her little boy close.

Maggie and Mikey Gordon

"Where's my little all-star?" Frank Gordon called as he opened the back door and stepped into the kitchen. Twenty-five-month-old Mikey, grinning from ear to ear, ran to greet his father. "There's my tough guy," Frank said, scooping Mikey up and swinging him over his head. Mikey laughed and crowed gleefully: "Daddy home!"

Four-year-old Maggie looked up hopefully from the kitchen table, where she was coloring. "Daddy, look what I drew!" she exclaimed, waving one of her pictures in the air. But Frank was already running off into the living room after Mikey. "Here I come!" yelled Frank, and when he caught Mikey he picked him up and tossed him in the air. Mikey squealed with delight.

"Be careful now," Christine called. "You don't want him to bump his mouth again."

"Women!" Frank said to Mikey. "They don't understand us men, do they, Tiger?"

"No!" said Mikey emphatically, shaking his head, without understanding exactly why.

"Anything good happen today?" Frank asked Christine as he came back into the kitchen to get a beer. Christine knew what this question meant. Frank wanted to know if anything special had happened with Mikey that day.

"Well, when I wasn't looking he figured out how to open up the vacuum cleaner and take the bag out. Then he wanted to see what was in it, so he ripped the bag open and dumped all the dirt on the floor. When I turned around, there he was with the empty bag upside down on his head! 'Party hat,' he kept saying. He must have been remembering Maggie's birthday, you know, with those big paper hats I made for the kids. Anyway, it was a real mess to clean up!"

Frank chuckled and shook his head. "What a kid!" he said.

"Oh, and Maggie said the funniest thing this morning . . . ." Christine's voice trailed off. Frank had already wandered away in search of Mikey. Christine sighed. She knew Frank didn't mean to ignore Maggie, but he was so involved with his son that sometimes he seemed only dimly aware of their little girl's existence.

Later that night, Christine tried to lead Mikey upstairs to bed. "No!" said Mikey, pulling his hand away and holding it tightly against his chest.

"Maybe he's not tired," Frank remarked from his seat in front of the TV.

"Frank, he's exhausted," Christine shot back. "But you get him so worked up he can't get to sleep."

"Yeah, yeah, it's always *my* fault," Frank answered irritably.

By now Christine had Mikey in her arms and was at the foot of the stairs. "No!" he said squirming to get down. "I do it!"

"Okay, sweetie. You do it yourself." Christine watched in amusement as he determinedly climbed the stairs alone, cautioning himself as he gripped the rails, "Careful. Hold on."

"Well, he's all settled in," Christine announced as she came downstairs after reading the children a story. She flopped down beside Frank on the sofa, slid off her shoes, and put her feet up. "Maggie's in bed, too. I told her she could listen to the Little Mermaid tape one more time."

"Quiet," said Frank. "This is a good program."

"You know," said Christine, "I wouldn't mind if once in a while we could talk at night instead of you shushing me so you can watch the damn TV."

"I talked before and what'd it get me? A lousy putdown, that's what."

"All I said was that Mikey was tired, and he was."

"It's the *way* you said it," Frank answered, hitting the off button on the remote. "OK. What is it? I know you got somethin' to say. So say it. Let's get it over with so I can have some peace."

"Yeah," Christine answered, standing up and looking angrily at her husband, "I've got something to tell you. I've been thinking about this a long time, but tonight you make me mad enough to be really sure. Helen's opening a new shop just for kids' clothes and she wants *me* to help manage it. And I'm gonna say yes whether you like it or not! What do you think of that?"

"Oh great! What is this? The new independence? The modern woman crap? It's those damn buying trips I let you go on. Give you an inch and you want a mile!"

"*I know* I can do it," Christine answered defiantly. "I've got it all figured out. Five mornings a week in the shop, and the rest at home where I can still do my sewing. I've even looked into day care for Mikey and Maggie."

"Dump the kids in day care?" Frank shouted, the veins on his neck standing out. "Now you've gone too far, Chrissie! What the hell kind of mother are you?"

"I'm a good mother! They'd only be there half-time. Maggie's already in nursery school three mornings a week anyway. Besides, this isn't just any old daycare center. It's run by experts on kids. People who teach at Brown."

"Screw experts! I don't want any eggheads messin' with my kids."

"Oh, Frank, that's ridiculous! I could bring in $20,000 a year between this new job and my sewing. And we could really use the money around here, the way you've been doing lately!"

As soon as the words were out of her mouth, Christine was sorry. It was true Frank's hours had been cut back at work, but that wasn't his fault. The construction business was slow all over the state. What a stupid, unfair thing to say, she thought. She was just about to tell him she was sorry, when suddenly she felt her head snap sideways. Frank had struck her across the face. Christine was stunned. It wasn't so much the pain, which was bad enough, but the shock that paralyzed her. Frank had never so much as raised a finger to her before.

"Mommy?" Through her pain and confusion Christine heard a little voice from the stairs. Horrified, she realized that Maggie must have heard the argument and gotten out of bed to see what was going on.

"Chrissie!" Frank said. "God, I didn't mean to. It just happened. When you said that . . . Look, we'll work this out, OK? Chrissie?"

Maggie loved day care from the very beginning. She was ecstatic to be going to "school" every day, instead of just three days a week, and she came home every day full of happy chatter. At first Mikey protested being left at day care in the mornings. He gradually got used to the new routine, though, and by the third week he looked forward to spending the mornings with his new friends. One thing that helped was an old Raggedy Ann doll someone had given Maggie when she was a baby. Mikey had found it in the toy box, and now he carried it with him everywhere and slept with it every night. He was oblivious to the doll's shabby condition and loved it passionately, perhaps because of the little red heart on its chest.

One morning Mikey came down to breakfast, toting Raggedy Ann with him as usual. Setting the doll beside his bowl of cereal, he began to eat noisily. His father seethed across the table. Finally, he reached out and picked up the toy.

"Mikey," Frank said. "you're a big boy now, and big boys don't play with dolls. Only girls and babies do. You don't want to be a baby, do you?" Mikey didn't understand what his father was saying. All he knew was that his favorite toy had just been taken from him. He let out a loud wail.

"Frank," Christine protested, "he's only two."

"Stay out of this, Chrissie," Frank snapped back. "It's that damn day care center, and I'm not gonna let it happen. I'm gonna put a stop to it right now."

Then more gently he said to Mikey, "Don't cry, Mikey. We'll go to the toy store and get you a great big red fire engine. The kind with lights that flash and a siren that goes off when you press a button. Would you like that, huh?"

Mikey stopped crying and wiped his face. For a few days he asked his mother where "Rang-ety" had gone. But soon he forgot all about the doll with the little red heart on its chest.

Meryl Polonius

A barrage of large raindrops spattered against the windows. Water overflowed from the rain gutter and gushed noisily onto the back steps. Sitting warm and dry on the kitchen floor, 15-month-old Meryl Polonius was oblivious to the weather that beat upon the house. For what seemed to Karen like the hundredth time, she was carefully inspecting the contents of the kitchen cabinets. Whenever she took out a pot or other utensil she would hold it up and exclaim, "Eh! Eh!" Besides something that sounded like "muh," which she used to refer to both her mother and her grandmother, "eh" was Meryl's only word. But she used it very expressively. "Eh?" she asked while pointing to some newfound object, obviously wanting to know what this strange and wonderful thing was. "Eh!" she demanded, holding up a set of sticky fingers, clearly wanting someone to hurry and clean this mess off.

Karen sat at the kitchen table, aimlessly twirling a lock of hair around her finger. She pored over the Sunday want ads, a red pen in her hand. "Let's see. 'ASSEMBLY LINE—light packaging—full-time days.' Forget that. 'CLERICAL—word processing and data entry.' Computers? Are you kidding? 'DELIVERY PERSON—must have own truck or van.' Fat chance. 'RECEPTIONIST—professional appearance essential.' Ha! All I've got to wear are jeans and tee-shirts!"

In the midst of this dreary round of pessimism, the kitchen door opened and Karen's mother burst in. "What weather!" she said to Karen, pushing the wet hair back from her face.

"Did you sell the house?" asked Karen, looking up from the paper.

"No. The snooty woman didn't like the color of the tile in the bathroom. And the husband saw that the chimney was leaking a little. 'What doesn't leak in monsoons like this?' I tried to tell him. But his mind was made up."

"Too bad," said Karen, turning back to her job search.

Karen and her mother were getting along a little better these days. The counselor at the Teen Mother Project had helped them work out some of their problems. At the second session they'd had together, Mrs. Polonius poured out her feelings of guilt over Karen's pregnancy. "I feel I failed you as a mother," she told Karen with tears in her eyes. "I wasn't much older than you when I got pregnant and had to marry your father. I of all people should have been able to guide you better. I'm sorry, honey, if I let you down." Karen had cried out of sheer relief that someone in the world really cared about her. She and her mother still disagreed on many subjects, but at least they could talk to each other now.

"See any interesting prospects?" Karen's mother asked, bending over her daughter's shoulder to see what she had circled in the paper. "Look at all these listings. There's got to be something here. Don't be too fussy, you know. It doesn't have to be the greatest job to start with. Just something to get you out of the house a little and meeting new people."

"I'm not being fussy!" Karen snapped. "It's just that I'm not qualified for anything. What do I know except housework and babies? Ha! That's it. I'll get a part-time job as a nursemaid!"

"What about these waitress jobs?" Karen's mother pressed on, ignoring both her daughter's sarcasm and the loud clanging of metal in the background as Meryl banged the lids of two pots together. "Here. 'WAITRESSES—immediate openings—full- or part-time—apply in person—The Green Door.' That's a nice place. What's wrong with that?"

"But I'm not experienced, Mom. That's what's wrong. They want experienced people."

"How do you know that if you don't try? You're bright and attractive. If I had a restaurant, you'd be just the kind of girl I'd want to hire."

Karen rolled her eyes. "Mom. Look. It says immediate. I'm not ready immediately. I don't have a sitter lined up for Meryl. And she's so cranky and difficult it's gonna be hard to find anyone who wants the job."

"Well, I may have the answer to that," Karen's mother said, cutting off her daughter's last excuse. "Arlene Springer down at the office told me about this wonderful woman on Cragmont Street who takes care of children in her home. She's raised five children of her own, and one of them's a doctor. How much more qualified could she be? Just do me a favor, Karen, and apply at The Green Door. I think it could be perfect for you."

On another rainy January day, a year later, it was almost 5:00 when Karen arrived at Mrs. Jasper's house to pick up Meryl. Usually she was there by 4:30, right after her shift at The Green Door. But today she'd had to stop at the store, the checkout lines had been long, and the rain had slowed traffic to a crawl. Meryl was sitting on the floor in front of the TV when Karen came in.

"Ready to go home?" she asked Meryl, picking up her little yellow raincoat.

"No!" Meryl said and kept staring at the TV.

At first Mrs. Jasper had been reluctant to accept Meryl in her family day care. With her long list of allergies and shyness with other children, Mrs. Jasper thought this little girl might be too much of a problem. In the beginning Meryl was a problem. All day she followed Mrs. Jasper around, whining and pouting when urged to play with the other children. At home, Meryl's tantrums became steadily worse. Her behavior toward Karen was oddly ambivalent. Sometimes she seemed very angry at her; other times she would cling and demand to sit on her lap.

In time, however, Meryl settled down at Mrs. Jasper's house and became more interested in playing with the toys. Recently she had begun to play a make-believe game in which a family of stuffed bears acted out everyday activities. "Bye-Bye. Go work now. Don't cry, baby. Mommy be back." Most of her other favorite pastimes were quiet, solitary activities, like stringing large wooden beads. When she was finished, she would take her creation to Mrs. Jasper, requesting "Tie it, pwease," and then wear it around her neck for the rest of the day. Outdoors Meryl's behavior was equally reserved. When Mrs. Jasper installed a seesaw, Meryl was the only child who refused to try it out, although she quietly watched the other children from a safe distance. When Mrs. Jasper tried to coax her on, Meryl retreated to the sandbox, where she took up the more familiar activity of spooning sand into little plastic cups. But despite her reserve, Meryl had adapted to day care. She no longer gave Mrs. Jasper any trouble to speak of. Her whining and uncooperativeness tended to surface only when it was time to go home.

"No?" Karen asked Meryl as she stood holding out the yellow raincoat. "You don't want to come home with me? Don't you want to have your dinner? I know I'm a little late, but I got held up at the store. What if we have ice cream for dessert? Then will you come home with me?"

"No, I won't," answered Meryl.

Karen glanced over at Mrs. Jasper, who was busily picking up toys. Meryl didn't say no to her as often as she did to Karen. A few weeks before, Karen had asked Mrs. Jasper why she thought that was. Mrs. Jasper had put her arm around Karen's shoulders. "Children need to learn to mind, dear," she said kindly. "They know when you don't mean it. You just love her and mean what you say and Meryl will be fine." It sounded so simple. But for Karen it didn't come easily.

"Please, Meryl, come on," Karen tried again, doing her best to sound firm. "We'll have ice cream."

"Chocowat?" Meryl finally asked after considering the offer for several seconds. And when her mother nodded assent, she stood up so Karen could put on her coat. At least this time there wasn't a tantrum.

7 Toddler Language and Thinking

Language acquisition for this 2-year-old involves learning to sign rather than to speak.

Symbolic representation:
The use of ideas, images, or other symbols to stand for objects or events.

Language:
An abstract, rule-governed system of arbitrary symbols that can be combined in countless ways to communicate information.

M eryl was 16 months old before she finally said her first recognizable word. One day when Karen went into Meryl's room to get her up from her nap, Meryl announced with a serious look, "Mama." Karen was elated. "Mama! Yes, mama! I'm your mama!" she told Meryl, picking her up and giving her a hug that made the little girl squirm. Minutes later Karen was on the phone, sharing the news with her mother at work.

To parents, children's first words are among the most exciting milestones in their development. Language opens up new, more efficient ways to communicate. When parents ask their child a question or give an instruction, they can get a verbal response.

Emerging language is one example of a general capacity for **symbolic representation**—the use of ideas, images, sounds, or other symbols to stand for objects and events. The capacity for symbolic representation appears during a major transition period—the transition from infancy to childhood. This transition is called the *toddler period* because it coincides with the time when children learn to walk. The toddler period lasts from roughly 12 months of age to about 30 months of age.

Because language is such an important accomplishment of the toddler period, it is the primary focus of this chapter. (Many other important aspects of toddler cognition were discussed in Chapter 5.) **Language** is an abstract, rule-governed system of arbitrary symbols that can be combined in countless ways to communicate information. Language is not synonymous with speech. The sign language used by deaf people is a genuine language that can express any desired idea. In contrast, a bird mimicking speech is not displaying true language; to the bird, words are simply sounds that do not symbolize anything.

This chapter begins with a look at the various components of human language to give you some idea of what is involved in mastering a language. Next we examine the course of early language learning, including mastery of sound patterns, word meanings, grammar, and the social use of language. We then consider the relative contributions of the child and the environment to the process of language development. Finally, we discuss three nonlinguistic aspects of toddler cognitive development that are related to the emergence of symbolic representation—the development of gestures, pretend play, and understanding of iconic symbols such as pictures.

Questions to Think About As You Read

- How do nature and nurture interact in children's acquisition of language?
- How are cognitive and social development intertwined with language development?

THE COMPONENTS OF LANGUAGE

Language Development Milestones

When 2½-year-old Meryl hands Mrs. Jasper a string of beads and requests, "Tie it, pwease," her simple words reflect a major accomplishment. They show that Meryl is mastering the many conventions of language for combining sounds into meaningful words, and words into meaningful sentences. Meryl knows the sound combination /tai/ means to fasten two pieces of string together. She also knows that, for her sentence to make sense, the object *it* must follow the verb, not precede it. Meryl does not think of speech in terms of such rules, but she follows them nonetheless. She is also starting to follow conventions for how to word sentences in various social contexts, such as using *please* to make a request, especially of an adult. All this Meryl has mastered in the year since she spoke her first word. To understand the size of the task faced by language-learning toddlers, let's look more closely at the various components of language.

Sounds, Structure, Meaning, and Conversational Rules

All languages can be broken down into five major subsystems: *phonology, semantics, morphology, syntax,* and *pragmatics.* Becoming a competent speaker of a language requires learning all five.

Phonology refers to the system of sounds used in a language, the rules for combining those sounds to make words, and the use of stress and intonation in spoken sentences. Every language has its own set of **phonemes**—speech sounds that contrast with one another and can change the meaning of a word. For example, in English the sound /b/ in *bat* is a different phoneme from the sound /p/ in *pat,* which is why you immediately recognize these two words as different. Other languages include phonemes not used in English, such as the tongue-trilled /r/ in Spanish, the German /ch/ sounds, and the clicking sounds used in some African languages.

Semantics consists of the meanings of words and sentences. A sentence might be perfectly correct grammatically but nevertheless be confusing because it breaks semantic rules. For instance, if a preschooler told you "My daddy is having a baby," you would ask for clarification, even though the child's grammar is flawless, because the meaning of the word *daddy* is inconsistent with the meaning of the phrase *having a baby.*

Morphology is the system of rules for combining units of meaning to form words or to modify word meanings. The smallest meaningful units in a language are called **morphemes.** Many words are single morphemes, such as *child, language,* and *speak.* Other words consist of several morphemes. The word *unspeakable* has three morphemes: the prefix *un-* (meaning not), the root word *speak,* and the suffix *-able* (meaning capable of being done).

Syntax refers to the rules for organizing words into phrases and sentences. Following the rules of syntax allows speakers to form grammatical sentences and convey the meanings they intend. *The boy kissed the girl* and *The girl kissed the boy* are both grammatical sentences, but they mean different things because of their word order. *Kissed the girl the boy* is hard to interpret because it does not follow the usual rules of English syntax.

Pragmatics is the set of rules governing conversation and social use of language. It includes knowing how to use language to accomplish social goals. For example, there are various ways to make requests in English. If you wanted someone to open a window, you could say "Open the window!" or "Would you please open the window?" or "Can you open the window?" or even "It's hot in here." Native speakers of English know these can all be requests, varying in politeness and directness. Pragmatics also includes knowing how to adjust language to fit different social situations. You talk differently to your friends than to your professors, even to convey the same basic information. Similarly, if you were explaining how to play a game to a 5-year-old, your choice of words and sentence structure would be quite different than if you were speaking to an adult. In each case your language is guided by rules of pragmatics.

Productive and Receptive Skills

Another way to view what children master when they learn their native language is in terms of the mental skills required. Children need two sets of skills to be able to communicate effectively: **productive skills,** which are used to put ideas into words, and **receptive skills,** which are used to understand what other people say.

Many parents believe infants can grasp much of what they are told before they are able to talk. Parents tend to overestimate this ability in their babies, but they are correct that receptive skills emerge sooner than productive ones (Golinkoff et al., 1987). This can be seen in every aspect of language development, including phonology (Jusczyk, 1997). As a toddler Meryl could not pronounce the phoneme /l/. Her *l*'s sounded like *w*'s.

Phonology:
The system of sounds used in a language, the rules for combining those sounds to make words, and the use of stress and intonation in spoken sentences.

Phonemes:
Speech sounds that contrast with one another in a particular language and can change the meaning of a word.

Semantics:
The meanings of words and sentences.

Morphology:
The system of rules for combining morphemes to form words or to modify word meanings.

Morphemes:
The smallest meaningful units in a language.

Syntax:
The rules for organizing words into phrases and sentences.

Pragmatics:
The rules governing conversation and social use of language.

Productive skills:
Language skills used to put ideas into words.

Receptive skills:
Language skills used to understand what other people say.

One day Karen teasingly said to Meryl, "Wet's go!" Meryl responded, "No. Not wet's. Say *wet's*." Although Meryl mispronounced /l/, she could hear the difference between a correct and an incorrect pronunciation by someone else. Her receptive phonology was more advanced than her productive phonology. Similarly, young children understand words not yet in their active vocabularies, and they understand sentences much longer and more complex than the ones they speak.

MAJOR TASKS IN EARLY LANGUAGE LEARNING

Malcolm was an early talker; even at 8 or 9 months, he was constantly babbling strings of nonsense syllables that sounded startlingly like real speech. "Ah-ma-ka?" he might ask of DeeDee, his voice rising in a question as he jangled a set of car keys above his head. When DeeDee laughed and answered that those were indeed for the car, he bobbed his head, smiling as if he understood: "Ah-ka-ba-ba! Ah-ka-ba!"

To describe how children become able to communicate linguistically, we will look at how development proceeds in each subsystem of language. We will examine how children master the sound system of their native language *(phonology),* how they learn the meanings of individual words *(semantics),* and how they develop sets of rules about the structure of language—rules for modifying word meanings *(morphology)* and for organizing words into sentences *(syntax).* Finally, we consider how they learn to use language in socially appropriate ways *(pragmatics).*

Learning the Sound Patterns of a Language

One difficult aspect of learning a language is mastering its sound patterns. Think about your own experiences listening to foreign languages; the sounds probably blurred together, with no obvious pauses between words. Now imagine the task confronting children who do not even know words exist. Somehow, just by hearing others talk, they learn to recognize and produce the phonemes of their language. Ultimately, they break down the stream of speech sounds they hear into words, and they begin to produce recognizable words themselves.

Much progress toward mastering the sounds of a language occurs in the first year of life, even before babies produce words. During this time, dramatic changes in babies' vocalizations culminate in the production of speech sounds. This early period of **prelinguistic vocalization** can be divided into five stages (Menn and Stoel-Gammon, 1993).

In the first weeks of life, infants' only means of vocal communication is **crying.** As you learned in Chapter 4, crying is a reflexive vocalization that occurs automatically

Prelinguistic vocalization:
Sounds produced by infants during the first year of life, before they begin to speak.

Crying:
Reflexive vocalization that occurs automatically whenever an infant is overly aroused.

In the first stage of prelinguistic vocalization, infants can communicate only by crying.

whenever babies are overly aroused, but their cries vary somewhat depending on the nature of their discomfort.

At around 2 months, babies start to make sounds expressing pleasure and contentment. This behavior is called **cooing** because it involves many vowel sounds, especially /u/, and very few consonant sounds. Babies also begin to laugh and chuckle during the cooing stage.

At about 4 months, babies enter the stage of **vocal play.** During this stage, they seem to be trying out the range of their vocal abilities, and they produce sounds that vary greatly in pitch and loudness. They also begin to utter occasional simple syllables consisting of consonant-vowel combinations (*ba, ga, ma,* etc.) → Guttural sounds

The fourth stage, **canonical babbling,** begins at around 6 months. During this stage, babies' vocalizations sound increasingly like speech. Instead of isolated syllables, they begin to produce strings of syllables. At first, these strings consist mostly of one syllable repeated over and over (e.g., *ma-ma-ma-ma*). Later, strings of different vowel and consonant combinations become more common, with utterances like Malcolm's "Ah-ka-ba-ba."

During the canonical babbling stage, children are not yet imitating the particular phonemes of their native language. When Meryl, Malcolm, Maggie, and Mikey began to babble, they not only made sounds corresponding to English phonemes, they also made some sounds that are phonemes in other languages. Infants around the world initially babble similar sounds, despite being exposed to very different languages. However, they do not produce *all* the phonemes found in human speech, and the most frequent and infrequent sounds are fairly similar across languages (Locke and Pearson, 1992). This suggests that the early development of speech sounds is constrained by infants' physical limitations. Linguistic input from the environment becomes important during this stage, however. Deaf infants engage in vocal play very similar to that of babies who can hear, but they are slow to produce the clear consonant-vowel syllables of canonical babbling (Oller and Eilers, 1988). (The box on page 240 provides more information about language development of deaf infants.)

By 10 months or so, most infants progress to the fifth stage, **conversational babbling** or **jargon,** in which they begin to use adultlike stress and intonation, as Malcolm did when "asking" DeeDee about the car keys. Because of its stress and intonation, jargon sounds like conversational speech. It seems to include questions and statements, but without identifiable words. During this stage, there begin to be differences in the particular sounds babies produce, depending on the language they are acquiring (Boysson-Bardies and Vihman, 1991).

Between 10 and 12 months, most children start to make the transition from babbling to true speech. A few **protowords** may appear—vocalizations that seem to have consistent meanings for a child and are used in attempts to communicate, but do not closely resemble adult words in sound or meaning. Children's protowords are idiosyncratic; unlike real words, they usually do not make sense to strangers. Meryl's "eh" and "muh" are examples of protowords; Karen and her mother could understand what Meryl was trying to communicate with these sounds, but other people could not. Children's protowords and their first real words are constructed from a limited set of speech sounds appropriate to their native language, usually the same sounds that became predominant during the conversational babbling stage (Bloom, 1998). Interestingly, there is great similarity across languages in children's early pronunciation errors, suggesting continuing physical constraints on children's sound production. For example, English-speaking children frequently substitute a /t/ sound for a /k/ sound, as in saying *tat* for *cat*. The same error has been observed in children learning such disparate languages as German and Hindi (Locke and Pearson, 1992).

The developmental sequence involved in acquiring speech sounds during the first year of life suggests that two things are needed to prepare children to begin speaking. First, they must gain control over their speech apparatus—the mouth, lips, tongue, and vocal cords—enabling them to produce speech sounds intentionally. This process is aided

Cooing:
Prelinguistic vocalizations that consist largely of vowel sounds and express pleasure and contentment.

Vocal play:
Prelinguistic vocalizations that vary greatly in pitch and loudness, including occasional simple syllables.

Canonical babbling:
Prelinguistic vocalizations consisting of strings of syllables that sound increasingly like speech.

Child Development CD
Prelinguistic Vocalization

/dehart5

Early Detection of Hearing Impairment

Conversational babbling or jargon
Prelinguistic vocalizations in which infants use adultlike stress and intonation.

Protowords:
Vocalizations that seem to have consistent meanings for a child and are used in attempts to communicate, but do not closely resemble adult words in sound or meaning.

A CLOSER LOOK

LANGUAGE DEVELOPMENT OF DEAF CHILDREN

About 1 in 1,000 babies is born with a severe hearing impairment (Watkin and Baldwin, 1999). The process of language development for these babies differs in some ways from that experienced by hearing babies, but in other ways it is quite similar. Understanding the similarities and differences is useful not only for determining the most effective ways to foster the development of communication skills in deaf infants, but also for clarifying the roles of biology and the environment in language development.

Early in infancy deaf babies produce sounds very similar to those of hearing babies (Hoff, 2001). During the crying, cooing, and vocal play stages, their vocalizations do not differ from those of hearing infants in quantity or quality, and the timetable for these stages of prelinguistic vocalizations is similar. These early developments seem to depend on biologically built-in factors, rather than environmental input. Around 6 to 9 months, differences in vocalization begin to appear. As already mentioned, deaf infants are slow to produce the consonant-vowel syllables of canonical babbling (Oller and Eilers, 1988). From this point on, environmental input becomes increasingly important in the development of vocalization and eventually of spoken language. Over time, the amount of babbling produced by hearing infants increases, while the amount produced by deaf infants declines.

About 10 percent of deaf infants have deaf parents; usually these babies are exposed to formal sign language from birth (Hoff, 2001). For them, the development of sign language follows a course similar to the development of spoken language in hearing infants (Petitto, 2000). Beginning at 4 to 6 months, they engage in manual babbling, producing fragmentary hand movements that gradually come to resemble adult signs. At about the same age hearing infants speak their first words, deaf infants start to produce clear single-word signs (Capirci, Montanari, and Volterra, 1998). They also produce two-word combinations of signs, grammatical morphemes, and complex syntax on roughly the same timetable as hearing infants (Hoff, 2001).

Some researchers have argued that deaf infants' first signs emerge earlier than hearing infants' first words because the motor skills needed for manual signing develop earlier than those needed to control the vocal apparatus (Bonvillian and Folven, 1993). However, careful longitudinal observation of deaf and hearing infants with and without exposure to sign language has revealed great similarities in their early manual behavior. What some researchers (and parents) have interpreted as early signs are probably nonlinguistic gestures. Studies in which a distinction is made between true signs and nonlinguistic gestures have found no difference in the timing of first words and first signs (Capirci, Montanari, and Volterra, 1998).

Deaf babies who are not exposed to sign language early in development often create their own sign systems for communication, known as *homesign* (Morford, 1998). Homesign includes both pointing gestures and descriptive gestures, and these gestures are combined and modified in structured ways reminiscent of more formal languages. Homesign commonly includes nouns and verbs, variations in hand shape and motion that serve morphological functions, and ordering preferences similar to syntax. Although they are not as complex as formal spoken and sign languages, homesign systems provide some idea of the human brain's capacity to create a language in the absence of input from the environment.

considerably by brain development and by such physical changes as emergence of teeth and development of muscles in the tongue. Second, children must learn the phonemes of their particular language by paying close attention to the speech sounds they hear and beginning to imitate them. Only when they can recognize and produce appropriate speech sounds are they ready to combine sounds to make words.

Learning Words and Their Meanings

First Words Most children say their first identifiable words around their first birthday, although there is great variation in the exact age. First words usually refer to familiar persons *(mama)*, body parts *(nose, feet)*, animals *(doggie)*, and objects *(shoe, ball)*. Many children's early vocabularies are dominated by words referring to objects and people they regularly interact with (Bates, Bretherton, and Snyder, 1988; Dromi, 1999; Nelson, 1973). First words may also express feelings *(naughty, goodboy)*, movement *(up, down, allgone, byebye)*, and social commands that are not broken down into their component words *(gimmefive!)*. For example, as Malcolm watches a car disappear down the street, he might comment "bye" or "allgone"; although *allgone* is two words for adults, many

Toddlers' first words often refer to familiar objects, animals, or people.

toddlers treat it as one. Another common topic during the single-word phase is the concept *no.* Young toddlers often develop several ways to express this concept. In addition to the traditional "no," they might say "me" or "mine," meaning "No, *me* do it" or "No, that's *mine.*"

Children differ in the purposes for which they use their first words. Some initially use words mainly to *refer to objects and events;* their first words are mostly nouns, plus some verbs and adjectives. This is a **referential style** of word use. Other children initially use words mainly to *express social routines;* their first words are primarily pronouns, such as *me* or *mine,* and formulas, such as *stopit.* This is an **expressive style** of word use. These differences in how first words are used are related to other aspects of social and cognitive development (Bates et al., 1988; Goldfield and Snow, 1993). Referential children are more likely to be firstborn and tend to come from more educated families than expressive children (Nelson, 1973). Mothers of referential children often encourage labeling by asking their children many questions, while mothers of expressive children tend to use language more to direct their children's behavior (Olsen-Fulero, 1982). Referential children initially acquire words faster than expressive children do, but there is no difference in how grammatical their speech is (Clark, 1983).

Vocabulary Growth New words are acquired rather slowly during early toddlerhood; by 18 to 19 months, children have an average vocabulary of about fifty words (Bloom, 1998). In most children the rate of vocabulary growth increases dramatically at about 18 months of age, as shown in Figure 7.1. This sudden increase in word acquisition is known as the **vocabulary spurt.** Referential children, who are learning mostly nouns, show a more obvious vocabulary spurt than expressive children, who are adding roughly equal proportions of nouns and other kinds of words to their vocabularies (Goldfield and Reznick, 1990). Around the time of the vocabulary spurt, many English-speaking children also begin producing verbs to name actions and events (Tomasello and Kruger, 1992).

During the preschool years, children's vocabularies continue to increase rapidly, although the exact rate of growth is not certain. An early study suggested that the average

Referential style:
A style of early word use in which words primarily refer to objects and events.

Expressive style:
A style of early word use in which words primarily express social routines.

Vocabulary spurt:
A sudden increase in word acquisition at about 18 months of age.

Figure 7.1
ESTIMATES OF VOCABULARY GROWTH AS A FUNCTION OF AGE
This figure illustrates the slow initial growth of productive vocabulary, followed by a spurt in growth at about 18 months of age. The two scales indicate the uncertainty about the size of toddlers' and preschoolers' vocabularies. *(Source: Based on Carey, 1978; Miller, 1981; and Smith, 1926.)*

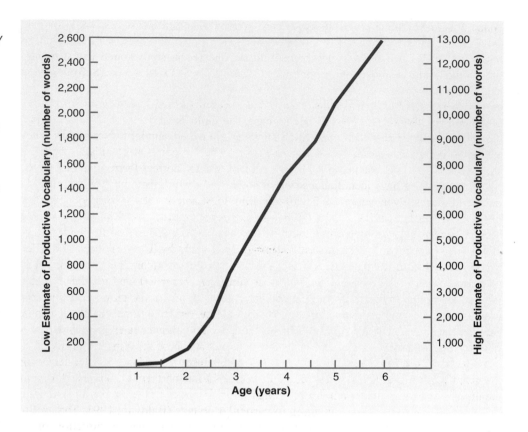

productive vocabulary—the number of words a child actually uses when speaking—was 1,222 for 3½-year-olds and 2,526 for 6-year-olds (Smith, 1926). More recent work has yielded much higher estimates—up to 8,000 to 14,000 words for the average 6-year-old (Carey, 1978). The actual number probably lies somewhere between these extremes. Productive vocabulary size is hard to measure because after the early stages there is no easy way to keep track of all the words a child actually uses.

Children's *receptive* vocabulary (words they can understand, even if they don't use them) is larger than their productive vocabulary. A truly remarkable growth in receptive vocabulary occurs between ages 1 and 6. During the preschool years, children learn on average 5.5 new words per day, resulting in a receptive vocabulary of around 10,000 words by the end of first grade and around 40,000 by the end of fifth grade (Anglin, 1993).

Children differ considerably in timing and rate of vocabulary growth. In one study, first words appeared at ages from 10 to 17 months, and the vocabulary spurt occurred at anywhere from 13 to 25 months (Bloom, 1993). Socioeconomic status has considerable impact on children's vocabulary development; children from low-income and working-class families show slower rates of vocabulary growth than children from middle-class and professional families (Fenson et al., 1994; Hart and Risley, 1995).

Processes of Word Learning Children's earliest words tend to be bound to the particular contexts in which they are learned (Dromi, 1999; Nelson, 1985). It is not until around the time of the vocabulary spurt that children start to use words to refer to *categories* of objects, people, and events. A milestone in language development comes when the child discovers that everything has a name (Gopnik and Meltzoff, 1987; Nelson, 1985). Now vocabulary building speeds up as the toddler begins to ask incessantly, "What that?"

The task of word learning is all the more complex because most of the words children learn are not often spoken separately. Usually children must pick out the critical group of sounds from a longer string. When DeeDee says to Malcolm, "Look at the ball *roll*," Malcolm must extract the new word *roll* from his mother's flow of speech. The ability to do this apparently emerges in infancy; one recent study found that 8-month-olds could group sounds from a continuous flow of speech into words (Saffran, Aslin, and Newport, 1996).

Toddlers sometimes make mistakes in the location of word boundaries, producing sentences like "Readit the book." In this case, the child has incorrectly concluded that the verb is *readit,* rather than *read.* Such mistakes are called **segmentation errors.** They are fairly common, especially where unstressed syllables come at boundaries between words (Gleitman and Wanner, 1982), but children usually correct them quickly.

Once toddlers have identified a string of sounds as a word, they must figure out what that word means. Even before age 2, children seem to be able to use the linguistic and non-linguistic context in which an unfamiliar word appears to make a quick and reasonably accurate guess as to its meaning (Carey, 1978; Woodward, Markman, and Fitzsimmons, 1994). This process is known as **fast mapping.** In a study by Tracy Heibeck and Ellen Markman (1987), 2- to 4-year-olds received brief exposure to unfamiliar terms for colors (*chartreuse, amaranth, maroon),* shapes (*oval, hexagon, trapezoid),* and textures (*coarse, fibrous, granular).* In each case, the experimenter used the unfamiliar term in contrast to a familiar one, such as *blue, round,* or *fuzzy* ("Bring me the chartreuse one. Not the blue one, the chartreuse one."). When the children were tested a few minutes later, even 2-year-olds showed comprehension of the unfamiliar terms, especially those referring to shapes.

The process of fast mapping is helped along by **joint attention**—the tendency for language-learning children and their adult conversation partners to share a focus of attention. Caregivers often talk about things their babies are already paying attention to, or try to direct the babies' attention to particular objects (Baldwin, 1991; Tomasello, 1988). Babies as young as 16 months are able to use such cues as direction of an adult's gaze to determine what object the adult is labeling (Akhtar and Tomasello, 1996; Baldwin et al., 1996).

Fast mapping can work only if children have built-in assumptions about the most likely meanings of unfamiliar words. Suppose DeeDee points to a large red ball and says the word *ball.* How can Malcolm figure out that *ball* is the name of the thing itself, not one of its qualities (color, shape, size) or DeeDee's action (pointing)? Some theorists suggest that children have an inborn tendency to perceive objects (Spelke and Newport,

Segmentation errors:
Mistakes in detecting boundaries between words in a sentence.

Fast mapping:
A process in which a young child uses context cues to make a quick and reasonably accurate guess about the meaning of an unfamiliar word.

Joint attention
The tendency for language-learning children and their adult conversation partners to share a focus of attention.

Joint attention with caregivers helps toddlers learn word meanings quickly.

Whole-object assumption:
Children's tendency to assume that unfamiliar words are names for objects rather than for attributes or actions.

Lexical contrast:
Children's tendency to assume that no two words have the same meaning.

Underextensions:
Language errors in which the meaning a child attaches to a word is too restricted.

Overextensions:
Language errors in which the meaning a child attaches to a word is too broad.

1998) and to assume unfamiliar words are names for objects rather than attributes or actions (Huttenlocher and Smiley, 1987; Woodward and Markman, 1998). This tendency is known as the **whole-object assumption.**

But what if DeeDee holds up the ball and says, "Look, Malcolm, it's red"? How does Malcolm figure out that *red* is not just another word meaning *ball?* Children also seem to have a built-in tendency to assume that no two words have the same meaning, and thus unfamiliar words must refer to things for which they do not already have labels (Clark, 1988, 1990; Markman, 1987). This assumption is known as **lexical contrast** (*lexical* means "pertaining to words"). When Malcolm hears *red* in reference to this ball, he assumes it contrasts in meaning with the word *ball,* which he already knows. As possible meanings for *red,* he therefore considers features for which he has no labels. When he hears *red* also applied to his toy fire truck, his overalls, and his new winter coat, he concludes that *red* must be the name for a particular color.

Errors in Early Word Learning Once toddlers isolate a word, they very seldom assign entirely the wrong meaning to it. Malcolm is not likely to decide *red* means any round object that bounces and scream "Red!" when he sees his brother's new basketball. Such errors are rare in toddlers' productive language but may be more common in their understanding of what others say.

Toddlers' semantic errors are usually errors of under- and overextension. **Underextensions** occur when a word is used correctly but in too restricted a way. Suppose Mikey is given a toy dump truck and told that it is a *truck.* If he then starts to use the word to refer to toy trucks only and not to full-sized trucks he sees on the road, he has an underextended concept of truck. In **overextensions,** toddlers make the opposite mistake. Because their definition of a certain word is not sufficiently restricted, they sometimes use it when it doesn't really apply. If Mikey initially uses *truck* to refer to *any* wheeled vehicle, he is overextending its meaning.

Underextensions are much less obvious than overextensions. When children overextend the meaning of a word, they use it in clearly inappropriate ways, such as calling a squirrel *kitty.* When they underextend the meaning of a word, they simply fail to use it where it could have been used. Careful observations of toddlers over time show that they do sometimes underextend word meanings. One 8-month-old boy responded to the word *shoes* by crawling to the shoes in a particular closet (Reich, 1976). Gradually he generalized the meaning of *shoes* to shoes in another closet, then to shoes left outside closets, and finally to shoes on people's feet. A similar pattern can be seen in a little girl who at first applied the word *car* only to cars moving on the street outside her living room window (Bloom, 1973). Six months passed before she extended the meaning to cars in other situations.

Overextensions are very common in toddlers' speech. The word *ball,* for example, is often applied to a range of relatively small, round objects, such as apples, melons, and eggs. Most overextensions of nouns refer to objects broadly similar in appearance, especially in shape (Clark, 1983). Children may overextend the same word in a variety of ways. One little boy used the word *Nunu* (the name of the family dog) to refer not only to all dogs but also to other animals, to furry slippers and coats, and even to black olives in a salad, which resembled the dog's nose (de Villiers and de Villiers, 1979). Toddlers also overextend verbs and other parts of speech. One toddler initially used the word *out* to refer to opening or closing a door. Later the child generalized the meaning of *out* to peeling fruit, shelling peas, and undoing shoelaces (Clark, 1973).

One study of language development in six children found that the rate of overextensions was very high in the initial stages of vocabulary building, but dropped dramatically as the toddlers learned more words (Kuczaj, 1982). This pattern makes sense; the more words children know, the more likely they are to know what word to use in a given context.

When children overextend a word, it does not necessarily mean they are unaware of the boundaries of the word's meaning. Suppose Mikey wants to call attention to a bus that just went by. If he knows the word *truck* but not the word *bus,* he might use *truck*

If Maggie knows the words cheese, truck, cookie, mama, kitty, dada, blankie, go, *and* milk, *how would she label the objects shown here? She might well call the first object* truck, *the next two* cookie, *and the third* cheese. *These labels are incorrect, but they represent smart mistakes because she has chosen the best words available. She would not be likely to label any of these objects* kitty *or* blankie.

instead of nothing at all. This example suggests that toddlers may sometimes *knowingly* produce overextensions. They use a word in a wrong context not because they're unaware it doesn't quite fit, but because it is the word in their vocabulary that comes closest to what they want to say. In these cases the child is searching for the right word and is very responsive to corrective feedback from adults ("No, that's not a truck; that's a bus"). Receiving feedback following errors of overextension is one of the most effective ways for children to learn new words (Merriman, 1986).

Studies of *receptive* overextension show that toddlers have more knowledge of word meanings than their rate of productive overextensions suggests. Even if Mikey called a bus *truck,* he could probably pick out the correct objects from a set of toys if asked "Where's the bus? Where's the truck?" (Clark, 1983). This implies that Mikey does have the concept *bus,* even though he doesn't know the word *bus* as well as he knows *truck.* He uses *truck* when he can't remember *bus* because trucks and buses have some features in common.

To summarize, toddlers' under- and overextensions of words follow a common pattern:

- When words are first learned, they tend to be used only in the specific contexts in which they were originally heard, resulting in underextensions (Carey, 1978).

- As children begin to explore the limits of word meanings (Does *ball* mean all round objects? Does *truck* mean anything with wheels?), overextensions occur.

- A toddler may *knowingly* overextend a word because it is the closest one available in his or her vocabulary.

- Finally, as children's vocabularies grow, the rate of overextensions declines.

Learning Morphological Rules

Children's first words are usually single morphemes: *Mommy, Daddy, milk, more, doggie, go, cookie, sock.* Each is a unit of language representing a single object, action, or quality. As language development proceeds, children gradually add **grammatical morphemes** to the words they speak—units of language that carry little meaning by themselves, but that change the meaning of words and sentences in systematic ways. English grammatical morphemes include prefixes, suffixes, auxiliary verbs, articles, and certain prepositions. For instance, an *-s* added to the end of most English nouns changes their meaning from singular to plural and is therefore a grammatical morpheme.

English-speaking children generally do not begin to use grammatical morphemes until after they start to combine words into sentences. However, many languages, such

Grammatical morpheme:
A unit of language that carries little meaning by itself, but that changes the meaning of words or sentences in a systematic way.

as Turkish and Russian, have more grammatical morphemes than English does—for example, different endings for nouns depending on whether they are used as subjects or objects in sentences. Children learning these languages add grammatical morphemes to words earlier than children learning English do, often before they begin to combine words into sentences (Hoff, 2001; Peters, 1995).

Order of Acquisition Roger Brown (1973) studied the learning of grammatical morphemes in three children he called Eve, Adam, and Sarah. He found that they acquired these morphemes in a consistent order, although their speed of acquisition varied considerably. The same pattern appeared in a cross-sectional study of a large group of children (de Villiers and de Villiers, 1978). First, children begin to add -s to nouns to form plurals and -ing to verbs to form present participles (as in *going* or *running*). Somewhat later, children start to use -ed to form past tense verbs (as in *jumped*) and -s to form the third person singular (as in *she sits*). Among the last grammatical morphemes to appear are those for contractions of the verb *to be* (the *'s* in *it's big,* or the *'re* in *they're playing*).

The order in which toddlers acquire grammatical morphemes has nothing to do with how often they hear each of these morphemes in the language spoken to them. Contrary to what you might expect, the most frequently heard morphemes are not acquired first (Brown, 1973). Instead, three other factors seem to govern the order of acquisition.

First, *grammatical complexity* plays a role. Brown (1973) suggested that morphemes that produce the simplest changes in a word's function in a sentence are learned first. By this he meant forms that are the closest to the active, declarative form of a verb (as *going* is to *go*) or to the base morpheme of a noun (as *socks* is to *sock*).

Second, *semantic complexity* is involved (Brown, 1973). The -ing that forms the present participle adds to the verb the quite simple idea of ongoing action. In contrast, adding an -s to a verb to form the third person singular (as in *she sits*) is more semantically complex even though it appears structurally simple. This is so because it adds several ideas: that we are talking about someone else, that only one person or object is referred to (*he, she,* or *it,* not *they*), and that the action takes place in the present.

Finally, the *phonological characteristics* of a morpheme—how it sounds—also influence when it is acquired. For example, Turkish children acquire some grammatical morphemes earlier than children learning other languages. Most Turkish grammatical morphemes are full syllables; many are word endings pronounced with considerable stress, which makes them more noticeable (Aksu-Koc and Slobin, 1985).

Productivity and Overregularization The acquisition of grammatical morphemes is of particular interest to developmentalists because it shows that language learning involves discerning rules. For instance, children do not learn the plural forms of nouns word by word. Instead, they learn a general rule about forming plurals: in English, add the suffix -s or -es and the noun becomes "more than one." In a classic study, Jean Berko (1958) showed how children apply morphological rules even to words they have never heard before. She taught children that an unusual birdlike creature was called a *wug*. Then she showed them a picture of two of these creatures and said: "Now there is another one. There are two____." (See Figure 7.2.) The children's task was to fill in the blank. Those who had acquired the rule of adding -s to form the plural readily answered "wugs." Berko's study shows the great *productivity* of

Figure 7.2
AN ITEM FROM BERKO'S
WUG STUDY

THIS IS A WUG.

NOW THERE IS ANOTHER ONE.
THERE ARE TWO OF THEM.
THERE ARE TWO _____.

language—the fact that it allows almost unlimited output because it is governed by general rules. As a result, we can take even an unfamiliar word and modify its meaning in ways others will understand.

Exceptions to morphological rules are potential stumbling blocks for children. Most English nouns become plural by adding -*s* or -*es,* but sometimes this rule does not apply (*mouse/mice, foot/feet*). Similarly, the usual way to form the past tense of English verbs is to add the suffix -*ed,* but irregular verbs do not follow this convention (*go/went, come/came*). You might think children would learn regular forms first and tackle the exceptions later, but this is not the usual pattern (Marcus et al., 1992). Instead, correct irregular past tenses and plurals often appear early, with the child saying *came, did, mice, feet,* and so on. Shortly thereafter an odd thing happens. The child starts to impose regular forms on irregular nouns and verbs so that *mice* becomes *mouses, feet* becomes *foots, came* becomes *comed,* and *did* becomes *doed.* These errors are called **overregularizations.** Overregularizations appear about the same time the child begins to use regular past tenses and plurals reliably. Apparently, the child learns the -*ed* and -*s* rules and applies them indiscriminately. Overregularizations do not completely replace the correct irregular forms, however. Most children use overregularized forms only occasionally— about 2.5 percent of the time for verbs (Marcus et al., 1992) and about 8 percent of the time for nouns (Marcus, 1995). By age 6 or 7, children use correct forms almost all the time (Cazden, 1968), although school-age children still occasionally produce incorrect irregular forms, such as "I *brang* my lunch."

Overregularization is an example of what developmentalists call a *growth error.* When overregularization appears, the number of mistakes a child makes in forming past tenses and plurals increases, which might seem like a setback in language development. However, the mistakes are due not to regression or loss of ability, but to the emergence of a more advanced way of thinking. Even though children who overregularize temporarily make more mistakes, they are in fact making progress toward understanding the morphological rules of their language.

Overregularization provides insight into the cognitive processes underlying language learning. When learning something complex, such as a language, children seem to search automatically for regularities. To find them, they must first learn a number of examples from which rules can be drawn. At this early stage they learn each regular and irregular form separately. From this pool of examples, they filter out the irregular ones and zero in on the patterns used most. They then begin to apply these rules in other cases, including irregular nouns and verbs. Gradually, they develop an understanding of which verbs and nouns are exceptions to the rules, and overregularizations fade out.

This learning process is clearly very complex, as anyone who has ever tried to master irregular forms in a second language knows. Yet preschoolers seem to accomplish it with little effort, just from hearing spoken language. Long before adulthood, morphological rules and most exceptions to them seem second nature to us, even though we may still be caught off guard when asked what the plural of *moose* is or whether the past tense of *fly* is ever *flied.* (It is, in the sentence "The batter flied out.") Our hesitation in answering such questions reminds us what a remarkable achievement it is for young children to master morphological rules.

Learning to Form Sentences

We noted earlier that *syntax* is a language's rules for organizing words into phrases and sentences. In any system of syntax, individual words each belong to a particular **form class,** such as nouns, verbs, and adjectives. In English, for instance, *dog* and *justice* are classified as nouns, *sit* and *believe* as verbs, and *lazy* and *purple* as adjectives. Syntactic rules specify how words belonging to various form classes can be combined to make phrases, clauses, and sentences.

One set of syntactic rules governs how phrases are formed. For example, an article and a noun make up a noun phrase, such as *the boy* or *a dog.* Other syntactic rules limit

Learning Syntactic Rules

Overregularizations:
Language errors in which a child applies a morphological rule to a word that is an exception to the rule.

Form class:
A category of words in a language that can fill similar syntactic roles in forming phrases and sentences.

the ways in which phrases can be put together to make sentences. For example, *A dog bit the boy* and *The boy bit a dog* are acceptable sentences in English, but *Bit the boy a dog* normally is not.

Form classes, phrases, and sentences are all highly abstract categories. Children cannot learn syntactic rules simply on the basis of noticing how specific words, like *dog* or *boy,* are used in sentences and then figuring out a rule for each individual word. Instead, children somehow extract and use rules involving these abstract categories from the particular, concrete examples of speech they hear. This is *not* to say that young children are consciously aware they are learning and using grammatical rules. It will be years before they are cognitively advanced enough to understand and talk explicitly about grammatical categories and rules.

A very important feature of syntactic rules is their productivity. Just as morphological rules allow for tremendous output in forming and modifying words, so syntactic rules allow for countless possible sentences just by placing different words in various roles. Once children can use the rules of syntax, their ability to create new meaningful sentences becomes virtually unlimited.

The One-Word Stage   When children first start saying recognizable words, they use only one word at a time. To an adult, a single word is often just a label for an object, action, or quality. To a toddler, a single word can be an attempt to communicate much more. For example, when Meryl says "mama," she may be simply labeling her mother, or she may be trying to express some idea related to Karen that an older child would express in a phrase or sentence (de Villiers and de Villiers, 1978). How to interpret Meryl's meaning depends on the context in which she says the word. If she says "mama" when Karen enters the room, she might be trying to communicate *Here is mama.* If she says "mama" after Karen leaves the house, she might be trying to express *I want my mama.* If she says "mama" while holding up Karen's purse, she might be trying to tell someone *This belongs to mama.* A word that conveys such extended meaning is called a **holophrase.** When a toddler says a single word, it is not always obvious whether it is just a label or whether it is intended to communicate a more complex meaning. To tell the difference, listeners must pay attention to context, including the child's gestures, facial expression, and tone of voice.

Holophrase:
A single word that conveys the meaning of a phrase or sentence.

Toddlers' early sentences often require considerable interpretation.

First Sentences   At 18 to 24 months of age, toddlers usually start to produce two-word sequences. This change typically occurs soon after the vocabulary spurt, but it is even more closely connected to the appearance of verbs in the child's vocabulary (Bloom, 1998). The earliest two-word sequences may not really be sentences. Often they seem to be expressing two separate ideas, one after the other. For example, psychologist Lois Bloom's daughter Allison said "daddy, car" on one occasion when her father left in the car. On another similar occasion, she said "car, daddy" (Bloom, 1973). In both cases, she paused between the two words, as if she were conveying two related, but separate thoughts ("There goes *daddy.* Daddy is in the *car.*"). Such a pause between words is not characteristic of true sentences. And since Allison spoke these two words in both possible orders, word order was apparently unimportant to what she wanted to say. In true English sentences, in contrast, word order *is* important. Thus, the first words toddlers speak in close succession may be a kind of transitional step from one-word statements to true sentences.

Toddlers' earliest true two-word sentences are usually composed of nouns, verbs, and adjectives. Few articles *(a, the)*, conjunctions *(and, or)*, or prepositions *(of, by)* appear, even though these words are common in adult speech. As we have mentioned, English-speaking toddlers at first do not add grammatical morphemes to words. They also ignore most auxiliary verbs, such as *can, may,* or *would.* When Maggie at 18 months wanted to express the idea *I can see the teddy bear,* she said simply: "See teddy." In this phase the child seems to omit words that are not essential to the central meaning of the sentence. This style of talking is called **telegraphic speech** because it sounds somewhat like the terse wording of a telegram. Telegraphic speech has been observed among children learning a wide range of languages, including German, Finnish, and Kaluli (a language spoken in Papua New Guinea) (Hoff, 2001).

Interestingly, young toddlers use telegraphic speech even when adults specifically model longer sentences for them (Brown and Fraser, 1963). When Christine repeatedly encouraged 18-month-old Maggie to say "I love my grandma," Maggie's words came out simply "Love gama." Using more than two words to express a single idea seemed to exceed her current cognitive capacity.

Although a child's earliest sentences are telegraphic, they are not arbitrary groupings of words. Most two-word sentences seem to express a relatively small set of basic meanings, listed in Table 7.1. The categories of meanings expressed at the two-word stage are remarkably similar across languages (Slobin, 1970). Out of context, children's two-word utterances are nearly as ambiguous as their one-word utterances. Adults must still rely heavily on context, gestures, facial expressions, and intonation to interpret what a child means. In our toddler vignette, 2-year-old Mikey greeted his father with a broad smile, outstretched arms, and a joyous "Daddy home!" Clearly, this was meant as a happy announcement that his father had returned. On another occasion, when Christine let Mikey talk to his father on the phone, he said sternly, "Daddy *home!*" with stress on the second word. Here his meaning seemed to be the command "Daddy, come home *now!*"

Telegraphic speech:
A toddler speech style in which words not essential to the meaning of a sentence are omitted.

Further Syntactic Development After children pass the two-word stage, their knowledge of syntax increases rapidly. Their sentences grow longer and become more grammatically complex. Brown (1973) divided early syntactic development into five stages based on increasing length of utterances:

- Stage I (average utterance length 1.0 to 2.0 morphemes) corresponds roughly to the two-word stage we have just described. During this stage, children begin to express simple semantic and syntactic relationships.

Table 7.1 Categories of Meanings Expressed in the Two-Word Stage

Meaning	Example
agent + action	Daddy sit
action + object	drive car
agent + object	Mommy sock
agent + location	sit chair
entity + location	toy floor
possessor + possession	my teddy
entity + attribute	crayon big
demonstrative + entity	this telephone

Source: Hoff, 2001; based on Brown, 1973.

- During Stage II (average utterance length 2.0 to 2.5 morphemes) children acquire basic grammatical morphemes, such as the suffix -s to form the plural.
- In Stage III (average utterance length 2.5 to 3.0 morphemes) variations on simple sentences appear, including questions ("Can I go?" "Where's Mommy?") and negation ("You can't come"; "It's not here").
- At Stage IV (average utterance length 3.0 to 3.5 morphemes), children begin to embed one sentence in another, producing various kinds of subordinate clauses ("I see what you made;" "I want you to do it").
- By Stage V (average utterance length 3.5 to 4.0 morphemes), children join simple sentences to form compound sentences ("I had cake and Daddy had ice cream").

Most children pass through Brown's five stages by the time they reach age 3½.

Learning to Use Language Socially

Communicative competence: The ability to use language in a socially appropriate way in a particular culture.

While children are acquiring the sound system, vocabulary, morphology, and grammar of their native language, they are also learning pragmatics—that is, how to use the language socially. In other words, they are acquiring not only linguistic competence, but also **communicative competence.** Linguistic competence involves syntactically and semantically correct use of a language. Communicative competence involves the ability to carry on conversations, to recognize and repair breakdowns in communication, and to use language in a socially appropriate way.

Some of the skills involved in communicative competence begin to appear in infancy, long before children speak their first words. As you learned in Chapter 6, caregivers respond to infants' early vocalizations, facial expressions, and gestures as if they were attempts at intentional communication. With the caregiver's assistance, infants develop skills that will be needed later on in conversation, such as turn-taking. The principle of taking turns with a conversational partner is well established by 1 year of age. Thereafter, children continue to develop more skill at timing their conversational turns and making *relevant* responses to what conversational partners say (Bryant, 2001).

By late in the first year of life, infants' vocalizations and gestures show clear communicative intent. Many babies point or use protowords to request out-of-reach objects. With communicative intent comes the possibility of communication failure, and children must learn to recognize when they are not being understood and how to make conversational repairs. Roberta Golinkoff (1986) studied communication failures between preverbal 11- to 18-month-olds and their mothers, often involving the mother's failure to understand a request from the baby. In such cases, the baby typically showed frustration but also attempted a conversational repair by repeating or altering the request—all by means of gesture, vocalization, facial expression, and behavior, since these babies were not yet using language fluently.

Pragmatics

Pragmatic skills continue to develop after true language appears. For instance, 2-year-olds will attempt to repair breakdowns in understanding during conversations with adults, thereby demonstrating an ability to tell whether they are successfully communicating (Anselmi, Tomasello, and Acunzo, 1986). They do this by responding appropriately to adults' requests for clarification, repeating or modifying statements that have not been understood. Toddlers are particularly likely to successfully clarify requests that have not been fulfilled, suggesting that their clarification ability may depend more on a desire to make sure their goals are met than on a real understanding of other people's communication needs (Shatz and O'Reilly, 1990).

Another aspect of pragmatic development is learning the social routines and conventions for communication and language use in one's native culture (Bryant, 2001). The particular routines and conventions to be taught vary, but across cultures caregivers provide considerable pragmatic instruction to young children. This instruction begins in infancy, before children even begin to use language, with the teaching of communicative routines. Examples common across many Western cultures include playing peekaboo

Japanese culture places a high value on sensitivity to others' feelings. Accordingly, Japanese toddlers receive extensive instruction in the use of polite language.

and teaching a baby to wave bye-bye. In Italy, for instance, babies are taught to wave *ciao* (New, 1988).

Once children begin to speak, adults teach them verbal routines. For example, mothers in the Kaluli culture of New Guinea use an imitation routine to teach infants how to speak appropriately and how to use language for various social purposes. They model what they want their language-learning children to say, ending these utterances with the word *elema,* which means "say it" (Schieffelin, 1990).

As children's language development proceeds, parents continue to provide instruction in pragmatic routines (Bryant, 2001). In middle-class American culture, these include greetings and leave-takings *(hi, how are you?, bye-bye),* politeness formulas *(please, thank you),* appropriate forms of address *(ma'am, sir, Mrs., Mr.),* and specific-occasion routines, such as what to say when trick-or-treating (Becker, 1994; Greif and Gleason, 1980). Parents also instruct children in qualitative aspects of speech, such as loudness ("Use your indoor voice"), tone of voice ("Don't talk to your sister like that!"), and clarity ("I can't understand you when you mumble"). Pragmatic instruction can be either direct or indirect, with prompting ("What's the magic word?") a particularly common strategy in middle-class American families (Becker, 1994; Gleason, Perlmann, and Greif, 1984).

In Japan, politeness formulas are more elaborate and numerous than in the United States, and Japanese mothers place even more emphasis on teaching them to toddlers than American mothers do (Clancy, 1986). To accomplish this, they use direct instruction, model the correct forms for children, point out politeness formulas used by other people and by storybook characters, and show great insistence in correcting their children when they do not use a needed expression. A common Japanese strategy for correcting children's insufficiently polite speech is to appeal to general rules for behavior, often pointing out that others will feel hurt or angry if the child does not speak politely.

THE CHILD AND THE ENVIRONMENT IN LANGUAGE DEVELOPMENT

In the brief year and a half of toddlerhood, most children progress from speaking a few isolated words to using a great many words in properly structured sentences. How can they accomplish the complex task of learning a language in such a short time? A long-standing debate exists between environmentalist and nativist theories of language

Environmentalist theories:
Theories that stress environmental factors in language acquisition.

Nativist theories:
Theories that stress inborn, biologically based factors in language acquisition.

More on Skinner

More on Chomsky

Language acquisition device (LAD):
Chomsky's term for innate capacities of the human brain that make language acquisition possible.

acquisition. **Environmentalist theories** center on factors in the child's environment that support language acquisition, including the language the child hears, the structure of social interactions, and the physical environment. **Nativist theories,** in contrast, center on inborn, biologically based factors within the child that make language acquisition possible.

The contemporary debate between environmentalist and nativist theorists goes back to an exchange between psychologist B. F. Skinner and linguist Noam Chomsky in the 1950s. In his book *Verbal Behavior* (1957), Skinner argued that adults instrumentally condition children to talk. According to Skinner, when babies babble, parents smile, pay attention, and talk to them in response. These responses reinforce infants for babbling. Babbling becomes more frequent, which raises the probability that babies will, just by chance, make sounds resembling words. When parents hear these wordlike sounds, they reinforce them in preference to nonword sounds. Babies respond by repeating sounds that are reinforced, and thus words enter the baby's repertoire of verbal behaviors. Skinner argued that grammar is acquired through similar reinforcement, with parents reinforcing grammatically correct statements and rejecting or showing confusion over incorrect ones.

At first glance, Skinner's account of language acquisition seems reasonable, but there are problems with his explanation. Parents do not actually provide much reinforcement and feedback for children's learning of grammar. Brown and Hanlon (1970) found that parents are much more likely to correct children's statements that are untrue than those that are grammatically incorrect. For instance, when Maggie says "Me put doggie chair," while placing a toy elephant on top of the sofa, Christine is apt to ignore her rough-edged grammar but tell her gently, "That's an elephant, honey, not a dog." This response is typical of most parents (Hirsh-Pasek, Treiman, and Schneiderman, 1984; Morgan and Travis, 1989). Despite this pattern of reinforcement, most children learn to use correct grammar anyway—even though they don't always use it to tell the truth.

In a review of Skinner's book, Chomsky (1957) offered a strong critique of Skinner's arguments. Chomsky contended that it was impossible to pack into a lifetime all the reinforcement episodes needed to learn language through instrumental conditioning. Children produce a large number of different sentences, which could not each have been learned separately through reinforcement. Even if imitation is added as a learning mechanism, it still explains only how children learn to repeat things they have heard. But children do not simply repeat other people's sentences. One of the most important features of language, Chomsky pointed out, is that children combine words to say things they have never heard anyone say. In principle, there is no limit to the novel sentences they can form.

Chomsky's critique of Skinner's book was so compelling that most developmentalists strongly agreed with his reasoning. This is not to say that they dismissed reinforcement and imitation as irrelevant to language learning. Reinforcement and imitation remain useful principles for explaining how some of the details of language are learned (Speidel and Nelson, 1989). Babies learn the sounds of their native language by imitating the speech they hear. Moreover, specific words must be learned by imitation, because the connection between a certain string of sounds and a certain meaning is entirely a matter of convention.

In contrast to Skinner's approach, Chomsky (1957) argued that all languages share structural characteristics, presumably because languages and the human brain evolved together. Our early ancestors fashioned language as they did because innate brain capacities led them to perceive and understand their world in certain ways. The same innate capacities allow toddlers to extract the rules of any language they hear, especially its syntax. Chomsky called these innate capacities the **language acquisition device (LAD).** He maintained that part of the brain is specially adapted for language learning. When a toddler is exposed to language, the LAD automatically focuses on the rules that govern it.

But just as there were limitations to Skinner's explanation of language acquisition, so there were limitations to Chomsky's. Chomsky focused on the question of how children acquire syntax and had little interest in the development of other aspects of linguistic and communicative competence. In addition, because of his emphasis on innate capacities, he ignored the social contexts in which language acquisition occurs.

Today no one holds a purely nativist or a purely environmentalist position on language acquisition. Instead, as in other nature-nurture issues, debate focuses on the relative contributions of inborn and environmental factors. Even researchers who are strongly oriented toward the environment admit that *something* must be built into the child's brain for language learning to be possible. And even the most nativist researchers acknowledge that environmental input is essential for language to be acquired. What is at issue is exactly what is built in biologically, what contribution the environment makes, and how the two sets of factors interact.

What the Child Brings to Language Acquisition

There is plenty of evidence that, as a species, humans are biologically predisposed to learn language. Language is learned so rapidly, so universally, and with so little explicit teaching that it is clear the process of language acquisition must have a biological basis. In addition, there is considerable similarity in the general processes of language acquisition across cultures, despite variations in linguistic structure and socialization practices (Slobin, 1985).

Evidence for Biological Underpinnings One indication of the biological underpinnings of language acquisition is the apparent existence of a critical or sensitive period early in life when language can be learned with the greatest ease (Lenneberg, 1967). Lenneberg and others have argued that this period is produced by developmental changes in the brain. Most likely, the various processes that contribute to early brain plasticity, discussed in Chapter 4, play a role in the critical or sensitive period for language (Bates, Thal, and Janowsky, 1992; Johnson, 1998). For example, several changes occur in the brain at about 8 to 9 months of age, including the establishment of long-range connections in the cerebral cortex and the emergence of adultlike patterns of metabolic activity. These changes may make possible such language-related skills as word comprehension and language-specific phonological development. At about the same time as the vocabulary spurt in the second year of life, there is a sharp increase in the density of synaptic connections, probably increasing memory and information-processing capacity. And by about age 4, when basic grammatical development is complete, synaptic density and the rate of brain metabolism begin to decline.

It is difficult to *prove* a truly critical period exists because it is rare to find a child who can serve as a test case—a child who has received no linguistic input early in life. One exception would be severely neglected children like Victor or Genie, discussed in Chapter 2. The difficulties these children had learning language as adolescents lend some support to the critical period hypothesis, although there is no way of knowing whether they were born with cognitive impairments. Another, less problematic test case is that of deaf children with hearing parents who begin to learn sign language after early childhood. Research by Elissa Newport (1990) suggests that the earlier deaf children begin to acquire sign language, the greater their ultimate fluency and grammatical proficiency.

Research on second language acquisition has produced similar findings. Jacqueline Johnson and Elissa Newport (1989) demonstrated that knowledge of English grammar among Chinese- and Korean-speaking adults depended on the age when they had first been exposed to English. Those who started to learn English before age 7 understood English grammar as well as native speakers of English. As the age of first exposure to English increased beyond age 7, the ultimate level of competence in English grammar decreased. (The box on page 255 discusses childhood bilingualism in more detail.)

Another indication that language acquisition has a biological basis is the fact that it is *species-specific*—an ability that all humans share as a result of their common genetic

Animal Communication

inheritance, but that is not found in members of other species. Many other species of animals (from honeybees to vervet monkeys to dolphins) have impressive communication abilities, but none of their communication systems is as abstract, flexible, or productive as human language. Attempts to teach chimpanzees to use sign language and other symbolic communication systems show that chimps probably have some symbolic abilities, but they cannot use rules of syntax to combine words into a wide variety of meaningful sentences (Lieberman, 1984; Premack, 1986). They may, however, be able to *understand* simple syntax and grasp the meaning of novel sentences made up of familiar words (Savage-Rumbaugh et al., 1993). Thus, their receptive language skills may surpass their productive ones, but they still do not come close to the language ability of humans.

Inborn Abilities and Constraints It is not yet clear exactly what the built-in characteristics are that make language acquisition possible, but researchers have proposed a number of ways the human brain might be prewired for language acquisition (Maratsos, 1998; Spelke and Newport, 1998.) Some of the proposed characteristics are *specific* to the domain of language learning abilities; others are more *domain-general* cognitive abilities.

Infants appear to have a number of abilities and predispositions that are inborn or develop in the first few months of life that help them detect information needed for language learning:

- Infants as young as 7 months apparently can detect rules and regularities in sequences of made-up words (Marcus et al., 1999).

- By 8 months infants appear to be able to segment words from a continuous stream of speech (Saffran et al., 1996).

- By 9 months, infants seem to be able to break down streams of speech into phrases and clauses; in laboratory experiments, they show preference for speech with pauses located at boundaries between phrases and clauses rather than within them (Hirsh-Pasek and Golinkoff, 1993; Jusczyk et al., 1992).

- Children may have a built-in predisposition to pay attention to perceptually salient stretches of speech, such as stressed syllables and beginnings and ends of words, which would help them zero in on many grammatical morphemes (Slobin, 1985).

Along with built-in abilities useful for interpreting language, the human brain may come equipped with certain *constraints* on the conclusions that can be drawn about language structure. It is hard to imagine how children could correctly work out all the rules in any language without such constraints. The range of possible rules that could be generated from the input is simply too broad. As a result, theorists have proposed that language learning must be governed by constraints that limit in advance what kinds of rules can be generated.

For instance, children's learning of syntax may be constrained by a predisposition to detect fairly broad syntactic categories common to all languages, such as nouns, verbs, subjects, objects, and grammatical phrases (Pinker, 1987). Although an infant's brain would not be specifically prewired to recognize *English* nouns, for example, the general concept of nouns could be built in, along with a range of possible rules for nouns.

Another built-in constraint that might assist in learning syntax is an assumption that words contain morphemes marking grammatical characteristics such as number, tense, and case (Newport, 1988). How these characteristics are marked varies from language to language, but children would be predisposed to look for some sort of morphology. Newport has found evidence that this particular constraint may be present during a critical period early in life, when language learning normally takes place. This evidence comes from the study of people who have learned American Sign Language (ASL) at various ages. Those who learn ASL as children are more likely to break it down into morphemes and make the same sorts of overregularization errors observed in children

APPLYING RESEARCH FINDINGS

Childhood Bilingualism

Most Americans think *bilingualism*—the ability to speak two languages—is relatively rare, but from a worldwide perspective *monolingualism*—speaking only one language—is the exception to the rule (Snow, 1993). Even in the United States, however, bilingualism is becoming increasingly prevalent. Nationally, about 17 percent of the school-age population speaks a language other than English at home; in some states, including New York, California, Texas, New Mexico, and Arizona, the percentage is much higher (U.S. Census Bureau, 2002b).

What is language development like for *native bilinguals*—children who grow up learning two languages simultaneously? Until about 18 months, children exposed to two languages tend to learn isolated words from each language; it is not clear to what extent they realize words in one language can be translated into the other (Taeschner, 1983). Once they start using grammatical morphemes and syntactic structures, however, they usually treat the languages as separate systems (de Houwer, 1995). Native bilinguals often mix their languages or switch back and forth between them, but the mixing is not random and does not indicate a lack of understanding of the boundaries between languages. Instead, it most often occurs when a child knows a word in only one language or when a concept is closely tied to experience in one language (Snow, 1993). Children exposed to two languages at home do not remain bilingual unless they have continued opportunities to use both languages. If they live in a country where only one of their languages is regularly spoken, they often begin to lose proficiency in the other language once they start school.

What effect does bilingualism have on linguistic and cognitive development? Native bilinguals tend to develop *metalinguistic awareness*, the ability to think about language as an arbitrary system, earlier than children who speak only one language (Hakuta and Diaz, 1985). There

is also evidence for greater cognitive flexibility in bilingual children (Peal and Lambert, 1962). Bilingual preschoolers do tend to show slower than average vocabulary growth in both languages (Snow, 1993). However, single-language vocabulary tests underestimate the total size of bilingual children's vocabularies. Especially early in development, the words they know in each of their languages tend to be somewhat different; when combined, their total vocabulary is often larger than that of monolingual children (Romaine, 1999).

In contrast to native bilinguals, some children learn one language at home and later learn a second in school. The outcome for these children depends on the type of exposure they receive to the second language. Elementary school foreign language instruction involving limited exposure to a second language is not very successful; children learn a second language from standard classroom instruction more slowly than adolescents or adults (Snow, 1993). Children are most likely to become truly bilingual if they participate in a *language immersion curriculum*, in which the second language is used for routine classroom interactions and instruction in other subjects.

Ideally, bilingual education programs should be designed to foster additive rather than subtractive bilingualism. *Additive bilingualism* involves learning a second language and staying proficient in the first; *subtractive bilingualism* involves learning a second language but losing proficiency in the first. One approach that seems to foster additive bilingualism is the *two-way immersion program* (Senesac, 2002). In this type of program, children who are native English speakers and children who are native speakers of another language, such as Spanish, are in classes together. For half of the day, instruction is in English; for the other half, it is in the second language. In this setting, both English and non-English speakers stand the greatest chance of becoming truly bilingual.

---

learning spoken languages. In contrast, those who learn ASL later in life tend to learn signs in a more holistic fashion and not to recognize many morphological markings.

Researchers have also proposed built-in constraints that may help in the learning of words (Behrend, 1990; Markman, 1987; Woodward and Markman, 1998). Two that we have already mentioned are inborn assumptions that unfamiliar words are the names for objects and that new words mean something different from words already known.

General cognitive abilities and constraints wired into the human brain may contribute to language learning as well. As discussed in Chapter 4, infants seem to have an inborn ability to perceive objects, motion, and other characteristics of the world, rather than a disorganized stream of sensory information. This ability gives them an early knowledge of things to which labels can be attached. General symbolic representation and memory abilities can also aid language learning, as suggested by several studies showing correlations between toddlers' language development and cognitive skills. Cecilia Shore (1986) found that 2-year-olds' ability to combine two or more words is related to their block-building, memory, and symbolic-play abilities. Similarly, the ability to string words

Bilingualism

The ability to combine words into sentences seems to be related to other combinatorial abilities, such as block building.

together into well-formed sentences is linked to improved capacity for remembering sequences, which occurs between ages 1 and 3. Alison Gopnik and Andrew Meltzoff (1987) found that 18-month-olds' vocabulary spurt is specifically connected to the development of mature object permanence and to the ability to sort objects into two categories.

In summary, human infants clearly come equipped with a general predisposition to learn language. They may also have a range of more specific built-in predispositions, abilities, and constraints that make language acquisition possible. In all likelihood, children bring a number of inborn factors, both linguistic and cognitive, to the task of acquiring language.

The Environment of Language Learning

Built-in abilities and constraints are not the whole story of language acquisition. Environment also plays a part; without exposure to language, after all, children cannot learn to speak. Moreover, the *nature* of the language environment seems to make a difference. For instance, the more parents interact linguistically with children when they are toddlers, the larger the children's vocabularies are by the time they start school (Hart and Risley, 1995). But what about the type of speech to which young children are exposed and the structure of their interactions with adults? Can these aspects of the language environment facilitate language learning by making linguistic rules and meanings easier to decipher?

Characteristics of Child-Directed Speech To answer this question, we must first look at exactly how adults talk to young children. A number of researchers have observed that adults modify their speech to toddlers in ways that might make it easier for children to acquire language (e.g., Snow and Ferguson, 1977; Pine, 1994). These speech modifications are known as **child-directed speech (CDS),** or **motherese,** even though many fathers and other adults use them also (Barton and Tomasello, 1994; Gleason, 1975). The following conversation between a mother and her 19-month-old daughter is a typical example of middle-class American CDS:

Mother: What should I draw first?

Child: Bi goggie.

Mother: A big doggie. All right. Is that big?

Child: Oggie bi. Bi gog.

Mother: What's this? What's this part of the doggie? Is that a big enough doggie?

Child: Bi goggie.

Mother: Well, I did make a big doggie. Look.

Child: Bi goggie.

Mother: You make a big doggie. Make a kitty.

Child: Kiki.

(Genishi and Dyson, 1984, p. 45)

English speakers' CDS differs from adult-directed speech in several ways (Cruttenden, 1994; Fernald, 1984; Snow, 1977):

- CDS is simpler grammatically and includes fewer grammatical errors.
- CDS is spoken in a higher than normal pitch, its intonations are more exaggerated, and it has fewer lapses in fluency.
- In CDS the boundaries between phrases and clauses are more clearly marked by pauses and intonation.
- CDS tends to focus more on objects and events discussed in the present tense, using concrete nouns. The adult frequently comments on what the child is doing or on what is going on around the child.
- CDS tends to be quite redundant. The mother in the preceding dialogue, for instance, finds many ways to repeat the words *big* and *doggie.*
- CDS typically includes many questions about objects and events.

Fathers' speech to young children tends to differ from mothers', at least when the father is a secondary caregiver. These fathers ask for more labels and explanations ("What's this?" "What does it do?"), and they use more advanced vocabulary words. They also ask for more repetitions and clarifications from the child (Masur and Gleason, 1980). One reason for this is that communication breakdowns are more frequent in children's conversations with secondary-caregiver fathers. These fathers are more likely than mothers to ignore children's utterances, and when they don't understand something their child says, they most often respond with a nonspecific request for clarification ("What?"). Mothers more often make a specific request for clarification ("Put it where?") (Tomasello, Conti-Ramsden, and Ewert, 1990). These differences most likely arise because secondary-caregiver fathers spend less time with their children than primary-caregiver mothers do. They are therefore less familiar with their children's speech and routines, and probably less tuned in to their communication needs. However, these fathers make a distinctive contribution to children's linguistic environments by readying them for the broader social world, in which clarity is important and in which not all speakers structure the conversation and adjust their speech as much as mothers do (Barton and Tomasello, 1994).

Siblings and other older children also adjust their speech to toddlers in many of the ways adults do. When asked to describe the rules of a game to a younger child, 4-year-olds make their sentences less complex, speak more slowly, and repeat more often than when describing the rules to an adult (Shatz and Gelman, 1973). Even 2- and

Child-directed speech (CDS) or motherese:
The modifications adults make in their speech when talking to young children.

Motherese

3-year-olds use shorter sentences and more repetition when talking to infant siblings than when talking to their mothers (Dunn and Kendrick, 1982b). However, siblings' speech to toddlers also differs from adults' speech in some ways. Siblings' speech adjustments to infants and toddlers are less sensitive than those made by adults. Siblings ask fewer questions, issue more directives, and put less emphasis on getting the younger child to talk (DeHart, 1990; Hoff-Ginsberg and Krueger, 1991; Tomasello and Mannle, 1985).

Impact of Child-Directed Speech   Now let's return to the question of whether CDS facilitates language learning. Studies have not found a relationship between CDS and *overall* rate of language acquisition (Newport, Gleitman, and Gleitman, 1977). However, certain *particular* characteristics of mothers' speech do seem to support their children's development of related syntactic structures (Hoff-Ginsberg, 1990). For example, English-speaking mothers who ask many questions, which makes auxiliary verbs especially salient, have children who use high numbers of auxiliary verbs. However, the language *model* provided by CDS is probably not its most important feature. Its effects on children's language development are more likely due to the chances it gives for active participation in conversations.

Cross-cultural research on how adults talk to children also sheds light on the role of CDS in language acquisition. Although there are many similarities in the features of CDS across languages (Fernald et al., 1989; Kuhl et al., 1997), there are also some differences. For example, English speakers exaggerate their pitch and intonation more when addressing young children than speakers of most other languages do. In some cultures, CDS is limited or nonexistent. The Kaluli people of New Guinea believe it is important for infants to hear what they call "hard speech"—the language spoken by adults. They do not use baby talk with infants and young children because they do not believe it is good to teach childish forms of language. Preverbal Kaluli babies are not considered capable of communicating on their own. Rather than speaking *to* their babies in a special way, Kaluli mothers often speak *for* their babies in dialogues with other people. The mother holds her baby facing away from her, moves the baby as if he or she were conversing, and speaks for the baby in a special, high-pitched voice. This style of inter-

When siblings are talking to toddlers, they make many of the same speech adjustments that adults do.

action is quite different from the middle-class American practice of face-to-face "conversations" with preverbal infants. Despite these differences from the way American mothers interact with their babies, Kaluli babies develop language on a timetable comparable to that of American babies (Schieffelin, 1990).

Some researchers have argued that CDS serves a primarily attentional or affective function in mother-child interaction—that is, mothers use it to capture their babies' attention and to communicate with them emotionally, but it has little or no direct impact on children's syntactic development (Newport, et al., 1977). It is true that even newborns attend more to CDS than to adult-directed speech and show a preference for listening to CDS (Cooper and Aslin, 1990; Fernald, 1985). However, there is some recent evidence that what babies prefer is not CDS per se, but the positive affect it communicates (Singh, Morgan, and Best, 2002). Both English- and German-speaking mothers vary their pitch and intonation in consistent ways to engage their babies in interaction and to soothe distressed infants (Papoušek, Papoušek, and Bornstein, 1985; Stern, Spieker, and MacKain, 1982). Brown (1977) suggested that CDS arises from parents' desires both to communicate with their infants, which leads to simplification, and to express affection toward them. In all likelihood, CDS serves more than one function in early parent-child relationships and in children's early language development.

CDS by itself does not explain children's language acquisition. It does simplify and structure the linguistic input children receive, which may be useful in syntactic development. The concrete, present-oriented nature of adult-child conversations may help children make connections between words and the things they refer to. The frequent questions and clear turn-taking provide opportunities for linguistic practice and learning conversational skills. Jerome Bruner (1983) suggested that the ways adults structure children's language environments should be considered a *language acquisition support system (LASS)*—a complement to Chomsky's LAD. Biology and environment interact in children's semantic and syntactic development, just as in their acquisition of the sounds of their language.

NONLINGUISTIC ASPECTS OF SYMBOLIC REPRESENTATION

In Piaget's view, the principal cognitive development of toddlerhood is the emergence of *symbolic thought*, the ability to let one thing stand for another that is not physically present. Symbols can be mental representations, or they can be words, objects, or actions. When Mikey forms a mental image of a piece of candy, he is using a symbol to represent an object he wants. When Meryl tells Mrs. Jasper "Mommy go work," she is using words as symbols for something that has already happened. When Malcolm pretends a paper plate is a steering wheel, he is using the plate and his actions as symbols for the real act of driving. When Maggie shows a newborn photo to her Aunt Sarah and proudly labels it "Baby Mikey!," she is using the photo as a symbol for her baby brother.

Implicit in Piaget's notion of symbols is the ability to manipulate symbols intentionally, creating new ideas and thoughts. In the case of linguistic symbols, children become able to combine words into sentences. This deliberate manipulation of symbols enables children to say anything imaginable. In Piaget's view, a toddler's first words are not really symbols, because they refer only to objects or events in the here and now. Not until a child begins to talk about things that are not currently present does he or she use language symbolically as Piaget defined the term. This point in language development usually occurs between 18 and 24 months of age—the age range that marks the last of Piaget's six sensorimotor stages, as we discussed in Chapter 5.

According to Piaget, the general symbolic abilities that emerge during toddlerhood are a developmental outgrowth of sensorimotor activities. In particular, Piaget emphasized the role of imitation in the development of a toddler's use of symbols. Consider the following observation he made of his daughter Jacqueline:

At 15 months Jacqueline was playing with a clown with long feet and happened to catch the feet in the low neck of her dress. She had difficulty in getting them out, but as soon as she had done so she tried to put them back in the same position. . . . As she did not succeed she put her hand in front of her, bent her forefinger at a right angle to reproduce the shape of the clown's feet, described exactly the same trajectory as the clown, and thus succeeded in putting her finger into the neck of her dress. She looked at the motionless finger for a moment, then pulled at her dress, without of course being able to see what she was doing. Then satisfied, she removed her finger and went on to something else.
(Piaget, 1962, p. 65)

Notice how Jacqueline imitates with the action of her finger the previous action of the clown's feet. This forerunner of mature symbolic representation helps to show the origins of this important new ability. By the end of the sensorimotor period, Piaget contended, children's imitations become more abbreviated. For example, rather than going through the whole process of imitating the clown's feet getting caught in her dress, Jacqueline at 20 months might simply flex her finger slightly to stand for the shape of the feet. She is now able to use a symbol that bears a much less obvious relationship to the thing being symbolized. Still later she will use words ("feet caught") to represent the incident with purely verbal symbols. Piaget maintained that the meaning of any symbol lies in the child's current schemes for interacting with the thing symbolized. Symbols do not represent things in themselves, but rather the child's present understanding of things.

Language development is a dramatic indication of toddlers' emerging representational skills. But, as our examples show, language is not the only way toddlers use symbols. Three other manifestations of symbolic representation that emerge during the toddler period are pretend play, the use of gestures, and understanding iconic symbols.

Toddlers' Pretend Play

Toddlers' emerging representational ability is especially obvious in their play. Several investigators have separately demonstrated an orderly sequence in the development of symbolic play during the toddler period (Belsky and Most, 1981; McCune, 1995; Striano, Tomasello, and Rochat, 2001). Initially, symbolic representation is seen in behaviors directed to the self. For example, a 16-month-old may pretend to drink from a toy

By the time they are 2 years old, most children can use substitute objects in pretend play—for example, using a block to represent a telephone.

cup. Later, toddlers direct such acts to others (as in pretending to feed a doll). By age 2, they can combine a series of such acts around a theme (such as building a fence with blocks around pretend animals).

As representational skills develop, toddlers are able to use decreasingly realistic objects as symbols in their play (Fein, 1981). Between 14 and 19 months, children's pretend play with *replica objects* (dolls, toy horses, toy cars) increases sharply, but their use of *substitute objects* (using a pillow to represent a baby, or a block to represent a car) is still rare. Between 19 and 24 months, the use of substitute objects greatly increases, and by 24 months most children can use one substitute object in a pretend scenario (using a block to feed a baby doll). *Double substitutions* (using a block as a bottle *and* a pillow as the baby) do not appear until later in the preschool period.

The social context has a definite effect on children's ability to engage in pretend play (Tomasello, Striano, and Rochat, 1999). Toddlers show more advanced forms of pretend play when they are pretending with other people than when they are pretending by themselves, particularly when the play partner is an older sibling or a parent. For example, children as young as 24 months have been observed to take on such complementary roles as mother and baby, teacher and pupil, and airplane pilot and passenger in play with their older brothers and sisters (Dunn and Dale, 1984). This more sophisticated play results partly from direction by the more skilled partner, but participation in these scenarios still requires the toddler to have some understanding of pretense and the partner's intentions. Another reason siblings elicit advanced forms of pretend play from toddlers is that they provide an opportunity for repeated enactment of the same scenario. The familiarity of both the sibling and the particular game of pretend makes possible fairly sophisticated role playing.

Toddlers' Use of Gestures

A second area in which emerging representational skills can be observed during toddlerhood is the use of gestures (Goodwyn and Acredolo, 1998; Petitto, 1992; Volterra and Erting, 1990). Simple *communicative gestures,* such as pointing, normally emerge at around 9 months. These early gestures are often accompanied by vocalizations, as when a baby points at a toy she cannot reach and whimpers. *Conventional social gestures* (such as waving bye-bye, nodding *yes,* and shaking the head *no*) usually appear between 9 and 12 months. But although these early gestures communicate meaning, they do not directly represent or symbolize actions or objects. That is, there is no resemblance between the gesture and what it communicates.

Baby Signs

Between 12 and 18 months, toddlers begin to produce *symbolic gestures,* which do directly represent some aspect of an action or object. For example, sniffing might be used to represent a flower and moving a thumb to the mouth to request a bottle. Symbolic gestures most often develop in the context of interactive routines between child and parent, or from the child's own interactions with objects (Goodwyn and Acredolo, 1998). For example, Linda Acredolo's daughter took the raised-arms gesture used in the parent-infant game "So Big!" and applied it to objects that were big in comparison to other, similar objects. Early symbolic gestures usually reflect the function of an object rather than its physical form, such as using a bouncing motion to represent a ball rather than indicating its round shape. Goodwyn and Acredolo (1998) found that toddlers tend to use symbolic gestures as requests earlier than they use them to label objects. Some children even combine symbolic gestures to make complicated requests. For instance, one little girl got her mother to let the dog out by panting and moving her hand as if turning a doorknob.

Another gestural advance during toddlerhood is the ability to coordinate divergent gestural and visual signals. Twelve-month-olds have trouble following an adult's pointing gesture if the adult is not looking and pointing in the same direction, but 17-month-olds can follow the direction of a point even if the adult is looking elsewhere. Similarly, 12-month-olds tend to look in the direction of an object they are pointing at, but 18-month-olds can look at a conversational partner even while pointing at something else. The emergence of the ability to coordinate divergent signals seems to correspond roughly to the emergence of true words (Masur, 1990).

As the ability to use gestures advances, the total frequency of a child's gestures first rises and then falls. From about 10 to 18 months, children gradually use more and more gestures. After 18 months the frequency of gestures declines, until it levels off around 24 months. The early increase in gesturing parallels the beginnings of word learning, while the later decline occurs about the same time as the vocabulary spurt. Some researchers suggest that, as vocabulary size increases, language begins to replace gesturing as the child's main channel of communication (Lock et al., 1990). But the early increase in gesturing that occurs at the same time as early word learning implies that gesturing is not just a precursor to language. Gesturing and language are apparently two separate systems that develop side by side. The fact that symbolic gestures appear around the same time as children's first words suggests that both reflect the toddler's emerging symbolic abilities.

The study of deaf children also reveals parallel development of gesture and language. Deaf children acquiring sign language produce gestures very similar to those produced by children who can hear. Deaf children's gestures are not more complex, despite their experience with signing (Petitto, 1992). In addition, they keep their linguistic signs and their gestures distinct; they do not mix or confuse them. Here again we see that gestures form a communication system that remains separate even after language has emerged.

Toddlers' Understanding of Iconic Symbols

Iconic symbols:
Symbols that closely resemble the things they represent.

The ability to use symbolic representation does not emerge all at once, as demonstrated by toddlers' difficulty making use of information from most **iconic symbols.** These are symbols that closely resemble whatever they are supposed to represent, such as pictures and scale models.

At 9 months, babies seem confused by pictures; when shown realistic color photos of objects, they try to grasp the objects portrayed in them (DeLoache, 2002). Twenty-month-olds no longer show this sort of manual exploration of pictures; they seem to understand that the objects portrayed are not physically present. However, toddlers have trouble using information contained in pictures. When shown a picture of a room and told that it shows where a toy is hidden, 2-year-olds are rarely able to find the toy in the actual room. This ability seems to develop fairly rapidly; by age 2½, children are able to find the toy about 80 percent of the time (DeLoache and Burns, 1994). Similar results are obtained when toddlers watch on a television screen as an experimenter hides an object in a neighboring room (Troseth and DeLoache, 1998). However, if they watch the same event *directly,* through a window into the room, even 2-year-olds can find the hidden object. The problem seems to be making a connection between the symbolic information contained in pictures or video and the real objects portrayed.

mhhe.com
/dehart5

Toddlers and Scale Models

Scale models are even more difficult for toddlers to comprehend (DeLoache, 2002; DeLoache, Miller, and Pierroutsakos, 1998). Three-year-olds can use information about a hidden toy's location in a scale model of a room to find the toy in the actual room, but 2½-year-olds have trouble with this task. One reason may be that toddlers find the miniature room so interesting as an object in its own right, they have trouble simultaneously thinking of it as symbolic of anything else. Interestingly, 2½-year-olds have no trouble with this task if they believe a scale model has been produced by shrinking a full-sized room or a full-sized room has been produced by making a scale model grow. This is accomplished by showing toddlers a hidden toy in a full-sized room or a model, then closing the door to the room and telling them that a special machine is going to shrink the room or make it grow. After several minutes of computer-generated sound effects and flashing lights on an instrument panel, the door is opened to reveal the predicted change in size. Under these conditions, 2½-year-olds readily find the toy, presumably because they do not have to take the extra step of thinking about the room they are seeing as a *symbol* of another, different-sized room.

ADVANCES AND LIMITATIONS OF TODDLERHOOD: AN OVERVIEW

In this chapter we have looked at the representational skills that emerge in toddlerhood—skills using ideas, images, sounds, and other symbols to stand for, or represent, objects and events. Infants who knew the world through *physical* actions have grown into toddlers who are capable of *mental* actions. Just as infants actively explored objects by grasping, manipulating, and combining them, so toddlers actively manipulate symbolic elements, such as words.

These representational abilities build on the emerging long-term memory skills discussed in Chapter 5 (Bauer, 1995). Storage of past experience and the ability to compare past and present are the foundation for symbolic representation. At the same time, emerging representational abilities dramatically enhance memory. Symbolic representation is an efficient way of summarizing experience for storage and retrieval.

The representational skills that emerge during toddlerhood provide the foundation for more elaborate social interactions, for pretend play, and for new kinds of problem solving. Representational skills allow toddlers to be dramatically more flexible in their behavior and to engage in much more planning of their actions than they could do as infants. These skills also enable them to think about the world in new, more complex ways. Consider a form of fantasy play that Mikey invented when he was $2\frac{1}{2}$. He pretended the living room couch was a boat, the rug an ocean, the coffee table an island, and an umbrella a fishing pole. Once when Maggie walked through the room, he complained to her crossly: "No walk water!" As we have seen, the ability to engage in make-believe play grows dramatically between the ages of 1 and 3. Developmental psychologist John Flavell (1985) has suggested that make-believe play marks the beginning of an important awareness in the child: the awareness that there is a distinction between appearance and reality.

Although many cognitive advances take place during the toddler period, toddlers' thinking is still constrained by a lack of logic in using their new mental skills, by limited memory abilities, and by difficulty distinguishing between what is real and what is not. Advances will be made in all of these areas during the preschool period that follows.

Chapter Summary

Introduction

Toddlerhood is the period from roughly 12 to 30 months of age. One of its major cognitive developments is the emergence of a capacity for **symbolic representation,** which includes **language.**

The Components of Language

The components of language include:

- **phonology,** the system of sounds used in a language;
- **semantics,** the meanings of words and sentences;
- **morphology,** the rules for combining units of meaning in words;
- **syntax,** the rules for organizing words into phrases and sentences; and
- **pragmatics,** the rules for the social use of language.

Children must develop two sets of skills to use language: **productive skills** for putting ideas into words and

receptive skills for understanding what other people say. In general, toddlers' receptive skills are more advanced than their productive skills.

Major Tasks in Early Language Learning

In the first year of life, children's vocalizations change dramatically, culminating in the ability to produce true speech. The five stages of **prelinguistic vocalization** are:

- reflexive **crying;**
- **cooing,** primarily vowel sounds expressing contentment;
- **vocal play,** when babies produce a range of sounds varying widely in pitch and volume;
- **canonical babbling,** when infants produce increasingly speechlike strings of syllables; and
- **conversational babbling,** with adultlike stress and intonation patterns.

Toddlers' first words often label many of the same everyday concepts, but children show differences in the *purposes* for which they use their first words. Some have a more **referential style,** others a more **expressive style.**

At first children learn new words slowly, but at about 18 months they usually show a **vocabulary spurt.** During the preschool years, their vocabularies grow rapidly, with receptive vocabulary outpacing productive vocabulary.

To learn words, toddlers must first separate them out from the stream of speech they hear and then assign meanings to them. Through the process of **fast mapping,** young children use context to make a quick guess about a word's meaning. This process may be aided by **joint attention,** the **whole-object assumption,** and **lexical contrast.**

Children's early word-learning errors consist mainly of **underextensions** and **overextensions** of word meanings.

After starting to learn single words, children begin to add **grammatical morphemes** to them. The order in which grammatical morphemes are acquired depends on

- grammatical complexity,
- semantic complexity, and
- phonological characteristics.

The acquisition of grammatical morphemes demonstrates that children are learning linguistic rules. The productivity of these linguistic rules leads to a particular type of error called **overregularization.**

Children's single-word utterances are often **holophrases,** conveying what an adult would say with an entire phrase or sentence. When children begin to construct two-word sentences, they produce **telegraphic speech,** including only the words necessary to convey the essential meaning. After children pass through the two-word stage, the grammatical complexity of their speech increases rapidly.

At the same time children are acquiring linguistic competence, they are also acquiring **communicative competence,** including the ability to carry on conversations, to repair communication breakdowns, and to use language in socially appropriate ways.

The Child and the Environment in Language Development

A long-standing debate exists between **environmentalist** and **nativist** explanations of language acquisition.

Human infants come equipped with a general predisposition to learn language. Various aspects of brain development probably contribute to an early critical or sensitive period for language acquisition. Infants also have a number of specific built-in predispositions, abilities, and constraints that make language acquisition possible.

Adults modify their speech toward toddlers in ways that may make it easier for children to learn language. Although the format of **child-directed speech (CDS)** varies across cultures, it includes several features that differentiate it from speech to adults:

- grammatical simplicity and few grammatical errors,
- exaggerated pitch and intonation,
- clear marking of phrase and clause boundaries,
- focus on present objects and events,
- redundancy, and
- frequent questions.

Nonlinguistic Aspects of Symbolic Representation

Toddlers' symbolic representation skills are reflected in other aspects of their development besides language, including pretend play, the use of gestures, and the beginnings of an understanding of iconic symbols.

Advances and Limitations of Toddlerhood: An Overview

Representational skills expand the flexibility of toddlers' thought and behavior. However, toddlers' thinking is still constrained by:

- a lack of logic,
- limited memory abilities, and
- difficulty distinguishing what is real and what is not.

Review Questions

Introduction

1. What major cognitive skill emerges during toddlerhood?

The Components of Language

2. List and explain the major components of language.

Major Tasks in Early Language Learning

3. Describe the stages of **prelinguistic vocalization.**

4. Describe the typical course of vocabulary development and explain the processes involved in word learning.
5. Describe the acquisition of **grammatical morphemes** and explain what it reveals about language development.
6. Summarize children's syntactic development from the one-word stage through complex sentences.
7. Explain what is involved in developing **communicative competence.**

**The Child and the Environment
in Language Development**

8. Discuss the possible contributions of biology and environment to children's language acquisition.

Nonlinguistic Aspects of Symbolic Representation

9. Trace the early development of pretend play, the use of gestures, and the understanding of iconic symbols.

**Advances and Limitations of Toddlerhood:
An Overview**

10. Summarize the cognitive advances of toddlerhood and the limitations that remain.

Application and Observation

1. Observe parents interacting with babies and young children of various ages. How does their speech to their children compare with their speech to other adults? How does it compare to the characteristics of child-directed speech described on pp. 256–258? How does it vary depending on the baby or child's age? Do you notice any differences between mothers' and fathers' speech? How do the children respond to the various interaction partners? What factors (both linguistic and nonlinguistic) might explain the parents' speech patterns and the children's responses?

2. Watch several television shows aimed at children of various ages and take note of the language and speech used by narrators and characters on the shows. To what extent is child-directed speech used? How does this vary among the shows? How do adults and children watching the shows differ in their responses to the style of language and speech used? Why?

3. If you have access to a baby book (yours or someone else's), look at the entries in it related to language development. What kinds of things did the person keeping the book find significant enough to record? How does the baby's development seem to compare to the pattern of development described in this chapter? (Keep in mind that entries in baby books don't always capture the first time a baby has done a certain thing and that mothers' memories aren't always accurate.) If you don't have access to a baby book, ask your mother about your own language development. (For example, what was your first word? What else does she remember about when you were learning to talk? Are there any family stories about unusual speech habits you had or funny things you said when you were little?)

4. Try out the Wug Test. Look up the original (Berko, 1958), draw your own pictures to go with some or all of the items, and administer it to several young children of different ages.

8 Toddler Social and Emotional Development

*A*s 12-month-old Mikey sits playing with toys a few feet from his mother, his attention is suddenly captured by a large wooden puzzle piece. It is a bright orange carrot with a cluster of emerald green leaves. Mikey grasps the wooden carrot with widened eyes. Then, in a smooth motion, he turns and extends the piece toward his mother. "Ya-ka!" he says with a broad smile. "Yes, sweetie, that's a carrot," Christine answers, smiling in return. "Do you like carrots?" "Ya-ka!" Mikey repeats happily.

A little more than a year later Mikey is with his mother at the university child study laboratory. Mikey has been presented with a series of problems to solve. The final problem is difficult. It requires him to weigh down a long board in order to lift candy through a hole in a Plexiglas box and hold the candy up long enough so he can get it (see photo on p. 282). Mikey attacks the problem eagerly, but it is beyond his cognitive abilities. He promptly calls upon Christine for help. She gives him clues and leads him step-by-step to see that he must weigh down the board with a large wooden block. Mikey cooperates with her suggestions and is ecstatic when he gets the candy. "I take it out!" he exclaims proudly.

Mikey has shown dazzling development in one year. At age 2, he is able not only to talk and solve quite challenging problems, but also to interact with others on a much more mature level than at age 1. The new social and emotional capacities that emerge during toddlerhood and the changes underlying them are major subjects of this chapter. We also explore how the quality of the parent-child relationship that formed during infancy and other influences pave the way for the adaptations the child makes during toddlerhood.

Developmentalists have increasingly recognized the importance of the toddler period. In the first 12 months, the regulation of excitement, emotions, and behavior is orchestrated by caregivers, though the infant plays an ever more active role. By the preschool period, children are expected to regulate and control themselves to a large extent. The toddler period is the transition during which control begins to be transferred from the parent to the child.

Toddlerhood is a period of other major developments as well. As you discovered in Chapter 7, important cognitive changes occur, especially the emergence of language and other forms of symbolic representation. There are also dramatic changes in the parent-child relationship. During toddlerhood, children move from almost complete dependence on their parents toward greater self-reliance. As toddlers begin to exert their own will, parents must learn to impose control when needed while still fostering independence and growth. Since this is also the period when children are beginning to develop a sense of self, the way parents handle the issue of autonomy at this time can greatly influence children's self-esteem and ultimately their capacity for flexible self-control.

In addition to moving toward greater self-reliance, toddlers start to acquire the rules, standards, and values of their society. As mentioned in Chapter 2, this important process is called **socialization** (Bugental and Goodnow, 1998; Maccoby, 1992). At first, socialization simply involves responding to the expectations parents and others in authority hold. In time, however, the child begins to *internalize* these standards—to incorporate them into the self (Grusec and Kuczynski, 1997). This second phase in the socialization process takes place in the preschool years and beyond, but it builds on experiences in toddlerhood (Kochanska et al., 2001). Learning the rules within the family (or within the day care setting) paves the way for more general respect for social order.

As children become more mobile, and as their learning of language opens up new means of communication, most parents in Western cultures greatly increase the demands they impose. Because children can now get into things and can understand the word *no,* parents start establishing rules. It has been reported that young toddlers (11 to 17 months) experience on average one prohibition from an adult every nine minutes (Power and Chapieski, 1986). At the same time, toddlers are weaned from the breast or bottle, and

Toddlerhood

Socialization:
The process by which children acquire the rules, standards, and values of a culture.

not long thereafter toilet training begins. In other words, during the toddler period, parents begin to expect compliance with social norms.

To summarize, toddlers in Western cultures face two important tasks:

- to move from near-total dependence on their parents toward greater self-reliance, and
- to begin complying with social rules and expectations.

Although children around the world confront these same two tasks, cultures vary in how the tasks are presented and how rapidly they are carried out (Rogoff et al., 1993). In some cultures—for example, in rural Filipino communities (Whiting and Edwards, 1988) and in Samoa (Mead, 1925/1939)—children are indulged fully until weaning and then rapidly socialized. In North America, the demands parents make regarding independence and compliance change gradually. Nevertheless, by about age 5, children are expected to do many things for themselves, to exert considerable control over their impulses, and to have a sense of appropriate and inappropriate behavior.

In this chapter you will learn much more about the major developments of toddlerhood. We begin by exploring two views of how the process of socialization occurs. To provide a more detailed idea of what children this age are like, we then examine the major ways toddlers differ from infants: their increased autonomy from parents and competence in social interaction, their more sophisticated understanding of the self and others, their beginning capacity to control themselves, and their broader range of emotions. Next we turn to parent-child relations during toddlerhood, focusing on the role parents play in encouraging toddlers' development. This leads to a discussion of individual adaptations, the roots of personality in toddlers. For example, what causes one toddler to be eager and cooperative, while another is persistently prone to tantrums? Finally, we address the issue of parental neglect and abuse of toddlers; although abuse can be directed at children of any age, toddlers are particularly frequent victims.

Increasingly mobile toddlers become experts at getting into things.

Questions to Think About As You Read

- How do their new behaviors and abilities change toddlers' relationships with others?
- What can parents do to help their children successfully negotiate the developmental challenges of toddlerhood?

TWO VIEWS OF SOCIALIZATION

Traditionally, socialization has been thought of as a process in which rules and values are imposed on an unwilling child by parents and other adults—socialization from the *outside*. Early forms of both psychoanalytic and social learning theories adopted such a view. More recently, many developmentalists have argued for a perspective that might be called socialization from the *inside*. Barbara Rogoff (1990) uses the term **appropriation** to convey the idea that children naturally take on the rules and values of their culture as part of their participation in relationships with caregivers. Let's look more closely at these two views of socialization.

Appropriation:
The process by which children naturally take on the rules and values of their culture through participation in relationships with caregivers.

Socialization from the Outside

In his early work, Freud saw the infant as a seething mass of biological drives and impulses. Society's job was to curb these innate impulses and channel them in acceptable directions. If parents blocked the expression of biological drives to a moderate degree, the child would learn to redirect this energy toward socially desirable goals. The

Sublimation:
Freud's term for the redirection of blocked biological drives and impulses.

end result would be compliance with the parents' wishes in order to maintain their love and nurturance. Freud called this redirecting of blocked biological drives **sublimation**. As long as the child was not excessively thwarted and overwhelmed by anxiety or anger, sublimation was a positive process, Freud believed.

Early social learning theorists shared Freud's view that social rules and values were actively imposed on children as they grew older. Some early social learning theorists suggested that children complied with these standards to maintain closeness with parents, who had been associated with reducing hunger and meeting other basic needs. The most common theme in the traditional social learning view, however, was the direct teaching of acceptable behavior by means of selective rewards and punishments. According to this perspective, children were rewarded for good behavior and punished for bad behavior. As a result, they learned to behave in ways approved of by their parents and others around them.

Contemporary social learning theorists put less emphasis on the direct and purposeful teaching of appropriate behavior than their predecessors did (Bandura, 1992; Mischel and Mischel, 1983). Instead, they underscore the importance of imitation and vicarious rewards and punishments that a child observes (those the child sees *others* experiencing). According to this view, children come to behave appropriately just by being exposed to desirable behavior in others whom they love or respect and by seeing those people socially rewarded for adhering to norms and values. Maggie, for instance, may observe Christine comforting a neighbor's child who has fallen and hurt himself. When the child's mother arrives, she thanks Christine profusely. From these observations Maggie learns a set of actions to be used with others in distress. She also learns that kindness is the right response in such a situation and that being kind may result in gratitude and praise. Note how modern social learning theorists emphasize the cognitions, or ideas and understanding, that Maggie acquires. They believe that once Maggie knows the behaviors considered appropriate in this situation, she will naturally tend to adopt them. Maggie, like all children, wants to be socially competent, and learning society's rules is one way of acquiring such competence. Here you can see how modern social learning theory is leaning increasingly toward the view of socialization from within.

Socialization from the Inside

Mary Ainsworth argued persuasively that socialization emanates from inside children (Ainsworth, Bell, and Stayton, 1974). She believed that in the natural course of events children *want* to comply with their parents' requests and expectations (see also Waters, Kondo-Ikemura, and Richters, 1990). This desire stems from our evolution as a group-living species. It is also encouraged by the social context in which children are embedded from birth (Bugental and Goodnow, 1998).

Malcolm, for example, has become a participant in smoothly operating relationships with his caregivers early in life. His behavior is organized around DeeDee, John, and Momma Jo, who represent bases of security for him. As a toddler, Malcolm naturally wants to maintain these close and harmonious relationships (Waters et al., 1990). There is no reason to assume that he will routinely resist the adults in his family or that they will have to force his compliance through punishment or threat of withholding love. Malcolm *enjoys* pleasing them and participating in partnerships with them. They have been reliable and responsive to him, and it makes sense that he wants to be responsive to them.

Ainsworth's research showed that most children do behave this way. Children whose caregivers were consistently responsive to them were found to be compliant as early as 12 months of age and tended to be secure in their attachments (Ainsworth et al., 1974). This tendency is also seen at age 2 (Frankel and Bates, 1990; Kochanska et al., 2001).

Most toddlers are of course negativistic at times. Even those who have secure relationships with their parents will periodically oppose parental wishes and demand their own way, at times with great intensity. One study showed that more than 90 percent of

Toddlers become socialized not just because their parents make them do things but also because they want to cooperate with and help their parents.

2-year-olds at times refused parental requests to put toys away (Klimes-Dougan and Kopp, 1999). For this reason, the toddler period is often called the *terrible twos*. As Erik Erikson (1963) argued, some negativism is a natural outcome of the toddler's expanding capabilities coupled with the movement toward greater self-reliance. When Mikey refuses to let Christine help him up the stairs, he is showing a normal desire to exercise his newfound skills and autonomy. Ainsworth's point is simply that a motivation toward cooperation and compliance is as natural in toddlers as the thrust toward independence is. Toddlers generally are oppositional when the adult request is counter to their own goals, not when they are seeking assistance from a parent (Schneider-Rosen and Wenz-Gross, 1990). When a toddler seems dedicated to thwarting his or her parents and consistently opposes or ignores most parental requests, a problem in the parent-child relationship is likely. This is not simply something in the toddler's nature. Later in this chapter you will read about several studies that demonstrate this point. But first let's arrive at a better picture of toddlerhood by looking at some major developments in this important period.

The Terrible Twos

MAJOR DEVELOPMENTS IN THE TODDLER PERIOD

In addition to starting to acquire the rules and values of society, there are several other important social and emotional developments in toddlerhood:

- increased independence from parents and increased self-reliance;
- increased awareness of the self and other people;
- increased sociability and more mature forms of social interaction;
- the beginnings of self-control; and
- a broader range of emotional responses.

Moving Toward Independence

One of the most obvious developmental changes in the toddler period is a decline in physical closeness and contact with caregivers. Mobile toddlers readily separate from their caregivers to play and explore. The distance a toddler ventures from a parent can

A CLOSER LOOK

THE ORGANIZATION OF BEHAVIOR

Research has revealed that it is not simply what toddlers do or even how often they show particular behaviors that is most revealing. Rather, it is the way behaviors are combined, the particular contexts in which they take place, the sequences in which they occur, and, especially, how they are organized with respect to caregivers that tell us the most about toddlers' functioning. Specific behaviors that are apparently the same may mean very different things at different times, in different circumstances, or in different combinations. And behaviors that outwardly appear very different from each other may have similar meanings or functions in different situations or at different ages. All of these factors must be considered in looking at the *organization of behavior*.

For example, in a classic study Inge Bretherton and Mary Ainsworth (1974) showed that young toddlers were quite interested in unfamiliar persons. They showed toys to them and even approached them with some frequency. This did not mean, however, that these toddlers saw strangers as equivalent to their caregivers or that 12-month-olds are not wary of strangers. After they approached the strangers, the children in this study almost always immediately retreated to their mothers. This sequence revealed the complexity of their social motivations; they found the strangers interesting, but also needed reassurance from their mothers after interacting with them. Simply observing that a toddler is wary or friendly toward a stranger does not reveal very much; to understand the significance of the toddler's behavior we would need to know how the stranger was behaving, whether the child's mother was present or not, and how the same child behaved toward other familiar and unfamiliar people in similar situations.

In another study, researchers looked at the play of 18-month-olds in two different conditions (Carr, Dabbs, and Carr, 1975). One was a typical playroom situation in which the caregiver sat in a chair watching the toddler. In the other, a screen was placed between the child and caregiver. The amount of play was greatly reduced in this circumstance. These toddlers vocalized a great deal to their mothers and occasionally looked around the screen to see them. Most interestingly, when the screen was not present, the toddlers did not in fact look at their mothers very often. The mere *possibility* of looking at them provided enough support to encourage play in children of this age.

Finally, in a very important study, Everett Waters (1978) demonstrated remarkable stability in patterns of attachment between 12 and 18 months. But it was not specific behaviors, such as contact seeking, vocalizing, crying, or looking at the mother, that were stable. For example, relationships that were secure remained secure, but toddlers manifested these differently than infants did. Most 12-month-olds were distressed by separations and strongly sought contact with their mothers upon reunion. They were readily comforted by this contact, which is why they were classed as secure. When these children were 18 months old, they were not nearly as distressed as they had been six months earlier, and they usually required only brief physical contact with their caregivers following brief separation. They manifested their security in the relationship primarily through positive greetings and active initiation of interaction. Even though there were great changes in specific behaviors across this time period, there was similarity in the *quality* of the behavioral organization with respect to the caregiver.

be quite substantial when the toddler initiates the separation (Rheingold and Eckerman, 1971). Occasionally, in the course of other activities, the toddler will return to the caregiver before going off again. But more often the child will merely show a toy or vocalize from a distance, as in our opening example of Mikey at age 1. As a young infant, Mikey needed *physical* contact to support his explorations, but he now relies more on *psychological* contact (Sroufe, 1995). Psychological contact can be maintained by interactions that do not involve physical touching, such as exchanges of words, smiles, and looks. Mikey's secure attachment to his parents, in toddlerhood as well as infancy, supports his explorations and mastery of the environment. But much more than in infancy, he can now draw support from cues across a distance, and this ability allows him to be more independent (Emde, 1992). This is an example of how the underlying *organization* of a child's behavior with regard to the caregiver can remain consistent over time, even though specific behaviors may change (see the box above).

Compared with infants, toddlers also show less distress in a laboratory setting when caregivers briefly leave them, and they settle down more quickly when their caregivers return (Sroufe, 1995). Apparently, by age 18 months, most children have acquired the expectation that contact with their caregiver will alleviate distress, making it possible for them to be comforted quickly. Moreover, when a caregiver prepares a toddler for separation by increasing interaction beforehand or by explaining the departure, the child is much less distressed (Lollis, 1990). Such efforts to reduce separation distress have little impact on infants, due in part to their cognitive and linguistic limitations.

At the same time toddlers are becoming more comfortable with separations from their caregivers, they are also actively experimenting with mastery over objects. Recall the incident in which 13-month-old Maggie explored the effects of throwing objects down the stairs. We pointed out that Maggie was not just repeating an action, but was actively experimenting with cause and effect. Through active experimentation Maggie learns to integrate her various capabilities in new and purposeful ways. She also learns that it is fun to explore and manipulate objects and that the possibilities for exploration are endless. Maggie's motivation to discover is fed by these experiences. Perhaps most important of all, she learns that *she* can do things, that *she* can be in charge. Charles Wenar (1976) calls this **executive competence.** As toddlers like Maggie begin to understand they can use things for their own ends, they start to develop a sense of personal agency, of knowing they are autonomous forces in the world.

Executive competence does not apply only to objects. Toddlers are quite capable of using adults, especially caregivers, as props for problem solving and mastery (Kopp, in press). They look to them for help as well as for information, as Mikey does with Christine to solve the lever problem in our chapter opening. An analysis of the coping strategies used by toddlers in challenging situations showed that most of them involve turning to the caregiver for support and assistance (Parritz, 1996).

Executive competence: The child's feeling that he or she is an autonomous force in the world, with the ability to influence the outcome of events.

Awareness of Self and Others

Awareness of their own self and increased understanding of the intentions, goals, and feelings of others are dramatic achievements of the toddler period. Together, these two achievements enable changes in social relationships with parents, peers, and others. Knowledge of one's own existence as a separate person emerges clearly in the toddler period. At the same time, in a coordinated manner, a greater awareness of others as independent agents evolves.

Awareness of Self Several lines of research suggest the existence of self-awareness in toddlers. First, self-awareness can be inferred from what we know about cognitive development. If toddlers can form mental representations of objects, they should be able to represent themselves mentally as people and actors.

Self-awareness in toddlers is also revealed by studies of children's reactions to their images in a mirror. Using a procedure introduced by Gordon Gallup in research with chimpanzees, children were shown their faces in a mirror (Amsterdam, 1972). Then, unobtrusively, a dab of rouge was placed on each child's face and the child was shown the mirror again. If the child reached directly to the spot of rouge, not in the reflection but on his or her own face, the child was assumed to know that he or she was the person in the mirror. This reaction was common by about 20 months of age and sometimes appeared by 18 months or a little earlier. Subsequent researchers have confirmed these findings. In one study, three-quarters of children between the ages of 21 and 24 months touched their rouge-marked noses when looking into a mirror, thus showing self-recognition. In contrast, only one-quarter of children ages 15 to 18 months and no children ages 9 to 12 months responded this way (Lewis and Brooks, 1978).

Self-recognition is closely tied to general cognitive development. The age at which a child with Down syndrome starts touching his or her rouge-marked nose when looking in a mirror is directly related to the child's degree of mental retardation. The more severe the retardation, the more delayed the youngster is in showing this sign of self-awareness (Cicchetti and Beeghly, 1990). At the same time, awareness of self promotes cognitive development, including the beginnings of autobiographical memory (Harley and Reese, 1999).

Self-Recognition

This child knows she is the little girl in the mirror.

The final indication of self-awareness in toddlers is the addition of "I" to their vocabularies, coupled with clear examples of self-assertion and will. "No! I do it!" Mikey says emphatically, squirming to get down from Christine's arms and climb the stairs by himself. During the toddler period children have a heightened awareness of their own intentions and often are determined to direct their own activity (Sander, 1975).

Understanding of Others Toddlers show an increased awareness and understanding of others in many ways. They try to get others to pay attention to an object they may be talking about, they show more emotion, including smiling, when a receptive partner is present, and they show some capacity to respond to the desires and intentions of another person (Carpenter et al., 1998; Moses et al., 2001; Sroufe, 1995). For example, when an experimenter pretended to dislike crackers by showing a disgusted expression, but to love broccoli, 18- to 19-month-olds offered broccoli to them, even though they themselves much preferred crackers (Repacholi, 1998).

Shortly after age one, toddlers recognize that others can do things they cannot (Wolf, 1982). By age two they recognize that both parties in a social exchange have separate roles; now, for example, toddlers can play a real game of hide-and-seek. When they were younger, they may have jumped out of hiding before they were found, as if the distinction between hider and seeker were blurred in their minds. At age two, waiting to be found may still be difficult for them, but at least they run in the opposite direction when the seeker comes near. This new recognition underlies the battles of will that tend to arise during toddlerhood. It also underlies the compromises arrived at when parents set limits. In our story, Mikey goes to bed when his mother tells him, but he insists on climbing the stairs by himself. He understands that he and his mother have independent wishes. As a result, their social interactions are more sophisticated.

A more advanced understanding of others affects interactions with peers as well. During the second year, toddlers come to understand the possession rule: the idea that if someone else already has possession of an object, that person has some claim on it. As a result, 24-month-olds try to take an object from a peer less often than do 18-month-olds, and they are more likely to negotiate over the object (Brownell and Brown, 1992). Twenty-four-month-olds are also more likely to relinquish an object when a peer who was playing with it earlier tries to take it away.

Social Referencing The increased understanding that others have feelings and desires allows toddlers to use cues from other people, such as facial expression and tone of voice, to interpret situations and guide their own behavior. This is referred to as **social referencing** (Moses et al., 2001). In a typical study of social referencing, 12-month-olds were enticed across a low table to the edge of a thick sheet of glass raised a foot above the floor (Sorce, Emde, and Klinnert, 1985). As the child peered over the edge of this variation of the visual cliff (see Figure 4.6), the mother was instructed either to smile broadly at the child or to show exaggerated fear. Most of the children whose mothers smiled crossed over the glass, but none of the children whose mothers showed fear were willing to take this risk. The youngsters apparently took their cues about the safety of the glass from their mothers' facial expressions.

Research shows that toddlers look to their caregivers as a social reference largely in ambiguous situations in which the right response is not clear (Moses et al., 2001). In one experiment, Megan Gunnar showed children ages 12 to 13 months a pleasant, an ambiguous, or a frightening toy. She asked each child's mother either to smile, suggesting the situation was positive, or to adopt a neutral face. As expected, a mother's smile encouraged play with the ambiguous toy, but it had no effect on behavior toward the other two playthings. The children consistently avoided the frightening toy regardless of a smile from the mother, and they generally approached the pleasant toy even if the mother looked neutral (Gunnar and Stone, 1984).

Research has shown that toddlers can also use emotional expressions of adults other than their caregivers to guide their behavior (Moses et al., 2001). A toddler's play with

Social referencing:
The use of cues from another person to interpret situations and guide behavior.

Child Development CD
Visual Cliff Studies

an object is influenced by whether an experimenter has previously expressed positive or negative emotion toward it. Experiments by Louis Moses show that this is not simply a generalized fear or joy response by the toddler but is specific to the experimenter's reaction to the object in question. For example, when the experimenter gives the toddler a toy but shows negative emotion toward a second toy, it does not influence the toddler's play with the toy he or she was given. The toddler looks at the experimenter when she expresses emotion to see which toy she is reacting to (see also Repacholi, 1998).

This and other sophisticated reactions to others increase dramatically between ages 1 and 2 years (Emde, 1992). We provided an example in our story of Malcolm. When he and Momma Jo are accosted by the teenagers, Malcolm does not know what to make of the situation at first. He uses cues from Momma Jo's face and voice to interpret the encounter as negative.

The Growth of Sociability

Supported by the rapid advances in their understanding of themselves and others, children become more sociable and competent in their interactions with adults and other children during the toddler period (Rubin, Bukowski, and Parker, 1998). Compared with infants, toddlers have a greatly expanded capacity to observe and interpret other people's actions, to imitate others, and to maintain sequences of social interaction. They are also keenly interested in interacting with others, including other toddlers.

Sharing Experiences One characteristic behavior of toddlers is their constant effort to share objects they discover with others. Toddlers persistently point at things, talk about them, and bring them to others for inspection (Emde, 1992). Such behavior is important both because it illustrates the general sociability of toddlers and because it reveals an increased ability to take another person's perspective. When Malcolm deliberately seeks out Momma Jo to show her some newfound treasure, he must understand that just because *he* sees the object, he cannot assume she sees it too, unless her attention is directed to it.

Related to the constant communication about discoveries is the toddler's frequent sharing of positive emotions with caregivers, called **affective sharing** (Emde, 1992; Saarni, Mumme, and Campos, 1998; Sroufe, 1995). When Mikey turns, smiles exuberantly, and extends the wooden puzzle piece toward his mother, happily exclaiming "Ya-ka!," he

Affective sharing:
The toddler's sharing of positive emotions with the caregiver.

Affective sharing is one way toddlers stay close to their caregivers as they become increasingly independent.

Toddlers like playing near each other, but they rarely coordinate their play or develop themes together.

is doing more than merely calling attention to an object; he is also sharing his pleasure. Toddlers show things to a variety of people, but automatic displays of newfound objects accompanied by happy smiles and vocalizations are directed almost exclusively to attachment figures.

Interaction Between Toddlers Part of moving out into the social world is the toddler's increased interest in interacting with other young children (Rubin et al., 1998). In the period between 15 and 24 months, children develop the ability to behave in a complementary manner with a peer. This allows the emergence of games between toddlers, often rooted in imitation (Brownell, 1990). One toddler does something, the other repeats the action, and the imitation continues back and forth, much to the delight of both children. There is much more complexity and positive emotion in interactions between toddlers than in interactions between infants (Brownell, 1990). Moreover, 2-year-olds clearly distinguish among playmates, and they interact with familiar partners in more complex ways than with unfamiliar partners (Rubin et al., 1998).

Most of the interactions between young toddlers are centered on objects (both children playing with the same set of blocks, for example) (Bronson, 1981). But two young toddlers who are playing with the same object rarely focus on the same theme (one may be using the blocks to build a tower, while the other is building an unrelated road). At three years of age, shared themes among playmates become somewhat more prominent, and social pretend play, in contrast to solitary pretend play, emerges (Howes, Unger, and Seidner, 1989). Social pretend play involves children acting out interrelated roles, such as doctor and patient or teacher and student. These new developments reflect the fact that 3-year-olds are much more capable of coordinated play than 2-year-olds are (Rubin et al., 1998).

The foundations for peer relationships and friendships are laid down in toddler interactions and the caregiver-infant interactions that preceded them. However, toddlers cannot yet be said to form true continuing relationships or genuine friendships with peers. Not until later in the preschool period do children start to differentiate friends from playmates, showing more reciprocity and more positive emotions with friends (Rubin et al., 1998). Along with this change will come the beginning of the concept of *friend* and an understanding that other people, their peers included, have rights as well as intentions.

The Beginnings of Self-Control and Self-Regulation

Complying with a parent's commands and directives calls upon the child's capacity to understand the parent's wishes and goals. It also calls upon the capacity for self-control, because at times the child must inhibit a desire or do something he or she does not want to do. Continuing to comply, even when the parent is not present, requires a further step—**internalization** of control, or incorporating the parent's standards of behavior into the self. Control does not become internalized until after the toddler period, but this process seems to be influenced by how toddlers respond to parents' directives.

Internalization:
Incorporating the parent's standards of behavior into the self.

To study the development of these capacities, Grazyna Kochanska and her colleagues observed more than 100 boys and girls at ages 14, 22, 33, and 45 months of age (Kochanska et al., 2001). They saw them in a variety of situations in which parents gave instructions to their children (for example, picking up toys, not touching a forbidden object). Even at 14 months, toddlers were beginning to show the capacity to respond to direct parental prohibitions, what Kochanska calls "The Don'ts." By 22 months, they were clearly able to respond to prohibitions. Somewhat slower to develop is the capacity to continue doing an unwelcome task, such as cleaning up. But both of these capacities move forward in the toddler period, with girls ahead of boys at the beginning. In fact, many children not only go grudgingly along with parental directives but show what Kochanska calls **committed compliance**—they enthusiastically do what parents wish. This form of compliance when parents are present predicts beginning internalization of control a year later at age 3.

Even researchers studying noncompliance, which increases during the toddler period to a peak at age 30 months, report positive changes during this period (Klimes-Dougan and Kopp, 1999). Toddlers move from simple refusal ("No, I don't want to") to "on-task" noncompliance ("after I play with this truck") and other forms of primitive negotiation. Thus, while young toddlers cannot yet control themselves, their understanding of parental wishes, an expanding array of options when conflict arises, and a desire to please their parents, which balances their strivings for independence, pave the way for self-control in the preschool years (see Chapter 10).

Committed compliance:
Children's enthusiastic compliance with parents' directives.

Emotional Changes

All the developments discussed so far are related to changes in the emotional capacities of toddlers (Saarni et al., 1998). A more mature awareness of other people, for example, is related to a new sensitivity to others' feelings, just as a growing awareness of the self is related to the emergence of new emotions involving self-consciousness, such as shame. The emotional developments of toddlerhood also make possible a new level of relating to other people and play a key role in the child's beginning acceptance of social rules and standards.

Feelings, Social Sensitivity, and the Beginnings of Morality By the middle of the second year, toddlers show a sensitivity to social demands—understanding, for example, that certain activities are forbidden (Kochanska, 1993). They may stop a forbidden behavior, hesitate, start and then stop, or, at times, engage in the behavior while looking at the caregiver. The beginnings of behavioral control, discussed above, are based upon this sensitivity and awareness of standards for behavior.

Such changes are guided by feelings available to toddlers (Saarni et al., 1998). For example, toddlers show an awareness of things that are not as they should be (Emde et al., 1991; Stipek, Recchia, and McClintic, 1992). This awareness is revealed in expressions of uncertainty or distress regarding a flawed object, or distress when an external standard is violated or cannot be met, as when they cannot do something they are told to do. Moreover, they begin to be sensitive to others who are in pain, for the first time approaching those who are distressed (Zahn-Waxler et al., 1992). This is an early sign of empathy.

At this stage, however, these emotional reactions remain quite primitive. They are usually undifferentiated—that is, similar regardless of the particular situation. The same reaction occurs when a parental rule is violated as when a performance standard is not met (as when peas persistently roll off a fork and onto the floor). These reactions reflect a generalized response to adult disapproval, best characterized as general arousal, often with a strong quality of uncertainty, and sometimes combining interest, upset, and amusement (Kochanska, 1993).

By the end of the second year toddlers react with specific negative feelings to their own transgressions, showing distress or **deviation anxiety** when they are doing, or are about to do, something forbidden (Kochanska, 1993). For example, if an experimenter prepares a doll so that the head falls off when the child plays with it, toddlers show a variety of negative emotions, along with verbalized concern and attempts at reparation (Cole, Barrett, and Zahn-Wexler, 1992). In more naturalistic research situations, they show spontaneous self-corrections when they catch themselves doing something bad, self-corrections that are often mediated by language (Londerville and Main, 1981). They might, for example, say "No, can't" and get back down from a shelf they had been told

Deviation anxiety:
The distress toddlers experience over doing something forbidden.

not to climb on. The standards involved in such situations are always externally imposed by adults, and the toddler's adherence to them almost always requires an adult presence. Still, awareness that there are standards and sensitivity to the reactions of others represent the early beginnings of conscience and morality (Emde et al., 1991; Kochanska, 1997).

Changing Emotions and New Emotions   During the toddler period some previously existing emotions are fundamentally changed. High levels of emotional arousal are now less likely to make a child behave in a disorganized way. As a result, toddlers become able to initiate and sustain raucous games. Mikey, for instance, can laugh uproariously while getting Frank to chase him, yet he is still able to keep running and decide where to flee.

Another factor underlying a fundamental change in existing emotions during the toddler period is the child's increasingly mature ability to differentiate the self and others. Mikey is aware not only that Christine is a specific separate person (as he knew at age 10 months), but also that he too is a separate, independent agent with a will of his own. This awareness gives him new ways of expressing both anger and joy toward his caregivers. Now he may deliberately oppose Christine when he becomes angry, expressing his defiance as a way of asserting his independent will. He may also run up and hug her even when he isn't upset, thereby showing *his* affection as a separate person toward *her* as a separate person. This is the prototype of love.

Important new emotions also arise during the toddler period, emotions that were totally absent in infancy. These include **shame** and what may be termed **positive self-evaluation**, a forerunner of pride. Shame is the sense of the self as exposed, vulnerable, and bad (Erikson, 1963). It is the toddler's new understanding of the self that makes shame possible. But because the sense of self at this age is still quite fragile, a toddler who is punished (even for some very specific misdeed) is vulnerable to feeling that the entire self is dissolving. This is especially true when the punishment is harsh or degrading. By the same token, toddlers are capable of feeling an all-encompassing sense of pleasure with the self, a cockiness that is qualitatively different from anything they displayed as babies. When Momma Jo praises 2-year-old Malcolm for putting on his own socks, his whole self seems to swell with joy. Later in the preschool period, when children begin to experience such emotional reactions in response to meeting standards they themselves have set, we see more genuine pride.

Michael Lewis calls the new emotions that emerge during the toddler period and the preschool years the **self-conscious emotions,** or secondary emotions, to distinguish them from the qualitatively different basic emotions of infancy, such as joy, fear, anger, and surprise (e.g., Lewis 1992; Lewis, Alessandri, and Sullivan, 1992). Unlike the basic emotions, the self-conscious emotions require some objective sense of self (including a sense of the self as an agent or doer of things), as well as some understanding of standards for behavior. Lewis has found, for example, that toddlers who can recognize themselves in a mirror are much more likely to show embarrassment than those who can't yet recognize their mirror image. Emotions such as embarrassment and shame, Lewis argues, clearly indicate an emerging sense of self, and at the same time they are critical for consolidating the self that is emerging. Experiencing connections between one's own actions and the feelings they give rise to is central to a sense of self.

PARENT-TODDLER RELATIONS

mhhe.com/dehart5

Parenting Toddlers

All the developmental changes we have outlined dramatically influence the parent-child relationship. On the one hand, they offer parents new sources of pleasure and new avenues for communication with children. On the other hand, they create new demands and challenges for caregivers. In this section, we look at the parents' role in the parent-toddler relationship. This sets the stage for discussing how the personalities and self-concepts of individual children begin to take shape in the toddler period.

Shame:
An emotion in which the self feels exposed, vulnerable, and bad.

Positive self-evaluation:
An emotion in toddlers that is the forerunner of pride.

Self-conscious emotions:
Emotions that require some objective sense of self and some understanding of standards for behavior.

The Parents' Tasks

At every stage of development, parents must adjust their own behavior to meet the needs posed by their child's current capacities and limitations. The rapid social, cognitive, and linguistic developments of toddlerhood make this adjustment particularly challenging for parents of 1- to 3-year-olds. It is known that between ages 1 and 2½ years there is an increase in the average amount of anger parents experience toward their children (Aber et al., 1999). Such changes are greater if the parents are experiencing high stress in their own lives. At the same time, a positive parent-child relationship at the onset of the period is protective, leading to more positive experiences with toddlers.

During the toddler period, parents face two major tasks:

"Do it myself!"

- to support their child's exploration of the world and
- to set appropriate limits for the child.

Parents carry out the first task by creating an arena in which children have space and support to develop. One way they do this is by participating in their toddlers' efforts to communicate with language and to share joy and excitement when discovering new things (Bloom and Tinker, 2001). Mikey's interactions with Frank and Christine provide good examples of this process. Frank and Christine respond to Mikey's nonsense words as if they conveyed real meaning, and they express delight when Mikey shows them the simplest of objects. At the same time, they allow Mikey to try things on his own and push his capacities to the limit, always being available to help if he exceeds his resources. You can see this in the way Christine handles the stair-climbing incident.

The second parental task, setting limits, is also critical to fostering toddlers' development. Most developmentalists believe that providing toddlers with limits is just as important as providing them with encouragement to master new skills. If toddlers can be confident their parents will impose limits when needed, they can explore their capacities freely, testing how far they will reach. The limits reassure the toddler that parents will not let their impulses go too far. The limits therefore provide a kind of safety zone in which development can take place. Parents may set limits through commands, comments, and questions, making use of the child's growing comprehension of language (Bugental and Goodnow, 1998). A dramatic increase in the number of instructions from both mothers and fathers occurs when the child is between 12 and 18 months old (Fagot and Kavanaugh, 1993). Toddlers have countless verbal experiences that help them learn to behave appropriately. When Karen asks Meryl, "Is that toothpaste *supposed* to be on the mirror?" and pauses to allow her to answer, Meryl learns more than where the toothpaste goes. She also learns that there are constraints on behavior and that there are right and wrong things to do. In addition, as social learning theorists emphasize, toddlers learn a great deal about limits by watching parents praise, reprimand, and correct siblings (Dunn, 1988).

The support and limit-setting provided to toddlers by parents create a structure within which children can develop their abilities in all areas. In the areas of cognitive and language development, the process by which parents support the child in new tasks by offering developmentally appropriate guidance, hints, and advice is often called **scaffolding** (Bruner, 1975). We have already seen early examples of scaffolding in parents' structuring of social interactions with their infants (Chapter 6) and in the frequent questions typical of child-directed speech. Christine's structuring of the lever task for Mikey is another good example of scaffolding. Parental support of toddlers' exploration and problem solving can also be regarded as a process of **guided self-regulation** (Sroufe, 1995). During the toddler period, children become increasingly able to regulate themselves, with appropriate help and guidance from their caregivers.

Notice that what is important here is the parents' *general* approach toward the child, not specific child-rearing practices. For instance, there is no evidence that the specific

Scaffolding:
The process by which parents support the child in new tasks by offering developmentally appropriate guidance, hints, and advice.

Guided self-regulation:
The ability of toddlers to regulate their own behavior with guidance from caregivers.

A toddler's first steps promote her advancing independence and lead to new challenges for her and her parents.

age at which a child is weaned or toilet trained has a major impact on development (Maccoby, 1992); however, there *is* evidence that general quality of care, in particular the consistency with which parents set limits and provide guidance, does make a difference in how well a child fares (Crockenberg and Litman, 1990; Erikson, Egeland, and Sroufe, 1985; Frankel and Bates, 1990; Parke and Buriel, 1998; Thompson, 1998). In one study, researchers found that a combination of control and supportive guidance produced a maximum of child compliance without compromising the child's assertiveness (Crockenberg and Litman, 1990). Negative control alone (prohibitions and criticism) led to defiance. This result supports the idea that "a young child's receptiveness to parental values is influenced not only by parental reactions to misbehavior but also by the broader emotional tone of their relationship" (Thompson, 1998, p. 81). What parents do to support and foster desirable behavior is at least as important as what they do to discourage undesirable behavior. In addition, the process of socialization from the inside—the toddler's desire to comply with parents' wishes and to accept their values and standards—is facilitated by warm, supportive family relationships (Kochanska, 1997).

Changes in Caregiving During the Toddler Period

Throughout the world the care of children often changes dramatically during the toddler period (Tronick, Morelli, and Ivey, 1992; Whiting and Edwards, 1988). In many cultures, when a child becomes mobile and stops nursing (often when a new baby is born), siblings, sometimes quite young themselves, take on much of the responsibility for the toddler's care and supervision. This practice is followed, for example, by the Efe foragers of central Africa (Tronick et al., 1992). In many cultures, such as that of the Gusii of East Africa, all adult kin, or even all adults in the community, assume a role in socializing children after infancy (Bugental and Goodnow, 1998; Whiting and Edwards, 1988).

Fathers

Even in Western industrialized cultures, marked changes in caregiving occur during toddlerhood. One change that has been studied extensively is the father's increasing involvement with the child. Fathers are much less involved with infants than mothers are, but this often changes somewhat during the toddler period, especially for boys (Amato, 1998; Lamb, 1997; Parke and Buriel, 1998). Fathers' behavior with toddlers is often quite different from that of mothers. Fathers are less often involved in care and nurturance and more often involved in challenging toddlers and in play (Lamb, 1997). In a recent study in Germany (Grossmann et al., 2002), such challenging by fathers in a playful context was related to the child's later ability to cope well with negative feelings. In general, research has shown that involvement with fathers in the early years predicts positive child outcomes above and beyond predictions based on mother-child relationships (Amato, 1998; Pierce, 1999). Fathers' influence has been most notable in the areas of self-esteem, empathy, education, and behavior problems.

The playful style of fathers, which we illustrated with our description of Frank's interaction with Mikey, is well suited to the child's general orientation at this age. Since a major task for toddlers is to evolve new ways of relating to parents that are more in keeping with growing independence, the father's input may be very helpful now. At the same time, the father's increased involvement with and emotional support of the toddler may ease the beginnings of psychological separation from the mother. Thus, having two caregivers with somewhat different styles of interaction, though not necessary for normal development, can have advantages for a young child.

INDIVIDUAL ADAPTATIONS: THE ROOTS OF PERSONALITY

As toddlers acquire more self-awareness and begin to experience a broader range of emotions, their individual developmental paths diverge even more than was the case in infancy. Some develop very positive attitudes and expectations about the self, while others do not have such feelings. Some show proficiency at handling their emotions, while others tend to be overwhelmed by them. Such individual differences affect how others respond to each child and how children themselves respond to others, as well as to opportunities and challenges. These individual styles of responding, or **patterns of adaptation,** form the roots of personality.

Patterns of adaptation:
Individual styles of responding to others and to the environment that form the roots of personality.

Becoming a Separate Person

An important starting point for the development of individual adaptations in toddlerhood is what Margaret Mahler called the **separation-individuation process** (Mahler, Pine, and Bergman, 1975). This term refers to the child's psychological separation from the caregiver, coupled with a growing awareness of being an individual. As children move away from the caregiver and experience doing things on their own, they increasingly realize they are independent and their actions are separate from the caregiver's. The way the connection with the caregiver supports this progress toward greater autonomy and a sense of self has been beautifully described by the philosopher Søren Kierkegaard:

Separation-individuation process:
Mahler's term for the child's psychological separation from the caregiver and growing awareness of being an individual.

> *The loving mother teaches her child to walk alone. She is far enough from him so that she cannot actually support him but she holds out her arms to him. She imitates his movements, and if he totters, she swiftly bends as if to seize him, so that the child might believe that he is not walking alone.... Her face beckons like a reward, an encouragement. Thus, the child walks alone with his eyes fixed on his mother's face, not on the difficulties in his way. He supports himself by the arms that do not hold him and constantly strives toward the refuge in his mother's embrace, little suspecting that at the very same moment he is emphasizing his need of her, he is proving that he can do without her, because he is walking alone. (1938, p. 85)*

The separation-individuation process does not proceed with equal smoothness for every child. In Erikson's theory a major factor affecting how smoothly it unfolds is the way parents impose limits on the child. According to Erikson (1963), when a toddler's sense of self begins to emerge and the child confronts parental limits, there is the potential either to develop a positive sense of independence and competence, based on feeling supported, or to feel shamed by parents and experience profound self-doubt. Thus, the defining issue for this stage in Erikson's theory is *autonomy versus shame and doubt.*

Another factor affecting how smoothly separation-individuation proceeds is the degree of basic trust the child has developed. When basic trust is strong, the toddler can seek autonomy and still feel secure. Louis Sander (1975) has described this way of reconciling toddlers' striving toward independence with their continuing need for closeness to and security from parents. He points out that toddlers' strivings toward autonomy are balanced by bids for a continuing emotional partnership with caregivers. If toddlers know they can reclaim the former closeness with the caregiver—if they have confidence that the attachment relationship is secure and that care remains available—they will feel free to explore their capacities to the fullest (Schore, 1994). Such confidence is a product of each child's history of interactions with the caregiver. The parent's reliability during infancy breeds a basic trust, which later enables the toddler to make initiatives toward independence.

You have seen this developmental process going well for both Mikey and Malcolm, and you can see evidence that it went well for Maggie as well. These toddlers have been able to become more autonomous while still maintaining psychological contact with their caregivers, as illustrated by Malcolm's behavior in the park with Momma Jo. Even when they do things against their parents' wishes and temporarily annoy them, they remain confident that closeness with the parents can be reclaimed. Their bids for independence do not threaten their strong emotional ties to their parents. Because their early attachment relationships were secure, they are certain of their parents' continued availability, readily reassured by them in times of stress, and accepting of the limits they have set. Like other toddlers who have had these positive experiences, Mikey and Malcolm are confident, eager, resourceful, and secure. Maggie's easy adjustment to Mikey's arrival when she was 2 and her willingness to join her parents in caring for him demonstrate her growing autonomy and her confidence in her closeness to her parents.

Toddler Autonomy

A more negative outcome is illustrated in our story of Meryl and can be seen in other toddlers who have experienced less secure relationships with their caregivers. When children are unduly anxious about the caregiver's availability, when autonomy is forced on them too early, or when their bids for independence are viewed negatively, self-reliance is compromised (Sroufe, 1995). This compromising of self-reliance can take many forms, including timidity and continued preoccupation with the caregiver, unremitting power struggles, persistent angry interactions, lack of emotional interest in mastery, and general emotional detachment. We have described some of these reactions in Meryl.

The Influence of Parent-Child Relationships

The Attachment History A number of longitudinal studies support the view of toddler social and emotional development we have just described (Fox and Calkins, 1993; Kochanska, 1997; Londerville and Main, 1981). These studies show a clear association between the quality of the infant-caregiver relationship and independent measures of how well the child later functions as a toddler.

In one study (Matas et al., 1978), children whose attachment to their mothers had been assessed at ages 12 and 18 months were seen again at age 2 years. The researchers presented the children with a series of four problems that required the use of simple tools. The first two problems were relatively easy; one involved using a long stick to push a lure from inside a tube, for example. The final two problems were more difficult. The last was the one we described Mikey solving at the beginning of this chapter: holding down the end of a board with a large wooden block to get candy out of a deep box. This problem is beyond the capacity of almost all 2-year-olds, but in this study each child's mother was present as a potential resource. The researchers looked at the quality of each toddler's problem solving, including emotional responses, enthusiasm, and ability to face challenges without quickly becoming frustrated. They also looked at the child's persistence and flexibility toward the task, and at his or her ability to call upon and accept the mother's help when needed. At the same time, the researchers examined the timing and clarity of the mother's clues and the degree of emotional support she provided.

Toddlers with a history of secure attachment show enthusiasm and persistence in solving problems, such as this lever task.

The findings were striking. As a group, 2-year-olds who had been securely attached as infants (and therefore confident of their caregiver's availability) were more enthusiastic in approaching the problems, showed more positive emotions and less frustration, were more persistent and flexible, and cooperated more with their mother to reach a solution. These differences were not related to earlier measures of temperament.

In contrast, many of the children who had experienced an insecure attachment during infancy showed a variety of maladaptive responses. Some were intermittently clingy and dependent or whiny and prone to tantrums, quickly becoming frustrated or embroiled in conflict with their mother while the problem to be solved faded into the background. This reaction was most common in children like Meryl with a history of anxious-resistant attachment. Other anxiously attached toddlers showed no enthusiasm or pleasure and little involvement in the problems. They either ignored or refused to act on their mother's suggestions. (For instance, when a mother said "Get the block," the child did get it but put it on the floor instead of on the board.) Such reactions were most common in children with a history of anxious-avoidant attachment.

Ongoing Parental Support It would not be appropriate to say the quality of the infant-caregiver attachment *caused* the differences observed among the toddlers in this study. More is involved in explaining toddlers' adaptations than the attachment aspect of the child's developmental history. Parental support and stimulation *during* the toddler period itself also promote positive functioning (Frankel and Bates, 1990; Kochanska, 1997; Silverman and Ragusa, 1990; Wachs et al., 1993). When caregivers are emotionally available and provide consistent and clear guidance, their toddlers tend to be more eager, persistent, and resourceful.

Consistency in parental behavior across a child's early years (Pianta, Egeland, and Erickson, 1989) makes it difficult to separate the impact of early parenting from that of later parenting (Lewis, 1997). Caregivers whose children were securely attached as infants were more likely to be supportive of their toddlers in the problem-solving situation just described (Sroufe, 1995). They tended to adjust their behavior depending on the particular demands of the situation and the child's needs. These caregivers allowed their toddlers to proceed on their own until they approached the limits of their resources. Then they calmly increased the number of clues they offered and eventually gave direct assistance if the child signaled a need for it. In this way the parents anticipated frustration and took steps to prevent it. Research has shown that such anticipatory behavior is more effective with toddlers than waiting for full-blown problems to arise (Spiker, Ferguson, and Brooks-Gunn, 1993).

In sharp contrast to this pattern, caregivers of children with a history of anxious-avoidant attachment failed to increase the amount of help they offered as their toddlers struggled to solve the problems in the study. Many remained rather uninvolved throughout the child's efforts, despite the increasing difficulty of the problems. The caregivers of children with a history of anxious-resistant attachment did increase the amount of help they gave, but that help became less and less appropriate and clear. Both caregiver and child became more frustrated and ineffective as the pressure of the situation mounted.

This failure to provide clear guidelines was very different from the actions of caregivers whose toddlers had been securely attached as infants. Such caregivers generally tend to be very clear in the help they give their children. In a parallel way, they are very clear in establishing limits, and they are firm in maintaining those limits once they are set. These differences in caregiver behavior during the toddler period are predictive of the child's later functioning (Erickson et al., 1985; Spiker et al., 1993; Sroufe, 1995).

The Active Role of the Child

By the toddler period, even more clearly than in infancy, the child's own characteristics play an important role in development. Some researchers emphasize the concept of temperament, arguing that inborn differences are critical (e.g., Kagan, 1998; Rothbart et al.,

2001). Various dimensions of behavior (intensity of response, fearfulness, etc.) do become more stable and consistent across this period (Rothbart and Bates, 1998), and the descriptions of various observers agree more about behavior in toddlerhood than in infancy (Vaughn et al., 1992). Such stability in behavior is in accord with the temperament concept. It also follows from the idea that by this age children have incorporated past regularities in experience into their understanding of the world, which then guides both expectations and behavior.

Temperament

Whether such emergent child characteristics are inborn, the product of experience, or, most likely, some combination of these, is not most critical. The important fact remains that as the child's behavior is more stable it has a greater influence on parents and a greater impact on the child's encounters with the world. Toddlers who are extremely inhibited, however they came to be that way, may have difficulty coping with new challenges (Nachmias et al., 1996). Toddlers perceived as difficult may receive more control and harsh discipline from their parents (Rothbart and Bates, 1998). In general, children with different characteristics may be more or less responsive to different kinds of parenting. For example, fearful toddlers are more compliant if their parents use gentle discipline (Kochanska, 1997). In contrast, oppositional toddlers may not be responsive to such gentle treatment. They are less likely to develop later aggression problems if parents are restrictive, rather than lax (Bates et al., 1998).

Considering attachment history, current parenting, and emerging child characteristics together gives a more complete picture than considering any one of these developmental influences alone. For example, inhibited toddlers have difficulty coping with challenges, but this is true only for those who also have a history of insecure attachment (Nachmias et al., 1996). Inhibited toddlers with secure attachment histories do not have coping problems, perhaps because their shyness reflects a cautious style rather than profound self-doubts.

Situational compliance:
Children's unwilling compliance with parents' directives due to fear or parents' control of the situation.

Another example comes from the work of Grazyna Kochanska. She contrasts **situational compliance** with committed compliance, discussed on page 277. In situational compliance, children comply only because they seem to feel little choice in the matter and don't really want to do whatever is being asked of them. In committed compliance, children eagerly carry out parental directives, and it is clear that they actually want to comply. Child fearfulness is related to the more superficial situational compliance, especially in prohibition ("Don't do that") situations. Committed compliance, in contrast, is more closely related to a history of secure attachment (Kochanska, 1997; Kochanska et al., 2001).

Toddlers with different temperament characteristics respond differently to the same situation. This toddler may react more warily to an unfamiliar person than other children the same age would.

In these and other ways attachment history, current parenting, and emerging child characteristics work in combination to guide development. Child characteristics can make the tasks of parents easier or more difficult. At times this leads to cycles involving parent and child. In one such cycle, toddlers who need more support and consistent handling (perhaps because of their attachment histories) are often those who are harder to care for and whose parents have more difficulty being consistent. As a result, the parents' responses tend to perpetuate the difficult aspects of these children. In another type of negative cycle, toddlers are rather detached from their parents, and at the same time the parents are emotionally distant, making cooperative partnerships increasingly unlikely.

We have illustrated the first of these negative cycles in our description of the relationship between Karen and Meryl. Meryl frequently resists her mother's wishes, throwing tantrums when Karen tries to insist, perhaps in part because of Karen's inconsistency. As a result, Karen often backs down and lets Meryl have her way, just to keep the peace. Here Meryl's behavior is clearly affecting her mother's behavior, and the reverse is also true. By vacillating and failing to set firm limits, Karen is inadvertently promoting Meryl's difficult behavior. And by being difficult, Meryl makes it hard for Karen to be consistent.

You can see an example of a more positive cycle in Mikey's development. By age 2, Mikey's tendency to be slow to warm up to new situations has diminished, due in part to Christine's continuing support and assistance in managing his reactions to novelty. In turn, his increasing capacity for coping with unfamiliar situations makes him easier to care for and increases his positive interactions with Christine, with Frank, and with others in his life. Although he at first responds somewhat warily to day care, he adjusts relatively quickly, thanks to this support.

Individual Adaptations and the Broader Developmental Context

The transactional model helps to show that parents are not solely responsible for the relationship that evolves with a child. Once a parent has started to respond to an infant in a certain way, the child's reactions often work to maintain the parent's style of caregiving and vice versa. In addition, parent and child do not exist in a vacuum. They are surrounded by a larger social environment that includes other adults and children in the family, as well as people and institutions with which the family comes in contact, as portrayed in our discussion of Bronfenbrenner's model in Chapter 2. This larger social environment can impose pressures and challenges or offer various kinds of support. Developmentalists increasingly stress the need to view child-caregiver interactions as partly a product of this broader social context (e.g., Bates et al., 1998; Bugental and Goodnow, 1998).

Developmentalists are especially interested in how the quality of care children receive is influenced by the quality of relationships between adults in the family, the amount of stress the family experiences, and the various forms of social support available to parents (Belsky, 1988; Parke and Buriel, 1998; Rutter, 2000). These factors interact, often aggravating or lessening one another's effects. For instance, the loss of a job or a serious illness may produce enough stress to tax a parent's capacity to emotionally support a child. However, if the parent has supportive relationships with other adults, that stress may be easier to cope with and its negative effects greatly reduced. Particularly important is the quality of parental relationships. For example, research shows that when a father is supportive of a mother, she is more affectionate and responsive toward their child (Belsky and Isabella, 1987; Easterbrooks and Emde, 1988). Without such psychological backing by the marital partner or someone else, a caregiver tends to take less pleasure in parenting and is more susceptible to its stresses (Pierce, 1999).

The potential effects of stress on the quality of child care is illustrated in a study by Byron Egeland and his colleagues (Vaughn et al., 1979). These researchers found that the quality of a child's attachment to the mother sometimes changed during the toddler period. A relationship classified as anxious when the child was 12 months of age might be classified as secure six months later, and vice versa. Significantly, a switch from an insecure to a secure attachment was linked to a reduction in disruptive life changes and stress experienced by the caregiver. This finding suggests that when parents have greater stability in their lives, they are better able to provide for the emotional needs of a child. It also suggests that a pattern of anxious attachment may be changed if circumstances change for the better. As is true at every phase of life, patterns of adaptation depend on current situations as well as developmental history and child characteristics.

[handwritten margin note: larger social environment-impose pressures & challenges / offer various kinds of support.]

PARENTAL ABUSE AND NEGLECT OF TODDLERS

Child Development CD
Child Maltreatment

Child Maltreatment

More than 2 million cases of physical battering, sexual abuse, and gross neglect of children are reported in the United States each year (Cicchetti and Lynch, 1995; U.S. Census Bureau, 2002b). Although parents may mistreat a child of any age, children under the age of 3 are particularly at risk of abuse and neglect. This is partly because toddlers can be very challenging, with their frequent efforts to assert their independence, often in ways that inconvenience or frustrate adults, and their tendency during explorations to get into things they shouldn't. An adult can easily misinterpret a toddler's behavior as intentionally contrary or naughty, and some may conclude that increasingly severe punishment is needed to set the child right. Others, overwhelmed by the parenting task, may give up early and neglect their child. Toddlers, for their part, have not yet learned how to avoid mistreatment or to meet their own needs, making them particularly vulnerable to abuse or neglect.

Problems Related to Child Maltreatment

Demonstrating consequences of maltreatment is sometimes difficult because other associated factors, such as poverty and family stress, may also influence children (Sameroff, 2000; Glaser, 2000). Certain correlates of maltreatment are quite well established, including aggression, social withdrawal, and other difficulties with peers (Cicchetti and Lynch, 1995; Egeland, 1997; Shields, Ryan, and Cicchetti, 2001). Problems of low self-esteem, difficulty maintaining a coherent sense of self, and problems describing one's own feelings and actions have been found (Cicchetti and Lynch, 1995). Emotional disturbances, including inability to experience pleasure, uncontrollable anger, and difficulty recognizing the emotional expressions of others, have also been reported (Pollak et al., 2000). In addition, there may be apathy in the face of challenges or difficulty balancing the desire to explore with the need to feel secure. Such problems may persist into later childhood or even into adulthood (Harmer et al., 1999). The most widely reported adult outcomes from child maltreatment are aggression, depression, and parenting problems (Egeland, Jacobvitz, and Sroufe, 1988; Mullen et al., 1996; National Research Council, 1993).

The psychological trauma from parental abuse has been linked to later abnormalities in brain development, especially in the right hemisphere (Schore, 2001a; Siegel, 2001). It also has been linked to Post-Traumatic Stress Disorder (see Chapter 15) and to dissociative problems (lapses in memory, behaving without awareness). This is especially true if the child also experienced disorganized attachment in infancy, which may have compromised the emergence of the self (Ogawa et al., 1997).

One reason the correlates of maltreatment are so varied is that it takes many forms, and each form has its own set of consequences (Egeland, 1997; Glaser, 2000). **Physical neglect** (failure to meet the child's basic needs for food, warmth, cleanliness, and medical attention) tends to produce devastating health consequences, a lack of competence in dealing with the world of objects, and major achievement problems in school (Egeland, 1997; National Research Council, 1993).

Physical abuse (deliberately causing the child physical injury) often promotes behavioral and emotional problems, including avoidant or disorganized attachment relationships (Egeland, 1997; Cicchetti and Lynch, 1995), lack of social sensitivity, aggressiveness with peers (Dodge et al., 1997; National Research Council, 1993; Egeland, 1997), and blunted emotions (Cicchetti and Lynch, 1995). A study by Ken Dodge and his colleagues (1997) is especially important because it shows that physical abuse predicts later aggressiveness, even after differences in children's temperaments and family characteristics such as income and marital stability are taken into account. These researchers have concluded that abuse leads to aggression by influencing both children's perceptions of other people, whom they tend to see as potentially hostile and threatening, and their social competency, which leads to failure in strategies for problem solving.

Emotional unavailability, which is often a result of depression in the parent, can be a particularly devastating form of maltreatment (Egeland, 1997; Glaser, 2000; National

Physical neglect:
Failure to meet a child's basic needs for food, warmth, cleanliness, and medical attention.

Physical abuse:
Deliberately causing a child physical injury.

Emotional unavailability:
A chronic lack of parental involvement and emotional responsiveness.

APPLYING RESEARCH FINDINGS

Do Abused Children Cause Their Own Maltreatment?

Some observers have suggested that negative child behavior is primarily responsible for the frequently reported association between aggression and harsh parental treatment. They point to the fact that maltreated toddlers who are placed in foster homes are often treated harshly by their new caregivers, as if there is something about these children that demands severe discipline. They conclude that it is child aggression that causes abuse, not abuse that causes child aggressiveness (Harris, 1998). We believe this conclusion is incorrect.

Is it possible to determine the direction of causality between maltreatment and child aggressiveness? A correlation at one point in time cannot answer the question. Harsh parenting and child aggression would be seen in the same families either way. In addition, each could support the other. Harsh treatment could lead to further problem behavior, which could lead to further harsh treatment, in what Gerald Patterson calls *coercive cycles* (Patterson and Dishion, 1988).

Only prospective, longitudinal studies, in which assessments of children and parents begin very early in the child's life, can resolve this issue. Such studies show that harsh parental discipline generally *precedes* negative child behavior, rather than the other way around, especially in very young children (Egeland, 1997; Egeland, Sroufe, and Erickson, 1983). Neither premature birth nor infant temperament predicts maltreatment, but parenting practices predict child aggressiveness well before the child is even capable of such behavior. One study found that parental violence predicted later child aggression better than the child's initial levels of aggression (Strassberg et al., 1994). Even spanking was related to aggressive reactions in children, although the rate of aggression was

much higher when the parents engaged in violent physical abuse (see Figure 8.1).

Why, then, are children who are abused at home frequently punished by teachers or abused again in foster care? The concepts of *appropriation* and *internal working models* help provide an explanation. Children appropriate, or take into themselves, aspects of the relationship systems that surround them. When they are part of a coercive system, they develop internal working models—expectations and attitudes about themselves and others—in keeping with such a system. They learn the role of victim, including provocative behaviors. They develop basic expectations about relationships that reflect their experience. These attitudes, expectations, and behaviors are carried forward into new relationships.

Another line of evidence that children can internalize a coercive relationship system comes from the finding that violence by a child's father toward the child's mother increases the likelihood of behavior problems, including aggression, in the child (Yates et al., in press). This is true even after factors such as violence against the child, poverty, and general life stress are taken into account. Clearly, the child cannot be held responsible for the father's abuse of the mother. It is much more likely that the father's abusive behavior influences the child's behavior. Apparently, a coercive relationship system is part of such children's developmental context, a way of life they learn.

Thus, it is true that abused children often are provocative and otherwise difficult. And provocative, difficult children often do elicit harsh responses from others. But this does not mean that they caused their own maltreatment in the first place.

Research Council, 1993). Over time, children who experience a chronic lack of parental involvement and emotional responsiveness show a marked decline in functioning, eventually becoming apathetic, devoid of joy or pleasure, and easily frustrated and upset.

Searching for Causes of Maltreatment

Although maltreatment of children is generally associated with parents who are poor, young, lacking in education, and unprepared for raising a child, it certainly is not confined to people with these characteristics (Cicchetti and Lynch, 1995). The problem crosses all ethnic, social class, and religious lines. Some abusing parents appear to outsiders to be devoted mothers or fathers. Most want to do well by their children but are unable to. The question is, why?

Characteristics of the Child In the past some researchers have proposed that abused children may have certain inherent characteristics that elicit mistreatment from adults (Harris, 1998). Prematurity, physical defects, and infant irritability and fussiness have all been suggested as causes of abuse. However, these suggestions were based on investigations made *after* child abuse was reported. In such studies, people's perceptions and

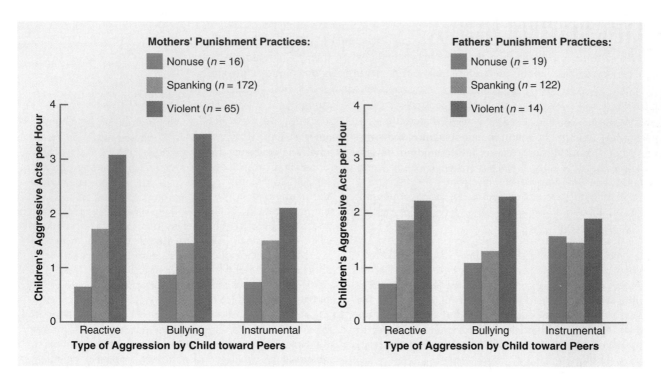

Figure 8.1
RELATIONSHIP BETWEEN PARENTAL PHYSICAL PUNISHMENT PRACTICES AND CHILD AGGRESSION *(Source: Strassberg et al., 1994, pp. 453–454.)*

memories might easily become distorted to help explain the known outcome. Sometimes, too, the consequences of abuse can be confused with its causes.

Much more dependable are the findings of *prospective* longitudinal studies, in which assessments of the children are made *before* abuse occurs. Such studies do not find a correlation between prematurity, early infant irritability, or any other measures of infant temperament and later child abuse (Pianta, Egeland, and Erickson, 1989). Moreover, only a very modest relationship has been found between complications of pregnancy or child-birth and a woman's subsequent mistreatment of her child. This modest relationship may not be one of cause and effect. Abusive mothers generally receive inadequate prenatal care, thus increasing the risk of childbearing complications. And some of the same factors that could prompt a woman to neglect her health during pregnancy could later prompt her to abuse her child (Glaser, 2000).

There is scant evidence that inherent characteristics of children are major causes of child abuse. In some cases, an infant who is ill and difficult to care for may add to the pressures on an already overstressed parent, resulting in mistreatment. But here the cause of the mistreatment is cumulative stress on the parent, not the child's nature. Of course, a maltreated infant may well become a difficult child, which can perpetuate the cycle of stress and maltreatment (Cicchetti and Lynch, 1995). But the child's contribution in this case is a learned set of behaviors, the product of a history of mistreatment. (For further discussion of whether abused children in some way elicit maltreatment, see the box on page 287.)

Characteristics of the Parent If child abuse cannot be explained by children's inherent characteristics, perhaps it can be explained by mental disturbance in the parents. Although this line of inquiry seems reasonable, it turns out not to be very productive. The vast majority of abusing parents suffer no psychotic disorder, and there is *no single personality trait* (such as extreme hostility) that abusive parents share. However, *a broad set of adult characteristics* is associated with child maltreatment, including low self-esteem, poor impulse control, doubts about personal power, negative emotions, and anti-social behavior (Cicchetti and Lynch, 1995; National Research Council, 1993).

Perhaps more important than the personality makeup of abusing parents are their thoughts and feelings about their child and child rearing. In one large-scale study, researchers interviewed and tested new mothers, most of them single, before they gave birth to their first baby and again during the child's infancy (Pianta et al., 1989). They found that those who later became abusers differed from nonabusers in two ways. First, they were less able to cope with the ambivalence and stress inherent in a first pregnancy. Second, they had significantly less understanding of what is involved in caring for a baby. When the inevitable difficulties of raising an infant arose, these mothers became more stressed and doubtful about their parenting abilities. Often they suspected the baby was being deliberately contrary. Thus, the stage was set for these unprepared mothers to start a pattern of child abuse. Similar factors probably also help to trigger abuse by fathers (National Research Council, 1993).

Further encouraging a downward spiral into child abuse is a parent's own experience of being maltreated (Harmer et al., 1999). Mothers and fathers who were abused themselves as children are, as a group, dramatically more likely to abuse their own children than are parents who were not abused. Apparently, the experience of abuse provides models of hostile and neglectful ways of dealing with stress. In their study of new mothers, Byron Egeland and his colleagues found that 30 percent of those with childhood histories of abuse maltreated their own child sometime during the child's early years. This percentage of abusers was far higher than the percentage in a nonabused comparison group from the same general population (Egeland et al., 1988).

However, not all parents who were maltreated themselves abuse their own children. In the same study, 30 percent of the mothers with histories of childhood abuse were observed to provide fully adequate care. Three key factors were found in the women who overcame their history of abuse: (1) many of them had compensated for their abusive parent by forming a stable, supportive relationship with some other adult during childhood; (2) many of them had undergone extensive psychotherapy; and (3) all of them were currently involved in a stable partnership. Apparently, a troubled past need not impair current parenting ability if a person has a chance to experience positive relationships and adequate social support.

The Environmental Context   Because parents are the caretakers of children and the more mature members of a family, they must bear the primary responsibility when child abuse occurs. Nonetheless, given the data on how a history of maltreatment and current high levels of stress can contribute to the abuse of children, it is shortsighted simply to blame the parents for abuse. As shown in Table 8.1, child abuse takes place within a larger context (Belsky, 1988; Cicchetti and Lynch, 1995). While it is found at every socioeconomic level, its likelihood increases with poverty, social isolation, and lack of education. (Glaser, 2000). In the large-scale study we mentioned earlier, less than half of the mothers who mistreated their children had adequate social support, as opposed to virtually all the mothers who provided adequate care (Pianta et al., 1989). Within low-income families, the greater the stress experienced (frequent household moves, job loss, serious illness, etc.), the greater the chances parents will mistreat their children.

Another part of the child abuse context in the United States is the level of violence our culture tolerates. Many of the heroes in our books and movies use violence of one form or another to right wrongs and to teach people lessons. This cultural acceptance of violence as a solution to problems is a likely contributor to child abuse (National Research Council, 1993). In the traditional culture of Japan and many Native American societies that placed great stress on harmony and personal restraint, the physical abuse of children was virtually unknown. In many traditional societies, moreover, nuclear families were not isolated, as they often are in the United States today; rather, they were part of an extended kin network. Research shows that the high degree of social support a close-knit network of kin provides can help prevent child abuse (Cicchetti and Lynch, 1995).

Table 8.1 The Context of Child Abuse and Neglect

Factors That Increase the Risk of Abuse	Factors That Decrease the Risk of Abuse
Long-term vulnerability factors 1. Poverty and ongoing stress 2. Parental history of abuse 3. Unfulfilled relationship needs 4. Lack of understanding of the child as a complex individual	*Long-term protective factors* 1. Nurturant care by someone in childhood 2. Good relationship with spouse 3. Awareness of one's own inner needs
Current challenges 1. Relationship instability 2. Violence, alcoholism, or drug abuse in the home 3. Lack of social support 4. Job loss or other acute stressors	*Short-term buffers* 1. Reduction in stress 2. Separation from abusive partner 3. Child entry into school 4. Crisis counseling

Source: Adapted from Belsky, 1988; Cicchetti and Olsen, 1990.

THE IMPORTANCE OF THE EARLY YEARS FOR SOCIAL, EMOTIONAL, AND NEUROLOGICAL DEVELOPMENT

Like all developmental periods, toddlerhood has its own special significance in the development of children. During this period, a primitive sense of self emerges, and the foundations of self-esteem, patterns of emotional expression and emotional regulation, and perhaps even the roots of morality are laid down.

Current views of socialization suggest that toddlers are particularly open (or vulnerable) to family and cultural influences. By participating in relationships with the people around them, toddlers begin to take in, or appropriate, the major patterns of thought, feeling, and behavior that exist in their world (Bugental and Goodnow, 1998). If the caregiving environment is supportive, toddlers come to view relationships as supportive, evolve a sense of self-worth, and are prepared to become empathic, responsive members of the community. If, however, toddlers experience abusive, neglectful, or rejecting caregiving, the seeds of low self-esteem are sown, and social relationships may come to be viewed as worthless or exploitative.

Experiences during toddlerhood are important not only at the social and emotional level, but also at the neurological level. As we discussed in Chapter 4, researchers now see the first years of life as a sensitive period in the development of the brain. Not only does brain development make possible new experiences, but experiences influence the development of the brain as well. Just as in the cognitive domain, brain development during infancy and toddlerhood has many implications for social and emotional development—and at the same time social and emotional experiences during the first years of life have implications for brain development.

As you learned in Chapter 4, brain development follows an orderly course. At birth the neurons of the brain are largely formed and in place. Certain neurological structures are "online," but many others are not, and various systems in the brain are not yet integrated (Schore, 2001b; Siegel, 2001). For example, the amygdala is at least partly functional very early, which allows for the primitive feeling states of the early months of life described in Chapter 6. But the connections between emotion centers and the cerebral cortex, which would allow integration of memories, expectations, and feelings, are not

Toddler Brain Development

yet in place early in infancy. You may recall that the hippocampus, a brain structure involved in memory consolidation, does not mature until late in the first year. As a result, young infants are not capable of linking a present experience to a past threat to produce a feeling of fear. In addition, the lack of coordination between the cerebral cortex and emotion centers of the brain keeps young infants from regulating their own emotions efficiently. The emotional and social-experiential functions of the brain tend to develop before its linguistic, autobiographical memory functions, and excitatory functions tend to develop before inhibitory functions. Not until late in the toddler period does the brain development occur that makes possible response flexibility, the balancing of excitation and inhibition, and the integration of emotion and memory (Schore, 2001b; Siegel, 2001).

Because these major brain developments are experience-dependent, they are critically influenced by what happens to the child. Brain structures that are available at birth may be largely hardwired and pretty much the same from child to child. However, the development that occurs after birth, especially connections between the cortex and other parts of the brain, is heavily dependent on the context in which the brain is developing.

experience-dependent

Although the focus in discussions of early brain development is often on cognitive stimulation, early experience, especially in the context of attachment relationships, also has implications for social and emotional development (e.g., Schore, 2001b). When caregivers respond to young children in a sensitive manner, when they are attuned to children's moods and feelings, when they coordinate their own behavior and emotions with those of their children, they may be promoting the development of well-integrated brains as well as becoming secure bases for their children. Responsive caregivers keep arousal within tolerable limits, they see to it that excitation is balanced by restraint, and they give their children repeated experiences of emotional stimulation followed by calming, gradually stretching the children's tolerance for emotional arousal. In so doing, they appear to actually tune emotional centers of the brain (Sroufe, 2000). Likewise, when parents help toddlers control their behavior, they may be helping to ensure a functional balance between excitatory and inhibitory systems.

On the other hand, constantly overstimulating a child, failing to provide assistance when the child's capacities are overloaded, abusing the child, or exposing the child to repeated trauma may compromise important features of brain development. For example, when infants experience ongoing trauma (abuse or frequent, intense attachment disruptions), the internal hormonal and neurotransmitter climate of their brains is disrupted. If this occurs at the end of the first year or the beginning of the second, when key brain structures are in a sensitive period of development, the sense of agency, coherence, and continuity of the self may be compromised (Schore, 2001a; Siegel, 2001). The child may be vulnerable to fundamental problems in emotionally connecting with others and to difficulties integrating various aspects of experience.

Certainly, the brain goes on developing after toddlerhood and retains some plasticity, or capacity to change, throughout life. Development is not fixed in the first 2½ years of life, even though early experiences remain very important influences later on. Early experience is not destiny. As you will learn in later chapters, there are many opportunities for positive change in the child as family circumstances improve and as children are influenced by a broader social world. However, development is always influenced by context, and what happens in the early years is part of the context for later development.

Chapter Summary

Introduction

Dramatic social and emotional developments occur during the toddler period. Toddlers in Western cultures face two important tasks:

- to move from dependence on parents toward greater self-reliance; and
- to begin complying with social rules and expectations.

Two Views of Socialization

Socialization has traditionally been viewed as the imposition of rules and standards on an unwilling child (*socialization from the outside*), but developmentalists have increasingly viewed socialization as a process that stems from children's internal desire to comply with their parents' requests and expectations (*socialization from the inside*).

Major Developments in the Toddler Period

Important social and emotional developments in toddlerhood include:

*   increased self-reliance and independence from parents;
*   increased awareness of the self and other people;
*   increased sociability and more mature forms of social interaction;
*   the beginnings of self-control; and
*   a broader range of emotional responses.

Compared with infants, who need physical contact with caregivers to support their exploration of the environment, toddlers rely more on psychological contact. The active experimentation made possible by this change fosters the development of **executive competence.**

During toddlerhood children become aware that their own behaviors are distinct from those of others—that is, they develop self-awareness. At the same time, they gradually come to realize that other people are independent agents, and they begin to use **social referencing** to interpret situations and guide their own behavior.

Toddlers' increased sociability is reflected in:

*   their use of **affective sharing** in interactions with caregivers, and
*   their increased interest and skill in interacting with other children.

Toddlers cannot yet control themselves, but they are beginning to respond to parents' directives. Their response to parental directives paves the way for the development of self-control. The extent to which they show **committed compliance** predicts how well they will later begin to internalize control.

Changes in emotional responses during toddlerhood include:

*   the emergence of **deviation anxiety,** which reflects sensitivity to the rules and expectations of adults; and
*   the appearance of **self-conscious emotions,** such as **positive self-evaluation,** embarrassment, and **shame.**

Parent-Toddler Relations

The developmental changes of toddlerhood create new demands and challenges for caregivers. During the toddler period, parents face two major tasks:

*   to support their child's exploration of the world, and
*   to set appropriate limits for the child.

Individual Adaptations: The Roots of Personality

An individual's **pattern of adaptation,** or style of responding to others and the environment, forms the roots of personality. The process of **separation-individuation** is an important starting point for the development of individual adaptations. The smoothness of this process is affected by the way parents impose limits on toddlers and the degree of basic trust toddlers have already developed.

Attachment history influences how well a child will function as a toddler. Securely attached infants show more positive and adaptive reactions to problem-solving situations than insecurely attached infants do. The *ongoing* quality of support and stimulation provided by parents also influences children's individual adaptations during the toddler period.

During toddlerhood, child characteristics become more stable and more consistent across situations. Considering child characteristics and attachment status together gives a more complete understanding of toddlers than considering either one alone.

The broader social context influences the quality of parent-child relationships. Important factors in this context during the toddler period include:

*   quality of relationships between adults in the family;
*   stress experienced by the family; and
*   social support available to parents.

Parental Abuse and Neglect of Toddlers

Children of all ages are abused, but toddlers are especially vulnerable to abuse, in part because they are challenging to care for.

Consequences of child maltreatment are far-reaching. The specific pattern of problems associated with maltreatment varies, depending on the form of maltreatment.

A variety of factors contribute to child maltreatment:

*   There is little evidence that inherent characteristics of the child elicit maltreatment from adults.
*   No *single* adult personality trait explains child abuse, but many abusive parents share a *pattern* of characteristics, including personality traits, thoughts and feelings about child rearing, and a history of abuse in their own childhoods.
*   Factors in the broader social context that contribute to child abuse include poverty, social isolation, lack of education, stress, the level of violence tolerated in the culture, and lack of supportive extended families.

The Importance of the Early Years for Social, Emotional, and Neurological Development

Toddlerhood has special significance in children's development because during this period the foundations of self-esteem, patterns of emotional expression and regulation, and the roots of morality are established. As the process of socialization begins, children are particularly open to family and cultural influences. Experiences during toddlerhood are also important at the neurological level, as important brain structures and systems are rapidly developing.

Review Questions

Introduction

1. What are the major developmental tasks of toddlerhood in Western cultures?

Two Views of Socialization

2. Explain the difference between socialization from the outside and socialization from the inside.

Major Developments in the Toddler Period

3. List the important social and emotional developments of toddlerhood.
4. How does toddlers' behavior change as they move toward increased independence?
5. How does awareness of the self and of other people increase during toddlerhood?
6. Discuss the developments that reflect toddlers' increased sociability and more mature forms of social interaction.
7. Explain how responses to parents' directives during toddlerhood are related to the development of self-control and self-regulation.

8. Describe the emotional changes of toddlerhood and explain how they are related to other aspects of development.

Parent-Toddler Relations

9. What are the major tasks of parents during toddlerhood?

Individual Adaptations: The Roots of Personality

10. How do attachment history and child characteristics influence individual adaptations during toddlerhood?

Parental Abuse and Neglect of Toddlers

11. Summarize the consequences and likely causes of child maltreatment.

The Importance of the Early Years for Social, Emotional, and Neurological Development

12. What special significance does toddlerhood have in children's development?

Application and Observation

1. Interview parents of toddlers and/or day care providers who work with toddlers about their experiences with this age group. How is toddlers' behavior different from that of infants or of older preschoolers? How are toddlers' needs different from those of younger and older children? What do parents or day care providers have to do differently in caring for toddlers, compared to caring for infants or older preschoolers?

2. Observe toddlers and parents interacting in a play group, a park, a store, a restaurant, or any other public setting with lots of families. What toddler behaviors do you see that reflect concepts covered in this chapter? How do the parents respond to these behaviors? What evidence do you see of limit-setting and encouragement of increasing independence?

3. Explore websites or books aimed at parents of toddlers. What issues do parents and advice-givers seem to be the most concerned about? What advice do the books or websites offer for dealing with toddlers?

How well does it match what you have learned about toddler development in the last two chapters?

4. Observe the reactions of 1- to 3-year-olds to seeing their reflections in a mirror. First, place the child in front of a full-length mirror, call his/her attention to the reflection, and ask "Who's that?" Repeat, if necessary, until you're sure the child has looked in the mirror, even if there is no sign of self-recognition. Next, inconspicuously apply lipstick to the child's nose by pretending to wipe his/her face. Then, place the child in front of the mirror and again call his/her attention to the reflection until you're sure s/he has looked in the mirror. Note each child's reactions to the reflection, with and without lipstick on the nose. What evidence of self-recognition and what emotional reactions did the child show? Ask the child's parents if s/he usually shows interest in mirrors. If so, how does s/he react to them? (If the child isn't interested in mirrors now, did s/he show interest in them at an earlier age?)

Part 3 Epilogue: Toddlerhood

Development in the toddler period builds on the achievements of infancy. For example, toward the end of the first year of life, advances in memory enable infants to recall past experiences and anticipate outcomes. When 10-month-old Mikey spotted a jar of seashells his mother and Maggie had collected, he remembered the interesting sound he had recently made by shaking this object. So he grasped and shook the jar again, anticipating the result. But note that seeing the jar was necessary to trigger this recollection in Mikey. At 10 months of age, he was not yet able to imagine the jar if it was not physically present. The ability to imagine—to *represent things mentally*—is an extremely important development of toddlerhood. Like all the major developmental changes of the toddler period, it builds on foundations established in infancy.

The Integrative Nature of Toddler Development

The *emergence of representational skills* is one of the milestones of toddler development. The ability to use words to stand for things that are not actually present is one of the most obvious representational skills that emerge in the toddler period. Another underlies the ability to infer things not actually experienced with the senses. If Maggie has a seashell in her hand and moments later it has disappeared, Mikey as a toddler can infer that Maggie must have put the shell somewhere. This is because he has stored a mental image of the shell and knows that the real shell still exists. The ability to store mental images of things also allows toddlers to imitate other people's actions long after they have seen them performed. In addition, representational skills enable toddlers to engage in symbolic play, letting one object stand for another, as when Mikey uses a block of wood as a toy car.

The emergence of representational skills also has profound consequences for social development. With representational skills comes an *awareness* of the self as an agent and an object. Children now understand that it is "I" who shakes this object, "I" to whom Mommy talks, "I" who wants to find a hidden object. This emerging awareness of self is accompanied by a *growing understanding of others* as independent agents with their own wishes and intentions. Mikey, for instance, now recognizes that his intentions (such as a desire to continue playing) may be different from those of his mother (who may want to put him to bed). Language helps Mikey communicate about this clash of intentions, exert his own autonomy, and find compromises (such as doing what his mother asks but going "by myself").

Representational skills also promote the *beginnings of self-control* in children. Malcolm starts to reach again for the leaf in the water, but he remembers Momma Jo's no-nonsense tone, and he stops himself. This is a common capacity in toddlers. Recent research indicates that brain mechanisms related to self-regulation, such as the ability to balance excitement and inhibition, are in place by the toddler period (Schore, 2001b).

New emotions arise as well during the toddler period. Recognizing the self as a separate, autonomous person, toddlers are now capable of having negative feelings about the self, of experiencing shame and vulnerability. By the same token, they are also capable of positive self-evaluations. When DeeDee hugs Malcolm and praises his actions after the incident with the teenage boys, we can imagine Malcolm's feeling of being valued, the forerunner of genuine pride. Differentiation of the self from others likewise enables toddlers to experience new interpersonal emotions, such as affection. Twelve-month-olds rarely give love pats to parents and dolls, but 18-month-olds often do so (Sroufe, 1995).

Development does not simply flow in one direction, with cognitive advances leading to changes in social and emotional life. The emerging sense of intentionality and self-direction, accompanied by the desire to share experiences, prompts advances in language development and representation too. "Engagement in a world of persons and objects" (Bloom and Tinker, 2001, p. vii) helps to motivate language acquisition. In the toddler period, as in all other periods, development is an integrated process, with each aspect influencing every other. Memory advances pave the way for the emergence of self-awareness. At the same time, the age at which self-awareness appears predicts later differences in autobiographical memory, as does the parent's style of elaborating stories with the child (Harley and Reese, 1999). Cognitive development enables new social achievements; at the same time, social understanding, including sensitivity to the intentions of others, fuels knowledge acquisition (Baldwin, 2000).

Parent-Toddler Relationships

Just as a toddler's growing autonomy fosters new emotions, it also helps bring about *major changes in the parent-child relationship.* Parents in our culture expect toddlers to show increasing self-reliance but also to begin complying with rules and limits. The child's process of taking in or appropriating these rules is an important foundation for moral development.

As increasingly active participants in parent-child relationships, toddlers exert a stronger force than infants in determining the course of those relationships. Although personality is certainly not fully formed in toddlerhood, children this age are less malleable than they were as babies. Toddlers have rather definite expectations about their parents' availability and actions, and these expectations in turn affect children's customary ways of responding.

Change in parent-child relationships is always possible, of course. Parents who were unresponsive or inconsistent toward their children as infants can make concerted efforts to turn the relationship around. These efforts at first may be puzzling to a toddler who doubts the parent's new availability and questions the new firmness. Such a toddler is likely to be whiny and negative, having learned that only such behavior brings the desired response from the caregiver. It takes time and resolve to change negative patterns of adaptation that have become established over months. In the end, however, even difficult toddlers generally respond to reassuring firmness from parents. We may be seeing the beginning of such a change in Meryl, helped along by the model of loving firmness Mrs. Jasper provides. Let's look more closely at Meryl's development in toddlerhood, as well as that of Maggie, Mikey, and Malcolm.

Four Children as Toddlers

All four of our children show normal development in terms of major toddler milestones. All are walking, talking, and becoming more autonomous in thought and behavior. Although Meryl is progressing more slowly than the other three, she is well within the normal range. Each child is also developing an individual style consistent with his or her past. Despite dramatic changes as they grow older, all four are building on foundations laid down in the prior developmental period.

You can see this clearly in Mikey. His early tendency to warm up slowly to new situations has moderated, and as a toddler he is taking his entry into day care in stride. Given his history of secure attachment, his mother's continuing nurturance and availability, and the high-quality day care program in which he is enrolled, this is not surprising. An additional in-

gredient in Mikey's positive adjustment is his father's strong interest in and involvement with him. Frank is proud of Mikey's boyish behavior; he enjoys being with his son and playing their physically active games together. The differences in Frank's and Christine's styles of interacting with Mikey are typical of mother-father differences. We also see in Frank the beginnings of a serious concern about gender-appropriate behavior. This is a common paternal influence in the socialization of boys.

Like Mikey, Maggie coped well with the developmental challenges of toddlerhood. She adjusted positively to Mikey's birth when she was 2, thanks in part to Christine's efforts to explain Mikey's feelings and behavior to her and to involve her in Mikey's care. As a result, Maggie and Mikey have developed a playful, comfortable sibling relationship. Supported by Christine's responsive care, Maggie has carried the easygoing, positive disposition she showed as an infant through toddlerhood and into early childhood. She adjusted even more readily than Mikey to day care, in part because she is older and in part because of her confidence and sociability.

But there is also growing trouble in the Gordon family. The increasing contrast in Frank's behavior toward Maggie and Mikey could have implications for both children's development. Partly because of the stress of Frank's reduced hours at work and partly because of their sharply differing views about women working outside the home, Christine and Frank are experiencing conflict. Maggie has already witnessed one episode of violence directed toward her mother. Frank and Christine also show less unity regarding parenting than many other couples do. What one thinks is good for the children, the other often opposes. Most troublesome of all, they frequently center their arguments on Mikey. How all of this will affect Mikey's and Maggie's future development bears watching.

Like Mikey and Maggie, Malcolm is developing well. As you might have expected of this robust baby, he has become a live wire of a toddler. He is exuberant, energetic, and into everything. The members of his family continue to view his liveliness very positively. Momma Jo delights in telling friends what a "pile of mischief" Malcolm gets into. For her, as for DeeDee and John, Malcolm is a source of great joy and pride. In a family with fewer social and psychological resources, Malcolm's style of responding might not be valued so highly. Notice, too, how the Williams's network of mutual caring and support more than makes up for the stresses they face as a moderate-income, urban, minority-group family. Malcolm reaps the benefits of this rich social network. DeeDee, John, Momma Jo, Denise, Teresa, and John, Jr., are all actively involved with him and contribute to his ongoing feelings of security and acceptance.

Things are not going as well for Meryl, who is in many ways a difficult toddler. She is lagging in achieving self-reliance, she is easily stressed and unusually needy of adult contact, she can be whiny and negative, and she is prone to tantrums. Meryl continues to be timid and hesitant in new situations, as when she refuses to try the new seesaw at Mrs. Jasper's house. In contrast to the moderation in Mikey's temperament, Meryl shows an increasing tendency to be slow to warm up. It was predictable that entering day care would be difficult for Meryl and a challenge to her relationship with Karen.

There are, however, some seeds of positive change for Meryl. Karen seems to be settling into a happier and more stable life. The détente with her own mother has been a big help. Karen can now draw on her mother's emotional support, counsel, and day-to-day assistance in caring for Meryl. Mrs. Jasper is also a model from whom she can learn. Karen clearly cares about Meryl and wants to be a good mother, as evidenced by her attentiveness to Mrs. Jasper's suggestions and the way she keeps trying despite her struggles with Meryl.

There are also signs of change in Meryl herself. We see her actively trying to cope with her anxieties through play. With the stuffed bears she works through her concerns about Karen's availability, thus creating feelings of mastery that may counteract vulnerable feelings. Such active mastery is made possible by the representational skills Meryl has developed. It is also supported by the increased stability in her life and the improved quality of care she is receiving. Perhaps these seeds of positive change will take root in Meryl's preschool years.

Early Childhood

Part 4 Four Children as Preschoolers

Malcolm Williams

"C'mon, Motor Man. You want this horse? Jump for it," John, Jr., told his little brother. Malcolm reached an arm as high as he could and jumped with all his might, but the toy horse remained just out of reach. "Now how you ever gonna make the pros with jumps like that, man?" JJ teased. "Let's see a real jump." This time Malcolm jumped so hard he fell over backward. "Gimme!" he yelled. "Gimme it."

"You give that horse to your brother right now!" said Momma Jo, as she strode into the room. "What are you tryin' to do, makin' him jump and fall all over the place? He's only 4 years old. Treat him like your brother, not your dog!"

"We were just havin' fun," JJ protested. "He didn't hurt himself none."

"I'm 4 an' a *half*," said Malcolm. "An' I'm gonna be the bestest basketball player ever!"

"Hey, Motor Man," said JJ, pretending to dribble a ball in front of Malcolm. Malcolm raised both arms and waved them frantically in a childish imitation of a guard blocking a shot. As Momma Jo looked on with mixed exasperation and amusement, the front door opened and John Williams walked in. "Daddy!" yelled Malcolm, running over to his father. "Hey, my man!" John Williams answered, holding out his hand for Malcolm to give him five. "What's happenin'?"

"We're playin' basketball," said Malcolm. "An' I'm the best!"

"Oh, yeah!" his father smiled. "I bet you are."

At dinner Malcolm was in high spirits. With great excitement he told about a model airplane he had seen flying in the park. "An' the plane goed straight up!" he exclaimed, his hand illustrating a steep upward climb. "An' then it goed round an' round an' round." Malcolm's whole body circled around to help make the point. "But how'd the plane do that, Daddy? Was there a little aminal inside it?"

"No, Malcolm, It's called remote control. The man with the plane had a box and when he pressed a button it sent out signals, and the signals told the plane what to do."

"Yeah," said JJ, "remote control. That's what Momma Jo's gonna get for you, Motor Man, to help slow you down some." The whole family laughed.

"You know," DeeDee said to John later, "we've gotta decide where to send Malcolm to school next year. If we're gonna send him to St. Dominic's with Teresa, Sister Carmen told me we should get the application in by next month."

"They're strict at St. Dom's," John answered, "and that would be good for Malcolm. I've always said that. And the tuition there isn't *that* high. If we can afford it for Teresa, we can find a way to manage for Malcolm, too. So let's just go with St. Dom's and not worry about it any longer. Why don't you pick up an application tomorrow when you drop Teresa off?"

"Hold still, Malcolm, while I take your picture," DeeDee said. "You look so grown up in your new school clothes."

"I gotta go to the bathroom, Momma," Malcolm complained, hopping up and down.

"This'll just take a second, honey. Stop holding yourself, Malcolm. You can go to the bathroom in a minute. There. That's better. Now you can run along. Teresa? Hurry up, sugar, or we're gonna be late!"

An hour later DeeDee stood with twenty-two other mothers in the large, sunny kindergarten room. "The mommas have to go now," she told Malcolm, placing a hand on each of his shoulders. "You be good and *mind* your teacher. Bye-bye, honey. You can tell me all about it tonight." And with that DeeDee turned and walked quickly out the door. Malcolm, in his new navy blue shorts and spotless white shirt, was left alone, wide-eyed with wonder, for his first day at school.

It didn't take Malcolm long to adjust to school. Every morning he was eager to be off. He loved having so many other children to play with. His "best friend in the whole world" was a large, good-humored, red-headed boy with a face full of freckles—Patrick Coleman, nicknamed Pug. As soon as Mrs. Hennessy, their teacher, announced recess, Malcolm and Pug would race to claim the two tricycles kept in the schoolyard. One day in October, they rushed out the door and climbed on the trikes as usual. Pug pedaled furiously down the path, but before Malcolm could get started April Kaid stepped in front of him.

"I wanna ride," she said. "It's my turn. Let me ride."

"I was here first!" Malcolm answered. "Get outa my way! It's my bike!"

"No, it's not!" said April, gripping the handlebar.

"Get outa my way," Malcolm repeated, trying to pry her fingers off the bike. When April refused to let go, Malcolm punched her in the chest. She wailed and ran to the teacher.

"What does she *mean*, 'a little hyperactive'?" John asked indignantly.

"Hyperactive indeed!" Momma Jo added. "That child's just full of pep, that's all. What he needs is a firm hand from a good teacher.

"Now, Momma Jo," DeeDee said, "Mrs. Hennessy *is* a good teacher. She said Malcolm is real smart and the other children like him. He just has to work harder at controlling himself. He's got so much energy, he gets impatient when he doesn't get his way. But he's gotta learn he can't hit kids."

"Well, look who's here," said John as Malcolm burst through the door with JJ. "Just the man we're talkin' about."

"Uh-oh, Motor Man. You're in for it now." JJ cautioned, walking off toward the kitchen, sniffing the aroma of supper in the oven, his basketball tucked under one arm.

"I went to see your teacher today," DeeDee said, "and she told me you hit a little girl."

"Yucky April Kaid!" Malcolm answered. "She wouldn't let go of my bike! I didn't mean to hurt her."

"It wasn't *your* bike, boy," Malcolm's father cut in sharply. "It belongs to the whole class. And even if it *was* your bike, you still shouldn't have hit her. Boys don't hit girls, you hear me? Your momma had to leave work to go see your teacher. I don't want that ever happenin' again!"

"OK, Daddy," said Malcolm, starting to sniffle as tears welled up in his eyes.

"Now you just dry up, boy," John admonished. "I mean dry up right now."

"Malcolm," DeeDee added, "you've gotta learn to share. You can't always get what you want and do what you want. Do you understand me?" Malcolm nodded slowly. "OK," his mother concluded. "Now go wash up for supper."

Maggie and Mikey Gordon

The boys stood back, gazing at their masterpiece. "Wow!" said Mikey in admiration. "That's tall!" The tower of blocks was indeed impressive. It stood as tall as the boys could reach, looking as if it might topple over at any minute.

"I'm gonna put this purple on the very top," Justin Davis announced, picking up a large pyramid-shaped block.

"No!" said Bryan Packer, pushing Justin's hand away. "I'm gonna put this one there!"

"I thought of it first!" Justin answered angrily, pushing Bryan back.

"Hey, I got it! Let's make a space station at the top!" Mikey suggested.

"Yeah! That's neat!" the others agreed, forgetting their tussle. "Go get the rocket ship!"

Once again Mikey had warded off a fight. He was so successful at defusing trouble that his teachers called him "the peacemaker." Mikey was one of the most popular children in his class, a friendly little boy with an infectious giggle.

"Mikey," called Sue, one of the preschool teachers. "Your mom's here. Time to go home."

"Gotta go," said Mikey to his friends, as he ran toward the door. Stopping abruptly, he darted to his cubby to get a drawing. "Look, Mom," he said proudly, running back to Christine. "Look how good I wrote my name on this!"

Christine knelt down to look at Mikey's artwork. "Oh, sweetie, that's great!" she said smiling at him. It seemed incredible he was already 4 and starting to learn his letters. Maggie had been a quick learner and an early reader, and Mikey was progressing nearly as fast. In another year they'd both be in school, and then Frank surely couldn't object if she increased her hours at the shop, Christine told herself. No, he'd find *some* reason to object, she thought wearily. But there was time to worry about that later. Right now she just had time to give Mikey lunch and go grocery shopping before it was time to pick Maggie up from first grade.

Two hours later, waiting in front of Maggie's school with the back of the minivan full of groceries, Christine found herself only half-listening to Mikey's morning adventures. She was thinking about what Maggie's teacher had said the night before at a parent conference. "Maggie's school work is fine," Mrs. Johnson had said. "She's one of the brightest children in the class. But she seems a bit subdued. Do you know if there's anything special bothering her?" Maggie *did* seem subdued lately, Christine reflected. When she got home from school she spent a lot of time hanging around watching Christine sew or work in the kitchen, instead of running out to play with the girls next door, as she'd done when she was in kindergarten. And the way Frank treated Maggie wasn't helping. Lately it seemed he paid attention to her only to tell her to be quiet or to criticize her. Well, it wouldn't do any good to point that out to him, Christine thought. He'd just get defensive. I'd better find a way to spend more time with Maggie and make sure she knows we still love her.

"Late as usual," Frank Gordon grumbled, sliding into his customary place at the head of the dinner table. "Pretty soon you're gonna be starving us till midnight."

"I'm sorry, Frank," Christine answered, trying to placate him. "But it's not *that* late. It's not even six o'clock."

"Yeah, but it's later and later every night. We're hungry, aren't we, kids?"

Maggie and Mikey stared down at the table. No one said a word.

"Well, *I'm* hungry," Frank persisted irritably, rising slightly so he could reach the platter of pork chops.

"Maggie, pass Daddy the biscuits, please, honey, and the butter. He should get them first."

"Yeah, I guess I'll have some of those," Frank remarked unenthusiastically. "But they're not as good as the ones you used to make from scratch. You kids remember when Mommy used to have time to bake good things for us?"

"I like *these* biscuits," piped up Mikey. "They're yummy!" As if to prove it, he placed an extra-large glob of butter in the steamy center of the biscuit he had just broken open.

"Thank you, Mikey," Christine answered. "Why don't you tell Daddy about the tower you built at school today?"

"Yeah!" said Mikey. "It was neat! It was so high it almost hit the ceiling! An' know what? When I was running Justin grabbed my pocket and almost ripped it off! Wanna see?" And he stood up to display the torn pocket flapping on the back of his jeans.

"You're gonna wait a long time for Mommy to fix *that*," Frank commented. "I've been waiting months for her to sew a lousy button on my shirt. But she doesn't have time to sew for us—just for a bunch of strangers!"

Mikey's face fell as he climbed back onto his chair. He began to fiddle with a bone on his plate. Across from him Maggie ate silently, eyes downcast. As Mikey hit the end of the bone with his finger, it flipped up and fell to the floor.

"Whoops," said Mikey, climbing down to look for the bone. Seconds later his face appeared above the tabletop. Clenching the bone between his teeth, he growled like a dog.

"Mikey," Christine laughed. "You silly boy."

Maggie giggled at Mikey's clowning. Even Frank stopped his griping and helped himself to another biscuit. Mikey got back up on his chair. Temporarily, the tension had eased.

"A man's got to feel like he's the provider, Chrissie. It's only natural. Your father was the same way. You made your bed when you decided to take that job. Now you've got to lie in it."

"But, Mom," Christine said, the phone propped between her ear and shoulder as she washed the dishes. "I've got *my* life, too. It shouldn't always be what Frank wants."

"If you ask me, your life is with Frank and the children. This job is only a sideline. Think of what's really important to you and work harder at being a good wife."

"I've gotta go, Mom. Frank's coming. I'll talk to you later."

"So your mom sided with me again," Frank said smugly as he sauntered into the kitchen for a beer.

"Oh, shut up," Christine answered. It seemed the more gingerly she treated Frank, the more belligerent he got. So she had made up her mind to just say what she thought.

"That's a hell of a way to talk to your husband," Frank shot back. "What's eatin' you?"

"Nothing. Just leave me alone, will you? I'm tired."

"You wouldn't be half so tired if you quit that stupid job of yours," Frank continued, spotting his opening.

"Look. Not tonight, OK? I'm not gonna be dragged into another argument with you."

"I'm not arguing," Frank answered. "I'm just tellin' ya what's what."

"Well, I wouldn't be half so tired," Christine snapped, "if you'd take one-tenth the effort you put into griping and put it into helping me around here!"

"Why should I help?" Frank persisted, popping open his beer. "It's your damn job to take care of the house and kids."

"Oh, so you don't live here, too?" Christine shouted. "You don't dirty the clothes or eat the food or mess up the bathroom or anything else, huh?"

At the top of the stairs Maggie and Mikey sat huddled together listening to their parents' voices growing louder and louder. Maggie twisted a strand of hair around and around her finger. Mikey hugged his legs tightly with both arms and rested his chin on one wrist.

"What are you doing, Mikey?" Christine asked as she made dinner the next day. Mikey was playing with trucks on the kitchen floor, as he often did, but this time the trucks were crashing into each other.

"The trucks just ran over a boy," Mikey answered.

Christine was disturbed. "That's an awful story, Mikey," she said. "Where are that little boy's mommy and daddy? They wouldn't let that happen."

"They was drivin' the trucks," Mikey explained, "an' the boy felled out by accident." Then he continued the make-believe drama. "Oh no! He got his leg broken! Here comes the ambilenz." He brought a white truck to a screeching halt, opened and closed its doors, and drove it off again quickly. "They take him to the hospital. They fix it!"

Christine just looked at Mikey, not knowing what to say.

Meryl Polonius

"Mommy, pick me up! I want to see what you doing."

"Not now, Meryl," Karen answered as she peeled carrots. "Why don't you go play with your farm?"

"Nooo!" whined Meryl, tugging the leg of Karen's pants. "I don't waaant to! Pick me up!"

"I'm peeling carrots, Meryl, and I can't keep doing it if I'm holding you. Now go and play."

"No!" said Meryl, hanging on Karen's pants now. "I want to seeee!"

"Now *stop* it, Meryl," Karen snapped, losing her temper. Don't be such a pest."

Meryl's face puckered. She ran to one of the kitchen chairs, put her head down, and began sobbing.

"Oh, Meryl. I'm sorry," Karen relented. "Come here, honey. It's OK. Mommy's sorry."

But Meryl was not to be appeased. "No!" she shouted, clenching her hands into tight fists. Before Karen could answer, the back door swung open and Joe Turner walked in. "Hi," he said, smiling at Karen, and then to Meryl, "What's the matter, honey?"

"Go 'way!" Meryl pouted. Then, turning her back, she started sucking her thumb.

"Don't ask me how my day was," Karen said, returning Joe's affectionate kiss. "This is the high point so far."

Karen and Joe had been living together for nearly a month. Seven months before, right after Meryl turned 3, another waitress had introduced them. A reporter for the local paper, Joe was seven years older than Karen. At first she had not been very interested. As far as looks were concerned, he was no Jeff. Even at 26 his hair was thinning, and Karen suspected he would soon have a fair-sized bald patch. But there was something about Joe that made Karen feel warm and comfortable. With him she didn't have to pretend to be anyone but herself. She grew to love Joe for making her feel so special, and for his genuine affection for Meryl.

"Do you think Meryl will ever get over these awful tantrums?" Karen asked doubtfully after yet another battle of wills over whether Meryl would brush her teeth before bed.

"Sure she will. Do you think ten years from now you'll have a teenager who stamps her feet and pouts?"

"Yes," laughed Karen. "That's *exactly* what I'm afraid I'll have! Seriously, what do you think I could do to stop the whining and tantrums? I must be doing *something* wrong."

"Well, I'm no expert on kids," Joe answered, "but you might try not waffling quite so much. You go back and forth a lot. First you tell her she can't have something, then you give it to her anyway. Next you tell her she can't sit on your lap, then you pick her up when she pouts. She's not gonna die if she doesn't get her way all the time, you know."

"I know," agreed Karen. "But when she gets upset I think I must be doing the wrong thing, so I turn around and do the opposite. I know it doesn't help. Mrs. Jasper told me that, too. She said I just have to mean what I say more."

"I think that's probably right," said Joe.

In the following weeks Karen watched how Joe dealt with Meryl. One day she overheard them in the kitchen. "I want another cookie!" Meryl demanded. "No," Joe said firmly, "not until dinner. Why don't you come help put the silverware away? Get the stool so you can see." In a voice sweet as an angel's Meryl answered, "Here I come!" Why is it so easy for him and so hard for me? Karen wondered.

"I think it's partly because she doesn't know any different with me," Joe said later. "Give it time, and mean what you say, like Mrs. Jasper said. Things will settle down."

And in time they did. After four months of the new living arrangement, Meryl was far more cheerful and cooperative. Karen thought Joe was the main reason. He read Meryl stories and played with her. To Meryl these pastimes were far more interesting than pouting and clinging. As the whining and tantrums declined, Karen became more confident in dealing with Meryl, which helped break the cycle they had been tangled in. The improvements in their relationship made Meryl's fourth birthday a real celebration for them all.

"I have a surprise for you, sweetie," Karen said to Meryl, as she put her to bed that night. "Joe and Mommy are getting married. That means we'll have another party—like a birthday party, but without the balloons and candles. And you'll get a new dress. What do you think of that?"

"Oh, boy!" said Meryl. "Can I have flowers?"

"Oh course," smiled Karen. "We'll get you flowers to wear in your hair."

"You know," said Joe after Meryl was in bed, "when we're married I'd like to adopt Meryl. I feel like her father already, and adoption would make it legal."

"Oh, Joe, that'd be wonderful!" Karen answered. "It'll make Meryl so happy! You know, I often wonder when she's going to ask about Jeff and why *he* didn't want to be her daddy. I'm even afraid someday she may want to look for him."

"Let's not worry about Jeff now," Joe said softly. "Right now I just want Meryl to know that I love her very much."

Meryl Polonius Turner stood shy and hesitant in the room full of kindergarten children. She looked down at her new shoes and began wiggling her toes.

"Would you like to come play in the store, Meryl?" Mrs. Schultz asked encouragingly.

Meryl walked slowly toward the teacher without saying a word and stood in the doorway. Inside were shelves with brightly colored boxes, just like a real supermarket. To one side was a counter with a toy cash register and even a conveyor belt. Two little girls toting bright red shopping baskets were busily inspecting the wares. One wore a long string of beads, the other a pair of large purple sunglasses. Meryl smiled slightly and glanced up at Mrs. Schultz.

"We need someone to work at the checkout counter, Meryl. Would you like to do that?"

Meryl walked quietly behind the counter. She pressed a button on the cash register and the drawer flew open, revealing a tray full of play money. Meryl's smile grew bigger. She had never seen such a wonderful play store before.

One of the shoppers approached Meryl with her purchases. "Do you have any coupons?" Meryl asked shyly, just as she had heard checkout clerks asking her mother.

The shopper looked disappointed. "No," she said, adjusting the sunglasses on her nose. "I just have money."

"Don't worry," said Meryl. "We *give* coupons." And she ripped some strips of paper from a brown bag.

"Thank you," said the shopper, smiling happily at Meryl. "My name is Amy."

From then on, Meryl and Amy were constant companions.

9 Cognitive Development in Early Childhood

*"M*ommy, who was born first, you or me?"
   "Daddy, when you were little, were you a little boy or a little girl?"
   "Why do they put a pit in every cherry? We have to throw the pit away anyway."
"When the sun sets into the sea, why isn't there any steam?"

These are questions actually asked by Russian preschool children (Chukovsky, 1941/1971). In every country, preschoolers—aged 2½ to 5—ask the same kinds of questions as they strive to understand their world. Some of their strange and humorous ideas stem from a simple lack of information. We might imagine intelligent aliens from another planet making some of these same errors because they didn't yet have all the relevant facts. However, young children's thinking is also *qualitatively* different from the thinking of adults, which is what makes it so interesting. Preschoolers' thinking is particularly fascinating because it possesses both mature and immature qualities. It is sufficiently different from adult thinking that we notice its magical elements. Yet it is similar enough to enable children to construct complex ideas and to allow us to observe developmental continuities. A major goal of this chapter is to explore both the cognitive skills and the cognitive limitations of preschoolers, pointing out the mature and the immature aspects of their thinking.

As you explore preschoolers' cognitive abilities, think about how they differ in fundamental ways from the cognitive abilities of infants and toddlers. As infants, children understand the world by perceiving and acting on it—by seeing, hearing, touching, tasting, and doing. In toddlerhood mental representation emerges, allowing children to think about things that aren't physically present. Toddlers can imagine the consequences of an action without actually carrying it out, and they develop the ability to combine symbols to express more complex ideas. Preschoolers try to understand the world at an even more advanced level, exploring how things work and why events take place. When Malcolm strives to grasp the workings of the remote-controlled plane, he is functioning in a way no toddler can. His idea that a small animal might be piloting the plane seems far-fetched to us, but it shows a remarkable advance over the ability he had as a toddler to think about causes and effects.

Despite the cognitive differences between a preschooler and a younger child, all the preschooler's new skills emerged from abilities possessed at earlier ages. Malcolm's ability to think of an explanation of the remote-controlled plane builds on the primitive perception of causality he possessed as a baby. New skills do not appear out of nowhere, but are built on abilities the child already has, as we suggested in Chapter 1.

Preschoolers want to know "why?" Many natural processes are mysterious and fascinating to them.

As you read this chapter, you will encounter several themes you have met before. First, during the preschool years children continue to be *active participants in their own development.* By this we mean not only that they actively explore the world, but also that they actively construct an understanding of it. Preschoolers progress from observing and describing events to trying to explain them. An important part of this active construction of understanding is a continued search for general patterns and rules. Just as toddlers search for patterns in forming early concepts, so preschoolers search for patterns in trying to master new cognitive challenges. For instance, when Malcolm uses overregularization to say the airplane "goed," he is using a general pattern found in English to understand how language works and to impose order on it.

Another familiar theme is the *continual interplay between children's developing capacities and the environment.* Preschoolers' advancing cognitive skills allow them to engage the environment in new ways and to draw forth new types of social interaction. At the same time, both adults and peers provide children with continual feedback about their efforts. When Meryl gets a positive response from Amy as she acts the part of clerk in the kindergarten store, she learns that her script for grocery shopping is shared by other children, which in turn helps to refine her general skill for social pretend play.

The issue of *specificity versus generality* becomes increasingly important in understanding children's cognitive abilities in early childhood. Both domain specificity and cultural specificity are significant issues during this period. Piaget attempted to describe and explain preschoolers' cognitive development in terms of general advances and limitations in logical reasoning. In contrast, many recent researchers have focused on children's acquisition of concepts and skills in specific domains. Furthermore, culture exerts an increasingly powerful influence on children's cognitive development during the preschool years, shaping both knowledge and reasoning processes.

Finally, this chapter contains the familiar theme of *cognitive limitations.* Despite their cognitive advances, young children still have significant limitations to their thinking. One limitation is *difficulty integrating multiple pieces of information.* When asked which of two cars is going faster, 4-year-old Mikey is likely to consider only which car is currently ahead, even if the car that is behind is rapidly narrowing the gap. This tendency to consider only one piece of information when multiple pieces are relevant is called **centration.** A second limitation is *difficulty distinguishing between appearance and reality.* When 3-year-olds look at a white object, look at it again through a blue filter, and then remove the filter, they think the object is really changing color, not just *appearing* to change (Flavell, Green, and Flavell, 1986). This tendency to define reality by surface appearance is called the **appearance-reality problem.** A third limitation is *difficulty managing attentional and memory processes.* Preschoolers show growing memory abilities in everyday situations, but they often have trouble with tasks that require memory strategies. Maggie is beginning to understand the value of such strategies when she holds on to her sweater after her mother tells her not to forget it as they prepare to leave the house. But preschoolers do not usually know about memory strategies, and even when they do they don't often use them.

Young children's cognitive limitations are not as extensive as was once thought, however. For example, Piaget argued that preschoolers' thought was characterized by **egocentrism,** an inability to take the perspective of another person. Today we know that egocentrism is not absolute in young children; when given relatively simple perspective-taking tasks, 4-year-olds can adopt another person's viewpoint in a limited way. Thus, whether young children display certain skills depends in part on the difficulty of the tasks they are given. Perspective-taking ability unfolds gradually during the preschool years and is applied in an increasing number of contexts. Understanding preschool cognitive development requires attention both to how new skills are gained and to how existing skills become more widely used.

This chapter explores preschoolers' cognitive abilities and limitations in three major sections. We start by examining general characteristics of preschoolers' reasoning, using as a starting point some topics originally studied by Piaget—reasoning about causation,

Centration:
The tendency to consider only one piece of information when multiple pieces are relevant.

Appearance-reality problem:
The tendency to define reality by surface appearances.

Egocentrism:
The inability to take the perspective of another person.

living and nonliving things, quantity, categories, and logical relations. In the second major section, we turn to the topic of preschoolers' attention and memory capabilities, exploring cognitive skills from an information-processing perspective. Finally, in the third major section, we take up the subject of social cognition—children's knowledge about and understanding of the social world.

Questions to Think About As You Read

- What can parents and preschool teachers do to foster preschoolers' cognitive development?
- How does cognitive development in early childhood prepare children for the start of formal education?

PRESCHOOLERS' REASONING ABILITIES

Preoperational period:
In Piaget's theory, the period from ages 2 to 7, characterized by an inability to use logical operations.

As we discussed in Chapters 1 and 5, Piaget was primarily interested in the development of children's logical reasoning abilities. He characterized ages 2 to 7 as the **preoperational period** because he believed that during this age range children cannot yet use logical operations in their reasoning. According to Piaget, their ability to use mental representation has taken them beyond the sensorimotor world of infancy, but their reasoning is not yet logically consistent or systematic.

Although subsequent research has contradicted many of Piaget's original conclusions, the questions he asked about children's cognitive development set an agenda for much of that research—and many of his original questions continue to be explored in some form today (Wellman and Gelman, 1998). For that reason, we will begin our discussion of cognitive development in early childhood by examining some aspects of preschoolers' reasoning originally studied by Piaget and tracing the directions more recent research on the same or related topics has taken.

Reasoning About Causation

Piaget was very interested in how children's causal reasoning changes as they grow older. In his early work, he used interviews to explore this topic. He asked children questions, such as why clouds move, and searched for developmental trends in their answers. Here are examples of children's responses at four different developmental levels typically seen between ages 3 and 10. (There is considerable variability in the ages at which children move from one level to the next.)

Level 1

Adult: What makes clouds move?
Child: When we move along they move along too.
Adult: Can you make them move?
Child: Yes.
Adult: When I walk and you are still, do they move?
Child: Yes.
Adult: And at night, when everyone is asleep, do they move?
Child: Yes.
Adult: But you tell me that they move when somebody walks.
Child: They always move. The cats, when they walk, and then the dogs, they make the clouds move.

(Piaget, 1930/1969a, p. 62)

Preschoolers tend to base their explanations of phenomena such as the movement of clouds on superficial appearances.

Level 2

Adult: What makes the clouds move along?
Child: God does.
Adult: How?
Child: He pushes them.
(Piaget, 1930/1969a, p. 63)

Level 3

Adult: What makes the clouds move along?
Child: It's the sun.
Adult: How?
Child: With its rays. It pushes the clouds.
(Piaget, 1930/1969a, p. 65)

Level 4

Adult: What makes the clouds move along?
Child: Because they have a current.
Adult: What is this current?
Child: It's in the clouds.
(Piaget, 1930/1969a, p. 72)

At the first level, characteristic of younger preschoolers, the child reports that when we move along the clouds move along too. Where did he or she get such a strange idea? To understand, think about how objects appear in relation to us as we walk along. Nearby objects, such as houses and trees, loom up closer as we approach them and recede into the distance after we pass them. This is not true of things that are very far away, however, such as the sun, the moon, and distant clouds; they never seem to get any closer or farther away as we change position. Young children often notice this phenomenon and interpret it to mean that the sun, moon, and clouds must be moving with them.

These children are using observations to construct an understanding of the world, but for children at this level, reality is defined by the superficial appearance of things. Because the moon *appears* to be keeping up with them as they walk, it must be moving too. As children grow older, their interpretations of what they observe change, and

[handwritten note in margin: 1. using observations to construct an understanding of the world, but for children @ this level, reality is defined by the superficial appearance of things]

with these changes comes a different understanding of the world. At causal reasoning level 2, children often appeal to an all-powerful force that controls objects and events. This omnipotent force may be called God, or perhaps Mommy or Daddy. At reasoning level 3 children begin using causes in nature to explain natural phenomena, but those causes may be quite improbable (the rays of the sun pushing clouds along, for instance). Finally, at level 4, children are approaching an adult explanation, even though their explanation is still incomplete.

Piaget did not find mature reasoning about causation until well into middle childhood, but other researchers have shown that the level of preschoolers' causal reasoning is influenced by the complexity and familiarity of the problems posed. Preschool children can quickly learn the cause-and-effect relationships that operate in very simple systems (Wellman and Gelman, 1998). For example, children as young as 3 can learn that putting a marble down one chute causes a Snoopy doll to appear, while putting it down another chute does not, and 5-year-olds can give reasonable explanations as to why this difference occurs (Bullock and Gelman, 1979). What's more, if young children are asked for explanations of things they are familiar with (such as how a bicycle works), their responses are more mature than when they are asked about unfamiliar things (Berzonsky, 1971). Such findings show that preschoolers have the skills to give good explanations if the things to be explained are simple and familiar.

One reason preschoolers sometimes explain things in ways adults find fanciful is that young children do not yet understand what a good explanation is. When they don't know the reason for something, they may invent one that seems far-fetched to adults. Preschoolers, in other words, lack an abstract idea of what constitutes a plausible cause. Acquiring an understanding of various specific causes gives them the foundation for developing this more mature and abstract concept.

Interestingly, at the same time children are beginning to develop an understanding of physical causality in the everyday world, they are also developing parallel but separate beliefs about magical processes (Rosengren and Hickling, 2000). Between ages 3 and 4 children begin to explain some seemingly impossible events as due to supernatural powers. However, they do not use magic as a general explanation for processes they don't understand. Instead, they use magical explanations mainly in certain specific situations, such as seeing a magician perform or getting toys from Santa Claus. Typically, these situations are labeled by parents, teachers, or older children as magical. Once children start school, their use of this sort of magical reasoning drops quickly, as their causal understanding and knowledge of the world increase and support for magical beliefs from parents, teachers, and peers declines.

Children and Magic

Reasoning About Living and Nonliving Things

Another aspect of children's reasoning Piaget was interested in was the ability to distinguish between living and nonliving things. Piaget (1929) claimed young children's thinking was characterized by **animism,** or a tendency to attribute life to nonliving things. In particular, he observed that young children often seemed to believe anything that moved was alive, including clouds and bicycles. Later researchers found preschoolers' thinking is not as animistic as Piaget believed, but children sometimes do have trouble deciding exactly where to draw the line between the categories *living* and *nonliving* (Flavell, Miller, and Miller, 2002). For example, their category of *living things* often includes animals of all types, but not plants.

Subsequent research on children's understanding of biological concepts has demonstrated that preschoolers do make clear distinctions in their reasoning about living and nonliving things. Children as young as age 3 recognize that animals move on their own and nonliving things move as the result of external forces, including human intervention (R. Gelman, 1990). By age 4 they have acquired a basic but incomplete theory of biology (Springer, 1999). They realize living things grow and nonliving things do not, whereas nonliving things become worn in ways that living things do not (Rosengren et

Animism:
The tendency to attribute life to nonliving things.

Preschoolers have some understanding of the differences between animate and inanimate objects, but their knowledge is still incomplete and prone to errors.

al., 1991). And they know living things reproduce and their offspring belong to the same species and tend to resemble them (S. Gelman and Wellman, 1991; Solomon et al., 1996; Springer and Keil, 1989). However, they do not yet understand all the implications of the *living/nonliving* distinction; for example, they may not realize fireflies will die if they are kept in a closed jar with no air holes. In addition, they have trouble understanding biological processes that violate their assumptions about the nature of living things, such as metamorphosis or seasonal color changes (Rosengren et al., 1991; Rosengren, Taylor, and DeHart, 1997). By about age 6 their understanding of the differences between living and nonliving things has become more specific, consistent, and coherent (Gimenez and Harris, 2002; Zhu and Fang, 2000).

Reasoning About Quantity

As an adult you understand many things about quantity. You have a concept of number and know how to count, add, and subtract. You know how to measure things, and you know what kinds of transformations change the amount of a substance (adding more juice to a glass or cutting a chunk off a roll of cookie dough) and what kinds do not (pouring juice from one glass to another or rolling a ball of cookie dough out flat). Preschoolers are just beginning to develop a knowledge of these concepts and principles. Centration, the appearance-reality problem, and memory limitations often seem to place limits on their understanding. We begin our examination of preschoolers' quantitative reasoning by looking at a group of concepts originally studied by Piaget, the concepts of conservation.

Concepts of Conservation   Concepts of **conservation** all include the general idea that the amount of something remains the same, or is conserved, despite changes in its form, shape, or appearance. Einstein's famous equation, $E = mc^2$, is a formula about the conservation of mass and energy that says that while mass can be transformed into energy and vice versa, their total amount is fixed, or conserved. A transformation from one to the other produces neither an increase nor a decrease in the total. To physicists this idea seems intuitive and obvious, but many adults find it difficult to grasp. In the same way, other concepts of conservation that seem obvious to adults are not at all obvious to preschoolers.

These concepts include:

Conservation:
The idea that the amount of something remains the same despite changes in its form, shape, or appearance.

- *Conservation of liquid volume*, the idea that the total amount of a liquid remains the same despite changes in shape when it is poured into different containers;

Child Development CD
Conservation Tasks

- *Conservation of number,* the idea that the number of items in a group remains the same despite repositioning of those items;
- *Conservation of mass,* the idea that quantity of matter remains the same despite changes in its shape (e.g., rolling a large ball of clay into a snake); and
- *Conservation of length,* the idea that the length of something remains the same regardless of whether it is straight, bent, or twisted (e.g., a coiled-up string pulled out full length does not grow any longer).

A mature understanding of the concepts of conservation usually does not emerge until middle childhood. Moreover, children do not grasp all of them at once. Some are learned well before others, as if children approach each one as a new problem. One of the first concepts of conservation acquired is conservation of liquid volume, which is discussed in detail in the box below.

It makes sense that the various concepts of conservation are learned one by one when you consider that whether a quantity is conserved after a transformation depends

A CLOSER LOOK

CONSERVATION OF LIQUID VOLUME

Piaget tested children's understanding of conservation of liquid volume by showing them two glasses the same size and shape containing equal amounts of water (Figure 9.1A). He asked which had more water, or if they had the same amount. Most children said they had the same, although some required small adjustments before declaring the amounts equal. Next, Piaget poured the water from glass *b* into glass *c*, which was taller and narrower (Figure 9.1B). He asked if glass *a* had more water, if *c* had more, or if both had the same. Young preschoolers almost invariably answered that *c* had more. When asked why, they pointed out that the water in glass *c* rose higher. This experiment shows that young children do not grasp that a volume of water remains the same regardless of the size and shape of the container into which it is poured.

This experiment illustrates two limitations on preschoolers' thought. First, children are misled by the appearance of the liquid in the glasses. By mistaking superficial appearance for reality, they manifest the *appearance-reality problem.* Second, by focusing on only the height to which the water rises, they show their tendency toward *centration.*

Children pass through several stages as they gradually overcome these limitations and develop more mature reasoning. In stage 1 (3- and 4-year-olds), children are *nonconservers.* They consistently judge the amount of liquid by its height. Note that nonconservers use a consistent rule to judge the amount: higher is more. This rule is inaccurate, but children in this stage are perfectly happy with it. Certain their answers are correct, they have no motivation to change their thinking.

In stage 2 (5- and 6-year-olds), children enter a *transitional* period. Now they are less decisive about which glass has more water. They may first say the taller one has more, but then wonder if the other has more because it is wider. They may also notice that if the water is poured back into its original glass, the two amounts once again look equal. Children in stage 2 seem aware their answers may be wrong, and they are motivated to find a consistent and correct basis for responding. Their uncertainty stems from their ability to bring new information to bear on the problem. Centration no longer limits their focus to just height or width; they can now sequentially consider more than one dimension (height, then width, then height again). For this reason they vacillate in making a decision. They are also able to use information about changes in the water (e.g., being poured back into the original glass), rather than merely considering how it looks at a particular moment.

In stage 3, *mature conservation,* children answer the experimenter's questions quickly, confidently, and correctly. To them the correct answer seems obvious, and the incorrect answers of younger children seem "dumb." They show no awareness that at a slightly younger age they gave similarly "dumb" answers. Conservation of liquid volume is usually understood at about age 7 and is one of the cognitive markers for the transition into middle childhood.

Children who have a mature understanding of conservation explain their answers with one of the following justifications (Goodnow, 1973; Peill, 1975):

- *Compensation* ("This one is higher, but it's narrower; the other is shorter, but wider. So they're both the same"),
- *Reversibility* ("When you pour it back, it'll be the same again"),
- *Identity* ("It's still the same water"), or
- *The nothing added or subtracted criterion* ("You only poured it into a different glass").

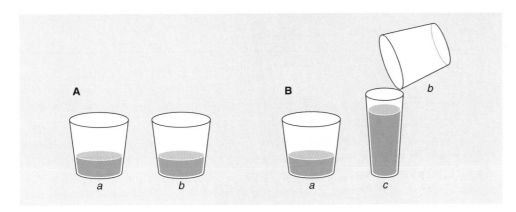

Figure 9.1
CONSERVATION OF LIQUID VOLUME
When glasses *a* and *b* are filled to equal heights, preschoolers judge that they have equal amounts of water. However, when the water in glass *b* is poured into glass *c*, which is taller and narrower, they judge glass *c* to have more water than glass *a*. This is an example of preschoolers' failure to conserve.

on the particular transformation. For instance, if you cut out 16 1-inch squares of paper and assembled them into different patterns, the area of those patterns would always be 16 square inches; area would be conserved. However, if you tied together the ends of a 22-inch piece of string and pulled the string into different shapes, the area within the string would vary greatly; it would *not* be conserved. If the string formed a circle, the area inside it would be 38.5 square inches. If the string formed a rectangle 1 by 10 inches, the area inside it would be only 10 square inches. With such seeming inconsistencies, it's no wonder that it takes time for children to master conservation.

There is some evidence that children's particular experiences affect the development of their understanding of various types of conservation. For example, children from pottery-making families in Mexico, who have fairly extensive experience handling clay, show an understanding of conservation of mass earlier than other children (Price-Williams, Gordon, and Ramirez, 1969).

Piaget believed that children's understanding of conservation depended on both physical maturation and experience in the world, and, therefore, efforts to teach preschoolers conservation would not be successful. Research testing this assumption confirmed that simply *explaining* concepts of conservation (for example, that the amount of water remains unchanged in the conservation of liquid volume task) to young children didn't work. However, when children were placed in learning situations designed to help them overcome specific cognitive limitations, they could often be taught to understand conservation concepts somewhat sooner than they normally would.

In one study, to help children overcome the appearance-reality problem, the containers in the conservation of liquid volume task were screened so that the children couldn't see how high the water rose when poured from one container to another (Bruner, Olver, and Greenfield, 1966). Screening the containers didn't improve 4-year-olds' performance; they typically failed to conserve when the containers weren't screened and responded randomly when they were. However, six-year-olds, who were in Piaget's transitional stage on the unscreened task, showed dramatically improved performance when the containers were screened, and they maintained their improvement even when the screen was removed. These children were probably on the verge of understanding conservation on their own; removing the distraction of contradictory visual information allowed them to grasp the underlying concept.

Thus, older preschoolers and young elementary school children can sometimes be trained to succeed on problems they wouldn't usually solve until a year or more later. For younger preschoolers, such learning is unstable because they haven't yet acquired a framework of understanding into which they can fit new conservation skills. A grasp of conservation is only one part of an overall cognitive system. As children attempt to solve problems and to understand how things work, their various cognitive abilities need to be coordinated within a framework that creates a consistent view of the world. Cognitive developments, in short, are interdependent, a fact that inhibits early acquisition of single skills.

Young children do not understand that changing the spatial arrangement of a group of objects does not change their number.

Concepts of Number During the preschool years, children make substantial progress in developing a *concept of number*—an awareness of how many items are present and how addition, subtraction, and rearrangement affect this number (Ginsburg, Klein, and Starkey, 1998). A grasp of this concept is necessary to solve conservation of number tasks.

In Piaget's original conservation of number task, a child is shown two rows of seven coins, arranged so they are the same length. The experimenter asks if one row has more coins or if they both have the same number. Once the child agrees they have the same number, the experimenter spreads the coins in one row out, making that row longer. Again the experimenter asks if one row has more or if they both have the same number of coins. Preschoolers typically respond that the longer row now has more coins; they seem to be overwhelmed by the *appearance* of the longer row and ignore the fact that no coins have been added to it or taken away from the shorter row.

Preschoolers' performance on conservation of number tasks improves considerably when the number of objects is small. On a conservation of number task using dolls and doll beds instead of coins, even 4-year-olds realized that simply rearranging the rows did not change the number, as long as each row contained only two or three items (Cooper, 1976).

Understanding the Effects of Addition and Subtraction. Other studies have demonstrated that preschoolers have some understanding of the effects of addition and subtraction on small numbers (Ginsburg et al., 1998). Rochel Gelman (1972) showed young children two plates, one containing a row of two toy mice, the other a row of three. The children were told they were going to play a game in which they had to identify the winning plate. Gelman pointed to the plate with three mice and said it would always be the winner, but she didn't say why. The children had to decide for themselves whether being a winner depended on number of mice or row length. Next, Gelman covered the plates and shuffled them. The children were then asked to uncover a plate and decide if it was the winner. Whenever a child identified the plate with three mice as the winner, he or she was given a small prize. After several rounds, Gelman surreptitiously changed the plate with three mice, either removing a mouse or moving the mice closer together or farther apart. Gelman found that even 3- and 4-year-olds defined the winning plate by number of mice, not row length. Almost no children thought changing the length of the three-mouse row meant the plate was no longer a winner. In fact, many failed to notice such a change, but almost all the children noticed *removal* of a mouse. The

mhhe.com
/dehart5

Preschoolers and Math

overwhelming majority doubted that a three-mouse plate with one mouse missing could still be a winner. The only way to fix things, they said, would be to add another mouse. Clearly, these children understood something about the effects of addition and subtraction on small numbers.

This understanding has been demonstrated in other studies as well. In one (Cooper, 1984), 2- to 7-year-olds were shown two groups of objects that were equal in number, differed by one, or differed by two. The experimenter then either added an object to one of the groups or took an object away. The children were then asked if either group now had more or less than the other.

All the children used a rule of some kind to determine their answers, and all showed some understanding that addition to a set *increases* its number and subtraction *decreases* its number. The rules used by children of different ages, however, varied in sophistication and effectiveness. The youngest children (2- and 3-year-olds) ignored the initial number of items in each group and always said a group added to now had more than the other group, and a group subtracted from now had less. Because of its lack of sophistication, this can be called a *primitive rule*. Most 4- and 5-year-olds used a *qualitative rule,* which took into account any initial difference between the two groups, but not the magnitude of the difference. It was as if they encoded the two groups in purely qualitative terms: *less than, equal to,* or *more than.* This rule led to errors when the initial groups differed by more than one. For instance, if the groups initially had five and seven, and one more was added to the smaller group, a child using this rule would mistakenly say the two groups had become equal. Finally, most 6- to 7-year-olds had developed a *quantitative rule* that took into account the magnitude of any difference between the initial groups—that is, the quantities involved. This enabled them to give consistently correct answers.

The use of these three rules is related to the development of conservation of number. Children who use the primitive rule do not show any grasp of number conservation, while many of those who use the qualitative rule appear to be transitional (at Piaget's stage 2). Those who use the quantitative rule exhibit number conservation and have reached Piaget's stage 3. This finding lends support to Piaget's belief that children's understanding of number conservation is related to their general understanding of numbers. But Piaget's perspective on this developmental process is probably not completely accurate. Many studies show that the acquisition of number concepts begins earlier than Piaget suggested and also extends longer (Ginsburg et al., 1998).

Learning to Count. Learning to count is a skill involving numbers that often begins in the early preschool years. Television programs like *Sesame Street* have helped to improve the counting skills of many young children in the United States. By the end of early childhood, most children can consistently count five or six objects accurately. Occasionally, younger preschoolers make strange errors in counting, revealing that their understanding of the process is not the same as an adult's. One young boy, for example, appeared to count correctly the fingers on one hand. However, when the researcher interviewing him held up his index finger and asked "How many is this?" the child replied, "four." A little probing revealed that he was using the number names as names for each of the fingers: the little finger was "one," the ring finger "two," the middle finger "three," the index finger "four," and the thumb "five."

Gelman and Gallistel (1978) identified five principles that children master in learning to count. One is the *one-to-one principle,* the idea that each member of a set to be counted is paired with one and only one number name. Two- and 3-year-olds have difficulty with this principle when counting more than three or four objects, despite attempts to keep track by pointing as they count. They count some objects more than once (often by saying the sequence of numbers faster than their fingers move), and they skip objects, especially when the objects are not arranged in a row.

Another principle involved in learning to count is the *stable-order principle,* the idea that number names occur in a certain order as they are paired with objects. In English the correct order is one, two, three, and so forth, but young children sometimes use idiosyncratic orders. For example, at age 2½ the son of one of the authors of this book consistently left out the number seven when counting. Young children use a stable order for counting smaller numbers (one to three), and then expand the range of their consistent order as they move through the preschool years. The rate of expansion and the development of later numerical skills is influenced by the counting system used in different cultures. The Oksapmin of Papua New Guinea use a counting system that depends on the names of body parts from the thumb on the right hand (corresponding to English *one*) through all the fingers, wrist, forearm, elbow (corresponding to English *eight*), and on across the body to the other hand. Although the concrete reference to the body may help in early learning of number names, it appears to slow the development of more abstract numerical skills (Saxe, 1982). In contrast, the Chinese counting system, which uses a more consistent naming system than English (e.g., *ten-one* rather than *eleven*) seems to accelerate the expansion of the counting range and the development of some abstract numerical skills (Miller et al., 1995).

The *cardinal principle* is a third rule in learning how to count. It holds that the final word in the counting sequence describes the total number of objects in the set. If there are four objects in a set, the child would count "one, two, three, *four*" and then say that the total number of objects is four. Based on her own research and the work of others, Karen Wynn (1990) concluded that children use the cardinal principle after about age 3½. Three-year-olds often appear to use it when counting two or three objects, but not for larger numbers. They can generally count a set of four objects correctly, for example, but when asked how many objects there are, they often count the objects again instead of saying "four" (Ginsburg et al., 1998). Use of the cardinal principle is more evident at age 4. When given a conservation of number task, 4-year-olds sometimes seem to miscount intentionally to make the result of their counting consistent with their judgment that the longer row has more objects. It makes sense to do this only if they are using the cardinal principle.

A fourth principle in learning to count is the *abstraction principle*. This is the idea that any set of objects is countable. Although the abstraction principle has not been the direct focus of any research, young children have been asked to count a variety of different things, including imaginary things, and they always seem to find the task plausible. They are also willing to group together different kinds of things in a set to be

Learning to count is an important part of preschoolers' developing understanding of quantity.

counted, such as grouping together and counting animate and inanimate objects. These informal findings suggest children understand the abstraction principle from an early age.

Finally, learning to count involves the *order-irrelevant principle,* the idea that it does not matter in what order things are counted. When young children are asked to count a set of objects more than once, they frequently count them in a different order the second time, as if they know the order does not make any difference. By age 5, many children are able to state explicitly that order is irrelevant (Flavell et al., 2002).

Developmentalists have debated exactly how children's understanding of these five principles develops. Some researchers argue that children grasp them at some level even before they start to count (Gallistel and Gelman, 1990). This is often interpreted to mean the principles are innate. Others say counting behaviors and skills develop first, and from them children extract the principles (Fuson, 1988; Siegler, 1991). In any case, we know that by the end of the preschool period, children understand the five principles involved in counting and apply them appropriately.

Concepts of Measurement Piaget believed learning about conservation was required to understand measurement. Yet preschoolers show an intuitive grasp of measurement before they correctly solve conservation problems, just as they show an intuitive grasp of number concepts and counting. For example, preschoolers will divide a string in half by grasping it near the center and adjusting it until the length of the two segments is equal (Miller, 1984), and they will form two equal groups of cookies by dividing a large group a pair at a time (Cooper, 1984).

Young children make measurement errors when the appearance of two equal quantities makes them look unequal, as when two strings of equal length are laid down side by side, one straight and the other wavy. In the absence of misleading perceptual information, preschoolers frequently perform reasonably well on simple measurement tasks. However, preschoolers' understanding of measurement, like their understanding of addition and subtraction, appears to be *qualitative* (Flavell et al., 2002). That is, under the right circumstances, they can make correct judgments about *relative* size and number (which of two sticks is longer, which plate has more cookies, etc.). But they are not yet able to combine this ability with their counting skills to arrive at precise, truly *quantitative* measurements (Case, 1998), and they do not yet have a grasp of abstract units of measurement, such as inches and meters.

Summing Up We can summarize what we've discussed about quantitative concepts in preschool children with four basic points:

- Preschoolers do not usually display an understanding that quantities are conserved despite changes in appearance, in part because they tend to focus on one aspect of a stimulus (height of water in a glass, length of a row of objects).

- Teaching can lead to stable acquisition of a new cognitive skill, but probably not before the child has a cognitive framework for the skill.

- Preschoolers show considerable sophistication in reasoning about *small* numbers.

- Preschoolers' quantitative reasoning is immature but not random; they seem to follow rules in solving quantitative problems, and the nature of their rules changes with development.

Reasoning About Classes and Logical Relations

Piaget's research on preschoolers' emerging logical reasoning focused on three skills:

- **classification,** the ability to group things by shared characteristics, such as size or shape;

- **seriation,** the ability to arrange things in a logical progression, such as smallest to largest or oldest to newest; and

Classification:
The ability to group things by shared characteristics, such as size or shape.

Seriation:
The ability to arrange things in a logical progression, such as from oldest to newest.

Transitive inference:
The ability to infer the relation between two objects by knowing their respective relations to a third.

Class:
Any set of objects or events that are treated as the same in certain ways because they have features in common.

- **transitive inference,** the ability to infer the relation between two objects by knowing their respective relations to a third.

As was the case with quantitative reasoning skills, Piaget underestimated preschoolers' classification, seriation, and transitive inference skills, and more recent research has given us a more complete picture of their abilities in these areas. However, these skills are only beginning to develop in early childhood, and preschoolers are hampered in using them by centration, the appearance-reality problem, and memory limitations.

Classification   When Joe Turner empties the dishwasher and puts glasses away in one cupboard, plates in another, and silverware in a drawer, he is organizing these items into classes. A **class** is any set of objects or events that are treated as the same in certain ways because they have features in common. If, after watching Joe, Meryl takes one of her toy spoons and puts it in the silverware drawer, we can say she seems to understand the class *silverware.*

When do children first display classification skills? Infants show a primitive form of classification when they treat stimuli as the same on the basis of shared characteristics. Before they are 2, toddlers sometimes sort objects on the basis of common properties (Gopnik and Meltzoff, 1987). However, not until the preschool years are children consistently able to make simple classifications when asked to do so.

Piaget studied classification in preschoolers by giving them different colored shapes and instructing them to sort those that went together into separate groups (Inhelder and Piaget, 1964). In the simplest form of this task there were only two colors (e.g., red and blue) and two shapes (e.g., circles and squares). Piaget found that the youngest preschoolers would sometimes sort correctly along one dimension (shape *or* color). For instance, they might put all the red circles and squares in one pile and all the blue ones in another. It was not unusual for 3-year-olds to start sorting on the basis of color and then switch suddenly by matching the shape of the last object added to a pile. Older preschoolers were more consistent in their sorting, until by age 5 they were quite good at classifying along one dimension. Even the 5-year-olds, however, still focused on only a single characteristic (e.g., color). Ten-year-olds, in contrast, would sort using both dimensions simultaneously, putting all the blue squares in one pile, all the blue circles in another, all the red squares in a third, and all the red circles in a fourth. Piaget saw this difference between preschoolers and older children as another example of preschoolers' centration.

Later research has shown that this centration is not completely rigid, however. Two-dimensional sorting can be encouraged in preschoolers by giving them experience classifying objects (Watson, Hayes, and Vietze, 1979). But preschoolers seldom use two-dimensional classification spontaneously to organize objects in their everyday worlds. Although training can to some extent overcome centration on a single dimension, young children return to this narrower focus in situations that differ from the training examples.

When preschoolers are given explicit rules to use in sorting things, they show some of the same limitations Piaget observed, but they can sort consistently along one dimension at an earlier age. In a series of studies (Zelazo, Frye, and Rapus, 1996; Zelazo and Reznick, 1991; Zelazo, Reznick, and Piñon, 1995), Philip Zelazo and his colleagues told young children rules for sorting pictures into

This preschooler has no trouble sorting blocks either by color or by shape, but sorting them by both color and shape at the same time would be beyond her present abilities.

two boxes (e.g., fish versus birds, things that make noise versus things that are quiet). They found that 2½-year-olds can generally tell which box a picture belongs in if asked (e.g., "Is this a bird? Or is this a fish?"). But when children this young are given a rule to use in sorting ("If it's a bird, then it goes in this box. If it's a fish, then it goes in that box."), they tend to sort the pictures more or less randomly. This is true even if they are given extra help, including reinforcement, category labels for the pictures, and frequent reminders of the rule. Three-year-olds can follow sorting rules consistently, but they have difficulty switching from one rule (such as color) to another (such as shape). By age 4, children not only can follow one rule consistently, they also can switch to a new rule without difficulty.

Seriation   Piaget was interested in children's ability to do seriation tasks because he believed it reflected an underlying cognitive skill required to appreciate numbers and to measure effectively. Piaget (1952) studied seriation by asking children to arrange a group of sticks in a row from smallest to largest (see Figure 9.2). If the children succeeded in organizing the sticks into an orderly progression, they were given another stick of intermediate length to insert into the sequence. Piaget discovered that young preschoolers could find the largest and smallest sticks in a group, but they had great difficulty constructing an ordered series of seven sticks. By age 6 or 7, most children could easily construct such a series and could also insert an additional stick in the correct place.

Interestingly, because of the way they approach seriation tasks, preschool children do much better when there are only three or four sticks to be put in a series (Blevins and Cooper, 1986). If you were given this task, you would probably start by finding the smallest stick and putting it on the left, finding the next smallest and putting it second, and so on until all the sticks had been arranged. This planned course of action requires that you grasp the nature of a seriated set before you begin. Such an overall plan guiding each move is not apparent in the behavior of young children, even when they are organizing only a small number of sticks. Instead, preschoolers seem to use a trial-and-error strategy, arranging the sticks more or less at random and then checking to see if the results look right. Such a strategy works for a small number of sticks, which can be arranged in a limited number of ways. But with a larger number, there are far more alternatives, and the trial-and-error approach is less likely to succeed.

Preschoolers' approaches to seriation tasks illustrate some of the cognitive limitations characteristic of this age. Preschoolers cannot conceive of the relationship between members of an ordered set that is not visually present; they must see the whole array to know if it is right. This is the appearance-reality problem in a slightly different form. Young children's attempts to order a set of seven sticks show evidence of centration. The array in Figure 9.2B, produced by a preschooler, looks seriated if you focus only on the tops. It is as if this child could not coordinate information from the two ends simultaneously and focused on the tops alone.

Transitive Inference   If you know that *A* equals *B* and that *B* equals *C,* you can conclude by transitive inference that *A* and *C* are also equal. Transitive inference can be used to reason about inequalities as well. If you know that Mikey is taller than Bryan, and Bryan is taller than Justin, you know by transitive inference that Mikey is the tallest of the three.

In Piaget's initial studies of transitive inference, children could not solve such problems until middle childhood (Piaget, 1970), but later research found evidence of earlier skill in this area (Bryant and Trabasso, 1971; Riley and Trabasso, 1974). Tom Trabasso and his colleagues showed that even 4-year-olds can succeed at transitive inference problems if they are trained to remember the premise conditions (such as *Mikey is taller than Bryan* and *Bryan is taller than Justin*). Trabasso trained young children to remember five premise pairs, all involving relationships between pairs of real objects. It takes a long time to get 4-year-olds to master five pairs, but in the end they can answer questions such as "Who is taller, Mikey or Justin?," even though they have never been directly

Preschoolers and Classification

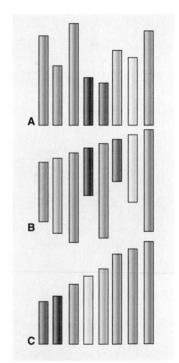

Figure 9.2
DEVELOPMENT OF SERIATION
When young preschoolers are asked to order a set of sticks from smallest to largest, they frequently produce a random order such as that shown in A. Older preschoolers sometimes centrate on the top ends of the sticks and produce an arrangement like that in B. Usually between 5 and 7 years of age, children can produce the correct ordering shown in C.

taught that relationship. Preschoolers do have a much harder time with this task than school-age children do, partly because of the memory demands it involves and partly because centration makes it difficult for them to coordinate the information from multiple premise pairs.

Distinguishing Between Appearance and Reality

Throughout our discussion of the general characteristics of preschoolers' thought we have given many examples in which children are misled by surface appearances. The development of the ability to distinguish between appearance and reality is also an area of research in its own right. In one of the earliest studies of this topic, children 3 to 6 years old got to know a cat named Maynard, and then researchers put a dog mask over Maynard's head (DeVries, 1969). The children were then asked questions like, "What kind of animal is it now? Would this animal eat dog food or cat food? Does it bark or meow?" Three-year-olds frequently seemed to believe that the mask changed the identity of the animal, whereas 5- and 6-year-olds did not.

John Flavell and his colleagues have conducted many studies in which they investigated children's understanding of the appearance-reality distinction (e.g., Flavell, Green, and Flavell, 1986, 1990). In these studies, they showed children objects that looked like other objects, such as a sponge that looked like a rock, and had children view things through colored filters, which made them appear to change color. They asked children what the objects looked like and what they really were. Despite great efforts to ensure children understood the questions, 3-year-olds consistently interpreted the appearance of an object as reality. Chinese children respond to appearance-reality tasks the same way as American children, suggesting the problem is not some peculiarity in the way the questions are worded in English (Flavell et al., 1983). The fact that other researchers have failed in attempts to train 3-year-olds to make the appearance-reality distinction further strengthens Flavell's findings (Taylor and Hart, 1990).

However, a number of studies have shown that preschoolers' limitations in this area are not as pervasive as originally thought. In one set of studies, children were presented with food that they had previously seen contaminated in some way, but that currently looked fine (Siegel and Share, 1990). For example, they watched a cockroach being removed from a glass of juice and were asked if the juice was now all right to drink. Children as young as 2½ said it was not drinkable, even though it looked fine. In another study, 3-year-olds were observed to use the word *real* to distinguish between toys and the real objects they represent, and the word *really* to differentiate between imaginary events and events that really happened (Woolley and Wellman, 1990). Clearly, even young children are starting to distinguish between appearance and reality, although in most situations their view of reality is dominated by appearances. By the end of the preschool years this difficulty is largely overcome. Five- and 6-year-olds still have a lot to learn about reality, but their view of it is no longer dominated by the way things look at the moment.

PRESCHOOLERS' ATTENTION AND MEMORY ABILITIES

Sensory register:
The part of memory where incoming information from one of the five senses is stored very briefly.

Short-term or working memory:
The part of memory where consciously noted information is stored for 10 to 20 seconds.

Long-term memory:
The part of memory where information is stored for a long time.

The focus in this section is on topics central to information-processing approaches, including the abilities to select and attend to information, to store it in memory, and to retrieve it. According to many information-processing theorists, information from the environment goes through various processing steps, as shown in Figure 9.3 (Atkinson and Shiffrin, 1968). First it enters a **sensory register**, where it is stored very briefly (less than 1 second for visual information). Whatever information is consciously noted moves to **short-term** or **working memory**, which is of more limited capacity than the sensory registers but holds information longer (usually 10 to 20 seconds). Some of the information in working memory then moves to **long-term memory**, which has a very large

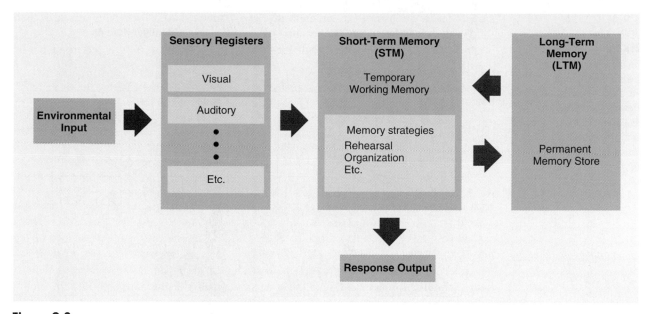

Figure 9.3
AN INFORMATION-PROCESSING MODEL

In this model of human information processing, information enters the sensory registers, which have a large capacity. Information here fades in less than 1 second, but before it fades some is transferred to short-term memory, and part of this information is transferred to long-term or permanent memory. *(Source: Adapted from Atkinson and Shiffrin, 1968.)*

capacity and can hold information for a very long time. Using memory strategies (such as rehearsing material, organizing it into categories, or relating it to other things) tends to increase the likelihood that information will be stored in long-term memory.

The information-processing model in Figure 9.3 can be used to help define attention and memory skills. **Attention skills** are the processes that control the transfer of information from the sensory register to working memory, while **memory skills** are the processes that retain information in working memory (short-term storage), transfer it to long-term memory, or both. Attention skills and memory skills may have a central role in cognitive development, as we saw in our discussion of working memory in Chapter 5.

In this section we focus on the development of attention and memory skills in preschoolers. Keep in mind that information-processing theorists believe that changes in attention and memory skills help to explain the changes in thinking and reasoning we have already discussed. For example, acquiring concepts of conservation can be explained in terms of developmental changes in what information is attended to and how that information is processed.

Attention skills:
Processes that control the transfer of information from a sensory register to working memory.

Memory skills:
Processes that retain information in working memory and/or transfer it to long-term memory.

Deploying Attention

In Maggie's kindergarten class the teacher is talking about the names of different shapes. Maggie is paying no attention to the teacher but instead is watching a red-tailed hawk that is hunting in a field outside the window. The teacher notices that Maggie is looking out the window and says gently, "Maggie, pay attention."

Maggie, of course, *has* been paying attention, but to the hawk, not to her teacher. Her problem is failure to focus on the right thing. Maggie is not alone in experiencing this problem. The tasks of selecting information to attend to, staying focused on it, and ignoring irrelevant stimuli all pose challenges to preschoolers because their attentional systems are not yet fully developed.

In a classic study, Elaine Vurpillot (1968) showed children pairs of houses like those in Figure 9.4 and asked them to determine if the two houses were the same. Half of the

Figure 9.4

DEVELOPMENT OF VISUAL ATTENTION

Children were asked if the houses were the same or different. Preschoolers compared only a few of the windows, whereas older children scanned back and forth more systematically. *(Source: Vurpillot, 1968.)*

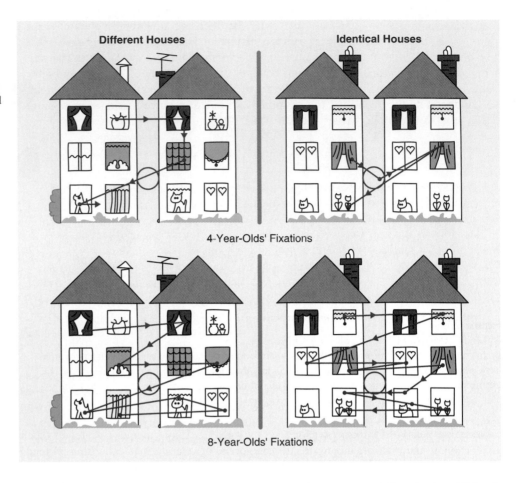

Preschoolers and Television

house pairs were identical, while the other half had features that differed. The children's eye movements were filmed as they made their judgments so that the researchers could tell what parts of the houses they looked at. The preschoolers in this study made more errors than older children because they did not use systematic, organized strategies in their scanning. As a result, they sometimes missed important information—in this case, some of the windows.

In other situations young children scan *more* information than they need to (Miller, 1990). In one study, children were shown twelve pictures, six of animals and six of household objects. The pictures were arranged on a board with twelve windows, one picture inside each window. The researcher asked the children to remember only the animal pictures and told them they could open each window as often as they wanted to memorize the picture inside it. The most efficient strategy, after finding the six animal pictures, would be to open only the windows covering those pictures. But preschoolers, unlike older children, did not use this selective behavior. They continued to open all twelve windows during the entire time they had for memorizing the pictures. As in Vurpillot's study, the preschoolers failed to direct their attention in an organized and effective way.

Although preschoolers seem less advanced than older children in focusing their attention, they have made progress compared with toddlers. When Daniel Anderson and Stephen Levin (1976) observed 2- to 4-year-olds watching *Sesame Street,* they found that the youngest children spent the least amount of time viewing the TV screen. This was especially true when toys were placed in the room. The younger children often wandered around, playing with the toys and talking with other people, while the older children were more likely to divide their attention between the television and the toys.

Preschoolers generally lack understanding of the nature of attention and strategies for maintaining attention and shutting out distractions (Flavell and Miller, 1998). For example, 4-year-olds do not usually recognize that focusing attention on one thing, such as trying to identify the people in a group picture or listening to a friend talk, means they will not be able to attend simultaneously to something else, such as the characteristics of the picture frame or instructions being given by the teacher. During the preschool years, children become increasingly skilled at deploying their attention, but not until middle childhood do they conceive of attention as a limited resource that must be deployed selectively (Miller, 1985; Miller and Harris, 1990).

Preschoolers' Memory

One Friday evening when Mikey was 3, his parents decided to go to the beach the next day. Mikey was very excited but did little planning for the trip. If Christine hadn't made a list of what to take along, Mikey would have forgotten most of his favorite toys. Three years later, when Mikey was 6, another trip to the beach was planned. This time Mikey thought about what he wanted to take and hoped he wouldn't forget anything. When he saw Christine putting together a number of things to take, he gathered his toys and added them to the pile. Three years later, when Mikey was 9, he often went to the beach on summer days. At this age, Mikey was much more organized in his efforts to remember. The night before, on his own, he would place his kite and fishing gear at the front door to make sure he would see them on his way out.

This example illustrates many key features of memory development. Young preschoolers are often oblivious to the memory demands of a situation. Thinking about the need to remember doesn't occur to them, even though they may be devastated if they forget something important to them. By the end of the preschool years, children are often aware that a particular task requires remembering, but they are not very good at generating a plan to facilitate memory. Mikey at age 6 simply copied his mother's strategy by adding to her pile. Although Mikey didn't generate his own plan, he at least recognized his mother's plan was effective. Finally, by age 9, Mikey spontaneously used intentional memory strategies: he put the things he wanted to take in a place where he knew he'd see them. In this section we focus on the aspects of memory development that occur during the preschool years.

Abilities and Limitations   In their daily activities preschoolers demonstrate both **recognition memory** (the ability to perceive a particular stimulus as familiar) and **free recall** (the ability to spontaneously pull information out of long-term memory for current use). Sometimes preschoolers' skills at recognition and recall are quite impressive. For example, at age 3 Mikey could recognize a wide variety of construction vehicles and equipment, from backhoes to stone crushers to excavators and road rollers. Malcolm at 5 could rattle off the names and home cities of basketball teams that his mother had trouble recalling. Studies verify that preschoolers often absorb a tremendous amount of information in the course of normal activities, such as a trip to an amusement park (Hamond and Fivush, 1991). As we mentioned in Chapter 5, it is during the preschool years that *autobiographical memory* emerges, and most people's earliest memories date from around age 3½ or 4.

In laboratory settings, preschoolers do best on *recognition* memory tasks, particularly those involving memory for spatial location, such as games like *Concentration* and *Memory* (Schneider and Bjorklund, 1998). One reason for their strong performance on these tasks is that visual/spatial memory skills are more highly developed than verbal memory skills in early childhood (Schumann-Hengsteler, 1992).

However, preschoolers usually perform poorly compared with older children and adults when asked to *recall* things like a set of pictures or numbers (Flavell et al., 2002). Consider how they do on a digit span test, in which numbers of increasing length are read at a rate of one digit per second and they must repeat the numbers out loud. The

Recognition memory:
The ability to perceive a particular stimulus as familiar.

Free recall:
The ability to spontaneously pull information out of long-term memory.

Autobiographical memory emerges in early childhood and is fostered by conversations with parents about past events.

longest number preschoolers can remember averages only four digits, compared with five digits for 6- to 8-year-olds, six digits for 9- to 12-year-olds, and eight digits for college students (Chi, 1978).

There are several explanations for this poor performance. There is some evidence that speed of information processing—and therefore the amount of information that makes it from the sensory register into short-term memory—increases throughout childhood and into adulthood (Schneider and Bjorklund, 1998). In addition, preschoolers may be less familiar with the number names they are asked to remember, and they may be less able to use intentional memory strategies. When preschoolers know as much about a topic as older children do, and when the task prevents the use of memory-enhancing strategies, preschoolers sometimes remember as well as older children. For example, in one study people were asked if they recognized pictures of cartoon characters viewed the previous day, when they had not been told they would be given a memory test. In this situation, preschoolers remembered just as well as older children and even adults (Chi and Ceci, 1987). But when people are *instructed* to remember material, older children and adults almost always perform better than preschoolers, partly because they know better how to go about remembering (Flavell et al., 2002).

Sometimes young children do use memory strategies, especially when simple strategies are fairly obvious (Schneider and Bjorklund, 1998). In one study, researchers hid a toy dog under one of several containers, asked preschoolers to remember where the toy was, and then left the room and observed the children through a one-way mirror (Wellman, Ritter, and Flavell, 1975). Even 3-year-olds sometimes used memory strategies, such as staring at the correct container, moving it away from the others so it was easy to recognize, or resting their hand on it. But preschoolers' occasional active efforts to memorize information or to search systematically for something are the exceptions rather than the rule.

In most cases, preschoolers perform significantly worse on memory tasks than older children because their memory strategies are still so limited (Schneider and Bjorklund, 1998). Most children younger than 5 do not spontaneously rehearse information—that is, they don't go over it several times in their minds to encourage retention. Whatever memory strategies preschoolers initially use tend to be limited, context-specific, and inconsistently applied. With further development, these strategies become more general and more consistent, and memory performance improves.

Adult Involvement in Children's Memory Performance The adults in preschoolers' lives are often involved in various ways in the formation and retrieval of children's memories. By prompting children to talk about past events, parents foster the emergence of autobiographical memory and influence its contents (Harley and Reese, 1999). Parents and other adults can also influence preschoolers' memory performance by suggesting simple memory strategies that children would not typically think of on their own, such as rehearsing a list of items to be remembered or placing an item near the door so it won't be forgotten on the way to preschool.

Vygotsky's concept of the zone of proximal development, introduced in Chapter 1, provides a perspective for viewing adult involvement in children's memory storage and retrieval. Recall that the zone of proximal development focuses on the gap between a child's current performance and potential performance with guidance by someone more skilled. Vygotsky emphasized the role of more knowledgeable others in helping children make progress within their zones of proximal development by building on skills they already have. For example, preschool children who are asked to remember a set of

Child Development CD
Piaget vs. Vygotsky

pictures may simply look at the pictures and do nothing else. It is not that they are totally unaware that there are things that can be done to improve memory; it is usually just that they don't know what to do. However, if an adult suggests repeatedly going through the set and saying the name of each picture out loud, most preschoolers are able to make use of the suggestion and improve their performance on the memory task.

Adults' influence on young children's memory has practical implications for preschoolers' reliability as witnesses—for example, in suspected cases of sexual abuse. A question that often arises in such cases is whether child witnesses are recalling events that really happened to them or whether they are recalling events interviewers have put into their heads. Asking a leading question just once isn't usually enough to change a young child's memory (Saywitz et al., 1991), but *repeatedly* asking suggestive questions can be influential, especially when the questioning occurs some time after the event.

This was shown in a study by Stephen Ceci and colleagues (White, Leichtman, and Ceci, 1997). Preschool children witnessed a game and were questioned about it a month later by two adults who had not seen it. The adults were told to use whatever strategies they thought would elicit accurate reports. Before questioning the children, they were told some things that *might* have happened in the game, but this information was true only half the time. When the adults were correctly informed, the children accurately reported 93 percent of the events from the game. But when the adults were incorrectly informed, about one-third of 3- and 4-year-olds claimed to recall one or more pieces of false information. Apparently, the adults formed hypotheses about what had happened and these influenced what they said in the interviews, to the point that they sometimes got children to corroborate false information.

This study suggests that adults with hypotheses about what a child experienced sometimes make inadvertent suggestions when questioning the child. Reviewing highly publicized cases, Ceci found that interviewers often pursue their suspicions about a child's experiences, even when the child initially denies them (Ceci and Bruck, 1998). If an interviewer makes a suggestion repeatedly, a young child can be swayed to believe it, even if it isn't true.

Research on young children's suggestibility has important policy implications. Adults must be careful how they interview child witnesses. When interviewers believe an accused person is guilty, they may convey that belief in their questions and may get children to corroborate it, even if it is false. The more an interviewer persists in suggesting events, the more credible and less hesitant the child's corroboration becomes (White et al., 1997). Interviewers often praise children for reporting events that match their own beliefs and reprimand them for sticking to another story. They may also tell young witnesses that other children have already confirmed their suspicions, creating additional pressure (Ceci and Bruck, 1998). Stricter guidelines for interviewing child witnesses are needed to prevent inappropriate questioning.

The susceptibility of preschoolers to repeated suggestions does not mean their testimony is always suspect. Young children's testimony is most likely to be accurate if: (1) they are asked concrete but open-ended questions that do not suggest a certain answer, (2) they are reminded that the adult questioning them doesn't know what happened, and (3) they receive moderate levels of social support from the questioner (Saywitz and Lyon, 2002).

Child Witnesses

SOCIAL COGNITION

The improvements in memory skills and other aspects of thinking that occur during the preschool years have an impact on children's understanding of the social world, or **social cognition.** During the preschool period children start to learn how other people think and feel, what their motives and intentions are, and what they are likely to do. They begin to understand that other people's perspectives sometimes differ from their own, which helps them communicate more effectively. Also aiding communication is the

Social cognition:
A child's understanding of the social world.

general understanding preschoolers acquire about how various social exchanges are supposed to be carried out. All this new knowledge about the social world enables children to respond more appropriately to other people and to relate to them in more mature ways. More mature social relationships, in turn, provide children with additional knowledge that fosters their cognitive growth. Thus, the development of social cognition is an excellent example of how cognitive and social development are interdependent, constantly influencing each other.

Egocentrism in Preschoolers

As we mentioned in the introduction to the chapter, Piaget believed preschoolers' thought was characterized by egocentrism, the inability to understand others' perspectives. Egocentrism is a cognitive limitation that appears at all levels of development (Elkind, 1978), but it is most obvious and most often studied in preschoolers. One of the authors of this book once saw a 4-year-old girl put her fingers in her ears and ask her father, "Can you hear me?" When he responded "No," she raised her voice and asked, "Can you hear me now?" There are two illustrations of egocentrism in this example. First, the little girl apparently believed that because she put her fingers in her ears she made it hard for her father to hear. She was demonstrating *perceptual egocentrism* by not differentiating her own perceptual experience from that of her father. Second, when the father answered "No" to the child's first question, she repeated the question more loudly, showing lack of awareness that his response meant her father must have heard her. Here the little girl demonstrated *cognitive egocentrism* by failing to take into account her father's cognitive perspective and realize that he was only teasing her. Examples of perceptual egocentrism abound in the preschool period. One day 4-year-old Maggie asked Christine if she could call her grandmother to tell her about her new shoes. "Look, Grandma," Maggie said into the receiver, as she held up one foot. "Aren't they beautiful?"

Piaget used an ingenious research technique called the Three-Mountain Task to study perceptual egocentrism. In this task, children were first allowed to inspect all sides of a large model of a mountain range (see Figure 9.5). Then they were asked to pick out a picture of the model that showed it as viewed by a person sitting on the model's opposite side. Four-year-olds had trouble with this task, and it was not until age 9 to 10 that children reliably picked the correct picture. However, the Three-Mountain Task is complex and places considerable memory demands on children. On simpler tasks, preschoolers give indications that their perceptual egocentrism is not complete. For example, when shown a block that is red on one side and white on the other, they can often correctly identify the color viewed by a person looking at the opposite side.

Cognitive egocentrism is also common in preschoolers. Young children assume, for example, that others have the same knowledge and beliefs that they do. Suppose a young preschooler sees cookies being hidden in a crayon box, and then a second child enters the room (Moses and Flavell, 1990). When asked what the second child thinks is in the box, the first child will answer "cookies," not "crayons." Apparently, a young preschooler can't adopt the other child's perspective. Because the first child *knows* there are cookies in the box, he or she can't imagine another person answering anything else. This

Figure 9.5

PIAGET'S THREE-MOUNTAIN TASK

In this task, a child sits in position 1, looking at this three-mountain display. When asked which picture, (A), (B), or (C), demonstrates how the display would look to a child sitting in position 4, preschoolers often incorrectly select their own view (C) rather than correctly choosing (A).

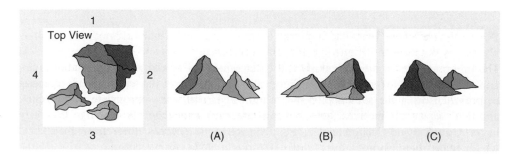

egocentrism may be closely connected to difficulties with the appearance-reality distinction. Preschoolers behave as if the way the world appears to them is reality, and so their own perspective *must* be shared by everyone else.

Cognitive egocentrism also includes knowledge about others' desires and wishes. It can be seen in a study John Flavell conducted by asking children ages 3 to 6 to select gifts for various people—their mother, their father, a brother or a sister if they had one, their teacher, and themselves (Flavell et al., 1968). The gifts to choose from included silk stockings, a necktie, a toy truck, a doll, and an adult book. Three-year-olds showed clear egocentrism by often selecting dolls and trucks for their mothers and fathers. They failed to differentiate their own desires from those of adults. If they wanted a doll or a truck, they presumed everyone else wanted one too.

But this study also showed the gradual progress older preschoolers make in overcoming egocentrism. Unlike the 3-year-olds, the 4-year-olds seemed aware that everyone in the world might not want what they want, although they still had trouble taking an adult's perspective and picking an appropriate gift. Interestingly, the 4-year-olds were more egocentric in making a gift choice for a teacher than for a parent, perhaps because they knew more about what parents buy for themselves. It was not until age 5 that 50 percent of the children chose appropriate gifts for everyone on the list; and it was not until age 6 that *all* the children chose appropriately. Thus, during the preschool period, children come to realize others may have desires different from their own, and they begin to take another person's perspective in trying to determine what that person's wishes might be.

Flavell has analyzed the cognitive components needed to overcome egocentrism and to take another's perspective (Flavell et al., 2002). First, children must realize that other people have thoughts, viewpoints, and desires that may differ from their own. Flavell calls this a *knowledge of existence of alternate viewpoints*. Second, children must realize it can be useful to consider another's perspective, that doing so can facilitate social interaction and communication. Flavell calls this an *awareness of need to consider other viewpoints*. Finally, children must become skilled at *social inference*. They must be able to read another person's actions and imagine that person's point of view.

The same cognitive components enable children to understand others' feelings and emotions. Very early signs of sensitivity to other people's feelings are not indications children truly comprehend what others feel. For instance, the social referencing of early toddlerhood, in which children take cues from the caregiver's face in novel situations, involves only a primitive awareness of the caregiver's feelings. Not until about age 4 is there strong evidence that children interpret facial expressions as belonging to general categories, such as "feels good" and "feels bad" (Shantz, 1975). More finely tuned interpretations of other people's feelings take substantially longer to develop. Even adults often have trouble with the inference part of this process. They recognize the existence of other people's feelings and the need to assess them, but they aren't always correct in deducing what those feelings are. In preschoolers, the emerging ability to grasp other people's feelings does not mean this new skill is regularly used. Its use is still quite limited (Flavell et al., 2002). We will return to the topic of understanding others' feelings when we discuss the development of empathy in Chapter 10.

The Child's Theory of Mind

During the preschool years children are constructing an understanding not only of physical reality but also of the human mind and such concepts as *knowing, wanting, thinking, remembering,* and *intending*. This understanding of the mind and mental operations constitutes the child's **theory of mind.** The term *theory* may seem excessive when referring to preschoolers' understanding of the mind, but it really is appropriate here. Young children's grasp of the mind goes beyond *empirical knowledge* (knowledge based on experience and observation in the physical world) to include *theoretical knowledge* (explanations based on constructs that cannot be directly observed).

Theory of mind:
An understanding of the mind and mental operations.

Preschoolers' Theory of Mind

In developing a theory of mind, children come to understand five fundamental principles, according to developmental psychologist John Flavell (Flavell et al., 2002). The first principle is simply that *minds exist*. Babies do not understand the existence of minds, even though they may be able to distinguish things that have minds (living things capable of moving and experiencing the world) from things without minds (inanimate objects) (Flavell, 1999; Wellman and Gelman, 1992). During the toddler period children start referring to mental states such as feelings and desires, which tells us they have begun to grasp the notion that minds exist. Thus, this important first principle is established even before the preschool years.

The second principle in the child's theory of mind is that *minds have connections to the physical world*. That is, what people think, feel, know, and want is linked to the objects and events around them. Substantial improvement in this understanding occurs between the ages of 2 and 3. For example, 3-year-olds (but not 2-year-olds) know that if something is hidden in a container, someone who has looked in the container *knows* it is there, whereas someone who hasn't looked doesn't know (unless that person saw the object being hidden or has been told where it is) (Pratt and Bryant, 1990). But though 3- and 4-year-olds know that what is in the mind has connections to the physical world, their understanding of the nature of those connections is very limited. They still make mistakes in predicting the kind of experiences needed to know certain things, and they also make errors in predicting how particular kinds of knowledge will influence behavior (Flavell et al., 2002).

The third principle that children come to understand is that *minds are separate and different from the physical world*. For example, 3-year-olds know the mind can fantasize about things that don't really exist (Wellman and Estes, 1986). They know that if one child has a cookie and another is thinking about a cookie, only one of those cookies can actually be seen and touched. This new understanding of mental events makes children less fearful of imagined ghosts and monsters, although such fears are not entirely gone. Even adults, after all, are often apprehensive after seeing ghosts and monsters in a horror film (Flavell et al., 2002).

Fourth, children come to understand the principle that *minds can represent objects and events accurately or inaccurately*. Understanding this idea requires that children reflect on mental representations, so it is not usually grasped by 2- and 3-year-olds. Four- and 5-year-olds, however, clearly exhibit some understanding of it. In one study, children heard a story about a boy who put some candy in a blue cabinet, and while he was out playing his mother moved it to a green cupboard (Wimmer and Perner, 1983). The children were asked where the boy would look for the candy when he came back. Three-year-olds predicted the green cupboard (where they knew the candy really was), but 4- and 5-year-olds predicted the blue cabinet (where they knew the boy *thought* it was). Apparently, 4- and 5-year-olds are able to reflect on the accuracy of the boy's beliefs and predict how a false belief will affect his behavior. Notice that the belief-reality distinction involved in this example is very similar to the appearance-reality distinction discussed earlier, and the two distinctions show similar developmental patterns (Flavell, 1999).

Finally, children come to understand a fifth principle: that *minds actively interpret reality and emotional experiences*. The beginnings of this understanding are revealed in success on tasks that involve false beliefs, like the one in the study just described. Preschoolers are very limited in this understanding, however. They tend to treat mental representations as passively acquired copies of real events, not as actively constructed *ideas* about reality. Even children as old as 8 believe everyone who hears the same message, regardless of their ages, will understand it in the same way (Montgomery, 1993). Similarly, it is not until well into middle childhood that children become aware that emotional responses are influenced not just by what happens but also by a person's prior feelings and expectations (Gnepp, 1989).

Developmental psychologists widely agree that children acquire a theory of mind from their experiences in the world, especially their social experiences (Flavell, 1999). For example, children with multiple siblings seem to understand the belief-reality

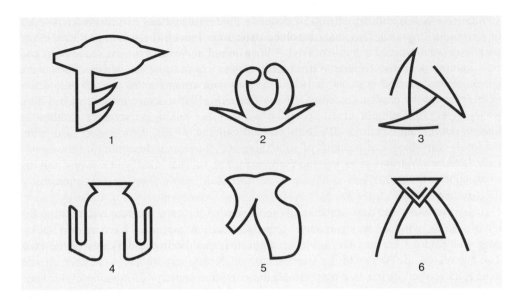

Figure 9.6
PICTURES ON BLOCKS IN GLUCKSBERG AND KRAUSS'S COMMUNICATION EXPERIMENT
Preschoolers had great difficulty communicating orally the nature of these abstract designs. When simpler geometric shapes in different colors were used, preschoolers could communicate much more effectively. *(Reprinted from "What do people say after they have learned to talk? Studies of the development of referential communication,"* Merrill-Palmer Quarterly, 13, *1967 by S. Glucksberg and R. M. Krauss by permission of the Wayne State University Press.)*

distinction sooner than other children. In the next section you will see how social experiences help preschoolers overcome egocentrism, in a process closely linked to developing a more mature theory of mind.

Communication and the Decline of Egocentrism

Communicating with others involves more than simply having a vocabulary and knowing how to put words together. It also involves an understanding of how to participate in conversations. How much information do others require to understand your meaning? Which of your ideas must you spell out in detail and which can your listeners infer? How do you know when clarifications are needed? Children start to understand these aspects of communication during the preschool period. One way to conceptualize their progress in this area is to think of it as part of a general decline in egocentrism.

Of course, how egocentric a young child's speech is often depends on the complexity of the communication task. This was demonstrated in a study by Sam Glucksberg and Robert Krauss (1967), who had two children sit on opposite sides of a screen, with identical sets of blocks in front of them. Each block had on it one of the abstract designs shown in Figure 9.6. The children's task was to stack the blocks in exactly the same order without either of them seeing what the other was doing. One of the children was given the job of describing each block to the other so that the second child could pick it out of the pile and add it to his or her stack. Four- and 5-year-olds performed very poorly on this task because they gave so many egocentric and uninformative descriptions: "A curved part of a pipe," the child might say, or simply "The first one." Often, the children seemed to ignore the fact that neither of them could see what the other was talking about, as in the following exchange:

> Speaker: It's a bird.
> Listener: Is this it?
> Speaker: No.
> (Glucksberg, Krauss, and Higgins, 1975, p. 321)

These results do not mean preschoolers can *never* analyze what a listener needs to know to understand their meaning. In more conducive circumstances they *can* convey their ideas to others in ways that are understood. For instance, when the abstract figures on the blocks in Glucksberg and Krauss's study were replaced with simple geometric shapes in different colors (a yellow circle, a blue square, etc.), preschoolers were much more successful at describing them to another child. In another study, preschoolers spontaneously adapted the amount of detail in their explanations to suit the knowledge of particular listeners. This study involved exposing 4-year-olds to a staged accident in which an adult spilled a cup of punch. When asked a week later why the empty cup was in the room, the children varied their answers depending on whether they were speaking to the adult who had knocked the cup over or to another person who knew nothing about the previous accident (Menig-Peterson, 1975). As we mentioned in Chapter 7, 4-year-olds simplify their speech when they are talking to younger children or infants (Dunn and Kendrick, 1982b; Shatz and Gelman, 1973). Preschoolers also spontaneously vary their clarifications of something they have said depending on the age of their listener (Warren-Leubecker and Bohannon, 1983). They clarify one way if talking to an adult and another way if talking to another child, again showing an awareness of the listener's needs.

If preschoolers do have some ability to vary what they say in accordance with a listener's needs, why did they perform so poorly in early experiments like that of Glucksberg and Krauss? The answer, as we've suggested, may lie in the difficulty of the task. The figures on the blocks in the Glucksberg and Krauss experiment were abstract and hard to describe. Such a task may use all the cognitive capacity of a young child, leaving nothing for use in determining an appropriate wording. As a result, the child lapses into egocentric wording that does not take into account the listener's needs (Shatz, 1978).

The studies of children's communication skills demonstrate an important distinction that can be helpful in understanding seemingly contradictory research evidence on cognitive development: the **competence-performance distinction.** Simply put, there is often a difference between what children—and adults, for that matter—are *capable* of doing under optimal circumstances (competence) and how they actually *do* on a particular task (performance). Every time you get back an exam and say to yourself, "That grade doesn't reflect what I really know," you're experiencing a version of the competence-performance distinction. Performance is often affected by the cognitive demands of tasks and of the environments in which they are being attempted.

Which tasks and environments are best to use for studying cognitive development depends on whether the goal is to determine children's maximum skill—competence—or their more typical performance. Competence in a particular domain or on a particular task is best measured by limiting other cognitive demands in the environment as much as possible. On the other hand, to find out how children *typically* perform, it is better to

Competence-performance distinction:
The difference between what children are capable of doing under optimal circumstances and how they actually do on a particular task.

Preschoolers adjust their speech to their conversation partner. For example, they use simpler terms when talking to younger children than with peers or adults.

make sure they are in an environment with all the demands and distractions usually found in a natural setting. For example, in a laboratory task Malcolm might be able to settle a disagreement with a peer more maturely than he settled the disagreement with April. But in a natural setting like a playground, where many cognitive demands are simultaneously occurring (the argument itself, shouted suggestions from friends, the perceptual distraction of other children at play), resorting to force is a course of action that many 5-year-olds would take.

Limited Cognitive Resources and Communication

One of the ways preschoolers are able to communicate and interact with others effectively, despite their limited cognitive resources, is through the use of scripts for common routines (Myles-Worsley, Cromer, and Dodd, 1986; Nelson and Gruendel, 1979; Schank and Abelson, 1977). A **script** is an abstract representation of a sequence of actions needed to accomplish some goal. Most preschoolers have scripts for a variety of routines they experience in their daily lives, such as eating at a fast-food restaurant, going to a birthday party, or shopping in a supermarket. Here is a conversation between two 4-year-olds that shows they have acquired the basics of a "talking on the phone" script:

Script:
An abstract representation of the sequence of actions needed to accomplish some goal.

Gay: Hi.
Daniel: Hi.
Gay: How are you?
Daniel: Fine.
Gay: Who am I speaking to?
Daniel: This is your daddy. I need to speak to you.
Gay: All right.
Daniel: When I come tonight, we're gonna have peanut butter and jelly
           sandwich, uh, at dinnertime.
Gay: Uhmmm. Where're we going at dinnertime?
Daniel: Nowhere. But we're just gonna have dinner at 11 o'clock.
Gay: Well, I made a plan of going out tonight.
Daniel: We're going out.
(Nelson and Gruendel, 1979, p. 76)

Preschoolers and Scripts

Preschoolers quickly learn the format of a birthday party: you arrive, you play games, you have cake and ice cream. This format is an example of a script.

Katherine Nelson, one of the researchers who recorded this conversation, believes such scripts can be learned either by firsthand experience or by observation of others. Meryl's "going shopping" script, seen in the story that precedes this chapter, was probably acquired by watching her mother and checkout clerks at the supermarket. Notice that a script only occasionally involves *specific* words or actions (such as singing "Happy Birthday"). More often, what is acquired is a *general* idea of the appropriate things to say and do; learning a script is more complex than just memorizing exactly what one saw or did.

When young children communicate with adults instead of with peers, a knowledge of scripts is probably less essential. Usually the adult ensures that the dialogue progresses smoothly, that intended meanings are understood, and that confusions are clarified (Ellis and Rogoff, 1986). This is another example of the role of more knowledgeable others within the zone of proximal development. In peer interactions, in contrast, children must monitor and coordinate their own conversations. A shared understanding of the scripts for various activities can greatly facilitate communication.

APPLYING RESEARCH FINDINGS

School Readiness

An issue of interest to parents, teachers, researchers, and policy-makers alike is the question of how to judge children's readiness for school. Cognitive development in early childhood, including improvements in attention, memory, and reasoning skills, helps to prepare children for the demands of formal education. Measures of broad cognitive skills, such as visual discrimination and auditory memory, do predict later academic achievement (Kurdek and Sinclair, 2001). However, school readiness extends far beyond the cognitive domain.

School readiness is often assumed to be reflected in children's performance on several key preacademic skills: knowing the letters of the alphabet, colors, and shapes, and being able to count to 20 and write their own names. Many preschool programs devote considerable time to teaching these skills, and school districts are increasingly likely to test children on them as they enter kindergarten (Meisels, 1999). Although these skills are easy to assess, there is little evidence that *by themselves* these isolated skills predict children's success in school. However, they do tend to be associated with demographic factors that *are* correlated with success in school. For example, preschool mastery of these skills is associated with gender (girls > boys), race and ethnicity (Asian > white > Black > Hispanic), language spoken at home (English-speaking > non-English-speaking), mother's education, family structure (two-parent homes > single-parent homes), and family income (U.S. Census Bureau, 2002b).

Interestingly, when American kindergarten teachers were asked in a large-scale national survey what children need to be ready for kindergarten, they ranked the following characteristics as most important: (1) being physically healthy, rested, and well-nourished, (2) being able to communicate needs, wants, and thoughts verbally, and (3) being enthusiastic and curious about new activities (NCES, 1993). There is increasing evidence that work-related social skills, such as listening to instructions, cooperation,

and self-control, are good predictors of school success, even when socioeconomic status and kindergarten academic achievement are controlled for (McClelland, Morrison, and Holmes, 2000).

In short, school readiness includes much more than the specific preacademic skills often assumed to be essential for success in kindergarten (Meisels, 1999). School readiness includes aspects of social development (e.g., ability to play and learn in a group), emotional development (e.g., self-control, confidence, willingness to try new things), language development (e.g., ability to understand directions and express needs), motor development (e.g., self-help skills, fine motor skills), and intellectual and academic development (e.g., ability to focus on an activity for 10–15 minutes, problem-solving skills) (CEED, 2001).

Parents can do much to help prepare children for starting school. Reading to children fosters literacy-related skills and communicates that reading is a valued and enjoyable activity. Exposing children to a variety of environments and activities helps to build their base of knowledge about the world. Encouraging physical activity and making sure children get good nutrition and adequate rest enhance health and physical stamina. Arranging experiences with other children and adults outside the family helps to prepare children for the social demands of school. Providing responsive caregiving and a structured environment helps children develop self-management skills and emotional resources needed to function in classroom environments.

Finally, at least as important as children's readiness for school is the readiness of schools for the children they serve (Pianta, Rimm-Kaufman, and Cox, 1999). Children's chances of educational success are increased if their school's curriculum is developmentally appropriate, if the relationship between school and home is strong and positive, and if the school responds appropriately to children's individual and cultural differences.

AN OVERVIEW OF PRESCHOOL COGNITIVE DEVELOPMENT

As we suggested at the beginning of the chapter, children enter the preschool period with a number of cognitive advantages over infants and toddlers, as well as several important cognitive limitations. Building on the sensorimotor abilities acquired in infancy and the mental representation skills that emerged during toddlerhood, they begin to reason in ways that are qualitatively different from the ones they used earlier. Their new thinking skills help prepare them for the beginning of formal education, as discussed in the box on page 330. Cognitive advances during the preschool years include:

School Readiness

- emerging understanding of causation, especially in simple or familiar systems;
- an ability to make clear distinctions between living and nonliving things;
- a qualitative understanding of many concepts related to quantity and an ability to reason about small numbers;
- a beginning understanding of classification and other logical relations;
- gradual development of the ability to distinguish between appearance and reality;
- expanding attention and memory skills; and
- steadily increasing understanding of others' perspectives and thoughts.

By the end of the preschool years, children have overcome some of the cognitive constraints that were present at the beginning of the period. They are no longer greatly affected by the appearance-reality problem, and their tendency toward centration has greatly declined. They are still hampered by their relative lack of strategies for effective deployment of attentional and memory resources. However, most of the abilities that will continue to develop during middle childhood are present in at least primitive form.

Chapter Summary

Introduction

Preschoolers' thinking differs in fundamental ways from that of infants and toddlers, but they still have three main cognitive limitations:

- difficulty integrating multiple pieces of information;
- difficulty distinguishing between appearance and reality; and
- difficulty managing attentional and memory processes.

Preschoolers' Reasoning Abilities

Piaget characterized the period from ages 2 to 7 as the **preoperational period.** The issues he explored set an agenda for research on cognitive development.

- Piaget did not find mature reasoning about causation until middle childhood, but more recent research suggests preschoolers can understand causation in simple systems and familiar processes.
- Piaget believed preschoolers tended to attribute life to nonliving things; more recent research shows that children begin to make clear distinctions between living and nonliving things by age 3.
- A mature understanding of **conservation** does not emerge until middle childhood. For each type of conservation, children pass through *nonconserver* and *transitional* stages on the way to *mature conservation.*
- New cognitive skills can sometimes be taught to children sooner than they would otherwise acquire them, but only if they already have a cognitive framework into which the new skills can be integrated.
- Preschoolers have some understanding of the effects of addition and subtraction on small numbers, but they do not develop *quantitative rules* for carrying out these processes until ages 6 to 7.
- Learning to count depends on mastering the *one-to-one, stable-order, cardinal, abstraction,* and *order-irrelevant principles.*
- Preschoolers have an intuitive, qualitative concept of measurement, but they cannot yet make precise, truly quantitative measurements.

- Piaget originally underestimated preschoolers' **classification, seriation,** and **transitive inference skills;** more recent research gives us a more complete picture of their abilities in these areas.
- Preschoolers gradually develop the ability to distinguish between appearance and reality. Early on, their problems in this area are not as pervasive as once thought. By age 6 they have largely overcome this limitation.

Preschoolers' Attention and Memory Abilities

Preschoolers have a number of attentional and memory limitations, but they gradually develop **attention** and **memory skills** that help them master other cognitive tasks.

- Preschoolers user fewer strategies for deploying attentional resources than older children do; they scan less systematically and are more distracted by irrelevant information.
- In everyday life, preschoolers exhibit good **recognition memory** and **free recall.** In laboratory settings, they do best on recognition tasks, especially those involving spatial location.
- Preschoolers' memory limitations can be explained by their slow information-processing speed, their limited knowledge base, and their lack of memory strategies.
- Adults are often involved in the formation and retrieval of children's memories. Their influence has practical implications for preschoolers' reliability as witnesses.

Social Cognition

Improvements in memory and other cognitive skills during the preschool years increase children's understanding of the social world.

- Piaget characterized preschoolers' thought as **egocentric.** There is ample evidence of both *perceptual* and *cognitive* egocentrism in preschoolers' thinking, but it is not as absolute as Piaget believed.
- Children's **theory of mind** is based on an understanding of five fundamental principles:

- minds exist;
- minds have connections to the physical world;
- minds are separate and different from the physical world;
- minds can represent objects and events accurately or inaccurately; and
- minds actively interpret reality and emotional experiences.

- The development of children's communication skills during the preschool years reflects declining egocentrism. Seemingly contradictory results of studies of children's communication skills demonstrate the **competence-performance distinction.**
- An understanding of **scripts** allows preschoolers to make the most of limited cognitive resources, especially when interacting with other children.

An Overview of Preschool Cognitive Development

Cognitive advances during the preschool years include:

- emerging understanding of causation, especially in simple or familiar systems;
- an ability to make clear distinctions between living and nonliving things;
- a qualitative understanding of many concepts related to quantity and an ability to reason about small numbers;
- a beginning understanding of classification and other logical relations;
- gradual development of the ability to distinguish between appearance and reality;
- expanding attention and memory skills; and
- steadily increasing understanding of others' perspectives and thoughts.

One major constraint remaining at the end of the period is a relative lack of attention and memory strategies. Most of the abilities that will continue to develop during middle childhood are present in at least primitive form.

Review Questions

Introduction

1. What major cognitive limitations do preschoolers have?

Preschoolers' Reasoning Abilities

2. How did Piaget characterize the preschool period?
3. Compare Piaget's ideas about preschoolers' causal reasoning and understanding of living and nonliving things to more recent research findings.

4. Trace the development of children's understanding of **conservation.**
5. What do preschoolers understand about number and measurement?
6. Summarize preschoolers' understanding of **classification** and other logical relations.
7. What difficulties do preschoolers have with the **appearance-reality problem?**

Preschoolers' Attention and Memory Abilities

8. Describe preschoolers' attentional limitations.
9. Summarize preschoolers' memory strengths and weaknesses.

Social Cognition

10. To what extent do preschoolers show evidence of **egocentrism?**

11. Describe the development of preschoolers' **theory of mind.**
12. Explain how **scripts** help preschoolers make the most of their cognitive resources.

An Overview of Preschool Cognitive Development

13. What are the major cognitive advances made during the preschool years?

Application and Observation

1. Try out Piaget's conservation of liquid volume and conservation of number tasks, described on pages 309–312, with several children between the ages of 3 and 12. How does their performance compare to each other's and to Piaget's findings?

2. Watch an episode of *Sesame Street* or another educational television show aimed at preschoolers and analyze how and to what extent it fits preschoolers' cognitive abilities. Take note of *(a)* aspects of the show that seem to be designed with preschoolers' existing cognitive skills in mind and *(b)* what cognitive skills the show seems to be trying to teach. (For greater insight into how the show actually fits children's cognitive abilities, watch the show with a preschooler and take note of his or her behavior in response to it.)

3. Visit a toy store and look at toys and games labeled as appropriate for preschoolers (3- to 6-year-olds). How well do the recommended ages correspond to what you have learned about preschoolers' cognitive skills? What specific cognitive abilities and limitations seem to have been taken into consideration in designing and recommending toys for this age group? How are the toys different from those intended for younger and for older children?

4. Observe young children in a preschool or day care setting, taking particular note of behavior that sheds light on their cognitive development. What evidence do you see of memory or attentional limitations, appearance-reality problems, counting and other quantitative reasoning, classification skills, understanding of (or trying to figure out) causality, the use of scripts, or advances/limitations in social cognitive reasoning?

10 Social and Emotional Development in Early Childhood

335

F ive-year-old Mikey stands in line with twenty other kindergartners, just ahead
of Benito and Richie, two of his neighborhood friends. The three boys are
eager to be out on the playground, but they wait for the teacher to swing open
the door. Then, without pushing, they walk out quietly but quickly with the class.
Once outside in the bright October sunshine, their self-restraint breaks down.
Shouting with glee, they race toward the play equipment. "Hey! It's a boat!"
Mikey calls, pointing to a large climbing structure in the center of a sand-filled
area. The structure, made of wood, ropes, and old tires, looks nothing like a boat,
but its placement in the middle of the sand inspires the boys' imaginations.
"C'mon!" Mikey urges, and the other two scramble up behind him. They play
joyously for a time, taking turns being captain. Just when their excitement has
begun to subside, Benito yells in mock alarm: "Oh, no! We're sinkin'! Swim for
it!" With that, he jumps into the sand and begins flailing his arms and legs.
Laughing and shouting, the others jump off too, and the trio makes its way to
"shore."

This episode, drawn from a detailed observational study of preschool behavior (Sroufe
et al., 1984), illustrates much about the social achievements of early childhood. First,
children between the ages of 2½ and 5 experience a *dramatically expanding world*. In
industrialized cultures, day care, preschool, and kindergarten take them increasingly away
from home and parents; in many nonindustrialized cultures, starting at about age 2
children spend much of their time in mixed-age groups of children, rather than with their
mothers (Whiting and Edwards, 1988). In these new settings young children are propelled by a natural curiosity to explore. No one has to tell Mikey and his friends to play
on the climbing structure. The motivation and ideas for their activities come from
themselves. Notice too how the boys' world is enlarged by their rich interactions with
one another. Early childhood is the age when true peer relationships emerge. This capacity for relationships with peers will expand and become more elaborate throughout
childhood.

Second, early childhood is a time of *notable developments in self-reliance, self-
control and self-regulation* (Kochanska, Murray, and Harlan, 2000; Kochanska et al.,
2001). Toddlers are not expected to direct their own activities or control their own
impulses without adult guidance. Yet just a few years later children are routinely expected
to tolerate minor delays and frustrations; to control aggressive impulses, such as pushing,

*During early childhood,
children's social worlds expand
and peers become increasingly
important.*

shoving, and hitting; and not to need constant supervision. These new expectations have significant effects on children's developing self-concepts. Whether Mikey thinks of himself as capable or incapable, kind or mean, stems in part from how he meets adults' expectations for self-regulation.

Third, during early childhood youngsters begin to *explore adult roles.* Mikey and his friends take turns being captain of a ship, a role they have heard about in stories and seen on television. This exploration of roles takes place during play, especially social fantasy play. Typically, preschoolers try out the roles of adults they are close to or see often: mother, father, teacher, grocery store clerk, police officer, and so forth. All over the world, children use play to act out both culturally universal adult activities, such as cooking food and caring for children, and culturally specific activities important among adults in their own culture, which might include going to work in an office in North America or paddling canoes and fishing in the South Pacific (Farver and Shin, 1997).

A major theme of this chapter is the *organization and coherence of preschoolers' behavior.* Children's emerging capacities fit together and support one another. For example, the capacity for play supports the capacity for early peer relationships, and vice versa. At the same time, the behavior of individual children becomes increasingly coherent and distinctive; they manifest characteristic styles of responding and clear expectations concerning themselves and others. It is no exaggeration to say that by age 5 a personality has formed.

This chapter explores the social and emotional changes that occur in early childhood. We begin with a closer look at some of the hallmarks of early childhood development we just introduced: the child's expanding world, the move toward greater independence, and the unfolding of self-control and self-management. We then turn to other areas of development that are important in the preschool years, including young children's sense of self, their peer relationships, their emotions, their play, and the influence of their parents.

Questions to Think About As You Read

- How are social, emotional, and cognitive development interrelated in the preschool years?
- What can preschool and day care teachers do to foster healthy social and emotional development in early childhood?

SOME HALLMARKS OF EARLY CHILDHOOD SOCIAL AND EMOTIONAL DEVELOPMENT

The Child's Expanding World

One of the major changes of early childhood is expansion of the child's world. The majority of North American children in this age group spend time outside their homes in day care, preschool, or kindergarten. Experiences at school and in day care can be extremely important. For example, a young child's general adjustment, competence with peers, and complexity of play have all been found to be related to the quality of day care and relationships with teachers (e.g., Peisner-Feinberg et al., 2001; Pianta and Steinberg, 1992).

Child Development CD
Exploration in Early Childhood

Peers also exert an increasing influence during the preschool years. Peer relationships become a central arena for developing and expressing certain new capacities, such as an understanding of fairness and reciprocity (mutual give-and-take).

Because peer relationships are so important, we devote an entire section of this chapter to them.

Sibling relationships, too, become increasingly important. Like parents, older siblings can provide a unique framework within which preschoolers' development takes place. For instance, young preschoolers can engage in joint fantasy play with a nurturant older sibling in a way they cannot do with their mothers (Boer and Dunn, 1992). They also listen carefully to conversations between their mothers and older siblings, as shown by the fact that their interruptions are much more often relevant to what is being said than are the interruptions of 2-year-olds (Dunn and Shatz, 1989). Thus, some of what children learn from siblings is acquired indirectly by watching and listening to them interacting with others. We will discuss sibling relationships more extensively in Chapter 12.

All the new arenas of development that emerge during the preschool years influence one another. Experiences with preschool teachers, for example, influence peer relationships, as do the skills and understanding developed in relating to siblings (DeHart, 1999). At the same time, successful peer relationships can promote better relationships with siblings (Kramer and Gottman, 1992) and tend to elicit more positive responses from teachers.

Moving Toward Greater Self-Reliance

Accompanying the preschooler's entry into a broader world is the development of greater self-reliance. All developmental theorists see this as an important achievement. Psychoanalytic theorists emphasize the child's sense of independent purposefulness, which Erikson (1963) called **initiative.** Social learning theorists, such as Albert Bandura (1997), emphasize the child's growing **self-efficacy,** or sense of being able to do things on his or her own as a result of repeated experiences of mastery.

Greater self-reliance is supported by several capacities of 3- and 4-year-olds:

- motor skills such as climbing and manipulating objects that allow them to do many things for themselves;

- language and other cognitive abilities that enable them to think, plan, and solve problems in ways they could not do as toddlers;

Initiative:
Erikson's term for a child's sense of independent purposefulness.

Self-efficacy:
The sense of being able to do things effectively on one's own.

Some children need a great deal of support and contact from their preschool teachers.

- a growing ability to tolerate delays and frustrations, to stick to a task despite obstacles and setbacks; and

- an emerging capacity for imagination and fantasy play that allows preschoolers to maintain a sense of power in a world generally controlled by adults—an important psychological foundation for strivings toward independence.

Some children, however, have trouble moving toward greater independence. They may hover near teachers or require a great deal of encouragement to meet simple challenges (Sroufe, Fox, and Pancake, 1983). For them, infantile dependency is hard to leave behind. We see this problem in Meryl as a 3-year-old when she clings to Karen in everyday situations. Meryl is not just showing normal **instrumental dependency,** a need for help from adults when trying to solve complex problems or perform difficult tasks. She is also showing **emotional dependency,** an atypical need for continual reassurance and attention from adults (Sears, Maccoby, and Levin, 1957). Emotionally dependent children need such contact not just when they are upset, but virtually all the time. We discuss the origins of such problems in a later section.

Self-Control and Self-Regulation

At a family picnic, Frank is organizing a race between 2-year-old Maggie and her cousins. The children are to run across the yard, touch the big oak tree, and then run back to the starting line. Frank gives the signals "Ready . . . get set . . ." But before he can say "go," Maggie bolts off toward the oak tree, and the other two girls quickly follow. It takes five tries before Frank can get all three girls to wait until they hear the word "go." Are they just not listening to his instructions, or are they really having trouble following them?

A developmental psychologist could tell the greatly exasperated Frank that the second explanation is correct. The ability to inhibit a physical action until given a signal to proceed is something that emerges gradually during the preschool years (Thompson, 1998). The Soviet psychologist A. R. Luria (1961) studied this ability in children ages 2 through 4. When a green light came on, the children were to press a rubber bulb held in one hand, and when a red light came on, they were not to press. The 2-year-olds made many mistakes, pressing for red lights as well as for green. Not until age 4 could most children reliably inhibit a response to the wrong color. And it is not just that 4-year-olds understand the instructions better. The 2-year-olds realize they are not supposed to press on red, but somehow they just can't stop themselves. The ability to inhibit an action until a "go" signal is given is one aspect of the broader abilities of **effortful control** and **self-regulation.** Effortful control refers to the ability to suppress some strong behavior, such as slowing down when running or talking more quietly (Kochanska, Murray, and Harlan, 2000; Rothbart and Bates, 1998). Self-regulation includes effortful control as well as children's ability to direct their own activities and adjust their behaviors and emotional expression to fit the situation. The larger abilities are major developments of the preschool period (Kopp, 1992).

Psychologist Eleanor Maccoby (1980) has listed some other signs of self-control and self-management that emerge by the end of the preschool period. Many of these involve the ability to reflect on one's own actions—that is, to monitor and direct those actions as needed. Most also involve being able to inhibit actions, delay gratification (wait for rewards), tolerate frustration, and adjust behavior to situational demands. According to Maccoby, compared with younger preschoolers, older preschoolers are better able to:

- weigh future consequences when deciding how to act;

- stop and think of possible ways around an obstacle blocking a goal;

- control emotions when goal-directed activities are blocked, thus greatly decreasing the likelihood of tantrums;

Instrumental dependency:
A young child's normal need for adult help in solving complex problems or performing difficult tasks.

Emotional dependency:
A child's atypical need for continual reassurance and attention from adults.

Effortful control:
The ability to suppress strong behaviors.

Self-regulation:
Children's ability to direct their own activities, to adjust behavior to fit situations, and to exercise effortful control.

- concentrate—that is, block out irrelevant thoughts, sights, and sounds and focus instead on what is needed to reach a desired objective; and
- do more than one thing at a time, as long as they are not incompatible or highly complex behaviors.

These abilities are not *fully* developed by the end of the preschool period; further advances will occur later. Nevertheless, the preschool years are a time of great progress in exercising management and control over the self. We will return to the topic of control over the self when we discuss emotional regulation.

THE DEVELOPING SELF

The cognitive advances of the preschool period discussed in Chapter 9 have a profound effect on the development of a child's sense of self. It is during this time that children start to be aware of themselves as persons (Eder and Mangelsdorf, 1997). They know that minds exist, that they have a mind, and that they are a particular person. Partly because of their new capacity for thinking about categories, they see themselves as boys or girls—like one parent in gender and unlike the other. In this section we discuss these and other changes in self-understanding that occur during the preschool period.

Changes in Self-Understanding

Late in toddlerhood children become able to represent the self mentally. But this mental representation involves *immediate* experiences, one at a time (*I am eating an apple, I am sitting on the swing, I am walking up the stairs,* etc.) (Fischer, Shaver, and Carnochan, 1990). Not until the preschool period do cognitive advances enable the child to represent a variety of different experiences and *alternate* among them. A preschooler can mentally move back and forth among particular experiences, between particular experiences and more general ones (getting ready for bed last night versus what bedtime is like in general), and between past and present (Harter, 1998). This ability to represent alternative experiences can also be seen in fantasy play. In the following example, a preschooler, J., is playing with several figures in a dollhouse:

> "He has to go upstairs, Mommy."
> Then, to the Mommy doll, "Watch, Mommy."
> (J. releases the figure so it falls down the steps.)
> "He fell down, Mommy. He's crying, Mommy. He's a boo boo on his head."
> (J. makes crying sound effects for the figure.)
> "Ouch, ouch, I hurt my head."
> (Wolf, 1990, p. 24)

Notice how the child alternates between the role of observer and the role of the doll. This ability to move mentally back and forth among different experiences makes for a much more comprehensive sense of self (Fischer, Shaver, and Carnochan, 1990; Harter, 1998).

Dennie Wolf (1990) has described another capacity that underlies preschoolers' expanding sense of self. Children can now uncouple various aspects of experience. They can, for example, pretend and at the same time *observe* themselves pretending. Similarly, they can look at themselves in a mirror and know *that is me,* at the same time being aware that *I am watching myself.* This capacity makes the sense of self significantly more mature.

But the preschooler's sense of self is still limited. Children this age have trouble understanding they are the same person when they feel different in different situations (e.g., nice in one situation, mean in another) (Fischer, Shaver, and Carnochan, 1990). They cannot coordinate disparate experiences into a unified sense of self (Eder and

Mangelsdorf, 1997). Simultaneous understanding of different aspects of the self, understanding the selves of others, and self-reflection must all await later childhood and adolescence.

Self-Constancy and Self-Representation

By internalizing parents' rules, challenging those rules (and feeling guilty), and then once again achieving harmony with parents, preschoolers experience what Louis Sander (1975) calls **self-constancy**—a sense that the self endures despite temporary disruptions in relationships.

> **Self-constancy:**
> A sense that the self endures despite temporary disruptions in relationships.

To understand the emergence of a sense of self-constancy, picture Malcolm, who has just turned 3. He is eyeing the window blind cords, which he loves to play with but is forbidden to touch. DeeDee, who is cleaning a nearby closet, glances over at him. Malcolm is aware not only of his own intention to pull on the cords, but also of his mother's knowledge of that intention. He reaches for the cords and begins to pull them vigorously, knowing full well that his mother sees his actions as both bad and deliberate (Emde and Buchsbaum, 1990; Kochanska, 1993). "Malcolm!" says DeeDee sharply. "Stop that right now!" This response is just what Malcolm expected. Malcolm also understands that the self who has just done wrong and is being scolded is the same self who a moment before was in harmony with DeeDee. Equally important, Malcolm knows he can reinstate the former harmony by making up with his mother—for example, by saying he is sorry. This is an early form of the concept of reversibility, discussed in Chapter 9—an understanding that the effects of a transformation can later be undone. A 3-year-old can engage in such advanced thinking only in well-practiced, concrete situations. Nevertheless, the ability to do so is very important. It allows Malcolm to understand the continuity of his self in relation to his mother.

Preschoolers like Malcolm also start to think of themselves as having dispositions—ways of being—that are consistent through time (Eder and Mangelsdorf, 1997). Such thoughts about the self are referred to as **self-representation.** All children acquire this ability, but not all come to think of the self in exactly the same way. Each child develops a particular view of the self based on his or her unique experiences, perhaps especially those with attachment figures. Most young children, but not all, think of the self as good and kind and likable, and as competent and effective in the world. These positive thoughts and feelings about the self, as assessed in puppet play, predict preschoolers' later social competence in third grade (Verschueren, Buyck, and Marcoen, 2001).

> **Self-representation:**
> Thoughts about the self.

Positive thoughts and feelings about themselves develop as young children begin to see themselves as competent and take pride in their accomplishments.

Gender and the Self

Gender is a central organizing theme in development. It plays a key role in the way people define and experience their worlds. In all cultures, parents and others treat boys and girls differently and expect different things from them (Whiting and Edwards, 1988). Because of this, children learn cultural stereotypes regarding male and female behaviors and characteristics. This learning begins early and is pervasive (Ruble and Martin, 1998). It manifests itself in children's activities, preferences, and social styles (Bem, 1989; Fagot, Leinbach, and O'Boyle, 1992; Serbin, Powlishta, and Gulko, 1993; Theimer, Killen, and Stangor, 2001). Even among preschoolers, gender is so salient that a child's most advanced thinking is often applied to it. Preschoolers label and categorize different activities in terms of gender (Fagot et al., 1992), they remember modeled behaviors better when they are "gender-appropriate" (Bauer, 1993), and in general they use gender as a basis for organizing information (Serbin et al., 1993).

Gender is a key aspect of the preschooler's emerging self-concept (Ruble and Martin, 1998). Being a boy or a girl is central to the definition of the self. Development of a gender-based self-concept involves three steps:

Sex-typed behavior:
Actions that conform to cultural expectations about what is appropriate for boys and for girls.

Gender-role concept:
Knowledge of cultural stereotypes regarding males and females.

- First, children gradually adopt **sex-typed behavior**—actions that conform to cultural expectations about what is appropriate for boys and for girls.

- Second, children simultaneously acquire **gender-role concepts**—a beginning knowledge of the cultural stereotypes regarding males and females.

- Finally, children develop an emotional commitment to their particular gender.

Changes in Sex-Typed Behavior The development of sex-typed behavior occurs in a series of phases. By age 2, children already show gender-related preferences in toys. Boys have learned to play largely with trucks and cars, while girls have learned to gravitate toward soft, cuddly toys (Ruble and Martin, 1998; Serbin et al., 1993). Such early learning probably results from imitation, reinforcement, and direct guidance from parents (Leaper, 2000). These early preferences are not absolute, however, as illustrated in our story of 2-year-old Mikey's attachment to Raggedy Ann. At this young age, children in all cultures have a limited understanding of gender-related behaviors. They have learned that certain objects go with mommies or daddies (e.g., lipsticks versus neckties), but they do not yet understand the broader categories of gender, nor do they know that they share a gender with one of their parents.

By age 3 or 4, children know a great deal more about "gender-appropriate" objects and activities (Ruble and Martin, 1998; Serbin et al., 1993; Theimer et al., 2001). They exhibit *categorical* thinking about what is male and what is female, having a rather firm idea about which occupations, activities, and behaviors belong to each. In addition, they begin to show much more sex-typed behavior. For example, preschool girls around the world show more interest in and nurturance toward babies than do their male peers (Whiting and Edwards, 1988). Preschool girls also generally prefer to play with one other child at a time, in contrast to boys' preference for group activities (Benenson, 1993).

Studies of how sex-typed behavior is learned in the United States show that it pervades our society. Even when their children are babies, most American parents dress boys and girls in different clothing, decorate their rooms differently, give them different playthings, and interact with them differently (Fagot et al., 1992). Parents encourage sex-typed play beginning in toddlerhood by reacting more positively to play with "gender-appropriate" toys (Ruble and Martin, 1998). Differential treatment of boys and girls increases during the preschool years (Maccoby, 1990). If children behave in gender-inconsistent ways, parents and peers are often quick to give negative feedback.

Judith Langlois illustrated this by getting preschoolers to play with "gender-inappropriate" toys and then inviting their mothers, fathers, or peers to watch (Langlois and Downs, 1980). Mothers were often accepting of the "cross-gender" play, but fathers and peers were not. Fathers had the strongest negative reactions, especially to the sight of their sons playing with "feminine" toys. Just as Frank encouraged Mikey to shun girls' toys, so other preschoolers are channeled into sex-typed behaviors.

Sex-typed behavior becomes very common in early childhood.

Developing Gender-Role Concepts By age 4 or 5, children start to learn more abstract cultural beliefs about gender differences (Bem, 1989; Serbin et al., 1993); that is, they begin to acquire gender-role concepts. Learning gender-role concepts is based partly on cognitive maturation, and partly on countless experiences of being told and shown what is considered appropriate for boys or for girls. From these experiences young children begin to abstract more generalized ideas about gender (Leaper, 2000; Ruble and Martin, 1998).

Gender-role concepts are well ingrained in adults. In our culture, as in many others, males are viewed as more aggressive, competitive, self-confident, and ambitious, while females are seen as more emotional, kind, interpersonally sensitive, and domestic (Ruble and Martin, 1998). (A more complete list of gender stereotypes found in North American culture is given in Table 10.1.) These gender stereotypes can be summed up by saying that the male role is *instrumental* (men are viewed as geared to getting things done), while the female role is *expressive* (women are seen as oriented toward feelings). As early as age 3, children show some awareness of gender stereotypes, and by age 5 their knowledge of gender stereotypes is typically high (Serbin et al., 1993).

The marked increase in sex-typed behavior and growing understanding of gender differences during the preschool period help encourage a rather strict gender segregation in the classroom and on the playground (Maccoby, 1990; Serbin et al., 1993). The fact that we see Maggie, Mikey, Malcolm, and Meryl playing with other children of their own gender is no accident. Children this age know they are boys or girls, they know these are categories of people, and they see themselves as members of one category or the other (Ruble and Martin, 1998; Serbin et al., 1993). In addition, they tend to attribute positive attributes to their own gender and negative attributes to the opposite gender (Ruble and Martin, 1998).

Understanding Gender Constancy One important aspect of children's developing sense of gender is an understanding of **gender constancy**—the fact that gender is permanent despite changes in age, dress, hairstyle, or behavior (Bem, 1989; Ruble and Martin, 1998). Three-year-olds know they are boys or girls, and they know the characteristics and activities usually associated with their gender, but they may still be unsure whether changes in superficial characteristics (such as boys wearing dresses and playing with dolls or girls cutting their hair short and playing with footballs) can produce a

Child Development CD
Preschoolers and Gender Roles

Gender constancy:
The understanding that gender is permanent despite superficial changes.

Table 10.1 Some Characteristics Regarded as Stereotypically Masculine and Feminine by North American College Students

Masculine Characteristics	Feminine Characteristics
Independent	Emotional
Aggressive	Home-oriented
Skilled in business	Kind
Mechanical aptitude	Cries easily
Outspoken	Creative
Acts as a leader	Considerate
Self-confident	Devotes self to others
Takes a stand	Needs approval
Ambitious	Gentle
Not easily influenced	Aware of others' feelings
Dominant	Excitable in a major crisis
Active	Expresses tender feelings
Makes decisions easily	Enjoys art and music
Doesn't give up easily	Tactful
Stands up under pressure	Feelings hurt
Likes math and science	Neat
Competitive	Likes children
Adventurous	Understanding

Source: Ruble, 1983.

change in gender. This uncertainty is related to the appearance-reality problem discussed in Chapter 9.

The earliest age at which children show an understanding of gender constancy depends on how it is assessed (Ruble and Martin, 1998). When researchers made gender-inappropriate changes in hairstyle and dress to a drawing of a boy or a girl, and then asked preschoolers, "If the child did this would he (or she) still be a boy (or a girl)?" very few said gender remained the same despite these changes in appearance (Emmerich et al., 1977). But it is possible the children assumed that because these were just drawings, the experimenter could change the figure's gender at will. Sandra Bem (1989) designed a study to see if preschoolers would make the same error regarding real children. She showed them photographs of actual male and female toddlers, first nude with sexual anatomy visible, then dressed in clothing considered appropriate for the other sex. Almost half the 3- to 5-year-olds and more than half the girls knew the child's gender remained unchanged even when dress changed. Moreover, three-quarters of those who knew the difference between male and female genitals passed the gender constancy test. Similarly, when preschoolers are asked whether they themselves would change gender if they changed their style of dress, virtually none say yes (Ruble and Martin, 1998).

An understanding of gender constancy is related to the concepts of conservation discussed in Chapter 9. The child eventually grasps that gender remains the same despite superficial transformations (changes in hairstyle and dress). The fact that a grasp of gender constancy begins to emerge before an understanding of other conservation concepts suggests the great importance of gender to young children.

Explaining Sex-Typed Behavior and Gender-Role Development Several different explanations have been proposed for the development of sex-typed behavior and gender-role concepts:

- Social learning theorists explain these developments in terms of the rewards and punishments children experience when they behave in sex-typed and non-sex-typed ways and children's observations of how mothers, fathers, and other community members behave.

- Cognitive theorists see gender-role learning as an example of children's emerging understanding of categories, scripts, and schemas. When children grasp the categories *male* and *female* and learn something about the objects and activities associated with each one, they begin to apply this knowledge to themselves as a member of one category or the other.

- **Gender schema theory** brings together the social learning and cognitive positions (Serbin et al., 1993). According to this theory, children use their cognitive abilities to form a concept or schema of male and female characteristics, with the content of the schema based on their particular social learning histories.

- Psychoanalytic theory emphasizes developmental changes in relationships with parents. In striving to be like the parent of the same gender, a child adopts that parent's behaviors, attitudes, and values.

Gender schema theory:
The theory that children form a concept or schema of male and female characteristics, with the content of the schema based on their particular social learning histories.

separateness vs. connectedness

In a variation of psychoanalytic theory, Nancy Chodorow (1989) has argued that boys define their masculinity by contrasting themselves with their mothers, whereas girls define their femininity in terms of similarities with their mothers. This leads boys to define themselves in terms of separateness and to have more concern with people's differences and their own individuality. Girls, in contrast, define themselves in terms of connectedness, see people in terms of their similarities, and have a stronger capacity for sensing the feelings of others.

Social learning theorists emphasize the differing experiences of boys and girls. Two powerful influences on the development of sex-typing and gender concepts are the activities encouraged for boys and girls and the ways parents converse with them. In an interesting experiment, Campbell Leaper (2000) had groups of 4-year-old boys and girls play with both trucks and tracks and dolls and dishes with their parents present. The activity greatly influenced the play for both boys and girls; they played more independently with the trucks and more socially and cooperatively with the dolls. Leaper argues that, since sex-typed activities are usually encouraged, the two genders normally practice very different skills. Other research shows that when parents converse with their children about the past, they talk more about social events and emotions with girls than with boys (Buckner and Fivush, 2000). Such experiences make it unsurprising that girls come to talk more about emotions and recall more emotional aspects of events than do boys.

SOCIAL DEVELOPMENT: THE NEW WORLD OF PEERS

Peers are of great interest even to toddlers, as we discussed in Chapter 8. By age 2 children often show the rudiments of social turn-taking (Rubin et al., 1998). They speak to or show something to another child, wait for a response, and then repeat the cycle. Most of this early turn-taking, however, centers on objects, and toddlers really respond to each other's specific intentions only occasionally (Bronson, 1981). Not until the preschool period, as children's mastery of language grows, do their peer interactions become sustained and highly coordinated (Brownell, 1990; Hartup, 1992).

Two illustrations vividly contrast toddlers' and preschoolers' peer interactions. The first is a "conversation" between two boys, 13 and 15 months of age. Bernie, the younger, initiates the exchange by turning and looking at Larry, who has been watching him while mouthing a toy. Bernie then "speaks" to Larry:

> Bernie: Da . . . Da.
> Larry: (Laughs very slightly as he continues to look.)

mhhe.com
/dehart5

Preschoolers and Peers

According to psychoanalytic theory, children identify with parents of the same gender and strive to be like them.

Bernie: Da.

Larry: (Laughs more heartily this time.)

The same sequence of Bernie saying "da" and Larry responding with laughter is repeated five more times. Then Larry looks away and offers an adult a toy. Bernie pursues him.

Bernie: (Waving both hands and looking directly at Larry.) Da!

Larry: (Looks back at Bernie and laughs again.)

The sequence of "da" followed by laughter is repeated nine more times. Finally, Bernie turns away abruptly and toddles off. Larry laughs once more in a forced manner and then silently watches Bernie depart.

(Mueller and Lucas, 1975, p. 241)

The second conversation is between a boy and a girl, both 5 years old. The boy is testing the girl's competence, and the girl is rising to the challenge:

Boy: Can you carry this? (Shows girl a toy fish.)

Girl: Yeah, if I weighed 50 pounds.

Boy: You can't even carry it. Can you carry it by the string?

Girl: Yeah. Yes I can. (Lifts fish overhead by string.)

Boy: Can you carry it by the nose?

Girl: Where's the nose?

Boy: That yellow one.

Girl: This? (Carries it by the nose.)

Boy: Can you carry it by its tail?

Girl: Yeah. (Carries it by tail.)

Boy: Can you carry it like this? (Shows how to carry it by fin.)

Girl: (Carries it by fin.) I weigh 50 pounds about, right?

Boy: Right.

(Garvey, 1977, p. 59)

Although Bernie and Larry are socially competent for toddlers, perhaps because they are longtime acquaintances, there is a world of difference between their interaction and that of the 5-year-olds. The 5-year-olds can share a fantasy, make up rules for a game, respond to each other's questions, demonstrate novel procedures, and in general coordinate their behaviors in ways far beyond the abilities of any pair of 1-year-olds.

Competence with Peers

Successful entry into a peer group and competence with peers are complex matters. They cannot be gauged just by measuring the amount of contact a child has with other children. If a child's contacts are mostly aggressive or consistently asymmetrical, with the child always in the role of follower, even a large number of contacts doesn't imply social competence. Conversely, sometimes playing alone doesn't mean lack of social competence (Coplan et al., 2001). Playing alone is different from hovering near a group of other children but being unable to join in. Even children who are rated socially competent by their teachers or who are popular with peers will at times play by themselves in group settings (Rubin et al., 1998), especially when they are engaged in quiet, constructive play such as drawing or building things (Coplan et al., 2001).

A convergence of measures is generally needed to gauge a child's competence with peers. Detailed observational studies show that children who engage and respond to peers with positive feelings, who are of interest to peers and highly regarded by them, who can take the lead as well as follow, who are able to sustain the give-and-take of peer interaction, and who are able to form a reciprocal friendship will be judged by teachers and other observers as having social competence (LaFreniere and Dumas, 1995; Vaughn et al., 2000; Vaughn and Waters, 1981). These various measures of social competence are usually in agreement, which is not surprising because they tend to foster one another (Rubin et al., 1998; Sroufe et al., 1984). For example, when children engage peers in positive ways, they are better liked, and that popularity can encourage additional positive behaviors that keep attracting peers (Denham and Holt, 1993). In contrast, children who often behave aggressively and frequently display negative emotion are unpopular (Arsenio, Cooperman, and Lover, 2000; Ladd and Burgess, 2001).

Our chapter-opening example illustrated what socially competent preschoolers are like, especially the positive emotions that such children express toward peers. Mikey conveyed his excitement about seeing the climbing structure as a boat through his tone of voice, his posture, and his facial expression. If he had suggested the boat idea in a flat, matter-of-fact way, the other two boys might have ignored it. But Mikey's enthusiastic "Hey! It's a boat!" brought the other two running. His enthusiasm captured their interest and was contagious. This ability to have fun and to share that fun with others is one reason such a child is popular with peers (Sroufe et al., 1984).

Early Friendships

Preschoolers not only prefer certain other children to play with; interviews and detailed observational studies have shown that they form partnerships with one another that may last for a year or more (Park, Lay, and Ramsay, 1993). These early peer relationships may endure partly because adults promote them and partly because the children involved are continually in contact with each other at day care or preschool. Nevertheless, by age 4 or so, children have considerable capacity to maintain friendships through their own efforts (Hartup, 1992; Rubin et al., 1998; Vaughn et al., 2000).

Young friends behave differently with each other than they do with nonfriends (Hartup, 1992; Hartup and Laursen, 1993). They have more frequent positive exchanges and are more cooperative in problem-solving tasks. When placed in experimental conflict situations—with, for example, each partner being told a different set of rules for a game—friends also disagree with each other more often than mere acquaintances do. However, these conflicts are less heated, result in fairer solutions, and do not cause the children to separate. Being able to continue a relationship despite conflicts offers important opportunities to learn how to be together (Hartup and Laursen, 1993).

The Importance of Peer Relationships

Early relationships with peers are important for several reasons. As we mentioned in Chapter 2, the peer group is a major setting for learning about the concepts of fairness, reciprocity, and cooperation. It is also a critical setting for learning to manage interpersonal aggression, as the episode between Malcolm and April illustrates. In peer groups children learn a great deal about cultural norms and values, such as gender roles, as well.

Peer interactions become sustained and coordinated during early childhood, and children begin to show clear playmate preferences and form genuine friendships.

Finally, experiences within the peer group, whether positive or negative, can greatly affect a child's self-concept and future dealings with others. Perhaps for this reason, how well a child gets along with peers is one of the strongest predictors of later success. It is related to levels of adjustment, psychological problems, and even school achievement (e.g., Buhs and Ladd, 2001; Rubin et al., 1998; Teo et al., 1996).

Increased peer interactions can sometimes help children overcome developmental problems. For instance, when socially withdrawn preschoolers were given the opportunity to interact one-on-one with somewhat younger children in a series of special play sessions, they became more outgoing in their regular classrooms (Furman, Rahe, and Hartup, 1979). Having a chance to interact successfully with a peer seemed to enhance both social skills and confidence about peer relations. Interacting with a more competent, but tolerant, same-age peer (or even an older sibling) would also be expected to enhance social competence. Another remedial approach, effective to some extent, is directly teaching socially isolated children interaction skills (Mize and Ladd, 1990).

EMOTIONAL DEVELOPMENT

Preschoolers' Emotions

Because all areas of development are interrelated, it is not surprising that emotional changes during the preschool years are as dramatic as cognitive and social ones. These changes include a growing understanding of emotions and their causes, a rapidly expanding capacity for regulating emotional experiences (part of a general increase in self-regulation), and the further development of the self-evaluative emotions (Eisenberg et al., 1993; Lewis, 1992; Sroufe, 1995).

Young Children's Understanding of Emotion

By the preschool period, children have learned a great deal about emotion and emotional expression (Saarni, Mumme, and Campos, 1998). For example, their understanding and use of emotional words expands rapidly (Ridgeway, Waters, and Kuczaj, 1985). About half of all toddlers use the word *good,* but only about 7 percent use the word *sad.* By age 6, children consistently use such words. They also understand complex emotional concepts such as *jealous, proud, embarrassed,* and *miserable.* Preschoolers' reading of positive emotions in natural settings shows close agreement with that of adults, although they are still not very good at interpreting the range of negative emotions others may express (Fabes et al., 1994). Preschoolers also have trouble distinguishing what people *really* feel from what they *appear* to feel. This is not surprising, given their struggle with the appearance-reality distinction. Thus, young children have no difficulty distinguishing between pictures of happy and sad faces, but they have great difficulty understanding that someone who is sad may put on a happy face (e.g., to protect someone else's feelings) or that someone who is really happy may not show happiness (e.g., Friend and Davis, 1993).

During the preschool period children acquire a better understanding of the causes of emotions. By age 4 they know emotions are influenced not only by what happens, but also by what people expect to happen or think happened. For example, 4-year-olds know that a girl may be sad if she *mistakenly* thinks she isn't going to get a prize she wants (Harris, 1994). But if the girl doesn't look sad, children this age would typically be confused about how she feels. It is not until between ages 5 and 8 that children are able to integrate situational cues and visible expressions of emotion to infer how someone else feels.

The Growth of Emotional Regulation

Emotional regulation includes the capacities to control and direct emotional expression, to maintain organized behavior in the presence of strong emotions, and to be guided by emotional experiences. All these capacities expand significantly during the preschool years. Some of them are revealed in preschoolers' increasing ability to tolerate frustration.

Emotional regulation:
The capacities to control and direct emotional expression, to maintain organized behavior in the presence of strong emotions, and to be guided by emotional experiences.

Tolerating Frustration An important aspect of emotional regulation is the ability to tolerate frustration—that is, to avoid becoming so upset in a frustrating situation that emotions get out of control and behavior becomes disorganized. This ability begins to appear by about age 2 and expands dramatically throughout the preschool years (Bridges and Grolnick, 1995; Eisenberg et al., 1994; van Lieshout, 1975). When confronting a frustrating situation, such as an attractive toy that is inaccessible, older preschoolers are less angry and tantrum-prone than younger children are. They also stay engaged with the problem despite their frustration, and they make more constructive responses, such as seeking direct help.

This emerging capacity affects relationships with parents. Defiance of parents' requests and passive noncompliance with them decline markedly between the ages of 2 and 5 (Kuczynski and Kochanska, 1990). Children are increasingly able to tolerate the frustration of being asked to do something counter to their own wishes. They also begin to learn how to use negotiation to resolve such a conflict (Klimes-Dougan and Kopp, 1999).

Another form of tolerance for frustration is **delay of gratification,** the ability to forgo an immediate reward, such as a small piece of candy, despite strong desire for it, in order to have a better reward later. With support from an adult, preschool children can usually endure the frustration of delaying gratification. The wait may not be easy for them, but most manage to get through it. The ability to delay gratification will expand in the middle childhood years to the point where the child can wait even in the absence of adult help (Mischel, Shoda, and Rodriguez, 1989).

Delay of gratification:
The ability to forgo an immediate reward in favor of a better reward at a later time.

Researchers are not yet sure why tolerance for frustration improves so noticeably during the preschool years. Children are probably becoming able to suppress their feelings to some extent, making them *appear* less upset (Maccoby, 1980). At the same time, they are learning strategies that help them limit the buildup of tension that tends to accompany frustration. For instance, in experiments in which attractive toys are locked inside a Plexiglas box, some preschoolers distract themselves by turning to other activities. This strategy redefines the situation as one in which the inaccessible toy is no longer the central focus of attention (e.g., Wolf, 1990). Undoubtedly, such strategies help reduce tension and make the situation more bearable.

Showing Flexibility in Emotional Expression The ability to exert self-control over emotions would be a mixed blessing if children couldn't adjust its level to suit particular situations. Some situations demand a great deal of self-restraint, while others allow children to be as impulsive and expressive as they want. The ability to adapt to these

Preschoolers can maintain organized behavior when working on hard problems. They can carry out activities that require several steps and do not lead to immediate rewards.

Ego resiliency:
The ability to modify self-restraint to adapt to changing circumstances.

different situations is called **ego resiliency** because the ego, or self, is showing the capacity to be flexible in its control over the expression of impulses and feelings (Block and Block, 1980). Mikey is showing ego resiliency in the scene at the start of the chapter. He is able to line up quietly when the teacher requests, but he also runs, shouts, and plays gleefully during outdoor recess. Like all ego-resilient children, Mikey can be spontaneous and expressive in some settings, reserved and self-disciplined in others (Sroufe, 1995).

Internalizing Standards The awareness of standards that dawned in the toddler period advances markedly in the preschool years. In addition, these standards become more fully *internalized* or adopted by the self (Kochanska et al., 2001). Once the child has internalized standards, he or she will comply with parents' prohibitions even when the parents aren't present (Bugental and Goodnow, 1998; Kochanska et al., 2001). If an experimenter gets a preschool child to do something against a parent's rules when the parent is not there, the child will typically show signs of distress and may confess to the parent when the parent returns (Emde and Buchsbaum, 1990). Another indication of the internalization of standards is concern for other people. In their third year children not only respond emotionally to mishaps they cause or witness, but also seek to make reparations (Cole, Barrett, and Zahn-Waxler, 1992).

Internalization is also a cornerstone of moral development (Turiel, 1998) and the development of a conscience. Children begin to understand that some behaviors are right and others are wrong (Emde et al., 1991). Preschoolers also begin to understand the concept of cheating (Kochanska, 1997). While they may find it difficult not to cheat in the face of a desirable prize, they often can control themselves for a time. Likewise, in doll play in which the experimenter has introduced moral issues (one doll wants to take something from another doll or one doll is distressed), preschoolers often show concern. They may, for example, tell the distressed doll they are sorry. Four-year-olds do this more than 3-year-olds and 5-year-olds do it more than 4-year-olds.

By age 4 children view *moral* transgressions, such as hitting someone or not sharing, as more serious than *conventional* transgressions, such as eating ice cream with your fingers. They make such judgments more independently from adults than do younger children (Smetana, Schlagman, and Adams, 1993). It is as if they have internalized not just standards of behavior but also a sense that certain standards entail moral obligations.

Parents encourage this change in preschool children by changing their socialization techniques as the preschool period progresses (Power and Manire, 1992). Instead of direct, at times strong, controls ("No, no! Don't hit!"), they begin to use indirect external controls ("What a good boy to let Bobby play with your new boat!"), and finally, they start to encourage internal self-regulation ("I'm counting on you to divide up those cookies fairly"). Encouraging self-regulation also involves reasoning and persuasion; the parent might explain *why* a certain distribution is fair and just. Research suggests that when parents provide information about rules and values and underscore that information through their own consistent behavior, young children are more likely to behave responsibly in the parents' absence (Power and Manire, 1992).

The Self-Evaluative Emotions

Internalization of standards affects the emotional experiences of preschoolers. Children can now feel genuine *guilt* and *pride*, two emotions that involve evaluating the self against internalized standards (Saarni, Mumme, and Campos, 1998; Sroufe, 1995). These emotions are different from the beginnings of shame and pride that toddlers experience. For example, preschoolers' guilt reactions occur not because of what their parents do or say, but because they themselves *know* they have done something wrong. Guilt no longer arises only from a fear of being punished; it is also due to an undermining of self-esteem caused by failure to live up to an internalized standard (Kochanska, 1993). Preschoolers' guilt reactions are also more organized than toddlers' shame—they are not just global, all-encompassing states of anxiety—and they occur more as a result of *particular* behaviors. The specificity that characterizes preschoolers' guilt allows the attempts at making up that we discussed earlier.

Likewise, true pride is distinguished from toddlers' joy in mastery because it is based on self-evaluation. Toddlers often show just as much pleasure when an adult solves a problem as when they solve it, but preschoolers are usually happier when they find the solution themselves (Stipek, Recchia, and McClintic, 1992). Children perceive that they have done a good job, and consequently feel proud. Pride reactions are more common and stronger when the problem solved or the task accomplished is difficult than when it is easy (Lewis et al., 1992). This tells us that preschool children evaluate the complexity of what they are trying to do and have their own standards of performance.

Emotional Development, Aggression, and Prosocial Behavior

Aggression refers to negative acts intended to harm others or their possessions, while **prosocial behavior** refers to positive feelings and acts directed toward others, with the intention of benefiting them (Eisenberg and Fabes, 1998). Both types of behavior are closely related to emotional regulation. When Malcolm acts aggressively toward April, hitting her to get possession of the tricycle, he is letting go of self-restraint and acting on impulse. Aggression often involves relinquishing self-control and spontaneously lashing out, although at times it can be deliberate and calculating. Refraining from aggression frequently involves self-management. Prosocial behavior also involves self-management, but in a different way. To be kind or helpful to someone else, you must often make a conscious effort to put aside your own desires and enter into the other person's point of view. This requires a substantial amount of self-regulation. Thus, as the capacities for self-management and emotional regulation unfold in children, we would expect to see changes in both aggression and prosocial behavior. In fact, this is exactly what happens.

Aggression:
Negative acts intended to harm others or their possessions.

Prosocial behavior:
Positive feelings and acts directed toward others, with the intention of benefiting them.

Preschoolers and Aggression

Instrumental aggression:
Aggression used as a means to get something.

Hostile aggression:
Aggression aimed solely at hurting someone else.

Empathy:
The ability to experience the emotions of another person.

Altruism:
Acting unselfishly to aid someone else

Developmental Changes in Aggression When 12-month-old Maggie roughly pushes away her mother's hand to get at her favorite toy, she is not really being aggressive. Although her behavior is assertive and purposeful, she does not intend to cause physical or psychological harm. This intent is central to true aggression; only when Maggie is cognitively advanced enough to appreciate the consequences of her actions can she engage in genuine aggression (Maccoby, 1980). This ability develops sometime during toddlerhood, when representational thought emerges. During toddlerhood we see an increase in angry outbursts in response to constraints imposed by parents, as well as in negative behavior directed toward peers. Such negative behaviors actually reach their peak in toddlerhood and the early preschool period (Coie and Dodge, 1998). However, much of the negative peer interaction of toddlers is object-centered, as when two children pull on a plaything in order to possess it (Howes, 1988). Not until the preschool period, when children better understand the self as an agent and the concept of fairness, does true interpersonal aggression become common. The aggression that arises now includes actions whose only purpose is to cause another person distress (Hartup and Laursen, 1993; Maccoby, 1980). By this age, too, there is consistency in the level of aggression found in individual children (Coie and Dodge, 1998).

During the late preschool and early elementary school years aggressive behavior changes. Children's overall level of physical aggression declines because of a drop in **instrumental aggression,** the use of physical aggression as a means to get something (Hartup and Laursen, 1993). Malcolm is engaging in instrumental aggression when he tries to wrestle the tricycle from April's grip. Older children are much less likely to become involved in such a squabble because they have learned alternative ways to settle disputes over objects.

Although instrumental aggression declines sharply in middle childhood, **hostile aggression**—aggression aimed solely at hurting someone else—does not (Coie and Dodge, 1998). Most acts of hostile aggression during middle childhood are concerned with getting even. Children lash out when they perceive that their rights have been violated or their egos threatened. Over the elementary school years hostile aggression changes dramatically in form. Both boys and girls become more prone to verbal insults and various kinds of threats than to hitting. However, there are important differences between boys and girls in the ways they express aggression and the functions it serves for them in the peer group (Crick, Casas, and Ku, 1999). We will discuss these differences in Chapter 12.

The Development of Empathy and Altruism Two related forms of prosocial behavior are empathy and altruism. **Empathy** (sensing the emotions of another person) underlies **altruism** (acting unselfishly to aid someone else). When empathy is aroused, children are more willing to be helpful, or altruistic, toward others (Eisenberg and Fabes, 1998).

Both empathy and altruism follow a developmental course parallel to that of aggression, because the same cognitive factors underlie all three. To engage in true aggression, altruism, or empathy, children must understand they are independent agents responsible for their own actions. They must also grasp that their actions can cause feelings in other people that are different from the feelings they themselves are experiencing.

Researchers have suggested that the development of empathy and altruism has three phases (Hoffman, 1979; Zahn-Waxler et al., 1992). In the first phase, during infancy, the child shows a *primitive capacity for empathy* by crying when another person is distressed. But the child as yet has little understanding of who is actually upset. On hearing another baby cry, 8-month-olds will often crawl to their own mothers and seek contact with them (Hoffman, 1979). Apparently, the distinction between self and other is not yet clear in infants' minds, and contagious crying results.

In the second phase, during early toddlerhood, advances in the concepts of self and others enable the child to engage in *more purposeful helping behaviors.* Children may hug or pat another child who is crying, bring their mothers over to the crying youngster, or bring the child a favorite toy. But these actions do not really take into account the needs of the other child. Instead, toddlers do what would be helpful to themselves in that situation: They bring their *own* mothers or their *own* favorite toys.

In phase three, during early childhood, the *capacity to take the perspective of others,* and with it the *capacity to respond to others' needs,* increase dramatically (e.g., Radke-Yarrow and Zahn-Waxler, 1984; Zahn-Waxler et al., 1992). Although these capacities are widespread among preschoolers, actual displays of helping are relatively rare in natural settings. The fact that children can experience another person's distress does not guarantee they will immediately offer comfort or assistance to someone who is upset (Kestenbaum, Farber, and Sroufe, 1989), perhaps because they know adults will often help.

Instrumental aggression is common among preschoolers who have started to develop concepts of fairness and possession but have not yet learned other ways to settle disputes over objects.

How have researchers discovered these stages in the development of empathy and altruism? The work of Marion Radke-Yarrow deserves special mention because it shows how naturalistic observations and laboratory studies can be used together (e.g., Radke-Yarrow and Zahn-Waxler, 1984). Radke-Yarrow asked mothers to record in detail their children's reactions to others' distress in everyday settings. Because of possible bias in mothers' reports, assistants sometimes observed and recorded the same incidents. In addition, Radke-Yarrow supported all her findings with laboratory experiments.

Not only did Radke-Yarrow's data reveal the developmental phases just outlined, they also suggested that a parent's style of caregiving greatly influences a child's prosocial behavior. In keeping with a social learning perspective, a young child's tendency to feel empathy is related to experience with nurturant caregivers who provide models of empathy and helpfulness toward others. Just telling the child not to hurt other people is apparently not enough. The parent must clearly state the consequences for the victim, explain to the child principles and expectations regarding kindness, and convey the entire message with intensity of feeling about the issues involved. Not surprisingly, the kind of caring, nurturant parent who provides these types of lessons also tends to foster a secure attachment in young children. In accord with Bowlby's theory, security of attachment in infancy predicts a high level of empathy and prosocial behavior in the preschool years (Kestenbaum et al., 1989). By experiencing an empathic caregiving relationship beginning in infancy, children not only learn how to be cared for, but how to care as well. Children with secure attachment histories bring forward a basic responsiveness to others, which, in turn, is related to fewer behavior problems in elementary school (Hastings et al., 2000).

The frequency of prosocial behavior increases through the preschool years and later in childhood (Eisenberg and Fabes, 1998). Boys and girls are equally likely to show helpful behavior to others in need, but girls appear to show more kindness, concern, and consideration (Hastings et al., 2000).

THE ROLE OF PLAY IN PRESCHOOL DEVELOPMENT

Preschool Play

Play is the province of children. Once their more fundamental needs have been met—that is, whenever they aren't eating or sleeping or seeking attention from adults—children will play, often for hours on end. Even emotionally disturbed children play, although the quality of their play is notably affected. The absence of play is considered a sign of extreme abnormality (see Chapter 15). No one has to teach children to play; they do so naturally. No one has to reward children for playing; play is its own reward.

Play serves important functions for children. It is a means by which they can be active explorers of their environments, active creators of new experiences, and active participants in their own development. Play is a laboratory in which children learn new skills and practice behaviors and concepts that lie at the very edge of their capacities (Lillard, 1993). Play is also a child's social workshop, an arena for trying out roles alone and with other children, and for expanding and preserving a sense of self. For preschoolers, play is also an arena for emotional expression, often concerned with important themes and feelings from everyday life (Fischer, Shaver, and Carnochan, 1990). Let's look more closely at the emotional function of play before turning to some of play's social functions.

Play and Mastery of Conflict

By the preschool years play becomes the child's foremost tool for dealing with conflict and mastering whatever is frightening or painful. This was shown in a film Jeanne Block and her colleagues at Berkeley made during the civil disturbances of the 1960s. The sandbox play of children at that time was filled with police and civilians in conflict. Similarly, the play and drawings of children growing up in the midst of the Israeli-Palestinian conflict are filled with threatening and violent images (Elbedour et al., 1997). We illustrated the importance of play as a vehicle for expressing a young child's current anxieties in our story about Mikey. In Mikey's make-believe drama, which is based on an actual case observation (Rosenberg, 1984), the little boy is caught in the midst of his parents' crashing cars, just as Mikey is caught in the middle of Frank and Christine's persistent clashes. Similarly, one 4-year-old's mother observed her daughter dwelling on a recent fear in her play. The day after she was scared by a large dog, she pretended to be a dog terrorizing a group of dolls. She barked ferociously while crawling on the floor and then reassured the dolls by saying, "It's OK. He won't hurt you." In such ways preschoolers work their anxieties into play and thereby master them.

Play is also an arena for working through ongoing developmental issues. Consider how children resolve the issue that arises when they realize they have less power than their parents. This resolution is often worked out in play (Breger, 1974; Wolf, 1990). In play the child can safely turn the tables and become the powerful one. A common game preschoolers initiate with parents is "you be the baby and I'll be the mommy (or daddy)." The child might say: "Now you go right to bed!" (Parent: "Can I read?") "No, you have to go right to sleep!" The power roles are reversed in play, and the parent is charmed, not infuriated.

Pretend solutions are usually a healthy outlet for preschoolers. Because they involve active confrontation of a problem, they provide a prototype for more mature solutions in later years. With further development, pretend or play solutions must be left behind, but they represent the beginnings of active mastery of conflict. Imaginary companions and "personified objects" (a doll or stuffed toy that the child frequently talks to) also are quite common in the preschool years, somewhat more so for firstborns and only children (Gleason, Sebanc, and Hartup, 2000). Such pretend play partners seem to fulfil a useful function for the children who have them.

A history of parental support and nurturance can help children find these healthy resolutions to issues and conflicts. Preschoolers whose parents are nurturant and supportive tend to engage in fantasy play that is more flexible and elaborate, and they are

Social pretend play gives preschoolers a chance to try out adult roles and work through fears and conflicts.

more likely to bring negative themes to successful resolution (Rosenberg, 1984). As Rosenberg repeatedly observed in case studies of children with histories of secure attachment, Mikey brings the issue of being caught in the midst of parental conflict to a satisfactory close ("He got his leg broken! Here comes the ambilenz. They take him to the hospital. They fix it!"). Likewise, researchers sometimes present separation scenarios to preschoolers, using puppets, doll play, or stories; for example, the child becomes lost in the woods while being tended by a baby sitter. Children with histories of secure attachment much more frequently complete the story by having the parents come and find them than do children with anxious attachment histories (Bretherton and Munholland, 1999). Such pretend dramas and their resolutions are an adult's entrée to the child's inner world and an indicator of positive adaptation during the preschool period.

Role Playing

Another important function of preschoolers' play is providing an opportunity to try out social roles and cultural values. In play, children can be mommies and daddies, doctors, police officers, or robbers. In play, they can act out their aspirations as well as their fears. Dressing up in grown-up clothes and playing at grown-up jobs are also important parts of identifying with parents and exploring gender roles.

Cultural factors influence the quantity, form, and themes of young children's social fantasy play. In one study, Jo Ann Farver and Yoolim Lee Shin (1997) studied social fantasy play among Korean-American and European-American 4-year-olds enrolled in three different preschools. During free play at school, the Korean-American children engaged in less social fantasy play than the European-American children did, apparently because such activity was not encouraged at their preschool and no props for fantasy play were provided. In an experimental setting where props for fantasy play were provided, the Korean-American and European-American children engaged in equal amounts of social fantasy play, but the content and form of their play differed. Korean-American children's play focused on everyday activities and family relationships, and they tended to be nonconfrontational and to minimize conflict in their play. In contrast, European-American children's play focused on fantasy themes and danger, and they were more likely to assert themselves and reject their partner's ideas and behaviors. These differences reflect differences in cultural values. The Korean-American children came from immigrant families in which group harmony and interdependence were emphasized, whereas the European-American children came from families in which the mainstream American culture's emphasis on individuality and self-expression was more prominent.

Social fantasy play is normal and healthy for preschoolers. In fact, the more a young child engages in social fantasy play and the more flexible and elaborate that play is, the more socially competent the child is likely to be, as judged by teachers (Connolly and Doyle, 1984; Rosenberg, 1984). There are several possible explanations for this correlation. Elaborate social fantasy play may provide opportunities to develop social skills, social competence may make elaborate social fantasy play possible, or the same general social cognitive skills may underlie both social competence and social fantasy play. Whatever the explanation, skill at social fantasy play is an indicator of a preschooler's overall quality of adjustment.

THE PARENTS' ROLE IN EARLY CHILDHOOD DEVELOPMENT

The social and emotional development and behavior of preschoolers is related both to their history of earlier care and to the care they receive during the preschool period (e.g., Sroufe, 1988; DeMulder et al., 2000; Landry et al., 2001). In the following section, we take a look at some aspects of parenting that are important at this age.

Important Aspects of Parenting in the Preschool Period

Some of the same qualities of parenting that are important for infants and toddlers remain important for preschoolers. These include parental warmth, emotional responsiveness, and sharing of positive feelings with the child. For example, preschoolers whose parents are emotionally responsive tend to show empathy for others and to engage in prosocial behavior (Fabes et al., 1994). Similarly, parents who are emotionally responsive, accept their child's autonomy, and often share positive feelings tend to have preschoolers who are socially competent with peers and cooperative with their parents (Clark and Ladd, 2000; Kochanska and Aksan, 1995; LaFreniere and Dumas, 1995). Such correlations do not prove cause and effect, but their consistency with infant studies certainly suggests that parental warmth and responsiveness are important.

Certain parental qualities become newly important during the preschool years, largely because children's needs and abilities are changing. For instance, consistency in the parents' approach to discipline, agreement between the parents concerning child-rearing practices, and low levels of marital conflict tend to be more important for preschoolers than for younger children (Block and Block, 1980; Frosch and Mangelsdorf, 2001; LaFreniere and Dumas, 1995). This may be because the expanded cognitive abilities of preschoolers cause them to become confused by inconsistencies and to be more aware of conflict.

As children's abilities and needs change during the preschool period, the developmental tasks they face also change, and with those changes come related changes in the parents' tasks. These new sets of tasks are summarized in Table 10.2. Just as in toddlerhood, parents must gradually give children more responsibility, while remaining available to step in and help if the children's resources are exceeded. According to Erikson, the preschool period is a time when children may attempt to do too much as they strive for mastery. If parents frequently ridicule or punish a preschooler's failures, the child may experience pervasive feelings of guilt (Erikson, 1963). Thus, parents must neither push preschoolers too fast nor thwart their efforts. This role is similar to the one parents played when the child was a toddler, but now they are dealing with a much more mature and competent youngster. Parents must also try to display clear roles and values in their own actions and show the flexible self-control they hope to promote in their child.

Some of the characteristics of parents who raise well-adjusted preschoolers are summed up in what Diana Baumrind (1967) calls **authoritative parenting.** Authoritative parents are nurturant, responsive, and supportive, yet they also set firm limits for

Authoritative parenting:
A parenting style in which the parents are nurturant, responsive, and supportive, yet set firm limits for their children.

Table 10.2 Tasks For Preschoolers and Their Parents

Parents' Tasks	Children's Tasks
Nurturance	Accepting care and developing trust
Training and channeling of physical needs	Complying and controlling self
Teaching and skill training	Learning
Orienting child to family and peers	Developing a general understanding of the social world
Promoting interpersonal skills and control of emotion	Role taking
Guiding formation of goals, plans, and aspirations	Achieving self-regulation
Transmitting cultural values	Developing a sense of right and wrong

Source: Adapted from Clausen, 1968.

their children and hold them to high standards. Their preschoolers typically have a number of positive qualities: they are energetic, emotionally responsive to peers, curious, and self-reliant.

Other parenting styles that Baumrind has identified are not generally associated with such positive characteristics in children. One is **permissive parenting,** in which the parents totally fail to set firm limits or to require appropriately mature behavior. This pattern is associated with children who are impulsive, low in self-control, and lacking in self-reliance. Another parenting style associated with problems is **authoritarian parenting.** Authoritarian parents are unresponsive to their children's wishes and inflexible and harsh in controlling their children's behavior. This pattern is related to apprehension, frustration, and passive hostility in European-American children throughout childhood and into adolescence (Baumrind, 1991).

The meaning and impact of parenting practices seem to depend somewhat on cultural context (Greenfield and Suzuki, 1998). For example, effective parents in traditional

Parenting Styles

Permissive parenting:
A parenting style in which parents fail to set firm limits or to require appropriately mature behavior of their children.

Authoritarian parenting:
A parenting style in which parents are unresponsive, inflexible, and harsh in controlling behavior.

Authoritative parenting involves setting firm limits for children, but also being responsive and communicative.

Chinese-American families show many characteristics of Baumrind's authoritarian parenting category, including parental control, directiveness, and strictness. However, at the same time they show many characteristics of authoritative parenting, such as reasoning with children about misbehavior. These seemingly contradictory characteristics of traditional Chinese parenting reflect the Chinese concepts of *chiao shun* ("training"/"teaching appropriate behaviors") and *guan* ("to govern"/"to care for or love")(Chao, 1994). Children in these families do not typically show the negative outcomes of authoritarian parenting seen in European-American children. It appears that the categories of authoritarian and authoritative parenting may not be as meaningful in traditional Chinese culture as they are in European-American culture.

In addition, researchers have recently found that nonabusive physical punishment is associated with heightened child aggression in European-American families, but not in African-American families (Deater-Deckard et al., 1996). This difference may be due to differences in how physical punishment is used or what other parenting behaviors are associated with it; for instance, African-American parents usually do not combine physical punishment with a withdrawal of love, as European-American parents often do (Parke and Buriel, 1998). Even in African-American families, when discipline is unduly harsh and coercive, especially when accompanied by lax guidance, it is related to later aggression and other conduct problems (Kilgore, Snyder, and Lentz, 2000).

Different styles of parenting may be appropriate in different contexts, as we suggested in Chapter 2 (Parke and Buriel, 1998). More controlling, strict, and even authoritarian parenting appears to be more common in dangerous inner-city neighborhoods, and it is not clear that such parenting practices have negative consequences in these contexts. Some studies suggest that they are even associated with more positive outcomes among the urban poor (Baldwin, Baldwin, and Cole, 1990). One likely explanation for this finding is that parental control and directiveness in dangerous settings is associated with care and concern and is not experienced by children as rejection.

Less successful styles of parenting can be associated with negative situations in the parents' lives, such as high levels of stress or marital conflict. At the same time, such negative family situations can have direct adverse effects on children. For instance, preschool children are quite vulnerable to conflict between their parents, as can be seen in Maggie's reaction to her parents' fighting. Marital conflict has been shown to be related to negative play with peers, anxiety about parents' whereabouts, and an increased level of behavioral problems (Frosch and Mangelsdorf, 2001; Katz and Gottman, 1993). The particular effects on children may depend on the form of marital conflict they experience. Lynn Katz and John Gottman (1993) have found that mutually hostile patterns of parental interaction are associated with aggression and related problems in children, while a pattern in which the father becomes angry and withdrawn is associated with such problems as anxiety.

Child Development CD
Divorce and Child Development

Divorce may also have a negative impact on preschool children because they are now cognitively mature enough to grasp the anger and incompatibility between the parents, but not yet mature enough to understand the marital breakup is not their fault (Hetherington and Stanley-Hagan, 1999). When Judith Wallerstein and Joan Kelly (1982) interviewed a large number of $3^{1}/_{2}$- to 6-year-olds following their parents' divorce, they found that self-blame was preschoolers' predominant response. Younger children would probably not be capable of such a reaction. In Chapter 12 we will say more about the effects on children of marital conflict and divorce.

Identification with Parents

Identification:
The process by which children strive to be like their parents in thoughts and feelings as well as in actions.

Psychoanalytic theory holds that children strive to be *like* their parents, not only in actions but in thoughts and feelings as well. This process is called **identification.** As young children become aware of parent-child power differences, identification with their parents allows them to feel more potent rather than powerless. Historically, psychoanalysts have argued that children identify most strongly with the parent of the same sex, and that this is the basis for the child's sense of gender. Our own view is that relationships with *both* parents, and the parents' relationship with each other, all may influence the preschool child's emerging sense of self.

Identification isn't possible until a child has some ability to *understand* the parents' attitudes and feelings, as well as observing their actions. This is why identification doesn't become apparent until the preschool period, when such cognitive ability emerges. It is also no accident that the appearance of identification coincides with the appearance of true interpersonal aggression, true empathy for others, and a marked increase in self-regulation. All of these developmental changes are intimately connected. Self-control, for example, partly involves internalizing parental standards and using them as guides for behavior. Such internalization is at the heart of the identification process.

Cognitive readiness to identify with parents and accept their beliefs, rules, and values may not be enough to ensure that this process occurs. There is general agreement that internalization of the parents' rules and values is also influenced by the quality of the parent-child relationship. A relationship that facilitates internalization probably involves certain cognitive elements, such as clear communication (Grusec and Goodnow, 1994). At the same time, a loving, supportive relationship may provide an important motivational and emotional framework for internalization (Kochanska, 1997). For example, when parents overemphasize their power in teaching rules to children, the children can feel very anxious about prohibitions and fail to internalize them (Hoffman, 1994). Coercive techniques may get a child to comply with the parent's rules, but more positive approaches bring enthusiastic cooperation. When parents are clear in conveying rules and explain the reasons for them, they generate only moderate anxiety in children and therefore promote genuine acceptance of the rules.

Given that the quality of the parent-child relationship may affect the internalization of rules, it isn't surprising that security of attachment during infancy and toddlerhood is related to a child's openness to socialization and identification with family norms and values during the preschool years. Everett Waters has drawn upon social learning theory, cognitive developmental theory, and Bowlby's attachment theory to explain this connection (Waters et al., 1991). In keeping with our Chapter 8 discussion of socialization from the inside, Waters argues that securely attached infants are already committed to the family system long before they understand the rules. When the rules are then conveyed to them as preschoolers—through prohibitions, praise, and so forth—their reaction is, "If that's the system, that's for me." In other words, a positive orientation toward socialization and family rules is part of secure children's attachment relationships.

In early childhood there is both change and continuity in parent-child relationships—change because of the child's development and continuity because the foundation laid earlier in the relationship remains.

THE COHERENCE OF BEHAVIOR AND DEVELOPMENT

A major theme of this book is that child behavior and development is coherent, orderly, and logical. There is sense in the way various influences combine to shape the child, in the way each child develops interrelated characteristics, and in the way one phase of development paves the way for the next. Coherence in behavior and development exists from the beginning of life, but it becomes even more apparent during the preschool period.

The Coherence of the Self

Coherence can be seen very clearly in the individual characteristics of preschool children. Clusters of characteristics go together in a logical, meaningful way (Eder and Mangelsdorf, 1997). For instance, children who have high self-esteem also tend to have flexible self-control, to show more prosocial behavior, and to be better liked by peers (Sroufe, 1983). Those who are rated as more socially competent by teachers or who are better liked by peers engage in more social play, show more positive feelings toward other children, are less aggressive, and are more well-regulated emotionally (Arsenio et al., 2000; Howes, 1990; Rubin et al., 1995). In contrast, children who show hostility do not show much concern for others or prosocial behavior (Eisenberg and Fabes, 1998; Hastings et al., 2000), nor is prosocial behavior common among children who are highly dependent on their preschool teachers (Sroufe et al., 1983). Once again, the various characteristics make sense together. Children do not display a random assortment of disconnected traits; instead, their behavior reflects a logical and coherent underlying self. By the end of the preschool years it is possible to see children as having distinctive personalities.

The Coherence of Behavior Over Time

Just as there is logic and coherence in a preschooler's current behavior, so there is logic and coherence in how the child's behavior has developed over time. For example, children who had secure attachments in infancy are also able to use their parents as a secure base in the preschool years (Vaughn and Waters, 1990). Preschoolers with a history of secure attachment in infancy vary in such characteristics as their social involvement and activity levels, but they tend to share certain positive patterns of behavior (Sroufe, 1983). They have high self-esteem, are popular with peers, and show little negative emotion or hostile aggression. This is not to say that these preschoolers never use force; in fact, they tend to be quite assertive and sometimes display instrumental aggression in struggles over objects (Sroufe, 1983; Maccoby, 1980). However, they do not *seek* to injure other children either in response to frustration or without obvious provocation. Generally, they are empathic toward their peers, and they have a greater capacity for forming friendships than preschoolers with a history of anxious attachment (Kerns, 1996; Kestenbaum et al., 1989). They also tend to show more self-reliance, more curiosity, greater flexibility, and more positive emotions in interacting with peers (Arend, Gove, and Sroufe, 1979; Sroufe, 1983; Sroufe et al., 1984).

A very different profile is typical of preschoolers with a history of anxious-resistant attachment. These children have difficulty sustaining the give-and-take of peer interaction and often wind up neglected by peers. They have low self-esteem and little capacity for flexible self-management (Sroufe, 1983). They also have a great need for support and contact with teachers, often hovering near them (Sroufe, 1988; Sroufe et al., 1983). They show less prosocial behavior toward peers than children with secure attachment histories, not because they are hostile but because their immaturity and low tolerance for stress make them unable to do so. For example, one 4-year-old, on seeing another child with a cut lip, clapped his hand over his own mouth and climbed up on a teacher's lap (Kestenbaum et al., 1989). Such children also are frequent targets of bullying by peers.

Preschoolers with histories of anxious-avoidant attachment show yet another profile. They are often emotionally isolated or hostile and aggressive toward other children

(Sroufe, 1983). Some of these children show aggression that is calculated and without immediate provocation. For instance, in response to a playmate's remark that she had a stomachache, one little girl jabbed her fist into the other child's stomach. When the playmate complained, "That hurt!" the girl punched her again (Troy and Sroufe, 1987). Lying, blaming others, and behaving defiantly are also common in these children. Yet these same antisocial children also show strong dependency needs. Through their negative behaviors they elicit much guidance, support, and discipline from teachers (Sroufe and Fleeson, 1988), and they spend more time than their classmates sitting on teachers' laps during group activities (Sroufe et al., 1983). During group activities or when it's time to go home, their efforts to seek contact with the teacher often have a desperate quality. But when greeted by a teacher or when very upset, they deliberately turn away.

This pattern of behavior is complex, but its developmental link to anxious-avoidant attachment is coherent and understandable. The hostility toward or isolation from peers, the desperate dependency on adults, coupled with avoidance of adults when contact with them is appropriate, can all be interpreted as reflecting low self-esteem, general mistrust, and unresolved needs for nurturance arising from profound doubts about the availability of care beginning early in life.

Explaining Developmental Coherence

The coherence of young children's behavior over time is partly due to the fact that many influences on children continue to exert themselves in much the same ways they have in the past. Among these consistent influences is the amount of support children receive from parents. Research shows that there is substantial consistency in the level of parental support over time (Pianta, Egeland, and Erickson, 1989). Children who were nurtured and encouraged but given reasonable limits as toddlers tend to be treated in a similarly appropriate way as preschoolers. Moreover, parents who provided a secure base for exploration in infancy are more likely to encourage and support relationships with peers in preschool (Lieberman, 1977).

Another influence on preschool children that helps explain the coherence of their behavior over time is the fact that they are becoming increasingly consistent forces in

Individual differences in children's emotional responses and social behavior become increasingly prominent and stable during the preschool period.

their own development. By the preschool period, parents and other observers describe particular children as behaving in fairly consistent ways (e.g., Aksan et al., 1999; Kochanska et al., 2000; Vaughn et al., 1992). Moreover, research shows that preschool children have developed consistent expectations about their social worlds (Bretherton and Munholland, 1999; Main and Hesse, 1990; Sroufe, 1990). Some preschoolers routinely expect other people to be responsive to them, whereas others routinely expect the opposite. These consistent expectations and patterns of behavior are powerful influences. They tend to elicit certain reactions from others, and those reactions, in turn, reinforce how the child thinks and acts.

For example, parents, and even unfamiliar adults, show less positive emotions toward a difficult child than toward the child's siblings (Bugental, Blue, and Lewis, 1990). This less positive reaction can, in turn, help maintain the original difficultness. Similarly, other children do not like aggressive children and frequently reject them as playmates (Rubin et al., 1998; Sroufe, 1983). This rejection may encourage further aggression on the part of the disliked children.

Just like parents and peers, preschool teachers also respond in ways that reinforce the emerging personalities of young children (Sroufe and Fleeson, 1988). With children who are well managed, self-reliant, and sociable, teachers are warm and accepting. They hold age-appropriate standards for such youngsters and expect them to comply with their directives with little external control. At the same time, they directly promote the acceptance of these children by peers (White and Kistner, 1992). These responses, not surprisingly, tend to further encourage the very behaviors the children originally displayed.

In contrast, preschool teachers are quite controlling of children who are timid or impulsive (often those with histories of anxious-resistant attachment, like Meryl). They also make allowances for such children, accept their immature behavior, and are very nurturant toward them, much as one would be with a younger child. Once again, the teachers' responses tend to support the original patterns. With aggressive or hostile children (often with histories of avoidant attachment), teachers are controlling and at times even angry. They rarely expect compliance, and they discipline these children often. Since they do not expect these children to exert self-control, the children are not encouraged to manage themselves. Thus, although teachers can have a positive influence on children with troubled histories, the behavior of such children often works against them, eliciting responses from teachers that confirm the children's negative expectations about themselves (Sroufe and Fleeson, 1988).

Stability and Change in Individual Behavior

Personality may be thought of as a structure that evolves over the early years of life. At its base is the history of responsiveness and care provided during infancy and toddlerhood, a history that leads to a particular attachment relationship. The quality of the attachment relationship, in turn, predicts certain aspects of a child's behavior during the preschool period and also apparently forms the basis for later resilience in the face of adversity (see the box on page 363). The power of a secure attachment relationship seems to lie in promoting a beginning sense of self-worth and an abiding sense of relatedness or connection to others, which Erikson calls *basic trust*.

Resilience

In subsequent periods, parents of securely attached children build upon this base by supporting their children's independent initiatives, by promoting self-control, and by maintaining a clear parental presence through emotional support and demands for appropriate behavior. The parents, in other words, develop a system for exerting control over their children that doesn't stifle the children's efforts at exploration and autonomy. This *control system* (in addition to the attachment relationship) is another avenue by which parents influence their children's personality development.

The quality of the control system that parents establish predicts different behaviors in children than the quality of the attachment relationship does. For instance, attention and activity problems in elementary school are related to parents' failure to maintain appropriate boundaries between themselves and their child and to support the child's

A CLOSER LOOK

RESILIENCE

Even in the face of adversity, some children seem to do well (Werner and Smith, 2001). Likewise, following times of developmental difficulty, some children bounce back and again function well. Both of these circumstances have been used as examples of *resilience*. The term is certainly an apt description for such cases. But how are they to be explained?

In the history of developmental psychology, such children were first referred to as "invulnerable" or "invincible." E. James Anthony (1974) wrote that some children were like glass, easily shattered. Others—the "invulnerable"—were more like steel, with adversity simply bouncing off them. These terms carried the unfortunate implication that some children were not affected by adversity. It also suggested that these children inherently had "the right stuff." Thus, "invulnerability" suggested a fixed trait of the child, a part of his or her inborn nature. To some extent, *resilience* is still often applied in this traitlike way. In a prime example of circular reasoning, resilience is sometimes used simultaneously as evidence and explanation for children's positive functioning—that is, Why are these children doing well? Because they are resilient. How do we know they are resilient? Because they are doing well. The question remains, Why are they doing well?

Research shows that resilience is not a magical trait that some children have from birth. Rather, it is a capacity that develops over time in the context of a supportive environment (Masten, 2001). Some children do cope better with stress than others, but these tend to be children with histories of secure attachment and ongoing parental support (Pianta, Egeland, and Sroufe, 1990). Likewise, when troubled preschoolers whose functioning improves are compared with other children whose problems persist, differences in their early histories are found. Those troubled 4-year-olds who improve more often have supportive early histories including secure attachments (Sroufe, Egeland, and Kreutzer, 1990). Similarly, children whose functioning improves between middle childhood and adolescence are distinguished from those who continue to struggle by an early supportive history, current parental support, or both (Sroufe, Carlson, and Levy, 1998). When these factors are taken into account, little mystery remains.

It is the case that some children cope better with difficulty and adversity than others. It makes sense to describe them as resilient. But such a capacity is best understood as a developmental outcome, not as an inborn trait.

development of self-control and self-management (Carlson, Jacobvitz, and Sroufe, 1995). Not surprisingly, measures of the quality of early attachment *combined* with later measures of parental guidance in self-control predict a child's behavior much better than either set of measures does alone (e.g., Sroufe et al., 1999; Teo et al., 1996).

When personality is viewed as a developmental structure that is built up over time, it becomes clear that early experiences or temperament do *not* directly cause the child's behavior in the preschool period. Nor is it the case that the child's typical patterns of behavior cannot change. Fundamental change in children is always possible. For instance, since the quality of care a preschooler currently receives affects how well that child functions, improvement in care during the preschool years will have positive consequences for a child's behavior, even for a child who was anxiously attached earlier. As was the case at younger ages, the social support available to parents and the level of stress they experience are critical to the quality of the child care they provide. Across various cultural groups, measures of parental stress and social support have been shown to be related to the degree of security a young child feels, the quality of the parent-child relationship, and the child's acceptance by peers (e.g., Jennings, Stagg, and Connors, 1991; Melson, Ladd, and Hsu, 1993; Nakagawa, Teti, and Lamb, 1992). In the Minnesota longitudinal study, the single best predictor of change from anxious attachment in infancy to confident functioning in kindergarten was the mother's formation of a stable, supportive partnership during the intervening years, as we mentioned in Chapter 2 (Erickson, Egeland, and Sroufe, 1985). We can see these processes at work in the changes in Meryl's behavior during the preschool years.

Even though fundamental change in a child is always possible, it becomes more difficult as personality increasingly stabilizes. In infancy, assessments of caregiving received

APPLYING RESEARCH FINDINGS

Investing in Preschoolers

Since children's basic personality characteristics and the core of their self-esteem emerge by the end of the preschool period, growth-enhancing experiences during early childhood should be quite valuable, an investment in the child. This idea has inspired many intervention programs for preschoolers at developmental risk from economically disadvantaged environments. Contrary to early expectations, intervention programs do not primarily affect IQ scores. Although programs do tend to boost test scores temporarily, these effects fade within a few years after the program ends. What is of more lasting benefit is the empowering of youngsters who participate in high-quality preschool programs. These children tend to develop greater self-esteem, more positive attitudes toward education, and a stronger belief in themselves as able learners—factors that can continue to affect them even into adulthood. They also, in fact, do better in school.

An example of the long-lasting effects of intervention can be seen in the High/Scope Perry Preschool Project. The developers of this very successful program conducted a genuine experiment. They identified 123 young African-American children living in poverty and randomly assigned 58 of them to the program group. The other 65 served as controls. The long-term effects were dramatic, as shown in Figure 10.1. Compared with participants in the control group, young adults who had experienced the intervention program as preschoolers were significantly more likely to have at least a twelfth-grade education, to earn a steady income, to own their own home, and to have stayed off welfare and out of trouble with the law. These positive results translate into important economic benefits for society as a whole. The cost of the program was just a little over $12,000 per child, but society gained back more than $88,000 per child in savings on the cost of schooling (children in the program had less need for special education), welfare, involvement in the legal system, and settlements for victims of crimes, as well as in taxes these children later paid (see Figure 10.2).

Such long-term benefits result only from preschool programs of high quality. The High/Scope Project was a model of early-childhood education. It included two years of daily preschool classes in which the children participated in selecting their own learning activities in an environment rich with materials. Such child-initiated learning activities were vital to the program's success because they encouraged the empowering of the children (Schweinhart, Weikart, and Larner, 1986). The High/Scope Project also included weekly visits to the children's homes, which gave parents an opportunity to learn about what their children were doing in the classroom, to witness first-hand their children's progress and skills, and to discover how they could help. Parents were encouraged to become active participants in supporting their children's development. Active involvement of the parents is central to the long-term success of early-childhood intervention because it can continue long after the preschool program is over. Other factors that contribute to a successful program are a stable staff, a low child-teacher ratio, and a fairly long duration (Schweinhart and Weikart, 1993). In general, quality of out-of-home care during the preschool years has been found to be related to children's later cognitive and socioemotional adjustment (Peisner-Feinberg et al., 2001).

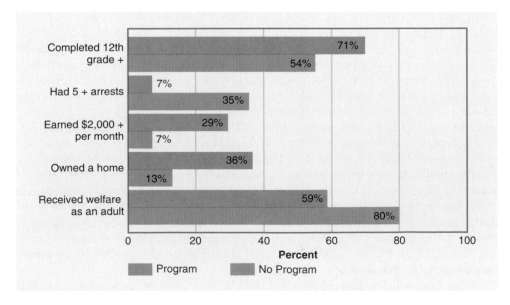

Figure 10.1
HIGH/SCOPE PERRY
PRESCHOOL PROJECT:
MAJOR FINDINGS AT AGE 27
*(Source: Schweinhart and
Weikart, 1993, p. 54.)*

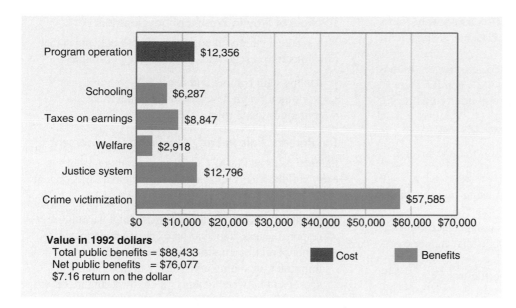

Figure 10.2
HIGH/SCOPE PERRY
PRESCHOOL PROJECT:
PUBLIC COST AND
ECONOMIC BENEFIT PER
PARTICIPANT
*(Source: Schweinhart and
Weikart, 1993, p. 55.)*

or other environmental measures often predict later behavior better than measures of the infant's own current behaviors do. By the preschool years, this is no longer so clearly the case. Assessments of preschoolers (apart from caregivers) predict later behavior quite well, even through adolescence and early adulthood (Sroufe, Carlson, and Shulman, 1993). Developmental history has now become part of the child, and a distinctive personality is emerging and becoming stable. In subsequent periods, behavior will be even more stable, with certain patterns like aggressiveness becoming very difficult to change. For these reasons, researchers have become increasingly interested in early intervention to change maladaptive behaviors. Such interventions are the topic of the box on page 364.

Preschool Intervention

Chapter Summary

Introduction

The social achievements of early childhood include:

- experiencing a dramatically expanding world;
- notable developments in self-reliance, self-control, and self-regulation;
- exploration of adult roles; and
- increasingly coherent and individually distinctive behavior.

Some Hallmarks of Early Childhood Social and Emotional Development

In early childhood, children's social worlds expand as a result of:

- attending day care, preschool, and kindergarten;
- expanded peer influence; and
- increasing importance of sibling relationships.

Increases in self-reliance during the preschool years are supported by developments in:

- motor skills;
- language and cognitive abilities;
- ability to tolerate frustration; and
- capacity for imagination and fantasy play.

Signs of preschoolers' growing self-control and self-management include increased abilities to:

- weigh future consequences;
- think of ways around obstacles;
- control emotions when goal-directed activities are blocked;
- concentrate; and
- do more than one thing at a time.

The Developing Self

Preschool cognitive development has a strong impact on the development of a sense of self.

- Children become increasingly able to include a variety of different experiences in their representation of self and to uncouple different aspects of experience.

- Children develop a sense of **self-constancy,** begin to think of themselves as having particular dispositions, and begin to evaluate the self.
- Children develop a gender-based self-concept as they adopt **sex-typed behavior,** acquire a **gender-role concept,** and develop a sense of **gender constancy.**

Social Development: The New World of Peers

In early childhood, peer relationships include several important features:

- Interactions with peers become increasingly sustained and coordinated.
- Individual differences in social competence emerge.
- Children begin to form friendships that endure over time.
- Peer relationships provide opportunities for development.

Emotional Development

Preschoolers' emotional development is as dramatic as their cognitive and social development.

- Children's understanding of emotions and their causes increases.
- Children's **emotional regulation** increases, including their ability to tolerate frustration and to be appropriately flexible in controlling emotions and impulses.
- Children begin to internalize standards for behavior into the self.
- Self-evaluative emotions, such as guilt and pride, emerge.
- True interpersonal **aggression** and **prosocial behavior** emerge and increase in frequency.

The Role of Play in Preschool Development

Play serves a variety of cognitive, emotional, and social functions for preschoolers, providing opportunities for:

- dealing with conflict and fear;
- working through developmental issues; and
- trying out social roles.

The Parents' Role in Early Childhood Development

Parents' roles and tasks change in several ways during early childhood as children's developmental tasks change.

- Some parenting qualities that were important to infants remain so in early childhood, including warmth, responsiveness, and sharing of positive feelings.
- Other parenting qualities become increasingly important, including consistency in discipline and agreement between parents on child-rearing methods.
- Differences in parenting style begin to have an impact on children's functioning and future development.
- Preschool cognitive advances make possible **identification** with parents.

The Coherence of Behavior and Development

Coherence in behavior and development becomes increasingly apparent in early childhood.

- Children's behavior begins to reflect a logical and coherent underlying self.
- Children's development shows coherence over time, due to attachment history, consistency of ongoing parental influence, and consistency in their own behavior and expectations.
- Fundamental change is always possible for children, but becomes increasingly difficult as personality stabilizes.

Review Questions

Introduction

1. What are the major social achievements of early childhood?

Some Hallmarks of Early Childhood Social and Emotional Development

2. How do children's social worlds expand in the preschool years?
3. Explain the increases in self-reliance, self-control, and self-management that occur in early childhood.

The Developing Self

4. Summarize the development of preschoolers' sense of self and explain how cognitive development is involved in this process.

5. Explain what is involved in children's development of a gender-based self-concept.

Social Development: The New World of Peers

6. How do children's peer relationships change during the preschool years?

Emotional Development

7. What major emotional developments occur during the preschool years?
8. Explain how preschoolers' cognitive and emotional development are related.

The Role of Play in Preschool Development

9. What functions does play serve for preschoolers?

The Parents' Role in Early Childhood Development

10. How do parents' roles and tasks change during early childhood?

The Coherence of Behavior and Development

11. Discuss how coherence in behavior and development increases during early childhood.

Application and Observation

1. Examine parenting books and/or parenting magazines for advice on disciplining young children. What issues do the books or articles focus on? What discipline techniques are most frequently suggested? How do the recommended techniques relate to Baumrind's parenting categories? What short- and long-term effects would the recommended techniques seem likely to have on preschoolers' behavior and development?

2. Interview children from 3 to 7 years old about their understanding of gender roles, using a task modeled on the Sex Role Learning Index (Serbin et al., 1993). Find pictures of five items traditionally associated with the masculine gender role in our culture and five traditionally associated with the feminine gender role—a mixture of toys and items used by adults is best. Tell the child *"I'm going to show you pictures of some things, and we're going to put them into three piles: things for girls, things for boys, and things for both girls and boys."* Show the pictures to the child in random order. For each picture, say *"This is a picture of a/an_____. Who would use a/an_____to_____ —girls? boys? or both girls and boys?"* Then let the child put it in the pile s/he has chosen. When you have gone through all the cards, pick up the cards the child has placed in the *"both"* pile and get the child to sort them into the *"boy"* and *"girl"* piles by saying, *"You said these things are for both girls and boys, but who would use a/an_____ to_____more—girls? or boys?"* Count the number of cards the child initially places in the *"both"* pile to score her/his gender role flexibility. Count the number of traditionally masculine objects the child *ends up* placing in the *"boy"* pile and the number of traditionally feminine objects the child *ends up* placing in the *"girl"* pile to score his/her knowledge of traditional gender roles. What differences and similarities are there in the children's responses? How do they compare to the information in this chapter about children's understanding of gender roles? How would you explain the responses of the particular children you interviewed?

3. Visit a toy store and look at toys and games intended for preschoolers (3- to 6-year-olds). To what extent do the toys and games seem to be gender-typed? How is it indicated that a particular toy is intended for boys or for girls? What toys are aimed mainly at boys? Mainly at girls? At both boys and girls? How do these three groups of toys differ? What kinds of play activities would be fostered by the toys aimed at boys, by those aimed at girls, and by those that seem to be gender-neutral?

4. Observe young children in a preschool or day care setting, taking particular note of behavior that sheds light on their social development. First, take note of overall patterns in their behavior—e.g., what they're doing, who's playing together, whether they're playing in groups or in pairs, how the teacher or other adults are involved with them. Next, select a few children for closer observation and note individual differences in their behavior—e.g., activity level, choice of playmates, amount of interaction with other children, amount and type of aggression, amount and type of pretend play.

Part 4 Epilogue: Early Childhood

Development continues at a very rapid pace during the preschool period, ages 2½ through 5. Preschoolers don't just learn more skills and information; they also undergo qualitative changes in how they think and act. Although development always builds on what has gone before, 5-year-olds are fundamentally different people from 2-year-olds. Five-year-olds use language fluently, in contrast to the two- or three-word sentences of the toddler. Five-year-olds also reason about the world in ways far beyond 2-year-olds' capacities. Although 5-year-olds' explanations for things often charm us with their magical qualities, the very fact that they are so preoccupied with how things work sets them distinctly apart from children who are only 2. In independence from parents, 5-year-olds are also markedly different from toddlers, who are just discovering their autonomy. Similarly, 5-year-olds exert a degree of self-management absent in children three years younger. Five-year-olds are in some ways more similar to adults than to 2-year-olds. For instance, whereas a 5-year-old can easily learn to use a phone to make an emergency call, a 2-year-old cannot be expected to master this skill.

Compared with toddlers, preschoolers have a more advanced ability to represent things mentally. Preschoolers can imagine combinations of things that they have never actually experienced. After spotting some candy on a shelf that is too high to reach, a preschooler might imagine stacking some nearby boxes to form a makeshift set of steps. Representational skills of this sort account for more effective problem solving. The child can "see" the solution without having directly experienced it before and without engaging in a random trial-and-error approach.

Preschoolers' cognitive advances support their social and emotional development. Improvements in language and the ability to take another person's perspective are the basis for rapid advances in peer relationships. Representational skills and imagination make possible fantasy play, which in turn helps the child to resolve conflicts, practice new skills, and try out social roles. Representational skills, along with the ability to categorize things, allow children to conceive of themselves as boys or girls. Representational skills also enable identification with parents, and they con-tribute to the child's growing ability to delay gratification, inhibit responses, tolerate frustration, and otherwise exert self-control.

Cognitive advances also help promote changes in the parent-child relationship. As a child's language and thinking abilities become more advanced, parents begin to rely more on reasoning to influence behavior. They also expect a preschooler to act more maturely, partly because they believe that the child "knows better" by this age. These expectations help encourage the very behaviors the parents want.

At the same time cognitive advances are influencing social and emotional development, the reverse is also taking place. How a preschooler interacts with and feels about other people greatly affects opportunities for cognitive stimulation and growth. For instance, involvement with peers fosters expansion of a child's knowledge and affords opportunities to practice language and other cognitive skills.

Different aspects of development are intimately connected. When we see a change in a child's way of thinking and reasoning, we usually see a parallel change in the child's social and emotional life. For example, preschoolers begin acquiring abstract representations—scripts—of the sequences involved in familiar experiences, such as going to a birthday party. In a parallel fashion, they also develop abstract representations of themselves with others—generalized expectations about how others are likely to respond to them, called internal working models. The various aspects of human development do not proceed in isolation. Each is linked to the others; development is organized and coherent.

Stability and Change in Individual Development

Individual development is characterized by logical coherence and by continuity over time. By the end of the preschool period we see individual adaptations that have evolved from the adaptations that emerged during infancy and toddlerhood. These individual adaptations, or personalities, are intimately related to the caregiving system in which the child has been raised, although temperament also plays a part. By the preschool period, however, temperament and experience, whatever their respective roles, have both become incorporated into the total child.

368

Continuity in development persists beyond the preschool period. For instance, there is evidence for a link between a child's degree of self-control as a preschooler and his or her self-control between the ages of 7 and 23 (Block, 1987). For girls, the correlation between self-control at age 4 and self-control years later is particularly strong. Researchers have even been able to predict the likelihood of teenage drug abuse from earlier measures of self-control versus impulsiveness. In a similar vein, psychologist Walter Mischel has found that measures of a 5-year-old's ability to delay gratification can be used to predict aspects of behavior at 12 years of age (Mischel, Shoda, and Rodriguez, 1989).

Complex issues are involved in conducting such longitudinal studies. Often the researchers must look at very different behaviors over time, behaviors appropriate to the child's developmental level and the particular situation (Sroufe, 1988). Nevertheless, as developmental research becomes more conceptually sophisticated, increasing evidence of a marked continuity in individual development is emerging. Children are not chalkboards to be erased and written on anew. Current development unfolds in a logical fashion from what has gone before.

One factor contributing to this developmental continuity over time is stability in the care the child receives. Parents who provide for a child's needs in one developmental period are likely to continue meeting the child's needs in subsequent periods partly because of continuity in the social support available to them. Conversely, parents who have trouble being adequately responsive at one stage of their child's development are likely to continue to have problems with parenting unless their circumstances change. We have repeatedly emphasized the importance of life circumstances for the caregiving system. If stresses on parents diminish, or if their social support is strengthened, the child will probably begin to function better.

Another factor contributing to continuity in children's adaptations is the fact that, with age, children increasingly shape their own environments. This may be partly because certain aspects of behavior (e.g., general activity level) are stable by the preschool age and may lead to different kinds of experiences. More important, we believe, is the fact that youngsters develop expectations, and their approach to the world based on those expectations often makes the expectations come true. For instance, imagine two children in a preschool classroom, each asking another child to play (Sroufe, 1988). When the first child is turned down, she is devastated by what she perceives to be a personal rejection. She retreats to a corner, where she sits alone, convinced nobody likes her. The second child receives a similar refusal, but rather than feeling rejected he simply moves on to another potential playmate, who accepts his invitation, and the two play happily. These children are clearly creating different environments for themselves on the basis of different expectations

and outlooks. Both have the cognitive capacity to recognize that their invitation was declined, but the rejection has different meanings to them; they interpret it in different ways. Thus, by the preschool period, children, through their various experiences, have formed expectations about the self and others that greatly influence how they act. These distinctive expectations, which are very general in nature, are central to the child's personality.

How a preschooler's expectations affect the caregiving system is particularly important to maintaining the child's style of thinking and acting. Consider an infant who shows a pattern of anxious-resistant attachment—Meryl, for example. Because of inconsistent care she has developed the expectation that contact with her mother may not always give her comfort in times of stress. As a result, she is anxious in new situations, easily upset, and hard to reassure. Research suggests that such a child is also likely to be whiny, prone to tantrums, and difficult to control, often becoming locked in power struggles with the parent (Gove, 1983). Meryl as a toddler and young preschooler strongly resisted Karen's efforts to impose limits on her. Such a child requires unusually clear, firm, and consistent handling in order to change her negative expectations, yet this was precisely what was difficult for Karen to provide in the first place. To break the negative cycle an intervention program may be needed, for parents sometimes need help to believe they can ultimately master the child's behavior.

Does all this mean that personality is fixed by early childhood? No, certainly not. The success of intervention programs underscores the fact that fundamental change in behavior is always possible. It is especially likely during periods of major developmental reorganization, when children acquire new ways of integrating and using the capacities they have. Developmentalists would single out the toddler period, early childhood, adolescence, and early adulthood as periods of notable reorganization. Fundamental change in behavior can occur at any time, however—often spurred, as we said earlier, by changing life circumstances. Meryl again provides a good example. The arrival of Joe Turner makes a real difference in her life. Not only does Meryl respond well to Joe's firm, authoritative parenting, she also benefits from the greater confidence and satisfaction Joe inspires in Karen as a mother. At the same time, Meryl is fortunate to have a kindergarten teacher who helps create change-producing experiences for her by gently guiding her toward involvement with peers. With this help she is able to make a solid connection in the peer group.

Four Children as Preschoolers

Despite the fundamental changes that have taken place in Meryl, she is still distinctly different from Malcolm, Mikey, and Maggie, who are also different from one another. Each is developing in his or her own unique way, the product of a certain biology and specific past and present experiences. Let's review the progress each has made during the preschool period.

Mikey is tackling the developmental issues of the preschool period with ease. He is a capable, self-reliant child who shows all the signs of readiness for school. He is interested in cognitive activities and is responsive to his preschool teachers. At the same time, he has moved smoothly into the world of peers, becoming a peer leader who is liked by others.

Even with all these positive developments, however, Mikey may encounter some problems. Because he is such a bright, sensitive, perceptive child, he is vulnerable to internalizing the conflicts between his mother and father, which are now intensifying. The role of peacemaker we see him playing is not really a new one for Mikey. Earlier, Christine and Frank used Mikey's behavior as an excuse to become distracted from their differences, as happened in the episode at the breakfast table when Mikey was a baby. Now Mikey deliberately distracts them from their arguments with his words and antics. Although his awareness of interpersonal tension is impressive in a child this age, it is also worrisome. Mikey is too young to be mediating conflicts between others, especially between his parents. He is essentially assuming responsibility for his parents' needs rather than the other way around. This role reversal is a burden for any child (Minuchin, 1988). Unless the marital conflicts are resolved, Mikey may face difficulties.

Maggie also progressed well for the most part during her preschool years. At age 4, she eagerly embraced the new challenges and opportunities provided by being in day care every day. Her easygoing, adaptable disposition and her secure attachment history provided her with some protection against the potential negative impacts of the growing conflict between her parents. However, the difference in Frank's treatment of her and Mikey has sown a seed of potential trouble. In addition, she has witnessed more of the friction between her parents than Mikey has, and by the end of her preschool years she shows signs of internalizing their conflict in the form of anxiety and social withdrawal that is uncharacteristic of her. Exacerbating the situation for her is the fact that Christine seems too preoccupied and overwhelmed by her own struggles to be as available and supportive to her as in the past. Because of Maggie and Mikey's loving, positive sibling relationship, they are able to serve as sources of comfort and support to each other, but in the long term they will also need support from their parents if they are to continue to develop in positive ways.

Malcolm, the active, precocious toddler, has become a lively and engaging preschooler. He is curious, confident, and full of energy and good humor. His language and thinking skills are well developed when he enters kindergarten. Being very outgoing, Malcolm quickly makes friends at school.

At home Malcolm's social environment continues to be warm and supportive, while still providing him with clear-cut standards of behavior. His mother, father, and grandmother nicely illustrate Baumrind's authoritative parenting: high expectations and firm limits combined with a great deal of love. Their handling of the incident over the tricycle on the playground is a case in point. DeeDee, John, and Momma Jo cherish Malcolm, including his great exuberance. Behavior that to others might seem slightly hyperactive is to them an indication that he is simply full of pep. Yet they do not take Malcolm's physical aggression lightly. They demand of him more self-control and concern for other people. In a family less able to handle Malcolm and less willing to go to bat for him, this incident could have been a negative turning point. But instead, Malcolm's parents take the event in stride and turn it into a valuable learning experience for him. We can imagine Malcolm in the future striving to heed what his parents have said by resolving peer conflicts more peacefully. If the Williams family continues to be this supportive of Malcolm's development, we would expect him to continue to flourish as he enters middle childhood, a time that poses special challenges for minority-group children in urban neighborhoods.

The preschool period for Meryl, as we have said, marks a significant turnaround. She is showing more independence and self-management. When functioning at her best (as in the pretend shopping scenario when she first meets Amy), she seems every bit as competent as Mikey, Maggie, and Malcolm. This notable improvement is probably due in large part to Meryl's more stable and responsive home environment. In offering Karen his love and support, Joe Turner has helped her become a more effective parent. Now potentially stressful situations with Meryl seem more benign to Karen. She can respond to Meryl more firmly and consistently, following the model Joe provides. Joe has also made a direct contribution to Meryl's improvement by handling her in an affectionate but authoritative way. In these new circumstances, Meryl has become more cooperative, self-reliant, and confident about herself. She is breaking away from the overly passive, weak, and dependent profile often found in children with a history of anxious-resistant attachment.

We cannot say Meryl is suddenly an entirely different person, however. Her new self shows clear continuities with her past self. She is perhaps no longer a difficult child, but she is still initially hesitant with peers, she is still reluctant to try new things, and transitions continue to be hard for her. Under stress she may revert to her earlier patterns, but, given time, she can adapt well to new situations. As with our three other children, we can be optimistic about Meryl's ultimate adjustment to school.

Our stories are simplified composites of actual cases. The life of any child is more complicated and difficult to understand than the cases we present here. Nevertheless, the coherence in individual development that we describe in each case is supported by an emerging body of research.

Middle Childhood

Part 5 Four Children in Middle Childhood

Malcolm Williams

"Here are your arithmetic tests," announced Mrs. Khan to her class of fourth graders. "Four of you scored 90 or above: Gretchen, Andrea, Kevin, and Malcolm." Malcolm felt a glow of pride as the teacher handed him his paper. He sneaked a look at Tammy Wilson, who sat diagonally in front of him. She had been watching Malcolm, but she quickly turned away as soon as he glanced in her direction. She stared down at the paper on her desk and her face broke into a smile. Malcolm quickly turned back to his own paper. He wanted to look at Tammy again, but he didn't dare. His friends would tease him to death if they knew he liked her.

The rest of the afternoon dragged endlessly for Malcolm. By 3:02 he was in his coat and hurrying down the stairs, trying as best he could not to break the "no running" rule. Down the hall, past the cafeteria, right at the bulletin board; the short walk to freedom seemed endless. Malcolm could feel the cool March air rushing in through the open door. The breeze was like a shot of adrenaline to him. Veering around the other children he raced out the door and down the path, his math test flapping in his grip.

"Hey, Malcolm! Wanna shoot some hoops?" shouted Andy, a neighborhood friend.

"I gotta get home!" yelled Malcolm over his shoulder, never slowing his pace.

Despite Malcolm's excitement at getting a good grade on the test, doing well in school was not really new for him. Malcolm could be an excellent student when he applied himself. He was nowhere near as diligent as his sister Teresa, but his quick mind and enthusiasm for learning earned the praise of his teachers. "If he would just channel more of that energy into his school work," Mrs. Khan told DeeDee, "Malcolm would be at the top of the class." But channeling his energies into any one thing for long didn't come easily to Malcolm. He was a child with as many interests as there were hours in the day. Collections of everything imaginable cluttered his untidy

room. It seemed that every week he was announcing something else he wanted to do when he grew up. His whole family took great pleasure in Malcolm's endless plans and projects. They were convinced that this child, with his buoyant high spirits, was very special.

"Momma Jo!" called out Malcolm loudly, as he ran up the steps two at a time, still clutching his arithmetic test. "Momma Jo!"

"What is it?" Momma Jo asked. "What's got you so near burstin'?"

"Look!" said Malcolm excitedly, stopping at last to catch his breath, and he extended the precious, now crumpled sheet of paper to his grandmother.

"Well, will you look at that! No wonder you're so proud of yourself!"

"It was one of the best grades in the whole class!" Malcolm added.

"I wouldn't expect any less from such a bright child as you," Momma Jo answered. "Now come on here into the kitchen and tell me all about it. Your momma and daddy are gonna be so proud of you when they get home!"

The next two years of Malcolm's life passed quickly. In sixth grade he was still doing well at school, though concentration remained a problem he constantly worked on. Malcolm also stayed popular with his classmates. Because he was filled with enthusiastic schemes for having fun, other children liked him and followed his lead. Malcolm's best friends were three other boys from his neighborhood, Andy, Leon, and Curtis. After school they would usually head for the park. If the weather was bad, they would often congregate in Malcolm's room to sort through their basketball cards. DeeDee marveled at how grown-up they were becoming.

Given how independent Malcolm normally was, it seemed strange when he starting asking John to give him a ride to school in the morning on his way to work. Malcolm himself was a little embarrassed by this new arrangement, and he made his father drop him off a block from school. He didn't want the other kids to think he was a baby, coming to school with his daddy. But he wanted to avoid at all costs a group of older boys who hung out near the video arcade. They had been hassling him on the way to school for weeks now. Malcolm was not about to tell his parents what the problem was. If his father tried to interfere, it would only make things worse.

One morning when John had dropped him off, Malcolm spotted an older boy in an alley across the street, throwing something into a trashcan. Normally Malcolm would have walked on by, but something about the boy's furtive glances piqued his curiosity. When the boy had left, Malcolm crossed the street and looked in the can. There, under a pile of newspapers, wrapped in a plastic bag, was a .22-caliber handgun. Malcolm checked the gun and found it wasn't loaded. He stood there for a minute, his mind racing. Then he wrapped the gun up again and stuffed it in his pocket. He just had time before school to hide it in a hole in an old cement wall in the alley.

At lunch he told Andy about his discovery. They ate quickly and managed to slip out of the school cafeteria and around the corner to the alley before anyone noticed they were gone. Excitedly, Malcolm pulled the gun out of its hiding place.

"Let 'em mess with me," he said, referring to the boys who hung out near the video arcade. "I know how to take care of myself!"

"What ya got?" asked Eric Sanders, coming up behind Malcolm and Andy and peering over their shoulders. "Hey, Malcolm, you're not supposed to have a gun! You're gonna get in trouble!"

"It's just for self-defense, turkey," Malcolm answered. "Everybody has a right to self-defense. It's in the Constitution. C'mon, Andy. Let's go. Eric's being a jerk."

"It's against the *rules*," Eric called out loudly. "You know what Mr. Espinosa told us!"

"Will you slow down, Malcolm. I can't understand what you're saying." John Williams sat on the edge of a desk at the post office, listening into the phone.

"It was just for self-defense, Daddy. Honest it was. To show those gang kids I'm not afraid of them. Only Eric *told* on me. He told one of the teachers. I can't believe he did that! You just don't tell on your friends!" Malcolm's voice sounded on the verge of tears.

"OK, Malcolm, OK. I get the picture. Now put your principal back on the phone. We'll talk more about this when I get to school."

"Do you know how serious what you did was, Malcolm?" DeeDee asked him as she and John sat at the kitchen table with their son that evening.

"Yes," Malcolm answered, his head hanging, his voice soft and contrite.

"*Why* was keeping that gun so bad, no matter what the reason?" DeeDee pressed him.

"Cause people could get hurt."

"*You* could've gotten hurt—not necessarily by the gun, but by those gang kids if they thought you had a *loaded* gun! Do you know that?" DeeDee's face was filled with concern.

"Yes, ma'am."

"What if that gun had been used in a crime?" John put in sternly. "You're lucky you didn't end up in trouble with the police. You're lucky Mr. Espinosa understood the situation and let you off as lightly as he did."

"I don't feel lucky. I hate Eric. I hate all white people. You can't trust 'em."

DeeDee put a hand on Malcolm's shoulder and looked at him. "Let me ask you something," she said softly. "What color are the boys who've been hassling you?"

"Black," answered Malcolm, fingering a small hole in the knee of his jeans.

"So you don't put down all black people just because those boys are bad. Why do you put down all white people because of Eric? Anyway," DeeDee added, "Eric may have only been doing what he thought was right. You *did* break an important rule, you know."

"Naah, he didn't think it was right," Malcolm answered scornfully. "He was just tryin' to get me in trouble. He wanted to get back at me cause I called him a jerk. He's not so big on followin' the rules, ya know. He cheats on his spelling tests. I've seen him."

"Well, it's not always easy to live up to what we think is right," answered DeeDee. "Sometimes we all disappoint ourselves that way. White or black, it makes no difference. The important thing is that we learn from our mistakes."

"I guess so," said Malcolm grudgingly. "But Momma, when a white guy's a jerk, he's the biggest jerk of all."

DeeDee smiled and shook her head. Some lessons are learned in small steps, she thought.

Maggie and Mikey Gordon

"Would you read the next page for us please, Mikey?" Mrs. Clayton requested.

Mikey swung his gaze back from the window when he heard his name. He looked confused, then embarrassed. "Jimmy . . . ran . . . with . . . the . . . kite," he began hesitantly.

"Mikey, Katie just read that part," Mrs. Clayton corrected gently, as the other children started to giggle. "Begin at the top of the next page, please."

Mikey flushed and fumbled to turn the page. Everyone's eyes were on him. What's wrong with this child? Mrs. Clayton wondered as she showed Mikey where to start. On days like this he hardly seemed the same little boy who had started out as one of the best readers in her second-grade class. Mrs. Clayton was also concerned about Mikey's relationships with his classmates. He no longer seemed to be a leader. On the playground he was usually content to follow what the other boys suggested. "I'm a little worried about Mikey," Mrs. Clayton told Christine at a parent-teacher conference toward the end of the school year. "Sometimes he's his old fun-loving self. But other times he seems moody, even a bit lost. Is everything OK at home?"

"Things are fine at home," Christine answered quickly. But she knew in her heart that her marriage was going from bad to worse and Mikey was a barometer of the conflict. Frank stayed out late two or three nights a week. When he came home he had always been drinking heavily, and when he was drunk he was surly. Christine treated him gingerly, but that only seemed to make things worse.

One day in March, Frank's boss called at lunchtime to ask where Frank was. Christine, taken aback, blurted out a story about a possible doctor's appointment. She sensed that Frank's boss knew she was lying. That night, when she asked Frank where he had been, he said it was none of her damn business. "But you'll lose your job!" Christine shouted.

"That's *my* business," Frank answered. Then he laughed and looked at Christine with contempt. "What the hell's the difference? You don't need my paycheck. You're doing just fine at your high and mighty shop!"

These days Frank and Christine rarely talked except to argue. Mikey, sensing the widening rift between his parents, began to fill the tense silences with hilarious imitations of his teachers. He also began praising one parent to the other. When he was with his mother, he would talk excitedly about what he had done with his dad; when he was with his father, he talked in glowing terms about his mom. But even these poignant efforts had no effect on Christine and Frank. The gap between them had become a chasm. There was no bridging it now.

The voices came to Mikey as if in a dream. His parents were arguing, yelling angrily at each other. The voices grew louder and more filled with emotion. Eight-year-old Mikey could feel himself drawn out of sleep. He lay in bed with his eyes wide open. This wasn't a dream. It was real life. Mikey got out of bed and pulled his door open. Maggie sat huddled in her nightgown at the top of the stairs. She glanced at Mikey and then looked back down the stairs. Mikey sat down beside her, and she put her arm around him. "They're going to kill each other this time," Maggie whispered in her 10-year-old wisdom. "This is really a bad one."

The trouble had started hours earlier, as Frank sat drinking with four of his buddies at the Riverside Tavern. Sam had made a comment about men who couldn't handle their wives. The others had laughed and starting ribbing Frank. What was it like being married to such a feminist? George wanted to know. When Frank protested, Pete pointed out that Christine had him well trained. Then Phil began to speculate about all the buying trips Christine had been taking to New York. "Ya never know what she might get into down there," he went on relentlessly. By the time Frank left he was very drunk and very humiliated. As soon as he walked through the door he let the anger spill out.

"What do you want me to *do*?" Christine pleaded, knowing she shouldn't try to reason with him when he was in this condition.

"Be the wife you're supposed to be, damn it! Don't think I don't know what goes on in New York!"

"Frank, that's crazy! I rush back home the same day just to try to keep you happy!"

"Don't call me crazy!" Frank shouted and pushed her against the wall.

"That's it! I've had it!" Christine shouted back, and she ran to the hall and started up the stairs. As she looked up she was startled to see Mikey and Maggie silently watching, with strangely calm expressions on their faces. "Get your coats," she instructed sharply. "And be quick about it! We're going to Grandma's." Two weeks later Christine filed for divorce.

The next year, while the divorce proceedings dragged on, was a difficult time for Christine and the children. They moved in with her mother, who insisted she was rattling around all alone in her house and would enjoy the company. But it was crowded, with no room for all of their things, and Grandma wasn't used to the commotion the children brought with them. Christine was working full-time at the shop and sewing in the evening, trying to keep herself busy and save up enough for their own place. Although her mother lived across town from their old house, Christine didn't want to make Mikey and Maggie change schools in the middle of the year. So every morning she drove them to school on her way to work, and every afternoon her mother picked them up. It was hard to have friends over after school, and there wasn't much to do at Grandma's anyway, with no swings or tree house in the backyard and Grandma watching her talk shows on TV all the time.

At first Maggie spent every afternoon watching TV with her grandmother. She didn't seem to mind not seeing her friends, and Christine worried that she was still so withdrawn. But the anxiety Christine had noticed in her the last few years seemed to be easing day by day. When school let out for the summer, she spent hours in the hammock in the backyard reading. In the fall she started sixth grade. She seemed to welcome the change to middle school and quickly made friends there. She spent more and more time with her new friends Nicole and Jessica, who lived down the street and rode the bus with her every day. She was still quiet and serious most of the time, but she threw herself into her schoolwork, talked enthusiastically about her new teachers, and started violin lessons at school so she could join the orchestra.

Mikey took the separation from his friends in the old neighborhood much harder and arranged to go home after school with Richie to play on his computer as often as he could. Some days he seemed lethargic and depressed, other days he was ready to pick a fight with anyone at the slightest provocation. His schoolwork continued to suffer, and it was only by promising to have him tutored over the summer that Christine kept him from having to repeat third grade. He resisted the change to a new school in the fall, and many mornings he fought with Christine about going to school at all. It was harder for him to go to Richie's house now that they were no longer in the same school, and Mikey spent many afternoons in his room, working on model cars and airplanes. When Christine tried to talk to him about the divorce, he would pick at his fingernails and mutter one-word responses. Finally his new teacher mentioned to Christine that the school counselor was starting a support group for children with divorced parents. Despite Mikey's protests, Christine insisted he go, and it seemed to be helping. He was slowly growing more talkative and cheerful and spending less time alone in his room. Despite these improvements, worries lay just beneath the surface. Mikey couldn't shake the idea that somehow *he* was to blame for the divorce. He kept thinking that somehow he had let his parents down. His secret dream was that one day they would get back together.

Mikey continued to see Frank nearly every weekend. Frank delighted in taking his son fishing, camping, and to baseball games. Maggie was often left out of these father-son outings, but she didn't seem to mind very much. She told Christine she didn't want to stay at her father's house and would rather spend time with her and Grandma. Christine reflected that Frank hadn't shown much interest in Maggie in years anyway, so the new arrangement wasn't that much of a change. More than anything, Maggie seemed relieved that her father was gone.

"So how's it goin' at home?" Frank asked his son as the two settled into a booth at Burger King one Saturday a few months after the divorce was finalized.

"OK, I guess," said Mikey unenthusiastically.

"Hey, what's the matter? We're still going fishing this weekend, aren't we?"

"Sure," said Mikey, brightening a little.

"Good. Cause there's someone I want you to meet, and she's coming along. Her name's Nancy. She works in the office at my company. You'll like her. She's OK."

Mikey looked blankly at his father, as if he understood the words but couldn't quite figure out what they meant.

"Hey, aren't you gonna eat the rest of those fries?" Frank asked, reaching over to help himself.

Meryl Polonius Turner

This sumer I got a new bruther. He crys a lot. Mom seys all babys cry. Sumtimes I make a fase and he stops crying. Wen he gets biger I will show him my toys. I like haveing a bruther moste of the time.

"Oh, that's very good!" Karen exclaimed after reading the story Meryl had written on her first day in third grade. "And look, you've done a picture of the whole family! There you are holding daddy's hand and here I am holding little Joey. You even drew my fuzzy blue bedroom slippers. Are they really that big and blue?"

"They're pretty big, Mom," Meryl said, considering the picture soberly.

"Well, we'll just have to hang this right up on the refrigerator where everyone can see it."

"You can take down the one with the pussy willows to make room," Meryl suggested. "That one's old and I don't like it very much any more. I can draw a lot better now."

Karen was astounded at how much better Meryl did everything these days. Around the house Meryl was a real little helper. She would stand by with the soap and towel when Karen gave Joey his bath. She meticulously set the table for dinner, making sure the silverware was neatly aligned. Meryl's second-grade teacher had called her "a joy to have in the class." She worked hard in school, listened carefully, and cooperated well with others. Karen could hardly believe this was the same little girl who used to throw such terrible tantrums.

But looking beneath the surface, Karen could see threads from Meryl's past. Meryl was still shy with strangers and hesitant in new situations. Take the time Joe tried to teach her to ride a bicycle. Meryl had just turned six and was starting first grade. Other children her age were riding two-wheelers, and Joe thought it was time for Meryl to learn how to ride one too. But she stubbornly refused to let him remove the training wheels from her bike. "I'll fall off!" she insisted. "I *know* I'll fall off!" Joe removed the training wheels anyway and coaxed her to give it a try. He ran alongside until she was riding smoothly and then let go of the bike. Meryl stopped pedaling and slowed to a wobble. "You've got to keep pedaling!" Joe shouted from behind her. "You can't just *sit* there! Pedal!" Meryl slowed almost to a standstill and crashed to the ground. Sobbing, she got up and limped away toward home. "Don't be a quitter, honey," Joe called after her. Meryl just kept walking. Joe was afraid she might never try riding a bike again.

But Meryl surprised him. She learned to ride a bike her own way. In the weeks that followed she studied other children on their bikes. She watched them pedal, mount and dismount, turn corners, and stop. Then one day shortly before Christmas she suddenly announced to Joe, "I'm ready to ride my bike now." Joe took the bike out again and Meryl gingerly climbed on. "Don't let go this time," she instructed. "You promise?" Joe assured her he would run along right beside her, holding onto the back of the seat until she told him to let go. Within a week she was riding with confidence, as if she had been doing it for years. The following spring she tried roller skating. At first she would inch her way from tree to fencepost, clutching at anything that could give her support. But soon she was skating with remarkable skill, even taking the cracks and bumps in stride. It seemed as if every month now she was ready to try something new.

What pleased Karen the most was Meryl's friendship with Amy. The two girls played together every chance they got. Amy would call Meryl on Saturday morning and they would make plans for the weekend.

"Why don't you come over here and we can play in the pool. My Dad's fixing it up today."

"OK. I'll bring my Barbie and her beach stuff."

Later that day the two would be back at Meryl's asking if Amy could stay for dinner. Soon they would be calling Amy's mother to ask if Amy could stay overnight. Because both girls had blonde hair, strangers sometimes asked them if they were sisters. "No," Meryl and Amy giggled, putting their arms around each other's shoulders. "We're just *best friends*."

The summer after Meryl finished fourth grade, the Turner family moved into a new house. Meryl was delighted with her new room. She and Amy spent hours picking out a new bedspread and curtains and deciding what color to paint the walls. But Meryl's favorite part of the house was the area under the back deck. It was high enough for a 10-year-old to stand up in but much too low for an adult. Meryl and Amy called it their apartment. They hung old blankets from the deck for walls, and they posted a sign that said in large letters: "PRIVATE. KEEP OUT! NO BOYS ALLOWED!" When 2-year-old Joey dared to peek in, the girls immediately shooed him away despite his tears and protests. That summer everything seemed perfect to Karen. Two beautiful children, a house of their own—finally, some of the good things in life. Neither she nor Joe realized what a heavy strain a large mortgage could place on their marriage and family.

"Meryl, honey, are you going to stay in *all* Saturday? It's so nice out. Why don't you call Amy and see what she's up to?"

Meryl briefly looked up from the picture she was drawing of a mother dog and her puppies. "Amy's probably over at that dumb Rita Martinez's house," Meryl said jealously. "She's always over there, and Rita can never do anything cause she always has to take care of her stupid little brother and help clean the house and stuff. I don't like her much anyway. She's Mexican."

"What has being Mexican got to do with whether you like her?" asked Karen. She tried to think of family conversations that might have triggered this sudden prejudice. All she could remember was something Joe had said about not being able to understand two new Mexican workers at the newspaper loading dock. "If they come to this country they should at least *try* to learn English," he'd grumbled. Could remarks like that have influenced Meryl?

With a forced smile, Karen returned to the original subject. "Why don't you just ride your bike over to Rita's and see if all three of you can play together?" Karen was worried that Meryl had been spending so much time alone lately. Often she stayed in her room for hours, sprawled on the floor with her crayons spread around her, slowly and carefully drawing. Puppies with their mothers was a frequently repeated theme. But what worried Karen even more was the way her daughter was talking right now. The old negative, insecure Meryl was emerging again.

"I'm busy," answered Meryl, turning back to her drawing and picking up a brown crayon. "And anyway," she added with a touch of bitterness, "who needs *them?*"

Karen knew her daughter too well to think this change had sprung from nowhere. Whenever there were problems that touched on Meryl's life, she tended to withdraw and become more inhibited. Karen wondered if it might be because things were so tense between Joe and herself. Joe and Karen were finding it hard to make their monthly mortgage payment. Their credit cards were charged to the limit. Their bills were piling up. They talked and worried about money almost every day. Even grocery shopping had become an ordeal because they agonized over everything they bought. Did they really *need* that bag of cookies? Could they get Meryl to eat the no-name brand of peanut butter? Their anxiety was clearly starting to have an effect on Meryl.

One evening Joe exploded because Karen had splurged on steak for dinner.

"I was only trying to do something a little special!" Karen protested, her voice quivering.

"Will you stop whining?" Joe shouted. "I'm sick of being the only adult around here!"

"Just because you don't show your feelings doesn't make you an adult!" Karen shot back.

"Fine! Let's just sell this damn house! I'm fed up with living this way!"

Meryl, who was sitting at the kitchen table, visibly shrank. Later she told her mother she had a stomachache and shut herself in her room. It was then that Karen knew she and Joe somehow had to solve this problem. Gradually they began to talk about it more rationally. They decided they really loved the house and wanted to keep it. The best solution would be for Karen to find a job. After some thought, Karen settled on getting a real estate license and going to work with her mother. The idea buoyed her spirits, and she threw herself into studying for the exam. It was a happy day the following April when she took her first clients house hunting.

But the best part for Karen was the change she could see in Meryl. Meryl was thrilled with her mother's new business. She was constantly asking questions, poring over Karen's book of listings, and saying which houses she thought were the prettiest. Meryl's friendship with Amy was also rekindled. The turning point came one Saturday morning when Meryl went over to Rita's to work on a school project with Amy and Rita. Meryl had felt nervous at first, but Rita's warm, outgoing mother had put her at ease. By the end of the morning the three girls were laughing and talking as they worked together at the kitchen table. From then on, both Amy and Meryl often went to Rita's. They enjoyed spending time with the large, close-knit Martinez family.

"*Yo ayudo mis amigas,*" Meryl said to Karen one evening as they cleared away the dinner dishes. "That means 'I help my girlfriends' in Spanish. Mrs. Martinez told me. And Rita told me some other Spanish words. *Perro* means dog, and *gato* means cat, and *casa* means house."

"I know some Spanish too," said Karen, smiling and brushing back a lock of Meryl's hair. "*Te amo.* Do you know what that means? It means I love you."

11 Cognitive Development in Middle Childhood

M r. Jones went to a restaurant and ordered a pizza for dinner. When the waiter asked if he wanted it cut into six or eight pieces, Mr. Jones said: "You'd better make it six. I could never eat eight!"

"Please stay out of the house today," Susie's mother said. "I have a lot of work to do." "Okay," replied Susie as she walked to the stairs. "Where do you think you're going?" her mother asked. "Well," said Susie, "if I can't stay in the house, I'll just play in my room instead."

Mr. Barley teaches first grade. One day when his class was talking about religion, Mr. Barley asked how many of the children were Catholic. When Bobby didn't raise his hand, the teacher said, "Why, Bobby, I thought you were Catholic too." "Oh no," said Bobby. "I'm not Catholic; I'm American."

These three jokes are taken from a study of children's humor conducted by Paul McGhee (1976). If they don't strike you as hilarious, that is because you are no longer in middle childhood. The typical 8- or 9-year-old finds them very funny. The first joke involves a misunderstanding about conservation; Mr. Jones apparently thinks the amount of pizza increases if it is cut into more slices. The other two jokes involve misunderstandings about classification. Susie is confused about the relationship between the subordinate concept of *room* and the larger concept of *house;* Bobby doesn't realize he can be classified as both a Catholic and an American at the same time. Each of these errors in reasoning is conquered during middle childhood, which is why children this age find these jokes funny; the punch lines deal with skills 8- or 9-year-olds have recently acquired. Preschoolers, in contrast, do not find these jokes funny because they don't understand that Mr. Jones, Susie, and Bobby have made errors in reasoning.

Between the ages of 5 and 8 children become fascinated with telling jokes and riddles. Theories of development provide various explanations for this new fascination. A social learning explanation is that children begin to spend more time with their peers, and jokes and riddles are part of what they share in the peer group. Being good at telling jokes and riddles is usually rewarded with social approval, which motivates children to

In cultures around the world, children are expected to assume increased responsibility when they reach middle childhood.

develop this skill. A Piagetian explanation is that children this age have acquired the cognitive abilities needed to master the format of jokes and riddles and to understand their humor. Because they take great pleasure in exercising these newfound abilities, joke and riddle telling blossoms. An information-processing explanation is that between the ages of 5 and 8 all the various skills needed to understand and tell jokes have become practiced and refined enough for children to integrate them into an effective joke-telling system. A sociocultural explanation is that joke telling and humor are highly valued in North American culture. Children experience many examples of adults and other children telling jokes and making humorous remarks in day-to-day interaction, and they gradually begin to participate in this cultural practice. In searching for the roots of cognitive changes during middle childhood, we will use a combination of all four of these approaches.

Piaget saw age 7 as a major cognitive turning point. At around this time, he argued, children make the important transition from *preoperational* thinking to more advanced *concrete operational* thought. Recent research suggests that the transition from early to middle childhood does not involve as dramatic a transformation in cognitive abilities as Piaget thought. Instead, the major cognitive developments of middle childhood appear to involve refinement and more widespread use of skills that existed in primitive form during the preschool years.

Other theorists have noted that in many cultures around the world children begin to be treated differently somewhere between ages 5 and 7, a change often referred to as the *5 to 7 year shift* (Sameroff and Haith, 1996). In some cultures, children of this age are given increased responsibility, such as caring for younger siblings. In many religious and legal traditions, children are considered to have reached the age of reason and accountability for their own actions at around this age. In most industrialized countries, children begin formal schooling at this time. All of these changes suggest widespread adult recognition of important changes in children's cognitive abilities.

Among the cognitive changes between early and middle childhood, several stand out as particularly important. During these years, children show improvements in:

Child Development CD
Transition to Middle Childhood

- capacity for logical, systematic thinking using multiple pieces of information, due in part to a marked decline in centration;

- ability to perceive underlying reality despite superficial appearance;

- domain-specific knowledge or *expertise;*

- information-processing capacity and control over attention and memory; and

- **metacognition,** the ability to think effectively about their own knowledge and processes of thought.

Metacognition:
The capacity to think about thinking.

Despite these advances, elementary school children still face cognitive limitations. First, even with increases in domain-specific knowledge, *they still lack the broad base of knowledge that adults possess.* This absence of information sometimes makes their reasoning seem immature. For instance, the summer Mikey turned 10, he and his friends decided to build a raft out of pieces of styrofoam held together by large thumbtacks. The raft fell to pieces as soon as they launched it in a nearby stream, much to their disappointment. What the boys lacked was information about appropriate ways to hold structures together against the forces exerted on them.

Second, because elementary school children have only recently acquired some of their thinking skills, *they sometimes have trouble using a skill they possess as part of a larger problem-solving system.* For instance, when Meryl was 8 she was perfectly capable of taking another person's perspective, but she didn't always do so when playing checkers with Joe. In her struggle to figure out what move to make next, she often forgot to look at Joe's moves from *his* viewpoint—namely, as strategies to lure her into making moves that were to *his* advantage. As a result, Meryl fell into Joe's traps again and again.

Finally, *elementary school children cannot reason maturely about abstract and hypothetical problems.* Their reasoning tends to be confined to the concrete here and now. For example, if 9-year-old Malcolm were given the hypothetical problem "What would you do if your remote control car wouldn't run?," he could not construct a comprehensive picture of all the things that *might* be wrong and then systematically propose how to test each one, both alone and in various combinations. In case of a real problem with his car, Malcolm would make reasonable attempts to solve it, but his efforts would not be organized to address each possibility in a systematic way.

As you read this chapter, you will learn much more about both the cognitive advances and the cognitive limitations of middle childhood. Elementary school children are far more competent than preschoolers are, but their thinking still has many immature aspects. The emergence of adultlike thinking across a broad range of contexts must await adolescence.

In exploring the cognitive world of middle childhood, we begin with an in-depth look at three areas in which major advances are made: concepts of conservation, classification skills, and memory abilities. In each case, you will see how capacities that emerged during the preschool period set the stage for later, more mature accomplishments. Next, we turn to social factors that can facilitate cognitive development during middle childhood. Here we focus on the roles of both peers and adults in promoting cognitive growth. We then discuss individual differences in cognitive functioning, especially as measured by IQ tests. Finally, we consider the significance of culture in intelligence testing and school achievement.

Questions to Think About As You Read

- What are the connections between social interaction and cognitive development in middle childhood?
- How do the real-world demands placed on children this age, at home and at school, allow for and foster cognitive development?

MAJOR COGNITIVE DEVELOPMENTS OF MIDDLE CHILDHOOD

Conservation Concepts

Child Development CD
Conservation Tasks

Although preschoolers sometimes show the beginnings of a grasp of concepts of conservation (the fact that quantities remain the same despite superficial transformations to them), they have trouble reasoning about them. They are greatly hampered by both centration and the appearance-reality problem. They do not realize that the transformations made during conservation tasks are reversible. During middle childhood, these earlier limitations are largely overcome. By age 10, most children exhibit an understanding of conservation of physical quantities such as number, length, area, mass, and displaced liquid volume, and they are able to use this understanding in a variety of circumstances. Figure 11.1 shows tasks for assessing children's knowledge of these conservation concepts.

Piaget argued that the same logical skills allow an understanding of *all* types of conservation. In his view, children acquire some of these concepts before others simply because they learn the characteristics of different kinds of quantities at different times. Table 11.1 on page 384 shows the ages at which 50 percent of American children succeed at different conservation tasks. Because this table is based on a large number of studies, many with different criteria for having attained conservation, a range of ages is shown for each task. Cross-cultural research has also revealed some differences in the ages at which children in different cultures are able to perform conservation tasks. The box on page 384 provides more details on these findings.

These changes in children's ability to solve conservation tasks illustrate a more general pattern of development: when abilities first emerge they are fragile, require substantial cognitive resources, and are used in a limited range of contexts. With additional experience they become more robust, require fewer cognitive resources, and are used in a broader range of contexts. During middle childhood, understanding of conservation of physical quantities becomes automatic and is a piece of knowledge that can be used in solving other problems.

An understanding of conservation requires children to look beyond the physical characteristics of things and to reason logically about what transformations mean. To do so, they must understand the difference between **contingent truth** and **necessary truth** (Inhelder and Piaget, 1964; Moshman and Timmons, 1982). Contingent truth is dependent or *contingent* on empirical observations. When you look out the window, observe drops of water falling, and conclude that it is raining, you are deducing a contingent truth. In contrast, a necessary truth is based on logical necessity apart from what you observe with your senses. If a twisting line to get into a movie is straightened out, you know by logical necessity that your wait to get in will not become longer, even though the line now looks longer, because no more people have been added.

In grasping the necessary truth that number is conserved despite a change in spacing, elementary school children are overcoming the appearance-reality problem that constrained them as preschoolers. They are no longer deceived by superficial appearance, such as the length of a movie line, and can think about the underlying reality. Still, there are limitations to their thinking. During middle childhood, understanding of necessary truth tends to be limited to concrete characteristics, such as the number of people in a

Contingent truth:
Knowledge that depends on empirical observations, on information gathered through the senses.

Necessary truth:
Knowledge that is based on logical necessity, apart from information gathered through the senses.

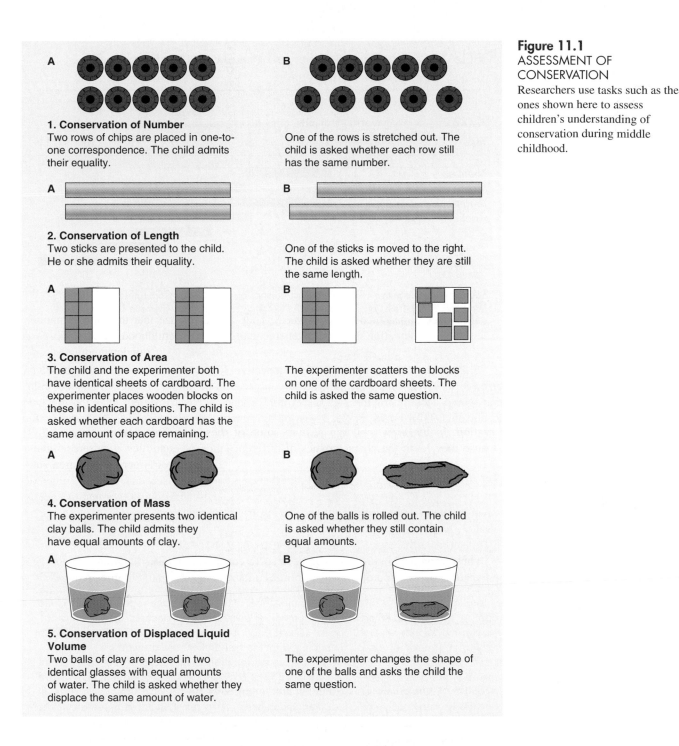

Figure 11.1
ASSESSMENT OF
CONSERVATION
Researchers use tasks such as the
ones shown here to assess
children's understanding of
conservation during middle
childhood.

A / **B**

1. Conservation of Number
Two rows of chips are placed in one-to-one correspondence. The child admits their equality.

One of the rows is stretched out. The child is asked whether each row still has the same number.

2. Conservation of Length
Two sticks are presented to the child. He or she admits their equality.

One of the sticks is moved to the right. The child is asked whether they are still the same length.

3. Conservation of Area
The child and the experimenter both have identical sheets of cardboard. The experimenter places wooden blocks on these in identical positions. The child is asked whether each cardboard has the same amount of space remaining.

The experimenter scatters the blocks on one of the cardboard sheets. The child is asked the same question.

4. Conservation of Mass
The experimenter presents two identical clay balls. The child admits they have equal amounts of clay.

One of the balls is rolled out. The child is asked whether they still contain equal amounts.

5. Conservation of Displaced Liquid Volume
Two balls of clay are placed in two identical glasses with equal amounts of water. The child is asked whether they displace the same amount of water.

The experimenter changes the shape of one of the balls and asks the child the same question.

line or the volume of liquid in a container. Children this age find it hard to grasp necessary truths related to more abstract concepts. We'll return to this issue later, when we talk about classification.

An Information-Processing Approach to Conservation   Piaget believed that the ability to solve conservation problems resulted from a fundamental shift in children's ability to reason logically. Information-processing theory offers a different explanation based on changes in the mental procedures, or rules, children follow to arrive at their solutions. Problem solvers do not *consciously* follow these rules; they use them implicitly. But as the rules change, so do the kinds of solutions reached.

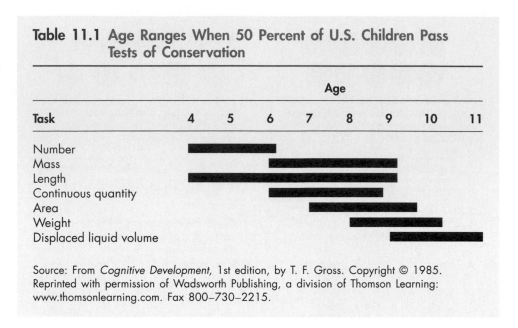

Table 11.1 Age Ranges When 50 Percent of U.S. Children Pass Tests of Conservation

Task	Age							
	4	5	6	7	8	9	10	11
Number								
Mass								
Length								
Continuous quantity								
Area								
Weight								
Displaced liquid volume								

Source: From *Cognitive Development*, 1st edition, by T. F. Gross. Copyright © 1985. Reprinted with permission of Wadsworth Publishing, a division of Thomson Learning: www.thomsonlearning.com. Fax 800–730–2215.

Taking an information-processing perspective, Robert Siegler and his colleagues analyzed 3- to 9-year-olds' performance on conservation of number tasks and deduced rules that would account for the patterns of performance seen at different ages (Siegler and Robinson, 1982). For example, 3-year-olds' immature errors seemed to be based on the rule, *The longer one always has more.* In contrast, the rule that many 6-year-olds seemed

A CLOSER LOOK

CULTURE AND THE EMERGENCE OF CONSERVATION CONCEPTS

When researchers assess the ages at which concepts of conservation emerge among children in industrialized cultures, they find patterns very similar to those in the United States and western Europe. In fact, some Asian children seem to understand conservation slightly earlier than American and European children (Gardiner and Kosmitzki, 2002). In traditional cultures that lack formal schooling, however, a lag of one or more years in the development of conservation concepts is frequently found (Dasen and Heron, 1981). In one early study, only 50 percent of 10- to 13-year-olds in Senegal correctly solved a conservation of liquid volume problem (Greenfield, 1966). Some studies in traditional societies have even found adults who fail to exhibit an understanding of conservation.

These results do not suggest that people in nonindustrialized cultures have major cognitive deficits. Instead, there is considerable evidence for two other explanations. One is that researchers conducting studies in traditional cultures may encounter communication problems. This was suggested in a study of Nova Scotian children who were tested in English for their understanding of concepts of conservation (Nyitii, 1982). Those who spoke English at school and Micmac (an Algonquin Indian language) at home lagged behind their peers who spoke English both at home and at school. However, when each group was tested in the language they spoke at home, no differences were found. Thus, at least part of the reported delay in the development of conservation concepts in nonindustrialized cultures may be due to subtle difficulties in understanding what the researchers are asking.

Another explanation is that cultures that lack formal schooling do not provide the same opportunities to learn about conservation concepts, or about test taking, as industrialized cultures. As a result, children in these cultures are slower to develop these skills. If this theory is right, providing supplemental learning experiences for these children should help close the gap between them and their peers in industrialized cultures. Research shows that this is often what happens. In one study, children from the Baoule culture in west Africa were trained to perform cognitive tasks similar to conservation tasks (Dasen, Ngini, and Lavallée, 1979). Then they were given conservation tests. The training did not entirely eliminate the age difference in understanding conservation, but it did dramatically reduce it. Apparently, normal youngsters in middle childhood in all cultures have the cognitive skills needed to rapidly develop an understanding of conservation if given the opportunity to do so.

An understanding of conservation allows children to reason about many quantitative concepts.

to follow was, *Ignore everything else and count.* Almost all 7- to 9-year-olds seemed to apply the mature rule, *The quantities will be different only if something is added or subtracted.* Both the 3-year-olds and the 6-year-olds treated the problem as one involving a contingent truth; they had to look at the lengths of the rows or count the number of objects to decide whether the quantities were the same or different. Only the oldest children recognized that the problem involved a necessary truth: number cannot change unless something is added or subtracted.

Similar sets of rules could be written to describe children's performance at different ages on other types of conservation tasks. The most mature rule would always entail an understanding of the logical necessity inherent in the problem. The content of less mature rules would vary depending on the particular conservation concept involved, because different physical dimensions and transformations have to be considered. For conservation of liquid volume problems, for example, children have to attend to the height and width of a column of liquid, rather than the length of a row and the spacing between objects. A rules approach to solving such problems tends to draw attention to these differences. It isn't surprising that children at first treat each kind of problem differently and don't develop the various concepts of conservation all at the same time. Only after children understand the logical necessity entailed in different kinds of conservation problems can they fully appreciate the similarity between them.

Summing Up Conservation Concepts Whether children's performance on conservation problems is explained using a Piagetian or an information-processing framework, several things are clear:

- Some concepts of conservation emerge during the preschool years, but not until middle childhood do children acquire a large set of conservation concepts and use them confidently in measurement and reasoning about concrete quantities.

- At least within industrialized cultures, the various concepts of conservation are acquired in a predictable order.

- Once children can consistently solve conservation problems, they are soon able to explain their answers in terms that show they understand conservation as a necessary truth.

- Once children understand conservation, they can think logically about many quantitative issues. For instance, conservation concepts are prerequisites for performing well on many elementary school arithmetic problems.

Figure 11.2
HIERARCHICAL
CLASSIFICATION
This hierarchy is part of the classification system for mammals. Each intersection represents a class (e.g., the class of domesticated dogs, which is composed of the subordinate classes of golden retrievers and all other domesticated dog breeds). An understanding of the relationships between subordinate and superordinate classes develops during middle childhood.

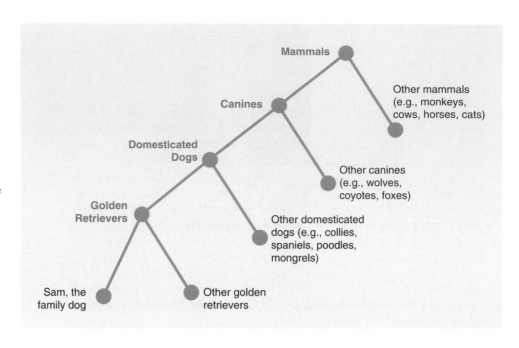

Hierarchical classification:
A classification system in which items are categorized using a hierarchy of subordinate and superordinate classes.

Matrix classification:
A classification system in which items are categorized simultaneously along two independent dimensions, such as shape and color.

Classification Skills

As we discussed in Chapter 9, preschoolers can readily sort things along one dimension, such as separating red blocks from blue ones. But Piaget maintained that children could not understand the relationships among categories in a more complex classification system until the concrete operational period. One such system is **hierarchical classification,** in which items are categorized using a hierarchy of subordinate and superordinate classes. Another is **matrix classification,** in which items are categorized simultaneously along two independent dimensions, such as shape and color.

Hierarchical Classification Hierarchical classification is often used to organize bodies of knowledge. Consider how we organize our knowledge of animals (see Figure 11.2). Sam, the Gordon family's dog, is a golden retriever, a type of domesticated dog belonging to a category called canines, along with other species such as wolves, jackals, and coyotes. Canines, in turn, are classified as a type of mammal, which is a type of animal. As we move up this hierarchy of classification, each term is broader and more inclusive. Notice, too, that each higher class is composed of all the classes under it in the hierarchy. The concept *domesticated dog,* for example, is produced by adding all the various breeds of dog together (golden retriever, poodle, cocker spaniel, etc.). For this reason, Piaget said that hierarchical classification involves the *addition* of classes. The addition of classes, in Piaget's theory, is a concrete operation.

Piaget used a task called *class inclusion* to test whether children understood hierarchical classification. In this task, a child is presented with a group of objects—say, six petunias and three begonias. The researcher makes sure the child knows that petunias and begonias are both flowers. The child is then asked, "Are there more petunias or more flowers?" Surprisingly, most 6-year-olds say there are more petunias. They seem to be comparing the two subordinate classes, petunias and begonias. Not until age 8 do most children start to give the correct answer by comparing one of the subordinate classes (petunia) to the superordinate class (flower).

Why do 6-year-olds fail the class-inclusion test? They seem to have trouble thinking about petunias simultaneously belonging to *two* classes—a subordinate one and a superordinate one. You can think of this as a kind of centration, one of the limitations of preschool thought. Of course, the fact that children don't pass the class-inclusion test doesn't mean they're unable to learn anything about hierarchical classification. By age

5 or 6, Mikey certainly knew Sam was a golden retriever and a golden retriever was a type of dog. But children this age lack a genuine understanding of a hierarchy's structure and its logical implications.

Typically, such genuine understanding is still absent even when children begin to answer the class-inclusion question correctly. For instance, during much of middle childhood, most youngsters don't yet realize that a subclass, by definition, cannot contain more elements than its superordinate class. Ellen Markman (1979) demonstrated this in a study of children age 9 and older. When she asked them the class-inclusion question about objects they could see, most answered correctly. However, when she asked them a *hypothetical* question about classification hierarchies ("Suppose we added 100 more petunias; would there be more petunias or more flowers?"), children younger than 11 often gave the wrong answer. Apparently, not until children are approaching adolescence do they grasp the more abstract, logical structure of classification hierarchies. In the earlier years of middle childhood, a knowledge of hierarchical classes seems to be tied to concrete objects and situations. An 8-year-old knows there are more flowers than petunias because he or she *sees* that petunias form a smaller group. Such knowledge, in other words, is based on contingent, not necessary, truth.

Interestingly, when the superordinate term is a naturally occurring **collection** rather than an abstract class, youngsters in early middle childhood have an easier time thinking about the relationship between levels in the system. A collection is an entity with subparts that go together because of their proximity, such as a forest of trees, a bouquet of flowers, or a flock of birds. Markman and her colleagues asked 6- and 7-year-olds the standard class-inclusion question versus a modified version using a collection instead of a superordinate class (Markman and Siebert, 1976). For instance, the child might be shown a picture of a forest with twenty oaks and ten pines and asked, "Are there more oaks or more trees here?" or, alternatively, "Which has more, the oaks or the forest?" Quite often 6- and 7-year-olds were able to answer the second type of question correctly, even though they failed on the first. Apparently, use of the collective term *forest* helped them to consider different levels simultaneously in this classification system. So, like conservation, class inclusion first appears as a skill in very specialized circumstances and then, during middle childhood, becomes a more generalized and useful skill for constructing knowledge.

If shown this picture and asked "Are there more daisies or more flowers here?," 6-year-olds would tend to answer incorrectly, "More daisies." If asked "Which has more, the daisies or the bouquet?," they would be more likely to answer correctly, "The bouquet."

Collection:
A naturally occurring entity with subparts that go together because of their proximity.

Matrix Classification Hierarchical classification is very useful for organizing some kinds of information, but other data are better organized in a matrix system. Suppose you want to organize bolts for sale in a hardware store. The bolts come in a range of diameters and lengths. You might arrange them in a set of drawers so that the top row has bolts one-quarter inch in diameter, the second row has bolts three-eighths inch in diameter, the third row has bolts one-half inch in diameter, and so on, working downward in order of increasing diameter. Similarly, you would put the shortest bolts in the first column of drawers at the left, the next longer size in the second column, and so forth, until the longest bolts were in the column at the far right. In the end you would produce a matrix of diameter times length. The bolts in each cell of the matrix would be the product of the diameter assigned to that particular row and the length assigned to that column. Piaget's term for the mental operation involved in forming such a matrix was *multiplication* of classes: one classification dimension (diameter) is multiplied by another (length). Like addition of classes, multiplication of classes is a concrete operation in Piaget's theory.

One way researchers study the development of matrix classification is to ask children to sort objects that differ along two or more dimensions, as we mentioned in Chapter 9. For instance, a child might be given a pile of blocks that are small and large, red and green, and asked to put the blocks into piles so that all the blocks in each pile go together. Preschoolers typically sort along one dimension only (size *or* color), as if

Figure 11.3
MATRIX COMPLETION
The objects in this matrix classification scheme are sorted by shape and color. One way to assess a child's understanding of matrix classification is to ask what the shape and color of the missing object should be.

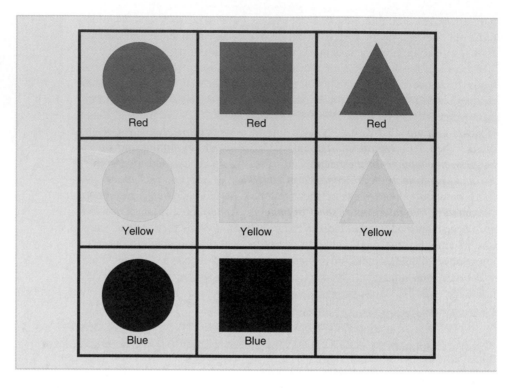

centration keeps them from noticing the other dimension. During the transition between early and middle childhood, children frequently first sort the blocks along one dimension and then subdivide the two resulting piles along the second dimension. This behavior suggests that they *notice* both dimensions but can handle only one at a time. By age 8 or 9, children approach this task much as adults do, sorting along both dimensions simultaneously to produce a classification matrix.

A second way to assess children's understanding of matrix classification is to ask them to place objects in a partly completed matrix. This task is illustrated in Figure 11.3, which shows a matrix classification system for circles, squares, and triangles of three different colors. A number of studies have confirmed Piaget's findings that preschoolers tend to complete the matrix with an object that is correct along only one of the two dimensions—they choose another red triangle, for example, or another blue square (Jacobs and Vandeventer, 1971). In contrast, by age 8, most children find such matrix classification problems easy to solve.

Six- and 7-year-olds can be trained to solve such problems by using a two-step strategy of dealing first with one dimension and then the other (Resnick, Siegel, and Kresh, 1971). This strategy allows children to overcome the constraints of centration by focusing on only one dimension at a time. It also gives them a ready-made approach to the problem so that they do not have to formulate their own plan for solving it. But even though 6- and 7-year-olds can learn how to follow the two-step procedure, they don't use it on their own in other situations.

Summing Up Classification Skills We can summarize the development of classification skills in children by reviewing a few key points:

- Children begin to classify objects very early in life, but it is not until middle childhood that they make effective use of classification when organizing information—for example, to answer class-inclusion questions correctly.

- A major reason why performance on classification tasks improves during middle childhood is that children this age largely overcome centration and become able to focus on more than one dimension or level at a time.

- Elementary school children make great progress in classification skills, but they still do not entirely grasp the logical necessity of classification structures. Their understanding of classification is not abstract but is applied to concrete objects and situations. In other words, it derives from contingent, not necessary, truth.

Information-Processing Abilities

One evening after dinner, 10-year-old Meryl sits at the kitchen table studying for a spelling test. In the same room, the dishwasher is running and Karen is talking with her mother on the telephone as she cleans the kitchen. In the living room, Joe and little Joey are engaged in raucous play. Meryl sits with her hands over her ears as she reads through a story presenting the spelling words. When she is finished, she takes out a sheet of paper and carefully copies each word. Then she practices writing each one five times. Finally, she turns to her mother, who has just hung up the telephone, and says, "Mom, can you test me on my spelling words?" Karen sits down next to her and reads the words one at a time for Meryl to spell out loud.

As Meryl's behavior demonstrates, children show major improvements in their ability to process information between early and middle childhood. Both attentional and memory abilities improve, and children gain a clearer understanding of their own information-processing abilities and what strategies they can use to improve their attentional and memory performance. These advances have implications for virtually every area of cognitive development.

Attentional Abilities Compared with preschoolers, 6- to 11-year-olds show greatly improved abilities to control their attention. As we discussed in Chapter 9, preschoolers have difficulty selecting information to attend to, staying focused on it, and ignoring irrelevant stimuli; during middle childhood, performance improves in all of these areas. Most school-aged children increasingly recognize that attention is a limited resource that can be intentionally directed to particular sources or types of information (Flavell and Miller, 1998). At the same time, they actually become more systematic, organized, and selective in directing their attention (Flavell et al., 2002). A major reason for their improved performance is that they develop increasingly sophisticated and effective strategies for directing and maintaining attention, and they begin to use them more consistently. For example, Meryl can concentrate on her spelling words in spite of the noise from the dishwasher, her mother's telephone conversation, and the noise from the living room, but she also realizes that covering her ears will help her shut out these sounds and focus attention on her task. Perhaps the most important attentional improvement in middle childhood is a growing flexibility in deploying attention, depending on the situation. Children now begin to realize that in some situations it is more adaptive to attend to all available information and in others it is more adaptive to be selective, and they adjust how they pay attention accordingly (Flavell et al., 2002).

Not all children are equally successful at directing and maintaining their attention on tasks and information that are not interesting to them. Individual differences in attentional skills become increasingly noticeable and important during middle childhood. Attention deficit disorders are often diagnosed during the elementary school years, in part because the school environment demands greater attentional abilities than most preschool settings. We will return to the topic of attention deficit disorders in Chapter 15.

Child Development CD
Attention Deficit Disorder

Memory Abilities Meryl's behavior demonstrates some of the improvements in memory abilities in middle childhood. She now knows which strategies are most likely to help her learn her spelling words, and she has become quite good at applying them. Children's memory skills are also useful on tasks unrelated to school, as seen in Chapter 9 when Mikey was trying to remember what to take to the beach. At age 6 he was not

During middle childhood, children's ability to focus attention on a task in spite of distractions increases greatly.

very good at generating a plan to help him remember, but at age 9 he could do so quite well. The night before, on his own, he placed his kite and fishing gear by the front door so he would see them on his way out and remember to take them. Virtually all elementary school children become better at using their memory capabilities and more aware of the nature of memory and how it works.

To explore the major aspects of memory that develop during middle childhood, we will use a framework suggested by John Flavell (Flavell et al., 2002), who has studied memory development extensively. Flavell's framework includes four factors: *memory capacity, knowledge, memory strategies,* and *metamemory.*

Memory Capacity. Memory capacity involves the amount of information that can be held in the various memory stores introduced in Chapter 9 (sensory register, short-term memory, long-term memory) and the space available for carrying out mental processes during memory storage and retrieval (Flavell et al., 2002; Schneider and Bjorklund, 1998). The capacity of long-term memory is virtually unlimited. However, short-term memory and the sensory register both have a limited capacity, which continues to increase from early to middle childhood.

The most widely accepted explanation for these increases in memory capacity is an increase in the speed and efficiency of processing information (Schneider and Bjorklund, 1998). As processing speed and efficiency increase, the volume of information that can be handled also increases. Thus, the increases in memory capacity seen in middle childhood are best described as increases in *functional* capacity (Flavell et al., 2002). These increases are probably due in part to neurological development, such as continued myelination of neurons in the cerebral cortex, and in part to practice, which makes mental processes more automatic (Kail, 1991; Schneider and Bjorklund, 1998).

There appear to be few age differences in the amount of information that can be held in the sensory register, but there is a substantial increase with age in the amount of information that is transferred from the sensory register to short-term memory (Schneider and Bjorklund, 1998). The most likely explanation for this change is an increase in information-processing speed. Information remains in the sensory register for less than one second before it decays. Because older children process information more rapidly than younger children do, they are able to move more of it from the sensory register to short-term memory before it is lost.

As we mentioned in Chapter 9, improvements also occur in short-term memory as children grow older. When presented with a string of digits to hold in short-term memory, the average 5-year-old can retain four of them, the average 7-year-old five, the average 9-year-old six, and the average adult seven (Dempster, 1981). At first glance, it may appear that these increases reflect a simple increase in the total capacity of short-term memory. However, it turns out that speed of processing is involved, even in improvements on this simple memory task (Schneider and Bjorklund, 1998). For example, memory for digits varies for speakers of different languages. As early as age 4, Chinese speakers can remember longer strings of digits than English speakers, probably because Chinese number words are shorter and can be articulated more quickly than English number words (Geary et al., 1993). Bilingual speakers sometimes show differences in digit span in their two languages; in one study, Welsh schoolchildren whose second language was English had longer digit spans in English, which has shorter number words, than in Welsh (Ellis and Hennelly, 1980).

Chess experts of elementary-school age do better than adult chess novices at remembering arrangements of pieces that might occur during a chess game. The children's knowledge of chess enhances their memory abilities.

Knowledge. Another aspect of memory that changes during middle childhood is the total amount of knowledge held in long-term storage. Piaget called this *memory in the wider sense* (Piaget and Inhelder, 1973), referring to the vast networks of accumulated information that people store in memory during their lives.

Such knowledge greatly affects what children are able to learn and remember. Elementary-school-aged children often show enhanced memory for information from domains in which they are highly knowledgeable. In one study, children who were expert chess players did better than adult chess novices at remembering arrangements of pieces on a chess board that might occur during an actual game (Chi, 1978). However, when the pieces were arranged randomly on the board, the child chess experts had no advantage. Knowledge of a specific domain appears to confer a memory advantage by providing a framework for the organization, storage, and retrieval of information.

The organizational framework that knowledge provides also enables children this age to make inferences about new information, and these inferences in turn seem to help them better understand and recall new information. Scott Paris (1975) studied this process by presenting children with brief stories like this one:

> *Linda was playing with her new doll in front of her big red house. Suddenly she heard a strange sound coming from under the porch. It was the flapping of wings. Linda wanted to help so much, but she did not know what to do. She ran inside the house and grabbed a shoe box from the closet. Then Linda looked inside her desk until she found eight sheets of yellow paper. She cut up the paper into little pieces and put them in the bottom of the box. Linda gently picked up the helpless creature and took it with her. Her teacher knew what to do.*

Paris then asked the following eight yes-or-no questions:

1. Was Linda's doll new?
2. Did Linda grab a matchbox?
3. Was the strange sound coming from under the porch?
4. Was Linda playing behind her house?
5. Did Linda like to take care of animals?
6. Did Linda take what she found to the police station?
7. Did Linda find a frog?
8. Did Linda use a pair of scissors?

Questions 1 through 4 can be answered directly from information in the paragraph, but questions 5 through 8 require inferences based on knowledge about the connection between behavior and feelings, where teachers are normally found, which animals have wings, and how paper is usually cut. Paris found that elementary school children automatically make these kinds of inferences in the process of storing and remembering information. He also found that this inference drawing, or **constructive memory,** is an aid to recall. In one study, how well children did on inference questions predicted how well they later remembered information about a story (Paris and Upton, 1976). Apparently, if children can integrate new information into meaningful structures already stored in memory, they are more likely to make inferences about it and be able to recall it later.

The ability to engage in constructive memory exists in preschoolers to some extent (Paris and Upton, 1976), but it is hard to demonstrate in children this young because of their limited general knowledge and often illogical inferences. In middle childhood, constructive memory becomes increasingly prominent as children's knowledge base expands and their inferences become more accurate. Children this age are also better at integrating information from different senses (e.g., spoken words and pictures), can integrate data more rapidly, and are less distracted by irrelevant information (Ackerman, 1984). By age 11, the constructive memory processes that children use seem much like those of adults (Kail, 1990). Here we see another example of middle childhood as a time of expanding and refining the cognitive skills that began to emerge in an earlier period of development.

Mnemonic Strategies. The increasing use of **mnemonic strategies** during middle childhood also fosters memory improvements. Mnemonic strategies are simply intentional, goal-directed behaviors designed to improve memory (the term *mnemonic* is derived from the Greek word for memory). Mikey used a mnemonic strategy when he put the things he wanted to take to the beach by the front door. Mnemonic strategies that have been studied in children include **rehearsal, organization,** and **elaboration.** *Rehearsal* involves repeating information over and over, as you do to keep a telephone number in mind before dialing it. *Organization* involves arranging information to be recalled into meaningful categories, such as remembering what you need to buy at the grocery store by grouping the items by their location in the store. *Elaboration* involves creating a meaningful connection between items to be remembered, either verbally or visually, such as remembering that you need to buy a hammer and a pane of glass at the hardware store by picturing the hammer breaking the glass.

Robert Kail and John Hagen (1982) summarized the development of children's mnemonic strategies as follows:

- Five- and six-year-olds do not spontaneously use mnemonic strategies often. They may feel it is important to remember something, but they seldom turn this motivation into a deliberate effort to improve memory.
- The period between 7 and 10 years of age seems to be a transitional stage during which use of mnemonic devices expands. Exactly when a particular strategy emerges depends on its nature and the context in which it is used.
- Beginning at about age 10, children show the first signs of using mnemonic devices consistently and effectively. This tendency increases over the next several years, until by adolescence youngsters are quite good at using deliberate strategies to help themselves remember.

Researchers studying memory development have identified three types of deficiencies in children's use of memory strategies (Schneider and Bjorklund, 1998):

- **mediation deficiencies,** in which children are unable to use a strategy even when adults suggest it;
- **production deficiencies,** in which children do not use a strategy spontaneously but can use it when instructed to do so; and

Constructive memory:
Inferences drawn in the process of storing and remembering information.

Mnemonic strategies:
Intentional, goal-directed behaviors designed to improve memory.

Rehearsal:
The mnemonic strategy of repeating information over and over.

Organization:
The mnemonic strategy of arranging information to be recalled into meaningful categories.

Elaboration:
The mnemonic strategy of creating a meaningful connection between items to be remembered, either verbally or visually.

Memory Strategies

Mediation deficiencies:
Problems in mnemonic strategy use in which children are unable to use a strategy even when adults suggest it.

Production deficiencies:
Problems in mnemonic strategy use in which children do not use a strategy spontaneously, but can use it when instructed to do so.

- **utilization deficiencies,** in which children use a strategy spontaneously but without benefit to their memory performance.

These types of deficiencies appear at different stages of a child's acquisition of a memory strategy and at different ages for different strategies (Flavell et al., 2002; Schneider and Pressley, 1997). Mediation deficiencies occur when the child has not yet acquired the strategy in question. Preschoolers show mediation deficiencies for most memory strategies, including simple ones like rehearsal, but even older elementary school children show mediation deficiencies for complex strategies, such as elaboration. Production deficiencies occur when the child is in the midst of acquiring a strategy. They are very common in elementary school children's use of a variety of memory strategies, but they are also sometimes seen in adolescents for complex or infrequently used strategies. Utilization deficiencies occur when the child has acquired a strategy but has not yet had much practice using it. They are seen throughout childhood and adolescence, for simpler strategies at the younger ages and more complex strategies at the older ages.

In one of the earliest studies of children's use of mnemonic strategies, researchers asked 5-, 7-, and 10-year-olds to memorize a set of pictures (Flavell, Beach, and Chinsky, 1966). During the time between seeing the pictures and taking the recall test, the children were watched to see if they used verbal rehearsal. The older children were much more likely to use rehearsal than the younger ones; only 10 percent of the 5-year-olds rehearsed, compared with 60 percent of the 7-year-olds and 85 percent of the 10-year-olds.

In another study researchers investigated what effect training in rehearsal would have on memory performance of first graders who did not spontaneously rehearse (Keeney, Cannizzo, and Flavell, 1967). The children were told to whisper the names of objects to be remembered over and over until it was time for a recall test. After training, these children used rehearsal 75 percent of the time, and their memory performance improved to the level of first graders who spontaneously rehearsed. Finally, the children were given a new set of pictures to remember and told that they did not have to rehearse any longer; instead, they could do whatever they wanted to remember the new pictures. Over half of the children reverted to not rehearsing, and their performance declined.

Although rehearsal is regularly seen from age 7 or 8 on, there continue to be important developmental changes in its use. When 7- to 10-year-olds are presented with a list of words to remember with a five-second pause between words, the younger children rehearse almost as much as the older children, but the younger ones often limit their rehearsal to the word just presented, whereas the older ones rehearse some of the previously heard words as well (Ornstein, Naus, and Stone, 1977). This tells us that 9- and 10-year-olds have more effective rehearsal strategies than 7- and 8-year-olds do. Still, their strategies are not as flexible as those of adolescents and adults. For example, when told that they will be given ten cents for remembering some of the words in a list and only one cent for remembering others, they do not rehearse the more valuable words more, as adults do (Cuvo, 1974).

Research on children's use of organization and elaboration as mnemonic strategies has found that these strategies tend to emerge somewhat later than rehearsal, and it takes longer for children to become completely proficient in their use (Flavell et al., 2002; Schneider and Pressley, 1997). The ability to use organization and elaboration spontaneously and effectively continues to improve throughout adolescence and into the college years (Brown et al., 1983). One reason these strategies develop more slowly than rehearsal is that they require more memory and processing resources, and until they are well practiced the processing cost of using them tends to outweigh the memory benefits.

Metamemory.   A fourth aspect of memory that develops during middle childhood is **metamemory,** or knowledge about memory and memory processes. When you think about the need to remember and how to go about remembering, you are using metamemory capabilities. When you know your own strengths and weaknesses in remembering (e.g., good at remembering faces, poor at remembering names), you are also using

Utilization deficiencies:
Problems in mnemonic strategy use in which children use a strategy spontaneously, but without benefit to their memory performance.

During middle childhood, children become consistent in using mnemonic strategies, such as rehearsal, to memorize information they need to remember later, such as how words are spelled.

Metamemory:
Knowledge about memory and memory processes.

Table 11.2 Children's Predictions of the Number of Items They Could Remember and Their Actual Performance

	Mean Predicted Memory Span	Mean Actual Memory Span
Preschool	7.21	3.50
Kindergarten	7.97	3.61
Second grade	6.00	4.36
Fourth grade	6.14	5.50

Source: Flavell, Friedrichs, and Hoyt, 1970.

metamemory. In addition, metamemory allows you to monitor your own memory performance. It is what enables you to know when you have learned a certain fact. Like other *metacognitive* skills—the ability to think about thinking—metamemory shows substantial advancement during middle childhood.

John Flavell and his colleagues examined the development of one component of metamemory by asking children of different ages to predict how many pictures they would be able to remember (Flavell, Friedrichs, and Hoyt, 1970). On the first trial each child was shown only one picture. That picture was then covered and the child was asked if he or she could remember it. On each subsequent trial the number of pictures was increased, to a maximum of ten. In the first phase of the experiment, the children were not actually required to remember the pictures, just to say whether they thought they could remember them. In the second phase, actual recall tests were given. Table 11.2 shows both the children's self-predictions and their actual performance. Notice that the preschoolers and kindergarteners were quite poor at remembering, the second graders were better, and the fourth graders were quite good. Notice, too, that the preschoolers and kindergartners were far off in their predictions of how many pictures they could remember. They estimated about twice as many as they actually recalled, whereas the second graders made fairly accurate predictions, and the fourth graders made very accurate ones. Other researchers have similarly found that older children are much better at predicting what they will be able to remember (Schneider and Bjorklund, 1998). Apparently, knowledge about one's own memory capabilities increases greatly during middle childhood.

Similar improvements occur in other metamemory skills across the elementary school years (Flavell and Wellman, 1977; Wellman, 1985). For instance, school-age children become increasingly good at knowing when a particular mnemonic strategy has worked. The fact that first graders who have been trained to use rehearsal often revert to *not* rehearsing when left to remember on their own suggests they do not yet realize this strategy improves their memory performance. They lack the metamemory skill of monitoring how well they are doing on a set of memory tasks. Thus, metamemory may be an important factor in using mnemonic devices. Once children realize mnemonic strategies improve recall, they are more likely to use them.

This is true even though mnemonic devices do not improve memory as much when they are first tried out as when they are more practiced (Flavell et al., 2002). Apparently, when a mnemonic device is new to a child, using it consumes so much operating space in short-term memory that little space is left for information storage. Why, then, does the child persist in using the strategy? The same question could be asked about walking. When a child first tries to walk, great effort is required, and walking is not as successful a way to get around as crawling. Yet the child continues to try until walking is mastered. For the use of mnemonic strategies, as well as for walking, the keys to persistence may be encouragement from others and the inner motivation to become competent at a new skill.

The fact that the development of metamemory becomes most apparent from second grade on does not mean that younger children have no metamemory capabilities. Flavell believes metamemory begins to emerge during the preschool years, but these beginnings are greatly overshadowed by the dramatic progress made later. For instance, even kindergartners and first graders know that increasing the number of items to be remembered makes a memory task harder; they are aware, in other words, that certain factors can influence memory performance (Kreutzer, Leonard, and Flavell, 1975). Yet these same children are very poor at predicting how much they will remember when presented with increasing amounts of information to recall. It is as if they have trouble making use of the bits of metamemory knowledge they possess.

Among older children, in contrast, metamemory knowledge is much more extensive. When presented with a memory task, many 5- and 6-year-olds can think of only one strategy to help them remember, but older children can think of many more (Kreutzer, Leonard, and Flavell, 1975). In addition, as we mentioned earlier, older children are far more likely to use memory strategies without prompting from adults. Thus, the developmental pattern for metamemory adds to our picture of middle childhood as a time when cognitive skills that began to emerge earlier are refined, elaborated, and made into more effective practical tools.

Summing Up Improvements in Information-Processing Abilities Children's attentional and memory abilities improve considerably during middle childhood. These improvements seem to be based in part on increased speed of processing, due to neurological development. However, a more important change in information-processing abilities during these years is increasing control and flexibility, which seems to be due mainly to expanded metacognitive understanding and a growing knowledge and use of attentional and memory strategies.

SOCIAL INTERACTION AND COGNITIVE DEVELOPMENT

Seven-year-old Mikey, Benito, and Richie are building a fort out of large cardboard boxes in Mikey's backyard. The boys want to add a lookout tower on one side. But when they cut a large hole in the top of one of the boxes, the edges aren't strong enough to support the tall box they want to put on top. The boys consider the problem, each offering ideas on how to make the structure stronger. Just as they are about to try Richie's idea, Frank walks by. "That's not gonna work," he advises. "Let me show you what to do . . . Okay, Mikey, try that piece over there . . ."

Elementary school children's cognitive development is greatly influenced by interaction with both adults and peers (Rogoff, 1998). Adults most often provide children with **didactic learning experiences,** in which a knowledgeable teacher who has already mastered a problem teaches a particular solution to a learner. Didactic learning experiences occur at home as well as at school—for example, when parents teach children procedures for household chores or show them how to do a homework problem. In the preceding episode Frank is providing a didactic learning experience for the boys because he is deliberately teaching them something they don't yet know.

Under certain circumstances, children can also provide each other with didactic learning experiences. However, they are more likely to provide **cooperative learning experiences,** in which learners at approximately the same level of knowledge and skill interact, share ideas, and discover solutions on their own. Before Frank arrived, Mikey, Richie, and Benito were engaged in a cooperative learning experience as they worked together to solve their construction problem.

Didactic learning experience: A situation in which a knowledgeable teacher who has already mastered a problem teaches a particular solution to a learner.

Cooperative learning experience: A situation in which learners at approximately the same level of knowledge and skill interact, share ideas, and discover solutions on their own.

Teachers provide many didactic learning experiences for elementary school children.

Both didactic and cooperative learning experiences can foster children's cognitive development. Which type of experience is likely to be more effective depends on characteristics of the learners and the teachers, the nature of the material to be learned, and the cultural norms for learning and teaching that prevail in a particular setting. In this section we look at how both didactic and cooperative learning experiences foster cognitive development in middle childhood.

Didactic Learning Experiences

In a didactic learning situation the teacher is responsible for structuring the learning experience for the learner. One important way teachers do this is by *scaffolding* (Bruner, 1975), a process we introduced in Chapter 8 to describe the ways parents support toddlers in new tasks. In middle childhood, the process of scaffolding is much the same as in toddlerhood. The teacher provides support to the learner by observing the learner's behaviors and offering guidance, hints, and advice. As the learner advances, the teacher's strategies progressively change to encourage the mastery of increasingly complex understandings (Cazden, 1983).

Children as well as adults use scaffolding in didactic learning situations. Of course, the age of the teacher is a significant factor in the effectiveness of scaffolding, because selecting effective scaffolding approaches requires metacognitive awareness of what the learner thinks and understands. Shari Ellis and Barbara Rogoff (1986) demonstrated this when they studied teaching styles of elementary school children and adults. All the children in this study (both the learners and the child teachers) were 8 or 9 years old, and all the adults were women with children this age. The learners had to master a complex classification task in which photographs of common objects were sorted into categories. Ellis and Rogoff identified three things the teachers needed to do to be successful: they had to see that the learners sorted the photos into the appropriate categories, they had to help the learners understand the underlying classification scheme, and they had to manage the social interactions between themselves and the learners. Ellis and Rogoff found that the child teachers tended to focus simply on getting the learners to accomplish the sorting task. They concentrated less than the adult teachers did on communicating the underlying classification scheme, even though they understood it. Apparently, the job of coordinating all three tasks was too complex for children this age. As a result, the child teachers were less effective than the adult teachers at helping the learners master the classification scheme.

However, didactic learning experiences provided by peers can sometimes foster cognitive development. Research by Frank Murray (1972) provides one example. Murray paired children who understood conservation with children who did not and asked the pairs to reach consensus about various conservation questions. Even though the children were similar in age, it was a didactic learning situation because one of them already knew the correct answers and was deliberately teaching the other. In this situation, the nonconserving children were able to learn about conservation from their peers. The consensus reached by the children almost invariably favored conservation, and when the previously nonconserving children were later tested alone, they continued to give correct responses to conservation questions.

Cooperative Learning Experiences

Cooperative Learning

Children can also learn from their peers in cooperative situations that do not involve a more knowledgeable child intentionally teaching a less knowledgeable one. This was shown in studies by a group of Swiss researchers, in which children cooperated on a broad range of tasks over an extended time (Mugny, Perret-Clermont, and Doise, 1981). These researchers found that interaction with a *less* knowledgeable peer could promote cognitive progress. In one case, a child who couldn't yet solve number conservation problems, but who understood one-to-one correspondence and could count accurately, interacted with a child who was less advanced in these areas. Through discussing number conservation problems with the less competent child, the more advanced one acquired a grasp of this concept.

Researchers have identified several factors that seem to be particularly important in facilitating cognitive advancement in cooperative learning situations among peers (Cooper and Cooper, 1984; Forman, 1982):

- the task to be mastered should be concrete, rich in relevant information, and not too complex;
- the information available must be somewhat ambiguous, able to support at least two different conclusions;
- the peers must see reaching a consensus as a goal of their interaction, rather than just expressing diverse opinions with no intention of agreeing on a solution; and
- the children should know each other and have a smooth system of interaction.

Under these conditions, elementary school children can be quite good at helping each other learn.

As we mentioned in our discussion of scaffolding, children become increasingly effective at teaching one another with age, partly because they become increasingly able to understand what other children are thinking. Catherine Cooper and her colleagues looked at age as a factor in learning from peers in a study of 5- to 12-year-olds at a Montessori school that particularly encouraged peer interactions as a means of promoting learning (Cooper, Marquis, and Edwards, 1986). The researchers concluded that effective didactic and cooperative peer learning emerge early in middle childhood, but improvements occur with age. Because of their increased metacognitive skills, older elementary school children are better able to plan long-term collaborative projects, to engage in more elaborate and extended arguments, to offer more effective teaching approaches, and to progressively adjust the guidance they provide as teachers.

Explaining the Effects of Social Interaction

Both Piaget's and Vygotsky's theories of cognitive development address the issue of how social interaction helps children make cognitive progress. Piaget's perspective applies more to cooperative learning situations than to didactic ones. For Piaget, cognitive development occurs within the individual, and social interaction provides experiences that help children construct their understanding of reality. Piaget believed that interaction with peers is especially useful because the similar status of peers makes it easy for children

When peer interaction is encouraged as a legitimate way to learn, both didactic and cooperative peer learning become more elaborate and effective during middle childhood.

to notice discrepancies between their own ideas and those of their peers. Resolving such discrepancies is one way children make progress in figuring out how the world works. In contrast, when an adult expresses an idea different from a child's own, the new idea may be accepted as correct on the basis of the adult's authority, but it will not be integrated into the rest of the child's knowledge system.

Vygotsky's approach applies more to didactic learning situations than to cooperative ones. Vygotsky saw cognitive development as a fundamentally social process in which children internalize knowledge that is shared among people in their culture. As we mentioned in Chapter 1, Vygotsky did not believe children have to construct their understanding of reality themselves; instead, they can benefit from the knowledge already gained by those around them. Interaction with adults is particularly useful in this process. In Vygotsky's theory, a more knowledgeable teacher provides guidance for a less knowledgeable learner—hints, feedback, scaffolding—within the learner's zone of proximal development.

Piaget and Vygotsky focused on different ways social interaction and cognitive development are related, and their theories are useful for explaining different aspects of children's cognitive development. Just as children benefit from both didactic and cooperative learning experiences, both Piaget's and Vygotsky's ideas can help us understand the social context in which cognitive development occurs.

Child Development CD
Piaget vs. Vygotsky

INDIVIDUAL DIFFERENCES IN INTELLIGENCE

So far in this chapter we have focused on cognitive developments that most children of elementary school age share. In this section we shift our focus to cognitive *differences* among children. We discuss cognitive differences in more depth in this chapter than in earlier ones because a child's level of intellectual competence takes on special importance when he or she enters school. In fact, many theories of intelligence, and most widely used methods of measuring it, have focused on school-related tasks and abilities.

Intelligence Testing and Concepts of Intelligence

The first modern intelligence test was developed in France at the beginning of the twentieth century. Administrators of the Paris public schools wanted a way to differentiate normally intelligent children from those requiring special help. The minister of education called upon Alfred Binet, a well-known French psychologist, and his colleague Theodore Simon to develop a reliable test. (Jean Piaget later received his first exposure to children's cognitive performance when he took a job developing test items for Binet.)

Intelligence Theory and Testing

To be included in Binet and Simon's test, items had to predict school performance, and the likelihood they would be answered correctly had to increase with the test-taker's age. The test items chosen included word definitions, arithmetic problems, verbal reasoning tasks, questions on general information, and tasks requiring an understanding of spatial relationships. For each type of item, the questions were placed in order from easiest to hardest.

Lewis Terman of Stanford University published an English version of Binet and Simon's test in 1916. This test, called the Stanford-Binet, was designed for children between the ages of 3 and 18, and an updated version of it is still widely used today. Scoring of the test involved the concept of **mental age (MA),** a measure of a child's level of intellectual development. For instance, a child who correctly answered as many questions as the average 12-year-old would be said to have a mental age of 12. Mental age was divided by the child's chronological age (CA) and multiplied by 100 to produce an **intelligence quotient,** or **IQ** (MA/CA $\times$ 100 = IQ). A child with a mental age of 12 who was also 12 years old would be exactly average and would be assigned an IQ of 100 (12/12 $\times$ 100 = 100). If this child was only 10, however, mental age would be above chronological age and the child's IQ would be above average (12/10 $\times$ 100 = 120). By the same token, the IQ of a 14-year-old who had a mental age of 12 would be below average (12/14 $\times$ 100 = 86). This method of computing IQ scores is no longer used, but IQ scores are still determined by comparing a child's performance with the performance of others the same age.

Notice how Binet's approach entails a *unitary* concept of intelligence. In other words, he considered intelligence to be a *general* cognitive capability that can be measured by a single IQ score. In early twentieth-century England, an educational psychologist named Charles Spearman (1927) was also sympathetic to the concept of a general reasoning ability, which he labeled *g*. In Spearman's view, performance on an intellectual task depended not only on *g* but also on knowledge, abilities, and aptitudes *specific* to the particular problem or question at hand. Performance in a college algebra class, for instance, would be determined in part by general intelligence and in part by specific aptitude for math.

Many contemporary intelligence tests are based on a combination of Binet's and Spearman's conceptions of intelligence. One example is the widely used Wechsler scales, which include separate tests for ages 4 to 6, ages 6 to 16, and adults. The Wechsler scales provide IQ scores that summarize overall performance, reflecting Binet's global approach to intelligence. However, they are made up of *verbal* subtests (including vocabulary, arithmetic, and general information) and *performance* subtests (including mazes, block design, and object assembly). The test taker also receives separate verbal and performance subscores, a procedure that acknowledges Spearman's stress on specific abilities in addition to general intelligence.

Broadening the Definition of Intelligence

Although Binet and Spearman differed in the number of specific abilities they thought were involved in intelligence, their approaches emphasized the same *kind* of mental abilities—those useful in school. Other researchers have argued that these abilities do not represent the full range of human intelligence and that intelligence should be defined more broadly. Underlying recent attempts to define intelligence more broadly is the idea that intelligence is what allows us to adapt successfully to situations. In this way these newer theories of intelligence have something in common with Piaget's view.

The newer theories address skills for adaptation not just in academic and formal problem-solving settings, but in a wide variety of other contexts as well. In fact, some psychologists believe it is useful to make a distinction between the kind of intelligence that allows a person to perform well in school and on IQ tests, and the kind of intelligence that enables someone to solve problems in everyday settings. The first can be called **academic intelligence,** the second **practical intelligence** (Sternberg and Grigorenko, 2000). Academic and practical intelligence do not necessarily go together. A high level of one does not guarantee a high level of the other. They can develop independently and at times may even conflict with each other (Sternberg et al., 2001b). This general point is important to all the newer theories of intelligence that try to broaden

Mental age (MA):
On an intelligence test, a measure of a child's level of intellectual development.

Intelligence quotient (IQ):
A measure of intelligence based on a comparison of a child's performance with the performance of others the same age; originally, mental age divided by chronological age.

Child Development CD
Brazilian Street Vendors' Math Skills

Academic intelligence:
Intellectual capacity as measured by performance on tasks typically encountered in school or on standard IQ tests.

Practical intelligence:
Intellectual capacity as reflected in successful performance in natural, everyday, nonschool settings.

One of the competences in Gardner's theory of multiple intelligences is bodily-kinesthetic intelligence.

Gardner's Multiple Intelligences

how intelligence is defined. Being highly intelligent in one way does not necessarily mean a person will be highly intelligent in another.

Gardner's Theory of Multiple Intelligences Howard Gardner (1983, 1999) argues that humans have a number of different intellectual competences, which he calls intelligences. He defines an intelligence as "an ability or set of abilities that permits an individual to solve problems or fashion products that are of consequence in a particular cultural setting" (Walters and Gardner, 1986, p. 165). Thus, each kind of intelligence allows members of our species to adapt to the many demands and challenges human societies create. Gardner believes each kind of human intelligence develops more or less independently and may draw on its own area of the brain.

On the basis of existing research on human abilities and brain functions, Gardner has proposed eight intellectual competences that appear basic, autonomous, and universal enough to be considered intelligences. However, he cautions that his list should not be considered complete. These eight are *linguistic intelligence* (skill in understanding and using language), *musical intelligence* (skill in the creation of music), *logical-mathematical intelligence* (skill in logical thinking and reasoning about quantities), *spatial intelligence* (skill in understanding how patterns and objects are laid out in space), *bodily-kinesthetic intelligence* (skill in anything involving complex body movement), *intrapersonal intelligence* (skill in understanding one's own feelings and motives), *interpersonal intelligence* (skill in understanding feelings and behaviors of others), and *naturalist intelligence* (skill in understanding features of the environment). Notice that only three of these intelligences—linguistic, logical-mathematical, and spatial—are addressed in traditional IQ tests.

Gardner makes several points about these eight intelligences. First, a person's level of competence in each depends not only on biological endowment, but also on socialization and education. A child can be *taught* to be a more competent gymnast or juggler, for example, although innate ability also enters into his or her performance. Second, culture determines both how a given competence will be fostered (in one culture a musically gifted child might learn to play the banjo, in another the sitar) and which competences will be most stressed (e.g., logical-mathematical intelligence is highly valued in technologically advanced societies). Third, high competence in one area does not imply high competence in others. A child prodigy may show unusual ability in one intellectual domain, while being average or below average in others. There are even rare individuals called *savants* who are extremely retarded in all areas of intellectual functioning except for one small island of remarkably superior skill.

Sternberg's Triarchic Theory   Psychologist Robert Sternberg (1985) took another intriguing approach to broadening the concept of intelligence. Whereas Gardner focused on recognizing different *types* of intelligence (linguistic, musical, interpersonal, etc.), Sternberg analyzed the various factors that contribute to making a particular behavior intelligent or not. Sternberg's approach is called a *triarchic theory* because he sees intelligent behavior as governed by three factors.

The first factor in Sternberg's theory is the *componential element* of intelligence. This refers to the many information-processing skills used in solving problems, such as attending to, storing, retrieving, and manipulating information. Children who are highly proficient at using these components of intelligence usually do well on traditional IQ tests.

The second factor that governs intelligence in Sternberg's theory is the *experiential element*—prior knowledge that affects how a person approaches a problem. For example, the first time you used a computerized library catalog you probably carefully read the instructions, cautiously tried out a few examples, and proceeded very slowly. Now, however, you can probably use a computerized catalog efficiently, without stopping to read instructions or take trial runs. The intelligent thing to do has changed with experience. Likewise, behavior that is intelligent for a preschooler may not be intelligent for an older child. Experience changes which choices and actions are intelligent.

Finally, Sternberg sees intelligence as governed by a *contextual element*—the set of circumstances in which a choice is made or an action is taken. It is intelligent behavior to check the spark plugs in an engine that won't start, but it is not intelligent to check them in an overheated engine. Similarly, the cultural context makes a difference in determining what is intelligent and what is not. For example, certain Indian tribes in the Pacific Northwest traditionally held events called *potlatches* in which the host gave away or destroyed huge quantities of surplus food and other valuable items (blankets, animal skins, canoes, pieces of copper). To those of us who live in a society where "saving for a rainy day" is considered prudent, this behavior seems foolish. But among the tribes who practiced it, potlatching was perfectly intelligent. It was a way of converting surpluses into personal prestige (the host of a potlatch was greatly admired) and of redistributing wealth from those who had plenty to those who did not (the recipients of potlatch gifts included people in economic need). Thus, the intelligence of behavior cannot be assessed outside the cultural context in which it occurs.

To summarize, Sternberg's theory helps us to see that intelligence is more than just the cognitive skills typically measured on standard IQ tests. Intelligent behavior is also governed by experience and context. If tests of intelligence fail to consider all these factors, they will probably not be very good at predicting how intelligently a person will behave in his or her everyday environment.

Despite the value of newer theories of intelligence such as Gardner's and Sternberg's, no methods for assessing nonacademic intelligence are as well established as the standard IQ tests. For now, children's IQs are much more likely to be tested than their practical intelligence. Moreover, the research on individual differences in children's intelligence has largely examined differences in performance on IQ tests.

Explaining IQ Differences

As we discussed in Chapter 1, IQ differences are the result of complex interactions between genetic and environmental influences. Clearly, *many* genes are involved; no single gene, or small set of genes, makes one person more or less intelligent than another. The expression of these genes is influenced by interactions with other genes and with the environment at every level from the cellular to the social and physical contexts in which a child grows up.

Many combinations of genetic and environmental factors can depress intelligence through their impacts on brain development, as you have already learned. Genetic defects, prenatal exposure to alcohol or other teratogens, malnutrition before or after birth, and inadequate social and cognitive stimulation early in life can all disrupt brain development, leading to cognitive deficits. Other combinations of factors can enhance intelligence. Genetic inheritance can limit a developing individual's susceptibility to harmful environmental influences. Good nutrition can prevent neurological defects before birth and promote brain development after birth. A stimulating environment and high caregiver expectations can maximize cognitive functioning.

It is probably not possible to quantify precisely the relative influences of heredity and environment on intelligence. For one thing, the extent of environmental influences seems to depend in part on the individual's genetic inheritance. Studies with rats have demonstrated that the impacts of environmental deprivation or enrichment vary, depending on the rats' genetic characteristics (Gottlieb, 2001). Whether rats come from a strain bred to be slow or fast at learning mazes (*maze-dull* versus *maze-bright*) makes a difference in how they respond to deprived and enriched environments. Enriched environments produce greater improvements in maze-learning performance in maze-dull rats than in maze-bright rats, and deprived environments have stronger negative impacts on maze-dull rats than on maze-bright rats. We will discuss issues of environmental deprivation and enrichment related to human intelligence in the next section.

The Stability of IQ

Children's scores on intelligence tests do not remain perfectly stable over time. Several longitudinal studies have found that fluctuations in IQ scores of 15 or more points between ages 3 and 18 are not unusual (Honzik, McFarlane, and Allen, 1948; Sontag, Baker, and Nelson, 1958). This is not particularly surprising when you consider that IQ represents a *test score,* not an intrinsic trait of a child. However, as children grow older, their IQ scores become increasingly stable (Sternberg, Grigorenko, and Bundy, 2001). They also become increasingly good predictors of adult IQ, as shown in Figure 11.4. By the elementary school years, intelligence tests seem to measure relatively stable aspects of cognitive functioning. This stability is probably due to the combined effects of genetic makeup and a fairly constant rearing environment.

But what happens if the rearing environment changes? Enriching a very deprived environment early in life *can* make a difference in performance on IQ tests, especially if the enrichment is pervasive and long-lasting. Studies of children adopted from orphanages

Figure 11.4
CORRELATIONS BETWEEN ADULT AND CHILD/ ADOLESCENT IQ SCORES
From early childhood to late adolescence, IQ scores become increasingly predictive of adult IQ. *(Source: Bloom, 1964.)*

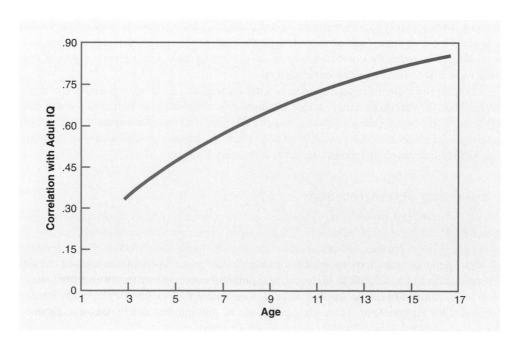

before age 2 show increases in mean IQ scores from the mentally retarded range (typically 50–80) at the time of adoption to the normal range (around 100) in later childhood (Dennis, 1973; O'Connor et al., 2000). For these children, every aspect of the environment—nutrition, health care, social interaction, cognitive stimulation—changed dramatically and permanently when they were adopted. Impacts on IQ scores from preschool intervention programs for children from low-SES families are generally less dramatic and more transient. Typically, children's IQ scores increase significantly by the end of the intervention program, but within a few years these gains disappear (Lazar et al., 1982; Ramey and Ramey, 1998). However, one intervention program that began in infancy and provided full-time child care throughout the preschool years produced increases in IQ scores that remained significant when the participants reached age 21 (Campbell et al., 2001). The difference in that case seemed to be that the program started earlier, lasted longer, and was more extensive than most preschool intervention programs. Just as giving a malnourished child a balanced diet for just a year would not produce sustained physical growth, so providing a time-limited cognitive intervention does not lead to sustained intellectual growth.

How Meaningful Are IQ Scores?

Ever since IQ scores were introduced, people have debated their value. If one child gets 100 on an IQ test and another gets 120, what exactly does that tell us about these two children? The controversy over IQ scores centers on issues of cultural bias and the question of just what an IQ score can predict.

The Issue of Cultural Bias   How well do you think you would perform on Binet's original intelligence test? Since this test was given in French, you would probably do very poorly if you aren't fluent in French. And even if you are, some of the general information questions asked at the turn of the century might be obscure today. Any IQ test is the product of a certain culture, and knowledge of that culture affects how well a test taker does.

There are also more subtle ways cultural background can influence performance on an IQ test. Cultures vary considerably in their definitions of intelligence and in the particular cognitive skills they value (Goodnow, 1976; Greenfield, 1997). They also vary in what they consider the right way to perform certain cognitive tasks. For example, if you were asked to sort items into categories, you would probably not think of putting a knife and an orange together, but members of Africa's Kpelle tribe would do so because a knife is used to cut an orange (Glick, 1975). Thus, a person who is not a member of the cultural group for which an intelligence test was designed may answer items on that test incorrectly for reasons that have nothing to do with low overall intelligence.

The interpersonal setting in which a test is given can also introduce cultural bias. Children tested by a member of another racial or ethnic group may feel uncomfortable and do less well than if they were tested by a member of their own group. Even the interpersonal format of an IQ test, in which a child is asked questions by an adult who already knows the answers to them, is unfamiliar to children from many cultural backgrounds. Consider the following exchange, from a testing session with a 5-year-old lower-middle-class African-American child:

Tester:	What is a stove?
Child:	You cook. That's what you writing down?
Tester:	Yeah. I'm writing down what you say so I can remember it later.
Child:	(incredulously) 'Cause you don't know what it's for?

(Miller-Jones, 1989, p. 362)

To overcome the problem of cultural bias, a number of psychologists tried to develop IQ tests that were either **culture-free** (with no culture-based content) or **culture-fair** (appropriate for all the cultures in which it is used). One attempt at a culture-free test is Raven's Progressive Matrices Test, which requires the use of multiplication of classes to complete a matrix of unfamiliar visual designs. Because the problems on this test are presented visually

Culture-free IQ test:
An IQ test entirely free of culture-based content.

Culture-fair IQ test:
An IQ test that is appropriate for all the cultures in which it is used.

and do not involve language, it was thought they would be almost free of cultural bias. As it turns out, this is not the case. In fact, performance differences between some cultural groups are actually greater for this test than for verbal IQ tests, perhaps because test-taking experience increases familiarity with solving matrix completion problems (Sternberg, 1985).

The unsuccessful efforts to develop a culture-free IQ test have led developmentalists to conclude that intelligence is not an inherent cognitive potential independent of a person's environmental experiences. Rather, intelligence *always* exists in an environmental context, and unfamiliarity with a particular context affects how intelligent a person appears. This is an example of the performance-competence distinction we introduced in Chapter 9. Intelligence testing may or may not elicit evidence of a person's maximum level of competence. How well it achieves this goal depends on the cultural appropriateness of the test and the familiarity and comfort of the testing situation for the person being tested. Thus, intelligence tests are an effective means of comparing the abilities of people *within* the same culture or subculture, but for comparisons *across* cultures, IQ tests must be interpreted cautiously.

High-Stakes Testing

What IQ Scores Can Predict When we say that IQ tests are good for comparing abilities within the same cultural group, we must qualify that statement even further. In general, IQ tests are fairly good predictors of a person's success in school, at least in the schools created by the culture that developed the tests (Sternberg et al., 2001a). This makes sense when you consider that prediction of school performance is the purpose for which IQ tests were originally developed.

As for what else IQ scores are good at predicting, one longitudinal study found a moderate correlation between IQ in childhood and later occupational success (McCall, 1977). Childhood IQ scores may be best at predicting success in occupations that require abstract thought (Ghiselli, 1966). In adulthood, IQ scores are better predictors of success in job-training programs than of actual job performance (Wagner, 1997; Wigdor and Garner, 1982). This suggests that these tests are poorer measures of practical intelligence than of school-related skills.

CULTURE AND SCHOOL ACHIEVEMENT

Child Development CD
First Grade Around the World

In most parts of the world, children start formal education somewhere between the ages of 5 and 7, the beginning of middle childhood. By this age, in the course of daily activities, they have already acquired knowledge and skills that should be useful in school. For example, they are fluent speakers of their native language, they understand many things about quantity and number, and they have developed some logical reasoning abilities. Yet the transition to formal education is not always easy. Many children have difficulty applying their informal knowledge of language, number, and logic to more formal classroom tasks, such as learning to read and do math.

Decontextualized thought:
A cognitive skill needed to solve problems that are abstract, self-contained, and removed from any immediate context.

One reason this transition is sometimes difficult is that it involves a shift to **decontextualized thought**—learning to solve problems that are abstract, self-contained, and removed from any immediate context (Donaldson, 1978). Instead of using their informal skills to solve concrete, everyday problems, children in school must learn to deal with problems that seem to have little connection to their lives outside the classroom.

Cultural Mismatch

The transition to school is often particularly hard for children who come from cultural backgrounds different from that of the school they attend, for many of the same reasons that contribute to cultural bias in IQ testing (Skinner et al., 1998). For instance, the format of social interaction expected at school may be unfamiliar to such children. In one study, Shirley Brice Heath (1983) found that white middle-class preschoolers were accustomed to being asked many questions at home, especially *test questions* to which the adult already knew the answers ("What color is that?" "Where's your nose?" "What do cows say?").

Black lower-class preschoolers, in contrast, heard far fewer questions at home, and the questions they were asked served different functions and required different kinds of responses than the white middle-class parents' test questions did. The three most common types of questions they heard were *analogy questions* ("What's that like?"), *story-starter questions* ("Did you see Jimmy's dog yesterday?"—to which an appropriate answer would be "What happened to Jimmy's dog?"), and *accusation questions* ("What's that all over your face?"). When the black children entered school, their teachers often perceived them to be unresponsive and slow. Clearly, the white children's experience with test questions allowed them to respond in ways that better matched the expectations of their teachers.

Research with other minority groups, including Polynesian children in Hawaii, Native American children, and East Indian children in England, has revealed similar examples of cultural mismatch between children's usual style of interacting with adults and the style expected in school (Phillips, 1983; Tharp, 1994; Yates, 1987). Cultural mismatch can also sometimes be seen in differences between parents' and teachers' ideas about educational goals and curriculum content and in contrasting value systems at home and at school (Reese and Gallimore, 2000; Trumbull et al., 2001). For example, children from immigrant Asian and Latino families are often faced with a contrast between *collectivistic* values at home and *individualistic* values at school. (Collectivistic values emphasize the goals and well-being of the family and the community over those of the individual; individualistic values focus on the goals and well-being of individuals rather than those of groups.) Cultural mismatch can affect not only how easily children make the transition to school but also how much they derive from the school experience. Cultural mismatch may help explain why achievement test score averages for African American, Latino, and Native American children are lower than for whites, and why their dropout and school failure rates are higher (Gallimore and Goldenberg, 2001; Neisser, 1986; Slaughter-Defoe et al., 1990).

Many attempts are being made to decrease cultural mismatch between children and schools. On a small scale, Heath (1981) was able to convince some teachers to use questioning strategies more familiar to their pupils, at the same time introducing the children to the unfamiliar test questions they would continue to encounter in school. On a larger scale, programs have been developed to help Hawaiian, Native American, and Latino children bridge the cultural divide between home and school (Gallimore and Au, 1997; Trumbull et al., 2001).

Native Hawaiian Education

Cultural Differences in Math Achievement

The role school experiences play in children's achievement may be clearer if we consider a different example of a low-achieving group. Overall, children in the United States do consistently worse than children in many other countries on measures of math and science achievement. For instance, studies comparing the math achievement of American, Japanese, and Chinese children show that achievement differences appear as early as first grade and increase in size during the elementary school years (Stevenson, 1995). No one suggests that American children have learning deficiencies compared with children in other countries. Instead, researchers and teachers assume that cultural differences in values and classroom practices must be the cause.

International Math Achievement Tests

Some researchers have tried to discover the respective roles that heredity and environment play in the development of ethnic differences in math performance. Although genetic explanations have been proposed (e.g., Herrnstein and Murray, 1994; Lynn, 1982), the evidence for them is not compelling (Stevenson et al., 1985). More important contributing factors seem to be the kind of math instruction children receive and the attitudes they learn from both peers and adults (Resnick, 1995; Stevenson, 1995; Stevenson and Lee, 1990).

American parents and teachers tend to attribute children's success or failure in math to inborn abilities. In contrast, in China and Japan, math performance—whether high or low—is attributed to effort and work habits (Stevenson, 1995). This approach tends to build children's confidence that they can do well in math if they really try. Oddly enough, despite their poor group performance, American children tend to think math is easy, and

Native American children often encounter a cultural mismatch between the styles of interaction they experience at home and those expected at school.

both they and their parents believe they are exceptionally good at math. Chinese and Japanese children are more likely to say they find math challenging, and they and their parents tend to rate their math ability as only average.

There are also differences in what goes on during math instruction in American and Asian classrooms (Lee, Graham, and Stevenson, 1996). Both Japanese and Chinese teachers spend more time on math instruction and assign more homework than American teachers do. Perhaps more important, the *processes* by which math is taught differ. Asian teachers explain math problems in detail, direct more attention to the principles underlying the problems and less to mechanical computational procedures, and analyze and correct individual students' errors carefully, thus encouraging them to learn from their failures as well as their successes (Stigler and Perry, 1990). A mistake is seen as an opportunity to gain further insights into how numbers work, not as a reason to feel defeated or worse at math than peers. In addition, Japanese children learn much of their math in cooperative learning settings in which mastering skills, not outperforming others, is the primary goal. They are also encouraged to explore a variety of ways to solve a problem rather than focusing on repeated practice of one correct strategy (Stevenson, 1995). This approach tends to make them more creative mathematical thinkers than their American counterparts, whose learning of math is much more by rote and repetition.

A number of changes in mathematics instruction are currently being tried in an effort to improve the overall math performance of American youngsters. These changes incorporate many of the key elements of math instruction used in Japanese schools (Stevenson, 1995). For instance, more classroom time is being spent in small, cooperative groups, with more emphasis placed on the group's success than on the performance of individual students. These new programs also stress communication of the value of mathematics and of the benefits of exploring alternative solutions to problems (Resnick, 1995; Slavin, 1990).

One response to reports of low educational achievement test scores by American children has been a movement to require more frequent standardized testing in public schools, with more severe consequences for students and schools if they do not achieve specified goals. Some issues associated with this approach are discussed in the box on page 407.

AN OVERVIEW OF MIDDLE CHILDHOOD COGNITIVE DEVELOPMENT

Middle childhood is a time when children face new demands on their cognitive abilities in new situations, including formal schooling. As you have seen in the research findings we have discussed in this chapter, the cognitive changes from early to middle childhood

APPLYING RESEARCH FINDINGS

High-Stakes Testing

In recent years states have increasingly adopted various forms of high-stakes testing, in which both individual students and entire schools and school systems are evaluated on the basis of standardized achievement tests. For individual students, performance on the tests may determine whether or not they are allowed to move on to the next grade and ultimately whether they are allowed to graduate. At the institutional level, test results are used to rate the success of individual schools or entire school systems, often with financial consequences if performance does not improve over time.

High-stakes testing programs have generally been started in response to concerns about falling educational standards or poor student performance. The assumption underlying high-stakes testing is that simply making schools accountable for the success or failure of their students, without necessarily providing additional resources, would raise standards and improve student performance. However, there is little scientific evidence for the validity of this assumption, and high-stakes testing programs can have negative consequences at both the individual and the institutional level.

One negative effect for both schools and students is that high-stakes testing seems to narrow the curriculum as teachers are pushed to "teach to the test" (Jones, 2001; Perreault, 2000; Stecher and Barron, 2001). Teachers and parents commonly report that considerable class time must be devoted to preparing students for the tests, not only by teaching relevant material but also by giving practice tests. As a result, less time is left for valuable educational activities such as active student involvement in time-intensive projects, art and music, and field trips. In addition, the tests tend to overemphasize decontextualized skills, rather than the ability to apply skills in practical contexts (Stecher and Barron, 2001).

High-stakes testing also has negative impacts on both student and teacher motivation and attitudes toward school (Jones, 2001; Perreault, 2000). Teachers report increased stress both for themselves and for their students. In addition, spending large amounts of time preparing for and administering achievement tests tends to reduce student engagement in school, which is a key element in educational effectiveness (Jones, 2001). By discouraging student engagement, high-stakes testing may actually work against its stated goal of making schools more effective.

Finally, there is mounting evidence that high-stakes testing has a disproportionately negative impact on students who are at risk for a variety of reasons (Smith, 2001). In some states, as test scores have improved, dropout rates have increased dramatically. This appears to be partly due to students dropping out after failing tests required for high school graduation and partly due to the cumulative effects of being held back in earlier grades after poor performance on achievement tests. Students with any sort of special needs tend to be at a disadvantage when taking high-stakes tests, and there has been much debate about how to accommodate them. For all of the reasons discussed in the chapter, high-stakes tests are particularly problematic for students whose cultural background does not match the dominant culture in a school district. At this point, there is no evidence that high-stakes testing improves the quality of education or increases student learning in any but the narrowest sense.

are not revolutionary, but more a matter of refinement of skills that began to emerge in the preschool years. As children refine their cognitive skills, they also become able to use them more and more flexibly and to apply them in a wider range of situations.

Children's increasing ability to reason logically, their growing knowledge base, their increased information-processing capacity, and their growing metacognitive understanding all contribute to major advances on a wide range of cognitive tasks. In addition to conquering Piaget's conservation tasks, they develop a range of classification skills and a growing repertoire of attentional and memory strategies. They acquire the reasoning abilities needed to successfully deal with the demands of schoolwork and other increased responsibilities.

To a greater extent than in earlier periods of development, individual differences in cognitive abilities become significant. Social interactions with peers and adults influence the course and level of children's cognitive development. Culture has an ever greater impact on the particular cognitive skills they value and pursue, the uses to which their skills are put, and the ways their skills are measured.

By age 12, children have come a long way from their preschool cognitive abilities, but they have not yet achieved adultlike competence in several areas:

- Despite the considerable amount of knowledge they have acquired, they still lack the broad knowledge base they will have in adulthood.

- They still sometimes have trouble combining their cognitive skills into a larger problem-solving system.
- They cannot yet reason maturely about abstract and hypothetical problems.

Mastery of these cognitive limitations awaits the further development that will occur during adolescence.

Chapter Summary

Introduction

Piaget saw age 7 as a major transition point from *preoperational* to *concrete operational* thought, and other theorists have taken note of a *5- to 7-year shift* in many cultures. However, recent research suggests the major cognitive developments of middle childhood involve refinement and more widespread use of skills that existed in primitive form during the preschool years.

Major cognitive advances of middle childhood include increases in the following:

- Capacity for logical, systematic thinking using multiple pieces of information, due in part to a marked decline in centration.
- Ability to perceive underlying reality despite superficial appearance.
- Domain-specific knowledge or *expertise.*
- Information-processing capacity and control over attention and memory.
- Ability to think effectively about their own knowledge and processes of thought, a capacity called **metacognition.**

Cognitive limitations that remain in middle childhood include the following:

- Children still lack the broad knowledge base of adults.
- They sometimes have trouble using a newly acquired skill as part of a larger problem-solving system.
- They cannot reason maturely about abstract or hypothetical questions.

Major Cognitive Developments of Middle Childhood

During middle childhood, children develop a mature understanding of conservation.

- Some concepts of conservation emerge during the preschool years, but only in middle childhood do children acquire a large set of conservation concepts and use them confidently.
- At least in Western cultures, the various concepts of conservation are acquired in a predictable order.
- When children can consistently solve conservation problems, they are soon able to explain their answers in terms that show they understand conservation as a **necessary truth.**

- Once children understand conservation, they can think logically about many quantitative issues.

Children's understanding of both **hierarchical classification** and **matrix classification** improves greatly during middle childhood.

- Children begin to classify objects very early in life, but not until middle childhood do they make effective use of classification to organize information.
- Performance on classification tasks improves during middle childhood because children overcome the limitations imposed by centration.
- Elementary school children make great progress in classification skills, but they still do not entirely grasp the logical necessity of classification structures.

Children show major improvements in both attentional and memory abilities between early and middle childhood.

- School-aged children become increasingly systematic, organized, selective, and flexible in directing their attention. Individual differences in attentional abilities become apparent during these years.
- Memory development during middle childhood involves changes in four areas: memory capacity, knowledge, memory strategies, and **metamemory.**

Social Interaction and Cognitive Development

Elementary schoolchildren can learn from both **didactic** and **cooperative learning experiences.**

- Didactic learning experiences can be provided by either adults or more knowledgeable peers.
- Cooperative learning experiences are most likely to promote cognitive advances if the task is concrete, information-rich, and not too complex; the information available is somewhat ambiguous; the peers see reaching a consensus as a goal of their interaction; and the children know each other.
- Children become increasingly effective at teaching one another with age, but learning among peers is not always as effective as learning from a knowledgeable adult.
- Piaget's and Vygotsky's theories provide different explanations for how social interaction fosters cognitive development.

Individual Differences in Intelligence

Individual differences in cognitive abilities take on special significance when children enter school.

- Psychologists have had varying conceptions of intelligence, some seeing it as a *general* capacity, others as made up of separate, independent mental abilities.
- Attempts to broaden the definition of intelligence include Gardner's theory of multiple intelligences and Sternberg's triarchic theory.
- Researchers agree that individual differences in intelligence are a product of interaction between heredity and environment. Stability of IQ scores increases with age, probably reflecting relatively stable influences of both genes and environment.
- Because intelligence tests are prone to cultural bias, they are effective for comparing the abilities of people *within* cultures, but not across cultures.

Culture and School Achievement

- Although children have already acquired a variety of useful cognitive abilities before they enter school, the transition to school requires them to develop a new set of **decontextualized abilities.**
- For children from many minority groups, there may be a mismatch between their usual way of interacting with adults and the style of interaction expected in school, which can contribute to school achievement problems.
- American children lag behind Japanese and Chinese children in math achievement. Contributing factors include cultural differences in attributions about math performance, attitudes toward math, and processes of math instruction.

Review Questions

Introduction

1. What are the major cognitive advances and limitations of middle childhood?

Major Cognitive Developments of Middle Childhood

2. How does children's understanding of conservation change during middle childhood?
3. How does children's understanding of classification improve during middle childhood?
4. How do children's attentional abilities change from early to middle childhood?
5. How do changes in memory capacity, knowledge base, **mnemonic strategies,** and **metamemory** contribute to memory development in middle childhood?

Social Interaction and Cognitive Development

6. How do **didactic** and **cooperative learning experiences** advance children's cognitive development?

Individual Differences in Intelligence

7. Explain the various ways that psychologists have conceptualized intelligence.
8. What roles do heredity and environment, including culture, play in the development of intelligence?

Culture and School Achievement

9. How are culture and school achievement related?

Application and Observation

1. Try some of the conservation tasks described on page 383 with children of various ages. How does their performance compare to each other's and to Piaget's findings?
2. Try Paris's constructive memory task described on pages 391–392 with children of various ages (and/or with college students). Are there age differences in how children and/or adults respond to this task? What do their answers tell you about the development of memory skills and general knowledge base?
3. Observe an elementary school classroom during math class. How does what you see in the classroom

compare to what is described in the research on American and Asian math achievement and instruction?

4. Interview several teachers and parents of elementary school-aged children about their experiences with standardized testing, especially with state achievement tests. How has the introduction or expansion of such tests affected the curriculum, class activities, and time use during the school year? How have children reacted to the testing? What effects, positive or negative, has testing had on the school and on children's educational experiences?

12 Social and Emotional Development in Middle Childhood

411

en-year-old Malcolm and his buddies Andy, Leon, and Curtis pass Tammy Wilson on the sidewalk with her friends Vanessa and Lorraine. It is as if two powerful force fields have collided. The girls fall silent; the boys act cool. Vanessa nudges Tammy. Tammy slaps her arm away and looks straight ahead. Lorraine suppresses a giggle. As each group goes its own way, Vanessa turns around and yells: "Hey, Malcolm, Tammy likes you!" Tammy covers her face and runs up the street. Malcolm's buddies turn on him: "Uuuh-ahh, Malcolm, you sweet on her!" "Yeah! Malcolm got a girlfriend!" "Why don't you go kiss her, Malcolm!" Malcolm shoves them and shouts defensively, "No way, man! Get outa here." Laughing, shouting, and playfully fighting, the boys proceed to the candy store.

Latency period:
Freud's term for middle childhood, the period in which sexual urges lie relatively dormant.

Middle childhood was once considered an uneventful phase of development. Given the whirlwind changes of infancy, toddlerhood, and early childhood, this view was understandable. The physical growth of school-age children slows to a few inches per year, and their cognitive and social advances no longer seem so dramatic. Freud went so far as to label middle childhood a **latency period.** He believed children's sexual urges lay relatively dormant at this time, awaiting their great awakening in adolescence. Others took Freud's view to mean that little of social or emotional importance happened during middle childhood. Partly for this reason, social and emotional development in middle childhood remained one of the least studied topics in child psychology until the last three decades.

This lack of attention to middle childhood was unfortunate. To ignore any period of development creates serious gaps in our knowledge of how children grow. Ignoring middle childhood also hindered our ability to understand how youngsters handle the critical challenges of adolescence, because developmental outcomes in adolescence build on earlier outcomes. But perhaps most important of all, research into middle childhood has shown very clearly that this is *not* an uneventful time. Critical social and emotional development occurs from ages 6 through 12.

Erik Erikson (1963) argued that the major issue of middle childhood is the challenge of starting to master adult skills and the feelings fostered by success and failure. Success at meeting this challenge brings what Erikson called a **sense of industry**—that is, a basic belief in one's own competence, coupled with a tendency to initiate activities, to seek out learning experiences, and to work hard to accomplish goals. You saw examples of a sense of industry in our vignettes about Meryl, Malcolm, and Maggie. These children and their friends felt pride in being able to carry out projects, and they were busy setting new challenges and objectives for themselves. The fantasy play of the preschool period does not produce a sense of industry. Instead, concrete achievements in the real world, such as success in school, and effective coping with problems lead to deep feelings of competence and self-worth (Harter, 1998). Repeated failure to master new skills, in Erikson's view, leaves a child with feelings of incompetence and inferiority.

Sense of industry:
In Erikson's theory, the basic belief in one's own competence.

What Erikson describes is part of a broader task of middle childhood: *forming a coherent self-concept* by pulling together various experiences—as a social partner, an initiator, a boy or a girl, a problem solver, and so forth. In other words, in middle childhood a self-image with many dimensions becomes consolidated in the child's mind (Harter, 1998; Wolf, 1990). Just as children can consider multiple aspects of a problem with increasing ease in middle childhood, they can also coordinate multiple characteristics into an integrated concept of the self.

Middle childhood is also marked by *major developments in peer relations*, including formation of loyal friendships and development of genuine understanding of what it means to be part of a group and adhere to group norms. Meryl and Amy's "apartment" and Malcolm's strong belief that peers shouldn't tell on each other reflect these developmental changes.

Finally, middle childhood is a time of *growing understanding of emotions*. Children gain increased understanding of the complexity of emotions and the rules for displaying

Acquiring a sense of industry is a basic developmental task of middle childhood. One way children negotiate this task is by participating in projects that allow them to practice adult skills.

them. Their deepening emotional understanding combines with their cognitive and social advances to support their moral development.

We begin this chapter by stepping inside the minds of school-age children to observe the new ways they think about themselves and others. We then look at changes in peer relationships during middle childhood, as well as developments in the understanding of emotions. Finally, we examine the major contexts of development in middle childhood, including the family and the school.

Questions to Think About As You Read

- How are social, emotional, and cognitive development related in middle childhood?
- What are the contributions of family and peers to school-aged children's development?

THE INNER WORLD OF THE SELF

During middle childhood, developmental changes lay the groundwork for assembling a more complete, mature, and better integrated view of the self. This more mature view includes what is called the **psychological self**—a concept of the self that is made up of psychological characteristics, such as mental abilities and customary ways of feeling. To be aware of these psychological characteristics, elementary school children must consider various aspects of their experiences together and see them all as part of the same inner self (Harter, 1998; Wolf, 1990).

Psychological self:
A concept of the self that is made up of psychological characteristics, such as mental abilities and customary ways of feeling.

The Emergence of the Psychological Self

When psychologist John Broughton (1978) questioned children of different ages about the self, he found that preschoolers tend to think of the self not in psychological terms, but as a concrete entity, often synonymous with the brain or the head. Consequently, they tend to think of nonhumans—dogs, cats, and perhaps even flowers and trees—as having selves. Preschoolers often tie even their concepts of their own selves to their bodies, and they tend to distinguish themselves from others in terms of physical traits. "I'm different from Madeline because I have brown hair," a 5-year-old might explain. Similarly, when preschoolers are asked to list things about themselves, they usually dwell on physical activities. "I play on the swings," a 4-year-old might say, or "I go to nursery school" (Harter, 1998).

It is not until middle childhood that the concept of self becomes more psychological. Now children increasingly describe themselves in terms of inner thoughts, feelings, abilities, and attributes (Broughton, 1978; Harter, 1998; Selman, 1980). Meryl at age 9 described herself this way: "I'm kind, I'm helpful, I love to draw, I'm a good artist, I sometimes feel shy." Underlying such changes in children's self-descriptions are changes in their thinking about the nature of selves in general. This overall view of the self is called a **metatheory of the self.** To conclude she is kind, 9-year-old Meryl might consider acts of kindness to her friends, her little brother, her neighbor's cat, and Joe's elderly grandmother, and tie them all together as arising from a single characteristic. Such thinking is clearly more mature than the preschooler's focus on specific physical traits.

This is not to say that older children don't sometimes include physical features in their self-descriptions. When they do, it is often because they have compared themselves with others and identified features that stand out as different. Thus, Meryl might describe herself as having the blondest hair of anyone in her class. This more sophisticated outlook brings with it a firmer understanding of the self's uniqueness. As one of Broughton's 10-year-old study participants explained, "I am one of a kind. . . . There could be a person who looks like me or talks like me, but no one who has every single detail I have. Never a person who thinks exactly like me" (Broughton, 1978, p. 86). The capacity to coordinate various self-representations is the hallmark of the development of the self in middle childhood (Harter, 1998).

Psychologist Robert Selman (1980) showed how the emergence of a child's sense of an inner, private self parallels a growing awareness that all people have internal thoughts and feelings that are often hidden from others and sometimes even from themselves. Selman explored this topic by presenting children with dilemmas such as this one:

> *Tom has just saved some money to buy Mike Hunter a birthday present. He and his friend Greg go downtown to try to decide what Mike will like. Tom tells Greg that Mike is sad these days because his dog Pepper ran away. They see Mike and decide to try to find out what Mike wants without asking him right off. After talking to Mike for a while the kids realize that Mike is really sad because of his lost dog. When Greg suggests he get a new dog, Mike says he can't just get a new dog and have things be the same. Then Mike leaves to run some errands. As Mike's friends shop some more they see a puppy for sale in the pet store . . . Tom and Greg discuss whether to get Mike the puppy . . . What do you think Tom will do? (p. 175)*

Selman then presented a number of questions related to the story. Did Mike mean what he said? Can someone say something and not mean it? Did you ever think you'd feel one way and then find out you felt another? How can this happen? Can you ever fool yourself?

Selman found that very young children do not seem to distinguish between people's inner psychological experiences and their external words and actions. Many 5-year-olds conclude Tom should not buy Mike a puppy because Mike doesn't want another dog. They say they know this because Mike told Tom so. In contrast, by age 8 or 9 an understanding of the internal self usually emerges. Now children recognize that what people say and do need not conform to what they think and feel. Mike may insist he doesn't want a puppy, and he may even make himself believe this. Yet inside he could want a

Metatheory of the self:
Children's understanding of the nature of selves in general.

new dog very much. Such insights into the private, psychological self show children make great strides in self-understanding during middle childhood.

The Development of the Social Self

Another advance in self-understanding that occurs in middle childhood is development of what is often called the **social self**—an awareness that the self is intimately tied to other people (Damon and Hart, 1988). During the elementary school years, children's ability to adopt this perspective increases significantly. For one thing, children begin to incorporate social group membership into their self-descriptions. When asked to tell about himself, 10-year-old Mikey identifies himself as a fifth grader, a Boy Scout, and a member of a Little League team. The emergence of references to social group membership tells us that children this age increasingly place the concept of self in a social context.

Closely linked to the inclination to define the self in terms of relationships with others is the tendency to use others as a source of information in evaluating the self. This is called **social comparison.** The use of social comparison gradually increases during middle childhood. In one set of experiments, 5- to 10-year-olds were given feedback about their own and other children's performance on difficult tasks (Ruble, 1983). The researchers found that youngsters did not begin to compare their own performance to that of others until age 7 or 8, and did not consistently and systematically use social comparison in making self-assessments until age 9 or 10.

The use of social comparison in evaluating the self depends on several things. One is the *decline in centration* that marks the end of the preschool period. Until children are able to consider their own performance *and* someone else's at the same time, it is very hard for them to make social comparisons of any kind. Social comparison is also based on a *normative understanding of ability*—that is, the capacity to think about ability partly in terms of what most children can do. With a normative understanding of ability, a child is naturally inclined to look to others when assessing his or her own skills. Finally, the use of social comparison depends on the *cultural context*. In some cultural settings it is encouraged, in others it is not. Even the purpose for which social comparisons are made can depend on the cultural context. For example, Israeli kibbutz children, who are socialized to value group cooperation, use social comparison as a guide to how close they are

Social self:
An awareness that the self is intimately tied to other people.

Social comparison:
The tendency to use others as a source of information in evaluating the self.

Social comparison becomes important in children's self-assessments during middle childhood.

to mastering a task, whereas urban Israeli children use social comparison more as a gauge of who did better (Butler and Ruzany, 1993).

The Developing Sense of Gender

The sense of gender, including gender stereotypes, is another aspect of the self that continues to develop during middle childhood (Beal, 1994; Ruble and Martin, 1998; Serbin, Powlishta, and Gulko, 1993). By the end of elementary school, children know fully the activities, occupations, and personality traits considered appropriate for males and females in their culture—in other words, they have firm notions about what being a boy or a girl means (Beal, 1994). Often, they have adopted the cultural stereotypes of boys as more *instrumental* and girls as more *expressive,* as discussed in Chapter 10 (Davies and Lindsay, 2001).

Knowledge of gender stereotypes has a powerful influence on children's perceptions and memories (Liben and Signorella, 1993). In one study, children were given stereotyped information about a specific boy and girl and were then shown videos of the two children that contradicted the stereotypes (McAninch et al., 1993). When questioned later, they remembered the children as conforming to the stereotypes, not deviating from them. For example, they attributed to the girl in the video shy behaviors that were not in fact shown. This finding is in keeping with the emergence of constructive memory, discussed in Chapter 11.

Child Development CD
Gender Differences in Middle Childhood

Elementary school children apply gender stereotypes to themselves more than preschoolers do (Ruble and Martin, 1998). For instance, their preferences for activities tend to conform to traditional gender roles (Serbin et al., 1993). If children deviate from those traditional preferences, they often criticize themselves (Bussey and Bandura, 1992). Other aspects of their behavior match gender stereotypes too. Elementary school boys, for example, are more assertive in entering groups, whereas girls are more attentive to new group members (Borja-Alvarez, Zarbatany, and Pepper, 1991).

Several factors can influence how strict or flexible children are in conforming to gender stereotypes. In general, boys are more strongly sex-typed than girls, who tend to show more gender flexibility (Frey and Ruble, 1992; Katz and Ksansnak, 1994). Thinking about gender usually becomes more flexible with age and cognitive development (Serbin et al., 1993). For instance, as children mature they are more likely to say that hammers and rifles, dishes and brooms might be used by either sex, and that both boys and girls could be adventurous and cruel or weak and gentle. Socialization factors can also influence the flexibility of gender-related thinking. Having a mother of higher socioeconomic status who engages in nontraditional roles is related to more flexibility, as is having important people in one's life who think more flexibly about gender (Katz and Ksansnak, 1994; Serbin et al., 1993). In any case, gender influences all aspects of social behavior. We will examine one example of this later in the chapter when we discuss the impact of marital conflict on children.

Personal Effectiveness and Self-Management

A final aspect of the self that develops in middle childhood is children's beliefs that they can master and prevail in challenging circumstances, and that their successes come from resources within (Harter, 1998; Oettingen et al., 1994; Skinner, 1990). For instance, Susan Harter (1980) found that most preschoolers believe their physical and cognitive accomplishments result from their own efforts, but social success is chancier. When asked, "How do you find a friend?" a preschooler might answer, "You go and ring someone's doorbell" or "Maybe a policeman can help you." In contrast, most school-age children feel social successes, like physical and cognitive ones, depend on their own actions. As one 10-year-old girl replied when asked how you get someone to like you, "You talk to them and play with them and be nice to them."

As children develop a sense of personal effectiveness, they also develop capacities to cope with stress and emotionally challenging situations (Saarni, Mumme, and Campos,

1998). Compared with preschoolers, they are better at tolerating aversive emotions, viewing a stressor in different ways, and recruiting social support. They also can better tolerate delays in attaining goals (Mischel et al., 1989). For instance, when given the choice of accepting a small reward immediately or waiting for a much larger one later, and when told that certain actions carried out in the meantime will shorten the waiting period, school-age children tend to busy themselves with the prescribed behaviors and are able to wait substantial amounts of time. This ability to delay gratification increases markedly between ages 5 and 12.

All of the changes just described are referred to as changes in **executive functioning,** because in one way or another they involve changes in the capacity to plan and organize behavior that occur during middle childhood. Researchers believe that increases in executive functioning at this time are supported by increased myelination of the frontal lobes of the cerebral cortex and greater coordination between the frontal lobes and other parts of the brain, based on proliferating synaptic connections (Janowsky & Carper, 1996).

Executive functioning:
The capacity to plan and organize behavior.

PEER RELATIONSHIPS IN MIDDLE CHILDHOOD

Peer groups become increasingly important in middle childhood, rivaled only by the family as children's major developmental setting (Hartup, 1992). The importance of the peer group derives partly from the sheer amount of time elementary school children spend with peers. By age 11, time spent with peers usually surpasses time spent with family (Rubin, Bukowski, and Parker, 1998).

Middle-childhood peer groups are important for other reasons as well. One is *the unique learning experiences peer groups provide* (Keller and Edelstein, 1993). Because adult-child relationships are based to some extent on power and obedience (the adult has the right to *tell* the child what to do), they are limited in what they can teach children about such things as reciprocity and cooperation. In the peer group, in contrast, relationships are more nearly equal (the word *peer* means equal standing), and they are guided by principles of sharing and fairness. This equality makes the peer group highly conducive to learning about rules and expectations that will guide behaviors with others later in life. Peer relations may be especially important for learning to regulate aggression and for understanding the principles of loyalty and equity, important foundations for moral development (Hartup, 1992; Keller and Edelstein, 1993; Rubin et al., 1998). When Malcolm and Andy debate how to get even with Eric, or when Meryl and Amy discuss how to share a new toy, they are tackling principles best learned within the peer group.

Another reason peer groups are important is that *they promote interaction and conflict negotiation skills.* Elementary school children must work to make peers grasp what they are thinking and feeling, and to see other children's points of view. Through such efforts toward mutual understanding, children gain in social competence throughout middle childhood. In fact, measures of peer competence in middle childhood predict later ability to negotiate conflicts in romantic relationships, and they do so better than measures of childhood experiences with parents (Collins and Madsen, 2002).

Advances That Enable More Complex Peer Relations

A number of advances made during middle childhood make possible increasingly complex peer relationships. One important advance underlying more mature peer relations is *a greater ability to understand the perspectives, needs, and feelings of others.* For instance, 9-year-old Meryl can understand how Amy feels when she forgets her lunch one day. When Meryl offers Amy half her own lunch, she is not simply following a rule about sharing. Instead, she knows sharing is the helpful, kind thing to do; she shares to address a need and inequality; and she shares on a personalized basis. Thus, the

Peer groups provide a major arena for learning about reciprocity, cooperation, and fairness.

capacity to consider others' feelings leads to a marked advance in prosocial behavior, as well as to more mature peer relations.

A second advance related to more mature peer relations is *the ability to grasp more complex rules regarding interpersonal behavior.* For example, different situations require different behavior toward others. At age 11, Malcolm knows that when one of his best friends buys a bag of candy, he can help himself to a piece, as long as he doesn't take more than his fair share. However, helping himself would not be acceptable behavior with a boy he hardly knows. Malcolm also understands that he and his best friends can laugh, elbow, and playfully shove each other while working on a joint project at home, but a joint project at school requires much more restrained behavior.

A final factor contributing to more mature peer relations is *a growing ability to communicate feelings and wishes* with words rather than actions. When preschoolers want a toy another child has, they often express their desire for it by trying to grab it. Elementary schoolers are much less likely to display such instrumental aggression (Coie and Dodge, 1998). Instead, they typically try to negotiate or appeal to group norms, such as sharing, to get what they want. Similarly, when someone offends them, elementary school children can communicate their displeasure verbally rather than physically. Compared with preschoolers, they are much more likely to hurl verbal insults intended to cause psychological distress (Maccoby, 1980; Thorne, 1986). This trend makes sense in light of developmental changes in understanding of self and others. For instance, Eric will be insulted by being called a jerk only if he wants to see himself as competent and well liked. At the same time, only if Malcolm is able to consider Eric's feelings about receiving such an insult will he understand how much the taunt can hurt. In middle childhood, girls become especially likely to use verbal aggression. They display less physical aggression than boys, but more **relational aggression**—attempts to hurt another person by damaging a relationship. This form of aggression includes attempts to exclude peers from activities, to damage their reputations, and to gossip about their negative characteristics or behavior (Crick et al., 2001). This form of aggression requires considerable sophistication.

Relational aggression: Attempts to hurt another person by damaging a relationship.

Five Major Developments in Peer Relations

Peer relations change in several ways during middle childhood:

- Children begin to expect more from friends, including loyalty and understanding.
- Children start to form networks of friends, or peer groups.
- Children learn to coordinate their allegiance to individual friends with their functioning in a group.
- Adhering to peer group norms becomes increasingly important.
- Clear boundaries for interaction with members of the opposite sex develop.

Let's look at each of these developments.

Forming Loyal Friendships

Interviewer: Why is Caleb your friend?
Tony (a preschooler): Because I like him.

During middle childhood, the capacity for loyal and intimate friendships increases.

Interviewer: And why do you like him?
Tony: Because he's my friend.
Interviewer: And why is he your friend?
Tony: (slowly and emphatically, with mild disgust) Because ... I ... chosed ...
*   him ... for ... my ... friend.*
(Rubin, 1980, p. 34)
Interviewer: Why is Shantel your friend?
Lakisha (age 10): Shantel tells me things she wouldn't tell anyone else. Like, if
she was mad at some of the other kids, she would tell me. And some kids wouldn't
do that. I think it's nice that she shares her secrets with me.

Although preschoolers routinely label other children as friends, these relationships lack the reciprocal support and loyalty, the shared closeness and common interests of genuine friendships. Not until middle childhood do more mature ideas and expectations about friendship develop (Keller and Edelstein, 1993; Selman, 1980). This is one of the major social accomplishments of the period. By the end of the elementary school years most children are involved in what psychiatrist Harry Stack Sullivan (1953) called *chumships*—very close and personal friendships, such as the one between Meryl and Amy.

Child Development CD
Friends in Middle Childhood

The deepening of peer relationships in middle childhood is related to various advances in children's thinking (Hartup, 1992; Keller and Edelstein, 1993). During the elementary school years children come to understand how friends support each other. No longer do they define a friend simply as "someone I like" or "someone I play with a lot." Friends are now seen as people who help and share with each other, especially in times of need. They are evaluated in terms of their personal traits. This is how one 10-year-old girl explained why another child was not her friend:

(Why don't you make friends with Bernadette?) "'Cause we had a fight, a big
one." (Why can't you make up?) ... "'Cause we're not good friends and I don't
like her that much. She's not my kind of person. She's not my taste." (What's your
taste?) "I like nice people. If they're not kind then they're not a friend."
(Weinstock, quoted in Damon, 1977, p. 158)

Children this age also come to understand that conflict is a part of friendship and may even strengthen it (Hartup and Laursen, 1993). When asked if an argument would end a friendship, 10-year-old Lakisha thought for a while and replied: "No. Actually, you probably would be even better friends because you would understand each other better." Some less confident children think relationships with peers are more fragile, that other

APPLYING RESEARCH FINDINGS

Understanding Intergroup Conflict

Gang violence is a problem in every large American city, often involving school-age children. Even if they are not gang members by age 11 or 12, most youngsters in tough urban neighborhoods have witnessed gang-related beatings, knifings, and shootings. The problem of intergang violence is complex, but research suggests it is fostered by competition for scarce resources (McDonald, 1988). In deprived areas, gangs strive to get ahead by whatever means they can and aggressively retaliate against anyone trespassing on their territory or getting in their way.

The power of competition for resources to breed intergroup conflict was demonstrated in a classic study by Muzafer and Carolyn Sherif (Sherif and Sherif, 1953; Sherif et al., 1961). The Sherifs recruited 11- and 12-year-old boys to attend a summer camp and divided them into two groups, housed at different campsites. As the members of each group worked together on tasks requiring cooperation, they developed a strong sense of group identity. Soon the two groups—neither one knowing what the other was doing—adopted group names (Eagles and Rattlers) and made group flags and banners. Coordinating their activities toward desirable goals transformed strangers into two very cohesive groups.

The Sherifs next demonstrated how conflict between groups could be provoked by putting the Eagles and Rattlers in competition for limited resources. They organized a series of contests between the groups and gave the winners valuable prizes. At first, competitive pressures caused upheaval in each group. Group members blamed each other for losses, and angry confrontations often resulted.

This reaction soon faded. Each group emerged more unified than ever and focused its hostility on the other group. Intergroup bickering, name calling, fights, and raids rapidly became the norm. This phase of the study revealed some ways intergroup prejudices and hatreds develop.

Ending the intergroup warfare proved far from easy. Asking each group to see the other's good side met with no success, nor did getting the groups together for shared activities such as picnics, fireworks displays, and movies. These social events dissolved into chaos as the Eagles and Rattlers hurled food and insults at each other. The one strategy that did work was a series of bogus emergencies. The camp truck mysteriously broke down and had to be repaired for food to be delivered. An unexplained leak had to be found or the water system would be shut down. Resolving these staged difficulties required cooperation among *all* the campers. Intergroup conflict sharply decreased, and friendships began to form across group lines. When enemies are forced to pull together for their common good, they often begin to see each other in a more favorable light.

This lesson in reducing intergroup conflict among school-age boys has application to reducing intergang violence. If gang members can be encouraged to work together on projects benefiting the whole community—building a playground, painting a mural, refurbishing a recreation center—hostilities between the gangs may decline. Even athletic events can reduce rivalries, if teams are made up of members of both gangs, rather than pitting one gang against another.

children will not like them very long if they argue with them (Sroufe, Carlson, and Shulman, 1993). However, by the end of middle childhood, all children have the capacity to think about friendship in much more complex ways than they could in the preschool years. They now recognize that the essence of friendship is mutual understanding and caring, as well as shared outlooks and interests (Hartup, 1992).

Children behave differently with friends than with mere acquaintances (Laursen, Hartup, and Koplas, 1996). Compared with nonfriends, friends are more positive and reciprocal, show more emotional intensity and understanding, are more likely to phrase ideas in mutual terms ("Let's do it this way," "Let's make sure it's straight"), and are more concerned with equity in how rewards are distributed (Rubin et al., 1998). They are just as likely to experience conflict, but they resolve conflict differently. Friends are more likely than nonfriends to resolve conflicts in a way that will preserve their relationship—for example, by emphasizing fairness (Laursen, Hartup, and Koplas, 1996). Ample research shows that having friends plays an important role in children's well-being, at times offsetting the negative consequences of a harsh home environment or negative child characteristics such as aggressiveness (Deater-Deckard, 2001; Ladd and Burgess, 2001; Schwartz et al., 2000).

Forming Peer Groups If beginning peer relationships are the hallmark of the preschool years, *friendship networks* are the hallmark of middle childhood (Hartup,

1992). Like conceptions of friendship, conceptions of the peer group also change with age. Preschoolers have very little understanding of groups as such. They have little sense of peer group members sharing a collective identity, only rudimentary feelings of "us" versus "them." By the end of the elementary school years, however, children have a well-defined sense of "groupness" and readily distinguish between those inside and outside their group. This understanding develops partly because of cognitive advances and partly because of experience belonging to groups. Teams, clubs, scout troops, school classes, and other formal and informal groups become an increasingly important part of children's social life during the elementary school years. This orientation toward group membership includes the beginnings of gang involvement for boys in many urban neighborhoods. The box on page 420 describes a classic study of boys' group behavior that helps to explain the appeal and functioning of middle-childhood and adolescent groups in general and urban gangs in particular.

School-age boys tend to form peer groups that are built on shared activities and competition.

Elementary school children tend to play with relatively stable clusters of friends. These groups are usually smaller for girls, with each girl having one or two best friends (Maccoby, 1990). This tendency is in keeping with the stress that school-age girls place on intimacy, sharing of confidences, and mutual support. Boys' peer groups, in contrast, tend to be larger, with an emphasis on loyalty and shared activities.

Boys and girls do different kinds of things in their peer groups (Shulman, Elicker, and Sroufe, 1994). Boys often engage in joint building activities and competitions, such as skateboard contests. These activities allow a great deal of individual self-expression and emphasize dominance, as the boys vie to be the leader or the winner. There is often considerable physical intimacy in boys' peer groups—playful pushing and wrestling, for example, but there is little emotional or verbal intimacy. Boys are more likely than girls to participate in team sports, which involve formal rules and coordination of a large number of people. Girls' groups, in contrast, are more cohesive and more oriented toward accord and toward verbal and emotional intimacy. Many girls' activities, such as planning a skit, support a great deal of talking; frequently talking itself *is* the activity. Loyalty may be achieved more quickly in a girls' peer group. One group of girls in the Minnesota day camp study refused to say who they liked best in their group because they had made a pact to say they liked each other exactly the same (Shulman et al., 1994).

Coordinating Friendship and Group Interaction Learning to coordinate close friendships and interaction within a group is important because both types of social involvement provide children with valuable experiences. Trust and reciprocity are the lessons of close friendships, while cooperation, coordination of activities, and adherence to rules and norms are the primary lessons of the peer group. Both close friendships and acceptance by peer groups are related to feelings of self-worth and lack of loneliness in children (Parker and Asher, 1993; Rubin et al., 1998). Typically, friendship and group interaction supplement each other; friendships promote integration into a group, and functioning in the group is a rich context for sharing between friends (Shulman et al., 1994; Sroufe et al., 1993).

Even when two socially competent friends are functioning within a group, the special relationship between them is apparent in the way they behave toward each other. It is as if an invisible membrane surrounds them even when they are some distance apart and mingling with other children. This is not the case for children who are less socially competent (Shulman et al., 1994). Some fail to stay connected with their friend when playing in a group, or the friend leaves them behind—the membrane around them ruptures. Other pairs of friends steer clear of peer groups entirely. They form an exclusive relationship, playing apart from others. Apparently the membrane around them is too rigid, allowing no involvement with the outside world.

Adhering to Peer Group Norms During middle childhood, children become very concerned about enforcing **peer group norms,** or rules of conduct. Strict adherence to norms is common in children this age. You saw one example in Malcolm's amazement that Eric could break the code against telling on peers.

Major peer group norms during middle childhood include fairness, equity, and sharing, perhaps because they help maintain group harmony and cohesiveness (Hartup, 1992; Rubin et al., 1998). School-age children splitting a treat, such as a large candy bar or a plate of cookies, will often struggle mightily to make sure everyone receives *exactly* the same amount. However, fairness sometimes requires that things be divided unequally, if the distribution is based on performance (Graziano, 1984). Mikey and his Little League teammates might decide that whoever scored the most runs in winning a game deserves the last slice of the pizza they are sharing to celebrate. If no one had clearly made a larger contribution to winning, the boys would probably rigidly enforce the equity standard. Sharing is another strictly adhered-to rule in middle childhood. By about age 8 or 9, sharing becomes closely tied to fairness and rectifying inequalities. Amy, for example, may say it's only fair to allow Rita to join in some of the bike hikes she and Meryl take.

Because peer group norms usually agree with the moral values of the larger culture, peer relationships are an important arena for promoting moral development (Damon, 1988; Keller and Edelstein, 1993). Adults may teach children how they are expected to behave, but peers do much to ensure that those expectations are carried out. Friends and playmates tell each other when they are doing wrong, and children who refuse to follow the rules are often ostracized. Thus, the peer group is one of the mainstream culture's great watchdogs and enforcers. Partly through peer group vigilance, cultural norms and values become deeply ingrained.

Maintaining Gender Boundaries One area of socialization in which the peer group's influence stands out is maintaining boundaries between the sexes (Ruble and Martin, 1998). Elementary school children are diligent in their efforts to ensure that children do not stray too far across gender lines, at least in public settings. Chase games between the sexes may be acceptable, but a boy who tries to enter a girls' game of jump rope is usually shunned by the girls and ridiculed by the boys. Similarly, a girl who hovers near the boys usually gets a negative reaction from both sexes. Barrie Thorne (1986) has called these rituals of teasing and ostracism **border work,** because the children are defending the borders of their gender-segregated groups. This is what Malcolm's friends are doing in the scene at the beginning of the chapter. Their teasing keeps Malcolm from showing any reciprocal liking for Tammy.

Gender segregation is common in middle childhood. Some cultures impose gender boundaries—for example, by having boys live in a separate village (Beal, 1994; Whiting and Edwards, 1988). In Western cultures the segregation is largely left up to the children, and maintaining this separation may be what accounts for the animosity (at least on the surface) between boys and girls (Underwood, Schockner, and Hurley, 2001). In the Minnesota day camp study, 10-year-olds interacted exclusively with members of the opposite sex during only 6 percent of their free time (Sroufe, Bennett, et al., 1993). Even when groups of boys and girls interacted, physical boundaries between the sexes were maintained. One function gender segregation appears to serve is to protect young children from premature sexual contact.

This is not to say that elementary school children have no contact with members of the opposite sex. A great deal of such contact occurs, but only within the limits of peer

Peer group norms:
Informal rules governing the conduct of children within a peer group.

Border work:
The rituals of teasing and ostracism with which elementary school children maintain the boundary between their gender-segregated peer groups.

Table 12.1 Knowing the Rules: Under What Circumstances is it Permissible to Have Contact with the Other Gender in Middle Childhood?

Rule:	The contact is accidental.
Example:	You're not looking where you're going and you bump into someone of the other gender.
Rule:	The contact is incidental.
Example:	You go to get some lemonade and wait while two children of the other gender get some. (There should be no conversation.)
Rule:	The contact involves some clear and necessary purpose.
Example:	You may say, "Pass the lemonade" to persons of the other gender at the next table. No interest in them is expressed.
Rule:	An adult compels you to have contact.
Example:	A teacher says, "Go get that map from X and Y and bring it to me."
Rule:	You are accompanied by someone of your own gender.
Example:	Two girls may talk to two boys, though physical closeness with your own partner must be maintained and intimacy with the others is disallowed.
Rule:	The interaction or contact is accompanied by disavowal of any interest in or liking for members of the other gender.
Example:	You call members of the other gender ugly, hurl some other insult at them, or (more commonly for boys) push them or throw something at them as you pass by.

Source: Sroufe, Bennett, et al., 1993.

group rules (Elicker, Englund, and Sroufe, 1992; Sroufe, Bennett, et al., 1993). These rules are unwritten, and adults do not teach them (many adults, in fact, seem to have forgotten them), but most children know them well. For example, children usually consider it inappropriate to interact with children of the opposite sex, especially when a single child is the odd girl or boy out in an other-gender group. However, there *are* exceptions to this norm, such as when a teacher requires such contact. This and other rules of acceptable opposite-sex contact are listed in Table 12.1. In general, school-age children consider it acceptable to interact with members of the other gender only when they have a suitable excuse.

Girls or boys who routinely fail to maintain gender boundaries are less popular with other children and are rated as less socially competent by adult observers (Ruble and Martin, 1998). Following peer group rules appears to be a sign of competence and adjustment during middle childhood, and it forecasts successful functioning in mixed-gender peer groups during adolescence (Sroufe, Egeland, and Carlson, 1999).

Status and Acceptance in the Peer Group

Not all children are popular with peers. A research technique called **sociometrics** (literally, "social measurement") is used to measure children's peer status—the extent to which they are accepted by their peers. Sociometric techniques involve asking children to name others they especially like or don't like to play with. Some children are frequently named as liked and are well accepted by their peers. Others are consistently named as disliked and are characterized by researchers as *rejected* (Rubin et al., 1998; Rudolph and Asher, 2001). Rejected children are often viewed by peers, teachers, and other observers as aggressive or mean. Still other children are rarely named as either liked or disliked. These children, who seem to be of little interest to peers, are characterized by researchers as

Sociometrics:
A research technique used to measure peer status.

Children's status and acceptance among their peers is often evident in their behavior on the playground.

neglected (Brendgen et al., 2001; Rubin et al., 1998). Neglected children tend to be ineffective with peers and dependent on teachers, but generally they are not hostile (Sroufe, 1983). A subgroup of these children, who are submissive and low in assertiveness, often become chronic victims of aggressive children (Schwartz, Dodge, and Coie, 1993). The distinctions among accepted, rejected, and neglected children are very powerful, predicting later social behavior in important ways (Brendgen et al., 2001; Deater-Deckard, 2001; Rubin et al., 1998; Rudolph and Asher, 2001).

Although many unpopular children feel lonely or victimized by peers, not all of them do (Rubin et al., 1998; Schwartz et al., 1993). Unpopular children's feelings about their low peer status depend on multiple factors. For example, intense loneliness is associated with a *combination* of isolation from the group, friendlessness, and low peer acceptance, not one of these factors alone (Rubin et al., 1998). Similarly, aggressive children, especially those who exhibit instrumental aggression and bullying, are more likely to be rejected, and the combination of aggression and rejection is strongly associated with maladjustment (Coie and Dodge, 1998; Rubin et al., 1998). Aggressive children who are *not* rejected are better adjusted, no doubt because of other positive characteristics (Hymel, Bowker, and Woody, 1993).

During elementary school a child's popularity with peers becomes quite stable, reflecting children's growing capacity to think of others in terms of enduring traits and to form stable expectations about them (Brendgen et al., 2001; Coie and Dodge, 1998; Hartup, 1992). A child's status among peers is also perpetuated by his or her own behavior. This was suggested in a study in which third and fourth graders were carefully observed on the playground (Ladd, 1983). Rejected children spent the most time isolated from others or engaged in negative behavior such as aggression. Neglected children spent more time watching others playing; they merely stood on the sidelines and didn't participate. Popular children spent much of their time in relatively large, heterogeneous play groups that included their friends and other popular youngsters. Thus, the children's behavior reinforced their status among peers. Established patterns of behavior and peer reactions may carry over into new settings. In one study, when children rated high or low in peer acceptance were placed in a new group of youngsters, these new peers soon viewed them the same way their previous peers had (Dodge et al., 1986). Apparently, the children continued to behave in ways that encouraged certain peer responses.

Chapter 12 Social and Emotional Development in Middle Childhood   **425**

How well an elementary school child functions with peers and is accepted by them strongly predicts adjustment in adolescence and mental health in adulthood (Deater-Deckard, 2001; Rudolph and Asher, 2001; Sroufe et al., 1999). For this reason, researchers have tried to find ways to improve the status of unpopular children. One approach has been to change their expectations about how peers will react to them, which in turn causes them to change their behavior toward their peers. For example, when researchers assured rejected children that the members of a new group would like them before entering them into that group, the children in the new group did in fact accept them more (Rabiner and Coie, 1989). Another approach has been to focus directly on changing key aspects of unpopular children's behavior toward peers. For example, children may be trained to perceive other people's intentions more accurately (and not jump to the conclusion that others are hostile to them) or to regulate their own emotions better. Compared with children who have not received this sort of training, the trained youngsters attribute more appropriate intentions to their peers and manage themselves better (Deater-Deckard, 2001). However, we do not yet know how long the effects of such interventions last.

Social Skills Training

EMOTIONAL DEVELOPMENT IN MIDDLE CHILDHOOD

Even though children experience all the basic human emotions by the end of the preschool period, emotional development still continues at a rapid pace during middle childhood. During this period, children go beyond experiencing emotions such as guilt and pride to *understanding* these emotions and their causes (Saarni et al., 1998).

The Changing Understanding of Emotion

During middle childhood, children *become increasingly able to understand the complexity of emotion-arousing situations* (Saarni et al., 1998). Preschoolers tend to say many events would make them happy, whereas older children have a more differentiated view (Saarni et al., 1998). Elementary school children know, for example, that different features of the same situation could make them happy *and* sad. They also know that emotional experience depends not only on what happens to them in the present but also on their previous thoughts, feelings, and expectations (Gnepp, 1989). A preschooler would say that a child expecting a big prize would be happy to receive a small one, but an older child would know this situation is likely to cause disappointment.

School-age children can also *take particular situations into account when determining an appropriate emotional response* (Strayer, 1993). For instance, children this age say they would be less angry at another child for stealing their cat if they knew the child's cat was lost and his or her parents refused to get another one. Similarly, school-age children show a growing understanding that emotions may vary in the same situation depending on the outcome, that different children may experience different emotions in the same circumstances, and that they themselves may experience different reactions at different times (Gnepp and Klayman, 1992).

Finally, elementary school children know a great deal about *display rules* for emotions (Underwood, Coie, and Herbsman, 1992). They know it is sometimes better not to show your feelings, such as not showing disappointment when given a gift you don't like or anger when a teacher calls on someone else. Because elementary school children become increasingly adept at masking emotions, it is not always easy to tell exactly what they are feeling (Saarni et al., 1998).

These changes in emotional understanding seem to be related to *increases in true empathy* for others. School-age children move beyond simply becoming distressed when someone else is feeling hurt, sad, or angry. Now they are able to feel along with the other person, and they do so more and more as they grow older (Fabes, Eisenberg, and Eisenbud, 1993; Strayer, 1993).

Emotional, Social, and Cognitive Bases of Moral Development

Cognitive advances, social relationships, and emotional development all work together to foster moral development in middle childhood. The advances in children's thinking described in Chapter 11 support a deepening of moral concerns and a greater understanding of moral issues. As children move away from a focus on their own perspective and centration on one aspect of a situation, they are increasingly able to consider other people's feelings, even the feelings of several others simultaneously. Whereas a 4-year-old would say that a boy who pushes another child off a swing feels happy because he got the swing for himself, an 8-year-old would expect the boy to have mixed feelings and to be aware that the other child may be unhappy (Arsenio and Kramer, 1992). Such consideration for other people's feelings is a major factor in moral growth.

The combined influence of cognitive, social, and emotional development is demonstrated in a set of studies in which European children were given a realistic moral dilemma to solve. The dilemma was between keeping a promise to meet a best friend who needed to talk or going to a movie with a new child in the neighborhood who was going to pay for all the treats (Keller and Edelstein, 1993). Most 7-year-olds said a child faced with this decision would choose the movie, but 67 percent of 12-year-olds said the child would choose to keep the promise to the friend. Important changes in thinking, feeling, and interacting with others underlie this change. Many 7-year-olds said the child might feel at least a little bad about going to the movie, but it was because they thought the friend might be angry or have nice toys the child wouldn't get to play with. Older children, in contrast, based their preference for meeting the friend on the importance of both the friendship and the promise. They believed that a promise should be kept and that loyalty is part of being a best friend. At the same time, they became able to evaluate and consider the feelings of the other two children. Thinking of the friend waiting at home, for example, would make them feel bad. Note, however, that the older children's more mature moral thinking is not just the result of cognitive advances that allow them to understand other people's feelings better. Their emotional experiences in friendships and their commitment to them also help them to understand others' feelings. A moral sense, in other words, derives partly from participation in close relationships (Keller and Edelstein, 1993; Turiel, 1998).

The particular moral principles children adopt are largely a product of their culture. When young Chinese children are presented with the moral dilemma just described, they use a different reason than young Western children to support the choice of going to the movie; they say the child would go to the movie because it is important to show caring and acceptance toward a new child (Keller et al., 1998). Such reasoning probably derives from the Chinese concern with interpersonal harmony and the welfare of others. However, as Chinese children grow older, they increasingly emphasize the importance of friendship in making this moral decision and say the child would opt for showing loyalty to the best friend. For Chinese children, a consistency between moral thinking and moral behavior (*doing* the same thing your reasoning tells you is right) often emerges earlier than in Western children. Even the 7-year-old Chinese children were sure they had made the right moral choice, whereas the young European children were uncertain.

CONTEXTS OF DEVELOPMENT IN MIDDLE CHILDHOOD

As in all other periods of development, the changes of middle childhood take place within various contexts. We have already discussed the context of the peer group, but family, school, and after-school care are also important developmental contexts.

The Family

Parents and siblings are both powerful influences on children's development. In our examination of the family context during middle childhood, we'll consider first the nature of parent-child relationships and then the influence of siblings.

Parents tend to give school-age children increased responsibility and expect them to carry out tasks with limited supervision.

Parent-Child Relationships Relationships with parents change markedly during middle childhood, partly due to children's advancing cognitive abilities. Because school-age children are more competent and better able to exert self-control, parents begin to give them more responsibilities, including household chores (Bugental and Goodnow, 1998). At the same time, parents are less inclined to use physical coercion and more likely to use reasoning to get their children to do what they should. Children, in turn, have a greater understanding of parents' behavior, including reasons for discipline (Turiel, 1998). In fact, 10-year-olds and their parents show considerable agreement regarding the kind of infractions that require serious punishment. Dangerous behaviors and moral transgressions are seen as calling for more serious discipline than violating social conventions.

As in peer relations, there is now more concern for equity and fairness in the parent-child relationship. In general, the parent-child system moves toward more shared responsibility for children's behavior. Parents no longer explicitly direct children in a continuous way. Children now have a general knowledge of what they should do, and parents expect children to follow those internalized guidelines for behavior. However, the parents' role as *monitors* of behavior remains critically important (Parke and Buriel, 1998). The hallmark of effective parenting in this period is keeping track of children's whereabouts and activities and providing supervision and direction when needed.

Parental influences take on new forms in middle childhood. Parents not only influence children by modeling behaviors and providing direct reinforcement, as they did in earlier years; now they also influence them by how they supervise and what they expect of them. This can be seen in gender socialization (Huston, Carpenter, and Atwater, 1986; Ruble and Martin, 1998). Parents tend to allow boys more freedom to explore and encourage them to do things on their own, whereas they tend to encourage girls to stay close to home and be more involved in domestic activities. Similarly, parents are more likely to expect sons to be ambitious, hardworking, achievement-oriented, and assertive, and more likely to expect daughters to be nurturant, kind, unselfish, and loving. In keeping with these expectations, girls tend to place high value on socially oriented goals, such as showing concern for other people and being liked in return. When a girl's own achievements jeopardize her social acceptance, she is more likely than a boy to experience anxiety and show a drop in her level of performance.

Parenting Styles and Child Development Researchers who have studied parenting styles have found that certain parental characteristics are closely related to differences in children's behavior (Parke and Buriel, 1998). Parental responsiveness and the child's perception that parents are available for them promote development in middle childhood, as they did earlier (Kerns et al., 2000). In general, parenting characterized by warmth, support, and a reasoning approach to discipline is consistently associated with such positive child characteristics as cooperativeness, effective coping, low levels of behavior problems, strongly internalized norms and values, a sense of personal responsibility, and high levels of moral reasoning (Hardy, Power, and Jaedicke, 1993; Walker and Taylor, 1991). Such findings apply to both mothers and fathers (Amato, 1998). In contrast, absence of parental warmth and reliance on power-assertive discipline (shouting, physical punishment) are associated with negative child characteristics, such as aggression, noncompliance, and projecting blame for negative outcomes onto other people (Parke and Buriel, 1998; Weiss et al., 1992). Controlling, intrusive parenting is associated with the belief in children that their efforts make little difference (Ginsberg and Bronstein, 1993).

Such correlations do not prove the parental behaviors *cause* the child characteristics. It may be that the child's characteristics elicit a certain style of response from the parents. In other words, there may be an influence from child to parent, as well as from parent to child. Some studies examining interaction sequences between parents and children have shown children do play a role in maintaining negative encounters (e.g., Vuchinich, Bank, and Patterson, 1992). But this is not the whole story. When researchers assess parenting style before the child is old enough to display stable behavioral characteristics, they find that how the parents act is generally related to how the child acts at a *later* age. One study found that harsh discipline by parents predicted later child aggression, even when other potential causes of aggression (temperament, social class, marital violence) were statistically controlled (Weiss et al., 1992). It has also been found that teaching alternative parenting techniques to parents who discipline harshly can help improve the behavior of their children (e.g., Dishion and Bullock, 2002; Patterson and Capaldi, 1991). Such work suggests that certain parental characteristics do influence children. The box on page 429 presents additional evidence for parental influence on children's development.

It turns out to be important to look at *clusters* of parenting characteristics, rather than isolated traits, because a particular trait may have different effects depending on what other traits are present. For example, parental permissiveness may lead children to be either sociable and expressive or disobedient, irresponsible, and lacking in persistence, depending on the other characteristics that go with it (Becker, 1964). Being relatively permissive with a child in a context of clear rules, careful supervision, and modeling of nurturance and respect has different meaning than being permissive in a context of hostility, ambiguous rules, and lack of attention. The first suggests a pattern of high positive regard, the second a pattern of neglect.

mhhe.com/dehart5

Parenting Styles

In recent decades researchers have identified clusters of characteristics in parents that are consistently associated with particular outcomes in children. One such effort is Diana Baumrind's work, discussed in Chapter 10. As you may recall, Baumrind (1967, 1991) identified three major patterns among parents of preschoolers:

- *authoritative parents,* who are nurturant and responsive, set firm limits and demand maturity of their children, rely on discipline techniques based on reasoning, and take care to respect the child's point of view;

- *authoritarian parents,* who are harsh in their discipline and rigid in enforcing rules, and seldom try to understand the child's point of view; and

- *permissive parents,* who are somewhat nurturant but fail to maintain firm limits and standards.

A follow-up study of the children in Baumrind's original preschool research, conducted when they were 8 and 9, showed that authoritative parenting continued to be associated with positive outcomes in middle childhood (Baumrind, 1989). School-age

A CLOSER LOOK

DO PARENTS MATTER?

In *The Nurture Assumption,* Judith Rich Harris (1998) contended that parenting practices have little or no influence on children's personality development and peers have a great deal of influence. She also suggested that any apparent parental influence is only the influence of genes shared by parents and children. A closer look at several lines of research reveals clearly that parenting is of great importance in children's development and that this influence is not reducible to the role of genes.

Monkey Research
It is not feasible to do human experiments to test the relative impacts of parental behavior and genes, but studies with monkeys help to untangle these influences. Lynn Fairbanks (1989) found that the amount of time an infant vervet monkey was held predicted how much she would hold her own babies when she grew up. This result held even after controlling for how much the monkey's mother held all her babies (a good estimate of genetic influence) and how much she held a current baby. Stephen Suomi (1995) provided even more convincing evidence in an experiment in which newborn rhesus monkeys were randomly assigned to foster mothers varying in nurturance. Infants adopted by highly nurturant mothers grew up to be more nurturant than those raised by nonnurturant adopted mothers, regardless of the nurturance of their biological mothers. In later studies Suomi showed that, when placed with nurturant foster mothers as infants, even monkeys having an anomaly in a gene often associated with impulsiveness did not grow up to be distractible and hyperactive. In fact, they were the leaders of the troop (Suomi, 2002).

Parent Behavior versus Parent Traits
Much research shows a correlation between harsh parental treatment of children and child aggression, which could be interpreted as due to shared genes. However, Patterson and Dishion (1988) have shown that harsh treatment by parents predicts children's aggressiveness far better than assessments of parental aggressiveness as a trait. Another parenting variable, lack of monitoring, also predicts aggression, and here possible genetic interpretations are not so obvious.

Changing Parental Behavior
Several studies show that when researchers intervene to promote more responsive and appropriate parental behavior, child behavior problems decrease and academic achievement and other aspects of competence increase (e.g., Cowan and Cowan, 2002; Dishion and Bullock, 2002). This provides clear and direct human evidence that parenting matters. Other studies have shown caregiver depression to be related to negative child outcomes. However, results depend on when the caregiver is depressed. Infants show more problems if caregivers are actively depressed during their first year of life than if they are depressed earlier or later (Dawson and Ashman, 2000), yet the same genetic vulnerability should apply regardless of timing. In addition, changes in parental depression (or drug problems or life stress) are associated with changing child behavior problems (Egeland et al., 1990).

Nonobvious Relationships
Often the links between parenting and child outcome are not obvious. That is, the outcome is not identical or even similar to the parenting behavior. The connection between parental monitoring and child aggression is one example. Another is the link between avoidant attachment and later dependency. Parent rejection of an infant's attempts to gain physical closeness has been consistently associated with avoidant attachment. This finding by itself could be explained genetically; perhaps the parent passes on a genetic tendency to dislike physical closeness to the infant. But this would not explain why these children later spend more time on their preschool teachers' laps and in other behaviors that are strongly dependent.

Predicting Peer Relationships
Peers are important in children's development, as documented throughout this textbook. However, experiences with parents routinely predict later peer experiences. Moreover, parenting and peer experiences together predict child outcomes far better than peer experiences alone. Finally, as you will see in Chapter 14, experiences with peers and parents predict different aspects of later development.

children raised in authoritative homes tended to score higher in **agency**—the tendency to take initiative, rise to challenges, and try to influence events. Interestingly, girls who scored high on agency tended to have argumentative interactions with their parents, especially their fathers, but argumentative interactions were not associated with increased agency for boys. Baumrind proposes that argumentative encounters may balance pressures toward conformity and give girls the extra push they need to be self-assertive.

Baumrind's parenting styles are not the only ones that have been identified. Eleanor Maccoby and John Martin (1983) offered a framework emphasizing two factors:

Agency:
The tendency to take initiative, rise to challenges, and try to influence events.

frequency of parent-child conflict over goals, and degree of balance in how parent and child resolve disagreements. According to Maccoby and Martin, the best developmental outcomes occur when conflicts over goals are relatively infrequent and neither the parent nor the child always prevails. Like Baumrind's authoritative parents, these parents are responsive to their children and willing to negotiate with them, but they also require the children to respect their views.

Several factors encourage harmonious parent-child relationships. Cognitive development supports school-age children's ability to comply with parents' wishes in many situations. As children move into middle childhood, they have a greater understanding of the legitimacy of parents' authority. They grasp the fact that parents have more experience than they do and that parents' decisions are usually intended for their own good. But more than cognitive advances must be involved in this developmental process, or else all children of school age would have the kind of relationship with their parents that Maccoby and Martin describe. One additional factor may be the empathy shown by caring, responsive parents. Children who see that their parents understand their feelings learn not only how to show concern for others but also a complementary set of roles characteristic of close relationships (Sroufe and Fleeson, 1988). As a result, these children are more disposed to seek harmony with their parents.

Parent-child relationships in middle childhood draw upon the prior history of interaction. If parents have been responsive earlier, now they can draw on the child's store of confidence in their concern and sensitivity (Maccoby and Martin, 1983). Thus, the quality of a parent-child relationship tends to perpetuate itself, for several reasons. The expectations parents and children form about each other color the meaning attributed to behavior. For instance, children who early in life come to expect parental rejection may interpret even supportive behavior as a sign of rejection. Some research has shown that the frequency of coercive exchanges between parents and children is predicted by both the child's and the parents' negative expectations (MacKinnon-Lewis et al., 1994). In addition, certain kinds of behavior elicit responses that encourage more of the original behavior (Vuchinich, Bank, and Patterson, 1992). For example, if parents treat a child harshly and the child responds by becoming irritable, that irritability is likely to bring on more punitiveness from the parents. Likewise, a child who expects parental support and responds positively to parental encouragement is likely to inspire more supportive behavior from his or her parents.

Family Violence, Conflict, and Divorce A climate of violence, conflict, or disruption in a family affects children's development. Harsh physical abuse has been shown in numerous studies to be related to later negative behavior in children (Cicchetti and Toth, 1998; Shields and Cicchetti, 2001). For example, physically abused children studied at a summer camp were found to have lower self-esteem, to withdraw more from peers, and to engage in less prosocial behavior than other children from comparable socioeconomic backgrounds (Cicchetti and Lynch, 1995). Even if children aren't physically abused themselves, violence in the family, especially physical abuse of the mother, is still associated with a variety of child problems, including aggression and withdrawal (Christopoulos et al., 1987). These apparent consequences of family violence hold true even when socioeconomic status, life stress, and direct maltreatment of the child are statistically controlled (Yates et al., in press).

Child Development CD
Divorce and Child Development

Children are also affected by a climate of nonviolent conflict in the family and by divorce (Hetherington and Kelly, 2002; Parke and Buriel, 1998). Divorce typically is preceded by a history of conflict, and often the conflict continues even after the divorce. The impact of divorce on children is influenced by the level of conflict between parents and especially by how the conflict is managed (Grych and Fincham, 2001; Hetherington and Kelly, 2002). Ending parental conflict tends to moderate negative consequences of divorce, such as troubled peer relationships and school problems (Grych and Fincham, 2001; Hetherington and Clingempeel, 1992). Children who had behavior problems before a divorce are more likely to continue to have them after a divorce, but even after controlling for predivorce behavior problems, consequences of divorce still remain (Hetherington and Kelly, 2002). Much of this effect appears to be due to changes in children's level of security in the conflict-laden divorce context (e.g., Shelton et al., 2001), to changes in parents' controllingness and intrusiveness, or to withdrawal and lax discipline following divorce (e.g., Madden-Derdich and Leonard, 2001).

Divorce is difficult for children of any age; however, some studies show that the impact may be greater for younger children (Parke and Buriel, 1998; Zill, Morrison, and Corio, 1993). One reason may be that older children and adolescents are better able to understand disagreements and conflicts between adults and less likely to blame themselves for them. Also, if divorce occurs when children are older, they may have had a period of conflict-free parenting early in life.

It was once thought that the consequences of divorce were greater for boys than girls, probably because boys exhibit more obvious and immediate reactions, such as increased aggression and problems of impulse control. But girls also exhibit negative reactions, of a different kind (Hetherington and Kelly, 2002; Parke and Buriel, 1998). When their parents divorce, girls are more likely to become anxious, inhibited, and withdrawn. Maggie's reaction to her parents' conflict and divorce illustrates this response. Since such reactions do not disrupt the home or classroom, they are more likely to be ignored or overlooked. This does not mean girls are less troubled by divorce, however. In fact, girls may react more negatively than boys to remarriage by the mother (Hetherington and Kelly, 2002). Also, the negative impact of divorce on girls may be more delayed than for boys, sometimes not becoming apparent until adolescence (see Chapter 14).

The differential socialization of girls and boys seems to result in different reactions to parental conflict and different consequences from it (Davies and Lindsay, 2001; Kerig, 1998). Boys seem to respond more in terms of perceived threat, and such reactions predict their later behavior problems. To reestablish their autonomy and assertiveness in the face of this threat they act out in an aggressive or delinquent manner. Girls, being more oriented toward connection to others, are constrained from such overt expressions. Thus, they strive to repair the disharmony, with the result often being anxiety and depression as their efforts fail. The extent of these problems is related to the degree of self-blame they experience for the conflict of divorce.

There are some ways divorce can have a special impact on boys. Since mothers are more likely than fathers to receive custody of children after a divorce, boys may miss the role modeling, sex-role socialization, and disciplinary functions a father often provides. They may also respond more negatively than girls to living with the opposite-sex parent. Fortunately, negative effects of a father's absence can be reduced if the mother is not overly anxious and restrictive toward her son, and if she approves of the father as a role model for him (Hetherington and Clingempeel, 1992). More important than the specific type of custody arrangement (mother custody, father custody, joint custody) is cooperation and harmony between divorced parents (Parke and Buriel, 1998).

It is important to point out that studies of the long-term effects of divorce on children have found that many children whose parents divorce develop well (Hetherington and Kelly, 2002). In fact, an extensive literature review suggests that children growing up in families with joint physical custody following divorce generally have no more notable problems than children from nondivorced families (Bauserman, 2002). Factors that promote good outcomes include ongoing contact with both parents, an end to parental conflict, cooperation between parents concerning child care, emotional well-being of the custodial parent, and good relationships in any stepfamilies created after a divorce (Hetherington, Bridges, and Insabella, 1998; Hetherington and Kelly, 2002; Parke and Buriel, 1998). A good relationship with the custodial parent seems to be of special importance, no doubt because the child spends so much time with this parent. Thus, the fact that Mikey and Maggie both have good relationships with Christine at the time of their parents' breakup should help them through this developmental crisis.

Dealing with siblings helps children learn that close relationships often involve a mixture of positive and negative feelings and can endure despite conflict.

When divorce puts an end to severe marital conflict and makes parental cooperation possible, children usually fare better than those in conflict-ridden two-parent homes. The best advice to divorcing parents is to reduce their mutual hostility as much and as quickly as they can. If each parent maintains a warm and close relationship with the children, good adjustment is even more likely (Parke and Buriel, 1998). The meaning children attach to divorce is also a critical factor. When a child feels abandoned by one parent and blamed by the other, negative consequences are likely.

Sibling Relationships

Sibling Relationships Sibling relationships have a special place in the network of influences affecting child development (Eisenberg and Fabes, 1998). Because relationships among siblings continue throughout life and are often deeply emotional, they are in some ways similar to parent-child relationships. By the end of middle childhood, youngsters rate alliances with both parents and siblings as more enduring and reliable than those formed with people outside the family (Buhrmester and Furman, 1990). But siblings are far closer to each other in status than parents and children are, making sibling relationships in some ways more similar to those among peers. However, sibling and peer relationships also differ in important ways. First, there is usually a greater age disparity between siblings than between friends, which tends to give one of the siblings more power and privileges than the other. Second, sibling relationships often cross gender boundaries, whereas in middle childhood primary friendships rarely do.

Emotional Qualities of Sibling Relationships. Sibling relationships generally involve a mixture of positive and negative feelings. Competition among siblings for their parents' attention and approval is common, especially when both children are boys, or when at least the older one is male (Dunn, Slomkowski, and Beardsall, 1994; Stoneman and Brody, 1993). Sibling strife based on social comparison intensifies after about age 8, when children develop the cognitive skills needed to compare themselves with others. Elementary-school-aged children do not seem to have a higher *number* of conflicts with siblings than with peers, but that may be only because they spend less time with their siblings. When the amount of time siblings and peers spend socially engaged with each other is considered, the *rate* of conflict is higher for siblings (DeHart et al., 1998; Hartup and Laursen, 1993). In any case, by late middle childhood, children themselves *feel* that they have more conflicts with their siblings (Buhrmester and Furman, 1990). Children also feel that sibling conflict more often results in coercive tactics and intense emotion (Hartup and Laursen, 1993; Vespo, 1997).

Intermixed with this rivalry and conflict between siblings are strong positive feelings. Younger siblings see older ones not only as controllers but also as facilitators. Older siblings often help younger ones solve a problem or perform some task. Older siblings, for their part, may resent their younger siblings, but they also feel nurturant toward them (Dunn et al., 1994). Thus, Maggie resents the attention Mikey receives from Frank, but she also tries to shield him from their parents' fighting; and although Meryl initially feels some jealousy of her baby brother, she cares for him and fusses over him as well.

The overall quality of sibling relationships varies greatly from case to case. Important factors influencing that quality include closeness in age, gender composition, stress experienced by either sibling, the children's personalities, and preferential treatment by parents (Brody, 1998). For example, sibling pairs tend to show greater competition when either parent behaves preferentially or more affectionately toward one sibling (Brody, Stoneman, and McCoy, 1992). The quality of sibling relationships, whether intensely conflictual or relatively harmonious, tends to remain somewhat stable from early through middle childhood (Dunn et al., 1994).

The Importance of Sibling Relations. The emotional ambivalence common in sibling relations offers an important learning opportunity for children. It teaches them how to deal with anger and aggression in an ongoing relationship. When siblings fight and become angry, they cannot simply end their relationship. Siblings who are in conflict must somehow work things out and continue to live with each other. As a result, sibling relationships are an excellent place to learn that expressing anger toward someone you are close to does not necessarily threaten mutual attachment in the long run (DeHart, 1999).

Sibling relationships are also important because of the mutual support they can provide. The close tie between siblings is probably what underlies reports that these relationships often help children weather parental divorce, as it did for Maggie and Mikey (Jenkins, 1992). Similarly, research suggests that sibling relationships may compensate somewhat for poor peer relationships (East and Rook, 1992).

Other benefits of sibling relations depend on the children's relative ages. For instance, in many cultures older siblings, especially sisters, are assigned the role of caring for younger siblings (Zukow-Goldring, 2002). This caregiving role helps prepare the older children for parenting, and it increases the number of people to whom infants become attached. In dominant U.S. culture, with the growing number of families in which both parents work, care of younger siblings sometimes falls to older children by default. And even when parents are home, older children often look after their younger siblings informally and help them learn new things. Such situations provide older siblings with experience in role taking, in nurturance toward others, and in teaching skills (Eisenberg and Fabes, 1998).

Adopting the role of boss may also help older siblings practice leadership skills and enhance their social confidence. One study found that in families in which the typical bickering between siblings occurred in a framework where the older child was definitely in charge, these older children were more competent with peers than were firstborns from families in which this role relationship was blurred (Marvinney, 1988).

Younger siblings, too, can benefit from a relationship in which the older sibling is usually the boss. In dealing with an older sibling who is bossier and more punitive than parents and more inclined to induce dependency, younger siblings learn how to negotiate with and accept help from other people. Younger siblings also appear to look to older siblings as models. For example, gender role qualities of firstborns, as reflected in their attitudes and activities, predict these qualities in secondborns three years later, even after accounting for the secondborns' initial qualities and for parental effects (McHale et al., 2001).

Conflictual sibling relationships have been shown to contribute to children's maladjustment (Stocker et al., 2002)—even more so in combination with rejecting parenting (e.g., Garcia et al., 2000). Gerald Patterson and his colleagues (Bank, Patterson, and

Reid, 1996) have proposed a *sibling amplifier model* for child aggressiveness. In this model, the consequences of harsh discipline and poor monitoring from parents are amplified when sibling relationships are conflictual. This outcome may occur because aggressive patterns are further developed between siblings and carried outward to peer relationships, or because children in these relationships lack the social support found in positive sibling relationships.

The School

Child Development CD
First Grade Around the World

The period from age 5 to age 7 is a momentous time for children in many parts of the world because this is when they start formal schooling. With the initial step inside a school classroom, children's lives change dramatically. No longer are play and good behavior all that is expected of them. Now they must formally begin to learn the body of knowledge that adults deem important to master. For at least the next twelve years, many children will be at school six hours a day, five days a week, nine months a year (more in many Asian and European countries). If influence is related to sheer length of exposure, school is certainly a major factor in many children's lives.

Socialization in the Classroom   Children learn many things in the classroom beyond the subjects specifically taught. North American schools often promote competitiveness and individualism, but curricula have also been designed to encourage cooperation and prosocial behavior (Eisenberg and Fabes, 1998). Schools sometimes provide opportunities for cross-ethnic contact and friendships unavailable in a child's own neighborhood. For example, research has shown that, in ethnically diverse schools, interracial friendships increase between kindergarten and third grade (Howes and Wu, 1990).

Mainstream cultural norms and values are repeatedly reinforced by the way schools organize activities and distribute rewards (Ruble and Martin, 1998). When children are required to line up on hearing a bell ring; when they must refrain from running in the hallways, walking through the bushes in the schoolyard, or making too much noise at lunch; when they must do their assignments neatly, on time, and as the teacher instructs, they are being taught such cultural values as hard work, achievement motivation, respect for private property, obedience to authority, punctuality, neatness, and compliance with rules. Teachers also encourage competition and social comparison in children by stressing each student's academic progress relative to that of classmates. The school, in short, is a very powerful agent of socialization. At school, children are drilled in many of the values and behaviors that the dominant culture expects them to adopt.

The arrangement of a classroom and the structure of its activities can communicate powerful messages about the values children are expected to adopt.

Boys and girls may have very different experiences at school, which may support cultural stereotypes. Girls are more likely than boys to fit the stereotype of the model pupil (well-behaved, compliant, nondisruptive), but teachers tend to interact more with boys, to give boys more positive and useful feedback on their performance, and to give girls more criticism (Beal, 1994; Sadker, 1999). At the same time, boys speak up more in class than girls do. Ironically, high-achieving girls may be the most criticized of all. In one study of fifth graders, the teacher gave girls who were high achievers the least praise and positive feedback and the most disparaging remarks of any group of students. When boys are criticized, it is usually for misbehavior or lack of neatness rather than for lack of scholastic ability. Moreover, teachers tend to attribute boys' poor performance to insufficient effort and girls' poor performance to low aptitude (Dweck et al., 1978). Thus, there is reason to believe that many North American schools subtly discourage intellectual achievement in girls.

Gender Bias in Schools

The main areas in which gender differences in intellectual achievement are regularly found in our society are math and science. In a comprehensive study of gender differences, Maccoby and Jacklin (1974) found that around age 12 or 13 boys begin to do better in math than girls, even though in elementary school boys and girls show similar levels of mathematical ability. However, even in elementary school, girls think they are worse in math than in reading (Freedman-Doan et al., 2000).

Child Development CD
Gender Differences in Math and Science

These gender differences diminish when the classroom teaching style is made more "female-friendly"—that is, when the atmosphere is warm and nurturing, with less emphasis on social comparison and competition (American Association of University Women, 1998). Some classroom practices have been found to be especially important for promoting achievement in girls (Eccles, Wigfield, and Schiefele, 1998). If math and science are taught with an emphasis on cooperation and an applied or person-centered perspective, girls generally fare better than if the emphasis is on competition and a theoretical/abstract perspective.

Influences on School Achievement and Adjustment   An elementary school child's classroom adjustment and academic success are not just important in their own right but are actually predictive of good mental health (Roeser and Eccles, 2001). Because of its overall importance in children's development, researchers have wondered what factors influence school success.

Many studies have shown that the quality of schools, including classroom climate, influences students' school success and motivation (Roeser and Eccles, 2001). Warmth and supportiveness of staff, stress on academic, goal-oriented lessons, and efficient organization seem to be critical factors. In one study, Michael Rutter (1981) showed that certain school factors accounted for ongoing achievement of London schoolchildren, after personal aptitude was accounted for. In particular, schools that emphasized academic achievement, provided incentives for good performance, and had skilled teachers who allowed students to assume responsibilities tended to turn out pupils with above average records and few behavior problems. In contrast, children assigned to lower quality schools faced an increased risk of performing poorly both scholastically and socially. Other research shows that noninteractive teaching strategies and required public self-evaluation of performance are related to lower performance expectations in children (Oettingen et al., 1994).

Other factors are also involved in school adjustment and achievement (Jimerson, Egeland, and Teo, 1999; Pianta and Steinberg, 1992; Teo et al., 1996). Association with well-adjusted, academically motivated peers has a positive impact. A history of nurturant support from parents and a well-organized home environment also seem to be important. These family factors strongly predict both achievement and school adjustment, and such effects hold even after IQ and earlier achievement are statistically controlled (Teo et al., 1996). Research also shows that when teachers praise children for their effort, as opposed to telling them how smart they are, motivation to learn is enhanced (Mueller and Dweck, 1998).

Parents and school staff often wonder whether starting a child in school a year late or repeating a grade will benefit that child's academic performance and school adjustment. Contrary to what many people believe, neither practice is supported by research. By late elementary school, children who have been held back a year are no better off academically than similarly low-performing children who were not held back, even though they've had an extra year of schooling. In addition, they tend to be less well adjusted (Jimerson et al., 1997).

After-School Care

After-School Care

Because of the prevalence of single-parent and two-career families, researchers have become interested in the after-school care of children (e.g., Posner and Vandell, 1994; Vandell and Ramanan, 1991). They are especially concerned about latchkey children, those who let themselves into the house after school and care for themselves until their parents get home. How well these children fare depends in part on their socioeconomic status. Few drawbacks of self-care have been found for middle- and upper-middle-class children, perhaps because any negative impact is offset by economic advantages or indirect parental supervision (Vandell and Ramanan, 1991). For children of poverty, however, significant time in after-school self-care is associated with academic and behavioral problems (Galambos and Maggs, 1991; Posner and Vandell, 1994).

THE COHERENCE OF DEVELOPMENT IN MIDDLE CHILDHOOD

Development in middle childhood is coherent in the same three ways as in early childhood:

- *Coherent sets of influences*—Various influences tend to channel development in a broadly similar direction and to be mutually reinforcing. For example, parents, peers, and teachers all tend to promote differences in boys' and girls' experiences.

- *Coherence of individual adaptations*—The various characteristics of an individual child are not randomly assembled, but fit together in a way that makes sense.

- *Coherence of development over time*—Development in middle childhood has continuity with the past. Although children's individual differences reflect current influences, they tend to be predictable from preceding periods of development.

Coherent Sets of Influences

Family, peers, and school, the major agents of socialization in middle childhood, are not independent of each other. They are an interacting set of forces, and because they affect one another, the influences they exert on the child tend to be similar in certain ways.

Competence with peers, for example, is a major issue in middle childhood and a barometer of the child's overall functioning. As such, it predicts other aspects of functioning, such as later achievement and adjustment at school (Brendgen et al., 2001; Teo et al., 1996). Peer competence may influence sibling and parent-child relationships (Kramer and Gottman, 1992; Vuchinich, Bank, and Patterson, 1992), and it is strongly related to the child's sense of well-being (Rudolph and Asher, 2001). However, peer competence itself is influenced by other contexts of development. Peer problems have been linked to a history of low school achievement (Teo et al., 1996), and competence with peers is predicted by the quality of sibling relationships (Marvinney, 1988). Parents, too, influence peer relationships. They do so directly through encouragement, support, training, advice, and the general quality of the parent-child relationship (Lollis and Ross, 1992; MacKinnon-Lewis et al., 1994; Vuchinich, Bank, and Patterson, 1992). Parents also influence peer relationships indirectly (Parke and Ladd, 1992). For instance, when parents are depressed, under a great deal of stress, or having marital problems, those factors can indirectly take a toll on how well their children interact with peers, as seen in Mikey's, Maggie's, and Meryl's reactions to conflict between their parents.

Likewise, a child's adjustment at school affects adjustment in other contexts. Poor school adjustment can be a source of family conflict and problems with peers, just as good school adjustment can have the opposite impact. At the same time, school adjustment is influenced by a host of factors outside the classroom. Children like school better if they are getting along with teachers and peers, but

Peer competence is a good indicator of a child's overall functioning in middle childhood.

the attitudes and problems they bring with them to school influence others' reactions to them and are strongly related to achievement (Ladd and Burgess, 2001; Oettingen et al., 1994). Teachers (and frequently peers as well) like children less if they have behavior problems, are very dependent, or have poor school attitudes (Nelson-LeGall and Jones, 1990). These characteristics, in turn, are influenced by family stress and social support, as well as by parental involvement with the school (Garcia et al., 2000; Grolnick and Slowiaczek, 1994; Teo et al., 1996). Thus, school adjustment influences each of the other major contexts of child development as well as being influenced by them. As a result, children tend to be exposed to a set of interrelated influences that are similar in quality and tone.

The Coherence of Individual Adaptations

The distinctive characteristics of children—their individual patterns of adaptation—also are coherent. Children who are effective in the peer group tend to be popular with peers; to form close, loyal friendships; to coordinate friendship and group demands; and to maintain gender boundaries (Sroufe, Bennett, et al., 1993). Likewise, individual differences in peer functioning, harmony of parent-child relationships, and adjustment to school are often closely related (Teo et al., 1996). In Chapter 10 we described how behavior in the preschool years was coherent enough that we can speak of the emergence of personality. Such coherence is increased in middle childhood. Both observers and children themselves see characteristics as more enduring and integrated at this age than was previously true (Harter, 1998; Shiner, 1998). Now it makes sense to speak not just of a child who shows certain behaviors in a particular context, but of a more generally kind child or a socially competent child—broader characteristics that transcend isolated circumstances.

The Coherence of Development Over Time

There is also coherence in how individual patterns of adaptation develop over time. Socially competent toddlers who are securely attached to their caregivers tend to become preschoolers who are competent with peers. In turn, these preschoolers usually go on to be popular and well adjusted in elementary school. In fact, with age, children's current characteristics become increasingly predictable from their past characteristics (Sroufe et al., 1993).

The coherence of individual development over time was shown in the Minnesota day camp study. Counselors unfamiliar with campers' attachment histories judged those who had been securely attached to be more socially skilled, more inclined to form friendships, more self-confident, and less dependent. Other observers confirmed the counselors' judgments. They also found that children with secure attachment histories spent less time alone, less time with counselors, and more time with other children than did youngsters who had been anxiously attached as infants and toddlers (Elicker et al., 1992; Sroufe et al., 1999). Moreover, those with secure attachment histories spent more time in groups of same-gender peers and were more effective in these peer groups. Other researchers report that children who have been securely attached are less often ridiculed or excluded from group activities in middle childhood (Grossmann and Grossmann, 1991).

In the Minnesota study, there were also differences in the nature of friendships among children with histories of secure and anxious attachments (Shulman et al., 1994). Children with secure attachment histories tended to choose each other as friends, and their friendships were likely to be reciprocal rather than one-sided. Moreover, a close friendship among secure children did not prevent them from functioning in the larger peer group. These friends often spent time together in groups, and their play together also included other children.

Developmentalists seek to explain why such continuity exists in patterns of adaptation over time. The quality of early attachment does not inevitably cause certain kinds of peer relations in middle childhood; some anxiously attached infants later become competent with peers. In part, it may be a matter of the stability of parental influence over time. If parents who promote secure attachment in infants and toddlers go on to support peer relationships when their children are in school, secure attachment becomes correlated with peer effectiveness in middle childhood.

However, continuity in parents' influence is probably not the whole story. Attachment assessments predict middle-childhood behavior even after current family support is accounted for (Sroufe, Egeland, and Kreutzer, 1990). Factors within the child—skills, experiences, personal beliefs, and social expectations formed early in life and carried forward into middle childhood—also enter the picture. From their relationships with caregivers, securely attached toddlers acquire positive beliefs and expectations about the self and others that help them master the challenge of social give-and-take as preschoolers and form a basis for tackling the tasks of friendship and peer group functioning in middle childhood. Feelings of self-worth, a sense of social effectiveness, and positive expectations regarding others all move the child toward closer and more complex relationships. These feelings and expectations about the self and others that originate in early attachment experiences are what Bowlby (1973) referred to as *internal working models* (discussed in Chapter 6).

These drawings were made by 8-year-olds with varying attachment histories. The drawing at top left was made by a child who was securely attached as an infant. It is colorful and full of life, and the figures are grounded, complete, well proportioned, rich in detail, and individuated. The drawing at top right was made by a child with a history of avoidant attachment. This picture includes an incomplete self-portrait (far right); the rest of the figures are not grounded and have an aggressive aspect. The drawing at right, made by a child with a mixed anxious attachment history, is skillfully drawn yet has an ominous quality. The child and his brother are shut up in the black tower, and the mother (lower right) is placed under the ground though in reality she is not dead.

Internal working models of the self and others are reflected in school-age children's stories and drawings (Bretherton and Munholland, 1999; Fury, Carlson, and Sroufe, 1997; McCrone et al., 1994). When asked to tell stories about pictures of peer interaction, children with secure attachment histories talk about cooperation and successful negotiation of conflict. On sentence-completion tests, these children project positive attitudes ("Other kids . . . are fun to be with"). When asked to draw a picture of their family, secure children show connections among family members, appropriate sizing of the figures, and expression of positive emotions (Fury et al., 1997). As the examples above show, such drawings are often quite different from those of children with anxious attachment histories.

Connections between internal working models and behavior are illustrated in the behavior of aggressive children. Such children frequently interpret others' actions as hostile, especially when cues are ambiguous and they feel threatened. These misinterpretations are not produced by cognitive deficits. Instead, they fit the children's histories of anxious-avoidant attachment and harsh treatment (Suess, Grossmann, and Sroufe, 1992; Weiss et al., 1992). In other words, these children apparently perceive hostility in others because they have previously experienced hostility and rejection. Moreover, their aggressiveness tends to elicit angry responses from others, making their experiences self-perpetuating. Nonaggressive peers, in fact, expect that others will be more angry at aggressive children in ambiguous situations (Trachtenberg and Viken, 1994). Thus, children's thinking and behavior derive from their experiences and are tied together in middle childhood.

Children certainly can change during middle childhood. A bright child who does well academically may get a boost in self-esteem by receiving positive feedback from teachers. Sometimes a gifted and caring teacher is responsive to children despite their behavior problems and poor attitudes, and this has been shown to make a difference in the child's level of problems (Ladd and Burgess, 2001). Peers may also respond favorably to some special skill or talent a child has. Family circumstances may change, leading to changes in children (Egeland et al., 1990). Once a child's self-esteem is raised and behavior changes, feedback from others may become more positive, and the child's attitude toward school may improve.

Chapter Summary

Introduction

Middle childhood was once considered an uneventful time, labeled a **latency period** by Freud. But critical social and emotional development occurs during these years. Erikson saw developing a **sense of industry** as the central task of middle childhood. Other important developments include:

- forming a coherent self-concept;
- major developments in peer relations; and
- growing understanding of emotions.

The Inner World of the Self

During middle childhood, major developments in children's concept of the self occur:

- The **psychological self** emerges, along with a growing awareness of others' internal thoughts and feelings.
- The **social self** develops, as children begin to define themselves in terms of social tendencies and groups they belong to, and their use of **social comparison** increases.

- Children's sense of their own gender and knowledge of gender stereotypes increase.
- Children's sense of personal effectiveness and ability to manage their own feelings and behavior increase.

Peer Relationships in Middle Childhood

Peer groups become an important developmental setting during middle childhood because:

- children this age spend increasing time with peers;
- peers provide unique learning experiences; and
- peers challenge children to develop interaction skills.

Advances that enable increasingly complex peer relationships in middle childhood include:

- the tendency to think of others in terms of their psychological traits;
- a greater ability to understand the perspective, needs, and feelings of others;
- the ability to grasp more complex rules regarding interpersonal behavior; and

- a growing ability to communicate feelings and wishes with words rather than with actions.

Five major developments in peer relations during middle childhood are:

- formation of loyal friendships;
- formation of networks of friends, or peer groups;
- coordination of allegiance to individual friends with functioning in a group;
- increased importance of adhering to peer group norms; and
- development of clear boundaries for interaction with members of the opposite sex.

Children's level of peer acceptance becomes relatively stable during the elementary school years, and it has implications for their current and future mental health.

Emotional Development in Middle Childhood

During middle childhood, children go beyond *experiencing* emotions to *understanding* emotions and their causes. They become increasingly able to:

- understand complexity of emotion-arousing situations;
- take particular situations into account when determining appropriate emotional responses;
- understand and apply display rules for emotions; and
- feel true empathy for others.

Emotional development, combined with cognitive advances and experience in social relationships, fosters moral development in middle childhood.

Contexts of Development in Middle Childhood

The family remains an important developmental context in middle childhood.

- Relationships with parents change markedly.
- Parenting style has considerable impact on children's behavior and development.
- Family violence, conflict, and divorce all have impacts on children's development. The effects of divorce vary somewhat depending on the age and sex of the child.
- Sibling relationships continue to be an important context for development, especially for learning how to deal with conflict in an ongoing relationship.

School becomes an important developmental context during middle childhood.

- School provides an important context for socialization in cultural values, especially gender-role learning.
- School achievement and adjustment are influenced by both family and school factors and predict later mental health.
- After-school care arrangements are also important, with their impact depending to some extent on children's socioeconomic status.

The Coherence of Development in Middle Childhood

Development in middle childhood is coherent for three reasons:

- coherent sets of influences,
- coherence of individual adaptations, and
- coherence of development over time.

Review Questions

Introduction

1. What are some major social and emotional developments in middle childhood?

The Inner World of the Self

2. How does a child's concept of the self change from early to middle childhood?

Peer Relationships in Middle Childhood

3. Summarize the developmental advances that allow increasingly complex peer relations in middle childhood.
4. What major developments occur in peer relations during middle childhood?
5. What is known about peer status and acceptance in middle childhood?

Emotional Development in Middle Childhood

6. How does children's understanding of emotions change during middle childhood?

Contexts of Development in Middle Childhood

7. How do parent-child relationships change during middle childhood?
8. How does parenting style affect children's behavior and development?
9. How do family violence, conflict, and divorce affect children's development?
10. What roles do sibling relationships play in development in middle childhood?
11. How do schools affect children's development?

The Coherence of Development in Middle Childhood

12. Explain how coherence of development is demonstrated in middle childhood.

Application and Observation

1. Interview children of various ages from preschool to middle school about their ideas on the subjects of friendships and peer status. Spend a few minutes getting acquainted with each child, so that s/he is comfortable talking with you. Then tell the child that you'd like him/her to tell you a little bit about his/her friends, and ask the child questions such as the following: (*a*) How many friends do you have? What are their names? (*b*) How do you know when someone is your friend? What makes a friend different from someone you just know? (*c*) What do you and your friends do together? (*d*) Do you have a best friend? What is her/his name? (*e*) What makes a best friend different from your other friends? (*f*) Do you ever argue with your friends? What do you argue about? (*g*) What do you do to settle an argument with a friend? When you have an argument with a friend, is that person still your friend later? (*h*) Who is the most popular person in your class at school? What is that person like? Why do you think that person is popular? *Things to look for:* How do the children's age and gender seem to affect their answers? What about individual differences (personality, interests, etc.)? How typical are each child's responses for his/her age and gender?

2. Observe elementary-school-aged children in an unstructured situation such as the school playground

and compare the behavior you observe to the information in this chapter. What gender differences do you see in activities or group size? Do you see evidence of gender boundaries? Can you pick out children who seem to be popular, neglected, or rejected?

3. Observe elementary-school-aged children playing an adult-organized team sport. How do the children interact with each other and with the adults who are present? How does the presence of adults (coaches, parents, other spectators) seem to affect the children's behavior? How do social, emotional, and cognitive development during middle childhood contribute to children's ability to participate in team sports? What would children be most likely to learn from experiences in this setting (positive or negative)?

4. Observe an elementary school classroom for part of a school day. What might children be learning in the classroom beyond the formal educational curriculum? What kinds of adult–child and child–child interactions do you see? What values and norms are being reinforced? Do you see evidence of the gender differences in school experience described in this chapter?

Part 5   Epilogue: Middle Childhood

Significant development continues during middle childhood, roughly ages 6 through 12, although the changes taking place are not always as obvious as in earlier periods. Physical growth has slowed to a few inches yearly and is no longer as dramatic as in infancy and toddlerhood. Now the major developmental changes are largely internal, having to do with the child's ways of thinking and feeling. These internal changes may not be apparent to casual observers, but they are nevertheless of great importance, both in their own right and because they pave the way for the far-reaching changes of adolescence.

Like all developmental periods, middle childhood involves qualitative change—major developmental reorganizations that boost children to higher levels of social and cognitive functioning. One such major reorganization occurs between the ages of 5 and 7, as children become able to reason systematically, using more than one piece of information. These changes are supported by continued development of the brain, especially maturation of the frontal lobes of the cortex. By age 8 or 9, children have acquired most of the basic tools of thinking and reasoning. They come to grasp the logic of concrete operations carried out on objects. They understand most conservation rules with enough flexibility to effectively use measuring devices, such as rulers and measuring cups. Children age 8 and older also understand hierarchical classifications. If they are shown a group of objects that consists of toy dogs and toy cats, they know that there are fewer dogs than animals present, because they grasp that *dog* is a subclass of *animal*. Similar advances occur in the area of social cognition, or understanding of people. Youngsters are now much better at taking the perspective of others. They can also coordinate their knowledge of the various social categories that apply to people. For instance, a girl whose father is a doctor would now understand that she can be both a patient and a daughter to him at the same time.

The age of 8 is also a milestone in self-understanding. By this age children are beginning to view the self in psychological terms. They realize that who they are is based partly on what they think and feel, not just on their physical traits. At the same time, they begin to compare themselves with others in order to appraise their own abilities, and they realize that how other people respond to them can depend on their own actions.

Advances in peer relations accompany this new view of the self. By age 8 children have a more mature view of friendship than preschoolers do. They begin to recognize that the basis of friendship lies in loyalty and mutual support, not just in the sharing of toys. With this advancement, relationships with peers take on much deeper meaning. In fact, the formation of close chumships is one of the hallmarks of this age. In their interactions with friends, school-age children adhere very closely to peer group norms. Equity, fairness, and reciprocity are cardinal principles of their relationships. Because of this, peer relationships in middle childhood play an important role in moral development (Damon, 1988). In addition, school-age children have a new understanding of the legitimacy of authority, including parental authority. This understanding, coupled with their greater desire to conform to norms and values, helps make the job of parenting easier than it was before. Markus and Nurius (1984) have summed up these many social advances this way: (1) school-age children acquire a relatively stable and comprehensive understanding of the self, (2) they acquire a refined understanding of how the social world works; and (3) they acquire a set of standards and expectations regarding their dealings with others.

As in other developmental periods, all these changes are intimately interconnected. For example, school-age children can solve classification problems and understand conservation in large part because they can now consider two aspects of a problem simultaneously (the height *and* the width of a glass, for instance). This same capacity underlies their ability to unify different aspects of the self and to make social comparisons—that is, to understand their own behavior and that of others at the same time. Advances in different areas of development are also mutually influencing and supportive. For example, the cognitive ability to understand different perspectives and to take on different roles helps school-age children interact more maturely with peers. At the same time, interactions with peers provide experiences that foster these cognitive skills. Social and cognitive development, in other words, always proceed together, with each helping to make possible advances in the other.

Our discussions of cognitive and social development may have implied that cognitive advances occasionally occur a little earlier than social ones. This unintended implication is partly the product of researchers' goals. Cognitive researchers often look for the first appearance of a particular skill, whereas social researchers often search for the age at which a certain ability is regularly used. Time and experience are typically needed before a new capacity is used often. Thus, in their everyday behaviors children may not always show their highest potential levels of functioning.

Unevenness in Development

Repeatedly we have stressed the orderliness and coherence of human development, whether we are talking about general developmental changes or the life of an individual child. But this doesn't mean that development proceeds in a lockstep fashion, with related changes always occurring together. Sometimes there seems to be an unevenness in development, as when a change that we would expect to occur at a certain age is delayed. You saw, for instance, that children in nonindustrialized cultures generally pass tests of conservation concepts later than children in industrialized cultures do. For them there is a lag in achieving this developmental milestone, in part because their lack of formal schooling sharply reduces opportunities to learn about and practice these skills. Such unevenness in development can also occur for reasons that have nothing to do with a child's culture. When Meryl was a preschooler, for example, her social development lagged somewhat behind her cognitive progress. This is not unusual. In fact, even within the same domain—cognitive *or* social—closely related developmental milestones may not be reached simultaneously. Thus, a 6-year-old who grasps the concept of conservation of number may not necessarily also grasp conservation of liquid volume. As we mentioned in Chapter 5, Piaget called this phenomenon *décalage*.

In addition to the unevenness in general developmental changes, unevenness occurs in the progress of individual lives. Individual children experience ups and downs. Life goes well for a time, but then a child appears to be struggling. You saw this pattern especially in the development of Meryl, Maggie, and Mikey during their school-age years. It occurs in the lives of all children and in adults as well. These ups and downs in the quality of individual adaptations are *not* incoherent and illogical. They make sense in terms of what is happening to the child at a particular time. The child may be responding to external circumstances, such as conflict in the family or a poor environment at school, or to internal changes, such as illness. Pulling back and retrenching before moving forward again may even be the typical way in which children make developmental progress. Parents often notice that their children consolidate already acquired skills before tackling new ones. In fact, much of middle childhood can be

viewed as a period of consolidation, a gathering of potentials to be used during adolescence. Such a view of middle childhood gives new meaning to the concept of latency that Freud attached to this period.

Four Children in Middle Childhood

Our four children have continued to develop during middle childhood, often predictably, but sometimes taking unexpected turns. Although all have developed normally, each has encountered problems at times. These problems illustrate the continuing need of school-age children for care, understanding, and guidance from adults.

For Maggie and Mikey Gordon, the elementary school years are a very stressful time because of their parents' escalating conflict leading to divorce. It is complicated to assess the impact of the divorce on Maggie and Mikey—even to say whether it has been good or bad for them. On the one hand, things were going poorly before the separation. The conflict between Christine and Frank had become intense, and Maggie and Mikey were both suffering ill effects at home and at school. Despite their best intentions, Christine and Frank could not shelter their children from such a troubled marriage. On the other hand, the divorce was very hard on Mikey because he loved both his parents and desperately wanted them to stay together. Even more than most children, a child like Mikey feels responsible for the breakup. Isn't he supposed to be the peacemaker, the one who keeps conflicts from getting out of control? His parents' divorce means he has failed in this role. Fortunately, Mikey is old enough to begin to understand the divorce is not his fault, but he will need help to come to this realization. Since both parents care deeply for Mikey, and Christine is the kind of parent who talks to him about his feelings, we can be optimistic that Mikey will ultimately pull through this developmental crisis.

In the long run, in fact, the divorce may in some ways be harder on Maggie because it has shown so clearly the extent to which her father favors Mikey. She would probably feel more resentment toward Mikey if she did not have a close sibling relationship with him and if Christine had not worked so hard to reassure her that she was loved despite her father's indifference. She copes largely by denying any interest in activities with her father and by becoming very involved with friends and schoolwork. The effects on her are different from those on Mikey, but they are no easier to deal with.

It is tempting to see Frank's behavior as the cause of the Gordons' troubles. He is the one with the drinking problem, and he is also totally unsupportive of his wife's desire for a career outside the home. Ultimately, he is responsible for his violent behavior against Christine. From a systems perspective, however, causes cannot be attributed solely to one person. Any relationship is the product of two individual histories (Sroufe and Fleeson, 1986). Christine's contribution partly stems from the fact that she was raised to take care of men. Her mother's only advice when the marriage became rocky was to work harder at being a good wife. It is also difficult for Christine to ask that her own needs be met; she has been taught to be self-sacrificing. To cope with the mounting resentment Frank feels about her job, she strives to keep her working life separate from her home life. As Frank's self-esteem is increasingly damaged by Christine's business success and his own reduced income, Frank criticizes Christine ever more sharply. She responds by trying to mollify him. This reaction feeds the system as much as Frank's tendency to blame her does. And both of them, in their own ways, put Mikey and Maggie in the middle.

Malcolm's development during this period is nowhere near as conflict-ridden as Mikey's and Maggie's. Middle childhood for Malcolm seems to be a busy, productive, generally fun-filled time. But the incident in which Malcolm finds the gun illustrates how normal, healthy children can sometimes get in trouble and cause their parents concern. The lovable exuberance Malcolm exhibits when bounding up the stairs and his unthinking impulsiveness in taking the gun both stem from the same high-spirited energy. Malcolm hits upon the idea of keeping the gun in a naive effort to defend himself against a gang of older boys. We see him becoming very upset about Eric's telling on him. But this is Malcolm's nature. He will not be upset for long. The incident will pass, and Malcolm will be fine again. In fact, he has probably learned some important lessons from it.

In Malcolm's life we also see the special challenges that urban children face: gangs to be dealt with going to and from school, incidents that foster interracial mistrust. Malcolm is fortunate that he does not have to deal with the additional challenge of a poor-quality school. His teacher and principal recognize his talents despite his occasional impulsive behavior and difficulty concentrating. At the same time, we once again see the benefits of Malcolm's large and constantly supportive family. Many ears listen to his reports of school achievements; many voices guide him when he gets into trouble. All this serves to encourage positive development in Malcolm.

Meryl also seems to be getting some good support at home. She has become a much more competent and self-confident child than we would have predicted from her infant and toddler periods. She takes the arrival of her baby brother in stride and even seems to blossom in the role of big sister. She is generally doing well at school and has formed the normal close friendships characteristic of middle childhood. The only times we see vestiges of the old, hesitant Meryl are under conditions of stress. Amy befriends Rita, and Meryl loses her confidence; Karen and Joe have a period of tension, and Meryl becomes withdrawn. But even during the time of family problems, Meryl works in her own way toward bolstering herself psychologically. We find her in her room drawing pictures of mother dogs caring for their puppies. As Karen and Joe resolve their difficulties, Meryl brightens once again and regains her confidence. With each developmental period she seems to be getting stronger.

Adolescence

Part 6 Four Children in Adolescence

Malcolm Williams

Malcolm could barely contain his excitement. He'd just been offered an after-school job at Kroger's. Now he'd have money to hang out with his friends, buy cool clothes, and—most important—take Felicia out. But Malcolm knew he'd have to convince his parents. He'd start by pointing out he was almost 16, certainly no longer a kid. By the time his daddy was 16, he'd already had several jobs. Besides, jobs were good for keeping guys off the street. Not that Malcolm wanted to join a gang, but it was a good point to bring up anyway. And he'd have to promise to keep his grades up.

Malcolm took the steps two at a time and pushed open the door. All right! His parents weren't home yet. That meant he could win over Momma Jo first, and have her behind him when he talked to them. In his eagerness to convince Momma Jo, Malcolm's words spilled out rapidly, and Momma Jo had trouble following what he was saying. By the time she was putting it all together, DeeDee and John walked in. Oh no, thought Malcolm. Now I have to work on all three at once.

When Malcolm had presented his case, his father still looked doubtful. He felt Malcolm had been a little less serious about his schoolwork lately. Momma Jo saw John's expression. "I remember you nearly burstin' with pride when you showed me your first pay slip," she said.

"Momma, I'm not saying a job wouldn't be good for Malcolm," John answered. "I'm just concerned about him handling all the responsibilities that go with it."

"Oh, I'll be responsible, Daddy," Malcolm assured him. "I won't ever be late for work cause they dock your pay and . . ."

"Listen to me, man," John cut in sharply. "I'm not talking about being late for work. I'm talking about your responsibilities right here at home. You're got to keep your grades up and do your chores around the house."

"Oh, I know that," said Malcolm quickly. "Sure, I'll do all those things. I'm not gonna goof off and mess up goin' to college. But I can do those things and have a job."

"What do you say we let him take the job on a trial basis?" DeeDee suggested. "If his grades slip or his chores don't get done, the job goes—no second chances."

"That sounds OK to me," John said, "as long as he holds the hours to fifteen a week, no more. And remember what your momma said—no second chances."

"All riiiight!" crowed Malcolm. "Y'all are cool!" He hugged his mother and Momma Jo and knocked fists with his father. Then he charged out of the kitchen to call the manager at Kroger's. Hallelujah, he thought, I got me a job!

The next morning Malcolm jumped out of bed, surging with energy. Looking in the mirror, he noticed with satisfaction his developing muscles and the facial fuzz marking the beginnings of a small mustache. I'm a man with style, he thought. Felicia, you one lucky lady!

When Malcolm came down to breakfast, he was ready for the affectionate teasing his family usually gave him about his clothes. This time it was his mother. "My, my! I'd think you were entering a fashion show!"

"You like my outfit?" Malcolm grinned. "I kind of appreciate it myself." And with that he slid into his chair and began to wolf down his breakfast.

"Well, since you're so handsome," DeeDee continued, "maybe you'd like to come along this weekend to show yourself off at the church retreat."

Malcolm's spoonful of cereal froze midway to his mouth. "I told you I didn't want to go to that thing! Why would I want to spend a whole weekend hanging out with old folks? Anyway, I'll probably be working Saturday morning. Mr. Lacey and I are gonna figure out my hours today."

DeeDee shook her head in resignation. "Well, I'm not leaving you here entirely on your own," she said. "I guess I'll see if JJ can stay over Saturday night."

"That's cool with me," Malcolm answered, digging into his cereal again. He knew his 27-year-old brother was not about to give him any trouble over his plans with Felicia.

Saturday Malcolm was relieved when his brother showed up dressed to go out. "Hey, man," JJ said, "I ain't gonna daddy you or nothin' cause I know this is a chance that don't come along too often. But whatever you do, don't have the neighbors callin' over here and don't let me know what you're plannin'. That way, when I tell Momma everything was cool, I won't have to lie. You got that?"

"Got it," agreed Malcolm. "No problem."

"And another thing, Motor Man," JJ added, as he headed for the door, "Daddy asked me how much I thought you knew about not pickin' up any nasty germs when you're out prowlin' with the ladies. I told him you was a man with brains who knew just what to do. Am I right?"

"Hey, I ain't *dumb*," Malcolm answered. "They been talkin' about that in school since seventh grade! I'm not gonna get no AIDS. Besides we ain't gonna do nothin'."

"Yeah, well, whatever," said JJ, reaching for the doorknob. "Just remember, it's latex or later, my man. Those are your only options." And with that he left for his own date. As soon as JJ was gone, Malcolm ran to the phone and nervously dialed Felicia's number.

True to his word, Malcolm kept up his grades and did his chores despite his job. In fact, he seemed to thrive on the workload. It forced him to think more about how he used his time. If he found himself with a few spare hours now, he would get a head start on some upcoming project instead of watching television. DeeDee was impressed with this new maturity, and with Malcolm's growing interest in the world beyond girls, sports, and clothes. Especially when family conversation turned to racial prejudice or unfair treatment of the poor, Malcolm joined in eagerly, expressing passionate views.

One evening in March of Malcolm's junior year, his father brought up a redevelopment plan the mayor's office was proposing. Many area residents feared low-income families would be forced out of the neighborhood as property values and rents rose. Malcolm was indignant at the thought. How could they let people be pushed out of their homes just because a bunch of yuppies wanted to move in? "We have to *fight* this," he nearly shouted at his father.

"That's why the Community Action Committee is holding an open meeting Tuesday night," John answered. "If you feel so strongly about it, why don't you come with me and let the mayor's staff know your views?"

"You *bet* I will," said Malcolm. "I'm not gonna let 'em get away with this!"

"But first you better read up on the subject," John advised, passing Malcolm all the clippings and information about the project he had accumulated.

"Right!" said Malcolm. "By Tuesday night I'll know this plan inside and out."

On Tuesday Malcolm and his father had front-row seats at the meeting. Malcolm was fascinated by the discussion. He leaned forward, soaking up every word. Finally, he bravely raised his hand. The committee chair nodded, and Malcolm rose to his feet. "I've lived in this neighborhood all my life," he began in a clear, strong voice, "and I think that some change would be a good thing, but it's got to be *fair*. That low-income project you're talking about building over on Melrose would be pushing poor people out of the center of the neighborhood. My grandma's 82, and if she had to get to the stores and back from Melrose, I don't think she could make it. And another thing, my father always says diversity is what made this country great. Well, doesn't that apply to communities too? All kinds of people living together is what'll make this neighborhood a good place to live."

As Malcolm sat down, he was surprised to hear a murmur in the audience and then loud applause. John placed his hand on Malcolm's shoulder and smiled proudly. "Good for you, son," he said softly. "You're gonna make your mark." Yeah, I am, thought Malcolm. I'm gonna make a difference. With growing pride in himself, Malcolm resolved to fight the odds and make an impression on the world.

Maggie And Mike Gordon

"Hey, Maggie! Are you actually *using* that computer or what?" Jessica's voice startled Maggie out of a dream involving a prom limo and Justin Carlucci. "Huh? Yeah, of course I'm using it. I've gotta finish this paper before I go to work," Maggie answered sleepily. Jessica sighed. "Well, hurry up. People are *waiting*." "Sorry," Maggie mumbled. "I'll hurry."

Maggie tried to focus on the screen, but the words swam together. I've *got* to wake up, she thought. This paper is already two days late, and the last thing I need is a bad English grade my junior year. It was such a hassle using the library computers, but when she'd asked if they could get a computer for Christmas, Christine had said, "Not this year." When Maggie had started her job at the mall, she'd hoped to save enough to pay at least half the cost of a computer, but it seemed the money just evaporated. By the time she bought a few clothes and went to a couple of movies with her friends, she barely had enough left for lunch money. She just had to find a way to get more hours, so when her boss asked her to stay late to close the store, she couldn't very well say no. Caffeine, that's what I need, thought Maggie. But if I go to the vending machine, someone'll grab this computer. She glanced at the clock . . . time to go to work. Oh well, this paper will just have to be *three* days late.

Christine gazed out the window at the dreary November scenery. The best part of buying trips to New York was the peace and quiet on the train. Now that Helen was about to retire, she usually sent Christine by herself, and Christine loved it. It gave her a chance to think, and there was always plenty to think about. Maggie and *Mike*—he refused to answer to "Mikey" these days—were growing up fast. And money was a constant concern, even though she budgeted carefully. Two years ago, Christine had finally managed to buy a small house a few blocks from her mother's place. Now Mike and Maggie could have friends over and play their music without disturbing Grandma.

The kids helped out as much as they could. Maggie's job meant she paid most of her own expenses. And Mike's mechanical talent saved money on home and car repairs. When the family's ancient van acted up, Christine marveled at his ability to figure out what was wrong. Saturday she'd commented at breakfast that the van didn't sound right, and Mike immediately quizzed her, to narrow down what the problem might be. "What do you mean, it doesn't sound right?" he asked. "Well, it sounds like it's going to start, but then it takes a long time to turn over," she explained. "Do you have enough gas?" he asked. "Almost a full tank." "Does it ever make a real loud grinding noise?" "No, nothing like that." "Then it's probably your spark plugs or alternator. I'll check 'em." And by the end of the day he'd figured out what was wrong.

Really, the kids were doing pretty well after a few rough years. When Frank had remarried four years ago, Maggie had refused to go to the wedding and had taken an instant dislike to Frank's new wife. But Christine had to admit Frank and Nancy had handled the situation well, always inviting Maggie to do things, even though she kept turning them down. Frank had started to call Maggie and take her out for ice cream. He said this was something he'd decided to do at Alcoholics Anonymous. Christine thought it might be Nancy's influence, but she didn't care. Frank was paying more attention to Maggie than he had since she was a baby. When Frank and Nancy's son Nicholas had been born three years before, Maggie's interest in the baby had overcome her dislike for Nancy, and she had started to spend time with them.

At first Mike had refused to believe his father and Nancy were getting married, and he'd objected when Frank included Nancy in their weekend outings. Nancy's son Matt was Mike's age, and Frank had tried hard to get the boys together. But Mike had hated Matt from the beginning, and he bitterly resented the preferential treatment he felt Nancy gave Matt. When Nicholas was born, Mike's resentment had deepened. He called him "that obnoxious little brat" and would see his father only if he left Nick at home.

Still, things had been pretty calm lately. Maggie continued to be a star at school, always on the honor roll and involved in orchestra and endless after-school activities. Her friendships with Jessica and Nicole had endured, and she had a constantly widening circle of other friends. Christine worried a little because she was so unsure of herself with boys. She always seemed to have a crush on some boy who barely knew she existed or thought of her only as a friend. Her latest was Justin Carlucci, junior class president. Justin had dated Jessica last summer, and he worked on the school newspaper with Maggie, but Christine saw no sign of romantic interest. Maggie was already agonizing over whether to invite Justin to her birthday party in February, not wanting to throw herself at him but hoping he'd have such a good time at the party he'd ask her to the prom. Right now Christine's main concern about Maggie was that she was spending so much time at her job, and Christine suspected her grades might be slipping.

Mike had done well in middle school, but since he'd started high school, he'd been hanging out with a new crowd of friends who dressed, talked, and acted tough. Christine worried that criticizing them might only make Mike defensive and cement the friendships further. She knew he'd started smoking on the sly, and she was sure he was drinking beer at parties and had probably tried pot. It also bothered her that Mike was spending so much time alone in his room. She knew he wasn't doing schoolwork. His math and science grades were fair, but his grades in English and history were barely passing. When she mentioned these problems to Frank, he laughed and said he'd been just like that at Mike's age.

Maybe she'd talk to Dave about Mike, thought Christine. Dave was an old friend of her brother-in-law Dan. She'd met him the previous summer when he stopped by Dan and Paula's house one evening. He was an electrician, divorced, with three grown sons. Christine had immediately liked his sense of humor and friendly, outgoing personality. They'd started seeing each other, and now Dave ate dinner with them several nights a week and occasionally stayed over when Mike and Maggie were with Frank. Just thinking about him made her smile; she loved the way he treated her and the children. Dave had brought up the subject of marriage more than once, but Christine wasn't sure she was ready for that step. It had taken her so long to build her own identity, the thought of being someone's wife again made her a little nervous. Dave kept reminding her that he wasn't Frank, and their relationship was certainly different from her relationship with Frank. Dave seemed genuinely interested in her job and always wanted to hear all about her buying trips; once he'd even met her in New York for a weekend. Mike often sat in the living room with Dave after dinner, watching sports on TV and talking. In fact, Christine reflected, she found out more about her son from Dave than from Mike himself. She wasn't so sure how Maggie felt; she was polite to Dave, but when he ate with them, she often excused herself after dinner and went to her room.

Dave smiled when Christine told him her suspicions about what Mike was doing behind that door with the large PRIVATE sign on it. He felt it was perfectly normal for a 14-year-old boy to spend time by himself listening to loud music. "If I were you," he advised, "I'd be more worried about his new friends. If Mike really wants to go to college, he'd better stop hangin' out with kids who are goin' nowhere and pull his grades up. He needs a push in the right direction." Christine sighed. Mike had developed an uncanny ability to tune her out when she started talking about schoolwork or his friends, and Frank wasn't likely to be much help. She hated to drag Dave into this, but maybe he could get through to Mike.

As it turned out, Dave had plenty of chances to influence Mike. Christine and Dave got engaged that Christmas and married in March. Christine had known there would be adjustments when Dave moved in, but she was unprepared for Maggie's reaction. Every conversation involving Maggie and Dave became a battle of wills, with Maggie resisting Dave's opinions and wishes on every conceivable subject. Maggie had worked long hours during the holiday season, and her midyear grades had plummeted. Maggie's job had been the topic of heated discussion all winter, and Maggie had kept working only by promising to cut back her hours and keep up with her studies. But when third quarter grades came out, there was no improvement. Christine looked at the grade report and shook her head sadly. "I'm really disappointed in you, Maggie. You're going to have to quit your job until you can get your grades back up," she told her daughter. "You can't make me quit!" Maggie blurted out. "I *need* that money! I can handle it, I promise!" "I'm sorry, Maggie, but you've already had your chance. Your spring grades are important for getting into college. You have to call your manager and tell her you're quitting." "It's all *your* fault!" Maggie cried, turning on Dave. "Mom always let me work before *you* moved in! I'm gonna go live with Dad. *He* won't make me quit!" After several phone conversations confirmed that Frank agreed Maggie should quit work until her grades improved, she resigned herself to staying with Christine and living with reduced finances. The extra studying she needed to do gave her a good excuse to avoid Dave, and an uneasy truce reigned.

"Did you know that early reptiles had large fins that soaked up solar heat and helped keep them warm?" Mike reached for a third piece of chicken and another helping of mashed potatoes. "I learned that in biology today."

Christine smiled with pleasure and amusement. Ever since her son had entered Mr. Yamoto's sophomore biology class in the fall, he had become an endless source of such information. What a difference a teacher can make, she thought. Mike pored over books on animal physiology and behavior as if they were sports magazines.

"Aren't you interested in learning any *human* biology?" Maggie asked. Well into her senior year, she had recently announced she wanted to major in biology and go to medical school. She had worked hard and brought her grades up, and

Christine agreed she could go back to work. Frank had helped her get a summer job in the construction company office, and she had kept working there part-time during the school year. Just the week before she had been accepted at Boston College, with substantial financial aid.

"Sure I am," said Mike defensively. "I bet you didn't know that if you take a human heart out of the body and put it in the right kind of fluid, it'll keep beating on its own."

Maggie rolled her eyes. "Leave it to you to bring up something like that at the dinner table."

That summer Mr. Yamoto helped Mike get a job at the marine biology station where he worked when school was out. Long conversations with Mr. Yamoto driving to and from the station each day filled Mike's head with dreams of the future. *He* would end the ravages of pollution on marine life. *He* would invent new methods of farming the seas. The entire world might be saved by one of his discoveries!

That summer Mike confided his ambitions to Dave as they worked in the backyard vegetable garden. Mike broached the subject hesitantly, fearing Dave might react to the idea of a science career just as his father would. Frank always referred to scientists as eggheads. To Mike's delight, Dave was enthusiastic. "Gee, Mike," he said as they cleared out the pea patch to make room for more spinach, "That sounds great! You've got the stuff to do whatever you want if you put your mind to it. You know, I got off on the wrong track in high school, messin' around with a lot of losers, and I've always regretted it. I could have done more with my life if I'd buckled down and gone to college. But my dad didn't think it was important, so I didn't get the push I needed. Not that I've done so bad, but I'd do things differently if I were your age again."

Mike was struck by the wistfulness in Dave's voice. He had never thought Dave would confide in him like this, and he had never imagined he would feel so comfortable telling him the things he had.

At the start of junior year, Mike worked out a plan for getting into college, with help from Mr. Yamoto and his guidance counselor. Mike wanted to go to Amherst, where Mr. Yamoto had gone. But he knew his family could never afford it without a scholarship. Mike doggedly tackled the program he had set for himself, and his grades soon reflected his hard work. He forged ahead with renewed determination, the goal of a scholarship firmly in mind.

Hoping to appear well rounded to the admissions committee, Mike went out for wrestling, much to his father's delight. Mike was number one in his weight class at his school, but he often lost in competition with other schools. "Where's your killer instinct, Gordon?" the wrestling coach complained. "Yeah, yeah. I'll get 'em next time," Mike would answer. But to him, doing well at wrestling was just a means to an end, putting him one step closer to Amherst.

Mike dated very little; he went to parties and dances and would ask girls out once or twice, but that was as far as he let things develop. He felt girls were trying to crowd him, wanting some kind of steady commitment, and he wasn't ready for that. "The next thing you know she'll be talkin' about getting married," Mike once remarked about a girl who seemed especially attracted to him. "And I don't want any part of that right now. I've got big plans."

"There's a letter for you on the table," Christine said to her son as he walked through the back door late one afternoon in March of his senior year. "It's from Amherst."

"Did you open it?" Mike asked excitedly.

"No, of course not. It's addressed to you. But it's thick. That's a good sign."

Mike's diligence in school had paid off. He'd already been accepted at his two backup colleges. Nervously, he tore open the envelope. A gigantic grin spread across his face. "I made it!" he shouted ecstatically. "I got a scholarship! Mom, look! This is all we have to pay. Can we afford that? Can we?" Christine hurried over for a look. "Fantastic!" she beamed. "Between your father and me, we can do it."

It was a proud family that watched Mike graduate from high school in June. Christine and Maggie, who had just finished her sophomore year at Boston College, sat with Dave and Grandma in the front row. Beside them were Frank, Nancy, Matt, and Nick. As he walked up to receive his diploma and a special award in science, Mike looked over the audience and beyond as if toward the future. Not quite 18—barely a fourth of the way into his life—he smiled with the joy of someone eagerly awaiting new experiences.

Meryl Polonius Turner

"Close the door," Meryl said to Amy as they hurried into Meryl's bedroom, backpacks clutched in their arms. "I don't want my little brother snooping. He'd tell Mom for sure."

Amy shut the door, locking it for good measure. "I don't know what you're so worried about. It's *your* hair. At fourteen you have a right to do what you want with it."

Meryl reached into her backpack and pulled out a small cardboard box. "Drop of Sun" the carton read in pale blue letters beneath the picture of a glamorous woman with long, light-blond hair. "Return to the natural blond you were born with," Meryl read out loud. "The golden glow of soft, healthy, natural-looking hair kissed by the sun."

"Anyway," Amy continued, "your mom's never even gonna notice. It says natural-looking, doesn't it? I mean, you're blond already, Mer. So who's gonna notice a little lighter? It'll be just like the sun did it."

"I don't know," answered Meryl. "What if it turns my hair, like, *real* platinum? Everyone will notice then. They'll stare at me like I'm a freak or something. I already get stared at because my arms are so long."

"What's wrong with your arms?" asked Amy, lying back on the bed and unwrapping a piece of gum. "They match your legs. And long legs are sexy. Everybody knows *that*."

"Uh-oh!" Meryl exclaimed, jumping up and looking out the window. "There's my mom. I'd better hide this stuff."

Ever since Meryl had turned 13, her mother suddenly seemed like an obstacle blocking all the things she wanted to do. "Sometimes my mom is so *clueless!*" Meryl confided to Amy. "She just doesn't understand *anything!*" This new view led to frequent arguments between Meryl and Karen, especially about boys. When Meryl was asked out on her first date to the movies, Karen was reluctant to let her go. Meryl had been to mixed-sex parties, but never on a date alone with a boy before. "But Mom, you've just *got* to let me go," Meryl pleaded. "All my friends date. I'll be so embarrassed if you won't let me! Don't you see how unfair you're being?"

Karen searched for a compromise, suggesting Joe could drive Meryl and her date to the movies. Meryl was horrified. "Have *Dad* drive us?" she asked in disbelief. "Don't you know *anything*, Mom?" Finally Karen yielded to the inevitable, but she remained strict about when Meryl could go out and what time she had to be home.

"Amy's parents don't have all these dumb rules," Meryl complained. "She comes in whenever she wants. And she doesn't have to say where she's going, like some kind of prisoner or something."

"Well, we're not Amy's parents," Karen answered. "Dad and I do things differently."

"But Mom, I'm *fourteen!*" Meryl protested.

"That's just it. You're very grown up for 14, but you're still only 14. You're not old enough to make all your own rules yet. Teenagers can get into trouble if they're left to do anything they please."

"Just because *you* got pregnant, you think *I'm* going to!" Meryl blurted out. "It's not fair of you not to trust me because of something *you* did."

"It's not that I don't trust you, honey," Karen answered, knowing there was some truth to what her daughter said. "You handle yourself real well, and I'm proud of you. But I do worry. You've been seeing a lot of Jim lately, and I just think you could slow things down a bit."

Meryl often got angry during these talks with her mother, but she felt better afterward. Sometimes a few hours later she would seek her mother out to talk about other things on her mind. She might tell Karen about a fight between two of her friends, how dumb one of her teachers was, or how she just *had* to have a new sweater for Saturday night. And more and more often, Meryl would turn the conversation to her biological father. She wanted to know what he looked like, what Karen had felt about him, why he didn't want to get married, and where he might be now. Karen answered all these questions as honestly as she could, but sometimes they disturbed her. One night she asked Joe if he thought all this interest in Jeff was all right.

"Don't worry about it," Joe answered. "It's only natural. And it's no big deal to me. I know Meryl loves me, even if I am sometimes so *clueless*." Karen laughed at Joe's imitation of Meryl's favorite phrase. Having him in her life to share things with made all the difference.

Karen's concerns about Meryl and Jim didn't last long. That summer they broke up. At first Meryl was hurt and sank into what she described as the deepest depression ever experienced. But when she found out Jim was dating Barbie, her hurt turned to anger. "How could he go out with *her*?" she asked Amy. "Everyone knows her reputation!" By the end of the summer, Jim seemed to have been forgotten. Meryl began dating other boys and going out in mixed-sex groups. She was having more fun than ever, and her confidence was growing. The self-consciousness that had dogged her in the past seemed to be fading. Then another blow came. One afternoon Karen asked Meryl why she hadn't seen Amy for a while. Meryl replied bitterly, "She only wants to be with *Bill* these days. She never wants to be with *me* anymore. And when she's not with Bill, she just stays home."

"Well, maybe something's bothering her, honey," Karen answered sympathetically. "It could be all the trouble her parents have been having. But she's still your best friend, you know. You just have to work on getting her to open up."

"That's just it, Mom," Meryl persisted. "She doesn't act like a best friend. We used to tell each other *everything*. Now when I ask her what's wrong, she just says she doesn't want to talk about it. It's like she doesn't trust me anymore, and I don't know why. I've never blabbed secrets to anybody, not *ever*."

"Well, give her time, Meryl. She can't cut herself off from her best friend forever."

In time Meryl did find out what was wrong with Amy. She was pregnant. Her parents wanted her to have an abortion, but Amy wasn't sure. Finally she relented, but afterward she hardly seemed like the same person. The girl who had been so full of energy and self-assurance was now apathetic and depressed. In the spring Amy's family moved to Los Angeles. Meryl and Amy exchanged e-mail for a while but gradually grew apart. Meryl was devastated by this loss. It was some time before she had another friend as close as Amy.

"How can you eat that lettuce?" asked 17-year-old Meryl, looking at her mother incredulously. "Don't you know about the terrible conditions of the farm workers?"

"You're right," said Karen, feeling slightly guilty. "But what's summer without salads?"

"Don't you think that's hypocritical, Mom?" Meryl asked. "I mean, if you think farm workers are being exploited, you shouldn't give money to the guys who are exploiting them."

Karen felt trapped. She knew her daughter had a point and she was pleased with Meryl's convictions. But Meryl could be so dogmatic. Last week when Meryl had attacked the morality of making big commissions selling houses, Karen had been totally exasperated. Where was that sweet little girl who used to be so proud of her mother the real estate lady? When Karen tried to explain that real estate agents often worked long hours on deals that didn't pay off, Meryl shook her head self-righteously and walked out of the room, sipping her diet soda.

"It's just a stage," Karen said to Joe. "It's all part of growing up . . . isn't it?"

"Don't ask me," Joe answered. "I'm just that dumb city editor who persists in covering trite local news when people in Third World countries are starving to death."

Despite occasional frustration over Meryl's intense convictions, Karen and Joe had much to be proud of in their daughter. The talent for art she had shown in childhood had blossomed. Her sketches and watercolors were exhibited in citywide art shows, and a few pieces had even been sold. Meryl was in charge of set design for the senior class play, and she threw herself into the project with enthusiasm, spending long hours attending to every detail. On opening night, when Meryl took a shy bow at the end of the performance, Karen felt so proud it brought tears to her eyes.

Meryl began to think about being an art teacher. "If you want to teach," Joe suggested, "it wouldn't be a bad idea to practice talking in front of a group. When I was your age, I had a great time on the debate team." Meryl looked at him as if he had just told her to walk to San Francisco. "The *debate* team?" she asked in disbelief. "No way I'm going to volunteer to give a speech!"

Pursuing the idea of teaching, Meryl applied to Fresno State. She planned to major in art and get a teaching certificate. When she received her acceptance, the whole family celebrated. Two of Meryl's friends were going there too, and the three girls decided to share an apartment near campus.

"You know, honey," Karen said to Meryl later, when all the excitement had died down, "I've been thinking about my own future lately. I'd like to take some business courses, and Fresno State's the perfect place. How would you feel about bumping into your mom on campus?"

"I think that'd be great, Mom!" Meryl said with genuine pleasure. "With all that business sense of yours, you should definitely go for it!"

"Thanks," said Karen, smiling and putting an arm affectionately around Meryl's shoulder. "Did I ever tell you how lucky I am to have a daughter like you?"

13 Physical and Cognitive Development in Adolescence

*F*ourteen-year-old Mike stood before the mirror, combing his hair for the
third time. He wanted to look good for the party tonight. Finished, he
stood back and tried to appraise himself impartially. He was too short,
that was for sure. With a father over six feet tall, how could he still be only
five feet seven? And his arms were so scrawny they looked like a girl's! Mike
pulled his shoulders back and flexed his muscles. It was no use. He was still
skinny. He decided to put on a long-sleeved shirt over his favorite blue tee
shirt. Of course, everyone would look at him funny for wearing a shirt like that
on such a hot night, even if he did roll up the sleeves. All the kids would know
he was trying to hide his scarecrow arms. Would the other guys give him a
hard time? Ben and Doug might. As much as he wanted to be accepted by
them, he had to admit they weren't like real friends. Real friends didn't jump at
every chance to put a guy down, like Ben and Doug did. Well, it was better
than still hanging out with wimps like Richie and Benito. Mike took one last
critical look in the mirror, adjusted his collar, and walked out the door.

Adolescence, the period from roughly age 12 through the late teens, is a time of dramatic and far-reaching change. It is characterized by an especially close connection
between physical and psychological development, as demonstrated in Mike's great concern about his physical appearance. During this time new cognitive skills also emerge,
such as the ability to reason about hypothetical situations. These new skills contribute
to many aspects of social development, including changes in adolescents' concepts of
self and others, their ability to conceptualize human thoughts and feelings, their views
of friendship and family relationships, and their moral reasoning. In the next two chapters we will discuss these and other changes that come with adolescence.

Adolescence acquired the status of a unique developmental period only in the early
1900s (Grotevant, 1998). Before then, reproductive maturity marked entry into adulthood, not into a transitional phase between childhood and adulthood. The view of adolescence as a preadult period of development was partly inspired by the work of G. Stanley Hall (1904). Hall saw adolescence as a time when all earlier developmental issues
were reworked, a period when storm and stress were inevitable because of rapid physical changes. Many psychologists now question this conflict-ridden view of adolescence,
but Hall made an enduring contribution by recognizing adolescence as a separate developmental period during which biological changes play a key role.

The period labeled adolescence in our society is now longer than it was in Hall's
day, partly because puberty occurs earlier and partly because people now need more years
of schooling to prepare for most adult occupations. At the beginning of the twentieth
century, most young people in the United States left school after the eighth grade. By
the middle of the century, most adolescents received at least some high school education, but few went on for further education. Today, over 60 percent of all 18- and 19-
year-olds are enrolled in school, most in college or other postsecondary education (U.S.
Bureau of the Census, 2002b). These additional years in school have lengthened the transition between childhood and adulthood.

Because adolescence covers so many years, it makes sense to divide it into substages
(Grotevant, 1998). In each of these substages, young people face a different set of challenges and opportunities, and their thinking and behavior differ considerably across them:

**mhhe.com
/dehart5**

**Postsecondary
Education Statistics**

- *Early adolescence* covers the years from the beginning of puberty to about age 13
  and includes most of the major physical changes of adolescence and accompanying
  changes in relationships with parents and peers.

- *Middle adolescence* (ages 14 to 16) is a time of increasing independence and
  preparation for adult occupations or further education. Some young people enter
  adult roles directly from middle adolescence.

- *Late adolescence* (age 17 to early adulthood) is a time of continued preparation for
  adulthood, usually in college or other educational settings.

Early adolescence brings its own distinctive set of developmental issues, quite different from those faced in middle and late adolescence.

We devote the first section of this chapter to biological changes because of the impact they have on other areas of development during adolescence. An understanding of the physical transformations associated with adolescence sets the stage for understanding other aspects of adolescent development, both cognitive and social. We then go on to explore some of the changes in thinking that adolescents experience. Finally, we look at two aspects of adolescent social cognition: the adolescent form of egocentrism and the development of moral reasoning.

Questions to Think About As You Read

- How are physical, cognitive, and social development interrelated during adolescence?
- How well does the education system meet the developmental needs of adolescents?

BIOLOGICAL CHANGES DURING ADOLESCENCE

The dramatic biological changes that occur in adolescence are apparent to everyone. Teenagers experience accelerated growth, more rapid than at any other time since infancy. Accompanying this spurt in growth are changes in body shape and proportions, such as development of broader shoulders in boys and wider hips in girls. At the same time, significant changes take place in the structure and function of the brain, which may have important implications for cognitive development. The biological changes of

Pubertal Development

puberty also have major impacts on social development. Partly because of changes in physical appearance, teenagers stop thinking of themselves as children, and parents begin to expect more mature and responsible behavior from them. Increased sexual urges and the capacity for reproduction are issues that both teenagers and their families must face. Finally, variations in the age at which physical changes occur have a major impact on how teenagers view themselves and how they relate to others.

Puberty: Norms and Individual Differences

Puberty is the period during which a child changes from a sexually immature person to one who is capable of reproduction. For girls, the clearest indication that this change has occurred is **menarche,** the onset of menstruation. In the United States and western Europe, the average age of menarche is generally between 12 and 13 years (Coleman and Coleman, 2002). However, a girl has not reached true reproductive maturity until she begins to ovulate, which is usually not until several months after menarche. For boys, the critical change marking puberty is **spermarche,** the first ejaculation of mobile sperm. Because this event is not as noticeable as menarche, it is hard to specify an average age for it. Tests for the presence of live sperm in the urine indicate that most boys in the United States reach spermarche by age 14 (Brooks-Gunn and Reiter, 1990).

Puberty is best thought of not as a single event, but as a more extended period when sexual organs and other sexual characteristics are developing rapidly (Connolly, Paikoff, and Buchanan, 1996). By the time menarche or spermarche occurs, an adolescent's body has already been changing for several years. The major noticeable changes of puberty usually occur over a span of about four years, but the total duration of puberty may actually be longer. The first hormonal changes can begin as early as age 7 or 8, and the latest phases can continue into the midteens. In most cases, girls begin puberty about two years earlier than boys (Brooks-Gunn and Reiter, 1990; Rogol, Roemmich, and Clark, 2002).

Even within each sex the timing of puberty varies considerably. The onset is influenced by heredity, nutrition, stress, and exercise, all of which vary from one individual to the next. For example, girls who are serious ballet students or competitive runners or gymnasts often experience delayed puberty (Bale, Doust, and Dawson, 1996; Vadocz, Siegel, and Malina, 2002). Some research suggests that psychosocial factors, especially family conflict, may also influence the timing of puberty, at least for girls. In several studies, higher levels of family conflict have been associated with earlier menarche, whereas higher levels of parental warmth have been associated with later menarche (Graber, Brooks-Gunn, and Warren, 1995; Moffitt et al., 1992; Steinberg and Morris, 2001). The most likely explanation for these findings is that the stress associated with family conflict affects levels of crucial hormones.

Defining the normal range for beginning and completing puberty is really a statistical task. James Tanner, a highly respected researcher in this field, defines *normal* as the range experienced by 95 percent of the population (Tanner, 1990). According to this definition, it is normal for menstruation to begin as early as age 9 or as late as age 16, and it is normal for sperm production to start as early as age 10 or as late as age 19. However, youngsters who mature earlier or later than most of their peers, even though they fall within the normal range, may encounter special psychological issues. We will discuss these issues later in the chapter.

The average age at which puberty occurs has been decreasing for at least the last 100 years. Girls in the United States and western Europe now begin menstruating about two years earlier than their great-grandmothers did (Tanner, 1990). Boys, too, show signs of an earlier onset of puberty (Herman-Giddens, Wang, and Koch, 2001). This generational change is most likely due to improvements in health and nutrition. A recent large-scale study found evidence that girls in the United States are showing signs of pubertal development, such as pubic hair and breast development, at earlier ages than in the past (Herman-Giddens et al., 1997). Interestingly, the average age of menarche does not appear to have changed in the last 30 years or so; instead, for many girls the length of time it takes to complete pubertal development seems to be increasing. The reasons for this shift are not yet clear. It may be related to recent increases in childhood obesity, since higher body fat levels are associated with higher levels of female hormones (Kaplowitz et al., 2001).

Cross-cultural research supports the idea that improved health and nutrition are major causes of earlier puberty. Around the world, girls in industrialized countries tend to reach menarche sooner than girls in developing countries, where malnutrition and chronic disease are more common. The median age at menarche in North America, western Europe, and Japan is about 12.5 to 13.5 years; in Africa and New Guinea, it is 14 to 17 years. Similar differences are found across income levels within cultures. In such widely separated parts of the world as Hong Kong, Tunisia, South Africa, and the United States, girls from higher-income families reach menarche earlier than girls from lower-income families (Eveleth and Tanner, 1976; Hauspie, Vercauteren, and Susanne, 1997). When groups with adequate nutrition are compared, however, there do not seem to be large ethnic differences in the age at which puberty begins or the rate at which it progresses. In the United States, for example, fairly small differences have been found in age at menarche for African-American, Asian-American, and European-American girls. However, African-American girls are more likely than European-American girls to show early signs of pubertal development before age 8 (Herman-Giddens et al., 1997).

Hormonal Control of Puberty

Puberty is the final stage in a much longer process of sexual development. Remember from Chapter 3 that sexual differentiation begins soon after conception. Whether a fertilized egg becomes male or female depends on the presence or absence of a Y chromosome, which in turn governs the amount of male hormones, or *androgens,* the embryo produces. An abundance of androgens triggers the development of male sex organs, and a relative lack of androgens allows female organs to develop.

After birth, levels of sex hormones drop precipitously, and they stay low through infancy and early childhood. During middle childhood, sex hormones once again begin to influence physical development. Androgen levels in both boys and girls actually begin to rise several years before most of the external signs of puberty appear—usually between ages 6 and 8 (Rogol et al., 2002; Spear, 2000). This early increase in androgen levels is called **adrenarche** because the androgens involved come from the **adrenal glands,** small glands located above the kidneys that produce androgens and other hormones related to stress, metabolism, and reproduction. Eventually, rising levels of adrenal androgens result in some of the earliest outward signs of puberty in both boys and girls, such as the growth of pubic and underarm hair. They may also be associated with mood changes and the beginnings of sexual attraction (Herdt and McClintock, 2000).

Several years later the levels of sex hormones produced by the **gonads,** or sex glands, begin to rise. This increase in gonadal sex hormones is called **gonadarche.** The male gonads are the testes, which produce androgens. The female gonads are the ovaries, which produce female hormones called *estrogens* and *progesterone,* as well as small amounts of androgens. Rising levels of these hormones eventually make reproduction possible; they also contribute to many of the obvious changes in physical appearance associated with puberty, such as growth of the penis and testicles in boys and breast development in girls.

Complex feedback systems involving various glands are responsible for regulating levels of both adrenal and gonadal hormones. Figure 13.1 shows how the gonadal hormone feedback loop works; a similar feedback loop regulates levels of adrenal androgens. The **pituitary gland,** a small structure at the base of the brain often referred to as the *master gland,* plays a central role in the feedback systems. The pituitary gland in turn is affected by hormones from a part of the brain known as the **hypothalamus.** These brain hormones, known as *releasing factors,* turn the production of pituitary hormones on and off. Some of the pituitary hormones are called **gonadotropins** because they travel through the bloodstream and affect hormone output from the gonads. The levels of sex

Adrenarche:
The increase in adrenal androgen levels in middle childhood.

Adrenal glands:
Small glands located above the kidneys that produce androgens and other hormones related to stress, metabolism, and reproduction.

Gonads:
The sex glands: testes in men and ovaries in women.

Gonadarche:
The increase in gonadal sex hormone levels at puberty.

Pituitary gland:
A small gland at the base of the brain that plays a major role in regulating the hormonal output of other glands.

Hypothalamus:
A part of the brain that regulates many body functions, including the production of pituitary hormones.

Gonadotropins:
Pituitary hormones that affect hormone output by the gonads.

Figure 13.1
GONADAL HORMONE
FEEDBACK LOOP
Levels of sex hormones are
regulated by a feedback system
composed of the hypothalamus,
pituitary gland, and gonads.
*(Source: Adapted from
"Hypothalamic pituitary
regulation of puberty in man:
Evidence and concepts derived
from clinical research," by
M. M. Grumbach, J. C. Roth,
S. I. Kaplan, and R. P. Kelch, in
Control of the onset of puberty by
M. M. Grumbach, G. D. Grave,
and F. H. Mayer (eds.).
Copyright © 1974 by John Wiley
& Sons, Inc. Reprinted by
permission of John Wiley &
Sons, Inc.)*

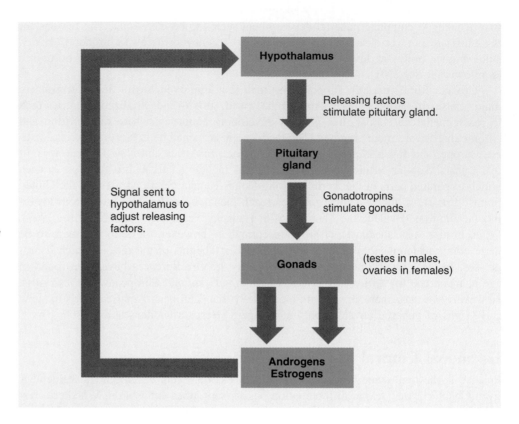

hormones in the blood provide signals to the hypothalamus, which modifies its activities accordingly and affects output from the pituitary gland. This complex control system functions even before birth. Through middle childhood it works to keep sex hormones at low levels (Rogol, 2002).

At the end of middle childhood the brain directs first the adrenal glands and then the gonads to step up production of sex hormones. How the brain knows it is time to begin puberty is not yet understood. One explanation, the *critical weight hypothesis* (Frisch and Revelle, 1970), was based on data suggesting that menarche occurs at a relatively constant weight and the adolescent growth spurt in both sexes is weight-related. However, menarche seems not to be controlled by weight per se, but by factors *related* to weight, such as proportion of fat to lean tissue (Frisch, 1991). This would explain the prevalence of delayed menarche in ballet dancers and certain kinds of athletes, whose intense physical training may result in low levels of body fat. It also explains why nutritional factors would be involved in the trend toward earlier menarche and in cross-cultural and social class differences in age at menarche. Some researchers now suspect that subtle changes in the body's metabolism provide signals to the brain that trigger the stepped-up production of sex hormones (Spear, 2000).

Regardless of what brings about increased output of sex hormones at the end of middle childhood, that increase starts the changes we call puberty. Rising levels of sex hormones circulate in the blood, becoming available to cells throughout the body. When the concentrations of these hormones reach a critical threshold, cells that are receptive to them change their growth patterns. Androgens and estrogens are present in the blood throughout childhood, but not until their concentrations rise to some critical level do the physical changes of adolescence begin.

Changes in Appearance at Puberty

Among the physical changes of puberty are the development of **secondary sex characteristics**—physical features that differentiate adult males from adult females but

Secondary sex characteristics:
Physical features that differentiate adult males from adult females but are not directly involved in reproduction.

Table 13.1 Stages of Puberty

Stage	Pubic Hair Development	Female Breast Development	Male Genital Development
1	No pubic hair.	Elevation of papilla (nipple) only.	Penis, scrotum, and testes stay in the same proportion to body size as in early childhood.
2	First pubic hair, which is sparse, long, and slightly pigmented, appears, usually at base of penis or along labia.	Breast buds appear. The breast and papilla are elevated slightly in a small mound.	Scrotum and testes enlarge and scrotum darkens.
3	Hair darkens, becomes coarser and more curled; remains sparse but spreads over the midsection of the pubic region.	Breast and areola continue to enlarge, but there is no separation of their contours.	Penis grows, primarily in length, and scrotum and testes continue to grow.
4	Hair development is completed, but area covered is still smaller than in adults.	Areola and papilla elevate above the mound of the breast to form a secondary mound.	Growth of penis includes width and enlargement of glans; scrotum continues to grow and darken.
5	Quantity and area covered reach adult proportions.	Papilla continues to project, but areola recesses to the general contour of the breast.	Genitals attain adult size and shape.

Source: Adapted from Tanner, 1962.

are not directly involved in reproduction. Secondary sex characteristics include new distributions of muscle and fat tissue, the growth of hair on certain parts of the body, the development of breasts in females, and the lowered pitch of the male voice. Major secondary sex characteristics are often used as markers for various stages of puberty. For instance, Tanner (1962) identified five stages of puberty on the basis of pubic hair and genital development in boys, and pubic hair and breast development in girls (see Table 13.1). The development of the various secondary sex characteristics does not always occur at the same rate. For instance, a male might be at stage 4 for genital development but only at stage 2 for the development of pubic hair.

Most adolescents also experience noticeable changes in their skin and sweat glands. The skin becomes rougher and more oily, and acne may develop. The sweat glands enlarge and become more active, especially in the underarm and genital areas, resulting in new body odors.

Another physical change that occurs near the beginning of adolescence is a marked spurt in growth. Figure 13.2 shows that increases in height slow substantially during the late preschool years and early middle childhood. Across this age range, the average height of girls and boys is virtually identical (Tanner, 1990). Then the growth spurt for girls begins, at an average age of 10.5 years. For boys, the spurt starts a couple of years later, on average at age 12.5 years. The adolescent growth spurt reaches its peak about a year and a half after it begins. The peak rate of growth for boys is greater than the peak rate for girls, which partly explains why they end up on average about two and a half inches taller.

Growth occurs near the ends of bones in rings of cartilage called *epiphyseal growth plates*. Adolescent skeletal growth ceases when increased amounts of sex hormones cause calcification of the cartilage involved in this process. Different patterns of skeletal growth among adolescent boys and girls partially account for the gender-related differences in body

Figure 13.2
GROWTH RATES FOR BOYS AND GIRLS
The rate of growth, which is at its maximum in infancy, declines through childhood and is followed by a spurt in adolescence. The growth spurt for males is greater than for females, and their growth continues over a longer period of time, which is why they end up taller on average. (*Source: Tanner, Whitehouse, and Takaishi, 1966.*)

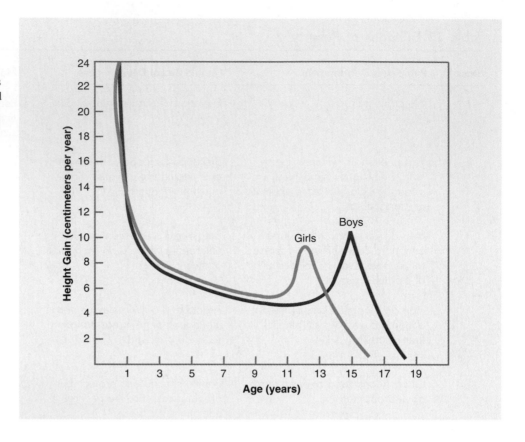

shape. The classic male growth pattern leads to broader shoulders, narrower hips, and longer legs relative to torso. The classic female growth pattern leads to narrower shoulders, broader hips, and shorter legs relative to torso (see Figure 13.3). Differences in the amount and distribution of body fat also contribute to gender differences in body shape. During adolescence, girls develop fat deposits on the thighs, hips, buttocks, and upper arms. Overall, the percentage of body fat increases for girls and decreases for boys (Rogol et al., 2002).

During the adolescent growth spurt the arms and legs grow before the torso does in both boys and girls. This growth pattern, which makes the limbs seem temporarily out of proportion to the rest of the body, is one source of self-consciousness among teenagers. Meryl expresses this concern to Amy in the story that precedes this chapter. The torso growth that follows usually brings the body back into normal proportions.

In addition to increases in height, adolescents experience increases in weight, strength, and endurance. Part of the weight gain comes from growth in both the size and number of muscle cells. As a result, adolescents become stronger than they were as children, although males experience a greater increase in strength than females do (Rogol et al., 2002). During adolescence the heart and lungs also develop in ways that contribute to increased endurance and allow for participation in more demanding competitive sports.

The growth patterns we have described are but a sampling of the physical changes that occur during puberty, meant to illustrate what a dramatic transformation occurs at this time. In just a few years youngsters change from looking like children to looking like young adults. In the process, they gain new physical capacities, perhaps most importantly the capacity for sexual reproduction. All these physical changes help propel adolescents toward a new set of social roles.

Neurological Changes at Puberty

Mounting evidence suggests that the brain also undergoes substantial change around the time of puberty. It is not yet clear what causes these neurological changes. They may be

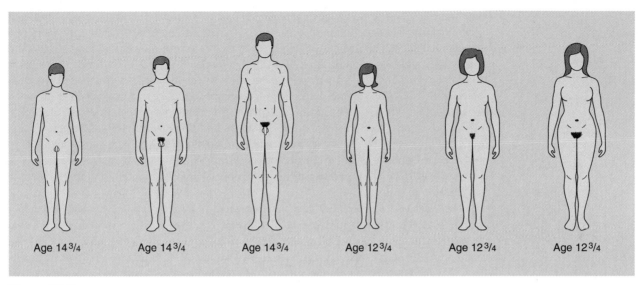

Age 14³/₄   Age 14³/₄   Age 14³/₄   Age 12³/₄   Age 12³/₄   Age 12³/₄

Figure 13.3
DEVELOPMENTAL DIFFERENCES IN SAME-AGE BOYS AND GIRLS
The three males in this figure are all the same age (14³/₄ years), as are the three females (12³/₄ years), but they are in different stages of development. These pictures illustrate the different patterns of growth for males and females and different rates of development within gender.
(Source: Tanner, 1962.)

produced partly by hormonal changes and partly by experience during earlier developmental periods. In any case, by the end of adolescence the brain seems to be a somewhat different organ than it was in childhood. Between childhood and adulthood the brain shows two major changes:

- a decline in **plasticity,** or the ability of brain regions to take on new functions, and
- an increase in efficiency of brain functioning.

As discussed in Chapter 4, brain plasticity is high at birth and gradually declines as various brain regions take on specialized functions. Declining plasticity can be seen in the fact that adults have more difficulty recovering from brain injuries than children do, in part because functions previously performed by damaged parts of their brains are less readily taken over by undamaged parts. Further evidence for decreased plasticity comes from the decline in language-learning abilities between childhood and adulthood. As mentioned in Chapter 7, success at second-language learning begins to decline gradually in middle childhood and drops off sharply around the time of puberty (Johnson and Newport, 1989). Both these lines of evidence suggest the brains of young children have a marked capacity for reprogramming, some of which is lost by adulthood.

One change that may contribute to the loss of plasticity is **hemispheric specialization,** the process by which certain brain functions become localized in either the right or left side of the cerebral cortex. In most adults, for example, language is primarily a function of the left hemisphere, and spatial abilities are primarily a function of the right hemisphere. The process of hemispheric specialization has already begun at birth, but it is thought to be completed in most people around the time of puberty. Adults vary in their extent of hemispheric specialization, and one factor that may contribute to this variability is age at puberty. Several researchers have found evidence of greater hemispheric specialization among late maturers than among early maturers, but they have not found consistent differences in cognitive functioning between the two groups (Newcombe, Dubas, and Baenninger, 1989; Waber, 1977).

Another change that probably contributes even more to loss of plasticity is a decrease in the number of synapses, or connections among brain cells, in the cerebral cortex. As

Plasticity:
The ability of brain regions to take on new functions.

Adolescent Brain Development

Hemispheric specialization:
The process by which certain brain functions become localized in either the right or left side of the cerebral cortex.

mentioned in Chapter 4, synapses are overproduced in infancy and then gradually begin to be eliminated in childhood. Postmortem examinations have shown a sharply decreased density of synapses between ages 15 and 20 in the regions of the cerebral cortex involved in language and higher-order thinking skills (Huttenlocher, 2002). Brain imaging studies have also found a rapid growth just before puberty in the same regions of the cortex, followed by a loss of volume during adolescence, presumably as synapses are eliminated (Durston et al., 2001; Thompson et al., 2000). In keeping with these findings, electronic brain scans show that between the ages of 10 and 14 there is roughly a 50 percent drop in the energy being used in these brain regions (Chugani, 1994). Since substantial energy is needed to send messages from one brain cell to another, this decrease in energy use could arise partly from a pruning of brain synapses—that is, the elimination of synapses that are not needed.

The decrease in synapses does not represent a loss of brain function; instead, it allows for more efficient functioning of the synapses that remain. Another process that increases efficiency of brain functioning is *myelination,* or the formation of myelin sheaths around nerve fibers, as discussed in Chapter 4. The process of myelination is thought to be completed in many areas of the cerebral cortex during adolescence (Graber and Petersen, 1991).

These findings suggest that environment may be in many ways as important for brain development during adolescence as during the first few years of life. Activities and experiences during the adolescent years have a potentially powerful influence on the architecture of the brain at maturity because they determine which synapses will be eliminated and which will be retained.

Developmental studies of sleep patterns also support the idea that the brain changes at puberty (Sampaio and Truwit, 2001). Children aged 2 to 11 spend about twice as much time as adults do in *deep sleep,* a state characterized by extremely slow brain waves. Then, between the ages of 11 and 14, the amount of deep sleep declines to adult levels. We do not know what prompts this nighttime change in brain-wave patterns. One possibility is that deep sleep somehow helps the brain recover from its metabolic activities during the day. If the brain becomes more efficient at the time of adolescence, its amount of metabolic activity would decline, as would the need for deep sleep. Changes in sleep patterns during adolescence are discussed further in the box on page 463, along with their implications for teenagers' daytime schedules and functioning.

mhhe.com
/dehart5

Adolescents and Sleep

Let's summarize the findings about changes in the brain at puberty. Apparently, during early adolescence the brain becomes more efficient at certain tasks, which may play a role in the changes in cognitive abilities that occur during adolescence. Greater efficiency comes at the price of a decrease in plasticity; after adolescence, the brain cannot adapt as readily to new demands, such as learning a new language or recovering from damage.

Impacts of Pubertal Change

The physical changes of puberty have a powerful impact on adolescents' psychological functioning, behavior, and relationships with others. In fact, some of the behavioral changes of adolescence are tied more closely to these physical changes than to chronological age or level of cognitive development. The impact of puberty on adolescents depends partly on its timing—that is, whether it occurs early, on schedule, or late compared with the majority of their peers.

Puberty and Body Image Body image is strongly affected by puberty and its timing (Petersen, 1987; Rosenblum and Lewis, 1999; Tobin-Richards, Boxer, and Petersen, 1983). In early adolescence, boys who are more physically mature have a more positive body image and perceive themselves as generally more attractive than boys who are less physically mature. One reason for this is that boys who have passed puberty have an athletic advantage because of the increased height and muscle development that come with puberty.

A CLOSER LOOK

ADOLESCENT SLEEP PATTERNS

Although the relative amount of deep sleep apparently declines during adolescence, the *overall* amount of sleep needed does not seem to change, contrary to the assumptions of many parents, teachers, and school administrators. In a longitudinal study, Mary Carskadon and her colleagues (1980) observed youngsters in a sleep laboratory during six consecutive summers, beginning when they were 10, 11, or 12 years old. They expected that the length of time the participants would sleep at night would decline as they got older until it reached the adult average of 7.5 to 8 hours by the time they were in their late teens. Instead, they found that the average sleep length of 9.2 hours per night stayed constant from late childhood through adolescence, as long as the study participants were allowed a constant 10-hour opportunity for sleep.

Another surprising finding of this study was that midday sleepiness increased during puberty and stayed high through late adolescence, even though study participants were allowed what ought to be enough hours for sleep. One reason for the increase in sleepiness during the day is that adolescents typically show a shift in their timing of sleep, preferring to stay up later at night and sleep later in the morning than they did in middle childhood (Wolfson and Carskadon, 1998).

Parents often attribute this shift to adolescent contrariness or bad habits such as staying up to watch television, listen to music, or talk to friends on the telephone. However, there is evidence of a biological basis for this change. Carskadon and her colleagues have found that the preference for staying up late and sleeping late is related to physical indicators of puberty, rather than simply to age (Carskadon and Acebo, 1993). In addition, they have demonstrated that during puberty a shift occurs in the timing of daily secretion of *melatonin*, a hormone associated with the onset of sleep (Carskadon et al., 1997).

Although the *need* for sleep does not seem to decline during adolescence, the *actual* amount of sleep adolescents get does decline (Wolfson and Carskadon, 1998). Teenagers in North America and Europe consistently report that they do not get enough sleep. Most studies have found that elementary-school-age children average about 10 hours of sleep a night; by age 16 the average is less than 7.5 hours per night.

One major factor in adolescents' sleep deficits is early morning start times for school. In many school districts, middle school starts earlier than elementary school and high school starts earlier than middle school. One longitudinal study that followed students across the transition to high school found that an earlier school start time was associated with a loss of sleep for most students (Carskadon, 2002). Studies in the United States, Europe, and South America have found that adolescents consistently sleep longer on weekends when they do not have to get up for school, and the difference between weekend and weeknight sleep length increases with age (Andrade and Menna-Barreto, 2002; Szymczak et al., 1993; Wolfson and Carskadon, 1998). School schedules are obviously not the only factor in adolescents' sleep patterns; after-school and evening jobs, homework, social activities, and family routines also contribute.

In a large study of high school students in Rhode Island, Wolfson and Carskadon (1998) found that inadequate sleep and irregular sleep schedules were associated with a variety of problems, including academic difficulties, behavior problems, and depressed mood, in addition to daytime sleepiness. These findings suggest that although "adolescent sleepiness is so widespread that it almost seems normal" (Wolfson and Carskadon, 1998, p. 885), inadequate sleep can have serious implications for adolescent development and well-being.

For girls, in contrast, puberty tends to have a negative effect on body image, mostly because of the increase and redistribution of body fat at this time. Girls in early adolescence generally have a poorer body image than boys of the same age and tend to think of themselves as too heavy (Dornbusch et al., 1987; Richards et al., 1990; Rosenblum and Lewis, 1999). Girls who are well ahead of their peers in physical development have the most negative self-perceptions, even more so than girls who lag behind. Among early adolescent girls, those who are about *average* in physical development generally have the most positive body image and the greatest feelings of attractiveness.

Studies in both the United States and Sweden have found that early-maturing girls remain dissatisfied with their height and weight throughout adolescence, perhaps because they tend to differ from their peers in height and weight in ways that are a disadvantage at every age (Simmons, Carlton-Ford, and Blyth, 1987; Stattin and Magnusson, 1990). In sixth grade, they are taller and heavier than most of their classmates, both male and female. By tenth grade, they are generally shorter and heavier than late-maturing girls,

Interest in the opposite sex increases around the time of puberty.

who have continued to grow taller but have not yet acquired the added body fat that follows puberty. The early-maturing girls thus are less likely to fit the cultural ideal of the slender, long-legged woman. This difference in height and weight between early- and late-maturing girls persists into adulthood (Brooks-Gunn and Reiter, 1990).

The one physical change of puberty that seems to have a positive effect on girls' body image is breast development (Brooks-Gunn and Reiter, 1990). In sixth and seventh grade, girls who have passed menarche think they are too tall and weigh too much, but they are more satisfied with their figures than girls who have not reached menarche. What these early maturers actually seem to be expressing satisfaction with is their relatively advanced breast development (Simmons, Carlton-Ford, and Blyth, 1987). Breast development probably has such a strong impact on body image because of the strong sexual significance of female breasts in our culture and the fact that breast development is more obvious to other people than many of the other changes of puberty.

Puberty and Social Relationships Puberty is associated with increased interest in the opposite sex and an increased likelihood of dating and sexual activity. Roberta Simmons and her colleagues (1987) found that girls who had reached puberty by sixth and seventh grades considered themselves more popular with boys and were more likely to be dating than girls who had not yet reached puberty. Young adolescents of both sexes who are further along in puberty are more likely to date and talk on the telephone with members of the opposite sex (Petersen, 1987). These behaviors may be due partly to increased sexual interest as a result of higher androgen levels (Smith, 1989) and partly to increased sexual attractiveness. Timing of puberty also affects relationships with the opposite sex. One Swedish study found that early-maturing girls were more likely than late-maturing girls to have a steady boyfriend and sexual experience by midadolescence and to experience an unwanted pregnancy by the end of adolescence (Stattin and Magnusson, 1990).

Puberty also affects parent-child relationships. When children reach puberty, conflicts with their mothers often increase (Laursen, Coy, and Collins, 1998; Papini and Sebby, 1987; Steinberg, 1989). Near the end of puberty, adolescents report increased feelings of autonomy from their parents (Simmons, Carlton-Ford, and Blyth, 1987; Steinberg, 1987). The timing of puberty makes a difference; mother-son conflict tends to be greatest for early-maturing boys (Steinberg, 1987), and early-maturing girls often have an unusually prolonged period of conflict with their parents (Hill et al., 1985). Puberty is more likely to be associated with increased feelings of autonomy for late-maturing adolescents, particularly girls. This shows that parents consider chronological age as well as pubertal status in allowing their children more independence. We will discuss changes in parent-child relationships during adolescence more extensively in Chapter 14.

Puberty and Problem Behaviors Various problem behaviors become more common at puberty, especially in early-maturing girls. Simmons and her colleagues (1987) found increased problem behaviors and decreased academic performance in sixth- and seventh-grade girls who had passed menarche. In Sweden, Stattin and Magnusson (1990) found heightened rates of truancy, academic trouble, drug and alcohol use, running away, and shoplifting among early-maturing girls. Studies in Finland have found that early-maturing girls are more likely than late-maturing girls to smoke and drink on a regular basis (Aro and Taipale, 1987; Dick et al., 2000). Interestingly, one study in New Zealand found

The physical changes associated with puberty occur at widely varying ages, and differences in their timing pose emotional challenges for both boys and girls.

early-maturing girls only showed an increase in problem behaviors at puberty if they attended coeducational high schools, perhaps because of contact at school with older boys (Caspi et al., 1993). Some researchers have also found early-maturing boys at heightened risk of problem behaviors, including delinquency, drug and alcohol use, truancy, and early sexual activity (Williams and Dunlop, 1999).

Timing of Puberty and Overall Adjustment As we have seen, the age at which puberty occurs has an impact on many aspects of an adolescent's development, with girls and boys affected differently. For girls, early maturers are at a disadvantage compared with late maturers, at least during adolescence. For boys, in contrast, late maturers are likely to experience more problems in the short term.

In addition to the various negative effects we have already mentioned, early-maturing girls tend to have lower self-esteem and are at greater risk for a variety of emotional problems than are late-maturing girls (Simmons and Blyth, 1988). The long-term effects of early maturation for girls are not completely clear. One study suggests early-maturing girls develop coping skills during adolescence that result in greater psychological flexibility in adulthood (Peskin, 1973). However, the problem behaviors of some early-maturing girls can have lasting impacts. For example, Stattin and Magnusson (1990) followed the participants in their study into adulthood and found that early-maturing girls had a tendency to have children earlier and to complete fewer years of education.

Late-maturing boys tend to be less popular and less self-confident than early maturers during adolescence; they are often regarded by their peers as childish, bossy, tense, and restless (Graber et al., 1997; Jones, 1957). In adulthood they are frequently viewed as impulsive and nonconforming, but also insightful and creative. Early-maturing boys, in contrast, are often viewed as competent, poised, and successful as adolescents, but in adulthood tend to become inflexible and conventional (Livson and Peskin, 1980). The characteristics that contributed to their social success in adolescence become less useful in adulthood.

This pattern of different effects for boys and girls makes sense if the key issue in the timing of puberty is being in step with the physical development of one's peers. Early-maturing girls, who can reach puberty as young as age 9, and late-maturing boys, who can reach puberty as late as age 19, are the *most* out of step developmentally. It is thus not surprising that these two groups seem to encounter the most negative consequences of puberty.

Direct and Indirect Effects of Puberty The causal connections between puberty and adolescent behavior are complex (Brooks-Gunn, Graber, and Paikoff, 1994). Sexual maturity alone does not produce the effects we have discussed; social factors are also extremely important. Puberty produces both unseen internal and visible external physical changes. The internal changes directly affect adolescents' feelings and behaviors through the influences of hormones—increasing sexual desire, for example. The external changes affect feelings and actions too, through their impact on adolescents' body image and the reactions they trigger in others. For example, parents may perceive physically mature teenagers as more personally responsible, while members of the opposite sex may find them more sexually attractive. These reactions in turn can powerfully influence adolescents' behavior.

How adolescents and others react to the changes of puberty depends on the meaning attached to those changes, which is partly a product of culture. For example, ballet students regard late maturation and the elongated, slender body type that results as particularly advantageous (Brooks-Gunn, 1987), and the emphasis placed on weight by adolescent girls in the United States seems to vary from one community to another (Richards et al., 1990). Reactions to puberty, in other words, are not universal but depend on the particular context in which these physical changes occur.

CHANGES IN THINKING DURING ADOLESCENCE

Adolescence is a time when youngsters acquire important new cognitive skills. Some developmentalists, such as Piaget, see these new skills as marking the transition to a qualitatively different period of development (Case, 1998; Moshman, 1998). Although these researchers believe the skills of adolescence are built on those of childhood, they tend to focus on how adolescent thinking differs from thinking earlier in life. In contrast, other developmentalists put more stress on continuity with the past. They see the cognitive accomplishments of adolescence as logical and steady progressions from the skills of middle childhood (Keating, 1980; Siegler, 1978). However, there is general agreement that during adolescence youngsters become much more mature in their reasoning and problem-solving abilities.

One major change is that *adolescents can apply logical thinking to the possible* (what *might* exist), *not just to the real* (what *does* exist). In one investigation of this change, children were shown poker chips of several colors, one of which was then hidden in the experimenter's hand (Osherson and Markman, 1975). The experimenter said, "Either the chip in my hand is green or it is not green," and the children were asked to decide if this statement was true or false. Elementary-school-aged children had great difficulty answering the question. They kept trying to determine if the chip was green; upon discovering they couldn't do so, they said there was no way to answer the question. These children seemed wedded to a *contingent* notion of truth; to know if the experimenter's words were true, they thought they had to *see* what was in his hand. Adolescents can break free of this focus on concrete things perceived by the senses. They are able to consider the possibilities contained in the statement (the chip may be green or it may be some other color) and examine their logical implications. Using this more abstract perspective, adolescents correctly conclude that the statement involves a *necessary* truth.

A second cognitive advance in adolescence is *the ability to think about relationships among mentally constructed concepts*—that is, among abstract concepts that are built up from the more concrete things perceived by the senses. Number, for instance, is an abstract, mentally constructed concept drawn from more concrete, observable concepts: one, two, three, and so on. Elementary school children can form *individual* abstract concepts, but they have trouble reasoning about the logical relationships between them. The adolescent's newfound ability to think about such relationships is evident in a variety of contexts. For instance, an elementary school child might define an abstract concept such as morality by focusing on specific behaviors— not stealing, telling the truth, obeying parents. In contrast, an adolescent understands that morality entails interrelations among subordinate concepts such as honesty, fairness, and kindness. Because of their ability to think this way, teenagers have a more mature grasp of such abstract concepts as identity, justice, religion, society, and friendship. The ability to think about relationships among abstract concepts also gives adolescents even more capacity for *metacognition*— thinking about thinking—than they had in middle childhood (Flavell et al., 2002). This capacity reveals itself in improved strategies for memory and problem solving and in increased ability to explain their own thought processes (Reich, Oser, and Valentin, 1994). In addition, it shows up in teenagers' heightened introspection and focus on their own thoughts (Elkind, 1967).

A third major advance is that *adolescents' thinking becomes even more logical and systematic than it was in childhood.* These improved powers of reasoning increase adolescents' ability to construct logical arguments and see fallacies in others' logic—a development that does not always endear them to parents. Using their new abilities to think about the possible as well as the actual and to reason about relationships among abstract concepts, adolescents can engage in what Piaget referred to as **hypothetico-deductive reasoning.** This ability allows adolescents to think of hypothetical solutions to a problem (ideas about what *might* be) and formulate a systematic plan for deducing which of these solutions is correct. Consider the car repair problem facing Mike in the story that precedes this chapter. He can solve this problem because he is knowledgeable about engines and because he lays out the possible reasons for the malfunction and then deduces what symptoms would differentiate one possibility from another.

Hypothetico-deductive reasoning is also useful in situations that require thinking about possible consequences of various courses of action. Research on adolescents' competence to consent to medical treatment has shown that by age 14 children can weigh the consequences of proposed treatments, consider multiple relevant factors such as treatment advantages and disadvantages, and arrive at a rational decision (Weithorn and Campbell, 1982). Younger children tend to focus on one or two particularly salient features of a proposed treatment, such as pain or duration, and to have trouble coordinating multiple factors that need to be considered.

Developmentalists are still trying to determine what underlies the cognitive changes of adolescence. One explanation is contained in Piaget's theory of formal operations. Because Piaget's ideas have had such an influence on the field, we will describe them in some detail.

Hypothetico-deductive reasoning:
The ability to think of hypothetical solutions to a problem and to formulate a systematic plan for deducing which of these solutions is correct.

Advances in logical reasoning abilities allow adolescents to become increasingly skilled and often passionate at debating both real and hypothetical issues.

Piaget's Theory of Formal Operations

Piaget attributed the cognitive advances of adolescents to their developing ability to use principles of propositional logic, which he called **formal operations.** Propositional logic involves combining individual statements or *propositions* to reach logical conclusions, as in the following example: "All A's are B. X is an A. Therefore, X is a B." Principles of propositional logic can be applied to statements based in reality: "All mammals are warm-blooded. Whales are mammals. Therefore, whales are warm-blooded." But they can also be applied to hypothetical or fanciful statements: "All wonkets have three eyes. Cleo is a wonket. Therefore, Cleo has three eyes."

Piaget argued that formal operations allow adolescents to think more abstractly and systematically than ever before. Elementary school children can use logic to reason about concrete situations, but they have trouble with problems based on hypothetical situations, especially if the situations are contrary to fact. Adolescents are able to think about the logical implications in a problem, whether or not it is grounded in reality. For example, adolescents would have no trouble answering the following question: "If all dogs were green, and I had a dog, would it be green too?" (Ault, 1983). Younger children would tend to object that dogs cannot be green. They would have trouble getting beyond the fact that the situation portrayed in the problem did not match their concrete experience.

Piaget did not believe formal operations needed to be taught. Instead, he maintained that adolescents develop the ability to understand and apply formal operations as a result of their own reasoning and experimentation. Once this ability has developed, adolescents can use it to solve problems and expand their understanding of the world.

Piaget believed the cognitive skills that constitute formal operations are qualitatively different from any skills the child has had in the past. However, he saw these skills as produced by the same processes of adaptation and equilibration that produced earlier cognitive structures. Thus, cognitive structures and abilities change, but not the underlying processes of development.

Piaget's Experiments

Piaget built his theory of formal operations on extensive research into adolescents' reasoning abilities, in which youngsters of different ages conducted science experiments. The youngsters were given an apparatus (such as a pendulum) or a set of materials (such as chemicals that could be combined to produce a certain reaction). Their task was to manipulate these items in any way they wished to determine how they worked. Piaget found that adolescents approached and understood these tasks in markedly different ways than elementary school children did.

To give you a clearer sense of the basis for Piaget's ideas about formal operations, we will look at three of his experiments. As you read about them, notice the general cognitive abilities they demonstrate. The first experiment shows the ability to reason about relationships among abstract concepts; the second one shows the ability to isolate variables that may be having an effect on results; and the last one shows the ability to combine a number of different factors in a systematic way. Piaget believed all these abilities resulted from adolescents' use of formal logical reasoning.

The Law of Floating Bodies Study In the law of floating bodies study, youngsters were given objects of different sizes and materials, along with a large container of water. They were asked to classify the objects according to whether they would float or sink and to explain their classification. Then they were given a chance to experiment with each object in the water and describe what they had learned.

At the beginning of middle childhood (ages 6 to 7) children were often wrong in their hypotheses about what would float and what would not. When given a chance to experiment and draw more accurate conclusions, their reasoning was often unsystematic, illogical, and incomplete. Here are some examples (Inhelder and Piaget, 1955/1958, pp. 26–27):

Child 1: (explaining why a large piece of wood floats) Because this plank is bigger and it came back up. (Interviewer: And why does the ball come up?) *Because it's smaller.*

Child 2: (explaining why certain items sink) They are little things. (Interviewer: Why do the little ones go to the bottom?) *Because they aren't heavy; they don't swim on top because it's too light. (Later the same child says that a metal key sinks "because it's too heavy to stay on top.")*

Child 3: (explaining why a candle sinks) Because it's round. (Interviewer: And why does the wooden ball stay on top?) *Because it's round too.*

These examples highlight the self-contradictions in young children's explanations. The children seemed to focus on an object's most obvious features (large, small, round, etc.), regardless of the question being asked or the answers they had previously given.

Somewhat older children (7 to 10 years old) tried to avoid self-contradictions. They frequently expressed the idea that light objects float and heavy ones sink. When reminded that some very light objects sink and some very heavy ones float, they groped for an overall explanation that would accommodate these facts. Here is how two older elementary school youngsters tackled the problem (Inhelder and Piaget, 1955/1958, pp. 29, 35):

Child 1: (explaining why the ball floats): It stays on top. It's wood. It's light. (Interviewer: And this key?) *It goes down. It's iron. It's heavy.* (Interviewer: Which is heavier, the key or the ball?) *The ball.* (Interviewer: Why does the key sink?) *Because it's heavy.* (Interviewer: And the nail?) *It's light but it sinks anyway. It's iron and iron always goes under.*

Child 2: (explaining why the wooden ball floats while the iron key sinks) Wood isn't the same as iron. It's lighter; there are holes in between. (Interviewer: And steel?) *It stays under because there aren't any holes in between.*

Notice that both these children were quite good at predicting what would float and what would sink. But when confronted with the fact that some light objects sink, the first child offered an explanation that simply appealed to empirical knowledge ("iron *always* goes under"). This child was struggling toward an understanding that some things can be "heavy" and still feel relatively light. The second child had moved a step further by developing an implicit notion of an object's density (weight per unit of volume) but could not yet articulate the concept maturely.

More mature explanations come in adolescence. This older adolescent described the principle in very adultlike terms (Inhelder and Piaget, 1955/1958, p. 44):

Adolescent: (explaining why the key sinks despite the fact that it is relatively small and light) With the same volume the water is lighter than the key. (Interviewer: How would you prove that?) *I would take some modeling clay, then I would make an exact pattern of the key and I would put water inside it. It would have the same volume of water as the key . . . and it would be lighter.*

This example illustrates how the cognitive skills of adolescents are built upon those developed in middle childhood. Elementary school children have acquired the concepts of volume and weight, which is why they are able to solve conservation problems. An understanding of density is based on an understanding of the *ratio* of weight to volume. Understanding a ratio involves the ability to think about relationships among mentally constructed concepts (in this case the concept of weight and the concept of volume). During adolescence, youngsters become able to see how two or more mentally constructed concepts can be related to produce a third, even more abstract, concept. Thus, they grasp that the ratio of weight to volume yields the concept of density.

The Pendulum Study   The pendulum study measured ability to investigate the effects of a single variable while holding all other factors constant (Inhelder and Piaget, 1955/1958).

Figure 13.4
APPARATUS FOR PIAGET'S
PENDULUM PROBLEM
The pendulum problem uses a
simple apparatus consisting of a
string, which can be shortened or
lengthened, and a set of varying
weights. Other variables to be
considered are the height of the
release point and the force with
which the pendulum is pushed.
(*Source: Inhelder and Piaget,
1955/1958, p. 68.*)

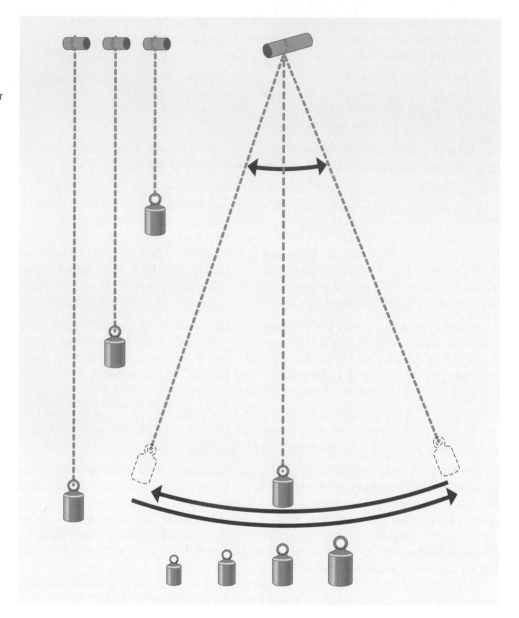

Here youngsters had to figure out which of four factors determines the period of a
pendulum—the time it takes to complete a swing from one side to the other and back.
As shown in Figure 13.4, the four factors were the length of the pendulum's string,
the weight of the pendulum, the height from which the pendulum is released, and the
force with which the pendulum is pushed.

The solution to this problem is contrary to most adults' intuitions: the length of the
string is the *only* factor that influences the period of the pendulum's swing. Because the
correct answer is unlikely to be guessed, the pendulum problem provides a good way to
demonstrate adolescents' skills in experimentation and logical deduction. Elementary
school children do not isolate each of the variables; therefore, they draw wrong conclusions. Adolescents systematically test each factor while holding the others constant, an
approach that enables them to discover the right answer.

The All Possible Combinations Study   In another of Piaget's experiments, children
and adolescents had to try all possible combinations of five colorless liquids to determine which combinations turned yellow (Inhelder and Piaget, 1955/1958). Four of the

liquids were in large flasks numbered 1 through 4. The fifth, labeled *g,* was in a smaller bottle with an eyedropper in it. The experimenter first showed the youngsters a flask containing an unidentified liquid (actually a combination of liquids 1 and 3). To this he added a few drops of *g,* and the liquid in the flask turned yellow. The participants were then asked to reproduce the yellow color in as many ways as possible using the five liquids.

Elementary school children typically took the small bottle and placed a few drops from it in flasks 1 through 4. When nothing happened, they usually realized liquids from more than one flask must first be mixed together, but their approach to finding the right combination was haphazard. If they stumbled on the 1 + 3 + *g* combination through trial and error, they generally stopped their search, not thinking some other combination might also produce yellow. (In fact, 1 + 3 + 2 + *g* produced yellow, too.)

In contrast, youngsters in midadolescence or older adopted a systematic approach and tried all possible combinations. After working through the two-liquid combinations (1 + *g,* 2 + *g,* etc.), they proceeded to the three-, four-, and five-liquid ones, trying to avoid repeats while not missing any. These older subjects readily discovered the two combinations that worked.

Is Piaget's View Correct?

Piaget's *description* of adolescent reasoning abilities has proven to be quite accurate. Other researchers have found similar age-related changes in performance on the tasks Piaget designed, as well as on other kinds of problem-solving tasks (Keating, 1980; Neimark, 1982). However, as was the case for infancy and childhood, there has been criticism of Piaget's *explanation* of adolescents' new cognitive skills. Researchers have not found strong evidence to support Piaget's idea that adolescents' advances in reasoning are based on mastery of specific principles of formal logic. Various other explanations for those changes have been proposed, but there is still no consensus about how they are best explained (Keating, 1990; Moshman, 1998).

We also lack consensus as to whether the ability to deal with propositional logic is entirely new to adolescents. Elementary school children have been found to be quite good at solving simple, concrete logical problems like the following: "If Jack washes the dishes, then his father will be very pleased. If Jack's father is very pleased, then Jack gets 50 cents. Jack washes the dishes. Does Jack get 50 cents?" (Brainerd, 1978). Such findings call into question Piaget's belief that the cognitive skills of adolescence are qualitatively different from anything possessed before.

How Pervasive Are Formal Operations? A major question about Piaget's theory is how pervasive formal operations are in the thinking of adolescents. Skill at using formal operations appears to develop gradually, rather than all at once. Some researchers have suggested that a distinction should be made between the levels of expertise in formal operations commonly demonstrated in early adolescence and in late adolescence (Kuhn et al., 1977). In early adolescence, the capacity for formal operational thought seems to be present, but not yet fully developed or consistently applied. Young teenagers often use formal reasoning on some tasks or in some situations, but not others—a type of thinking that has been characterized as *emergent formal operations.* By middle or late adolescence, some young people show evidence of mature, consistent use of formal reasoning in problem solving—in other words, of *consolidated formal operations.*

However, this use of formal reasoning does not appear to be universal. A number of studies have shown that many adolescents (and even many adults) do not normally use formal operations to solve problems. On tests of the ability to use formal operations, only about one-third of adolescents and adults pass (Capon and Kuhn, 1979; Keating, 1980). In one study, only 32 percent of 15-year-olds and 34 percent of 18-year-olds were even beginning to use formal operations, and only 13 and 19 percent, respectively, used them in mature ways (Epstein, 1979). Generally speaking, the higher the scholastic ability and performance of a teenager, the more likely he or she is to use this kind of thinking (Shayer, 1980).

Adolescents' increased skill with formal logic, as studied by Piaget, is particularly useful in scientific reasoning.

In addition, formal operations seem to be more culture-bound than the earlier cognitive abilities in Piaget's theory. They represent a form of reasoning that is most useful and most valued in cultures with an orientation toward science and technology. Across cultures, some secondary school education appears to be a prerequisite for the emergence of formal operations (Shea, 1985). Researchers using standard Piagetian tasks have found little evidence of formal operations in cultures that do not emphasize formal schooling, scientific thought, and technological sophistication (Dasen and Heron, 1981). However, characteristics of formal operational thought, such as hypothesis testing and logical inference, have been observed among people in nonindustrialized cultures when they are engaged in tasks that are meaningful to them, such as hunting by Kalahari Desert tribesmen (e.g., Tulkin and Konner, 1973).

Defenders of Piaget say that the lack of pervasiveness of formal operations reflects the distinction between competence and performance that we introduced in Chapter 9. Some psychologists argue that the gap between competence and performance captures a significant characteristic of adolescent thought; teenagers who possess the skills of formal operations may fail to use them for a number of reasons. They may not recognize that these abilities are appropriate to a particular situation. They may lack the specific knowledge needed to use higher-level reasoning (as in the case of a teenager who knows nothing about engines trying to repair a car by aimless fiddling). They may be inattentive to the demands of a situation, they may experience information overload, or they may be overwhelmed by emotional factors or the need to arrive at a quick solution. Piaget himself (1972) suggested that adults may use formal operational thought only when dealing with domains in which they have high interest and expertise. The cross-cultural findings raise the issue of competence versus performance in a different way. Although human beings as a species are capable of developing and using formal operations, it may not always be adaptive or necessary to do so. Formal operations, as Piaget measured them, are needed mainly for scientific and mathematical reasoning and are of little use in other contexts.

Can Formal Operations Be Taught? As we saw in Chapter 11, Piaget was not entirely correct in his belief that the cognitive skills of a given developmental period cannot be taught. Researchers have had some success teaching the concrete operation of conservation to very young elementary school children, particularly those in a transitional phase with regard to this skill. Efforts to teach formal operations have met with similar success, mostly with youngsters in late middle childhood and adolescents who do not show formal operational reasoning on a pretest (Beilin, 1980; Inhelder, Sinclair, and Bovet, 1974). Using the same training procedures with younger children often has no effect, unless they are of above-average intelligence (Case, 1974). High intelligence may be associated with early onset of formal operational skills.

Edith Neimark (1982) has argued that training in formal operations is sometimes effective because the procedures encourage existing competencies to be displayed, rather than teaching new skills. This view is consistent with the frequent finding that adolescents and adults fail to exhibit their highest level of reasoning because of limitations on performance rather than lack of skills. You can see this quite clearly in a study in which adults were presented with an experiment similar to the all possible combinations problem (Pitt, 1983). Even physical science professors performed badly when they were simply given the equipment and encouraged to find the solution. Both they and other participants performed much better when asked to plan a strategy before beginning to gather data. Thus, training studies of formal operations may tell us more about how to get people to perform at their peak ability than about the development of new competencies.

Are Formal Operations Related to Academic Performance? Another question psychologists have raised is whether formal operations are useful to academic performance. Since performance on formal operational tasks is related to measures of intelligence, and since measures of intelligence predict performance in school (as you know from Chapter 11), it is not surprising that tests of formal operations can be used to predict school success. However, assessments of formal operations provide different insights into cognitive skills than IQ tests do. For one thing, tests of formal operations predict performance in science and math better than they predict overall academic performance (Cooper and Robbins, 1981).

Researchers have found that explicit training in formal operations can improve students' grades in science classes. In one British study, a group of adolescents spent two years learning science from a curriculum that emphasized formal operational reasoning, beginning at age 12. At the end of the curriculum, they had better formal operational skills than a control group, but they scored no better on a science achievement test. Over time, however, their superior reasoning skills seemed to pay off, and they did earn better science achievement scores in subsequent years (Shayer and Adey, 1992, 1993).

Even simple exposure to formal operational tasks, without explicit instruction in the principles involved, may have a similar effect. In one study, 53 percent of the students in an introductory college astronomy class failed to use formal operations consistently on an initial test. Half of these students then completed a set of laboratory exercises that required the collection and evaluation of data but included no explicit instruction in formal operational skills. The other half received only supplemental audiovisual material. The students who completed the laboratory exercises not only showed greater improvement on a posttest of formal operations, but also received higher average grades in the course (Cooper and Robbins, 1981).

Other Approaches to Adolescent Cognition

As we mentioned earlier, Piaget's theory is not the only explanation for the widely observed changes in adolescent cognitive abilities. Other accounts have centered on adolescents' information-processing abilities and on the influence of cognitive socialization.

Information-Processing Explanations Research on adolescents' information-processing abilities consistently indicates continuing improvement in attention and memory skills. Typically, major advances are seen between middle childhood and early adolescence (roughly between ages 8 and 12), with smaller further advances between early and late adolescence (Keating, 1990).

Compared with younger children, adolescents are better at both **selective attention** (focusing attention on relevant information despite distractions) and **divided attention** (paying attention to two tasks at the same time) (Higgins and Turnure, 1984; Schiff and

Selective attention:
Focusing attention on relevant information despite distractions.

Divided attention:
Paying attention to two tasks at the same time.

Knopf, 1985). Some research suggests that attentional skills continue to improve through late adolescence; in one study 12-year-olds did markedly better than 8-year-olds on a divided-attention task, and 20-year-olds outperformed the 12-year-olds (Manis, Keating, and Morrison, 1980).

Both short- and long-term memory also improve from middle childhood to adolescence. Short-term memory can be measured by the ability to recite back a string of digits read by an experimenter. As mentioned in Chapter 11, performance on this task improves slightly between age 9 and adulthood; 9-year-olds can typically recall a string of six digits, while adults can typically recall seven (Dempster, 1981). Adolescents' short-term memory skills also appear to give them an advantage over younger children on some problem-solving tasks, such as analogies (e.g., "Sun is to day as _____ is to night."). Studies by Robert Sternberg and his colleagues focused on the processes used by third graders, sixth graders, ninth graders, and college students to solve analogy problems. The third and sixth graders did worse than the ninth graders and college students, apparently because they had trouble keeping in mind all the information needed to solve the problem (Sternberg and Nigro, 1980). In the area of long-term memory, adolescents are better than younger children at intentionally memorizing material and recalling it later in situations such as school tests (Flavell et al., 2002; Schneider and Bjorklund, 1998).

One question about adolescent memory improvements is to what extent they are due to increases in memory capacity and to what extent they are due to improvements in memory processes. Increased efficiency of brain functioning in early adolescence may result in a modest increase in capacity, but most researchers agree that improved memory processes play a larger role in adolescent memory advances (Kail and Bisanz, 1992). Development of metamemory and increased sophistication in using mnemonic strategies account for much of the improvement in memory processes. Adolescents are better than younger children at recognizing when they need to use a mnemonic strategy, at selecting an appropriate strategy, and at actually deploying it. Adolescents spontaneously use complex memory strategies, such as elaboration, that are seldom seen in middle childhood. They are more planful in their use of memory strategies and more flexible at changing strategies when appropriate (Plumert, 1994). They are also better at using external memory aids and outside sources of information to solve problems—for example, taking notes, writing themselves reminders, and remembering where to find information they need for solving a particular problem (Flavell et al., 2002; Schneider and Bjorklund, 1998).

mhhe.com
/dehart5

Memory Strategies

Adolescents are far better than younger children at intentional memory tasks, such as learning lines for a play.

However, adolescents still show some metamemory limitations. Although they use memory strategies readily, they do not always recognize which strategy is most appropriate to use on a particular memory task or in a particular situation (Schneider and Pressley, 1997). For example, high school and college students often construct complicated mnemonic devices for remembering material for an exam (such as figuring out a word that can be formed from the first letters of the major cognitive advances of adolescence), rather than using a conceptually based method that would actually result in better long-term memory for the material.

Another factor in adolescent advances in both memory and attentional processes may be an increase in available cognitive processing capacity, as proposed by Robbie Case (1985). Case attributed this increased capacity partly to **automatization** of basic cognitive processes. As adolescents become increasingly practiced at attentional and memory tasks, these processes become less effortful and more automatic. As basic cognitive processes become more automatic, adolescents have more cognitive resources available to devote to more complex cognitive tasks. A good example of automatization is learning to drive. When you first started driving, chances are you devoted most of your attention to making sure each task involved in driving was done accurately and in sequence. Coordinating gas pedal, clutch, and brake, steering, checking the rearview mirror, watching oncoming traffic, and keeping track of where you were trying to go may at times have resulted in an information overload. As you gained experience and confidence as a driver, however, these tasks became increasingly automatic, until they seemed like second nature. Today you probably use the processing capacity freed up by this automatization for such additional activities as conversing with passengers, singing along with the radio, juggling fast-food containers, and thinking about what you need to do when you get to your destination.

Automatization:
The tendency for basic cognitive processes to become less effortful and more automatic with practice.

Another factor that may help explain adolescents' increased cognitive sophistication is their expanding knowledge base. Compared with younger children, adolescents have a larger store of general knowledge and a greater likelihood of extensive specialized knowledge in particular areas. As we discussed in Chapter 11, extensive knowledge in a specific domain leads to improved performance on memory tasks in that domain, even for children (Chi, 1978). During early and middle adolescence, specialized abilities and skills become increasingly prominent (Keating, 1990). The result is that teenagers' apparent level of cognitive sophistication is likely to vary, depending on what content area is being tested.

However, adolescents' knowledge base does not always have a positive impact on their cognitive functioning and education. Especially in technical and scientific areas, adolescents often have strong misconceptions that are amazingly resistant to correction (Carey, 1986; diSessa, 1988). Within specific domains, such as physics, their knowledge is often fragmented and not part of a coherent theory.

Cognitive Socialization **Cognitive socialization** refers to the influence of social environment on the development of cognitive skills. Social environment includes not only influences in the immediate environment, such as interactions with friends, family, and teachers, but also influences from the larger social, economic, and cultural contexts. Recent thinking and research in this area have been heavily influenced by the ideas of Vygotsky, as we discussed in earlier chapters. Compared with the Piagetian and information-processing approaches, relatively little research has been done on the impact of cognitive socialization on adolescents' thinking. However, there is evidence that social factors do play an important role, and the practical implications of cognitive socialization are considerable (Keating, 1990).

Cognitive socialization:
The influence of social environment on the development of cognitive skills.

To begin with, individual social interaction plays a key role in the cognitive advances of adolescence. Adolescents do not simply invent principles of logical reasoning and effective approaches to problem solving on their own. Instead, especially during early adolescence, discussion with others, individually or in small groups, seems to foster the emergence of higher-order thinking skills (Newmann, 1991; Rogoff, 1998). Some of this

Child Development CD
Piaget vs. Vygotsky

improvement occurs through direct instruction, as when a parent or teacher suggests a strategy for memorizing material for a test. But the reason for much of the impact of social interaction is that it provides a setting for trying out ideas, responding to opposing points of view, and learning to evaluate the soundness of arguments and evidence.

At the broader social level, schools play the most obvious role in adolescents' cognitive socialization. Much of the research into the impact of schooling on adolescent thinking has emphasized achievement-test results. This research has prompted much concern about test score declines in the United States and deficits in American teenagers' performance compared with that of adolescents in other industrialized countries (Keating, 1990; Stevenson, 1995). Unfortunately, the emphasis on improving achievement-test scores may have contributed to educational practices that work against the development of higher-order cognitive skills. For example, one of the best ways to foster critical thinking and mastery of subject matter is to provide extensive opportunities for substantive student-teacher discourse. However, in typical secondary school classrooms, less than 10 percent of instructional time is devoted to such discourse (Goodlad, 1984). (For a discussion of how schools can encourage the development of critical thinking, see the box below.)

A variety of other cultural factors are also involved in adolescents' cognitive socialization. Some researchers have argued that television has an impact on cognitive functioning, by means of both its content and the format in which it presents information (Keating, 1990). Many commercials, for example, present large amounts of information,

Critical Thinking

APPLYING RESEARCH FINDINGS

Fostering Critical Thinking

Researchers and educators alike have expressed concern about American adolescents' critical thinking skills in a variety of areas, including science, math, and social studies (Linn, Songer, and Eylon, 1996; Newmann, 1991; Resnick, 1986). In theory, adolescent cognitive advances should lead to increased critical thinking, but it is clear this does not always happen.

Critical thinking involves three key elements: (1) understanding a problem in more than a superficial way; (2) logically analyzing the problem and its possible solutions; and (3) selecting an appropriate solution. Adolescents' cognitive *competence*—their enhanced knowledge base, memory abilities, and logical thinking skills—should allow them to do these things. However, as with formal operations, their *performance* often does not reach expected levels.

Many attempts have been made to teach critical thinking to adolescents. The focus has been on specific skills, such as solving logic problems or using memory strategies. Unfortunately, evaluation of these programs has usually involved testing students' ability to solve the same kinds of problems on which they were trained. There is little evidence that these skills generalize to other kinds of problems, to other content areas, or to nonclassroom settings (Keating, 1990).

Daniel Keating, a psychologist who studies adolescent thinking and its connection to education, argues that critical thinking should be seen as a *disposition*—a general approach to problem solving—rather than a set of specific skills. Looked at in this way, the task of teaching critical thinking is to encourage students to adopt a new way of looking at the world. According to Keating, this

process begins long before adolescence; basic reading and math skills and knowledge in core subject areas provide a foundation on which critical thinking can be built.

Keating suggests that success in encouraging critical thinking in adolescents depends on four factors. First, the *process* of critical thinking should be embedded in the teaching of *content*, or expertise in particular domains. Critical thinking is an abstract ability, but it must be taught in concrete contexts. Trying to teach critical thinking skills as a separate subject is ineffective and does not help students see critical thinking as a general disposition. Teaching content knowledge without reference to critical thinking fosters a tendency to accept information uncritically.

Second, adolescents must be convinced of the value of critical thinking. Teachers and parents need to show adolescents practical applications for critical thinking, talk explicitly about its value, and model its use in their own problem solving.

Third, adolescents need opportunities to practice critical thinking. One of the best settings for practice is extended discussions with others who can challenge their reasoning and push them to provide clarification and evidence. Teachers and parents can serve this function better than peers, but many adolescents have limited opportunity for this kind of discussion with adults.

Fourth, adolescents need to be encouraged to explore subjects in depth over time. This sort of exploration fosters critical thinking by expanding students' knowledge bases and providing opportunities to practice critical thinking. Unfortunately, the typical American high school curriculum is too fragmented to allow for this sort of extended study.

much of it irrelevant, in a short period of time; the effect is to discourage critical thinking and reasoned decision making. The frequent shifts of topic and the rapid pace at which information is presented on television encourage a style of information processing that is in many ways the opposite of what schools typically seek to develop in their students. Experience with other media, such as computers and video games, may also have an impact on adolescents' thinking processes and, perhaps more important, on which cognitive skills they perceive to be most useful. A genuine understanding of adolescents' day-to-day cognitive skills depends in part on further study of these issues.

SOCIAL COGNITIVE CHANGES OF ADOLESCENCE

The new cognitive skills of adolescence do much more than simply allow teenagers to think more systematically and with more mature logic when solving problems in math and science. These same skills also have an impact on adolescents' reasoning in the social domain. For instance, their effects can be seen in a new kind of egocentrism that develops during adolescence and in the new ways that adolescents are able to reason about moral issues.

Adolescent Egocentrism

Egocentrism involves failure to distinguish one's own point of view from a more objective conception of reality. As you saw in Chapter 9, 4-year-olds have trouble understanding others' perspectives and assume that others' thoughts and desires are the same as their own. The cognitive development of middle childhood frees youngsters from this early egocentrism. However, new cognitive abilities of adolescence, including the ability to think about thinking and to consider abstract possibilities, give rise to a new form of egocentrism. **Adolescent egocentrism** involves teenagers' assumption that they are the focus of everyone's attention and that their experiences, thoughts, and feelings are unique. Mike's behavior as he gets ready for the party in our example at the beginning of the chapter illustrates this type of egocentrism.

In describing adolescent egocentrism, David Elkind (1967) stresses the concept of an **imaginary audience.** By this he means teenagers' unjustified concern that they are the focus of others' attention. Because adolescents can think about other people's thoughts, they can consider what others might be thinking of *them.* You saw an example of such self-consciousness in Meryl's certainty that the whole world was staring at her long arms. Notice how Meryl's cognitive ability interacted with her awareness of the physical changes of puberty. These physical changes are a major source of concern for adolescents and are one reason they turn their thoughts to others' opinions of them. This kind of egocentrism may help explain adolescents' desire for privacy; teens who believe others are viewing them negatively want privacy to escape their imaginary audiences. Oddly enough, the imaginary audience also helps explain why adolescents are sometimes loud and boorish, thus drawing real attention to themselves. If they think others are already observing them critically, behaving badly should not make any difference.

Another aspect of adolescent egocentrism described by Elkind is the **personal fable**—teenagers' belief that they are unique and no one has ever before had the same thoughts or feelings they are having. Elkind (1978) gives the example of the adolescent girl who says to her mother, "You just don't know how it feels to be in love!" The girl is convinced her emotions are beyond the capacity of anyone else (especially adults) to understand. The personal fable can also include feelings of invulnerability to risks and physical dangers. Teenagers' belief in their own uniqueness often extends to a sense that bad things will not happen to them. For example, they may discount the likelihood that they will have an accident if they drive too fast or that they will get pregnant or catch a sexually transmitted disease if they engage in unprotected sex.

One reason adolescents develop this egocentric viewpoint is that their new cognitive skills allow them to think about concepts with which they have little actual experience,

Adolescent egocentrism:
Teenagers' assumption that they are the focus of everyone's attention and that their experiences, thoughts, and feelings are unique.

Imaginary audience:
Teenagers' unjustified concern that they are the focus of others' attention.

Personal fable:
Teenagers' exaggerated belief in their own uniqueness.

The physical changes of puberty, combined with adolescents' newfound ability to imagine what others are thinking, often lead to a preoccupation with physical appearance.

Moral realism:
In Piaget's theory, the stage in which children treat morality as absolute and moral constraints as unalterable.

Autonomous morality:
In Piaget's theory, the stage in which children see morality as relative to the situation.

Moral Development

such as sex and romantic love. However, because many of these issues are quite personal, they seldom discuss them with adults. Lacking a broad perspective for viewing their new thoughts and feelings, they come to the conclusion that these thoughts and feelings are unique to them. Eventually, communication with close friends helps dispel personal fables. By midadolescence, when youngsters have a better understanding that many of their thoughts and feelings are shared by others, they begin to lose the sense of being different from everyone else.

Other factors besides reasoning skills may be associated with the emergence of adolescent egocentrism. Various researchers have found egocentrism in high school and college students to be associated more clearly with interpersonal understanding or with the process of forming a personal identity than with formal operational reasoning (Jahnke and Blanchard-Fields, 1993; O'Connor and Nikolic, 1990). Perhaps the self-concerns and social demands associated with identity development heighten adolescents' sense of being at center stage and of being unique. (We will discuss issues of identity development further in Chapter 14.)

Moral Reasoning

Another area in the social domain affected by the cognitive advances of adolescence is *moral reasoning*—the process of thinking and making judgments about the morally right course of action in a given situation. Piaget (1932/1965) included the development of moral reasoning within his broad theory of cognitive development. Later, Lawrence Kohlberg (1969) expanded on Piaget's approach, producing a six-stage model of the development of moral reasoning.

Piaget's Model Piaget's model begins with an amoral stage, which is characteristic of children until about age 7. During the concrete operations period, the stage of **moral realism** emerges. Children at this stage treat morality as absolute and moral constraints as unalterable. They see behavior as either totally right or totally wrong, and they believe in *immanent justice,* a kind of inherent retribution. If they break a moral precept, they think God or some other moral authority will make bad things happen to them. When asked to judge whether an action is right or wrong, they base their answer on the consequences of the action and tend to ignore the intentions of the actor.

Piaget's next stage, **autonomous morality,** is usually attained in late childhood or early adolescence. Now children see morality as relative to the situation. In judging whether a particular action is right or wrong, they consider intentions as well as consequences. Youngsters at this stage recognize the possibility of diverse opinions on moral standards and no longer see moral rules as absolute. Instead, they consider them the result of social agreement and subject to change.

Piaget believed moral development is a direct consequence of cognitive development and increased social experience. For instance, as centration declines, children become able to consider consequences and intentions simultaneously when judging the morality of an act. In adolescence, the ability to consider one's own and others' opinions systematically makes possible recognition of different moral viewpoints and the idea that moral rules are based on social agreement.

Kohlberg's Model Kohlberg's model of moral development is broadly similar to Piaget's, although Kohlberg divided development into more stages. Kohlberg derived his stages by presenting individuals of different ages with moral dilemmas to solve. Table 13.2 gives an example of one of these dilemmas, along with examples of responses

Table 13.2 Kohlberg's Heinz Dilemma and Representative Responses

Dilemma:

In Europe, a woman was near death from a special kind of cancer. There was one drug that the doctors thought might save her. It was a form of radium that a druggist in the same town had recently discovered. The drug was expensive to make, but the druggist was charging ten times what the drug cost him to make. He paid $200 for the radium and charged $2,000 for a small dose of the drug. The sick woman's husband, Heinz, went to everyone he knew to borrow the money, but he could only get together about $1,000, which is half what it cost. He told the druggist that his wife was dying and asked him to sell it cheaper or let him pay later. But the druggist said: "No, I discovered the drug and I'm going to make money from it." So Heinz got desperate and broke into the man's store to steal the drug for his wife. Should the husband have done that?

Preconventional Morality

Stage 1—Obedience and Punishment Orientation
Pro— "If you let your wife die, you'll get in trouble. You'll be blamed for not spending the money to save her and there'll be an investigation of you and the druggist for your wife's death."
Con—"You shouldn't steal the drug because you'll be caught and sent to jail if you do. If you do get away, your conscience would bother you thinking how the police would catch up with you at any minute."

Stage 2—Hedonistic and Instrumental Orientation
Pro— "If you do happen to get caught, you could give the drug back and you wouldn't get much of a sentence. It wouldn't bother you much to serve a little jail term, if you have your wife when you get out."
Con—"He may not get much of a jail term if he steals the drug, but his wife will probably die before he gets out, so it won't do him much good. If his wife dies, he shouldn't blame himself; it wasn't his fault she has cancer."

Conventional Morality

Stage 3—Good-Boy, Nice-Girl Orientation
Pro— "No one will think you're bad if you steal the drug, but your family will think you're an inhuman husband if you don't. If you let your wife die, you'll never be able to look anybody in the face again."
Con—"It isn't just the druggist who will think you're a criminal; everyone else will too. After you steal it, you'll feel bad thinking how you've brought dishonor on your family and yourself; you won't be able to face anyone again."

Stage 4—Authority or Law-and-Order Orientation
Pro— "If you have any sense of honor, you won't let your wife die because you're afraid to do the only thing that will save her. You'll always feel guilty that you caused her death if you don't do your duty to her."
Con—"You're desperate and you may not know you're doing wrong when you steal the drug. But you'll know you did wrong after you're punished and sent to jail. You'll always feel guilt for your dishonesty and lawbreaking."

Postconventional or Principled Morality

Stage 5—Social Contract Orientation
Pro— "You'd lose other people's respect, not gain it, if you don't steal. If you let your wife die, it would be out of fear, not out of reasoning it out. So you'd just lose self-respect and probably the respect of others too."
Con—"You would lose your standing and respect in the community and violate the law. You'd lose respect for yourself if you're carried away by emotion and forget the long-range point of view."

Stage 6—Hierarchy of Principles Orientation
Pro— "If you don't steal the drug and let your wife die, you'd always condemn yourself for it afterward. You wouldn't be blamed and you would have lived up to the outside rule of the law, but you wouldn't have lived up to your own standards of conscience."
Con—"If you stole the drug, you wouldn't be blamed by other people but you'd condemn yourself because you wouldn't have lived up to your own conscience and standards of honesty."

Sources: Kohlberg, 1969, p. 379; Rest, 1979.

According to Kohlberg, during adolescence most people begin to relate moral judgments to the laws of society and concerns about harm to others.

Preconventional morality:
In Kohlberg's theory, moral reasoning based on fear of punishment or desire for reward.

Conventional morality:
In Kohlberg's theory, moral reasoning based on opinions of others or formal laws.

Postconventional or principled morality:
In Kohlberg's theory, moral reasoning based on abstract principles underlying right and wrong.

typical of each of Kohlberg's six stages. Responses are assigned to stages on the basis of the reasons given for the choice that is made, not on the basis of the choice itself. At each stage, both "pro" and "con" choices are possible.

Kohlberg's first two stages constitute the period of **preconventional morality**—a period when moral judgments are not based on social conventions, rules, or laws. During stage 1, good behavior is based on desire to avoid punishment from external authority. Kohlberg called this the *obedience and punishment orientation.* In stage 2, good is whatever satisfies one's own needs, even indirectly, as in helping others so they will help you. Actions are motivated by a desire for reward or benefit. Kohlberg called this the *hedonistic and instrumental orientation,* meaning an orientation toward obtaining pleasure and getting what one wants.

In the next two stages, the period of **conventional morality,** moral judgments are based on internalized standards arising from concrete experience in the social world. Kohlberg called this reasoning conventional because it focuses either on opinions of others or on formal laws. In stage 3, the goal is to act in ways others will approve of. Actions are motivated more by a fear of disapproval than by a fear of punishment. This motivation is called the *good-boy, nice-girl orientation.* In stage 4, the basis of moral judgments shifts to doing one's duty as prescribed by society's laws. Concerns about possible dishonor or concrete harm to others replace concerns about others' disapproval. Kohlberg called this the *authority or law-and-order orientation.*

The last major period in Kohlberg's model is called **postconventional** or **principled morality.** In this period, people transcend conventional reasoning and focus on more abstract principles underlying right and wrong. In the first stage of this period, stage 5, the goal is to meet one's obligation to help keep society running smoothly. Particular laws may be seen as somewhat arbitrary, but they are nevertheless deemed important because they allow people to live together in reasonable harmony. At this stage, actions are motivated by a desire to maintain self-respect and the respect of peers. Kohlberg called this the *social contract orientation.* In the sixth and final stage of moral reasoning, the goal is to make decisions on the basis of the highest relevant moral principles. At this level of thinking, rules of society are integrated with dictates of conscience to produce a hierarchy of moral principles. Concern shifts to avoiding self-condemnation for violating one's own principles. Kohlberg called this stage the *hierarchy of principles orientation.*

How are Kohlberg's stages of moral reasoning related to Piaget's stages of cognitive development? You might guess that children at the preoperational level (ages 2 to 6) would be in the period of preconventional morality, that youngsters at the level of concrete operations (ages 7 to 12) would be in the period of conventional morality, and that adolescents at the level of formal operations (over age 12) would be in the period of postconventional morality. These are very reasonable guesses, but they turn out to be wrong. The emergence of each of Kohlberg's levels of moral reasoning seems to lag behind the cognitive skills needed for that kind of thinking. Kohlberg (1976) concluded that preconventional morality (stages 1 and 2) is characteristic of most children until about age 9, and that most adolescents and adults are at the conventional morality level (stages 3 and 4). One long-term longitudinal study found that stage 3 moral reasoning (concern about other people's disapproval) peaks in midadolescence and then declines, whereas stage 4 moral reasoning (concern about doing one's duty) increases dramatically in later adolescence and young adulthood (Colby et al., 1983). Very few people reach the postconventional level of moral reasoning.

Child Development CD
Adolescent Moral Development

Criticisms of Kohlberg's Model The most common objection to both Piaget's and Kohlberg's models of moral development is that measures of moral reasoning are often related only weakly or not at all to actual moral behavior (Rest, 1983). Thus, adolescents may talk about doing their duty and following established rules, but when it comes to a real-life situation, they may ignore these rules.

Others have objected to the idea that the form of moral reasoning can be separated from the content of moral judgments (see Rest, 1983). What matters in Kohlberg's model is not the particular solution a person offers in response to a moral dilemma, but the reasoning behind the solution. Critics question whether the content of a moral choice can be ignored in assessing a person's level of moral thinking.

Kohlberg's theory of moral reasoning has also been criticized for the method used to gather the data on which it is based. Questions have been raised about the method's reliability (Kurtines and Greif, 1974). Will a child evaluated one day by a particular researcher be assessed at the same moral level a few days later when scored by someone else? This problem has been exacerbated by frequent revisions in Kohlberg's scoring system as well as in the theoretical framework used to support it (Rest, 1983). Some think that a different approach to assessment may be preferable. For instance, James Rest (1983; Rest et al., 1999) developed an objectively scored test of moral reasoning that overcomes many of the limitations inherent in Kohlberg's method.

One of the most controversial challenges to Kohlberg's approach is the contention that it is biased against women. Carol Gilligan (1982) argues that women tend to respond to moral dilemmas on the basis of concepts such as caring, personal relationships, and interpersonal obligations, which are likely to be scored at the stage 3 level. Men, in contrast, tend to appeal to abstract concepts, such as justice and equity, which are likely to be scored at stage 5 or 6. These general patterns are believed to result from the ways males and females are socialized in our culture. In response to Gilligan's criticism, the most recent version of Kohlberg's scoring system was revised to reduce bias against responses based on caring for others (Colby et al., 1983).

Connections between gender and moral reasoning seem to be more complex than Gilligan's analysis suggests. One review of research found no consistent gender differences in the stages at which people were scored on Kohlberg's dilemmas (Walker, 1984). In fact, when sex differences are found, women actually tend to score higher than men (Thoma, 1986; Wark and Krebs, 1996). It is also clear that both males and females consider issues related to *both* caring and justice in their moral reasoning; which orientation they use depends to some extent on the situation and the type of dilemma they are asked to resolve (Galotti, 1989; Walker, 1989; Wark and Krebs, 1996). Some researchers have found that women often give *priority* to care-based issues and men give priority to justice-based issues. In a study in which college students were asked to talk about real-life moral dilemmas they had faced, women more often reported dilemmas involving issues of care, while men more often reported dilemmas involving issues of justice (Wark and Krebs, 1996). In any case, Gilligan's questions have highlighted a formerly neglected aspect of moral reasoning and broadened the issues considered in moral development research.

A final criticism of Kohlberg's theory is that it is culture-specific, reflecting concerns about individualism peculiar to middle-class groups in complex, urban societies (Snarey, 1985). Members of more traditional cultures tend to be scored at lower stages on Kohlberg's dilemmas, even though their responses reflect the moral concerns of their own cultures (Edwards, 1982). For example, many traditional cultures are more *collectivist* than North American and western European cultures. That is, the well-being of the group is assumed to be of greater importance than the well-being of any one individual. In collectivist cultures, meeting one's obligations to family and community and submitting to the authority of elders are often considered the highest moral principles. In Kohlberg's system, however, reasoning along those lines tends to be scored at stage 3 or 4. These findings, along with Gilligan's criticisms, emphasize the need to consider socialization history and cultural context in evaluating the development of moral reasoning.

AN OVERVIEW OF ADOLESCENT PHYSICAL AND COGNITIVE DEVELOPMENT

The physical changes that occur during adolescence are a good example of *qualitative* change; puberty produces a *transformation* in a young person's physical appearance and a *reorganization* of his or her functioning. In turn, these physical changes have far-reaching implications for other areas of an adolescent's life. As we have seen in this chapter, physical and cognitive development are closely interrelated during adolescence. Neurological development appears to contribute to the emergence of increasingly efficient and abstract thought. This higher-order thinking makes adolescents self-reflective, painfully aware of the many changes occurring in their bodies, and at times preoccupied with how they appear to others. As was the case throughout childhood, cognitive development is also inextricably connected with social development. Our examination of adolescent social cognition has provided some insight into the connections between cognitive and social development in adolescence. We will explore this connection further in Chapter 14.

By the end of adolescence, cognitive abilities have also undergone substantial changes that can be considered qualitative in nature, though they build on and expand many abilities already present in middle childhood. The major cognitive advances of adolescence include:

- logical thinking is now applied to the possible, not just to the real;
- the ability to think about relationships among mentally constructed concepts emerges, producing major advances in attentional and memory skills; and
- adolescents' thinking becomes even more logical and systematic than it was in childhood.

Even with these advances, certain cognitive limitations remain. Many of these limitations involve the inconsistent application of recently acquired cognitive abilities. Not all adolescents show evidence of logical, systematic, abstract thinking abilities. Even adolescents who *do* have such abilities do not always apply them in situations in which they would be appropriate. Although adolescents have command of a wider range of memory strategies than younger children do, they do not always apply them effectively. Finally, adolescents' knowledge base is continuing to expand, but it is still not as broad as it will be in adulthood, which can contribute to errors of reasoning.

Chapter Summary

Introduction

Adolescence, the period from roughly age 12 through the late teens, is characterized by an especially close connection between physical and psychological development and between cognitive and social development.

Adolescence can be divided into three substages, each with its own challenges and opportunities:

- early adolescence (ages 12–14),
- middle adolescence (ages 15–17), and
- late adolescence (age 18–early 20s).

Biological Changes During Adolescence

There is considerable individual and group variation in the timing of **puberty.**

- Puberty usually begins about two years earlier in girls than in boys.
- For each sex, the timing of puberty is influenced by heredity, nutrition, stress, and exercise.
- The average age at which puberty occurs has been decreasing for at least the last 100 years, probably due to improvements in health and nutrition.
- Girls tend to reach puberty sooner in industrialized countries than in developing countries.

Puberty is the final stage in a process of sexual development that begins before birth.

- A complex feedback system regulates levels of sex hormones in the body, keeping them low through most of middle childhood.
- At the end of middle childhood the brain directs the **adrenal glands** and the **gonads** to step up production of sex hormones, which produces the physical changes of puberty.

The physical changes of puberty include:

- the development of **secondary sex characteristics,**
- changes in skin and sweat glands, and
- a noticeable spurt in growth.

Mounting evidence indicates that the brain changes substantially during adolescence, resulting in:

- decreased **plasticity** and
- increased efficiency in brain functioning.

These changes in the brain include:

- completion of **hemispheric specialization;**
- a decrease in the number of synapses in the cerebral cortex; and
- completion of myelination in many areas of the cerebral cortex.

The physical changes of puberty have both direct and indirect impacts on other areas of adolescents' lives, including body image, social relationships, and problem behaviors. The impact of these changes differs for boys and girls and for early- and late-maturing adolescents.

Changes in Thinking During Adolescence

Several important cognitive advances occur in adolescence.

- Logical thinking is now applied to the possible, as well as to the real.
- The ability to think about relationships among mentally constructed concepts emerges.
- Adolescents' thinking becomes even more logical and systematic than it was in childhood.

Piaget attributed the cognitive advances of adolescents to their developing ability to use principles of propositional logic, or **formal operations.** He based his theory on studies of adolescents' reasoning as they conducted various science experiments.

Piaget's description of adolescent reasoning abilities has proven to be quite accurate, but his explanation of their new skills has been criticized.

- Formal operational thinking develops more gradually and is less pervasive among older adolescents than Piaget thought.
- Formal operations are more culture-bound than the earlier stages of Piaget's theory.
- Contrary to Piaget's expectations, training in formal operations is effective under some circumstances, perhaps because it encourages the display of already existing competencies rather than teaching entirely new skills.

Research on adolescents' information-processing abilities indicates continuing improvement in attention and memory skills, due to:

- increased capacity,
- improved cognitive strategies,
- **automatization** of basic mental processes, and
- expanded knowledge base.

The cognitive socialization approach emphasizes the influence of social environment on cognitive development.

- Individual social interaction plays a role in the emergence of higher-order thinking skills.
- Schools provide a major setting for cognitive socialization.
- Television and other cultural influences also have an impact on adolescents' thinking processes and on which cognitive skills they value.

Social Cognitive Changes of Adolescence

The ability to think about thinking and to consider abstract possibilities give rise to **adolescent egocentrism,** involving both the **imaginary audience** and the **personal fable.**

Adolescent cognitive advances also lead to increased maturity in reasoning about moral issues.

- Piaget believed that children progressed from **moral realism** to **autonomous morality** by adolescence.
- Kohlberg's theory of moral reasoning consists of three broad levels: **preconventional morality, conventional morality,** and **postconventional** or **principled morality.** Most adolescents have reached the stage of conventional morality.
- Stage theories of moral reasoning have been criticized because of the weak connection between moral thought and moral action, the methods used to assess moral reasoning, and possible gender and cultural biases.

An Overview of Adolescent Physical and Cognitive Development

The physical changes of adolescence are a good example of *qualitative* change; in turn they have far-reaching implications for other areas of an adolescent's life.

Even with the cognitive advances of adolescence, certain cognitive limitations remain, mostly involving inconsistent application of recently acquired cognitive abilities:

- Not all adolescents show evidence of logical, systematic, abstract thinking abilities.
- Adolescents who *do* have such abilities do not always apply them when they would be appropriate.
- Although adolescents have a wider range of memory strategies than younger children do, they do not always apply them effectively.
- Adolescents' knowledge base is continuing to expand, but it is still not as broad as it will be in adulthood.

Review Questions

Introduction

1. When did adolescence first come to be regarded as a distinct period of development and how has it changed since then?

Biological Changes During Adolescence

2. What factors influence the timing of **puberty?**
3. Explain the operation of the hormonal systems that control pubertal change.
4. Summarize the changes in appearance associated with puberty.
5. What neurological changes are associated with puberty?
6. Summarize the impacts of pubertal change on body image, social relationships, and problem behaviors for both early- and late-maturing boys and girls.

Changes in Thinking During Adolescence

7. What are the major cognitive advances of adolescence?

8. How did Piaget explain adolescent cognitive development?
9. What improvements in information-processing abilities occur during adolescence?
10. What impact does the social environment have on cognitive development in adolescence?

Social Cognitive Changes of Adolescence

11. How do the cognitive advances of adolescents affect their reasoning in the social domain?
12. What does research on adolescents' moral reasoning reveal?

An Overview of Adolescent Physical and Cognitive Development

13. What cognitive limitations remain at the end of adolescence?

Application and Observation

1. Try Piaget's pendulum task with children and adolescents from middle school age up (and possibly with adults too). Give the people doing the task a length of string and several metal washers of various sizes and tell them that their task is to experiment with these materials and determine which of the four factors listed on p. 470 determines the time it takes for a pendulum to complete a swing. After they've had a chance to experiment, have them tell you what they've discovered and ask them to explain their reasoning.

2. Interview several high school students, parents, and teachers about the issue of adolescent sleep needs and school start times. Find out if your local school district has modified or considered modifying start times to take the issue of students' sleep needs into account. What issues are involved in making such a decision? What factors might weigh against making secondary school start times later?

3. Give Kohlberg's Heinz dilemma to children, adolescents, and adults of various ages and both genders. What similarities and differences do you find across groups? How do people react to the task and its particular constraints?

4. Watch several TV shows or movies that are centered on adolescent characters and look for evidence of the adolescent reasoning patterns and issues related to pubertal development described in this chapter.

14 Social and Emotional Development in Adolescence

I just have all these feelings and things inside. . . . The feelings are so strong, and my parents don't understand. They won't let me do anything. I'm afraid that by the time I'm old enough to do the things I need to do—by the time they'll let me—I won't have the feelings anymore.

These words, spoken by a 15-year-old girl during an interview with one of the authors of this book in the 1960s, illustrate how timeless the social and emotional issues of adolescence are. Adolescence is a wonderful time, filled with new feelings, increased self-awareness, and a sense of unlimited horizons to explore. But it is also a very challenging time. Early in adolescence the emerging sense of self is not yet firmly established and at times may seem so changeable that a young person may wonder who he or she really is. The preceding statement reflects these challenges. This teenager worries her strong feelings will disappear before she has a chance to act on them. Her parents remain important in her life, but she feels they cannot understand her situation and she cannot really share all her new thoughts and emotions with them. She also expresses frustration with the boundaries her parents continue to set for her as she moves toward greater independence.

To a large extent, this young woman is in the midst of reworking many issues she faced in earlier developmental periods. Issues of trust, autonomy, competence, and a sense of self are all confronting her again. This time the issues are more challenging, for she has to work through them not only with her parents but also with peers who are in the throes of adolescence with her. However, she has cognitive and emotional resources to draw on that were not available to her when she encountered the same issues earlier in childhood.

In reworking these issues, adolescents face four important developmental tasks. One major task is *establishing a personal **identity**—*a sense of an integrated, coherent, goal-directed self. Identity development is a complex process, involving an understanding of the self, of one's relationships with others, and of one's values and roles in society. Erikson (1981) believed establishing a personal identity was the central task of adolescence.

A second major task of adolescence is *achieving a new level of closeness and trust with peers.* This task also includes integration into the more complex, mixed-gender peer network of this period (Hartup and Stevens, 1999; Sroufe, Egeland, and Carlson, 1999).

A third major task is *acquiring a new status in the family.* In white, middle-class families, relationships with parents generally become more equal as the child grows more

Identity:
A sense of an integrated, coherent, and goal-directed self.

Changes in family roles at adolescence vary from one cultural group to another. In Mexican-American families, parent–child relationships often remain quite formal and asymmetrical.

independent and responsible. Family ties are not severed; connections with parents merely take a different form (Collins, 1997). The exact nature of the change in family roles that occurs at adolescence varies across cultural groups, however (Grotevant, 1998). In Asian and Mexican families who have recently immigrated to the United States, for example, parent–child relationships tend to remain quite formal, with children enjoying little power even after adolescence (Cooper, 1999).

A fourth major task of adolescence is *moving toward a more autonomous stance toward the larger world.* This includes taking personal responsibility for schoolwork and perhaps finding a job and becoming more financially independent. It also includes anticipating future adult roles and making career choices. These changes cannot be made simply by following parental wishes and plans; teenagers must make decisions themselves and actively translate them into practice.

In summary, adolescents continue the process of becoming separate individuals while remaining connected to others (Steinberg and Morris, 2001). They elaborate and evolve a distinctive self-system while also elaborating a social network that now includes romantic partners as well as parents and friends. In the remainder of this chapter, we examine each of these tasks of adolescence in detail.

Questions to Think About As You Read

- How does the environment influence the ways teenagers address the major developmental issues of adolescence?
- How is individual functioning of adolescents related to their earlier developmental history?

THE SOCIAL WORLD OF ADOLESCENCE: AN OVERVIEW

How Stormy Is Adolescence?

Many people believe the challenges of adolescence make it an inevitably stormy and stressful period. Psychologists G. Stanley Hall and Anna Freud are among those who claimed inner turmoil and disruption are necessary to becoming a separate, autonomous person. They argued that a difficult break with parents is essential to forging an independent identity. But other psychologists believe the struggle of adolescence has been greatly exaggerated (Steinberg and Morris, 2001). They point out that most teenagers get along well with their parents and families that functioned well before a child reached puberty tend to continue functioning well afterward (Collins, 1997; Steinberg and Morris, 2001). As with many controversies, both perspectives turn out to have some merit. Adolescence can be stormy or peaceful, with the degree of turmoil varying considerably across age groups, individuals, and different domains of teenagers' lives. Not all adolescents experience storm and stress, but adolescence is on the whole more challenging than other periods of development (Arnett, 1999; Cicchetti and Rogosch, 2002).

Many studies that support the storm and stress view have investigated younger adolescents, whereas those that support a more harmonious view of parent–child relationships have generally looked at the later teenage years. Early adolescence seems to be a unique subphase of development when youngsters experience more turmoil, parents more stress and dissatisfaction, and families more conflict than at any other time (Steinberg and Morris, 2001). A longitudinal study, cataloguing the daily emotional experiences of youth from fifth through twelfth grade, showed less positive emotion and more unstable emotional states in early adolescence (Larson et al., 2002). From the tenth grade on, emotional life was both more stable and more positive. Likewise, in the early teenage period, parents and teens differ greatly in their positions about how much independence and responsibility the adolescents are ready to have, but they are in greater accord later (Collins et al., 1997).

How stormy or peaceful the teenage years are also depends partly on the particular developmental history and personal characteristics of the individual involved. High levels of stress and conflict during adolescence are often part of a generally difficult developmental pathway. Behavior and adjustment problems are most common among adolescents who have had similar problems earlier in childhood (Caspi and Moffitt, 1991; Cicchetti and Rogosch, 2002). Also, the number of changes being experienced at the same time (new schools, changing pubertal status, and so forth) has an effect on the stressfulness of the period (Steinberg and Morris, 2001).

Whether adolescence seems stormy or peaceful further depends on what aspects of it are considered. Teenagers do report more negative moods than younger children, especially in early adolescence (Cicchetti and Rogosch, 2002). In one study, nearly half the teenagers interviewed reported feeling unhappy (Rutter et al., 1976). But this unhappiness reflects mainly *inner* turmoil, not overt conflict with others. Teenagers and parents argue most about mundane matters such as appearance, homework, phone or stereo use, and household chores. There is seldom much conflict over basic values and beliefs (Collins, 1997). Very few teenagers (3 percent of females and 5 to 9 percent of males) express outright rejection of their parents (Rutter et al., 1976). Most continue to have positive feelings toward their parents, even though they may not *express* them as much as they did in childhood. The majority of teenagers continue to get along with their parents, to be influenced by them, and to respect the need for the limits they set (Collins, 1997; Steinberg and Morris, 2001).

Thus, although stress and conflict may occur during adolescence, they are far from the only themes of this period. The typical family conflicts arise out of normal self-assertion, not rebellion and defiance. Parents for a time may see their child as "impossible" or "lost." But this period soon gives way to a realignment in which the adolescent carves out a new place within the family, a new stance toward the world, and a new sense of self-awareness (Steinberg and Morris, 2001). Moreover, even while becoming more autonomous from parents, most teenagers remain emotionally connected to them and highly value their relationships with them (Collins, 1997).

In many cultures, the transition from childhood to adulthood is clearly marked by formal ceremonies called rites of passage, such as this Apache puberty ritual.

A Cross-Cultural Perspective on Adolescence

Even though adolescent conflict with parents is seldom severe or prolonged, teenagers' *inner* sense of unrest can be very unsettling (Cicchetti and Rogosch, 2002). The nature of modern Western societies may help to explain these negative inner feelings. Complex, industrialized democracies demand skilled and knowledgeable adults. Young people must learn a great deal before taking on the responsibilities and privileges of adulthood, making for a protracted period of dependency on parents, often lasting into the twenties or beyond. During this time, young people are also expected to delay full entry into adult sexual roles. Although they are physically no longer children, they have much more to learn and are not yet ready to be launched into the world of adults. The sense of being in a no-man's-land between childhood and adulthood can give rise to feelings of ambiguity, impatience, and frustration.

In nonindustrialized cultures the transition to adult roles begins much earlier than in our own. From an early age, children in these cultures are given responsibilities such as caring for younger siblings or helping in the fields (Whiting and Edwards, 1988). When anthropologist Margaret Mead studied Samoan culture in the 1920s, she found that adolescence was not a stressful period, but a time of gradually maturing interests and activities (Mead, 1925/1939). Samoans began the transition to adulthood early and let it proceed gradually. Mead's description of some aspects of Samoan culture has been questioned (Freeman, 1983), but her insights about the cultural basis of adolescence are still considered valid (Coté, 1992; Grotevant, 1998).

In other traditional cultures the transition to adulthood is much more abrupt. Among the Gusii of Kenya, for example, children are given greatly expanded duties in a short period of time (Whiting and Edwards, 1988). Societies with abrupt adolescent transitions often have special ceremonies, called **puberty rites** or **rites of passage,** to mark entry into new adult roles. Children anticipate these rites for years in advance and know exactly when they will be considered adults.

Puberty rites/rites of passage: Ceremonies that mark the transition from childhood to adulthood.

People in our own society also expect young people to start acting like adults quite abruptly, but the timing of this transition is ambiguous. Adolescents receive conflicting messages about their status and are allowed to take on different adult responsibilities at widely varying ages. In most states they can drive a car and work at age 16, they can vote and serve in the military at age 18, but they cannot legally drink until age 21. Families also vary in their expectations about when adolescents should be on their own, earning a living and acting grown-up. In some families, the key transition is graduation from high school, in some it is graduation from college, and in others it is landing a first permanent job. This ambiguity, which is a product of our culture and the different demands placed on people who pursue different careers, creates special challenges for adolescents and their parents.

One factor that can increase tension between parents and teens is immigrant status (Steinberg and Morris, 2001). Since young people are more quickly influenced by the dominant culture, discrepancies in values between parents and teens may increase over time. This has been found to be true for Vietnamese but not for Mexican immigrants in Southern California, presumably because of the size and influence of the Mexican-American community in that part of the country (Phinney, Ong, and Madden, 2000).

DEVELOPMENT OF THE SELF

The Self-Concept During Adolescence

Adolescents' progress toward a personal identity involves continuing changes in their self-concepts, which have been developing since early childhood. Just as younger and older teenagers differ in how they think and reason, they also differ in how they view themselves.

Changes from Middle Childhood to Adolescence Studies in which adolescents produce descriptions of themselves reveal several ways self-concepts change from middle childhood to adolescence (Damon and Hart, 1988; Harter, 1998; Steinberg and Morris, 2001). First, self-concepts become more *differentiated.* Rather than seeing themselves as always having certain traits, teenagers evolve a more complex picture that takes situations into account. For instance, an adolescent might say, "I generally follow the rules, *except* when my dad is being unfair to me." At the same time, self-concepts become differentiated across various relationships, settings, and areas of competence. An adolescent's self-description might include the following assessments: "I'm pretty grouchy with my family, but I'm more easy-going with my friends. I usually do what I'm supposed to at school, but when I go out, I know how to have a good time. I do well in my classes, but I'm not so good at sports."

Second, teenagers' self-concepts become more *individuated,* or distinct from the self-concepts of others. Younger children often describe themselves in terms of similarities with peers, but adolescents describe themselves more in terms of what makes them different from others. This tendency begins in middle childhood and becomes more noticeable in early adolescence. Teens define themselves more in terms of personal beliefs and standards and less in terms of social comparison, as was the case in middle childhood (Steinberg and Morris, 2001).

Third, teenagers' self-concepts begin to *focus on how they interact with others.* Elementary school children's self-concepts are social in the sense that they compare themselves with others. Young adolescents' self-concepts focus more on traits that "define [their] place and manner of operating in the social network" (Damon and Hart, 1988, p. 64). Adolescents' self-descriptions often include statements such as: "I'm not very popular at school," "I like to take charge of things with my friends." "People like me because I'm friendly."

Fourth, teenagers increasingly view themselves as *self-reflective*—capable of thinking about and evaluating the self. Because they see themselves in this increasingly introspective manner, they believe they can make their own choices about values and behaviors.

Fifth, adolescents increasingly think of the self as a *coherent* system made up of diverse but integrated parts. They are able to put together various aspects of a self-concept and make sense of it, despite seeming contradictions. This achievement is supported by the cognitive advances described in Chapter 13. Their increased logical powers and ability to coordinate multiple viewpoints allow adolescents to reconcile diverse aspects of the self and behavior in different situations. Their new capacities to reflect on the self and consider a range of alternatives make it possible to examine the self at present, relate that self to past behavior, and project the self into the future. As a result, the self becomes more cohesive and unified than ever before.

Changes in self-concept from middle childhood to adolescence are illustrated in Table 14.1, which shows young people's answers to questions regarding physical, social, and psychological aspects of themselves. These answers illustrate several important points. They demonstrate adolescents' increasing emphasis on styles of interaction with others and decreasing emphasis on comparison with others. They reflect a growing introspection, an inclination to search for a deeper understanding of the self (Montemayor, Adams, and Gullotta, 1990). While 9-year-olds list unquestioned truths about themselves ("I go to Marcy School; I have lots of friends"), adolescents often see themselves in terms of questions: "Am I liberal? Am I conservative? Am I classifiable at all?" (Harter, 1990). They show an increasing tendency for self-concepts to be guided by belief systems, plans, and ideologies. This makes the sense of self coherent and lays the groundwork for a mature personal identity.

Changes from Early to Late Adolescence Research on changing self-concepts during the teenage years supports the view that there are subphases of adolescent development. Young adolescents (ages 12–13) have an understanding of the self that is well

Table 14.1 Self-Descriptions in Childhood and Adolescence

Middle Childhood
"I'm bigger than most kids."
"I like sports. . . . That's what most boys like."
"I feel proud when my parents cheer and let me know I did good."
"They can't read the hard books but I can."

Early Adolescence
"I wear glasses and kids make fun of me."
"I'm in terrific shape . . . everybody I meet respects me for it."
"I play sports. . . . All the kids like athletes."
"I treat people well and don't get into too many fights over stupid things. . . . I'll always have friends when I need them."
"I'm shy. . . . I don't have lots of friends, but the ones I have are good ones."
"I can understand them. Like when they have problems, they come to me to talk about it."

Late Adolescence
"I don't have many things. . . . It's not fair to have a lot of things when some people don't have anything."
"I go to church every Sunday because I want to be a faithful Christian."
"It's good to be beautiful but only if it's real and not false."
"If more people did what we did the world would be a better place."
"I'm proud of being a good reader. . . . It helps you in learning a lot."

Source: Damon and Hart, 1988.

advanced over that of elementary school children. However, by late adolescence (age 17 and up) there are further qualitative advances in how the self is viewed (Steinberg and Morris, 2001).

Evidence that older adolescents have a more sophisticated self-understanding than younger adolescents comes partly from the research of Robert Selman (1980) mentioned in Chapter 12. You may remember that Selman told study participants a story about a boy named Mike whose dog, Pepper, had run away. Two of Mike's friends were trying to decide whether to buy him a new dog for his birthday. Selman probed children's and adolescents' concepts of the self by asking what they believed the thoughts and feelings of someone in Mike's position would be. He found that young adolescents understand the self can sometimes manipulate inner experiences. "I can fool myself into thinking I don't want another puppy," one young teenager explained. However, it wasn't until later adolescence that youngsters started to grasp the notion of conscious and unconscious levels of experience. Here is how one older teenager described these levels in Mike:

He might feel at some level that it would be unloyal to Pepper to just go out and replace the dog. He may feel guilty about it. He doesn't want to face these feelings, so he says no dog. (Interviewer: Is he aware of this?) *Probably not.* (Selman, 1980, p. 106)

Another aspect of self-understanding that differentiates early from late adolescence is increased knowledge of how different aspects of the self are tied together into an integrated whole. Young teenagers make a start in this direction in their ability to link together their past and future selves when giving self-descriptions (Damon and Hart, 1988). They know, for example, that they do not always behave the same way and that at times they act in ways they do not really feel. They recognize contradictions in the self and may have a sense of phoniness (Broughton, 1978). But it is only in later adolescence that youngsters are able to unify contradictory aspects of the self by explaining

Older adolescents have a more integrated sense of self than younger adolescents, along with a much greater understanding of individuals' uniqueness and separateness.

those contradictions (Harter, 1998; Steinberg and Morris, 2001). For instance, a 15-year-old might say he is talkative with his friends, but quiet with his family, and not be able to give a reason for this difference. An older teenager might offer an explanation based on situational factors: "I am really talkative with my friends because they are treating me like a person. My family doesn't listen to what I say, so I just don't like talking to hear myself speak" (Damon, 1983, p. 318).

The Declining Fragility of the Self   Many of the changes in self-concept from early to late adolescence reflect an overall decline in the fragility of the self—that is, a decline in the degree to which the self is tentative and uncertain. As a sense of self emerges, it is at first very fragile. Like scientists who have just formulated a new theory, teenagers are unsure about the validity of the new self, and other people can easily challenge it (Harter, 1998). No wonder young adolescents appear to their parents to be much less open than they were as children. Teenagers feel they must be careful not to disclose too much, or else the new sense of self that is emerging might somehow be lost.

The feeling that the self is fragile is linked to several other beliefs and behaviors of young teenagers. First, it is tied to a concern that the self is transparent and readily scrutinized by others, which gives rise to the *imaginary audience* discussed in Chapter 13. Second, it partly explains the expressions of physical invulnerability that are part of the *personal fable.* Imagining oneself to be indestructible can provide a defense against feelings of vulnerability that come with a tentative and uncertain sense of self. Third, it helps account for young teenagers' strict conformity in dress and hair style. Such conformity enables adolescents to hide their fragile sense of individual uniqueness, while expressing their belonging to a distinct group. Finally, the fragility of the self underlies the young adolescent's tendency to fantasize different roles. Just as play provided a safe haven for the preschooler to work through conflicts, so fantasies allow the adolescent to experiment with possible new dimensions of the self before actually committing to them. As grandiose as these fantasies can be (Malcolm will end poverty; Mike will save the marine world), they are part of a healthy adolescent idealism and may serve as beacons drawing the young person forward.

In time the fragile sense of self that emerges in early adolescence becomes more firmly established. Through interactions with others, performance at school, and experiences in the larger world, teenagers' tentative beliefs about the self are increasingly confirmed and they become less self-conscious (Harter, 1998). In several studies, researchers have used the Imaginary Audience Scale to demonstrate a decline over time in the belief

Table 14.2 Items from the Imaginary Audience Scale (IAS)

1. You have looked forward to the most exciting dress-up party of the year. You arrive after an hour's drive from home. Just as the party is beginning, you notice a grease spot on your trousers or skirt. (There is no way to borrow clothes from anyone.) Would you stay or go home?

   ———Go home.
   ———Stay, even though I'd feel uncomfortable.
   ———Stay, because the grease spot wouldn't bother me.

2. Let's say some adult visitors came to your school and you were asked to tell them a little bit about yourself.

   ———I would like that.
   ———I would not like that.
   ———I wouldn't care.

3. It is Friday afternoon and you have just had your hair cut in preparation for the wedding of a relative that weekend. The barber or hairdresser did a terrible job and your hair looks awful. To make it worse, that night is the most important basketball game of the season and you really want to see it, but there is no way you can keep your head covered without people asking questions. Would you stay home or go to the game anyway?

   ———Go to the game and not worry about my hair.
   ———Go to the game and sit where people won't notice me very much.
   ———Stay home.

4. If you went to a party where you did not know most of the kids, would you wonder what they were thinking about you?

   ———I wouldn't think about it.
   ———I would wonder about that a lot.
   ———I would wonder about that a little.

Source: Elkind and Bowen, 1979, pp. 40–41.

that others are scrutinizing the self. (Items from this scale are shown in Table 14.2.) Self-conscious answers generally peak at age 12 or 13 (Elkind and Bowen, 1979).

The decline in self-consciousness in later adolescence goes hand in hand with a growing ability for accurate self-appraisal, including personal weaknesses as well as strengths. Thus, twelfth graders are able to size up both their good and bad points realistically and integrate them into a coherent and stable sense of self. It is not surprising, then, that in general young people show a rise in self-esteem across the adolescent years (Twenge and Campbell, 2001).

The Concept of Personal Identity

By late adolescence, development of the self has advanced to the point that formation of a personal identity becomes possible. A personal identity is more than just a self-concept. Forming a personal identity requires integrating into a coherent whole past experiences, ongoing personal changes, and society's demands and expectations for the future (Grotevant, 1992; Moshman, 1999).

A personal identity includes the values, principles, and roles an individual has adopted as his or her own. The process of identity formation typically includes selecting and preparing for a career, reevaluating religious and moral beliefs, working out a political ideology, and adopting social roles, including those related to sexuality, marriage, and parenthood (Harter, 1990). Much of this work goes on in early adulthood, but it begins in adolescence (Steinberg and Morris, 2001).

Adolescent Identity Development

Commitment to ideology is often a hallmark of late adolescence.

James Marcia (1980) writes that identity refers to a *structure* of abilities, beliefs, and past experiences regarding the self. "The better developed this structure is, the more aware individuals appear to be of their own strengths and weaknesses. The less developed this structure is, the more confused individuals seem to be about their own distinctiveness from others and the more they have to rely on external sources to evaluate themselves" (p. 159).

Identity formation builds on the integrated self-concept that typically develops by late adolescence. It is based in part on the cognitive abilities that emerge during adolescence, such as the ability to reason about relations among abstract concepts. In addition, relationships with other people are essential to the process of identity formation.

Erik Erikson referred to the struggle teenagers encounter when trying to establish their personal identities as an **identity crisis.** When they take on this challenging task, adolescents are caught in the middle of two changing systems (Sprinthall and Collins, 1995). One is their own biological system, with its hormonal changes and resulting transformations in the body. This system is linked to new sexual urges, as well as new ways of thinking and reasoning. The other is the social system in which the adolescent lives. Parents and other adults are making new demands that are not always clear or consistent. Often the teenager is expected to behave maturely, almost like an adult, yet many restrictions continue to be imposed as if he or she were still a child. All these changes and contradictions push adolescents to reassess their notions about themselves and their place in the world. Despite the discomfort that this need for reassessment can create, Erikson maintained that adolescence is the ideal time for experimenting with various possible roles and identities, before adulthood requires serious commitments to a particular occupation or ideology.

Individual Differences in Identity Formation Adolescents vary in how easily they establish a personal identity. Some feel overwhelmed by the task or retreat from it. Some get there by fits and starts; for others it is relatively smooth sailing. By late adolescence, many young people have yet to complete the process. James Marcia (1980; Marcia et al., 1993) has described four categories of *identity status,* based on whether or not adolescents have passed through a period of identity exploration and whether or not they have committed to an adult identity. Marcia's four categories are *identity diffusion* (no exploration or commitment), *foreclosure* (commitment without exploration), *moratorium*

Identity crisis:
In Erikson's theory, the struggle that teenagers experience when trying to establish their personal identities.

(exploration without commitment), and *identity achievement* (exploration followed by commitment).

Adolescents in a state of **identity diffusion** are not engaged in active exploration of roles and values, and they have made no serious commitments to an adult identity. They seem so overwhelmed by the possibilities of life that they cannot find direction. Young people in this group have no long-range goals but live for the moment, for immediate pleasures. Identity diffusion is normal in early adolescence, but some young people have difficulty moving beyond it.

Foreclosure involves commitment to a set of roles and values without going through a period of crisis or exploration. Teenagers in this group have not struggled to reconcile incompatible aspects of the self or to evolve their own goals and purposes. Instead, they have simply accepted the roles that others, most often their parents, have prescribed for them. For all of us, *some* aspects of personal identity are defined by our families and communities (Grotevant, 1992; Spencer and Markstrom-Adams, 1990). But for adolescents who take the route of identity foreclosure, their sense of who they are is dictated by someone else. This can compromise development. On the other hand, in the case of immigrant families, adhering closely to parents' traditional values may be necessary (Cooper, 1999).

Adolescents who are in **moratorium** are in the midst of actively exploring options for a personal identity but have not yet committed to any of them. Moratorium is the least stable identity status (Marcia et al., 1993). It is the developmentally appropriate identity status for middle adolescence, but it can become problematic if it continues into adulthood.

Identity achievement occurs when a person commits to a particular set of roles and values following a period of active exploration (Moshman, 1999). Adolescents in this group are confident about the consistency and continuity of the self, and equally confident that others see these same qualities in them. Identity achievement is seldom reached before late adolescence or early adulthood.

Across the adolescent years, there is a fairly steady increase in the percentage of young people who can be classified as identity achievers and a decrease in the percentage who are in a state of identity diffusion (Kroger, 2000). Keep in mind, however, that a person's identity status is not always consistent in all domains of life. College students are most likely to have reached identity achievement in the area of vocational choice, but they are often still in a state of diffusion or foreclosure regarding religious beliefs and political ideologies.

Researchers have found some interesting correlations between identity status and other characteristics (Berzonsky and Kuk, 2000; Kroger, 2000). Identity achievers tend to have the highest self-esteem, followed by those in moratorium, those who adopt foreclosure, and finally those floundering in identity diffusion. Identity achievers are more goal-oriented, choose more demanding college majors, show greater cognitive sophistication, and take more personal responsibility for their actions than those in other identity statuses. Identity achievers report low levels of anxiety, but self-reported anxiety is lowest for those in foreclosure and highest for those in moratorium (Waterman, 1992). Those in identity diffusion tend to have more academic and social problems, including drug abuse (Berzonsky and Kuk, 2000).

According to Erikson, two sets of ingredients are needed to consolidate an optimal sense of personal identity. First, adolescents must carry forward from middle childhood an inner confidence about their competence and ability to master new tasks, along with a sense of basic trust, autonomy, and initiative from earlier developmental periods. The second set of ingredients Erikson saw as critical to optimal identity formation is ample opportunity to experiment with new roles, both in fantasy and in practice, coupled with support in this effort from parents and other adults. There is some research evidence that warm, supportive parents who encourage communication and resolution of differences do foster identity formation and self-development in adolescents (Baumrind, 1989; Grotevant and Cooper, 1998; Steinberg and Morris, 2001).

Identity diffusion:
Identity status in which there has been no active exploration of roles and values and no commitment to an adult identity.

Foreclosure:
Identity status in which commitment has been made to a set of roles and values without a period of exploration.

Moratorium:
Identity status in which a person is in the midst of exploring options for a personal identity, but has not yet committed to any of them.

Identity achievement:
Identity status in which a person has committed to a set of roles and values following a period of active exploration.

Group Differences in Identity Formation Although identity formation is by definition an individual matter, there are some group differences in how the process unfolds. For instance, gay and lesbian adolescents, as a group, have to contend with more social disapproval than their heterosexual peers. Ritch Savin-Williams (1990), who has extensively studied gay and lesbian youth, points out that negative community attitudes pose a great challenge to these young people's identity formation and self-acceptance. Research suggests that gay and lesbian youths who express their sexual orientation openly, even in the face of social stigma, pass identity formation milestones at developmentally appropriate ages and show greater self-esteem than those who maintain secrecy (Dubé and Savin-Williams, 1999).

Identity development also appears to proceed differently for young women and young men (Patterson, Sochting, and Marcia, 1992). During adolescence, the interpersonal domain, especially as it relates to future marriage and family roles, is more prominent in girls' identity exploration than in boys' (Kroger, 2000). Girls and boys show equal concern about occupational issues, but girls show more concern than boys about how to balance career and family demands (Archer and Waterman, 1994). Erikson believed identity issues had to be resolved before the intimacy issues of early adulthood, but there is some evidence that young women deal with identity and intimacy simultaneously rather than sequentially (Marcia et al., 1993). Because of this pattern, the process of identity formation is in some ways more complex for girls than for boys (Kroger, 2000).

Members of ethnic minority groups also face distinctive challenges of identity formation (Markstrom-Adams, 1992). Minority youth are confronted by two often conflicting sets of cultural values—those of their ethnic community and those of the larger society. Deciding which aspects of each set of values to incorporate into their personal identities can be difficult. Identifying too closely with the values of the dominant culture may invite ostracism in their ethnic community, but identifying too closely with the values of their own community may limit opportunities for success in the larger society. As one 15-year-old girl of mixed ethnic background complained to an interviewer about one of her white friends: "She doesn't understand I have one foot in the white world and one foot in the black world, and she can't accept that I have to be solid in the black world" (Sroufe, Carlson, and Shulman, 1993).

Identity development poses particular challenges for adolescents who belong to ethnic minorities, especially if they are biracial or multiracial.

Perhaps as a result of these difficulties, minority adolescents appear more likely than white adolescents to avoid or cut short identity exploration (Cooper, 1999; Markstrom-Adams, 1992). In a number of studies, researchers have found higher rates of foreclosure for African-American, Hispanic, and Native American youth than for whites (Spencer and Markstrom-Adams, 1990; Streitmatter, 1988). Foreclosure is an understandable response to the complexities of the task facing these adolescents. When, despite challenges, minority youth achieve a secure ethnic identity, positive attitudes toward their own group, a sense of effectiveness, and higher self-esteem appear to follow (Carlson, Uppal, and Prosser, 2000).

PEER RELATIONSHIPS IN ADOLESCENCE

Peer relationships change during the adolescent years in important ways, and their impact on other areas of development grows:

Child Development CD
Peer Relations in Early Adolescence

- *The cognitive advances of adolescence make possible a deeper, more mature understanding of others* that parallels gains in self-understanding. Friendships grow deeper as teenagers acquire the cognitive potential for mutual exploration and discovery.

- *Involvement with peers becomes increasingly critical to progress in self-understanding;* adolescents discover their inner feelings largely through close relationships with peers.

- *Peer group membership contributes to the development of personal identity.* The group of friends to which an adolescent belongs helps define who he or she is, and peer groups offer chances to try out various roles.

- As new types of peer groups emerge during adolescence, *friendships with same-sex peers pave the way for romantic relationships.*

These changes mean peer relationships become more complex in adolescence. Youngsters must not only coordinate close friendships with same-sex peers and function in same-sex groups as they did in middle childhood, they must also coordinate same-sex and opposite-sex friendships and function in mixed-sex groups. How adolescents respond to these new challenges depends in part on their developmental history. Longitudinal research shows that those who effectively negotiated the tasks of middle-childhood peer relationships, including maintaining boundaries between the sexes, are more effective in mixed-sex groups and in general better able to meet the complex challenges of adolescent peer relationships (Sroufe et al., 1993; Sroufe et al., 1999).

Advances in Understanding Others

Understanding the self and understanding others go hand in hand, so it is not surprising that an adolescent's advances in self-awareness are accompanied by a growing sense of what others are like. Teenagers know they have inner motives, and they deduce that others do too. As they come to see themselves as having coherent selves, they also recognize the coherence of others' personalities.

Robert Selman's (1980) research shows that understanding of others is generally at the same level as self-understanding. When asked questions about Mike, his dog Pepper, and his friend Tom, adolescents in their midteens consider the feelings of both Mike and Tom in this situation, and they know each boy will make inferences about the intentions of the other. As one 15-year-old explained it: "Mike will understand what Tom was trying to do, and even if he doesn't like the dog, he'll appreciate that Tom thought he would" (Selman, 1980, p. 106). Here we see a grasp of other people's thoughts and feelings that closely matches the youngster's depth of understanding about the self. Selman's ideas about the link between self-understanding and understanding of others are summarized in Table 14.3.

Table 14.3 Stages in Understanding Self and Others

Level	Concept of Persons	Concept of Relationships
0: *Egocentric perspective taking* (under 6 years)	*Undifferentiated:* Confuses internal (feelings, intentions) with external (appearance, actions) characteristics of others.	*Egocentric:* Fails to recognize that self and others have different feelings and thoughts as well as different external characteristics.
1: *Subjective perspective taking* (ages 5–9)	*Differentiated:* Distinguishes feelings and intentions from actions and appearances.	*Subjective:* Recognizes people may feel and think differently but limited concept of how they affect each other.
2: *Self-reflective or reciprocal perspective taking* (ages 7–12)	*Second-person:* Can reflect on own thoughts and realizes that others can do so as well; realizes appearances may be deceptive about true feelings.	*Reciprocal:* Puts self in others' shoes and realizes others may do same, but others' and own perspectives are assumed not to influence each other.
3: *Mutual perspective taking* (ages 10–15)	*Third-person:* Knows that self and others act and reflect on effects of action; recognizes own subjective perspective and realizes it fits into own more general attitudes and values.	*Mutual:* Can imagine another's perspective on self and own actions, coordinates other's and own view; sees relationships as ongoing mutual sharing of social satisfaction or understanding.
4: *In-depth and societal-symbolic perspective taking* (ages 12–adult)	*In-depth:* Recognizes that people are unique, complex combinations of their own histories; realizes that people may not *always* understand their own motivations (i.e., that there may be unconscious psychological processes).	*Societal-symbolic:* Realizes people may form perspectives on each other at different levels, from shared superficial information or interests to common values or appreciation of abstract moral, legal, or social notions.

Source: Selman, 1980.

The Nature of Adolescent Friendships

Developmental changes in understanding the self and others underlie changes in the nature of friendship from childhood to adolescence. Compared with younger children, teenagers have a much greater capacity for true *mutual understanding* (Hartup and Stevens, 1999). Elementary school children grasp the importance of give-and-take between friends, but they do not fully understand each other as persons. In contrast, because adolescents are increasingly aware of their own unique feelings, they recognize that others also have unique feelings. This may explain why adolescents often seek friends who are similar to themselves in important ways, such as behavior, academic orientation, or, especially in the case of African-American youth, ethnic identity (Hamm, 2000; Steinberg and Morris, 2001).

Partly because of their growing capacity for true mutual understanding, teenage friends want to share their inner experiences and life histories (Buhrmester, 1998). This desire for *self-disclosure* accounts for the many hours they spend talking with each other, either on the phone or face-to-face. As three teenagers described this aspect of friendship:

> "A friend is a person you can talk to—you know, show your feelings. And he'll talk to you."
> "Someone you can tell your problems and she'll tell you her problems."
> "You can tell a friend everything." (Youniss, 1980, pp. 181–182)

When important inner feelings are shared between friends, their relationship deepens. We illustrated this in our story of Meryl, whose relationship with Amy has deepened over time into the type of friendship we are describing. The distress she feels when Amy no longer confides in her reflects the significance she places on mutual understanding and self-disclosure between friends. A close relationship like Meryl and Amy's is said to be characterized by *intimacy*. Intimacy includes self-disclosure, understanding of each other's feelings, and knowledge of each other's personality characteristics and preferences (Collins and Repinski, 1994). From middle childhood to middle adolescence, young people show an increased capacity and desire for intimacy, and they increasingly report that they have intimate friends (Buhrmester, 1998; Hartup and Stevens, 1999; Rubin, Bukowski, and Parker, 1998).

Related to the growth of intimacy is a deeper *commitment* between teenage friends. Because adolescents have an increased understanding that friends share experiences and extend themselves for one another, their friendships tend to be more loyal and faithful than those among younger children (Buhrmester, 1998; Phillipsen, 1999). As a result, across adolescence friendships become more stable and long-lasting (Degirmencioglu, Urberg, Tolson, and Richard, 1998).

Another aspect of commitment is the ability to keep confidences, to refrain from telling something a friend told you in private. This ability is very important to teenagers, as this adolescent confirms:

> *Friends can keep secrets together. They can trust that you won't tell anybody else. If you tell somebody something, they won't use it to get revenge on you when you get in a fight. You talk about things you wouldn't tell other people. (Youniss, 1980, p. 181)*

In adolescents' descriptions of friendship, words like *trust, faith,* and *believe in* are mentioned again and again. The preciousness of inner feelings to an adolescent, who is so newly aware of them, demands absolute loyalty from friends. The highly sensitive nature of these feelings makes teenagers very vulnerable to betrayal. Mutual understanding and emotional intimacy help create the trust needed to make teenage friendships work, but some degree of initial trust is needed before adolescents can share their inner experiences and build mutual understanding and closeness with peers.

The nature of friendship continues to change over the course of the teenage years. Increased intimacy and commitment appear in early to midadolescence; during later adolescence another qualitative advance occurs. In keeping with their ability to integrate diverse aspects of the self, *older teens are able to coordinate a broader range of friends.* Friendships no longer need to be so exclusive, as pairs of friends accept each other's need to establish relationships with other people and to grow through these experiences. In late adolescence, patterns of friendship come closer to those found among adults, as the number of friends considered close decreases (Hartup and Stevens, 1999).

Although teenage boys as well as girls experience increased intimacy and commitment in friendships, there are some gender-related differences in the nature of friendships during adolescence (Hartup and Laursen, 1993). Teenage girls report more frequent intimate interactions with same-sex friends than boys do, and they have more intimate knowledge of their friends (Buhrmester, 1998; Collins and Repinski, 1994). However, girls also report about twice as many disagreements with friends, which often involve interpersonal issues of the "he said/she said" variety: "And Stephen said that you said that I was showing off just because I had that blouse on" (Hartup and Laursen, 1993). Girls also report more often than boys do that negative feelings persist following a disagreement. This may reflect greater intimacy in girls' relationships, or it may simply mean that boys and girls have different ideas about what disagreements mean for a friendship. Finally, boys are more likely than girls to report

Adolescent girls have more frequent intimate interactions with their friends, both positive and negative, than boys do.

conflicts over friends pressuring them to do things, while girls are more likely to report conflicts involving betrayal of secrets (Cooper and Cooper, 1992).

Changes in the Nature of Peer Groups

Not only does the nature of friendship change in adolescence, but the nature of peer groups changes as well (Rubin et al., 1998). The importance of being in a group increases dramatically from childhood to early adolescence. For younger adolescents, conformity to group norms is highly valued, and there is often antagonism to those outside one's own group (Gavin and Furman, 1989). In early adolescence it is also important to belong to a popular group. These behaviors and outlooks diminish markedly by late adolescence.

Clique:
A close-knit group of a few friends who are intimately involved with each other.

Crowd:
A group that is larger, less exclusive, and more loosely organized than a clique.

Two group structures important in adolescence are the *clique* and the *crowd*. A **clique** is a close-knit group of a few friends, usually of the same gender; who are intimately involved with each other and spend a great deal of time together (Brown, 1990). Girls' cliques often are more tightly organized and more oriented to sharing of intimacies and to mutual social support (Henrich et al., 2000). The clique is the dominant peer-group structure during adolescence. The mixed-gender **crowd** is larger, less exclusive, and more loosely organized than the clique, and it offers a broader range of informal contacts. Crowds tend to be identified by the interests, abilities, attitudes, style of dress, and by reputations and stereotypes shared by their members (Steinberg and Morris, 2001). In one study of three hundred Australian high school students, there were forty-four cliques (composed of three to nine members each) and only twelve crowds (Dunphy, 1963). The crowds were made up of cliques, but not every clique was part of a crowd. One way crowds affect adolescents is by providing norms of behavior for their members and by influencing the ways adolescents view themselves and others (Steinberg and Morris, 2001).

Youngsters' concepts of cliques and crowds change over time, as their cognitive abilities become more sophisticated. Sixth graders can readily describe who belongs to various cliques in their class, but they tend to label them on the basis of concrete characteristics, such as what they do at recess ("the jump rope group") or who their leader is ("Jessica's group"). Older adolescents are more likely to characterize crowds by their general dispositions or interests (Kinney, 1999; Stone and Brown, 1999).

Interestingly, teenagers' characterizations of crowds seem to be based more on *reputation* than on actual behavior (Brown, Mory, and Kinney, 1994). Most middle-school and high-school students can readily list the major crowds in their school (e.g., "populars," "jocks," "brains," "normals," "burnouts") and describe what people in each of these crowds are like. However, these crowd descriptions turn out not to be particularly accurate reflections of reality. Individuals who are identified by themselves or others as belonging to a particular crowd are far from uniform in dress, behavior, or attitudes. In addition, when adolescents are asked to choose which characteristics on a list fit a particular crowd at their school, there is limited consensus (Brown, Lohr, and Trujillo, 1990). Adolescents also tend to exaggerate the positive characteristics of their own crowd and crowds that are socially close to theirs, and they feel better about themselves if they view their crowd as high status (Steinberg and Morris, 2001). At the same time, they emphasize negative characteristics of crowds that are socially distant. Crowd labels and descriptions seem to function as caricatures or shorthand characterizations of various groups. These caricatures make it easier for adolescents to understand the various social identities available to them, to predict peer behavior, and to identify potential friends and foes (Brown et al., 1994).

Interestingly, adolescents are often reluctant to assign themselves to any one crowd. In response to researchers' questions about which crowd they belong to, they often say, "I really don't belong to any one crowd," or "I have friends in several crowds" (Brown et al., 1994). In one study, one-third of the high school students surveyed said that they belonged to two or more crowds (Youniss, McLellan, and Strouse, 1994).

During adolescence, the importance of both cliques and crowds first increases and then declines (Connolly and Goldberg, 1999; Rubin et al., 1998). Membership in cliques peaks in early adolescence, around eighth grade, and falls off during high school. Older adolescents' social life is more likely to be organized around specific friendships and romantic relationships than around membership in a clique. Clearly identifiable crowds also appear in early adolescence, often beginning with a differentiation between the popular crowd and everyone else (Kinney, 1993). Through early high school, crowds become more differentiated, as individuals become identified with various extracurricular activities and academic tracks. As they progress through high school, however, adolescents tend to attach decreasing importance to belonging to an identifiable crowd. By senior year, crowds typically become less prominent, and the boundaries between them often begin to break down (Strouse, 1999).

These patterns are related to the tasks confronting youngsters in different phases of adolescence. In early adolescence, clique and crowd membership provides teenagers with both a social identity and a reliable setting for social interaction and friendship formation. Later on, as adolescents develop a sense of individual identity and become more confident about their social skills and ability to make friends, these functions lose their importance.

Dating and Sexual Activity

Dating and sexual activity are usually offshoots of crowd activities. Few adolescents begin dating before they participate in crowds. Fewer than 10 percent of youngsters date before age 12, but 90 percent are dating by age 16 (Savin-Williams and Berndt, 1990). Intimacy in heterosexual relationships lags behind. It is only in later adolescence, by about twelfth grade, that emotional intimacy in male-female relationships surpasses that of same-sex relationships (Buhrmester and Furman, 1987; Hartup and Stevens, 1999). Intimate male–female relationships may play an important role in identity formation. They may also facilitate further development of empathy and prosocial behavior; relating to someone different from yourself can increase sensitivity to the needs of others. These same functions may also be served by the relationships of gay and lesbian couples (Diamond, Savin-Williams and Dubé, 1999).

Sexual intimacy is another dimension of peer relations that emerges in adolescence. Adolescent sexual activity has increased in the United States in the last few decades, but the size of the increase is not entirely clear. The sensitive nature of the topic makes it difficult to get a reliable estimate of the percentage of teenagers who are sexually active. For a variety of reasons, teenagers may either overstate or understate their actual experience.

Adolescent Sexual Behavior

Much of the increase in adolescent sexual intercourse apparently occurred from the 1960s to the 1980s (Dreyer, 1982). During that time, the percentage of high school boys who were sexually active doubled; for girls, the percentage quadrupled. The increase in adolescent girls' sexual activity was accompanied by an increase in the pregnancy rate among unmarried teenagers, as we discussed in Chapter 2.

Child Development CD
Teen Pregnancy and Childbearing

Recent nationwide surveys suggest the rate of sexual intercourse remains relatively low in early adolescence but increases substantially through middle and late adolescence (Abma et al., 1997; Centers for Disease Control and Prevention, 2002a; Sonenstein et al., 1998). In a recent nationwide survey of high school students, under 35 percent of ninth graders reported they had ever had sexual intercourse; by twelfth grade, about 60 percent said they had (Centers for Disease Control and Prevention, 2002a). (See Figure 14.1.) Other studies suggest that by age 19 about 75 percent of females and 85 percent of males have had intercourse (Abma et al., 1997; Sonenstein et al., 1998). In most studies, more boys than girls report they have had intercourse; however, this difference tends to narrow with age. There is considerable variation in rates of sexual activity reported by adolescents in different parts of the country, in rural and urban areas, and in different ethnic and racial groups. African-American teenagers, especially boys, become

Figure 14.1
PERCENTAGE OF HIGH
SCHOOL STUDENTS WHO
SAID THEY HAVE HAD
SEXUAL INTERCOURSE, 2001
*(Source: Centers for Disease
Control and Prevention, 2002a.)*

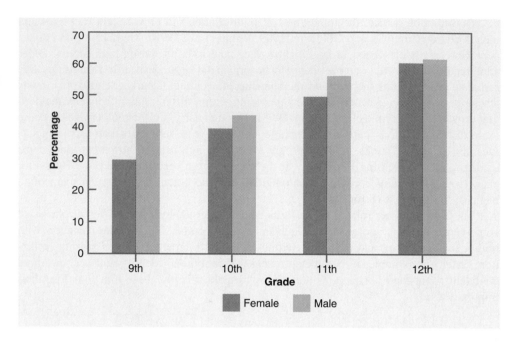

sexually active earlier than white or Hispanic teenagers and continue to show higher rates of sexual activity throughout adolescence (Centers for Disease Control and Prevention, 2002a).

The Relative Influence of Peers

A topic of great interest to parents and researchers alike is the influence of peers on the behavior and development of adolescents. During adolescence, the trend toward spending increasing time with peers continues (Steinberg and Morris, 2001). One study found that, not counting time in class, high school students spend more than twice as much time with peers as with parents and other adults (29 percent vs. 13 percent) (Csikszentmihalyi and Larson, 1984). Teenagers, especially in early adolescence, adopt a style of dress and behavior that sets them apart from other age groups and indicates identification with the peer group. Surveys find that as young teens become more autonomous from parents, they grow more dependent on peers (Harter, 1998; Bukowski, Sippola, and Newcomb, 2000). They come to see peers as a more important source of intimacy than parents (Collins, 1997). This increased involvement with peers may help youngsters carve out a more mature relationship with their parents. It also allows them to maintain a distance from adult roles and commitments while gaining the interpersonal experience needed to prepare them for adulthood.

Peer influence can be positive or negative. Sometimes peers promote academic achievement and prosocial behavior (Steinberg and Morris, 2001). On the other hand, attraction to peers who show problem behavior can lead young people to problems themselves. Research shows that for a time at the transition to middle school, teens are sometimes attracted to older aggressive boys. This is especially true for girls (Bukowski et al., 2000).

The degree of conformity to the peer group changes during the years from middle childhood to late adolescence, peaking in early adolescence (Steinberg and Morris, 2001). This was shown in a study in which youngsters of various ages were asked to decide which two lines in a set were the same length. Some were told that peers had chosen pairs of lines that were obviously *un*equal. As shown in Figure 14.2, 12- to 13-year-olds went along with the incorrect opinions of peers much more than 7- to 8-year-olds did. By age 16 to 17 the conformity of early adolescence had declined, and by age 19 to 21 it was no greater than it had been in middle childhood (Costanzo, 1970). Similar findings

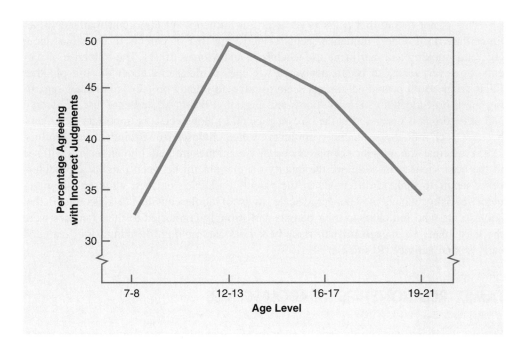

Figure 14.2
CHANGES IN CONFORMITY
TO PEERS WITH AGE
Young people of different ages
were asked to decide which lines
in a set were the same length,
and some were told peers had
chosen obviously *un*equal lines.
The tendency to go along with
incorrect judgments peaked in
early adolescence.

emerged from another study in which youngsters were given hypothetical situations that involved opposing pressures from parents and peers (Berndt, 1979). Young adolescents experienced the most conflict, finding it hard to decide which side to go along with.

This pattern makes sense when you consider that young adolescents have well-developed social-comparison skills but are still very self-conscious about what others think of them. Older adolescents, by contrast, have largely outgrown the imaginary-audience phase. Because they no longer feel that others are always scrutinizing them critically, they aren't so uncomfortable about being a bit different from other people. Excessive conformity, like excessive self-consciousness, is something most teenagers eventually outgrow.

Even during early adolescence some youngsters are more conforming than others. Teenagers who have a medium level of status with their peers are more likely to conform than either high-status or low-status teenagers, perhaps because they feel they will gain in group acceptance by going along with others (Sprinthall and Collins, 1995). The source of peer influence also makes a difference in whether a particular adolescent conforms. In general, teens are more influenced by friends, especially long-term friends, than by mere acquaintances (Hartup, 1992). For example, friends are more likely than acquaintances to be similar in their drug-related behavior. Even adolescents who have only recently become friends exert a noticeable influence on one another. Teenagers who become friends during a school year are more similar at the end of that year than they were at the beginning (Berndt, 1999). All this suggests that Christine has good reason to be concerned when 14-year-old Mike starts hanging out with a tough crowd.

Parents and peers tend to influence different aspects of a teenager's life. Peers have the greatest impact on superficial behaviors, such as dress and mannerisms. Parents, in contrast, retain substantial influence on adolescents' basic beliefs and values. This pattern of dual influence was shown in a classic study in which ninth to eleventh graders were presented with hypothetical teenage dilemmas (Brittain, 1963). Sometimes they were told what parents thought the teenager in the dilemma should do; other times they were told what peers advised. Each participant was then asked how the dilemma should be resolved. Many responded with their own judgments, although often the views of parents and peers were influential. Peer opinions were most influential in matters dealing with status in the peer group, whereas parental judgments were most influential in matters involving important life decisions, education, and ethics. More recent studies agree with this general split in influence during the teenage years (Sprinthall and Collins, 1995).

This is not to say that peers never exert an influence on important matters; sometimes they do. Friends' influence seems to outweigh that of parents in decisions about cigarette smoking and marijuana use (Steinberg and Morris, 2001). The influence of parents, however, seems to be greater when it comes to decisions about the use of other illicit drugs. Both peers and parents seem to have an impact on teenage choices regarding the use of alcohol (Savin-Williams and Berndt, 1990). (Adolescents' use of alcohol and other drugs is discussed in the box on page 507.) However, it is important to remember that peer influences generally diminish by late adolescence (Sprinthall and Collins, 1995), whereas the influence of parents usually continues into adulthood, as you will see in the next section. In addition, the quality of relationship between parents and adolescents seems to make a difference in the parents' influence on their children's involvement in risky behaviors. One large-scale study of adolescent health risks found that adolescents who felt close to their parents and strongly connected to their families were the least likely to engage in such risky behaviors as smoking, drinking, drug use, and early sexual activity (Resnick et al., 1997).

National Adolescent Drug Use Study

FAMILY RELATIONSHIPS IN ADOLESCENCE

Despite the increasing significance of peers in teenagers' lives, the family remains a critical context for development during adolescence. For example, parents can directly support development by allowing adolescents to explore new roles and values, by tolerating self-expression, and by discussing different views, while still providing guidelines when needed. At the same time, relationships with parents, in both the past and the present, indirectly influence development by influencing the quality of peer relationships (Sroufe et al., 1999; Steinberg and Morris, 2001). Teens from supportive families have more positive friendships and are in general more socially competent. Positive family relationships also can lessen any negative impact from peers.

The parents' role in the transition from childhood to adulthood is analogous to their role in the transition from infancy to childhood. Toddlers and adolescents are not just becoming more independent of their parents, they are also becoming connected to their parents in new ways. During toddlerhood, the child's assertiveness and the parents' setting of limits lead the child to a new understanding of the boundaries between self and others. Gradually, the toddler comes to see the self not as an extension of the parent, but as a separate person who is linked to the parent through strong emotional ties. Similarly, the adolescent's new level of self-assertion and the parents' mix of accepting and challenging this behavior promote a new level of mutual understanding. By late adolescence or early adulthood, sons and daughters have usually gained renewed respect for their parents (Collins, 1997). It is not the adoration of a young child, but it is a powerful connection nonetheless.

The Changing Family Structure

Parenting Adolescents

During adolescence, a child's changing level of understanding plays a role in bringing about changes in family relationships. The cognitive skills that permit hypothetical thinking and exploration of inconsistencies also allow teenagers to anticipate how parents will counter their arguments, to note imperfections in parents' behavior, and to conceive of other ways the family might function (Powers, Hauser, and Kilner, 1989). Adolescents may resent an unsatisfactory family situation because they can now see what *might* be. Teenagers also have a new understanding of parent–child relationships and parental authority. By late adolescence they see mutual tolerance and respect as the basis of interactions between themselves and their parents, and they see their power as closer to that of their parents than in childhood (Nucci, Camino, and Sapiro, 1996). No longer will adolescents simply accept parental dictates without being given reasons and a chance for input. This can pose special problems when parents are intolerant of disagreement, as is common in many immigrant families (Phinney et al., 2000).

Most teens accept parents' authority with regard to moral, legal, and social issues, but at the same time they hold that they should have increasing authority over dress, activities, and other personal issues. This appears to hold across ethnic groups (Nucci et al., 1996; Smetana, 2000).

Pressure from adolescents for change in the family structure was shown in a classic study of several thousand 14- to 16-year-olds, 80 percent of whom said they wanted their parents to be less restrictive and to allow them more independence (Douvan and Adelson, 1966). More recent studies of teenagers reflect the same desire for redefinition of the parent–child relationship away from unilateral parental authority toward cooperative negotiation (Collins et al., 1997).

Most parents make appropriate changes in response to these pressures from their children. For example, parents generally grant more autonomy as children move through the teen years, although this depends on circumstances (Bumpus, Crouter, and McHale, 2001). Firstborns tend to be allowed more independence than secondborns and boys, especially in homes with traditional gender role attitudes, tend to be granted more autonomy than girls. Asian-American parents grant less autonomy than European-American parents. Despite such differences, the amount of conflict over this issue is similar across these groups (Fuligni, 1998).

APPLYING RESEARCH FINDINGS

Adolescent Drug and Alcohol Use

Much attention has been focused on teenagers' use of alcohol and other drugs. Since 1975, researchers at the University of Michigan have tracked teenage drug use in annual surveys of high school seniors from across the United States. These surveys indicate that drug and alcohol use increased during the 1970s, began to decline around 1980, and increased again during the 1990s (see Table 14.4 on page 508). However, the 2000 data suggest that drug use has leveled off and may be starting to decline again (Johnston, O'Malley, and Bachman, 2002).

Use of illicit drugs by high school seniors is now about as high as it was when the surveys began. After several years of increases, the percentage of seniors who say they have tried any illicit drug remained stable from 1997 through 2000 (see Figure 14.3 on page 508). Over the same period, experimentation was down slightly for marijuana, LSD, inhalants, and cocaine, though not for PCP and heroin (both used very infrequently by this age group). Cigarette smoking declined somewhat after five years of increases. Still, 63 percent of seniors had tried cigarettes, and 21 percent were daily smokers.

Alcohol remains by far the most widely used drug among high school students. In 2000, 80 percent of seniors reported experience with alcohol, a percentage that has remained quite stable since 1975. However, only 50 percent had consumed alcohol in the past thirty days; this figure has declined notably since 1980. Only about 3 percent of seniors used alcohol on a daily basis, but 32 percent had been drunk in the last month.

Since 1991 the annual nationwide surveys have also included eighth and tenth graders. Alarmingly, by eighth grade a fairly high number of students have already tried one or more drugs. In the 2000 survey, more than a quarter (27 percent) of eighth graders had tried at least one illicit drug. More than half (52 percent) had tried alcohol, and 25 percent had been drunk at least once. Forty-one percent had tried cigarettes, and 15 percent had smoked in the past month.

The surveys reveal clear ethnic differences in drug use (Johnston, O'Malley, and Bachman, 2002). In eighth grade, Hispanic-Americans have the highest usage rates for nearly all drugs. By twelfth grade, however, it is whites who are most likely to use alcohol, cigarettes, and most illegal drugs. In twelfth grade, Hispanics have the highest rates only for cocaine. The difference between eighth and twelfth grades can be explained partly by Hispanics' higher high school dropout rates. Drug users are especially likely to quit high school and not be included in the twelfth-grade survey. At all three grade levels studied, African-American students are less likely than whites or Hispanics to use illegal drugs, alcohol, or tobacco. In twelfth grade, for example, they are *much* less likely than whites to be daily cigarette smokers (7.5 percent versus 24 percent) or binge drinkers (12 percent versus 35 percent). Since the differences between whites and African-Americans are already present in eighth grade, they cannot be readily explained by high school dropout rates.

Teenagers' attitudes toward drugs have generally paralleled drug use rates. As drug use increased during the 1990s, students' disapproval of drug use and their perception of its riskiness generally declined, especially for marijuana and cocaine. However, since 1998, there have been slight increases in the percentage of students who disapproved of drug use at all three grade levels. Johnston and his coauthors suggest that this shift in attitudes can be explained by shifts in media attention and health education efforts.

Table 14.4 Percentage of High School Seniors Reporting Use of Alcohol, Cigarettes, or Illicit Drugs in the Previous Thirty Days, 1975–2000*

Substance	1975	1980	1985	1990	1995	2000
Alcohol	68.2	72.0	65.9	57.1	51.3	50.0
Cigarettes	36.7	30.5	30.1	29.4	33.5	31.4
Marijuana	27.1	33.7	25.7	14.0	21.2	21.6
Inhalants	N/A	2.7	3.0	2.9	3.2	2.2
Cocaine	1.9	5.2	6.7	1.9	1.8	2.1
LSD	2.3	2.3	1.6	1.9	4.0	1.6
PCP	N/A	2.3	1.3	0.4	0.6	0.9
Heroin	0.6	0.2	0.3	0.2	0.6	0.7

*These data are drawn from interviews of a nationally representative sample.
SOURCE: Johnston, O'Malley, and Bachman, 2002.

A longitudinal study by Laurence Steinberg (1981) demonstrates the process by which a more symmetrical parent–child relationship develops during adolescence. In Steinberg's study, families with sons were visited several times as the boys passed from middle childhood through puberty. At each visit, the parents and son were given a problem to solve jointly, such as planning a vacation together. As the boys entered puberty, the parent–child interactions during these problem-solving discussions changed considerably. Sons deferred to their mothers less. Mothers and sons interrupted each other more, responded less to each other's opinions, interacted more contentiously and rigidly, and offered fewer explanations for their views. During this period the fathers typically stepped in and asserted their opinions strongly, and the boys continued to defer to them. After the peak of puberty had passed, family interactions became more flexible again. Mothers interrupted less often, and sons became more willing to justify their thinking. The sons' relative dominance in these discussions was now greater than the mothers', but still less than the fathers'. This finding does not necessarily imply that mothers have less power in the family than their older adolescent sons do. It may simply mean that mothers are increasingly willing to be open to their teenagers' points of view. Research does show that teenagers spend more time with their mothers than their fathers, confide in them more, and feel more accepted by them (Collins, 1997; Collins and Russell, 1991). Mothers are also more self-disclosing toward their teenagers than fathers are, and they encourage more closeness (Cooper and Cooper, 1992).

Figure 14.3
PERCENTAGE OF HIGH SCHOOL SENIORS WHO HAVE USED ANY ILLICIT DRUG, 1975–2000
(Source: Johnston, O'Malley, and Bachman, 2002.)

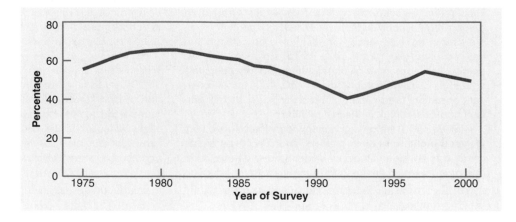

Like toddlers, adolescents must evolve new ways of relating to parents that combine increasing separateness with continued closeness. Mothers and daughters often remain particularly close.

In any case, during adolescence patterns of family interaction change, and both parent and child recognize greater symmetry in their relationship (Feldman and Gehring, 1988; Steinberg and Morris, 2001). However, the emergence of this new power structure often involves conflict and stress. One reason for this conflict, especially during early adolescence, is that the parents' appraisal of the child's cognitive capacities lags behind the child's advances (Collins, 1997; Smetana, 1995). The child may be ready to share decision making before the parents realize it, necessitating realignment of the parents' perceptions with the child's actual abilities. Mismatches between parents' and children's expectations are greatest in early adolescence and gradually decline as the relationship goes through a series of realignments (Collins et al., 1997). These realignments often come more easily with laterborn children than with firstborns, probably because parents are more prepared for laterborns' adolescent changes (Hill, 1988). Fortunately, the relatively high levels of parent–child conflict seen in early adolescence generally do not last long. As parents and teenagers work out a new understanding of each other, conflict declines (Montemayor and Hanson, 1985).

Parenting Patterns and Adolescent Development

As power relationships in the family become more symmetrical, the tasks of parenting change. Parents of adolescents must respond to their children's new ways of thinking and new strivings for self-expression and influence by granting them more autonomy (Bumpus et al., 2001). This does not mean parents let their sons and daughters do whatever they want; adolescent development goes best when parents stay involved with their teens and continue to impose limits on them (Baumrind, 1989; Collins, 1997). Guidance and feedback generally replace demands and directives, as the parents gradually turn over more responsibility to the emerging adult.

Many of the parenting qualities that were important in earlier periods of development continue to be important now. Warmth, support, authoritativeness, and continued supervision are linked to positive outcomes (Baumrind, 1989; Brendgen et al., 2001; Sampson and Laub, 1994; Steinberg and Morris, 2001). In particular, adolescents who receive authoritative parenting tend to be more psychologically mature, have a stronger orientation toward achievement, and do better in school than those from authoritarian or permissive homes. Likewise, consistency between parents in the controls they employ and their responsiveness to their children is also associated with positive development in teenagers, including higher self-esteem (Johnson, Shulman, and Collins, 1991). Erratic and harsh parental treatment is strongly correlated with aggressive behavior and delinquency in adolescents (Sampson and Laub, 1994).

One of the parenting features that has been found to be most consistently related to teen adjustment is *monitoring*—that is, knowing about and attending to sons' and daughters' activities (Brendgen et al., 2001; Kerr and Stattin, 2000; Pettit et al., 1999). At times this refers to direct supervision, as in being present during after-school hours. At other times, by midadolescence, it is more indirect, perhaps involving phone check-ins. It may even be that simple knowledge about the young person's activities and companions plays a key role (Kerr and Stattin, 2000). There is generally a movement toward self-monitoring on the part of the maturing adolescent, with the parent monitoring this process.

There is some variation among ethnic groups in the connection between parenting style and adolescent outcomes. In a large study of an ethnically diverse group of adolescents, Larry Steinberg and his colleagues (1994) found that authoritative parenting is generally positive and neglectful or disengaged parenting is generally negative for adolescents, regardless of their ethnicity. However, *authoritarian* parenting was more likely to be associated with positive outcomes for Asian-American adolescents than for European-American adolescents. As we mentioned in Chapter 10, this difference probably reflects variability in the cultural meaning of parenting practices that are part of the authoritarian parenting category, such as parental control over adolescents' decisions. In a traditional Asian-American family, for example, respect for parents' authority is valued much more highly than in many other North American families.

Researchers have explored links between parenting practices and adolescent development by observing interactions between parents and teenagers as they discussed dilemmas, solved problems, or planned activities (Collins et al., 2000; Hauser and Bowlds, 1990; J. Sroufe, 1991). In one such study, adolescents' maturity and identity achievement were strongly predicted by the extent of warmth, support, and positive emotion in their families (Powers et al., 1983). Apparently, it is not enough for parents simply to prod teenagers into exploring alternatives and questioning opinions. For this kind of cognitive challenge to encourage identity achievement, it must take place within a warm and supportive family context. Under these circumstances, such challenges come across not as criticism, but as a sign of the parents' interest and respect.

The importance of parental support and responsiveness was also suggested in a study by Hal Grotevant and Catherine Cooper (1986), who observed teenagers and their parents jointly planning a vacation. They found that teenagers whose parents responded to their feelings, accepted disagreements, and initiated compromises were more likely to perform at a relatively high level on two key tasks involved in identity achievement: (1) exploring alternatives regarding the self, and (2) perceiving and coordinating different points of view. In a later study, the young people from these supportive families were also more successful at mutual negotiation with peers (Cooper and Cooper, 1992). Since these were correlational studies, we cannot draw conclusions about cause and effect from them. Perhaps a teenager's ability to explore alternatives and coordinate different viewpoints helps encourage parental support and responsiveness as much as the other way around. However, recent longitudinal studies show that differences in identity exploration and social competence are predicted by parenting patterns years earlier (Collins et al., 2000). All of these findings are in keeping with a social construction view of self-development, which stresses the importance of supportive relationships.

Not only do parents influence adolescents' behavior, but different adolescents elicit different responses from their parents. A good fit between parent and child facilitates a harmonious relationship during adolescence.

Bidirectional Influences

Although parents clearly affect their children and the quality of their development, children also have an impact on their parents and on patterns of interaction in the family (Cooper and Cooper, 1992; Steinberg and Morris, 2001). Different children seem to bring out different parenting responses, just as different parenting styles seem to foster different reactions in children.

For example, bidirectional influences can be seen in developmental differences between males and females. During the teenage years girls not only experience greater self-consciousness and lower self-esteem than boys, but they also tend to seek autonomy in different ways (Harter, 1998; Kroger, 2000). One study in England found that adolescent girls primarily seek recognition of their emerging uniqueness within the family, whereas boys often struggle to escape the family's confines (Coleman, 1974). In addition, parents allow their sons greater freedom to be away from home and have more concerns about their daughters' sexual behavior, suggesting bidirectional influences (Block, 1979; Bumpus et al., 2001). Apparently, an interaction of the parents, the child, and the child's gender gives rise to significant differences in patterns of development.

The Impact of Divorce on Adolescents

In Chapter 12 we discussed the impact of divorce on children. There are some important additional findings concerning adolescents and divorce:

Child Development CD
Divorce and Child Development

- Adolescents from divorced and remarried families are at increased risk for behavior problems, drug and alcohol use, early sexual activity, adolescent pregnancy, and poor school performance, even when income level is controlled for (Hetherington, Bridges, and Insabella, 1998).

- Divorce can prompt a *sleeper effect*—a result that is not apparent at the time of the marital breakup but shows up some years later, often during adolescence (Chase-Lansdale and Hetherington, 1990; Furstenberg, 1990).

- Normative tasks of adolescence, such as achieving intimate relationships and moving toward autonomy, seem to be especially difficult for young people from divorced or remarried families (Hetherington et al., 1998).

- While divorce and remarriage clearly are risks for adolescents, leading to a two-fold increase in the risk of notable problems, many and perhaps even most youth from such families do well (Hetherington et al., 1998).

During adolescence there are continuing differences in the effects of divorce on males and females, just as during the childhood years (Hetherington and Stanley-Hagan, 1999). The consequences of divorce appear more slowly and take different forms in girls than in boys. Girls are more likely to experience academic difficulties, distress, and dissatisfaction with the family's situation, whereas boys are more likely to show problem behavior (Allison and Furstenberg, 1989). There is some evidence girls are at higher risk than boys for dropping out of high school and having long-term economic problems (Hetherington, 1999).

Studies of teenagers in single-parent homes show that it is not simply the absence of a father that has negative effects. Adolescents living in remarried families have a similar risk for problems as those from divorced, single-parent families (Hetherington et al., 1998). Conflict between step-parents and teens, especially stepdaughters, remains high in adolescence and often increases. A stable male presence may be beneficial, especially for boys, but it is not always so.

Absence of a father through divorce appears to have different consequences than loss of a father through death. This was illustrated in a classic study by Mavis Hetherington (1972), who looked at 13- to 17-year-old girls from families with both mother and father at home, from divorced families in which the mother had child custody and had never remarried, and from mother-headed families in which the father had died. Hetherington found that girls from father-absent homes were just as sex-typed in their behavior as girls from homes with a father present. However, the girls with absent fathers tended to show difficulties in their opposite-sex relations, the form of which varied depending on whether the father's absence was due to death or divorce. In general, girls whose fathers had died were shy and hesitant with males, whereas daughters of divorced fathers tended to be sexually forward.

Hetherington (1988) speculated that the attitudes and behaviors of the mothers involved may largely account for these differences. Many of the divorced mothers were still hostile toward their former husbands, recalled their marriages with bitterness, and were generally dissatisfied with life. Some of their daughters may have therefore concluded that happiness depends on being successful with men. However, because they lacked experience with males in the family, their approach to this goal was often inappropriate. In sharp contrast, the widows tended to cling to happy memories of their husbands, to the point where they may have painted idealistically perfect images of them. As a result, their daughters may have felt too awed by males to approach them. These are only hypotheses, but it is clear that the *meaning* a girl attaches to the loss of her father can be very important.

Siblings in Adolescence

Sibling relationships are emotionally charged early in adolescence, but they become less conflictual and less influential in later adolescence as teens separate in some ways from the family (Hetherington et al., 1999; Steinberg and Morris, 2001). Nonetheless, they remain important relationships throughout the teen years. On the one hand, positive sibling relationships are associated with school competence, sociability, and feelings of positive self-worth (Steinberg and Morris, 2001). Such positive relationships can help children cope with divorce and can compensate for difficulties making or keeping friends (Updegraff and Obeidallah, 1999). They may also provide unique opportunities for learning to deal with the opposite gender. Girls, for example, appear to learn control tactics from their brothers (Updegraff, McHale, and Crouter, 2000). In general, there is evidence that positive sibling experiences are taken forward into peer relationships (Steinberg and Morris, 2001). Finally, sibling relationships may promote individuality. In defining themselves as different from each other and in eliciting different treatment from their parents, siblings each develop unique qualities (Feinberg and Hetherington, 2000).

On the other hand, negative sibling relationships can spur the development or intensification of problem behavior (Steinberg and Morris, 2001). For example, negative sibling coalitions can promote aggression and other deviant behavior and can undermine parenting (Bullock and Dishion, 2000).

Whether adolescent sibling relationships are positive or negative appears to be influenced in part by the degree of warmth and harmony in the parent–teen relationship (Bussell et al., 1999) and in part by the history of the siblings' own relationship (Dunn et al, 1994). One important finding is that teens who experience parental rejection are more aggressive with their siblings (Steinberg and Morris, 2001).

ADOLESCENTS IN THE BROADER WORLD

During adolescence, developmental contexts beyond the home and peer group, including school and the workplace, become increasingly important. School and work are often intimately tied to both family and friends; peer relationships and family life greatly influence how well adolescents perform in the classroom and on the job (Cairns, Cairns, and Neckerman, 1989; Entwisle, 1990; Steinberg and Morris, 2001). School and work, in turn, provide opportunities for interactions with peers, and for shared pride and conflict within the family. School and the workplace are also vital proving grounds for an adolescent's developing sense of identity; accomplishments in the classroom and on the job give teenagers feelings of competence and allow them to explore and anticipate future roles.

Adolescents at School

In some ways middle schools and high schools support adolescent development. Students are given increasing responsibility for mastering course material, such as completing homework assignments and doing special projects on their own. Occasionally, there are courses in which young people can explore diverse opinions on social issues through class discussion. Being exposed to peers from diverse backgrounds, as occurs especially in public schools, can also encourage adolescents to perceive different points of view.

But schools also have some negative influences on adolescents. The peer culture at school rewards popularity and athletic performance far more than scholastic achievement (Entwisle, 1990). For some students, peers even encourage academic failure. Associating with potential dropouts is one clear predictor of dropping out of school oneself (Cairns, Cairns, and Neckerman, 1989).

Generally speaking, grades decline during adolescence. This may be due in part to harder classes and stricter grading, but it is also tied to transitions from one school to another, which is often linked to loss of friends (Eccles, Lord, and Buchanan, 1996; Entwisle, 1990). In one study, young adolescents who remained in the same school from kindergarten through eighth grade received better grades than those who switched to a junior high school at the age of 12 (Simmons and Blyth, 1988). The critical variable underlying this difference was the amount of change experienced—in this case, adjustment to a new school. Other kinds of changes can also prompt a decline in academic performance. Youngsters who are in the midst of puberty or who are being affected by other sudden turns in their lives are most likely to suffer a drop in school grades.

Adolescents differ in their beliefs about what factors contribute to academic achievement (Little et al., 1995; Weiner, Kun, and Benesh-Weiner, 1980). Some teenagers are convinced success in school depends on their actions. They are said to have an **internal locus of control.** Others think grades are largely a matter of factors outside them, such as luck or teacher favoritism, and nothing they do will make a difference. They are said to have an **external locus of control.** Students with an external locus of control also tend to believe their ability is fixed and won't be changed by effort and hard work (Henderson and Dweck, 1990). Not surprisingly, such attitudes influence school performance.

Internal locus of control:
The belief that success depends on one's own efforts.

External locus of control:
The belief that success depends on factors outside one's control.

The transition to middle school or junior high is stressful for most adolescents, often accompanied by a drop in grades and upheaval in their social world.

Child Development CD
Gender Differences in Math and Science

Gender also influences achievement at school (Entwisle, 1990). Girls are often socialized away from feelings of *instrumental competence* (having the ability to accomplish things) and toward feelings of helplessness when confronted with a challenge (Block, 1979). For instance, parents tend to believe adolescent boys have more natural talent for math, and they convey this belief to their children (Parsons, Adler, and Kaczala, 1982). Girls usually have lower expectations for success at math and a variety of other tasks, despite the fact that overall they earn better grades than boys (Entwisle, 1990). When girls fail, they are more likely than boys to attribute their failure to something they cannot change, such as innate lack of ability (Henderson and Dweck, 1990). This prompts them to give up trying more readily than boys. In addition, success at academic tasks doesn't always give girls as much pride as it does boys.

One developmental hazard unique to the teen years is dropping out of school. Approximately 12 percent of students leave school before graduating from high school (U.S. Department of Education, 2000). Early exit from school is associated with an array of problems, including delinquency and later unemployment (Jimerson et al., 2000). Many factors are related to dropping out, including a history of poor achievement, lack of student involvement at school, and lack of parental involvement (Keith et al., 1998; Mahoney and Stattin, 2000). Some of these are markers of a process that has been underway for a long time. Not only do achievement problems in early elementary school and early grade retention predict dropping out, but one longitudinal study showed that dropouts could be predicted with 77 percent accuracy by age 3 (Jimerson et al., 2000). Principal predictors were lack of emotional support and responsive care from parents, along with stressful family lives. Such factors predict later lack of school involvement by both students and parents.

Adolescents at Work

Another setting in which teenagers can experience success or failure is the workplace. About 60 percent of high school sophomores and 75 percent of high school seniors have a part-time job, averaging sixteen to twenty hours a week (Fine, Mortimer, and Roberts, 1990). Over half of adolescents with jobs work in the retail sector, including restaurants and fast-food outlets; another one-quarter work in the service sector, particularly in health care settings, such as nursing homes (National Research Council, 1998). Nearly 10 percent are employed in agriculture, not counting many who work on their family farms without being paid. Teenage girls are almost as likely to have a job as boys are, although girls continue to be paid less than boys. Adolescents from lower-income families have a lower than average rate of employment, but those who are employed tend to work longer hours and have more dangerous jobs than middle-class teenagers (National Research Council, 1998). Adolescents from ethnic minority groups also have low employment rates. African-American teenagers are about half as likely to have a job as white teenagers are, but the lowest employment rate of all (about 12 percent) has been found among some immigrants from Southeast Asia.

mhhe.com
/dehart5

Adolescent Employment

Working can provide a number of benefits for adolescents, but it also poses substantial risks. Whether a job has a positive or negative impact on a teenager depends on a number of factors, perhaps most importantly the number of hours worked. The box on page 515 provides a closer look at the risks and benefits of employment for adolescents.

THE COHERENCE OF DEVELOPMENT IN ADOLESCENCE

As in other age periods, the coherence of adolescent development takes several forms. First, *the various aspects of individual development fit together in a coherent way.* There are close links between the quality of parent–child relationships, peer relationships, and school functioning. For example, teens whose friendships are more intimate and supportive become increasingly involved at school, while those who are less competent with

A CLOSER LOOK

THE BENEFITS AND RISKS OF ADOLESCENT EMPLOYMENT

Working can benefit adolescents in several ways (Fine, Mortimer, and Roberts, 1990; National Research Council, 1998). A job can contribute to self-esteem and a sense of personal identity by allowing adolescents to feel they are doing something useful. The pay they earn makes them more independent from their parents and gives them experience managing money. By forcing teens to budget time, make choices, and take responsibility, a part-time job can foster maturity. Jobs can teach valuable skills, and working during adolescence is associated with more continuous employment and higher wages after high school graduation. Low-income minority youth who have jobs during adolescence are more likely to graduate from high school and attend college than those who don't (Leventhal, Graber, and Brooks-Gunn, 2001).

However, jobs for adolescents also pose risks (Fine, Mortimer, and Roberts, 1990; National Research Council, 1998). The work available is often routine and impersonal, with teenagers seldom feeling close to adult coworkers and often not really enjoying their jobs. Working also has impacts on other areas of adolescents' lives. High school students with jobs report fewer close peer relationships, less involvement in school activities, less enjoyment of school, lower grades, less positive relationships with parents, and higher rates of substance use than those without jobs (Pickering and Vazsonyi, 2002; Post and Pong, 2000; Wu, Schlenger, and Galvin, 2003).

One critical factor in determining whether the benefits of working outweigh the risks is the number of hours spent at work. In a large-scale survey of American high school students, those who worked the most during the school year reported the worst school performance, the least investment in education, and the most psychological distress, delinquency, drug and alcohol use, and autonomy from parents (Steinberg and Dornbusch, 1991). Negative effects were apparent for students working only eleven to fifteen hours weekly, and they increased from there. Interestingly, the benefits of working do not increase with the number of hours worked but are present even for adolescents who work only a few hours a week.

Many adolescents face relatively high health and safety risks on the job, regardless of the number of hours worked (National Research Council, 1998). Some of the industries employing large numbers of adolescents have relatively high rates of worker injury and death. For example, clerks in fast-food restaurants and convenience stores are at greater than average risk of being injured or killed in a robbery, and agricultural workers face risks from exposure to chemicals and dangerous machinery. Adolescents have an on-the-job injury rate nearly twice that of adults—about 4.9 injuries per 100 full-time-equivalent workers for adolescents, compared with 2.8 per 100 for adults. About one hundred thousand adolescents receive emergency treatment for injuries on the job each year, and at least seventy die from work-related injuries. Work-related injuries are highest for adolescents employed in retail stores and restaurants, manufacturing, and construction; the highest rates of adolescent work-related deaths are found in agriculture, retail settings, and construction.

These heightened risks are partly due to characteristics of adolescent workers, including inexperience and developmental factors. For example, adolescents who feel invulnerable may underestimate physical dangers or ignore safety precautions. But characteristics of the workplace also contribute. Equipment designed for use by adults may be too large, heavy, or complex to be safely operated by many teenagers. Adolescent workers often do not receive adequate supervision or training in health and safety issues. Finally, current child labor laws do not provide adequate protection against work in hazardous settings for adolescents, particularly those who are 16 and older and those who work in agriculture.

peers become less involved and are more likely to drop out of school (Jimerson et al., 2000).

Second, *there is coherence in the course of individual development over time,* with connections between how well a youngster functions in adolescence and how well he or she functioned in earlier developmental periods. Detailed longitudinal observation of children in nursery school and summer camp settings shows substantial continuity of individual functioning across childhood and adolescence. For instance, peer functioning in middle childhood predicts relationships in the teenage years, and dependency and lack of effectiveness in entering the peer group in the preschool period predict similar problems in adolescence. Even differences in the quality of attachment assessed in infancy are predictive: those who were securely attached are, as a group, dramatically less dependent, form more intimate friendships, and are more effective in the peer group as teenagers (Sroufe et al., 1993; Sroufe et al., 1999). Such differences are not caused in a simple way by early attachment history. Rather, attachment history tends to set a child on a developmental pathway that often continues because it is supported by later circumstances.

This is not to say that the quality of a person's adjustment cannot change with age. During adolescence, some young people become better adjusted than they were before, while for others the opposite is true. But such changes do not come about unexpectedly. Developmentalists see them as understandable reactions to changes in the environments in which the youngsters grow.

Despite the challenging developmental tasks encountered during adolescence, most young people pass through the teenage years relatively unscathed and emerge prepared to deal with the demands of adulthood. A minority of teenagers are overwhelmed by the demands of adolescence and develop serious problems, some of which will be discussed in Chapter 15. But for most, adolescence is a time of great change but only transitory turmoil.

Chapter Summary

Introduction

Major developmental tasks of adolescence include:

- establishing a personal **identity,**
- achieving a new level of closeness and trust with peers,
- acquiring a new status in the family, and
- gaining greater autonomy in the world outside the family.

The Social World of Adolescence: An Overview

Adolescence is often considered a stormy period, but the amount of actual turmoil depends on:

- whether early or late adolescence is being considered,
- what domain of life is examined, and
- a variety of individual differences.

Culture plays a role in how difficult the transition from childhood to adulthood is.

Development of the Self

Between middle childhood and adolescence self-concepts become increasingly differentiated, individuated, concerned with social interaction, self-reflective, and coherent.

From early to late adolescence additional changes in self-concept are seen, including:

- increased understanding of conscious and unconscious levels of experience,
- increased knowledge of how different aspects of the self form an integrated whole, and
- an overall decline in the fragility of the self.

Forming a personal identity involves integrating into a coherent whole past experiences, ongoing changes, and society's expectations for the future.

Marcia described four categories of identity status, based on whether or not identity exploration and commitment to a particular identity had occurred:

- **identity diffusion,**
- **foreclosure,**
- **moratorium,** and
- **identity achievement.**

The process of identity development varies somewhat, depending on gender, ethnicity, and sexual orientation.

Peer Relationships in Adolescence

During adolescence, peer relationships are connected with other aspects of development:

- The cognitive advances of adolescence allow deeper understanding of others.
- Involvement with peers becomes increasingly critical to progress in self-understanding.
- Peer group membership contributes to the development of personal identity.
- Involvement with same-sex peers paves the way for close opposite-sex relationships.

The nature of friendship changes from middle childhood to adolescence, with increasing emphasis on mutual understanding, self-disclosure, intimacy, and commitment. It continues to change during adolescence, as older teens become able to coordinate a broader range of friends.

During adolescence the nature of peer groups changes as **cliques** and **crowds** form. The importance of these groups increases in early adolescence and later declines.

Romantic relationships also develop during adolescence:

- Dating and sexual activity usually emerge from crowd activities in middle adolescence.
- Male–female relationships surpass same-sex friendships in intimacy in late adolescence.
- Intimate male–female relationships may play a role in identity formation and facilitate development of empathy and prosocial behavior.

- The rate of sexual activity increases dramatically in middle and late adolescence.
- There are gender and ethnic differences in rates of sexual activity.

The relative influence of peers and parents changes over the course of adolescence:

- Peer influence increases in early adolescence and then declines.
- Peers and parents tend to influence different areas of adolescents' lives.
- Parental influence remains strong into adulthood.

Family Relationships in Adolescence

Patterns of interaction within the family change during adolescence:

- Adolescents' increasing cognitive skills and physical maturity lead them to push for greater autonomy, but parents' perceptions often lag behind their children's development.
- Realignments in parent–child relationships are often accompanied by conflict.
- Parent–child relationships become increasingly symmetrical during adolescence.

Parenting style continues to make a difference in developmental outcomes during adolescence, even though the tasks of parenting change when children reach adolescence:

- Warm, authoritative parenting seems to foster particularly positive outcomes in adolescents' development.
- There are some ethnic differences in how parenting style affects development.

Parental divorce continues to affect children's development during adolescence:

- Adolescents from single-parent families and stepfamilies are at heightened risk for a variety of problems.
- Some effects of divorce are not apparent at the time of the marital breakup but show up some years later, often during adolescence.
- Divorce continues to affect boys and girls somewhat differently.
- Negative effects of divorce are not due simply to the absence of the father.

Sibling relationships become less conflictual and less influential during adolescence, as teens begin to separate from the family. However, both positive and negative sibling relationships have impacts on adolescent development.

Adolescents in the Broader World

During adolescence, developmental contexts beyond the home and peer group, such as school and the workplace, become increasingly important:

- Schools have both positive and negative impacts on adolescent development.
- Gender and **locus of control** influence adolescents' experience and achievement in school.
- Working can increase adolescents' self-esteem and feelings of autonomy, but it also poses risks.

The Coherence of Development in Adolescence

The coherence of adolescent development takes three forms:

- The various aspects of individual development fit together in a coherent way.
- There is coherence in individual development over time.
- Individuals' level of adjustment can change in response to changes in their environment.

Review Questions

Introduction

1. What are the major developmental tasks of adolescence?

The Social World of Adolescence: An Overview

2. What factors influence the level of storm and stress present during adolescence?

Development of the Self

3. How does self-concept change from middle childhood to adolescence and from early to late adolescence?
4. What individual and group differences are there in the process of identity formation?

Peer Relationships in Adolescence

5. How are peer relationships related to other areas of development during adolescence?
6. How do friendships, peer groups, and romantic relationships change over the course of adolescence?
7. How does the influence of peers compare with that of parents during adolescence?

Family Relationships in Adolescence

8. How do family structure and interaction patterns change during adolescence?
9. How do parenting patterns, divorce, and sibling relationships affect adolescent development?

Adolescents in the Broader World

10. What influences do school and work have on adolescent development?

The Coherence of Development in Adolescence

11. How does development in adolescence show coherence?

Application and Observation

1. Interview several adolescents about peer groups at their school. What identifiable crowds are there? What characteristics do members of each crowd have? Do they perceive themselves as belonging to a particular crowd? Is it possible for students to be part of more than one crowd? To what extent do members of different crowds associate with each other?

2. Interview several adolescents about their work experience and/or reflect on your own experience with adolescent employment. What benefits does working have for them (or did it have for you)? What problems does/did it create? What benefits or problems have they/you seen for other adolescents with jobs? How does their/your experience compare to the research cited in this chapter?

3. Watch several TV shows or movies that are centered on adolescent characters and pay attention to how they depict adolescent social life. How do their portrayals of adolescents' relationships with family, peers, friends, and romantic partners compare to the evidence from research on adolescent social development?

4. Observe adolescent social interaction at a school event, such as a football or basketball game, or at a mall or other public gathering place. How do the interactions you observe compare to the information presented in this chapter? What age and gender differences do you see? What difference do the setting and the presence or absence of adults seem to make?

Part 6 Epilogue: Adolescence

Adolescence can be thought of as a second revolution in human development—the first occurring during the toddler period, when a child emerges from an infant. During adolescence, a child is transformed into a young adult. Qualitative advances can be seen in all developmental areas. Among the most obvious are the physical changes. Just as toddlers lose their former babyish shape, so adolescents lose the look of children. Not only do they grow taller, heavier, and stronger, but their body proportions change and secondary sex characteristics develop. For males this includes a broadening of the shoulders, enlargement of the genitals, and growth of hair on various parts of the body. For females it includes widening of the hips, development of breasts, and the growth of pubic and underarm hair. Both sexes, of course, acquire the capacity for reproduction.

Equally important are the cognitive changes of adolescence. Teenagers are able to consider hypotheticals, to engage in "what-if" thinking about possibilities. (What if all the lakes in this country became polluted? What if I were in charge of planning the first colony in space?) This enables them to make inferences in the absence of direct experience. Teenagers can also draw tentative conclusions while they gather more data to assess an idea. School-age children, in contrast, generally think their first conclusion *must* be right, and they seldom search out additional information to make a more thorough assessment. Adolescents can also reason more systematically than younger children can. They are able to proceed step by step to logical conclusions. As a result, they can understand abstractions such as $A = 2X$ with as much certainty as they know the sun is shining. Finally, adolescents can embrace multiple viewpoints. They can take one perspective and then consider several others, examining the differences among them.

Taken together, these new abilities represent a major qualitative advancement that sets adolescents' thinking apart from that of elementary school children. Essentially, older adolescents have the cognitive capacities of adults, even though their thinking skills are still unseasoned by adult experience. Twenty years from now you will think about many things differently because of all you have learned in life, but the basic tools you use to solve problems and think about the world will be much the same as those you have already acquired.

Along with the cognitive changes of adolescence come dramatic changes in self-understanding. Adolescents can reflect on the nature of the self—its history, its uniqueness, its complexity. They also develop much greater feelings of autonomy, which is why psychoanalytic theorists refer to adolescence as a second individuation. The first individuation occurs in toddlerhood, when children come to understand their basic separateness from parents. In adolescence, the individuation process is carried much further. Now young people come to understand they have inner feelings that even parents can't know. Accompanying this important individuation is a *deidentification* with parents. Teenagers are moving toward their own ideals, goals, and values, their own unique characters. In Erik Erikson's terms, they are establishing a sense of personal identity, a knowledge of who they are as separate from their parents and of what their place in the world is. Adolescence is especially critical in Erikson's theory because teenagers must rework all previous developmental issues—trust, autonomy, initiative, industry—in light of their newly emerging identity.

A growing sense of identity and self-awareness inevitably brings changes in an adolescent's relationships with others. Consider peer relationships. Although sharing and loyalty are often seen in childhood friendships, the intimacy and self-disclosure among pairs of adolescent friends put their relationships in a different league. At first these close relationships are most often with friends of the same gender, but gradually heterosexual contact develops. By late adolescence, most teens are not only dating but are also forming intimate relationships with members of the opposite sex. This is a marked change from the strict segregation by gender that occurred during the elementary school years.

As relationships with peers change and mature, so do relationships with parents. In mainstream American culture (although not nearly so much in traditional Asian, Latino, or Native American families), early adolescence may be a period of new assertiveness on the youngster's part, which can produce increased conflict with parents and distancing from them (Cooper, 1999). This new assertiveness is in some ways analogous to the contrariness of toddlers as they try to establish themselves as separate people, while still staying connected to parents in new, more mature ways. Both the toddler's behavior and that of the young teenager seem to be an important part of individuation in Western culture. Then, following each of these phases, there comes a period of realignment with parents. The 3-year-old becomes more cooperative and more self-confident. The older adolescent accepts the parents on a new level, and the relationship between them becomes more symmetrical. The parents are now advisers, counselors, and sounding boards more than controllers and disciplinarians. This new, more mature relationship is carried forward to young adulthood.

Four Teenagers, Four Themes

All the dramatic developmental changes just mentioned are apparent in our four teenagers. Malcolm, Maggie, Mike, and Meryl each show advances in thinking and self-reflection. This can be seen in Meryl's discussions of her relationship with Amy and in her concerns for migrant workers, in Mike's new concern about the environment, especially the marine environment, in Maggie's reflections on balancing her job and schoolwork, and in Malcolm's growing political idealism and thoughts about social justice. At the same time, each displays a new self-assertiveness with parents, especially during early adolescence. Meryl tells her parents that they just don't understand, that things are different now; Mike insists that his mother stop calling him Mikey, a name that to him is embarrassingly babyish; Maggie refuses to accept her mother's decision about quitting her job and contradicts her stepfather at every turn, and Malcolm flatly refuses to go on the church retreat, no matter how hard his parents and grandmother try to persuade him. The peer relationships of these young people also show the typical adolescent changes, although Mike and Maggie seem to be getting involved in dating more slowly than the others.

Despite their typical adolescent characteristics, Malcolm, Maggie, Mike, and Meryl also have distinctive personalities arising from their different temperaments, life histories, circumstances, and genders. In looking at their similarities and differences in the rest of this epilogue, we return to some of the major themes of this book. The lives of our four teenagers are useful aids in summarizing these themes.

Normative Versus Individual Development

Mike illustrates many of the normative features of adolescent development—that is, the features that most teenagers share. His desire for privacy early in adolescence, his broadening interest in the world, and the great pride he takes in his first summer job are all common among youngsters his age. Academic problems early in adolescence, like those Mike experiences, are also fairly frequent, although his were probably compounded by his parents' divorce and his father's remarriage. Mike, however, pulls himself through these difficult years. His solid early care, the continued involvement of his parents, and the special interest of his stepfather and a gifted teacher all help him to turn out fine. You can think of these factors as reinforcing one another. The biology teacher is able to ignite a spark because Mike already has a positive image of his own intellectual abilities, an image fostered by years of being told by his family that he is smart and capable. The biology teacher is partly reacting to positive characteristics that he sees in Mike—characteristics that Mike's parents encouraged by their love for and interest in him.

Maggie also illustrates several aspects of normative development. Her continuing friendships with Jessica and Nicole, her expanding interest in boys, her growing assertiveness with her parents, and her increasing ability to understand and cope with contradictory feelings are all typical adolescent characteristics. In addition, her heavy involvement with her part-time job is typical of American adolescents today. Her individual development is heavily influenced by her parents' divorce and her mother's remarriage. Like many girls in this situation, she shows some delayed effects from the divorce and reacts negatively at first to her stepfather. The intensity with which she throws herself into her schoolwork and extracurricular activities probably reflects in part her continuing struggle to come to terms with her parents' divorce and to prove herself worthy of their love. Her uncertainty about her attractiveness to boys and her tendency to become infatuated with boys who are not interested in her may also stem from her father's relative lack of attention to her through much of her childhood. However, the solid early care she has received, her continuing positive relationship with her mother, and her own capacity to adapt to change all help her to deal with the challenges adolescence brings to her.

Malcolm's movement toward independence and his growing concern for questions of right and wrong are also fairly typical of his age group. But Malcolm places his own distinctive stamp on these adolescent changes. His flamboyant nature and boundless enthusiasm are predictable from his history. We would have a hard time believing that Malcolm would ever become a socially isolated, hesitant, pessimistic teenager. For him, life is full speed ahead—getting a job, dating, spending time with friends, becoming involved in political activities. Asserting himself and embracing the future seem to pose little problem. Malcolm retains the tendency toward impulsiveness that he showed throughout childhood. But because he cares about himself and others, the impulsiveness will probably not get out of hand. He may make mistakes, as we all do, but he is likely to learn from them and work to make things right.

Meryl, too, has become a fine young person. To be sure, she still has vestiges of shyness and hesitancy in new situations.

When her body first starts maturing, she feels awkward and self-conscious. Even in later adolescence she steers away from certain kinds of self-exposure, such as joining the debating team. Still, she handles relationships with peers well. Her relationship with Amy clearly illustrates the loyalty, commitment, and self-disclosure typical of adolescent friendships. When allowed to select extracurricular activities of special interest to her (doing artwork, being set director for the senior class play), she shows much persistence and competence. She is growing in self-confidence day by day. She also has a plan for her future and looks forward to college. It is particularly noteworthy that Meryl breaks a two-generation pattern by not becoming pregnant as a teenager. We see the contributions of grandmother, mother, and daughter to this accomplishment—Mrs. Polonius by facing her own guilt and building a strong relationship with Karen; Karen by building a close and open relationship with Meryl; and Meryl by carving out her own identity, developing good relationships with peers, and making wise choices.

Our four teenagers, then, have much in common because of the similar issues they face. All reflect the general or normative trends in adolescent development. Yet each has an individual style of tackling developmental tasks. For instance, although they all assert their independence from their parents, they do so in distinctive ways: Mike by spending time alone behind his closed bedroom door marked PRIVATE; Maggie by throwing herself into her studies and her part-time job; Malcolm by loudly announcing his plans and opinions; and Meryl by informing her mother that they are not the same people, even though she stays close to Karen through frequent conversations. Thus, Mike, Maggie, Malcolm, and Meryl illustrate how general trends and individual adaptations both characterize development.

The Interaction of Social and Cognitive Development

Another theme of this book that is illustrated in the stories of our four adolescents is the continual interaction of social development and cognitive development, with each supporting the other. For instance, Malcolm's cognitive abilities to coordinate multiple perspectives, to think in terms of abstract concepts such as fairness and justice, and to contemplate the future and his place within it allow him to participate in political events in a new way. At the same time, participation in the political process stimulates Malcolm's cognitive development, encouraging him to think more deeply about social issues. This give-and-take between the social and cognitive realms of development can be seen over and over. An individual's social relationships and other life experiences both influence and are influenced by cognitive advances.

Stability and Change in Individual Development

A third theme of this book concerns stability and change in individual development. The stories of our four children were constructed to illustrate both of these processes. Of the four youngsters, Malcolm has shown the most stability, the most continuity in his ways of responding from one developmental period to the next. This is largely because he has experienced the most continuity in care. For him there was no divorce, no new father, no move to a new home, no other major stress; hence, his development has made fairly continuous progress.

Meryl, Maggie, and Mike, in contrast, have had notable changes in their individual adaptations as their life circumstances have changed. Meryl has done better than we might have expected earlier in her life, and Mike and Maggie have had more problems. Still, they continue to be in many ways the same people throughout their various developmental periods. For instance, the hesitancy Meryl showed in early childhood can still be glimpsed in her teenage years, even though she has learned to cope well with her initial shyness in new situations. We can easily picture Malcolm standing to make a speech at his first political meeting, but this is something we cannot imagine Meryl doing. For Mike and Maggie, too, the past has never been completely discarded, not even during their most difficult developmental periods. Their fundamental belief in themselves as competent, valuable persons, a belief forged in infancy and early childhood, has served them well in disruptive and challenging times. As with Meryl, Mike's and Maggie's early life experiences have remained with them—transformed, to be sure, by later experiences, but never completely erased.

A final point to add in thinking about stability and change in human development is that who a person becomes is never inevitable, even given a certain general set of life circumstances. Thus, if we started Malcolm's life over in the same family, he would probably not turn out exactly as he is today. Every life has twists and turns, and complex multiple influences. We would expect that if Malcolm started over in the same family he would still end up exuberant and self-confident, but these characteristics can be expressed in many different ways. Recall the model of branching developmental pathways we talked about in Chapter 1, a model we represented by a tree. A proliferation of smaller branches lies at the end of each major branch. As a result, two pathways almost exactly alike in the beginning can lead to a diversity of possible outcomes.

The Contexts of Development

The importance of developmental contexts in shaping children's lives has been a fourth major theme of this book. One critical context is the family, which time and again has affected the fates of our four children. Without Joe and Karen finding each other and marrying, without Christine and Frank's conflict and eventual divorce, and without ongoing social support in Malcolm's family, adolescence would have been quite different for these four young people.

Broader contexts beyond the family also exert powerful influences. Relationships with peers, teachers, and others take on new significance as teenagers come to better understand themselves and establish their places in the world. Societal, cultural, and economic contexts also continue to be important. For instance, Meryl's artistic expression is influenced in part by cultural ideas about appropriate areas of achievement for females. Maggie's aspirations to attend medical school reflect new educational opportunities for young women that have opened up in the last generation. Similarly, Mike's interest in marine biology is influenced by current ecological concerns in North American society, and Malcolm's interest in minority politics is in part a product of the economic and social realities of his community. The difference between the broader social context in which Malcolm is developing, and the broader social contexts of Meryl, Maggie, and Mike, can be seen in one of the arguments Malcolm gives in favor of a part-time job. Of our four teenagers, only he would mention avoidance of gang involvement as a reason for working after school.

Beyond these direct influences of context, there are indirect influences as well. Contextual factors often affect children through their impact on parents. The beneficial counseling that Karen received ultimately benefited Meryl. Frank Gordon's employment problems contributed to his drinking, his lowered self-esteem, and the tension in his marriage, and through these effects they influenced Mike and Maggie. Mike and Maggie were also influenced indirectly by the cultural factor of expanding work roles for women, because this factor encouraged their mother to pursue a career outside the home and contributed to the conflict in their parents' marriage (as well as adding to their mother's self-esteem and therefore to her confidence as a parent). Meryl, too, was indirectly influenced by this same cultural factor, but in her case it produced *less* family conflict and a positive role model of a working woman for her to emulate.

Moving Toward Adulthood

All four of our adolescents are reasonably well adjusted. Because their developmental contexts have been sufficiently supportive, they have managed to handle developmental issues favorably. Each is now on the threshold of young adulthood. All have the aptitude, the means, and the motivation for higher education, and a college degree will serve them well as they make their ways in today's complex world. We can be optimistic that they will face no more than the normal struggles in coping with future challenges. None is seriously disturbed, and serious psychiatric problems do not seem likely in their futures. Could it have been otherwise if life had gone differently for them? We turn to this question in our final chapter.

Disorders and Resiliency

CHAPTER 15
Developmental Psychopathology

15 Developmental Psychopathology

The four children we have been following—Mike, Maggie, Malcolm, and Meryl—represent basically healthy patterns of development. To be sure, each child has faced difficulties, had problems, and shown vulnerabilities, as we all do. Mike has a tendency to feel more responsibility than is sometimes appropriate, especially when things go wrong in important relationships. Maggie has learned to withdraw and throw herself into work to escape stresses in relationships, and she is uncertain in relationships with the opposite sex. Malcolm can at times be impulsive, and others do not always appreciate his exuberant style. He also faces the challenge of being a young male in a tough urban environment. Meryl is still somewhat shy and hesitant, and she has difficulty adapting to new situations. Friends sometimes view her as unduly sensitive and lacking in self-confidence. Still, in late adolescence all four are purposeful and well directed in meeting their goals, successful in dealing with other people, and sufficiently competent at managing their own lives.

But what if they had received less nurturance and guidance from their families? Would Mike have been vulnerable to adolescent depression? Could Maggie have developed an eating disorder? Might Malcolm have been labeled hyperactive and had serious attention problems at school? Would Meryl have suffered a severe anxiety disorder? Although it is difficult to answer these hypothetical questions, studies of children who have developed emotional problems suggest that teenagers like Mike, Maggie, Malcolm, and Meryl might have turned out differently in less supportive circumstances. Such studies show that children who develop emotional problems are often not qualitatively different from our four children in their initial characteristics. What tips the balance for them are life histories that are more demanding in critical ways and provide poor support for important aspects of development.

It is also interesting to ask whether other youngsters, more prone to emotional or behavioral problems, would have developed them given the *same* experiences as our four children. This question emphasizes a child's genetic or biological vulnerability. For instance, perhaps a child with a strong biological predisposition to depression would have suffered depression during adolescence if confronted with the same life challenges as those faced by Mike. Most researchers who study emotional and behavioral problems believe that such genetic factors always interact with environment (Rutter, 1991).

The subfield of developmental psychology concerned with emotional and behavioral disorders is called **developmental psychopathology.** (The term *pathology* refers to any marked deviation from a normal, healthy state.) Developmental psychopathology is the study of the origins and course of such disorders, whenever they may occur (Cicchetti and Cohen, 1995; Rutter and Sroufe, 2000; Sroufe and Rutter, 1984). It includes:

- the study of disturbed children,
- the developmental roots of adult disorders, and
- the patterns that disorders follow after they emerge.

Developmental psychopathology stresses all the major themes of this book: the importance of developmental contexts, the interaction of genes and environment, the role of past development in current developmental outcomes, and the orderliness of development despite changes over time.

Studying psychopathology from a developmental perspective has enriched our understanding of emotional and behavioral disorders in several ways. First, *it has encouraged us to explore both the origins of abnormal behavior and the ways abnormal behavior changes over time.* Like other aspects of development, abnormality is not static. For example, young children may manifest depression through irritability, while adolescents are more likely to show depressed mood and report feelings of hopelessness.

Second, *it has focused attention on children who seem to be on a path to developing some disorder yet somehow manage not to develop it* (Masten and Coatsworth, 1995; Sroufe, 1997). Such cases of *resilience* provide clues to how to prevent or treat disorders in their early stages. If we can discover what protective factors help these children

Developmental psychopathology: The study of the origins and course of emotional and behavioral disorders.

avoid emotional and behavioral problems, perhaps we can foster these same conditions for others who are at similar risk.

Third, *it encourages us to explore how disorders may have their roots in the ways individuals resolve (or fail to resolve) the major developmental issues all people face* (Sroufe, 1989). Developmental psychopathologists look for the precursors of disorders within the developmental challenges that are most salient at a given age (secure attachment in infancy, increased independence in the preschool period, close peer relationships in middle childhood, and so on). If development goes awry in these critical areas, future problems seem more likely. The key tasks in this search are to define important developmental issues, to identify normal patterns of resolving them, and to describe deviations from these normal patterns. In this way, developmental psychopathology brings together the study of normal and abnormal development.

We focus on these three features of the developmental perspective in the first major section of this chapter. Here we take a closer look at how developmental psychopathologists think about and analyze emotional and behavioral disorders. In the next section we look at various approaches to explaining psychopathology—first those that emphasize biological factors, then those that emphasize environmental factors. This section ends with a discussion of how the developmental perspective combines and integrates all the other views. Then, in the third section of the chapter, we consider some specific developmental disorders that can arise in childhood or adolescence. Finally, we review how the study of developmental psychopathology emphasizes all the major themes of this book.

Questions to Think About As You Read

- What are the different ways that psychological problems can emerge?
- What roles do heredity and environment play in the development of various disorders?
- What problems should parents and teachers be particularly concerned about at each stage of development?

A DEVELOPMENTAL PERSPECTIVE ON PSYCHOPATHOLOGY

A major goal of developmental approaches to psychopathology is to understand why some children who are at risk for developing an emotional or behavioral disorder actually develop it, while others at similar risk do not. Put another way, developmental psychopathologists are interested in both the *risk factors* for emotional and behavioral disorders and the *protective factors* that help people avoid them.

Risk Factors and Protective Factors

Determining factors that place people at risk for developing an emotional or behavioral disorder is a central task for developmental researchers. As you learned in Chapter 3 in connection with prenatal development, a **risk factor** is any factor that increases the likelihood of a negative developmental outcome. For example, childhood risk factors for developing criminal behavior as an adult include persistent aggression, a low IQ, harsh treatment by parents, and parents who engage in criminal activity, who are poorly educated, and/or who have been hospitalized for psychiatric illness (Farrington, 1995; Rutter, 1997). As this list suggests, a risk factor may be genetic (such as a biological parent with a disorder that has a known genetic component), familial (such as a hostile emotional climate in the home), socioeconomic (such as poverty and its associated stress), cultural (such as frequent exposure to a delinquent subculture), or developmental (such as anxious

Risk factor:
Any factor that increases the likelihood of a negative developmental outcome.

Table 15.1 Risk Factors for Child Psychiatric Disorders

Health History
Prematurity
Birth complications
Illnesses
Accidents

Demographic Factors
Low family income
History of parental unemployment
Low parental education
Minority status
Unstable family structure
Large family size

Adverse Conditions
Poverty
Neglect
Abuse
Chaotic family life
Mental illness in parent
Alcoholism in parent
Parental conflict
Social isolation

Stressful Life Events
Serious illness or accidents involving immediate family
Death of parents
Divorce of parents
Remarriage of parents
Trauma (rape, witnessing violence, etc.)
Repeated hospitalization
Foster care
Frequent moves

attachment in infancy or peer rejection in childhood) (Masten and Coatsworth, 1995; Sroufe, 1997). In other words, all five of the contexts of development that we discussed in Chapter 2 must be considered in assessing the risk of psychopathology. (See Table 15.1 for a summary of risk factors for psychiatric disorders in children.)

To understand the significance of risk factors, you must realize that risk is a statistical concept that applies to *groups* of people. We cannot say that a *particular* child who has experienced harsh parental treatment is destined to become a criminal. In fact, most of the people in an at-risk category will *not* develop the particular problem behavior for which they are at risk. Consider schizophrenia, a condition that first appears in young adulthood and is characterized by extremely disordered thinking and severe social withdrawal. The rate of schizophrenia in the general population is only 1 percent. Among people with one biological parent who is schizophrenic, the rate more than triples, rising to 3.7 percent (somewhat higher if related disorders are taken into account) (Farone and Tsuang, 1988). These are the people considered at heightened risk for developing schizophrenia. But note that the vast majority of them—over 95 percent—will *not* develop schizophrenia. Being in the at-risk category in no way guarantees succumbing to the disorder. All it means is that, as a group, these people face a greater risk than the general population.

Since risk factors do not guarantee the development of a disorder, it is generally inappropriate to assume that they are *causes*. Many risk factors may not be causal at all but may simply be associated with other circumstances that contribute to a disorder.

Poverty, for instance, is a risk factor for emotional or behavioral problems. Children who are poor are more likely to develop such problems than children whose parents are financially secure, all other things being equal. But poverty itself is probably not a direct cause of disorders. Rather, it is likely that stress and other factors related to poverty are what make people who are poor more vulnerable (McLoyd, 1998).

While the presence of a single risk factor often has limited predictive power, the presence of several risk factors is usually much more predictive (Masten and Coatsworth, 1995; Sameroff, 2000; Yoshikawa, 1994). As we discussed in Chapter 3, multiple risk factors greatly increase the chances of negative outcomes. As a result, two or three or four risk factors occurring together predict a negative outcome far more strongly than does each factor occurring alone. For example, children with two alcoholic parents are far more likely to develop problems than children with only one alcoholic parent (Earls, 1994; Earls et al., 1988).

Often it is the sheer number of risk factors, not the specific factors present, that predicts a negative outcome. For instance, the presence at age 8 of *any* three (or more) of the risk factors listed earlier for adult criminal behavior strongly predicts the development of such behavior in adulthood (Farrington, 1995). In fact, 75 percent of children who have three or more of these risk factors are convicted of offenses more serious than traffic violations by age 32. Similarly strong predictive power has been found in multiple risk factors for poor school performance and social maladjustment (Sameroff, 2000).

The ways risk factors combine to encourage psychological problems can be quite complex. There is not just one pathway to most disorders. Different combinations of risk factors can lead to the same disorder. Psychopathologists say that multiple causes, in varying combinations, lead to a *final common pathway* to a disorder. Conversely, the same factors may place people at risk for a number of different disorders. For instance, conduct problems, harsh parental treatment, and incompetence with peers in middle childhood are risk factors for a range of negative outcomes in adulthood, including depression, alcoholism, criminal behavior, and schizophrenia (Robins and Price, 1991; Zoccolillo, 1993). Even a very specific risk factor, like having a schizophrenic biological parent, is associated with multiple disorders, including antisocial behavior (Sameroff, 2000).

These linkages illustrate the complexity of causation and the need to consider transformations and branching pathways over the course of development. Problems are expressed in different ways at different stages of development, and the same pattern at one age may diverge into different outcomes over time. For example, misconduct in middle childhood may elicit reactions from others that lead to a loss of self-esteem and feelings of rejection that could later contribute to depression.

Whether risk factors lead to serious emotional or behavior problems is also influenced by the presence of **protective factors**—factors that promote or maintain healthy development (Glick and Zigler, 1990; Sameroff, 2000). Protective factors serve as buffers, counteracting the effects of risk factors and sometimes preventing a disorder from arising (Masten and Coatsworth, 1995; Werner and Smith, 2001). For instance, in line with other researchers, Michael Rutter (1979) has reported that the presence of three or more common risk factors predicts a 75 percent rate of problem behavior. However, if the protective factor of a loving, dependable parent is simultaneously present, the rate of problem behavior is only 25 percent.

Thus, the route from risks to emotional and behavioral disorders is rarely direct and straight. Many twists and turns are possible along the way, including turns in a positive direction. Such an idea was presented in Bowlby's tree model, which was discussed in Chapter 1. This web of influences underscores the need to consider the *total context* of development when assessing child problems.

Protective factor:
Any factor that promotes or maintains healthy development.

/dehart5

Resilience

Assessing Normal and Abnormal Behavior

In addition to its focus on how risk factors and protective factors combine to influence development, the developmental perspective on psychopathology has other important features.

The presence of a loving, dependable parent early in life is one of the most important protective factors against later psychological and behavioral disorders.

mhhe.com /dehart5

Assessing Childhood Problems

One is its view that normal and abnormal behavior must be considered together because disorders often have their roots in the ways normal developmental issues are handled. Thus, to understand the origins of problem behaviors, developmental psychopathologists look at how people resolve the major developmental challenges we have discussed throughout this book. When attachment is insecure in infancy, when emerging autonomy is compromised in toddlerhood, when self-management and peer competence are not acquired by middle childhood, serious problems can result.

It is not always easy to tell when a particular child's development deviates far enough from expected patterns to be considered abnormal. A behavior that *seems* problematic may turn out not to be a major cause for concern. Many seemingly problematic behaviors are in fact fairly typical at certain ages (Wenar, 1994). For example, lying is common among small children, but it drops off after age 6 for girls and age 8 for boys. Temper outbursts are common throughout childhood, especially for boys. Disturbing dreams are quite common for girls when they enter school and for boys and girls just prior to adolescence. Hallucinations, however, are not common at *any* age.

Such information is very important in judging the significance of a particular behavior for present and future adjustment. Common problems are less cause for worry than uncommon ones. For instance, a high activity level by itself, without aggression or other symptoms, is not a major cause for concern when found in a preschool boy. In fact, about 50 percent of parents of preschool boys say their sons are unusually active. Similarly, food finickiness is fairly common at age 3 and is unlikely to predict anorexia at age 15. Sensitivity, shyness, and specific fears, by themselves, are also normal in young children and probably do not predict later pathology.

Other, less common behavior patterns, however, are strongly linked to later disorders. Conduct problems are a clear warning sign, especially a combination of aggression, lying, stealing, and defiance that persists into middle childhood. Another important warning sign is difficulty with peers—not just occasional squabbles with friends, which is relatively common, but persistent unpopularity with other children. Even though unpopularity is not generally considered pathological by itself, it is one of the strongest predictors of a range of adult disorders (Rubin, Bukowski, and Parker, 1998; Robins, 1978).

From a developmental perspective, the link between peer problems and later maladjustment is understandable. Because forming a close friendship and becoming an active member of a same-gender peer group are major tasks of middle childhood, incompetence with peers at this age represents a major adaptational failure. In addition, unsuccessful peer relations in middle childhood leave a person unprepared for close relationships later in life (Sroufe, Egeland, and Carlson, 1999). Close and supportive relationships, in turn, are a major protective factor, reducing the likelihood of pathology and buffering children against the effects of problems that do arise (Sroufe and Rutter, 1984). For instance, having family and friends who are willing and able to offer social support is associated with more rapid and complete recovery for people hospitalized with a major psychiatric disorder (Glick and Zigler, 1990). Lack of close relationships, conversely, leaves a person more vulnerable.

Change and Stability Over Time

Another feature of the developmental perspective on psychopathology is its focus on patterns of change and stability in behavior over time. Such patterns were clearly revealed in a study by Lee Robins (1966, 1978), who was able to obtain data about a large number of children who had been seen at a child guidance clinic in St. Louis. Years later, Robins studied these same people to see how well they had fared as adults. Some of the results were surprising.

Robins did find that psychiatric problems in childhood were in general related to problems in adulthood, showing continuity in development and links from past to present. For instance, 34 percent of the children who had been seen at the clinic had serious adult disorders, whereas only 8 percent of a control group from the same neighborhoods did. Moreover, only 20 percent of the children from the clinic were free of problems as adults, compared with 57 percent of the controls.

The exact links between childhood and adult problems varied greatly, however, depending on the particular disorders involved. Sometimes the links were very direct. For example, among the children classified as *sociopaths* (people who behave irresponsibly, with no concern for others and no signs of remorse for their misdeeds), 94 percent had been arrested by adulthood (versus 17 percent of the controls) and 70 percent had major adult problems such as alcoholism, criminal convictions, and psychosis. Looking at this link from the other direction, virtually *all* the diagnosed adult sociopaths had shown sociopathic behavior when they were children.

In other cases the links between childhood and adult problems were more complex and difficult to foresee. For instance, adult schizophrenia, a disorder often marked by severe withdrawal and social isolation, was not generally associated with these same symptoms in childhood. Instead, adult schizophrenics often showed conduct disorders as children, behaviors such as overaggressiveness or antisocial tendencies. Depression in adulthood has also been found to be linked to conduct disorders in childhood, especially among females (Robins and Price, 1991).

Finally, Robins discovered that some childhood problems were *not* strongly linked to adult disorders. For example, children who were shy and anxious (so-called *internalizing* children) were no more likely to have problems in adulthood than children from the control group. Thus, we might be optimistic that a child like Meryl will not go on to become a troubled adult.

To summarize, although some childhood disorders show rather simple continuity with adult disorders, many do not. Some childhood problems typically disappear with time, while others evolve into very different forms in later years. Development is often characterized by transformations over time, rather than by simple continuity. Still, all of these links between childhood problems and adult psychopathology are meaningful.

EXPLAINING PSYCHOPATHOLOGY

Over the years, various models of psychopathology have been proposed (Lazare, 1973). A **model** is a framework for explaining why things happen, a set of ideas and assumptions about causes and effects. Models of psychopathology focus on the *etiology* of psychological disorders—the conditions that produce them. Some models of psychopathology focus mainly on the biological underpinnings of emotional and behavioral problems, while others focus mainly on environmental factors. These two approaches are not incompatible. In fact, most researchers believe that psychological disorders often involve a complex interplay of biology and environment.

Model:
A framework for explaining why things happen, a set of ideas and assumptions about causes and effects.

Biological Perspectives

The Traditional Medical Model The traditional medical model draws an explicit analogy between psychological disorders and physical illnesses. It holds that psychological disorders should be considered mental illnesses. Just as diabetes, for example, results from a deficiency in the body's production of insulin, a psychological disturbance is thought to be caused by some underlying structural or physiological malfunction in some part of the brain.

Certain mental disorders do fit the medical model. For instance, *general paresis,* an irreversible deterioration of all mental and physical processes, has been traced to an attack

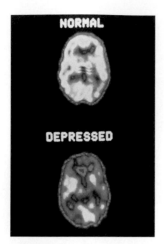

Depressed and normal adults show different patterns of cerebral cortex activity, but these differences do not necessarily mean that a disorder is primarily physiological.

on the body's organs, including the brain, by the bacteria that cause syphilis. Similarly, *autism,* a condition characterized by a range of severe cognitive deficits and unresponsiveness to other people, also appears to be the result of biological abnormality (Travis and Sigman, 2000). However, for most behavioral and emotional problems, especially those of children, biological factors are better viewed as contributors than as causes.

Modern Neurological and Physiological Models Modern neurological and physiological models of psychopathology focus on these contributing biological factors, especially chemical imbalances in the brain. These imbalances involve either neurotransmitters (chemicals that govern the transfer of signals from one nerve cell to another) or other chemicals that control the activities of neurotransmitters (Pennington and Welsh, 1995). The evidence that chemical imbalances are involved in some psychological disorders is often quite impressive. For example, researchers have found lower-than-normal levels of certain brain chemicals in people who are depressed. Drugs used to alleviate depression raise the levels of these chemicals, while substances that lower their levels cause a recurrence of depressive symptoms (Harrington, 1994).

Although it is tempting to say in this case that chemical deficiencies cause depression, determining cause is difficult because biological and environmental factors are mutually influencing. For instance, studies of young monkeys show that changes in the levels of these same brain chemicals occur following permanent separation from a parent (McKinney, 1977). The levels of these chemicals are also influenced by the quality of care the young monkey has received (Kraemer, 1992). Thus, depression and changes in brain chemistry may be a chicken and egg situation, in which it is impossible to say which comes first. It may be more appropriate to consider unusual brain chemistry as a correlate or *marker* of a disorder, rather than a cause. This is true even if symptoms of depression can be relieved by a drug that returns brain chemistry to normal. Although chemical imbalances may be associated with these symptoms, faulty brain chemistry is not necessarily their initial cause.

Genetic Models Researchers who take a genetic perspective on psychopathology assume that some people inherit a genetically based predisposition to develop emotional and behavioral problems. Since genes express themselves through activities within the cells of the body, genetic models of psychopathology can be thought of as a subclass of neurological and physiological models.

Virtually no modern behavior geneticist believes single genes directly cause complex disorders such as schizophrenia (Mash and Wolfe, 2002; Siminoff, McGuffin, and Gottesman, 1994). A single defective gene could not account for the distribution of schizophrenia found in families. If one dominant gene caused this disorder, the children of two schizophrenic parents would have at least a 75 percent chance of inheriting the condition; if one recessive gene were the root of the problem, schizophrenia would occur in all youngsters with two schizophrenic parents. The actual statistics are very different. When both the mother and father have the disorder, only 25 to 35 percent of their children develop it, even though in these cases children are also dealing with very atypical environments. Such a pattern suggests the inherited component of schizophrenia is *polygenic*—that is, arising from several genes acting together.

How do scientists know that *any* genetic component is involved in schizophrenia? Couldn't the greater incidence of schizophrenia in children born to and raised by schizophrenic parents be caused as easily by environment? To eliminate this possibility, researchers often study children born to schizophrenic women but raised by nonschizophrenic adoptive parents. Such studies show that these children have a greater chance of developing schizophrenia than adopted children born to women who do not have the disorder (Siminoff, McGuffin, and Gottesman, 1994). Environmental factors could still be at work here. Adopted children with a schizophrenic biological mother might have experienced more detrimental intrauterine environments or less adequate preadoption care. Such early environmental factors might partly account for these children's higher susceptibility to schizophrenia. Still, the preponderance of evidence from adoption studies, twin studies, and other genetic research makes a good case for a hereditary factor in schizophrenia. A similar case has also been made for some forms of adult depression (Harrington, 1994).

This is not to say that environmental forces play no role in schizophrenia and depression (Cannon, Mednick, and Parnas, 1990; Cadoret et al., 1990). Even identical twins, with their identical genetic makeup, are only 20 to 60 percent *concordant* for schizophrenia, depending on the study (Gottesman, 1991). This means that even if one twin develops the disorder, the other twin often does not. As a result of such findings, modern genetic models of psychopathology generally emphasize a combination of genetic and environmental influences (Rutter and Silberg, 2002).

Environmental Perspectives

Sociological Models Sociological models of psychopathology stress the social context surrounding children who develop a disorder (Cadoret et al., 1990). When studying depression, for instance, a researcher who takes a sociological perspective would look at the depressed person's social situation. Has the person lost a loved one recently? Moved to a new community? Been cut off from important sources of social support? Therapy might take the form of helping the person become more involved with others.

Many disorders besides depression have been approached from a sociological viewpoint, including hyperactivity and attention problems. Some observers have argued that the sedentary and regimented environment of most schools in the United States and the rapid-fire, overstimulating nature of the surrounding culture contribute to the problems of young children (de Grandpre, 1999; McGuiness, 1989). According to these critics, when a child has a problem sitting still and paying attention at school, we should look to the school situation or to the particular classroom, as well as the pressure put on children. Notice how sharply this view contrasts with the biological perspective. Proponents of neurological and physiological models would look for some kind of brain dysfunction in a child who is persistently fidgety and inattentive at school. The sociological perspective, in contrast, assumes the surrounding context is the heart of the problem.

Behavioral Models Like sociological models, behavioral models focus on environmental factors, but instead of emphasizing a child's general social situation, behavioral

The behavioral model focuses on changing children's behaviors, regardless of whether they reflect serious disturbance or simple misbehavior.

models look at specific rewards, punishments, and modeled behaviors (Bandura, 1986). In the case of a hyperactive child, for instance, behaviorists would look at how teachers and classmates respond to the child's behavior. The assumption is that the child's disruptive behavior persists because it is reinforced by the outcomes it produces. The child may get attention for acting up in class, and even negative attention can be rewarding to some children. The recommended treatment involves changing the environmental contingencies—that is, the connections between the child's behaviors and their consequences. The environment must be restructured so that the child is rewarded only for appropriate responses, not disruptive ones.

This form of treatment can be effective. When hyperactive children are rewarded for staying in their chairs, paying attention, and completing assignments (usually with points or tokens they can exchange for desirable items such as candy), their behavior at school improves (O'Leary and O'Leary, 1977). This procedure can even be applied successfully to an entire classroom of disruptive children. Likewise, training parents to be consistent and moderate in discipline leads to significant reductions in children's aggressive behavior at home (Dishion, French, and Patterson, 1995).

The earliest behavioral models of psychopathology assumed that a child's symptoms *are* the disorder. In other words, when a child is hyperactive and disruptive in the classroom, those negative behaviors themselves are the problem. There is no need to dig any deeper in a search for hidden causes within the child. More recently, this classic behavioral approach has been altered to take into account internal cognitive processes, which include a child's expectations, beliefs, and ways of viewing the world (Bandura, 1997; Kendall, 2000). Therapists who use this newer cognitive behavioral approach would try to teach hyperactive children some basic cognitive skills to help them behave appropriately in a variety of situations (Kendall, 2000). For example, these children might be taught things they could routinely say to themselves ("Slow down, take your time") to encourage thinking before acting. The goal is for the results of the therapy to carry over, or *generalize,* to settings other than the one in which treatment took place.

Psychodynamic Models Psychodynamic models of psychopathology have evolved over the years from Sigmund Freud's psychoanalytic theory. Like medical models, they assume that disturbed behavior is a manifestation of underlying causes. Psychodynamic models, however, do not regard those causes as physical in nature. Instead, the underlying causes are assumed to be thoughts and feelings—fears, anxieties, conflicts, irrational beliefs and outlooks—produced by life experiences. This is why psychodynamic therapists believe it is not enough simply to treat the behavioral symptoms of a problem. In their view, if you treated a hyperactive boy only by rewarding him for acceptable behavior, you would be ignoring the core of his problem. You would be leaving untouched the underlying factors—fear of abandonment, perhaps, or distress at tension between his parents—that are producing his negative actions. Advocates of this approach make a clear distinction between primary and secondary causes. A boy may be disruptive in the classroom because of the attention this gets him (secondary cause), but he may be seeking the attention because of conflict at home (primary cause).

To understand better how a psychodynamic perspective compares with other perspectives on psychopathology, consider a woman who is deeply depressed after her husband dies (Lazare, 1973). Those who adopt a medical model would be concerned with diagnosing her problem, determining whether depression runs in her family, and assessing how she has responded to medical treatments (drugs, electric shock therapy) if she has ever suffered from depression before. Those with a sociological perspective would look at her overall social context (her current living arrangements, the number of friends she has) to see if it is adequate to meet her needs. Behaviorists would focus on the specific sources of positive reinforcement she has lost with the death of her husband, and they might help her develop other sources of reward and satisfaction in her life.

In contrast to all these, only psychodynamic therapists would probe her inner thoughts and feelings for causes that are rooted in her history of life experiences. What was the nature of her relationship with her husband? Did it mirror any earlier relationships, such as the one she had with her father, who perhaps died when she was a teenager? Was the woman ambivalent about her father? Had she adequately mourned his loss? Does she somehow feel responsible for his death and her husband's? Is she unable to express her anger toward her husband for leaving her by dying?

Family Models Family models take yet another perspective in the effort to search the environment for the causes of psychopathology. This view holds that, while one person in a family is usually identified as having the problem, in fact that person's symptoms are a reflection of disturbance in the larger family system (Wagner and Reiss, 1995; Sroufe and Fleeson, 1988). In one family, for example, the hyperactive son was labeled the problem, but a look at the entire family revealed that the problem was much broader. The boy's father devoted all his energies to caring for his dependent parents, felt burdened by the further responsibility of a wife and three children, and was totally unable to express his own needs for care and nurturance. The mother, who felt neglected by her husband, got what little satisfaction she could from the antics of her hyperactive son. The son, in turn, served as a foil for the other two children, who were models of deportment, mature beyond their years. Notice how all the behavioral pieces of this family fit together into an interconnected whole. The problem cannot be understood by looking at only one of the family members, because the behavior of each person is encouraging and supporting that of the others.

This perspective is supported by findings on the role of life stress and social support in child development, as well as by research on parental conflict and psychopathology. Witnessing parental violence, for example, is associated with later behavior problems of boys, even after controlling for stress and poverty (Yates et al., in press).

The Developmental Perspective

The developmental perspective draws upon and integrates all the models we have described. It assumes that genetic and other biological influences, the family, socioeconomic and cultural contexts, and past developmental history all influence the development of emotional and behavioral problems just as they influence normal development (Cadoret et al., 1990; Robins and Rutter, 1990; Sameroff, 2000; Sroufe, Carlson, et al., 1999).

In the case of a child like Meryl, a developmental perspective would consider a wide range of possible factors contributing to her hesitancy in new situations: her biological makeup, learned cultural norms of appropriate female behavior, her mother's inconsistency in reinforcing more positive responses, insecurity stemming from ambivalent care

Family theorists focus on the entire family, including how each member reflects the family system, not just on the child with obvious symptoms.

experienced during infancy, and the early conflict between Karen and her mother, which encouraged Karen to develop unrealistic expectations for Meryl. A developmental perspective would also explore how Meryl's basic style of behavior changed over time in response to changes in her surroundings. As Karen's life stabilized, as she worked out problems with her mother and developed a supportive relationship with Joe, she became more confident and consistent in handling Meryl, and Meryl responded by becoming more confident and capable.

The developmental perspective has proven extremely helpful in pulling together the factors that contribute to far more serious emotional problems than Meryl's. For example, Remi Cadoret and his colleagues (1990) found that a number of childhood environmental factors predicted depression in a sample of adopted children followed to adulthood, even after depression in the biological parents was statistically controlled for. These factors included poverty, parental illness, early deprivation of parenting, and, especially, delayed placement in a permanent adoptive home. The researchers also demonstrated an interaction of biology and environment. A combination of biological vulnerability and delayed placement in an adoptive home predicted depression far better than either factor alone.

Evidence for the power of the developmental perspective also comes from a Finnish study of adopted children (Tienari et al., 1990). The researchers examined the quality of adoptive homes, as well as each child's genetic risk for schizophrenia (measured by whether the biological mother was schizophrenic). The results of the study are summarized in Table 15.2. As you can see, children of schizophrenic mothers were more likely than other children to develop psychotic disorders, which suggests a genetic influence. Yet none of the children in supportive adoptive homes became psychotic, even when they were in the genetic risk group. In fact, psychological disorders of all types were much more likely to develop when the adoptive families functioned poorly. Thus, it appears to be a combination of genetic *and* environmental risk that leads to psychotic disorders.

Juvenile depression is another serious disorder for which the developmental perspective has helped to integrate biological and environmental causes (Garber, 2000; Harrington, 1994). Developmental psychopathologists have noticed a marked rise in depression following puberty, which suggests that hormonal changes and other biological factors may be involved. At the same time, they have observed that significantly more teenage girls than boys are depressed. Perhaps this is partly because girls in our culture

Table 15.2 The Role of Adoptive Family Functioning and Genetic Risk in Psychological Disorders of Adoptees

| | Adoptive Family Ratings | | | | | | | |
| | Total Number | | Healthy | | Neurotic | | Severe Dysfunction | |
Adoptee Diagnosis	At Risk*	Control**	At Risk	Control	At Risk	Control	At Risk	Control
Healthy	58	67	41	35	11	21	6	11
Neurotic	34	41	7	11	12	16	15	14
Borderline syndrome and severe personality disorder	26	17	2	1	6	8	18	8
Psychotic	8	1	0	0	3	0	5	1

*Biological mother is schizophrenic.
**No known genetic risk.
Source: Tienari et al., 1990.

are more likely to be socialized toward feelings of helplessness. Other factors contributing to juvenile depression are loss of one's mother, especially before age 11, and emotional distance from parents in early childhood (Duggal et al., 2001; Harris, Brown, and Bifulco, 1990). Thus, a developmental explanation of depression must incorporate biological factors, cultural influences, developmental history, and the youngster's immediate environment, such as home life and friends.

SOME CHILDHOOD DISORDERS

Psychological disorders that usually appear first in childhood or adolescence are listed in Table 15.3 (American Psychiatric Association, 2000). In this section we consider six of them: *autism and related disorders, conduct disorders, attention deficit/hyperactivity disorder, anxiety disorders, depression,* and *anorexia nervosa.* For most childhood disorders, both biological and environmental causes have been proposed, although the evidence supporting each is not always equally compelling. Autism is the one childhood disorder about which developmentalists are in agreement that biological factors are largely responsible. The other disorders are open to a number of explanations.

Autism and Related Disorders

You are visiting a home for children with severe developmental disorders. On a couch across from you an 8-year-old boy sits rhythmically rocking forward and back. Occasionally he starts to perform a strange, ritualistic flicking of his fingers in front of his face. All the while he seems oblivious of you. As you approach him, however, his rocking intensifies. He does not speak to you, nor does he have any communicative language. When you sit on the couch a short distance from him, he hurriedly rises and goes to a corner of the room, where he again starts to rock and flick his fingers, this time furiously.

Aaron is a handsome 12-year-old boy with a performance IQ score in the normal range and a verbal IQ score slightly below normal. He attends middle school and spends part of his day in a special education classroom and part of his day in regular classes. He started to talk very late; now his vocabulary and grammar are nearly normal for his age, but the intonation of his speech is peculiar and what he says is not always socially appropriate. He enjoys working with computers and is very skilled at solving computer problems. He is obsessed with Star Trek *and can identify all the ships from all the* Star Trek *movies and television shows. He does not like loud noises and is bothered by the way many fabrics feel against his skin. His motor development is quite delayed, and he walks with a peculiar, clumsy gait.*

Autism and Related Disorders

Both of these boys have been diagnosed with **autism,** which is classified by the American Psychiatric Association (2000) as a *pervasive developmental disorder* because it is so severe. Its symptoms are always apparent by the age of 3. As you can see by the descriptions, however, the severity of the disorder varies considerably. Full-blown autism is only one of several **autistic spectrum disorders**—a range of related pervasive developmental disorders with overlapping symptoms and varying severity. The extreme syndrome shown by the first child is quite rare, affecting only 4 in 10,000 children (Lord and Rutter, 1994). When the entire range of autistic spectrum disorders is considered, the frequency rises to 6 in 1,000. This is a greater incidence than was previously recognized, probably because of increased awareness of the condition and an appreciation of the full range of related disorders (Medical Research Council, 2002).

Because autism is often diagnosed during toddlerhood, some physicians and parents of autistic children have suggested that childhood immunizations received in the second

Autism:
A rare, severe developmental disorder, featuring a powerful insistence on sameness, extreme social isolation, and severe language deficits.

Autistic spectrum disorders:
A range of related pervasive developmental disorders with overlapping symptoms and varying severity.

Table 15.3 Disorders Usually First Diagnosed in Infancy, Childhood, or Adolescence*

Attention-Deficit and Disruptive Behavior Disorders

Attention-Deficit/Hyperactivity Disorder
Characterized by prominent symptoms of inattention and/or hyperactivity-impulsivity.

Disruptive Behavior Disorders
Conduct Disorder
   Characterized by a pattern of behavior that violates the basic rights of others or major age-appropriate societal norms or rules.
Oppositional Defiant Disorder
   Characterized by a pattern of negativistic, hostile, and defiant behavior.

Pervasive Developmental Disorders
Characterized by severe deficits and pervasive impairments in multiple areas of development, including impairment in reciprocal social interaction and communication, as well as the presence of stereotyped behavior, interests, and activities.
Includes *Autistic Disorder, Asperger's Disorder,* and *Childhood Disintegrative Disorder.*

Mental Retardation
Characterized by significantly subaverage intellectual functioning (IQ of approximately 70 or below) with onset before age 18 and concurrent deficits or impairments in adaptive functioning. Separate categories for *Mild, Moderate, Severe,* and *Profound Mental Retardation.*

Feeding and Eating Disorders of Infancy or Early Childhood
Characterized by persistent disturbances in feeding and eating.
Includes *Pica, Rumination Disorder,* and *Feeding Disorder of Infancy or Early Childhood.*
(*Anorexia Nervosa* and *Bulimia* are included under adult disorders.)

Tic Disorders
Characterized by vocal and/or motor tics.
Includes *Tourette's Disorder, Chronic Motor or Vocal Tic Disorder,* and *Transient Tic Disorder.*

Elimination Disorders
Includes *Encopresis* (repeated passage of feces into inappropriate places) and *Enuresis* (repeated voiding of urine into inappropriate places).

Communication Disorders
Characterized by difficulties in speech or language.
Includes *Expressive Language Disorder, Mixed Receptive-Expressive Language Disorder, Phonological Disorder,* and *Stuttering.*

Motor Skills Disorder
Developmental Coordination Disorder
Characterized by motor coordination that is substantially below that expected given the person's chronological age and measured intelligence.

Learning Disorders
Characterized by academic functioning substantially below that expected given the person's chronological age, measured intelligence, and age-appropriate education.
Includes *Reading Disorder, Mathematics Disorder,* and *Disorder of Written Expression.*

Other Disorders of Infancy, Childhood, or Adolescence
Separation Anxiety Disorder
   Developmentally inappropriate and excessive anxiety concerning separation from home or attachment figures.
Reactive Attachment Disorder of Infancy or Early Childhood
   Markedly disturbed and developmentally inappropriate social relatedness that occurs in most contexts and is associated with extremely abnormal patterns of care.
Selective Mutism
   Consistent failure to speak in specific social situations despite speaking in other situations.
Stereotypic Movement Disorder
   Repetitive, seemingly driven, and nonfunctional motor behavior that markedly interferes with normal activities and may result in bodily injury.

year of life, especially the combination measles, mumps, and rubella vaccine, were causing infants to develop autism. However, large-scale studies in several countries have found no evidence of a causal link between immunization and autism (Madsen et al., 2002; Medical Research Council, 2002).

According to Leo Kanner (1943), who first identified autism, the core features of the disorder are:

- a powerful insistence on preserving sameness in the environment;
- extreme social isolation, or autistic aloneness; and
- severe language deficits.

The first of the core features of autism could account for the ritualistic behaviors often seen in autistic children, such as the repetitive body rocking and finger-flicking in the preceding example. The constant level of stimulation provided by such behaviors helps to maintain sameness in the environment. Autistic children apparently have difficulty regulating input from their senses, and any new stimulus can cause them great distress (Lord and Rutter, 1994). As a result, they have trouble making sense of their experiences and are easily overwhelmed by them. Even a small change of routine that most people would hardly notice (putting the child's chair in a different place, offering him or her milk in a different cup) can provoke a tantrum.

The second feature, autistic aloneness, means that autistic children recoil from contact with others. As babies they do not cuddle when held by their parents. Nor do they babble, make eye contact, or engage in social smiling, imitation, or other forms of social play (Lord and Rutter, 1994). Their attachment relationships are often grossly abnormal and may include intense preoccupation with objects. This withdrawal from social interaction seems to be related to the sensory overload to which autistic children are prone. Apparently, interacting with others is very confusing and upsetting for children who can't make sense out of simple stimuli.

The third symptom, severe speech deficits, means that autistic children do not use language normally in spontaneous communication (Lord and Rutter, 1994; Travis and Sigman, 2000). Children with the most severe forms of autism are often mute, and many who do speak are *echolalic*—that is, they repeat words and phrases they hear with no concern for their meaning. Children with less severe forms of the disorder often speak with peculiar intonation and have great difficulty with *pragmatics*—the social use of language. Autistic children often have great trouble

Autistic children often have severe difficulty with social interaction.

learning even simple abstract concepts, such as *larger than,* even though they appear to have normal memories for routine information, such as where particular toys are kept.

Autistic children seem to have particular difficulty with social cognition. Some researchers have referred to this difficulty as **mind blindness,** a deficit in development of a theory of mind (see Chapter 9). Even beyond what might be expected given their other difficulties, those with severe autism are unable to understand the concept of mind or the intentions, beliefs, and thoughts of others. They show little interest in what others are seeing or feeling (Baron-Cohen, 2000; Siegel, 1999).

There are other pervasive developmental disorders that show only some of the features of autism. Children with **Asperger's syndrome,** for example, show many of the same odd preoccupations and social deficits as autistic children, but their cognitive and language skills are superior (Mash and Wolfe, 2002). They have more motor coordination problems than autistic children, who generally are quite motorically skilled.

Although the exact causes of autistic spectrum disorders are still not known, it is clear that they have a neurological basis (Lord and Rutter, 1994; Travis and Sigman,

Mind blindness:

Deficits in understanding the concept of mind or the intentions, beliefs, and thoughts of others.

Asperger's syndrome:

An autistic spectrum disorder characterized by odd preoccupations, social deficits, and motor coordination problems, but superior cognitive and language skills.

2000). Brain imaging studies have found an array of abnormalities in several areas of the brain, including various lobes of the cerebral cortex, the cerebellum, and certain limbic structures (Mash and Wolfe, 2002). Many autistic children develop signs of brain pathology such as seizures as they get older (Lord and Rutter, 1994; Mash and Wolfe, 2002). The cause of these neurological differences is not yet clear, though autism is statistically related to various prenatal complications, such as exposure to rubella.

There is also increasing evidence for genetic factors, most likely involving multiple genes (Travis and Sigman, 2000). If one of a pair of monozygotic twins is autistic, the other is also likely to be; however, this is not true for dizygotic twins. It was once thought that autism did not run in families, in part because it is rare to find more than one child in a family with full-blown autism. However, when the full range of autistic spectrum disorders is considered, it is far more common to find multiple cases in the same immediate or extended family.

It is hard to be optimistic about the long-term adjustment of most autistic children (Lord and Rutter, 1994). Only a very small percentage of those with the most severe form of the disorder, who are unable to communicate with language and have IQ scores under 50, can live outside institutions as adults. For those with normal nonverbal intelligence and some language skills, the outlook is better (Mash and Wolfe, 2002). Given extensive, highly structured treatment, about half of them attain marginally adequate adjustment. However, even autistic adults who hold down jobs and are relatively independent generally continue to have social impairments; as a result, they seldom marry.

Conduct Disorders

Mark is a bright, capable 11-year-old, but he is also a daredevil and a loner. A favorite activity is racing his all-terrain vehicle through the woods. Younger boys are at times attracted to Mark's daring antics (such as sneaking into adult bookstores), but friendships between Mark and others are always short-lived. Mark was referred for treatment because for two years he had been ransacking and robbing houses. He is a "master of the sincere lie" and is viewed by professionals as unreachable. A routine of his, which ultimately got him caught, was to show up back at the scene of his latest robbery and offer to help put the house back in order. "His manner was one of sincere concern, and he asked for no favors in return." (Adapted from Wenar, 1990, pp. 231–32)

**mhhe.com
/dehart5**

Conduct Disorders

Conduct disorder:
A persistent pattern of repeatedly violating either age-appropriate social norms or the basic rights of others.

Mark's behavior fits a diagnosis of **conduct disorder,** a persistent pattern of repeatedly violating either age-appropriate social norms or the basic rights of others. Children who engage in drug abuse and violent acts, as well as those who chronically lie, cheat, run away from home, or show disregard for others, fall into this category. Juvenile delinquency, a legal concept that includes chronic truancy, vandalism, stealing, or otherwise breaking the law, is also subsumed under conduct disorders (Yoshikawa, 1994).

Mental health professionals distinguish among degrees of conduct disorder, from mild to severe, depending on the extent to which the child's actions harm other people (American Psychiatric Association, 2000). They also distinguish between conduct disorders that involve aggressive behavior and those that do not, as well as between children who are able to form normal bonds of friendship and affection *(socialized)* and those who seem to have no feelings for others *(undersocialized)*. Although it is hard to say for sure from the brief description of Mark, his conduct disorder would probably fit the *nonaggressive, undersocialized* pattern. He ransacks the houses he robs in a destructive manner, but he does not seek physical confrontations with the owners. He does not seem to have formed any real friendships, even with other delinquent youths. We would view his behavior with even more alarm if it included acts of deliberate interpersonal violence (such as setting fire to houses in which people were sleeping). We would be less likely to view him as emotionally disturbed if he exhibited antisocial behavior as part of peer group activities, though the behavior would still be of great concern.

Conduct disorder is one of the most frequent diagnoses given to children, especially boys, who are referred to mental-health centers (Mash and Wolfe, 2002). These problems are also among the most persistent (Dodge, 2000; Robins and Price, 1991; Rutter, 1997; Yoshikawa, 1994). When aggression and antisocial behavior begin early, they are very stable across the childhood years and predict problems in adulthood. Such a pattern is referred to as a **life-course-persistent conduct disorder** (Moffitt, 1993). In contrast, **adolescent-limited conduct disorders** are those that first appear in adolescence; individuals who fit this pattern often do not go on to have chronic problems.

In contrast to autism, conduct disorder does not fit a biological model very well; the evidence is much stronger for the role of environmental factors. Nonetheless, possible biological causes have been proposed. In adults, researchers report that high levels of aggression are associated with low levels of the neurotransmitter serotonin (Mash and Wolfe, 2002) and possible genetic differences (Rutter, 1997). A genetic component has been suggested for children as well, but the link between heredity and misbehavior is tenuous and may be accounted for by differences in IQ and other factors (Mash and Wolfe, 2002; Plomin, Nitz, and Rowe, 1990; Yoshikawa, 1994). Others argue that the persistence of the problem, along with difficulties in language, impulse control, and planfulness, suggests a neuropsychological deficit (Moffitt, 1993). However, no specific mechanisms have been demonstrated.

A large number of studies have found a link between conduct disorders and a negative family environment, including poverty and stress, conflict between the child's parents, and parents' hostility toward, rejection of, or abuse of the child (Dishion, French, and Patterson, 1995; Dodge, 2000; Farrington, 1995; Rutter, 1997; Werner and Smith, 2001; Yoshikawa, 1994). Similarly, therapists working with hard-core offenders attest to their histories of early mistreatment, and large-scale interview studies further support the frequency of this relationship (Kruttschnitt, Heath, and Ward, 1986). Of course, such correlational data cannot tell us for certain whether a negative family environment causes conduct disorders, but the fact that these same findings consistently appear is very suggestive. Moreover, the correlation between child aggression and parental mistreatment of the child is greater than the correlation between child aggression and parents' overall aggressiveness, as measured by standard psychological scales (Patterson and Dishion, 1988). This implies that how parents treat children, and not simply the genes they pass on, fosters the development of conduct disorders.

The great cultural differences in violence also suggest a prominent role for environment, as opposed to genetic or innate neurological causes of conduct problems (Mash and Wolfe, 2002). There are cultures in which interpersonal violence is rare, such as the Lepcha in the Indian Himalayas, where there was no authenticated case of homicide over a 200-year period. The United States leads all industrialized nations by far in violent behavior, but there are nonindustrialized cultures with even higher rates of violence. In the United States itself there are notable community variations, with a clear role for poverty and stress.

Prospective, longitudinal data often can make a contribution to questions of etiology. In the Minnesota Longitudinal Study, 180 children were followed from before birth. Various influences on development, such as prenatal care, early neurological status, temperament, and language and cognitive development, were assessed age by age. This study confirmed the distinction between life-course-persistent and adolescent-limited conduct disorders. Those who entered the pathway to conduct problems early and stayed on it had prior histories characterized by inadequate care, including avoidant attachment and maltreatment, chaotic home environments, high family stress, and a climate of violence (Aguilar et al., 2000; Yates et al., in press). Histories of those whose problems emerged in adolescence were not distinguishable from those who never showed conduct problems. There was no support for the idea that the life-course-persistent group had an inherent neurological deficit. The early measures of neurological status, temperament, and language and cognitive development did not distinguish them. They did have certain cognitive problems, but these emerged well after the start of their conduct problems and may be a

Life-course-persistent conduct disorder:
A conduct disorder that begins early, is stable across the childhood years, and predicts problems in adulthood.

Adolescent-limited conduct disorder:
A conduct disorder that first appears in adolescence and does not predict problems in adulthood.

reflection of general maladaptation. Some children may have out-of-balance activation and inhibitory systems in their brains, but it is not at all clear that they were born that way.

Early detection and intervention may be critical to stemming the development of a conduct disorder. Once a conduct disorder has been allowed to progress across the childhood years, the problem is usually very difficult to treat (Yoshikawa, 1994). Patterson and his colleagues have had some success using behavioral approaches to break the negative cycles between parents and aggressive children (Dishion, French, and Patterson, 1995). Also impressive have been efforts at early intervention and prevention with young children at high risk for conduct disorders. Successful programs have the following characteristics in common:

- they last at least two years;
- they provide high-quality infant day care or preschool for the child;
- they provide emotional support and developmental information for the parents; and
- they address the family's broader context, via educational and vocational counseling, for instance (Yoshikawa, 1994).

Attention Deficit/Hyperactivity Disorder

Brad was always in trouble. His neighbors were mad at him, both because he trampled their flowers as he ran home from school and because he poured milk down the pockets of their new pool table "just to see what would happen." Brad's teachers were also upset because he was constantly whistling and generally disrupting the classroom. He couldn't seem to follow instructions or complete assignments because his attention kept wandering. Often he would fidget with objects and accidentally break them. Brad's parents were at their wits' end. They had tried everything, from bargaining to belts, but they couldn't make him shape up. Yet he was a bright child with an IQ of 125. He was not malicious and he had a good sense of humor, along with an infectious grin. One day the lifeguard pulled him off the bottom of the community pool. It turned out he wasn't drowning; he was just trying to pull out the plug because he thought it would be funny to see all those kids in the pool with no water!

The currently used term for Brad's problem is **attention deficit/hyperactivity disorder (AD/HD)** (American Psychiatric Association, 2000). Children diagnosed with this disorder are a heterogeneous group; they do not represent a single type (Jacobvitz et al., 1990; Mash and Wolfe, 2000). Some are impulsive; others are not. Some are more easily distracted than others and have a harder time concentrating. All have some kind of attention-related or motivational difficulty (Barkley, 1997; Landau, Lorch, and Milich, 1992; Taylor, 1994). These children especially have trouble with maintaining attention when given routine tasks and with controlling their behavior. They appear careless and hurried, and their schoolwork is often sloppy, incomplete, or superficial. Many also seem restless and fidgety. This restlessness prompts them to do things that get them in trouble, such as whistling in class. Although these children are sociable, they also have persistent difficulties with peers (Campbell, 2000).

This condition is common, with estimates for its prevalence ranging from 3 to 5 percent of all children (Mash and Wolfe, 2002). The incidence is higher in boys, up to 9 percent. About half of the children referred to clinics show symptoms typical of AD/HD.

It is often quite difficult to distinguish AD/HD children from those with conduct disorders. As many as half the children fitting the diagnosis of AD/HD also fit that of conduct disorders (Taylor, 1994). Such a situation, in which children fit the diagnostic criteria for two or more disorders, is referred to as **comorbidity** (Caron and Rutter, 1991). It may mean that the child actually has two disorders or that one set of problems leads to another. On the other hand, it may just mean that distinct psychiatric disorders are

Child Development CD
Attention Deficit Disorder

mhhe .com
/dehart5

AD/HD

Attention deficit/hyperactivity disorder (AD/HD):
A behavior pattern exhibited by children of normal intelligence that is characterized by extremely high activity levels coupled with attention-related difficulties.

Comorbidity:
A pattern of symptoms that fits more than one disorder.

Exuberant activity such as this usually does not indicate a disorder. Children with AD/HD also typically have severe difficulty managing their impulses and maintaining their arousal at a moderate level.

rare in childhood. Regardless, the family situation of a child showing both sets of problems is worse, as is the child's prognosis (Taylor, 1994). We will discuss the issue of comorbidity further later in the chapter.

Causes of AD/HD Children with AD/HD problems are quite heterogeneous, and causes also are likely to be varied, with different factors being more prominent for different children. Proving a particular cause is complex, because what may appear to produce the problem (e.g., irritable parents or some anomalous brain wave pattern) may be an outcome instead.

Biological theories for the causes of AD/HD have received by far the greatest amount of attention (Barkley, 1997; Mash and Wolfe, 2002), although none has been clearly supported. There is some support for a role for genes, more so than for conduct disorders, but far less so than for autism (Mash and Wolfe, 2002). In this case, one particular gene has been given particular attention. DRD4, the dopamine transporter gene, is thought to interfere with the neurotransmitter dopamine and thereby lead to less ability to inhibit behavior. However, monkey studies show that this particular defect is only associated with problems in certain rearing conditions, so an interaction between genes and environment is suggested (Suomi, 2002).

There also is some evidence for differences between AD/HD and non-AD/HD children in functioning in regions of the brain known to underlie attention capacities, especially during tests of attention (Barkley, 1997; Mash and Wolfe, 2002). However, such differences would be expected during attentional tasks in *any* child who was not paying attention and perhaps even at rest in a child with a long history of attentional problems. There are no studies showing that such differences measured in infancy predict later problems. Similarly, although medication often reduces the symptoms of hyperactivity, this does not necessarily mean that the disorder has an organic cause. By analogy, tranquilizers can reduce symptoms of anxiety that are totally environmental in origin.

Recent research has implicated family and other environmental factors as contributors to AD/HD, especially parental criticism and overstimulation (Taylor, 1994). In one study, researchers examined intrusiveness and overstimulating interactions, such as provoking a child who already is frustrated (Carlson, Jacobvitz, and Sroufe, 1995). The researchers reasoned that if parents provoke and stimulate when their young children are in need of calming, the youngsters might later be unable to regulate their own arousal and might thus be prone to attention problems and hyperactivity. This hypothesis was borne out, with predictions of future problems being successfully made from patterns of care experienced as early as 6 months of age. The children who developed these problems had *not* been overactive or distractible as infants.

One small group, however, did show signs of motor immaturity as newborns. Interestingly, there was no overlap between these children and the larger group that experienced overstimulating care. This suggests that there may be more than one pathway to AD/HD. Another important finding of this study was that, up to the third grade, children could be deflected from the path leading to attention problems. Increased stability in the parents' lives and more supportive treatment of the child led to a reduction in symptoms. Overall, this study suggested that AD/HD is a *developmental construction,* rather than a biological condition—that is, that it is produced by a combination of factors in a child's developmental history.

Whatever the origins of AD/HD, this problem poses real challenges for parents (Campbell, 2000). We can easily imagine a cycle in which the reactions of the parents and of the child feed each other, prompting the child to become ever more difficult and the parents to become ever more exasperated.

Treatment and Prognosis A common treatment for AD/HD is the use of a stimulant drug, most often Ritalin (methylphenidate). It may strike you as strange that stimulants are given to hyperactive children. Why would doctors want to speed up their physiological processes? Some people have argued that a *paradoxical drug effect* is involved—that the stimulants are actually slowing these children down instead of speeding them up. They suggest that this effect occurs because Ritalin offsets a biochemical deficiency in the brains of hyperactive children. If there were no biochemical deficiency, they reason, how could Ritalin have any positive results? On the basis of this argument, hundreds of thousands of AD/HD children have been given stimulants (see Figure 15.1), with at least 1.5 million using medication regularly today (Mash and Wolfe, 2002).

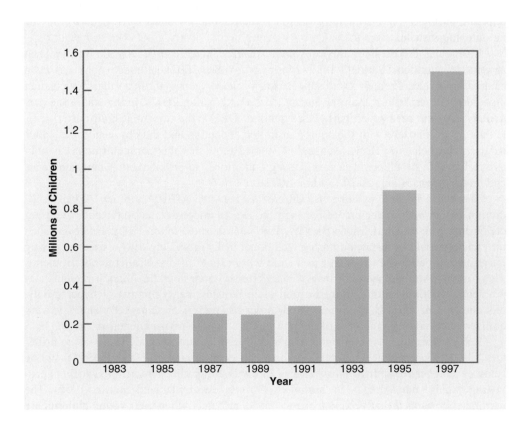

Figure 15.1
CHILDREN TREATED WITH RITALIN IN THE UNITED STATES, 1983–1997
(Sources: de Grandpre, 1999; U.S. Drug Enforcement Administration.)

A thorough review of the evidence, however, reveals that this argument has at least three flaws (de Grandpre, 1999; Jacobvitz et al., 1990; Taylor, 1994). First, there is nothing paradoxical about the effects of stimulants on AD/HD children. Stimulants do not slow these youngsters down. On the contrary, their activity levels increase in unconstrained situations (such as a playground), their heart rates and blood pressures rise, and their general energy levels are boosted. But stimulants also enhance these children's abilities to concentrate, sustain attention, and persist at routine tasks, which is probably why it appears they are slowing them down. These are the same effects that stimulants have on normal children and adults (Peloquin and Klorman, 1986). Second, the fact that stimulants can improve the performance of AD/HD children does not indicate a biochemical need for them. There are no dependable neurophysiological indicators as to which children will respond best to Ritalin and similar drugs. Third, there is reason to doubt the long-term effectiveness of stimulants. Most studies that show favorable results are short-lived—only four to six weeks in duration. Long-term studies show no lasting improvement in academic achievement or peer relationships, and no reduction in problem behavior in later years (Safer, 2000; Weiss and Hechtman, 1986).

Behavioral therapies, which reinforce the child for appropriate behavior or teach cognitive strategies for self-control, offer alternatives to medication. These alternatives have been successful at reducing symptoms in particular settings, such as the classroom (Kendall, 2000). Behavioral treatment with medication has been shown to be more effective than medication alone, and most researchers believe that medication should only be used as one part of a more comprehensive treatment program (Mash and Wolfe, 2002).

It is only partly true that most AD/HD children grow out of this disorder. Recent studies show that many of them continue to have problems through adolescence, although the problems may take different forms than they did in childhood. Typical problems among adolescents with AD/HD include underachievement at school, immaturity, and work-related problems, rather than hyperactivity (Taylor, 1994). Such problems are no less common in adolescents who have been treated over the years with stimulant drugs (Jacobvitz et al., 1990). To us this raises more doubts about the wisdom of medication, although others might say it suggests a need to continue drug treatment through the teenage years.

Before stimulants are taken for such a long period, however, it is critical to evaluate their long-term effects on the body. Stimulant drug treatment is associated with suppression of growth in both weight and height, perhaps due to influences on growth hormone (Jensen and Garfinkel, 1988). This fact raises concerns about reproductive development in children treated during adolescence and about the long-term health consequences for kidneys and the cardiovascular system.

Anxiety Disorders

Donny was an impeccably dressed 8-year-old who tested in the gifted range on the Stanford-Binet IQ test. His behavior matched his dress. He avoided dirt and messiness of any kind. He would even turn down chocolate milk because it might spill on his tie; playing with finger paint was out of the question. The play he did engage in was excessively precise and orderly. He would lay out the buildings for an airport in exact alignment. He also had an array of irrational fears. He was frightened, for example, that spiders might come out of the toilet and bite him, even though he realized that this was impossible. Not surprisingly, Donny was overtly anxious. At times he talked rapidly with pursed lips; other times he wrung his hands.

Janice also showed anxiety, although in different ways. She was always upset when her mother dropped her off at kindergarten. She spent much of the day hovering near the teacher, hoping for attention. When the teacher tried to encourage her to play with the other children, she remained on the sidelines, never joining the activities. Her face constantly bore a worried expression and her

mhhe.com /dehart5

Anxiety Disorders

eyes seemed perpetually filled with tears. She had chronic stomachaches, and when it came time for first grade, she refused to go to school at all.

Both of these children would probably be diagnosed as having an *anxiety disorder* (Vasey and Ollendick, 2000; Warren and Sroufe, in press). Donny would be said to suffer from **generalized anxiety disorder,** characterized by very general and pervasive worries and fears. Janice's problem would probably be labeled **separation anxiety disorder**—excessive anxiety precipitated by separation from someone to whom the child is emotionally attached.

Anxiety disorders are less frequently seen at clinics than conduct disorders or AD/HD, yet population surveys show that they affect up to 8 percent of children (Klein, 1994). Perhaps many of these youngsters are not brought in for treatment because parents consider their problems less serious than other, more disruptive problems of childhood. They may also assume these children will eventually outgrow their fears and anxieties, and in this assumption they are often right. Compared with conduct disorders and hyperactivity, anxiety disorders are more likely to show **spontaneous remission**—that is, to go away without professional help. Moreover, anxiety disorders are generally not predictive of serious problems in adulthood.

Despite a great deal of speculation, there is only modest evidence that anxiety disorders in children are caused mainly by biological factors (Mash and Wolfe, 2002). As with AD/HD, research centers around a particular gene, particular neurotransmitter systems (e.g., the GABA-ergic system), and particular regions of the brain (those related to fear responses) (Mash and Wolfe, 2002). The gene in question is the serotonin transporter (5-HTT) because this transmitter is linked to anxiety reactions and responds to antidepressant medication. So far, evidence is slender that this accounts for many of the anxiety problems of children. In general, it is not known whether brain and biochemical differences are merely reflections of anxiety states or predisposing factors.

There is also modest evidence for factors in the family environment as causes. For example, anxiously overinvolved parents and high levels of family stress have been linked to anxiety disorders in boys (Mash and Wolfe, 2002). In the Minnesota Longitudinal Study, a history of anxious/resistant attachment in infancy predicted anxiety disorders at age 17 (Warren et al., 1997). These children seem to have formed an internal working model of the world as unpredictable or threatening and of themselves as unable to influence events.

Anxiety disorders are generally quite responsive to a variety of treatments (Bernstein and Borchart, 1991; Vasey and Ollendick, 2000; Wenar, 1994). Both behavioral and psychodynamic therapies are more successful than simply waiting for the problem to go away by itself. All effective treatments of school refusal (another category of anxiety disorder) involve getting the child back into the classroom as soon as possible. Focusing on the parents' anxiety also seems useful in such cases, for this seems to be a key to the problem.

Depression

It is now recognized that children, as well as adults, may suffer from depression (Garber, 2000; Harrington, 1994). This has been appreciated only in recent decades because young children often show such problems through somatic complaints (headaches, stomachaches), irritable mood, and social withdrawal (American Psychiatric Association, 2000), rather than motor slowing and obvious despondency. It is also difficult to diagnose because it frequently co-occurs with other problems, such as anxiety disorders or AD/HD. In fact, it is difficult to distinguish anxiety disorders from depression, especially in children. Nonetheless, it is estimated that 2 percent of children, and up to 8 percent of adolescents, qualify for the diagnosis (Mash and Wolfe, 2002).

Current research suggests that depression in children may be distinctive from adult-onset depression (Harrington, 1994; Harrington, Rutter, and Fombonne, 1996). Childhood depression is most strongly associated with a history of psychosocial adversity,

Generalized anxiety disorder:
A disorder characterized by very general and pervasive worries and fears.

Separation anxiety disorder:
Excessive anxiety precipitated by separation from someone to whom the child is emotionally attached.

Spontaneous remission:
The disappearance of a disorder without professional treatment.

Childhood Depression

It is normal for young children to cling to parents in times of threat. But if this child continues to be so preoccupied with contact, it may be a sign of an anxiety disorder.

including stress, anxious attachment, and physical or sexual abuse (Duggal et al., 2001). Family studies and twin studies provide rather clear evidence for a genetic factor in adult depression, but less so for childhood depression. Moreover, for adults there is an established biological marker. When given a chemical called dexamethasone, most nondepressed adults show a decrease in the stress hormone cortisol in the bloodstream. Depressed adults do not show this change. However, neither this marker nor any other distinguishes depressed from nondepressed children (Harrington, 1994). Depression does run in families, but the transmission may be psychosocial as well as genetic. Perhaps a vulnerability to anxiety or depression is inherited, but certain family stressors are required for their expression (Mash and Wolfe, 2002).

Although antidepressant medication is increasingly used in treating childhood depression, such a practice may not be justified, at least in isolation. Attending to the surrounding life context that may have contributed to the depression is also important.

Anorexia Nervosa

When Alma came in for consultation, she looked like a walking skeleton, scantily dressed in shorts and halter, with her legs sticking out like broomsticks, every rib showing, and her shoulder blades standing up like little wings. . . . Alma's arms and legs were covered with soft hair, her complexion had a yellowish tint, and her dry hair hung down in strings. Most striking was the face—hollow like that of a shriveled-up old woman with a wasting disease. . . . Alma insisted that she looked fine and there was nothing wrong with her being so skinny (Bruch, 1979, pp. 2–3).

mhhe.com /dehart5

Eating Disorders

Alma suffers from **anorexia nervosa,** a serious eating disorder characterized by extreme reduction in food intake and loss of at least 25 percent of original body weight. No physical illness accounts for this dramatic weight loss. Individuals with anorexia deliberately starve themselves. This intentional weight loss is accompanied by a highly distorted body image (Tyrka, Graber, and Brooks-Gunn, 2000). No matter how emaciated they become, persons with anorexia are convinced they are still overweight. The more unrealistic their belief, the more difficult the problem is to treat (Leon and Phenan, 1985). Reassurances, admonitions, even threats from concerned friends or relatives in no way weaken their resolve. Many eat almost nothing and exercise excessively. Others occasionally go on eating binges, but then induce vomiting to avoid gaining weight—a practice called **bulimia.** This self-abuse can produce very serious physical side effects. Between 6 and 10 percent of anorexics die from medical complications or suicide (Mash and Wolfe, 2002).

Anorexia nervosa:
A serious eating disorder characterized by extreme reduction in food intake and loss of at least 25 percent of normal body weight.

Anorexia nervosa is primarily a disorder of adolescent girls and young adult women, and it is much more common in the middle class than in the lower socioeconomic classes (Attie, Brooks-Gunn, and Petersen, 1990). Girls with anorexia are often bright, academically successful, and viewed as perfect young ladies—neatly dressed, well-mannered, and compliant (Wenar, 1994). In fact, a perfectionist tendency is one clue to the cause of this disorder, as we will discuss shortly.

Bulimia:
Eating binges followed by self-induced vomiting to avoid weight gain.

Child Development CD
Adolescent Eating Disorders

Biological theories of anorexia include the possibility of a dysfunctional hypothalamus (the brain region that regulates hunger and affects the production of hormones) or abnormal levels of the neurotransmitter serotonin, but there is little evidence to support biological causation. Although girls with anorexia often suffer hormone imbalances, which can cause their menstrual cycles to cease, these abnormalities seem to be more effect than cause (Steinhausen, 1994). Concentration camp victims who were starved for long periods showed many of the same hormonal and menstrual symptoms. If a girl with anorexia does gain appropriate weight, her hormonal and menstrual functioning will return to normal. Still, the physiological changes that occur with anorexia may maintain the problem and interfere with treatment (Mash and Wolfe, 2002).

Psychological theories of anorexia have emphasized early sexual abuse (Shapiro and Rosenfeld, 1987) or overinvolved, overentangled families (Minuchin, Rosman, and Baker, 1978). Parents in some cases expect the child to be perfect and do not allow her

Girls with anorexia often have severely distorted body images.

to question the status quo or express anger. They demand absolute compliance in return for nurturance, and they repeatedly suggest that the child could be "just a little bit better." The girl comes to feel that her life, her self, even her body are not her own. Over-controlled, she is left without a sense of autonomy (Wenar, 1994). In adolescence, she confronts her parents indirectly by asserting control over how much she eats. For this small victory of causing her parents worry and making them feel helpless to change her, she pays an enormous price.

You may wonder why an adolescent girl focuses on food in an effort to assert some autonomy in her life. Part of the answer is cultural (Tyrka et al., 2000). Girls in North America today are barraged with images of extreme thinness—on television, in music videos, in magazines and advertisements. Our culture associates extreme thinness with beauty, affluence, and success. Not surprisingly, this is the image to which troubled girls often aspire (Mash and Wolfe, 2002).

Anorexia nervosa is quite difficult to treat because of the girl's entrenched belief that she is not too thin and perhaps should become even thinner. However, there is some evidence that behavioral therapies may be effective in the short run and that family therapy may have longer-term success with younger, less chronic patients. Multifaceted programs are currently advocated (Tyrka et al., 2000; Steinhausen, 1994). A first goal of any treatment is to get the patient eating again, but the long-term aim is to help her believe that she has a right to self-expression, including the expression of anger, and that as a person she has worth.

Comorbidity

In contrast to the situation for children's physical diseases and for adults' psychiatric disorders, comorbidity is the rule for childhood psychological problems. With the exception of autism, children showing each of the problems just discussed often also qualify for other diagnoses. Anorexia overlaps greatly with depression. Depression overlaps with each of the others. One study reported that 75 percent of children seen for depression also met criteria for another disorder (Harrington, 1994). Fully half also qualified for AD/HD, conduct disorder, *and* an anxiety disorder. Anxiety disorders also are comorbid with a host of other child problems.

This widespread comorbidity may have several causes. One issue may be the limited ways in which children manifest problems. Difficulty concentrating, for example, is one criterion for AD/HD, depression, and generalized anxiety disorder. It also is a hallmark for post-traumatic stress disorder, another anxiety disorder that is rooted in a history of abuse or trauma. Another possibility is that childhood problems do not represent distinct syndromes at all. Research often suggests that broad classes of problems may be a better way to group children. The imposition of more specific categories, while useful for communication among professionals and for conducting research, may distort the situation regarding childhood problems. It may reflect the medical model of psychopathology more than actual findings from research (Sroufe, 1997).

CHILDHOOD DISORDERS AND DEVELOPMENT

The study of developmental psychopathology calls attention to major themes of this book, including the integrated nature of development, the child as an active force in development, stability and change over time, the complexity of developmental pathways, the interaction of biology and environment, and the importance of considering the total context of development. The disorders we have reviewed underscore these themes and also shed light on normal development.

Autism, for instance, sheds light on normal development by highlighting the degree to which human beings are social animals who depend on emotional communication. Autistic children are striking in their lack of these fundamental human characteristics. They shun contact with others, including other children, and fail to form normal attachments to adults. At the same time, autism underscores the integrated nature of development. The autistic child's profound language and cognitive handicaps are coupled with equally severe social and emotional ones. Cognitive limitations make social interaction difficult. Withdrawal from social interaction deprives autistic children of experiences that promote cognitive development, which in turn inhibits social understanding.

Conduct disorders illustrate the developmental theme of continuity over time. Signs of aggression and antisocial behavior often appear in the preschool years and may persist through middle childhood into adolescence and beyond (Moffitt, 1993). The most compelling explanation for this continuity is that children play active roles in their own development. Children with conduct disorders behave in ways that elicit negative, even punitive, feedback from other people, which only serves to perpetuate their problems. But just as there is continuity in the development of conduct disorders, so there is variation in the ways in which they unfold. Conduct disorders illustrate the principle of branching pathways, in that they predict a wide range of adult problems, including depression, schizophrenia, and alcoholism, as well as criminal behavior.

Attention deficit/hyperactivity disorder highlights the theme of transformations over the course of development. The condition tends to proceed from overactivity in childhood to academic failure and problems of impulse control in adolescence. AD/HD also illustrates how similar behavioral patterns may result from multiple pathways. In some cases, the origins of AD/HD seem to lie in patterns of care and other early life experiences, but in other cases they are rooted more in cultural or biological factors.

Anxiety disorders seem to result from difficulty negotiating the developmental issues that all children face. These disorders illustrate the usefulness of considering disturbed behavior as a deviation from normal development. Separation anxiety, for instance, is a normal part of development and becomes pathological only when it lingers as the child grows older, preventing him or her from becoming more autonomous from parents. Specific fears are also normal in early childhood. They are pathological only when they become pervasive and interfere with functioning in many areas of the child's life. These difficulties negotiating developmental issues are not irreversible. In fact, anxiety disorders often disappear on their own without treatment.

Anorexia nervosa is another illustration of a failure to negotiate a developmental issue that all children face. This disorder can best be seen as a delayed and self-destructive attempt to establish autonomy. Anorexia also illustrates the complexity of developmental pathways. Food finickiness in the early years does not predict anorexia in adolescence. But parental overcontrol of the child (especially overcontrol of her expressions of anger and other impulses) and parental overinvolvement (including a sexualized relationship with the father) do place girls at risk for this disorder.

Other disorders of childhood and adolescence illustrate the complex interaction of biologically based and environmental risk factors and protective factors in the development of psychopathology. For instance, when adultlike depression arises in a youngster and persists to adulthood, you might assume the child has a genetic or physiological vulnerability to this disorder. But even in these cases, environmental factors (especially early losses, such as the death of a parent) often also play a part. Not all children with a family history of depression develop this disorder, nor do all children who have experienced early losses. For all disorders, we must consider the total context of development.

Chapter Summary

Introduction

Developmental psychopathology includes:

- the study of disturbed children,
- the developmental roots of adult disorders, and
- the patterns disorders follow after they emerge.

Studying psychopathology from a developmental perspective has enriched our understanding by:

- encouraging exploration of the origins of abnormal behavior and how it changes over time,
- focusing attention on resiliency, and
- encouraging exploration of roots for disorders in major developmental issues.

A Developmental Perspective on Psychopathology

Developmental psychopathologists are interested in both **risk factors** for emotional and behavioral disorders and **protective factors** that help people avoid them.

Meaningful links between childhood and adult psychological problems exist, but they are not always straightforward. Development often involves transformations over time, rather than simple continuity.

Explaining Psychopathology

Various **models** of psychopathology have been proposed, some focusing mainly on biological factors, others mainly on environmental factors.

Models emphasizing a biological perspective include:

- the traditional *medical model,* which draws an explicit analogy between psychological disorders and physical illnesses;

- *neurological and physiological models,* which focus on chemical imbalances in the brain; and
- *genetic models,* which focus on genetically based predispositions to develop emotional and behavioral problems.

Models emphasizing an environmental perspective include:

- *sociological models,* which stress the social context surrounding children who develop a disorder;
- *behavioral models,* which focus on specific rewards, punishments, and modeled behaviors;
- *psychodynamic models,* which focus on thoughts and feelings produced by life experiences; and
- *family models,* which assume a child's symptoms are a reflection of disturbance in the larger family system.

The *developmental perspective* draws upon and integrates aspects of all of these models.

Some Childhood Disorders

Autism is one of the most severe and rare childhood disorders. Other **autistic spectrum disorders** are less rare.

- Autism is characterized by a powerful insistence on preserving sameness in the environment, extreme social isolation, and severe language deficits.
- Autism is probably caused by some as-yet-unidentified biological factor.
- Even with treatment, the long-term prognosis for children with full-blown autism is bleak. For children with other autistic spectrum disorders, the outlook is better.

Conduct disorders are one of the most common childhood psychological diagnoses, especially for boys.

- They involve a persistent pattern of repeatedly violating either age-appropriate social norms or the basic rights of others and may be either *aggressive* or *nonaggressive, socialized* or *undersocialized.*
- Conduct disorders that begin early in childhood are more difficult to treat and more predictive of adult problems than those that appear in adolescence.
- Negative family environments seem to play a major role in the development of conduct disorders.
- Early intervention is important in treating conduct disorders.

Attention deficit/hyperactivity disorder (AD/HD) is a commonly diagnosed disorder, but children with this diagnosis are a heterogeneous group.

- Children with AD/HD have attentional problems; other common problems include impulsiveness, restlessness, difficulties with self-control, and trouble with peers.
- AD/HD is often assumed to have a biological cause, but it is not clear if brain chemistry features are a cause or a consequence of the problem. Family and environmental factors may also be involved.
- Children with AD/HD are commonly treated with stimulant drugs, but it is not clear that these are effective in the long term. A combination treatment seems most effective.

Anxiety disorders are relatively common, but children with these disorders are less likely to be referred for treatment than children with conduct disorders or AD/HD.

- Compared with other disorders, anxiety disorders are more likely to show **spontaneous remission** and less likely to predict adult problems.
- There is more evidence for family factors than for biological ones as causes for anxiety disorders in children.
- Both behavioral and psychodynamic therapies are effective treatments.

Childhood depression differs from adult depression in several ways:

- Symptoms of childhood depression are different from those found in adults.
- Childhood depression is more closely tied to psychosocial adversity.
- There is no clear genetic component and no biological marker for depression in children.
- Antidepressant medication may not be the most appropriate treatment for childhood depression.

Anorexia nervosa is a serious eating disorder characterized by extreme reduction in food intake and loss of at least 25 percent of original body weight.

- It is primarily found among middle-class adolescent girls and young adult women.
- Family and psychological factors are the most likely causes of anorexia.
- It is difficult to treat, but behavioral and family therapy can help.

Comorbidity is very common in children with psychological problems.

Childhood Disorders and Development

The study of developmental psychopathology calls attention to major themes of this book:

- the integrated nature of development,
- the child as an active force in development,
- stability and change over time,
- the complexity of developmental pathways,
- the interaction of biology and environment, and
- the importance of considering the total context of development.

The disorders reviewed in this chapter underscore these themes and also shed light on normal development.

Review Questions

Introduction
1. What issues are covered by **developmental psychopathology**?
2. How does a developmental approach enhance understanding of psychological problems?

A Developmental Perspective on Psychopathology
3. How do **risk factors** and **protective factors** in childhood predict adult psychological problems?
4. What kinds of connections have been found between childhood and adult psychological problems?

Explaining Psychopathology
5. What are the underlying assumptions of the *medical, neurological and physiological, genetic, sociological, behavioral, psychodynamic,* and *family models* of psychopathology?
6. How does a developmental perspective combine the assumptions of the other models?

Some Childhood Disorders
7. Discuss the symptoms, most likely causes, and most effective treatments for **autism** and related disorders,

conduct disorders, attention deficit/hyperactivity disorder, anxiety disorders, childhood depression, and **anorexia nervosa.**

8. Why is **comorbidity** common among children with psychological problems?

Childhood Disorders and Development

9. How does the study of developmental psychopathology shed light on the nature of more general developmental processes?

Application and Observation

1. Search the web for information on one of the psychological disorders discussed in this chapter. Try to find several websites with different intended audiences (students, parents, teachers, pediatricians, etc.) and different types of sponsors (universities, government agencies, professional organizations, parent advocacy groups, commercial websites, etc.). What differences and similarities do you see across the websites? How does the information and advice on the websites compare to the material found in this chapter?

2. Interview campus counselors or residence hall staff members on the issue of eating disorders on your campus. How prevalent are they? What problems do they create for students (those with eating disorders and others around them)? What help is available to students on your campus with this problem? What is being done on your campus to educate students about eating disorders?

3. Observe children with AD/HD or autistic spectrum disorders in an individual or group setting (a special education class, inclusive classroom, after-school program, etc.). What do you notice that seems distinctive about their behavior? How does their behavior compare with that of typically developing children of the same age?

4. Interview teachers or parents of children with one of the psychological disorders discussed in this chapter. What particular challenges does the disorder create for the children, their peers, their teachers, and their families? How have the parents/teachers and the children dealt with the disorder? What would they most like other people to understand about the disorder? What kinds of treatments and/or educational practices have they found most and least helpful?

Part 7 Epilogue: Psychopathology and Individual Lives

As a way of summarizing the material we've discussed on developmental psychopathology, let's return to the four children we've followed throughout the book and assess their degree of vulnerability to various disorders.

Malcolm Williams

Malcolm represents an interesting case because of all the things that might have gone wrong in his development. Conduct disorders, especially the gang-socialized type, are very common among boys raised in inner cities, yet for solid reasons we portrayed Malcolm as making a positive social adjustment. He did occasionally show bad judgment, as when he kept a gun he found, but he seemed to learn from these experiences and he matured well. He also had no serious problems due to his high activity level, his exuberant style, his tendency to be impulsive, and his inclination to keep shifting his attention from one thing to another. He learned to keep these characteristics within appropriate bounds. The warmth and firm guidance from his caring family were critical factors leading him to such a good outcome (Masten and Coatsworth, 1995). Malcolm's development is quite similar to that of some well-functioning inner-city boys in the Minnesota Longitudinal Study.

But wait, you may be saying to yourself. Isn't attention deficit/hyperactivity disorder something that a child either has or doesn't have? How can we suggest that Malcolm avoided this diagnosis simply because his parents so strongly supported him? We can say this precisely because such disorders are not givens; they aren't something that children either are or are not born with. Instead, these problems are developmental constructions that depend on the interaction of internal and external factors (Sroufe, 1997). In Malcolm's case, firm guidance and limits provided by his family allowed him to acquire an adequate degree of self-control. Even failure at school is not something we should think of as always stemming from innate characteristics. In the Minnesota Longitudinal Study, being required to repeat kindergarten was not predicted by IQ or early language comprehension tests. Instead, it was predicted by social and emotional factors, such as a child's attachment history.

Another problem that *might* have arisen for Malcolm is school refusal during the period of middle childhood when he was having trouble with gang members on his way to school. But if this had happened, it would have stemmed from a serious external conflict, not from anxiety over leaving home. Any form of internalizing disorder would be out of character for Malcolm, who is filled with a sense of personal ability and confidence. The overcontrol and perfectionism of the person with anorexia or the hopelessness and self-contempt of the depressed adolescent would not make sense in his case. Likewise, adult schizophrenia would be unlikely to develop in Malcolm. He shows none of the precursors of it. He is successful socially and academically; there is no history of family psychopathology and no disturbed pattern of family interaction. Although our present state of knowledge doesn't allow us to rule out the possibility of later disorders, Malcolm seems well on his way to good adult adjustment, with only the normal ups and downs everyone has.

Meryl Polonius Turner

Meryl is in many ways the opposite of Malcolm. As is common for females in our culture, she has been socialized toward internalizing problems. School refusal and other forms of anxiety disorder were possibilities for her. Indeed, during the early preschool years she showed signs of such problems: she had great difficulty adapting to new situations, and she tended to become greatly upset under stress. As a female, especially with her tendency to internalize stress, she might also have been at risk for anorexia nervosa or depression.

However, many factors in Meryl's life worked against her developing these disorders. When Karen met Joe and her life stabilized, Meryl's development underwent a critical turnaround. Increasingly, her parents helped her become a self-sufficient and autonomous person. In her adolescence, Karen and Joe tolerated Meryl's normal pushing away from them— criticism, argumentativeness, and other forms of deidentification. At the same time, they provided Meryl with a great deal of nurturance, supporting her and helping her learn to seek support when she needed it. Karen and Joe's own relationship modeled the vital role social support can play in alleviating stress. Although they had their periods of marital tension, they were able to talk about and resolve their conflicts, and Meryl

553

was not made to feel responsible when things went wrong. All this served a child like Meryl well. We therefore described her as becoming more competent and confident in herself, thereby moving away from the path toward adult depression. Meryl's developmental path parallels that of several children, most of them girls, whom we have studied.

Given her history, the possibility of any adult conduct disorder would be very remote for Meryl. It would be inconceivable, for example, to see Meryl headed for a career of violent crime. Aggressive, antisocial behavior is simply not congruent with the personality or style of coping illustrated by Meryl (Robins, 1966). Neither would adult schizophrenia be likely for someone like Meryl. For girls there may be a link between adult schizophrenia and certain internalizing symptoms, primarily withdrawal (Watt et al., 1984). But nothing in Meryl's history suggests risk for extreme disorder. Most important, she shows social competence and academic success, which together indicate that serious adult disorders are unlikely.

For a person like Meryl, however, we might expect that new situations would continue to be challenging. If confronted with a crisis, she might respond at first by becoming disorganized. But then, with effort, she is likely to cope effectively. Another area of challenge for her might be close relationships with men. We could imagine Meryl being quite demanding of the men in her life. But with her keen sensitivity to others and desire for closeness, she would also give a great deal.

Maggie and Mike Gordon

Maggie and Mike experienced prolonged parental conflict and eventual divorce. They both showed more adjustment problems in adolescence than either Malcolm or Meryl did, but the nature of their problems was different.

Maggie was primarily a witness to the conflict and occasional physical violence between her parents, but for the most part she avoided getting caught between them. This was possible in part because of Frank's intense involvement with Mike and relative lack of interest in her during early and middle childhood. Long before Christine and the children moved out of the house, Frank had been fairly uninvolved in Maggie's life. Witnessing the intense conflict between her parents— particularly the physical conflict—put Maggie at heightened risk for a variety of problems, including both aggressiveness and withdrawal. Like other girls, Maggie was at most immediate risk for internalizing problems, such as anxiety and depression, in the immediate aftermath of Frank and Christine's divorce. But during adolescence there was potential for a delayed reaction to the divorce that could have taken the form of problem behaviors as well.

Maggie did show signs of both anxiety and withdrawal during the years of conflict between her parents and right after the separation. However, she was able to turn to her mother and grandmother for support and appeared to bounce back

more quickly than Mike after her parents divorced. Involvement in schoolwork, extracurricular activities, and new friendships also provided a refuge for her after the divorce. Her strong performance in school was primarily a reflection of her positive adjustment, but Maggie's push to excel in school and in her part-time job as an adolescent may also reflect a need to prove her worth to her father and herself. In adolescence, she reacted to her father's remarriage by essentially ignoring him and his new wife for a while, but eventually she responded positively to Frank's attempts to become more involved in her life. Her mother's remarriage provided a challenge to her, and her adjustment to her stepfather was rocky, but only for a brief time. Through all of the changes in her family, Maggie's history of support and solid early adaptation served as protective factors (Masten and Coatsworth, 1995; Werner and Smith, 2001).

With a less positive developmental history and fewer sources of current support, Maggie might have been vulnerable to a number of more severe problems. Both anxiety disorders and depression would have been possibilities for her, given her internalizing response to her parents' conflict and divorce. She could also have been vulnerable to eating disorders, especially given her strong desire to achieve and her desire to make her father notice her. Under slightly different circumstances, her problematic relationship with her father might also have placed her at risk for problem behaviors, especially early sexual activity or promiscuity.

As an adult, Maggie may continue to be concerned about her attractiveness to men, and she may well continue to seek reassurance of her basic worth through academic achievement and overdoing it at work. Her tendency to throw herself into work to escape conflict may also cause her problems in her personal life. But at the end of adolescence Maggie is well adjusted, academically successful, and likely to be able to draw on her personal resources and her network of family and friends for support when needed.

Mike was burdened with his parents' relationship, and during their period of intense conflict he felt it was up to him to keep the family together. His mother leaned on him at times, and for a while he feared that his father might be turning most of his attention to his new wife and son. Such factors can be associated with conduct disorders, hyperactivity, and depression.

At one time or another, Mike did show behavior congruent with some of those disorders. Still, we never intended to portray him as seriously disturbed, nor would we anticipate any serious adult disorders for him. As is the case for Maggie, his positive history of secure attachment and early competence would serve as protective factors during stressful periods (Masten and Coatsworth, 1995; Werner and Smith, 2001).

Mike at first showed more of a tendency toward internalizing symptoms than Malcolm would have done in his situation. Remember how responsible he felt for his parents' separation and how in the year following the breakup of the marriage he became less outgoing. But then, with the divorce and his father's remarriage, he began to express his pain in acting-out behaviors. This is in keeping with cultural patterns of socialization for boys. Frank Gordon's son was not going to sit around moping and having stomachaches for long. It is hard to say how likely it would have been for a teenager like Mike to continue down the path toward conduct disorders, perhaps eventually abusing drugs or alcohol. Without the strong support he received from his mother, his stepfather, and his high school biology teacher, and the continuing interest shown by his father, it would have been much less likely for things to work out so well for Mike. Unfortunately, we have other cases in our research in which cumulative stress and lack of support have resulted in disorders.

Some would argue that alcoholism, conduct disorders, and schizophrenia are genetically related to one another (Wender and Klein, 1986). If so, Frank's lapse into alcohol abuse during the rockiest time of his first marriage, coupled with Mike's brief bouts of misconduct during early adolescence, might mean that Mike is at higher than normal risk for adult schizophrenia. But many factors counteract these negative warning signs: Mike's solid developmental beginnings, his good adjustment, and his ongoing social support all work in his favor.

As for how a person like Mike will later face the roles of partner and father, we might expect him to have doubts about his ability to provide for a partner. After all, his father was unable to meet his mother's emotional needs, and Mike himself experienced a sense of failure filling the gap. Emotionally caring for a parent is a big task for a child. Doubts about his own caretaking abilities might also arise when Mike eventually becomes a parent. Still, he appears to have overall positive self-esteem; doubts and lack of confidence do not predominate in his general self-image. A basic commitment to family life will probably help Mike be successful as a partner and a parent. He will certainly have some vulnerabilities as he faces these adult tasks, as everyone does, but he also has particular strengths that he can bring to these challenges.

Conclusion: Psychopathology and Normal Development

Developmental psychopathology is the study of deviations from normal development that seriously impair a person's functioning and result in disordered patterns of behavior. Developmental psychopathologists seek to understand the origins and course of such deviations as well as the factors that promote the return to normal developmental pathways. As it turns out, the same principles and influences found to be important in the study of normal development are critical for understanding pathological development. These include the interplay of biology and environment, the surrounding rings of contextual influence (social support, poverty, cultural expectations, etc.), and the person's previous developmental history.

Glossary

Academic intelligence Intellectual capacity as measured by performance on tasks typically encountered in school or on standard IQ tests.

Accelerated longitudinal design A type of longitudinal study in which researchers simultaneously follow several age groups over a period of time.

Accommodation In Piaget's theory, the process of modifying an existing strategy or skill to meet a new demand of the environment.

Adaptation A change in a species that increases chances of survival in a particular environment. In Piaget's theory, the process by which children change in order to function more effectively in their environment.

Adaptational theory Bowlby's developmental theory, which integrates ideas from evolutionary, psychoanalytic, and cognitive theories to explain the development and impact of early attachment relationships.

Adolescent egocentrism Teenagers' assumption that they are the focus of everyone's attention and that their experiences, thoughts, and feelings are unique.

Adolescent-limited conduct disorder A conduct disorder that first appears in adolescence and does not predict problems in adulthood.

Adrenal glands Small glands located above the kidneys that produce androgens and other hormones related to stress, metabolism, and reproduction.

Adrenarche The increase in adrenal androgen levels in middle childhood.

Affective sharing The toddler's sharing of positive emotions with the caregiver.

Agency The tendency to take initiative, rise to challenges, and try to influence events.

Aggression Negative acts intended to harm others or their possessions.

Allele One of several alternate forms of a particular gene.

Altruism Acting unselfishly to aid someone else.

Amniocentesis Withdrawal of amniotic fluid for the purpose of testing for chromosomal abnormalities.

Amniotic sac The fluid-filled sac that surrounds and protects the embryo and the fetus.

Amygdala A brain structure involved in memory formation and emotional responses.

Androgens Male sex hormones.

Animism The tendency to attribute life to nonliving things.

Anorexia nervosa A serious eating disorder characterized by extreme reduction in food intake and loss of at least 25 percent of normal body weight.

Anoxia A disruption in the baby's oxygen supply during or just after birth.

Anxious attachment Patterns of attachment in which the infant is not confident of the caregiver's availability and responsiveness and cannot use the caregiver as a secure base for exploration.

Anxious-avoidant attachment An attachment pattern in which the infant readily separates from the caregiver but avoids contact after a brief separation.

Anxious-resistant attachment An attachment pattern in which the infant separates from the caregiver reluctantly but shows ambivalence toward the caregiver after a brief separation.

Apgar scale A scale for rating a baby's well-being shortly after birth.

Appearance-reality problem The tendency to define reality by surface appearances.

Appropriation The process by which children naturally take on the rules and values of their culture through participation in relationships with caregivers.

Asperger's syndrome An autistic spectrum disorder characterized by odd preoccupations, social deficits, and motor coordination problems, but superior cognitive and language skills.

Assimilation In Piaget's theory, the process of applying an existing capability without modification to various situations.

Associative learning Learning that certain stimuli or events tend to go together or to be associated with one another.

Attachment An enduring emotional tie between infant and caregiver.

Attention deficit/hyperactivity disorder (AD/HD) A behavior pattern exhibited by children of normal intelligence that is characterized by extremely high activity levels coupled with attention-related difficulties.

Attention skills Processes that control the transfer of information from a sensory register to working memory.

Attunement Caregivers' adjustment of the stimulation they provide in response to signs from the infant.

Authoritarian parenting A parenting style in which parents are unresponsive, inflexible, and harsh in controlling behavior.

Authoritative parenting A parenting style in which the parents are nurturant, responsive, and supportive, yet set firm limits for their children.

Autism A rare, severe developmental disorder, featuring a powerful insistence on sameness, extreme social isolation, and severe language deficits.

Autistic spectrum disorders A range of related pervasive developmental disorders with overlapping symptoms and varying severity.

Autobiographical memory Enduring memory of one's own past.

Automatization The tendency for basic cognitive processes to become less effortful and more automatic with practice.

Autonomous morality In Piaget's theory, the stage in which children see morality as relative to the situation.

Axons Long neuron structures that branch at the end and relay electrical impulses to other neurons.

Behavioral reorganization A change in the way a developing child organizes and uses his or her capabilities; one way in which qualitative change occurs.

Bidirectional effects Two-way developmental influences between family members.

Binocular depth cues Visual cues for depth and distance resulting from the fact that visual information reaches the brain from two eyes.

Blastocyst The hollow, ball-like structure into which a zygote develops in the first week following conception.

Bonding The parent's initial emotional tie to the newborn.

Border work The rituals of teasing and ostracism with which elementary school children maintain the boundary between their gender-segregated peer groups.

Brainstem The part of the brain that controls reflexes and basic survival functions.

Bulimia Eating binges followed by self-induced vomiting to avoid weight gain.

Canalization The extent to which genes constrain environmental influences on particular traits.

Canonical babbling Prelinguistic vocalizations consisting of strings of syllables that sound increasingly like speech.

Categorical perception Perceiving stimuli that vary along a continuum as belonging to distinct categories.

Centration The tendency to consider only one piece of information when multiple pieces are relevant.

Cephalocaudal development The principle that development proceeds from the head downward.

Cerebellum A brain structure involved in motor control and balance.

Cerebral cortex The brain's thin, highly convoluted outer layer.

Cesarean section Delivery of a baby by surgical incision in the abdomen and uterus of the mother.

Child-directed speech (CDS) or motherese The modifications adults make in their speech when talking to young children.

Chorionic villus sampling A technique for analyzing the fetus's genetic makeup using cells from the developing placenta.

Chromosomal abnormality Any genetic defect that occurs when errors in meiosis produce sperm or egg cells with incorrect numbers of chromosomes or with damaged chromosomes.

Chromosome Threadlike structures in which the organism's genetic instructions are stored, composed of DNA and located in the nucleus of each cell.

Circular reaction A behavior that produces an interesting event, initially by chance, and is repeated.

Class Any set of objects or events that are treated as the same in certain ways because they have features in common.

Classical conditioning A learning process in which a new stimulus comes to elicit an established reflex response through association with an old stimulus.

Classification The ability to group things by shared characteristics, such as size or shape.

Clique A close-knit group of a few friends who are intimately involved with each other.

Cognitive socialization The influence of social environment on the development of cognitive skills.

Cohort effect In a cross-sectional study, a difference between age groups due to a peculiarity in one of the groups being studied rather than to a general developmental difference.

Collection A naturally occurring entity with subparts that go together because of their proximity.

Committed compliance Children's enthusiastic compliance with parents' directives.

Communicative competence The ability to use language in a socially appropriate way in a particular culture.

Comorbidity A pattern of symptoms that fits more than one disorder.

Competence-performance distinction The difference between what children are capable of doing under optimal circumstances and how they actually do on a particular task.

Concrete operational period Piaget's term for the period when children begin to use logical operations to reason about concrete objects.

Conduct disorder A persistent pattern of repeatedly violating either age-appropriate social norms or the basic rights of others.

Congenital (birth) defect Any abnormality that is present at birth.

Conservation The idea that the amount of something remains the same despite changes in its form, shape, or appearance.

Constructive memory Inferences drawn in the process of storing and remembering information.

Contingencies The relationships between events and their consequences.

Contingent truth Knowledge that depends on empirical observations, on information gathered through the senses.

Conventional morality In Kohlberg's theory, moral reasoning based on opinions of others or formal laws.

Conversational babbling or jargon Prelinguistic vocalizations in which infants use adultlike stress and intonation.

Cooing Prelinguistic vocalizations that consist largely of vowel sounds and express pleasure and contentment.

Cooperative learning experience A situation in which learners at approximately the same level of knowledge and skill interact, share ideas, and discover solutions on their own.

Coordination of schemes A goal-directed chain of behaviors.

Correlational methods Research methods that allow researchers to examine relationships among factors but not to draw conclusions about causes and effects.

Critical period A limited time during which some part of a developing organism is susceptible to influences that can bring about specific and permanent changes.

Crossing over An exchange of corresponding segments of genetic material between homologous chromosomes during meiosis.

Cross-sectional study A study comparing groups of people of different ages at the same time.

Crowd A group that is larger, less exclusive, and more loosely organized than a clique.

Crying Reflexive vocalization that occurs automatically whenever an infant is overly aroused.

Cued recall A type of memory in which a familiar stimulus triggers recall of stored information.

Culture A system of beliefs, attitudes, values, and guidelines for behavior shared by a group of people.

Culture-fair IQ test An IQ test that is appropriate for all the cultures in which it is used.

Culture-free IQ test An IQ test entirely free of culture-based content.

Décalage Piaget's term for inconsistencies in a child's cognitive development across different domains.

Decontextualized thought A cognitive skill needed to solve ploblems that are abstract, self-contained, and removed from any immediate context.

Deferred imitation Imitation of observed behavior after time has elapsed, indicating an infant's ability to store a representation of the behavior in memory.

Delay of gratification The ability to forgo an immediate reward in favor of a better reward at a later time.

Dendrites Short, branching neuron structures that receive electrical impulses from other neurons.

Development Age-related changes that are orderly, cumulative, and directional.

Developmental psychopathology The study of the origins and course of emotional and behavioral disorders.

Deviation anxiety The distress toddlers experience over doing something forbidden.

Didactic learning experience A situation in which a knowledgeable teacher who has already mastered a problem teaches a particular solution to a learner.

Differentiation A developmental process in which structures and functions become increasingly specialized.

Dishabituation Increased attention to a new stimulus after habituation to a previous stimulus.

Disorganized-disoriented attachment A type of anxious attachment in which the infant shows contradictory features of several patterns of anxious attachment or appears dazed and disoriented.

Divided attention Paying attention to two tasks at the same time.

Dizygotic twins Fraternal twins, the result of the fertilization of two ova by two different sperm.

Ecological validity The degree to which experimental findings in the laboratory generalize to the outside world.

Ectoderm Cells that form the central nervous system, sensory organs, and skin.

Effortful control The ability to suppress strong behaviors.

Ego Freud's term for the self; the part of the mind whose major role is to find safe and appropriate ways to express instinctual drives.

Ego resiliency The ability to modify self-restraint to adapt to changing circumstances.

Egocentrism The inability to take the perspective of another person.

Elaboration The mnemonic strategy of creating a meaningful connection between items to be remembered, either verbally or visually.

Embryo The term applied to the developing organism during weeks 3 through 8 of prenatal development.

Embryoblast A group of cells at one end of the blastocyst that develops into the embryo.

Embryonic induction A chemical interaction between the cells of different tissues that triggers developmental changes in the embryo.

Emotion A state of feeling that arises when a person evaluates an event in a particular way.

Emotional dependency A child's atypical need for continual reassurance and attention from adults.

Emotional regulation The capacities to control and direct emotional expression, to maintain organized behavior in the presence of strong emotions, and to be guided by emotional experiences.

Emotional unavailability A chronic lack of parental involvement and emotional responsiveness.

Empathy The ability to experience the emotions of another.

Endoderm Cells that develop into internal organs such as the stomach, liver, and lungs.

Environmentalist theories Theories that stress environmental factors in language acquisition.

Equilibration In Piaget's theory, a self-regulatory process that produces increasingly effective adaptations.

Estrogen A female sex hormone.

Ethology A field of study relying on observation of species in their natural habitats, in order to understand patterns of behavior and their functions.

Evolution The development of species through structural changes over time.

Executive competence The child's feeling that he or she is an autonomous force in the world, with the ability to influence the outcome of events.

Executive functioning The capacity to plan and organize behavior.

Experience-dependent synaptogenesis Synapse formation in response to environmental input specific to an individual.

Experience-expectant synaptogenesis Synapse formation in response to input that can be expected in virtually any environment typical for a particular species.

Experiment A study in which researchers control conditions and systematically manipulate one or more factors so as to rule out all influences except the one(s) being investigated.

Explicit or declarative memory Memory that is conscious, involves mental representation of images or ideas, and can be explicitly stated or declared.

Expressive style A style of early word use in which words primarily express social routines.

External locus of control The belief that success depends on factors outside one's control.

Family day care A day care setting in which a group of children is cared for in the home of a nonrelative.

Fast mapping A process in which a young child uses context cues to make a quick and reasonably accurate guess about the meaning of an unfamiliar word.

Fetal alcohol syndrome (FAS) A constellation of problems found among babies born to heavy drinkers.

Fetus The term applied to the developing organism during weeks 9 through 38 of prenatal development.

Fixation Failure to resolve the major issues of a psychosexual stage, resulting in repeated symbolic reliving of those issues.

Foreclosure Identity status in which commitment has been made to a set of roles and values without a period of exploration.

Form class A category of words in a language that can fill similar syntactic roles in forming phrases and sentences.

Formal operational period Piaget's term for the period when children gain the ability to reason systematically about abstract issues and hypothetical problems.

Formal operations In Piaget's theory, a set of principles of formal logic on which the cognitive advances of adolescence are based.

Fovea The central region of the retina where fine detail and color are primarily detected.

Free recall The ability to spontaneously pull information out of long-term memory.

Gamete A mature reproductive cell (egg or sperm).

Gender constancy The understanding that gender is permanent despite superficial changes.

Gender-role concept Knowledge of cultural stereotypes regarding males and females.

Gender schema theory The theory that children form a concept or schema of male and female characteristics, with the content of the schema based on the child's particular social learning history.

Gene A segment of DNA that contains the code for producing a particular protein.

Generalized anxiety disorder A disorder characterized by very general and pervasive worries and fears.

Genome The complete DNA sequence for an organism.

Genotype An individual's genetic makeup.

Germ cells The cells from which eggs and sperm are produced.

Glial cells Brain cells that provide structural support and nourishment for neurons.

Gonadarche The increase in gonadal sex hormone levels at puberty.

Gonadotropins: Pituitary hormones that affect hormone output by the gonads.

Gonads The sex glands-the ovaries and testes.

Grammatical morpheme A unit of language that carries little meaning by itself, but that changes the meaning of words or sentences in a systematic way.

Greeting reactions Positive reactions of infants when the caregiver appears.

Guided self-regulation The ability of toddlers to regulate their own behavior with guidance from caregivers.

Habituation The decrease in attention that occurs when the same stimulus is presented repeatedly.

Hemispheric specialization The process by which certain brain functions become localized in either the right or left side of the cerebral cortex.

Heterozygous Carrying two different alleles for a particular trait.

Hierarchical classification A classification system in which items are categorized using a hierarchy of subordinate and superordinate classes.

Hippocampus A brain structure that integrates sensory information and is essential to memory formation.

Holophrase A single word that conveys the meaning of a phrase or sentence.

Homologues Two chromosomes that form one of the twenty-three pairs of human chromosomes and resemble each other in size, shape, and the types of genes they carry.

Homozygous Carrying two identical alleles for a particular trait.

Hormone A chemical produced in the body that regulates physiological processes.

Hostile aggression Aggression aimed solely at hurting someone else.

Hypothalamus A part of the brain that regulates many body functions, including the production of pituitary hormones.

Hypothesis A testable proposition, often developed to check the validity of a theory.

Hypothetico-deductive reasoning The ability to think of hypothetical solutions to a problem and to formulate a systematic plan for deducing which of these solutions is correct.

Iconic symbols Symbols that closely resemble the things they represent.

Id Freud's term for the part of the mind that consists of primitive drives and instincts.

Identification The process by which children strive to be like their parents in thoughts and feelings as well as in actions.

Identity A sense of an integrated, coherent, and goal-directed self.

Identity achievement Identity status in which a person has committed to a set of roles and values following a period of active exploration.

Identity crisis In Erikson's theory, the struggle that teenagers experience when trying to establish their personal identities.

Identity diffusion Identity status in which there has been no active exploration of roles and values and no commitment to an adult identity.

Imaginary audience Teenagers' unjustified concern that they are the focus of others' attention.

Imitative learning A way of learning new behaviors by copying others' behaviors.

Implicit or procedural memory Memory that is unconscious, involves memory for procedures or skills, and does not lend itself to explicit statement.

Individual development (1) Individual variations around the normative course of development; (2) continuity within a child's developmental pathway.

Infantile amnesia Adults' inability to recall events from infancy.

Information-processing theory A theory that seeks to explain human thought processes by comparing them to the workings of a computer.

Initiative Erikson's term for a child's sense of independent purposefulness.

Inner speech Children's inaudible directives to themselves, used for behavior regulation.

Instrumental aggression Aggression used as a means to get something.

Instrumental dependency A young child's normal need for adult help in solving complex problems or performing difficult tasks.

Instrumental or operant conditioning Learning in which behaviors are influenced by their consequences.

Intelligence quotient (IQ) A measure of intelligence based on a comparison of a child's performance with the performance of others the same age; originally, mental age divided by chronological age.

Internal locus of control The belief that success depends on one's own efforts.

Internal working model An infant's generalized expectations about the social world, including caregiver responsiveness, the infant's own ability to obtain care, and the nature of social relationships.

Internalization Incorporating the parent's standards of behavior into the self.

Joint attention The tendency for language-learning children and their adult conversation partners to share a focus of attention.

Kinetic depth cues Visual cues in which information about depth and distance is carried in the motion of objects.

Language An abstract, rule-governed system of arbitrary symbols that can be combined in countless ways to communicate information.

Language acquisition device (LAD) Chomsky's term for innate capacities of the human brain that make language acquisition possible.

Latency period Freud's term for middle childhood, the period in which sexual urges lie relatively dormant.

Lexical contrast Children's tendency to assume that no two words have the same meaning.

Life-course-persistent conduct disorder A conduct disorder that begins early, is stable across the childhood years, and predicts problems in adulthood.

Limbic system A collection of brain structures involved in physiological regulation, sensory integration, memory formation, and emotional responses.

Longitudinal study A study following a group of subjects over a period of time.

Long-term memory The part of memory where information is stored for a long time.

Low birth weight Referring to a baby weighing less than 2500 grams at birth.

Matrix classification A classification system in which items are categorized simultaneously along two independent dimensions, such as shape and color.

Maturation Age-related physical changes guided by a genetic plan.

Mediation deficiencies Problems in mnemonic strategy use in which children are unable to use a strategy even when adults suggest it.

Meiosis The process of cell division by which egg and sperm cells are formed.

Memory skills Processes that retain information in working memory and/or transfer it to long-term memory.

Menarche The onset of menstruation.

Mental age (MA) On an intelligence test, a measure of a child's level of intellectual development.

Mesoderm Cells that become the muscles, skeleton, and blood.

Metacognition The capacity to think about thinking.

Metamemory Knowledge about memory and memory processes.

Metatheory of the self Children's understanding of the nature of selves in general.

Mind blindness Deficits in understanding the concept of mind or the intentions, beliefs and thoughts of others.

Mitosis The process of cell division by which the body grows and repairs itself, in which the genetic material from the parent cell is duplicated in each daughter cell.

Mnemonic strategies Intentional, goal-directed behaviors designed to improve memory.

Model A framework for explaining why things happen, a set of ideas and assumptions about causes and effects.

Modeling Learning by imitating others' behavior, especially behavior that has been observed to have positive consequences.

Monozygotic twins Identical twins, the result of the division of a single fertilized egg into two separate units during its early cell division.

Moral realism In Piaget's theory, the stage in which children treat morality as absolute and moral constraints as unalterable.

Moratorium Identity status in which a person is in the midst of exploring options for a personal identity, but has not yet committed to any of them.

Morphemes The smallest meaningful units in a language.

Morphology The system of rules for combining morphemes to form words or to modify word meanings.

Myelination Formation of myelin sheaths around nerve fibers, which helps to speed conduction of electrical impulses.

Nativist theories Theories that stress inborn, biologically based factors in language acquisition.

Natural experiment An observational method in which researchers compare groups of people who differ naturally on the factors being studied.

Natural selection The process by which traits that are well adapted to an environment are selected through reproduction and become increasingly common in a species.

Naturalistic observation A research method in which naturally occuring behavior is observed in everyday settings.

Necessary truth Knowledge that is based on logical necessity, apart from information gathered through the senses.

Neonate The technical term for a baby during the first month of life.

Neo-nativist A contemporary developmental theorist who believes infants have a wide range of innate abilities and knowledge.

Neural tube A tube running from the head to the tail of the embryo, which will develop into the brain and spinal cord.

Neurogenesis Formation of neurons.

Neurons Nerve cells.

Nonexperimental methods Research methods in which information about behavior is collected without manipulating the factors thought to be influencing it.

Normative development The general changes and reorganizations in behavior that virtually all children share as they grow older.

Object permanence The understanding that objects continue to exist when they are out of sight.

Organization The mnemonic strategy of arranging information to be recalled into meaningful categories.

Organogenesis The formation of organs and other major body structures.

Orienting response The response when a stimulus is first presented, involving both behavioral and physiological changes.

Overextensions Language errors in which the meaning a child attaches to a word is too broad.

Overregularizations Language errors in which a child applies a morphological rule to a word that is an exception to the rule.

Ovulation Release of an ovum into one of the fallopian tubes, the passages that lead into the uterus.

Ovum An egg cell.

Patterns of adaptation Individual styles of responding to others and to the environment that form the roots of personality.

Peer group norms Informal rules governing the conduct of children within a peer group.

Perception The process by which the brain interprets information from the senses, giving it order and meaning.

Permissive parenting A parenting style in which parents fail to set firm limits or to require appropriately mature behavior of their children.

Personal fable Teenagers' exaggerated belief in their own uniqueness.

Phenotype An individual's observable traits.

Phonemes Speech sounds that contrast with one another in a particular language and can change the meaning of a word.

Phonology The system of sounds used in a language, the rules for combining those sounds to make words, and the use of stress and intonation in spoken sentences.

Physical abuse Deliberately causing a child physical injury.

Physical neglect Failure to meet a child's basic needs for food, warmth, cleanliness, and medical attention.

Pictorial depth cues Visual cues that can be used to depict depth and distance in two-dimensional pictures.

Pituitary gland A small gland at the base of the brain that plays a major role in regulating the hormonal output of other glands.

Placenta A mass of tissue that supplies oxygen and nutrients to the embryo and carries away waste products.

Plasticity The capacity for different areas of the brain to take on new functions.

Polygenic Influenced by multiple gene pairs.

Positive self-evaluation An emotion in toddlers that is the forerunner of pride.

Postconventional or principled morality In Kohlberg's theory, moral reasoning based on abstract principles underlying right and wrong.

Practical intelligence Intellectual capacity as reflected in successful performance in natural, everyday, nonschool settings.

Pragmatics The rules governing conversation and social use of language.

Preadapted Equipped at birth with built-in capacities that make it possible to understand the environment and form social relationships.

Preconventional morality In Kohlberg's theory, moral reasoning based on fear of punishment or desire for reward.

Prelinguistic vocalization Sounds produced by infants during the first year of life, before they begin to speak.

Premature Referring to a baby born less than thirty-five weeks after conception.

Prenatal period The period of development prior to birth.

Preoperational period In Piaget's theory, the period from ages 2 to 7, characterized by an inability to use logical operations.

Preparedness The genetic predisposition to learn certain behaviors.

Prereaching Early spontaneous arm movements, sometimes made in response to an object.

Primary circular reaction A circular reaction involving an infant's own body.

Private speech Audible speech that children direct to themselves in regulating their own behavior.

Production deficiencies Problems in mnemonic strategy use in which children do not use a strategy spontaneously, but can use it when instructed to do so.

Productive skills Language skills used to put ideas into words.

Prosocial behavior Positive feelings and acts directed toward others, with the intention of benefiting them.

Protective factor Any factor that promotes or maintains healthy development.

Protowords Vocalizations that seem to have consistent meanings for a child and are used in attempts to communicate, but do not closely resemble adult words in sound or meaning.

Proximodistal development The principle that development proceeds from the center of the body outward.

Psychoanalytic theory Any theory of development derived from the ideas of Freud.

Psychological self A concept of the self that is made up of psychological characteristics, such as mental abilities and customary ways of feeling.

Puberty The period during which a child changes from a sexually immature person to one who is capable of reproduction.

Puberty rites/rites of passage Ceremonies that mark the transition from childhood to adulthood.

Pursuit eye movements The smooth, continuous eye motions used to track a moving object.

Qualitative change A developmental change involving a fundamental transformation in an ability or characteristic.

Quantitative change A developmental change involving an increase in the amount of an existing ability or characteristic.

Random assortment The shuffling of chromosomes from the mother and the father that occurs during meiosis when homologues separate in preparation for cell division.

Recall Active retrieval of information from memory.

Receptive skills Language skills used to understand what other people say.

Reciprocity True social interactions involving mutual exchanges between partners.

Recognition memory A type of memory in which a particular stimulus is perceived as familiar.

Recognitory assimilation A form of visual mastery in which the infant recognizes a familiar stimulus and assimilates it to an established scheme.

Referential style A style of early word use in which words primarily refer to objects and events.

Reflex An automatic, inborn response to a particular stimulus.

Rehearsal The mnemonic strategy of repeating information over and over.

Reinforcement Any event following a behavior that increases the likelihood the behavior will be repeated.

Relational aggression Attempts to hurt another person by damaging a relationship.

Retina The light-sensitive surface at the back of the eye.

Risk factor Any factor that increases the likelihood of a negative developmental outcome.

Saccadic eye movements The rapid, jerky eye movements that occur when the gaze is shifted to a new object.

Scaffolding The process by which parents support the child in new tasks by offering developmentally appropriate guidance, hints, and advice.

Schemes In Piaget's theory, cognitive structures that can be applied to a variety of situations.

Script An abstract representation of the sequence of actions needed to accomplish some goal.

Secondary circular reaction A circular reaction involving the effects of an infant's behavior on an external object.

Secondary sex characteristics Physical features that differentiate adult males from adult females but are not directly involved in reproduction.

Secure attachment A pattern of attachment in which the infant is confident of the caregiver's availability and responsiveness and can use the caregiver as a secure base for exploration.

Secure-base behavior Behavior in which the infant uses the caregiver as a base for exploration.

Segmentation errors Mistakes in detecting boundaries between words in a sentence.

Selective attention Focusing attention on relevant information despite distractions.

Self-conscious emotions Emotions that require some objective sense of self and some understanding of standards for behavior.

Self-constancy A sense that the self endures despite temporary disruptions in relationships.

Self-efficacy The sense of being able to do things effectively on one's own.

Self-regulation: Children's ability to direct their own activities, to adjust behavior to fit situations, and to exercise effortful control.

Self-representation Thoughts about the self.

Semantics The meanings of words and sentences.

Sense of industry In Erikson's theory, the basic belief in one's own competence.

Sensitive care A caregiving style in which the caregiver attends to the infant's needs and responds to them promptly and effectively.

Sensitive period A time when particular experiences are especially important for development.

Sensitive period hypothesis The idea that certain kinds of experience are especially important at particular points in development.

Sensorimotor period Piaget's term for the first two years of life, when awareness of the world is limited to what can be known through sensory awareness and motor acts.

Sensory register The part of memory where incoming information from one of the five senses is stored very briefly.

Separation anxiety disorder Excessive anxiety precipitated by separation from someone to whom the child is emotionally attached.

Separation distress Negative reactions of infants when the caregiver temporarily leaves.

Separation-individuation process Mahler's term for the child's psychological separation from the caregiver and growing awareness of being an individual.

Seriation The ability to arrange things in a logical progression, such as from oldest to newest.

Sex chromosome abnormalities A type of chromosomal abnormality that occurs when a baby receives an abnormal number of sex chromosomes.

Sex chromosomes In humans, the twenty-third pair of chromosomes, which determine genetic gender. Females normally have two X chromosomes, males one X chromosome and one Y chromosome.

Sex-linked traits Recessive genetic traits that are carried on the X chromosome and are commonly expressed only in males.

Sex-typed behavior Actions that conform to cultural expectations about what is appropriate for boys and for girls.

Shame An emotion in which the self feels exposed, vulnerable, and bad.

Shape constancy The ability to perceive an object as constant in shape, even though its image on the retina changes shape when the object is viewed from different angles.

Shaping Reinforcing gradually closer approximations of a target behavior.

Short-term or working memory The part of memory where consciously noted information is stored for 10 to 20 seconds.

Single-gene (Mendelian) disorder Any disorder produced by inheritance of a single gene.

Situational compliance Children's unwilling compliance with parents' directives due to fear or parents' control of the situation.

Size constancy The ability to perceive an object viewed from different distances as constant in size even though its image on the retina grows larger or smaller.

Social cognition A child's understanding of the social world.

Social comparison The tendency to use others as a source of information in evaluating the self.

Socialization The process by which children acquire the rules, standards, and values of a culture.

Social learning theory A theory that emphasizes the learning of behaviors through associations with different kinds of consequences, especially in a social context.

Social referencing The use of cues from another person to interpret situations and guide behavior.

Social self An awareness that the self is intimately tied to other people.

Sociocultural theory A theory that emphasizes the role of social interaction and specific cultural practices in the development of cognitive skills.

Socioeconomic status (SES) The grouping of people within a society on the basis of income, occupation, and education.

Sociometrics A research technique used to measure peer status.

Somatic cells The cells that make up the body, not including egg and sperm cells.

Spermarche The first ejaculation of mobile sperm.

Spontaneous remission The disappearance of a disorder without professional treatment.

Stereotypic leg movements Rhythmic, repetitive leg movements elicited automatically when an infant reaches a certain level of excitement.

Strabismus A condition in which the eyes are misaligned and do not function together.

Stranger distress Negative reactions of infants to strangers.

Subcultures Groups whose beliefs, attitudes, values, and guidelines for behavior differ in some ways from those of the dominant culture.

Subject attrition In a longitudinal study, the loss of participants over time.

Sublimation Freud's term for the redirection of blocked biological drives and impulses.

Superego Freud's term for the conscience; the part of the mind that has internalized rules and values governing behavior.

Survey research Research in which information is collected using interviews or questionnaires.

Symbolic or representational thought In Piaget's theory, the ability to make one thing stand for another.

Symbolic representation The use of ideas, images, or other symbols to stand for objects or events.

Synapses Connections between neurons.

Synaptogenesis Formation of synapses, or connections between neurons.

Syntax The rules for organizing words into phrases and sentences.

Telegraphic speech A toddler speech style in which words not essential to the meaning of a sentence are omitted.

Temperament An individual infant's general style of behavior across contexts.

Teratogen A substance in the environment that can cause physical malformations during prenatal development.

Tertiary circular reaction A circular reaction involving purposeful, trial-and-error experimentation with a variety of objects.

Thalamus A brain structure that relays sensory information to the cerebral cortex.

Theory An organized set of ideas about how things operate, an attempt to explain past findings and predict future ones.

Theory of mind An understanding of the mind and mental operations.

Transactional model Sameroff's model describing the cumulative effects of ongoing two-way influences between children and parents.

Transitive inference The ability to infer the relation between two objects by knowing their respective relations to a third.

Trimesters Three-month periods that correspond to changes in the mother's experience of pregnancy.

Trophoblast The cells in the blastocyst that form the basis of the embryo's life-support system.

Ultrasound A technique that produces a computer image of a fetus by bouncing sound waves off it.

Umbilical cord A cord containing blood vessels that connects the embryo with the placenta.

Underextensions Language errors in which the meaning a child attaches to a word is too restricted.

Utilization deficiencies Problems in mnemonic strategy use in which children use a strategy spontaneously, but without benefit to their memory performance.

Very low birth weight Referring to a baby weighing less than 1500 grams at birth.

Visual acuity The degree to which one can see fineness of detail.

Vocabulary spurt A sudden increase in word acquisition at about 18 months of age.

Vocal play Prelinguistic vocalizations that vary greatly in pitch and loudness, including occasional simple syllables.

Whole-object assumption Children's tendency to assume that unfamiliar words are names for objects rather than for attributes or actions.

Working memory The information-processing capacity available at any one time.

Zone of proximal development Vygotsky's term for the gap between a particular child's current performance and potential performance with guidance from someone more skilled.

Zygote The cell resulting from the union of a sperm cell with an ovum.

References

Aber, J. L., Belsky, J., Slade, A., and Crnic, K. (1999). Stability and change in mothers' representations of their relationships with their toddlers. *Developmental Psychology, 35,* 1038–1047. [8]

Abma, J., Chandra, A., Mosher, W., Peterson, L., Piccinino, L. (1997). Fertility, family planning and women's health: New data from the 1995 National Survey of Family Growth. *Vital Health Statistics 23,* No. 19. [14]

Ackerman, B. (1984). Storage and processing constraints on integrating story information in children and adults. *Journal of Experimental Child Psychology, 38,* 64–92. [11]

Ackerman, B., Schoff, K., Levinson, K., Youngstrom, E., and Izard, C. (1999). The relations between cluster indexes of risk and promotion and the problem behaviors of 6- and 7-year-old children from economically disadvantaged families. *Developmental Psychology, 35,* 1355–1366. [2]

Accornero, V. H., Morrow, C. E., Bandstra, E. S., Johnson, A. L., and Anthony, J. C. (2002). Behavioral outcome of preschoolers exposed prenatally to cocaine: Role of maternal behavioral health. *Journal of Pediatric Psychology, 27,* 259–269. [3]

Aguilar, B., Sroufe, L. A., Egeland, B., and Carlson, E. (2000). Distinguishing the early-onset/persistent and adolescence-onset antisocial behavior types: From birth to 16 years. *Development and Psychopathology, 12,* 109–132. [15]

Ainsworth, M. (1967). *Infancy in Uganda.* Baltimore: Johns Hopkins University Press. [6]

Ainsworth, M., and Bell, S. (1974). Mother-infant interaction and the development of competence. In K. Connolly and J. Bruner (Eds.), *The growth of competence* (pp. 97–118). New York: Academic Press. [6]

Ainsworth, M., Bell, S., and Stayton, D. (1974). Infant-mother attachment and social development: Socialization as a product of reciprocal responsiveness to signals. In M. Richards (Ed.), *The integration of the child into the social world* (pp. 99–135). Cambridge, England: Cambridge University Press. [1], [8]

Ainsworth, M., Blehar, M., Waters, E., and Wall, S. (1978). *Patterns of attachment.* Hillsdale, NJ: Erlbaum. [6]

Aitken, K., and Trevarthen, C. (1997). Self/other organization in human psychological development. *Development and Psychopathology, 9,* 653–677. [6]

Akhtar, N., and Tomasello, M. (1996). Two-year-olds learn words for absent objects and actions. *British Journal of Developmental Psychology, 14,* 79–93. [7]

Aksan, N., Goldsmith, H., Smider, N., Essex, M., Clark, R., Hyde, J., Klein, M., and Vandell, D. (1999). Derivation and prediction of temperamental types among preschoolers. *Developmental Psychology, 35,* 958–971. [10]

Aksu-Koc, A. A., and Slobin, D. I. (1985). The acquisition of Turkish. In D. I. Slobin (Ed.), *The crosslinguistic study of language acquisition: Vol. 1. The data* (pp. 839–880). Hillsdale, NJ: Erlbaum. [7]

Alessandri, S. M., Bendersky, M., and Lewis, M. (1998). Cognitive functioning in 8- to 18-month-old drug-exposed infants. *Developmental Psychology, 34,* 565–573. [3]

Alexander, G. R., Kogan, M., Bader, D., Carlo, W., Allen, M., and Mor, J. (2003). US birth weight/gestational age-specific neonatal mortality: 1995–1997 rates for whites, hispanics, and blacks. *Pediatrics, 111,* e61–66. [3]

Allison, P., and Furstenberg, F., Jr. (1989). How marital dissolution affects children: Variations by age and sex. *Developmental Psychology, 25,* 540–549. [14]

Amato, P. (1998). More than money? Men's contributions to their children's lives. In A. Booth and A. Crouter (Eds.), *Men in families: When do they get involved? What difference does it make?* (pp. 241–278). Mahwah, NJ: Lawrence Erlbaum Associates. [8], [12]

American Academy of Pediatrics. (2000). Evaluation of the newborn with developmental anomalies of the external genitalia. *Pediatrics, 106,* 138–142. [3]

American Association of University Women. (1998). *Gender gaps: Where schools still fail our children.* Washington, DC: AAUW Educational Foundation. [2], [12]

American Psychiatric Association (2000). *Diagnostic and statistical manual of mental disorders DSM-IV-TR (Text Revision).* Washington, DC: Author. [15]

Ames, A. (1951). Visual perception and the rotating trapezoidal window. *Psychological Monographs* (Series No. 324). [4]

Ames, E.W., and Chisholm, K. (2001). Social and emotional development in children adopted from institutions. In Bailey, D. B., Jr., Bruer, J. T., Symons, F. J., and Lichtman, J. W. (Eds.). *Critical thinking about critical periods* (pp. 129–148). Baltimore: Paul H. Brookes. [2]

Amsterdam, R. (1972). Mirror self-image reactions before age two. *Developmental Psychobiology, 5,* 297–305. [8]

Anderson, D., and Levin, S. (1976). Young children's attention to *Sesame Street. Child Development, 47,* 806–811. [9]

Anderson, R. N. (2002). *Deaths: Leading causes for 2000.* National Vital Statistics Reports, 50(16). Hyattsville, MD: National Center for Health Statistics. [2]

Andrade, M., and Menna-Barreto, L. (2002). Sleep patterns of high school students living in Sao Paulo, Brazil. In M. A. Carskadon (Ed.), *Adolescent sleep patterns: Biological, social, and psychological influences* (pp. 118–131). New York: Cambridge University Press. [13]

Anglin, J. M. (1993). Vocabulary development: A morphological analysis. *Monographs of the Society for Research in Child Development, 58*(10, Serial No. 228). [7]

Anisfeld, M. (1991). Neonatal imitation: Review. *Developmental Review, 11,* 60–97. [4]

Anisfeld, M. (1996). Only tongue protrusion modeling is matched by neonates. *Development Review, 16,* 149–161. [4]

Annas, G. J., and Elias, S. (1999). Thalidomide and the Titanic: Reconstructing the technology tragedies of the twentieth century. *American Journal of Public Health, 89,* 98–101. [3]

Anselmi, D., Tomasello, M., and Acunzo, M. (1986). Young children's responses to neutral and specific contingent queries. *Journal of Child Language, 13,* 135–144. [7]

Antell, S. E., and Keating, D. P. (1983). Perception of numerical invariance in neonates. *Child Development, 54,* 695–706. [5]

Anthony, E. J. (1974). The syndrome of the psychologically invulnerable child. In E. J. Anthony and C. Koupernik (Eds.), *The child in his family: Children at psychiatric risk* (pp. 529–545). New York: Wiley. [10]

Apgar, V. (1975). A proposal for a new method of evaluation of a newborn infant. *Anesthesia and Analgesia, 32,* 260–267. [3]

Archer, S., and Waterman, A. (1994). Adolescent identity development: Contextual perspectives. In C. B. Fisher and R. Lerner (Eds.), *Applied developmental psychology* (pp. 76–100). New York: McGraw-Hill. [14]

Arend, R., Gove, F., and Sroufe, L. A. (1979). Continuity of individual adaptation from infancy to kindergarten: A predictive study of ego-resiliency and curiosity in preschoolers. *Child Development, 50,* 950–959. [1], [10]

Arnett, J. (1999). Adolescent storm and stress, reconsidered. *American Psychologist, 54,* 317–326. [14]

Aro, H., and Taipale, V. (1987). The impact of timing of puberty on psychosomatic symptoms among fourteen- to sixteen-year-old Finnish girls. *Child Development, 58,* 261–268. [13]

Arsenio, W., Cooperman, S., and Lover, A. (2000). Affective predictors of preschoolers' aggression and peer acceptance: Direct and indirect effects. *Developmental Psychology, 36*, 438–448. [10]

Arsenio, W., and Kramer, R. (1992). Victimizers and their victims: Children's conceptions of the mixed emotional consequences of moral transgressions. *Child Development, 63*, 915–927. [12]

Ashmead, D. H., and Perlmutter, M. (1980). Infant memory in everyday life. In M. Perlmutter (Ed.), *New directions for child development: No. 10. Children's memory* (pp. 1–16). San Francisco: Jossey-Bass. [5]

Aslin, R. N. (1981). Development of smooth pursuit in human infants. In D. F. Fischer, R. A. Monty, and J. W. Senders (Eds.), *Eye movements: Cognition and visual perception* (pp. 31–51). Hillsdale, NJ: Erlbaum. [4]

Aslin, R. N., and Banks, M. S. (1978). Early visual experience in humans: Evidence for a critical period in the development of binocular vision. In H. L. Pick, Jr., H. W. Leibowitz, J. E. Singer, A. Steinschneider, and H. W. Stevenson (Eds.), *Psychology: From research to practice* (pp. 227–239). New York: Plenum Press. [4]

Aslin, R. N., Pisoni, D. B., and Jusczyk, P. W. (1983). Auditory development and speech in infancy. In P. H. Mussen (Series Ed.), M. M. Haith and J. J. Campos (Eds.), *Handbook of child psychology: Vol. 2. Infancy and developmental psychobiology* (4th ed., pp. 573–687). New York: Wiley. [4]

Aslin, R. N., and Salapatek, P. (1975). Saccadic localization of peripheral targets by the very young human infant. *Perception and Psychophysics, 17*, 293–302. [4]

Atkinson, J., and Braddick, O. (1989). Development of basic visual functions. In A. Slater and G. Bremner (Eds.), *Infant development* (pp. 3–41). Hove, U.K.: Erlbaum. [4]

Atkinson, R. C., and Shiffrin, R. M. (1968). Human memory: A proposed system and its control processes. In K. W. Spence and J. T. Spence (Eds.), *The psychology of learning and motivation: Advances in research and theory* (Vol. 2). New York: Academic Press. [9]

Atkinson, R. C., and Shiffrin, R. M. (1969). Storage and retrieval processes in long-term memory. *Psychological Review, 76*, 179–193. [1]

Attie, I., Brooks-Gunn, J., and Petersen, A. C. (1990). A developmental perspective on eating disorders and eating problems. In M. Lewis and S. M. Miller (Eds.), *Handbook of developmental psychopathology* (pp. 409–420). New York: Plenum Press. [15]

Ault, R. L. (1983). *Children's cognitive development* (2nd ed.). New York: Oxford University Press. [13]

Bai, J., Wong, F. W., Bauman, A., and Mohsin, M. (2002). Parity and pregnancy outcomes. *American Journal of Obstetrics and Gynecology, 186*, 274–278. [3]

Bachevalier, J. (1991). Cortical versus limbic immaturity: Relationship to infantile amnesia. In M. R. Gunnar and C. A. Nelson (Eds.), *Minnesota Symposia on Child Psychology: Vol. 24. Developmental Behavioral Neuroscience* (pp. 129–153). Hillsdale, NJ: Erlbaum. [5]

Bailey, J. M., Bobrow, D., Wolfe, M., and Mikach, S. (1995). Sexual orientation of adult sons of gay fathers. Developmental Psychology, 31, 124–129. [2]

Baillargeon, R. (1987). Object permanence in 3- and 4-month-old infants. *Developmental Psychology, 23*, 655–664. [5]

Baillargeon, R. (1991). Reasoning about the height and location of a hidden object in 4.5- and 6.5-month-old infants. *Cognition, 38*, 13–42. [5]

Baillargeon, R. (1993). The object concept revisited: New directions in the investigation of infants' physical knowledge. In C. E. Granrud (Ed.), *Visual cognition and perception in infancy* (pp. 265–315). Hillsdale, NJ: Erlbaum. [5]

Baillargeon, R. (1994). How do infants learn about the physical world? *Psychological Science, 3*, 133–140. [5]

Baillargeon, R., and DeVos, J. (1991). Object permanence in young infants: Further evidence. *Child Development, 62*, 1227–1246. [5]

Baillargeon, R., and Hanko-Summers, S. (1990). Is the top object adequately supported by the bottom object? Young infants' understanding of support relations. *Cognitive Development, 5*, 29–53. [5]

Baillargeon, R., Needham, A., and DeVos, J. (1992). The development of young infants' intuitions about support. *Early Development and Parenting, 1*, 69–78. [5]

Baird, P., Sadovnik, A., and Yee, I. (1991). Maternal age and birth defects: A population study. *Lancet, 337*, 527–530. [3]

Baker, L., and Daniels, D. (1990). Nonshared environmental influences and personality differences in adult twins. *Journal of Personality and Social Psychology, 58*, 103–110. [1]

Baldwin, A., Baldwin, C., and Cole, R. (1990). Stress-resistant families and stress-resistant children. In J. Rolf, A. Masten, D. Cicchetti, K. Neuchterlein, and S. Weinraub (Eds.), *Risk and protective factors in the development of psychopathology* (pp. 257–280). New York: Cambridge University Press. [10]

Baldwin, D. (2000). Interpersonal understanding fuels knowledge acquisition. *Current Directions in Psychological Science, 9*, 40–45. [8]

Baldwin, D. A. (1991). Infants' contribution to the achievement of joint reference. *Child Development, 62*, 875–890. [7]

Baldwin, D. A., Markman, E. M., Bill, B., Desjardins, R. N., and Irwin, J. M. (1996). Infants' reliance on a social criterion for establishing word-object relations. *Child Development, 67*, 3135–3153. [7]

Bale, P., Doust, J., and Dawson, D. (1996). Gymnasts, distance runners, anorexics body composition and menstrual status. *Journal of sports medicine and physical fitness, 36*, 49–53. [13]

Bandstra, E. S., Morrow, C. E., Anthony, J. C., Accornero, V. H., and Fried, P. A. (2001). Longitudinal investigation of task persistence and sustained attention in children with prenatal cocaine exposure. *Neurotoxicology and Teratology, 23*, 545–559. [3]

Bandura, A. (1986). *Social foundations of thought and action: A social cognitive theory.* Englewood Cliffs, NJ: Prentice-Hall. [15]

Bandura, A. (1992). Social cognitive theory. In R. Vasta (Ed.), *Six theories of child development:*

Revised formulations and current issues (pp. 1–60). London, England: Jessica Kingsley. [8]

Bandura, A. (1997). *Self efficacy: The exercise of control.* New York: Freeman. [1], [10], [15]

Bandura, A., Ross, D., and Ross, S. A. (1961). Transmission of aggression through imitation of aggressive models. *Journal of Abnormal and Social Psychology, 63*, 575–582. [1]

Bank, L., Patterson, G. R., and Reid, J. B. (1996). Negative sibling interaction patterns as predictors of later adjustment problems in adolescent and young adult males. In G. H. Brody (Ed.), *Sibling relationships: Their causes and consequences* (pp. 197–229). Norwood, NJ: Ablex. [12]

Banks, M. S., and Salapatek, P. (1983). Infant visual perception. In P. H. Mussen (Series Ed.), M. M. Haith and J. J. Campos (Eds.), *Handbook of child psychology: Vol. 2. Infancy and developmental psychobiology* (4th ed., pp. 435–571). New York: Wiley. [4]

Barkley, R. (1997). Behavioral inhibition, sustained attention, and executive function: Constructing a unifying theory of ADHD. *Psychological Bulletin, 121*, 65–94. [15]

Baron-Cohen, S. (2000). Theory of mind and autism: A review. *International Review of Research in Mental Retardation, 23*, 170–184. [15]

Barr, H. M., and Streissguth, A. P. (2001). Identifying maternal self-reported alcohol use associated with fetal alcohol spectrum disorders. *Alcoholism, Clinical and Experimental Research, 25*, 283–287. [3]

Barr, R., Desilets, J., and Rotman, R. (1991). The normal crying curve: Hoops and hurdles. In B. Lester (Ed.), *Biological and social aspects of infant crying.* New York: Plenum Press. [4]

Barrera, M. E., and Maurer, D. (1981). Recognition of mother's photographed face by the three-month-old. *Child Development, 52*, 558–563. [4]

Barton, M. E., and Tomasello, M. (1994). The rest of the family: The role of fathers and siblings in early language development. In C. Gallaway and B. J. Richards (Eds.), *Input and interaction in language acquisition* (pp. 109–134). Cambridge, England: Cambridge University Press. [7]

Bassuk, E. L., and Rosenberg, L. (1990). Psychological characteristics of homeless children and children with homes. *Pediatrics, 85*, 257–261. [2]

Bates, E., Bretherton, I., and Snyder, L. (1988). *From first words to grammar: Individual differences and dissociable mechanisms.* New York: Cambridge University Press. [7]

Bates, E., Thal, D., and Janowsky, J. W. (1992). Early language development and its neural correlates. In I. Rapin and S. Segalowitz (Eds.), *Handbook of neuropsychology* (pp. 69–110). Amsterdam: Elsevier. [7]

Bates, J. (1980). The concept of difficult temperament. *Merrill-Palmer Quarterly, 26*, 299–319. [4]

Bates, J., Dodge, K. Pettit, G., and Ridge, B. (1998). Interaction of temperamental resistance to Control and restrictive parenting in the development of externalizing behavior. *Developmental Psychology, 34*, 982–995. [8]

Battles, H. B., and Wiener, L. S. (2002). From adolescence through young adulthood: Psychosocial adjustment associated with long-term survival of HIV. *Journal of Adolescent Health, 30,* 161–168. [3]

Bauer, P. (1993). Memory for gender-consistent and gender-inconsistent event sequences by twenty-five-month-old children. *Child Development, 64,* 285–297. [10]

Bauer, P. J. (1995). Recalling past events: From infancy to early childhood. *Annals of Child Development, 11,* 25–71. [7]

Bauer, P. J., and Dow, G. A. (1994). Episodic memory in 16- and 20-month-old children: Specifics are generalized but not forgotten. *Developmental Psychology, 30,* 403–417. [5]

Bauer, P. J., Hertsgaard, L. A., and Dow, G. A. (1994). After 8 months have passed: Long-term recall of events by 1- to 2-year-old children. *Memory, 2,* 353–382. [5]

Baumrind, D. (1967). Child care practices anteceding three patterns of preschool behavior. *Genetic Psychology Monographs, 75,* 43–88. [10], [12]

Baumrind, D. (1989). Rearing competent children. In W. Damon (Ed.), *Child development today and tomorrow* (pp. 349–378). San Francisco: Jossey-Bass. [2], [12], [14]

Baumrind, D. (1991). Parenting styles and adolescent development. In J. Brooks-Gunn, R. Lerner, and A. Petersen (Eds.), *The encyclopedia of adolescence* (pp. 746–758). New York: Garland. [10], [12]

Bauserman, R. (2002). Child adjustment in joint custody versus sole custody arrangements: A meta-analytic review. *Journal of Family Psychology, 16,* 91–102. [12]

Bayley, N. (1949). Consistency and variability in the growth of intelligence from birth to eighteen years. *Journal of Genetic Psychology, 75,* 165–169. [5]

Beal, C. (1994). *Boys and girls: The development of gender roles.* New York: McGraw-Hill. [12]

Becker, J. (1994). Pragmatic socialization: Parental input to preschoolers. *Discourse Processes, 17,* 131–148. [7]

Becker, W. (1964). Consequences of different kinds of parental discipline. In M. L. Hoffman and L. W. Hoffman (Eds.), *Review of child development research* (Vol. 1, pp. 169–208). New York: Russell Sage. [12]

Behrend, D. A. (1990). Constraints and development: A reply to Nelson (1988). *Cognitive Development, 5,* 313–330. [7]

Beilin, H. (1980). Piaget's theory: Refinement, revision, or rejection? In R. Kluwe and H. Spada (Eds.), *Developmental models of thinking* (pp. 245–260). New York: Academic Press. [13]

Beilin, H. (1994). Jean Piaget's enduring contribution to developmental psychology. In R. D. Parke, P. A. Ornstein, J. J. Rieser, and C. Zahn-Waxler (Eds.), *A century of developmental psychology* (pp. 257–290). Washington, DC: American Psychological Association. [1]

Bell, R. (1968). A reinterpretation of the direction of effects in studies of socialization. *Psychological Review, 75,* 81–95. [2]

Belsky, J. (2001). Emanuel Miller Lecture: Developmental risks (still) associated with early child care. *Journal of Child Psychology and Psychiatry and Allied Disciplines, 42,* 845–859. [2], [6]

Belsky, J. (1988). Child maltreatment and the emergent family system. In K. Browne, C. Davies, and P. Strattan (Eds.), *Early prediction and prevention of child abuse* (pp. 291–302). New York: Wiley. [8]

Belsky, J., Fish, M., and Isabella, R. (1991). Continuity and discontinuity in infant negative and positive emotionality: Family antecedents and attachment consequences. *Developmental Psychology, 27,* 421–431. [6]

Belsky, J., and Isabella, R. A. (1988). Maternal, infant, and social-contextual determinants of attachment security. In J. Belsky and T. Nezworski (Eds.), *Clinical implications of attachment* (pp. 41–94). Hillsdale, NJ: Erlbaum. [2], [8]

Belsky, J., and Most, R. K. (1981). From exploration to play: A cross-sectional study of infant free play behavior. *Developmental Psychology, 17,* 630–639. [7]

Bem, D., and Funder, D. (1978). Predicting more of the people more of the time: Assessing the personality of situations. *Psychological Review, 85,* 485–501. [1]

Bem, S. L. (1989). Genital knowledge and gender constancy in preschool children. *Child Development, 60,* 649–662. [10]

Benatar, D., and Benatar, M. (2001). A pain in the fetus: Toward ending confusion about fetal pain. *Bioethics, 15,* 57–76. [4]

Bendersky, M., and Lewis, M. (1998). Arousal modulation in cocaine-exposed infants. *Developmental Psychology, 34,* 555–564. [3]

Benenson, J. (1993). Greater preference among females than males for dyadic interaction in early childhood. *Child Development, 64*(2), 544–555. [10]

Bengtson, V. L. (2001). Beyond the nuclear family: The increasing importance of multigenerational bonds. *Journal of Marriage and the Family, 63,* 1–16. [2]

Berko, J. (1958). The child's learning of English morphology. *Word, 14,* 150–177. [7]

Berndt, T. (1979). Developmental changes in conformity to peers and parents. *Developmental Psychology, 15,* 608–616. [14]

Berndt, T. (1999). Friends' influence on children's adjustment to school. In W. A. Collins and B. Laursen (Eds.), *Minnesota Symposia on Child Psychology: Vol. 30. Relationships as developmental contexts: Festschrift in honor of Willard W. Hartup* (pp. 85–107). Mahwah, NJ: Erlbaum. [14]

Bernstein, G., and Borchart, C. (1991). Anxiety disorders of childhood and adolescence: A critical review. *Journal of the American Academy of Child and Adolescent Psychiatry, 30,* 519–532. [15]

Bertenthal, B. I., and Clifton, R. K. (1998). Perception and action. In W. Damon (Series Ed.), D. Kuhn, and R. S. Siegler (Vol. Eds.), *Handbook of child psychology: Vol. 2. Cognition, perception, and language* (5th ed., pp. 51–102). New York: Wiley. [4]

Berzonsky, M. (1971). The role of familiarity in children's explanations of physical causality. *Child Development, 42,* 705–715. [9]

Berzonsky, M., and Kuk, L. (2000). Identity status, identity processing style, and the transition to university. *Journal of Adolescent Research, 15,* 81–98. [14]

Bhana, N., Ormrod, D., Perry, C. M., and Figgitt, D. P. (2002). Zidovudine: A review of its use in the management of vertically-acquired pediatric HIV infection. *Paediatric Drugs, 4,* 515–553. [3]

Bjork, E. L., and Cummings, E. M. (1984). Infant search errors: Stage of concept development or stage of memory development. *Memory and Cognition, 12,* 1–19. [5]

Bjorklund, D. F. (1997). The role of immaturity in human development. *Psychological Bulletin, 122,* 153–169. [4]

Bjorklund, D. F., and Pellegrini, A. D. (2002). *The origins of human nature: Evolutionary developmental psychology.* Washington, DC: American Psychological Association. [2]

Blevins, B., and Cooper, R. G. (1986). The development of transitivity of length in young children. *Journal of Genetic Psychology, 147,* 395–405. [9]

Block, J. (1987, April). Longitudinal antecedents of ego-control and ego-resiliency in late adolescence. Paper presented at the biennial meeting of the Society for Research in Child Development, Baltimore. [10]

Block, J. H. (1979). *Personality development in males and females: The influence of different socialization.* Master Lecture Series of the American Psychological Association, New York. [14]

Block, J. H., and Block, J. (1980). The role of ego-control and ego-resiliency in the organization of behavior. In W. A. Collins (Ed.), *Minnesota Symposia on Child Psychology: Vol. 13. Development of cognition, affect, and social relations* (pp. 39–101). Hillsdale, NJ: Erlbaum. [10]

Bloom, B. S. (1964). *Stability and change in human characteristics.* New York: Wiley. [11]

Bloom, L. (1973). *One word at a time: The use of single word utterances before syntax.* The Hague: Mouton. [7]

Bloom, L. (1993). *The transition from infancy to language: Acquiring the power of expression.* Cambridge, England: Cambridge University Press. [7]

Bloom, L. (1998). Language acquisition in its developmental context. In W. Damon (Series Ed.), D. Kuhn, and R. S. Siegler (Vol. Eds.), *Handbook of child psychology: Vol. 2. Cognition, perception, and language* (5th ed., pp. 309–370). New York: Wiley. [7]

Bloom, L., and Tinker, E. (2001). The intentionality model and language acquisition. *Monographs of the Society for Research in Child Development, 66,* (Ser. No. 267) 1–91. [8]

Boer, F., and Dunn, J. (1992). *Children's sibling relationships: Developmental and clinical issues.* Hillsdale, NJ: Erlbaum. [10]

Bonvillian, J. D., and Folven, R. J. (1993). Sign language acquisition: Developmental aspects. In M. Marschark and M. D. Clark (Eds.), *Psychological perspectives on deafness* (pp. 229–265). Hillsdale, NJ: Erlbaum. [7]

Booth, A., and Crouter, A. C. (Eds.) (1998). *Men in families: When do they get involved?* Mahwah, NJ: Erlbaum. [2]

Borja-Alvarez, T., Zarbatany, L., and Pepper, S. (1991). Contributions of male and female guests and hosts to peer group entry. *Child Development, 62,* 1079–1090. [12]

Bornstein, M. H. (1978). Chromatic vision in infancy. In H. W. Reese and L. P. Lipsitt (Eds.), *Advances in child development and behavior* (Vol. 12, pp. 117–182). New York: Academic Press. [4]

Bornstein, M. H., and Sigman, M. D. (1986). Continuity in mental development from infancy. *Child Development, 57,* 251–274. [5]

Bornstein, M. H., Tamis-LeMonda, C. S., Tal, J., Ludemann, P., Toda, S., Rahn, C. W., Pecheux, M. G., Azuma, H., and Vardi, D. (1992). Maternal responsiveness to infants in three societies: The United States, France, and Japan. *Developmental Psychology, 63,* 808–821. [6]

Bowlby, J. (1969/1982). *Attachment and loss* (2nd ed.). New York: Basic Books. [6]

Bowlby, J. (1973). *Separation.* New York: Basic Books. [1], [6], [12]

Bowlby, J. (1988). *A secure base: Parent-child attachment and healthy human development.* New York: Basic Books. [6]

Boysson-Bardies, B., and Vihman, M. M. (1991). Adaptation to language: Evidence from babbling and first words in four languages. *Language, 67,* 297–319. [7]

Bradley, R. H., and Corwyn, R. F. (2002). Socioeconomic status and child development. *Annual Review of Psychology, 53,* 371–399. [2, 5]

Brainerd, C. J. (1978). *Piaget's theory of intelligence.* Englewood Cliffs, NJ: Prentice-Hall. [13]

Brazelton, T. B. (1962). Crying in infancy. *Pediatrics, 29,* 40–47. [4]

Brazelton, T. B. (1973). *Clinics in developmental medicine: No. 50. Neonatal behavioral assessment scale.* Philadelphia: Lippincott. [4]

Brazelton, T. B., Koslowski, B., and Main, M. (1974). The origins of reciprocity: The early mother-input interaction. In M. Lewis and L. Rosenblum (Eds.), *The effect of the infant on its caregiver.* (pp. 49–76). New York: Wiley. [6]

Breger, L. (2000). *Freud: Darkness in the midst of vision.* New York: Wiley. [1]

Breger, L. (1974). *From instinct to identity: The development of personality.* Englewood Cliffs, NJ: Prentice-Hall. [2], [10]

Brendgen, M., Vitaro, F., Bukowski, W., Doyle, A., and Markiewicz, D. (2001). Developmental profiles of peer social preference over the course of elementary school: Associations with trajectories of externalizing and internalizing behavior. *Developmental Psychology, 37,* 308–320. [12], [14]

Bretherton, I., and Ainsworth, M. D. S. (1974). Responses of one-year-olds to a stranger in a strange situation. In M. Lewis and L. Rosenblum (Eds.), *The origins of fear* (pp. 131–164). New York: Wiley. [8]

Bretherton, I., and Munholland, K. (1999). Internal working models in attachment relationships: A construct revisited. In J. Cassidy and P. Shaver (Eds.), *Handbook of attachment* (pp. 89–111). New York: Guilford. [10], [12]

Bridges, L., and Grolnick, W. (1995). The development of emotional self-regulation in infancy and early childhood. In N. Eisenberg (Ed.), *Social development: Review of child development research* (pp. 185–211). Thousand Lakes CA: Sage. [6], [10]

Brittain, C. (1963). Adolescent choice and parent-peer cross pressures. *American Sociological Review, 28,* 385–391. [14]

Brody, G. H. (1998). Sibling relationship quality: Its causes and consequences. *Annual Review of Psychology, 49,* 1–24. [2], [12]

Brody, G., Stoneman, Z., and McCoy, J. K. (1992). Associations of maternal and paternal direct and differential behavior with sibling relationships: Contemporaneous and longitudinal analyses. *Child Development, 63,* 82–92. [12]

Bronfenbrenner, U. (1979). *The ecology of human development.* Cambridge, MA: Harvard University Press. [2]

Bronfenbrenner, U., and Evans, G. W. (2000). Developmental science in the 21st century: Emerging questions, theoretical models, research designs and empirical findings. *Social Development, 9,* 115–125. [2]

Bronfenbrenner, U., and Morris, P. A. (1998). The ecology of developmental processes. In W. Damon (Series Ed.) and R. M. Lerner (Vol. Ed.), *Handbook of child psychology: Vol. 1. Theoretical models of human development* (5th ed., pp. 993–1028). New York: Wiley. [2]

Bronson, G., and Pankey, W. (1977). On the distinction between fear and wariness. *Child Development, 48,* 1167–1183. [6]

Bronson, W. (1981). *Toddlers' behavior with agemates: Issues of interaction, cognition and affect.* Norwood, NJ: Ablex. [8], [10]

Brooks-Gunn, J. (1987). Pubertal processes and girls' psychological adaptation. In R. M. Lerner and T. T. Foch (Eds.), *Biological-psychosocial interactions in early adolescence* (pp. 123–153). Hillsdale, NJ: Erlbaum. [13]

Brooks-Gunn, J., and Furstenberg, F. (1986). The children of adolescent mothers: Physical, academic, and psychological outcomes. *Developmental Review, 6,* 224–251. [2]

Brooks-Gunn, J., Graber, J., and Paikoff, R. (1994). Studying links between hormones and negative affect: Models and measures. *Journal of Research on Adolescence, 4,* 469–486. [13]

Brooks-Gunn, J., Han, W., and Waldfogel, J. (2002). Maternal employment and child cognitive outcomes in the first three years of life: The NICHD study of early child care. *Child Development, 73,* 1052–1072. [2]

Brooks-Gunn, J., Klebanov, P., Smith, J. R., and Lee, K. (2001). Effects of combining public assistance and employment on mothers and their young children. *Women and Health, 32,* 179–210. [2]

Brooks-Gunn, J., and Reiter, E. O. (1990). The role of pubertal processes. In S. S. Feldman and G. R. Elliott (Eds.), *At the threshold: The developing adolescent* (pp. 16–53). Cambridge, MA: Harvard University Press. [13]

Broughton, J. (1978). Development of concepts of self, mind, reality, and knowledge. *New Directions for Child Development, 1,* 75–100. [12], [14]

Brown, A. L., Bransford, J. D., Ferrara, R. A., and Campione, J. C. (1983). Learning, remembering, and understanding. In P. H. Mussen (Series Ed.), J. H. Flavell and E. M. Markman (Vol. Eds.), *Handbook of child psychology: Vol. 3. Cognitive*

development (4th ed., pp. 183–218). New York: Wiley. [11]

Brown, B. (1990). Peer groups and peer cultures. In S. Feldman and G. Elliot (Eds.), *At the threshold: The developing adolescent* (pp. 171–196). Cambridge, MA: Harvard University Press. [14]

Brown, B. B., Lohr, M. J., and Trujillo, C. M. (1990). Multiple crowds and multiple lifestyles: Adolescents' perceptions of peer group characteristics. In R. E. Muuss (Ed.), *Adolescent behavior and society: A book of readings* (pp. 30–36). New York: Random House. [14]

Brown, B. B., Mory, M. S., and Kinney, D. (1994). Casting adolescent crowds in a relational perspective: Caricature, channel, and context. In R. Montemayor, G. R. Adams, and T. P. Gullotta (Eds.), *Personal relationships during adolescence* (pp. 123–167). Thousand Oaks, CA: Sage. [14]

Brown, G. (1999). Optimizing expression of the common human genome for child development. *Current Directions in Psychological Science, 8,* 37–41. [2]

Brown, J. V., Bakeman, R., Coles, C. D., Sexson, W. R., and Demi, A. S. (1998). Maternal drug use during pregnancy: Are preterm and fullterm infants affected differentially? *Developmental Psychology, 34,* 540–554. [3]

Brown, L. K., Lourie, K. J., and Pao, M. (2000). Children and adolescents living with HIV and AIDS: A review. *Journal of Child Psychology and Psychiatry and Allied Disciplines, 41,* 81–96. [3]

Brown, R. (1973). *A first language: The early stages.* Cambridge, MA: Harvard University Press. [7]

Brown, R. (1977). Introduction. In C. E. Snow and C. A. Ferguson (Eds.), *Talking to children: Language input and acquisition* (pp. 1–27). Cambridge, England: Cambridge University Press.

Brown, R., and Fraser, C. (1963). The acquisition of syntax. In C. N. Cofer and B. Musgrave (Eds.), *Verbal behavior and learning: Problems and processes.* (pp. 158–196) New York: McGraw-Hill. [7]

Brown, R., and Hanlon, C. (1970). Derivational complexity and order of acquisition. In J. R. Hayes (Ed.), *Cognition and the development of language.* (pp. 11–54) New York: Wiley. [7]

Brownell, C. A. (1990). Peer social skills in toddlers: Competencies and constraints illustrated by same-age and mixed-age interaction. *Child Development, 61,* 838–848. [8], [10]

Brownell, C. A., and Brown, E. (1992). Peers and play in infants and toddlers. In V. B. Van Hasselt and M. Hersen (Eds.), *Handbook of social development: A lifespan perspective* (pp. 183–200). New York: Plenum. [8]

Bruch, H. (1979). *The golden cage: The enigma of anorexia nervosa.* New York: Vintage Books. [15]

Bruer, J. (1999). *The myth of the first three years.* New York: Free Press. [4]

Bruner, J. S., (1983). *Child's talk.* New York: Norton. [7]

Bruner, J. S. (1975). The ontogenesis of speech acts. *Journal of Child Language, 2,* 1–19. [8], [11]

Bruner, J. S., Olver, R. R., and Greenfield, P. M. (1966). *Studies in cognitive growth.* New York: Wiley. [9]

Bryant, J. B. (2001). Language in social contexts: Communicative competence in the preschool years. In J. B. Gleason (Ed.), *The development of language* (5th ed., pp. 213–253). [7]

Bryant, P. E., and Trabasso, T. R. (1971). Transitive inferences and memory in young children. *Nature, 232,* 456–458. [9]

Buchacz, K., Cervia, J. S., Lindsey, J. C., Hughes, M. D., Seage, G. R., Dankner, W. M., Oleske, J. M., and Moye, J. (2001). Impact of protease inhibitor-containing combination antiretroviral therapies on height and weight growth in HIV-infected children. *Pediatrics, 108(4),* E72. [3]

Buchanan, C. M., Maccoby, E. E., and Dornbusch, S. M. (1991). Caught between parents: Adolescents' experience in divorced homes. *Child Development, 62,* 1008–1029. [2]

Buckner, J., and Fivush, R. (2000). Gender themes in family reminiscing. *Memory, 8,* 401–412. [10]

Buckner, J. C., Bassuk, E. L., Weinreb, L. F., and Brooks, M. G. (1999). Homelessness and its relation to the mental health and behavior of low-income school-age children. *Developmental Psychology, 35,* 246–257. [2]

Bühler, C. (1930). *The first year of life* (P. Greenberg and R. Ribin, Trans.). New York: John Day. [4]

Bugental, D., Blue, J., and Lewis, J. (1990). Caregiver beliefs and dysphoric affect directed to difficult children. *Developmental Psychology, 26,* 631–638. [10]

Bugental, D. B., and Goodnow, J. J. (1998). Socialization processes. In W. Damon (Series Ed.) and N. Eisenberg (Vol. Ed.), *Handbook of child psychology: Vol. 3. Social, emotional, and personality development* (5th ed., pp. 389–462). New York: Wiley. [8], [10], [12]

Buhrmester, D. (1998). Need fulfillment, interpersonal competence and the developmental contexts of early adolescent friendship. In W. Bukowski, and A. Newcomb (Eds.), *The company they keep: Friendship in childhood and adolescence* (pp. 158–185). New York: Cambridge University Press. [14]

Buhrmester, D., and Furman, W. (1987). The development of companionship and intimacy. *Child Development, 58,* 1101–1113. [14]

Buhrmester, D., and Furman, W. (1990). Perceptions of sibling relationships during middle childhood and adolescence. *Child Development, 61,* 1387–1398. [12]

Buhs, E., and Ladd, G. (2001). Peer rejection as an antecedent of young children's school adjustment: An examination of mediating processes. *Developmental Psychology, 37,* 550–560. [10]

Bukowski, W., Sippola, L., and Newcomb, A. (2000). Variations in patterns of attraction to same- and other-sex peers during early adolescence. *Developmental Psychology, 36,* 147–154. [14]

Bullock, B., and Dishion, T. (2002). Sibling collusion and problem behavior in early adolescence: Toward a process model for family mutuality. *Journal of Abnormal Child Psychology, 30,* 143–153. [14]

Bullock, M., and Gelman, R. (1979). Preschool children's assumptions about cause and effect: Temporal ordering. *Child Development, 50,* 89–96. [9]

Bumpus, M., Crouter, A., and McHale, S. (2001). Parental autonomy granting during adolescence: Exploring gender differences in context. *Developmental Psychology, 37,* 163–173. [14]

Bussell, D., Neiderhiser, J., Pike, A., Plomin, R., Hetherington, E. M., Carroll, E., and Reiss, D. (1999). Adolescents' relationships to siblings and mothers: A multivariate genetic analysis. *Developmental Psychology, 35,* 1248–1259. [14]

Bussey, K., and Bandura, A. (1992). Self-regulatory mechanisms governing gender development. *Child Development, 63,* 1236–1250. [12]

Butler, R. (1953). Discrimination learning by rhesus monkeys to visual exploration motivation. *Journal of Comparative and Physiological Psychology, 46,* 95–98. [2]

Butler, R., and Ruzany, N. (1993). Age and socialization effects on the development of social comparison motives and normative ability assessment in kibbutz and urban children. *Child Development, 64,* 532–543. [12]

Butler, S. C., Berthier, N. E., and Clifton, R. K. (2002). Two-year-olds' search strategies and visual tracking in a hidden displacement task. *Developmental Psychology, 38,* 581–590. [5]

Butterworth, G. (1977). Object disappearance and error in Piaget's stage IV task. *Journal of Experimental Child Psychology, 23,* 391–401. [5]

Cabrera, N. J., Tamis-LeMonda, C. S., Bradley, R. H., Hofferth, S., and Lamb, M. E. (2000). Fatherhood in the twentieth-first century. *Child Development, 71,* 127–136. [2]

Cadoret, R. J., Troughton, E., Merchant, L. M., and Whitters, A. (1990). Early life psychosocial events and adult psychosocial symptoms. In L. Robins and M. Rutter (Eds.), *Straight and devious pathways from childhood to adulthood* (pp. 300–313). Cambridge, England: Cambridge University Press. [1], [15]

Cairns, R. B., Cairns, B. D., and Neckerman, H. J. (1989). Early school dropout: Configurations and determinants. *Child Development, 60,* 1437–1452. [14]

Calkins, S., Fox, N., and Marshall, T. (1996). Behavioral and physiological antecedents of inhibition in infancy. *Child Development, 67,* 523–540. [6]

Campbell, F., and Ramey, C. (1994). Effects of early intervention on intellectual and academic achievement: A follow-up study of children from low income families. *Child Development, 65,* 684–698. [5]

Campbell, F. A., Pungello, E. P., Miller-Johnson, S., Burchinal, M., and Ramey, C. T. (2001). The development of cognitive and academic abilities: Growth curves from an early childhood educational experiment. *Developmental Psychology, 37,* 231–242.

Campbell, S. (2000). Attention deficit/hyperactivity disorder. In A. Sameroff, M. Lewis, and S. Miller (Eds.), *Handbook of developmental psychopathology* (2nd ed.), pp.383–402. New York: Plenum. [15]

Campos, J. J., Bertenthal, B. I., and Kermoian, R. (1992). Early experience and emotional development: The emergence of wariness of heights. *Psychological Science, 3,* 61–64. [4]

Campos, J. J., Hiatt, S., Ramsay, D., Henderson, C., and Svejda, M. (1978). The emergence of fear on the visual cliff. In M. Lewis and L. Rosenblum (Eds.), *The development of affect* (pp. 149–182). New York: Wiley. [4]

Camras, L., Oster, H., Campos, J., Campos, R., Ujiie, T., Miyake, K., Wang, L., and Meng, Z. (1998). Production of emotional facial expressions in European American, Japanese, and Chinese infants. *Developmental Psychology, 34,* 616–628. [6]

Camras, L. A., Oster, H., Campos, J. J., Miyake, K., and Bradshaw, D. (1992). Japanese and American infants' responses to arm restraint. *Developmental Psychology, 28,* 578–583. [6]

Canfield, R. L., and Haith, M. M. (1991). Active expectations in 2- and 3-month-old infants: Complex event sequences. *Developmental Psychology, 27,* 198–208. [5]

Canfield, R. L., and Smith, E. G. (1996). Number-based expectations and sequential enumeration by 5-month-old infants. *Developmental Psychology, 32,* 269–279. [5]

Cannon, T. D., Mednick, S. A., and Parnas, J. (1990). Two pathways to schizophrenia in children at risk. In L. Robins and M. Rutter (Eds.), *Straight and devious pathways from childhood to adulthood* (pp. 328–350). Cambridge, Eng.: Cambridge University Press. [15]

Capirci, O., Montanari, S., and Volterra, V. (1998). Gestures, signs, and words in early language development. In J. M. Iverson and S. Goldin-Meadow (Eds.), *The nature and function of gesture in children's communication. New Directions for Child Development,* No. 79 (pp. 45–60). San Francisco: Jossey-Bass. [7]

Capon, N., and Kuhn, D. (1979). Logical reasoning in the supermarket: Adult females' use of a proportional reasoning strategy in an everyday context. *Developmental Psychology, 15,* 450–452. [13]

Carey, S. (1978). The child as word learner. In M. Halle, J. Bresnan, and G. A. Miller (Eds.), *Linguistic theory and psychological reality.*(pp. 264–293) Cambridge, MA: MIT Press. [7]

Carey, S. (1986). Cognitive science and science education. *American Psychologist, 41,* 1123–1130. [13]

Carlson, C., Uppal, S., and Prosser, E. (2000). Ethnic differences in processes contributing to the self-esteem of early adolescent girls. *Journal of Early Adolescence, 20,* 44–67. [14]

Carlson, E. (1998). A prospective longitudinal study of attachment disorganization/ disorientation. *Child Development, 69,* 1107–1128. [6]

Carlson, E., Jacobvitz, D., and Sroufe, L. A. (1995). A developmental study of inattentiveness and hyperactivity. *Child Development, 66,* 37–54. [10], [15]

Caron, C., and Rutter, M. (1991). Comorbidity in child psychopathology: Concepts, issues, and research strategies. *Journal of Child Psychology and Psychiatry, 32,* 1063–1079. [15]

Carpenter, M., Akhar, N., and Tomasello, M. (1998). Fourteen- to 18-month-old infants differentially imitate intentional and accidental actions. *Infant Behavior and Development, 21,* 315–330. [8]

Carr, S., Dabbs, J., and Carr, T. (1975). Mother-infant attachment: The importance of the mother's visual field. *Child Development, 46,* 331–338. [8]

Carskadon, M. A. (2002). Factors influencing sleep patterns of adolescents. In M. A. Carskadon (Ed.), *Adolescent sleep patterns: Biological, social, and psychological influences* (pp. 4–26). New York: Cambridge University Press. [13]

Carskadon, M. A., and Acebo, C. (1993). A self-administered rating scale for pubertal development. *Journal of Adolescent Health Care, 14,* 190–195. [13]

Carskadon, M. A., Acebo, C., Richardson, G. S., Tate, B. A., and Seifer, R. (1997). Long nights protocol: Access to circadian parameters in adolescents. *Journal of Biological Rhythms, 12,* 278–289. [13]

Carskadon, M. A., Harvey, K., Duke, P., Anders, T. F., and Dement, W. C. (1980). Pubertal changes in daytime sleepiness. *Sleep, 2,* 453–460. [13]

Carver, L. J., Bauer, P. J., and Nelson, C. A. (2000). Associations between infant brain activity and recall memory. *Developmental Science, 3,* 234–246. [5]

Case, R. (1974). Structure and strictures: Some functional limitations on the course of cognitive growth. *Cognitive Psychology, 6,* 544–573. [13]

Case, R. (1985). *Intellectual development: Birth to adulthood.* New York: Academic Press. [5], [13]

Case, R. (1998). The development of conceptual structures. In W. Damon (Series Ed.), D. Kuhn, and R. S. Siegler (Vol. Eds.), *Handbook of child psychology: Vol. 2. Cognition, perception, and language* (5th ed., pp. 745–800). New York: Wiley. [9], [13]

Caspi, A., and Elder, G. H. (1988). Emergent family patterns: The intergenerational construction of problem behavior and relationships. In R. Hinde and J. Stevenson-Hinde (Eds.), *Relationships within families: Mutual influences* (pp. 218–240). Oxford, England: Oxford University Press. [2]

Caspi, A., Lynam, D., Moffitt, T., and Silva, P. (1993). Unraveling girls' delinquency: Biological, dispositional, and contextual contributions to adolescent misbehavior. *Developmental Psychology, 29,* 19–30. [13]

Caspi, A., and Moffitt, T. E. (1991). Individual differences are accentuated during periods of social change: The sample case of girls at puberty. *Journal of Personality and Social Psychology, 61,* 157–168. [14]

Castilla, E. E., Ashton-Prolla, P., Barreda-Mejia, E., Brunoni, D., Cavalcanti, D. P., Correa-Neto, J., Delgadillo, J. L., Dutra, M. G., Felix, T., Giraldo, A., Juarez, N., Lopez-Camelo, J. S., Nazer, J., Orioli, I. M., Paz, J. E., Pessoto, M. A., Pina-Neto, J. M., Quadrelli, R., Rittler, M., Rueda, S., Saltos, M., Sanchez, O., and Schuler, L. (1996). Thalidomide, a current teratogen in South America. *Teratology, 54,* 273–277. [3]

Cazden, C. (1983). Peekaboo as an instructional model: Discourse development at school and at home. In B. Brain (Ed.), *The sociogenesis of language and human conduct: A multidisciplinary book of readings* (pp. 33–58). New York: Plenum Press. [11]

Cazden, C. (1968). The acquisition of noun and verb inflections. *Child Development, 39,* 438–443. [7]

Ceci, S. J., and Bruck, M. (1998). Children's testimony: Applied and basic issues. In W. Damon (Series Ed.) and I. E. Sigel and K. A. Renninger (Vol. Eds.), *Handbook of child psychology: Vol. 4.*

Child psychology in practice (5th ed., pp. 713–774). New York: Wiley. [9]

Center for Early Educational and Development (CEED). (2001). Questions about kids: Is my child ready for kindergarten? http://education.umn.edu/CEED/publications/questionsaboutkids/kindergarten.htm [9]

Centers for Disease Control and Prevention (1999). *Status of perinatal HIV prevention: U. S. declines continue.* http://www.cdc.gov/hiv/pubs/facts/perinatl.htm [3]

Centers for Disease Control and Prevention (2002a). *CDC Surveillance Summaries. Youth Risk Behavior Surveillance—United States, 2001.* MMWR 2002;51 (No. SS-04). http://www.cdc.gov/mmwr/PDF/ss/ss5104.pdf [3]

Centers for Disease Control and Prevention (2002b). *Why folic acid is so important.* http://www.cdc.gov/ncbddd/folicacid/ [3]

Chao, R. K. (1994). Beyond parental control and authoritarian parenting style: Understanding Chinese parenting through the cultural notion of training. *Child Development, 65,* 1111–1119. [10]

Charlesworth, W. R. (1994). Charles Darwin and developmental psychology: Past and present. In R. D. Parke, P. A. Ornstein, J. J. Rieser, and C. Zahn-Waxler (Eds.), *A century of developmental psychology* (pp. 77–102). Washington, DC: American Psychological Association. [1], [2]

Chase-Lansdale, L., and Hetherington, M. (1990). The impact of divorce on life-span development. In D. Featherman and R. Lerner (Eds.), *Life span development and behavior* (Vol. 10, pp. 105–150). Orlando, FL: Academic Press. [14]

Chasnoff, I. J., Anson, A., Hatcher, R., Stenson, H., Iaukea, K., and Randolph, L. A. (1998). Prenatal exposure to cocaine and other drugs: Outcome at four to six years. *Annals of the New York Academy of Sciences, 846,* 314–328. [3]

Chavkin, W., Kristal, A., Seabron, C., and Guigli, P. E. (1987). The reproductive experience of women living in hotels for the homeless in New York City. *New York State Journal of Medicine, 87,* 10–13. [2]

Chen, J., and Goldsmith, L. T. (1991). Social and behavioral characteristics of Chinese only children: A review of research. *Journal of Research in Childhood Education, 5,* 127–139. [2]

Chen, Z., and Siegler, R. S. (2000). Across the great divide: Bridging the gap between understanding of toddlers' and older children's thinking. *Monographs of the Society for Research in Child Development, 65* (2, Serial No. 261). [1]

Chervenak, F. A., Isaacson, C., and Mahoney, M. J. (1986). Advances in the diagnosis of fetal defects. *New England Journal of Medicine, 315,* 305–307. [3]

Chi, M. T. H. (1978). Knowledge structure and memory development. In R. S. Siegler (Ed.), *Children's thinking: What develops?* Hillsdale, NJ: Erlbaum. [9], [11], [13]

Chi, M. T. H., and Ceci, S. J. (1987). Content knowledge: Its role, representation, and restructuring in memory development. In H. W. Reese and L. Lipsett (Eds.), *Advances in child development and behavior.* New York: Academic Press. [9]

Chipuer, H. M., Plomin, R., Pedersen, N. L., McClearn, G. E., and Nesselroade, J. R. (1993).

Genetic influences on family environment: The role of personality. *Developmental Psychology, 29,* 110–118. [2]

Chiriboga, C. A. (1998). Neurological correlates of fetal cocaine exposure. *Annals of the New York Academy of Sciences, 846,* 109–125. [3]

Chodorow, N. (1989). *Feminism and psychoanalytic theory.* New Haven: Yale University Press. [10]

Chomsky, N. (1957). *Syntactic structures.* The Hague: Mouton. [7]

Christopoulos, C., Cohn, D. A., Shaw, D. S., Joyce, S., Sullivan-Hanson, J., Kraft, S. P., and Emery, R. E. (1987). Children of abused women: I. Adjustment at time of shelter residence. *Journal of Marriage and the Family, 49,* 611–619. [12]

Chugani, H. T. (1994). Development of regional brain glucose metabolism in relation to behavior and plasticity. In G. Dawson and K. W. Fischer (Eds.), *Human behavior and the developing brain* (pp. 153–175). New York: Guilford. [13]

Chukovsky, K. (1941/1971). *From two to five.* (M. Morton, Trans. and Ed.). Berkeley, CA: University of California Press.

Church, M. W., Crossland, W. J., Homes, P. A., Overbeck, G. W., and Tilak, J. P. (1998). Effects of prenatal cocaine on hearing, vision, growth, and behavior. *Annals of the New York Academy of Sciences, 846,* 12–28. [3]

Cicchetti, D., and Beeghly, M. (1990). *Down Syndrome: A developmental perspective.* Cambridge, England: Cambridge University Press. [3], [6], [8]

Cicchetti, D., and Cohen, D. (1995). Development and psychopathology. In D. Cicchetti and D. Cohen (Eds.), *Developmental processes and psychopathology* (Vol. 1, pp. 3–20). New York: Cambridge University Press. [15]

Cicchetti, D., and Lynch, M. (1995). Failures in the expectable environment and their impact on individual development: The case of child maltreatment. In D. Cicchetti, and D. J. Cohen (Eds.), *Developmental psychopathology, Vol. 2: Risk, disorder, and adaptation* (pp. 32–71). New York: Wiley. [8], [12]

Cicchetti, D., and Olsen, K. (1990). The developmental psychopathology of child maltreatment. In M. Lewis and S. Miller (Eds.), *Handbook of developmental psychopathology* (pp. 261–279). New York: Plenum Press. [8]

Cicchetti, D., and Rogosch, F. (2002). A developmental psychopathology perspective on adolescence. *Journal of Consulting and Clinical Psychology, 70,* 6–20. [14]

Cicchetti, D., and Toth, S. L. (1998). Perspectives on research and practice in developmental psychopathology. In W. Damon (Series Ed.) and I. E. Sigel and K. A. Renninger (Vol. Eds.), *Handbook of child psychology: Vol. 4. Child psychology in practice* (5th ed., pp. 479–483). New York: Wiley. [12]

Cicchetti, D., Toth, S., and Lynch, M. (1995). Bowlby's dream comes full cycle: The application of attachment theory to risk and psychopathology. *Advances in Clinical Child Psychology, 17,* 1–75. [6]

Clancy, P. (1986). The acquisition of communicative style in Japanese. In B. Schieffelin and E. Ochs

(Eds.), *Language socialization across cultures* (pp. 213–250). Cambridge, England: Cambridge University Press. [7]

Clark, E. V. (1973). What's in a word? On the child's acquisition of semantics in his first language. In T. E. Moore (Ed.), *Cognitive development and the acquisition of language* (pp. 65–110). New York: Academic Press. [7]

Clark, E. V. (1983). Meanings and concepts. In P. H. Mussen (Ed.), *Handbook of child psychology* (Vol. 3, 4th ed.): J. H. Flavell and E. M. Markman (Eds.), *Cognitive development* (pp. 787–840). New York: Wiley. [7]

Clark, E. V. (1988). On the logic of contrast. *Journal of Child Language, 15,* 317–335. [7]

Clark, E. V. (1990). On the pragmatics of contrast. *Journal of Child Language, 17,* 417–432. [7]

Clark, K., and Ladd, G. (2000). Connectedness and autonomy support in parent-child relationships: Links to children's socioemotional orientation and peer relationships. *Developmental Psychology, 36,* 485–498. [10]

Clausen, J. (1968). Perspectives on childhood socialization. In J. Clausen (Ed.), *Socialization and society* (pp. 130–181). Boston: Little, Brown. [10]

Clements, P., and Seidman, E. (2002). The ecology of middle grades school and possible selves: Theory, research, and action. In T. M. Brinthaupt and R. P. Lipka (Eds.), *Understanding early adolescent self and identity: Applications and interventions* (pp. 133–164). Albany, NY: State University of New York Press. [2]

Clifton, R., Muir, D. W., Ashmead, D. H., and Clarkson, M. G. (1993). Is visually guided reaching in early infancy a myth? *Child Development, 64,* 1099–1110. [4]

Cohen, L. B., and Campos, J. (1974). Father, mother, and stranger as elicitors of attachment behaviors in infancy. *Developmental Psychology, 10,* 146–154. [2]

Cohen, L. B., and Younger, B. A. (1984). Infant perception of angular relations. *Infant Behavior and Development, 7,* 37–47. [5]

Coie, J., and Dodge, K. (1998). Aggression and antisocial behavior. In W. Damon (Series Ed.) and N. Eisenberg (Vol. Ed.), *Handbook of child psychology: Vol. 3. Social, emotional, and personality development* (5th ed., pp. 779–862). New York: Wiley. [10], [12]

Colby, A., Kohlberg, L., Gibbs, J., and Lieberman, M. (1983). A longitudinal study of moral judgment. *Monographs of the Society for Research in Child Development, 48*(1-2, Serial No. 200). [13]

Cole, P. M., Barrett, K. C., and Zahn-Waxler, C. (1992). Emotional displays in two-year-olds during mishaps. *Child Development, 63,* 314–324. [8], [10]

Coleman, J. (1974). *Relationships in adolescence.* London: Routledge & Kegan Paul. [14]

Coleman, L., and Coleman, J. (2002). The measurement of puberty: A review. *Journal of Adolescence, 25,* 535–550. [13]

Coley, R. L., and Chase-Lansdale, P. L. (1998). Adolescent pregnancy and parenthood: Recent evidence and future directions. *American Psychologist, 53,* 152–166. [2]

Collins, W. A. (1990). Parent-child relationships in the transition to adolescence: Continuity and change in interaction, affect, and cognition. In R. Montemayor, G. Adams, and T. Gullotta (Eds.), *Advances in adolescent development: Vol. 2. From childhood to adolescence* (pp. 103–110). Newbury Park, CA: Sage. [1]

Collins, W. A. (1997). Relationships and development during adolescence: Interpersonal adaptation to individual change. *Personal Relationships, 4,* 1–14. [14]

Collins, W. A., Laursen, B., Mortensen, N., Luebker, C., and Ferreira, M. (1997). Conflict processes and transitions in parent and peer relationships: Implications for autonomy and regulation. *Journal of Adolescent Research, 12,* 178–198. [14]

Collins, W. A., Maccoby, E., Steinberg, L., Hetherington, E. M., and Bornstein, M. (2000). The case for nature and nurture. *American Psychologist, 55,* 218–232. [14]

Collins, W. A., and Madsen, S. D. (2002, April). Relational roots of romance: Beyond "chumships." In S. Shulman and I. Seiffge-Krenke (Co-Chairs), *Antecedents of the quality and stability of adolescent romantic relationships.* Symposium presented at the biennial conference of the Society for Research on Adolescence, New Orleans. [12]

Collins, W. A., and Repinski, D. J. (1994). Relationships during adolescence: Continuity and change in interpersonal perspective. In R. Montemayor, G. R. Adams, and T. P. Gullotta (Eds.), *Personal relationships during adolescence* (pp. 7–36). Thousand Oaks, CA: Sage. [14]

Collins, W. A., and Russell, G. (1991). Mother-child and father-child relationships in middle childhood and adolescence: A developmental analysis. *Developmental Psychology, 11,* 99–136. [14]

Colombo, J., and Frick, J. (1999). Recent advances and issues in the study of preverbal intelligence. In Anderson, M. (Ed.), *The development of intelligence* (pp. 43–71). Hove, England: Psychology Press. [5]

Conel, J. L. (1939–1963). *The postnatal development of the human cerebral cortex (7 vols.).* Cambridge, MA: Harvard University Press. [4]

Conger, R. D., Elder, G. H., Jr., Lorenz, F. O., Simons, R. L., and Whitbeck, L. B. (1994). *Families in troubled times: Adapting to change in rural America.* New York: Aldine de Gruyter. [2]

Connolly, J. A., and Doyle, A. (1984). Relation of social fantasy play to social competence in preschoolers. *Developmental Psychology, 20*(5), 797–806. [10]

Connolly, J., and Goldberg, A. (1999). Romantic relationships in adolescence: The role of friends and peers in their emergence and development. In W. Furman, B. Brown, and C. Feiring (Eds.), *The development of romantic relationships in adolescence* (pp. 266–290). New York: Cambridge University Press. [14]

Connolly, S. D., Paikoff, R.L., and Buchanan, C. M. (1996). Puberty: The interplay of biological and psychosocial processes in adolescence. In G. R. Adams, R. Montemayor, and T. Pl Gullotta (Eds.), *Psychosocial Development During Adolescence: Progress in Developmental Contextualism* (pp. 259–299). Thousand Oaks, CA: Sage. [13]

Connor, E. M., Sperling, R. S., Gelber, R., Kiselev, P., Scott, G., O'Sullivan, M. J., VanDyke, R., Bey, M., Shearer, W., Jacobson, R. L., Jimenez, E., O'Neill, E., Bazin, B., Delfraissy, J.-F., Culnane, M., Coombs, R., Elkins, M., Moye, J., Stratton, P., and Balsley, J. (1994). Reduction of maternal-infant transmission of human immunodeficiency virus Type 1 with Zidovudine treatment. *New England Journal of Medicine, 331,* 1173–1180. [3]

Cooper, C. R. (1999). Multiple selves, multiple worlds: Cultural perspectives on individuality and connectedness in adolescent development. In A. S. Masten (Ed.), *Minnesota Symposia on Child Psychology: Vol. 29. Cultural processes in child development* (pp. 25–59). Mahwah, NJ: Erlbaum. [14]

Cooper, C. R., and Cooper, R. G. (1984). Peer learning discourse: What develops? In S. Kuczaj (Ed.), *Discourse development: Progress in cognitive development* (pp. 77–97). New York: Springer-Verlag. [11]

Cooper, C. R., and Cooper, R. G. (1992). Links between adolescents' relationships with their parents and peers: Models, evidence, and mechanisms. In R. D. Parke and G. W. Ladd (Eds.), *Family–peer relationships: Modes of linkages* (pp. 135–158). Hillsdale, NJ: Erlbaum. [14]

Cooper, C. R., Marquis, A., and Edwards, D. (1986). Four perspectives on peer learning among elementary school children. In E. C. Mueller and C. R. Cooper (Eds.), *Process and outcome in peer relationships* (pp. 269–300). New York: Academic Press. [11]

Cooper, R. G. (1976, April). *The role of estimators and operators in number conservation.* Paper presented at the Southwestern Psychological Association, Albuquerque. [9]

Cooper, R. G. (1984). Early number development: Discovering number space with addition and subtraction. In C. Sophian (Ed.), *Origins of cognitive skills.* Hillsdale, NJ: Erlbaum. [9]

Cooper, R. G., and Robbins, R. R. (1981). The effect of cognitive skills on learning astronomy. *Proceedings of the 1980 Frontiers in Education Conference.* Houston, TX: Southwest Astronomy and Astrophysics Society. [13]

Cooper, R. P., and Aslin, R. N. (1990). Preference for infant-directed speech in the first month after birth. *Child Development, 61,* 1584–1595. [7]

Coplan, R., Gavinshi-Molina, M., Lagace-Seguin, D., and Wichmann, C. (2001). When girls versus boys play alone: Nonsocial play and adjustment in kindergarten. *Developmental Psychology, 37,* 464–474. [10]

Cornelius, M. D., Ryan, C. M., Day, N. L., Goldschmidt, L., and Willford, J. A. (2001). Prenatal tobacco effects on neuropsychological outcomes among preadolescents. *Journal of Developmental and Behavioral Pediatrics, 22,* 217–225. [3]

Corman, H. H., and Escalona, S. K. (1969). Stages of sensorimotor development: A replication study. *Merrill-Palmer Quarterly, 15,* 351–361. [5]

Coscia, J. M., Christensen, B. K., Henry, R. R., Wallston, K., Radcliffe, J., and Rutstein, R. (2001). Effects of home environment, socioeconomic status, and health status on cognitive functioning in children with HIV-1 infection. *Journal of Pediatric Psychology, 26,* 321–329. [3]

Costanzo, P. (1970). Conformity development as a function of self-blame. *Journal of Personality and Social Psychology, 14,* 366–374. [14]

Coté, J. E. (1992). *Adolescent storm and stress: An evaluation of the Mead-Freeman controversy.* Hillsdale, NJ: Erlbaum. [14]

Cowan, C. P., and Cowan, P. A. (2000). *When partners become parents: The big life change for couples.* Mahwah, NJ: Erlbaum. [2]

Cowan, P. A., and Cowan, C. P. (2002). What an intervention design reveals about how parents affect their children's academic achievement and behavior problems. In J. Borkowski, S. Landesman Ramey, and M. Bristol-Power (Eds.), *Parenting and the child's world* (pp. 75–98). Mahwah, NJ: Erlbaum. [12]

Cowan, W. M. (1979). The development of the brain. *Scientific American, 241,* 113–133. [3]

Cox, M. J., Owen, M. T., Lewis, J. M., and Henderson, V. K. (1989). Marriage, adult adjustment, and early parenting. *Child Development, 60,* 1015–1024. [6]

Cox, M. J., Owen, M. T., Henderson, V. K., and Margand, N. A. (1992). Prediction of infant-father and infant-mother attachment. *Developmental Psychology, 28,* 474–483. [6]

Cox, M. J., and Paley, B. (1997). Families as systems. *Annual Review of Psychology, 48,* 1997, 243–267. [2]

Crick, N., Casas, J., and Ku, H. (1999). Relational and physical forms of peer victimization in preschool. *Developmental Psychology, 35,* 376–385. [10]

Crick, N., Nelson, D., Morales, J., Cullertonsen, C., Casas, J., and Hickman, S. (2001). Relational victimization in childhood and adolescence: I hurt you through the grapevine. In *Peer harassment in school: The plight of the vulnerable and victimized* (pp. 196–214). New York: Guilford. [12]

Crockenberg, S. (1981). Infant irritability, mother responsiveness and social support influences on the security of infant-mother attachment. *Child Development, 52,* 857–865. [6]

Crockenberg, S., and Litman, C. (1990). Autonomy as competence in 2-year-olds: Maternal correlates of child defiance, compliance, and self-assertion. *Developmental Psychology, 26,* 961–970. [8]

Crook, C. (1987). Taste and olfaction. In P. Salapatek and L. Cohen (Eds.), *Handbook of infant perception: Vol. 1. From sensation to perception* (pp. 237–264). Orlando, FL: Academic Press. [4]

Crouter, A. C., and McHale, S. M. (1993). Temporal rhythms in family life: Seasonal variation in the relation between parental work and family processes. *Developmental Psychology, 29,* 198–207. [2]

Crouter, A. C., Perry-Jenkins, M., Huston, T. L., and McHale, S. M. (1987). Processes underlying father involvement in dual-earner and single-earner families. *Developmental Psychology, 23,* 431–440. [2]

Crowe, K., and von Baeyer, C. (1989). Predictors of positive childbirth experience. *Birth, 16,* 59–63. [3]

Cruttenden, A. (1994). Phonetic and prosodic aspects of Baby Talk. In C. Gallaway and B. J. Richards (Eds.), *Input and interaction in language acquisition* (pp. 135–152). Cambridge, England: Cambridge University Press. [7]

Cummings, E. M., and Davies, P. T. (2002). Effects of marital conflict on children: Recent advances and emerging themes in process-oriented research. *Journal of Child Psychology and Psychiatry and Allied Disciplines, 43,* 31–63. [2]

Cunningham, F. G., Gant, N. F., Leveno, K. J., Clark, S. L., Hauth, J. C., and Wenstrom, K. D. (2001). *Williams obstetrics* (21st ed.). New York: McGraw-Hill. [3]

Curtiss, S. (1977). *Genie: Psycholinguistic study of a modern day wild child.* New York: Academic Press. [2]

Cuvo, A. J. (1974). Incentive level influence on overt rehearsal and free recall as a function of age. *Journal of Experimental Child Psychology, 18,* 167–181. [11]

Csikszentmihalyi, M., and Larson, R. (1984). *Being adolescent.* New York: Basic Books. [14]

Dalaker, J. (2001). *Poverty in the United States:2000.* Current Population Reports, P60–214. Washington, DC: U.S. Census Bureau. [2]

Dalton, S. S., and Tharp, R. G. (2002). Standards for pedagogy: Research, theory and practice. In G. Wells and G. Claxton (Eds.), *Learning for life in the 21st century: Sociocultural perspectives on the future of education* (pp. 181–194). Malden, MA: Blackwell. [2]

Damon, W. (1977). *The social world of the child.* San Francisco: Jossey-Bass. [12]

Damon, W. (1983). *Social and personality development.* New York: Norton. [14]

Damon, W. (1988). *The moral child.* New York: Cambridge University Press. [12]

Damon, W., and Hart, D. (1988). *Self-understanding in childhood and adolescence.* Cambridge, Eng.: Cambridge University Press. [12], [14]

Dasen, P. R., and Heron, A. (1981). Cross-cultural tests of Piaget's theory. In H. Triandis and A. Heron (Eds.), *Handbook of cross-cultural psychology: Vol. 4. Developmental psychology.* (pp. 295–342). Boston: Allyn & Bacon. [1], [5], [11], [13]

Dasen, P. R., Ngini, L., and Lavallée, M. (1979). Cross-cultural training studies of concrete operations. In L. Eckensberger, Y. Poortinga, and W. Lonner (Eds.), *Cross-cultural contributions to psychology* (pp. 94–104). Amsterdam: Swets & Zeitlinger. [11]

Datta-Bhutada, S., Johnson, H. L., and Rosen, T. S. (1998). Intrauterine cocaine and crack exposure: Neonatal outcome. *Journal of Perinatology, 18,* 183–188. [3]

Davies, P., and Lindsay, L. (2001). Does gender moderate the effects of marital conflict on children? In J. Grych and F. Fincham (Eds.), *Interparental conflict and child development: Theory, research and applications* (pp. 64–97). New York: Cambridge University Press. [12]

Dawson, G., and Ashman, S. B. (2000). On the origins of a vulnerability to depression: The influence of the early social environment on the development of psychobiological systems related to risk for affective disorder. In C. Nelson (Ed.), *Minnesota Symposia on Child Psychology: Vol. 31. The effects of early adversity on neurobehavioral development* (pp. 245–279). Mahwah, NJ: Erlbaum. [12]

Dayton, G. O., Jr., and Jones, M. H. (1964). Analysis of characteristics of fixation reflexes in infants by use of direct current electrooculography. *Neurology, 14,* 1152–1156. [4]

Deater-Deckard, K. (2001). Annotation: Recent research examining the role of peer relationships in the development of psychopathology. *Journal of Child Psychology and Psychiatry, 42,* 565–579. [12]

Deater-Deckard, K., Dodge, K. A., Bates, J. E., and Pettit, G. S. (1996). Physical discipline among African American and European American mothers: Links to children's externalizing behaviors. *Developmental Psychology, 32,* 1065–1072. [10]

DeCasper, A. J., and Fifer, W. (1980). Of human bonding: Newborns prefer their mothers' voices. *Science, 208,* 1174–1176. [2], [4]

DeCasper, A. J., and Spence, M. J. (1986). Prenatal maternal speech influences newborn's perception of speech sounds. *Infant Behavior and Development, 9,* 133–150. [3]

Degirmencioglu, S., Urberg, K., Tolson, J., and Richard, P. (1998). Adolescent friendship networks: Continuity and change over the school year. *Merrill-Palmer Quarterly, 44,* 313–337. [14]

de Grandpre, R. (1999). *Ritalin nation.* New York: Norton. [15]

de Haan, M. (2001). The neuropsychology of face processing during infancy and childhood. In C. A. Nelson and M. Luciana (Eds.), *Handbook of developmental cognitive neuroscience* (pp. 381–398). Cambridge, MA: MIT Press. [4]

de Haan, M, and Nelson, C. (1999). Brain activity differentiates face and object processing in 6-month-old infants. *Developmental Psychology, 35,* 1113–1121. [6]

DeHart, G. B. (1990). *Young children's linguistic interaction with mothers and siblings.* Unpublished doctoral dissertation, University of Minnesota.

DeHart, G. B. (1999). Conflict and averted conflict in preschoolers' interactions with siblings and friends. In W. A. Collins and B. Laursen (Eds.), *Minnesota Symposia on Child Psychology: Vol. 30. Relationships as developmental contexts: Festschrift in honor of Willard W. Hartup* (pp. 281–303). Mahwah, NJ: Erlbaum. [2], [10], [12]

DeHart, G., Kucharczak, K., Lim, K., Ghazanfari, S., Duffy, L., and Johnson, S. (1998, May). Social engagement and sibling and friend conflict in early and middle childhood. Poster presented at the annual conference of the American Psychological Society, Washington, DC. [12]

de Houwer, A. (1995). Bilingual language acquisition. In P. Fletcher and B. MacWhinney (Eds.), *The handbook of child language* (pp. 219–250). Oxford, England: Basil Blackwell. [7]

Delaney-Black, V., Covington, C., Templin, T., Ager, J., Martier, S., and Sokol, R. (1998). Prenatal cocaine exposure and child behavior. *Pediatrics, 102,* 945–950. [3]

DeLoache, J. S. (2002). The symbol-mindedness of young children. In W.W. Hartup and R. A. Weinberg (Eds.), *Minnesota Symposia on Child Psychology: Vol. 32. Child psychology in retrospect and prospect: In celebration of the 75th anniversary of the Institute of Child Development* (pp. 73–101). Mahwah, NJ: Erlbaum. [7]

DeLoache, J. S., and Burns, N. M. (1994). Early understanding of the representational function of pictures. *Cognition, 52,* 83–110. [7]

DeLoache, J. S., Miller, K. F., and Pierroutsakos, S. L. (1998). Reasoning and problem solving. In W. Damon (Series Ed.), D. Kuhn, and R. S. Siegler (Vol. Eds.), *Handbook of child psychology: Vol. 2. Cognition, perception, and language* (5th ed., pp. 801–850). New York: Wiley. [7]

Dempster, F. N. (1981). Memory span: Sources of individual and developmental differences. *Psychological Bulletin, 89,* 63–100. [11], [13]

DeMulder, E., Denham, S., Schmidt, M., and Mitchel, J. (2000). Q-sort assessment of attachment security during the preschool years: Links from home to school. *Developmental Psychology, 36,* 274–282. [10]

Denham, S., and Holt, R. (1993). Preschoolers' likeability as cause or consequence of their social behavior. *Developmental Psychology, 29,* 271–277. [10]

Dennis, W. (1973). *Children of the creche.* New York: Appleton-Century-Crofts. [11]

Dennis, W., and Dennis, M. C. (1940). The effect of cradling practices upon the onset of walking in Hopi children. *Journal of Genetic Psychology, 56,* 77–86. [4]

de Villiers, J. G., and de Villiers, P. A. (1978). *Language acquisition.* Cambridge, MA: Harvard University Press. [7]

de Villiers, P. A., and de Villiers, J. G. (1979). *Early language.* Cambridge, MA: Harvard University Press. [7]

DeVries, R. (1969). Constancy of generic identity in the years three to six. *Monographs of the Society for Research in Child Development, 34* (Serial No. 127). [9]

de Weerth, C., van Geert, P., and Hoijtink, H. (1999). Intraindividual variability in infant behavior. *Developmental Psychology, 35,* 1102–1112. [6]

de Wolff, M., and van Ijzendoorn, M. (1997). Sensitivity and attachment: A meta-analysis on parental antecedents of infant attachment. *Child Development, 68,* 571–591. [6]

Diamond, A. (1988). Abilities and neural mechanisms underlying A performance. *Child Development, 59,* 523–527. [5]

Diamond, A., Cruttenden, L., and Neiderman, D. (1994). A, not B with multiple wells: 1. Why are multiple well sometimes easier than two wells? 2. Memory or memory + inhibition? *Developmental Psychology, 30,* 192–205. [5]

Diamond, L., Savin-Williams, R., and Dubé, E. (1999). Sex, dating, passionate friendships, and romance: Intimate peer relations among lesbian, gay, and bisexual adolescents. In W. Furman and B. Brown (Eds.), *The development of romantic relationships in adolescence* (pp.175–210). New York: Cambridge University Press. [14]

Diamond, M. C. (1991). Environmental influences on the young brain. In Gibson, K. R., and Petersen, A. C. (Eds.), *Brain maturation and cognitive development: Comparative and cross-cultural perspectives* (pp. 107–124). New York: Aldine De Gruyter. [4], [5]

Dick, D. M., Rose, R. J., Viken, R. J., and Kaprio, J. (2000). Pubertal timing and substance use: Associations between and within families across

late adolescence. *Developmental Psychology, 36,* 180–189. [13]

diSessa, A. A. (1988). Knowledge in pieces. In G. Forman and P. Pufall (Eds.). *Constructivism in the computer age* (pp. 49–71). Hillsdale, NJ: Erlbaum. [13]

Dishion, T., and Bullock, M. (2002). Parenting and adolescent problem behavior: An ecological analysis of the nurturance hypothesis. In J. Borkowski, S. Landesman Ramey, and M. Bristol-Power (Eds.), *Parenting and the child's world* (pp. 231–250). Mahwah, NJ: Erlbaum. [12]

Dishion, T., French, D., and Patterson, G. (1995). The development and ecology of antisocial behavior. In D. Cicchetti and D. Cohen (Eds.), *Developmental psychopathology* (Vol. 2, pp. 421–471). New York: Wiley. [15]

Dodge, K. (2000). Conduct disorders. In A. Sameroff, M. Lewis, and S. Miller (Eds.), *Handbook of developmental psychopathology* (2nd ed.), pp. 447–466. New York: Plenum. [15]

Dodge, K. A., Pettit, G. S., and Bates, J. E. (1997). How the experience of early physical abuse leads children to become chronically aggressive. In D. Cicchetti and S. L. Toth (Eds.), *Rochester symposium on developmental psychology: Vol. 8. Developmental perspectives on trauma: Theory, research, and intervention* (pp. 263–288). Rochester, NY: University of Rochester Press. [8]

Dodge, K. A., Pettit, G. S., McClaskey, C. L., and Brown, M. M. (1986). Social competence in children. *Monographs of the Society for Research in Child Development, 51* (2, Serial No. 213). [12]

Doi, T. (1992). On the concept of *amae. Infant Mental Health Journal, 13,* 7–11. [1], [2]

Donaldson, M. (1978). *Children's minds.* New York: Norton. [11]

Dornbusch, S. M., Gross, R. T., Duncan, P. D., and Ritter, P. L. (1987). Stanford studies of adolescence using the National Health Examination Study. In R. M. Lerner and T. T. Foch (Eds.), *Biological-psychosocial interactions in early adolescence* (pp. 189–205). Hillsdale, NJ: Erlbaum. [13]

Douvan, E., and Adelson, J. (1966). *The adolescent experience.* New York: Wiley. [14]

Dozier, M., Stovall, C., Albus, K., and Bates, B. (2001). Attachment for infants in foster care: The role of caregiver state of mind. *Child Development, 72,* 1467–1477. [6]

Dreyer, P. (1982). Sexuality during adolescence. In B. Wolman (Ed.), *Handbook of developmental psychology* (pp. 559–601). Englewood Cliffs, NJ: Prentice-Hall. [14]

Dromi, E. (1999). Early lexical development. In M. Barrett (Ed.), *The development of language* (pp. 99–131). Hove, East Sussex, U.K.: Psychology Press. [7]

Dubé, E., and Savin-Williams, R. (1999). Sexual identity development among ethnic sexual-minority male youth. *Developmental Psychology, 35,* 1389–1398. [14]

Dubrovina, I., and Ruzska, A. (1990). *The mental development of residents in a children's home.* Moscow: Pedagogics. [2]

Duggal, S., Sroufe, L. A., Egeland, B., and Carlson, E. (2001). Depression in childhood and adolescence. *Development and Psychopathology, 13,* 143–164

Dunham, P., and Dunham, F. (1990). Effects of mother-infant social interactions on infants' subsequent contingency task performance. *Child Development, 61,* 785–793. [6]

Dunn, J. (1988). *The beginning of social understanding.* Cambridge, MA: Harvard University Press. [2], [8]

Dunn, J. (1993). *Young children's relationships: Beyond attachment.* Newbury Park, CA: Sage. [2]

Dunn, J., and Dale, N. (1984). I a Daddy: Two-year-olds' collaboration in joint pretend with sibling and with mother. In I. Bretherton (Ed.), *Symbolic play and the development of social understanding* (pp. 131–158). New York: Academic Press. [7]

Dunn, J., and Kendrick, C. (1982a). Interaction between young siblings: Association with the interaction between mother and firstborn child. *Developmental Psychology, 17,* 336–343. [2]

Dunn, J., and Kendrick, C. (1982b). The speech of two- and three-year-olds to infant siblings: "Baby talk" and the context of communication. *Journal of Child Language, 9,* 579–595. [7], [9]

Dunn, J., and Plomin, R. (1990). *Separate lives: Why siblings are so different.* New York: Basic Books. [1]

Dunn, J., and Shatz, M. (1989). Becoming a conversationalist despite (or because of) having an older sibling. *Child Development, 60,* 399–410. [10]

Dunn, J., Slomkowski, C. L., and Beardsall, L. (1994). Sibling relationships from the preschool period through middle childhood and early adolescence. *Developmental Psychology, 30,* 315–324. [12]

Dunn, J., Slomkowski, C., Beardsall, L., and Rende, R. (1994). Adjustment in middle childhood and early adolescence: Links with earlier and contemporary sibling relationships. *Journal of Child Psychology and Psychiatry and Allied Disciplines, 35,* 491–504. [14]

Dunphy, D. (1963). The social structure of urban adolescent peer groups. *Sociometry, 26,* 230–246. [14]

Dunson, D. B., Colombo, B., and Baird, D. D. (2002). Changes with age in the level and duration of fertility in the menstrual cycle. *Human Reproduction, 17,* 1399–1403. [3]

Durston, S., Hulshoff Pol, H. E., Casey, B. J., Giedd, J. N., Buitelaar, J. K., and van Engeland, H. (2001). Anatomical MRI of the developing human brain: What have we learned? *Journal of the American Academy of Child and Adolescent Psychiatry, 40,* 1012–1020. [13]

Dweck, C. S., Davidson, W., Nelson, S., and Erra, B. (1978). Sex differences in learned helplessness: II. The contingencies of evaluation feedback in the classroom: III. An experimental analysis. *Developmental Psychology, 14,* 268–276. [12]

Earls, F. (1994). Oppositional-defiant and conduct disorders. In M. Rutter, E. Taylor, and L. Hersov (Eds.), *Child and adolescent psychiatry* (pp. 308–329). London: Blackwell. [15]

Earls, F., Reich, W., Jung, K., and Cloninger, R. (1988). Psychopathology in children of alcoholic and antisocial parents. *Alcoholism: Clinical and Experimental Research, 12,* 481– 487. [15]

East, P. L., and Rook, K. S. (1992). Compensatory patterns of support among children's peer relationships: A test using school friends, nonschool friends, and siblings. *Developmental Psychology, 28,* 163–172. [12]

Easterbrooks, M. A. (1989). Quality of attachment to mother and to father: Effects of perinatal risk status. *Child Development, 60,* 825–830. [6]

Easterbrooks, M. A., and Emde, R. N. (1988). Marital and parent-child relationships: The role of affect in the family system. In R. Hinde and J. Stevenson-Hinde (Eds.), *Relationships within families: Mutual influences* (pp. 83–103). Oxford, England: Oxford University Press. [8]

Eccles, J., Lord, S., and Buchanan, C. (1996). School transitions in early adolescence: What are we doing to our young people? In J. Graber, J. Brooks-Gunn, and A. Petersen (Eds.), *Transitions through adolescence* (pp. 251–284). Mahwah, NJ: Erlbaum. [14]

Eccles, J., Wigfield, A., and Schiefele, U. (1998). Motivation to succeed. In W. Damon (Series Ed.) and N. Eisenberg (Vol. Ed.), *Handbook of child psychology: Vol. 3. Social, emotional, and personality development* (5th ed., pp. 1017–1095). New York: Wiley. [12]

Eder, R., and Mangelsdorf, S. (1997). The emotional basis of early personality development: Implications for the emergent self-concept. In R. Hogan, J. A. Johnson, and S. R. Briggs (Eds.), *Handbook of personality psychology* (pp. 209–240). Orlando, FL: Academic Press. [10]

Edwards, C. P. (1982). Moral development in comparative cultural perspective. In D. A. Wagner and H. W. Stevenson (Eds.), *Cultural perspectives on child development* (pp. 248–279). San Francisco: Freeman. [13]

Egeland, B. (1997). Mediators of the effects of child maltreatment on developmental adaptations in adolescence. In D. Cicchetti and S. Toth (Eds.), *Rochester Symposium on Developmental Psychopathology: Vol. 8. Developmental perspectives on trauma: Theory, research, and intervention. on the developmental process* (pp. 403–434). Rochester, NY: University of Rochester Press. [6], [8]

Egeland, B., Jacobvitz, D., and Sroufe, L. A. (1988). Breaking the cycle of abuse: Relationship predictions. *Child Development, 59,* 1080–1088. [8]

Egeland, B., Kalkoske, M., Gottesman, N., and Erickson, M. (1990). Preschool behavior problems: Stability and factors accounting for change. *Journal of Child Psychology and Psychiatry, 31,* 891–909. [12]

Egeland, B., and Sroufe, L. A. (1981). Developmental sequelae of maltreatment in infancy. In D. Cicchetti and R. Rizley (Eds.), *New directions in child development: Developmental approaches to child maltreatment* (pp. 77–92). San Francisco: Jossey-Bass. [2], [6]

Egeland, B., Sroufe, L. A., and Erickson, M. (1983). Developmental consequences of different patterns of maltreatment. *Child Abuse and Neglect, 7,* 459–469. [8]

Eimas, P. D. (1985). The perception of speech in early infancy. *Scientific American, 204,* 66–72. [4]

Eimas, P. D., and Quinn, P. C. (1994). Studies on the formation of perceptually based basic-level categories in young infants. *Child Development, 65,* 903–917. [5]

Eimas, P. D., Siqueland, E. R., and Jusczyk, P. W. (1971). Speech perception in infants. *Science, 171,* 303–306. [4]

Eisenberg, N., and Fabes, R. (1998). Prosocial development. In W. Damon (Series Ed.) and N. Eisenberg (Vol. Ed.), *Handbook of child psychology: Vol. 3. Social, emotional, and personality development* (5th ed., pp. 701–778). New York: Wiley. [10], [12]

Eisenberg, N., Fabes, R. A., Bernzweig, J., Karbon, M., Poulin, R., and Hanish, L. (1993). The relations of emotionality and regulation to preschoolers' social skills and sociometric status. *Child Development, 64,* 1418–1438. [10]

Eisenberg, N., Fabes, R. A., Nyman, M., Bernzweig, J., and Pinuelas, A. (1994). The relations of emotionality and regulation to children's anger-related reactions. *Child Development, 65,* 109–128. [10]

Elbedour, S., Bastien, D., and Center, B. (1997). Identity formation in the shadow of conflict: Projective drawings by Palestinian and Israeli Arab children from the West Bank and Gaza. *Journal of Peace Research, 34,* 217–232. [10]

Elder, G. H., Jr. (1998). The life course and human development. In W. Damon (Series Ed.) and R. M. Lerner (Vol. Ed.), *Handbook of child psychology: Vol. 1. Theoretical models of human development* (5th ed., pp. 939–991). New York: Wiley. [2]

Elder, G. H., Jr. (1999). *Children of the Great Depression: Social change in life experience* (25th anniversary ed.). Boulder, CO: Westview Press. [1]

Elder, G. H., Jr., Caspi, A., and Burton, L. M. (1988). Adolescent transitions in developmental perspective: Historical and sociological insights. In M. Gunnar and W. A. Collins (Eds.), *Minnesota Symposia on Child Psychiatry: Vol. 21. Development during the transition to adolescence* (pp. 151–179). Hillsdale, NJ: Erlbaum. [2]

Elder, G. H., Jr., Caspi, A., and Downey, G. (1986). Problem behavior and family relationships: Life-course and intergenerational themes. In A. B. Sorensen, F. E. Weinert, and L. R. Sherrod (Eds.), *Human development and the life course: Multidisciplinary perspectives* (pp. 293–340). Hillsdale, NJ: Erlbaum. [2]

Elicker, J., Englund, M., and Sroufe, L. A. (1992). Predicting peer competence and peer relationships in childhood from early parent-child relationships. In R. Parke and G. Ladd (Eds.), *Family-peer relationships: Modes of linkage* (pp. 77–106). Hillsdale, NJ: Erlbaum. [12]

Elkind, D. (1967). Egocentrism in adolescence. *Child Development, 38,* 1025–1034. [13]

Elkind, D. (1978). Understanding the young adolescent. *Adolescence, 13,* 127–134. [9], [13]

Elkind, D., and Bowen, R. (1979). Imaginary audience behavior in children and adolescents. *Developmental Psychology, 15,* 38–44. [14]

Ellis, N. C., and Hennelly, R. A. (1980). A bilingual word-length effect: Implications for intelligence testing and the relative ease of mental calculation in Welsh and English. *British Journal of Psychology, 71,* 43–51. [11]

Ellis, S., and Rogoff, B. (1986). Problem solving in children's management of instruction. In E. C. Mueller and C. R. Cooper (Eds.), *Process and outcome in peer relationships.* New York: Academic Press. [9], [11]

Emde, R. N. (1985). The affective self: Continuities and transformations from infancy. In J. Call, E. Galenson, and R. Tyson (Eds.), *Frontiers of infant psychiatry (Vol. II).* [pp.] New York: Basic Books. [6]

Emde, R. N. (1992). Social referencing research: Uncertainty, self, and the search for meaning. In S. Feinman (Ed.), *Social referencing and the social construction of reality in infancy* (pp. 79–92). New York: Plenum Press. [8]

Emde, R. N. (1994). Individual meaning and increasing complexity: Contributions of Sigmund Freud and René Spitz to developmental psychology. In R. D. Parke, P. A. Ornstein, J. J. Rieser, and C. Zahn-Waxler (Eds.), *A century of developmental psychology* (pp. 203–231). Washington, DC: American Psychological Association. [1]

Emde, R. N., Biringen, Z., Clyman, R. B., and Oppenheim, D. (1991). The moral self of infancy: Affective core and procedural knowledge. *Developmental Review, 11,* 251–270. [8], [10]

Emde, R. N., and Buchsbaum, H. (1990). "Didn't you hear my mommy?" Autonomy *with* connectedness in moral self-emergence. In D. Cicchetti and M. Beeghly (Eds.), *The self in transition* (pp. 35–60). Chicago: University of Chicago Press. [10]

Emde, R. N., Gaensbauer, T., and Harmon, R. (1976). Emotional expression in infancy: A biobehavioral study. *Psychological Issues Monograph Series, 10* (Serial No. 37). [6]

Emde, R. N., Plomin, R., Robinson, J., Corley, R., DeFries, J., Fulker, D. W., Reznick, J. S., Campos, J., Kagan, J., and Zahn-Waxler, C. (1992). Temperament, emotion, and cognition at fourteen months: The MacArthur longitudinal twin study. *Developmental Psychology, 63,* 1437–1455. [6]

Emery, R. (1999). *Marriage, divorce, and children's adjustment* (2nd Ed.). Beverly Hills, CA: Sage. [2]

Emmerich, W., Goldman, K., Kirsh, K., and Sharabany, R. (1977). Evidence for a transitional phase in the development of gender constancy. *Child Development, 48,* 930–936. [10]

Engfer, A. (1988). The interrelatedness of marriage and the mother-child relationship. In R. Hinde and J. Stevenson-Hinde (Eds.), *Relationships within families: Mutual influences.* (pp. 104–118) Oxford, England: Oxford University Press. [2]

Entwisle, D. (1990). Schools and the adolescent. In S. Feldman and G. Elliot (Eds.), *At the threshold: The developing adolescent* (pp. 197–224). Cambridge, MA: Harvard University Press. [14]

Entwisle, D. R. (1994). Subcultural diversity in American families. In L. L'Abate (Ed.), *Handbook of developmental family psychology and psychopathology* (pp. 132–156). Oxford, England: Wiley. [2]

Epstein, H. T. (1979). Correlated brain and intelligence development in humans. In M. E. Hahn, C. Jensen, and B. C. Dudek (Eds.), *Development and evolution of brain size: Behavioral implications.* New York: Academic Press. [13]

Erickson, E. H. (1963). *Childhood and society* (2nd. ed.). New York: Norton. [1], [8]

Erikson, E. H. (1981). *Youth, change, and challenge.* New York: Basic Books. [14]

Erickson, M., Egeland, B., and Sroufe, L. A. (1985). The relationship between quality of attachment and behavior problems in preschool in a high risk sample. In I. Bretherton and E. Waters (Eds.), *Growing points in attachment theory and research. Monographs of the Society for Research in Child Development, 50* (1-2, Series No. 209), 147–186. [2], [8], [10]

Erikson, E. H. (1963). *Childhood and society* (2nd ed.). New York: Norton. [8], [10], [12]

Erickson, P. I. (1998). *Latina adolescent childbearing in East Los Angeles.* Austin, TX: University of Texas Press. [2]

Eveleth, P. B., and Tanner, J. M. (1976). *Worldwide variation in human growth.* London: Cambridge University Press. [13]

Fabes, R., Eisenberg, N., and Eisenbud, L. (1993). Behavioral and physiological correlates of children's reactions to others in distress. *Developmental Psychology, 29,* 655–663. [12]

Fabes, R., Eisenberg, N., Karbon, M., Bernzweig, J., Speer, A., and Carlo, G. (1994). Socialization of children's vicarious emotional responding and prosocial behavior. *Developmental Psychology, 30,* 44–55. [10]

Fagan, J. F., and McGrath, S. K. (1981). Infant recognition memory as a measure of intelligence. *Intelligence, 5,* 121–130. [5]

Fagot, B., and Kavanaugh, K. (1993). Parenting during the second year: Effects of children's age, sex and attachment classification. *Child Development, 64,* 258–271. [8]

Fagot, B., Leinbach, M., and O'Boyle, C. (1992). Gender labeling, gender stereotyping, and parenting behaviors. *Developmental Psychology, 28,* 225–230. [10]

Fairbanks, L. (1989). Early experience and cross-generational continuity of mother-infant contact in Vervet monkeys. *Developmental Psychobiology, 22,* 669–681. [6], [12]

Falbo, T., and Poston, D. L. (1993). The academic, personality, and physical outcomes of only children in China. *Child Development, 64,* 18–35. [2]

Fantz, R. L. (1958). Pattern vision in young infants. *Psychological Record, 8,* 43–47. [4]

Farkas, S., Duffett, A., and Johnson, J. (2000). *Necessary compromises: How parents, employers and children's advocates view child care today.* New York: Public Agenda. [6]

Farone, S., and Tsuang, M. (1988). Familial links between schizophrenia and other disorders: Psychopathology in offspring. *Psychiatry, 51,* 37–47. [15]

Farrington, D. (1995). The Twelfth Jack Tizard Memorial Lecture. The development of offending and antisocial behavior in childhood: Key findings from the Cambridge Study of Delinquent Development. *Journal of Child Psychology and Psychiatry, 36,* 929–964. [15]

Farver, J. A. M., and Shin, Y. L. (1997). Social pretend play in Korean- and Anglo-American preschoolers. *Child Development, 68,* 544–556. [10]

Fein, G. (1981). Pretend play in childhood: An integrative review. *Child Development, 52,* 1095–1118. [10]

Feinberg, M., and Hetherington, E. M. (2000). Sibling differentiation in adolescence: Implications for behavior genetic theory. *Child Development, 71,* 1512–1524. [14]

Feldman, S., and Gehring, T. (1988). Changing perceptions of family cohesion and power across adolescence. *Child Development, 59,* 1034–1045. [14]

Fenson, L., Dale, P. S., Reznick, J. S., Bates, E., Thal, D. J., and Pethick, S. J. (1994). Variability in early communicative development. *Monographs of the Society for Research in Child Development, 59* (Serial No. 242). [7]

Fernald, A. (1984). The perceptual and affective salience of mothers' speech to infants. In L. Feagans, C. Garvey, and R. Golinkoff (Eds.). *The origins and growth of communication* (pp. 5–29). Norwood, NJ: Ablex. [7]

Fernald, A. (1985). Four-month-olds prefer to listen to motherese. *Infant Behavior and Development, 8,* 181–195. [7]

Fernald, A., Taeschner, T., Dunn, J., Papouxek, M., de Boysson-Bardies, B., and Fukui, I. (1989). A cross-language study of prosodic modifications in mothers' and fathers' speech to preverbal infants. *Journal of Child Language, 16,* 477–501. [7]

Field, T. M. (2001). *Touch.* Cambridge, MA: MIT Press. [4]

Field, T. M., and Goldson, E. (1984). Pacifying effects of nonnutritive sucking on term and preterm neonates during heelstick procedures. *Pediatrics, 74,* 1012–1015. [4]

Fields, J., and Casper, L. M. (2001). *America's families and living arrangements: March 2000.* Current Population Reports, P60–213. Washington, DC: U.S. Census Bureau. [2]

Fine, G., Mortimer, J., and Roberts, D. (1990). Leisure, work, and mass media. In S. Feldman and G. Elliot (Eds.), *At the threshold: The developing adolescent* (pp. 225–252). Cambridge, MA: Harvard University Press. [14]

Fischer, G., Etzersdorfer, P., Eder, H., Jagsch, R., Langer, M., and Weninger, M. (1998). Buprenorphine maintenance in pregnant opiate addicts. *European Addiction Research, 4,* Suppl 1, 32–36. [3]

Fischer, K. (1980). A theory of cognitive development: The control and construction of hierarchies of skills. *Psychological Review, 87,* 477–531. [5]

Fischer, K. W., and Bidell, T. R. (1998). Dynamic development of psychological structures in action and thought. In W. Damon (Series Ed.) and R. M. Lerner (Vol. Ed.), *Handbook of child psychology: Vol. 1. Theoretical models of human development* (5th ed., pp. 467–561). New York: Wiley. [5]

Fischer, K. W., and Rose, S. P. (1994). Dynamic development of coordination of components in brain and behavior: A framework for theory and research. In G. Dawson and K. W. Fischer (Eds.), *Human behavior and the developing brain* (pp. 3–66). New York: Guilford. [5]

Fischer, K., Shaver, P., and Carnochan, P. (1990). How emotions develop and how they organize development. *Cognition and Emotion, 4,* 81–127. [10]

Fisher, C. B., Jackson, J. F., and Villarruel, F. A. (1998). The study of African American and Latin American children and youth. In W. Damon (Series Ed.) and R. M. Lerner (Vol. Ed.), *Handbook of child psychology: Vol. 1. Theoretical models of human development* (5th ed., pp. 1145–1207). New York: Wiley. [2]

Flaks, D. K., Ficher, I., Masterpasqua, F., and Joseph, G. (1995). Lesbians choosing motherhood: A comparative study of lesbian and heterosexual parents and their children. *Developmental Psychology, 31,* 105–114. [2]

Flavell, J. H. (1985). *Cognitive development* (2nd ed.). Englewood Cliffs, NJ: Prentice-Hall. [7]

Flavell, J. H. (1999). Cognitive development: Children's knowledge about the mind. *Annual Review of Psychology, 50,* 21–45. [9]

Flavell, J. H., Beach, D. H., and Chinsky, J. M. (1966). Spontaneous verbal rehearsal in a memory task as a function of age. *Child Development, 37,* 283–299. [11]

Flavell, J. H., Botkin, P. T., Fry, C. L., Wright, J. W., and Jarvis, P. E. (1968). *The development of role-taking and communication skills in children.* New York: Wiley. [9]

Flavell, J. H., Friedrichs, A. G., and Hoyt, J. D. (1970). Developmental changes in memorization processes. *Cognitive Psychology, 1,* 324–340. [11]

Flavell, J. H., Green, F. L., and Flavell, E. R. (1986). Development of knowledge about the appearance reality distinction. *Monographs of the Society for Research in Child Development, 51* (Serial No. 212). [9]

Flavell, J. H., Green, F. L., and Flavell, E. R. (1990). Developmental changes in young children's knowledge about the mind. *Cognitive Development, 5,* 1–27. [9]

Flavell, J. H., and Miller, P. H. (1998). Social Cognition. In W. Damon (Series Ed.), D. Kuhn, and R. S. Siegler (Vol. Eds.), *Handbook of child psychology: Vol. 2. Cognition, perception, and language* (5th ed., pp. 851–898). New York: Wiley. [9], [11]

Flavell, J. H., Miller, P. H., and Miller, S. A. (2002). *Cognitive development* (4th ed.). Upper Saddle River, NJ: Prentice-Hall. [5], [9], [11], [13]

Flavell, J. H., and Wellman, H. M. (1977). Metamemory. In R. B. Kail and J. E. Hagen (Eds.), *Perspectives on the development of memory and cognition* (pp. 3–30). Hillsdale, NJ: Erlbaum. [11]

Flavell, J. H., Zhang, X.-D., Zou, H., Dong, Q., and Qi, S. (1983). A comparison between the development of the appearance-reality distinction in the People's Republic of China and the United States. *Cognitive Psychology, 15,* 459–466. [9]

Fogel, A. (1993). *Developing through relationships.* Chicago: University of Chicago Press. [6]

Forbes, H. S., and Forbes, H. B. (1927). Fetal sense reaction: Hearing. *Journal of Comparative Psychology, 7,* 353–355. [4]

Forman, E. A. (1982). *Understanding the role of peer interaction in development: The contribution of Piaget and Vygotsky.* Paper presented at the meeting of the Jean Piaget Society, Philadelphia. [11]

Foster, G., and Williamson, J. (2000). A review of current literature on the impact of HIV/AIDS on children in sub-Saharan Africa. *AIDS, 14,* Suppl. 3, S275–284. [3]

Fox, N. A., and Calkins, S. D. (1993). Pathways to aggression and social withdrawal: Interactions among temperament, attachment, and regulation. In K. Rubin and J. B. Asendorpf (Eds.), *Social withdrawal, inhibition, and shyness in childhood* (pp. 81–100). Hillsdale, NJ: Erlbaum. [8]

Frankel, K. A., and Bates, J. E. (1990). Mother-toddler problem solving: Antecedents in attachment, home behavior, and temperament. *Child Development, 61,* 810–819. [8]

Frankenburg, W. K., and Dodds, J. B. (1967). The Denver developmental screening test. *Journal of Pediatrics, 71,* 181–185. [4]

Freedman-Doan, C., Wigfield, A., Eccles, J., Blumenfeld, P., Arbreton, A., and Harold, R. (2000). What am I best at? Grade and gender differences in children's beliefs about ability improvement. *Journal of Applied Developmental Psychology, 21,* 379–402. [12]

Freeman, D. (1983) *Margaret Mead and Samoa: The making and unmaking of an anthropological myth.* Cambridge, MA: Harvard University Press. [14]

Frey, K., and Ruble, D. (1992). Gender constancy and the "cost" of sex-typed behavior: A test of the conflict hypothesis. *Developmental Psychology, 28,* 714–721. [12]

Fried, P. A., Watkinson, B., and Gray, R. (1998). Differential effects on cognitive functioning in 9- to 12-year-olds prenatally exposed to cigarettes and marijuana. *Neurotoxicology and Teratology, 20,* 293–306. [3]

Friend, M., and Davis, T. (1993). Appearance-reality distinction: Children's understanding of the physical and affective domains. *Developmental Psychology, 29,* 907–913. [10]

Frisch, R. E. (1991). Puberty and body fat. In R. M. Lerner, A. C. Petersen, and J. Brooks-Gunn (Eds.), *Encyclopedia of adolescence* (Vol. 2, pp. 884–892). New York: Garland. [13]

Frisch, R. E., and Revelle, R. (1970). Height and weight at menarche and a hypothesis of critical body weights and adolescent events. *Science, 169,* 397–399. [13]

Frosch, C., and Mangelsdorf, S. (2001). Marital behavior, parenting behavior, and multiple reports of preschoolers' behavior problems: Mediation or moderation? *Developmental Psychology, 37,* 502–519. [10]

Fuligni, A., (1998). Authority, autonomy and parent-adolescent conflict and cohesion: A study of Adolescents from Mexican, Chinese, Filipino, and European backgrounds. *Developmental Psychology, 34,* 782–792. [14]

Furman, W., and Buhrmester, D. (1992). Age and sex differences in perceptions of networks of personal relationships. *Child Development, 63,* 103–115. [1]

Furman, W., Rahe, D., and Hartup, W. (1979). Rehabilitation of socially withdrawn preschool children through mixed age and same age socialization. *Child Development, 50,* 915– 922. [10]

Furstenberg, F. (1990). Coming of age in a changing family system. In S. Feldman and G. Elliot (Eds.), *At the threshold: The developing adolescent* (pp. 147– 170). Cambridge, MA: Harvard University Press. [14]

Fury, G., Carlson, E., and Sroufe, L. A. (1997). Children's representations of attachment relationships in family drawings. *Child Development, 68,* 1154–1164. [12]

Furstenberg, F., Brooks-Gunn, J., and Chase-Lansdale, L. (1989). Teenaged pregnancy and childbearing. *American Psychologist, 44,* 313–320. [2]

Fuson, K. C. (1988). *Children's counting and concepts of number.* New York: Springer-Verlag. [9]

Galambos, N., and Maggs, J. (1991). Children in self-care: Figures, facts and fiction. In J. Lerner and N. Galambos (Eds.), *Employed mothers and their children* (pp. 131–157). New York: Garland. [12]

Gallimore, R., and Au, K. H. (1997). The competence/incompetence paradox in the education of minority culture children. In M. Cole and Y. Engestroem (Eds.), *Mind, culture, and activity: Seminal papers from the Laboratory of Comparative Human Cognition* (pp. 241–253). New York: Cambridge University Press. [11]

Gallimore, R., and Goldenberg, C. (2001). Analyzing cultural models and settings to connect minority achievement and school improvement research. *Educational Psychologist, 36,* 45–56. [11]

Gallistel, C. R., and Gelman, R. (1990). The what and how of counting. *Cognition, 34,* 197–199. [9]

Galotti, K. M. (1989). Gender differences in self-reported moral reasoning: A review and new evidence. *Journal of Youth and Adolescence, 18,* 475–488. [13]

Garbarino, J. (2001). An ecological perspective on the effects of violence on children. *Journal of Community Psychology, 29,* 361–378. [2]

Garber, J. (2000). Development and depression. In A. Sameroff, M. Lewis, and S. Miller (Eds.), *Handbook of developmental psychopathology* (2nd ed.), pp. 467–490. New York: Plenum. [15]

Garcia, J., and Koelling, R. (1966). Relation of cue to consequences in avoidance learning. *Psychonometric Science, 4,* 123–124. [4]

Garcia, M., Shaw, D., Winslow, E., and Yaggi, K. (2000). Destructive sibling conflict and the development of conduct problems in young boys. *Developmental Psychology, 36,* 44–53. [12]

Garcia Coll, C. T., and Magnuson, K. (1999). Cultural influences on child development: Are we ready for a paradigm shift? In A. S. Masten (Ed.), *Minnesota Symposia on Child Psychology: Vol. 29. Cultural processes in child development* (pp. 1–24). Mahwah, NJ: Erlbaum. [2]

Gardiner, H. W., and Kosmitzki, C. (2002). *Lives across cultures: Cross-cultural human development* (2nd ed.). Needham Heights, MA: Allyn & Bacon. [5], [11]

Gardner, H. (1983). *Frames of mind: The theory of multiple intelligences.* New York: Basic Books. [11]

Gardner, H. (1999). *Intelligence reframed: Multiple intelligences for the 21st century.* New York: Basic Books. [11]

Garvey, C. (1977). *Play.* Cambridge, MA: Harvard University Press. [10]

Gavin, L., and Furman, W. (1989). Age differences in adolescents' perceptions of their peer groups. *Developmental Psychology, 25,* 827–834. [14]

Geary, D. C., Bow-Thomas, C. C., Fan, K., and Siegler, R. S. (1993). Even before formal instruction, Chinese children outperform American children in mental arithmetic. *Cognitive Development, 8,* 517–529. [11]

Gelman, R. (1972). The nature and development of early number concepts. In H. W. Reese (Ed.), *Advances in child development and behavior* (Vol. 7, pp. 116–167). New York: Academic Press. [9]

Gelman, R. (1990). First principles organize attention to and learning about relevant data: Number and the animate-inanimate object distinction. *Cognitive Science, 14,* 79–106. [9]

Gelman, R., and Gallistel, C. R. (1978). *The child's understanding of number.* Cambridge, MA: Harvard University Press. [9]

Gelman, S. A., and Wellman, H. M. (1991). Insides and essences: Early understandings of the nonobvious. *Cognition, 38,* 213–244. [9]

Genishi, C., and Dyson, A. H. (1984). *Language assessment in the early years.* Norwood, NJ: Ablex. [7]

Gennetian, L. A., and Miller, C. (2002). Children and welfare reform: A view from an experimental welfare program in Minnesota. *Child Development, 73,* 601–620. [2]

Ghiselli, E. E. (1966). *The validity of occupational aptitude tests.* New York: Wiley. [11]

Gibbons, A. (1998). Which of our genes make us human? *Science, 281,* 1432–1434. [2]

Gibson, E., Dembofsky, C. A., Rubin, S., and Greenspan, J. S. (2000). Infant sleep position practices 2 years into the "Back to Sleep" campaign. *Clinical Pediatrics, 39,* 285–289. [4]

Gibson, E. J., and Walk, R. D. (1960). The "visual cliff." *Scientific American, 202,* 64–71. [4]

Gibson, P. A. (2002). African American grandmothers as caregivers: Answering the call to help their grandchildren. *Families in Society, 83,* 35–43. [2]

Gilligan, C. (1982). *In a different voice: Psychological theory and women's development.* Cambridge, MA: Harvard University Press. [13]

Gimenez, M., and Harris, P. L. (2002). Understanding constraints on inheritance: Evidence for biological thinking in early childhood. *British Journal of Developmental Psychology, 20,* 307–324. [9]

Ginsburg, G., and Bronstein, P. (1993). Family factors related to children's intrinsic/extrinsic motivational orientation and academic performance. *Child Development, 64,* 1461–1474. [12]

Ginsburg, H. P., Klein, A., and Starkey, P. (1998). The development of children's mathematical thinking: Connecting research with practice. In W. Damon (Series Ed.) and I. E. Sigel and K. A. Renninger (Vol. Eds.), *Handbook of child psychology: Vol. 4. Child psychology in practice* (5th ed., pp. 401–476). New York: Wiley. [9]

Glaser, D. (2000). Child abuse and neglect and the brain—a review. *Journal of Child Psychology and Psychiatry, 41,* 97–116. [8]

Gleason, J. B. (1975). Fathers and other strangers: Men's speech to young children. In D. Dato (Ed.), *Georgetown University roundtable on language and linguistics*. Washington, DC: Georgetown University Press. [7]

Gleason, J. B., Perlmann, R. Y., and Greif, E. B. (1984). What's the magic word: Learning language through routines. *Discourse Processes, 6,* 493–502. [7]

Gleason, T., Sebanc, A., and Hartup, W. (2000). Imaginary companions of preschool children. *Developmental Psychology, 36,* 419–428. [10]

Gleitman, L. R., and Wanner, E. (1982). Language acquisition: The state of the state of the art. In E. Wanner and L. R. Gleitman (Eds.), *Language acquisition: The state of the art* (pp. 3–48). New York: Cambridge University Press. [7]

Glick, J. (1975). Cognitive development in cross-cultural perspective. In F. D. Horowitz (Ed.), *Review of child development research* (Vol. 4, pp. 595–654). Chicago: University of Chicago Press. [11]

Glick, M., and Zigler, E. (1990). Premorbid competence and the course and outcome of psychiatric disorders. In J. Rolf, A. Masten, D. Cicchetti, K. Neuchterlein, and S. Weintraub (Eds.), *Risk and protective factors in the development of psychopathology* (pp. 497–513). New York: Cambridge University Press. [15]

Glucksberg, S., and Krauss, R. M. (1967): What do people say after they have learned to talk? Studies of the development of referential communication. *Merrill-Palmer Quarterly, 13,* 309–316. [9]

Glucksberg, S., Krauss, R. M., and Higgins, E. T. (1975). The development of referential communication skills. In F. D. Horowitz (Ed.), *Review of child development research* (Vol. 4, pp. 305–345). Chicago: University of Chicago Press. [9]

Gnepp, J. (1989). Children's use of personal information to understand other people's feelings. In C. Saarni and P. L. Harris (Eds.), *Children's understanding of emotion*. Cambridge, Eng.: Cambridge University Press. [9]

Gnepp, J. (1989). Personalized inferences of emotions and appraisals: Component processes and correlations. *Developmental Psychology, 25,* 277–288.

Gnepp, J., and Klayman, J. (1992). Recognition of uncertainty in emotional inferences: Reasoning about emotionally equivocal situations. *Developmental Psychology, 28,* 145–158. [12]

Goldfield, B., and Reznick, J. S. (1990). Early lexical acquisition: Rate, content, and the vocabulary spurt. *Journal of Child Language, 17,* 171–183. [7]

Goldfield, B. A., and Snow, C. E. (1993). Individual differences in language acquisition. In J. B. Gleason (Ed.), *The development of language* (pp. 299–324). New York: Macmillan. [7]

Goldsmith, H., Buss, K., and Lemery, K. (1997). Toddler and childhood temperament: Expanded content, stronger genetic evidence, new evidence for the importance of environment. *Developmental Psychology, 33,* 891–905. [6]

Goldsmith, H., Lemery, K. S., Aksan, N., and Buss, K. A. (2000). Temperamental substrates of personality. In V. J. Molfese and D. L. Molfese (Eds.), *Temperament and personality development across the life span* (pp. 1–32). Mahwah, NJ: Erlbaum. [2]

Goldsmith, H., Lemery, K., Buss, K., and Campos, J. (1999). Genetic analyses of focal aspects of infant temperament. *Developmental Psychology, 35,* 972–985. [6]

Golinkoff, R. (1986). "I beg your pardon?": The preverbal negotiation of failed communications. *Journal of Child Language, 13,* 455–476. [7]

Golinkoff, R. M., Hirsh-Pasek, K., Cauley, K. M., and Gordon, L. (1987). The eyes have it: Lexical and syntactic comprehension in a new paradigm. *Journal of Child Language, 14,* 23–45. [7]

Goodlad, J. (1984). *A place called school*. New York: McGraw-Hill. [13]

Goodnow, J. J. (1973). Compensation arguments on conservation tasks. *Developmental Psychology, 8,* 140. [9]

Goodnow, J. J. (1976). The nature of intelligent behavior: Questions raised by cross-cultural studies. In L. Resnick (Ed.), *The nature of intelligence* (pp. 169–188). Hillsdale, NJ: Erlbaum. [11]

Goodwyn, S. W., and Acredolo, L. P. (1998). Encouraging symbolic gestures: A new perspective on the relationship between gesture and speech. In J. M. Iverson and S. Goldin-Meadow (Eds.), *The nature and function of gesture in children's communication. New Directions for Child Development*, No. 79 (pp. 61–73). San Francisco: Jossey-Bass. [7]

Gopnik, A., and Meltzoff, A. N. (1987). The development of categorization in the second year and its relation to other cognitive and linguistic developments. *Child Development, 58,* 1523–1531. [7], [9]

Gordon, F. R., and Yonas, A. (1976). Sensitivity to binocular depth information in infants. *Journal of Experimental Child Psychology, 22,* 413–422. [4]

Gottesmann, I. (1991). *Schizophrenia genesis*. New York: Freeman. [15]

Gottlieb, G. (1991). Experiential canalization of behavioral development: Theory. *Developmental Psychology, 27,* 4–13. [1], [2]

Gottlieb, G. (2001). A developmental psychobiological systems view: Early formulation and current status. In S. Oyama and P. E. Griffiths (Eds.), *Cycles of contingency: Developmental systems and evolution* (pp. 41–54). Cambridge, MA: MIT Press. [1], [2], [11]

Gould, E., Reeves, A. J., Graziano, M. S. A., and Gross, C. G. (1999). Neurogenesis in the neocortex of adult primates. *Science, 286,* 548–552. [4]

Gould, S. J. (2002). *The structure of evolutionary theory*. Cambridge, MA: Harvard University Press. [1]

Gove, F. (1983). *Patterns and organizations of behavior and affective expression during the second year of life*. Unpublished doctoral dissertation, University of Minnesota. [10]

Graber, J. A., Brooks-Gunn, J., and Warren, M. P. (1995). The antecedents of menarcheal age: Heredity, family environment, and stressful life events. *Child Development, 66,* 346–359. [13]

Graber, J. A., Lewinsohn, P. M., Seeley, J. R., and Brooks-Gunn, J. (1997). Is psychopathology associated with the timing of pubertal development? *Journal of the American Academy of Child and Adolescent Psychiatry, 36,* 1768–1776. [13]

Graber, J. A., and Petersen, A. (1991). Cognitive changes at adolescence: Biological perspectives. In K. Gibson and A. Petersen (Eds.), *Brain maturation and cognitive development* (pp. 253–280). New York: Aldine de Gruyter. [13]

Granrud, C. E. (1986). Binocular vision and spatial perception in 4- and 5-month-old infants. *Journal*

of Experimental Psychology: Human Perception and Performance, 37, 459–466. [4]

Grant, J. (1998). *Raising baby by the book: The education of American mothers*. New Haven, CT: Yale University Press. [2]

Gratch, G. (1975). Recent studies based on Piaget's view of object concept development. In L. B. Cohen and P. Salapatek (Eds.), *Infant perception: From sensation to cognition* (Vol. 2, pp. 51–99). New York: Academic Press. [5]

Gratch, G., Appel, K. J., Evans, W. F., LeCompte, G. K., and Wright, N. A. (1974). Piaget's Stage IV object concept error: Evidence of forgetting or object conception? *Child Development, 45,* 71–77. [5]

Graziano, W. (1984). The development of social exchange processes. In J. C. Masters and K. Yarkin-Levin (Eds.), *Boundary areas in social and developmental psychology* (pp. 161–189). New York: Academic Press. [12]

Green, N. S. (2002). Folic acid supplementation and prevention of birth defects. *The Journal of Nutrition, 132*(8, Suppl.), 2356S–2360S. [3]

Greenberg, M., and Crnic, K. (1988). Longitudinal predictors of developmental status and social interaction in premature and full-term infants at age two. *Child Development, 59,* 554–570. [2], [3]

Greenfield, P. M. (1966). On culture and conservation. In J. S. Bruner, R. R. Oliver, and P. M. Greenfield (Eds.), *Studies in cognitive growth* (pp. 225–256). New York: Wiley. [11]

Greenfield, P. M. (1997). You can't take it with you: Why ability assessments don't cross cultures. *American Psychologist, 52,* 1115–1124. [11]

Greenfield, P. M., and Suzuki, L. K. (1998). Culture and human development: Implications for parenting, education, pediatrics, and mental health. In W. Damon (Series Ed.) and I. E. Sigel and K. A. Renninger (Vol. Eds.), *Handbook of child psychology: Vol. 4. Child psychology in practice* (5th ed., pp. 1059–1109). New York: Wiley. [10]

Greenough, W. T., and Black, J. E. (1992). Induction of brain structure by experience: Substrates for cognitive development. In M. Gunnar and C. Nelson (Eds.), *Minnesota Symposia on Child Psychology: Vol. 24. Developmental behavioral neuroscience* (pp. 155–200). Hillsdale, NJ: Lawrence Erlbaum Associates. [4]

Greenough, W. T., Black, J. E., and Wallace, C. S. (1987). Experience and brain development. *Child Development, 58,* 539–559. [4]

Greif, E. B., and Gleason, J. B. (1980). Hi, thanks, and goodbye: More routine information. *Language in Society, 9,* 159–166. [7]

Grolnick, W. S., and Slowiaczek, M. (1994). Parents' involvement in children's schooling: A multidimensional conceptualization and motivational model. *Child Development, 65,* 237–252. [12]

Gross, R. T., Spiker, D., and Haynes, C. W. (Eds.) (1997). *Helping low birth weight, premature babies: The Infant Health and Development Program*. Stanford, CA: Stanford University Press. [5]

Gross, T. F. (1985). *Cognitive development*. Monterey, CA: Brooks/Cole. [11]

Grossmann, K., Grossmann, K. E., Fremmer–Bombik, E., Kindler, H., Scheuerer-Englisch, H., and

Zimmermann, P. (2002). The uniqueness of the child-father attachment relationship: Fathers' sensitive and challenging play as a pivotal variable in a 16-year longitudinal study. *Social Development, 11,* 307–331. [8]

Grossmann, K. E. (1999). Old and new internal working models of attachment: The organization of feelings and language. *Attachment and Human Development. Special Issue: Internal working models revisited, 1,*253–269. [6]

Grossmann, K. E., and Grossmann, K. (1991). Attachment quality as an organizer of emotional and behavioral responses in a longitudinal perspective. In C. M. Parkes, P. Marris, and J. Stevenson-Hinde (Eds.), *Attachment across the life cycle* (pp. 93–114). New York: Ruttledge. [12]

Grotevant, H. (1992). Assigned and chosen identity components: A process perspective on their integration. In G. Adams, R. Montemayor, and T. Gulotta (Eds.), *Adolescent identity formation* (pp. 73–90). Newbury Park, CA: Sage. [14]

Grotevant, H. (1998). Adolescent development in family contexts. In W. Damon (Series Ed.) and N. Eisenberg (Vol. Ed.), *Handbook of child psychology: Vol. 3. Social, emotional, and personality development* (5th ed., pp. 1097–1149). New York: Wiley. [13], [14]

Grotevant, H., and Cooper, C. (1986). Individuation in family relationships. *Human Development, 29,* 82–100. [14]

Grotevant, H., and Cooper, C. (1998). Individuality and connectedness in adolescent development: Review and prospects for research on identity, relationships, and context. In E. Skoe and A. von der Lippe (Eds.), *Personality development in adolescence* (pp. 81–98). London: Routledge & Kegan Paul. [14]

Grumbach, M. M., Roth, J. C., Kaplan, S. L., and Kelch, R. P. (1974). Hypothalamic-pituitary regulation of puberty in man: Evidence and concepts derived from clinical research. In M. M. Grumbach, G. D. Grave, and F. E. Mayer (Eds.), *Control of the onset of puberty.* New York: Wiley. [13]

Grusec, J., and Goodnow, J. (1994). Summing up and looking to the future. *Developmental Psychology, 30,* 29–31. [10]

Grusec, J. E., and Kuczynski, L. (Eds.), (1997). *Parenting and children's internalization of values: A handbook of contemporary theory.* New York: Wiley. [8]

Grych, J., and Fincham, F. (2001). Interparental conflict and child adjustment: An overview. In J. Grych and F. Fincham (Eds.), *Interparental conflict and child development: Theory, research, and application* (pp. 1-6). New York: Cambridge University Press. [12]

Grych, J., and Fincham, F. (2001). *Interpersonal conflict and child development: Theory, research, and application.* New York: Cambridge University Press. [2]

Guerri, C. (1998). Neuroanatomical and neurophysiological mechanisms involved in central nervous system dysfunctions induced by prenatal alcohol exposure. *Alcohol Clinical and Experimental Research, 22,* 304–312. [3]

Gunnar, M. (1994). Psychoendocrine studies of temperament and stress in early childhood. Expanding

current models. In J. Bates and T. Wachs (Eds.), *Temperament: Individual differences at the interface of biology and behavior* (pp. 175–198). Washington, DC: American Psychological Association. [6]

Gunnar, M. (2001). Effects of early deprivation: Findings from orphanage-reared infants and children. In C. Nelson and M. Luciana (Eds.) *Handbook of developmental cognitive neuroscience* (pp. 617–629). Cambridge MA: MIT Press. [6]

Gunnar, M., Mangelsdorf, S., Kestenbaum, R., Lang, S., Larson, M., and Andreas, D. (1989a). Stress and coping in early development. In D. Cicchetti (Ed.), *The emergence of a discipline: Vol. 1. Rochester Symposium on Developmental Psychopathology* (pp. 119–138). Hillsdale, NJ: Erlbaum. [6]

Gunnar, M., Mangelsdorf, S., Larson, M., and Hertsgaard, L. (1989b). Attachment, temperament, and adrenocortical activity in infancy: A study of psychoendocrine regulation. *Developmental Psychology, 25,* 355–363. [6]

Gunnar, M. R., Morison, S. J., Chisholm, K., Schuder, M. (2001). Salivary cortisol levels in children adopted from Romanian orphanages. *Development and Psychopathology, 13,* 611–628. [2]

Gunnar, M., and Stone, C. (1984). The effects of positive maternal affect on infant responses to pleasant, ambiguous, and fear-provoking toys. *Child Development, 55,* 1231–1236. [8]

Haith, M. M., and Benson, J. B. (1998). Infant cognition. In W. Damon (Series Ed.), D. Kuhn, and R. S. Siegler (Vol. Eds.), *Handbook of child psychology: Vol. 2. Cognition, perception, and language* (5th ed., pp. 199–254). New York: Wiley. [5]

Hakuta, K., and Diaz, R. (1985). The relationship between degree of bilingualism and cognitive ability: A critical discussion and some new longitudinal data. In K. E. Nelson (Ed.), *Children's language* (Vol. 5) (pp. 319–344). Hillsdale, NJ: Erlbaum. [7]

Hall, E., Perlmutter, M., and Lamb, M. E. (1982). *Child psychology today.* New York: Random House. [3]

Hall, G. S. (1904). *Adolescence.* New York: Appleton. [13]

Halpern, R. (1990). Poverty and early childhood parenting: Toward a framework for intervention. *American Journal of Orthopsychiatry, 6,* 6–18. [2]

Hamm, J. (2000). Do birds of a feather flock together? The variable bases for African American, Asian American and European American adolescents' selection of similar friends. *Developmental Psychology, 36,* 209–219. [14]

Hamond, N. R., and Fivush, R. (1991). Memories of Mickey Mouse: Young children recount their trip to Disney World. *Cognitive Development, 6,* 433–448. [5], [9]

Hamre, B. K., and Pianta, R. C. (2001). Early teacher-child relationships and the trajectory of children's school outcomes through eighth grade. *Child Development, 72,* 625–638. [2]

Han, W., Waldfogel, J., and Brooks-Gunn, J. (2001). The effects of early maternal employment on later cognitive and behavioral outcomes. *Journal of Marriage and the Family, 63,* 336–354. [2]

Hardy, D., Power, T., and Jaedicke, S. (1993). Examining the relation of parenting to children's coping with everyday stress. *Child Development, 64,* 1829– 1841. [12]

Harkness, S., and Super, C. M. (2002). Culture and parenting. In M. H. Bornstein (Ed.), *Handbook of parenting: Vol. 2. Biology and ecology of parenting* (2nd ed., pp. 253–280). Mahwah, NJ: Erlbaum. [2]

Harley, K., and Reese, E. (1999). Origins of autobiographical memory. *Developmental Psychology, 35,* 1338–1348. [5], [8], [9]

Harlow, H. F., and Harlow, M. K. (1966). Learning to love. *American Scientist, 54,* 244–272. [1], [6]

Harmer, A., Sanderson, J., and Mertin, P. (1999). Influence of negative childhood experiences on psychological functioning, social support, and parenting for mothers recovering from addiction. *Child Abuse and Neglect, 23,* 421–433. [8]

Harrington, R. (1994). Affective disorders. In M. Rutter, E. Taylor, and L. Hersov (Eds.), *Child and adolescent psychiatry* (pp. 330–350). London: Blackwell. [15]

Harrington, R., Rutter, M., and Fombonne, E. (1996). Developmental pathways in depression: Multiple meanings, antecedents, and end points. *Development and Psychopathology, 8,* 601–616. [15]

Harris, I. B. (1996). *Children in jeopardy: Can we break the cycle of poverty?* New Haven: Yale Child Study Center. [2]

Harris, J. R. (1998). *The nurture assumption: Why children turn out the way they do.* New York: Free Press. [8], [12]

Harris, P. L. (1994). The child's understanding of emotion: Developmental change and the family environment. *Journal of Child Psychology and Psychiatry, 35,* 3–28. [10]

Harris, T., Brown, G., and Bifulco, A. (1990). Loss of parent in childhood and adult psychiatric disorder: A tentative overall model. *Development and Psychopathology, 2,* 311–328. [15]

Harrison, L. J., and Ungerer, J. A. (2002). Maternal employment and infant-mother attachment security at 12 months postpartum. *Developmental Psychology, 38,* 758–773. [2]

Hart, B., and Risley, T. R. (1995). *Meaningful differences in the everyday experience of young American children.* Baltimore: Brookes. [5], [7]

Hart, C. H., Burts, D. C., and Charlesworth, R. (1997). *Integrated curriculum and developmentally appropriate practice: Birth to age eight.* Albany, NY: State University of New York Press. [2]

Harter, S. (1980). A model of intrinsic mastery motivation in children: Individual differences and developmental change. In W. A. Collins (Ed.), *Minnesota Symposia on Child Psychology: Vol. 13. Development of cognition, affect, and social relations* (pp. 215–255). Hillsdale, NJ: Erlbaum. [2], [12]

Harter, S. (1990). Self and identity development. In S. Feldman and G. Elliot (Eds.), *At the threshold: The developing adolescent* (pp. 352–387). Cambridge, MA: Harvard University Press. [14]

Harter, S. (1998). The development of self-representations. In W. Damon (Series Ed.) and N. Eisenberg (Vol. Ed.), *Handbook of child psychology: Vol. 3.*

Social, emotional, and personality development (5th ed., pp. 553–617). New York: Wiley. [10], [12], [14]

Hartup, W. (1992). Peer relations in early and middle childhood. In V. B. VanHasselt and M. Hersen (Eds.), *Handbook of social development: A lifespan perspective* (pp. 257–281). New York: Plenum Press. [10], [12], [14]

Hartup, W. (1999). Peer experience and its developmental significance. In M. Bennett (Ed.). *Developmental psychology: Achievements and prospects* (pp. 106–125). Philadelphia: Psychology Press. [2]

Hartup, W., and Laursen, B. (1993). Conflict and context in peer relations. In C. Hart (Ed.), *Children on playgrounds: Research perspectives and applications* (pp. 44–84). Albany: State University of New York Press. [10], [12], [14]

Hartup, W., and Stevens, N. (1999). Friendships and adaptation across the life span. *Current Directions in Psychological Science, 8,* 76–79. [14]

Hastings, P., Zahn-Waxler, C., Robinson, J., Usher, B., and Bridges, D. (2000). The development of concern for others in children with behavior problems. *Developmental Psychology, 36,* 531–546. [10]

Hatch, E. E., Palmer, J. R., Titus-Ernstoff, L., Noller, K. L., Kaufman, R. H., Mittendorf, R., Robboy, S. J., Hyer, M., Cowan, C. M., Adam, E., Colton, T., Hartge, P., and Hoover, R. N. (1998). Cancer risk in women exposed to diethylstilbestrol in utero. *Journal of the American Medical Association, 280,* 630–634. [3]

Hauser, S., and Bowlds, M. K. (1990). Stress, coping, and adaptation. In S. Feldman and G. Elliot (Eds.), *At the threshold: The developing adolescent* (pp. 388–413). Cambridge, MA: Harvard University Press. [14]

Hauser-Cram, P., Warfield, M. E., Shonkoff, J. P., Krauss, M. W., Sayer, A., and Upshur, C. C. (2001). Children with disabilities: A longitudinal study of child development and parent well-being. *Monographs of the Society for Research in Child Development, 66* (3, Serial No. 266) [3]

Hauspie, R. C., Vercauteren, M., and Susanne, C. (1997). Secular changes in growth and maturation: An update. *Acta paediatrica (Oslo, Norway:1992) Supplement, 423,* 20–27. [13]

Hayes, A. (1984). Interaction, engagement, and the origins of communication: Some constructive concerns. In L. Feagans, C. Garvey, and R. Golinkoff (Eds.), *The origins and growth of communication* [pp.]. Norwood, NJ: Ablex. [6]

Heath, S. B. (1989). Oral and literate traditions among Black Americans living in poverty. *American Psychologist, 44,* 367–373. [2]

Heath, S. B. (1981). Questioning at home and at school: A comparative study. In G. Spindler (Ed.), *Doing ethnography: Educational anthropology in action* (pp. 102–132). New York: Holt, Rinehart, and Winston. [11]

Heath, S. B. (1983). *Ways with words: Language, life, and work in communities and classrooms.* New York: Cambridge University Press. [11]

Heibeck, T. H., and Markman, E. M. (1987). Word learning in children: An examination of fast mapping. *Child Development, 58,* 1021–1034. [7]

Heinicke, C., and Westheimer, I. (1966). *Brief separations.* New York: International Universities Press. [6]

Hellström-Lindahl, E., and Nordberg, A. (2002). Smoking during pregnancy: A way to transfer the addition to the next generation? *Respiration, 69,* 289–293. [3]

Henderson, V., and Dweck, C. (1990). Motivation and achievement. In S. Feldman and G. Elliot (Eds.), *At the threshold: The developing adolescent* (pp. 308–329). Cambridge, MA: Harvard University Press. [14]

Henrich, C., Kupermine, G., Sack, A., Blatt, S., and Leadbeater, B. (2000). Characteristics and homogeneity of early adolescent friendship groups: A comparison of male and female clique and non-clique members. *Applied Developmental Science, 3,* 15–26. [14]

Herdt, G., and McClintock, M. (2000). The magical age of 10. *Archives of Sexual Behavior, 29,* 587–606. [13]

Herman-Giddens, M. E., Slora, E., J., Wasserman, R. C., Bourdony, C. J., Bhapkar, M. V., Koch, G. G., and Hasemeier, C. M. (1997). Secondary sexual characteristics and menses in young girls seen in office practice: A study from the Pediatric Research in Office Settings Network. *Pediatrics, 99,* 505–512. [13]

Herman-Giddens, M. E., Wang, L., and Koch, G. (2001). Secondary sexual characteristics in boys: Estimates from the National Health and Nutrition Examination Study III, 1988–1994. *Archives of Pediatrics and Adolescent Medicine, 155,* 1022–1028. [13]

Herrnstein, R. J., and Murray, C. (1994). *The bell curve: Intelligence and class structure in American life.* New York: Free Press. [11]

Hetherington, E. M. (1972). Effects of father absence on personality development in adolescent daughters. *Developmental Psychology, 7,* 313–326. [14]

Hetherington, E. M. (1988). Parents, children, and siblings: Six years after divorce. In R. Hinde and J. Stevenson-Hinde (Eds.), *Relationships within families: Mutual influences* (pp. 311–331). Oxford: Oxford University Press. [14]

Hetherington, E. M. (1999). Social capital and the development of youth from nondivorced, divorced, and remarried families. In W. A. Collins and B. Laursen (Eds.), *Minnesota Symposia on Child Psychology: Vol. 30. Relationships as developmental contexts: Festschrift in honor of Willard W. Hartup* (pp. 177–209). Mahwah, NJ: Erlbaum. [14]

Hetherington, E. M., Bridges, M., and Insabella, G. M. (1998). What matters? What does not? Five perspectives on the association between marital transitions and children's adjustment. *American Psychologist, 53,* 167–184. [2], [12], [14]

Hetherington, E. M., and Clingempeel, W. (1992). Coping with marital transitions: A family perspective. *Monographs of the Society for Research on Child Development, 57* (2–3, Serial No. 227). [12]

Hetherington, E. M., Henderson, S. H., Reiss, D., Anderson, E. R., Bridges, M., Chan, R. W., Insabella, G. M., Jodl, K. M., Kim, J. E., Mitchell, A. S., O'-Connor, T. G., Skaggs, M. J., and Taylor, L. C. (1999). Adolescent siblings in stepfamilies: Family

functioning and adolescent adjustment. *Monographs of the Society for Research in Child Development, 64* (4, Serial No. 259). [14]

Hetherington, E. M., and Kelly, J. (2002). *For better or for worse: Divorce reconsidered.* New York: W. W. Norton. [2], [12]

Hetherington, E. M., Reiss, D., and Plomin, R. (1994). *Separate social worlds of siblings: The impact of nonshared environment on development.* Hillsdale, NJ: Erlbaum. [1]

Hetherington, E. M., and Stanley-Hagan, M. (1999). The adjustment of children with divorced parents: A risk and resiliency perspective. *Journal of Child Psychology and Psychiatry and Allied Disciplines, 40,* 129–140. [2], [10], [14]

Hewlett, B. S., Lamb, M., Shannon, D., Leyendecker, B., and Schölmerich, A. (1998). Culture and early infancy among center African foragers and farmers. *Developmental Psychology, 34,* 653–661. [6]

Hiatt, S., Campos, J., and Emde, R. (1979). Facial patterning and infant emotional expression: Happiness, surprise, and fear. *Child Development, 50,* 1020–1035. [6]

Higgins, A., and Turnure, J. (1984). Distractibility and concentration of attention in children's development. *Child Development, 44,* 1799–1810. [13]

Hill, J. (1988). Adapting to menarche: Family control and conflict. In M. Gunnar and W. A. Collins (Eds.), *Minnesota Symposia on Child Psychology: Vol. 21. Development during the transition to adolescence* (pp. 43–77). Hillsdale, NJ: Erlbaum. [14]

Hill, J., Holmbeck, G., Marlow, L., Green, T., and Lynch, M. (1985). Menarcheal status and parent-child relations in families of seventh-grade girls. *Journal of Youth and Adolescence, 14,* 301–316. [13]

Hirsh-Pasek, K., and Golinkoff, R. M. (1993). Skeletal supports for grammatical learning: What infants bring to the language learning task. In C. K. R. Collier and L. P. Lipsitt (Eds.), *Advances in infancy research* (Vol. 8, pp. 299–338). Norwood, NJ: Ablex. [7]

Hirsh-Pasek, K., Treiman, R., and Schneiderman, M. (1984). Brown and Hanlon revised: Mothers' sensitivity to ungrammatical forms. *Journal of Child Language, 11,* 81–88. [7]

Hoff, E. (2001). *Language development* (2nd. ed.). Belmont, CA: Wadsworth. [7]

Hoff, E., Laursen, B., and Tardif, T. (2002). Socioeconomic status and parenting. In M. H. Bornstein (Ed.), *Handbook of parenting: Vol. 2. Biology and ecology of parenting* (2nd ed., pp. 231–252). [2]

Hoff-Ginsberg, E. (1990). Maternal speech and the child's development of syntax: A further look. *Journal of Child Language, 17,* 85–99. [7]

Hoff-Ginsberg, E., and Krueger, W. M. (1991). Older siblings as conversational partners. *Merrill-Palmer Quarterly, 37,* 465–481. [7]

Hoffman, L. W. (2000). Maternal employment: Effects of social context. In R. D. Taylor and M. C. Wang (Eds.), *Resilience across contexts: Family, work, culture, and community* (pp. 147–176). Mahwah, NJ: Erlbaum. [2]

Hoffman, M. (1979). Development of moral thought, feeling, and behavior. *American Psychologist, 34,* 958–966. [10]

Hoffman, M. (1994). Discipline and internalization. *Developmental Psychology, 30,* 26–28. [10]

Holden, C. (1996). Small refugees suffer the effects of early neglect. *Science, 274,* 1076–1077. [2]

Honzik, M. P. (1983). Measuring mental abilities in infancy: The value and limitations. In M. Lewis (Ed.), *Origins of intelligence: Infancy and early childhood* (2nd ed., pp. 67–105). New York: Plenum Press. [5]

Honzik, M. P., McFarlane, J. W., and Allen, L. (1948). The stability of mental test performance between two and eighteen years. *Journal of Experimental Education, 17,* 309–329. [11]

Hood, B., and Willatts, P. (1986). Reaching in the dark to an object's remembered position: Evidence for object-permanence in 5-month-olds. *British Journal of Developmental Psychology, 4,* 57–66. [5]

Hood, B., Carey, S., and Prasada, S. (2000). Predicting the outcomes of physical events: Two-year-olds fail to reveal knowledge of solidity and support. *Child Development, 71,* 1540–1554. [5]

Hopkins, B. (2000). Development of crying in normal infants: Method, theory and some speculations. In R. G. Barr, B. Hopkins, and J. A. Green (Eds.), *Crying as a sign, a symptom, and a signal* (176–209). London: MacKeith Press. [4]

Howe, M. L., and Courage, M. L. (1997). The emergence and early development of autobiographical memory. *Psychological Review, 104,* 499–523. [5]

Howe, N. (1991). Sibling-directed internal state language, perspective taking, and affective behavior. *Child Development, 62,* 1503–1512. [2]

Howes, C. (1988). Peer interaction of young children. *Monographs of the Society for Research in Child Development, 53*(Serial No. 217), 1–78. [10]

Howes, C. (1990). Can the age of entry into child care and the quality of child care predict adjustment in kindergarten? *Developmental Psychology, 26,* 292–303. [10]

Howes, C., Smith, E., and Galinsky, E. (1995). *The Florida Child Care Quality Improvement Study: Interim Report.* New York: Families and Work Institute. [6]

Howes, C., Unger, O., and Seidner, L. B. (1989). Social pretend play in toddlers: Parallels with social play and with solitary pretend. *Child Development, 60,* 77–84. [8]

Howes, C., and Wu, F. (1990). Peer interactions and friendships in an ethnically diverse school setting. *Child Development, 61,* 537–541. [12]

Huston, A. C., Carpenter, C. J., and Atwater, J. B. (1986). Gender, adult structuring of activities, and social behavior in middle childhood. *Child Development, 57,* 1200–1209. [12]

Huston, A. C., Duncan, G. J., Granger, R., Bos, J., McLoyd, V., Mistry, R., Crosby, D., Gibson, C., Magnuson, K., Romich, J., and Ventura, A. (2001). Work-based antipoverty programs for parents can enhance the school performance and social behavior of children. *Child Development, 72,* 318–336. [2]

Huttenlocher, J., and Smiley, P. (1987). Early word meanings: The case of object names. *Cognitive Psychology, 19,* 63–89.

Huttenlocher, P. R. (2002). *Neural plasticity: The effects of environment on the development of the cerebral cortex.* Cambridge, MA: Harvard University Press. [3], [4], [13]

Hymel, S., Bowker, A., and Woody, E. (1993). Aggressive versus withdrawn unpopular children: Variations in peer and self-perceptions in multiple domains. *Child Development, 64,* 879–896. [12]

Infant Health and Development Program. (1990). Enhancing the outcomes of low-birth-weight, premature infants. *Journal of American Medical Association, 263(22),* 3035–3042. [3]

Inhelder, B., and Piaget, J. (1955/1958). *The growth of logical thinking from childhood to adolescence.* New York: Basic Books. [13]

Inhelder, B., and Piaget, J. (1964). *The early growth of logic in the child.* London: Routledge & Kegan Paul. [9], [11]

Inhelder, B., Sinclair, H., and Bovet, B. (1974). *Learning and development of cognition.* Cambridge, MA: Harvard University Press. [13]

International Human Genome Sequencing Consortium. (2001). Initial sequencing and analysis of the human genome. *Nature, 409,* 860–921. [2], [3]

Isabella, R. A. (1993). Origins of attachment: Maternal interactive behavior across the first year. *Developmental Psychology, 64,* 605–621. [6]

Izard, C., and Malatesta, C. (1987). Perspectives on emotional development I: Differential emotions theory of early emotional development. In J. Osofsky (Ed.), *Handbook of infant development* (2nd ed., pp. 494–554). New York: Wiley. [6]

Jacobs, P. I., and Vandeventer, M. (1971). The learning and transfer of double classification skills by first graders. *Child Development, 42,* 149–159. [11]

Jacobson, J. L., Jacobson, S. W., and Sokol, R. J. (1994). Effects of prenatal exposure to alcohol, smoking, and illicit drugs on postpartum somatic growth. *Alcohol Clinical and Experimental Research, 18,* 317–323. [3]

Jacobson, S. W. (1979). Matching behavior in the young infant. *Child Development, 50,* 425–430. [4]

Jacobson, S. W., and Frye, K. F. (1991). Effect of maternal social support on attachment: Experimental evidence. *Developmental Psychology, 62,* 572–582. [6]

Jacobson, S. W., and Jacobson, J. L. (2000). Teratogenic insult and neurobehavioral function in infancy and childhood. In C. Nelson (Ed.), *Minnesota Symposia on Child Psychology: Vol. 31. The effects of early adversity on neurobehavioral development* (pp. 61–112). Mahwah, NJ: Erlbaum. [3]

Jacobvitz, D., Sroufe, L. A., Stewart, M., and Leffert, N. (1990). Treatment of attentional and hyperactivity problems in children with sympathomimetic drugs: A comprehensive review. *Journal of the American Academy of Child Psychiatry, 29,* 677–688. [15]

Jaffe, J., Beebe, B., Feldstein, S., Crown, C., and Jasnow, M. (2001). Rhythms of dialogue in infancy. *Monographs of the Society for Research in Child Development, 66,* Serial No. 265, 1–131. [6]

Jahnke, H., and Blanchard-Fields, F. (1993). A test of two models of adolescent egocentrism. *Journal of Youth and Adolescence, 22,* 313–326. [13]

Janowsky, J. S., and Carper, R. (1996). Is there a neural basis for cognitive transitions in school-age children? In A. J. Sameroff and M. M. Haith (Eds.), *The five to seven year shift: The age of reason and responsibility* (pp. 33–60). Chicago: University of Chicago Press. [12]

Jenkins, E. J., and Bell, C. C. (1997). Exposure and response to community violence among children and adolescence. In J. D. Osofsky (Ed.), *Children in a violent society* (pp. 9–31). New York: Guilford. [2]

Jenkins, J. (1992). Sibling relationships in disharmonious homes: Potential difficulties and protective effects. In F. Boer and J. Dunn (Eds.), *Children's sibling relationships* (pp. 125–138). Hillsdale, NJ: Erlbaum. [12]

Jennings, K., Stagg, V., and Connors, R. (1991). Social networks and mothers' interactions with their preschool children. *Child Development, 62,* 966–978. [10]

Jensen, J., and Garfinkel, B. (1988). Neuroendocrine aspects of attention deficit hyperactivity disorder. *Endocrinology and metabolism clinics of North America, 17,* 111–127. [15]

Jiao, S., Ji, G., and Jing, Q. (1986). Comparative study of behavioral qualities of only children and sibling children. *Child Development, 57,* 357–361. [2]

Jimerson, S., Carlson, E., Rotert, M., Egeland, B., and Sroufe, L. A. (1997). A prospective, longitudinal study of the correlates and consequences of early grade retention. *Journal of School Psychology, 35,* 3–25. [12]

Jimerson, S. R., Egeland, B., Sroufe, L. A., and Carlson, B. (2000). A prospective longitudinal study of high school dropouts: Examining multiple predictors across development. *Journal of School Psychology, 38,* 525–549. [14]

Jimerson, S., Egeland, B., and Teo, A. (1999). A longitudinal study of the trajectories of achievement: Factors associated with change. *Journal of Educational Psychology, 91,* 116–126. [12]

Johnson, B. M., Shulman, S., and Collins, W. A. (1991). Systemic patterns of parenting as reported by adolescents: Developmental differences and implications for psychosocial outcomes. *Journal of Adolescent Research, 6,* 235–252. [14]

Johnson, D. (2000). Medical and developmental sequelae of early childhood institutionalization in Eastern European adoptees. In C. Nelson (Ed.), *Minnesota Symposia on Child Psychology: Vol. 31. The effects of early adversity on neurobehavioral development* (pp. 113–162). Mahwah, NJ: Erlbaum. [2], [6]

Johnson, J. S., and Newport, E. L. (1989). Critical period effects in second language learning: The influence of maturational state on the acquisition of English as a second language. *Cognitive Psychology, 21,* 60–99. [7], [13]

Johnson, M. H. (1997). *Developmental cognitive neuroscience: An introduction.* Oxford, U.K.: Blackwell. [4], [5]

Johnson, M. H. (1998). The neural basis of cognitive development. In W. Damon (Series Ed.), D. Kuhn, and R. S. Siegler (Vol. Eds.), *Handbook of child psychology: Vol. 2. Cognition, perception, and language* (5th ed., pp. 1–49). New York: Wiley. [4], [5], [7]

Johnston, L. D., O'Malley, P. M., and Bachman, J. G. (2002). *Monitoring the Future national survey results on drug use, 1975–2001. Volume I: Secondary school students* (NIH Publication No. 02–5106). Bethesda, MD: National Institute on Drug Abuse. [1], [14]

Jones, L. V. (2001). Assessing achievement versus high-stakes testing: A crucial contrast. *Educational Assessment, 7,* 21–28. [11]

Jones, M. (1957). The later careers of boys who were early or late maturing. *Child Development, 28,* 113–128. [13]

Jones, S. S. (1996). Imitation or exploration: Young infants' matching of adults' oral gestures. *Child Development, 67,* 1952–1969. [4]

Jordan, B. (1993). *Birth in four cultures: A crosscultural investigation of childbirth in Yucatan, Holland, Sweden, and the United States.* Prospect Heights, IL: Waveland Press. [3]

Joseph, J. (2002). Twin studies in psychiatry and psychology: Science or pseudoscience? *Psychiatric Quarterly, 73,* 71–82. [1]

Jusczyk, P. W. (1997). *The discovery of spoken language.* Cambridge, MA: MIT. [7]

Jusczyk, P. W., Hirsh-Pasek, K., Kemler Nelson, D. G., Kennedy, L., Woodward, A., and Piwoz, J. (1992). Perception of acoustic correlates of major phrasal units by young infants. *Cognitive Psychology, 24,* 252–293. [7]

Kagan, J. (1984). *The nature of the child.* New York: Basic Books. [1], [6]

Kagan, J. (1992). Yesterday's premises, tomorrow's promises. *Developmental Psychology, 28,* 990–997. [6]

Kagan, J. (1998). Biology and the child. In W. Damon (Series Ed.) and N. Eisenberg (Vol. Ed.), *Handbook of child psychology: Vol. 3. Social, emotional, and personality development* (5th ed., pp. 177–235). New York: Wiley. [2], [8]

Kagan, J. (2000). Inhibited and uninhibited temperaments: Recent developments. In W. R. Crozier (Ed.), *Shyness: Development, consolidation and change* (pp. 22–29). New York: Routledge Falmer. [1]

Kagan, S., and Madsen, M. (1972). Experimental analyses of cooperation and competition of Anglo-American and Mexican children. *Developmental Psychology, 6,* 49–59. [2]

Kail, R. (1990). *The development of memory in children* (3rd ed.). New York: Freeman. [11]

Kail, R. (1991). Development of processing speed in childhood and adolescence. In W. Reese (Ed.), *Advances in child development and behavior* (Vol. 23, pp. 151–185). San Diego: Academic Press. [11]

Kail, R., and Bisanz, J. (1992). The information processing perspective on cognitive development in childhood and adolescence. In R. J. Sternberg and C. A. Berg (Eds.), *Intellectual development* (pp. 229–260). Cambridge, Eng.: Cambridge University Press. [13]

Kail, R., and Hagen, J. (1982). Memory in childhood. In B. B. Wolman (Ed.), *Handbook of developmental psychology* (pp. 350–363). Englewood Cliffs, NJ: Prentice-Hall. [11]

Kandall, S. R., Doberczak, T. M., Jantunen, M., and Stein, J. (1999). The methadone-maintained pregnancy. *Clinics in Perinatology, 26,* 173–183. [3]

Kanner, L. (1943). Autistic disturbances of affective contact. *Nervous Child, 2,* 217–250. [15]

Kaplan, H., and Dove, H. (1987). Infant development among the Ache of Eastern Paraguay. *Developmental Psychology, 23,* 190–198. [4]

Kaplowitz, P. B., Slora, E. J., Wasserman, R. C., Pedlow, S. E., and Herman-Giddens, M. E. (2001). Earlier onset of puberty in girls: Relation to increased body mass index and race. *Pediatrics, 108,* 347–353. [13]

Karen, R. (1994). *Becoming attached.* New York: Warner. [2]

Katz, L., and Gottman, J. (1993). Patterns of marital conflict predict children's internalizing and externalizing behaviors. *Developmental Psychology, 29,* 940–950. [10]

Katz, P., and Ksansnak, K. (1994). Developmental aspects of gender role flexibility and traditionality in middle childhood and adolescence. *Developmental Psychology, 30,* 272–282. [12]

Kaye, K., and Wells, A. J. (1980). Mothers jiggling and the burst-pause pattern in neonatal feeding. *Infant Behavior and Development, 3,* 29–46. [6]

Keating, D. P. (1980). Thinking processes in adolescence. In J. Adelson (Ed.), *Handbook of adolescent psychology* (pp. 211–247). New York: Wiley. [13]

Keating, D. P. (1990). Adolescent thinking. In S. S. Feldman and G. R. Elliott (Eds.), *At the threshold: The developing adolescent* (pp. 54–89). Cambridge, MA: Harvard University Press. [13]

Keen, R. (in press). Using perceptual representations to guide reaching and looking. In Nelson, C. A., Lockman, J. J., and Rieser, J. J. (Eds.), *Minnesota Symposia on Child Psychology: Vol. 33. Action as an organizer of learning and development.* Hillsdale, NJ: Lawrence Erlbaum Associates. [5]

Keeney, T. J., Cannizzo, S. R., and Flavell, J. H. (1967). Spontaneous and induced verbal rehearsal in a recall task. *Child Development, 38,* 953–966. [11]

Keith, T., Keith, P., Quirk, K., Sperduto, J., Santillo, S. and Killings, S. (1998). Longitudinal effects of parent involvement on high school grades: Similarities and differences across gender and ethnic groups. *Journal of School Psychology, 36,* 335–363. [14]

Keller, M., and Edelstein, W. (1993). The development of the moral self from childhood to adolescence. In G. Noam and T. Wren (Eds.), *The moral self* (pp. 310–336). Cambridge, MA: MIT Press. [12]

Keller, M., Edelstein, W., Schmid, C., Fang, F., and Fang, G. (1998). Reasoning about responsibilities and obligations in close relationships: A comparison across two cultures. *Developmental Psychology, 34,* 731–741. [12]

Kellman, P. J., and Arterberry, M. E. (1998). *The cradle of knowledge: Development of perception in infancy.* Cambridge, MA: MIT Press. [4]

Kellman, P. J., and Banks, M. S. (1998). Infant visual perception. In W. Damon (Series Ed.), D. Kuhn, and R. S. Siegler (Vol. Eds.), *Handbook of child psychology: Vol. 2. Cognition, perception, and language* (5th ed., pp. 103–146). New York: Wiley. [4]

Kellman, P. J., and Spelke, E. S. (1983). Perception of partly occluded objects in infancy. *Cognitive Psychology, 15,* 483–524. [5]

Kelly, S. J., Day, N., and Streissguth, A. P. (2000). Effects of prenatal alcohol exposure on social behavior in humans and other species. *Neurotoxicology and teratology, 22,* 143–149. [3]

Kendall, P. (2000). Guiding theory for therapy with children and adolescents. In P. Kendall (Ed.) *Child and adolescent therapy: Cognitive-behavioral procedures* (2nd ed., pp. 3–27). [15]

Kerig, P. (1998). Moderators and mediators of the effects of interparental conflict on children's adjustment. *Journal of Abnormal Child Psychology, 26,* 199–212. [12]

Kerns, K. (1996). Individual differences in friendship quality: Links to child-mother attachment. In W. Bukowski, A. Newcomb, and W. Hartup (Eds.), *The company they keep: Friendship in childhood and adolescence* (pp. 137–157). New York: Cambridge University Press. [10]

Kerns, K., Tomich, P., Aspelmeier, J., and Contreras, J. (2000). Attachment-based assessments of parent-child relationships in middle childhood. *Developmental Psychology, 36,* 614–626. [12]

Kerr, M., and Stattin, H. (2000). What parents know, how they know it and several forms of adolescent adjustment: Further support for a reinterpretation of monitoring. *Developmental Psychology, 36,* 366–380. [14]

Kessen, W. (1965). *The child.* New York: Wiley. [2]

Kessen, W. (Ed.). (1975). *Childhood in China.* New Haven,: Yale University Press. [2]

Kestenbaum, R., Farber, E., and Sroufe, L. A. (1989). Individual differences in empathy among preschoolers: Concurrent and predictive validity. In N. Eisenberg (Ed.), *Empathy and related emotional responses: No. 44. New directions for child development* (pp. 51–56). San Francisco: Jossey-Bass. [10]

Kierkegaard, S. (1938). *Purity of heart is to will one thing.* New York: Harper and Row. [8]

Kilgore, K., Snyder, J., and Lentz, C. (2000). The contribution of parental discipline, parental monitoring, and school risk to early-onset conduct problems in African American boys and girls. *Developmental Psychology, 36,* 835–845. [10]

King, M. C., and Wilson, A. C. (1975). Evolution at two levels in humans and chimpanzees. *Science, 188,* 107–116. [2]

Kinney, D. A. (1993). From "nerds" to "normals": Adolescent identity recovery within a changing social system. *Sociology of Education, 66,* 21–40. [14]

Kinney, D. (1999). From "headbangers" to "hippies": Delineating adolescents' active attempts to form an alternative peer culture. In J. McLellan and M. Pugh (Eds.), *The role of peer groups in adolescent social identity: Exploring the importance of stability and change* (pp. 21–35). San Francisco: Jossey-Bass. [14]

Kisilevsky, B., Hains, S., Lee, K., Muir, D., Xu, F., Fu, G., Zhao, Z., and Yang, R. (1998). The still-face effect in Chinese and Canadian 3- to 6-month-old infants. *Developmental Psychology, 34,* 629–639. [6]

Kisilevsky, B. S., Muir, D. W., and Low, J. A. (1992). Maturation of human fetal responses to vibroacoustic stimulation. *Child Development, 63,* 1497–1508. [4]

Kitchener, R. F. (1983). Developmental explanations. *Review of Metaphysics, 36,* 791–817. [1]

Klahr, D., and MacWhinney, B. (1998). Information processing. In W. Damon (Series Ed.), D. Kuhn, and R. S. Siegler (Vol. Eds.), *Handbook of child psychology: Vol. 2. Cognition, perception, and language* (5th ed., pp. 631–678). New York: Wiley. [1]

Klahr, D., and Wallace, J. G. (1976). *Cognitive development: An information-processing view.* Hillsdale, NJ: Erlbaum. [1]

Klaus, M., and Kennell, J. (1976). *Maternal infant bonding.* St. Louis: Mosby. [6]

Klein, R. (1994). Anxiety disorders. In M. Rutter, E. Taylor, and L. Hersov (Eds.), *Child and adolescent psychiatry* (pp. 351–374). London: Blackwell. [15]

Klimes-Dougan, B., and Kopp, C. (1999). Children's conflict tactics with mothers: A longitudinal investigation of the toddler and preschool years. *Merrill-Palmer Quarterly, 45,* 226–241. [8], [10]

Kline, M., Tschann, J., Johnston, J., and Wallerstein, J. (1989). Children's adjustment in joint and sole custody families. *Developmental Psychology, 25,* 1–9. [2]

Knight, W. G., Mellins, C. A., Levenson, R. L., Arpadi, S. M., and Kairam, R. (2000). Brief report: Effects of pediatric HIV infection on mental and psychomotor development. *Journal of Pediatric Psychology, 25,* 583–587. [3]

Kochanska, G. (1993). Toward a synthesis of parental socialization and child temperament in early development of conscience. *Developmental Psychology, 64,* 325–347. [8], [10]

Kochanska, G. (1997). Multiple pathways to conscience for children with different temperaments: From toddlerhood to age 5. *Developmental Psychology, 33,* 228–240. [8], [10]

Kochanska, G., and Aksan, N. (1995). Mother-child mutually positive affect, the quality of child compliance to requests and prohibitions, and maternal control as correlates of early internalization. *Child Development, 66,* 236–254. [10]

Kochanska, G., Coy, K., and Murray, K. (2001). The development of self-regulation in the first four years of life. *Child Development, 72,* 1091–1111. [8], [10]

Kochanska, G., Murray, K., and Harlan, E. (2000). Effortful control in early childhood: Continuity and change, antecedents, and implications for social development. *Developmental Psychology, 36,* 220–232. [10]

Kohlberg, L. (1969). Stage and sequence: The cognitive-developmental approach to socialization. In D. A. Goslin (Ed.), *Handbook of socialization theory and research* (pp. 347–481). Chicago: Rand McNally. [13]

Kohlberg, L. (1976). Moral stages and moralization: Cognitive-developmental approach. In R. Lickona (Ed.), *Moral development and behavior: Theory, research, and social issues* (pp. 31–53). Chicago: Rand McNally. [13]

Konner, M. (1991). *Childhood: A multicultural view.* Boston: Little, Brown. [2], [3]

Kopp, C. (1992). Emotional distress and control in young children. In N. Eisenberg and R. Fabes (Eds.), *Emotion and its regulation in early development. New Directions for Child Development* (pp. 41–56). San Francisco: Jossey-Bass. [10]

Kopp, C., (in press). Self-regulation in childhood. In N. Eisenberg (Ed.), N. Smelser and P. Baltes (Series Eds.), *International encyclopedia of the behavioral and social sciences.* New York: Pergamon. [8]

Koren, G., Nulman, I., Rovet, J., Greenbaum, R., Loebstein, M., and Einarson, T. (1998). Long-term neurodevelopmental risks in children exposed in utero to cocaine: The Toronto Adoption Study. *Annals of the New York Academy of Sciences, 846,* 306–313. [3]

Korner, A. F. (1990). The many faces of touch. In Barnard, K. E., and Brazelton, T. B. (Eds.), *Touch: The foundation of experience* (pp. 269–297). Madison, CT: International Universities Press. [4]

Korner, A. F., Hutchinson, C., Kopershi, J., Kraemer, H., and Schneider, P. (1981). Stability of individual differences of neonatal motor and crying patterns. *Child Development, 52,* 83–90. [4]

Kraemer, G. (1992). A psychobiological theory of attachment. *Behavioral and Brain Sciences, 15,* 493–511. [6], [15]

Kramer, L., and Gottman, J. (1992). Becoming a sibling: "With a little help from my friends." *Developmental Psychology, 28,* 685–699. [10], [12]

Kreppner, K. (2002). Retrospect and prospect in the psychological study of families as systems. In McHale, J. P., and Grolnick, W. S. (Eds.) *Retrospect and prospect in the psychological study of families* (pp. 225–257). Mahwah, NJ: Erlbaum. [2]

Kreutzer, M. A., Leonard, C., and Flavell, J. H. (1975). An interview study of children's knowledge about memory. *Monographs of the Society for Research in Child Development, 40,* (1, Serial No. 159). [11]

Kroger, J. (2000). *Identity development: Adolescence through adulthood.* Thousand Oaks, CA: Sage. [14]

Kruttschnitt, C., Heath, L., and Ward, D. (1986). Family violence, television viewing habits, and other violent criminal behavior. *Criminology, 24,* 201–233. [15]

Kuczaj, S. (1982). Children's overextensions in comprehension and production: Support for a prototype theory of object word meaning acquisition. *First Language, 3,* 93–105.

Kuczynski, L., and Kochanska, G. (1990). Development of children's noncompliance strategies from toddlerhood to age 5. *Developmental Psychology, 26,* 398–408. [10]

Kuhl, P. K., Andruski, J. E., Chistovich, I. A., Chistovich, L. A., Kozhevnikova, E. V., Ryskina, V. L., Stoyarova, E. I., Sundberg, U., and Lacerda, F. (1997). Cross-language analysis of phonetic units in language addressed to infants. *Science, 277,* 684–686. [7]

Kuhn, D., Langer, J., Kohlberg, L., and Haan, N. (1977). The development of formal operations in logical and moral judgment. *Genetic Psychology Monographs, 95,* 97–188. [13]

Kupersmidt, J. B., Shahinfar, A., and Voegler-Lee, M. E. (2002). Children's exposure to community violence. In A. M. La Greca, W. K. Silverman, E. M. Vernberg, and M. C. Roberts (Eds.) *Helping children cope with disasters and terrorism* (pp. 381–401). Washington, DC: American Psychological Association. [2]

Kurdek, L. A., and Sinclair, R. J. (2001). Predicting reading and mathematics achievement in fourth-grade children from kindergarten readiness scores. *Journal of Educational Psychology, 93,* 451–455. [9]

Kurtines, W., and Greif, E. G. (1974). The development of moral thought: Review and evaluation of Kohlberg's approach. *Psychological Bulletin, 81,* 453–470. [13]

Ladd, G., and Burgess, K. (2001). Do relational risks and protective factors moderate the linkages between childhood aggression and early psychological and school adjustment? *Child Development, 72,* 1579–1601. [10], [12]

Ladd, G. W. (1983). Social networks of popular, average, and rejected children in school settings. *Merrill-Palmer Quarterly, 29,* 283–308. [12]

LaFreniere, P., and Dumas, J. (1995). *Social competence and behavioral evaluation.* Los Angeles: Western Psychological Services. [10]

Lamb, M. E. (Ed.) (1997). *The role of the father in child development* (3rd ed.). New York: Wiley. [2], [8]

Lamb, M. E. (1998). Nonparental child care: Context, quality, correlates, and consequences. In W. Damon (Series Ed.) and I. E. Sigel and K. A. Renninger (Vol. Eds.), *Handbook of child psychology: Vol. 4. Child psychology in practice* (5th ed., pp. 73–133). New York: Wiley. [2]

Landau, S., Lorch, E., and Milich, R. (1992). Visual attention to and comprehension of television in attention-deficit hyperactivity disordered and normal boys. *Child Development, 63,* 928–937. [15]

Landry, S., Smith, K., Swank, P., Assel, M., and Vellet, S. (2001). Does early responsive parenting have a special importance for children's development or is consistency across early childhood necessary? *Developmental Psychology, 37,* 387–403. [10]

Landry, S. H., Denson, S. E., and Swank, P. R. (1997). Effects of medical risk and socioeconomic status on the rate of change in cognitive and social development for low birth weight children. *Journal of Clinical and Experimental Neuropsychology, 19,* 261–274. [2]

Langlois, J., and Downs, A. (1980). Mothers, fathers, and peers as socialization agents of sex-typed play behaviors in young children. *Child Development, 51,* 1217–1247. [10]

Larsen, W. J. (2001). *Human embryology* (3rd ed.). New York: Churchill Livingstone. [3]

Larson, R., Moneta, G., Richards, M., and Wilson, S. (2002). Continuity, stability, and change in daily emotional experience across adolescence. *Child Development, 73,* 1151–1165. [14]

Laucht, M., Esser, G., and Schmidt, M. H. (2001). Differential development of infants at risk for psychopathology: The moderating role of early maternal responsivity. *Developmental Medicine and Child Neurology, 43,* 292–300. [2]

Laursen, B., Coy, K. C., and Collins, W. A. (1998). Reconsidering changes in parent-child conflict across adolescence: A meta-analysis. *Child Development, 69,* 817–832. [13], [14]

Laursen, B., Hartup, W. W., and Koplas, A. L. (1996). Towards understanding peer conflict. *Merrill-Palmer Quarterly, 42,* 76–102. [12]

Lazar, I., Darlington, R. B., Murray, H., Royce, J., and Snipper, A. (1982). Lasting effects of early education. *Monographs of the Society for Research in Child Development, 47* (2-3, Serial No. 195). [11]

Lazare, A. (1973). Hidden conceptual models in clinical psychiatry. *New England Journal of Medicine, 288,* 345–350. [15]

Leaper, C. (2000). Gender, affiliation, assertion, and the interactive context of parent-child play. *Developmental Psychology, 37,* 381–393. [10]

Lee, S.-Y., Graham, T., and Stevenson, H. W. (1996). Teachers and teaching: Elementary school in Japan and the United States. In T. P. Rohlen and G. K. LeTendre (Eds.), *Teaching and learning in Japan* (pp. 157–189). New York: Cambridge University Press. [11]

Lemons, J. A., Bauer, C. R., Oh, W., Korones, S. B., Papile, L. A., Stoll, B. J., Verter, J., Temprosa, M., Wright, L. L., Ehrenkranz, R. A., Fanaroff, A. A., Stark, A., Carlo, W., Tyson, J. E., Donovan, E. F., Shankaran, S., and Stevenson, D. K. (2001). Very low birth weight outcomes of the National Institute of Child Health and Human Development Neonatal Research Network, January 1995 through December 1996. *Pediatrics, 107,* E1. [3]

Lenneberg, E. (1967). *Biological foundations of language.* New York: Wiley. [2], [7]

Leon, G., and Phenan, P. (1985). Anorexia nervosa. In B. Lahey and A. Kazdin (Eds.), *Advances in clinical child psychology* (Vol. 8, pp. 81–113). New York: Plenum Press. [15]

Leonard, S., Msall, M., Bower, C., Tremont, M., and Leonard, H. (2002). Functional status of school-aged children with Down syndrome. *Journal of Paediatrics and Child Health, 38,* 160–165. [3]

Leslie, A. M. (1984). Spatiotemporal continuity and the perception of causality in infants. *Perception, 13,* 287–305. [5]

Lester, B. M., LaGasse, L. L., and Bigsby, R. (1998). Prenatal cocaine exposure and child development: What do we know and what do we do? *Seminars in Speech and Language, 19,* 123–146. [3]

Leventhal, T., and Brooks-Gunn, J. (2000). The neighborhoods they live in: The effects of neighborhood residence on child and adolescence outcomes. *Psychological Bulletin, 126,* 309–337. [2]

Leventhal, T., Graber, J. A., Brooks-Gunn, J. (2001). Adolescent transitions to young adulthood: Antecedents, correlates, and consequences of adolescent employment. *Journal of Research on Adolescence, 11,* 297–323. [14]

LeVine, R. A. (1988). Human parental care: Universal goals, cultural strategies, individual behavior. In R. A. LeVine, P. M. Miller, and M. M. West (Eds.), *Parental behavior in diverse societies* (pp. 3–12). San Francisco: Jossey-Bass. [2, 5]

Levy, A. K. (1999). *Continuities and discontinuities in parent-child relationships across two generations:*

A prospective, longitudinal study. Unpublished doctoral dissertation, University of Minnesota. [2]

Lewis, M. (1992). The self in self-conscious emotions. Commentary on Stipek et al. *Monographs of the Society for Research in Child Development, 57* (Serial No. 226), 85–95. [8], [10]

Lewis, M. (1997). *Altering fate.* New York: Guilford. [6], [8]

Lewis, M., Alessandri, S. M., and Sullivan, M. W. (1992). Differences in shame and pride as a function of children's gender and task difficulty. *Child Development, 63,* 630–638. [8], [10]

Lewis, M., and Brooks, J. (1978). Self-knowledge and emotional development. In M. Lewis and L. Rosenblum (Eds.), *The development of affect* (pp. 205–226). New York: Plenum Press. [8]

Liben, L., and Signorella, L. (1993). Gender-schematic processing in children: The role of initial interpretations of stimuli. *Developmental Psychology, 29,* 141–149. [12]

Liberman, A. M., Harris, K. S., Hoffman, H. S., and Griffith, B. C. (1957). The discrimination of speech sounds within and across phoneme boundaries. *Journal of Experimental Psychology, 54,* 358–368. [4]

Lieberman, A. F. (1977). Preschoolers' competence with a peer: Relations with attachment and peer experience. *Child Development, 48,* 1277–1287. [10]

Lieberman, P. (1984). *The biology and evolution of language.* Cambridge, MA: Harvard University Press. [7]

Lillard, A. S. (1993). Pretend play skills and the child's theory of mind. *Child Development, 64*(2), 348–371. [10]

Linn, M. C., Songer, N. B., and Eylon, B.-S. (1996). Shifts and convergences in science learning and instruction. In D. C. Berliner and R. C. Calfee (Eds.), *Handbook of educational psychology* (pp. 438–490). New York: Macmillan. [13]

Lipsitt, L. P. (1990). Learning and memory in infants. *Merrill-Palmer Quarterly, 36,* 53–66. [4]

Little, T., Oettingen, G., Stetsenko, A., and Baltes, P. (1995). Children's action-control beliefs about school performance: How do American children compare with German and Russian children? *Journal of Personality and Social Psychology, 69,* 686–700. [14]

Livson, N., and Peskin, H. (1980). Perspectives on adolescence from longitudinal research. In J. Adelson (Ed.), *Handbook of adolescent psychology* (pp. 47–98). New York: Wiley. [13]

Lobel, M. (1994). Conceptualizations, measurement, and effects of prenatal maternal stress on birth outcomes. *Journal of Behavioral Medicine, 17,* 225–272. [3]

Lock, A., Young, A., Service, V., and Chandler, P. (1990). Some observations on the origins of the pointing gesture. In V. Volterra and C. J. Erting (Eds.), *From gesture to language in hearing and deaf children* (pp. 42–55). New York: Springer. [7]

Locke, J. L., and Pearson, D. M. (1992). Vocal learning and the emergence of phonological capacity: A neurobiological approach. In C. A. Ferguson, L. Menn, and S. Stoel-Gammon (Eds.), *Phonological development* (pp. 91–129). Timonium, MD: York Press. [7]

Lollis, S. (1990). Maternal influence on children's separation behavior. *Child Development, 61,* 99–103. [8]

Lollis, S., and Ross, H. (1992). Parents' regulation of children's peer interactions: Direct influences. In R. D. Parke and G. W. Ladd (Eds.), *Family-peer relationships: Modes of linkage* (pp. 255–281). Hillsdale, NJ: Erlbaum. [12]

Londerville, S., and Main, M. (1981). Security of attachment, compliance, and maternal training methods in the second year of life. *Developmental Psychology, 17,* 289–299. [8]

Lord, C., and Rutter, M. (1994). Autism and pervasive developmental disorders. In M. Rutter, E. Taylor, and L. Hersov (Eds.), *Child and adolescent psychiatry* (pp. 569–593). Oxford, Eng.: Blackwell. [15]

Luria, A. R. (1961). *The role of speech in the regulation of normal and abnormal behavior.* New York: Pergamon Press. [10]

Lwin, R., and Melvin, D. (2001). Paediatric HIV infection. *Journal of Child Psychology and Psychiatry and Allied Disciplines, 42,* 427–438. [3]

Lynn, R. (1982). IQ in Japan and the United States shows a growing disparity. *Nature, 297,* 222–223. [11]

Lyons-Ruth, K., Connell, D. B., Grunebaum, H. U., and Botein, S. (1990). Infants at social risk: Maternal depression and family support services as mediators of infant development and security of attachment. *Child Development, 61,* 85–98. [6]

Maccoby, E. E. (1980). *Social development.* New York: Harcourt Brace Jovanovich. [10], [12]

Maccoby, E. (1990). Gender and relationships. *American Psychologist, 45,* 513–520. [10], [12]

Maccoby, E. E. (1992). The role of parents in the socialization of children: An historical overview. *Developmental Psychology, 28,* 1006–1017. [8]

Maccoby, E. G., and Jacklin, C. N. (1974). *The psychology of sex differences.* Stanford, CA: Stanford University Press.

Maccoby, E. E., and Martin, J. A. (1983). Socialization in the context of the family: Parent-child interaction. In P. H. Mussen (Series Ed.) and E. M. Hetherington (Vol. Ed.), *Handbook of child psychology: Vol. 4. Socialization, personality, and social development* (4th ed., pp. 1–101). New York: Wiley. [12]

MacFarlane, A. (1975). Olfaction in the development of social preferences in the human neonate. *Parent-infant interaction. CIBA Foundation Symposium 33.* Amsterdam: CIBA Foundation. [4]

Mackinnon-Lewis, C., Volling, B., Lamb, M., Dechman, K., Rabiner, D., and Curtner, M. (1994). A cross-contextual analysis of boys' social competence: From family to school. *Developmental Psychology, 30,* 325–333. [12]

Madden-Derdich, D., and Leonard, S. (2001). Parent-child relationships: The moderating influence between interparental conflict and child adjustment. Poster presented at the biennial meeting of the Society for Research in Child Development, Minneapolis, MN. [12]

Madsen, K. M., Hviid, A., Vestergaard, M., Schendel, D., Wohlfahrt, J., Thorsen, P., Olsen, J., and

Melbye, M. (2002). A population-based study of measles, mumps, and rubella vaccination and autism. *New England Journal of Medicine, 347,* 1477–1482. [15]

Madsen, M. (1971). Development and cross-cultural differences in cooperative and competitive behavior of young children. *Journal of Cross-Cultural Psychology, 2,* 365–371. [2]

Mahler, M., Pine, R., and Bergman, A. (1975). *The psychological birth of the human infant.* New York: Basic Books. [8]

Mahoney, J., and Stattin, H. (2000). Leisure activities and antisocial behavior: The role of structure and social context. *Journal of Adolescence, 23,* 113–127. [14]

Main, M. (1991). Metacognitive knowledge, metacognitive monitoring, and singular (coherent) vs. multiple (incoherent) models of attachment: Findings and directions for future research. In C. M. Parkes, J. Stevenson-Hinde, and P. Marris (Eds.), *Attachment across the life cycle* (pp. 127–159). New York: Routledge. [6]

Main, M., and Hesse, E. (1990). Parents' unresolved traumatic experiences are related to infant disorganized attachment status: Is frightened and/or frightening parental behavior the linking mechanism? In M. T. Greenberg, D. Cicchetti, and E. M. Cummings (Eds.), *Attachment in the preschool years* (pp. 161–182). Chicago: University of Chicago Press. [6], [10]

Main, M., and Solomon, J. (1990). Procedures for identifying infants as disorganized/ disoriented during the Ainsworth Strange Situation. In M. T. Greenberg, D. Cicchetti, and E. M. Cummings (Eds.), *Attachment in the preschool years* (pp. 121–160). Chicago: University of Chicago Press. [6]

Mandler, J. M. (1998). Representation. In W. Damon (Series Ed.), D. Kuhn, and R. S. Siegler (Vol. Eds.), *Handbook of child psychology: Vol. 2. Cognition, perception, and language* (5th ed., pp. 255–308). New York: Wiley. [5]

Mandler, J. M., and McDonough, L. (1993). Concept formation in infancy. *Cognitive Development, 8,* 291–318. [5]

Mandler, J. M., and McDonough, L. (1995). Long-term recall of event sequences in infancy. *Journal of Experimental Child Psychology, 59,* 457–474. [5]

Mandler, J. M., and McDonough, L. (1996). Drinking and driving don't mix: Inductive generalization in infancy. *Cognition, 59,* 307–355. [5]

Mangelsdorf, S., Gunnar, M., Kestenbaum, R., Lang, S., and Andreas, D. (1990). Infant proneness-to-distress temperament, maternal personality, and mother-infant attachment: Associations and goodness of fit. *Child Development 61,* 820–831. [6]

Manis, F. R., Keating, D. P., and Morrison, F. J. (1980). Developmental differences in the allocation of processing capacity. *Journal of Experimental Child Psychology, 29,* 156–169. [13]

Mans, L., Cicchetti, D., and Sroufe, L. A. (1978). Mirror reactions of Down syndrome infants and toddlers: Cognitive underpinnings of self-recognition. *Child Development, 49,* 1247–1250. [1]

Maratsos, M. (1998). The acquisition of grammar. In W. Damon (Series Ed.), D. Kuhn, and R. S. Siegler (Vol. Eds.), *Handbook of child psychology: Vol. 2.*

Cognition, perception, and language (5th ed., pp. 421–466). New York: Wiley. [7]

Marcia, J. (1980). Identity in adolescence. In J. Adelson (Ed.), *Handbook of adolescent psychology* (pp. 159–187). New York: Wiley. [14]

Marcia, J. E., Waterman, A. S., Matteson, D. R., Archer, S. L., and Orlofsky, J. L. (1993). *Ego identity: A handbook for psychosocial research.* New York: Springer-Verlag. [14]

Marcus, G. F. (1995). Children's overregularization of English plurals: A quantitative analysis. *Journal of Child Language, 22,* 447–460. [7]

Marcus, G. F., Pinker, S., Ullman, M., Hollander, M., Rosen, T. J., and Xu, F. (1992). Overregularization in language acquisition. *Monographs of the Society for Research in Child Development, 57* (4, Serial No. 228). [7]

Marcus, G. F., Vijayan, S., Bandi Rao, S., and Vishton, P. M. (1999). Rule learning by seven-month-old infants. *Science, 283,* 77–80. [7]

Markman, E. M. (1979). Classes and collections: Conceptual organization and numerical abilities. *Cognitive Psychology, 11,* 395–411. [11]

Markman, E. M. (1987). How children constrain the possible meanings of words. In U. Neisser (Ed.), *Concepts and conceptual development: Ecological and intellectual factors in categorization* (pp. 255–287). Cambridge, England: Cambridge University Press. [7]

Markman, E. M., and Siebert, J. (1976). Classes and collections: Principles of organization in the learning of hierarchical relations. *Cognition, 8,* 227–241. [11]

Markstrom-Adams, C. (1992). A consideration of intervening factors in adolescent identity formation. In G. Adams, T. Gullotta, and R. Montemayor (Eds.), *Adolescent identity formation* (pp. 173–192). Newbury Park, CA: Sage. [14]

Martin, J. A., Park, M. M., and Sutton, P. D. (2002). *Births: Preliminary data for 2001.* National Vital Statistics Reports, 50(10). Hyattsville, MD: National Center for Health Statistics. [3]

Markus, H., and Nurius, P. S. (1984).

Marvin, R., and Pianta, R. (1992). Relationship-based approaches to assessment of children with motor impairments. *Infants and Young Children, 4,* 33–45. [6]

Marvinney, D. (1988). *Sibling relationships in middle childhood: Implications for social-emotional development.* Unpublished doctoral dissertation, University of Minnesota, Minneapolis. [12]

Mash, E., and Wolfe, D. (2002). *Abnormal child psychology* (2nd ed.) New York: Wadsworth. [15]

Masten, A. (2001). Ordinary magic: Resilience processes in development. *American Psychologist, 56,* 1–12. [10]

Masten, A. S., and Coatsworth, D. (1995). Competence, resilience, and psychopathology. In D. Cicchetti and D. Cohen (Eds.), *Developmental processes and psychopathology* (Vol. 1, pp. 715–752). New York: Cambridge University Press. [15]

Masten, A. S., Miliotis, D., Graham-Bermann, S. A., Ramirez, M., and Neemann, J. (1993). Children in homeless families: Risks to mental health and development. *Journal of Consulting and Clinical Psychology, 61,* 335–343. [2]

Masten, A., Morison, P., Pellegrini, D., and Tellegen, A. (1990). Competence under stress: Risk and protective factors. In J. Rolf, A. Masten, D. Cicchetti, K. Neuchterlein, and S. Weintraub (Eds.), *Risk and protective factors in the development of psychopathology* (pp. 236–256). Cambridge, England: Cambridge University Press. [2]

Matas, L., Arend, R., and Sroufe, L. A. (1978). Continuity of adaptation in the second year: The relationship between quality of attachment and later competence. *Child Development, 49,* 547–556. [2], [8]

Matheny, A., Riese, M., and Wilson, R. (1985). Rudiments of infant temperament: Newborn to 9 months. *Developmental Psychology, 21,* 486–494. [4]

Matthews, A., Ellis, A. E., and Nelson, C. A. (1996). Development of pre-term and full-term infant ability of AB, recall memory, transparent barrier detour, and means-ends tasks. *Child Development, 67,* 2658–2676. [5]

Mattson, S. N., and Riley, E. P. (1998). A review of the neurobehavioral deficits in children with fetal alcohol syndrome or prenatal exposure to alcohol. *Alcohol Clinical and Experimental Research, 22,* 279–294. [3]

Maurer, D., and Lewis, T. L. (2001). Visual acuity and spatial contrast sensitivity: Normal development and underlying mechanisms. In C. A. Nelson and M. Luciana (Eds.), *Handbook of developmental cognitive neuroscience* (pp. 237–251). Cambridge, MA: MIT Press. [4]

Maurer, D., and Maurer, C. (1988). *The world of the newborn.* New York: Basic Books. [4]

Maurer, D., and Salapatek, P. (1976). Developmental changes in the scanning of faces by young infants. *Child Development, 47,* 523–527. [4]

Masur, E. F. (1990). Gestural development, dual-directional signaling, and the transition to words. In V. Volterra and C. J. Erting (Eds.), *From gesture to language in hearing and deaf children* (pp. 18–30). New York: Springer. [7]

Masur, E., and Gleason, J. B. (1980). Parent-child interaction and the acquisition of lexical information during play. *Developmental Psychology, 16,* 404–409. [7]

McAdoo, H. P. (2002). African American parenting. In M. H. Bornstein (Ed.), *Handbook of parenting: Vol. 4. Social conditions and applied parenting* (2nd ed., pp. 47–58). Mahwah, NJ: Erlbaum. [2]

McAninch, C., Manolis, M., Milich, R., and Harris, M. (1993). Impression formation in children: Influence of gender and expectancy. *Child Development, 64,* 1492–1506. [12]

McCall, R. B. (1977). Childhood IQs as predictors of adult educational and occupational status. *Science, 197,* 482–483. [11]

McCall, R. B. (1981). Nature-nurture and the two realms of development: A proposed integration with respect to mental development. *Child Development, 52,* 1–12. [2]

McCall, R. B., and Carriger, M. S. (1993). A meta-analysis of infant habituation and recognition memory performance as predictors of later IQ. *Child Development, 64,* 57–79. [5]

McClelland, M. M., Morrison, F. J., and Holmes, D. L. (2000). Children at risk for early academic problems: The roles of learning-related social skills. *Early Childhood Research Quarterly, 15,* 307–329. [9]

McCrone, E., Egeland, B., Kalkoske, M., and Carlson, E. (1994). Relations between early maltreatment and mental representations of relationships assessed with projective story telling in middle childhood. *Development and Psychopathology, 6,* 99–120. [12]

McCune, L. (1995). A normative study of representational play in the transition to language. *Developmental Psychology, 31,* 198–206. [7]

McDonald, K. (1988). *Sociobiological perspectives on human development.* New York: Springer-Verlag, Inc. [12]

McDonald, S. D., Ferguson, S., Tam, L., Lougheed, J., and Walker, M. C. (2003). The prevention of congenital anomalies with periconceptional folic acid supplementation. *Journal of obstetrics and gynaecology Canada, 25,* 115–121. [3]

McGhee, P. E. (1976). Children's appreciation of humor: A test of the cognitive congruency principle. *Child Development, 47,* 420–426. [11]

McGuffin, P., Riley, B., and Plomin, R. (2001). Toward behavioral genomics. *Science, 291,* 1232–1249. [1]

McGuinness, D. (1989). Attention deficit disorder: The emperor's new clothes, animal "pharm," and other fiction. In S. Fisher and R. Greenberg (Eds.), *The limits of biological treatments for psychological distress: Comparisons with psychotherapy and placebo* (pp. 151–187). Hillsdale, NJ: Erlbaum. [15]

McHale, S. M., and Crouter, A. C. (1996). The family contexts of children's sibling relationships. In G. H. Brody (Ed.), *Sibling relationships: Their causes and consequences* (pp. 173–195). Norwood, NJ: Ablex. [2]

McHale, S., Updegraff, K., Helms-Erickson, H., and Crouter, A. (2001). Sibling influences on gender development in middle childhood and early adolescence: A longitudinal study. *Developmental Psychology, 37,* 115–125. [12]

McKenzie, B. E., Skouteris, H., Day, R. H., Hartman, B., and Yonas, A. (1993). Effective action by infants to contact objects by reaching and leaning. *Child Development, 64,* 415–429. [4]

McKinney, W. (1977). Animal behavioral/biological models relevant to depression and affective disorders in humans. In J. Schulterbrandt and A. Raskin (Eds.), *Depression in childhood.* New York: Raven Press. [15]

McLoyd, V. (1990). The impact of economic hardship on black families and children: Psychological distress, parenting, and socioemotional development. *Child Development, 61,* 311–346. [2]

McLoyd, V. (1998). Children in poverty: Development, public policy, and practice. In W. Damon (Series Ed.) and I. E. Sigel and K. A. Renninger (Vol. Eds.), *Handbook of child psychology: Vol. 4. Child psychology in practice* (5th ed., pp. 135–208). New York: Wiley. [2], [15]

McLoyd, V., Jayaratne, T. E., Ceballo, R., and Borquez, J. (1994). Unemployment and work interruption among African American single mothers: Effects on parenting and adolescent socioemotional functioning. *Child Development, 65,* 562–589. [2]

McMillan, J. A., DeAngelis, C. D., Feigin, R. D., and Warshaw, J. B. (Eds.). (1999). *Oski's pediatrics: Principles and practice* (3rd ed.). Philadelphia: Lippincott-Williams and Wilkins. [3]

Mead, M. (1925/1939). *Coming of age in Samoa.* New York: William Morrow. [8], [14]

Medical Research Council (2002). Autism Web Site. http://www.mrc.ac.uk/index/public-interest/public-topical_issues/public-autism_main_section [3]

Meisels, S. J. (1999). Assessing readiness. In R. C. Pianta and M. J. Cox (Eds.), *The transition to kindergarten* (pp. 39–66). Baltimore, MD: Paul H. Brookes. [2], [9]

Melson, G. F., Ladd, G. W., and Hsu, H. (1993). Maternal support networks, maternal cognitions, and young children's social and cognitive development. *Child Development, 64*(5), 1401–1417. [10]

Meltzoff, A. N. (1988). Infant imitation and memory: Nine-month-olds in immediate and deferred tests. *Child Development, 59,* 217–225. [5]

Meltzoff, A. N., and Moore, M. K. (1977). Imitation of facial and manual gestures by human neonates. *Science, 198,* 75–78. [4]

Meltzoff, A. N., and Moore, M. K. (1989). Imitation in newborn infants: Exploring the range of gestures imitated and the underlying mechanisms. *Developmental Psychology, 25,* 954–962. [6]

Meltzoff, A. N., and Moore, M. K. (1999). Persons and representation: Why infant imitation is important for theories of human development. In J. Nadel and G. Butterworth (Eds.), *Imitation in infancy* (pp. 9–35). [4]

Mendelson, M. J. (1990). *Becoming a brother: A child learns about life, family, and self.* Cambridge, MA: MIT Press. [2]

Menig-Peterson, C. L. (1975). The modification of communicative behavior in preschool-aged children as a function of the listener's perspective. *Child Development, 46,* 1015–1018. [9]

Menn, L., and Stoel-Gammon, C. (1993). Phonological development: Learning sounds and sound patterns. In J. B. Gleason (Ed.), *The development of language* (pp. 65–113). New York: Macmillan. [7]

Merriman, W. E. (1986). Some reasons for the occurrence and eventual correction of children's naming errors. *Child Development, 57,* 942–952. [7]

Mick, E., Biederman, J., Faraone, S. V., Sayer, J., and Kleinman, S. (2002). Case-control study of attention-deficit hyperactivity disorder and maternal smoking, alcohol use, and drug use during pregnancy. *Journal of the American Academy of Child and Adolescent Psychiatry, 41,* 378–385. [3]

Milewski, A. E. (1978). Young infants' visual processing of internal and adjacent shapes. *Infant Behavior and Development, 1,* 359–371. [4]

Miller, G. A. (1981). *Language and speech.* San Francisco: Freeman. [7]

Miller, K. (1984). Child as the measure of all things: Measurement procedures and the development of quantitative concepts. In C. Sophian (Ed.), *Origins of cognitive skills.* Hillsdale, NJ: Erlbaum. [9]

Miller, K. F., Smith, C. M., Zhu, J., and Zhang, H. (1995). Preschool origins of cross-national differences in mathematical competence: The role of number naming systems. *Psychological Science, 6,* 56–60. [9]

Miller, P. H. (1985). Metacognition and attention. In D. L. Forest, M. Pressley, G. E. MacKinnon, and T. G. Waller (Eds.), *Metacognition, cognition, and human performance* (Vol. 2). New York: Academic Press. [9]

Miller, P. H. (1990). The development of strategies of selective attention. In D. F. Bjorklund (Ed.), *Children's strategies: Contemporary views of cognitive development.* Hillsdale, NJ: Erlbaum. [9]

Miller, P. H., and Harris, Y. R. (1990). Preschoolers' strategies of attention on a same-different task. *Developmental Psychology, 24,* 628–633. [9]

Miller-Jones, D. (1989). Culture and testing. *American Psychologist, 44,* 360–366. [11]

Mindell, J. A. (1993). Normal sleep patterns in infancy. In M. A. Carskadon (Ed.), *Encyclopedia of sleep and dreaming* (pp. 302–304). New York: Macmillan. [4]

Minuchin, P. (1988). Relationships within the family: A systems perspective on development. In Robert A. Hinde and J. Stevenson-Hinde (Eds.), *Relationships within families: Mutual influences* (pp. 7–26). Oxford, England: Oxford University Press. [2], [10]

Minuchin, S., Rosman, B., and Baker, L. (1978). *Psychosomatic anorexia nervosa in context.* Cambridge, MA: Harvard University Press. [15]

Mischel, H., and Mischel, W. (1983). The development of children's knowledge of self-control strategies. *Child Development, 54,* 603–619. [8]

Mischel, W., Shoda, Y., and Rodriguez, M. (1989). Delay of gratification in children. *Science, 244,* 933–937. [10], [12]

Mittendorf, R. (1995). Teratogen update: Carcinogenesis and teratogenesis associated with exposure to diethylstilbestrol (DES) in utero. *Teratology, 51,* 435–445. [3]

Mix, K. S., Huttenlocher, J., and Levine, S. C. (2002). Multiple cues for quantification in infancy: Is number one of them? *Psychological Bulletin, 128,* 278–294. [5]

Mize, J., and Ladd, G. (1990). A cognitive-social learning approach to social skill training with low-status preschool children. *Developmental Psychology, 26,* 388–398. [10]

Moffitt, T. (1993). Adolescent-limited and life-course-persistent antisocial behavior: A developmental taxonomy. *Psychological Review, 100,* 674–701. [15]

Moffitt, T. E., Caspi, A., Belsky, J., and Silva, P. A. (1992). Childhood experience and the onset of menarche: A test of a sociobiological model. *Child Development, 63,* 47–58. [13]

Molitor, N., Joffe, L., Barglow, P., Benveniste, R., and Vaughn, B. (1984, April). *Biochemical and psychological antecedents of newborn performance on the Neonatal Behavioral Assessment Scale.* Paper presented at the International Conference on Infant Studies, New York. [6]

Money, J., and Ehrhardt, A. A. (1972). *Man and woman, boy and girl.* Baltimore: Johns Hopkins University Press. [3]

Montemayor, R., Adams, G., and Gullotta, T. (Eds.). (1990). *From childhood to adolescence.* Newbury Park, CA: Sage. [14]

Montemayor, R., and Hanson, E. (1985). A naturalistic view of conflict between adolescents and their parents and siblings. *Journal of Early Adolescence, 5,* 23– 30. [14]

Montgomery, D. E. (1993). Young children's understanding of interpretive diversity between different-aged listeners. *Developmental Psychology, 29,* 337–345. [9]

Moore, K. L. (1974). *Before we are born.* Philadelphia: Saunders. [3]

Morelli, G. A., Rogoff, B., Oppenheim, D., and Goldsmith, D. (1992). Cultural variation in infants' sleeping arrangements: Questions of independence. Developmental Psychology, 28, 604–613. [2], [4], [6]

Morford, J. P. (1998). Gesture when there is no speech model. In J. M. Iverson and S. Goldin-Meadow (Eds.), *The nature and function of gesture in children's communication. New Directions for Child Development,* No. 79 (pp. 101–116). San Francisco: Jossey-Bass. [7]

Morgan, B., and Gibson, K. R. (1991). Nutrition and environmental interactions in brain development. In Gibson, K. R., and Petersen, A. C. (Eds.), *Brain maturation and cognitive development: Comparative and cross-cultural perspectives* (pp. 91–106). New York: Aldine De Gruyter. [4]

Morgan, J. L., and Travis, L. L. (1989). Limits on negative information in language input. *Journal of Child Language, 16,* 531–552. [7]

Morrongiello, B. A., and Rocca, P. T. (1990). Infants' localization of sounds within hemifields: estimates of minimum audible angle. *Child Development, 61,* 1258–1270. [4]

Moses, L., Baldwin, D., Rosicky, J., and Tidball, G. (2001).Evidence for referential understanding in the emotions domain at twelve and eighteen months. *Child Development, 72,* 718–735. [8]

Moses, L. J., and Flavell, J. H. (1990). Inferring false beliefs from actions and reactions. *Child Development, 61,* 929– 945. [9]

Moshman, D. (1998). Cognitive development beyond childhood. In W. Damon (Series Ed.), D. Kuhn, and R. S. Siegler (Vol. Eds.), *Handbook of child psychology: Vol. 2. Cognition, perception, and language* (5th ed., pp. 947–978). New York: Wiley. [13]

Moshman, D. (1999). *Adolescent psychological development: Rationality, morality, identity.* Mahwah, NJ: Erlbaum. [14]

Moshman, D., and Timmons, M. (1982). The construction of logical necessity. *Human Development, 25,* 309–323. [11]

Msall, M. E., Bier, J. A., LaGasse, L., Tremont, M., and Lester, B. (1998). The vulnerable preschool child: The impact of biomedical and social risks on neurodevelopmental function. *Seminars in Pediatric Neurology, 5,* 52–61. [3]

Mueller, C., and Dweck, C. (1998). Praise for intelligence can undermine children's motivation and performance. *Journal of Personality and Social Psychology, 75,* 33–52. [12]

Mueller, E., and Lucas, T. (1975). A developmental analysis of peer interaction among toddlers. In M. Lewis and L. A. Rosenblum (Eds.), *Friendship and peer relations* (pp. 223–257). New York: Wiley. [10]

Mugny, G., Perret-Clermont, A. N., and Doise, W. (1981). Interpersonal coordinations and sociological differences in the construction of the intellect. In G. M. Stephenson and J. M. Davis (Eds.), *Progress in applied social psychology* (Vol. 1, pp. 315–343). New York: Wiley. [11]

Mullen, P., Martin, J., Anderson, S., Romans, S., and Herbison, G. (1996). The long-term impact of the physical, emotional, and sexual abuse of children: A community study. *Child Abuse and Neglect, 20,* 7–21. [8]

Murray, F. B. (1972). The acquisition of conservation through social interaction. *Developmental Psychology, 6,* 1–6. [11]

Myers, N. A., Clifton, R. K., and Clarkson, M. G. (1987). When they were very young: Almost threes remember two years ago. *Infant Behavior and Development, 10,* 123–132. [5]

Myles-Worsley, M., Cromer, C. C., and Dodd, D. H. (1986). Children's preschool script construction: Reliance on general knowledge as memory fades. *Developmental Psychology, 22,* 22–30. [9]

Nachman, S. A., Lindsey, J. C., Pelton, S., Mofenson, L., McIntosh, K., Wiznia, A., Stanley, K., and Yogev, R. (2002). Growth in human immunodeficiency virus-infected children receiving ritonavir-containing antiretroviral therapy. *Archives of pediatrics and adolescent medicine, 156,* 497–503. [3]

Nachmias, M., Gunnar, M., Mangelsdorf, S., Parritz, R. H., and Buss, K. (1996). Behavioral inhibition and stress reactivity: The moderating role of attachment security. *Child Development, 67,* 508–522. [8]

Nakagawa, M., Teti, D., and Lamb, M. (1992). An ecological study of child-mother attachments among Japanese sojourners in the United States. *Developmental Psychology, 28,* 584–592. [10]

Nassogne, M. C., Gressens, P., Evrard, P., and Courtoy, P. J. (1998). In contrast to cocaine, prenatal exposure to methadone does not produce detectable alternations in the developing mouse brain. *Brain Research. Developmental Brain Research, 110,* 61–67. [3]

National Association for the Education of Young Children. (1998). *Accreditation criteria and procedures of the national association for the education of young children—1998 edition.* Washington, DC: NAEYC. [2]

National Center for Education Statistics (NCES). (1993). *Fast response survey system: Kindergarten teacher survey on student readiness.* Washington, DC: U.S. Department of Education. [9]

National Research Council. (1993). *Understanding child abuse and neglect.* Washington, DC: National Academy Press. [8]

National Research Council (1998). *Protecting youth at work: Health, safety, and development of working children and adolescents in the United States.* Washington, DC: National Academy Press. [14]

Needham, A., and Baillargeon, R. (1993). Intuitions about support in 4.5-month-old infants. *Cognition, 47,* 121–148. [5]

Neimark, E. D. (1982). Adolescent thought: Transition to formal operations. In B. B. Wolman and G.

Strickler (Eds.), *Handbook of developmental psychology* (pp. 486–502). Englewood Cliffs, NJ: Prentice-Hall. [13]

Neisser, U. (1986). *The school achievement of minority children: New perspectives.* Hillsdale, NJ: Erlbaum. [11]

Nelson, C. (1994). The neural bases of infant temperament. In J. Bates and T. Wachs (Eds.), *Temperament: Individual differences at the interface of biology and behavior.* (pp. 47–82) Washington DC: American Psychological Association Press. [6]

Nelson, C. A. (1995). The ontogeny of human memory: A cognitive neuroscience perspective. *Developmental Psychology, 31,* 723–738. [5]

Nelson, C. A. (1998). The nature of early memory. *Preventive Medicine, 27,* 172–179. [5]

Nelson, K. (1973). Structure and strategy in learning to talk. *Monographs of the Society for Research in Child Development, 38*(1 and 2, Serial No. 149). [7]

Nelson, K. (1985). *Making sense: The acquisition of shared meaning.* New York: Academic Press. [7]

Nelson, K. (1993). The psychological and social origins of autobiographical memory. *Psychological Science, 4,* 7–14. [5]

Nelson, K., and Gruendel, J. (1979). At morning it's lunchtime: A scriptal view of children's dialogues. *Discourse Processes, 2,* 73–94. [9]

Nelson, K., and Ross, G. (1980). The generalities and specifics of long-term memory in infants and young children. In M. Perlmutter (Ed.), *New directions for child development: No. 10. Children's memory* (pp. 87–101). San Francisco: Jossey-Bass. [5]

Nelson-LeGall, S., and Jones, E. (1990). Cognitive-motivational influences on the task-related, help-seeking behavior of black children. *Child Development, 61,* 581–589. [12]

New, R. S. (1988). Parental goals and Italian infant care. In R. A. LeVine, P. M. Miller, and M. M. West (Eds.), *Parental behavior in diverse societies. New Directions for Child Development* (No. 40, pp. 51–63). [7]

Newcombe, N., Dubas, J. S., and Baenninger, M. (1989). Associations of timing of puberty, spatial ability, and lateralization in adult women. *Child Development, 60,* 246–254. [13]

Newell, A., and Simon, H. A. (1961). Computer simulation of human thinking. *Science, 134,* 2011–2017. [1]

Newell, M. L., and Gibb, D. M. (1995). A risk-benefit assessment of zidovudine in the prevention of perinatal HIV transmission. *Drug Safety, 12,* 274–282. [3]

Newman, C. G. H. (1986). The thalidomide syndrome: Risks of exposure and spectrum of malformations. *Clinics in Perinatology, 13,* 555–573. [3]

Newmann, F. M. (1991). Higher order thinking in the teaching of social studies: Connections between theory and practice. In J. Voss, D. Perkins, and J. Segal (Eds.), *Informal reasoning and education* (pp. 381–400). Hillsdale, NJ: Erlbaum. [13]

Newport, E. L. (1988). Constraints on learning and their role in language acquisition. *Language Sciences, 10,* 147–172. [7]

Newport, E. L. (1990). Maturational constraints on language learning. *Cognitive Science, 14,* 11–28. [7]

Newport, E. L., Gleitman, H., and Gleitman, L. R. (1977). Mother, I'd rather do it myself: Some effects and noneffects of maternal speech style. In C. E. Snow and C. A. Furguson (Eds.), *Talking to children: Language input and acquisition.*(pp. 109–150) Cambridge, England: Cambridge University Press. [7]

NICHD Early Child Care Research Network (1997). The effects of infant child care on infant-mother attachment security: Results of the NICHD study of early child care. *Child Development, 68,* 860–879. [6]

NICHD Early Child Care Research Network. (2001). Nonmaternal care and family factors in early development: An overview of the NICHD Study of Early Child Care. *Journal of Applied Developmental Psychology, 22,* 457–492. [2], [6]

Nordhaus, B., and Solnit, A. (1990). Adoption, 1990. *Zero to three. National Center for Clinical Infant Programs, 10,* No. 5, 1–4. [6]

Norton, A. J., and Glick, P. C. (1986). One parent families: A social and economic profile. *Family Relations, 35,* 9–18. [2]

Novak, M., O'Neill, P., Beckley, S., and Suomi, S. (1992). Naturalistic environments for captive primates. In E. Gibbons, E. Wyers, and E. Waters (Eds.), *Naturalistic habitats in captivity.* (pp.236–258). New York: Academic Press. [6]

Nucci, L., Camino, C., and Sapiro, C. (1996). Social class effects on Northeastern Brazilian children's conceptions of areas of personal choice. *Child Development, 67,* 1223–1242. [14]

Nussbaum, R. L., McInnes, R. R., and Huntington, F. W. (2001). *Thompson and Thompson genetics in medicine* (6th ed.). Philadelphia: Saunders. [3]

Nyitii, R. M. (1982). The validity of cultural differences explanations for cross-cultural variation in the rate of Piagetian cognitive development. In D. A. Wagner and H. W. Stevenson (Eds.), *Cultural perspectives on child development* (pp. 146–165). San Francisco: Freeman. [11]

Oakes, L. M. (1994). The development of infants' use of continuity cues in their perception of causality. *Developmental Psychology, 30,* 869–879. [5]

Oakes, L. M., and Cohen, L. B. (1990). Infant perception of a causal event. *Cognitive Development, 5,* 193–207. [5]

O'Callaghan, M. F., Borkowski, J. G., Whitman, T. L., Maxwell, S. E., and Keogh, D. (1999). A model of adolescent parenting: The role of cognitive readiness to parent. *Journal of Research on Adolescence, 9,* 203–225. [2]

O'Connor, B. P., and Nikolic, J. (1990). Identity development and formal operations as sources of adolescent egocentrism. *Journal of Youth and Adolescence, 19,* 149–158. [13]

O'Connor, T., Bredenkamp, D., and Rutter, M. (1999). Attachment disturbances and disorders in children exposed to early severe deprivation. *Infant Mental Health Journal, 20,* 10–29. [6]

O'Connor, T., and Croft, C. (2001). A twin study of attachment in preschool children. *Child Development, 72,* 1501–1511. [6]

O'Connor, T. G., and Rutter, M. (2000). Attachment disorder behavior following early severe deprivation: Extension and longitudinal follow-up. *Journal of the American Academy of Child and Adolescent Psychiatry, 39,* 703–712. [2]

O'Connor, T. G., Rutter, M., Beckett, C., Keaveney, L., and Kreppner, J. M. (2000). The effects of severe privation on cognitive competence: Extension and longitudinal follow-up. *Child Development, 71,* 376–390. [11]

Oettingen, G., Little, T., Lindenberger, U., and Baltes, P. (1994). Causality, agency, and control beliefs in East versus West Berlin children: A natural experiment of the role of context. *Journal of Personality and Social Psychology, 66,* 579–595. [12]

Ogawa, J., Sroufe, L. A., Weinfield, N., Carlson, E., and Egeland, B. (1997). Development of the fragmented self: Longitudinal study of dissociative symptomatology in a nonclinical sample. *Development and Psychopathology, 9,* 855–880. [8]

O'Leary, K. D., and O'Leary, S. (1977). *Classroom management: The successful use of behavior modification* (2nd ed.). New York: Pergamon Press. [15]

Oller, D. K., and Eilers, R. (1988). The role of audition in babbling. *Child Development, 59,* 441–449. [7]

Olsen-Fulero, L. (1982). Style and stability in mother conversational behavior: A study of individual differences. *Journal of Child Language, 9,* 543–564. [7]

Olsho, L. W., Schoon, C., Sakai, R., Turpin, R., and Sperduto, V. (1982). Preliminary data on frequency discrimination in infancy. *Journal of the Acoustical Society of America, 71,* 509–511. [4]

Ornoy, A., Segal, J., Bar-Hamburger, R., and Greenbaum, C. (2001). Developmental outcome of school-age children born to mothers with heroin dependency: Importance of environmental factors. *Developmental medicine and child neurology, 43,* 668–675. [3]

Ornstein, P. A., Naus, M. J., and Stone, B. P. (1977). Rehearsal training and developmental differences in memory. *Developmental Psychology, 13,* 15–24. [11]

Osherson, D. N., and Markman, E. M. (1975). Language and the ability to evaluate contradictions and tautologies. *Cognition, 2,* 213–226. [13]

Osofsky, J. D. (1997). *Children in a violent society.* New York: Guilford. [2]

Oster, H., Hegley, D., and Nagel, L. (1992). Adult judgments and fine-grained analyses of infant facial expressions: Testing the validity of *a priori* coding formulas. *Developmental Psychology, 28,* 1115–1131. [6]

Overton, W. F. (1998). Developmental psychology: Philosophy, concepts, and methodology. In W. Damon (Series Ed.) and R. M. Lerner (Vol. Ed.), *Handbook of child psychology: Vol. 1. Theoretical models of human development* (5th ed., pp. 107–188). New York: Wiley. [1]

Papini, D., and Sebby, R. (1987). Adolescent pubertal status and affective family relationships: A multivariate assessment. *Journal of Youth and Adolescence, 16,* 1–15. [13]

Papouxek, H. (1967). Experimental studies of appetitional behavior in human newborns and infants. In H. W. Stevenson, E. H. Hess., and H. L. Rheingold (Eds.), *Early behavior: Comparative and developmental approaches* (pp. 249–277). New York: Wiley. [2], [4]

Papouxek, M., Papouxek, H., and Bornstein, M. H. (1985). The naturalistic vocal environment of young infants: On the significance of homogeneity and variability in parental speech. In T. Field and N. Fox (Eds.), *Social perception in infants.* (pp. 269–297). Norwood, NJ: Ablex. [7]

Papouxek, H., Papouxek, M., and Koester, L. (1986). Sharing emotionality and sharing knowledge: A microanalytic approach to parent-infant communication. In C. Izard and P. Read (Eds.), *Measuring emotion in infants and young children* (pp. 93–122). New York: Cambridge University Press. [6]

Paris, S. G. (1975). Integration and inference in children's comprehension and memory. In F. Restle, R. Shiffrin, J. Castellan, H. Lindman, and D. Pisoni (Eds.), *Cognitive theory* (Vol. 1, pp. 223–244). Hillsdale, NJ: Erlbaum. [11]

Paris, S. G., and Upton, L. (1976). Children's memory for inferential comprehension. *Child Development, 47,* 660–668. [11]

Park, K. A., Lay, K., and Ramsay, L. (1993). Individual differences and developmental changes in preschoolers' friendships. *Developmental Psychology, 29,* 264–270. [10]

Parke, R. D., and Buriel, R. (1998). Socialization in the family: Ethnic and ecological perspectives. In W. Damon (Series Ed.) and N. Eisenberg (Vol. Ed.), *Handbook of child psychology: Vol. 3. Social, emotional, and personality development* (5th ed., pp. 463–552). New York: Wiley. [2], [8], [10], [12]

Parke, R. D., and Ladd, G. W. (Eds.) (1992). *Family-peer relationships: Modes of linkage.* Hillsdale, NJ: Lawrence Erlbaum Associates. [12]

Parke, R. D., and Stearns, P. (1993). Fathers and child rearing: A historical analysis. In G. H. Elder, Jr., J. Modell, and R. D. Parke (Eds.), *Children in time and place: Developmental and historical insights* (pp. 147–170). New York: Cambridge University Press. [2]

Parker, J., and Asher, S. (1993). Friendship and friendship quality in middle childhood: Links with peer group acceptance and feelings of loneliness and social dissatisfaction. *Developmental Psychology, 29,* 611–621. [12]

Parritz, R. H. (1996). A descriptive analysis of toddler coping in challenging circumstances. *Infant Behavior and Development, 19,* 171–180. [8]

Parritz, R. H., Mangelsdorf, S., and Gunnar, M. R. (1992). Control, social referencing, and the infant's appraisal of threat. In S. Feinman (Ed.), *Social referencing and the social construction of reality in infancy* (pp. 209–228). New York: Plenum. [6]

Parsons, J., Adler, T., and Kaczala, C. (1982). Socialization of achievement attitudes and beliefs: Parental influences. *Child Development, 53,* 310–321. [14]

Pascalis, O., de Schonen, S., Morton, J., Deruelle, C., and Fabre-Grenet, M. (1995). Mothers' face recognition by neonates: A replication and an extension. *Infant Behavior and Development, 18,* 79–86. [4]

Patterson, C. J. (2002). Lesbian and gay parenthood. In M. H. Bornstein (Ed.), *Handbook of parenting:*

Vol. 3. Being and becoming a parent (2nd. ed., pp. 317–338). Mahwah, NJ: Erlbaum. [2]

Patterson, G. R., and Capaldi, D. (1991). Antisocial parents: Unskilled and vulnerable. In P. Cowan and E. M. Hetherington (Eds.), *Family transitions* (pp. 195–218). Hillsdale, NJ: Erlbaum. [12]

Patterson, G. R., and Dishion, T. J. (1988). Multilevel family process models: Traits, interactions, and relationships. In R. Hinde and J. Stevenson-Hinde (Eds.), *Relationships within families: Mutual influences* (pp. 283–310). Oxford, England: Oxford University Press. [8], [12], [15]

Patterson, S. J., Sochting, I., and Marcia, J. E. (1992). The inner space and beyond: Women and identity. In G. R. Adams, T. P. Gullotta, and R. Montemayor (Eds.), *Adolescent identity formation* (pp. 9–24). Newbury Park, CA: Sage. [14]

Peal, E., and Lambert, W. E. (1962). The relation of bilingualism to intelligence. *Psychological Monographs, 76,* 1–23. [7]

Pederson, D., Gleason, K., Moran, G., and Bento, S. (1998). Maternal attachment representation, maternal sensitivity, and the infant-mother attachment relationship. *Developmental Psychology, 35,* 1379–1388. [6]

Pederson, D., and Moran, G. (1996). Expressions of the attachment relationship outside of the strange situation. *Child Development, 67,* 915–927. [6]

Peill, E. J. (1975). *Invention and the discovery of reality.* New York: Wiley. [9]

Peisner-Feinberg, E., Burchinal, M., Clifford, R., Culkin, M., Howes, C., Kagan, S., and Yazejian, N. (2001). The relation of preschool child-care quality to children's cognitive and social emotional trajectories through second grade. *Child Development, 72,* 1534–1553. [10]

Peloquin, L., and Klorman, R. (1986). Effects of methylphenidate on normal children's mood, event-related potentials, and performance in memory scanning and vigilance. *Journal of Abnormal Psychology, 95,* 88–98. [15]

Pennington, B., and Welsh, M. (1995). Neuropsychology and developmental psychopathology. In D. Cicchetti and D. Cohen (Eds.), *Developmental processes and psychopathology* (Vol. 1, pp. 254–290). New York: Cambridge University Press. [15]

Perreault, G. (2000). The classroom impact of high-stress testing. *Education, 120,* 705–710. [11]

Perry-Jenkins, M., Repetti, R. L., and Crouter, A. C. (2000). Work and family in the 1990s. *Journal of Marriage and the Family, 62,* 981–998. [2]

Peskin, H. (1973). Influence of the developmental schedule of puberty on learning and ego functioning. *Journal of Youth and Adolescence, 2,* 273–290. [13]

Peters, A. M. (1995). Strategies in the acquisition of syntax. In P. Fletcher and B. MacWhinney (Eds.), *The handbook of child language* (pp. 462–483). Oxford, England: Basil Blackwell. [7]

Petersen, A. C. (1987). The nature of biological-psychosocial interactions: The sample case of early adolescence. In R. M. Lerner and T. T. Foch (Eds.), *Biological-psychosocial interactions in early adolescence* (pp. 35–61). Hillsdale, NJ: Erlbaum. [13]

Petitto, L. A. (1992). Modularity and constraints in early lexical acquisition: Evidence from children's early language and gesture. In M. Gunnar and M. Maratsos (Eds.), *Minnesota Symposia on Child Psychology: Vol. 25. Modularity and constraints in language and cognition* (pp. 25–58). Hillsdale, NJ: Erlbaum. [2], [7]

Petitto, L. A. (2000). The acquisition of natural signed languages: Lessons in the nature of human language and its biological foundations. In C. Chamberlain and J. P. Morford (Eds.), *Language acquisition by eye* (pp. 41–50). Mahwah, NJ: Erlbaum. [7]

Pettit, G., Bates, J., Dodge, K., and Meece, D. (1999). The impact of after-school peer contact on early adolescent externalizing problems is moderated by parental monitoring, perceived neighborhood safety, and prior adjustment. *Child Development, 70,* 768–778. [14]

Phillips, D., and Adams, G. (2001). Child care and our youngest children. *Future of children: Caring for infants and toddlers,11,* 35–51. [6]

Phillips, S. U. (1983). *The invisible culture: Communication in classroom and community on the Warm Springs Indian Reservation.* New York: Longman. [11]

Phillipsen, L. (1999). Associations between age, gender, and group acceptance and three components of friendship quality. *Journal of Early Adolescence, 19,* 438–464. [14]

Phinney, J., Ong, A., and Madden, T. (2000). Cultural values and intergenerational value discrepancies in immigrant and non-immigrant families. *Child Development, 71,* 528–539. [14]

Piaget, J. (1929). *The child's conception of the world.* New York: Harcourt, Brace. [9]

Piaget, J. (1930/1969). *The child's conception of physical causality.* Totowa, NJ: Littlefield, Adams. [9]

Piaget, J. (1952). *The child's conception of number.* New York: Humanities Press. [6], [9]

Piaget, J. (1972). Intellectual evolution from adolescence to adulthood. *Human Development, 15,* 1–12. [13]

Piaget, J. (1932/1965). *The moral judgment of the child.* New York: Free Press. [13]

Piaget, J. (1952/1963). *The origins of intelligence in children.* New York: Norton. [5]

Piaget, J. (1962). *Play, dreams, and imitation in childhood.* New York: Norton. [4], [5], [7]

Piaget, J. (1970). Piaget's theory. In P. H. Mussen (Ed.), *Carmichael's manual of child psychology.* New York: Wiley. [9]

Piaget, J., and Inhelder, B. (1973). *Memory and intelligence.* New York: Basic Books. [11]

Pianta, R., Egeland, B., and Erickson, M. (1989). The antecedents of maltreatment: Results of the Mother-Child Interaction Research Project. In D. Cicchetti and V. Carlson (Eds.), *Child maltreatment* (pp. 203–253). New York: Cambridge University Press. [8]

Pianta, R., Egeland, B., and Erickson, M. (1989). The effects of maltreatment on the development of young children. In D. Cicchetti and V. Carlson (Eds.), *Child maltreatment* (pp. 647–684). New York: Cambridge University Press. [10]

Pianta, R., Egeland, B., and Sroufe, L. A. (1990). Maternal stress and children's development:

Prediction of school outcomes and identification of protective factors. In J. Rolf, A. Masten, D. Cicchetti, K. Neuchterlein, and S. Weintraub (Eds.), *Risk and protective factors in the development of psychopathology* (pp. 215–235). New York: Cambridge University Press. [10]

Pianta, R. C., Rimm-Kaufman, S. E., and Cox, M. J. (1999). An ecological approach to kindergarten transition. In R. C. Pianta and M. J. Cox (Eds.), *The transition to kindergarten* (pp. 3–12). Baltimore, MD: Paul H. Brookes. [2], [9]

Pianta, R. C., Sroufe, L. A., and Egeland, B. (1989). Continuity and discontinuity in maternal sensitivity at 6, 24, and 42 months in a high-risk sample. *Child Development, 60,* 481–487. [8]

Pianta, R., and Steinberg, M. (1992). Teacher-child relationships and the process of adjusting to school. In R. Pianta (Ed.), *Beyond the parent: The role of other adults in children's lives. New directions for child development* (pp. 61–80). San Francisco: Jossey-Bass. [10], [12]

Pickering, L. E., and Vazsonyi, A. T. (2002). The impact of adolescent employment on family relationships. *Journal of Adolescent Research, 17,* 196–218. [14]

Pierce, S. L. (1999). *The role of fathers and men in the development of child and adolescent . externalizing behavior.* Unpublished doctoral dissertation, University of Minnesota. [8]

Piers, M. (1978). *Infanticide.* New York: Norton. [2]

Pine, J. M. (1994). The language of primary caregivers. In C. Gallaway and B. J. Richards (Eds.), *Input and interaction in language acquisition* (pp. 15–37). Cambridge, England: Cambridge University Press. [7]

Pinker, S. (1987). The bootstrapping problem in language acquisition. In B. MacWhinney (Ed.), *Mechanisms of language acquisition* (pp. 399–441). Hillsdale, NJ: Erlbaum. [7]

Pinker, S. (1994). *The language instinct.* New York: Harper Collins. [2]

Pitt, R. B. (1983). Development of a general problem-solving schema in adolescence and early adulthood. *Journal of Experimental Psychology— General, 112,* 547–584. [13]

Plomin, R. (1994). *Genetics and experience.* Thousand Oaks, CA: Sage. [6]

Plomin, R., DeFries, J. C., McClearn, G. E., and Rutter, M. (1997). *Behavior genetics* (3rd ed.). New York: Freeman. [1], [2], [3]

Plomin, R., Emde, R., Braungart, J., Campos, J., Corley, R., Fulker, D., Kagan, J., Reznick, J. S., Robinson, J., Zahn-Waxler, C., and DeFries, J. (1993). Genetic change and continuity from fourteen to twenty months: The MacArthur Longitudinal Twin Study. *Child Development, 64,* 1354–1376. [6]

Plomin, R., Nitz, K., and Rowe, D. C. (1990). Behavioral genetics and aggressive behavior in childhood. In M. Lewis and S. M. Miller (Eds.), *Handbook of developmental psychopathology* (pp. 119–134). New York: Plenum Press. [15]

Plumert, J. (1994). Flexibility in children's use of spatial and categorical organizational strategies in recall. *Developmental Psychology, 30,* 738–747. [13]

Plunkett, J., Meisels, S., Stiefel, G., Pasicke, P., and Roloff, D. (1986). Patterns of attachment among preterm infants of varying biological risk. *Journal of the American Academy of Child Psychiatry, 25,* 794–800. [6]

Pollak, S., Cicchetti, D., Hornung, K., and Reed, A. (2000).Recognizing emotion in faces: Developmental effects of child abuse and neglect. *Developmental Psychology, 36,* 679–688. [8]

Posada, G., Jacobs, A., Carbonell, O., Alzate, G., Bustamante, M., and Arenas, A. (1999). Maternal care and attachment security in ordinary and emergency contexts. *Developmental Psychology, 35,* 1379–1388. [6]

Posner, J., and Vandell, D. (1994). Low-income children's after-school care: Are there beneficial effects of after-school programs? *Child Development, 65,* 440–456. [12]

Post, D., and Pong, S. (2000). Employment during middle school: The effects on academic achievement in the U. S. and abroad. *Educational Evaluation and Policy Analysis, 22,* 273–298. [14]

Power, T., and Chapieski, M. (1986). Childrearing and impulse control in toddlers: A naturalistic investigation. *Developmental Psychology, 22,* 271–275. [8]

Power, T., and Manire, S. (1992). Child rearing and internalization: A developmental perspective. In J. Janssen and J. Gerris (Eds.), *Childrearing: Influence on moral and prosocial development* (pp. 101–123). Amsterdam: Swets & Zeitlinger. [10]

Powers, S., Hauser, S., and Kilner, L. (1989). Adolescent mental health. *American Psychologist, 44,* 220–208. [14]

Powers, S., Hauser, S., Schwartz, J., Noam, G., and Jacobson, A. (1983). Adolescent ego development and family interaction: A structural-developmental perspective. In H. Grotevant and C. Cooper (Eds.), *New directions for child development: No. 22. Adolescent development in the family* (pp. 5–25). San Francisco: Jossey-Bass. [14]

Pratt, C., and Bryant, P. (1990). Young children understand that looking leads to knowing (so long as they are looking in a single barrel). *Child Development, 61,* 973–982. [9]

Prechtl, H., and Beintema, D. (1964). *Clinics in developmental medicine: No. 12. The neurological examination of the full-term newborn infant.* London, England: Heinemann. [4]

Premack, D. (1986). *Gavagai! or the future history of the animal language controversy.* Cambridge, MA: MIT Press. [7]

Price-Williams, D. R., Gordon, W., and Ramirez, M. (1969). Skill and conservation: A study of pottery-making children. *Developmental Psychology, 1,* 769. [9]

Provence, S. (1989). Infants in institutions revisited. *Zero to Three, 9,* 1–4. [2]

Putallaz, M., Costanzo, P. R., Grimes, C. L., and Sherman, D. M. (1998). Intergenerational continuities and their influences on children's social development. *Social Development, 7,* 389–427. [2]

Rabiner, D., and Coie, J. (1989). Effect of expectancy inductions on rejected children's acceptance by unfamiliar peers. *Developmental Psychology, 25,* 450–457. [12]

Radke-Yarrow, M., and Zahn-Waxler, C. (1984). Roots, motives, and patterns in children's pro-social behavior. In E. Staub, D. Bar-Tal, J. Karylowski, and J. Reykowski (Eds.), *Origins and maintenance of pro-social behaviors* (pp. 155–176). New York: Plenum Press. [10]

Rakic, P. (1995). Corticogenesis in human and nonhuman primates. In M. S. Gazzaniga (Ed.), *The cognitive neurosciences* (pp. 127–145). Cambridge, MA: MIT Press. [3], [4]

Rakic, P. (2002). Adult neurogenesis in mammals: An identity crisis. *Journal of Neuroscience, 22,* 614–618. [4]

Ramey, C. T., and Ramey, S. L. (1998). Early intervention and early experience. *American Psychologist, 53,* 109–120. [11]

Ratliff-Schaub, K., Hunt, C. E., Crowell, D., Golub, H., Smok-Pearsall, S., Palmer, P., Schafer, S., Bak, S., Cantey-Kiser, J., O'Bell, R. (2001). Relationship between infant sleep position and motor development in preterm infants. *Journal of developmental and behavioral pediatrics, 22,* 293–299. [4]

Reese, L., and Gallimore, R. (2000). Immigrant Latinos' cultural model of literacy development: An evolving perspective on home-school discontinuities. *American Journal of Education, 108,* 103–134. [11]

Reich, K., Oser, F., and Valentin, P. (1994). Knowing why I now know better: Children's and youth's explanations of their worldview changes. *Journal of Research on Adolescence, 4,* 151–173. [13]

Reich, P. A. (1976). The early acquisition of word meaning. *Journal of Child Language, 3,* 117–123. [7]

Repacholi, B. (1998). Infants' use of attentional cues to identify the referent of another person's emotional expression. *Developmental Psychology, 34,* 1017–1025. [8]

Resnick, L. B. (1986). *Education and learning to think.* Washington, DC: National Research Council. [13]

Resnick, L. B. (1995). Inventing arithmetic: Making children's intuition work in school. In C. A. Nelson (Ed.), *Minnesota Symposia on Child Psychology: Vol. 28. Basic and applied perspectives on learning, cognition, and development* (pp. 75–101). Hillsdale, NJ: Erlbaum. [11]

Resnick, L. B., Siegel, S. W., and Kresh, E. (1971). Transfer and sequence in learning double-classification skills. *Journal of Experimental Child Psychology, 11,* 139–149. [11]

Resnick, M. D., Bearman, P. S., Blum, R. W., Bauman, K. E., Harris, K. M., Jones, J., Tabor, J., Beuhring, T., Sieving, R. E., Shew, M., Ireland, M., Bearinger, L., and Udry, J. R. (1997). Protecting adolescents from harm: Findings from the National Longitudinal Study on Adolescent Health. *Journal of the American Medical Association, 278,* 823–832. [14]

Rest, J. (1979). *Development in judging moral issues.* Minneapolis: University of Minnesota Press. [13]

Rest, J. (1983). Morality. In P. H. Mussen (Series Ed.), J. H. Flavell and E. M. Markman (Vol. Eds.), *Handbook of child psychology: Vol. 3. Cognitive*

development (4th ed., pp. 920–990). New York: Wiley. [13]

Rheingold, H. L., and Eckerman, C. O. (1971). Departures from the mother. In H. R. Schaffer (Ed.), *The origins of human social relations* (pp. 186–223). New York: Academic Press. [8]

Richards, M., Boxer, A., Petersen, A., and Albrecht, R. (1990). Relation of weight to body image in pubertal girls and boys from two communities. *Developmental Psychology, 26,* 313–321. [13]

Richardson, G. A. (1998). Prenatal cocaine exposure: A longitudinal study of development. *Annals of the New York Academy of Sciences, 846,* 144–152. [3]

Richman, A. M., Miller, P. M., and LeVine, R. A. (1992). Cultural and educational variations in maternal responsiveness. *Developmental Psychology, 28,* 614–621. [6]

Ridgeway, D., Waters, E., and Kuczaj, S. (1985). Acquisition of emotion-descriptive language: Receptive and productive vocabulary norms for ages 18 months to 6 years. *Developmental Psychology, 21,* 901–908. [10]

Riley, C. A., and Trabasso, T. (1974). Comparatives, logical structures, and encoding in a transitive inference task. *Journal of Experimental Child Psychology, 45,* 972–977. [9]

Robins, L. (1966). *Deviant children grown up.* Baltimore: Williams and Wilkins. [15]

Robins, L. (1978). Sturdy childhood predictors of adult antisocial behavior: Replications from longitudinal studies. *Psychological Medicine, 8,* 611–622. [15]

Robins, L., and Price, R. (1991). Adult disorders predicted by childhood conduct problems: Results from the NIMH epidemiologic catchment area project. *Psychiatry, 54,* 116–132. [15]

Robins, L., and Rutter, M. (1990). *Straight and devious pathways from childhood to adulthood.* Cambridge, Eng.: Cambridge University Press. [15]

Rode, S., Chang, P., Fisch, R., and Sroufe, L. A. (1981). Attachment patterns of infants separated at birth. *Developmental Psychology, 17,* 188–191. [6]

Rodning, C., Beckwith, L., and Howard, J. (1989). Characteristics of attachment organization and play organization in prenatally drug-exposed toddlers. *Development and Psychopathology, 1,* 227–289. [6]

Roeser, R., and Eccles, J. (2001). Schooling and mental health. In A. Sameroff, M. Lewis, and S. Miller (Eds.), *Handbook of developmental psychopathology,* 2nd Ed. (pp. 135–156). New York: Kluwer Academic/ Plenum. [12]

Roffwarg, H. P., Muzio, J. N., and Dement, W. C. (1966). Ontogenetic development of the human sleep-dream cycle. *Science, 152,* 604–619. [4]

Rogoff, B. (1990). *Apprenticeship in thinking: Cognitive development in social context.* New York: Oxford University Press. [1], [8]

Rogoff, B. (1998). Cognition as a collaborative process. In W. Damon (Series Ed.), D. Kuhn, and R. S. Siegler (Vol. Eds.), *Handbook of child psychology: Vol. 2. Cognition, perception, and language* (5th ed., pp. 679–744). New York: Wiley. [1], [11], [13]

Rogoff, B., Mistry, J., Goncu, A., and Moiser, C. (1993). Guided participation in cultural activity by toddlers and caregivers. *Monographs of the Society for Research in Child Development, 58* (Serial No. 236). [8]

Rogol, A. (2002). Androgens and puberty. *Molecular and Cellular Endocrinology, 198*, 25–29. [13]

Rogol, A., Roemmich, J. N., and Clark, P. A. (2002). Growth at puberty. *Journal of Adolescent Health, 31*, 192–200. [13]

Rohlen, T. P., and LeTendre, G. K. (1996). *Teaching and learning in Japan.* New York: Cambridge University Press. [2]

Roisman, G., Padron, E., Sroufe, L. A., and Egeland, B. (2002). Earned-secure attachment status in retrospect and prospect. *Child Development, 73*, 1204–1219. [6]

Romaine, S. (1999). Bilingual language development. In M. Barrett (Ed.), *The development of language* (pp. 251–275). Hove, East Sussex, U.K.: Psychology Press. [7]

Rose, S. A., and Feldman, J. R. (1995). Prediction of IQ and specific cognitive abilities at 11 years from infancy measures. *Developmental Psychology, 31*, 685–696. [5]

Rose, S. A., and Feldman, J. R. (1997). Memory and speed: Their role in the relation of infant information processing to later IQ. *Child Development, 68*, 630–641. [5]

Rosenberg, D. M. (1984). *The quality and content of preschool fantasy play: Correlates in concurrent social-personality function and early mother-child attachment relationships.* Unpublished doctoral dissertation, University of Minnesota. [10]

Rosenblith, J., and Sims-Knight, J. (1985). *In the beginning: Development in the first two years.* Belmont, CA: Brooks/Cole. [3]

Rosenblum, G. D., and Lewis, M. (1999). The relations among body image, physical attractiveness, and body mass in adolescence. *Child Development, 70*, 50–64. [13]

Rosengren, K. S., Gelman, S. A., Kalish, C. W., and McCormick, M. (1991). As time goes by: Children's early understanding of growth in animals. *Child Development, 62*, 1302–1320. [9]

Rosengren, K. S., and Hickling, A. K. (2000). Metamorphosis and magic: The development of children's thinking about possible events and plausible mechanisms. In K. S. Rosengren, C. N. Johnson, and P. L. Harris (Eds.), *Imagining the impossible: Magical, scientific, and religious thinking in children* (pp. 75–98). New York: Cambridge University Press. [9]

Rosengren, K. S., Taylor, M. G., and DeHart, G. B. (1997, April). Variability in children's reasoning about biological change. In J. D. Coley and G. Hatano (Chairs), *Flexibility in early reasoning about living things.* Symposium presented at the biennial meeting of the Society for Research in Child Development, Washington, DC. [9]

Rothbart, M., Ahadi, S., Hershey, K., and Fisher, P. (2001). Investigations of temperament at three to seven years: The Children's Behavior Questionnaire. *Child Development, 72*, 1394–1408. [6]

Rothbart, M., and Bates, J. (1998). Temperament. In W. Damon (Series Ed.) and N. Eisenberg (Vol. Ed.), *Handbook of child psychology: Vol. 3. Social, emotional, and personality development* (5th ed., pp. 105–176). New York: Wiley. [6], [8], [10]

Rothbaum, F., Weisz, J., Pott, M., Miyake, K., and Morelli, G. (2000). Attachment and culture: Security in the United States and Japan. *American Psychologist, 55*, 1093–1104.

Rothbaum, F., Weisz, J., Pott, M., Miyake, K., and Morelli, G. (2000). Attachment and culture: Security in the United States and Japan. *American Psychologist, 55*, 1093–1104. [1], [2]

Rovee-Collier, C. (1993). The capacity for long-term memory in infancy. *Current Directions in Psychological Science, 2*(4), 130–135. [5]

Rovee-Collier, C., and Gekoski, M. J. (1979). The economics of infancy: A review of conjugate reinforcement. In H. W. Reese and L. P. Lipsitt (Eds.), *Advances in child development and behavior* (Vol. 13, pp. 195–255). New York: Academic Press. [4]

Rubin, K. H. (1998). Social and emotional development from a cultural perspective. *Developmental Psychology, 34*, 611–615. [2]

Rubin, K. H., Bukowski, W., and Parker, J. G. (1998). Peer interactions, relationships, and groups. In W. Damon (Series Ed.) and N. Eisenberg (Vol. Ed.), *Handbook of child psychology: Vol. 3. Social, emotional, and personality development* (5th ed., pp. 619–700). New York: Wiley. [2], [8], [10], [12], [14], [15]

Rubin, K. H., Coplan, R., Fox, N., and Caplan, S. (1995). Emotionality, emotional regulation, and preschoolers' social adaptation. *Development and Psychopathology, 7*, 49–62. [10]

Rubin, Z. (1980). *Children's friendships.* Cambridge, MA: Harvard University Press. [12]

Ruble, D. (1983). The development of social-comparison processes and their role in achievement-related self-socialization. In E. T. Higgins, D. N. Ruble, and W. W. Hartup (Eds.), *Social cognition and social development: A sociocultural perspective* (pp. 134–157). Cambridge, England: Cambridge University Press. [10], [12]

Ruble, D., and Martin, C. (1998). Gender development. In W. Damon (Series Ed.) and N. Eisenberg (Vol. Ed.), *Handbook of child psychology: Vol. 3. Social, emotional, and personality development* (5th ed., pp. 933–1016). New York: Wiley. [2], [10], [12]

Rudolph, K., and Asher, S. (2001). Adaptation and maladaptation in the peer system. In A. Sameroff, M. Lewis, and S. Miller (Eds.), *Handbook of developmental psychopathology*, 2nd Ed. (pp. 157–176). New York: Kluwer Academic/Plenum. [12]

Rush, D., and Callahan, K. R. (1989). Exposure to passive cigarette smoking and child development: A critical review. *Annals of the New York Academy of Sciences, 562*, 74–100. [3]

Rutter, M. (1979). Protective factors in children's responses to stress and disadvantage. In M. Kent and J. Rolf (Eds.), *Primary prevention of psychopathology: Vol. III. Social competence in children* (pp. 49–74). Hanover, NH: University Press of New England. [15]

Rutter, M. (1981). Epidemiological-longitudinal approaches to the study of development. In W. A. Collins (Ed.), *Minnesota Symposia on Child Psychology: Vol. 15. The concept of development* (pp. 105–144) Hillsdale, NJ: Erlbaum. [12]

Rutter, M. (1991). Nature, nurture, and psychopathology: A new look at an old topic. *Development and Psychopathology, 3*, 125–136. [15]

Rutter, M. (1997). Antisocial behavior: Developmental psychopathology perspectives. In D. Stoff, J. Breiling, and J. Maser (Eds.), *Handbook of antisocial behavior* (pp. 115–124). New York: Wiley. [15]

Rutter, M. (2000). Psychosocial influences: Critiques, findings, and research needs. *Development and Psychopathology, 12*, 375–406. [8]

Rutter, M., Grahan, P., Chadwick, O., and Yule, W. (1976). Adolescent turmoil: Fact or fiction? *Journal of Child Psychology and Psychiatry, 17*, 35–56. [14]

Rutter, M., Kreppner, J. M., and O'Connor, T. G. (2001). Specificity and heterogeneity in children's responses to profound institutional privation. *British Journal of Psychiatry, 179*, 97–103. [2]

Rutter, M., Quinton, D., and Hill, J. (1990). Adult outcome of institution-reared children: Males and females compared. In L. Robins and M. Rutter (Eds.), *Straight and devious pathways from childhood to adulthood.* (pp. 135–157) Cambridge, England: Cambridge University Press. [6]

Rutter, M., and Silberg, J. (2002). Gene-environment interplay in relation to emotional and behavioral disturbance. *Annual Review of Psychology, 53*, 463–490. [15]

Rutter, M., and Sroufe, L. A. (2000). Developmental psychopathology: Concepts and challenges. *Development and Psychopathology, 12*, 265–296. [15]

Rymer, R. (1993). *Genie: An abused child's flight from silence.* New York: Harper Collins. [2]

Saarni, C., Mumme, D., and Campos, J. (1998). Emotional development: Action, communication, and understanding. In W. Damon (Series Ed.) and N. Eisenberg (Vol. Ed.), *Handbook of child psychology: Vol. 3. Social, emotional, and personality development* (5th ed., pp. 237–309). New York: Wiley. [6], [8], [10], [12]

Sadker, D. (1999). Gender equity: Still knocking at the classroom door. *Educational Leadership, 56*, 22–26. [2], [12]

Safer, D. (2000). Are stimulants overprescribed for youths with ADHD? *Annals of Clinical Psychiatry, 12*, 55–62. [15]

Saffran, J. R., Aslin, R. N., and Newport, E. L. (1996). Statistical learning by 8-month-old infants. *Science, 274*, 1926–1928. [7]

Sagi, A., van IJzendoorn, M., Aviezer, O., Donnell, F., and Mayseless, O. (1994). Sleeping out of home in a kibbutz communal arrangement. *Child Development, 65*. [6]

Salapatek, P., and Kessen, W. (1966). Visual scannings of triangles by the human newborn. *Journal of Experimental Child Psychology, 3*, 155–167. [4]

Salls, J. S., Silverman, L. N., and Gatty, C. M. (2002). The relationship of infant sleep and play positioning to motor milestone achievement. *American Journal of Occupational Therapy, 56*, 577–580. [4]

Sameroff, A. (2000). Developmental systems and psychopathology. *Development and Psychopathology, 12*, 297–312. [8]

Sameroff, A. (2000). Dialectical processes in developmental psychopathology. In A. Sameroff, M.

Lewis, and S. Miller (Eds.), *Handbook of developmental psychopathology* (2nd ed.), pp. 23–40. New York: Plenum. [15]

Sameroff, A. J., and Chandler, M. (1975). Reproductive risk and the continuum of caretaking casualty. In F. D. Horowitz, E. M. Hetherington, S. Scarr-Salapatek, and G. Siegel (Eds.), *Review of child development research* (Vol. 4, pp. 187–244). Chicago: University of Chicago Press. [2]

Sameroff, A. J., and Fiese, B. H. (2000). Transactional regulation: The developmental ecology of early intervention. In Shonkoff, J. P., and Meisels, S. J. (Eds.), *Handbook of early childhood intervention* (pp. 135–159). New York: Cambridge University Press. [2]

Sameroff, A. J., and Haith, M. M. (Eds.) (1996). *The five to seven year shift: The Age of Reason and Responsibility*. Chicago: University of Chicago Press. [2], [11]

Sampaio, R. C., and Truwit, C. L. (2001). Myelination in the developing human brain. In C. A. Nelson and M. Luciana (Eds.), *Handbook of developmental cognitive neuroscience* (pp. 35–44). Cambridge, MA: MIT Press. [4], [13]

Sampson, P. D., Streissguth, A. P., Bookstein, F. L., Little, R. E., Clarren, S. K., Dehaene, P., Hanson, J. W., and Graham, J. M., Jr. (1997). Incidence of fetal alcohol syndrome and prevalence of alcohol-related neurodevelopmental disorder. *Teratology, 56*, 317–326. [3]

Sampson, P. D., Streissguth, A. P., Bookstein, F. L., and Barr, H. M. (2000). On categorizations in analyses of alcohol teratogenesis. *Environmental Health Perspectives, 108*, Suppl. 3, 421–428. [3]

Sampson, R., and Laub, J. (1994). Urban poverty and the family context of delinquency: A new look at structure and process in a classic study. *Child Development, 65*, 523–540. [14]

Sander, L. W. (1975). Infant and caretaking environment. In E. J. Anthony (Ed.), *Explorations in child psychiatry* (pp. 129–165) York: Plenum Press. [6], [8], [10]

Sastry, B. V. (1991). Placental toxicology: Tobacco smoke, abused drugs, multiple chemical interactions, and placental function. *Reproduction, Fertility, and Development, 3*, 355–372. [3]

Savage-Rumbaugh, E. S., Murphy, J., Sevcik, R. A., Brakke, K. E., Williams, S. L., and Rumbaugh, D. M. (1993). Language comprehension in ape and child. *Monographs of the Society for Research in Child Development, 58* (3–4, Serial No. 233). [7]

Savin-Williams, R. (1990). *Gay and lesbian youth*. New York: Hemisphere. [14]

Savin-Williams, R., and Berndt, T. (1990). Peer relations during adolescence. In S. S. Feldman and G. R. Elliott (Eds.), *At the threshold: The developing adolescent* (pp. 277–307). Cambridge, MA: Harvard University Press. [14]

Saxe, G. B. (1982). Developing forms of arithmetic operations among the Oksapmin of Papua New Guinea. *Developmental Psychology, 18*(4), 583–594. [9]

Saywitz, K. J., Goodman, G. S., Nicholas, E., and Moan, S. F. (1991). Children's memories of a physical examination involving genital touch: Implications for reports of child sexual abuse.

Journal of Consulting and Clinical Psychology, 59, 682–691. [9]

Saywitz, K. J., and Lyon, T. D. (2002). Coming to grips with children's suggestibility. In M. L. Eisen (Ed.), *Memory and suggestibility in the forensic interview* (pp. 85–113). Mahwah, NJ: Erlbaum. [9]

Scarr, S. (1998). American child care today. *American Psychologist, 53*, 95–108. [6]

Scarr, S. (1997). The development of individual differences in intelligence and personality. In H. W. Reese and M. D. Franzen (Eds.), *Biological and neuropsychological mechanisms: Life-span developmental psychology* (pp. 1–22). Mahwah, NJ: Erlbaum. [1]

Scarr, S., and McCartney, K. (1983). How people make their own environments: A theory of genotype-environment effects. *Child Development, 54*, 425–435. [2]

Schaffer, H. R., and Callender, M. (1959). Psychological effects of hospitalization in infancy. *Pediatrics, 24*, 528–539. [6]

Schank, R. C., and Abelson, R. (1977). *Scripts, plans, goals, and understanding*. Hillsdale, NJ: Erlbaum. [9]

Schellscheidt, J., Oyen, N., and Jorch, G. (1997). Interactions between maternal smoking and other prenatal risk factors for sudden infant death syndrome (SIDS). *Acta Paediatrica, 86*, 857–863. [3]

Schieffelin, B. B. (1990). *The give and take of everyday life: Language socialization of Kaluli children*. New York: Cambridge University Press. [7]

Schiff, A., and Knopf, I. (1985). The effects of task demands on attention allocation in children of different ages. *Child Development, 56*, 621–630. [13]

Schleidt, M., and Genzel, C. (1990). The significance of mother's perfume for infants in the first weeks of their life. *Ethology and Sociobiology, 11*, 145–154. [4]

Schneider, B., Atkinson, L., and Tardif, C. (2001). Child-parent attachment and children's peer relations: A quantitative review. *Developmental Psychology, 37*, 86–100. [6]

Schneider, M., and Moore, C. F. (2000). Effect of prenatal stress on development: A nonhuman primate model. In C. Nelson (Ed.), *Minnesota Symposia on Child Psychology: Vol. 31. The effects of early adversity on neurobehavioral development* (pp. 201–244). Mahwah, NJ: Erlbaum. [3]

Schneider, W., and Bjorklund, D. F. Memory. (1998). In W. Damon (Series Ed.), D. Kuhn, and R. S. Siegler (Vol. Eds.), *Handbook of child psychology: Vol. 2. Cognition, perception, and language* (5th ed., pp. 467–521). New York: Wiley. [5], [9], [11], [13]

Schneider, W., and Pressley, M. (1997). *Memory development between two and twenty*. (2nd ed.) Mahwah, NJ: Erlbaum. [11], [13]

Schneider-Rosen, K., and Wenz-Gross, M. (1990). Patterns of compliance from eighteen to thirty months of age. *Child Development, 61*, 104–112. [8]

Schore, A. N. (1994). *Affect regulation and the origin of the self: The neurobiology of emotional development*. Hillsdale, NJ: Erlbaum. [1], [2], [6], [8]

Schore, A. (2001a). The effects of early relational trauma on right brain development, affect

regulation and infant mental health. *Infant Mental Health Journal, 22*, 201–269. [8]

Schore, A. N. (2001b). Effects of a secure attachment relationship on right brain development, affect regulation and infant mental health. *Infant Mental Health Journal, 22*, 7–66. [2], [4], [8]

Schuengel, C., Bakermans-Kranenburg, M., and van Ijzendoorn, M. (1999). Frightening maternal behavior linking unresolved loss and disorganized infant attachment. *Journal of Consulting and Clinical Psychology, 67*, 54–63. [6]

Schumann-Hengsteler, R. (1992). The development of visuo-spatial memory: How to remember location. *International Journal of Behavioural Development, 15*, 455–471. [9]

Schwartz, D., Dodge, K., and Coie, J. (1993). The emergence of chronic peer victimization in boy's play groups. *Child Development, 64*, 1755–1772. [12]

Schwartz, D., Dodge, K., Pettit, G., and Bates, J. (2000). Friendship as a moderating factor in the pathway between early harsh home environment and later victimization in the peer group. *Developmental Psychology, 36*, 646–662. [12]

Schweinhart, L. J., and Weikart, D. P. (1993). Success by empowerment: The High/Scope Perry Preschool Study through age 27. *Young Children, 49*(1), pp. 54–58. [10]

Schweinhart, L. J., Weikart, D. P., and Larner, M. (1986). Consequences of three preschool curriculum models through age 15. *Early Childhood Research Quarterly, 1*, 15–45. [10]

Sears, R. R., Maccoby, E. E., and Levin, H. (1957). *Patterns of child rearing*. Evanston, IL: Row, Peterson. [10]

Seligman, M. E. P. (1970). On the generality of the laws of learning. *Psychological Review, 77*, 406–418. [4]

Selman, R. (1980). *The growth of interpersonal understanding*. New York: Academic Press. [12], [14]

Senesac, B. V. K. (2002). Two-way bilingual immersion: A portrait of quality schooling. *Bilingual Research Journal, 26*, 85–101. [7]

Serbin, L. A., Powlishta, K. K., and Gulko, J. (1993). The development of sex typing in middle childhood. *Monographs of the Society for Research in Child Development, 58*(2, Serial No. 232). [10], [12]

Shaffer, D. R. (1985). *Developmental psychology: Theory, research, and applications*. Monterey, CA: Brooks/Cole. [3]

Shantz, C. U. (1975). The development of social cognition. In E. M. Hetherington (Ed.), *Review of child development research* (Vol. 3). Chicago: University of Chicago Press. [9]

Shapiro, E. G., and Rosenfeld, A. (1987). *The somatizing child: Diagnosis and treatment of conversion and somatization disorders*. New York: Springer-Verlag. [15]

Shatz, M. (1978). The relation between cognitive processes and the development of communication skills. In C. B. Keasy (Ed.), *Nebraska Symposium on Motivation, 1977*. Lincoln: University of Nebraska Press. [9]

Shatz, M., and Gelman, R. (1973). The development of communication skills: Modifications in the speech of young children as a function of listening. *Monographs of the Society for Research in Child Development, 38* (5, Serial No. 152). [7], [9]

Shatz, M., and O'Reilly, A. W. (1990). Conversational or communicative skill? A reassessment of two-year-olds' behaviour in miscommunication episodes. *Journal of Child Language, 17,* 131–146. [7]

Shayer, M. (1980). Piaget and science education. In S. Modgil and C. Modgil (Eds.), *Toward a theory of psychological development* (pp. 699–731). Windsor, England: NFER Publishing Co. [13]

Shayer, M., and Adey, P. (1992). Accelerating the development of formal thinking in middle and high school students III: Testing the permanency of effects. *Journal of Research in Science Teaching, 29,* 1101–1115. [13]

Shayer, M., and Adey, P. (1993). Accelerating the development of formal thinking in middle and high school students IV: Three years after a two-year intervention. *Journal of Research in Science Teaching, 30,* 351–366. [13]

Shea, J. D. (1985). Studies of cognitive development in Papua New Guinea. *International Journal of Psychology, 20,* 33–61. [13]

Shelton, K., Hambright, S., Miles, C., and Harold, G. (2001). Marital conflict, emotional security, parent-child security and adolescent adjustment: A longitudinal assessment. Poster presented at the biennial meeting of the Society for Research in Child Development, Minneapolis, MN. [12]

Sherif, M., Harvey, O., White, B., Hood, W., and Sherif, C. (1961). *Intergroup conflict and cooperation: The Robbers Cave experiment.* Norman: University of Oklahoma Press.

Sherif, M., and Sherif, C. (1953). *Groups in harmony and tension.* New York: Harper and Row. [12]

Shields, A., and Cicchetti, D. (2001). Parental maltreatment and emotion dysregulation as risk factors for bullying and victimization in middle childhood. *Journal of Clinical Child Psychology, 30,* 349–363. [12]

Shields, A., Ryan, R., and Cicchetti, D. (2001). Narrative representations of caregivers and emotional dysregulation as predictors of maltreated children's rejection by peers. *Developmental Psychology, 37,* 321–337. [8]

Shiner, R. (1998). How shall we speak of children's personalities in middle childhood? A preliminary taxonomy. *Psychological Bulletin, 124,* 308–332. [12]

Shonkoff, J. P., and Phillips, D. A. (Eds.) (2000). *From neurons to neighborhoods: The science of early childhood development.* Washington, DC: National Academy Press. [2], [4]

Shore, C. (1986). Combinatorial play, conceptual development, and early multi-word speech. *Developmental Psychology, 22,* 184–190. [7]

Shulman, S., Elicker, J., and Sroufe, L. A. (1994). Stages of friendship growth in preadolescence as related to attachment history. *Journal of Social and Personal Relationships, 11,* 341–361. [12]

Shultz, T. R., and Zigler, E. (1970). Emotional concomitants of visual mastery in infants: The effects of stimulus movement on smiling and vocalizing. *Journal of Experimental Child Psychology, 10,* 390–402. [6]

Shwalb, D. W., and Shwalb, B. J. (Eds.) (1995). *Japanese childrearing: Two generations of scholarship.* New York: Guilford. [2]

Shweder R. A., Goodnow, J., Hatano, G., LeVine, R. A., Markus, H., and Miller, P. (1998). The cultural psychology of development: One mind, many mentalities. In W. Damon (Series Ed.) and R. M. Lerner (Vol. Ed.), *Handbook of child psychology: Vol. 1. Theoretical models of human development* (5th ed., pp. 865–937). New York: Wiley. [2]

Siegel, D. (1999). *The developing mind.* New York: Guilford. [15]

Siegel, D. (2001). Toward an interpersonal neurobiology of the developing mind. *Infant Mental Health Journal, 22,* 67–94. [4], [8]

Siegel, M., and Share, D. (1990). Contamination sensitivity in young children. *Developmental Psychology, 26,* 455–458. [9]

Siegler, R. S. (1998). *Children's thinking* (3rd ed.). Englewood Cliffs, NJ: Prentice-Hall. [1],[5], [9]

Siegler, R. S. (1978). The origins of scientific reasoning. In R. S. Siegler (Ed.), *Children's thinking: What develops?* (pp. 109–149). Hillsdale, NJ: Erlbaum. [13]

Siegler, R. S., and Robinson, M. (1982). The development of numerical understandings. In H. W. Reese and L. P. Lipsett (Eds.), *Advances in child development and behavior* (Vol. 16, pp. 241–312). New York: Academic Press. [11]

Silverman, I., and Ragusa, D. (1990). Child and maternal correlates of impulse control in 24-month-old children. *Genetic Psychology Monographs, 116,* 435–473. [8]

Siminoff, E., McGuffin, P., and Gottesman, I. (1994). Genetic influences on normal and abnormal development. In M. Rutter, E. Taylor, and L. Hersov (Eds.), *Child and adolescent psychiatry* (pp. 129–151). London: Blackwell. [15]

Simmons, R., and Blyth, D. (1988). *Moving into adolescence: The impact of pubertal change and school context.* New York: Aldine/Hawthorne. [13], [14]

Simmons, R. G., Carlton-Ford, S. L., and Blyth, D. A. (1987). Predicting how a child will cope with the transition to junior high school. In R. M. Lerner and T. T. Foch (Eds.), *Biological-psychosocial interactions in early adolescence* (pp. 325–375). Hillsdale, NJ: Erlbaum. [13]

Simon, T. J. (1997). Reconceptualizing the origins of number knowledge: A "non-numerical" account. *Cognitive Development, 12,* 349–372. [5]

Simons, R. L., Lorenz, F. O., Conger, R. D., and Wu, C. (1992). Support from spouse as mediator and moderator of the disruptive influence of economic strain on parenting. *Child Development, 63,* 1282–1301. [2]

Simons, R. L., Whitbeck, L. B., Conger, R. D., and Wu, C. (1991). Intergenerational transmission of harsh parenting. *Developmental Psychology, 27,* 159–171. [2]

Singer, L., Arendt, R., Farkas, K., Minnes, S., Huang, J., and Yamashita, T. (1997). Relationship of prenatal cocaine exposure and maternal postpartum psychological distress to child developmental outcome. *Developmental Psychopathology, 9,* 473–489. [3]

Singer, L., Brodzinsky, D., Ramsay, D., Steir, M., and Waters, E. (1985). Mother-infant attachment in adoptive families. *Child Development, 56,* 1543–1551. [6]

Singer, M. I., Anglin, T. M., Song, L. Y., and Lunghofer, L. (1995). Adolescents' exposure to violence and associated symptoms of psychological trauma. *Journal of the American Medical Association, 273,* 477–482. [2]

Singh, L., Morgan, J. L., and Best, C. T. (2002). Infants' listening preferences: Baby talk or happy talk? *Infancy, 3,* 365–394. [7]

Sinnott, J. M., Pisoni, D. B., and Aslin, R. N. (1984). A comparison of pure tone auditory thresholds in human infants and adults. *Infant Behavior and Development, 6,* 3–17. [4]

Skinner, B. F. (1957). *Verbal behavior.* New York: Appleton-Century-Crofts. [7]

Skinner, D., Bryant, D., Coffman, J., and Campbell, F. (1998). Creating risk and promise: Children's and teachers' co-constructions in the cultural world of kindergarten. *The Elementary School Journal, 98,* 297–310. [11]

Skinner, E. A. (1990). Development and perceived control: A dynamic model of action in context. In M. R. Gunnar and L. A. Sroufe (Eds.), *Minnesota Symposia on Child Psychology: Vol. 23. Self processes in development* (pp. 167–216). Hillsdale, NJ: Erlbaum. [12]

Skodak, M., and Skeels, H. M. (1949). A final followup study of one hundred adopted children. *Journal of Genetic Psychology, 75,* 85–125. [1]

Slater, A. (1989). Visual memory and perception in early infancy. In A. Slater and G. Bremner (Eds.), *Infant development* (pp. 43–71). Hillsdale, NJ: Erlbaum. [4]

Slater, A., and Bremner, G. (Eds.). (1989). *Infant development.* Hillsdale, NJ: Erlbaum. [4]

Slater, A., Johnson, S. P., Brown, E., and Badenoch, M. (1996). Newborn infant's perception of partly occluded objects. *Infant Behavior and Development, 19,* 145–148. [5]

Slater, A., Mattock, A., and Brown, E. (1990). Size constancy at birth: Newborn infants' responses to retinal and real size. *Journal of Experimental Child Psychology, 49,* 314–322. [4]

Slaughter-Defoe, D. T., Nakagawa, K., Takanishi, R., and Johnson, D. (1990). Toward cultural/ecological perspectives on schooling and achievement in African- and Asian-American children. *Child Development, 61,* 363–383. [11]

Slavin, R. E. (1990). Comprehensive cooperative learning models: Embedding cooperative learning in the curriculum and school. In S. Shlomo (Ed.), *Cooperative learning: Theory and research* (pp. 261–283). New York: Praeger. [11]

Slobin, D. I. (1970). Universals of grammatical development in children. In G. B. Flores d'Arcais and W. J. Levelt (Eds.), *Advances in psycholinguistics* (pp. 178–179). Amsterdam: North-Holland. [7]

Slobin, D. I. (1985). *The crosslinguistic study of language acquisition: Vol. 2. Theoretical issues.* Hillsdale, NJ: Erlbaum. [7]

Smetana, J. G. (1995). Context, conflict, and constraint in adolescent-parent authority relationships. In M. Killen and D. Hart (Eds.), *Morality in everyday life: Developmental perspectives* (pp. 225–259). Cambridge, England: Cambridge University Press. [14]

Smetana, J. (2000). Middle-class African American Adolescents' and parents' conceptions of parental authority and parenting practices: A longitudinal investigation. *Child Development, 71,* 1672–1686. [14]

Smetana, J. G., Schlagman, N., and Adams, P. W. (1993). Preschool children's judgments about hypothetical and actual transgressions. *Child Development, 64*(1), 202–214. [10]

Smith, D. (2001, December). Is too much riding on high-stakes tests? *Monitor on Psychology, 32(11),* 58–59. [11]

Smith, E. A. (1989). A biosocial model of adolescent sexual behavior. In G. R. Adams, R. Montemayor, and T. P. Gullotta (Eds.), *Biology of adolescent behavior and development* (pp. 143–167). Newbury Park, CA: Sage. [13]

Smith, K. (2000). *Who's minding the kids? Child care arrangements: Fall 1995.* Current Population Reports, P70-70. Washington, DC: U.S. Census Bureau. [2]

Smith, M. E. (1926). An investigation of the development of the sentence and the extent of vocabulary in young children. *University of Iowa Studies in Child Welfare, 3*(5). [7]

Snarey, J. R. (1985). Cross-cultural universality of social-moral development: A critical review of Kohlbergian research. *Psychological Bulletin, 97,* 202–232. [13]

Snow, C. E. (1977). The development of conversation between mothers and babies. *Journal of Child Language, 4,* 1–22. [7]

Snow, C. E. (1993). Bilingualism and second language acquisition. In J. B. Gleason and N. B. Ratner (Eds.), *Psycholinguistics* (pp. 392–416). Ft. Worth: Harcourt Brace Jovanovich. [7]

Snow, C. E., and Ferguson, C. A. (Eds.). (1977). *Talking to children: Language input and acquisition.* Cambridge, England: Cambridge University Press. [7]

Solomon, G. E. A., Johnson, S. C., Zaitchik, D., and Carey, S. (1996). The young child's conception of inheritance. *Child Development, 67,* 151–171. [9]

Sonenstein, F. L., Ku, L., Lindberg, L. D., Turner, C. F., and Pleck, J. H. (1998). Changes in sexual behavior and condom use among teenaged males: 1988 to 1995. *American Journal of Public Health, 88,* 956–959. [14]

Sontag, L. W., Baker, C. T., and Nelson, V. L. (1958). Mental growth and personality development: A longitudinal study. *Monographs of the Society for Research in Child Development, 23,* (2, Whole No. 68) [11]

Sorce, J., Emde, R., and Klinnert, M. (1985). Maternal emotional signaling: Its effect on the visual cliff behavior of 1-year-olds. *Developmental Psychology, 21,* 195–200. [8]

Sostek, A. M., and Anders, T. F. (1981). The biosocial importance and environmental sensitivity of infant sleep-wake behaviors. In K. Bloom (Ed.), *Prospective issues in infancy research.* Hillsdale, NJ: Erlbaum. [4]

Spangler, G., and Grossmann, K. (1993). Biobehavioral organization in securely and insecurely

attached infants. *Child Development, 64,* 1439–1450. [6]

Spear, L. P. (2000). The adolescent brain and age-related behavioral manifestations. *Neuroscience and Biobehavioral Reviews, 24,* 417–463. [13]

Spearman, C. (1927). *The abilities of man.* New York: Macmillan. [11]

Speidel, G. E., and Nelson, K. E. (1989). *The many faces of imitation in language learning.* New York: Springer. [7]

Spelke, E. S., and Newport, E. L. (1998). Nativism, empiricism, and the development of knowledge. In W. Damon (Series Ed.) and R. M. Lerner (Vol. Ed.), *Handbook of child psychology: Vol. 1. Theoretical models of human development* (5th ed., pp. 275–340). New York: Wiley. [5], [7]

Spencer, M. B., and Markstrom-Adams, C. (1990). Identity processes among racial and ethnic minority children in America. *Child Development, 61,* 290– 310. [14]

Spiker, D., Ferguson, J., and Brooks-Gunn, J. (1993). Enhancing maternal interactive behavior and child social competence in low birth weight, premature infants. *Developmental Psychology, 29,* 754–768. [8]

Spitz, R. A. (1945). Hospitalism: An inquiry into the genesis of psychiatric conditions in early childhood. *Psychoanalytic Study of the Child, 1,* 53–74. [2]

Springer, K. (1999). How a naive theory of biology is acquired. In M. Siegal and C. C. Petersen (Eds.), *Children's understanding of biology and health* (pp. 45–70). New York: Cambridge University Press. [9]

Springer, K., and Keil, F. C. (1989). On the development of biologically specific beliefs: The case of inheritance. *Child Development, 60,* 637–648. [9]

Sprinthall, N. A., and Collins, W. A. (1995). *Adolescent psychology: A developmental view* (3rd ed.). New York: McGraw-Hill. [14]

Sroufe, J. (1991). Assessment of parent-adolescent relationships: Implications for adolescent development. *Journal of Family Psychology, 5,* 21–45. [14]

Sroufe, L. A. (1983). Infant-caregiver attachment and patterns of adaptation in preschool: The roots of maladaptation and competence. In M. Perlmutter (Ed.), *Minnesota Symposia on Child Psychology: Vol. 16. Development and policy concerning children with special needs* (pp. 41–83). Hillsdale, NJ: Erlbaum. [10], [12]

Sroufe, L. A. (1988). The role of infant-caregiver attachment in development. In J. Belsky and T. Nezworski (Eds.), *Clinical implications of attachment* (pp. 18–38). Hillsdale, NJ: Erlbaum. [6], [10]

Sroufe, L. A. (1989). Pathways to adaptation and maladaptation: Psychopathology as developmental deviation. In D. Cicchetti (Ed.), *Rochester Symposia on Developmental Psychopathology* (Vol. 1, pp. 13–40). Hillsdale, NJ: Erlbaum. [15]

Sroufe, L. A. (1990). A developmental perspective on day care. In N. Fox and G. G. Fein (Eds.), *Infant day care: The current debate* (pp. 51–59). Norwood, NJ: Ablex. [6], [10]

Sroufe, L. A. (1995). *Emotional development: The organization of emotional life in the early years.*

New York: Cambridge University Press. [6], [8], [10]

Sroufe, L. A. (1997). Psychopathology as an outcome of development. *Development and Psychopathology, 9,* 251–268. [15]

Sroufe, L. A. (2000). Early relationships and the development of children. *Infant Mental Health Journal: Special edition in honor of Louis Sander, 21,* 67–74. [6], [8]

Sroufe, L. A. (2002). From infant attachment to promotion of adolescent autonomy: Prospective, longitudinal data on the role of parents in development. In J. Borkowski, S. Ramey, and M. Bristol-Power (Eds.), *Parenting and the child's world* (pp.187–202). Mahwah, NJ: Lawrence Erlbaum Associates. [6]

Sroufe, L. A., Bennett, C., Englund, M., Urban, J., and Shulman, S. (1993). The significance of gender boundaries in preadolescence: Contemporary correlates and antecedents of boundary violation and maintenance. *Child Development, 64,* 455–466. [12]

Sroufe, L. A., Carlson, E., and Levy, A. (1998, February). Competence as a developmental construct. Presented at the biennial meeting of the Society for Research on Adolescence, San Diego. [10]

Sroufe, L. A., Carlson, E., Levy, A., and Egeland, B. (1999). Implications of attachment theory for developmental psychopathology. *Development and Psychopathology, 11,* 1–13. [15]

Sroufe, L. A., Carlson, E., and Shulman, S. (1993). The development of individuals in relationships: From infancy through adolescence. In D. C. Funder, R. Parke, C. Tomlinson-Keesey, and K. Widaman (Eds.), *Studying lives through time: Approaches to personality and development* (pp. 315–342). Washington, DC: American Psychological Association. [10], [12], [14]

Sroufe, L. A., Egeland, B., and Carlson, E. A. (1999). One social world: The integrated development of parent-child and peer relationships. In W. A. Collins and B. Laursen (Eds.), *Minnesota Symposia on Child Psychology: Vol. 30. Relationships as developmental contexts: Festschrift in honor of Willard W. Hartup* (pp. 241–261). Mahwah, NJ: Erlbaum. [2], [10], [12], [14], [15]

Sroufe, L. A., Egeland, B., and Kreutzer, T. (1990). The fate of early experience following developmental change: Longitudinal approaches to individual adaptation in childhood. *Child Development, 61,* 1363–1373. [10], [12]

Sroufe, L. A., and Fleeson, J. (1988). The coherence of family relationships. In R. A. Hinde and J. Stevenson-Hinde (Eds.), *Relationships within families: Mutual influences* (pp. 27–47). Oxford, Eng.: Oxford University Press. [2], [10], [12], [15]

Sroufe, L. A., Fox, N., and Pancake, V. (1983). Attachment and dependency in developmental perspective. *Child Development, 54,* 1615–1627. [10]

Sroufe, L. A., Jacobvitz, D., Mangelsdorf, S., DeAngelo, E., and Ward, M. J. (1985). Generational boundary dissolution between mothers and their preschool children: A relationship systems approach. *Child Development, 56,* 317–325. [2]

Sroufe, L. A., and Pierce, S. (1999). Men in the family: Associations with juvenile conduct. In G.

Cunningham (ed.), *Just in time research: Children, youth and families* (pp 19–26). Minneapolis: University of Minnesota Extension Services. [2]

Sroufe, L. A., and Rutter, M. (1984). The domain of developmental psychopathology. *Child Development, 55,* 17–29. [15]

Sroufe, L. A., Schork, E., Motti, F., Lawroski, N., and LaFreniere, P. (1984). The role of affect in emerging social competence. In C. Izard, J. Kagan, and R. Zajonc (Eds.), *Emotion, cognition, and behavior* (pp. 289–319). Oxford, Eng.: Oxford University Press. [10]

Sroufe, L. A., Waters, E., and Matas, L. (1974). Contextual determinants of infant affective response. In M. Lewis and L. Rosenblum (Eds.), *The origins of fear* (pp. 49–72). New York: Wiley. [6]

Starkey, P., and Cooper, R. G. (1980). Perception of number by human infants. *Science, 210,* 1033–1035. [5]

Starkey, P., and Gelman, R. (1982). The development of addition and subtraction abilities prior to formal schooling in arithmetic. In T. Carpenter, J. J. Noser, and T. Romberg (Eds.), *Addition and subtraction: A cognitive perspective.* Hillsdale, NJ: Erlbaum. [9]

Starkey, P., Spelke, E. S., and Gelman, R. (1983). Detection of one-to-one correspondence by human infants. *Science, 222,* 179–181. [5]

Stattin, H., and Klackenberg-Larson, I. (1991). The short- and long-term implications for parent-child relations of parents' prenatal preferences for their child's gender. *Developmental Psychology, 27,* 141–147. [2]

Stattin, H., and Magnusson, D. (1990). *Pubertal maturation in female development.* Hillsdale, NJ: Erlbaum. [13]

Stecher, B. M., and Barron, S. (2001). Unintended consequences of test-based accountability when testing in "milepost" grades. *Educational Assessment, 7,* 259–281. [11]

Stein, A. H., Susser, M., Saenger, G., and Marolla, F. (1975). *Famine and human development: The Dutch hunger winter of 1944/45.* New York: Oxford University Press. [3]

Steinberg, L. (1981). Transformations in family relations at puberty. *Developmental Psychology, 17,* 883–850. [14]

Steinberg, L. (1987). Single parents, step parents and the susceptibility of adolescents to antisocial peer pressure. *Child Development, 58,* 269–275. [13]

Steinberg, L. (1989). Pubertal maturation and parent-adolescent distance: An evolutionary perspective. In G. R. Adams, R. Montemayor, and T. P. Gullotta (Eds.), *Biology of adolescent behavior and development* (pp. 71–97). Newbury Park, CA: Sage. [13]

Steinberg, L. (1990). Autonomy, conflict, and harmony in the family relationship. In S. Feldman and G. Elliot (Eds.), *At the threshold: The developing adolescent* (pp. 255–276). Cambridge, MA: Harvard University Press. [14]

Steinberg, L. (2002). *Adolescence* (6th Ed.). New York: McGraw-Hill. [14]

Steinberg, L., and Dornbusch, S. (1991). Negative correlates of part-time employment during adolescence: Replication and elaboration. *Developmental Psychology, 27,* 304–313. [14]

Steinberg, L., and Morris, A. (2001). Adolescent development. *Annual Review of Psychology, 52,* 83–110. [13], [14]

Sternberg, R. J., and Nigro, G. (1980). Developmental patterns in the solution of verbal analogies. *Child Development, 51,* 27–38. [13]

Steinberg, L. D., Lamborn, S. D., Darling, N., Mounts, N. S., and Dornbusch, S. M. (1994). Over-time changes in adjustment and competence among adolescents from authoritative, authoritarian, indulgent, and neglectful families. *Child Development, 65,* 754–770. [14]

Steiner, J. E. (1979). Human facial expressions in response to taste and smell stimulation. In H. W. Reese and L. P. Lipsitt (Eds.), *Advances in child development and behavior* (Vol. 13, pp. 257–295). New York: Academic Press. [4]

Steinhausen, H. (1994). Anorexia and bulimia nervosa. In M. Rutter, E. Taylor, and L. Hersov (Eds.), *Child and adolescent psychiatry* (pp. 425–440). London: Blackwell. [15]

Steinhausen, H. C., and Spohr, H. L. (1998). Long-term outcome of children with fetal alcohol syndrome: Psychopathology, behavior, and intelligence. *Alcohol Clinical and Experimental Research, 22,* 334–338. [3]

Stephens, T. D., and Brynner, R. (2001). *Dark remedy: The impact of thalidomide and its revival as a vital medicine.* Cambridge, MA: Perseus. [3]

Stern, D. N. (1985). *The interpersonal world of the infant.* New York: Basic Books. [6]

Stern, D. N., Spieker, S., and MacKain, K. (1982). Intonation contours as signals in maternal speech to prelinguistic infants. *Developmental Psychology, 18,* 727–735. [7]

Sternberg, R. J. (1985). *Beyond IQ: A triarchic theory of human intelligence.* New York: Cambridge University Press. [11]

Sternberg, R. J., and Grigorenko, E. L. (2000). Practical intelligence and its development. In R. Bar-On and J. D. A. Parker (Eds.), *The handbook of emotional intelligence: Theory, development, assessment, and application at home, school, and in the workplace* (pp. 215–243). San Francisco: Jossey-Bass/Pfeiffer. [11]

Sternberg, R. J., Grigorenko, E. L., and Bundy, D. A. (2001a). The predictive value of IQ. *Merrill-Palmer Quarterly, 47,* 1–41. [11]

Sternberg, R. J., Nokes, C., Geissler, P. W., Prince, R., Okatcha, F., Bundy, D. A., and Grigorenko, E. L. (2001b). The relationship between academic and practical intelligence: A case study in Kenya. *Intelligence, 29,* 401–418. [11]

Stevenson, H. W. (1995). Mathematics achievement of American students: First in the world by the year 2000? In C. A. Nelson (Ed.), *Minnesota Symposia on Child Psychology: Vol. 28. Basic and applied perspectives on learning, cognition, and development* (pp. 131–149). Hillsdale, NJ: Erlbaum. [11], [13]

Stevenson, H. W., and Lee, S. (1990). Contexts of achievement: A study of American, Chinese, and Japanese children. *Monographs of the Society for Research in Child Development, 55,* (1–2, Serial No. 221). [2], [11]

Stevenson, H. W., Stigler, J. W., Lee, S., Lucker, G. W., Kitamura, S., and Hsu, C. (1985). Cognitive performance and academic achievement of Japanese, Chinese, and American children. *Child Development, 56,* 718–734. [11]

Stevenson-Hinde, J. (1991). Temperament and attachment: An eclectic approach. In P. Bateman (Ed.), *Development and integration of behaviour: Essays in honour of Robert Hinde* (pp. 315–329). Cambridge, Eng.: Cambridge University Press. [6]

Stigler, J. W., and Perry, M. (1990). Mathematics learning in Japanese, Chinese, and American classrooms. In J. W. Stigler, R. A. Shweder, and G. Herdt (Eds.), *Cultural psychology* (pp. 328–353). New York: Cambridge University Press. [11]

Stipek, D., Recchia, S., and McClintic, S. (1992). Self-evaluation in young children. *Monographs of the Society for Research in Child Development, 57* (Serial No. 226). [8], [10]

Stocker, C., Burwell, R., and Briggs, M. (2002). Sibling conflict in middle childhood predicts children's adjustment in early adolescence. *Journal of Family Psychology, 16,* 50–57. [12]

Stone, M., and Brown, B. (1999). Identity claims and projections: Descriptions of self and crowds in secondary school. In J. A. McLellan and M Pugh (Eds.), *The role of peer groups in adolescent social identity: Exploring the importance of stability and change* (pp. 7–20). San Francisco: Jossey-Bass. [14]

Stoneman, Z., and Brody, G. (1993). Sibling temperaments, conflict, warmth, and role asymmetry. *Child Development, 64,* 1786–1800. [12]

Strassberg, Z., Dodge, K., Pettit, G., and Bates, J. (1994). Spanking in the home and children's subsequent aggression toward kindergarten peers. *Development and Psychopathology, 6,* 445–462. [8]

Strayer, J. (1993). Children's concordant emotions and cognitions in response to observed emotions. *Child Development, 64,* 188–201. [12]

Streissguth, A. P., and O'Malley, K. (2000). Neuropsychiatric implications and long-term consequences of fetal alcohol spectrum disorders. *Seminars in Clinical Neuropsychiatry, 5,* 177–190. [3]

Streissguth, A. P., Sampson, P. D., and Barr, H. M. (1989). Neurobehavioral dose-response effects of prenatal alcohol exposure in humans from infancy to adulthood. *Annals of the New York Academy of Sciences, 562,* 145–158. [3]

Streitmatter, J. L. (1988). Ethnicity as a mediating variable of early adolescent identity development. *Journal of Adolescence, 11,* 335–346. [14]

Striano, T., Tomasello, M., and Rochat, P. (2001). Social and object support for early symbolic play. *Developmental Science, 4,* 442–455. [7]

Strouse, D. (1999). Adolescent crowd orientations: A social and temporal analysis. In J. A. McLellan and M Pugh (Eds.), *The role of peer groups in adolescent social identity: Exploring the importance of stability and change* (pp. 7–20). San Francisco: Jossey-Bass. [14]

Sue, S., and Okazaki, S. (1990). Asian-American educational achievements: A phenomenon in search of an explanation. *American Psychologist, 45,* 913–920. [2]

Suess, G. J., Grossmann, K. E., and Sroufe, L. A. (1992). Effects of infant attachment to mother and father on quality of adaptation in preschool: From dyadic to individual organization of self. *International Journal of Behavioral Development, 15,* 43–66. [12]

Sullivan, H. S. (1953). *The interpersonal theory of psychiatry.* New York: Norton. [12]

Suomi, S. J. (1977). Development of attachment and other social behaviors in rhesus monkeys. In T. Alloway, P. Pliner, and L. Krames (Eds.), *Advances in the study of communication and affect: Vol. 3. Attachment behavior* (pp. 197–224). New York: Plenum Press. [2], [6]

Suomi, S. (1995). Influence of attachment theory on ethological studies of biobehavioral development in nonhuman primates. In S. Goldberg, R. Muir, and J. Kerr (Eds.) *Attachment theory: Social, developmental, and clinical perspectives* (pp. 185–201). Hillsdale, NJ: The Analytic Press. [6], [12]

Suomi, S. (2002). Parents, peers and the processes of socialization in primates. In J. Borkowski, S. Ramey, and M. Bristol-Power (Eds.), *Parenting and the child's world* (pp. 265–282). Mahwah, NJ: Lawrence Erlbaum Associates. [6], [12], [15]

Suomi, S. J., and Harlow, H. F. (1971). Abnormal social behavior in young monkeys. In J. Helmuth (Ed.), *Exceptional infant: Vol. 2. Studies in abnormalities* (pp. 483–529). New York: Brunner/Mazel. [6]

Suomi, S. J., Harlow, H., and McKinney, W. (1972). Monkey psychiatrists. *American Journal of Psychiatry, 128,* 41–46. [6]

Super, C. M. (1976). Environmental effects on motor development: A case of African infant precocity. *Developmental Medicine and Child Neurology, 18,* 561–567. [4]

Susman-Stillman, A., Kalkoske, M., and Egeland, B. (1996). Infant temperament and maternal sensitivity as predictors of attachment sensitivity. *Infant Behavior and Development, 19,* 33–47. [6]

Swanson, M. W., Streissguth, A. P., Sampson, P. D., and Olson, H. C. (1999). Prenatal cocaine and neuromotor outcome at four months: Effect of duration of exposure. *Journal of Developmental and Behavioral Pediatrics, 20,* 325–334. [3]

Szymczak, J. T., Jasinska, M., Pawlak, E., and Swierzykowska, M. (1993). Annual and weekly changes in the sleep-wake rhythm of school children. *Sleep, 16,* 433–435. [13]

Taeschner, T. (1983). *The sun is feminine: A study on language acquisition in bilingual children.* Berlin: Springer-Verlag. [7]

Takahashi, K. (1990). Are the key assumptions of the "Strange Situation" procedure universal? A view from Japanese research. *Human Development, 33,* 23–30. [6]

Tanner, J. M. (1962). *Growth at adolescence.* New York: Lippincott. [13]

Tanner, J. M. (1990). *Foetus into man: Physical growth from conception to maturity.* (Revised and enlarged ed.). Cambridge, MA: Harvard University Press. [1], [13]

Taussig, H. B. (1962). A study of the German outbreak of phocomelia: The thalidomide syndrome. *Journal of the American Medical Association, 180,* 1106–1114. [3]

Taylor, E. (1994). Syndromes of attention deficit and overactivity. In M. Rutter, E. Taylor, and L. Hersov (Eds.), *Child and adolescent psychiatry* (pp. 285–307). London: Blackwell. [15]

Taylor, H. G., Klein, N., and Hack, M. (2000). School-age consequences of birth weight less than 750 g.: A review and update. *Developmental Neuropsychology, 17,* 289–321. [3]

Taylor, M., and Hart, B. (1990). Can children be trained in making the distinction between appearance and reality? *Cognitive Development, 5,* 89–99. [9]

Teo, A., Carlson, E., Mathieu, P., Egeland, B., and Sroufe, L. A. (1996). A prospective longitudinal study of psychosocial influence on achievement. *Journal of School Psychology, 34,* 285–306. [10], [12]

Teti, D. M., and Gelfand, D. M. (1991). Behavioral competence among mothers of infants in the First year: The mediational role of maternal self-efficacy. *Child Development, 62,* 918–929. [6]

Tharp, R. G. (1994). Intergroup differences among Native Americans in socialization and child cognition: An ethnogenetic analysis. In P. M. Greenfield and R. R. Cocking (Eds.), *Cross-cultural roots of minority child development* (pp. 87–105). Hillsdale, NJ: Erlbaum. [11]

Tharp, R. (1989). Psychocultural variables and constants: Effects on teaching and learning. *American Psychologist, 44,* 349–359. [2]

Theimer, C., Killen, M., and Stangor, C. (2001). Young children's evaluations of exclusion in gender-stereotypic peer contexts. *Developmental Psychology, 37,* 18–27. [10]

Thelen, E. (1981). Rhythmical behavior in infancy: An ethological perspective. *Developmental Psychology, 17,* 237–257. [4]

Thelen, E. (1986). Treadmill-elicited stepping in seven-month-old infants. *Child Development, 57,* 1498–1506. [4]

Thelen, E. (1995). Motor development: A new synthesis. *American Psychologist, 50,* 79–95. [4]

Thelen, E., Corbetta, D., Kamm, K., Spencer, J. P., Schneider, K., and Zernicke, R. F. (1993). The transition to reaching: Mapping intention and intrinsic dynamic. *Child Development, 64,* 1058–1098. [4]

Thoma, S. J. (1986). Estimating gender differences in the comprehension and preference of moral issues. *Developmental Review, 6,* 165–180. [13]

Thoman, E. B., and Whitney, M. P. (1989). Sleep states of infants monitored in the home: Individual differences, developmental trends, and origins of cyclicity. *Infant Behavior and Development, 12,* 59–75. [4]

Thomas, A., and Chess, S. (1977). *Temperament and development.* New York: Brunner/Mazel. [6]

Thompson, P. M., Giedd, J. N., Woods, R. P., MacDonald, D., Evans, A. C., and Toga, A. W. (2000). Growth patterns in the developing brain detected by using continuum mechanical tensor maps. *Nature, 404,* 190–193. [13]

Thompson, R. (1998). Early sociopersonality development. In W. Damon (Series Ed.) and N. Eisenberg (Vol. Ed.), *Handbook of child psychology: Vol. 3. Social, emotional, and personality development* (5th ed., pp. 553–617). New York: Wiley. [6], [8], [10]

Thompson, R. A., and Nelson, C. A. (2001). Developmental science and the media: Early brain development. *American Psychologist, 56,* 5–15. [4]

Thorne, B. (1986). Girls and boys together . . . but mostly apart: Gender arrangements in elementary schools. In W. Hartup and Z. Rubin (Eds.), *Relationships and development* (pp. 167–184). Hillsdale, NJ: Erlbaum. [12]

Tienari, P. L., Lahti, I., Sorri, A., Naarala, M., Moring, J., Kaleva, M., Wahlberg, K-E., and Wynne, L. (1990). Adopted away offspring of schizophrenics and controls. In L. Robins and M. Rutter (Eds.), *Straight and devious pathways from childhood to adulthood* (pp. 365–379). Cambridge, England: Cambridge University Press. [15]

Tobin, J. J., Wu, D. Y. H., and Davidson, D. H. (1989). *Preschool in three cultures.* New Haven: Yale University Press. [2]

Tobin-Richards, M., Boxer, A., and Petersen, A. (1983). The psychological significance of pubertal change: Sex differences in perceptions of self during early adolescence. In J. Brooks-Gunn and A. Petersen (Eds.), *Girls at puberty: Biological and psychological perspectives* (pp. 127–154). New York: Plenum Press. [13]

Tomasello, M. (1988). The role of joint attentional processes in early language development. *Language Sciences, 10,* 69–88. [7]

Tomasello, M., Conti-Ramsden, G., and Ewert, B. (1990). Young children's conversations with their mothers and fathers: Differences in breakdown and repair. *Journal of Child Language, 17,* 115–130. [7]

Tomasello, M., and Kruger, A. C. (1992). Joint attention on actions: Acquiring verbs in ostensive and non-ostensive contexts. *Journal of Child Language, 19,* 311–333. [7]

Tomasello, M., and Mannle, S. (1985). Pragmatics of sibling speech to one-year-olds. *Child Development, 56,* 911–917. [7]

Tomasello, M., Striano, T., and Rochat, P. (1999). Do young children use objects as symbols? *British Journal of Developmental Psychology, 17,* 563–584. [7]

Trachtenberg, S., and Viken, R. (1994). Aggressive boys in the classroom: Biased attributions or shared perceptions. *Child Development, 65,* 829–835. [12]

Travis, L., and Sigman, M. (2000). A developmental approach to autism. In A. Sameroff, M. Lewis, and S. Miller (Eds.), *Handbook of developmental psychopathology* (2nd ed.), pp. 641–656. New York: Plenum. [15]

Tronick, E. Z., Morelli, G. A., and Ivey, P. K. (1992). The Efe forager infant and toddler's pattern of social relationships: Multiple and simultaneous. *Developmental Psychology, 28,* 568–577. [2], [6], [8]

Troseth, G. L., and DeLoache, J. S. (1998). The medium can obscure the message: Young children's understanding of video. *Child Development, 69,* 950–965. [7]

Troy, M., and Sroufe, L. A. (1987). Victimization among preschoolers: Role of attachment relationship history. *Journal of the American Academy of Child and Adolescent Psychiatry, 26,* 166–172. [10]

Truby-King, F. (1937). *Feeding and care of baby* (rev. ed.). Oxford, Eng.: Oxford University Press. [2]

Trumbull, E., Rothstein-Fisch, C., Greenfield, P. M., and Quiroz, B. (2001). *Bridging cultures between home and school: A guide for teachers with a special focus on immigrant Latino families.* Mahwah, NJ: Erlbaum. [11]

Tulkin, S. R., and Konner, M. J. (1973). Alternative conceptions of intellectual functioning. *Human Development, 16,* 33–52. [13]

Turiel, E. (1998). The development of morality. In W. Damon (Series Ed.) and N. Eisenberg (Vol. Ed.), *Handbook of child psychology: Vol. 3. Social, emotional, and personality development* (5th ed., pp. 863–932). New York: Wiley. [10], [12]

Twenge, J., and Campbell, W. K. (2001). Age and birth cohort differences in self-esteem: A cross-temporal meta-analysis. *Personality and Social Psychology Review, 5,* 321–344. [14]

Tyrka, A., Graber, J., and Brooks-Gunn, J. (2000). The development of disordered eating In A. Sameroff, M. Lewis, and S. Miller (Eds.), *Handbook of developmental psychopathology* (2nd ed.), pp. 607–624. New York: Plenum. [15]

UNAIDS (2002). *AIDS epidemic update: December 2002.* http://www.unaids.org [3]

Underwood, M., Coie, J., and Herbsman, C. (1992). Display rules for anger and aggression in school-age children. *Child Development, 63,* 366–380. [12]

Underwood, M., Schockner, A., and Hurley, J. (2001). Children's responses to same- and other-gender peers: An experimental investigation with 8-, 10-, and 12-year-olds. *Developmental Psychology, 37,* 362–372. [12]

Updegraff, K., McHale, S., and Crouter, A. (2000). Adolescents' sex-typed friendship experiences: Does having a sister versus a brother matter? *Child Development, 71,* 1597–1610. [14]

Updegraff, K., and Obeidallah, D. (1999). Young adolescents' patterns of involvement with siblings and friends. *Social Development, 8,* 52–69. [14]

U.S. Census Bureau. (1995). *Statistical abstract of the United States* (115th ed.). Washington, DC: U.S. Government Printing Office. [2]

U.S. Census Bureau. (1999). *Statistical abstract of the United States* (119th ed.). Washington, DC: U.S. Government Printing Office. [2]

U.S. Census Bureau (2002a). Historical Poverty Tables—People, (Table) 20. Poverty Status of Related Children Under 6 Years of Age: 1969–2000. [2] <http://www.census.gov/hhes/poverty/hist-pov/hstpov20.html>

U.S. Census Bureau. (2002b). *Statistical abstract of the United States* (122nd ed.). Washington, DC: U.S. Government Printing Office. [2], [7], [8], [9], [13]

U. S. Census Bureau (2003). Historical Table. Primary Child Care Arrangements Used by Employed Mothers of Preschoolers: 1985 to 1999. [2] http://www.census.gov/population/socdemo/child/ppl-168/tabH-1.pdf

U.S. Conference of Mayors. (2002). *A status report on hunger and homelessness in America's cities.* Washington, DC: U.S. Conference of Mayors. [2]

U. S. Department of Education (2000). *Digest of educational statistics, 2000.* Washington, D. C. U. S. Government Printing Office. [14]

U.S. Department of Health and Human Services. (2001). *Women and smoking. A report of the Surgeon General.* Atlanta: U.S. Department of Health and Human Services, Centers for Disease Control and Prevention, National Center for Chronic Disease Prevention and Health Promotion, Office on Smoking and Health. [3]

Usher, J. A., and Neisser, U. (1993). Childhood amnesia and the beginnings of memory for four early life events. *Journal of Experimental Psychology: General, 122,* 155–165. [5]

Uzgiris, I. C., and Hunt, J. M. (1975). *Assessment in infancy: Ordinal scales of psychological development.* Champaign: University of Illinois Press. [5]

Vadocz, E. A., Siegel, S. R., and Malina, R. M. (2002). Age at menarche in competitive figure skaters: Variation by competency and discipline. *Journal of Sports Sciences, 20,* 93–100. [13]

Valsiner, J. (1998). The development of the concept of development: Historical and epistemological perspectives. In W. Damon (Series Ed.) and R. M. Lerner (Vol. Ed.), *Handbook of child psychology: Vol. 1. Theoretical models of human development* (5th ed., pp. 189–232). New York: Wiley. [1]

van Baar, A. L., Soepatmi, S., Gunning, W. B., and Akkerhuis, G. W. (1994). Development after prenatal exposure to cocaine, heroin, and methadone. *Acta Paediatrica Supplements, 404,* 40–46. [3]

van den Boom, D. (1989). Neonatal irritability and the development of attachment. In G. Kohnstamm, J. Bates, and M. Rothbart (Eds.), *Temperament in childhood* (pp. 299–318). New York: Wiley. [6]

Vandell, D., and Ramanan, J. (1991). Children of the National Longitudinal Survey of Youth: Choices in after-school care and child development. *Developmental Psychology, 27,* 637–643. [12]

Vanhatalo, S., and van Nieuwenhuizen, O. (2000). Fetal pain? *Brain and Development, 22,* 145–150. [3]

van IJzendoorn, M. (1995). The association between adult attachment representations and infant attachment, parental responsiveness, and clinical status: A meta-analysis on the predictive validity of the Adult Attachment Interview. *Psychological Bulletin, 113,* 404–410. [6]

van IJzendoorn, M., and de Wolff, M. (1997). In search of the absent father: Meta-analysis of infant-father attachment. *Child Development, 68,* 604–609. [6]

Van Lieshout, C. F. M. (1975). Young children's reactions to barriers placed by their mothers. *Child Development, 46,* 879–886. [10]

Vasey, M., and Ollendick, T. (2000). Anxiety. In A. Sameroff, M. Lewis, and S. Miller (Eds.), *Handbook of developmental psychopathology* (2nd ed.), pp. 511–530. New York: Plenum. [15]

Vaughn, B. E. (1979). *An ethological study of greeting behaviors in infants from six to nine months of age.* Unpublished doctoral dissertation, University of Minnesota. [6]

Vaughn, B., Azria, M., Krzysik, L., Caya, L., Bost, K., Newell, W., and Kazura, K. (2000). Friendship and social competence in a sample of preschool children attending Head Start. *Developmental Psychology, 36,* 326–338. [10]

Vaughn, B. E., and Bost, K. (1999). Attachment and temperament: Redundant, independent, or interacting influences on interpersonal adaptation and development? In J. Cassidy and P. Shaver (Eds.), *Handbook of attachment: Theory, research, and clinical applications.* (pp. 198–225). New York: Guilford. [6]

Vaughn, B. E., Egeland, B., Waters, E., and Sroufe, L. A. (1979). Individual differences in infant-mother attachment at 12 and 18 months: Stability and change in families under stress. *Child Development, 50,* 971–975. [6], [8]

Vaughn, B. E., Stevenson-Hinde, J., Waters, E., Kotsaftis, A., Lefever, G. B., Shouldice, A., Trudel, M., and Belsky, J. (1992). Attachment security and temperament in infancy and early childhood: Some conceptual clarifications. *Developmental Psychology, 28,* 463–473. [6], [8], [10]

Vaughn, B. E., and Waters, E. (1981). Attention structure, sociometric status, and dominance: Interrelations, behavioral correlates and relationships to social competence. *Developmental Psychology, 17,* 275–288. [10]

Vaughn, B. E., and Waters, E. (1990). Attachment behavior at home and in the laboratory: Q-sort observations and strange situation classifications of one-year-olds. *Child Development, 61,* 1965–1973. [6], [10]

Venter, J. C., Adams, M. D., Myers, E. W., Li, P. W., Mural, R. J., Sutton G. G., et al. (2001). The sequence of the human genome. *Science, 291,* 1304–1351. [2], [3]

Ventura, S. J., and Bachrach, C. A. (2000). Nonmarital childbearing in the United States, 1940–1999. National Vital Statistics Reports, 48(16). Hyattsville, MD: National Center for Health Statistics. [2]

Ventura, S. J., Matthews, T. J., and Hamilton, B. E. (2001). Births to teenagers in the United States, 1940–2000. National Vital Statistics Reports, 49(10). Hyattsville, MD: National Center for Health Statistics. [2]

Ventura, S. J., Peters, K. D., Martin, J. A., and Maurer, J. D. (1997). Births and Deaths: United States, 1996. Monthly Vital Statistics Report, 46(1), Supplement 2. Rockville, MD: National Center for Health Statistics. [2]

Verschueren, K., Buyck, P., and Marcoen, A. (2001). Self-representations and socioemotional competence in young children: A 3-year longitudinal study. *Developmental Psychology, 37,* 126–134. [10]

Vespo, J. (1997). *The nature of sibling conflict during middle childhood.* Poster presented at the Biennial Meeting of the Society for Research in Child Development, Washington, DC. [12]

Volling, B. L., and Belsky, J. (1992). The contribution of mother-child and father-child relationships to the quality of sibling interaction: A longitudinal study. *Child Development, 63,* 1209–1222. [2]

Volterra, V., and Erting, C. J. (Eds.). (1990). *From gesture to language in hearing and deaf children.* New York: Springer. [7]

Von Hofsten, C. (1977). Binocular convergence as a determinant of reaching behavior in infancy. *Perception, 6,* 139–144. [4]

Vuchinich, S., Bank, L., and Patterson, G. (1992). Parenting, peers, and the stability of antisocial behavior in preadolescent boys. *Developmental Psychology, 28,* 510–521. [12]

Vurpillot, E. (1968). The development of scanning strategies and their relation to visual differentiation. *Journal of Experimental Child Psychology, 6,* 632–650. [9]

Waber, D. P. (1977). Sex differences in mental abilities, hemispheric lateralization, and rate of physical growth at adolescence. *Developmental Psychology, 13,* 290–38. [13]

Wachs, T. (1991). Environmental considerations in studies of non-extreme groups. In T. Wachs and R. Plomin (Eds.), *Conceptualization and measurement of organism-environment interaction* (pp. 44–67). Washington, DC: American Psychological Association. [1]

Wachs, T., Bishry, Z., Sobhy, A., McCabe, G., Galal, O., and Shaheen, F. (1993). Relation of rearing environment to adaptive behavior in Egyptian toddlers. *Child Development, 64,* 586–604. [8]

Wachsler-Felder, J. L., and Golden, C. J. (2002). Neuropsychological consequences of HIV in children: A review of current literature. *Clinical Psychology Review, 22, 441–462.* [3]

Waddington, C. H. (1966). *Principles of development and differentiation.* New York: Macmillan. [2]

Waddington, C. H. (1957). *The strategy of the genes.* London: Allen and Unwin. [1]

Wagner, B. and Reiss, D. (1995). Family systems and developmental psychopathology: Courtship, marriage, or divorce? In D. Cicchetti, and D. Cohen (Eds.), *Developmental Psychopathology: Vol. 1. Theory and methods* (pp. 696–730). New York: Wiley. [15]

Wagner, C. L., Katikaneni, L. D., Cox, T. H., and Ryan, R. M. (1998). The impact of prenatal drug exposure on the neonate. *Obstetrics and Gynecology Clinics of North America, 25,* 169–194. [3]

Wagner, D. A., and Spratt, J. E. (1987). Cognitive consequences of contrasting pedagogies: The effects of Koranic preschooling in Morocco. *Child Development, 58,* 1207–1219. [1]

Wagner, R. K. (1997). Intelligence, training, and employment. *American Psychologist, 52,* 1059–1069. [11]

Wakschlag, L. S., and Hans, S. L. (2002). Maternal smoking during pregnancy and conduct problems in high-risk youth: A developmental framework. *Development and Psychopathology, 14,* 351–369. [3]

Walker, L., and Taylor, J. (1991). Family interactions and the development of moral reasoning. *Child Development, 62,* 264–283. [12]

Walker, L. J. (1984). Sex differences in the development of moral reasoning: A critical review. *Child Development, 55,* 677–691. [13]

Walker, L. J. (1989). A longitudinal study of moral reasoning. *Child Development, 60,* 157–166. [13]

Walker-Andrews, A. (1997). Infants' perception of expressive behaviors: Differentiation on multimodal information. *Psychological Bulletin, 121,* 437–456. [6]

Waller, H., Kojetin, B., Bouchard, R., Lykken, D., and Tellegen, A. (1990). Attitudes and values: A study of twins reared apart and together. *Psychological Science, 1,* 138–142. [1]

Wallerstein, J. S., and Kelly, J. B. (1982). *Surviving the breakup: How children and parents cope with divorce.* New York: Basic Books. [10]

Walters, J. M., and Gardner, H. (1986). The theory of multiple intelligences: Some issues and answers. In R. K. Wagner and R. J. Sternberg (Eds.), *Practical intelligence* (pp. 163–182). New York: Cambridge University Press. [11]

Wang, X., Tager, I. B., Van Vunakis, H., Speizer, F. E., and Hanrahan, J. P. (1997). Maternal smoking during pregnancy, urine cotinine concentrations, and birth outcomes. A prospective cohort study. *International Journal of Epidemiology, 26,* 978–988. [3]

Ward, M., and Carlson, E. (1995). Associations among adult attachment representations, maternal sensitivity, and infant-mother attachment in a sample of adolescent mothers. *Child Development, 66,* 69–79. [6]

Wark, G., and Krebs, D. (1996). Gender and developmental differences in real-life moral judgment. *Developmental Psychology, 32,* 220–230. [13]

Warren, S., Huston, L., Egeland, B., and Sroufe, L. A. (1997). Child and adolescent anxiety disorders and early attachment. *Journal of the American Academy of Child and Adolescent Psychiatry, 36,* 637–644. [15]

Warren, S., and Sroufe, L. A. (in press). Developmental issues. In T. Ollendick and J. March (Eds.), *Phobic and anxiety disorders in children.* New York: Oxford Univ. Press. [15]

Warren-Leubecker, A., and Bohannon, J. N. (1983). The effects of verbal feedback and listener type on the speech of preschool children. *Journal of Experimental Child Psychology, 35,* 540–548. [9]

Wasz-Höckert, O., Lind, J., Vuorenkoski, V., Partanen, T., and Valanne, E. (1968). *The infant cry. A spectrographic and auditory analysis. Clinics in developmental medicine 29.* London: Heinemann. [4]

Waterman, A. S. (1992). Identity as an aspect of optimal psychological functioning. In G. R. Adams, T. P. Gullotta, and R. Montemayor (Eds.), *Adolescent identity formation* (pp. 50–72). Newbury Park, CA: Sage. [14]

Waters, E. (1978). The stability of individual differences in infant-mother attachment. *Child Development, 49,* 483–494. [6], [8]

Waters, E., Kondo-Ikemura, K., Posada, G., and Richters, J. E. (1991). Learning to love: Mechanisms and milestones. In M. R. Gunnar and L. A. Sroufe (Eds.), *Minnesota Symposia in Child Psychology: Vol. 23. Self processes in development* (pp. 217–255). Hillsdale, NJ: Erlbaum. [1], [8], [10]

Waters, E., Matas, L., and Sroufe, L. A. (1975). Infants' reactions to an approaching stranger: Description, validation, and functional significance of wariness. *Child Development, 46,* 348–356. [6]

Waters, E., and Sroufe, L. A. (1983). A developmental perspective on competence. *Developmental Review, 3,* 79–97. [1]

Watkin, P. M., and Baldwin, M. (1999). Confirmation of deafness in infancy. *Archives of disease in childhood, 81,* 380–389. [7]

Watson, J. B. (1928). *Psychological care of infant and child.* New York: Norton. [1], [2], [4]

Watson, J. S., Hayes, L. A., and Vietze, P. (1979). Bidimensional sorting in preschoolers with an instrumental learning task. *Child Development, 50,* 1178–1183. [9]

Weiner, B., Kun, A., and Benesh-Weiner, M. (1980). The development of mastery, emotion, and morality from an attributional perspective. In W. A. Collins (Ed.), *Minnesota Symposia on Child Psychology: Vol. 13. Development of cognition, affect, and social relations* (pp. 103–129). Hillsdale, NJ: Erlbaum. [14]

Weinfield, N., Sroufe, L. A., Egeland, B., and Carlson, E. (1999). The nature of individual differences in infant-caregiver attachment. In J. Cassidy and P. Shaver (Eds.), *Handbook of attachment* (pp. 73–95). New York: Guilford Press. [6]

Weiss, B., Dodge, K., Bates, J., and Pettit, G. (1992). Some consequences of early harsh discipline: Child aggression and a maladaptive social information processing style. *Child Development, 63,* 1321–1335. [12]

Weiss, G., and Hechtman, L. (1986). *Hyperactive children grown up.* New York: Guilford Press. [15]

Weithorn, L. A., and Campbell, S. B. (1982). The competency of children and adolescents to make informed treatment decisions. *Child Development, 53,* 1589–1598. [13]

Wellman, H. M. (1985). A child's theory of mind: The development of conceptions of cognition. In S. R. Yussen (Ed.), *The growth of reflection in children* (pp. 169–203) New York: Academic Press. [11]

Wellman, H. M., Cross, D., and Bartsch, K. (1986). A meta-analysis of research on stage 4 object permanence: The A-not-B error. *Society for Research in Child Development Monographs, 51* (3, Serial No. 214). [5]

Wellman, H. M., and Estes, D. (1986). Early understanding of mental entities: A reexamination of childhood realism. *Child Development, 57,* 910–923. [9]

Wellman, H. M., and Gelman, S. A. (1992) Cognitive development: Foundational theories of core domains. In M. R. Rosenzweig and L. W. Porter (Eds.), *Annual review of psychology.* Palo Alto, CA: Annual Reviews. [9]

Wellman, H. M., and Gelman, S. A. (1998). Knowledge acquisition in foundational domains. In W. Damon (Series Ed.), D. Kuhn, and R. S. Siegler (Vol. Eds.), *Handbook of child psychology: Vol. 2. Cognition, perception, and language* (5th ed., pp. 523–573). New York: Wiley. [9]

Wellman, H. M., Ritter, K., and Flavell, J. H. (1975). Deliberate memory behavior in the delayed reactions of very young children. *Developmental Psychology, 11,* 780–787. [9]

Wenar, C. (1990). *Developmental psychopathology* (2nd ed.). New York: McGraw-Hill. [15]

Wenar, C. (1994). *Developmental psychopathology* (3rd ed.). New York: McGraw-Hill. [15]

Wenar, C. (1976). Executive competence in toddlers: A prospective, observational study. *Genetic Psychology Monographs, 93,* 189–285. [8]

Werler, M. M., Shapiro, S., and Mitchell, A. A. (1993). Periconceptual folic acid exposure and risk of occurrent neural tube defects. *Journal of the American Medical Association, 269,* 1257–1261. [3]

Werner, E., and Smith, R. (2001). *Journeys from childhood to midlife: Risk, resilience, and recovery.* Ithaca, NY: Cornell University Press. [6], [10], [15]

Wertsch, J. V., Del Río, P., and Alvarez, A. (1995). *Sociocultural studies of mind.* New York: Cambridge University Press. [1]

Wertsch, J. V., and Tulviste, P. (1994). Lev Semyonovich Vygotsky and contemporary developmental psychology. In R. D. Parke, P. A. Ornstein, J. J. Rieser, and C. Zahn-Waxler (Eds.), *A century of developmental psychology* (pp. 333–355). Washington, DC: American Psychological Association. [1]

White, A., Eldridge, R., and Andrews, E. (1997). Birth outcomes following zidovudine exposure in pregnant women: The Antiretroviral Pregnancy Registry. *Acta Paediatrica Supplements, 421,* 86–88. [3]

White, B. L., Castle, P., and Held, R. (1964). Observations on the development of visually directed reaching. *Child Development, 35,* 349–364. [4]

White, K., and Kistner, J. (1992). The influence of teacher feedback on young children's peer preferences and perceptions. *Developmental Psychology, 28,* 933–940. [10]

White, R. (1959). Motivation reconsidered: The concept of competence. *Psychological Review, 66,* 297–333. [2]

White, T. L., Leichtman, M. D., and Ceci, S. J. (1997). The good, the bad, and the ugly: Accuracy, inaccuracy, and elaboration in preschoolers' reports about a past event. *Applied Cognitive Psychology, 11 (special issue),* S37–S54. [9]

Whiting, B. B., and Edwards, C. P. (1988). *Children of different worlds.* Cambridge, MA: Harvard University Press. [8], [10], [12], [14]

Whiting, B., and Whiting, J. (1975). *Children of six cultures: A psycho-cultural analysis.* Cambridge, MA: Harvard University Press. [2]

Wickens, D. D., and Wickens, C. A. (1940). A study of conditioning in the neonate. *Journal of Experimental Psychology, 26,* 94–102. [4]

Wiesenfeld, A., Malatesta, C., and DeLoach, L. (1981). Differential parental response to familiar and unfamiliar infant distress signals. *Infant Behavior and Development, 4,* 281–295. [4]

Wigdor, A. K., and Garner, W. R. (Eds.). (1982). *Ability testing: Uses, consequences, and controversies.* Washington, DC: National Academy Press. [11]

Williams, J. M., and Dunlop, L. C. (1999). Pubertal timing and self-reported delinquency among male adolescents. *Journal of Adolescence, 22,* 157–171. [13]

Willinger, M., Ko, C.-W., Hoffman, H. J., Kessler, R. C., Corwin, M. J. (2000). Factors associated with caregivers' choice of infant sleep position, 1994–1998: The National Infant Sleep Position Study. *JAMA: Journal of the American Medical Association, 283,* 2135–2142. [4]

Wilson, M. (1989). Child development in the context of the Black extended family. *American Psychologist, 44,* 380–385. [2]

Wimmer, H., and Perner, J. (1983). Beliefs about beliefs: Representation and constraining function of wrong beliefs in young children's understanding of deception. *Cognition, 13,* 102–128. [9]

Winick, M. (1975). Effects of malnutrition on the maturing central nervous system. In W. J. Friedlander (Ed.), *Advances in neurology* (Vol. 13, pp. 193–246). New York: Raven Press. [3]

Winnicott, D. W. (1965). *The maturational processes and the facilitating environment.* New York: International Universities Press. [6]

Wolf, D. (1990). Being of several minds: Voices and versions of the self in early childhood. In D. Cicchetti and M. Beeghly (Eds.), *The self in transition: Infancy to childhood* (pp. 183–212). Chicago: University of Chicago Press. [10]

Wolf, D. (1982). Understanding others: A longitudinal case study of the concept of independent agency.

In G. Furman (Ed.), *Action and thought* (pp. 297–327). New York: Academic Press. [8], [12]

Wolff, P. H. (1987). *The development of behavioral states and the expression of emotions in early infancy: New proposals for investigation.* Chicago: University of Chicago Press. [4]

Wolfson, A. R., and Carskadon, M. A. (1998). Sleep schedules and daytime functioning in adolescents. *Child Development, 69,* 875–887. [13]

Woodward, A. L., and Markman, E. M. (1998). Early word learning. In W. Damon (Series Ed.), D. Kuhn, and R. S. Siegler (Vol. Eds.), *Handbook of child psychology: Vol. 2. Cognition, perception, and language* (5th ed., pp. 371–420). New York: Wiley. [7]

Woodward, A. L., Markman, E. M., and Fitzsimmons, C. M. (1994). Rapid word learning in 13- and 18-month-olds. *Developmental Psychology, 30,* 553–566. [7]

Woodward, S., McManis, M., Kagan, J., Deldin, P., Snidman, N., Lewis, M., and Kahn, V. (2001). Infant temperament and the brainstem auditory evoked response in later childhood. *Developmental Psychology, 37,* 533–538. [6]

Woolley, J. D., and Wellman, H. M. (1990). Young children's understanding of realities, nonrealities, and appearances. *Child Development, 61,* 946–961. [9]

Wright, J. D. (1990). Homelessness is not healthy for children and other living things. *Child and Youth Services, 14,* 65–88. [2]

Wu, L., Schlenger, W. E., Galvin, D. M. (2003). The relationship between employment and substance use among students aged 12 to 17. *Journal of Adolescent Health, 32,* 5–15. [14]

Wynn, K. (1992). Addition and subtraction by human infants. *Nature, 358,* 749–750. [5]

Wynn, K. (1990). Children's understanding of counting. *Cognition, 36,* 104–143. [9]

Yang, B., Ollendick, T. H., Dong, Q., Xia, Y., and Lin, L. (1995). Only children and children with siblings in the People's Republic of China: Levels of fear, anxiety, and depression. *Child Development, 66,* 1301–1311. [2]

Yarrow, M. R., Scott, P., de Leeuw, L., and Heinig, C. (1962). Childrearing in families of working and nonworking mothers. *Sociometry, 25,* 122–140. [2]

Yates, P. D. (1987). A case of mistaken identity: Interethnic images in multicultural England. In G. Spindler and L. Spindler (Eds.), *Interpretative ethnography of education: At home and abroad* (pp. 195–218). Hillsdale, NJ: Erlbaum. [11]

Yates, T., Dodds, M., Sroufe, L. A., and Egeland, B. (in press). Exposure to partner violence and child behavior problems: Controlling for child-directed abuse, child cognitive ability, family income, and life stress. *Development and Psychopathology.* [8], [12], [15]

Yates, W. R., Cadoret, R. J., Troughton, E. P., Stewart, M., and Giunta, T. S. (1998). Effect of fetal alcohol exposure on adult symptoms of nicotine, alcohol, and drug dependence. *Alcohol Clinical and Experimental Research, 22,* 914–920. [3]

Yonas, A., Cleaves, W., and Pettersen, L. (1978). Development of sensitivity to pictorial depth. *Science, 200,* 77–79. [4]

Yonas, A., and Granrud, C. E. (1985). Development of visual space perception in young infants. In J. Mehler and R. Fox (Eds.), *Neonate cognition: Beyond the blooming, buzzing confusion* (pp. 45–67). Hillsdale, NJ: Erlbaum. [4]

Yonas, A., and Hartman, B. (1993). Perceiving the affordance of contact in four- and five-month-old infants. *Child Development, 64,* 298–308. [4]

Yonas, A., and Owlsley, C. (1987). Development of visual space perception. In P. Salapatek and L. Cohen (Eds.), *Handbook of infant perception* (pp. 80–122). New York: Academic Press. [4]

Yoshikawa, H. (1994). Prevention as cumulative protection: Effects of early family support and education on chronic delinquency and its risks. *Psychological Bulletin, 115,* 28–54. [15]

Youniss, J. (1980). *Parents and peers in social development: A Sullivan-Piaget perspective.* Chicago: University of Chicago Press. [14]

Youniss, J., McLellan, J. A., and Strouse, D. (1994). "We're popular, but we're not snobs": Adolescents describe their crowds. In R. Montemayor, G. R. Adams, and T. P. Gullotta (Eds.), *Personal relationships during adolescence* (pp. 101–122). Thousand Oaks, CA: Sage. [14]

Zahn-Waxler, C., Radke-Yarrow, M., Wagner, E., and Chapman, M. (1992). Development of concern for others. *Developmental Psychology, 28,* 126–136. [8], [10]

Zaporozhets, A. V. (1965). The development of perception in the preschool child. *Monographs of the Society for Research in Child Development, 30* (Serial No. 100). [4]

Zelazo, P. D., and Reznick, J. S. (1991). Age-related asynchrony of knowledge and action. *Child Development, 62,* 719–735. [9]

Zelazo, P. D., Frye, D., and Rapus, T. (1996). An age-related dissociation between knowing rules and using them. *Cognitive Development, 11,* 37–63. [9]

Zelazo, P. D., Reznick, J. S., and Piñon, D. E. (1995). Response control and the execution of verbal rules. *Developmental Psychology, 31,* 508–517. [9]

Zelazo, P. R. (1983). The development of walking: New findings and old assumptions. *Journal of Motor Behavior, 15,* 99–137. [4]

Zhu, L., and Fang, F. (2000). Development of Chinese preschoolers' understanding of biological phenomena: Growth and aliveness. *International Journal of Behavioral Development, 24,* 105–110. [9]

Zill, N., Morrison, D., and Corio, M. (1993). Long-term effects of parental divorce on parent-child relationships, adjustment, and achievement in young adulthood. *Journal of Family Psychology, 7,* 91–103. [12]

Zoccolillo, M. (1993). Gender and the development of conduct disorder. *Development and Psychopathology, 5,* 65–78. [15]

Zukow-Goldring, P. (2002). Sibling caregiving. In M. H. Bornstein (Ed.), *Handbook of parenting: Vol. 3. Being and becoming a parent* (2nd ed., pp. 253–286). Mahwah, NJ: Erlbaum. [2], [12]

Acknowledgments

CHAPTER 3

Fig. 3.8: Reprinted from Before We Are Born, by K.L. Moore, 1974, W.B. Saunders Co. Copyright © 1974 with permission from Elsevier Science.

CHAPTER 4

Fig. 4.4: Sostek and Anders, 1981.

Fig. 4.10: From D. Mauer and P. Salapatek, "Developmental Changes in the Scanning of Faces by Young Infants," *Child Development,* 47, 1976. Reprinted with permission of the Society for Research in Child Development, University of Michigan.

Fig. 4.19: A. Slater and G. Bremner (eds.), Infant Development, p. 62. Copyright © 1989. Used by permission of Taylor & Francis, Inc.

CHAPTER 5

Fig. 5.2: Reprinted from *Cognitive Psychology,* Vol. 15, 1993, "Perception of Partly Occluded Objects in Infancy," by P.J. Kellman and E.S. Spelke. Copyright © 1970, with permission from Elsevier Science.

Fig. 5.3: From R. Baillargeon, "Object Permanence in 3-1/2 and 4-1/2 Month-Old Infants," Developmental Psychology, 23, 1987. Copyright © 1987 by the American Psychological Association. Reprinted with permission.

Fig. 5.5: R. Baillargeon, A. Needham, and J. DeVos, "The Development of Young Infants' Intuitions About Support," Early Development and Parenting, 1, 69–78. Copyright © 1992 by John Wiley & Sons, Ltd. Reproduced by permission of John Wiley & Sons Limited.

Fig. 5.7: Reprinted from Infant Behavior and Development, Vol. 7, 1984, "Infant Perception of Angular Relations," by L.B. Cohen and B.A. Younger. Copyright © 1984, with permission from Elsevier Science.

Table 5.2: From Bayley Scales of Infant Development (BSID) by N. Bayley, 1969. Reproduced with permission of The Psychological Corporation.

CHAPTER 6

Fig. 6.1: T.B. Brazelton, B. Koslowski, and M. Main (1974). "The Origins of Reciprocity: The Early Mother-Input Interaction," in M. Lewis and L. Rosenblum (eds.), The Effect of the Infant on its Caregiver, pp. 62–63. Used by permission of Dr. M. Lewis and Dr. L. Rosenblum.

Fig. 6.4: E. Waters, L. Matas, & L.A. Sroufe (1975). "Infants' Reactions to An Approaching Stranger: Description, Validation, and Functional Significance of Wariness," *Child Development,* 46, 348–356. Copyright © 1975 Society for Research in Child Development, Inc.

CHAPTER 7

Fig. 7.2: From J. Berko, "The Child's Learning of English Morphology," *Word,* 14, 154. Copyright © 1958. Used by permission of the International Linguistic Association, New York.

CHAPTER 8

Fig. 8.1: From Z. Strassberg, K. Dodge, G. Pettit, and J. Bates, "Spanking in the Home and Children's Subsequent Aggression Toward Kindergarten Peers," Development and Psychopathology, Vol. 6, 1994. Reprinted with permission of Cambridge University Press.

CHAPTER 9

Fig. 9.3: Reprinted from R.C. Atkins and R.M. Shiffrin, "Human Memory: A Proposed System and Its Control Processes," in K.W. Spence and J.T. Spence (eds.), The Psychology of Learning and Motivation: Advances in Research and Theory, Vol. 2, 1968. Copyright © 1984, with permission from Elsevier Science.

Fig. 9.4: Reprinted from Journal of Experimental, Child Psychology, Vol. 6, 1968, The Development of Scanning Strategies and Their Relation to Visual Differentiation," by B. Vurpillot. Copyright © 1968, with permission from Elsevier Science.

Fig. 9.6: From S. Glucksberg and R.M. Krauss, "What Do People Say After They Have Learned to Talk? Studies of the Development of Referential Communication," Merrill Palmer Quarterly. Reprinted from Merrill Palmer Quarterly, 13, No. 4 (1936), Wayne State University Press with permission of the Wayne State University Press.

CHAPTER 10

Fig. 10.1: L.J. Schweinhart & D.P. Weikart (1993). "Success by Empowerment: The High/Scope Perry Preschool Study Through Age 27," Young Children, p. 54. Used by permission of Educational Research Foundation.

Fig. 10.2: L.J. Schweinhart & D.P. Weikart (1993). "Success by Empowerment: The High/Scope Perry Preschool Study Through Age 27," Young Children, p. 55. Used by permission of Educational Research Foundation.

CHAPTER 11

Excerpts: From Scott G. Paris, "Integration and Interference in Children's Comprehension and Memory," in F. Restle, R. Shiffrin, J. Castellan, H. Lindman and D. Pisoni (eds.), Cognitive Theory, Vol. 1, 1975. Reprinted with permission.

Table 11.2: Reprinted from Cognitive Psychology, Vol. 1, No. 4, 1970, "Developmental Changes in Memorization Processes," by J.H. Flavell, A.G. Friedrichs, and J.D. Hoyt. Copyright © 1970, with permission from Elsevier Science.

CHAPTER 12

Table 12.1: L.A. Sroufe, C. Bennett, M. Englund, J. Urban, and S. Shulman (1993). "The Significance of Gender Boundaries in Preadolescence: Contemporary Correlates and Antecedents of Boundary Violation and Maintenance," *Child Development,* 64 (2) 455–466. Used by permission.

CHAPTER 13

Fig. 13.1: Adapted from "Hypothalamic pituitary regulation of puberty in man: Evidence and concepts derived from clinical research," by M.M. Grumbach, J.C. Roth, S.I. Kaplan, and R.P. Kelch, in *Control of the onset of puberty* by M.M. Grumbach, G.D. Grave, and F.H. Mayer (eds.). Copyright © 1974 by John Wiley & Sons. Inc. Reprinted by permission of Jonh Wiley & Sons, Inc.

Table 13.1: From J.M. Tanner, Growth at Adolescence, 1962. Reprinted with permission of Blackwell Publishing.

Fig. 13.2: J.M. Tanner, R.H. Whitehouse, & M. Takaishi, "Standards From Birth to Maturity for Height, Weight, Height Velocity, and Weight Velocity: British Children, 1965," Archives of Disease in Childhood, 41, 613–635. Copyright © 1966. Used by permission.

Fig. 13.3: From J.M. Tanner, Growth at Adolescence, 1962. Reprinted with permission of Blackwell Publishing.

Fig. 13.4: From The Growth of Logical Thinking: From Childhood to Adolescence by Jean Piaget and Barbel Inhelder. Copyright © 1958 by Basic Books, Inc. Reprinted by permission of Basic Books, a member of Perseus Books, L.L.C.

CHAPTER 14

Table 14.1: From William Damon and Daniel Hart, Self-Understanding in Childhood and Adolescence, 1988. Reprinted with the permission of Cambridge University Press.

Table 14.2: From D. Elkind and R. Bowen, "Imaginary Audience Behavior in Children and Adolescence," Developmental Psychology, 15, 1979. Copyright © 1979 by the American Psychological Association. Reprinted with permission.

Table 14.3: Reprinted from R. Selman, The Growth of Interpersonal Understanding, 1980, Academic Press. Copyright © 1980, with permission from Elsevier Science.

Fig. 14.2: From P. Costanzo, "Conformity Development as a Function of Self-Blame," Journal of Personality and Social Psychology, 14, 1970. Copyright © 1970 by the American Psychological Association. Reprinted with permission.

CHAPTER 15

Table 15.2: From "Adopted Away Off-Spring of Schizophrenics and Controls," by P.L. Tienair, et al., in Lee N. Robins and Michael Rutter (eds.) Straight and Devious Pathways From Childhood to Adulthood, 1990. Reprinted with the permission of Cambridge University Press.

Photo Credits

Name Index

Heibeck, T. H., 243
Heinicke, C., 211
Heinig, C., 62
Held, R., 143
Hellström-Lindahl, E., 102
Henderson, C., 150
Henderson, V. K., 208, 213, 513, 514
Hennelly, R.A., 391
Henrich, C., 502
Henry, R. R., 106
Herbison, G., 286
Herbsman, C., 425
Herdt, G., 457
Herman-Giddens, M. E., 456, 457
Heron, A., 25, 184, 185, 384, 472
Herrnstein, R. J., 406
Hershey, K., 215, 216, 283
Hertsgaard, L. A., 181, 216, 218
Hesse, E., 211, 212, 362
Hetherington, E. M., 10, 62, 64, 358, 430, 431, 511, 512
Hewlett, B. S., 53, 220–21, 222
Hiatt, S., 150, 204
Hickling, A. K., 308
Higgins, A., 473
Higgins, E. T., 327
Hill, J., 220, 464, 509
Hirsh-Pasek, K., 237, 252, 254
Hoff, E., 65, 240, 246, 249
Hoff-Ginsberg, E., 258
Hoffman, H. J., 142
Hoffman, H. S., 148
Hoffman, L., 62
Hoffman, M., 352, 359
Hoijtink, H., 216
Holden, C., 46
Hollander, M., 246
Holmes, D. L., 330
Holt, R., 347
Homes, P. A., 103
Honzik, M. P., 187, 402
Hood, B., 172, 173
Hoover, R. N., 104
Hopkins, B., 132
Hornung, K., 286
Howard, J., 100, 219
Howe, M. L., 183
Howe, N., 55
Howes, C., 221, 276, 352, 360, 434
Hoyt, J. D., 394
Hsu, H., 363
Huang, J., 101
Hughes, M. D., 105
Hunt, C. E., 142
Hunt, J. M., 168, 171
Huntington, F. W., 99, 99–100
Hurley, J., 422
Huston, A. C., 427
Huston, T. L., 62
Hutchinson, C., 132
Huttenlocher, J., 177, 244
Huttenlocher, P. R., 96, 128, 129, 130, 462
Hyer, M., 104
Hymel, S., 424

Iaukea, K., 101
Inhelder, B., 382, 391, 468, 469, 470, 473
Insabella, G. M., 62, 431, 511
Irwin, J. M., 243
Isaacson, C., 108
Isabella, R. A., 54, 212, 219, 285
Ivey, P. K., 51, 222, 280
Izard, C., 202, 204

Jacklin, C. N., 435

Jackson, J. F., 73
Jacobs, A., 212
Jacobs, P. I., 388
Jacobson, J. L., 102, 103
Jacobson, R. L., 105
Jacobson, S. W., 102, 103, 139, 213
Jacobvitz, D., 286, 289, 363, 542, 543, 545
Jaedicke, S., 428
Jaffe, J., 198
Jagsch, R., 103
Jahnke, H., 478
Janowsky, J. S., 417
Janowsky, J. W., 253
Jantunen, M., 103
Jasnow, M., 198
Jenkins, E. J., 59
Jenkins, J., 433
Jennings, K., 363
Jensen, J., 545
Ji, G., 72
Jiao, S., 72
Jimenez, E., 105
Jimerson, S., 435, 436, 514
Jing, Q., 72
Joffe, L., 219
Johnson, A. L., 103
Johnson, D., 46, 209, 220
Johnson, J., 221
Johnson, J. S., 461
Johnson, L. D., 509
Johnson, M. H., 129, 153, 173, 182, 253
Johnson, S. P., 171
Johnston, J., 64
Johnston, L. D., 38, 507, 508
Jones, E., 437
Jones, L. V., 404
Jones, M., 465
Jones, M. H., 143
Jones, S. S., 139
Jorch, G., 101
Jordan, B., 112
Joseph, 10
Joseph, G., 65
Juarez, N., 104
Jusczyk, P. W., 148, 237, 254

Kaczala, C., 514
Kagan, J., 7, 24, 49, 216, 217, 218, 283
Kagan, S., 70
Kahn, V., 216
Kail, R., 392, 474
Kairam, R., 105–6
Kalish, C. W., 308
Kalkoske, M., 219
Kamm, K., 143
Kandall, S. R., 103
Kanner, L., 539
Kaplan, H., 145
Kaplan, S. L., 458
Kaplowitz, P. B., 457
Karen, R., 44
Katikaneni, L. D., 101, 103
Katz, L., 358
Katz, P., 416
Kaufman, R. H., 104
Kavanaugh, K., 279
Kaye, K., 199
Keating, D. P., 176, 466, 471, 473, 474, 475, 476
Keen, R., 172
Keeney, T. J., 393
Keil, F. C., 309
Keith, T., 514
Kelch, R. P., 458
Keller, M., 417, 419, 422, 426

Kelley, J., 64, 430, 431
Kellman, P. J., 147, 148, 153, 171
Kelly, J. B., 358
Kelly, S. J., 102
Kemler Nelson, D. G., 254
Kendall, P., 534, 545
Kendrick, C., 53, 258, 328
Kennedy, L., 254
Kennell, J., 207
Kerig, P., 431
Kermoian, R., 150
Kerns, K., 360, 428
Kerr, M., 510
Kessen, W., 68, 72, 143
Kessler, R. C., 142
Kestenbaum, R., 205, 218, 353, 360
Kierkegaard, S., 281
Kilgore, K., 358
Killen, M., 342
Kilner, L., 506
Kindler, H., 280
King, M. C., 48
Kinney, D. A., 502, 502, 503
Kiselev, P., 105
Kisilevsky, B. S., 147, 222
Kistner, J., 362
Kitchener, R. P., 6
Klackenberg-Larson, I., 53
Klahr, D., 15
Klaus, M., 207
Klayman, J., 425
Klein, A., 312
Klein, D., 554
Klein, N., 111
Klein, R., 546
Kleinman, S., 102
Klimes-Dougan, B., 271, 276, 349
Kline, M., 64
Klinnert, M., 274
Klorman, R., 545
Knight, W. G., 105–6
Knopf, I., 473–74
Ko, C.-W., 142
Koch, G., 456
Kochanska, G., 9, 268, 270, 276, 277, 278, 280, 282, 283, 284, 336, 339, 341, 349, 350, 351, 356, 359, 362
Koelling, R., 140
Koester, L., 196–97, 198, 199
Kogan, M., 110
Kohlberg, L., 478, 479, 479
Kondo-Ikemura, K., 270
Konner, M. J., 69, 112, 472
Kopershi, J., 132
Koplas, A. L., 420
Kopp, C., 271, 273, 276, 339, 349
Koren, G., 101, 103
Korner, A. F., 132, 133
Korones, S. B., 111
Koslowski, B., 198, 199
Kosmitzki, C., 184, 384
Kotsaftis, A., 219, 284
Kozhevnikova, E. V., 258
Kraemer, G., 217, 532
Kraemer, H., 132
Kramer, L., 338, 436
Kramer, R., 426
Krauss, M. W., 99
Krauss, R. M., 327, 328
Krebs, D., 481, 482
Kreppner, K., 46, 52, 55
Kresh, E., 388
Kreutzer, M A., 395
Kreutzer, T., 363, 438
Kristal, A., 67

Subject Index